Capital Investment
and
Financial Decisions

Fifth Edition

Capital Investment and Financial Decisions

Fifth Edition

Haim Levy and Marshall Sarnat

Prentice Hall
New York London Toronto Sydney Tokyo Singapore

First published 1978
Second Edition published 1982
Third Edition published 1986
Fourth Edition published 1990

This Fifth Edition first published 1994 by
Prentice Hall International (UK) Ltd,
Campus 400, Maylands Avenue
Hemel Hempstead
Hertfordshire, HP2 7EZ
A division of
Simon & Schuster International Group

Typeset in 10/12 Times by
Mathematical Composition Setters Ltd, Salisbury, Wiltshire

Printed and bound in Great Britain at
the University Press, Cambridge

Library of Congress Cataloging-in-Publication Data

Levy, Haim.
    Capital investment and financial decisions / Haim Levy and
Marshall Sarnat. — 5th ed.
        p. cm.
    Includes bibliographical references and index.
    ISBN 0-13-115882-1
    1. Capital investments. 2. Business enterprises—Finance.
I. Sarnat, Marshall. II. Title.
HG4028.C4L48 1993
658.15—dc20   93-25792
                                                         CIP

British Library Cataloguing in Publication Data

A catalogue record for this book is available from the
British Library

ISBN 0-13-115882-1

---

1 2 3 4 5   98 97 96 95 94

Contents

Part I Capital Budgeting, 1

1 The Goal of the Firm, 3

2 Capital Budgeting: An Overview, 20

3 The Economic Evaluation of Investment Proposals, 34

Part II Risk and Uncertainty, 211

Introduction, 212

8 Foundations of Risk Analysis, 215

9 Measuring Risk, 236

10 Applications of Risk Analysis, 268

11 Decreasing Risk by Diversification: The Portfolio Approach, 291

12 The Capital Asset Pricing Model and Arbitrage Pricing Theory, 315

Part II Suggestions for Further Reading, 367

Part III Long-term Financial Decisions, 369

Introduction, 370

13 Financial Leverage, 371

14 Capital Structure and Valuation, 401

15 Bankruptcy Risk and the Choice of Financial Structure, 448

16 Defining the Cost of Capital, 478

21 Mergers, 677

22 International Financial Management, 708

Part III Suggestions for Further Reading, 747

Preface

'Some questions can be decided even if not answered'

Mr. Justice Brandeis

This book is about financial policy with special emphasis on the allocation of a firm's long-term capital resources. Investment and financing decisions, which for better or for worse, fix the future course of the firm, have a great deal in common: they refer to a highly uncertain future, they must be made on the basis of incomplete information, and only a few of the relevant variables are controllable. But perhaps the salient characteristic of such decisions is that they cannot be avoided. 'No decision' is itself a 'decision'.

Under these circumstances, Mr. Justice Brandeis' famous dictum regarding cases before the Court, provides an appropriate motto for the financial manager, whose objective is not to answer the unanswerable, but rather to spell out an operational framework for reaching the *best attainable* financial decisions. The book is a product of our underlying conviction that the theory of finance can provide such guidelines for practical financial management. To paraphrase John Maynard Keynes (the leading economic theorist of his generation, and a highly successful investor as well), the theory of finance... 'is a method rather than a doctrine... a technique of thinking which helps its possessor to draw correct conclusions'. Accordingly, we have emphasized the practical application of financial theory in uncertain environments.

The fifth edition of the book reflects the changes which have taken place in recent years in the economy as well as in the theory of finance. Apart from polishing and correcting errors, the main changes in the fifth edition can be summarized as follows:

1. A Chapter on short-term working capital management has been added (Chapter 7).
2. Real world examples have been incorporated throughout the textbook to enhance the student's understanding of the material presented as well as increase the student's awareness of the material being discussed.

3. Consistent with the current low inflationary environment inflation has been incorporated in the relevant chapters rather than an entire chapter being devoted to the topic.
4. New problems have been added to every chapter.
5. The relevant changes in the U.S. tax code have been incorporated.
6. The discussion of capital market theory has been updated to reflect current and ongoing research in the area.
7. Boxed articles from the financial media are quoted, emphasizing the relevance of the studied material.

As was true for the first, second, third and fourth editions, the emphasis throughout the book is on the practical application of the modern theory of finance to realistic corporate decisions. To facilitate this goal numerous problems and mini-cases have been appended at the end of each chapter. In the fifth edition some problems have been eliminated and many have been added to reflect current trends and conditions. Although instructors and students differ widely in their tastes, probably everyone will want to spend some time discussing the end-of-chapter questions and problems. We have tested the problems in our own classes, but room for improvement surely remains; and we would appreciate hearing of your experience with the problems and the suggested solutions that appear in the revised Teachers' Manual.

The book is suitable as a core text for courses in Corporate Financial Theory and Policy. The approach reflects our belief that the 'technique of thinking' called financial management can best be obtained by considering the long-term problems of capital investment, financial structure, cost of capital and dividend policy. However, in recognition of the large variance in teaching methods and programs, the book has been designed to provide a highly flexible teaching instrument. It can be used for courses in capital budgeting, engineering economics and applied micro-economics, as well as for financial management.

Finally, a word to the student who has carelessly wandered into this preface: a finance course can be a challenging experience, as well as a lot of fun, just as writing this book has been for us. Unnecessary complexities and mathematical formulations have been ruthlessly weeded out. If you have an eye for a graph and don't have an aversion for numerical examples, you are well prepared to understand the text and perhaps, to improve it as well.

There remains the pleasant task of acknowledging the generous help of colleagues and friends. Our appreciation goes to Michael Adler, Fred Arditti, Moshe Ben-Horin, S. Benninga, Sasson Bar-Yosef, Mary Broske, David Cohen, Wanda Denny, R. Dunbar, S. Ekern, D. Galai, David Goldenberg, M. Gordon, P. Geleff, G. Grundy, G. Harpaz, G. S. Hatjoullis, R. Holtgrieve, Yoram Kroll, A. Levy, R. Mesznik, B. Rapp, R. Rundfelt, W. Sharpe, Lata Shanker, R. Stapleton, George Sapiro, R. Westerfield, and R. Wubbels for critical comments and suggestions on various chapters. We also wish to thank Moshe Smith, Zvi Lerman, Rogelio Saenz, Jim Craig, Mates Beja, Marcia Don, June Dilevsky, Ronnie Zuckerman, Robert Brooks, K. Bi, H. Pratt, V. Etimov, K. C. Lim, Charles Mann and D. Gregory who provided excellent assistance in the preparation of various editions of this book. Special thanks go to D. Gunthorpe, who provided excellent assistance in the preparation of the fifth edition. Once again, we wish to thank Cathy Peck and Henry Hirschberg of Prentice Hall, who by now have become experts in financial management, or at least in handling the authors of textbooks on that august subject with good humor and great skill. Finally we would like to thank Ester Tuval, Kerry Deyoung, Jerry Graves and Hyla Berkowitz for the excellent typing job.

H.L.
M.S.

Frequently Used Formulae

PROJECT PROFITABILITY MEASURES

Present value:

$$PV = \sum_{t=1}^{n} S_t/(1 + k)^t \qquad \text{(Chap. 3)}$$

Net present value:

$$NPV = \sum_{t=1}^{n} S_t/(1 + k)^t - I_0 \qquad \text{(Chap. 3)}$$

Internal rate of return: the value R which solves the equation

$$\sum_{t=1}^{n} S_t/(1 + R)^t = I_0 \qquad \text{(Chap. 3)}$$

Payback rate of return:

$$R_p = S/I_0 = R\left/\left[1 - \left(\frac{1}{1 + R)}\right)^n\right]\right. \qquad \text{(Chap. 4)}$$

(where S is a constant cash flow and $R = IRR$) \qquad (Chap. 6)

Accounting (total) rate of return:

$$R_t = (S - D)/I_0 = R\left/\left[1 - \left(\frac{1}{1 + R}\right)^n\right]\right. - \frac{1}{n} \qquad \text{(Chap. 6)}$$

Accounting (average) rate of return:

$$R_a = \frac{S - D}{I_0/2} = 2R\left/\left[1 - \left(\frac{1}{1 + R}\right)^n\right]\right. - \frac{2}{n} \qquad \text{(Chap. 6)}$$

_____ **DISCOUNT RATES**

After-tax weighted average cost of capital (WACC):

$$k = (S_L/V_L)k_e + (1 - T_c)r(B_L/V_L) \qquad \text{(Chap. 16)}$$

Cost of capital of levered firm k_L^* and unlevered firm k_U^*:

$$k_L^* = k_U^*\left[1 - \frac{T_c B_L}{V_L}\right] \qquad \text{(Chap. 16)}$$

Cost of equity (Gordon's Model):

$$k_e = d/P_0 + g \qquad \text{(Chaps 16, 17)}$$

Cost of debt: k_d^* which solves:

$$P_0 = \sum_{t=1}^{n} \frac{(1 - T_c)C_t}{(1 + k_d^*)^t} + \frac{Pn}{(1 + k_d^*)^n} \qquad \text{(Chap. 17)}$$

Cost of equity (CAPM approach):

$$k_e = r + (E(x_m) - r)\beta \qquad \text{(Chap. 17)}$$

_____ **VALUATION OF FIRMS**

In the absence of taxes: $V_L = V_U$ (Chap. 14)

With corporate taxes only: $V_L = V_U + T_c B_L$ (Chap. 14)

With corporate and personal taxes:

$$V_L = V_U + B_L\left[1 - \frac{(1 - T_c)(1 - T_g)}{(1 - T_p)}\right] \qquad \text{(Chap. 14)}$$

_____ **PORTFOLIO FORMULAE**

Mean return: $E(x) = \sum_{i=1}^{n} Pr_i x_i$ (Chap. 9)

Variance: $\sigma_x^2 = \sum_{i=1}^{n} Pr_i(x_i - E(x))^2$ (Chap. 9)

Standard deviation: $\sigma_x = \sqrt{\sigma_x^2}$ (Chap. 9)

Covariance of stocks x and y: $\text{Cov}(x, y) = E(xy) - E(x)E(y)$ (Chap. 9)

Correlation of x and y:

$$-1 \leqslant R_{x,y} = \frac{\text{Cov}(x, y)}{\sigma_x \sigma_y} \leqslant +1 \qquad \text{(Chap. 9)}$$

Portfolio mean: $E_p = \sum_{i=1}^{n} P_i E(x_i)$ \qquad (Chap. 11)

Portfolio variance: $\sigma_p^2 = \sum_{j=1}^{n} \sum_{i=1}^{n} P_i^2 \sigma_i^2$ \qquad (Chap. 11)

Beta (β): $\beta_i = \frac{\text{Cov}(x_i, x_m)}{\sigma_m^2}$ \qquad (Chap. 12)

EQUILIBRIUM FORMULAE

Capital market line (CML): $E_p = r + \left(\frac{E(x_m) - r}{\sigma_m} \right) \sigma_p$ \qquad (Chap. 12)

(where (E_p, σ_p) are the mean and standard deviation of *efficient* portfolios)

Security market line (SML)

$E(x_i) = r + (E(x_m) - r)\beta_i$ holds for all risky assets \qquad (Chap. 12)

OPTIONS FORMULAE

Call option bounds:

$$S_0 \geqslant C \geqslant \max[0, S_0 - E_x/(1 + r)] \qquad \text{(Chap. 19)}$$

Put–call parity:

$$C = S_0 + P - E_x/(1 + r) \qquad \text{(Chap. 19)}$$

Black and Scholes formula:

$$C = S_0 N(d_1) - E_x e^{-rt} N(d_2)$$

where

$$d_1 = \frac{\ln(S_0/E_x) + (r + \sigma^2/2)t}{\sigma\sqrt{t}} \quad \text{and} \quad d_2 = d_1 - \sigma\sqrt{t} \qquad \text{(Chap. 19)}$$

(where $C =$ call price, $P =$ put price, $E_x =$ exercise price, $S_0 =$ current asset price on which an opinion is written, $t =$ time to maturity, and $N =$ the cumulative normal distribution).

Frequently Used Symbols

RISK SYMBOLS

σ^2	Variance of returns
$c = \sigma/E$	Coefficient of variation of returns
σ_m^2	'Market portfolio' variance
σ_p^2	Portfolio variance
σ	Standard deviation of returns
β (beta)	Systematic risk (in portfolio context)
λ (lambda)	Market price of risk $= (E(x_m) - r)/\sigma_m^2$

VALUATION SYMBOLS

V_U	Market value of unlevered firm (also $V_U = S_U$)
S_U	Market value of equity of unlevered firm
V_L	Market value of levered firm
B_L	Market value of debt
S_L	Market values of equity of levered firm (by definition, $V_L \equiv B_L + S_L$)
P_t	Market value of stock at time t

OTHER SYMBOLS

t	Time (year)
S_t	Cash flow received at the end of year t
I_0	Initial investment
n	Project's economic life
D_t	Depreciation in year t
W	Working capital
d_t	Cash dividend paid in year t
EPS	Earnings per share
g	Annual growth rate of dividend
C_t	Coupon payment
U	Utility function
σ_{ij}	Covariance of returns on assets i and j
R_{ij}	Correlation of returns on assets i and j
L	Leverage measured by debt/equity ratio
e	2.718 (base for natural logarithms)
L_t	Lease payment in year t
P_i	The portfolio investment proportion in the ith security
P_r	The investment proportion in the riskless asset ($\Sigma\, P_i + P_r = 1$)
$\displaystyle\sum_{i=1}^{n}$	The sum of all elements from 1 to n
$q(t, k)$	Present value of \$1 received at the end of year t and discounted at $k\%$
$Q(n, k)$	Present value of annuity for n years discounted at $k\%$
Rev	Revenue

Part I

Capital Budgeting

Introduction

Part I is devoted to the basic elements of the firm's capital budgeting process: project evaluation, the importance of the time element, and the principles underlying the composition of the cash flow. Alternative goals of the firm are discussed in Chapter 1 which also presents the arguments on behalf of our choice of wealth maximization. Chapter 2 gives an overview of the investment decision-making process; while Chapter 3 focuses attention on the crucial role played by the timing of future cash flows. Chapter 4 sets out the theoretical arguments on behalf of the net present value method of appraising alternative investment proposals. Chapter 5 is devoted to a discussion of the principles underlying the firm's estimate of the relevant pre-tax cash flows of an investment project, as well as the impact of corporate taxes on these flows. Chapter 6 examines the traditional measures of investment worth. Chapter 7 is devoted to short-term financing and concludes Part I.

1

The Goal of the Firm

ARTICLE 1

Reebok Holders Reject Plan for Panel To Set Salaries, but It Gets Sizable Vote

BOSTON – Reebok International Ltd. shareholders rejected a proposal to form an independent committee to set executive pay, but the proposal won a sizable 26.9% of the shares voted.

Reebok management opposed the proposal, and put it on the shareholder ballot only after being ordered to do so in March by the Securities and Exchange Commission. The proposal was made by the New York City Employees Retirement System, which has about $20 billion in pension funds.

New York City Comptroller Elizabeth Holtzman called the vote 'a shot across the bow for Reebok and other major companies where there is lackluster performance and skyrocketing executive compensation.' She said that the proposal's 'impressive showing' should send a 'strong signal to Reebok that we want to see compensation linked to performance.'

The footwear company said that its chairman and chief executive officer, Paul Fireman, and his wife, who own about 18% of the company's stock, and other Reebok executives abstained from voting their shares on the measure.

The fund had called for restricting the compensation committee to outside board members, people who don't work for the company or aren't significant suppliers or customers, among other conditions. Reebok had insisted that it already has an independent executive compensation committee.

Mr. Fireman, who was paid $14.8 million in 1990, has been a target of criticism in the widening debate over executive compensation. However, as a result of a change in his compensation plan, Mr. Fireman's pay dropped to $2 million in 1991.

Ms. Holtzman wouldn't say whether the fund would resubmit its proposal next year. But she noted that it received well above the 3% level of support the SEC considers significant enough to permit reintroduction of the same proposal next year.

Source: *Wall Street Journal*, May 6, 1992, p. c13.

A business firm is confronted with many decisions – some important and others less so. This book is devoted to a particular group of business decisions:

those which determine a firm's capital expenditures and their financing. Perhaps more than any single factor, the investment strategy adopted by the firm determines its future growth and profitability. Strategic (long-range) capital investment decisions, such as the decision to 'go international', diversify into new product lines or pursue an important innovation, can materially change the character of even the largest firm in a single decade. Future success depends not only on finding an appropriate investment strategy, but also on the way in which the strategy is implemented. Tactical (short-run) decisions, such as the decision to buy rather than lease equipment, are no less important than the most elaborately planned long-term strategy.

In discussing the goal of the firm, a distinction must be made between a firm which is owned and operated by its owners (a family firm called a sole proprietorship) and a corporation such as Reebok which is generally managed by someone other than the owner (or which is owned by many individuals or stockholders). There are many conflicting forces in a corporation – employees, stockholders (shareholders), institutional investors, and so on. While the goal of both family firms and corporations can be defined and analyzed, the corporate form of organization (like that of Reebok) is more realistic and also more complex. In particular, the managers of corporations (called agents) may act (undertake projects) which maximize their own welfare, but their actions may not necessarily maximize the welfare of the stockholders (called principals or owners). In this chapter, the goal of the firm is first defined and then some of the possible conflicts of interest are discussed.

ALTERNATIVE GOALS FOR THE FIRM

By its very nature, financial decision-making involves purposeful behavior, which implies the existence of a goal, or what is much more likely, some combination of goals. In the absence of an objective, the firm would have no criterion for choosing among alternative investment strategies and projects. Surely there is no need to tell the firm that two million dollars is better than one. Yet even this decision is not always that simple. For example, an investment strategy which promises two million dollars accompanied by the risk of possible bankruptcy should the venture go sour may not be preferable to a conservative strategy which offers a payoff of only one million dollars but permits the directors of the firm to sleep soundly at night.

Once the complexity of the financial decision-making process is recognized, it is fairly easy to assemble a large number of possible candidates for 'the goal of the firm'. A partial listing which has been mentioned over the years includes:

1. Maximization of profits.
2. Maximization of sales.
3. Survival of the firm.

4. Achieving a 'satisfactory' level of profits.
5. Achieving a target market share.
6. Some minimum level of employee turnover.
7. 'Internal peace', or no ulcers for management as this objective is often called.
8. Maximization of managerial perks and salaries.

Listing the possible objectives for the firm is an endless game, more likely to leave its players exhausted than enlightened. However, we think the essential point has been made: no single 'goal' can express *all* of the complexities of the decision process. Despite this, we shall see that a 'goal' for corporate decision-making which serves as a foundation for the firm's critically important investment, financing, and dividend decisions can be found.

Since the first four goals listed above are the most frequently cited, let us now subject them to closer scrutiny. Following this, we spell out an appropriate goal which will enable us to feel somewhat more comfortable in discussing the numerous other candidates for 'goal of the firm'.

MAXIMIZING PROFITS

Almost every introductory textbook in economics, and especially those in price theory, assumes (apparently as self-evident) the goal of profit maximization.[1] Though appealing to many economists, upon reflection it is clear that this highly simplified model of corporate behavior rests squarely on the assumption that future profits are known with *certainty*. Taking the maximization of profits as the corporation's objective implies that when the firm chooses among alternative strategies, it can forecast with certainty all of the relevant future revenues and costs, and hence profit, associated with each policy. However, reality is not so accommodating. Even if we are willing to accept the assumption of 'certainty', the goal of profit maximization is at best ambiguous. Consider the following problem.

What profit should the firm maximize? Short-run profits (say next year's) or long-run profits over the next decade? To illustrate the problem, let us assume that the firm is confronted with two alternative investment strategies. If it adopts strategy A, the firm will earn a net profit of $10,000 a year for ten years:

---

1. The simplest model states that the firm should seek the output q which maximizes the function:

$$\pi = qp - C(q)$$

where π denotes net profit, q the number of units that the firm produces, $C(q)$ the total production cost, which changes with the level of output, and p equals the price of each unit sold.

Applying the 'maximum profit' goal, the firm should seek to produce that quantity q which maximizes its total profits, π.

	Strategy A					
Year	1	2	3	...	9	10
Net profit	10,000	10,000	10,000	...	10,000	10,000

On the other hand, adopting the alternative investment strategy B will yield the following stream of profits:

	Strategy B									
Year	1	2	3	4	5	6	7	8	9	10
Net profit	0	0	0	20,000	30,000	40,000	50,000	50,000	50,000	50,000

Which strategy should the firm choose in order to maximize its profits? Since the firm is an 'on-going' organization, it is almost intuitively obvious that profits in the long run (i.e., over the entire ten-year period) and not just the profits in the first year, or over some arbitrary number of years, are relevant.

The maximization of long-run profits, however, implies the need to reduce the stream of future receipts and outlays to some common denominator so that meaningful comparisons can be made. And while this is no easy task, the technique of discounting future cash flows, which is developed in Chapters 3 and 4, provides a neat solution to this problem. In the jargon of this approach, the firm should choose that strategy which maximizes the discounted *present value* of the stream of long-run profits (see Chapter 3). However, the simplicity and elegance of the present value solution should not obscure the fact that the goal of maximizing long-run profits is neither simple nor obvious once we relax the assumption of certainty and assume a more realistic setting in which uncertainty regarding future cash flows prevails. Given the highly uncertain environment in which most firms operate, a number of alternative objective functions have been proposed — the maximization of sales or market share being perhaps the best known.

Many firms tend to state their objective solely in terms of total sales or market share.[2] The possible explanation for this tendency is straightforward: market share is often a very good 'proxy' for profits, since market share and profits often move together. In a study of fifty-seven companies, Buzzell, Gale and Sultan[3] found a positive correlation between a firm's market share and its profitability (see Figure 1.1). On the average, an increase of 10% in market share was accompanied by an increase of about 5% in the pre-tax return on

2. The best known theoretical proponent of this approach is William J. Baumol. See his *Business Behavior, Value, and Growth*, New York, Macmillan, 1959.
3. See Robert D. Buzzell, Bradley T. Gale and Ralph G. M. Sultan, 'Market Share — A Key to Profitability,' *Harvard Business Review*, January/February 1975.

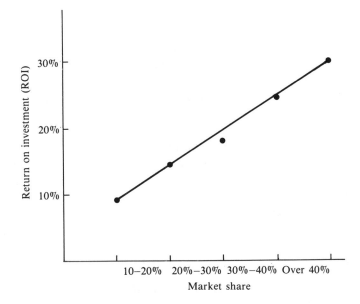

Figure 1.1 The relationship between pre-tax return on investment and market share. *Source*: R. D. Buzzell, B. T. Gale, and R. G. M. Sultan, 'Market Share – A Key to Profitability', *Harvard Business Review*, January/February, 1975, p. 98. Copyright 1974 by the President and Fellows of Harvard College; all rights reserved.

investment. Although one can find many possible explanations for this relationship, one thing is clear; the goals 'maximize profit' and 'maximize sales', or 'maximize market share', are closely related.

_____ SURVIVAL

'Survival' is another alternative which is often mentioned as the goal of the firm. Clearly, this objective cannot stand alone. If the firm's goal is purely to survive, why not invest all of its resources in short-term government securities (T-Bills) which guarantee an almost perfectly certain fixed income and therefore would also guarantee survival. However, when a businessperson speaks of 'survival' as a motivating policy goal, he or she is probably referring to the avoidance of 'very great' risks. Thus it is true that many firms will prefer to avoid a chance of earning even exceptionally high profits if the particular project endangers the financial stability of the firm. In this context the objective of business survival can be recast in terms of a goal of 'safety first'. Such an approach would identify some minimum level which the firm must meet at all costs. For example, assume that $100,000 is required to service the firm's annual debt payments. A 'safety-first' rule would be to *minimize* the probability of earnings falling below $100,000.

SATISFACTORY PROFITS _____

Explorations along the boundaries of economics and psychology have led to the development of an organizational or behavioral approach. The firm is viewed as a complex pattern of personal relationships. Perhaps the best-known advocate of such an approach is Herbert Simon, the Nobel Prize winner in economics, who in a variety of publications developed what has proved to be a very influential concept of the firm and its goals. [4]

Although Simon agrees that the concept of a goal is indispensable to organization theory, he emphasizes that the object of corporate action is seldom single-valued. In his view, the decision-making mechanism is imperfect; the firm is confronted by the necessity to choose among alternatives without knowing exactly the outcomes of each choice. Not knowing the *best* alternative, the decision-maker does not seek a maximum profit, but is content with some satisfactory level of profit. Or as Simon has put it, businesspeople (the organization) cannot maximize profits; they can only hope to *satisfice*. Thus in Simon's view it is 'satisficing' rather than maximizing behavior which characterizes the business firm.

Treating the firm as a complex organization has much to recommend it. There are many situations in which it is more fruitful to view decision-making as the search for courses of action which satisfy a number of constraints rather than as the pursuit of a single-valued goal such as profit maximization. This is especially true in the realistic setting of uncertainty. But its strength is also its weakness: the major drawback of the approach is its complexity, that is the large number of variables which must be considered. Thus greater organizational realism is acquired, but only at a price – in this instance the ease with which these types of models can be used to explain and predict corporate action.

WEALTH MAXIMIZATION _____

Although business motivation is admittedly very complex, a study by Robert Lanzillotti revealed that management is generally concerned with: [5]

1. Long-run profitability.
2. Stability.

Although these goals appear to be inconsistent – attempts to increase profits often involve greater risks, i.e., less stability – a way must be found to combine them if our definition of the goal of the firm is to reflect accurately the

4. See, for example, Herbert A. Simon, *Administrative Behavior*, 2nd edn, Macmillan New York, 1957, and his 'On the Concept of Organizational Goals,' *Administrative Science Quarterly*, June 1964. Somewhat similar views have been expounded by R. M. Cyert and J. G. March, *A Behavioral Theory of the Firm*, Prentice Hall, Englewood Cliffs, N.J., 1963.
5. See Robert F. Lanzillotti, 'Pricing Objectives in Large Companies,' *American Economic Review*, December 1958, pp. 921–40.

objectives of business management. One way out of this dilemma is to assume that management takes as its goal the maximization of shareholders' wealth, or alternatively stated, the maximization of the market value of its existing common stock.[6] Although anyone who has ever attended a board meeting is not likely to underestimate the ability of management to act in its own interest, maximizing the financial well-being of the shareholders is not necessarily incompatible with management's interests. On the contrary, it may well be an optimal strategy for maximizing management's welfare as well.

Taking shareholders' wealth as the firm's goal has the important advantage of permitting us to combine the profitability and riskiness of alternative courses of action into one quantitative measure. Consider a case of two firms, A and B, with identical expected profits (say $1 per share of common stock). Now assume that firm B expects to earn its profit by a very risky undertaking, e.g., financing a textbook on corporate investment. In such a case, the price (market value) of the common stock of firm A will be higher than that of firm B, since both offer investors the same expected future earnings, but one of

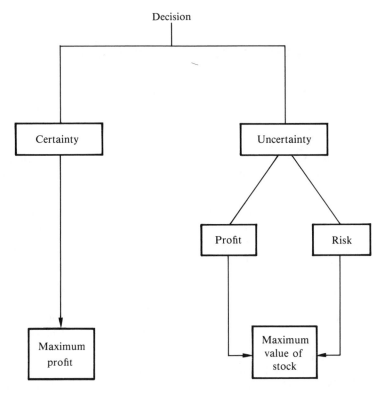

Figure 1.2

6. The formal equivalence between wealth maximization and the maximization of the market value of a firm's common stock is shown in Appendix 14A.

them has a much higher risk. The situation is more complex if we assume the more realistic case in which the risky venture also offers *higher* expected earnings. For example, suppose that the firm can earn $1 per share with certainty, or alternatively, $2 per share with a 90% probability, but that there also exists a 10% chance that the firm will go bankrupt. The decision in this case is not easy. Is the additional $1 of profit sufficient to offset the 10% chance of going bankrupt? The answer depends upon the market's evaluation of the risk-return tradeoff implicit in this venture. If the greater expectation of return outweighs the increase in risk, we expect the price of the stock to rise if the project is undertaken. Conversely, for the case in which the riskiness outweighs the increase in expected returns, we would expect the share price to fall. Thus defining the goal of the firm in terms of market value of the stock implies an effort on the part of management to seek an optimum balance between risk and profitability, which is consistent with much of the theory and empirical evidence on the motivation of corporate action.

Figure 1.2 summarizes the general decision problem faced by the firm. In the unrealistic case in which the results of all decisions are known in advance with

Tenneco Settles Lawsuit That Alleged Holders Were Misled on Firm's Finances

HOUSTON – Tenneco Inc. agreed to settle a class-action shareholder lawsuit out of court.

Terms of the settlement, which is subject to court approval, weren't disclosed. But sources familiar with the negotiations said Tenneco agreed to pay out most of a $65 million provision the company had set aside to cover the litigation.

In the suit, investors alleged Tenneco executives misled them about the company's financial condition. Besides the company, the suit named James Ketelsen, Tenneco's chairman, and James Ashford, former president of Tenneco's JI Case unit. Through a spokeswoman, Mr. Ketelsen declined to comment. Mr. Ashford couldn't be reached.

Several suits were consolidated into a class-action suit here in the U.S. District Court for the Southern District of Texas, covering holders who purchased shares from April 2, 1990, to Dec. 31, 1991.

The holders charged that despite a slump in the market, Tenneco continued to ship Case products to retailers at high volumes to pump up revenue to which the executives' compensation was tied. Unsold, the farm and construction equipment sat on Case lots, causing a buildup of inventories and problems with cash flow, the shareholders said.

Due in large part to Case's dismal performance, Tenneco reported a 1991 loss of $732 million, including restructuring charges and the £65 million fourth-quarter provision set aside to cover the possible costs of the shareholders' suit and certain other pending litigation. An attorney for the plaintiffs declined to comment on the amount of the settlement.

Mr. Ashford resigned from Tenneco a year ago, citing personal reasons. Mr. Ketelsen, 61 years old, will step down as Tenneco chairman effective with the company's annual meeting next month. The company is in the midst of a $2 billion restructuring and has already seen a 50% dividend cut, layoffs and asset sales.

In New York Stock Exchange trading yesterday, Tenneco fell $1.50 to $37.375. *Source: Wall Street Journal*, June 26, 1992, p. A4.

BP's Horton Quits as Chief And Chairman
Move Follows Board Talks On Direction of Firm; U.S. Issue Price Tumbles

LONDON — Robert Horton resigned abruptly as chairman and chief executive officer of British Petroleum Co. after meeting with board members who expressed 'numerous concerns about the way the company was going,' a BP official said.

The announcement sent the price of BP's American depositary receipts plunging 9.7% in New York, amid fears that BP's dividend would be cut. BP's ADRs were quoted at $48.375 apiece in late New York Stock Exchange trading, down $6 on heavy volume. The resignation announcement came after the close of trading in London, where BP shares had risen five pence (nine cents) to 243 pence.

Company insiders said Mr. Horton's departure was largely the result of 'personality clashes' with the board and other top executives and isn't likely to bring a radical change in BP strategy. Nonetheless, the announcement follows a yearlong slide in earnings accompanied by a steep drop in BP's share price, from a high of 367 pence last year to 238 pence in recent days in London trading.

Source: *Wall Street Journal*, June 26, 1992, p. A3.

---

certainty, the goal of the firm should be the maximization of the firm's long-run profit. However, when uncertainty prevails, as it always does in the real world, the firm must consider risk as well as profits, and therefore choose that combination of risk and profit which maximizes the market value of its stock. Those firms who place greater emphasis on the goal of 'survival' can be viewed as giving a very large weight to risk, but this is not necessarily inconsistent with the goal of maximizing the market value of the firm's common stock.

It is fairly obvious from the news article on Tenneco Inc. that the managers did not act in the best interest of the stockholders. They are reported to have 'pumped up' the revenue of the firm artificially. Although it is not obvious that the managers acted illegally, their intent was to maximize accounting revenue since their compensation was tied to this variable.

As shown in article 3, however, we see that the chief executive officer and chairman of British Petroleum Co. quit after a period of declining earnings and drop in the firm's stock price. To avoid such situations, some chief executive officers refrain from undertaking projects which are risky (and may cause a decline in earnings) even if the projects are desirable from the stockholders' point of view.

Both articles demonstrate the separation of ownership and management of a firm and the conflict of interest that can arise. Clearly, achieving the goal of the firm stated in Figure 1.2 is not an easy and unambiguous task.

AGENCY CONSIDERATIONS: MOTIVATING MANAGEMENT

Indeed, it has long been felt that the separation of management from ownership in the modern corporation may affect corporate objectives. The delegation of decision-making authority from owners (the 'principals') to managers (the 'agents') has become the subject of what is now called 'agency theory'. Agency theory deals with potential conflicts of interest between outside shareholders and management. Three major types of potential conflict have been identified:

1. Management may utilize corporate resources to provide themselves 'perks' (e.g., superfluous executive jets, first-class air travel, etc.) or embark upon expansions ('empire building') which are not in the shareholders' best interests.
2. Management may have shorter time horizons than shareholders. For example, a manager may favor short-term projects, with early returns, at the expense of those which mature too late to influence promotion.
3. Management and owners may differ as to the evaluation of risk.

In this context two principal factors can be identified as effective means for reducing the potential conflict between management and shareholders. First, owners may establish incentive compensation plans for executives which are tied to shareholders' objectives. Second, the ever-present threat of takeover is often a powerful mitigating influence on managerial behavior.

The question of whether shareholders' economic welfare is or is not a principal concern of management is clearly an empirical question. One study[7] which examined the goals of a sample of 326 management-controlled firms in the United States over the period 1967–75, indicates that maximization of stock price (i.e., shareholders' wealth maximization) is the dominant goal of such corporations.

Additional evidence supporting the wealth maximization hypothesis can be found in the growing tendency of firms to reward executives on the basis of stock price appreciation. Recognition that earnings per share (EPS) often have very little impact on stock price has led some firms (for example, Sears Roebuck, Borden, Combustion Engineering and Emhart) to tie their executive compensation plans to performance measures that create shareholder value in the form of increased prices of their common stock.[8]

Now more than ever, the compensation paid to chief executive officers (CEOs) is receiving considerable public scrutiny. While H. B. Atwater, the CEO of General Mills, Inc., feels that the current structure is working 'pretty well', many others believe that the CEOs should be more closely monitored and regulated. Indeed, the early 1990s is characterized by lawsuits being filed against some CEOs and 'no votes' being cast by major shareholders against the re-election of the existing board of directors (see article 4).

While the academic view is correct, the problem is how to achieve the goal. If, indeed, the manager acts like an owner, then the organization is similar to

7. Ali M. Fatemi, James S. Ang, and Jess H. Chua, 'Evidence Supporting Shareholder Wealth Maximization in Management Controlled Firms,' *Applied Economics*, February 1983.
8. *Business Week*, 2 April 1984, p. 67.

Voices of Protest

In today's compensation free-for-all, everybody has an opinion about changing CEO pay. Here are a few of them

BACK IN THE OLD DAYS, say a few years ago, chief executives compensation was strictly an issue between the CEOs and their boards of directors. Chief executives suggested the pay, the boards passed it. Except for a shareholder or two at the annual meeting – often dismissed as cranks – nobody complained much about it.

These days, there is a compensation free-for-all. Everybody, it seems, has an opinion about pay policy at the top, and how it should be changed. The trouble is, people can't quite agree – even on whether pay is too high.

Here are the views of several new players in the compensation game – two congressmen, an institutional investor, an individual investor and a professor – who are all grappling for a role in setting pay levels. Here also are the views of a chief executive and senior manager, whose pay would be affected by those crying for change.

The Representative

'A company doesn't exist exclusively for the executives, but also for the employees and the community.' *Martin Sabo*

The Academics

'The major problem with CEO pay is how to make managers more like owners. It's just that simple.' *Michael Jensen*

The Chief Executive

'From what I can see, I think the thing basically is working pretty well.' *H. B. Atwater*

The Institutional Investor

This year, 'you will see numerous "no" votes at numerous companies. It's small but spreading.' *Sarah Teslik*

Source: *Wall Street Journal*, April 22, 1992, p. R6.

---

a family firm with no conflict of interest. Constructing a compensation scheme which forces the CEO to act as an owner, however, is not a simple task.

In this book we assume that the goal of the firm is to maximize the value of the firm, which translates into maximizing the stock price, but it should be kept in mind that agency costs must be considered.

Over 90% of the one thousand largest U.S. manufacturing firms used a bonus plan to compensate their CEO. Moreover, most of the firms used some long-term (four to five year) contract based on a base salary and some incentive scheme (such as stock options).[9] Figure 1.3 shows the CEO's compensation breakdown for 1985 and 1991. First, note that the total compensation more than doubled in six years reaching $1.7 million in 1991. Second, the base salary component of total compensation declined to 35% from 52% with stock options playing an important role in managerial compensation in the 1990's.

The effectiveness of stock options as a compensation vehicle is debatable. Article 5, from *Fortune* magazine, best describes the pros and cons surrounding the use of stock options.

---

9. For more details see H. Fox, 'Top Executive Bonus Plans,' *The Conference Board*, New York, 1980, and D. Gunthorpe and H. Levy, 'The Separation of Ownership and Control and Potential Social Costs,' *Journal of Law and Public Policy*, 1992.

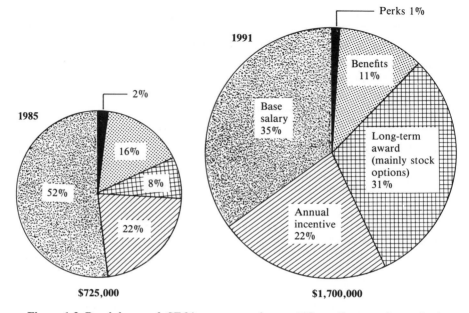

Figure 1.3 Breakdown of CEO's compensation at 282 medium- to large-sized firms, 1985 and 1991. *Source*: *Fortune*, April 6, 1992. p. 62.

ARTICLE 5

A standard option gives an executive the right but not the obligation to buy company shares for ten years at the market price on the day the options were granted, though usually he must wait two to four years before he may exercise them. The incentive seems straightforward: the executive will work like mad to maximize his wealth by raising the stock price, and shareholders get the benefit.

Trouble is, it doesn't work very well. Options can be employed intelligently and effectively. But because they have built-in flaws and are often abused, their record of linking executives' interests with shareholders' is far from good. One reason is that the optionee doesn't put up any money. For most ordinary investors, the fear of loss is at least as strong a motivator as the hope for gain, but recipients of options face no risk. If the stock rises, teriffic; if it falls, they simply discard the worthless things. As compensation consultant James E. Carey puts it,

'From the participant's viewpoint, the option grant may seem like a no-risk wager in a game of craps called "the market."'

The CEO with options has another advantage over the ordinary investor: inside information. Knowing the company's prospects more intimately than anyone, he has a far better chance of choosing a peak in the stock price to exercise options and take his profit. There's nothing illegal about this. That's just the way it is.

And that is how options work when companies play fair. Many play otherwise. Suppose a company issues options to a CEO when the stock is at $50, and it then falls to $30. You might think it's only right for the optionee to be out of the money in that case, but some compensation committees instead take pity on him. They cancel those options and replace them with new ones at $30.

Source: *Fortune*, April 6, 1992, p. 61.

And abroad?

Across America the cry was inescapable as President Bush led all those CEOs on his ill-starred January tour of Japan: *Our guys make three times more than theirs — and look who's eating whose lunch. It's a scandal!* The U.S. executives were prepared with their riposte: *Don't be fooled. These Japanese CEOs get enough perks to make Queen Elizabeth weep — and their value is never reported.*

What's the truth?

The truth, in a sentence, is that Japanese and other non-U.S. CEOs do get perks by the truckload — the use of company-owned homes and vacation retreats, club memberships — but their value does not close the pay gap by a long shot. Conventional wisdom holds that this is a cause of America's competitiveness problems. But while runaway pay disspirits workers, there's no reason to think that just cutting it will, by itself, do much for U.S. competitiveness. Why not? The situation is analogous to that of the U.S. students who ranked near the bottom in an international survey of math skills but had the No. 1 opinion of themselves. In a system in which CEOs appoint their companies' directors, most of whom are other CEOs, pay is precisely the expression of what CEOs think of themselves. Like U.S. students, they should recalibrate their self-image. But that won't help the country unless they also perform better.

What's true of companies is true for countries: If the U.S. were beating the pants off its rivals, hardly anyone would care what its CEOs got paid. That's why just paying less isn't the answer, and paying for performance is.

Source: *Fortune*, April 6, 1992, p. 68.

Thus, while it is obvious that the CEO should be motivated to maximize the value of the firm, how to achieve this objective is not as obvious.

CEO compensation outside the U.S.

CEO's in Japan (the country which is currently seen as the major competitor of the U.S.) are reported to be making one-third of the compensation made by CEOs in the U.S.

As article 6 shows, though, the CEOs of non-U.S. firms may likewise receive more perks (e.g., large offices and expensive lunches) which makes compensation comparisons difficult. Two important points emerge from this article: first, when a firm is successfully 'beating the pants off its rivals', less attention is paid to the CEO's compensation. Second, and more important, in the U.S. the CEO generally nominates the board of directors (or at least recommends the board to shareholders) who in turn determine the CEO's compensation. Emerging in the 1990s, however, is resentment for this process (initiated primarily by large institutional investors), and legislation is currently being considered to regulate the compensation of CEOs.

SUMMARY

The appropriateness of a decision rule can only be evaluated when one knows the firm's objective or goal. Empirical evidence indicates that some firms state their objectives in terms of their sales or market share, while others emphasize profits. 'Safety' and 'survival' are also widely mentioned as goals of the firm. However, a careful examination of the empirical evidence shows that most firms appear to have multidimensional goals. The two most important factors appear to be profitability (or market share, which is highly correlated with profits) and risk (i.e., safety or survival). The selection of the combination of expected profit and risk which is appropriate for a firm's shareholders is not an easy task, but by taking shareholders' interests as the goal of the firm, an operational method can be found for incorporating *both* risk and profitability into the firm's goal function. The rest of this book is devoted to spelling out the financial decision rules which are implied by the assumed goal of wealth maximization.

SUMMARY TABLE

Possible goals of the firm

1. Maximization of profit: applies only to the case of certainty.
2. Maximization of expected profit: applies to uncertainty but ignores risk.
3. Maximization of market share: can be justified only as a proxy for profit maximization.
4. Maximization of margin: can be justified only as a proxy for risk minimization.
5. Survival: if this is the only goal, firms should close their business and invest in treasury bills.
6. 'Safety first': minimizing the probability that earnings fall below some disastrous level.
7. A combination of profit and risk: maximize profit subject to the constraint $P_r(X \leqslant D) \leqslant P$ when P is some probability (say 0.1), D stands for a disaster level of income, and X the firm's earnings (which is a random variable).
8. Herbert Simon's goal: 'satisficing' rather than maximizing.
9. All the above considerations indicate that firms should (a) maximize profit, and (b) minimize risk. Since in real life a project with high profit potential is characterized by a high degree of risk, management should weigh the return against risk and should select the set of projects which maximizes the value of the shareholders' wealth.

QUESTIONS AND PROBLEMS

1.1 Is the goal of maximizing the stock price good for society; that is, do the same actions that maximize stock prices also benefit society?

1.2 In a recent study of five hundred corporations Professor Jack Skeptic found that no one firm mentioned maximizing shareholders' wealth as an objective of the firm. On the contrary, most of the firms stressed profitability and risk as the key variables affecting their decision. Discuss the implications of these findings.

1.3 'We have no goals for the firm, we are too busy making money.' Why might this be a perfectly acceptable motto for a corporate president? Why might this same motto be unacceptable for the authors of a textbook on capital budgeting?

1.4 The table below gives the price and fixed and variable production costs as a function of the quantity produced (Q).

Quantity	Price ($)	Fixed cost ($)	Total variable cost ($)
0	–	100	0
10	5.50	100	20
20	5.25	100	30
30	5.00	100	50
40	4.75	100	80
50	4.30	100	110
60	3.50	100	160

(a) Calculate: marginal cost per unit; total revenue; total cost; marginal revenue per unit; and profit per unit for each quantity level.

(b) How many units should the firm produce? (Hint: note that quantity produced is fixed at increments of 10 units.) What is its profit at that level of production?

1.5 Assume: cost $= 4.5Q + 0.25Q^2$

Price $= 8 - \frac{1}{2}Q$ where Q is the quantity produced

(a) Compute the optimal output and maximum profit.

(b) Graph the cost, marginal cost and marginal revenue functions. (Hint: remember, total revenue = price × quantity produced.)

1.6 The table provides recent financial data of firms belonging to the food and lodging industry.

(a) Examine the hypothesis that there is a positive correlation between the two goals: return on common equity and profit margins. (Hint: correlation $\equiv \text{Cov}(x, y)/\sigma_x\sigma_y)$).

(b) Examine the hypothesis that return on common equity and market share of sales are positively correlated. First calculate the market share of each firm as a percentage of the total sales in the industry.

	Sales ($m)	Profit margins (%)	Return com. eqy.
ARA Services	874.2	2.7	12.5
Church's Fried Chicken	123.1	9.3	36.8
Gino's	146.0	3.0	10.9
Hilton Hotels	219.4	16.3	22.7
Holiday Inns	551.3	7.3	12.6
Host International	147.5	4.6	21.1
Howard Johnson	262.4	6.7	13.2
Hyatt	208.3	4.4	26.5
Marriot	582.1	4.3	12.1
McDonald's	793.7	10.5	25.4
Ramada Inns	154.2	2.7	6.7
Webb (Del. E.)	244.8	3.4	18.4
Industry composite	4,307.0	6.4	17.1

Source: Business Week.

1.7 The table reports sales, assets and net income of eight large oil companies in the United States for two consecutive years denoted by 1 and 2.

Firm	Sales ($000)		Assets ($000)		Net income	
	1	2	1	2	1	2
Exxon	54,126,219	60,334,527	38,453,336	41,530,804	2,422,964	2,763,000
Mobil	32,125,828	34,736,045	20,575,967	22,611,489	1,004,670	1,125,638
Texaco	27,920,499	28,607,521	18,926,026	20,249,143	930,789	852,461
Std. Oil (Cal.)	20,917,331	23,232,413	14,882,347	16,861,021	1,016,360	1,105,881
Gulf Oil	17,840,000	18,069,000	14,225,000	15,036,000	752,000	791,000
Std. Oil (Ind.)	13,019,939	14,961,489	12,884,286	14,109,264	1,011,575	1,076,412
Atlantic Richfield	10,969,091	12,298,403	11,119,012	12,060,210	701,515	804,355
Shell Oil	10,112,062	11,062,883	8,876,754	10,453,358	735,094	803,623
Total	187,030,969	203,302,281	139,942,728	159,911,289	8,574,967	9,322,370

Source: *Fortune 500.*

For each firm:

(a) Calculate the net income as a percentage of assets for each of the two years. Then calculate the average of this figure for the two years.

(b) Draw a scatter diagram with net income as a percentage of assets on the vertical axis and market share on the horizontal axis.

(c) Calculate the regression line and the correlation coefficient between the variables (net income and market share in percent). Is market share a good proxy for profit in the oil industry? (Hint: use the correlations coefficient.)

1.8 Firm A and firm B have the following rates of return (in percentages) on investment as reported on the past five years:

Firm A	Firm B
8.0	2.0
7.9	18.0
8.1	30.0
8.0	0.0
7.8	3.0

Is it possible that firm A is maximizing its stock price but firm B is not? Do the two firms have different goals?

1.9 Mr. Abel, the firm's manager of Conecos, receives the following compensation scheme: $20,000 a year as a fixed salary plus 2% of the annual sales. Do you think that this compensation scheme may induce a conflict of interest between Mr. Abel and the shareholders?

1.10 Recently, more CEOs are receiving a large part of their annual compensation in the form of the company stocks. Moreover, in most cases the CEO is not allowed to sell the stocks for some predetermined period, e.g., two years. Appraise this compensation policy in light of the fact that the shareholders' goal is to maximize the value of the firm.

1.11 Dambo Corporation compensates its CEO as follows: $250,000 a year plus $\frac{1}{2}\%$ of the annual net cash flow that the firm produces. Appraise this compensation policy. Does it create a conflict of interest between the agent and the principal?

SELECTED REFERENCES

Alchian, Armen A. and Woodward, Susan, 'Reflections on the Theory of the Firm,' *Journal of Institutional Theoretical Economics*, March 1987.

Baysinger, Barry and Butler, Henry, 'The Role of Corporate Law in the Theory of the Firm,' *Journal of Law and Economics*, April 1985.

Chrisman, J. J. and Carroll, A. B., 'Corporate Responsibility – Reconciling Economic and Social Goals,' *Sloan Management Review*, Winter 1984.

Collins, J. Markham and Bey, Roger P., 'The Master Limited Partnership: An Alternative to the Corporation,' *Financial Management*, Winter 1986.

Fama, Eugene F., 'Agency Problems and the Theory of the Firm,' *Journal of Political Economy*, 1980.

Findlay, M. Chapman, III and Whitmore, G. A., 'Beyond Shareholder Wealth Maximization,' *Financial Management*, Winter 1974.

Gibbons, M. R. 'The Interrelations of Finance and Economics: Empirical Perspectives,' *American Economic Review*, May 1987.

Jennergren, I. Peter, 'On the Design of Incentives in Business Firms – A Survey of Some Research,' *Management Science*, February 1980.

Jensen, M. C. and Meckling, W. H., 'Theory of the Firm: Managerial Behavior, Agency Costs and Ownership Structure,' *Journal of Financial Economics*, October 1976.

Kensinger, John W. and Martin, John D., 'Royalty Trusts, Master Partnerships and Other Organizational Means of "Unfirming the Firm",' *Midland Corporate Finance Journal*, Summer 1986.

Lanzillotti, F. Robert, 'Pricing Objectives in Large Companies,' *American Economic Review*, December 1958.

Moore, W. T., Christensen, D. G., and Roenfeldt R. L., 'Equity Valuation Effects of Forming Master Limited Partnerships,' *Journal of Financial Economics*, September 1989.

Osteryoung, J. S., 'A Survey into the Goals Used by Fortune's 500 Companies in Capital Budgeting Decisions,' *Arkon Business and Economic Review*, Fall 1973.

Porter, Philip K., Scully, Gerald W., and Slottie, Daniel J., 'Industrial Policy and the Nature of the Firm,' *Journal of Institutional Theoretical Economics*, March 1986.

Rappaport, A., 'A Fatal Fascination with the Short Run,' *Business Week*, 4 May, 1981.

Ross, Steven A., 'The Interrelations of Finance and Economics: Theoretical Perspectives,' *American Economic Review*, May 1987.

Seitz, N., 'Shareholder Goals, Firm Goals and Firm Financing Decisions,' *Financial Management*, Autumn 1982.

Simon H. A., *Administrative Behavior*, New York: Macmillan, 1957.

Spooner, M. C., 'Origin of Fundamental Analysis,' *Financial Analyst Journal*, July/August 1984.

Summers, Lawrence, 'On Economics and Finance,' *The Journal of Finance*, July 1985.

Williamson, Oliver, 'Perspectives on the Modern Corporation,' *Quarterly Review of Economics and Business*, Winter 1984.

2

Capital Budgeting:
An Overview

ARTICLE 7

U.S. Businesses Plan a 4.7% Boost In Capital Budgets

WASHINGTON – U.S. businesses plan to boost their plant and equipment spending by 4.7% this year, little changed from an April projection but still a turnaround from last year, when outlays fell 0.6%, the Commerce Department said.

The department's latest survey projected 1992 capital spending at $553.86 billion, up from $529.2 billion in 1991. The April report projected a 4.6% increase for this year.

These surveys are often off target, however. For example, 1991 spending was initially projected to be 2.5% above 1990.

Despite the encouraging predictions, analysts said businesses, especially manufacturers, are still cautious about increasing capital investment. Manufacturing companies plan a 2.4% cut in spending for 1992 after trimming outlays 4.7% in 1991.

Companies outside the manufacturing sector, however, are planning an 8.4% increase in capital spending, after a 1.6% gain last year.

Source: *Wall Street Journal*, June 15, 1992.

Article 7 shows that planned capital spending for 1992 was $553.86 billion; up 4.6% from 1991. What is capital spending? Why do firm's invest? Why do capital expenditures increase and/or decrease from year to year? As you can see from this article, the investment decisions of business enterprises involve large sums of money and have a significant impact on the investing firms and on the economy as a whole. In 1990, total business expenditures in the United States for new plant and equipment exceeded $530 billion.[1] As Figure 2.1 shows, this amount represents an increase of more than 86% over the $286.4 billion invested in 1980. Taken in the aggregate, these capital expenditures constitute the economy's link with the future; the current investment decisions made by individual firms are a major determining factor of tomorrow's output. To the firm, these decisions, which shape both the pattern and growth

1. U.S. Bureau of the Census, *Statistical Abstract of the United States: 1991*. Washington, D.C.

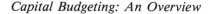

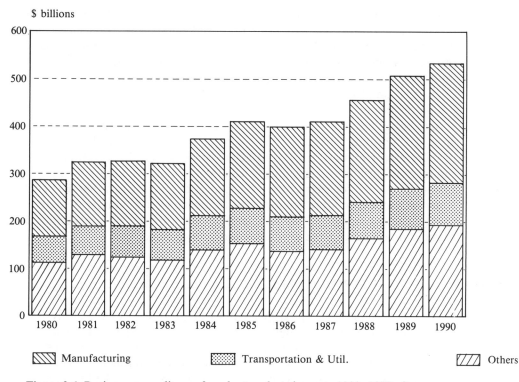

Figure 2.1 Business expenditures for plant and equipment, 1980–1990. *Source*:
U.S. Bureau of Census, *Statistical Abstract of the United States:
1991*, Washington, D.C.

of future output, constitute one of the most demanding challenges confronting
management, since in large measure the future benefits are irrevocably determined by today's capital budgeting decisions. In this chapter we sketch in
broad outline some of the considerations underlying these capital expenditure
decisions.

_____ **DEFINING CAPITAL EXPENDITURES**

What is a capital expenditure? In the typical capital investment decision
management makes a commitment of current resources in order to secure a
stream of benefits in future years. However, there is no sharp conceptual
difference between so-called capital and current expenditures; it is fair to say
that *all* of the firm's expenditures are made in expectation of realizing future
benefits. The firm is continuously confronted by the problem of deciding if a
proposed use of resources is worth while in terms of the prospective benefits.
However, when the time horizon is short, say less than one year (for example,
an increase in inventories or trade credit), *both* the costs and the benefits of
a given proposal can be set out in *current* dollars.

When, though, a significant period of time elapses between the outlay and the benefits, the problem of evaluating and comparing costs and benefits becomes more difficult. As a result, many firms apply formal capital budgeting procedures only to projects in which more than one year elapses between the initial investment outlay and the receipt of the project's final benefits. This distinction is completely arbitrary and reflects the underlying assumption that the timing of receipts can be ignored for time periods of less than one year.[2]

Many firms also limit their formal capital budgeting procedures to relatively large expenditures. This constraint is necessary if management time (a resource in short supply in most firms) is to be economized. The board of directors or capital appropriations committee is usually unwilling to discuss the merits of a proposed switch to electric pencil sharpeners despite the fact that the benefits from such an expenditure are expected to accrue over a number of years. Of course, the concept of a *relatively large* expenditure has no precise meaning outside the context of the particular problem at hand.

BREAKDOWN OF CAPITAL EXPENDITURES

Table 2.1 gives the total capital spending by major industries in billions of dollars for 1991 and projected figures for 1992. An increase in capital spending is normally accompanied by optimism and a decrease is generally interpreted as a sign of a recession. It is interesting that while the total spending is expected to increase in 1992 by 4.7% (which could be a good sign), the breakdown of the increase is not as promising since the increase is mainly in the commercial

Table 2.1 Capital spending by major industries ($billions)

	Actual total 1991	Anticipated total 1992
All Industries	529.20	553.86
Manufacturing	183.61	179.21
Durable	77.95	75.18
Nondurable	105.66	104.03
Mining	10.02	8.98
Railroad	5.92	7.41
Air Transp.	10.22	10.00
Other Transp.	6.55	7.14
Public Utilities	66.51	72.81
Commercial & Other	246.37	268.31

Source: *Wall Street Journal*.

2. Of course, the difference between a time lag of say six months and six years is not a difference of kind but only one of degree. However, in this context, it may be worth while to recall Norbert Wiener's remark that the difference between *fatal* and *medicinal* doses of strychnine is also only a matter of degree.

categories and public utilities. It is expected to decline in the manufacturing and mining categories and therefore may be a bad sign that more products consumed by the American consumer will be produced abroad. This can exacerbate the difficulty in the American economy, and, in particular, in the automotive industry.

THE CAPITAL BUDGETING PROCESS

Capital budgeting is a many-sided activity which includes: the formulation and articulation of long-term goals; searching for new and profitable uses for investment funds; the preparation of engineering, marketing and financial forecasts; the preparation of appropriation and control budgets and the integration of these budgets in the firm's information system; the economic evaluation of alternative projects; and the post-audit of the performance of past projects.

Long-term goals

A systematic approach to capital investment decisions requires the formulation of a set of long-term goals which can serve as a guide for managerial decisions. As already noted in Chapter 1, we assume throughout the book that management is concerned with maximizing the value of the firm's common stock. For the purposes of capital budgeting this means that other things being equal, management will strive to secure the highest net return on its capital investments which is compatible with the risks incurred. Of course, many investment projects cannot be described completely in terms of monetary costs and benefits: for example, a new cafeteria for the workers or an executive dining room. However, even in these cases a systematic calculation of the profitability of alternative investments can provide a benchmark for evaluating the otherwise intangible benefits.

Generating investment proposals

Another prerequisite for systematic capital management is so obvious that it is often neglected. A good investment proposal is not just born – someone has to suggest it. In the absence of a creative search for new investment opportunities even the most sophisticated evaluation techniques are worthless. In addition, someone within the firm must be willing to 'listen' to such proposals. In other words, a method must also be found for transferring proposals to the decision level. Clearly, the optimal method for identifying and generating investment proposals differs from industry to industry and even from firm to firm. A large chemical plant or electrical manufacturer is likely to have a well-equipped research and development division charged with the task of finding economically feasible and attractive uses for sophisticated new products or processes. In a small machine shop the search for investment possibilities may be less formal or structured. It often takes the form of an employees' 'suggestion box' or discussion during a coffee break. Article 8 relates a rather successful story of how employees and managers cooperate to create new ideas, projects and cost-cutting methods. Indeed, this perspective for systematic capital budgeting may be obvious but it is often neglected.

Working Together

A Manufacturer Grows Efficient by Soliciting Ideas From Employees

Eaton Gets Continuous Gains From a Team Approach And a System of Bonuses

Making a Die Last Longer

By Thomas F. O'Boyle

LINCOLN, ILL. – It's 7:30 a.m., time for the morning quiz at Eaton Corp.'s factory here. Ten union workers, each representing work teams, sit around a board-room table. 'What were our sales yesterday?' asks a supervisor at the head of the table. A worker, glancing at a computer printout, replies that they were $625,275. 'And in the month?' From another worker comes the response: $6,172,666.

The staccato review continues on to other vital statistics: the cost of materials and supplies used the day before; the cost of labor, shipping and utilities.

The aim of the exercise isn't simply to help workers understand the bottom line but also to get their help in enhancing it. Out on the shop floor minutes later, Glen Naugle, a worker, tells plant manager William Kelly how sandblasting welding electrodes, rather than machining them, would save $5,126 a year. It's the 193rd time in the past year that Lincoln workers have formally presented their ideas on improving operations to managers.

Savings Significant

The savings resulting from such suggestions total $1.4 million and helped Lincoln increase its first-quarter profit 30% from a year earlier. In the process, employees have earned $44,000 in 'Eaton

bucks,' credits they swap at the factory store for things like sporting goods. ...

It also explains why Main Street has surprised Wall Street this year. U.S. corporate profits rose 8% in the first quarter from the 1991 fourth period, the Commerce Department says, for the biggest such gain in four years. Eaton's own first-quarter results were 25% higher than Wall Street analysts had expected ...

Management shares extensive financial data with employees at the two plants to underscore the link between their performance and the factory's. At Kearney, a TV monitor in the cafeteria indicates how specific shifts and departments did the previous day against their cost and performance goals. Lincoln gets the message out via computer printouts. 'It gives you a sense of direction,' says Ricky Rigg, a metal fabricator, 'and makes you appreciate what you do more.' ...

There's noncash recognition as well. On a recent Wednesday, the Kearney plant held a lunchtime barbecue to mark the first shift's 365th consecutive day without any injuries. Plant Manager Dyer and his staff prepared the meal – hamburgers, hot dogs, potato salad and baked beans – while the first shift chowed down. *Source*: *Wall Street Journal*, June 5, 1992, p. 20.

Depending on the size and organization of the firm, formal requests for investment funds are made by heads of operating divisions or departments, often in conjunction with research and planning units. These requests are usually based explicitly on an expanding volume of sales of existing products, market research, technical engineering and methods studies, employee suggestions, significant changes in the competitive environment, and so on.

From the viewpoint of capital budgeting a broad interpretation of the term 'investment' is desirable. Thus the search for investment opportunities should encompass the acquisition of *existing* production and marketing facilities by means of a merger with another company as well as the expansion of the company's own facilities or the creation of an entirely new division. The problems created by business mergers are sufficiently different and important to warrant separate treatment. In many large companies trained specialists concentrate on discovering and analyzing the benefits of potential acquisitions of existing firms by the parent corporation. The need for specially trained staff reflects the complex legal, tax, financing, and accounting considerations attendant with external acquisitions.

Estimating cash flows and classifying projects

From the inception of the proposal, the expected costs and revenues generated by the project must be estimated. Often, the rough preliminary estimates which are prepared when the project is first defined have to be revised and refined when the proposal is incorporated in the firm's formal budget. Finally, on the eve of the actual budgeting decision, these revised estimates must be further refined and presented in the form of an appropriation request.

The relevant engineering, marketing and financial data must be compiled and collated from numerous departments and divisions throughout the firm. In the final stage, many of the cost estimates will be replaced by the actual offers made by supplying companies. However, the timing and magnitude of future cash flows usually retain their uncertainty throughout the budgeting process, and for that matter over the course of the project's life as well.

The estimation of cash flows is sufficiently important to warrant separate treatment, and Chapter 5 is devoted to a detailed examination of the principles underlying such forecasts. It may be well worth our while, however, to consider some alternative classifications of investment projects which can help the firm to develop standardized estimation and administration procedures for handling particular classes of proposals.

Let us consider briefly a few of the many possible ways of classifying investment projects.[3]

---

3. Of course, the 'best' classification scheme for some firms may be not to classify projects at all beyond their estimated profitability and probability of success. This is the practice in many smaller companies in which the executives are familiar with almost all aspects of the projects being considered. See National Association of Accountants, *Financial Analysis to Guide Capital Expenditure Decisions*, Research Report 43, July 1967, chapter 3.

By project size

The amount of cash resources required to implement the project provides a useful way of differentiating three classes of investments: major projects, regular capital expenditures, and small proposals. For example, one firm affords separate treatment to 'major projects', defined as initial expenditures of over $250,000. Another applies formal capital budgeting procedures to expenditures in excess of $5,000; while smaller projects are exempted from formal approval. Similarly, projects can be classified by the type of scarce resources used: land, key management personnel, floor space, and so on.

By type of benefit

Benefits can arise either from cost reductions, expansion of sales of existing products, expansion into new lines of business, risk reduction, or social overhead investments designed to improve general working conditions. Hot showers for workers, improved antipollution facilities, and perhaps even a contribution to the community welfare fund are examples of the latter type of investment.

By degree of dependence

Interdependence between two investment projects is another category and can arise for several reasons:

1. It may be technically impossible to undertake both investment A and investment B. Such investments are *mutually exclusive*, since the acceptance of one precludes the acceptance of the other. The early identification of mutually exclusive alternatives is crucial for a logical screening of investments; much effort, even more patience, and often money are wasted when two divisions independently investigate, develop and initiate projects which are recognized later as mutually exclusive. Numerous examples of such investments leap to mind: a basketball court and a swimming pool cannot be constructed on the same vacant lot; when a manufacturing plant is located near the sources of raw materials this may often mean that it cannot be close to the market; a power-generating plant can be nuclear or coal fired, but not both.

2. If the decision to execute the first investment increases the expected benefits from the second project, the proposals are said to be *complements*. For example, the construction of a water-recycling facility may have a positive impact on the profitability of a number of other projects.

3. If the acceptance of one project decreases the profitability of a second project they are said to be *substitutes*. Thus when a large razor-blade manufacturer such as Gillette contemplated the introduction of stainless steel blades, the forecasted revenue from the sale of new blades was offset, in part, by a decline in the expected sales of its conventional blades. No such consideration hampered Wilkinson Ltd, the British firm which first introduced stainless steel blades. Presumably Wilkinson assumed that the proceeds from razor blade sales were *economically independent* of the

revenue from their other line of ceremonial swords. (They ignored the possibility that naval officers who previously shaved with their Wilkinson swords would now switch to Wilkinson blades, thereby decreasing the replacement demand for the former.)

4. Economic independence or dependence must be distinguished from another type of interrelationship, namely *statistical independence* (or *dependence*). Two projects are said to be statistically dependent when increases (decreases) in the benefits from the one are accompanied by an increase (decrease) in the benefits of the second. Thus, the revenue from two lines of luxury goods (for example, caviar and Cadillacs) are likely to fluctuate together over time.[4]

By type of cash flow

Another type of classification is technical in nature but can prove useful when analyzing alternative measures of profitability. Here the forecasted cash flows of a project are examined and classified as either conventional or nonconventional. A conventional investment project is defined as one in which the initial outlay is followed by a stream of positive net receipts of the form: $- + + + ...$; or if the outlay takes place over a number of years, the cash flow has the form: $- - + + ...$. Some numerical examples will help to clarify the point. Consider the following investment projects whose cash flows are all of the conventional type.

Year	0	1	2	3	4	5
Project A	−100	+110	−	−	−	−
Project B	−100	−	−	−	+150	−
Project C	−100	+40	+40	+40	+40	+40
Project D	−100	−100	+80	+100	+50	+75

As can be seen from these examples, a conventional investment project is one whose cash flow has only one *change* in sign from a negative number to a positive number:[5] $- + + +$ or $- - + + +$ or $- +$. Hence projects with net terminal costs which have cash flows of the form $- + + + -$ are nonconventional since such projects have *two* changes in sign: the first following the initial investment outlay and the second preceding the terminal year. An example of a nonconventional project is provided by the case of a strip mining or quarrying project in which the company is required to restore the physical appearance of the concession after the supply of ore (stone) has been exhausted. Similarly, projects with initial positive receipts of the form $+ - + + +$ also have nonconventional cash flows. From the author's point

4. The statistical relationship among investment returns is an important factor when analyzing decisions under uncertainty, and is discussed in greater detail in Chapter 9.

5. From the borrower's point of view, a conventional loan also has a cash flow with only one change in sign but in reverse order, that is from the receipt to the negative repayments: $+ - -$, or $+ + - - -$, and so on.

of view, writing a textbook on capital budgeting provides an example of such a project; the initial receipt reflects the publisher's advance payment which precedes both the author's investment outlay and (hopefully) the later stream of royalties.

Many other classifications are possible. Some firms assign a priority rating to alternative proposals; classifying projects as 'urgent', 'required', 'desirable', and so on. Others classify investment alternatives by the location of the projects within the firm or within a division. The various classification schemes are *not* mutually exclusive; a firm can, and many do, use all of the above-mentioned classifications at one stage or another in their budgeting process.

THE ADMINISTRATIVE FRAMEWORK

A systematic approach to capital budgeting requires an administrative framework which facilitates the gathering and transferring of relevant information on alternative courses of action both for purposes of decision-making as well as for the control of expenditures, once these decisions have been reached. This requires a uniform set of procedures and forms which can be used to check project estimates for accuracy and against budget limits as well as to transfer the proposals to the decision level.

Figure 2.2 sets out a highly simplified flowchart for a typical investment proposal. The emphasis is on the importance of feedback from operating results both for control and for the future planning of new projects. The flowchart assumes that the firm employs a formal capital budget based on intensive financial planning. Practice, however, is far from uniform even among the medium-sized and large firms which typically budget their capital expenditures. Length of the budget period, definition of projects, evaluation techniques and administrative procedures vary greatly from firm to firm. Many firms divide their efforts between a long-term planning budget which rarely exceeds five years and a short-term one-year capital budget. The former is usually general in nature and often indicates *areas* of future interest rather than specific investment proposals. For example, the rough order of magnitudes of planned investment in fixed assets such as land, buildings and machines is projected by divisions, by product line or by manufacturing process. The short-term budget is more specific and includes the final estimates of the proposed projects. It is this budget which provides the cornerstone of the firm's control of its capital expenditures, and in fact, except in firms of very moderate size, some sort of short-term budget appears to be a necessity if management is to control its capital expenditures.

The post-completion audit of capital investment projects is one stage of the decision-making process which is often overlooked. Strictly speaking, the post-audit is not part of the current decision-making process since it refers to implemented projects. However, a systematic program of evaluating past decisions can contribute to the improvement of current decision-making by analyzing the patterns of past estimation errors by department, by personnel,

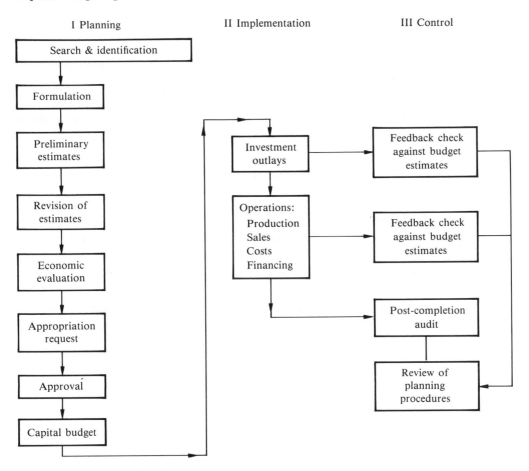

Figure 2.2 Project planning.

or by type of expenditure. The accumulated information can be extremely valuable in revising current forecasting and evaluation methods.

The post-audit is a necessary management tool because even the best laid plans of management may not have a happy ending. Although past mistakes cannot be undone, a careful analysis of the deviations of actual from planned performance may help to prevent history repeating itself. If investment outlays are consistently underestimated by 5–10%, a rule of thumb correction may be called for. In general, the post-audit can be a sobering and rewarding experience for most decision-makers.

_____ **SUMMARY**

This chapter has sketched out a broad overview of the capital budgeting process. A capital investment project can be distinguished from current expenditures by two features:

1. Such projects are relatively large.
2. A significant period of time (more than one year) elapses between the investment outlay and the receipt of the summary benefits.

As a result, most medium-sized and large firms have developed procedures and methods for dealing with these decisions. A systematic approach to capital budgeting implies:

1. The formulation of long-term goals.
2. The creative search for the identification of new investment opportunities.
3. Classification of projects and recognition of economically and/or statistically dependent (independent) proposals.
4. The estimation and forecasting of current and future cash flows.
5. A suitable administrative framework capable of transferring the required information to the decision level.
6. The controlling of expenditures and careful monitoring of crucial aspects of project execution.

Finally, a set of decision rules which can differentiate acceptable from unacceptable alternatives is required. It is to this key problem that we turn our attention in Chapter 3.

SUMMARY TABLE

Classification of investment projects

By project size
Small projects may be approved by departmental managers. More careful analysis, and approval by the board of directors, is needed for large projects of say $\$\frac{1}{2}$ million or more.

By type of benefit to the firm

1. An increase in cash flow.
2. A decrease in risk.
3. Indirect benefits (showers for workers, etc.).

By degree of dependence

1. Mutually exclusive projects: you can execute project A or project B, but not both.
2. Complementary projects: taking project A increases the cash flow of project B.
3. Substitute projects: taking project A decreases the cash flow of project B.

By degree of statistical dependence (discussion of these statistical relationships is in Chapter 10)

1. Positive dependence.
2. Negative dependence.
3. Statistical independence.

By type of cash flow

1. Conventional cash flow: only one change in the cash flow sign: for example $- + + + +$ or $+ - - - -$.
2. Nonconventional cash flows: more than one change in the cash flow sign, for example $+ - + + +$ or $- + - + + + +$.

_____ **QUESTIONS AND PROBLEMS**

2.1 Why is it necessary to assume a goal for the firm when applying capital budgeting methods?

2.2 Give two examples for each of the following types of investment projects:

(a) Mutually exclusive projects.
(b) Complementary projects.
(c) Substitute projects.
(d) Independent projects.

2.3 Define 'conventional' and 'nonconventional' projects.

2.4 Set out the cash flow generated by the following activities:

(a) Developing a new project requiring an investment of $800,000. This project will generate annual receipts of $250,000 for the next six years.
(b) A firm invests $3 million in a new project and expects annual receipts of $600,000 for the first three years and $900,000 during the last five years.
(c) Mr. Smith borrows $5,000 from the bank. The loan is repayable in seven equal annual instalments of $950 each.
(d) An investment of $75,000 in new equipment is expected to generate annual net receipts of $45,000 for four years starting at the third year.
(e) A firm takes a three-year loan of $100,000 which is to be repaid at the end of the third year in a lump sum payment of $130,000.

2.5 The Western Company is considering introducing a new product line. The required investment outlay is $650,000 this year and $550,000 the following year. The expected net receipts are $750,000 two years from now, $500,000 in the third year and $250,000 in the fourth year. In the fourth year the firm will have to invest an additional $600,000 to improve the product in order to generate net receipts of $400,000 in the fifth year and sixth year, and $500,000 in the seventh year. Set out the cash flow of this project.

2.6 'Improving capital investment decisions in practice is relatively simple; after all it all boils down to finding the correct decision rule.' Evaluate this statement.

2.7 Inquire at a corporation in your area as to their capital budgeting process. Be sure to have specific questions to identify and clarify the various stages of the process. Based on the information available, prepare a flowchart of this company's methodological approach to capital budgeting.

2.8 An electronics firm invented a new, high-quality 'Walkman' radio. More people will use 'Walkmans' in the future. The firm also produces batteries. Are these two products complements or substitutes?

2.9 In a given firm the chief executive officer insists on examining all potential investment projects. Due to time constraints, he cannot examine more than 100 projects a year.

(a) In 1992 the firm had 90 potential projects to evaluate.
(b) In 1993 the firm had 101 potential projects to evaluate.

What can be said about the project classifications in these two years?

2.10 There are two cars that a manufacturing firm is considering producing. They have the following cash flows:

	Year	
	t_0	t_1
Car A	− $10	$20
Car B	− $5	$10

However, if the firm decides to produce both cars then the combined cash flows are:

	Year	
	t_0	t_1
A + B	− $15	$30

How would you classify these two projects?

2.11 Answer problem 2.10 with the additional information that if both cars were produced, costs would be saved and hence the cash flows would be:

	Year	
	t_0	t_1
A + B	− $12	$25

2.12 Writing a textbook, the authors first write four chapters (one year's work) then send them to a few publishers. If the publishers like the chapters, a contract is offered. The author is paid advances upon signing the contract then works on the book for another year or two (with no income from the publisher). When the book is completed and sold the authors receive royalties. Write the cash flow signs of such a project. Is this a conventional project?

2.13 You deposit $1,000 in the bank and receive every six months $30 semi-annual interest. At the end of the second year you get back the principal. Is this a conventional project? Write the cash flows involved.

2.14 You receive a student loan of $5,000. After three years you return $700 a year for ten years. Write down the cash flows. Are the cash flows conventional? What are the bank's (lender) cash flows? Are the cash flows conventional from the lender's point of view?

SELECTED REFERENCES

Ang, J. S., 'A Graphical Presentation of an Integrated Capital Budgeting Model,' *Engineering Economist*, Winter 1978.

Bernanke, B. S., 'The Determinants of Investment: Another Look,' *American Economic Review*, Vol. 73, 1983.

Casey, Cornelius J. and Bartczak, Norman J., 'Cashflow – It's Not the Bottom Line,' *Harvard Business Review*, July–August 1984.

Churchill, Neil C., 'Budget Choice: Planning vs. Control,' *Harvard Business Review*, July/August 1984.

Dornbush, Rudiger, Fischer, Stanley, and Bossons, John, *Macroeconomics and Finance: Essays in Honor of Franco Modigliani*, Cambridge, Mass.: MIT Press, 1987.

Durand, D., 'Comprehensiveness in Capital Budgeting,' *Financial Management*, Winter 1981.

Hubbard, C. M., 'Flotation Costs in Capital Budgeting: A Note on the Tax Effect,' *Financial Management*, Summer 1984.

Larcker, D. F., 'The Perceived Importance of Selected Information Characteristics for Strategic Capital Budgeting Decisions,' *Accounting Review*, July 1981.

Meal, H. C., 'Putting Production Decisions Where They Belong,' *Harvard Business Review*, March/April 1984.

Petty, J. W., Scott, D. F. Jr., and Bird, M. M., 'The Capital Expenditure Decision-Making Process of Large Corporations,' *The Engineering Economist*, Spring 1975.

Pinches, G. E., 'Myopia, Capital Budgeting and Decision Making,' *Financial Management*, Autumn 1982.

Ross, Marc, 'Capital Budgeting Practices of Twelve Large Manufacturers,' *Financial Management*, Winter 1986.

Shapiro, Matthew D., 'Investment, Output and the Cost of Capital,' *Brookings Papers on Economic Activity*, Vol. 1 1986.

3

The Economic Evaluation of Investment Proposals

ARTICLE 9

CUSTOMER'S CHOICE
'Perfect Family Cars with the Budget in Mind'

1991 CORSICA
Loaded!
Over $12,800 new!

- Automatic
- A/C
- AM/FM stereo
- Power windows
- Tilt wheel
- Buckets & console

*Tax and tag to be paid in cash. 10.9% APR with approved credit, 60 months, deferred payments $9,761. Amount of finance: $7,500. Previous Short Term Lease

ONLY
$164
per month

AND ONLY
$388
down

$7888

1992 PONTIAC LEMANS
(2 or 4 Door)

These vehicles sell for over $10,800 new!

- Auto
- A/C
- Stereo
- Buckets & console

All lemans less 'than 12,000 miles'

*Tax and tag to be paid in cash. 10.9% APR with approved credit. 60 months, deferred payments $9,761. Amount to finance: $7,500. Previous short term lease.

Source: adapted from the *Gainesville Sun*, June 8, 1992, p. 8B.

As the advertisement in article 9 suggests, you can either get the 1992 Pontiac Lemans by paying $7,888 cash, or paying $164 per month for sixty months with a down-payment of $388. (Both alternatives involve taxes, title and transfer fees, but since they are the same for both, we can ignore them in this analysis.) Suppose that you have the cash readily available. What is the preferred alternative? To answer this question (which we solve in detail shortly), the concept of the time value of money must be introduced. Once this concept is understood, we turn our attention to a problem which lies at the very heart of the capital budgeting process – the economic evaluation of a project's desirability. This requires the stipulation of a decision rule for accepting or rejecting investment projects.

TIME VALUE OF MONEY

The expression 'time is money' is considered by many to be almost as American as apple pie. However, from the standpoint of investment analysis, its significance stems not from its national origin, but from the fact that a dollar received tomorrow is not equivalent to a dollar in hand today. And as the typical capital investment decision invariably involves the comparison of present outlays and future benefits, problems relating to the timing of receipts and outlays lie at the very heart of the capital budgeting process.

In order to focus attention on the implications of the time value of money for decision-making, let us initially assume that the costs and benefits of alternative investment projects are known with *certainty*. But even if the magnitudes of the relevant cash flows are known, attention must still be paid to their timing when weighing the desirability of an investment proposal. This will become clearer if we consider the following example of a project which requires an immediate investment outlay of $1,000, and which returns $1,100 with certainty exactly one year later. Does it pay to make such an investment, i.e., does it pay to give up $1,000 today in order to receive $1,100 one year hence? Clearly the answer depends on the alternative use we have for the $1,000. If, for example, we assume that we can earn 12% interest by depositing the $1,000 in a bank, the value of the deposit at the end of the year will be $1,120 ($1,000 × 1.12). And since $1,120 exceeds $1,100, the proposed investment is *not* desirable. On the other hand, if the bank pays only 8% interest, the value of the account at the end of the year will be $1,080. Since $1,080 is less than $1,100, the original proposal is worth while and, other things being equal, is preferred.

Clearly, an intelligent investment decision requires the comparison of alternatives; and it is the fact that money can always earn a positive return that lends importance to the time dimension of the typical capital investment project. A dollar given up today is not equivalent to a dollar received in the future as long as there exists the alternative of earning a positive return on the dollar in the interim.

Let us denote the relevant alternative annual rate of return which can be earned in the market, independent of the decision under consideration, by the letter k. What is the value of a dollar which will be received one year from now? To answer this question let us first check the *future value* (FV) of one dollar, i.e. principal plus accumulated interest at the end of the year. Given the alternative return k, the future value of a dollar is given by:

$$FV_1 = 1 \times (1 + k)$$

where FV_1 denotes the future value of one dollar at the end of year 1. If

$k = 10\%$ we have

$$FV_1 = 1 \times (1 + 0.10) = 1 + 0.10 = \$1.10$$

What is the future value of one dollar the end of two years?[1] As we have already noted, its value at the end of the first year will be $1.10, so that in the second year an additional 10% will be earned on $1.10 (not just on one dollar):

$$FV_2 = 1.10 + 0.11 = \$1.21$$

where FV_2 denotes the value at end of two years, or in symbols:

$$FV_2 = 1 \times (1 + k)(1 + k) = 1 \times (1 + k)^2$$

In general, the future value of one dollar at the end of n years will be

$$FV_n = 1 \times (1 + k)^n$$

Now let us take a concrete example and find the future of $1,000 after five years assuming that k is again equal to 10% each year. The relevant calculations are set out in Table 3.1. The future value at the end of two years is the same as that which we found using the formula for one dollar, multiplied of course by 1,000 ($1.21 \times 1,000 = \$1,210$). Similarly, the future value after three years is given by:

$$FV_3 = FV_2(1 + 0.10) = 1,210(1 + 0.10) = \$1,331$$

But as $FV_2 = FV_1(1 + k)$ and $FV_1 = V_0(1 + k)$ where V_0 denotes the amount invested at the beginning of the first year, we can set the same result as follows:

$$FV_3 = V_0(1 + k)^3$$

Applying this formula to the above example we obtain:

$$FV_5 = V_0 \times (1 + k)^5$$
$$= 1,000(1 + 0.10)^5 = \$1,611$$

Again V_0 denotes the amount invested at the beginning of the first year, which

Table 3.1 Future value calculations

Year	(1) Amount at beginning of year ($)	(2) Interest factor ($k = 10\%$)	(3) = (1) × (2) Future value ($)
1	1,000	1.10	1,100
2	1,100	1.10	1,210
3	1,210	1.10	1,331
4	1,331	1.10	1,464
5	1,464	1.10	1,611

1. Throughout the discussion we assume annual compounding; for the effects of alternative assumptions regarding the frequency of compounding, see Appendix 3A.

in this example is equal to $1,000. (Note that k denotes the alternative annual rate of return the firm can earn in the market. Later on we shall call this the firm's cost of capital. We use k and r interchangeably in this chapter where r stands for the annual interest rate.) Of course, this equation is a special version of the general formula for compound interest over time and can be applied to any amount of money using any interest rate. Thus if we want to know the future value to which V_0 dollars will accumulate in n years when it is compounded annually at some rate of interest r we can write:

$$V_n = V_0(1 + r)^n$$

In a world of electronic computers, the calculation of compound future values has been reduced to the mechanical reading of numbers from a table. Using the above compound interest formula we can easily generate the figures of Table 3.2 which gives the value of $(1 + r)^t$ for alternative values of r and t. The future value of any initial amount can be found by multiplying that amount by the relevant interest factor from Table 3.2. In our previous example we assumed a 10% compound rate and a five-year time horizon. The corresponding interest factor, 1.611, is found in line 5, column 10 of Table 3.2, and the future value of $1,000 at the end of five years is $1,611 as before:

$$1,000 \times 1.611 = \$1,611$$

It requires only a minor extension of the compound interest formula to derive the formula for *present value* (*PV*) rather than future value. Denoting V_0 by *PV* and dividing both sides of the formula $FV_n = PV(1 + r)^n$ by $(1 + r)^n$ we derive:

$$PV = \frac{FV_n}{(1 + r)^n}$$

which can be read as the present value (*PV*) of V dollars received at the end of n years (FV_n). As we have seen, this discounting of future sums is the opposite side of the compound interest formula. If we again assume that the firm's alternative annual rate of return is given by k, we can write the present value

Table 3.2 Compounded future value of $1

Year hence	1%	2%	3%	4%	5%	6%	7%	8%	9%	10%
1	1.010	1.020	1.030	1.040	1.050	1.060	1.070	1.080	1.090	1.100
2	1.020	1.040	1.061	1.082	1.102	1.124	1.145	1.166	1.188	1.210
3	1.030	1.061	1.093	1.125	1.158	1.191	1.225	1.260	1.295	1.331
4	1.041	1.082	1.126	1.170	1.216	1.262	1.311	1.360	1.412	1.464
5	1.051	1.104	1.159	1.217	1.276	1.338	1.403	1.469	1.539	1.611
6	1.062	1.126	1.194	1.265	1.340	1.419	1.501	1.587	1.677	1.772
7	1.072	1.149	1.230	1.316	1.407	1.504	1.605	1.714	1.828	1.949
8	1.083	1.172	1.267	1.369	1.477	1.594	1.718	1.851	1.993	2.144
9	1.094	1.195	1.305	1.423	1.551	1.689	1.838	1.999	2.172	2.358
10	1.105	1.219	1.344	1.480	1.629	1.791	1.967	2.159	2.367	2.594

formula as follows:

$$PV = \frac{FV_n}{(1+k)^n}$$

Applying this formula to our previous one-year example ($k = 10\%$) we get:

$$PV = \frac{FV_1}{1+k} = \frac{\$1.10}{1+0.10} = \$1$$

that is, the present value of $1.10 to be received at the end of one year is one dollar. Similarly, the present value of $1.21 to be received at the end of two years is equal to one dollar:

$$\frac{FV_2}{(1+k)^2} = \frac{\$1.21}{(1+0.10)^2} = \$1$$

The line of reasoning behind the formula is very simple: given the alternative of earning 10% on his money, an individual (or firm) should never offer (invest) more than $1,000 to obtain $1,100 with certainty at the end of the year. If he pays more, say $1,010, he could have reached a higher future value by investing the $1,010 at 10%:

$$\$1,010(1+0.10) = \$1,111 > \$1,100$$

Alternatively we can apply the present value formula directly by noting that:

$$PV = \frac{\$1,100}{1+0.10} = \$1,000 < \$1,010$$

The present value of $1,100 received one year hence is only $1,000, which is less than the proposed investment outlay of $1,010 and therefore the proposed investment is not worth while. Modern time-discounted methods for evaluating investment projects are straightforward generalizations of this future value–present value relationship.

NET PRESENT VALUE (*NPV*)

The net present value (*NPV*) method of evaluating the desirability of investments can be defined as follows:

$$NPV = \frac{S_1}{1+k} + \frac{S_2}{(1+k)^2} + \frac{S_3}{(1+k)^3} + \cdots + \frac{S_n}{(1+k)^n} - I_0$$

or

$$NVP = \sum_{t=1}^{n} \frac{S_t}{(1+k)^t} - I_0$$

where:

S_t = the expected net cash receipt at the end of year t
I_0 = the initial investment outlay[2]
k = the discount rate, i.e, the required minimum annual rate of return
     on new investment
n = the project's duration in years

An investment proposal's *NPV* is derived by discounting the future net cash receipts at a rate which reflects the value of the alternative use of the funds, summing them over the life of the proposal and deducting the initial outlay. The actual calculation can be reduced to a very simple procedure by using Table 3.3.[3] The 10% discount factors of Table 3.3 which are used to reduce the receipts to their present values are defined as follows:

$$q_{(1,10\%)} = \frac{1}{(1 + 0.10)} = 0.909$$

$$q_{(2,10\%)} = \frac{1}{(1 + 0.10)^2} = 0.826$$

$$q_{(3,10\%)} = \frac{1}{(1 + 0.10)^3} = 0.751$$

where the two subscripts of each q denote the year in which the dollar was received and the 10% discount rate, respectively. They also indicate the relevant line (year) and column (discount rate) of Table 3.3. Thus $q_{(6,8\%)}$ is found by taking the factor appearing in line 6 and the 8% column of Table 3.3, that is, $q(6,8\%) = 0.630$.

Table 3.2 Present value of one dollar

Year hence	1%	2%	4%	5%	6%	8%	10%
1	0.990	0.980	0.962	0.952	0.943	0.926	0.909
2	0.980	0.961	0.925	0.907	0.890	0.857	0.826
3	0.971	0.942	0.889	0.864	0.840	0.794	0.751
4	0.961	0.924	0.855	0.823	0.792	0.735	0.683
5	0.951	0.906	0.822	0.784	0.747	0.681	0.621
6	0.942	0.888	0.790	0.746	0.705	0.630	0.564
7	0.933	0.871	0.760	0.711	0.665	0.583	0.513
8	0.923	0.853	0.731	0.677	0.627	0.540	0.467
9	0.914	0.837	0.703	0.645	0.592	0.500	0.424
10	0.905	0.820	0.676	0.614	0.558	0.463	0.386

2. Since the investment outlay may stretch over an extended period, a more general formulation would be to define I_0 as the present value of the investment outlays.
3. A more complete table of present value factors is given in the appendix tables at the end of the book.

If we denote years by the letter t and discount (interest) rates by r, a general formula for calculating the discount factor of one dollar can be written:

$$q_{(t,r)} = \frac{1}{(1+r)^t}$$

The solution of the above equation, for selected values of t and r, generates Table 3.3. To find the present value of any given sum S received in any year t, we multiply S by the appropriate discount factor. In the case of a business firm the discount rate used, k, is the minimum required annual rate of return on new investment, or 'cost of capital' as it is often called:

$$S \times q_{(t,k)} = S \times \frac{1}{(1+k)^t} = \frac{S}{(1+k)^t}$$

The actual calculation of the present value of the receipts, using Table 3.3, can be illustrated by the three-year project example below.

Year (t)	Net receipt (S)	Discount factor $q_{(t,10\%)}$	Present value of cash flow
1	400	0.909	363.60
2	600	0.826	495.60
3	500	0.751	375.50
		Total	1,234.70
		Less: Initial outlay (I_0)	−1,000.00
		NPV	+234.70

In the case of an annuity (uniform annual receipts) the calculation can be facilitated further by using Table 3.4 which is merely a summation of the relevant annual discount factors of Table 3.3. Thus, to find the present value of a five-year one-dollar annuity at 10% discount, we multiply $1 dollar by the factor appearing in line 5 of the 10% column of Table 3.4, that is 3.791 which is a summation of the first five factors in the 10% column of Table 3.3.

Table 3.4 Present value of an annuity of one dollar

Year	1%	2%	4%	5%	6%	8%	10%
1	0.990	0.980	0.962	0.952	0.943	0.926	0.909
2	1.970	1.942	1.886	1.859	1.833	1.783	1.736
3	2.941	2.884	2.775	2.723	2.673	2.577	2.487
4	3.902	3.808	3.630	3,546	3.465	3.312	3.170
5	4.853	4.713	4.452	4.329	4.212	3.993	3.791
6	5.795	5.601	5.242	5.076	4.917	4.623	4.355
7	6.728	6.472	6.002	5.786	5.582	5.206	4.868
8	7.652	7.325	6.733	6.463	6.210	5.747	5.335
9	8.566	8.162	7.435	7.108	6.802	6.247	5,759
10	9.471	8.983	8.111	7.722	7.360	6.710	6.145

The calculation of the *NPV* of an annuity can be illustrated by considering the example of an investment which for an initial outlay of $1,000 offers a net receipt of $400 per year for three years. First we find the relevant discount factor for a three-year annuity and a 10% discount rate, that is the discount factor appearing in line 3 of the 10% column of Table 3.4: 2.487. The present value of the receipts is given by:

$$400 \times 2.487 = 994.80$$

Therefore the *NPV* of the project is negative, -5.20, since the initial investment outlay exceeds the present value of the receipts:

$$944.8 - 1,000 = -5.20$$

Before we can apply the *NPV* method of project evaluation as a decision rule the goal for the firm must be defined. Assuming that management desires *more* rather than *less* 'bang for its buck', the following decision rules should be adopted:

If the *NPV* is positive, accept the project
If the *NPV* is negative, reject the project

where the present values are calculated using a discount rate which reflects the alternative annual return which the firm can earn on the capital in the market. Thus the firm should execute projects with a positive *NPV* and reject those proposals whose *NPV*s are negative.[4] These decision rules follow directly from the assumption that firms operate to maximize the market value of their common stock, since under the assumed conditions of certainty the prices of all assets, including common stocks, are determined by their discounted present values.[5] These decision rules result in an *optimal* choice of projects, because under the assumed conditions no other group of projects can be found which will increase the value of the firm.

A graphical representation of NPV

The size of a project's *NPV* depends, among other things, on the discount rate. This dependence can be 'visualized' by using a simple graphical device called the *NPV profile*. Consider the following example of a $100 investment which generates a $200 receipt at the end of one year:

$$NPV = \frac{S_1}{1+k} - I_0 = \frac{200}{1+k} - 100$$

Figure 3.1 graphs the *NPV* of this project as a function of the discount rate. When the discount rate is zero (at the intercept on the vertical axis) the *NPV*

4. We ignore projects with zero *NPV* since by definition the firm is indifferent to such proposals.
5. A formal proof of this proposition was given by P. A. Samuelson, 'Some Aspects of the Pure Theory of Capital,' *Quarterly Journal of Economics*, May 1937, pp. 469–96.

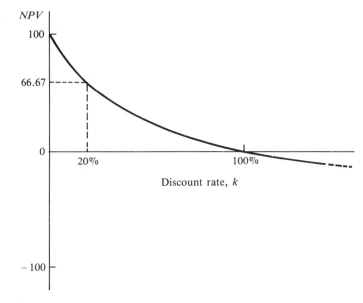

Figure 3.1

is given by:

$$NPV = \frac{200}{1 + 0} - 100 = 100$$

Conversely, if we let the discount rate become infinitely large, and approach infinity (∞), we get

$$NPV = \frac{200}{1 + \infty} - 100 = -100$$

If we set the discount rate equal to 100%, the *NPV* is exactly zero, which determines the intercept with the horizontal axis:

$$NPV = \frac{200}{1 + 1} - 100 = 0$$

These calculations determine three points on the *NPV* profile of the project which is drawn in Figure 3.1; the remaining points of the profile have been sketched in by permitting the discount rate to vary between zero and infinity.[6] From the diagram it is clear that the project's *NPV* is positive for all discount rates below 100%, and therefore should be accepted if the minimum required rate of return is less than 100%. For example if $k = 20\%$, the project has a positive *NPV* of $66.67:

$$NPV = \frac{200}{1 + 0.2} - 100 = 166.67 - 100 = \$66.67$$

6. We confine ourselves to positive values since the discount rate cannot be negative as long as money can earn a positive rate of interest in an alternative use.

The meaning of the *NPV* decision rule is clear. Assuming a 20% required annual rate of return, it pays the firm to invest $100 today in a one-year project if the return received at the end of the year exceeds $120. Since the project in question promises a return of $200, that is $80 in excess of the minimum required receipt ($120), the project should be accepted. The reader can also verify that the present value of the $80 profit is $80/1.2 = \$66.67$, which is the project's *NPV*.

Figure 3.2 generalizes the analysis for conventional multiperiod projects, that is, investment proposals having cash inflows in more than one year:

$$NPV = \sum_{t=1}^{n} \frac{S_t}{(1+k)^t} - I_0$$

When the discount rate (k) is equal to zero (at the intercept with the vertical axis), the *NPV* equals the algebraic sum of the stream of undiscounted net receipts minus the initial investment outlay:

$$\sum_{t=1}^{n} S_t - I_0$$

As the discount rate approaches infinity, the *NPV* reduces to $-I_0$. Since we have assumed conventional cash flows $(- + + + \cdots)$ the function slopes downward as the discount rate increases. For every increase in the discount rate the present value of the positive cash flow is decreased while the initial investment outlay remains unchanged, so that the project's *NPV* declines. Figure 3.2 shows that the project's *NPV* is positive, and therefore the proposal should be accepted for all discount rates (costs of capital) which are less than k.

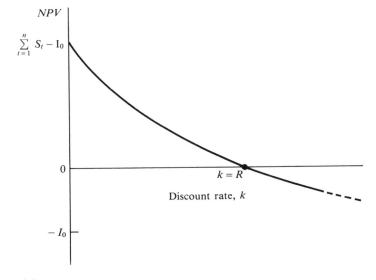

Figure 3.2

INTERNAL RATE OF RETURN

The *internal rate of return* (*IRR*) is another time-discounted measure of investment worth.[7] The IRR is defined as that rate of discount which equates the present value of the stream of net receipts with the initial investment outlay:

$$I_0 = \frac{S_1}{(1 + R)} + \frac{S_2}{(1 + R)^2} + \frac{S_3}{(1 + R)^3} + \cdots + \frac{S_n}{(1 + R)^n}$$

$$= \sum_{t=1}^{n} \frac{S_t}{(1 + R)^t}$$

where R denotes the internal rate of return (*IRR*). An alternative and equivalent definition of the *IRR* is 'the rate of discount which equates the *NPV* of the cash flow to zero':

$$\sum_{t=1}^{n} \frac{S_t}{(1 + R)^t} - I_0 = 0$$

The latter formula is somewhat more helpful in calculating the *IRR*, which for investments whose cash flows are received over a period of years, requires an iterative or 'trial and error' solution. The computational procedure is as follows: given the cash flows and investment outlay, choose a discount rate at random and calculate the project's *NPV*. If the *NPV* is positive, choose a *higher* discount rate and repeat the procedure; if the *NPV* is negative, choose a *lower* discount rate and repeat the procedure. (It may help to look back at Figure 3.1 to see this relationship.) The discount rate which makes the *NPV* = 0 is the *IRR*, and the procedure is completed.[8] Table 3.5 gives an example of such a calculation. Using an 8% discount factor the *NPV* is positive (+ 67.8) and therefore a higher rate, 15%, is chosen. This discount rate, however, results in a negative *NPV* (− 45.9) so that a discount rate which is lower than 15% but higher than 8% is required. A 12% discount rate reduces the project's *NPV* to zero so that by definition the project's *IRR* is 12%.

In cases of annuities, that is projects with equal annual receipts, Table 3.4 enables us to make a convenient short cut. To be more specific, in the case of constant cash flows per period, the *IRR* is given by the value R which solves the following formula:

$$\sum_{t=1}^{n} \frac{S}{(1 + R)^t} = I_0$$

7. Applied to the investment in real assets, this method is known under a variety of names including 'marginal efficiency of capital', 'discounted cash flow', 'investor's method', and so on. This is also the method which is used to compute the yield to maturity on a bond. The term 'internal rate of return' was first introduced by K. Boulding, 'The Theory of a Single Investment,' *Quarterly Journal of Economics*, May 1935, pp. 475–94.

8. For most projects, the *IRR* can be calculated by hand in a few minutes, but where necessary, standard computer programs are available to facilitate the calculations. Nowadays, however, the precise *IRR* can be easily obtained by employing a hand-held calculator.

Table 3.5 Calculation of *IRR* for a hypothetical project

Year	Net cash flow	Discount factor	Present value of cash flow
First iteration: 8% discount rate			
1	452	0.926	418.6
2	500	0.857	428.5
3	278	0.794	200.7
		PV of receipts	1,067.8
		Less: Initial outlay	−1,000.0
		NPV	+67.8
Second iteration: 15% discount rate			
1	452	0.870	393.2
2	500	0.756	378.0
3	278	0.658	182.9
		PV of receipts	954.1
		Less: Initial outlay	−1,000.0
		NPV	−45.9
Final iteration: 12% discount rate			
1	452	0.893	403.6
2	500	0.797	398.5
3	278	0.712	197.9
		PV of receipts	1,000.0
		Less: Initial outlay	−1,000.0
		NPV	0

where S is a constant, that is, $S_1 = S_2 = \cdots = S_n$. If we let $Q_{(n,k)}$ denote the discount factor in line (n) of Table 3.4, we can rewrite the *IRR* formula for an annuity as follows:

$$S \sum_{t=1}^{n} \frac{1}{(1+R)^t} = I_0 \quad \text{or} \quad SQ_{(n,R)} = I_0$$

Since the investment outlay (I_0) and the uniform annual receipt (S) are known, the discount factor Q can be determined by dividing S into I_0:

$$Q_{(n,R)} = \frac{I_0}{S}$$

The project's *IRR* is determined by looking along line n of Table 3.4 to find the column which includes this particular discount factor. Now let us apply the simplified annuity formula to a concrete example. Let

$S = \$20$ per year
$n = 7$ years
$I_0 = \$120$

First we find the discount factor,

$$Q_{(7,R)} = \frac{I_0}{S} = \frac{120}{20} = 6$$

A glance at line 7 of Table 3.4 shows that $Q_{(7,R)} = 6.002$ (which is approximately equal to 6) appears in the 4% column; hence the *IRR* of the annuity is approximately 4% per year.

Looking back at Figure 3.2, which graphs a project's *NPV* as a function of the discount rate, the *IRR* is located at the intercept with the horizontal axis, that is, at point *k*, since this is the rate of discount which reduces the *NPV* to zero (hence $k = R$). The reader can verify from this graph that for all $k < R$ the *NPV* is positive; conversely for all $k > R$ the *NPV* is negative. Unlike the *NPV* which may vary depending on the discount rate chosen, a project's *IRR* is fixed once and for all, independent of the discount rate. Thus the *IRR* decision rules must take the minimum required rate of return, *k*, explicitly into account:

If *R* is greater than *k*, accept the project.
If *R* is less than *k*, reject the project.

We again ignore the possibility of $R = k$ in which case the firm would be indifferent to the project.

AN ECONOMIC RATIONALE FOR THE *IRR* RULE

Although the *IRR* is easily calculated, its economic significance may not be intuitively obvious. What is the exact meaning of a 10% or 15% internal rate of return? Why must the *IRR* be higher than the opportunity cost of capital if the project is to be accepted? The answers to these questions can best be given within the context of a numerical example. Consider the cash flow to this hypothetical two-year investment proposal:

Year	0	1	2
Cash flow	−173.60	+100	+100

Dividing the uniform annual cash receipt (100) into the investment outlay (173.60) we find that the discount factor $Q_{(2,R)} = 1.736$. A glance at line 2 of Table 3.4 shows that this corresponds to an *IRR* of 10%. According to the *IRR* decision rule, that proposal should be accepted as long as the discount rate is less than 10%.

Common sense suggests that if the project earns 10% and we borrow the money needed to finance it at *less* than 10%, a profit will be made. That is, we will be able to repay the principal and interest out of the proceeds from the project and still have some money left. Should the bank demand more than 10%, the project's cash flow will be insufficient and a loss will be incurred; and if the interest rate exactly equals the project's *IRR*, the project will neither earn a profit nor suffer a loss, but will break even. If these relationships do not hold we may be in serious trouble because it would no longer be clear (to us at least) just why a project whose *IRR* is greater than *k* should be accepted.

To check the meaning of the *IRR* let us assume that the firm borrows from a bank the $173.60 necessary to implement the project, and that the bank charges 10% interest, that is an interest rate which just equals the project's *IRR*. If the *IRR* rule is to be meaningful, such a situation should result in a zero profit to the firm. Table 3.6 sets out the relevant transactions between the bank and the firm. At the end of this first year the firm pays the bank 10% interest on its loan of $173.60, that is $17.36, out of the cash proceeds from the project. But as the firm earned $100 from the project it is now able to repay part of the principal of the loan ($82.64) as well. At the end of the second year the interest payment to the bank in only $9.10 since the outstanding loan in the second year is only $90.96 ($10\% \times 90.96 \approx 9.10$). After paying the interest, $90.96 remains, which is just sufficient to repay the outstanding balance of the loan, so that the firm neither gains nor loses from the project (the small difference is due to rounding). We leave it to the reader to verify that had the bank charged 15% interest, the proceeds from the project would not have sufficed to pay the interest and principal on the loan. If we now generalize the arguments and substitute the minimum required rate of return (i.e., cost of capital[9]) for the interest rate on the bank loan, we can readily see the economic rationale for demanding $R > k$ as the necessary condition for accepting a project.

Now we are equipped with the tools to make the choice between the two alternatives given in the advertisement at the beginning of this chapter. If you invest $7,888 today by paying cash for the car, you save $164 every month plus $388 for the down-payment. What is the *IRR* on this investment? To answer this question we must solve the following equation:

$$7,888 = \sum_{t=1}^{60} \frac{164}{(1+R)^t} + 388$$

(Recall the down-payment is paid immediately and the monthly payment at the end of each month for sixty months.) We can rewrite this as:

$$7,500 = \sum_{t=1}^{60} \frac{164}{(1+R)^t}$$

Using a financial calculator, we find that R, the *IRR*, is about 0.937 on a

Table 3.6

	First year	Second year
Cash inflow	+100.00	+100.00
Interest payment	−17.36	−9.10
Payment of principal	−82.64	−90.96
Loan outstanding beginning of year	173.60	90.96
Loan outstanding end of year[a]	90.96	—

[a] $173.60 - 82.64 = 90.96$.

9. For further discussion of the cost of capital and its measurement, see Chapters 16 and 17.

monthly basis. On an annual basis it is 11.8% (that is, $1.00937^{12} - 1 = 0.118$). Recall that in 1992 the annual compounded interest rate paid on passbook savings accounts was approximately 3%, and on one-year certificate of deposits (i.e., CDs) approximately 5%. Therefore, if you had the cash in savings, you should pay for the car with cash (your savings) since you are earning less than 11.8%. Alternatively, if you did not have the funds necessary to purchase the car, and if your local financial institution's interest rate was less than 11.8% (indeed, the rate at many institutions during this same period was 9%), then you should purchase the car directly and finance it through a loan from your financial institution.

SUMMARY

In this chapter, problems associated with the time lag between a project's initial investment outlay and the receipt of the benefits have been examined. When evaluating the desirability of an investment proposal, consideration must be given to both the timing of the net receipts and to their magnitude, since a dollar invested today is not equivalent to a dollar received tomorrow, so long as there exists an alternative possibility of earning a positive return during the interim.

Two time-discounted methods of evaluating capital investment expenditures are defined. *Net present value* (*NPV*) is derived by discounting a project's cash receipts using the minimum required rate of return on new investment (cost of capital), summing them over the life of the proposal and deducting the initial investment outlay. *Internal rate of return* (*IRR*) is defined as that discount rate which equates the present value of the stream of net receipts with the initial outlay. All of the necessary calculations can be reduced to simple procedures by using present value tables which have been constructed for this purpose.

Assuming that the firm wishes to maximize the wealth of its shareholders, the following decision rules can be derived:

When the *NPV* is positive, accept the project.
When the *NPV* is negative, reject the project.

The following decision rules are associated with the *IRR* method:

When the *IRR* exceeds the discount rate, accept the project.
When the *IRR* is less than the discount rate, reject the project.

Since these two methods are closely related, we devote Chapter 4 to a comparison of their relative effectiveness in screening capital investment proposals.

Profitability measures

1.

$$NPV = \sum_{t=1}^{n} \frac{S_t}{(1+k)^t} - I_0$$

Accept a project if $NPV > 0$.

2. *IRR*: Solve for R from the equation:

$$\sum_{t=1}^{n} \frac{S_t}{(1+R)^t} = I_0$$

Accept a project if $R > k$.

Relationship between future value (*FV*) and present value (*PV*)

1. The future value of $1 invested for n years is:

$$FV = 1 \times (1+k)^n$$

2. The present value of $1 received n years from now is:

$$PV = \frac{1}{(1+k)^n}$$

3. The relationship between *FV* and *PV* is:

$$PV = \frac{FV}{(1+k)^n}$$

Continuous compounding and discounting (see Appendix 3A)

1. Continuous compounding of $1 received n years from now:

$$FV = 1e^{kn}$$

2. Continuous compounding of S_t dollars received (continuously) in time t for n years:

$$FV = \int_0^n S_t e^{kt} \, dt$$

3. Continuous discounting of $1 received n years from now:

$$PV = 1e^{-kn}$$

4. Continuous discounting of S_t dollars received (continuously) in time t for n years:

$$PV = \int_0^n S_t e^{-kt} \, dt$$

QUESTIONS AND PROBLEMS

3.1 Define the following terms:

(a) Time value of money.
(b) Present value.
(c) Future value.
(d) Internal rate of return (IRR).
(e) Net present value (NPV).

3.2 You are given the choice between $1,000 now or some amount of money one year from now.

(a) How large would the amount one year from now have to be for you to be indifferent between the two choices?
(b) Suppose that your choice is $1,100 one year from now. What does the answer to this question imply about the rate of interest during this time period?

3.3 How long does it take to double $100 if the interest rate is 8% compounded annually? How much would you get at the end of this period of time, if the $1,000 were an annual annuity?

3.4 If you decide to buy a house for which you have to pay $4,000 per year for eight years, and the interest rate is 10%, what is the equivalent price of the house if paid in a lump sum today?

3.5 Given the following cash flow:

Year:	0	1	2	3	4	5
	−3,352	1,000	1,000	1,000	1,000	1,000

(a) Calculate the net present value of the project using the following discount rates: 6, 10, 14, 15, 16, 20 and 24%.
(b) Graph the NPV of the project as a function of the discount rate.
(c) Find the internal rate of return, mathematically and graphically.

3.6 For each of the following investment projects, calculate:
(a) The net present value using a 15% discount rate.
(b) The internal rate of return.

Which project should be accepted?

Cash flow

Year	0	1	2	3	4	5	6	7
Project A	−4,564	1,000	1,000	1,000	1,000	1,000	1,000	1,000
Project B	−2,000	524.7	524.7	524.7	524.7	524.7	524.7	524.7
Project C	−21,000	3,000	3,000	3,000	3,000	3,000	3,000	3,000

3.7 For each of the following projects calculate:

(a) The net present value using a 20% discount rate.
(b) The internal rate of return.

Which project should be accepted given the stated decision rule?

Cash flow

Year:	0	1	2	3	4	5
Project A	− 370	−	−	−	−	1,000
Project B	− 240	60	60	60	60	−
Project C	− 263.5	100	100	100	100	100
Project D	− 200	56.8	56.8	56.8	56.8	56.8

3.8 For each of the following three projects, calculate:

(a) The net present value using a 16% discount rate.
(b) The internal rate of return.
(c) Graph the *NPV* of each project as a function of a discount rate. (Hint: calculate three points and draw the remaining segments of the curve in freehand.) Check your graphical answer with question (b).

Cash flow

Year:	0	1	2	3	4
Project A	− 800	350	350	350	100
Project B	− 70	40	25	25	25
Project C	− 20,000	2,000	8,000	14,000	4,466

3.9 A firm examines the following cash flow:

Year	0	1	2	3
Cash flow	−10,000	2,000	2,000	12,000

Assume a 12% cost of capital. Should the firm accept the project? Also, present the solution graphically.

3.10 Your business is expanding rapidly and as a result you are in need of additional capital. The bank offers you a loan under the following conditions: a loan of $100,000 repayable in five equal annual payments of $28,000 (the first payment at the end of the first year). Plot the *NPV* of the loan as a function of the discount rate by calculating the intercepts on the horizontal and vertical axis, and a third point of your own choice.

3.11 For each of the following projects:

(a) Calculate the net present value using a 10% discount rate.
(b) Calculate the internal rate of return.

Year:	0	1	2	3	4	5
Project						
A	− 50	17	17	17	17	17
B	50	−17	−17	−17	−17	−17
C	−100	−	−	−	100	−
D	0	5	5	5	5	5

3.12 The XYZ Corporation is evaluating the following two *mutually exclusive* projects:

Project A: Investment of $1,000, which generates an annual cash flow of $90 for the next 100 years.

Project B: Investment of $400, which generates an annual cash flow of $50 for the next 100 years.

Assume that the relevant discount rate (cost of capital) is 10%. Which of the projects should be preferred? Answer *without the use of the present value tables*.

3.13 Consider the following investments A through E all of which have a five-year expected life. These are the only investments available to the firm, and the cost of capital, k, is 10%.

Investment	Year					
	0	1	2	3	4	5
A	− 3,000	1,000	1,000	1,000	1,000	1,000
B	− 4,000	1,500	1,200	900	600	300
C	− 2,200	650	650	600	600	200
D	− 400	300	300	300	300	300
E	− 2,000	300	600	900	1,200	1,500

Assume that the cash flow of each of the above investments will be realized only if the investment is undertaken alone. For example, if investment A is chosen and B through E are rejected, then A's cash flow is as indicated above. However, if more than one investment is executed the following results will be realized:

(i) If A *and* B are both executed each cash flow will increase 10% while the initial investment will not be affected.

(ii) If B *and* C are executed each cash flow will decrease 15% while the initial investment will not be affected.

(iii) If A *and* C are executed the cash flow of each will increase by 30%; the initial investment outlay will not be affected.

(iv) If A, B, *and* C are executed, the initial investment outlay will not be affected but the cash flow of all three projects will increase by 7%.

(v) Executing A, B, C or any combination of these projects, excludes the possibility of choosing D or E.

(vi) If D *and* E are executed the cash flow of D will increase by 50%, the cash flow of E will decrease by 20% and the total initial investment of both projects (combined) will decrease by 10%.

Using the definition given in Chapter 2,

(a) Classify the investment combinations of A, B, C, D, and E as mutually exclusive, substitutes, complements or independent.

(b) Which investments should be undertaken and which should be rejected?

3.14 As a purchasing manager you determine that a specific machine will generate exactly $400 at the end of the first three years and then have no value. Four separate companies offer to sell this machine. Company 1 offers the machine for $1,000 today; company 2 offers the machine for $500 today and $500 at the end of the first year; company 3, understanding your preference for money today, offers the machine for $333 today and $333 at the end of the first and second year; company 4, desperate to sell you the machine, offers the machine for $250 today and $250 at the end of the next three years. For each offer, set up the cash flow stream and calculate the *IRR* and *NPV* (using 20% discount rate). Discuss the impact of time on investment outlay.

3.15 A project with a constant annual cash flow, $S_1 = S_2 = S_3 = \cdots = S_n = \$10.00$ has an *IRR* of $R = 20\%$. The initial investment is $41.92. What is the project's duration, n?

3.16 You take out a loan for $1,000 and have the following two options:

(i) Pay back the loan in annual instalments of $200 a year for the next 7 years, or
(ii) Pay back $1,600 at the end of the tenth year.

Your discount rate is 10%. Which alternative would you prefer? How would you change your answer if your discount rate were zero?

3.17 The initial outlay on project A is $I_0 = \$1,000$. The cash flow induced by this project is $S = \$800$ for one year only. Calculate the *IRR* of the project.

3.18 You have the following project:

Year	t_0	t_1	t_2
Cash flow	−$1,528	$1,000	$1,000

(a) Calculate the *IRR* of the project.
(b) You have no money to invest. Show that if the bank charges you an interest rate which is equal to the *IRR*, you exactly break even.

3.19 A firm faces the following project

Year	t_0	t_1	t_2
Cash flow	−$173.6	$100.00	$100.00

(a) Calculate the *IRR* of the project.
(b) Calculate the *NPV* of the project assuming a discount rate of 5%.
(c) You have no money, hence you intend to borrow $173.6 at 5%. Show that the cash flow is sufficient to return the principal and interest and still have some positive cash flow left. What is the *PV* of this cash flow?

3.20 Suppose that you have two projects, A and B. Project B's initial investment is twice the initial investment of project A. The cash flows of the projects are $S_B = 2S_A$, where S_B and S_A stand for the annual cash flows of projects B and A, respectively.

(a) State the NPV_B in terms of the NPV_A.
(b) Which project has the higher *IRR*?

3.21 It is given that the *IRR* of a project with a constant cash flow S for n years is positive. 'Hence the *NPV* of the project at a zero discount rate must be positive.' Do you agree? Prove your answer.

3.22 Suppose that an investment is evaluated by two partners, one of whom is American and the other German. They agree on the project's cash flows but one of them employs German marks and the other U.S. dollars. Suppose that a U.S.

dollar is worth 1.4 German marks:

(a) Do the partners get the same *IRR*?

(b) Do they get the same *NPV*?

3.23 In June 1992, Paul West, a Mitsubishi dealer, ran the following commercial:

> *'Pay for a new 1992 Mitsubishi Mirage $159.71 per month for sixty months or $7,694 cash, zero down-payment'.*

In 1992 the return on certificate of deposit was 4.5% a year. You could borrow from your bank at 8% per year for 5 years. You wish to buy the car. What is your best financing policy? Would you use the monthly payments offer or pay cash for the car?

APPENDIX 3A: CONTINUOUS COMPOUNDING AND DISCOUNTING

The fledgling, and perhaps the not so fledgling, student of finance is often puzzled by the bewildering variety of interest rates which banks and savings and loan associations offer on financial instruments. Many thrift institutions offer interest which is compounded semi-annually, quarterly or even daily. To this point we have assumed annual discounting, but to make sense out of the various offers we must adjust the interest formulas developed in the text to cover alternative assumptions regarding the frequency of compounding.

Obviously, for a given interest rate, the greater the frequency with which interest is earned, the higher the future value of the deposit, so that the investor is better off. Consider the following example. An individual deposits $100 in a bank for one year at an annual interest rate of 6%. The value of his account at the end of the year will be $100(1 + 0.06) = \$106$. Now, suppose the interest is compounded twice a year. In this case the value of the deposit at the end of the year is given by

$$100\left(1 + \frac{0.06}{2}\right)\left(1 + \frac{0.06}{2}\right) = 100\left(1 + \frac{0.06}{2}\right)^2 = \$106.10$$

The only difference between this calculation and the previous one is that in this instance the bank credits the account with $3 interest after six months have elapsed, so that for the next six months the investor earns 3% on $103 (and not on $100) or $3.09. The economic meaning of compounding within a given period is that the bank pays interest on the principal and the accumulated interest up to the compounding date. It follows that in the case of quarterly compounding the terminal value of the deposit is $100(1 + 0.06/4)^4$ and where interest is compounded daily the terminal value is $100(1 + 0.06/365)^{365}$. The maximum end-of-year value is achieved should the bank compound continuously; in this extreme case, the terminal value of the deposit equals $100 \times e^{0.06}$ (where e denotes the base of the natural logarithms).

These results can be generalized for deposits of any duration. The terminal value of the $100 deposit at the end of n years is given by the following formulas:

Annual compounding	$100(1 + 0.06)^n$
Semi-annual compounding	$100\left(1 + \dfrac{0.06}{2}\right)^{2n}$
Quarterly compounding	$100\left(1 + \dfrac{0.06}{4}\right)^{4n}$

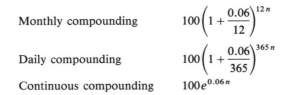

Monthly compounding $\qquad 100\left(1 + \dfrac{0.06}{12}\right)^{12n}$

Daily compounding $\qquad 100\left(1 + \dfrac{0.06}{365}\right)^{365n}$

Continuous compounding $\qquad 100e^{0.06n}$

Figure 3A.1 graphs the value of the deposit as a function of the frequency of compounding and of deposit duration. In this particular example, we have assumed an interest rate of 12%. However, it is worth noting that for short durations and for low interest rates the differences induced by the various compounding methods are negligible. In general, the higher the interest rate and the longer the duration, the greater is the impact of the compounding method. Thus when a bank declares that the annual interest of, say, 6% is compounded several times a year, this is tantamount to raising the simple interest rate.

Discounting more than once in a given period is the obverse of the frequency with

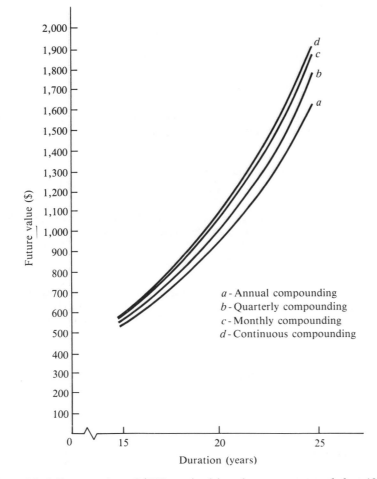

a - Annual compounding
b - Quarterly compounding
c - Monthly compounding
d - Continuous compounding

Figure 3A.1 Future value of $100 received in nth year compounded at 12%.

which interest is compounded. What is the value of $100 received one year from now? If the discount rate is 10%, the present value is equal to $100/(1 + 0.1)$, but if the cash flow is discounted twice a year, the present value is smaller, and equals $100/(1 + 0.1/2)^2$. In general, the value of $100 received n years from now, and discounted m times a year is $100/(1 + 0.1/m)^{mn}$. In the extreme case of continuous discounting, the present value is $100e^{-0.1n}$. In Table 3A.1 the present value of $100 received n years from now is calculated for several alternative assumptions regarding the frequency of compounding. These figures show that an increase in the frequency of compounding decreases the present value.

Formulae for future and present value: the continuous case

The value of $1 received n years from now and compounded m times each year is $1(1 + k/m)^{mn}$, where k denotes the cost of capital. As m approaches infinity, the future value of 1 dollar is given by:

$$\lim_{m \to \infty} 1\left(1 + \frac{k}{m}\right)^{mn} = e^{kn}$$

Similarly, if we invest S dollars instead of $1, the future value compounded continuously is $S \times e^{rn}$. Thus, where we deposit S_t continuously in the bank (at rate k) in period t, the future value of all these deposits compounded continuously is given by:

$$\int_0^n S_t e^{kt} \, dt$$

By the same token, the present value of $1 received n years from now and discounted at $k\%$, and compounded m times each year is $1/(1 + k/m)^{mn}$. As m approaches infinity, we get:

$$PV = \lim_{m \to \infty} \frac{1}{\left(1 + \dfrac{k}{m}\right)^{mn}} = \frac{1}{e^{kn}} = e^{-kn}$$

Similarly, the present value of S is given by Se^{-kn}. And where the cash flows are received continuously (S_t in period t), the present value is given by:

$$PV = \int_0^n S_t e^{-kt} \, dt$$

It is worth noting that for many firms the assumption that cash flows are received continuously is more realistic than the assumption that they are received at the end of the year, since the company incurs outlays and receipts more or less continuously throughout the year.

Table 3A.1 Present value of $100 received in the nth year discounted at 12%

	Year			
	1	5	10	20
Compounded annually	89.3	56.7	32.2	10.4
Compounded quarterly	88.8	55.4	30.6	9.4
Compounded monthly	88.7	55.0	30.2	9.2
Compounded continuously	88.7	54.9	30.1	9.1

3A.1 What is the future (terminal) value of $500 invested at 12% for five years if interest is:

(a) Compounded annually?
(b) Compounded semi-annually?
(c) Compounded quarterly?
(d) Compounded monthly?
(e) Compounded continuously?

3A.2 If you want to establish a fund of $6,000 for a trip around the world which you plan to take in three years, what would be the investment required now if money earns 8% compounded quarterly?

3A.3 You now have $2,500 in a savings account which earns 12% compounded semi-annually. How long will it take to accumulate:

(a) $5,000?
(b) $10,000?
(c) $12,500?
(d) $25,000?

3A.4 How much money will you have at the end of four years if you deposit $200 per month in a savings account at 12% interest compounded monthly?

3A.5 If you decide to buy a speedboat for which you will have to pay $90 per month for two years, how much can you afford to pay today for the speedboat if the annual interest rate is 12%?

3A.6 If you borrow $2,500 to be repaid over two-and-a-half years at an annual interest rate of 12%, what will be the monthly payment?

3A.7 What would be the annual rate of interest that an investor would earn if he were to pay $9,457 for a six-year program of quarterly receipts of $500?

3A.8 How long will it take to repay an 8% loan of $29,130 with semi-annual payments of $2,500?

3A.9 You are asked to examine the savings plans of three banks. The first bank offers interest of 8.2% compounded annually, the second bank offers 8% compounded quarterly, while the third one pays 7.8% compounded daily.

(a) On the assumption that you intend to put $1,000 in a bank now and let it remain for five years, which plan do you prefer? Explain.
(b) Does your answer change if the period of saving is ten years?

Ang, J. S. and Chua, J. H., 'Composite Measures for Evaluation of Investment Performance,' *Journal of Financial and Quantitative Analysis*, June 1979.
Ang, J. S. and Lai, T.-Y., 'A Simple Rule for Multinational Capital Budgeting,' *Global Finance Journal*, 1, 1989.

Benzion, U. and Yagil, J., 'On the Discounting Formula for a Stream of Independent Risky Cashflows,' *Engineering Economist*, Summer 1987.

Campbell, David R., Johnson, James M., and Savoie, Leonard M., 'Cashflow, Liquidity and Financial Flexibility,' *Financial Executive*, August 1984.

Chamber, D. R., Harris, R. S., and Pringle, J. J., 'Treatment of Financing Mix in Analyzing Investment Opportunities,' *Financial Management*, Summer 1982.

de la Mare, R. F., 'An Investigation into the Discounting Formulae Used in Capital Budgeting Models,' *Journal of Business Finance and Accounting*, Summer 1975.

Franklin, Peter J., 'The Normal Cost Theory of Price and the Internal Rate of Return Method of Investment Appraisal: An Integration,' *Journal of Business Finance and Accounting*, Spring 1977.

Golub, Steven J. and Huffman, Harry D., 'Cashflow – Why it Should be Stressed in Financial Reporting,' *Financial Executive*, February 1984.

Greenfield, R. L., Randall, M. R., and Woods, J. D., 'Financial Leverage and Use of the Net Present Value Investment Criterion,' *Financial Management*, Autumn 1983.

Hayes, R. H. and Garvin, D. A., 'Managing as if Tomorrow Mattered,' *Harvard Business Review*, May/June 1982.

Horvath, P. A., 'A Pedagogic Note On Intra-period Compounding and Discounting,' *Financial Review*, February 1985.

Jarrett, Jeffrey E., 'A Note on Investment Criteria and the Estimation Problem in Financial Accounting,' *Journal of Business Finance and Accounting*, Summer 1980.

4

Net Present Value versus Internal Rate of Return

ARTICLE 10

Economic Intelligence
A New Consensus for Investment

Debate may rage about the particulars of how to ensure America's future competitiveness, says C. Fred Bergsten, but there is powerful agreement on one issue: It's time for a national shift from consumption to investment. Bergsten, chairman of the bipartisan Competitiveness Policy Council established by the Administration and Congress, spoke with Fortune*'s John Labate.*

The public is realizing this is not your typical short-term, cyclical recession. People are looking at the longer sweep. Workers see that the average real wage today is more than 10% below what it was in 1970, and they know something is wrong.

Our council includes labor union presidents, corporate executives, and academics, and there is total consensus on the need to raise saving and investment in order to lift productivity. We've extrapolated that if productivity growth in the past 20 years had stayed where it was in the previous 20, per capita income in the country now would be about one-third higher. That is a stunning difference in the purchasing power of the average family.

The change in thinking began to develop more than a decade ago with a lot of rhetoric at the start of the Reagan period. The so-called supplyside measures were at least nominally aimed at that goal, but they failed miserably. Rising government spending swamped the pickup in federal revenues from the last recovery, and then the government cut taxes hugely. The budget deficits that ensued sharply reduced national savings.

The only way economists know to get the national saving rate up is by manipulating the government budget. So we should start by eliminating the deficit, which means balancing the budget, excluding the surpluses of Social Security and other trust funds.

It's less clear what to do about private saving — the rate fell during the 1980s despite incentives like IRAs and liberalized Keogh plans. But if you wanted to go whole hog, you would shift the entire basis of a tax system that now provides little real incentive for saving and investment. Whether you use carrots, such as exempting the earnings on savings from taxes, or sticks, such as a value-added tax, you have to tilt the balance. Nobody is against consumption, but to get a high and sustainable level later, you have to reduce its share now.

Source: Fortune, May 18, 1992, p. 22.

Three important points which are valid not only for the U.S. market, but also the United Kingdom, Germany and France (and indeed in all world markets) are discussed in the above article. The first is that if one wishes to consume more in the future, then one must consume less today – there is a tradeoff between present and future consumption. Second, in order to boost the economy one has to increase productivity: that is, for a given investment today production must result in greater net cash flows in the future. Alternatively stated, the net present value (*NPV*) of a project must increase. Third, the government can use either a 'carrot' (e.g., a lower the tax rate applicable to interest earned on savings) or a 'stick' (e.g., imposition of a tax on current consumption to make it less desirable) to increase savings. If personal savings increase, it may result in a reduction in interest rates which can stimulate investment by the corporate sector.

In this chapter, the tradeoff between present and future consumption as well as productivity and investment are discussed. We begin with a discussion of the differences between two concepts discussed briefly in the previous chapter: *NPV* and *IRR*.

It is already clear from the previous chapter that the net present value (*NPV*) and internal rate of return (*IRR*) methods of selecting capital investment proposals are closely related. Both are 'time-adjusted' measures of profitability: that is, they take the crucial element of timing into consideration. Even their mathematical formulas appear, at least on the surface, to be almost identical in form. However, unless the two investment criteria *invariably* lead to identical decisions, one cannot avoid having to choose between the two methods of measuring the desirability of capital investment proposals. With this in mind we now turn to the analysis and comparison of the *NPV* and *IRR* rules in order to determine which of the two is the *optimal* investment criterion for a wealth-maximizing firm. In order to focus attention on the crucial properties of the two decision criteria, we continue to abstract from risk, and therefore assume throughout this chapter that the magnitude and timing of investment outlays and receipts are known with perfect certainty.[1] This also permits us to postpone the discussion of the cost of capital (see Part III). Under the assumption of certainty, the cost of capital (discount rate) is simply the riskless rate of interest. We discuss how changes in productivity and interest rates may affect consumption and investment.

NPV vs. *IRR*: INDEPENDENT PROJECTS

If we limit the discussion to conventional projects (those having only one change in sign, for example − + + ···) which are economically independent of one another (that is, the selection of a particular project does not preclude

---

1. The assumption that all investments yield perfectly certain cash flows is unnecessarily restrictive. For the purpose of the comparison of *NPV* to *IRR*, it is sufficient to assume that all investments are homogeneous with respect to risk. Thus the acceptance of a particular project will not cause the market to reassess the riskiness of the firm.

the choice of the other) no problem arises. In this case, both the *NPV* and *IRR* rules lead to identical accept or reject decisions. Rather than simply stating this result as an axiomatic truth, however, it might be more convincing, especially to our more skeptical readers, if support of the claim that the two criteria lead to the same acceptance (or rejection) decisions were given. Of course, a number of specific examples could be examined which might remove some, but certainly not all, doubt. But conjuring up numerical examples, or 'proof by exhaustion' as it might be called, is a never-ending task. Fortunately for both the authors and the readers, the equivalence of the *NPV* and *IRR* rules with respect to conventional independent projects can readily be proven.

The equivalence can be seen in Figure 4.1, which again graphs the NPV of a conventional investment project as a function of the discount rate. Recall that the intercept with the horizontal axis, R, denotes the internal rate of return. (By definition, R is the discount rate which reduces the project's *NPV* to zero.) The graph shows that where the NPV is positive, for example using a discount rate (cost of capital) of k_1, R exceeds k_1. The *NPV*, which is measured by the height of the line connecting k_1 with the *NPV* function, is clearly positive and R lies to the right of k_1 along the horizontal axis. Conversely, where the *NPV* is negative, for example using the discount rate k_2, R is less than k_2. In sum, both methods result in identical accept/reject decisions; if the *NPV* criterion is fulfilled, the *IRR* criterion must also be satisfied, and vice versa. Thus a firm which is faced with the problem of screening acceptable

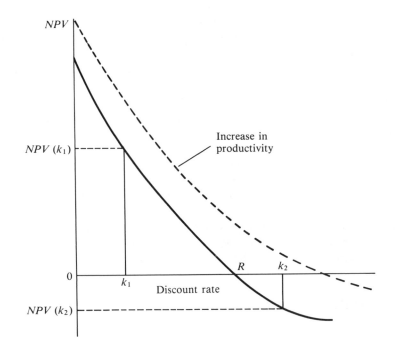

Figure 4.1

from unacceptable investment proposals will be indifferent as to which method is employed.

The mathematical proof of this equivalence is also straightforward. Let us assume that the project under consideration has a positive *NPV* and therefore should be accepted by the firm, that is:

$$\sum_{t=1}^{n} \frac{S_t}{(1+k)^t} - I_0 > 0 \quad \text{or} \quad \sum_{t=1}^{n} \frac{S_t}{(1+k)^t} > I_0 \tag{1}$$

The *IRR* of the *same* project is the value *R* which solves the following equation:

$$\sum_{t=1}^{n} \frac{S_t}{(1+R)^t} = I_0 \tag{2}$$

It follows that the left-hand side of equation (2), which equals I_0 must be smaller than the left-hand side of inequality (1) which is greater than I_0, and since by definition the numerators (S_t) are identical (and positive) in both instances this also implies that *R* must be greater than *k*, and conversely for the assumption of a negative *NPV*. Note that if the *NPV* is assumed to be zero, $R = k$, so that by both methods the firm will be indifferent to such a project. Hence for any conventional project, independent of the project's size or life, the *IRR* and *NPV* rules invariably lead to the same acceptance (rejection) signal.

Let us see how the article given at the beginning of this chapter suggests increasing investment and decreasing current consumption regardless of whether the *NPV* or *IRR* methods are employed. Suppose that the appropriate discount rate is k_2, then the project under consideration clearly should be rejected (see Figure 4.1). Since the project is rejected, the firm can distribute the initial cost of the investment denoted I_0 to the shareholders in the form of dividends (since these funds are not needed for the project). Suppose that the government enacts legislation to encourage savings, and as a result of the increase in savings (a large supply of funds) the interest rate falls from k_2 to k_1. Given this drop, the project becomes worth while and should be undertaken since the *NPV* is now positive (or $IRR > k_1$). This is exactly what the article suggests. Another suggestion is to increase productivity. What does this mean? It means that at the same cash outlay I_0 and same discount rate, the firm produces its output more efficiently, resulting in an increase in net income (see equation 1). Therefore, the *NPV* increases (see the dashed curve in Figure 4.1) and hence the project's *NPV* will be positive (or $IRR > k_2$) even at cost of capital k_2. This will, of course, increase investment and decrease present consumption (dividends).

NPV VERSUS *IRR*: DEPENDENT PROJECTS

While it is obvious that a change in government policy affects both *NPV* and *IRR*, these two methods do not always yield the same decision. In particular, a direct confrontation between the two time-adjusted methods of profitability analysis cannot be avoided once we drop the assumption of independence. As we noted in the previous chapter, mutually exclusive alternatives often crop up in a modern business enterprise; numerous examples exist of projects whose acceptance precludes the execution of another proposal. A five-story apartment building and a ten-story office building cannot both be built on the same plot of land; similarly, the purchase of a computer precludes the alternative of leasing the same computer.

The problems raised by such extreme dependency can be illustrated by considering the example of two one-year projects:

	Initial investment outlay	Net inflow at the end of the year
Project A	−10,000	12,000
Project B	−15,000	17,700

Since both projects have a one-year life their *IRR*s can be calculated directly, without recourse to present value tables or a financial calculator:

$$\frac{12,000}{1 + R_A} = 10,000, \text{ hence } IRR_A = 20\%$$

$$\frac{17,700}{1 + R_B} = 15,000, \text{ hence } IRR_B = 18\%$$

Assuming a cost capital $k = 10\%$ (discount factor = 0.909), the *NPV*s of the two projects are given by:

	Net inflow		Discount factor		Less: Initial outlay		*NPV*
Project A	12,000	×	0.909		−10,000	=	908
Project B	17,700	×	0.909		−15,000	=	1,089

Thus, despite the fact that project A has the higher internal rate of return, project B has the larger net present value:

	IRR	*NPV*
Project A	20%	908
Project B	18%	1,089

Now if the proposals are independent, both A and B are accepted, using either the *NPV* or the *IRR* rules, which is as it should be. But which of the two projects is the 'better buy'? If the firm is forced to choose between them, for example, if they are *mutually exclusive* alternatives, which of the two projects should be accepted? In such a case the method of analysis becomes crucial: if the firm uses the *NPV* criterion, project B will be chosen since it has the higher *NPV* (1,089 > 908); however, if the firm uses the *IRR* criterion, project A, which has the higher *IRR* (20% > 18%), will be preferred.

This paradoxical result reflects the fact that the two decision criteria do not necessarily rank projects the same. In the case of an independent proposal and no capital rationing, ranking is not important: in essence the firm is indifferent as to the 'order' in which projects are accepted, because the acceptance of one does not prevent the acceptance of the other. However, in the case of mutually exclusive investments, ranking becomes crucial. Only one of a group of mutually exclusive alternatives (presumably that with the highest rank) can be executed, and since the ranking depends on the investment criterion used, one can no longer be indifferent between the *NPV* and *IRR* methods.

To clarify the difference in ranking we have drawn the *NPV* curves for each of the above projects in Figure 4.2. The ranking of the projects by their internal rates of return is constant: 20% always exceeds 18%. On the other hand, the ranking of the projects by their net present values is not fixed.

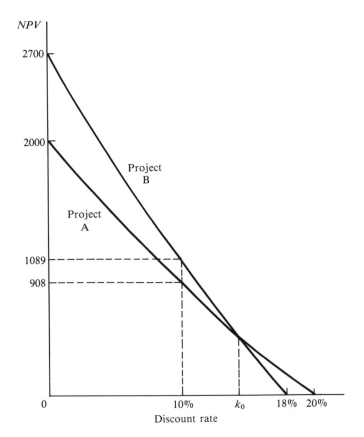

Figure 4.2

Figure 4.2 clearly shows that the *NPV* ranking depends on the discount rate assumed. For costs of capital greater than k_0 no contradiction arises: both the *IRR* and *NPV* methods rank project A first. However, for discount rates which are smaller than k_0 the two methods result in different rankings: project B has the higher *NPV* while project A has the higher *IRR*. In general, if the two functions intersect in the positive quadrant of the diagram, and such is the case in Figure 4.2, the dominance of one project over another by the *NPV* rule will not be absolute. As a result, there exists a range of values of the discount rate in which contradictory rankings can arise. In the following sections we attempt to provide an intuitively appealing argument for preferring the *NPV* ranking.

_____ **DIFFERENCES IN THE SCALE OF INVESTMENT**

Differences in the ranking of projects by the two methods may arise for a variety of reasons. Consider, for example, the cash flows of the following two projects:

Years:	0	1	2	3
Project A	−1,000	505	505	505
Project B	−11,000	5,000	5,000	5,000

If we assume a 10% discount rate, that is if we assume that the firm can acquire funds or find alternative uses for funds at 10%, both projects are acceptable by either the *IRR* or *NPV* methods since the *IRR*s of both exceed the cost of capital and therefore both projects also have positive net present values:

	IRR	NPV
Project A	24%	256
Project B	17%	1,435

Now let us assume that these two projects are mutually exclusive. If we invoke the *IRR* rule, project A with a 24% rate of return is preferable to project B which has only a 17% rate of return. However, by the *NPV* rule, project B should be preferred over project A since the former's *NPV* is larger. What is the reason for this disparity in the ranking of the projects? Figure 4.3 graphs the *NPV*s of the two projects as functions of the discount rate. As can be seen from the diagram, the functions intersect at a discount rate of 16.58%. The interpretation of the diagram is straightforward: given the necessity of making a choice between the two projects, the larger project will be preferred to the smaller one if the cost of capital is below 16.58%. The opposite holds

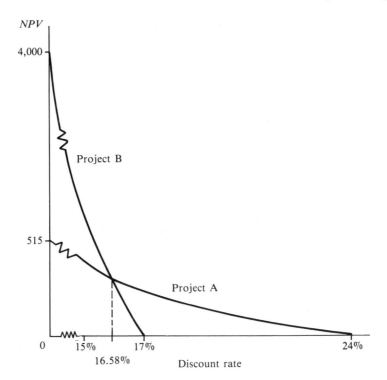

Figure 4.3

if the cost of capital is above 16.58%. In fact, for discount rates above 17%, only the smaller project is feasible; the *NPV* of project B becomes negative beyond this point.

The mathematics of capital budgeting aside, how can we account for the fact that for discount rates below 16.58% the *NPV* method gives priority to project B despite its relatively low rate of return? The source of this preference can be clarified by considering the *incremental* cash flow (see Table 4.1 and in Figure 4.4).

Initially, let us assume that the firm uses the *IRR* rule exclusively and therefore plans to execute project A. Now, add the additional profitable investment labelled 'B minus A'? If the answer is affirmative in favor of project B, the total investment will be A + (B − A) = B, that is to say the firm would shift from project A to project B. Choosing project B rather than project A

Table 4.1

	0	1	2	3
Project B	−11,000	5,000	5,000	5,000
Project A	−1,000	505	505	505
'B minus A'	−10,000	4,495	4,495	4,495

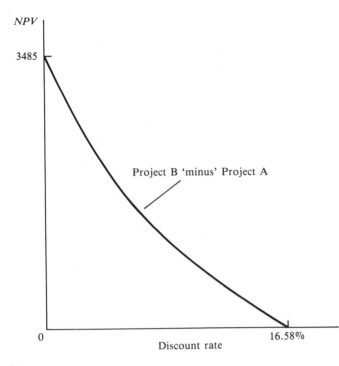

Figure 4.4

is tantamount to choosing a hypothetical project 'B minus A' which represents the *incremental* cash flow resulting from such a decision. Thus, the choice of the larger project B is equivalent to choosing the smaller project A plus an additional investment outlay of $10,000 on which $4,495 will be realized each year for three years. The internal rate of return on this incremental cash flow is 16.58%, and given a 10% cost of capital, this represents a profitable opportunity, and should be accepted.

Using the *IRR* criterion, the firm chooses project A, but as we have just seen would also like to accept the hypothetical cash flow 'B minus A'. This results in a total cash flow to the firm of A + (B − A) = B. Thus, the *IRR* rule when used properly (i.e, on an incremental basis) leads the firm to prefer project B, but this is precisely the project which has the higher *NPV*. In this example the superiority of the *NPV* rule has been established even though we used the *IRR* rule; that is, the *IRR* analysis has been contradicted using the *IRR* rule itself.[2]

To complete the analysis, it is worth noting that if the cost of capital is greater than 16.58%, it does not pay to make the additional commitment of

2. Of course, the above example could also be used to support the conclusion that a *modified IRR* method which systematically examines the incremental flows between all pairs of projects could be substituted for the *NPV* method. However, when nonconventional projects are introduced, even the modified version of the *IRR* fails to yield consistently correct results (see page 62).

resources and the hypothetical project 'B minus A' should be rejected. This is precisely what the *NPV* method prescribes: looking back at Figure 4.3 we note that the intersection of the two functions takes place at a discount rate of 16.58% which is the same as the *IRR* on the incremental cash flow (see Figure 4.4). This follows from the fact that the point of intersection represents a discount rate which *equates* the *NPV* of the two projects, and this is equivalent to the discount rate which equates their difference to zero. The latter, by definition, is the *IRR* on the *incremental* cash flow. To sum up, if the cost of capital is greater than 16.58% the firm should stick to project A (project B minus A should be rejected). But this is precisely the case in which the *NPV* of project A is greater than the *NPV* of project B (see Figure 4.3) so that again the *IRR* rule can be used to justify the use of the *NPV* criterion.

By *automatically* examining and comparing the incremental cash flows against the cost of capital, the *NPV* method ensures that the firm will reach the optimal *scale* of investment. The *IRR* criterion − which is expressed as a percentage rather than in terms of absolute dollar returns − ignores this important facet of an investment decision. The *IRR* method always prefers a 500% return on one dollar to a 20% return on one hundred dollars. To most of us (assuming a cost of capital below 20%) the optimal solution is to take advantage of both opportunities, but where a choice between the two must be made, few indeed would argue in favor of the *IRR* solution. Most individuals, as is true of most firms, have goals which are set out in terms of *absolute* returns, and not in percentage terms. And since the *NPV* reflects absolute returns, this ensures optimality when mutually exclusive choice situations arise.

The profitability index

Before going on to the other reasons for the difference in rankings, this might be a good place to pause to see if we can use the results of the previous section to analyse a very popular variant of the *NPV* criterion, the so-called profitability index.[3]

The profitability index is defined as the present value of the project divided by its initial outlay, that is

$$\text{Profitability Index} = \frac{\text{Present value of cash flow}}{\text{Initial investment}} = \frac{PV}{I_0}$$

The following decision rule is associated with the Profitability Index:

Accept the project if the index is greater than 1.
Reject the project if the index is less than 1.

Clearly, in the case of independent projects, the profitability index and the *NPV* criterion yield the same acceptance-rejection decision. If *NPV* > 0, we

---

3. For a critical analysis of the properties of the profitability index, see H. M. Weingartner, 'The Excess Present Value Index − A Theoretical Basis and Critique,' *Journal of Accounting Research*, Autumn 1963, pp. 213–24.

necessarily have $NPV = PV - I_0 > 0$, and therefore, $PV > I_0$. Dividing both sides by I_0 we get $PV/I_0 > 1$; that is, the profitability index is also greater than 1. Hence, if a project is acceptable by the *NPV* criterion it must also be acceptable by the profitability index.

For many people the profitability index is more intuitively appealing than the *NPV* criterion. The statement that a particular investment has an *NPV* of, say, $20 is not sufficiently clear to many people who prefer a relative measure of profitability. By adding the information that the project's initial outlay (I_0) is $100, the profitability index ($120/100 = 1.2$) provides a meaningful measure of the project's relative profitability in more readily understandable terms. It is then only a small step to convert the index of 1.2 to 20%.

However, once again problems can arise when mutually exclusive alternatives are considered. As we have seen in the previous section, one advantage of the *NPV* criterion over the *IRR* criterion in mutually exclusive choice situations stems from the fact that the *NPV* criterion reflects the *absolute* magnitudes of the investment proposals. The *IRR*, being a pure number, does not. But by converting the *NPV* criterion to a relative measure, the profitability index, which is itself a pure number, no longer reflects differences in investment scale, and as a result recreates the very paradox that the *NPV* criterion is designed to avoid. Consider, for example, the following two *mutually exclusive* proposals:

	Present value of cash flow	Initial investment outlay	Profitability index
Project A	100	50	2
Project B	1,500	1,000	1.5

According to the profitability index, project A, which has an index of 2, should be preferred. But it is equally clear that a firm which desires to maximize its absolute present value rather than percentage return would prefer project B, because the *NPV* of project B ($500) is greater than the *NPV* of project A ($50). Thus, while the profitability index may be useful for exposition, it should not be used as a measure of investment worth for projects of differing size when mutually exclusive choices have to be made.

TIMING OF THE CASH FLOW

The fact that the *NPV* rule takes differences in the scale of investments into account while the *IRR* rule does not might lead to the erroneous conclusion that if the initial investment outlays of two projects are the same, the *IRR* and *NPV* will rank the proposals in the same manner. The following example shows that even in the case of identical initial outlays the rankings by the *IRR* and by the *NPV* can differ.

		Cash flow	
	Initial outlay	First year	Second year
Project A	−100	20	120
Project B	−100	100	31.25
A minus B	0	−80	88.75

Assuming a cost of capital of 10% let us calculate the *NPV* and the *IRR* for these two projects.[4]

	NPV	*IRR*	
Project A	17.3	20%	
Project B	16.7	25%	
A minus B	0.6	10.9%	

Again a contradiction in the ranking arises. The *NPV* criterion ranks project A first, while the *IRR* criterion gives priority to project B even though both projects have identical initial outlays. Thus in this instance we cannot use the scale of investment argument to justify the choice of A; however, we can still use the same incremental technique.

Let us again assume that a firm uses the *IRR* criterion. If A and B are mutually exclusive, project B will be accepted and project A will be rejected. Before executing project B it is legitimate to ask whether or not it is worth while to add the incremental (hypothetical) investment 'A minus B'. Since the *IRR* of the incremental investment is 10.9% and therefore exceeds the cost of capital (10%), the hypothetical project should be accepted. But since B + (A − B) = A, it is tantamount to accepting project A: that is, the alternative with the higher *NPV*.

This result is illustrated in Figure 4.5. For discount rates below 10.9% the incremental investment 'A minus B' is acceptable, which coincides with the range over which project A has the higher *NPV*. Thus even when initial investment outlays are the same, the two methods can still yield contradictory ranking, and the *NPV* curves may still intersect (see Figure 4.5). In general, it is the failure of the *IRR* method to evaluate properly the alternative use of funds (it ranks projects *independently* of the cost of capital) which leads to differences in ranking. This can occur even if the projects have the same initial outlays and even the same lives, so long as they do not have identical annual cash

4. The *NPV* is calculated by using Table 3.3 (slight differences may occur when a financial calculator is used due to rounding). The *IRR* is calculated by 'trial and error' using the same table, or by a calculator. However, for the incremental cash flow (A − B) the *IRR* can be calculated directly as follows:

$$80/(1 + R) = 88.75/(1 + R)^2$$

which reduces to $80 = 88.75/(1 + R)$. Hence $R = 88.75/80 - 1 = 10.9\%$.

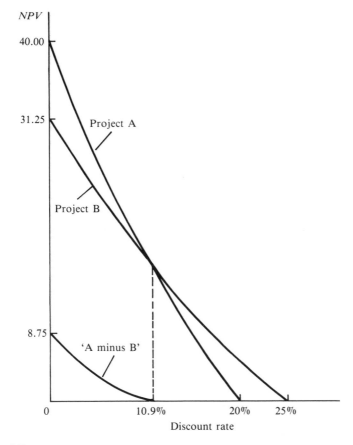

Figure 4.5

flows. (If they did, the projects themselves would, of course, be identical.) Any difference in the magnitude or timing of the cash flows can give rise to a difference in the rankings of projects by the two methods.

_____ **REINVESTMENT RATES**

How can one account for the superiority of the *NPV* rule even when differences in the scale of investment do not exist? The answer can be found by considering the element of time which is so crucial to investment analysis. Although both the *NPV* and the *IRR* take the time element into account, the time adjustment made in the *IRR* method is incorrect. This can be seen more clearly by examining the *implicit* assumptions made by the two methods regarding the 'reinvestment' of interim cash flows. The *IRR* tacitly assumes that a project's annual cash flows can be reinvested at the project's internal rate of return; the *NPV* method assumes that the cash flows can be reinvested at the firm's opportunity cost of capital.

Since these assumptions are implicit, a more formal demonstration can help to clarify the meaning and significance of the reinvestment rates. Consider any project with a given initial outlay I_0, a useful life of n years, and a stream of cash receipts $S_1, S_2, ..., S_n$. The internal rate of return (R) of this project is given by:

$$I_0 = \frac{S_1}{(1+R)^1} + \frac{S_2}{(1+R)^2} + \cdots + \frac{S_{n-1}}{(1+R)^{n-1}} + \frac{S_n}{(1+R)^n}$$

which can also be written as:

$$I_0 = \sum_{t=1}^{n-1} \frac{S_t}{(1+R)^t} + \frac{S_n}{(1+R)^n} \tag{1}$$

For simplicity, let us further assume that the same project has a positive *NPV*. Assuming a cost of capital equal to k, the *NPV* formula for the same project can be written as:

$$\sum_{t=1}^{n} \frac{S_t}{(1+k)^t} - I_0$$

hence:

$$I_0 < \frac{S_1}{(1+k)^1} + \frac{S_2}{(1+k)^2} + \cdots + \frac{S_{n-1}}{(1+k)^{n-1}} + \frac{S_n}{(1+k)^n}$$

or:

$$I_0 < \sum_{t=1}^{n-1} \frac{S_t}{(1+k)^t} + \frac{S_n}{(1+k)^n} \tag{2}$$

In order to make the reinvestment rates explicit, let us rewrite equations (1) and (2) in their future value forms. This is done by multiplying both sides of equation (1) by $(1+R)^n$:

$$I_0(1+R)^n = \sum_{t=1}^{n-1} S_t(1+R)^{n-t} + S_n \tag{3}$$

Similarly, we multiply both sides of equation (2) by $(1+k)^n$:

$$I_0(1+k)^n < \sum_{t=1}^{n-1} S_t(1+k)^{n-t} + S_n \tag{4}$$

Thus even if the initial investment outlays and the lives of the projects are the same, it is clear from these equations that the interim receipts are compounded forward (the other side of discounting) at different rates: R in the *IRR* formula, and k in the *NPV* formula.[5] This problem cannot be avoided, since it arises out of the very need to discount the cash flows of different time periods to some common denominator.

5. Except for one-year projects, in which case there is no need for compounding. In such cases the *NPV* and *IRR* rank conventional projects consistently as long as the initial outlays are the same.

The economic counterpart of these compounding rates is a 'reinvestment' rate, i.e., the time-discounting process which underlies both methods implicitly makes an assumption regarding the 'value' to the firm of the interim receipts. In the *NPV* method it is assumed, as it should be, that all receipts can be reinvested at the cost of capital k. If this does not hold true, the cost of capital has been incorrectly estimated. This makes sense, since by definition k should reflect the alternative use of funds, and in calculating the profitability of a project we want to evaluate it against that alternative use. This, of course, is the essence of the *NPV* calculation.

The *IRR* method, on the other hand, assumes reinvestment at the project's own internal rate of return R. This has no economic basis. If R does not equal k, and this is the only case where differences in ranking are of interest, assuming the future reinvestment of the interim proceeds at the rate R might be unrealistic to the extent that such high-return projects (in cases where $R > k$) simply may not be available in the future. But even if we could be certain of their physical availability, the *IRR*'s reinvestment assumption is still in error. Such high-return projects, if available, will always be executed if the cost of capital is equal to k, *independent* of the decision on the current project under consideration. It is an error, therefore, to 'credit' the current project with any benefits accruing from the reinvestment of the interim proceeds at rates of return above k. The *NPV* method isolates and evaluates the profitability of the current project alone, since the net present value of the proceeds reinvested at a rate of return *equal* to the cost of capital is zero.

Cost of capital values across years

The crucial importance of the reinvestment rate assumption can be made even more explicit if we assume that the firm expects the cost of capital to differ in future years. For simplicity, let us consider a case where the discount rate is expected to rise over time, so that $k_1 < k_2 < k_3 < \cdots < k_n$. Clearly, no change occurs in the internal rate of return calculation and equation (3) still holds. The interim proceeds are still assumed to be reinvested at the average rate of return R. But it is no longer clear that the *IRR* decision rule which relates the rate of return to the cost of capital can be used. Comparison of a single-valued rate of return with a series of discount rates $k_1, k_2, ..., k_n$ will not, in general, yield meaningful results. It is sufficient to consider an example of a three-year project with an internal rate of return equal to 15%, and the following costs of capital: $k_1 = 10\%$, $k_2 = 15\%$, and $k_3 = 20\%$. It is clear from this example that the *IRR* criterion does not lead to a clear accept–reject decision.

A similar problem does *not* arise with respect to the net present value method. Given the series of discount rates, the discounted cashflow of a three-year project can be formulated as follows:

$$I_0 \gtreqless \frac{S_1}{(1 + k_1)} + \frac{S_2}{(1 + k_1)(1 + k_2)} + \frac{S_3}{(1 + k_1)(1 + k_2)(1 + k_3)}$$

Multiplying both sides of this equation by $(1 + k_1)(1 + k_2)(1 + k_3)$ we obtain:

$$I_0(1 + k_1)(1 + k_2)(1 + k_3) \gtreqless S_1(1 + k_2)(1 + k_3) + S_2(1 + k_3) + S_3$$

Thus the *NPV* calculation remains meaningful even if we assume nonuniform short-term discount rates. The interim receipts are compounded forward (reinvested) in this case at the appropriate opportunity cost for each relevant period. The first-year receipts are reinvested during the second year at that year's cost of capital, k_2, and during the third year at k_3, and so on.

To sum up, the *NPV* method provides an optimal solution to the capital budgeting problem given the assumptions that future cash flows and the cost of capital (discount rate) are known. Both the *NPV* and *IRR* are weighted averages: the former using the appropriate short-term weights $k_1, k_2, ..., k_n$, while the latter method uses the inappropriate long-term rate of return R.

THE HORIZON PROBLEM

The reinvestment argument in favor of the *NPV* method which was set out above is completely general and holds even for cases where projects differ in their expected lives. However, the reinvestment problem, or horizon problem as it is often called, which arises when alternative investment projects have different lives, is of special interest and has been the subject of much dispute in the financial literature.[6]

Consider the following example of two mutually exclusive projects:

	Cash inflow				
	Initial outlay	First year	Second year	Third year	Fourth year
Project A	−100	120	−	−	−
Project B	−100	−	−	−	174

Assuming a 10% cost of capital, the *NPV* and *IRR* of the above two projects are:

	NPV	*IRR*
Project A	9	20%
Project B	19	15%

Once again, the *IRR* and *NPV* rankings are contradictory. As has already been shown, project B should be preferred because it has the higher *NPV*. What, then, is the horizon problem? Since project A earns its cash inflow of 120 at

6. The horizon problem in general, as well as the specific numerical example of the text, are due to Ezra Solomon, 'The Arithmetic of Capital Budgeting Decisions,' *Journal of Business*, April 1956.

the end of the first year, while in project B the cash inflow of 174 is not received until the end of the fourth year, it has been argued that the appropriate comparison is with the cash flow of the earlier project *repeated* three more times. Denoting the 'repetitive' project by A^*, we rewrite the cash flows as follows:

		Cash inflow			
	Initial outlay	First year	Second year	Third year	Fourth year
		120	120	120	
		−100	−100	−100	
Project A^*	−100	20	20	20	120
Project B	−100	—	—	—	174

Out of the cash flow of $120 received at the end of the first year, $100 is reinvested, so that the *net* cash flow is only $20. However, the reinvestment produces another cash inflow of $120 at the end of the second year, and so on. By repeating investment A we generate a new compound project A^* whose time horizon is identical lo that of project B, i.e., four years.

The *NPV* and *IRR* of projects A^* and B are:

	NPV	IRR
Project A^*	31.7	20%
Project B	19.0	15%

Thus, the paradoxical difference in ranking is resolved, and project A^* dominates project B by both the *IRR* and the *NPV* rules.

Is it proper to repeat project A until a common life is reached? The argument in favor of such a procedure rests on the fact that the cash flows of project A are realized earlier than those of project B so that the firm has 'extra' time to reinvest the money. *In general, this argument is not valid.* A firm whose cost of capital is 10% can, by definition, always raise money at this rate, and therefore can take advantage of an investment opportunity at the end of the first year, independent of the particular project (A or B) which it executes in the first year. However, three special cases are of interest.

1. What if the later investments are closely related to project A? For example, let us assume that the investment in the first year is only the initial stage of a larger project (such as the road for a factory which will be built in the following year). In such a case the cash flows of all of the components of the compound project should be combined, since in essence they constitute a single project. In fact, isolating the first year cash flow of such a project would be a conceptual error.

2. Another noteworthy possibility is the case in which proposals A and B utilize the same physical resource. For example, suppose that projects A and B are two alternative crops to be grown on the same acre of land. For simplicity, we assume that the amount of land is limited, and for some

reason the firm cannot sell this land. Project A is a one-year crop, for example cucumbers destined to be pickles, while Project B is a four-year crop, such as a fruit orchard. Once again a straightforward comparison of project A and B is conceptually incorrect. Only after equating the two time horizons will the comparison be meaningful. In this special case, we must consider the alternative uses of the land in the interim years, before comparing it with the four-year alternative.

3. Similarly, where replication is obvious, for example in technical cost minimization problems such as equipment replacement, equalization of time horizons is necessary. Replacement chains are discussed in Chapter 5.

A THEORETICAL JUSTIFICATION FOR NET PRESENT VALUE _____

In this section, we present a theoretically rigorous analysis of the advantages of *NPV* over *IRR*.[7] For simplicity the discussion is confined to two-period investments.[8] To simplify further the analysis, we initially examine the case of an investor, with given available resources W_0, who has to decide how much of his present wealth (W_0) to consume this year, and how much to invest in order to provide for consumption in the next year. But before continuing we can greatly facilitate matters by introducing the concept of an investment schedule. Thus, this analysis not only clarifies the difference between *NPV* and *IRR*, but also focuses on the relationship between current and future consumption as well as investment and interest rates discussed at the beginning of the chapter.

The investment schedule

Consider an investor with an initial endowment equal to W_0, who must decide how to divide his wealth between current consumption and investment in productive resources. As a first step, let us assume that he arrays all of his potential productive opportunities in descending order of profitability: that is, by their internal rates of return (see Table 4.2).

In a one-year investment in which the investment outlay takes place at the beginning of the year and the net cash receipt is received at the end of the year, a project's *IRR* is readily calculated by dividing the net receipt by the initial outlay, and then reducing the quotient by one. Assuming an initial endowment of $1,000, such a productivity schedule (which is also called the transformation curve) is illustrated in Figure 4.6.

Points W_0, *a*, *b*, *c*, and *d* represent the attainable combinations of current and future consumption, given the investor's initial endowment of $1,000 and

7. The discussion is based on the classic article by Jack Hirshleifer, 'On the Theory of Optimal Investment Decision,' *Journal of Political Economy*, August 1958.
8. The reader who wishes to generalize the analysis to the case of multiperiod investment should consult M. J. Bailey, 'Formal Criteria for Investment Decisions,' *Journal of Political Economy*, October 1959.

Table 4.2

Project	Required investment outlay	Net cash receipt at end of year	Internal rate of return
A	100	200	100%
B	100	150	50%
C	500	600	20%
D	300	315	5%

the four investment opportunities A, B, C, and D. For example, he can consume W_0 this year and nothing next year, but even though this alternative is physically available it cannot be recommended to an individual who desires to survive next year. On the other hand, if investment A is executed he can reach point *a* which denotes current consumption of $900 ($W_0$ less the required investment outlay of project A) and consumption of $200 next year which is the cash flow that project A produces in the second period. Similarly, by executing the other investment alternatives the individual can reach points *b*, *c*, and *d*.

To simplify the presentation, the attainable points of Figure 4.6 are connected to form the investment productivity curve W_0d. This is tantamount to assuming that the projects are infinitely divisible: that is, they can be broken down into very small components so that the investment alternatives can be

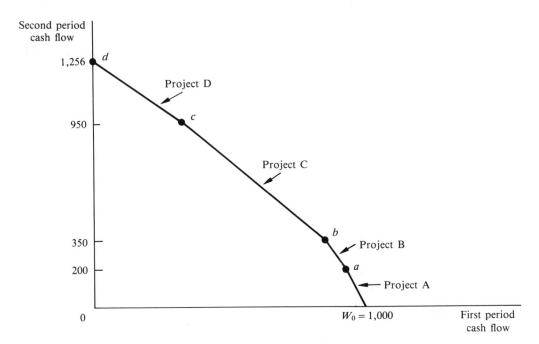

Figure 4.6

represented by a continuous curve instead of by a series of discontinuous points. The reader should also note that when moving from W_0 to d, the slope of the productivity curve declines, which reflects the fact that the projects have been arrayed in descending order of profitability from point W_0 to point d. Now, which projects should be accepted? In other words, which point on the investment productivity curve is optimal? Before we can answer this question a way must be found to represent the investor's tastes. This can be done by introducing another important tool of analysis, the *indifference curve*.

The meaning of indifference curves

Consider a rational[9] individual who is faced with the problem of choosing that combination of current and future consumption (C_0, C_1) which will maximize his satisfaction, where C_0 and C_1 denote cash flows (consumption) in the first and second periods respectively. One possible combination is represented by point M in Figure 4.7. Whenever a combination such as M is replaced by an alternative located in the direction of the arrow marked a, the satisfaction derived from the cash flow combination is increased: every movement along the line Ma increases current consumption without altering future consumption. Conversely, any movement in the direction of arrow b is undesirable, because consumption in the second period is reduced without any compensating increase in first period consumption, which is clearly to the individual's disadvantage. Since any movement in the direction of arrow b reduces the investor's satisfaction, while any movement in the direction of arrow a increases it, a point can be found between a and b (for example, N) at which the individual's satisfaction is neither increased nor decreased. If we substitute combination N for combination M, the first period cash flow increases and the second period

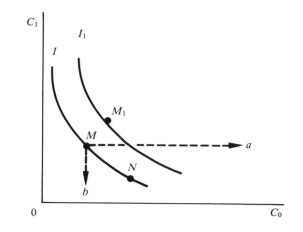

Figure 4.7

9. By 'rational' we simply mean that, other things being equal, such an individual prefers *more* to *less* consumption.

cash flow decreases; but, as we have assumed that the individual's satisfaction remains unchanged, the impact of the increase in C_0 on the individual's satisfaction is exactly offset by the decrease in C_1. Hence the investor is indifferent to the choice between the two consumption combinations represented by points M and N.[10] Other combinations of (C_0, C_1) can also be found which leave the individual indifferent: that is, with the same level of satisfaction which he derived from combination M. In principle, all such combinations can be plotted along an 'indifference curve' such as I of Figure 4.7. If we start with a point such as M_1, we can repeat the process and generate yet another indifference curve such as I_1, and so on until an entire indifference map is constructed which represents an investor's tastes with respect to current and future cash flows (consumption).

The indifference curves of Figure 4.7 decline from left to right, which indicates that the rational investor must be compensated by an increase in future consumption when his current consumption is reduced. The curves also have been drawn convex to the origin on the assumption that each additional decrease in current consumption requires increasingly larger increments of future consumption if the individual is to remain indifferent to the change.

Another important property of the indifference map is that the indifference curves of a single individual *cannot* intersect. This can be proved by examining Figure 4.8 in which two indifference curves I and I_1 of the *same* individual intersect at point Z. Since Z and Z_1 are located on the same indifference curve (I), the individual, by definition, must be indifferent between them. Z_2 and Z also lie on a single indifference curve (I_1), so that the individual is also

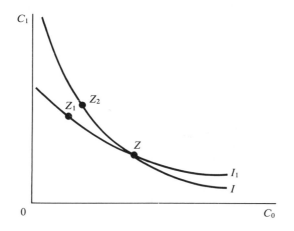

Figure 4.8

10. To facilitate the graphical representation the indifference curves of Figure 4.7 have been drawn as continuous curves, that is independent of the actual available alternatives. Clearly, no potential investment option may exist which permits an individual to achieve the consumption pattern represented by a point such as M or N. However, from the fact that both these points lie on the same indifference curve we can conclude that, had such alternatives been available, the individual would have been indifferent between them.

indifferent between these two alternatives. It follows that the individual must also be indifferent between Z_1 and Z_2, but this contradicts the assumption that the investor is rational, because Z_2 represents a larger cash flow in both periods.

An investor's final choice out of all available cash flow combinations depends on his tastes. He will choose that combination which allows him to reach the highest indifference curve: for the higher the curve, the greater his satisfaction or what is called in the economist's jargon 'utility'. Figure 4.9 superimposes an individual's indifference map on an opportunity set of alternative cash flow combinations denoted by points a, b, d, e, and f.

The individual would prefer a combination which would allow him to reach indifference curve I_5, but such a combination is not attainable (indifference curve I_5 does not intersect or touch any of the attainable points). The best that he can do, given the opportunity set, is to choose combination a, the option which lies on indifference curve I_3. As no other choice will permit him to reach a higher level of satisfaction (utility), the cash flow pattern represented by point a constitutes his *optimal* choice. Should he choose another alternative out of the available set, say point f, his satisfaction will fall since this option only permits him to reach indifference curve I_2, which represents a lower level of utility.

Can we infer from this analysis that no individual will ever prefer option f; or alternatively, does option a represent the optimal choice for all individuals? Because the shape of the indifference curves varies from one individual to another, it is conceivable that a second individual may have an indifference map, representing his individual preferences, in which the highest indifference curve touches point f rather than point a. In fact, depending on the shape of

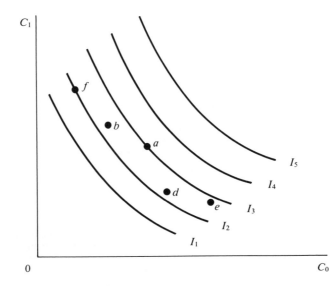

Figure 4.9

the curves, some other alternative may constitute the optimal choice for a particular individual. This is illustrated in Figure 4.10 which sets out the indifference curves of two *different* individuals. [11] From the shape of their indifference curves we can see that the individual whose tastes are represented by curve I_A would choose point *a* while the other would prefer point *f*.

The reader should note that the indifference curve I_A is steeper than curve I_B. This means that when his current consumption (C_0) is decreased by one unit, individual A requires a greater compensatory increase in future consumption (C_1). For individual B, on the other hand, a lower current consumption represents a lesser drawback, and therefore this individual requires a smaller compensating increase in future consumption in order to leave his level of satisfaction unchanged.

Optimal investment decisions

Now we are in a position to combine the concepts of an investment productivity curve and an indifference map in order to determine optimal investment policy for the individual or firm. Figure 4.11 superimposes the indifference curves of a hypothetical individual confronted by the investment opportunities which are summarized in the investment productivity curve W_0d. Note that his initial endowment equals W_0. From Figure 4.11 it is clear that the cash flow pattern (C_0^*, C_1^*) denoted by C^* permits the individual to reach his highest indifference curve (I_2). This occurs at the point of tangency between the productivity curve and an indifference curve. The *optimal* consumption combination also dictates the optimal investment policy: point C^* can be attained by consuming C_0^* in the current period and investing the amount $W_0 - C_0^* = I_0$

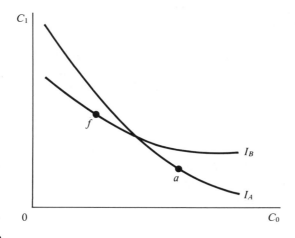

Figure 4.10

11. The reader should note that the intersection of the indifference curves of two *different* individuals does not contradict our previous proof that the indifference curves of the *same* individual cannot intersect.

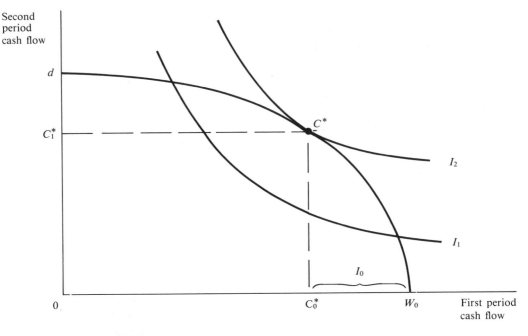

Figure 4.11

in order to provide a cash flow in the second period which is just sufficient to support a consumption of C_1^*.

Let us now apply the basic properties of this analysis to re-evaluate somewhat more rigorously the relationship of *NPV* to *IRR*. We shall start by assuming that all the alternative projects are independent of one another, and have conventional cash flows, i.e., the initial investment outlay in the first period is followed by a positive cash flow in the second period. Although the analysis is confined to two periods, the period which elapses between the investment outlay and the receipt of the cash flow can be as long or as short as required. For convenience we assume throughout that the investment horizon is one year.

The money market line

Consider an individual confronted by the net cash flows C_0 in period one and C_1 in the second period. Recalling the discussion in the text of the time element, the present value of these cash flows clearly is not $C_0 + C_1$ but rather the discounted sum:

$$PV = C_0 + \frac{C_1}{1+k}$$

where k denotes the individual's opportunity cost of capital which in a perfect market under conditions of certainty is also equal to the riskless interest rate for both borrowing and lending. For any given value of PV (for example $PV_1 = 1$) an infinite number of combinations of C_0 and C_1 can be found which yield this value. Hence we can write the following *linear* relationship (hence the name market line) between C_1 and C_0:

$$C_1 = PV_1(1 + k) - C_0(1 + k)$$

Since k is a constant, the intersection of this line with the vertical axis (future value) is the constant $PV_1(1 + k)$ and the slope of the line is given by $-(1 + k)$. All the combinations of cash flows (C_0, C_1) which lie on this line yield the same present value of consumption, which in this particular case is equal to PV_1. Now, suppose that we wish to find all the combinations (C_0, C_1) which yield a higher present value, say PV_2. In this case we substitute PV_2 for PV_1 in the above equation, thereby generating another line *with the same* slope, but with a higher intersection point on the vertical axis. By considering alternative values of PV we derive a family of parallel straight lines, each with the property that all combinations on a given line represent the same present value; hence, the name iso-PV or equal PV lines.

Let us examine the set of typical iso-PV lines drawn in Figure 4.12. Which PV line will the investor desire to reach? Obviously, he would prefer the highest line PV_3 since for every combination of (C_0, C_1) which is on the PV_2 (or PV_1) line, there is a combination (C_0, C_1) on PV_3 which yields higher consumption in the two periods: hence PV_3 is preferred to PV_2 and PV_1. But not all of these lines represent attainable cash flow combinations; the feasibility of an iso-PV line depends on the individual's initial endowment W_0, as well as the available investment opportunities (the investment productivity curve).

Figure 4.13 superimposes the investment productivity curve on a family of iso-PV lines. The initial endowment is denoted by point W_0 on the horizontal axis. The individual would prefer to reach line PV_4; however, none of the combinations (C_0, C_1) which lie on this line are attainable because this line lies

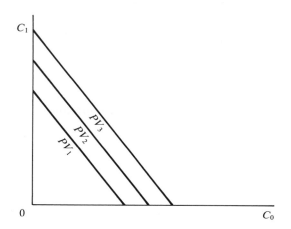

Figure 4.12

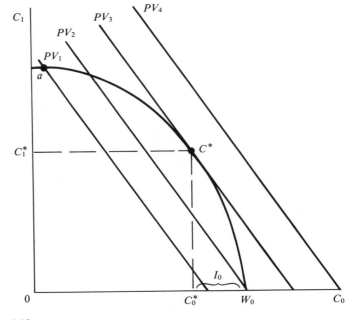

Figure 4.13

to the right of the investment curve. Point *a* is attainable, as he can invest part of his initial endowment and 'move' along the investment curve to this point. But will he choose this point? The answer is unequivocally negative, because point C^* which is also attainable (by investing I_0) represents a higher level of present value ($PV_3 > PV_1$). Given the productive investment opportunities and his initial endowment, the combination of net cash flows (C_0^*, C_1^*) denoted by point C^* and the current investment outlay I_0 required to achieve this combination are the best possible alternatives in the sense that they maximize the present value of the cash flows.

Before we analyze the investor's optimal choice, let us demonstrate the relationship of the present value of consumption and the net present value of investment. The present value of consumption is given by:

$$PV = C_0 + C_1/(1 + k)$$

The investor has an initial wealth of W_0, and invests I_0, therefore $W_0 - I_0 = C_0$ (see Figure 4.13). The present value of consumption can be rewritten by substituting $W_0 - I_0$ for C_0 as follows:

$$PV = W_0 - I_0 + C_1/(1 + k)$$

Since C_1 is the future cash flow arising due to the investment, $C_1/(1 + k) - I_0 = NPV$, hence:

$$PV = W_0 + NPV$$

From the last equation we see that by accepting all projects with positive

NPV we maximize *NPV*, hence maximizing the *PV* of consumption. Therefore, either reaching the highest *PV* line of consumption or maximizing the *NPV* from projects yields the same investment decision, namely, invest I_0 (see Figure 4.13).

Let us turn now to the choice of consumption mixes. Will an individual whose cost of capital is equal to *k* necessarily choose the cash flow (consumption) combination denoted by point C^*? To answer this question the individual's tastes (indifference map) must be taken into account and, moreover, the analysis must incorporate the fact that the individual is confronted with financial as well as productive investment opportunities. This is done in Figure 4.14 which superimposes the individual's indifference curve on the investment productivity curve and iso-*PV* line of Figure 4.13.

As shown in Figure 4.14, the individual invests the amount I_0 thereby reaching point C^*, the point of tangency between the highest attainable iso-*PV* line and the productivity curve. But the indifference curve which passes through point $C^*(I_1)$ lies below I_2, which is also attainable if financial alternatives are taken into account. Given his tastes (the shape of his indifference curves), the individual can reach a higher rate of satisfaction by lending the amount *L* at the opportunity cost of capital *k*. This is indicated by a movement along the iso-*PV* line to C^{**} at which point the iso-*PV* line is tangential to indifference curve I_2. The individual prefers lending to investing beyond point C^* because in period 2 he will receive $L(1 + k)$ in return for the loan; the effective rate of interest on the financial transaction *k*, therefore, is greater than the rate of

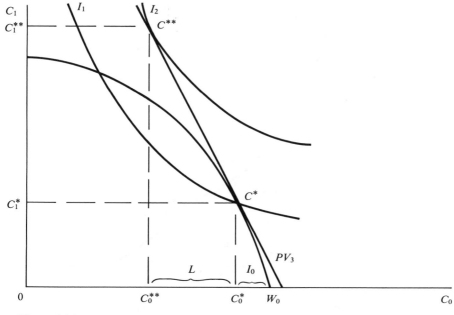

Figure 4.14

return on productive investment beyond this point as a comparison of the slopes of the investment curve and *NPV* line clearly shows.

Should the point of tangency with the indifference curve lie to the right of point C^*, the individual would again invest up to point C^* as before, but would borrow the amount B in order to increase his current consumption (see Figure 4.15).

Note that the indifference curves of Figure 4.15 have been drawn much steeper, which indicates that this individual gives high priority to current relative to future cash flows (consumption). However, despite this strong preference for current consumption, the individual in this case first takes advantage of his productive opportunities and invests I_0, that is up to the point C^*. The preferred consumption pattern is achieved by a financial transaction, in this instance borrowing. Finally, if an indifference curve is tangential to the investment productivity curve at point C^* itself, the individual neither borrows nor lends, and point C^* represents the optimum combination of cash flows (consumption).

Separation of investment and financing decisions

The striking feature of the analysis is that the optimal investment decision denoted by point C^* does *not* depend on the shape of the indifference curves. Whether the individual desires to redistribute his consumption over time by either borrowing or lending, the investment decision, as we have just seen, remains the same. The projects represented by the segments $W_0 C_0^*$ of the

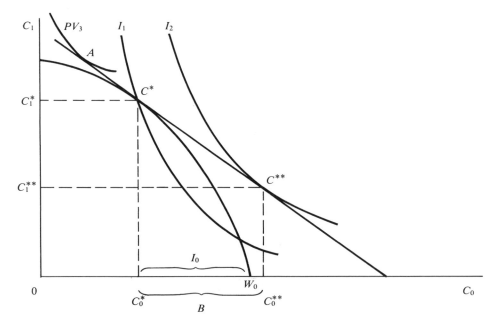

Figure 4.15

investment curve are accepted; this is the subset of all projects having a positive *NPV* at the cost of capital *k* which permits the individual to reach the highest attainable *PV* line. Thus, as long as the individual chooses investments so as to maximize *PV*, that is to reach the highest attainable iso-*PV* line, he also ensures that he will be able to maximize his satisfaction (utility) by redistributing (if necessary) his consumption over time by means of borrowing or lending. In this sense, the *NPV* rule is *optimal*; making investment decisions by the *NPV* rule maximizes *NPV*, reaches the highest *PV* line, and is therefore tantamount to the maximization of investors' utility as well.

The independence of investment and financing (i.e., borrowing or lending) decisions is called 'separation' and lies at the heart of the modern theory of finance. It is the existence of an efficient capital market which permits the individual (firm) to reach its productive investment decisions without *explicitly* considering its financial decisions. The property of separation leads to two important results: capital structure irrelevancy and dividend policy irrelevancy.

CAPITAL STRUCTURE IRRELEVANCY

Capital structure refers to the proportion of debt (bonds and bank loans) and equity (stocks and retained earnings) used by the firm in financing its investments. When a firm employs debt to finance some portion of an investment, we say that the firm is leveraged (or employs leverage). Is there an optimal mix of debt and equity (i.e., is there an optimal debt-to-equity ratio)? Is one debt-to-equity ratio preferred to another by some investors? Under the assumption of certainty, the answer is no. Capital structure (debt-to-equity ratio) is irrelevant which means a firm can arbitrarily choose its capital structure. Let us refer back to Figure 4.15. Suppose that the firm and not the individual borrows the amount *B*. In this case, all investments are financed by debt and in fact the firm borrows more than the amount needed for investment (i.e., $B > I_0$). Investors who have a tangency point at C^{**} are happy with this financing decision since utility is maximized for them at precisely this point. But suppose that there are other investors where the tangency point is to the left of C^{**}, say at point *A*. These investors do not like the amount of borrowing (leverage) employed by the firm. Will they sell their stock and hence decrease in the value of the firm? Absolutely not! Investors at point *A* can obtain the cash flows offered by the firm at point C^{**} and move along the line PV_3 to point *A* by lending money. This process is called 'undoing the leverage' employed by the firm. Given this opportunity to undo the leverage, there is no incentive for investors at point *A* to sell their stock. Of course, investors at point *A* have to expend a little more effort (lend money), but if we ignore transaction costs this extra effort is meaningless.

Similarly, if the firm decides to lend money at precisely point *A*, investors at this point are satisfied and investors who like to be at point C^{**} create 'home-made leverage' by borrowing themselves, and hence move along line

PV_3 to point C^{**}. In this case, investors at point B have to expend a little more effort in borrowing.

The conclusion is the following: regardless of the firm's financing mix (capital structure), all investors will maximize their utility by borrowing and lending. Capital structure is irrelevant. Although our analysis assumes perfect cetainty (the possibility of bankruptcy does not exist), there are two assumptions which are crucial in achieving this result. First, that individuals as well as firms can borrow and lend at the same interest rate (everyone moves along the same PV line); this means that home-made leverage and the firm's leverage are perfect substitutes. Second, that there are no transaction costs. The 'little effort' needed to create or undo the leverage employed by the firm has no economic value. In Chapter 14, we see that these two crucial assumptions are also needed to obtain capital structure irrelevancy in a world of uncertainty.

DIVIDEND POLICY IRRELEVANCY

An immediate result follows from the above discussion of the irrelevancy of capital structure: dividend policy is also irrelevant. Recall that by selecting the financial mix, the firm automatically decides its dividend policy. For example, in Figure 4.14, C_0^* and C_1^* are the dividends paid at the present time and in the future. Suppose an investor wants to receive a lower dividend today and a higher dividend in the future (e.g., C_0^{**} and C_1^{**} as shown in Figure 4.14). Does it mean that he will sell his stock in the firm and buy stock in another firm which meets his cash flow criteria? No, he will not. The investor can consume C^{**} if he deposits the amount L in the bank and therefore can obtain his optimal cash flow at point C^{**}. Once again, the ability of firms and individuals to move along the same PV line results in dividend policy being irrelevant. The investor can always individually adjust the firm's dividend policy by expending a little effort (borrow or lend).

In practice, dividend policy may be relevant since reality is uncertain and the economic content of dividends may be important (that is, dividends may have other uses such as signalling information to the market about the firm's future earnings potential and stability). Dividend policy in a world of uncertainty is discussed in Chapter 18.

NPV versus IRR: independent projects

Under the assumed condition of independence, does the internal rate of return rule also lead to the investment decision which maximizes investors' utility? The IRR criterion asserts that all projects with an IRR greater than k should be accepted. Then it also takes the opportunity cost of using the firm's capital resources into account. Looking back at Figure 4.6, it is clear that, by construction, the IRR of each project is given by the slope of the investment

productivity curve at the appropriate point.[12] Looking at Figure 4.15 the slope
of the investment curve at point C^* equals $-(1 + k)$ which is the slope of the
iso-PV line tangential to the curve at that point. Along the segment W_0C^* the
slope of the investment curve is greater than the slope of the PV lines; hence
the IRRs of all the projects on this segment are higher than the cost of capital
k, and therefore all these projects should be accepted by the IRR rule. By the
same token all projects which lie to the left of point C^* have IRRs which are
less than the cost of capital, and accordingly they should be rejected by the
IRR rule. But this is precisely the investment decision which maximizes the
investors' utility. Thus, in sum, both the NPV and IRR rules lead to an
optimal investment decision, in the sense that both lead to the acceptance/
rejection decision which maximizes investors' utility, that is, to the investment
decision which permits investors to reach their highest possible indifference
curves.

NPV versus *IRR*: mutually exclusive projects

When mutually exclusive proposals exist, the investment decision can no
longer be analyzed in terms of a single investment productivity function. If
two projects A and B are mutually exclusive, two investment curves must be
constructed: one which includes all of the independent projects, *plus project
A*; and a second which includes the independent projects *plus project B*. If
more than two projects are mutually exclusive, the number of possible investment curves increases accordingly so that the optimal investment curve, as well
as the optimal point, must be chosen.

Unlike the previous case of independence, when mutually exclusive projects
exist the NPV and IRR solutions no longer coincide: the NPV remains an
optimal rule, but the IRR may fail to yield the optimal investment decision.
To prove this contention let us consider the two investment curves A and B
of Figure 4.16.

Curve A represents all the independent projects, plus project A, and curve
B represents all the independent projects plus project B. This is tantamount
to assuming that A and B are the only two mutually exclusive proposals. We
continue to assume initial endowment of W_0. The IRR criterion cannot distinguish between alternatives A and B. In this example, if alternative A is chosen,
all projects up to point C_A should be accepted; if alternative B is chosen all
projects up to C_B should be accepted. But which alternative enables investors
to reach higher indifference (utility) curves? The IRR rule has no clear answer
to this crucial problem and hence cannot guarantee optimal results. The NPV
rule, on the other hand, provides a clear-cut answer to the question. The NPV
of alternative A is greater than that of B (recall that a higher PV line implies

12. For the first project, an outlay of $100 returns $200 in the second period, the IRR is given
by $100 = 200/(1 + R)$ or $1 + R = 200/100$, and $R = 100\%$. Since the slope of the new investment
curve in this segment is negative, we have $-(1 + R) = -200/100$; hence $R = 100\%$. In the continuous case the IRR of each additional dollar invested is measured by the slope of the investment
function at that point.

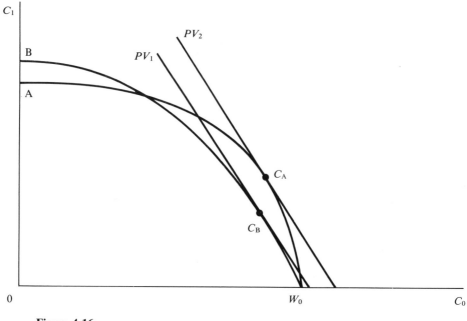

Figure 4.16

a higher *NPV*, and vice versa); it therefore permits a tangency with a higher indifference curve. Thus A is the optimal choice between the mutually exclusive alternatives A and B, and C_A is the optimal cut-off point for new investment.

Let us see how the policy suggested in the article at the beginning of the chapter may affect the individual's consumption pattern as well as the level of capital expenditure in the economy.

A. An increase in productivity

Consider Figure 4.17, which is similar to Figure 4.13. The optimal investment is I_0 and the level of current and future consumption is C_0^* and C_1^*, respectively.

The increase in productivity implies that current investment creates more cash flow, and hence the production function shifts to the right and the optimal point is C_p^* (where p stands for the improvement in productivity). Investment should increase by ΔI (i.e., from I_0 to $I_0 + \Delta I$). Of course, consumption today will decrease and future consumption will increase as suggested in the article. However, recall that these straightforward implications stem from the simplified analysis presented above. One obvious and critical issue exists: how to increase productivity? As we saw in the article on Eaton Corporation on page 24, some firms are striving to increase productivity through employee motivation, education, and creative compensation systems. Increasing productivity is not always such an easy task.

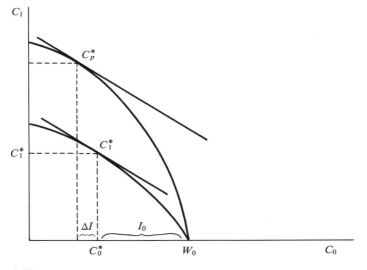

Figure 4.17

B. Increase personal savings in order to decrease interest rates

Suppose that, due to tax incentives offered by the government, investors increase their personal savings. This results in an increase in the supply of loanable funds which may result in a decrease in interest rates. In our framework, this drop in interest rates lowers the relevant discount rate employed for project evaluation (k). How does this affect the consumption/investment

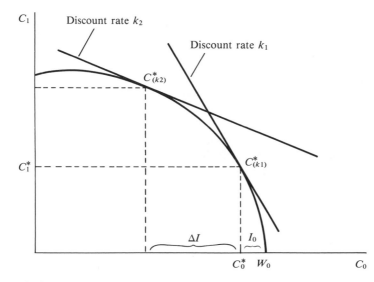

Figure 4.18

decision? Figure 4.18 examines the consumption/investment decision at two different discount rates.

Suppose that the discount rate falls from k_1 to k_2 and there is no change in productivity. In this case, the optimum point shifts from $C^*(k_1)$ to $C^*(k_2)$ (where the subscript indicates the discount rate) hence the investment of the firm should increase by ΔI: more capital expenditure and less consumption (dividend) are expected. While an increase in productivity should be motivated by each individual firm (see the example of Eaton Corp., page 24), an increase in savings accompanied by a decrease in interest rates could be stimulated by the government's use of savings incentives – the 'carrots' and 'sticks' we mentioned earlier.

NONCONVENTIONAL CASH FLOWS

Theoretically appropriate decision rules are often complicated, difficult to calculate and impractical to apply. The *NPV* decision criterion, however, is an exception to this rule. In all respects it is less complicated and easier to apply than the alternative *IRR* method. This is especially true once we drop the assumption of conventional cash flows. When nonconventional projects are considered, a proposal's *IRR* may not exist (that is, the calculation may result in imaginary numbers), or if it does, it may not be unique.

Absence of a real solution

Consider the following nonconventional cash flow:

Year	0	1	2
Cash flow	+100	− 200	+150

What is the *IRR* of this project? Should it be accepted by a firm whose cost of capital is 10%?

Anyone who attempts to solve the *IRR* by trial and error will exhaust most of his patience, as well as his computer budget, without success. The reason for this is simple; no 'real' *IRR* for this project exists. This can readily be seen by solving the following equation:

$$100 - \frac{200}{(1 + R)} + \frac{150}{(1 + R)^2} = 0$$

Dividing through by 100 (for simplicity only) and denoting $1/(1 + R)$ by x, we derive the following quadratic equation:

$$1.5x^2 - 2x + 1 = 0$$

The values of x which solve this equation are called the *roots* of the equation. If at least one real root exists, we can safely assert that there are values of x (and hence values of R) which equate the *NPV* to zero. If we cannot find real values of x which equate the formula to zero, this is tantamount to asserting that the *IRR* does not exist. Using the conventional formula for solving a quadratic equation[13] we get,

$$x_1 = \frac{2 + \sqrt{4 - 4(1.5)}}{3} = \frac{2 + \sqrt{-2}}{3}$$

$$x_2 = \frac{2 - \sqrt{4 - 4(1.5)}}{3} = \frac{2 - \sqrt{-2}}{3}$$

Since the square root of -2 is an *imaginary* rather than a real number, the *IRR* is also *imaginary*: that is, no real *IRR* exists. This is clear from Figure 4.19 which graphs the *NPV* of this nonconventional project as a function of the discount rate. At a zero discount rate, the *NPV* is simply the algebraic sum of the cash flow: $100 - 200 + 150 = 50$. As the discount rate approaches infinity, the *NPV* approaches 100. Between these values, the curve is U-shaped but always positive: that is, there is no positive discount rate at

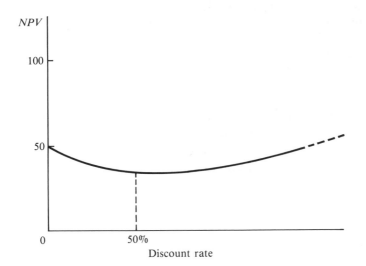

Figure 4.19

13. In general, a quadratic equation $ax^2 + bx + c = 0$ has two roots which we denote by x_1 and x_2, that is to say if we substitute either x_1 or x_2 in the above equation the value of the equation is equal to zero. x_1 and x_2 can be found by applying the standard formula:

$$x_1 = \frac{-b - \sqrt{b^2 - 4ac}}{2a} \quad \text{and} \quad x_2 = \frac{-b + \sqrt{b^2 - 4ac}}{2a}$$

In cases where $b^2 - 4ac < 0$, no real roots exist, and the function $ax^2 + bx + c$ can never intersect the horizontal axis of a diagram such as Figure 4.19.

which the *NPV* becomes zero. [14] As Figure 4.19 shows, the project in question is acceptable by the *NPV* criterion, at any cost of capital. Despite this the *IRR* rule cannot be applied because the *IRR* for such a project does not exist. Nor is this merely an intellectual curiosity; as we noted in Chapter 2, such nonconventional cash flows may be generated whenever a proposal which calls for an advanced payment or terminal costs is being evaluated.

Multiple solutions

In general, the *IRR* formula relates to *n* years and, therefore, has *n* roots. Thus there are always *n* values of *R* which solve the *IRR* equation. However, if the cash flow is conventional, only one of these values of *R* is a real number; the other *n* − 1 roots are imaginary numbers which are of importance in higher mathematics but have no economic meaning. In this sense we can say that a conventional project has a *unique* rate of return. The *NPV* function of such a proposal crosses the horizontal axis *once and once only*.

If the project is nonconventional, so that we are confronted by a cash flow which has more than one change in sign, the number of real solutions for the *IRR* can vary from zero to *m*, where *m* is the number of sign changes in the cash flow. [15] In our previous example we examined a case of a nonconventional but economically meaningful project which has no real *IRR*; we now turn to an example of a nonconventional project which has *more than one* real *IRR*.

Consider the following problem. A firm has an old machine which will produce a net return of $300 at the end of the first year, and $1,400 at the end of the second year. The current market value of this machine is zero. The firm is considering the alternative of replacing the old machine with a new one which costs $100, but which will produce a net return of $1,000 at the end of the first year, and only $200 at the end of the second year. The replacement problem requires the evaluation of the *incremental* cash flow stemming from the decision. The necessary data are summarized in the following table:

| | | Cash flow | |
		1st year	2nd year
New machine	−100	1,000	200
Old machine		300	1,400
Incremental flow[a]	−100	+700	−1,200

[a] Cash flow of new machine minus cash flow of old machine.

14. The mathematically inclined reader can readily verify that the function reaches a minimum at a discount rate of 50% by setting the first derivative equal to zero.

$$\frac{\partial NPV}{\partial x} = 3x - 2 = 0$$

Hence $x = \frac{2}{3}$ and since by definition $x = 1/(1 + R)$, $R = 50\%$.

15. The *maximum* number of real solutions is equal to the number of sign changes in the cash flow. See, for example, D. Teichroew, A. A. Robichek and M. Montalbano, 'An Analysis of Criteria for Investment and Financing Decisions under Certainty,' *Management Science*, January 1965.

Should the firm replace the old machine? Using the *IRR* rule, we first must solve the following equation for R:

$$-100 + \frac{700}{(1 + R)} - \frac{1,200}{(1 + R)^2} = 0$$

Dividing through by 100 and denoting $1/(1 + R)$ by x, the following must hold:

$$-12x^2 + 7x - 1 = 0$$

Solving this equation by the standard quadratic formula yields *two* real roots:

$$x_1 = \frac{-7 + \sqrt{49 - 48}}{-24} = \tfrac{1}{4}$$

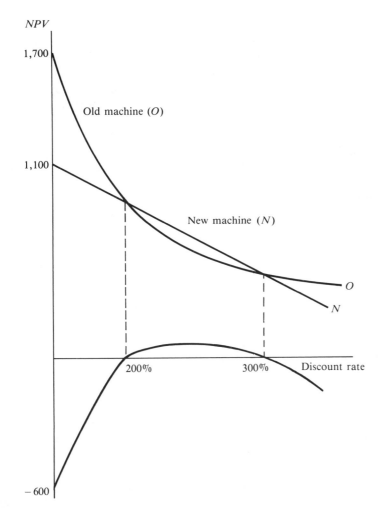

Figure 4.20

and since $x = 1/(1 + R)$:

$$R_1 = 300\%$$

Similarly,

$$x_2 = \frac{-7 - \sqrt{49 - 48}}{-24} = \tfrac{1}{3}, \text{ so that } R_2 = 200\%$$

Now, for sake of argument, assume that the cost of capital is 250%. Should the old machine be replaced? The *IRR* rule breaks down in such a case since contradictory answers are indicated depending on which rate of return is chosen:

$R_1 = 300\% > 250$; replace
$R_2 = 200\% < 250$; do not replace

Again, we have no way of discriminating between the two solutions.

The dilemma can be resolved by examining Figure 4.20 which plots the *NPV* profiles of the cash flows of the new machine and the old machine as well as the incremental cash flow of the replacement decision. The dual rate of return reflects the fact that the *NPV* functions of the old and new machines intersect *twice* – at discount rates of 200% and 300%. These rates are also, by definition, the internal rates of return of the incremental cash flow as they equate the *NPV* of the two alternatives. Applying the *NPV* rule to the diagram we note that for discount rates *between* 200% and 300%, the *NPV* of the new machine is greater than the *NPV* of the old machine and as a result the *NPV* of the incremental cash flow is positive over this range as well. Thus for these discount rates, the replacement is worth while. However, if the discount rate is below 200% or over 300%, the old machine should not be replaced.

CAPITAL RATIONING

Despite its name, a capital rationing situation can arise for a variety of reasons, not all of which are concerned with the capital market *per se*. Of course some far-reaching imperfection in the capital market may preclude a firm from raising additional debt and/or equity beyond some stipulated amount, but more often than not the restriction on the supply of capital reflects *noncapital* constraints or bottlenecks within the firm. For example, the supply of key personnel necessary to carry out the projects may be severely limited, thereby restricting the dollar amount of feasible investment. Similarly, considerations of management time may preclude the adoption of programs beyond some level. For example, the board of directors may insist on reviewing and approving all major projects, thereby limiting the overall scope of investment.

The impact of capital rationing can be classified by considering the two highly simplified cases drawn in Figure 4.21. Figure 4.21(a) graphs the familiar diagram from economic theory of the firm's demand for investment funds in a perfect capital market under certainty. For simplicity, the projects facing the firm are assumed to be independent and infinitely divisible, and therefore the opportunity set can be drawn as a continuous curve in descending order of the projects' internal rates of return.

Given the assumption of a perfect capital market with complete certainty, the supply of funds can be portrayed by the horizontal line drawn at the level of the riskless interest rate r_0, which is the cost of capital. The firm executes

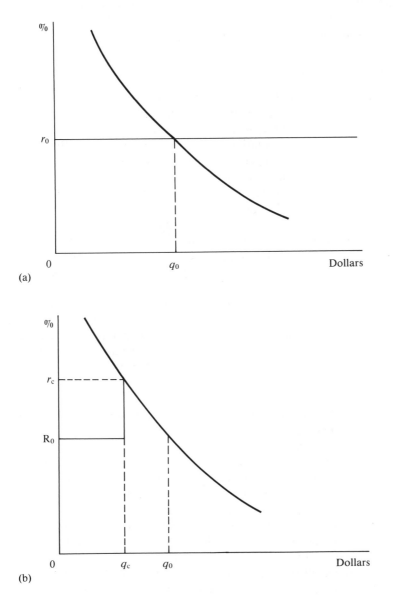

(a)

(b)

Figure 4.21

all projects with a positive *NPV* (i.e., those with an *IRR* greater than r_0), and the optimal initial outlay is denoted by $0q_0$. Figure 4.21(b) assumes that for some reason the firm is constrained to a total outlay of $0q_c$ dollars. Although the capital funds up to that amount are still made available at a cost of r_0, it is apparent that the opportunity cost or shadow price of the budget constraint is given by r_c which is considerably higher than r_0. If we add one dollar to the budget, the firm will earn r_c, and not r_0, on the additional investment. Hence the opportunity cost of funds is given by the internal rate of return of the marginal project. Thus r_c is the appropriate discount rate to be used in the *NPV* calculation.

A numerical example

We demonstrate in the following example how one can select the best set of projects in the case of capital rationing and how to find the cost of capital. Since we will consider mutually exclusive projects in the example, we therefore have a capital rationing situation and the use of *NPV* rather than *IRR* for the capital rationing case is imperative once we relax the assumption of independence and permit mutually exclusive projects. This can be clarified by considering a specific example. Consider the hypothetical case of the Gavka Company which is a subsidiary of the Brosh Investment Holding Company. Let us assume that each year the parent company allocates a *fixed sum* of $100,000 to Gavka which serves as the latter's *maximum* capital budget. Gavka is charged 8% interest per year on any funds which it utilizes, but $100,000 constitutes the effective ceiling on Gavka's annual capital expenditure budget.

Gavka faces four *independent* investment opportunities: Projects 1, 2, 3, and 4, but in each instance there are several alternative ways to execute the projects. These alternatives are designated by the letters a, b, or c. Since each project can be executed only once, the alternative ways of carrying out a particular project constitute *mutually exclusive* alternatives.

To simplify our calculations, let us further assume that the entire investment outlay is made immediately, that the equal annual net receipts are received at the end of each year, and that the project's terminal (scrap) values are zero. Table 4.3 summarizes the data available to Gavka on the four projects.

Given Gavka's budget constraint of $100,000, which projects should be executed and in which way, i.e., which of the alternative methods should be used to execute the accepted projects? Table 4.3 sets out three possible answers using three well-known decision rules: the *IRR*, *NPV* and profitability index (PV/I_0). As a first step, the *best* alternative is chosen out of the mutually exclusive sets of alternative ways to execute each project. The projects chosen by each evaluation method are set out in Table 4.4. Two striking features of the capital budgets can be readily discerned. First, all four projects are desirable in a world in which the cost of investment funds is 8%. However, the acceptance of the four projects by each method violates the budget constraint. More importantly, the actual projects chosen differ with each method. As we noted

Table 4.3 The Gavka company

	Initial investment outlay ($)	Annual net receipts ($)	Project's duration (in years)	IRR	NPV ($k = 8\%$)	Profitability index[a] ($k = 8\%$)
Project 1a	15,000	6,000	5	28.7	8,958	1.6
1b	7,000	4,000	3	32.7	3,308	1.5
Project 2a	50,000	17,000	5	20.8	17,881	1.4
2b	32,000	12,000	5	25.4	15,916	2.1
2c	45,000	15,000	5	19.9	14,895	1.3
Project 3a	70,000	20,000	8	23.2	44,940	1.6
3b	53,000	20,000	5	25.7	26,860	1.5
Project 4a	30,000	10,000	5	19.9	9,930	1.3
4b	33,000	9,000	8	21.6	18,723	1.6
4c	25,000	8,500	5	20.8	8,941	1.4

[a] Present value ÷ initial investment outlay ($PV \div I$).

Table 4.4 Projects chosen and total required outlay by method of evaluation

IRR	NPV $k = 8\%$	Profitability index
1b	1a	1a
2b	2a	2b
3b	3a	3a
4b	4b	4b
	Total required outlay	
$125,000	$168,000	$150,000

above, neither the *IRR* nor the profitability index is an appropriate measure of investment feasibility in mutually exclusive choice situations. Since Gavka is confronted by mutually exclusive choices, our attention will be focused on the *NPV* solution.

Since the budget constraint is violated (i.e., the total required outlay is $168,000), one project must be eliminated – in this instance project 3a. Thus the choice seems to be to execute projects 1a, 2a, and 4b: this entails a total initial outlay of $98,000 which satisfies the $100,000 budget constraint. However, a careful search indicates that even when one assumes an 8% discount rate, this solution is not correct since choosing projects 3a and 4a yields the highest *NPV* ($51,734) which satisfies the $100,000 constraint.[16] But is this solution correct? Applying the insights of Figure 4.21(b), it is clear that in a situation of capital rationing, 8% is not the true cost of the funds used. Given additional financing Gavka would also execute project 3a which has an *IRR* of over 23.2%. Furthermore, the choice between alternatives in the first

16. Using LINDO mixed integer linear programming yields this result.

three projects was made on the implicit assumption that Gavka's opportunity cost was only 8%, which clearly is not the case.

A way out of our dilemma can be found by applying the *NPV* method using the higher opportunity cost of financing and without violating the budget constraint. This can be done by a process of trial and error (see Table 4.5). The discount rate is raised, in the example to 16%, but the total investment outlay required ($150,000) still exceeds the $100,000 budget constraint. The discount rate is raised again, this time to 22%. At this rate, projects 1a, 2b, and 3b are chosen, and the required investment outlay satisfies the constraint. (Namely, at 22% these projects have the highest *NPV* in each category. We leave it to the reader to calculate the *NPV*.)

The striking feature of the solution using the 22% opportunity cost of funds, rather than the arbitrary 8% interest rate, is the significant difference in the composition of the projects chosen. Using the opportunity cost, projects 1a, 2b, and 3b are chosen; using the irrelevant 8% discount rate, the firm would prefer projects 3a and 4b.

Which solution is correct? The answer is straightforward. In the best possible world the budget constraint would be relaxed, Gavka would receive an additional $68,000 in investment funds, and would execute the *NPV* solution using an 8% discount rate (projects 1a, 2a, 3a, and 4b would be chosen). The marginal opportunity cost (shadow price) of an additional dollar is 8% and that is the appropriate discount rate. But in the assumed situation in which the $100,000 budget constraint is binding, the opportunity cost of the marginal dollar to Gavka, as the analysis of Figure 4.21(b) suggests, is much higher. Given additional funds, the company would execute a project with a rate of return in excess of 22%. Hence 22%, and not 8%, is the relevant opportunity cost (shadow price) to be applied in this case.

When the choice is more complicated, one can apply linear programming to solve for the optimum set of projects. This model is needed in the case of multiperiod projects with a constraint in each period. However, the solution in principle is similar to the one above; namely, the appropriate discount rate is determined by the future cash flows and by the constraints themselves.

Table 4.5 Projects chosen and total required
outlay by the *NPV* method of
alternative discount rates

$k = 8\%$	$k = 16\%$	$k = 22\%$
1a	1a	1a
2a	2b	2b
3a	3a	3b
4b	4b	—
	Total required outlay	
$168,000	$150,000	$100,000

This chapter has analyzed and compared two time-adjusted measures of investment worth: net present value (*NPV*) and the internal rate of return (*IRR*). Although both criteria give equivalent results with regard to independent conventional projects, they do not *rank* projects the same. This difference in ranking becomes crucial in mutually exclusive choice situations, that is when the firm must choose the best (presumably highest ranking) proposal out of two or more alternatives. *NPV* provides the more attractive criterion for the following reasons:

1. *NPV* reflects the *absolute* magnitude of the projects while the *IRR* does not. This is a point in the *NPV*'s favor, because the firm is concerned with absolute profits and not merely with the rate of profit. Similarly, this provides the reason for rejecting the profitability index as a measure of investment worth.
2. *NPV* implicitly assumes reinvestment of the interim proceeds at the cost of capital; the *IRR* assumes reinvestment at the project's own rate of return. Once again this is a point in favor of the *NPV* since projects which earn more than their opportunity cost would be accepted anyway, *independent* of the current investment decision. Hence, the investment worth of a current project should not be credited with returns on interim receipts in excess of the cost of capital.
3. The reinvestment assumption is of crucial importance if we assume a changing cost of capital in future years. Under such circumstances the *IRR* rule breaks down because the comparison of a single-valued rate of return with a series of different short-term discount rates is not meaningful.
4. Finally, the *NPV* is not only theoretically superior to the *IRR* but also has important technical advantages. When nonconventional cash flows are considered, a real solution for the project's *IRR* may not exist; or in other instances, more than one *IRR* may be found for a single project.

In summary, the *NPV* provides an optimal solution to the firm's capital budgeting problems on the assumption that the future cash flows and the appropriate cost of capital (discount rate) are known. The popularity of the *IRR* rule is in part psychological; a measure of investment worth which is set out in percentage terms is appealing to many executives. The rate of return can readily be compared with the cost of funds to yield a 'margin of profit'. This is a valid consideration and much can be said in favor of *presenting* the results of a feasibility study in a form which is preferred by management, that is in terms of the *IRR*. However, the intuitive appeal of the *IRR* should not be permitted to obscure the fundamental fact that when mutually exclusive decisions have to be made, they should be dictated by differences between the alternative proposals' net present values and not by their internal rates of return.

With this technical material under our belts, we turn in Chapter 5 to the 'real world' problem of applying our evaluation methods and decision rules to actual cash flows within the complex framework of a modern corporate organization.

Contrasting *NPV* and *IRR* rules

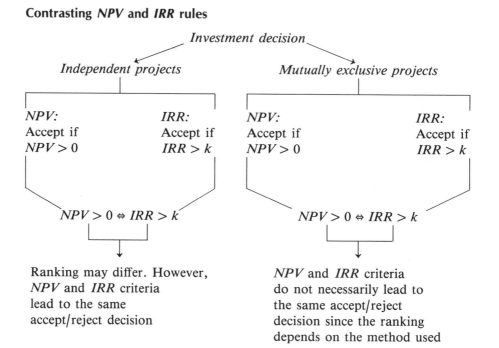

Reasons which may induce a difference in the ranking

1. Scale of investment is ignored by *IRR* rule.
2. Timing of cash flows.
3. Difference in the reinvestment assumption.

Theoretical justification of the *NPV* rule

1. Maximizes investor's utility.
2. Takes into account investment size.
3. Reinvests interim cash flows at the relevant rate.

Technical disadvantages of the *IRR* criterion

1. Nonconventional cash flow (no real *IRR* or more than one *IRR*).
2. Cost of capital may vary over time.

4.1 (a) The *NPV* and *IRR* criteria always lead to the same decisions, when the projects are conventional and independent. Prove this statement.

(b) The *NPV* and *IRR* may lead to different decisions when the projects are mutually exclusive. Explain.

4.2 Assume that you are confronted by the following three projects:

Year	0	1	2	3	4	5
				Cash flow		
Project A	−1,000	100	100	100	100	1,100
Project B	−1,000	264	264	264	264	264
Project C	−1,000	—	—	—	—	1,611

(a) Calculate the net present value of each of the above projects, assuming a 10% discount rate, and rank the projects.

(b) Calculate the internal rate of return for each of the above projects and rank the projects.

(c) Calculate the net present value of each of the projects using a 6% discount rate and rank the projects.

(d) Calculate the net present value of the projects assuming a 15% discount rate and rank the projects.

(e) Compare and explain the ranking which you obtained in parts (a)–(d) above using a diagram which graphs the *NPV* as a function of the discount rate.

4.3 Consider the following two *mutually exclusive* investment opportunities:

Year	0	1	2	3	4	5
Project A	− 48,700	17,000	17,000	17,000	17,000	17,000
Project B	− 31,600	12,000	12,000	12,000	12,000	12,000

(a) Calculate each project's net present value and internal rate of return. (Assume that the cost of capital is 8%.)

(b) Which of the two projects would be chosen according to the *IRR* criterion? Which according to the *NPV* criterion?

(c) How can you explain the differences in rankings given by the *NPV* and *IRR* methods in this case?

4.4 A company is confronted with the following two *mutually exclusive* investment opportunities:

Year	0	1	2	3	4
Project C	− 80,000	28,000	28,000	28,000	28,000
Project D	− 24,000	9,800	9,800	9,800	9,800

(a) Calculate the net present value of each of the above projects assuming a 10% discount rate.

(b) Calculate the internal rate of return of each project.

(c) Which of the two projects would be chosen according to the *NPV* criterion? Which according to the *IRR*?

(d) Describe the hypothetical cash flow 'C minus D' and calculate its *NPV* and *IRR*. Use this result to 'defend' the *NPV* decision.

(e) Graph the *NPV* of each project (including the project 'C minus D') as a function of the discount rate.

4.5 Consider the following two *mutually exclusive* projects:

Year	0	1	2
Project A	−10,000	6,700	5,700
Project B	− 2,000	1,900	900

(a) For each project, calculate the net present value, internal rate of return and the profitability index, assuming an 8% discount rate.

(b) Which of the two projects is preferred according to each of the three methods?

(c) How can you explain the differences in ranking given by the *NPV* criterion and the profitability index?

(d) Which of the two methods is the correct one?

(e) Calculate the internal rate of return of the project 'A minus B'. Does it confirm your answer to part (d)? Explain.

4.6 Having proven yourself to be a superior student (your choice of this course being a case in point) your university offers you a choice between an outright *gift* of $1,000 or a $7,000 *interest-free loan* to be paid back in seven equal annual instalments of $1,000 each. Assume that there is only one interest rate in the market, denoted by *r*.

(a) Which alternative would represent the optimal choice for you? Explain your decision.

(b) Under what circumstances would you reverse your choice? Be specific. (Use a graph to illustrate your answer.)

4.7 A corporation is examining the following two *mutually exclusive* investment proposals:

Proposal A: Initial outlay of $100,000 and receipts of $25,000 in the first year and $125,000 in the second year.

Proposal B: Initial outlay of $100,000 and receipts of $95,000 in the first year and $45,500 in the second year.

(a) Calculate each project's net present value and internal rate of return, assuming a cost of capital of 10%.

(b) Which of the two projects would be chosen according to the *NPV* criterion? Which according to the *IRR* criterion?

(c) How can you explain the differences in ranking given by the *NPV* and *IRR* methods *in this case*? Use the incremental cash flow 'A minus B' in your explanation.

(d) How would your answers to parts (a)–(c) be changed if you assume that the cost of capital is 16%? Be specific.

4.8 One of the main differences between the net present value and the internal rate of return methods lies in the implicit assumptions concerning the reinvestment of interim cash flows.

(a) Identify the implicit assumption in each of these methods.

(b) In the light of your answer to part (a), which method should be preferred? Explain your choice.

4.9 Under what assumptions will the *IRR* and *NPV* methods necessarily rank all projects in the same order of priority? Show your answer graphically.

4.10 Critically comment on the following statements:

(a) The problem of reinvestment rates can be avoided by considering only projects of the same duration.
(b) The problem of reinvestment does not exist when the two projects have the same duration and require the same investment outlay.
(c) The *IRR* method does not assume that interim receipts are reinvested.

4.11 The following cash flow represents an investment in an energy-saving machine for a firm faced with a cost of capital of 12%.

Year	0	1	2	3
Cash flow	−1000	400	500	600

(a) Calculate the project's *NPV* and *IRR*.
(b) Show numerically that if the firm borrows $1,000 at t_0 to pay for the investment at an interest rate which is equal to the project's *IRR*, it will end up with a zero cash balance at the end of the project.
(c) Show numerically that if the firm pays interest on the loan at the rate of $k\%$ per year ($k = 12\%$) and any cash which remains is used to pay the principal, then what is left at the end of the project will be exactly equal to the future value of the project's net present value.

4.12 Consider the following cash flows:

Year	0	1	2
Project A	500	−700	300
Project B	−60	120	−100

(a) Calculate the internal rate of return and the net present value (at a discount rate of 12%) for each project.
(b) Plot the *NPV* profile for each project as a function of the discount rate. Explain your results.

4.13 Consider the following cash flows:

Year	0	1	2
Project A	−40	130	−100
Project B	25	−140	160
Project C	−100	500	−600

(a) Calculate each project's *NPV* and *IRR* (assume a discount rate of 10%).
(b) Plot each project's *NPV* profile as a function of the discount rate. Indicate the intersections on both axes.
(c) What is the economic meaning of the *IRR* when a project has two rates of return?

4.14 The examination of a project revealed that it has two internal rates of return: 10% and 30%. Assume that the cost of capital is 15%. Should the firm accept the investment project? Explain your answer.

4.15 Part 1 The Olive Oil company is examining the following two *mutually exclusive* investment projects:

		Cash flow	
	Initial outlay	First year	Second year
Project A	−1,000	1,180	–
Project B	−1,000	–	1,300

(a) Calculate the net present value and the internal rate of return of each project. (Assume an 8% cost of capital.)
(b) Rank the projects according to each of the two methods.

Part 2 The Super Delux company was confronted by the following two *mutually exclusive* investment opportunities:

			Year		
	0	1	2	3	4
Project C	− 500	–	–	–	1,037
Project D	− 500	625	–	–	–

(a) Calculate each project's net present value and internal rate of return. (Assume that the cost of capital is 8%.)
(b) Which of the two projects would be chosen according to the *NPV* criterion? According to *IRR* criterion?
(c) How can you explain the difference in rankings in this case?
(d) Build a 'repetitive' project for the projects in this question and in question 4.2 above to show that the paradoxical difference in ranking can be resolved.

Part 3

(a) In view of your answers to parts (1) and (2) above, which of the two methods, in your opinion, provides the *optimal* decision in each of the cases? Explain and defend your choice.
(b) How would you qualify your answer in the absence of mutual exclusiveness, that is, if the projects were economically *independent*?

4.16 The Eastern Metals company is confronted with the following two-period independent projects:

Project	Required investment outlay ($)	Net cash receipts at end of year ($)
A	750,000	900,000
B	400,000	420,000
C	200,000	260,000
D	300,000	330,000
E	250,000	400,000
F	100,000	140,000

The firm has initial available resources of $2 million.

(a) Plot the productivity schedule of the firm.
(b) Calculate, and show on the graph, how much the firm can 'consume' next year if it 'consumes':
  (i) $350,000 this year
  (ii) $1,300,000 this year.

Which projects would it execute in each case?

4.17 Define the following terms:

(a) Rational individual.
(b) Indifference curve.
(c) Optimal choice.

4.18 An individual is indifferent between the following consumption combinations, which are in dollars:

This year	Next year
4,000	3,200
3,700	3,500
3,200	4,000
2,900	4,400

(a) Plot the indifference curve that represents the individual's tastes with respect to current and future consumption.
(b) What is the meaning of a *convex* indifference curve? Is the curve which you plotted in part (a) convex? Prove your answer.

4.19 1. 'I am indifferent between the consumption combinations ($2,200 this year; $2,500 next year) and ($2,600 this year; $2,000 next year).'
2. 'Consumption of $2,800 this year and $2,100 next year gives me the same satisfaction as consumption of $2,200 this year and $2,500 next year.'

Is it possible that both statements were made by the same individual? Prove your answer.

4.20 Illustrate graphically the two-period consumption–investment model for the case of independent projects.

(a) What are the equilibrium conditions when the only possibilities are investment and consumption?
(b) What are the equilibrium conditions when it is also possible to lend or borrow?

4.21 An investor with an initial endowment of $2,500 is confronted with the following two-period independent investment options:

Project	Required investment ($)	First-year receipts ($)
A	200	260
B	300	450
C	100	175
D	500	525
E	200	310
F	100	110
G	200	250
H	300	300
I	400	460
J	200	360

Assume that the investor's indifference curve is defined in the following manner: he requires compensation of 1.35 units of future consumption when his current consumption is decreased by one unit. Answer the following questions, assuming that there is no possibility to borrow or lend money.

(a) Plot the investor's productivity schedule.
(b) How much will the investor invest in production?
(c) What is the optimal consumption combination?
(d) Is it possible that the investor will choose to consume $1,300 this year? Explain.

4.22 Assume that the investor is allowed to lend and borrow at an interest rate of 20%. Answer the following questions with regard to the data in question 4.21.

(a) How much will the investor invest in production?
(b) What is the net present value of the investment chosen by the investor?
(c) What is the present value of the investor's total consumption in both periods?
(d) What is the future value of the investor's total consumption in both periods?

4.23 An investor with initial endowment of $2,000 is confronted with the same ten investment options that appeared in question 4.21. Assume that projects A, C, and G exclude projects H and J, that is if the investor decides to execute A, C, or G, he cannot execute H or J; likewise, if he chooses H or J he cannot choose A, C or G. Assume also that the interest rate is 20%.

(a) Illustrate graphically the two mutually exclusive investment (productivity) curves.
(b) Show and prove that the *NPV* rule gives the optimal investment decision in this case.
(c) How much will the investor invest in production? Which projects will he carry out?
(d) What is the present value of the total consumption in both periods?

4.24 'The two-period investment–consumption model gives a unique solution for the investment problem even when all the projects confronting the firm have the same *IRR*.'
Appraise, for both the case of independent projects and the case of mutually exclusive projects.

4.25 'One who is not concerned about future consumption need not bother investing in production.'
Appraise and prove your answer.

4.26 An investor with an initial endowment of $16,000 is confronted with the following productivity curve:

$$C_1 = 240\sqrt{(16,000 - C_0)}$$

where C_0 indicates consumption at present, and C_1 consumption in the future. Assume the interest rate (for borrowing and lending) is 20%. The investor's utility function, from which it is possible to derive his indifference curves, is defined as:

$$u(C_0, C_1) = C_0 \times C_1$$

Answer the following questions, using the two-period investment–consumption model:

(a) How much will the investor invest in production?
(b) What is the *NPV* of the investment chosen by the investor?
(c) What is the net present value of his total consumption?
(d) Does the investor borrow or lend in the capital market? Give a numerical answer.
(e) What is the optimal allocation of consumption for the two periods?

Illustrate your answers graphically.

4.27 Another investor with an initial endowment of $32,000 is confronted with the productivity curve defined as follows:

$$C_1 = 36\sqrt{(32,000 - C_0)}$$

where C_0 indicates consumption at present, and C_1 consumption in the future. Assume that the interest rate (for borrowing and lending) is 20%. The investor's utility function, from which it is possible to derive his indifference curves, is defined as:

$$u(C_0, C_1) = 12C_0^2 + 100C_0C_1$$

Answer the following questions, using the two-period model of investment–consumption:

(a) How much will the investor invest in production?
(b) What is the *NPV* of the investment chosen by the investor?
(c) What is the net present value of his total consumption in both periods?
(d) Does the investor borrow or lend in the capital market? Give a numerical answer.
(e) What is the optimal allocation of consumption for the two periods?

Illustrate your answer graphically.

4.28 Consider an investment in physical capital when the initial wealth W_0 is $100. The investment transformation curve between current consumption (C_0) and future consumption (C_1) is such that the marginal return on successive investments of

$10 is as follows:

Marginal investment ($)	Total return ($)	Marginal net return ($)
10	67.0	57.0
10	83.0	6.0
10	98.0	5.0
10	112.0	4.0
10	125.0	3.0
10	137.0	2.0
10	148.5	1.5
10	159.5	1.0
10	170.0	0.5
10	180.0	0.0

Assume that the borrowing and lending rate is 35% (i.e. $r = 0.35$).

(a) What is the optimal investment at time t_0? Show your solution on a diagram.

(b) Assume now that an individual has the following indifference curves between current and future consumption:

$$C_1 = a + \tfrac{1}{20}(C_0 - 100)^2 \qquad 0 \leqslant C_0 \leqslant 100$$

where a is a constant along any indifference curve. Determine the optimal amount to be borrowed or lent by the individual at time t_0 as well as his total consumption at t_0 and at t_1.

(c) Work out parts (a) and (b) once again, this time a assuming the following indifference curve:

$$C_1 = a + \tfrac{1}{20}(C_0 - 60)^2 \qquad 0 \leqslant C_0 \leqslant 60$$

Is there any change in the investment decision compared with parts (a) and (b)? Why?

4.29 Part 1 Consider a two-period investment productivity curve defined by the equation

$$C_1 = 300\sqrt{(12{,}000 - C_0)}$$

where C_0 is the current-period consumption and C_1 is the next-period consumption. The investor's initial endowment is $W_0 = \$12{,}000$.

(a) Draw the investment productivity curve in the (C_0, C_1) plane by calculating several points of the curve.

(b) What is the maximum attainable current consumption? What is the corresponding future consumption?

(c) What is the maximum investment that can be made in the current period? What are the corresponding consumption levels C_0 and C_1? What is the average return on investment?

(d) Suppose the investor with total endowment $W_0 = \$12{,}000$ decides to invest $4,900 in production. What are his consumption levels in the two periods, C_0 and C_1? Show the resulting two-period consumption strategy on your graph and indicate the production projects in which the individual invested his capital. What is his *average* return on investment? What is the marginal rate of return on investment?

Part 2 Now consider three investors whose indifference maps are described by the following two-period utility functions:

Investor A: $u(C_0, C_1) = C_0 + C_1$
Investor B: $u(C_0, C_1) = 3C_0 + C_1$
Investor C: $u(C_0, C_1) = C_0 \times C_1$

(Each indifference curve corresponds to some constant value of the utility function, $u(C_0, C_1) = $ constant.)

(a) Show graphically the optimum consumption combination that each investor will choose.
(b) Find the corresponding optimum consumption combination analytically.
(c) How much will each individual invest in production?
(d) What is the marginal rate of return on investment at the optimum point for each investor? What is the average rate of return of total investment?

Part 3 Now suppose that in addition to the investment productivity curve there is a perfect capital market in which all investors can borrow and lend at a constant rate of $r = 50\%$. Hence, 50% is in this case the cost of capital for all investors.

(a) Find analytically the optimum *production* policies of the three investors. Show your results graphically.
(b) What is the total amount invested by each investor in production?
(c) What is the marginal rate of return on production investments for each investor?
(d) What is the net present value of the optimum production strategy of each investor? What is the future value? What is the equation of the money market line through the optimum production point?
(e) Find analytically the optimum consumption combination of investor C. Indicate whether investor C acts as a borrower or a lender in the money market. What is the amount of borrowing or lending?
(f) Is investor C better off with or without the money market?

4.30 In the Bible we find the following text:

> The Lord shall open unto thee his good treasure, the heaven to give the rain unto thy land in his season, and to bless all the work of thine hand: and thou shalt lend unto many nations, and thou shalt not borrow. (Deuteronomy 28:12.)

Suppose that God opens his treasures to an investor and his initial wealth grows from W_0 to say $5W_0$. There is no change in the projects available and in the market interest rate. Show graphically a case where the investor changes, as a result of the increase in his wealth, from a borrower to a lender.

4.31 Two mutually exclusive projects have the following incremental cash flows:

	Initial outlay	Cash flow	
		Year 1	Year 2
Project A	−100	120	30
Project B	−100	40	140

Assuming a cost of capital of 20%, calculate the *NPV* and *IRR*. Show using incremental cash flows and the *IRR* decision rule that you choose the same project selected as with *NPV*.

4.32 The two-period production function is given by:

$$C_2 = 100 + 66\sqrt{(W_0 - C_1)} \text{ where } W_0 = \$1,000$$

(a) Draw a graph of the production function.

(b) Find the optimum investment when the riskless interest rate is 10%. What are the corresponding C_1 and C_2?

(c) What would be the optimum investment, and the corresponding C_1 and C_2 when the borrowing and the lending rate that the banks charge (or pay) is −10% (Assume zero inflation rate.) Do the conditions given in (c) describe equilibrium in the capital market? Explain.

(d) Assume that the interest rate is 10% and there is zero inflation (as described in (b) above). Now a neutral inflation rate of 10% for the next year is *fully anticipated*. What will be the impact of inflation on lenders' behavior and the production function? What changes does inflation cause in the optimum investment solution?

(e) Describe a case where investors have *different* marginal rates of substitution between consumption in the two periods, yet all reach identical investment and consumption decisions. In your answer assume $k = 10\%$ and zero inflation (i.e. corresponding to (b) above).

4.33 If two projects have the same initial investment outlay, the same economic duration and constant positive cash flows across years (but not the same cash flow for both projects) then the *NPV* and *IRR* must yield the same projects ranking. Do you agree with this assertion? Prove your answer.

4.34 Suppose that a firm faces two sets of projects: one set consists of A and B, and the other set consists of A^* and B, where A and A^* are mutually exclusive projects, and project B is the same project in the two sets.

(a) Draw the two production functions on the assumption that A and A^* are the most profitable projects in each set. Using these two production functions, show graphically a case when the *NPV* rule is a superior decision rule, dominating the *IRR* rule.

(b) Repeat (a) above when A (and A^*) are the projects with the lowest profitability in each set.

(c) Using these two production functions given in (b) above, show a case when the *NPV* and *IRR* yield the same investment decision.

4.35 Suppose that the firm invests $I_0 = 100$ and borrows \$50 at $r = 10\%$ per annum to finance the investment. The firm provides the shareholder with dividends of $d_0 = \$80$ today and of $d_1 = \$40$ next year. You do not like this financing policy because you prefer no leverage and dividends of $d_1 = \$95$ in the future. Show how dividend policy and capital structure are determined simultaneously in this case. Show how you 'undo' the leverage and obtain your optimum dividend cash flows.

APPENDIX 4A: CALCULATING THE OPTIMAL INVESTMENT–CONSUMPTION COMBINATION IN A TWO-PERIOD MODEL

Denoting by f the production function, we can find the optimal production strategy at the tangency point between f and the PV line by equating the slope of f to the slope of the PV line, i.e.:

$$\left(\frac{dC_1}{dC_0}\right)_f = -(1 + k)$$

To find the optimal borrowing, we equate the slope of the PV line to the slope of the indifference curve, thus

$$\left(\frac{dC_1}{dC_0}\right)_u = -(1+k)$$

where u denotes differentiation along a particular indifference curve corresponding to the value u of the utility function.

Example

Suppose that the productivity curve is defined as $C_1 = 250(18,000 - C_0)^{1/2}$ and the interest rate k is 25%, so that

$$\left(\frac{dC_1}{dC_0}\right)_f = -125(18,000 - C_0)^{-1/2} \qquad \text{and} \qquad -(1+k) = -1.25$$

Then:

$$\frac{-125}{(18,000 - C_0)^{1/2}} = -1.25$$

$$(18,000 - C_0)^{1/2} = 100$$

$$18,000 - C_0 = 10,000$$

$$\therefore C_0^* = 18,000 - 10,000$$

$$= \$8,000$$

If the initial endowment is \$18,000 then the investment in production is $I_0 = 18,000 - 8,000 = \$10,000$ and $C_1^* = 250(18,000 - C_0^*)^{1/2} = 250(10,000)^{1/2} = 250 \times 100 = \$\$25,000$.

The NPV of the investment is $C_1^*/(1+k) - I_0$ and the PV of the total consumption is:

$$\frac{C_1^*}{1+k} + C_0^* = \frac{25,000}{1.25} + 8,000 = \$28,000$$

The optimal consumption amounts (C_0^{**}, C_1^{**}) are determined by the point where the iso-PV line is tangential to the indifference curve, so that to find this point we have to equate the derivative of the indifference curve $(dC_1/dC_0)_u$ to the slope of the iso-PV line.

Suppose that $u(C_0, C_1) = 2C_0 \times C_1$. Then:

$$\left(\frac{dC_1}{dC_0}\right)_u = -\frac{\partial u(C_0, C_1)}{\partial C_0} \bigg/ \frac{\partial u(C_0, C_1)}{\partial C_1} = \frac{-2C_1}{2C_0} = -\frac{C_1}{C_0}$$

so that:

$$dC_1/dC_0 = -(1+k) \Leftrightarrow -C_1/C_0 = -1.25 \text{ or } C_1^{**} = 1.25C_0^{**}$$

Since this point lies on the same iso-PV lines as (C_0^*, C_1^*), then:

$$\frac{C_1^{**}}{1+k} + C_0^{**} = \frac{C_1^*}{1+k} + C_0^* = 28,000$$

or

$$\frac{1.25C_0^{**}}{1.25} + C_0^{**} = C_0^{**} + C_0^{**} = 2C_0^{**} = 28,000$$

$$\therefore C_0^{**} = \$14,000$$

$$\text{and} \quad C_1^{**} = 1.25C_0^{**} = 1.25 \times 14,000 = \$17,500$$

SELECTED REFERENCES

Beidlemen, C. R., 'Discounted Cash Flow Reinvestment Rate Assumptions,' *Engineering Economist*, Winter 1984.

Beranek, W., 'The AB Procedure and Capital Budgeting,' *Journal of Financial and Quantitative Analysis*, June 1980.

Bernardo, J. J. and Lanser, H. P., 'A Capital Budgeting Decision Model with Subjective Criteria,' *Journal of Financial and Quantitative Analysis*, June 1977.

Bernhard, R. H. and Norstrom, Carl J., 'A Further Note on Unrecovered Investment Uniqueness of the Internal Rate, and the Question of Project Acceptability,' *Journal of Financial and Quantitative Analysis*, June 1980.

Black, F., 'A Simple Discounting Rule,' *Financial Management*, Summer 1988.

Bradley, S. P. and Frey, C. S. Jr., 'Equivalent Mathematical Programming Models of Pure Capital Rationing,' *Journal of Financial and Quantitative Analysis*, June 1978.

Brick, J. R. and Thompson, H. E., 'The Economic Life of an Investment and the Appropriate Discount Rate,' *Journal of Financial and Quantitative Analysis*, December 1978.

Canada, J. R. and Miller, N. P., 'Review of Surveys on Use of Capital Investment Evaluation Techniques,' *Engineering Economist*, Winter 1985.

Canaday, R. E., Colwell, P. R., and Paley, H., 'Relevant and Irrelevant Internal Rates of Return,' *Engineering Economist*, Fall 1986.

Capettini, R., Grimlund, R. A., and Toole, H. R., 'Comment: The Unique, Real Internal Rate of Return,' *Journal of Financial and Quantitative Analysis*, December 1979.

Ederington, L. H. and Henry, W. R., 'On Costs of Capital in Programming Approaches to Capital Budgeting,' *Journal of Financial and Quantitative Analysis*, December 1979.

Emery, G. W., 'Some Guidelines for Evaluating Capital Investment Alternatives with Unequal Lives,' *Financial Management*, Spring 1982.

Gronchi, S., 'On Investment Criteria Based on Internal Rate of Return,' *Oxford Economic Papers*, March 1986.

Hajdasinski, M. M., 'A Complete Method for Separation of Internal Rates of Return,' *Engineering Economist*, Spring 1983.

Herbst, A., 'The Unique, Real Internal Rate of Return: *Caveat Emptor!*,' *Journal of Financial and Quantitative Analysis*, June 1978.

Hirshleifer, J. H., 'On the Theory of Optimal Investment Decisions,' *Journal of Political Economy*, August 1958.

Hoskins, Colin G., 'Benefit–Cost Ratio Ranking for Size Disparity Problems,' *Journal of Business Finance and Accounting*, 4(2), 1977.

Klammer, T. P. and Walker, A. C., 'The Continuing Increase in the Use of Sophisticated Capital Budgeting Techniques,' *California Management Review*, Fall 1985.

Ross, Stephen A., Spatt, Chester S., and Dybvig, Philip H., 'Present Values and Internal Rates of Return,' *Journal of Economic Theory*, August 1980.

Schwab, Bernard and Lusztig, Peter, 'A Comparative Analysis of the Net Present Value and the Benefit–Cost Ratios as Measures of the Economic Desirability of Investments,' *Journal of Finance*, June 1969.

Saphr, R. W., 'Basic Uncertainty in Capital Budgeting: Stochastic Reinvestment Rates,' *Engineering Economist*, Summer 1982.

Stapleton, R. C., 'The Acquisition Decision as a Capital Budgeting Problem,' *Journal of Business, Finance and Accounting*, Summer 1975.

Sundaresan, M., 'Consumption and Equilibrium Interest Rates in Stochastic Production Economics,' *Journal of Finance*, March 1984.

Sundem, G. L., 'Evaluating Capital Budgeting Models in Simulated Environments,' *Journal of Finance*, September 1975.

Tiffen, Mary, 'Dethroning the Internal Rate of Return: The Evidence from Irrigation Projects,' *Development Policy Review*, December 1987.

Weingartner, H. M., *Mathematical Programming and the Analysis of Capital Budgeting Problems*, Englewood Cliffs, N.J.: Prentice Hall, 1963.

Weingartner, H. M., 'Capital Rationing: Authors in Search of a Plot,' *Journal of Finance*, December 1977.

5

Using Cash Flows to Evaluate Investments

ARTICLE 11

AT&T to Adopt Rule On Tax Accounting, Sees Benefit in 1993

NEW YORK − **American Telephone & Telegraph** Co. said it plans to adopt a new accounting rule for income taxes that will give it a benefit of about $500 million next year.

AT&T said it plans to adopt the rule in the 1993 first quarter. The company indicated its estimated benefit in a filing with the Securities and Exchange Commission. The benefit will partly offset a big liability − the accumulated estimated cost of health benefits for retired employees. The liability also is the result of new accounting rules for corporations. AT&T previously estimated that cost at between $5.5 billion and $7.5 billion, to be taken next year as a non-cash charge against earnings.

The rule for income taxes requires companies to determine the amount of their deferred taxes based on the tax rates that will be in effect for years when taxes will be paid or refunds received. Like most other companies, AT&T will benefit because its deferred taxes were calculated on the basis of higher tax rates that were in effect when the deferrals were established. Its current deferred tax liability is about $1.5 billion.

Both rule changes, for income taxes and for retiree benefit costs, were issued by the Financial Accounting Standards Board. AT&T said that although they will affect net income, they won't affect cash flow. For 1991, AT&T reported earnings of $522 million; excluding major charges and gains, mainly costs associated with the acquistion of NCR Corp., net income was about $3.2 billion.

Source: *Wall Street Journal*, May 8, 1992.

Article 11 shows AT&T's estimated gain from changing accounting practices for income taxes is approximately $500 million in 1993. It also mentions that between $5.5 and $7.5 billion will be taken as a noncash charge against actual earnings next year. In addition, AT&T reports that it has changed retirement benefit costs and claims that, 'both rule changes ... will affect net income, they won't affect cash flows.'

What is the relevant measure of the profitability of a firm, or for that matter a project? Is accounting income relevant? If reported income increases or decreases but actual cash flows remain unchanged, are shareholders of the firm better or worse off (i.e., does the firm's value increase, decrease, or remain unchanged)? Why do taxes affect cash flows? How can AT&T realize a gain of $500 million by changing accounting practices?

In the two preceding chapters, alternative investment decision criteria were analyzed on the assumption that the annual cash flows are known. No attempt was made to determine how the future receipts and outlays should be defined or measured. The purpose of this chapter is to prepare the groundwork for the practical application of capital budgeting techniques. To this end we first examine the principles underlying the measurement of a project's cash flows; following this, the capital budgeting model will be applied to a recurring problem of great importance to most firms: the analysis of equipment replacement decisions. Then we discuss the impact of corporate taxes on a project's cash flows. We show that cash flows and not accounting income are relevant for decision making.

Although inflation rates are currently moderate (unlike the inflation rates in the 1970s and early 1980s), they still affect a firm's profitability and tax liability. We would be remiss if we did not at least mention the major impact inflation has on financial analysis. (After all, the double-digit inflation rates which characterized the 1970s and 1980s may plague us once again.) Therefore, in the last section of this chapter we discuss the impact inflation has on a firm's profitability.

_____ **INCREMENTAL CASH FLOWS**

Underlying modern financial analysis is the principle of *incremental cash flows*, which states that a project should be evaluated by considering all of the cash inflows and outflows induced by the investment. It follows that attention must be given to the magnitude and timing of the cash flows, rather than to the accounting concepts of income and expenses. To help clarify the cash flow principle let us consider an extreme hypothetical example. Assume that Avirone Aircraft Corporation signs a contract to supply five jet airplanes to Pan World Airlines in 1994. The contract is signed in 1992, and Pan World makes an advance payment of $20 million to help Avirone finance the project. On Avirone's financial statements, no profit from this contract will be reported in either 1992 or 1993. Only in 1994, when the jets are delivered to Pan World, will the profit (or loss) generated by this transaction be reflected in Avirone's accounts, that is to say the $20 million received in 1992 will not affect the accounting revenues of the project. Thus from the viewpoint of reported accounting earnings, Avirone Aircraft Corporation's decision to undertake such a project would not be influenced by the receipt of the advance payment.

Clearly, this does not make economic sense and in practice a firm will always prefer, other things being equal, to receive as large a cash advance as possible, thereby reducing the cost of financing the project. In order to reflect this important dimension of the decision process, modern time-adjusted investment criteria are based on cash inflows and outflows rather than accounting cash flows. Hence the exact timing of each component of the cash flow must be accurately determined if a proposal's full economic impact is to be gauged correctly.

The difference between the incremental cash flow and accounting concepts can also be illustrated by considering trade credit. Let us assume that the annual sales in 1992 of the ABC Company were $100,000, and that the company's policy was to offer two-year payment terms to its customers. The accounting department of the ABC Company will report gross revenues of $100,000 for the year. Now suppose that the total cost of producing and selling the product in question is $80,000 and that this outlay also occurred in 1992. The company's balance sheet for 1992 will include an entry *accounts receivable* of $100,000 and its income statement will report a profit of $20,000. However, from the viewpoint of capital budgeting, the impact on *NPV* is considerably smaller. Since the outlay of $80,000 occurs in 1992 no adjustment is required (for simplicity we assume that the costs were incurred on the first day of the year); but this is not true of the revenues from sales as they will only be realized in 1994, that is two years later. The calculation of the 'cash flow' profit is, therefore, as follows:

1992	1993	1994
− 80,000	−	+100,000

Obviously, the accounting and the cash flow profits are the same only for the trivial and unrealistic case of a zero discount rate (i.e., cost of capital). At all positive discount rates the cash flow profit will be smaller. For example, if we assume a 10% discount rate, the calculation of the discounted value of the profit is:

$$\frac{100,000}{(1.1)^2} - 80,000 = \$2,600$$

Thus the contribution to *NPV* is $2,600 and not $20,000. And as we have already noted, the *NPV* of cash flows is the relevant concept for the maximization of the value of the owners' equity.

Invoking the cash flow principle is not in itself sufficient to resolve all of the conceptual difficulties which plague the measurement of the costs and benefits of a typical investment project. Some of these problems can best be examined by considering yet another example. Suppose that the Pacific Electric Company is considering an investment in a new power unit, and that the gross cash inflows from this unit are expected to be $100,000 per year, while the annual cash outflows for fuel, labor, etc. are expected to be $75,000. In addition, the cost accounting department estimates that overhead costs of $20,000 per year should be charged to the new power unit. These costs include the new project's share of managerial salaries, general administrative expenses, etc. For simplicity, we shall assume that these overhead costs include $10,000 of *fixed costs*, that is costs which will be incurred even if the project is not implemented. An example of such a cost would be that fraction of the company president's salary which is allocated to investigating the feasibility of the new power unit. The remaining $10,000 is assumed to be variable costs, or costs that will be incurred only if the project is accepted. In addition, it has been estimated that the company's net receipts from its other power units will *decrease* by $5,000 per year should the new power unit be installed.

Table 5.1 summarizes the above information on the receipts and outlays of the proposed project. Clearly, the annual cash inflow of $100,000 is part of the project's cash flow, but it is not equally clear that all of the four outlays listed in Table 5.1 should be deducted from the inflow when calculating the project's net annual cash flow. In general, the fixed overhead expenses should *not* be deducted from the project's receipts as they do not represent an incremental cash outflow induced by the decision to invest in the new power unit. By definition, these fixed costs (president's salary, etc.) will remain the same, *independent* of the investment decision in question, and therefore they should not be 'charged' against the project. Variable overhead costs and the direct costs (fuel, labor, etc.) should be deducted since they do represent incremental outlays induced by the decision to invest in the new unit.

The last item of Table 5.1, the decrease in net receipts elsewhere in the firm, should also be deducted. By the incremental cash flow principle, this is a (negative) cash flow which occurs as a direct result of the decision to invest in the new unit. The fact that the change in the cash flow takes place with respect to other power units, or in another department, is relevant; we seek to measure the net change in the firm's *total* cash flow which will be induced by the decision to invest. Thus any impact of the new project on the cash flows of existing units is germane to the investment decision, and therefore should be reflected in the estimated cash flows of the new unit. Hence, when developing a new model car, Ford and General Motors try to introduce a model which will not compete with their existing models. A very 'successful' new car which drastically reduces revenues from the sales of existing models might prove a disaster, and therefore must be evaluated on an incremental cash flow basis if its true impact is to be reflected in the profitability calculation.

Initial investment outlay and depreciation

Having examined the underlying principle of incremental cash flows, let us now turn to some additional problems which can arise when determining a

Table 5.1 Annual receipts and outlays of new power unit (in dollars)

Annual inflow:	100,000
Annual outflow:	
Fuel, labor, etc.	75,000
Fixed overhead	10,000
Variable overhead	10,000
Decrease in net receipts from other power units	5,000

project's cash flows. Suppose, for example, that the XYZ Company acquires a machine which costs $10,000, has an expected economic life of ten years and is expected to produce a net annual cash inflow of S. The cash flows for such a machine can be written as follows:

	Years				
0	1	2	3	...	10
(−10,000)	S	S	S	...	S

Now, consider the problem confronting the company's accountant, who must allocate the project's revenues and costs to particular years in order to estimate the annual net profit in the annual report to the shareholders. To do this he must first calculate that part of the machine's original purchase price which erodes each year. The most popular solution to this problem is to divide the original cost of the machine by its expected economic life, thereby deriving the *depreciation* figure which must be deducted from the annual receipts when calculating the accounting profit for the year (allocating identical amounts of depreciation to each year of the project's economic life is called straight line depreciation). In our example, the annual depreciation expense is $1,000 ($10,000 \div 10 = 1,000$) and the net annual profit is S minus $1,000.

Obviously, the deduction of a depreciation allowance is a compromise between reality and the legal requirement to calculate an annual profit figure. However, when evaluating the profitability of a proposed capital investment one can (and should) ignore interim profits and consider the project's entire life as a single decision unit. Thus, in capital budgeting the allocation of costs to particular years can be ignored and attention can be focused on the cash flows at the precise time that they occur.

Since the machine in question is to be purchased and paid for at the outset of the project, an outlay of $10,000 at the beginning of the first year is taken into account, rather than deducting an allowance for depreciation of $1,000 in each of the next ten years. Clearly, the two alternative ways of handling the initial investment outlay are equivalent only for the special case in which the discount rate is equal to zero. In general the two methods differ, and in choosing a method of incorporating capital costs, we prefer to deduct the initial investment outlay when it is incurred because that is when the actual cash flow occurs. Since the capital cost is fully taken into account by deducting the initial investment outlay from the project's cash flow when calculating *NPV*, accounting depreciation should *not* be deducted from the net receipts S: deducting an annual depreciation allowance would double count investment costs.

Working capital

In addition to depreciable assets (buildings, machinery, etc.) investment in a new project often requires an investment in working capital (cash, inventories, etc.). The treatment of working capital requires special attention. Consider the following hypothetical example. Let:

I_0 = initial investment outlay
W = investment in working capital
S = annual net receipts
I_n = terminal (salvage) value of the depreciable assets
n = economic life of the project

The cash flow of such a project can be written as follows:

			Year		
0	1	2	3	...	n
$-(I_0 + W)$	S	S	S	...	$S + I_n + W$

Note that in the last year of the project's expected lifetime, the salvage (market) value of the investment in fixed assets and the total amount of working capital are added back to the cash flow of that year. This reflects the fact that the fixed assets may still have some value at the end of the project and the termination of the project releases the *entire* amount of funds which were previously tied up in working capital. [1]

Interest

Unlike accounting depreciation, interest often represents an actual cash outflow. Despite this, interest should *not* be deducted from the annual cash flow because the discounting process already takes the interest outlay into account. Should interest payments be deducted from the discounted cash flow, the interest charges would be double-counted (once in the numerator of the *NPV* equation and again in the denominator), and the project's net present value would be understated.

Opportunity costs

When estimating the cash flow of a proposed capital investment project, the 'opportunity' or 'alternative' costs, and not just the direct outlay costs, must

---

1. An alternative and fully equivalent way of handling the investment in working capital would be to exclude working capital from the initial outlay and to charge each year's cash flow with *imputed interest* (kW) using the cost capital k. The two methods are equivalent since the present value of the stream of imputed interest is exactly equal to the difference between W and $W/(1 + k)^n$.

The present value of a stream of annual outlays of kW for n years is given by:

$$-\left[\frac{kW}{1+k} + \frac{kW}{(1+k)^2} + \cdots + \frac{kW}{(1+k)^n}\right] = -\left[\frac{kW}{1+k}\left(1 - \frac{1}{(1+k)^n}\right) \Big/ \left(1 - \frac{1}{1+k}\right)\right]$$

$$= -\frac{kW}{k}\left[1 - \frac{1}{(1+k)^n}\right] = \frac{W}{(1+k)^n} - W$$

be taken into consideration. Consider, for example, the case of a firm which is evaluating a project which, among other things, requires 10,000 cubic feet of cold storage area. Let us further assume that the firm has 20,000 cubic feet of suitable storage space available, only half of which is currently being used for the firm's other products. Under the circumstances, what should be the storage cost (if any) which is assigned to the proposed project? The answer to this question is neither simple nor straightforward. If one adopts the incremental cash flow principle, it would appear, on the surface at least, that storage costs should *not* be charged. Clearly the firm already has the storage space available and therefore no additional cash outflow is incurred. But, suppose the firm can rent this space, say at a net annual rental of $20 per cubic foot. By executing the new project the firm suffers a loss of alternative income of $200,000 per year. In such a case the *opportunity cost* of using the storage space, that is $200,000, should be subtracted from the annual cash inflow of the new project. The problem is even more complicated if we assume that, for some reason, the firm cannot rent the unused storage space to outsiders. Here it would seem that in the absence of an alternative use (recall that only 10,000 cubic feet are currently being used) excess capacity exists whose opportunity cost is zero, and therefore no storage cost should be charged to the new project. However, if we are concerned with a project whose economic life is, say, ten years, we must, in fact, examine the possible alternative uses for the storage space over the entire ten-year period. If, for example, we expect the 'excess capacity' to disappear after the second year due to the expansion of the firm's other activities, the cost of acquiring additional storage space in the third and later years must be charged to the project under consideration. In such a case the storage cost is zero for two years, and positive from the third year onwards.

Similarly, the opportunity cost of using the limited services of key personnel may have to be estimated, especially if their involvement in the new project creates a need to hire additional people elsewhere in the firm. Despite the difficulties involved, a careful analysis of the opportunity costs of transferring existing assets (both human and physical) to the new project must be made in order to ensure that the overall return to the firm as a whole is reflected in the calculations.

Sunk costs

Sunk costs refer to those costs which have already been incurred, hence they are not incremental cash flows and should not affect future investment decisions. For example, consider an oil company which is deciding whether or not to drill a new oil well. The firm conducted a seismic test in 1992 at a cost of $10 million in an effort to estimate the oil reserves in a given tract of land. Given the results of this test, the firm estimated the expected cash flows (should it decide to drill for oil in 1992) to be: drilling investment $55 million, and net revenue from the oil field $10 million each year for the next ten years. The firm's cost of capital is 10%. The *NPV* of this project is:

$$NPV = -\$55 + \sum_{t=1}^{10} \frac{\$10}{(1.1)^t} = -\$55 + 61.45 = \$6.45 \text{ million}$$

Therefore, drilling should take place. However, if the cost of the seismic test is taken into consideration the *NPV* of this project would be:

$$NPV = -\$55 - 10 + \sum_{t=1}^{10} \frac{\$10}{(1.1)^t} = -\$3.55$$

and the project should not be undertaken. Since the firm has already spent the $10 million whether it drills or not, this sum represents a sunk cost and the investment decision should be considered independently of it. That is to say, the firm would be better off taking the investment (drilling) since, on an incremental basis, the *NPV* is positive. Sunk costs are not incremental cash flows and therefore should not be considered in the investment decision.

Salvage value

Sometimes, at the end of the project's life, assets have a positive value called salvage value. This value should be incorporated into the cash flows, as the following example demonstrates (for simplicity, we assume a world without taxes). Let:

I_0 = initial investment outlay in fixed assets = $100,000
W = investment in additional working capital = $25,000
CF = annual net cash receipts (cash receipts less cash expenses) = $35,000
I_n = salvage value of fixed assets = $2,000
n = economic life of the project = 5 years
k = the discount rate = 10%

Table 5.2 gives the cash flow for this project. Note that at the end of the project's expected life, the salvage (market) value of the fixed assets and the total amount of working capital are added to the cash flow of that year. Adding the salvage value reflects the fact that the fixed assets still have some market value at the end of the project. Adding the working capital to the cash flow at the end of the project, as explained before, reflects the fact that

Table 5.2 Project cash flow ($000)

	Year					
	0	1	2	3	4	5
Net annual receipts	—	35	35	35	35	35
Initial investment (depreciable assets)	(100)					2
Investment in working capital	(25)					25
Net cash flow	(125)	35	35	35	35	62
Present value at 10%	(125)	31.815	28.910	26.285	23.905	38.502
Net present value = $24.417						

termination of the project releases the entire amount of funds previously tied up in working capital.

EQUIPMENT REPLACEMENT DECISIONS

To this point, the cash flow analysis has been applied to conventional type capital budgeting decisions. In this section we extend the discussion to the closely related problem of optimal replacement. Consider a machine which costs $10,000, has a five-year life, and generates a net cash inflow of $5,000 a year. The firm is faced with the alternative of using the machine for five years, or selling it before the five years are up and replacing it with a new machine. Let us further assume that the market value of the old machine at the end of year t is as follows:

Year	Market value of old machine (I_n)
1	$8,000
2	7,000
3	6,000
4	2,000
5	0

On the basis of the above information the firm seeks to determine the optimal replacement period: but this requires the prior construction of the appropriate cash flow for each alternative course of action. Assuming a discount rate of 10% and that the machine is sold at the end of the first year, the net present value of this alternative (NPV_1) is given by:

$$NPV_1 = (-10,000) + \frac{5,000}{1.1} + \frac{8,000}{1.1} = \$1,818$$

Similarly, if the machine is sold after t years ($t = 2, 3, 4, 5$) the following NPV calculations are generated:

$$NPV_2 = (-10,000) + \frac{5,000}{(1.1)} + \frac{5,000}{(1.1)^2} + \frac{7,000}{(1.1)^2} = \$4,463$$

$$NPV_3 = (-10,000) + \frac{5,000}{(1.1)} + \frac{5,000}{(1.1)^2} + \frac{5,000}{(1.1)^3} + \frac{6,000}{(1.1)^3} = \$6,942$$

$$NPV_4 = (-10,000) + \frac{5,000}{(1.1)} + \frac{5,000}{(1.1)^2} + \frac{5,000}{(1.1)^3} + \frac{5,000}{(1.1)^4} + \frac{2,000}{(1.1)^4} = \$7,215$$

$$NPV_5 = (-10,000) + \frac{5,000}{(1.1)} + \frac{5,000}{(1.1)^2} + \frac{5,000}{(1.1)^3} + \frac{5,000}{(1.1)^4} + \frac{5,000}{(1.1)^5} = \$8,954$$

The above figures can be misleading. While using the machine for five years yields the highest net present value ($NPV_5 = \$8,954$), this does *not* necessarily mean that the optimal decision is to replace after five years. Since we are seeking the optimal replacement policy, one must compare different policies for *equal economic horizons*. For example, if we want to compare the policy of replacement every two years with the policy of replacement every four years, we must repeat the shorter cash flows for another two-year period if the comparison is to make economic sense. Repeating the two-year replacement option yields the following cash flow:

$$NPV = (-10,000) + \frac{5,000}{(1+k)} + \frac{5,000}{(1+k)^2} + \frac{5,000}{(1+k)^2}$$

$$+ \left[-\frac{10,000}{(1+k)^2} + \frac{5,000}{(1+k)^3} + \frac{5,000}{(1+k)^4} + \frac{7,000}{(1+k)^4} \right]$$

At a 10% discount rate, the *NPV* of the two-year replacement chain is equal to $8,151:

$$4,463 + \frac{4,463}{(1.1)^2} = \$8,151$$

which is, for example, preferable to a policy of replacing the machine at the end of four years ($NPV = \$7,215$). The crucial point in the above illustration is that in replacement problems one must consider the cash flows of alternative policies over *equal* time periods. Otherwise, the calculation discriminates against short replacement policies. In the above example, one might compare all five alternative replacement policies up to a common horizon of say, sixty years. Thus the policy to replace every year would be repeated sixty times, the policy to replace every two years would be repeated thirty times, and so on.[2]

Another way which will not change the policy ratings is to extend each policy to infinity. Note that the policy of annual replacement, extended to infinity, yields the following cash flow:

$$NPV_1 + \frac{NPV_1}{(1+k)} + \frac{NPV_1}{(1+k)^2} + \cdots = NPV_1 \sum_{t=0}^{\infty} \frac{1}{(1+k)^t}$$

$$= \frac{NPV_1(1+k)}{k}$$

$$= \frac{1,999.8}{0.1} = \$19,998$$

2. Changing the common horizon, say to 120 years, will not affect the ranking of alternatives as long as all alternatives are brought to the new *common* horizon.

Similarly, the two-year replacement policy extended to infinity yields:[3]

$$NPV_2 + \frac{NPV_2}{(1+k)^2} + \frac{NPV_2}{(1+k)^4} + \cdots = NPV_2 \sum_{t=0}^{\infty} \frac{1}{(1+k)^{2t}}$$

$$= NPV_2 \Big/ \left(1 - \frac{1}{(1+k)^2}\right) = 4{,}463 \Big/ \left(1 - \frac{1}{(1.1)^2}\right) = \$25{,}715$$

Applying the same approach, we can readily calculate the net present value for three-, four- and five-year replacement policies as well:

$NPV_3 = \$27{,}915$
$NPV_4 = \$22{,}761$
$NPV_5 = \$23{,}620$

Thus, in our particular example, the optimal policy would be to replace the machine every three years since it yields the greatest *NPV*.

PROJECTS WITH UNEQUAL LIVES: THE UNIFORM ANNUITY SERIES (UAS) _____

To this point, optimal replacement policy of equipment has been discussed using a specific case of mutually exclusive projects of unequal life.[4] For example, replacement of the machinery every two or four years may be considered as two mutually exclusive projects with unequal lives. The correct approach when choosing between such alternatives is simply to repeat the project with the shortest life until the two alternatives have equal lives, or to repeat both projects to infinity.

Another way to deal with mutually exclusive projects of unequal duration is to find the uniform annual series (*UAS*) of each alternative and then choose the project with the highest *UAS*. The *UAS* is defined as an *annuity* whose

---

3. If we repeat the same investment two years from now, we obtain the same NPV_2 but two years later, and consequently the net present value of the cash flow resulting from the second replacement is only $NPV_2/(1+k)^2$. Similarly, the net present value of the third replacement (four years from now) is $NPV_2/(1+k)^4$.

In general if we replace the machine every m years, we get:

$$NPV = NPV_m + \frac{NPV_m}{(1+k)^m} + \frac{NPV_m}{(1+k)^{2m}} \cdots = NPV_m \sum_{t=0}^{\infty} \frac{1}{(1+k)^{tm}}$$

Applying the formula for the summation of a geometric progression:

$$NPV = NPV_m \Big/ \left(1 - \frac{1}{(1+k)^m}\right)$$

4. The reader should be cautioned, once again, that the equalization of time horizons, and the equivalent alternative method of finding the uniform annuity series, are appropriate methods *if and only if* the relevant projects can be repeated indefinitely. Clearly, such an assumption may be appropriate for technical problems such as finding the optimal replacement period. However, it is equally clear that it would be a very unrealistic assumption for evaluating the construction of a plant design to produce a new chemical product, where economic life, due to obsolescence, competition, etc. may be less than a decade.

present value equals the *NPV* of the investment project in question:

$$NPV = \sum_{t=1}^{n} \frac{UAS}{(1+k)^t}$$

Hence:

$$UAS = NPV \bigg/ \sum_{t=1}^{n} \frac{1}{(1+k)^t}$$

Suppose that project A has a net present value of $200 and a life of ten years, then assuming a 9% discount rate its *UAS* is $31.16:

$$\$31.16 = 200 \bigg/ \sum_{t=1}^{10} \frac{1}{(1.09)^t}$$

$$200 = \sum_{t=1}^{10} \frac{31.16}{(1.09)^t}$$

Similarly, if project B's net present value is assumed to be $100 and its life is two years, its *UAS* will be $56.85 since:

$$100 = \sum_{t=1}^{2} \frac{56.85}{(1.09)^t}$$

Suppose that the above two projects are mutually exclusive. The two alternatives could be compared, if we assume that replication is an appropriate *assumption* in this instance, by repeating the two-year project five times or by repeating each into infinity. However, there really is no need to compare such replications: the *UAS* approach immediately shows that the shorter alternative is preferable. It yields a cash flow which is equivalent to an annuity of $56.85, and since we are assuming a case in which the projects can be repeated, $56.85 will be received in each year that the project is repeated. The ten-year project has a *UAS* of only $31.16 and hence it is inferior.

The *NPV* of the two-year project is $100 and its *UAS* for two years is a cash flow of $56.85. Since the *same* project can be repeated every two years, each replication creates an *NPV* which is identical to the original, i.e. present value of $100 and a cash flow of $56.85 each year. Hence we obtain an annuity of $56.85. The other project earns a *NPV* of $200 every ten years, but it only has an equivalent equal annual cash flow of $31.16. Thus the project with the shorter duration has a higher *NPV* on a comparable basis, namely for equal lives or when each project is repeated until infinity.

In the preceding section we solved the equipment replacement problem by extending each policy to infinity and calculating the appropriate *NPV* for each replacement policy. In the example in question the optimal policy is three-year replacement. Let us solve the same problem using the *UAS* approach. We have already found that:

$NPV_1 = \$1,818$ for one-year replacement
$NPV_2 = \$4,463$ for two-year replacement
$NPV_3 = \$6,942$ for three-year replacement
$NPV_4 = \$7,215$ for four-year replacement
$NPV_5 = \$8,954$ for five-year replacement

Since the assumed cost of capital is 10%, we can readily calculate the *UAS* for each replacement policy and then choose the strategy with the highest *UAS*. Applying the formula for the uniform annuity series yields:

$$UAS = NPV \Big/ \sum_{t=1}^{n} \frac{1}{(1+k)^t}$$

and plugging in the 10% discount rate ($k = 10\%$), we find:

$UAS_1 = 1,818 \div 0.909 = 2,000.00$ for a one-year replacement policy
$UAS_2 = 4,463 \div 1.736 = 2,570.85$ for a two-year replacement policy
$UAS_3 = 6,942 \div 2.487 = 2,791.31$ for a three-year replacement policy
$UAS_4 = 7,215 \div 3.170 = 2,276.03$ for a four-year replacement policy
$UAS_5 = 8,954 \div 3.791 = 2,361.91$ for a five-year replacement policy

Here too, the *UAS* approach identifies the optimal policy, i.e., replacement every three years.

Technically, the two equivalent methods (indefinite replication or *UAS*) involve the same number of calculations, but the *UAS* approach is for many people the more intuitively appealing. Repeating a project to infinity appears unrealistic; but despite their outward differences it should be recalled that both methods imply the same replication assumption.

IMPACT OF CORPORATE TAXES

So far we have ignored the effect that corporate taxes have on a project's cash flows. Tax rates vary not only between countries but also over time. Table 5.3 presents the highest marginal corporate and personal tax rates which prevailed in June 1992. In comparing these tax rates, a word of caution is warranted. The tax laws vary considerably in different countries due to state taxes, small business allowances, adjustments for double taxation, and so on. For example, unlike the United States, there is no double taxation in some countries on dividends paid to shareholders. The dual taxation in the U.S. stems, of course, from the fact that the earnings of a firm are first subject to corporate taxes, and when dividends are paid to shareholders the dividends are subject to personal taxes (hence the term double taxation). These differences make strict comparisons between countries imprecise. It does, however, give us a general idea of the structure of the tax burdens in different countries.

It is interesting to note, however, that the corporate tax structures of many countries are very similar, and for most countries range between 30% and

Table 5.3 Corporate and personal tax rates in various countries as prevailed in June 1992

Country	Corporate	Personal
United States	34%	31%
Canada	38%	29%
United Kingdom	35%	40% [b]
Japan	37.5%	50%
France	34%	56.4%
Italy	46.4% [a]	50%
Germany		51%
Australia	39%	47%
Austria	30%	50%
Israel	40%	48%
Hong Kong	17.5%	15%

[a] Represents a combined tax rate of corporate and local taxes.
[b] In June 1992 the basic personal income tax in the U.K. was 25%. A 40% marginal tax rate is paid on earnings above the threshold level (approximately £23,000).
Source: U.S. embassies of the appropriate country.

40%. The biggest difference rests in the personal tax rate structures of the various countries. With the exception of the United States and Canada, the personal tax rate is greater than the corporate tax rate. In this chapter, we generally employ the marginal tax rate in the United States of 34%.

To this point we have emphasized that investment decisions should be based on cash flows. Accounting conventions (for example, those affecting the allocation of depreciation expense over time) have been ignored. However, the accounting treatment of individual cost items, including depreciation expense, does influence the measurement and timing of the taxable income. Therefore, accounting conventions also affect the size and timing of corporate income tax payments, which of course are actual cash outflows. Moreover, because corporate taxes do not affect all investments to the same degree, project cash flows must always be expressed on an after-tax basis if meaningful comparisons are to be made.

Corporate taxes are a cash outflow and must be taken into account when evaluating a project's desirability. Suppose, for simplicity, that the corporate tax rate is $T_c\%$, the annual cash flow (before deducting depreciation) is CF_B, and the annual straight-line depreciation allowance is D. For simplicity, also assume that depreciation is the only factor which induces the difference between taxable income and the pre-tax cash flow: namely, all other revenues and expenses are on a cash flow basis. As noted earlier, depreciation is not an actual cash outflow and therefore is not subtracted from the annual cash flow. However, the tax deductibility of depreciation decreases the firm's tax liability and therefore the impact of depreciation is an element to be considered when calculating the company's after-tax cash flow.

The net after-tax cash flow equals the pre-tax cash flow (CF_B) minus taxes, where taxes are $T_c\%$ of the firm's taxable income:

$$\text{after-tax cash flow} = \text{pre-tax cash flow} - \text{corporate taxes}$$

which can be rewritten as:

$$CF_A = CF_B - T_c(CF_B - D) = (1 - T_c)CF_B + T_c D$$

where T_c = the corporate tax rate, D = the annual depreciation allowance, CF_B = the before-tax cash flow (which is assumed to be equal to the income before depreciation), and CF_A = the after-tax cash flow.

The after-tax cash flow is central to all financial decision problems and can be derived as follows:

Step 1: Calculate the project's net income by subtracting the depreciation allowance (D) from the pre-tax cash flow (CF_B).

Step 2: The tax rate (T_c) is then applied to the net income to derive corporate taxes.

Step 3: Deduct corporate taxes from the pre-tax cash flow, thereby deriving the after-tax cash flow (CF_A).

Table 5.4 shows the after-tax cash flow calculated for the following numerical example.

Annual cash flow (CF_B)
  (cash revenues less cash expenses) = \$400
Corporate tax rate (T_c) = 34%
Initial investment outlay (I_0) = \$1,000
Project's lifetime (n) = 10 years
Annual straight line depreciation (D) = \$100

As can be seen in Table 5.5 the after-tax cash flow is \$298, or:

$$CF_A = CF_B - T_c(CF_B - D)$$
$$CF_A = 400 - (0.34)300 = \$298$$

We can easily verify that the same result can be obtained using the depreciation tax shield ($T_c D$):

$$(1 - T_c)CF_B + T_c D = (0.66)400 + (0.34)100 = \$298$$

If we assume that the relevant after-tax discount rate is equal to 10%, the

Table 5.4 Example of after-tax cash flow

1. Annual pre-tax cash flow (CF_B)	\$400
2. Depreciation	100
3. Net income before tax [line (1) minus line (2)]	300
4. Corporate taxes [34% × line (3)]	102
5. After-tax cash flow (CF_A) [line (1) minus line (4)]	\$298

Table 5.5 Tax depreciation allowed under the accelerated cost recovery system (ACRS) (percentage of depreciable investment)

Year(s)	Tax depreciation schedules in recovery period class[a]					
	3-year	5-year	7-year	10-year	15-year	20-year
1	33.33	20.00	14.29	10.00	5.00	3.75
2	44.45	32.00	24.49	18.00	9.50	7.22
3	14.81	19.20	17.49	14.40	8.55	6.68
4	7.41	11.52	12.49	11.52	7.70	6.18
5		11.52	8.93	9.22	6.93	5.71
6		5.75	8.93	7.37	6.23	5.28
7			8.93	6.55	5.90	4.89
8			4.45	6.55	5.90	4.52
9				6.55	5.90	4.46
10				3.29	5.90	4.46
11					5.90	4.46
12					5.90	4.46
13					5.90	4.46
14					5.90	4.46
15					5.90	4.46
16					2.99	4.46
17–20						4.46
21						2.25

[a] Real property is depreciated using the straight-line method over 27.5 years for residential property and 31.5 years for nonresidential property.

project's *NPV* can be calculated as follows:

$$(6.145)298 - 1,000 = \$831$$

An additional tax factor should be mentioned. If a firm's equipment is expected to have any salvage value at the end of the project's lifetime and this value exceeds the equipment's book value (original sales price less accumulated depreciation), a corporate tax liability will be incurred on the profit (net of all removal costs) from the sale of such equipment. Starting with the 1986 tax year, corporate long-term capital gains are to be taxed as ordinary income, and are subject to a tax rate of 34%.[5] Prior to the 1986 tax reform, capital gains were taxed at a special corporate rate of 28%. Of course, the proceeds from the sale and any tax payment will appear at the end of the last year of the project's life. As a result, their present values tend to be small in relation to the project's *NPV*. However, when contemplating the replacement of machinery at the beginning or in the middle of a planned project, the impact of the proceeds from such sales can be significant. Tax payments generated by such sales can be crucial to the decision, and should not be overlooked.

Assume that a firm expects to be able to sell one of its machines at the end of its tenth year for $60,000 after paying all the removal costs of the

5. The corporate tax rate structure in the United States is actually a graduated structure (e.g., taxable income of $40,000 is taxed at 15%). We consider firms with income over $335,000 and hence a 34% tax rate.

equipment. The machine originally cost $1 million, but by the end of the ten years will have been fully depreciated: its book value will be zero. Since the net proceeds from the sale ($60,000) exceed the equipment's book value (zero), the firm will have to pay taxes on the $60,000 of recaptured depreciation:

$$\$60,000 - 0 = \$60,000$$

Applying the 34% tax rate, the firm will have to pay $20,400 ($0.34 \times 60,000 = 20,400$) in taxes on the 'profit' from the sale. As a result, the calculation of the net salvage value of the equipment, which will be added to the project's terminal cash flow at the end of year 10, is $39,600:

Proceeds from sale of equipment	$60,000
Less: Taxes on sale	$20,400
Net salvage value	$39,600

Project life and depreciation allowance

Historically, the period over which the firm was allowed to depreciate its assets for tax purposes was determined by the expected economic life of the asset. Nowadays, the direct relationship between the economic life of the project and its depreciable life has been completely abandoned. The depreciable life for tax purposes is now used to encourage (or discourage) firms to invest. There were, in the past, several accelerated depreciation methods which gave firms the benefit of relatively large early tax shield (T_cD) benefits. Starting in 1986, the assets are now classified according to their duration, and depreciation for tax purposes is calculated by the method known as the (modified) Accelerated Cost Recovery System (*ACRS*). For example, cars and tractors are in a five-year depreciable life category; most industrial equipment is in a seven-year category; industrial buildings are in a 31.5-year category, etc.

Once an asset is classified into the appropriate category, the modified depreciation allowance by the *ACRS* is given according to the rates given in Table 5.5.

Table 5.5 reveals that the first year depreciation percentage is smaller than the second year's depreciation percentage. This is so, since it is assumed that the asset is being purchased in the middle of the year, hence only half the depreciation in the first year is allowed. The firm is allowed to adopt straight-line depreciation, however, virtually always, a firm would be better off by applying the *ACRS* depreciation method.

Note that the asset's salvage value does not affect the allowed depreciation. If a firm purchased a machine for $100 with a salvage value of $40, at the end of the tenth year it could still depreciate all of the $100. However, when the machine is sold the firm will pay taxes on the difference between the market value and book value of the machine. Since 1986 the tax rate on capital gains is equal to the ordinary income tax rate (34%).

Investment tax credit

From time to time the U.S. government, and the governments of many other countries, offer a tax credit on the acquisition of certain kinds of capital equipment. The 1986 Tax Reform Act repealed the regular investment tax credit in the United States for assets placed in service after December 31, 1985. Such credits, however, remain one of the more important incentives offered by foreign countries to encourage new capital investments. Also, since the investment tax credit may be reinstituted in the United States, we would like the reader to be familiar with this notion. The purpose of such tax credits is to provide an incentive for new corporate investment. The investment credit is usually set as a percentage of the cost of the capital equipment – for example, 10% for qualifying assets. It works as follows. Assume a firm is contemplating a project that entails the purchase of $100,000 of new equipment with an expected duration of ten years. If the equipment qualifies for the investment credit, the firm will be able to deduct $10,000 from its tax bill. So long as the company has a current tax liability exceeding $10,000, the effective cost of the new equipment is reduced to $90,000, which serves as an added incentive to make the investment. Although practice varies, in most cases in order to avoid 'double benefits', the tax authorities force the firm to reduce the value of the asset for depreciation purposes by the amount of the tax credit. For example, if the firm uses straight-line depreciation, the annual depreciation allowance is $9,000:

$$\frac{(0.90)I_0}{10} = \frac{90,000}{10} = 9,000$$

The investment credit can be clarified by considering the following numerical example:

$$n = \text{project duration} = 10 \text{ years}$$
$$T_c = \text{corporate tax rate} = 34\%$$
$$k = \text{cost of capital} = 10\%$$
$$CF_t = \text{annual net receipt} = \$19,000$$
$$I_0 = \text{initial investment} = \$100,000$$
$$D_t = \text{annual depreciation (SLD)}$$
$$\text{without the tax credit} = \$10,000$$
$$(0.90)D_t = \text{annual depreciation (SLD)}$$
$$\text{with tax credit} = \$9,000$$

The annual after-tax cash flow without the 10% tax credit is:

$$(1 - T_c)CF_t + T_cD = (0.66)19,000 + (0.34)10,000 = \$15,940$$

and the project's *NPV* is:

$$NPV = \$15,940(DF_{10\%,10}) - \$100,000$$
$$= \$15,940(6.145) - 100,000$$
$$= -\$2,048.7$$

Since the *NPV* is negative, the project is unacceptable and the new equipment will not be purchased. But what happens to this particular decision if a 10% investment credit is granted? The annual after-tax cash flow becomes:

$$(1 - T_c)CF_t + (0.90)T_cD = 0.66 \times 19,000 + 0.9 \times 0.34 \times 10,000$$
$$= 0.66 \times 19,000 + 0.34 \times 9,000$$
$$= \$15,600$$

The project's *NPV*, taking the investment credit into account, is now positive:

$$NPV = 15,600(6.145) - 90,000 = \$95,862 - 90,000 = \$5,862$$

Since the *NPV* is positive, the project is acceptable, and the new equipment will be purchased.

This example illustrates how tax credits (and any other possible incentives) may encourage a firm to accept a project which would otherwise be rejected. When the economy is sluggish and the unemployment rate has soared, the government may establish tax incentives in order to increase total investment expenditures by making projects more profitable. When the economy overheats and there is fear that there will be high inflation, these tax incentives are eliminated in order to cool off the economy. Figure 5.1 demonstrates the impact of investment incentives on project profitability and the level of investment. With the tax incentives, project profitability rises and the demand curve for investment shifts from A to B. Assuming, for simplicity only, a constant

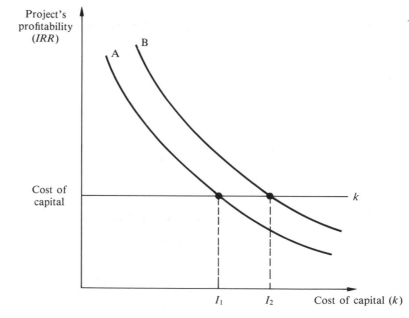

Figure 5.1

cost of capital of $k\%$, the investment expenditures rises from I_1 to I_2 which coincides with the above numerical example.

Formal and effective corporate tax rates

The 1986 tax reform set the formal corporate tax rate at 34%. Hence, throughout the book we employ this rate to calculate the post-tax cash flows. Before we end this chapter a word of caution is called for. Many firms pay a lower tax rate, hence projects which are characterized by a negative *NPV* with a 34% tax rate may have a positive *NPV* with a lower tax rate. In project evaluation the firm should always employ the effective actual tax rate and not the formal 34% rate.

Table 5.6 is reprinted from *The Wall Street Journal*. According to the study by Citizens for Tax Justice, the effective tax rate paid in 1987 by 250 of the nation's largest profit-making firms was only 22.1%, far below the 34% formal rate. Moreover, sixteen corporations which were very profitable, including the giants IBM and General Motor, received refunds, which meant a negative tax rate. While some of the firms disagree with these figures, it is equally clear that they paid less than 34% of their income in taxes. Most of the zero-tax firms had used carry-backs of tax breaks to get refunds on taxes paid in previous years. Over time, tax experts predict that those tax breaks will disappear and firms will indeed pay a tax rate closer to the formal 34% rate.

The lesson from Table 5.6 and the above discussion is that we shall probably see more acts by the Internal Revenue Service to avoid a situation of 'zero tax profitable corporations' in the future, and more effort by firms to find new legal loopholes in the tax code, such that they in effect pay a lower tax rate.

Table 5.6 Firms that paid no taxes in 1987 ($millions)

	Profits	Refund	Rate
General Motor	$2,396.2	($742.2)	−31.0%
IBM	2,932.7	(123.5)	−4.2
Aetna	1,010.5	(32.4)	−3.2
Baxter Travenol[a]	233.0	(32.0)	−13.7
Carolina P & L	536.3	(27.6)	−5.2
Illinois Power	344.5	(25.6)	−7.4
Corning	122.6	(16.3)	−13.3
Hewlett-Packard	405.0	(15.0)	−3.7
Ashland Oil	158.5	(11.8)	−7.5
Greyhound	62.9	(7.1)	−11.3
Ogden	55.7	(6.7)	−12.1
Sequa Corp.	42.3	(5.9)	−13.9
Pennzoil	76.8	(4.5)	−5.9
Goodyear Tire	573.7	(2.4)	−0.4
Consumers Power	384.3	(0.6)	−0.2
Gulf States Utilities	273.2	—	—
Total companies	**$9,608.2**	**($1,053.7)**	**−11.0%**

[a] Changed name to Baxter International in May 1988.
Source: The Wall Street Journal, September 23, 1988.

No matter what may be the outcome, the reader should keep in mind that the effective tax rate on each project – and not the formal rate – is the relevant one for project evaluation.

MEASURING PROFITABILITY IN AN INFLATIONARY ENVIRONMENT _____

In most financial analysis employed before the late 1960s, inflation or change in the price level was ignored. Ignoring inflation was due to the fact that the annual inflation rate was very low and not significantly different from zero for most years covering the period 1926–67. With the exception of the World War II years when the 9% inflation rate prevailed, in most other years inflation ran below 5%, and in many years it was even negative, e.g. 1932 (–10%), 1949 (–1.8%), etc.

However, in the late 1960s, and in particular during the 1970s, double-digit inflation erupted in most Western countries. This eruption of inflation focused everyone's attention on (a) the economic meaning of reported earnings, (b) the impact of inflation on project evaluation, and (c) the firm's decision-making process.

Indeed, the double-digit inflation rate caused losses for many firms, and in

Table 5.7 Percentage change in consumer prices (from the previous year)

Period	U.S.A.	U.K.	Japan	Canada
1967	2.9	2.5	4.0	3.5
1968	4.2	4.7	5.2	4.1
1969	5.4	5.3	5.4	4.5
1970	5.0	6.3	7.6	3.4
1971	4.3	9.5	6.1	2.8
1972	3.3	7.2	4.5	4.8
1973	6.2	9.2	11.8	7.6
1974	11.0	16.0	24.4	10.9
1975	9.1	24.3	11.8	10.8
1976	5.8	16.6	9.3	7.5
1977	6.5	15.8	8.0	8.0
1978	7.7	8.3	3.8	8.9
1979	11.3	13.4	3.6	9.1
1980	13.6	18.0	8.0	10.2
1981	10.3	11.9	4.9	12.5
1982	6.1	8.6	2.7	10.8
1983	3.2	4.6	1.8	5.8
1984	4.3	5.0	2.2	4.4
1985	3.6	6.1	2.1	3.9
1986	1.9	3.4	0.6	4.2
1987	5.3	4.1	–	4.4
1988	4.3	6.5	0.7	4.1
1989	4.7	5.0	1.0	3.7
1990	4.1	8.8	2.3	3.9
1991	5.3	–	2.2	6.8

Source: *International Economic Indicators*, U.S. Department of Commerce, various issues.

order to avoid high unemployment and encourage capital formation the United Kingdom and the United States (among other countries) established accelerated depreciation and investment tax credit schemes. These schemes have varied from time to time, depending on the condition of the economy, e.g. new investment expenditures and the unemployment level.

Table 5.7 illustrates the inflation level that prevailed in four major industrial countries during the years 1967–91. This table clearly reveals that the oil-crisis period (beginning in 1973) was characterized by double-digit inflation. In 1974 the inflation rate was 11% in the United States, 16% in the United Kingdom, 24.4% in Japan, and 10.9% in Canada. These high inflation rates prevailed up to 1981–82, a period when we notice a tendency for a sharp reduction in the inflation rate (see Table 5.7). In the late 1980s and early 1990s, inflation was negligible in Japan, 5.3% in the United States, 4.1% in the United Kingdom and 4.4% in Canada.

By the end of the 1980s inflation was expected to be in the neighborhood of 4–6%. While it is obvious that a 4–6% inflation rate would have a smaller impact on project evaluation in comparison with the double-digit inflation rates, it still has a significant impact that should not be ignored.

MEASURING THE RETURN ON FINANCIAL ASSETS UNDER INFLATION

For simplicity, let us assume an inflation of $h\%$ a year, and an annual nominal interest rate paid on savings accounts of $R_n\%$. Thus, for each $100 deposited, such accounts grow to $100 \times (1 + R_n)$ at the end of the year. However, as we have assumed an inflation rate of $h\%$ during the year, the value of one's savings in *real terms* (i.e., in terms of their purchasing power) is only $100(1 + R_n) \div (1 + h)$ at the end of the year. Clearly, if both the interest rate and the inflation rate are equal, say 5%, the account grows to $105 in nominal terms, but remains constant, $105/1.05 = 100, in terms of real purchasing power.

In general, the nominal future value of the savings (FV_n) at the end of the year is:

$$FV_n = \$100(1 + R_n)$$

and its *future* value in real terms, FV_{real}, is given by:

$$FV_{\text{real}} = FV_n \div (1 + h) = \$100(1 + R_n) \div (1 + h)$$

Since we are dealing with a one-year investment, the internal rate of return (*IRR*) in real terms, which we denote by R_{real}, is given by the following formulas:

$$\$100 = \frac{FV_{\text{real}}}{1 + R_{\text{real}}}$$

and

$$R_{real} = \frac{1 + R_n}{1 + h} - 1$$

Rates of return with taxes and inflation

Unfortunately, Uncle Sam does not readily agree to forgo his share in interest income, and as a result most of us have to pay income tax on our interest earnings. Suppose that the relevant personal income tax rate is $T_p = 0.31$, i.e. 31% of interest income goes to the tax collector. In this case where $T_p =$ the personal tax rate, the nominal future value (after one year) of $100 deposited at the beginning of the year grows, on an after-tax basis, to:

$$FV_n = 100[1 + R_n(1 - T_p)]$$

because only $R_n(1 - T_p)$ is left after making the income tax payment. And given an inflation rate of $h\%$, the future value after taxes is, in real terms:

$$FV_{real} = 100[1 + R_n(1 - T_p)] \div (1 + h)$$

In this instance, the after-tax *IRR* can be derived from the following equation:

$$\frac{FV_{real}}{1 + R_{real}} = \frac{\$100[1 + R_n(1 - T_p)/(1 + h)]}{1 + R_{real}} = \$100$$

Hence,

$$R_{real} = \frac{[1 + R_n(1 - T_p)]}{1 + h} - 1$$

Let us apply the formula to two cases – one with low inflation and one with high inflation – on the assumption that the personal tax rate T_p is 31%. Given the relatively low interest and inflation rates which prevailed during most of the 1950s and early 1960s, we have $R_n = 3\%$, $h = 1\%$, and the real after-tax rate of return was:

$$R_{real} = \frac{1 + 0.03(1 - 0.31)}{1.01} - 1 = 1.06\%$$

Now consider the after-tax *IRR* on savings in the early 1980s when there was high inflation. Assuming a 16% interest rate and 15% inflation, but retaining the same tax rate:

$$R_{real} = \frac{1 + 0.16(1 - 0.31)}{1.15} - 1 = -3.4\%$$

Thus, a negative real interest rate is obtained when inflation is high.

Inflation affects the reported earnings, borrowing and lending strategy of the firm as well as the firm's tax liability. Indeed, some firms change their inventory evaluation policy (i.e., FIFO and LIFO) to cope with the effects of inflation. However, since the late 1980s and early 1990s, inflation rates have been relatively low. We focus below on project evaluation and inflation when even a 3–5% inflation rate has a major affect.

PROJECT EVALUATION UNDER INFLATION

It is quite possible that a project that would be accepted in the absence of inflation may be rejected in an inflationary environment. Moreover, inflation may change the *ranking* of mutually exclusive projects, thereby altering the firm's investment priorities. For simplicity only, let us start with the case of 'neutral' inflation, in which gross income, labor costs, raw materials, prices, etc., all increase at the same rate, say $h\%$ a year. Also assume that the cost of capital in real terms, k_R, is 10%, so that an investment of $100 will only be attractive if the cash flow at the end of the year is $110 in *real* terms. The real net present value of such a project is, by definition, zero:

$$NPV = \frac{110}{1.1} - 100 = 0$$

If the cash flow in real terms is greater than $110, the project's *NPV* is positive and it would be accepted.

Now suppose that all prices (costs) are rising by 20% per year. What is the *minimum* required cash flow which will induce the firm to execute the project? Since the zero *NPV* cash flow, in the absence of inflation, is 110, the critical minimum required nominal cash flow, given an annual inflation rate of 20%, must be $(110) \times (1.20) = 132$. In other words, the cash flow must increase by 20% in order to preserve the project's previous *NPV*. Thus for a given 20% inflation, the minimum required nominal cash flow is 132; the real value of which remains $110(132/1.20) = 110$. Any net receipt in excess of 132 will generate a positive *NPV*.

Measuring a project's *NPV* in an inflationary environment can be done in one of two ways:

1. Reduce the nominal cash flow to *real* terms and then discount at the *real* cost of capital. In our example the *NPV* of the project is:

$$NPV = \frac{132/1.20}{1.1} - 100 = \frac{110}{1.1} - 100 = 0$$

2. Alternatively, the same result can be obtained by using the nominal cost of capital to discount the nominal cash flow. In the particular example, the nominal cost of capital is 32%, and the *NPV* of the project is given by,

$$NPV = \frac{132}{(1.2)(1.1)} - 100 = \frac{\$132}{1.32} - 100 = 0$$

As we have just seen, cash flows can be discounted either in nominal or in real (constant purchasing) terms. Correctly done, shifting from one method to the other will *not* affect a firm's investment decisions. To illustrate this point, consider a firm which invests I_0 dollars in order to obtain a future cash flow of $S_1, S_2, ..., S_n$, and for the moment, also assume the absence of depreciation and taxes. As before, all prices rise by $h\%$ per year and the real and nominal discount rates are k_R and k_N, respectively. Since S_t is the nominal cash flow in year t, it increases every subsequent year as a result of inflation. In order to calculate a project's *NPV* in real terms (i.e., in constant dollars), the nominal cash flows must first be deflated using the annual inflation rate. The real value of the first year cash flow is $S_1/(1 + h)$, and the real value of the second year cash flow is given by $S_2/(1 + h)^2$. The raising of the inflation term $(1 + h)$ to the second power reflects the underlying economic fact that prices rise at *compounded* rates. Hence, in general, the value, *in constant dollars*, of a nominal receipt S_t is given by the formula $S_t(1 + h)^t$; and the real *NPV* of a project, that is its *NPV* in dollars of *constant* purchasing power, is given by the formula:

$$NPV_R = \sum_{t=1}^{n} \frac{S_t/(1 + h)^t}{(1 + k_R)^t} - I_0$$

where NPV_R denotes the *NPV* in real terms.

Since real cash flows are in the numerator, the appropriate discount rate is k_R, the *real* rate. However, the shift to nominal discounting is straightforward. The above equation can be rewritten as follows:

$$NPV_N = \sum_{t=1}^{n} \frac{S_t}{(1 + k_R)^t(1 + h)^t} - I_0 = \sum_{t=1}^{n} \frac{S_t}{[(1 + k_R)(1 + h)]^t} - I_0$$

$$= \sum_{t=1}^{n} \frac{S_t}{(1 + k_N)^t} - I_0$$

where NPV_N denotes nominal net present value and k_N denotes the nominal discount rate.

Thus project analysis can be carried out in terms of either current (nominal) or real (constant) dollars. However, the project's *NPV* will be the same under both methods if, and only if, the real discount rate is applied to the constant dollar cash flows and the appropriate nominal rate is used to discount the cash flows in terms of current dollars. More specifically:

$$NPV_R = NPV_N \text{ if and only if } (1 + k_N) = (1 + k_R)(1 + h)$$

From this condition we can readily see that the nominal cost of capital equals the real cost of capital plus an adjustment for inflation:

$$k_N = k_R + h + k_R h$$

For example, suppose that one puts \$100 in the bank and obtains (in the absence of inflation) $k_R = 10\%$ in interest. With a 10% inflation one would now require a nominal interest rate of k_N in order to retain the same real income:

$$k_N = 0.10 + 0.10 + (0.10 \times 0.10) = 0.21 = 21\%$$

Since the investor earns 10% in the absence of inflation, he now requires 21%: 10% to compensate him for the loss of purchasing power of the principal; plus an additional 11%, which in real terms equals 10% ($0.11/1.1 = 0.10$). This is exactly the same rate of interest that he earned before the inflation. Hence, an interest rate of 21% fully compensates the investor for the 10% inflation.

INFLATION, TAXES, AND RANKING OF PROJECTS

An outstanding example of the differential impact of inflation on a project's cash flow is the depreciation tax shelter which is calculated on the basis of historical costs. The failure of the fiscal authorities to permit an upward adjustment of depreciation allowances, *for tax purposes*, produces the well-known negative impact of inflation on capital investment, even when the underlying inflationary process is neutral.

In the absence of inflation a project's after-tax cash flow in any year t is given by

$$(1 - T_c)(S_t - D_t) + D_t = (1 - T_c)S_t + T_c D_t$$

and its *NPV with no inflation* (denoted as NPV_{NI}) is:

$$NPV_{NI} = \sum_{t=1}^{n} \frac{(1 - T_c)S_t + T_c D_t}{(1 + k_R)^t} - I_0$$

In the absence of inflation, k_R is the firm's *real* cost of capital. If we now assume a neutral inflation of $h\%$ per year, the cash flow S_t increases each year by $h\%$ and the nominal cost of capital, k_N, becomes $(1 + k_R)(1 + h)$. Note, however, that the depreciation tax shelter $T_c D_t$ does *not* increase with inflation since it is calculated on the basis of historical costs. Hence the project's *NPV with inflation*, denoted as NPV_I, becomes:

$$NPV_I = \sum_{t=1}^{n} \frac{(1 - T_c)S_t(1 + h)^t + T_c D_t}{[(1 + k_R)(1 + h)]^t} - I_0$$

which can be rewritten as

$$NPV_I = \sum_{t=1}^{n} \frac{(1 - T_c)S_t}{(1 + k_R)^t} + \sum_{t=1}^{n} \frac{T_c D_t/(1 + h)^t}{(1 + k_R)^t} - I_0$$

Thus, given a *fully anticipated neutral* inflation in which all prices, including the nominal interest rate, rise at the rate of inflation, the discount rate becomes (in nominal terms) $(1 + k_R)(1 + h)$ where k_R denotes cost of capital in the absence of inflation. As before, one may first calculate the depreciation tax shield in constant dollars, $T_c D_t/(1 + h)^t$, and then discount it as the real rate; or alternatively, one may calculate all the cash flows in current dollars, and then apply the appropriate nominal discount rate: $(1 + k_R)(1 + h)$.

Since NPV_I (which is the correct measure of profitability with inflation) is less than NPV_{NI} (the correct measure in the absence of inflation), it is clear that even neutral inflation reduces a project's profitability via its negative impact on the depreciation tax shield.[6] And the greater the inflation rate, the greater is the gap between NPV_{NI} and NPV_I. Moreover, it is quite possible that NPV_{NI} is greater than zero while NPV_I is less than zero: so that a project which would have been accepted in the absence of inflation might be rejected under inflationary conditions. This reduction in NPV is also a function of the relative importance of labor and capital inputs. In general, the more capital-intensive the project, the larger will be the tax shelter. Since the real value of the latter is reduced by inflation, we expect capital-intensive projects to suffer more from inflation than otherwise comparable labor-intensive projects.

For example, suppose that a firm is considering three projects. Project A does not involve any initial investment (all machines and buildings are rented so there are annual rent payments but no initial outlay). Project B has an initial outlay (I_B) as does project C (I_C). All projects have a ten-year life and the firm uses straight-line depreciation. The cost of capital is 20% and the corporate tax rate is 34%.

Table 5.8 sets out the calculation of the project's net present values using the formula:

$$NPV = \sum_{t=1}^{n} \frac{(1 - T_c)S}{(1 + k)^t} + \sum_{t=1}^{n} \frac{T_c D}{(1 + k_R)^t} - I_0$$

In the absence of inflation, all three projects have the same NPV (in this case $1,000) so the firm is indifferent amongst them. Let us now assume a neutral inflation of $h\%$. As a result, S will increase annually by $h\%$ and the appropriate discount rate will also adjust to the inflation. As we have shown before, neutral inflation will *not* change the real value of the first term on the right-hand side of the NPV equation, but it does reduce the present value of the tax shield:

$$\sum_{t=1}^{10} \frac{T_c D_t}{[(1 + k_R)(1 + h)]^t}$$

Table 5.8 Net present values of three projects in the absence of inflation

	Projects		
	A	B	C
1. Initial investment outlay I_0	0.0	1,000.0	10,000.0
2. Project life	10.0	10.0	10.0
3. Depreciation ($D = I_0/n$)	0.0	100.0	1,000.0
4. Annual cash flow (S)	361.44	671.40	3,460.68
5. After-tax cash flow $(1 - T_c)S + T_c D$	238.55	477.12	2,624.05
6. $\sum_{t=1}^{10} \dfrac{(1 - T_c)S + T_c D}{(1 + k)^t}$	1,000.0	2,000	11,000
7. $NPV = (6) - (1)$	1,000.0	1,000.0	1,000.0

6. The reader should note that firms having fixed obligations (such as lease contracts) may gain from inflation since the real value of their fixed commitments decreases with inflation.

Clearly, the *NPV* of project A is not affected by inflation since $T_c D_t = 0$. However, we expect projects B and C to be adversely affected by inflation. The effect is particularly great in the case of project C since it involves a larger capital expenditure. To show this, we first calculate the appropriate nominal riskless discount rates for alternative inflation rates, assuming that the real rate is 20%:

Annual inflation rate (h)	$(1.20)(1 + h)$
4.17%	1.25
8.33%	1.30
12.50%	1.35
16.67%	1.40

Note that the discount factor for the tax shelter becomes $(1.20)(1 + h)$. The net present values of the three projects for each of the alternative inflation rates are given in Table 5.9. Although the *NPV* of project A is unaffected by inflation, the *NPV*s of projects B and C are decreased. The differential impact of inflation on a project's net present value is of crucial importance. A glance at Table 5.9 suffices to show that inflation can change a project's *NPV*; the magnitude of the change depends on its degree of capital intensity and the rate of inflation. Consider, for example, two projects D and L. The first is assumed to be capital intensive; the second, L, is labor intensive and has no investment in fixed assets. Let us further assume that in the absence of inflation, project D is preferred to project L, which is tantamount to assuming that project D has a higher *NPV*. If we introduce a neutral inflation, other things being equal,

Table 5.9 Net present value of three hypothetical projects with alternative inflation

		Projects		
		A	B	C
1. Investment outlay I_0		0.0	1,000.0	10,000.0
2. Present value of cash flow $(1 - T_c)S^a$		1,000.0	1,857.6	9,574.7
3. Depreciation (D_t)		0.0	100.0	1,000.0
4. Present value of tax shelter ($T_c D_t$)				
	$h = 4.17$	0.0	121.4[b]	1214.1
	$h = 8.33$	0.0	105.1	1051.3
	$h = 12.50$	0.0	92.3	923.1
	$h = 16.67$	0.0	82.1	820.7
5. Net present value (*NPV*)				
$[(2) + (4) - (1)]$	$h = 4.17$	1,000.0	979.0	788.8
	$h = 8.33$	1,000.0	962.7	626.0
	$h = 12.50$	1,000.0	949.9	497.8
	$h = 16.67$	1,000.0	939.7	395.4

[a] Discount at $k_R = 20\%$.

[b] $121.4 = 0.34 \times 100 \left[\sum_{t=1}^{10} \frac{1}{(1.2)(1.0417)} \right] = 34 \left[\sum_{t=0}^{10} \frac{1}{(1.25)^t} \right] = 34(3.571)$

where 3.571 is the *PV* of an annuity factor for ten periods at 25%.

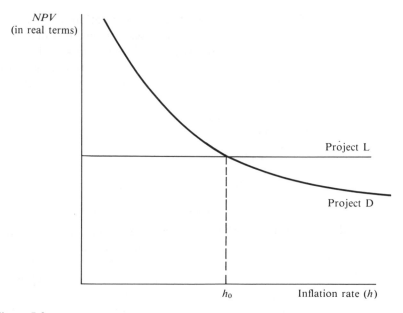

Figure 5.2

the *NPV* of project D decreases in *real* terms because the real value of its depreciation tax shield shrinks. The *NPV* of project L, however, does not change with inflation: it has no tax shield and, therefore, its entire cash flow rises proportionately at the inflation rate.

This situation is illustrated in Figure 5.2 which plots the *NPV*s of the two projects in relation to the inflation rate. For zero inflation and for all rates of inflation below h_0, project D has the higher *NPV*. But for the rates of inflation beyond $h\%$ the negative impact on the real value of the depreciation tax shelter becomes dominant, and beyond this point the labor-intensive project L has the higher *NPV*. Clearly, the ranking of the two projects depends upon the rate of inflation. And should the two projects happen to be mutually exclusive, an estimate of the rate of inflation must be made before the firm can choose between them.

SUMMARY

This chapter has examined the incremental principle underlying the definition of the major components of a project's cash flow. Special attention must be paid to the timing of receipts and outlays; and the handling of fixed and variable costs, accounting depreciation, working capital, interest expense, and opportunity costs. In general, a project's cash flows should reflect all of the cash flows generated by the investment decision, independent of whether they occur directly in the department in question, or elsewhere in the firm. Then we discussed the relevant cash flow for an important class of investment decision

– equipment replacement. While depreciation is not a cash flow, it is deductible for tax purposes. We therefore discussed the impact of corporate taxes on a project's cash flows, with particular emphasis on the depreciation tax shield. Finally, inflation affects the cash flows from the investor as well as the firm. Moreover, it may also affect the ranking of projects.

SUMMARY TABLE

A. Determining the project's cash flows

1. Apply the incremental cash flow principle (fixed costs are not incremental).
2. Include cash flows at the time they are incurred.
3. Include initial outlay at the time incurred.
4. Include working capital and return it at the end of the project's life.
5. Do not include interest in the numerator to avoid double-counting (it is included in the discount process, see Chapter 4).
6. Include opportunity costs (e.g. opportunity to rent vacant storage space).
7. Do not include sunk costs.

B. Equipment replacement decisions

1. Repeat each alternative such that all alternatives will have a common duration.
2. Or, repeat each alternative indefinitely and find *NPV* by the formula:

$$NPV = NPV_m \Bigg/ \left(1 - \frac{1}{(1 + k)^m}\right)$$

where *m* is the project's life, NPV_m is the net present value of one cycle, and *NPV* is the net present value for an infinite number of years.
3. Or, calculate the *UAS* by:

$$NPV = \sum_{t=1}^{n} \frac{UAS}{(1 + k)^t}$$

where *NPV* is calculated for one cycle.

C. After-tax cash flow

$$CF_A = (1 - T_c)CF_B + T_c D$$

where:

CF_A = after-tax cash flow
CF_B = before-tax cash flow
D = depreciation
T_c = corporate tax rate

D. Inflation and return on financial assets

1. Real rate of return with zero taxes:

$$R_{\text{real}} = \frac{1 + R_{\text{nominal}}}{1 + h} - 1$$

where h is the inflation rate.

2. Real rate of return with a tax rate T_p:

$$R_{\text{real,after-tax}} = \frac{1 + R_{\text{nominal}}(1 - T_p)}{1 + h} - 1$$

E. Relationship between nominal and real discount rates

1. Risky discount rate:

$$(1 + k_N) = (1 + k_R)(1 + h)$$

where k_N is the nominal discount rate, k_R is the real discount rate, and h is the inflation rate.

2. Interest rate:

$$(1 + r_N) = (1 + r_R)(1 + h)$$

where r_N is the nominal interest rate, and r_R is the real interest rate.

F. Project evaluation

1. In the absence of inflation:

$$NPV = \sum_{t=1}^{n} \frac{(1 - T_c)S_t}{(1 + k_R)^t} + \sum_{t=1}^{n} \frac{T_c D_t}{(1 + k_R)^t} - I_0$$

2. With $h\%$ inflation:

NPV in nominal terms (NPV_N)

$$NPV_N = \sum_{t=1}^{n} \frac{(1 - T_c)S_t(1 + h)^t}{(1 + k_N)^t} + \sum_{t=1}^{n} \frac{T_c D_t}{(1 + k_N)} - I_0$$

NPV in real terms (NPV_R)

$$NPV_R = \sum_{t=1}^{n} \frac{(1 - T_c)S_t}{(1 + k_R)^t} + \sum_{t=1}^{n} \frac{T_c D_t/(1 + h)^t}{(1 + k_R)^t} - I_0$$

and $NPV_N = NPV_R$ as long as we have the relationship in section E above.

G. Impact of inflation on a project's profitability

1. Decrease in profitability since $NPV_R < NPV$.
2. The ranking of projects may change in favor of less capital-intensive projects.

5.1 The Melany Boat Company builds fishing boats to order. The firm examined a proposal for building ten fishing boats for a large client. The initial outlay and receipt during the project's first year were expected to be $500,000 and $300,000, respectively. The terms of the contract permit the client to pay only 40% of the total receipts in the first year, 30% in the following year, and the remainder in the next year. Assume that the cost of capital is 12% and that there are no taxes.

(a) Calculate the accounting profit of the project.
(b) Calculate the cash flow profit of the project.

5.2 The Norton Loading Company is considering opening a new loading dock. In order to do so the company must purchase $280,000 of new equipment. The gross annual receipts are expected to be $250,000, and the annual costs of the new unit are estimated as follows:

Direct labor cost	$65,000
Fuel	50,000
Electricity	17,000
Direct administrative costs	23,000
Fixed overhead expense	26,000
General administrative cost (pro rata share of office expenses)	29,000

In addition, it has been estimated that the company's *net* receipts from its other loading docks will decrease by $25,000 per year when the new loading unit is installed. Assume no corporate taxes.

(a) Construct the net annual cash flow for the investment in the new loading dock. Explain your calculations.
(b) Assume that the new equipment's economic life is eight years, and a cost of capital of 16%. Is it worth while for the firm to open the new loading dock?

5.3 Mr. Jones is offered the opportunity to invest $5,000 with a promise of a return of $5,700 at the end of one year.
'I refused to make this investment,' Mr. Jones said. 'I had only $1,000 of my own, and for a $4,000 loan which I would have had to take, the bank wanted 10% interest so that my net return would have been only $5,300. Would you be satisfied with a 6% return in these days?' Appraise Mr. Jones's statement.

5.4 When Mr. Milford, the manager of the new computer unit, made his feasibility report on the proposed unit, he did not charge his own salary. 'I am not a new worker in the company,' Mr. Milford said. 'I used to be the manager of the laboratory and my deputy there took over my place.' Critically appraise Mr. Milford's logic.

5.5 A few years ago the Western Metals Company (WMC) was forced to discontinue operations of its export division owing to the closing of the foreign market for its particular product. While it would have been possible to sell limited amounts of the product on the local market, a careful feasibility study showed that such limited production could be carried on only at a loss, even if fixed costs were ignored. As a result of this study, production of the item was completely discontinued.

Recently, it became possible again to export the item in question, and in much larger amounts. In order to permit the expanded scale of production, WMC would have to acquire two additional machines. The cost of the two machines was $400,000 and $300,000, and the machines had expected economic lives of four and five years, respectively.

The company's production manager also pointed out that the division's old equipment had been transferred to the maintenance department and it would now be necessary to return it to the export division. While the book value of the old equipment was zero, the production manager estimated its market value at $150,000. He also stated that when the old equipment is transferred, WMC will have to acquire additional used equipment to replace it in the maintenance department. He estimated the cost of this equipment at $200,000. The production manager estimated that the old equipment still had a useful economic life of four years.

The expected receipts of the export department from the expanded scale of production were estimated at $600,000 per year.

Annual expenses were estimated as follows:

Raw materials	$40,000
Salaries	60,000
Other expenses	20,000
Fixed expenses of the company (120% of the salaries)	72,000
Straight-line depreciation	160,000
Total	$352,000

Renewed production would also require an additional $500,000 for working capital – principally inventories of raw materials and finished goods.

Assume that the cost of capital (i.e. minimum required rate of return) is 15% and that the company does *not* pay taxes.

Write a report to the president of WMC on the economic feasibility of reopening the export division.

5.6 Assume that the duration of a project is ten years (most of the equipment will serve ten years), but that a few machines will last for five years, while the buildings are expected to last for approximately twenty years. How is the cash flow affected by these facts?

5.7 The Palem Lock Company is using a new lathe which costs $120,000, has six years' duration and generates a net annual cash inflow of $42,000. The firm is faced with the alternative of using the lathe for the next six years or selling it before the six years are up and replacing it with a new lathe.

The finance manager asks you to determine the optimal replacement period for the lathe. You have the following information regarding the market value of the lathe:

End of year	Market value of old lathe
1	$100,000
2	85,000
3	75,000
4	60,000
5	32,000
6	6,000

Assume a 12% cost of capital and answer the following questions (ignoring corporate taxes):

(a) What is the optimal replacement policy for the firm?
(b) How would your answer to part (a) change if the lathe generated a net annual cash inflow of $60,000?
(c) What would your advice be to the finance manager if the lathe generated a net annual cash inflow of $24,000?

5.8 The United Carpenters Company is using a machine with a life expectancy of five years. The company is considering its replacement, and for this purpose has gathered the following data:

The purchase price of a new machine (P_0) is $97,000.
The market price of the machine at time t (P_t) and the operating expenses at time t (C_t) are estimated as follows:

Year (t)	Market value at end of year (P_t)	Operating expenses at t (C_t)
1	$70,000	$16,000
2	60,000	20,000
3	50,000	27,000
4	35,000	36,000
5	5,000	42,000

Note: The price for the last year is the salvage value. The operating expenses are calculated gross of depreciation and interest.
Assume that technological changes are not expected and therefore operating expenses and equipment prices will remain constant over time.
Assume also that the cost of capital is 15%, and that there are no taxes.

(a) On the assumption that the company only considers the possibility of purchasing new equipment, what is the optimal replacement policy?
(b) On the assumption that the company also considers the possibility of buying used equipment (machine), what is the optimal replacement policy? (Assume that there are no commissions on buying and selling, and therefore the selling price is equal to the buying price.)
(c) What would be your answer to part (a) if there were no possibility of selling used equipment?

5.9 Answer once again question 5.8(b) with the additional assumption that there is a $5,000 cost each time it incurs a transaction. Thus if the machine is sold and another is purchased the firm incurs transaction costs of $10,000. Compare your results with those of 5.8(b). How do you explain the difference? What would be the direction of change in optimal replacement policy if the transaction cost exceeds $5,000?

5.10 A textile manufacturing firm is attempting to calculate the optimal life of a piece of machinery. The firm's cost of capital is 10%. You have already calculated the

NPV for each of the five years of the asset's life.

Replacement policy	*NPV*
1	$2,210
2	5,102
3	7,321
4	8,942
5	11,297

Using the uniform annual series methodology, identify the optimal replacement policy.

5.11 'In the calculation of *NPV*, depreciation is not deducted from the net cash flow, despite the fact that depreciation is a real economic cost, and is also recognized by the tax authorities.' Critically evaluate this statement.

5.12 The Yellow Box Company is considering buying for $200,000 special equipment whose economic life span is expected to be eight years. The annual cash flow (before deducting taxes) generated by the equipment is expected to be $40,000. Assume that the corporate tax rate is 34% and the after-tax cost of capital is 8%.

(a) Set out the post-tax annual cash flow of the 'project', assuming straight-line depreciation.
(b) Should the firm buy the equipment? Support your answer.

5.13 'Taxes can't be all bad. Any increase in the corporate tax rate T_c will improve the profitability of the project, since the depreciation tax shield T_cD will also increase.' Evaluate this statement.

5.14 Assume an investment outlay of $200,000 which generates a net annual pre-tax cash flow of $56,000 for ten years.

(a) Calculate the pre-tax internal rate of return of this investment.
(b) Calculate the post-tax internal rate of return, assuming a 34% corporate tax rate. Assume straight-line depreciation.

5.15 In order to encourage investment in Puerto Rico, the government offers investors the incentives described in the following table taken from an advertisement in the *Wall Street Journal*.

Income tax calculation ($)	
Sales	10,000,000
Production worker payroll	1,700,000
Profit before tax but after depreciation (straight line)	1,000,000
Eligible incentives:	
(a) 5% production worker payroll deduction	85,000
(b) Income tax and property tax exception of partial rates	
Pre-tax income	1,000,000
Production worker payroll deduction	85,000
Adjusted taxable income	915,000

	Annual income tax calculation by period[a]			
Years	1–5	6–10	11–15	16–20
% tax exempt	90%	75%	65%	55%
% taxable income	10%	25%	35%	45%
Taxable income	$91,500	228,750	320,250	411,750
Calculated tax	$26,115	82,613	112,863	164,038
Effective tax rate	2.61%	8.26%	12.29%	16.40%

[a] Duration of tax exemption depends upon geographical zone in which the firm has been established.

Assume that you are considering the alternative of locating a plant either in Ohio or in Puerto Rico; the pre-tax financial characteristics of your project are as those described in the table. Find the post-tax internal rate of return of your project when your plant is located in Puerto Rico assuming an economic life of your project of $n = 5$ years and your firm is an all-equity firm. Also, you estimate that, should you decide to locate the plant in Ohio, the post-tax internal rate of return on your project will be 10%.

5.16 A firm purchased on January 1990 a machine which would last for four years. Depreciating the machine using straight-line depreciation over the four years yields an *NPV* of − $10. The firm is allowed to depreciate the machine under the *ACRS* depreciation method − the machine falls in the 3-year depreciation category (see Table 5.5). Calculate the net present value using the depreciation rates given in Table 5.5. Additional information you will need: initial investment = $100; cost of capital = 10%; tax rate = 34%; and the cash flows are constant over the four years.

5.17 The firm considers an investment which falls in the 3-year category for depreciation purposes (see Table 5.5). However, the financial manager estimates that the economic life of the investment is $n = 10$ years. The annual pre-tax cash flows are $S = \$30$, and the initial investment is $I_0 = \$100$. The corporate tax rate T_c is 34% and the after-tax cost of capital is $k = 10\%$. Should the firm undertake the investment?

5.18 The firm considers two options: (a) to buy a machine for $I_0 = \$100$ which induces a pre-tax cash flow of $S = \$50$ during the next four years; or (b) to buy the machine, use it for two years, and then sell the machine at the end of the second year at the estimated market price of $80. The firm cannot repeat its investment, namely it can only buy the machine once. The tax rate is 34% and the after-tax cost of capital is 10%. Which is the preferred option? Use the 3-year category from Table 5.5 for depreciation purposes.

5.19 'Neutral inflation doesn't change the firm's cost of capital or the real present value of its projects.' Critically evaluate this statement.

5.20 A textile firm is considering switching from hand looms to automatic machines. The new machines will allow the firm to reduce its labor and production costs by 50%. Without the change, annual sales and expenses for the next ten years are expected to be as follows:

Proceeds from sales	$30,000,000
Expenses (excluding depreciation)	$20,000,000
Depreciation (straight-line)	$2,000,000

The firm is considering acquiring machines which cost $40,000,000 and have an expected economic life of ten years. The introduction of the machines will increase expenses (excluding depreciation) to $10,000,000 annually, while sales will remain at the same level. The real cost of capital is 12%. Thus buying the machines *adds* $4,000,000 depreciation to the existing $2,000,000. The hand looms' market value is zero and has been fully depreciated. The firm pays 34% income tax. The predicted annual inflation rate for the next ten years is 9.83% annually.

Is it worth while for the firm to purchase the machines? (Assume that the acquisition of the machines is out of the firm's own capital.)

5.21 A French firm is considering an investment of $50,000,000 to set up a new production line. The economic life span of the machinery is ten years. The expected annual receipts from the investment are $20,000,000 and the annual expense (including straight-line depreciation) is $10,000,000. The real cost of capital is 15% and riskless interest rate is 10%. The firm's financial analysts predict an annual inflation rate of 10% for the next decade. Assume a 34% tax rate.

(a) Is it worth while for the firm to make the investment?
(b) How might your answer to (a) change if the tax authorities agree to accept depreciation expenses calculated on the basis of replacement costs rather than historical costs?

5.22 A petrochemicals firm is considering a $20,000,000 investment in a new product. Sales and expenses are expected to be as follows:

s = annual sales of $13,000,000
c = annual expenses $6,000,000 (before depreciation)
k = real cost of capital of 15%
T_c = corporate income tax rate of 34%
h = predicted annual inflation rate for the next ten years = 8.7%, hence the nominal discount rate is about 25%
n = economic duration of the equipment = 10 years

The firm has been offered the opportunity to sign a ten-year sales contract for its product, at a price *linked* to the increase in the consumer price index. Assume, therefore, that revenues and expenses will increase at the same rate over the ten-year period.

(a) Is it worthwhile for the firm to make the investment under the above assumptions?

The firm's advisors on the price of oil are divided in their opinion. One group says that because of the surplus of oil its price is not expected to increase any higher than the world inflation rate. Others estimate that, due to an increase in demand and a decrease in production, oil prices will increase at double the inflation rate.

(b) if you assume that oil prices grow at double the average inflation rate, how does this affect the feasibility of the project?

5.23 The firm employs either a nominal cost of capital of 30% or a real cost of capital of 10%. What is the implied inflation rate expected by the firm?

5.24 The firm's real cost of capital is $k_R = 10\%$. The firm invests $I_0 = \$100$ and in the absence of inflation receives $80 at the end of each of the next two years. Suppose now that we expect 10% inflation in the first year and 20% in the second.

(a) What is the firm's nominal cost of capital?
(b) Calculate the project's *NPV* using the nominal figure given in (a) above.
(c) Calculate the project's *NPV* using the real rate.

5.25 The firm considers a project whose investment is $I_0 = \$100$ which is depreciated in one year. The project's after-tax *NPV* (assuming a tax rate of 34%) is $20 and the project's economic life is one year. The firm's real cost of capital is $k_R = 10\%$. The above *NPV* was calculated on the assumption of no inflation. The firm is reluctant to accept the project since it expects a neutral inflation which may cause the project's *NPV* to be negative. What is the minimum inflation rate such that the *NPV* will be negative?

5.26 'Recently, inflation in the Western world was relatively low at only about 4% per year. In capital budgeting, therefore, one can ignore inflation, particularly for those projects with a long life.' Evaluate this statement. Demonstrate your answer with depreciation of $10,000 in the tenth year, a corporate tax rate of 34%, and a zero real cost of capital.

5.27 With inflation, a project's profitability is reduced since the depreciation tax shelter is calculated on a historical cost basis. In order to encourage investment, the government supplies a grant of $X. What should $X be such that a firm whose depreciation is $D = \$100$ for ten years and real cost of capital $k_R = 10\%$ will be exactly compensated for the erosion of profitability due to inflation. Assume a corporate tax rate of 34% and an inflation rate of 11% during the next ten years.

5.28 The value of the depreciation tax shield diminishes when inflation prevails. In order to encourage investment, the Heath government in the United Kingdom introduced a 100% depreciation allowance in the first year of the asset's life. For what inflation rate $h\%$ does the 100% depreciation allowance exactly offset the attrition of inflation? Assume firms use straight-line depreciation, that the cost of capital (in real terms) is 5%, and that the project's duration in five years ($n = 5$). Answer the same question assuming a project life of ten years ($n = 10$).

SELECTED REFERENCES

Angell, R. J. and Wingler, T. R., 'A Note on Expensing versus Depreciation under the Accelerated Cost Recovery System,' *Financial Management*, Winter 1982.

Arditti, F., 'A Note on Discounting the Components of an Income Stream,' *Journal of Finance*, June 1974.

Arditti, F. and Levy, H., 'Pre-tax and Post-tax Discount Rates,' *Journal of Business Finance*, Winter 1971.

Arthur, W. M., 'Reporting Economic – Not Accounting – Profit,' *Business Horizons*, March/April 1981.

Baran, A., Lakonishok, J., and Ofer, A. R., 'The Information Content of General Price Level Adjusted Earnings: Some Empirical Evidence,' *Accounting Review*, January 1980.

Barnea, Amir, Talmor, Eli, and Haugen, Robert A., 'Debt and Taxes: a Multiperiod Investigation,' *Journal of Banking and Finance*, March 1987.

Batrholdy, Jan, *Taxation and Financial Policy of Firms: Theory and Empirical Application to Canada*, Ottawa: Economic Council of Canada, 1987.

Beja, Avraham and Aharoni, Yair, 'Some Aspects of Conventional Accounting Profits in an Inflationary Environment,' *Journal of Accounting Research*, Autumn 1977.

Ben-Horim, M. and Levy, H., *Financial Management in an Inflationary Economy*, Financial Handbook, 6th edn, Chichester: Wiley, 1986.

Ben-Horim, M. and Levy, H., 'Inflation and the Trade Credit Period,' *Management Science*, June 1982.

Bierman, H. Jr. and Dukes, R. E., 'Limitations of Replacement Cost,' *Quarterly Review of Economics and Business*, Spring 1979.

Brennan, Michael J. and Schwartz, Eduardo S., 'Regulation and Corporate Investment Policy,' *Journal of Finance*, May 1982.

Brenner, Menachem and Venezia, Itzhak, 'The Effects of Inflation and Taxes on Growth Investments and Replacement Policies,' *Journal of Finance*, December 1983.

Chaney, P. K., 'Moral Hazard and Capital Budgeting,' *Journal of Financial Research*, Summer 1989.

Chang, Eric C. and Pinegar, Michael, 'Risk and Inflation,' *Journal of Financial Quantitative Analysis*, March 1987.

Chen, K. C. and Scott, Louis O., 'Uncertain Inflation and the Input–Output Choices of Competitive Firms,' *Quarterly Review of Economics and Business*, Autumn 1985.

Chen, Son-Nan, 'Capital Budgeting and Uncertain Inflation,' *Journal of Economics and Business*, August 1984.

Cheung, J. K., 'Depreciation, Debt and Equilibrium Tax Rates: A Reconsideration,' *Quarterly Review of Economics and Business*, Spring 1987.

Coen, Robert M., 'Investment Behavior, the Measurement of Depreciation and Tax Policy,' *American Economic Review*, March 1975.

Cooper, Ian and Franks, Julian R., 'The Interaction of Financing and Investment Decisions When the Firm has Unused Tax Credits,' *Journal of Finance*, May 1983.

Dammon, Robert M. and Senbet, Lemma W., 'The Effect of Taxes and Depreciation on Corporate Investment and Financial Leverage,' *Journal of Finance*, June 1988.

Day, Theodore E. 'Expected Inflation and the Real Rate of Interest: A Note' *Journal of Banking and Finance*, December 1985.

Fabozzi, F. J. and Shiffrin, L. M. 'Replacemnt Cost Accounting: Application to the Pharmaceutical Industry,' *Quarterly Review of Economics and Business*, Spring 1979.

Gee, K. P. and Peasnell, K. V., 'A Comment on Replacement Cost as the Upper Limit of Value to the Owner,' *Accounting and Business Research*, Autumn 1977.

Gentry, J. A., 'State of the Art of Short-Run Financial Management,' *Financial Management*, Summer 1988.

Haugen, Robert A. and Senbet, Lemma W., 'Corporate Finance and Taxes: A Review,' *Financial Management*, Autumn 1986.

Hochman, S. and Palmon, O., 'The Irrelevance of Capital Structure for the Impact of Inflation Investment,' *Journal of Finance*, June 1983.

Howe, K. M. and Lapan, H., 'Inflation and Asset Life: The Darby vs. the Fisher Effect,' *Journal of Financial and Quantitative Analysis*, March 1987.

Huang, Roger D., 'Financial Asset Returns, Inflation and Market Expectations,' *Research in Finance*, 5, 1985.

Hubbard, C. M., 'Flotation Cost in Capital Budgeting: A Note on the Tax Effect,' *Financial Management*, Summer 1984.

Jaffe, Jeffrey F., 'Inflation, the Interest Rate and the Required Rate of Return on Equity,' *Journal of Financial and Quantitative Analysis*, March 1985.

Jones, Charles P. and Wilson, Jack W., 'Stocks, Bonds, Paper and Inflation: 1870–1985,' *Journal of Portfolio Management*, Fall 1987.

Kaplan, R. S., 'Purchasing Power Gains on Debt: The Effect of Expected and Unexpected Inflation,' *Accounting Review*, April 1977.

Kim, M. K., 'Inflationary Effects in the Capital Investment Process: An Empirical Examination,' *Journal of Finance*, September 1979.

Kroll, Yoram, 'On the Differences Between Accural Accounting Figures and Cash Flows: The Case of Working Capital,' *Financial Management*, Spring 1985.

Lambrix, R. J. and Singhvi, S. S., 'How to Set Volume-Sensitive ROI Targets,' *Harvard Business Review*, March/April 1981.

Leech, S. A., Pratt, D. J., and Magill, W. G. W., 'Company Assets Revaluations and Inflation in Australia, 1950 to 1975,' *Journal of Business Finance and Accounting*, Winter 1978.

Lembke, V. C. and Toole, H. R., 'Differences in Depreciation Methods and the Analysis of Supplemental Current-Cost and Replacement Cost Data,' *Journal of Accounting Auditing and Finance*, Winter 1981.

Levy, H., 'The Connection Between Pre-tax and Post-tax Rates of Return,' *Journal of Business*, October 1968.

Levy, H. and Levy, A., 'Equilibrium under Uncertain Inflation: A Discrete Time Approach,' *Journal of Financial and Quantitative Analysis*, September 1987.

Levy, Haim and Brooks, Robert, 'Financial Break-even Analysis and the Value of the Firm,' *Financial Management*, Autumn 1986.

Logue, Dennis E. and Tapley, T. Craig, 'Performance Monitoring and the Timing of Cash Flows,' *Financial Management*, Autumn 1985.

Maloney, Kevin J. and Selling, Thomas I., 'Simplifying Tax Simplification: An Analysis of its Impact on the Profitability of Capital Investment,' *Financial Management*, Summer 1985.

Mandelker, Gershon and Tandon, Kishore, 'Common Stock Returns, Real Activity, Money and Inflation,' *Journal of International Money and Finance*, June 1985.

McCarty, D. E. and McDaniel, W. R., 'A Note on Expensing Versus Depreciation Under the Accelerated Cost Recovery Systems,' *Financial Management*, Summer 1983.

Moon, K. Kim and Young, Allen E., 'Inflation, the Value of the Firm and Firm Size,' *The Quarterly Review of Economics and Business*, Summer 1985.

Peavy, John W. III and Goodman, David, 'How Inflation, Risk and Corporate Profitability Affect Common Stock Returns,' *Financial Analysts Journal*, September/October 1985.

Pohlman, R. A., Santiago, E. S., and Markel, F. L., 'Cash Flow Estimation Practices of Large Firms,' *Financial Management*, Summer 1988.

Pindyck, Robert S., 'Risk, Inflation and the Stock Market,' *American Economic Review*, June 1984.

Piper, A. G., 'Reporting the Effects of Inflation in Company Accounts in the United Kingdom,' *Quarterly Review of Economics and Business*, Spring 1979.

Ro Byung, T., 'The Adjustment of Security Returns to the Disclosure of Replacement Cost Accounting Information,' *Journal of Accounting and Economics*, August 1980.

Samuelson, R. A., 'Should Replacement-Cost Changes be Included in Income?' *Accounting Review*, April 1980.

Schall, Lawrence D., 'Taxes, Inflation and Corporate Financial Policy,' *Journal of Finance*, March 1984.

Soenen, A. and Aggarwal, R., 'Cash and Foreign Exchange Management: Theory and Corporate Practice in Three Countries,' *Journal of Business, Finance and Accounting*, Winter 1989.

Steele, Anthony, 'A Note on Estimating the Internal Rate of Return from Published Financial Statements,' *Journal of Business Finance and Accounting*, Spring 1986.

Turnbull, S. M., 'Discounting the Components of an Income Stream: Comment,' *Journal of Finance*, March 1977.

6

Traditional Measures of Investment Worth

'You can't only look at your return on capital, especially if you're going into a foreign market.'

Fourth Executive: Your payback could be in two years or 20, and 20 years scares us to death. Instead, you look at the reasons for the investment. What are the opportunities? What are the threats if we don't do it?

'U.S. companies are doing themselves a terrible disservice with their myopic short-term focus.'

Fifth Executive: The demand for return is much more severe in this country than in others, and that comes out of our tendency to focus on short-term horizons. So in U.S. companies, people start walking away from capital expenditures if the payback is longer than a year. Japanese companies look at a capital investment and see markets penetrated, share captured and dominance achieved, not just a short-term return.

'Why do we put these payback demands on ourselves?'

Sixth Executive: I think it has to do with the United States being a country for the individual, with the ideal that if you work hard enough, claw your way to the top, you'll find the streets paved of gold.

In Japan, it's very different. You work together for the common good of your company, your country or whatever.

Our focus on the individual has a great deal of influence on maintaining self-serving short-term horizons.

Source: 'Harris Conversation for the 90s: A Discussion of a Select Group of Business Executives,' Fortune, April 20, 1992, p. 254.

The executives who discuss the American–Japanese competition in article 12 mention the payback investment decision rule. One executive claims that a twenty-year payback 'scares us to death.' A fifth executive is quoted in the article as saying that people start walking away from capital expenditure 'if the payback is longer than one year.' Another executive interviewed asks, 'Why do we put these payback demands on ourselves?'

What is the concept of payback? What is meant by the statement that Japanese firms have projects with longer payback periods than those of American firms? In the previous chapter we saw that the *NPV* criterion should be used for project evaluation. What is the relationship, if any, to the *NPV* and payback criterion? As we see from article 12, many businesspeople still use nondiscounted rules of thumb such as a simple payback formula (or accounting rate of return) when estimating the profitability of alternative investments. In this chapter, therefore, we change our perspective and focus attention on the perplexing question of why many business firms have persisted in using short-cut rules of thumb, rather than (or as a supplement to) one of the more sophisticated time-discounted decision rules. Here the analysis will be essentially *positive*, rather than normative: that is, we shall be using the tools at our disposal not to improve the decision-making process, but rather to account for, and hopefully understand, the observed behavior of many corporate executives.

RULES OF THUMB FOR PROJECT EVALUATION

One of the more pervasive facts of economic life has been the continued widespread use of a variety of short-cut rules of thumb to evaluate capital investment projects. Actual business practice suggests that the only effective limit on the number of differential methods employed has been the ingenuity of management in devising additional variants of existing profitability measures. But despite differences in detail, almost all of the popular rules of thumb fall into one of two broad classes: payback measures or undiscounted accounting rates of return.

Payback

Many firms still use a simple payback formula, that is the number of years required to recover the initial investment outlay from the project's future cash flows, as their index of an investment's desirability. For example, if a proposal requires an initial outlay of $1 million and is expected to give rise to a net cash flow of $250,000 per year for the next ten years, the project has a *four-year* payback. Had the expected annual cash flow been $500,000 per year, the payback period would be two years, and so on for any combination of investment outlay and cash receipts.

If we assume that all projects have equal annual receipts (as in the above mentioned examples) the payback can be calculated using the formula:

$$\text{Payback period} = \frac{\text{Initial investment outlay}}{\text{Annual cash receipts}}$$

Even if the receipts are expected to fluctuate over time, the payback period is still easily calculated by summing the receipts until the initial investment outlay is covered. For example, Table 6.1 sets out the cash flows of two projects, A and B. The former has a payback period of three years; summing the annual receipts of project B gives a somewhat larger payback of five years.

Table 6.1

Investment outlay	Project A ($1,000,000)	Project B ($1,000,000)
Net cash flow ($):		
First year	500,000	400,000
Second year	400,000	300,000
Third year	100,000	100,000
Fourth year	0	100,000
Fifth year	0	100,000
⋮	⋮	⋮
Tenth year	0	100,000
Payback (years)	3	5

The payback formula has some rather obvious defects. The formula does not take into consideration the time value of money; perhaps even more important, it concentrates solely on the receipts *within* the payback period: receipts in later years are ignored. Thus project A of Table 6.1 has a shorter payback, and therefore is presumably more desirable than project B, despite the fact that the internal rate of return of project A is zero while that of B is positive.

Finally, note that if n_p is the number of years until the investment is recovered, then $1/n_p$, the reciprocal of the payback period, measures the profitability. If the payback is four years, then $R_p = 1/n_p = 25\%$ is the profitability of the project. Thus, R_p is the payback profitability measure or the payback rate of return.

Some firms employ the discounted payback period, rather than the simple payback period. For example, suppose that we have the following cash flows:

Year	Cash flow
1	$100.00
2	100.00
3	81.70
4	100.00

Our initial investment is $200. Note that the discounted cash flows at a 20% discount rate are:

Year	Cash flow
1	$83.30
2	69.94
3	47.30
4	48.20

The payback period is two years, that is, we recover our initial investment at the end of the second year. The discounted payback period (which is about three years), like the *NPV* method, has the advantage of taking into consideration the time value of money. However, like the payback period, it has the disadvantage of not considering cash flows after the payback period: that is, after we have recovered our initial investment.

Accounting rate of return

Another widely used measure of investment profitability is the accounting rate of return. This rate of return is calculated by dividing a proposal's annual net profit (after deducting depreciation) by either the *total* or the *average* initial investment outlay:

$$\frac{\text{Accounting rate of return}}{\text{on } total \text{ investment}} = \frac{\text{Net annual profit}}{\text{Investment outlay}}$$

$$\frac{\text{Accounting rate of return}}{\text{on } average \text{ investment}} = \frac{\text{Net annual profit}}{\text{Investment outlay} \div 2}$$

Taking our previous example of a project with initial investment outlay of $1 million and annual net receipts of $250,000 for ten years, and assuming straight-line depreciation of $100,000 per year, the accounting rates of return on total and average investment are given by:

$$\frac{\text{ARR on total}}{\text{investment}} = \frac{250,000 - 100,000}{1,000,000} = 15\%$$

$$\frac{\text{ARR on average}}{\text{investment}} = \frac{250,000 - 100,000}{500,000} = 30\%$$

Once again we can note some very obvious defects of both versions of the accounting rate of return. As was true of payback, the accounting rate also neglects the timing of receipts: that is, no provision is made for discounting the future cash flows. Moreover, the accounting rate of return implicitly assumes *stable* cash receipts over time. Needless to say, this measure is particularly inappropriate where cash flows are expected to change over the life of the project.

--- **THE HISTORICAL RECORD**

Man's knowledge of the principles of compound interest can be traced back to the Old Babylonian period (circa 1800–1600 BC) in Mesopotamia, and present value tables not unlike the ones in this book can be found in the mathematical and early accounting literature of medieval Europe.[1] Despite this, time-discounted methods of project evaluation were not applied to *non-financial* investments until the nineteenth century when an American civil

1. For an informative and highly entertaining survey of the historical development of discounting, see R. H. Parker, 'Discounted Cash Flow in Historical Perspective,' *Journal of Accounting Research*, Spring 1968.

engineer, A. M. Wellington, anticipated many of the concepts of modern capital investment analysis in his work on the location of railways.[2] But as late as 1950, a study of twenty-five large electricity utilities reported that none of the firms surveyed used time-discounted methods: *all* of the firm's preferred the simple accounting rate of return on total assets as their measure of profitability.[3] Similarly, a 1950 field study[4] of corporate investment decisions in manufacturing firms found a marked preference for the use of nondiscounted payback periods; no firm surveyed reported the use of time-discounting when evaluating its capital expenditure programs.

It was not until the second half of the 1950s that U.S. business firms seriously began to consider the use of time-discounting for project evaluation. Since that time a virtual army of academic researchers has descended periodically upon the larger U.S. corporations in an effort to monitor the procedures and techniques which they use to evaluate capital investment proposals.[5] A sample of the findings of these surveys is given in Tables 6.2 and 6.3. Clearly, a preference for the use of rule of thumb evaluation methods continued well into the 1960s and the reliance on simple rules of thumb remains significant to this day.

Thus despite the theoretical arguments, presented in Chapters 3 and 4, 38% of the firms surveyed in 1970 relied on simple rule of thumb estimates of profitability for evaluating capital investments. Moreover, as both the surveys

2. Ibid., p. 62. Wellington's book, *The Economic Theory of the Location of Railways* (New York, Wiley, 1887) is discussed by M. B. Scorgie, 'Rate of return,' *Abacus*, September 1965, and by R. J. Stephens, 'A Note on an Early Reference to Cost–Volume Relationships,' *Abacus*, September 1965.
3. Michael Gort, 'The Planning of Investment: A Study of Capital Budgeting in the Electric Power Industry,' *Journal of Business*, April 1951 and July 1951.
4. See Walter W. Heller, 'The Anatomy of Investment Decisions,' *Harvard Business Review*, March 1951.
5. A far from exhaustive listing of such studies includes: Eugene F. Brigham, 'Hurdle Rates for Screening Capital Expenditure Proposals,' *Financial Management*, Autumn 1975; G. A. Christy, *Capital Budgeting: Current Practices and Their Efficiency*, Bureau of Business and Economic Research, University of Oregon, 1966; James M. Fremgen, 'Capital Budgeting Practices: A Survey,' *Management Accounting*, May 1973; Lawrence J. Gitman and J. R. Forrester Jr, 'A Survey of Capital Budgeting Techniques Used by Major US Firms,' *Financial Management*, Fall 1977; Donald Istvan, *Capital Expenditure Decisions: How They are Made in Large Corporations*, Bureau of Business Research, Indiana University, 1961; Thomas Klammer, 'Empirical Evidence of the Adoption of Sophisticated Capital Budgeting Techniques,' *Journal of Business*, July 1972; James C. T. Mao, 'Survey of Capital Budgeting: Theory and Practice,' *Journal of Finance*, May 1970; James H. Miller, 'A Glimpse at Practice in Calculating and Using Return on Investment,' *N.A.A. Bulletin*, June 1960; J. William Petty, David F. Scott Jr and Monroe M. Bird, 'The Capital Expenditure Decision-making Process of Large Corporations,' *The Engineering Economist*, Spring 1975; J. William Petty and David F. Scott Jr, 'Capital Budgeting Practices in Large American Firms: A Retrospective Analysis and Update,' *Financial Review*, March 1984; Lawrence D. Schall, Gary L. Sundem, and William R. Geijsbeek Jr, 'Survey and Analysis of Capital Budgeting Methods,' *Journal of Finance*, March 1978; and Jerry Viscione and John Neuhauser, 'Capital Expenditure Decisions in Moderately Sized Firms,' *Financial Review*, 1974.
    For a methodological critique of these studies, see Raj Agarwal, 'Corporate Use of Sophisticated Budgeting Techniques: A Strategic Perspective and a Critique of Survey Results,' *Interfaces*, April 1980; Allen Rappaport, 'A Critique of Capital Budgeting Questionnaires,' *Interfaces*, May 1979; and Meir, J. Rosenblatt and James V. Jucker, 'Capital Expenditure Decision-making: Some Tools and Trends,' *Interfaces*, February 1979.

Table 6.2 Project evaluation techniques

	Percentages used in			
	1976[a]	1970[b]	1964[b]	1959[b]
Discounting (*IRR*, *NPV* or profitability index)	66	57	38	19
Accounting rate of return	25	26	30	34
Payback or payback reciprocal	9	12	24	34
Qualitative methods		5	8	13
	100	100	100	100

[a] Based on *primary* evaluation technique used.
[b] Only *most* sophisticated method reported was counted.
Sources: for the years of 1970, 1964 and 1959: Klammer, Thomas, 'Empirical Evidence of the Adoption of Sophisticated Capital Budgeting Techniques,' *Journal of Business*, July 1972. For 1976: Gitman, Lawrence J. and Forrester Jr, John R., 'A Survey of Capital Budgeting Techniques Used by Major US Firms,' *Financial Management*, Fall 1977.

Table 6.3 Percentage of respondent firms using different types of capital budgeting methods

Discounted cash flow	Payback period	Accounting rate of return	Others	Percentage of firms using models (%)
Yes	Yes	Yes		28
Yes		Yes		8
Yes	Yes			16
Yes				28
	Yes	Yes		4
	Yes			2
		Yes		2
			Yes	12
				100

Source: Blume, E. M., Friend, I. and Westerfield, R., *Impediments to Capital Formation*, Rodney, L. White Center for Financial Research, December 1980.

reported in Tables 6.2 and 6.3 relate to very large U.S. corporations, the data probably *understate* the reliance on rules of thumb. Size and (observable) sophistication have a strong tendency to be positively correlated in the business world. It appears reasonable to conclude that many (if not most) business executives still use short-cut rules of thumb such as a payback formula or accounting rate of return when analyzing capital budgeting decisions.

The methods employed in project evaluation vary with the project classification. Table 6.4 summarizes the various methods employed by the project type. Though these figures are not directly comparable with the figures of Table 6.2, the results are similar. The proportion of firms using discounted methods as their primary method for project evaluation increases over time. However, it is interesting to note that in 1980, 23% of replacement projects have not been evaluated by any method, since they were classified as 'urgent', at least as management conceived them. The 'urgency' explanation is quite obvious in the case of the social expenditure category, but is less

Table 6.4 Project evaluation techniques

Most sophisticated primary evaluation standard used (classified by project type)	1980 survey percentage used in			1975 survey percentage used in		
	1980	1975	1970	1975	1970	1965
Replacement projects						
Discounting	56	45	28	56	35	21
Simple rate of return	7	14	21	8	13	15
Payback	4	8	10	6	12	12
Urgency	23	25	32	26	32	40
Total	90	92	91	96	92	88
Expansion – existing operations						
Discounting	75	62	44	72	47	30
Simple rate of return	10	16	28	13	24	30
Payback	5	9	14	10	18	19
Urgency	1	2	4	2	5	11
Total	91	89	90	97	94	90
Expansion – new operations						
Discounting	71	58	41	75	49	31
Simple rate of return	10	17	28	12	25	33
Payback	5	12	15	9	16	19
Urgency	1	1	2	1	3	6
Total	87	88	86	97	93	89
Foreign operations						
Discounting	72	59	45	71	44	32
Simple rate of return	11	20	27	11	24	26
Payback	3	8	14	8	14	18
Urgency	7	2	3	3	6	8
Total	93	89	89	93	88	84
Abandonment						
Discounting	55	47	36	n/a	n/a	n/a
Simple rate of return	10	14	20	n/a	n/a	n/a
Payback	4	5	8	n/a	n/a	n/a
Urgency	5	9	12	n/a	n/a	n/a
Total	74	75	76			
General and administrative						
Discounting	36	29	21	32	19	14
Simple rate of return	4	8	11	8	9	8
Payback	5	6	7	6	10	11
Urgency	32	32	36	37	43	46
Total	77	77	75	83	81	79
Social expenditures						
Discounting	14	14	10	16	10	8
Simple rate of return	2	2	4	2	2	2
Payback	1	1	1	1	1	1
Urgency	51	53	51	59	63	61
Total	68	70	66	78	78	78

The percentages are based on the response to a particular question. The difference between the percentage shown and 100% represents those who did not answer or checked 'other' on the questionnaires.
Source: Klamen, T. P. and Walker, M. C., 'The Continuing Increase in the Use of Sophisticated Budgeting Techniques,' *California Management Review*, Fall 1984.

understandable in project replacement decisions. Replacement, like any other new project, should be evaluated on a cash flow basis. Nevertheless, about one-third of the firms reporting the use of discounting also use other primary standards, e.g., payback or simple accounting rate of return method.

To summarize, it is equally clear from Tables 6.2, 6.3 and 6.4 that the use of time-discounting (principally the *IRR*) has been increasing over time. This shift to more sophisticated methods of project evaluation is not surprising. After an understandable lag, capital budgeting theory, developed in the 1950s, became the practice of business firms in the 1970s. Despite this trend, though, three nagging questions are raised by the empirical evidence:

1. How can we account for the persistence with which many knowledgeable businesspeople continue to use simple rule-of-thumb calculations?
2. What changes in the economic and business environment account for the observed shift to time-discounted methods?
3. How can we explain managements' preferences for the internal rate of return over other time-discounted methods such as *NPV*?

The remainder of the chapter is devoted to an attempt to answer each of these questions, but to do this we must first analyze the precise relationship between traditional rules of thumb and modern time-discounted methods of project evaluation.

RELATIONSHIP BETWEEN TRADITIONAL AND MODERN INVESTMENT ANALYSIS

As we have already noted, many businesspeople still use short-cut measures of investment worth when evaluating capital expenditures. Although it can readily be shown that the popular rules of thumb may distort investment decisions, they can provide close approximations of the discounted rate of return in a number of important situations.

Let us analyze the relationship between *IRR* and rules of thumb. (For the time being we shall do this ignoring taxes; corporate taxes are discussed in Appendix 6A.) In Chapter 3, an investment proposal's internal rate of return was defined as that rate of discount which equates the present value of the future net cash receipts generated by the proposal with the initial investment outlay:

$$I_0 = \frac{S_1}{(1 + R)} + \frac{S_2}{(1 + R)^2} + \cdots + \frac{S_n}{(1 + R)^n}$$

where:

R = internal pre-tax rate of return
I_0 = present value of the investment outlay
S_t = net pre-tax cash receipt in period t, before deducting depreciation expenses

Assuming equal future annual net receipts and zero terminal values, this formula can be rewritten as:

$$I_0 = \frac{S}{1+R} \times \left[1 + \frac{1}{(1+R)} + \frac{1}{(1+R)^2} + \cdots + \frac{1}{(1+R)^{n-1}} \right]$$

Summing the geometric progression within the square brackets and rearranging terms yields:

$$R = \frac{S}{I_0} - \frac{S}{I_0} \left(\frac{1}{1+R} \right)^n$$

Under these same two assumptions the reciprocal of an investment's payback period, R_p, can be defined as:

$$R_p = \frac{S}{I_0}$$

Comparing the definition of the payback reciprocal with the *IRR* formula clearly shows that the internal rate of return always lies below the payback reciprocal for all investment projects of finite duration, the margin of error being given by the expressions $(S/I_0)/(1+R)^n$. The margin of error depends not only on an investment proposal's expected economic life, but also on its internal rate of return. This can be seen by substituting the payback reciprocal into the *IRR* equation and rearranging terms:

$$R = R_p - R_p \left(\frac{1}{1+R} \right)^n$$

or

$$R_p = \frac{R}{1 - \left(\dfrac{1}{1+R} \right)^n}$$

The above relationship provides a convenient equation for carrying out a numerical analysis of the general relationship between the payback reciprocal and the internal rate of return.[6] The results of the numerical calculations are given in Table 6.5. An examination of the data confirms that the sign of the deviation is always positive (i.e., the payback reciprocal always exceeds the internal rate of return) and that for any given rate of return, the deviation decreases as an investment proposal's economic life increases.[7] However

---

6. For the purposes of this comparison, otherwise important differences between the internal rate of return and net present value investment criteria can be safely ignored. Strictly speaking, the use of the internal rate of return as a benchmark in the analysis is equivalent to assuming: (a) that no mutually exclusive investment alternatives exist, and (b) that the relevant discount rate does not change over time, cf. Chapter 4.

7. The percentage point deviations given in Table 6.5 were calculated by deducting R from R_p for each combination of R and n. For example, when $R = 10\%$ and $n = 10$ years, $R_p = 16.3\%$; the percentage point deviation, therefore, is given by $16.3 - 10 = +6.3$.

Table 6.5 Percentage point deviations of the payback reciprocal R_p from the internal rate of return for selected values of R and n

Internal rate of return R (%)	Project duration in n years								
	2	5	8	10	15	20	40	60	100
5	+48.8	+18.1	+10.5	+8.0	+4.6	+3.0	+0.8	+0.3	–
10	+47.6	+16.4	+8.7	+6.3	+3.2	+1.8	+0.2	–	–
15	+46.5	+14.8	+7.3	+4.9	+2.1	+1.0	+0.1	–	–
20	+45.4	+13.4	+6.1	+3.9	+1.4	+0.5	–	–	–
30	+43.5	+11.1	+4.2	+2.4	+0.6	+0.2	–	–	–
40	+41.7	+9.1	+2.9	+1.4	+0.3	–	–	–	–
50	+40.0	+7.6	+2.0	+0.9	+0.1	–	–	–	–
60	+38.5	+6.3	+1.4	+0.6	–	–	–	–	–

The symbol '–' represents deviations of less than 0.1 percentage points

Table 6.5 also clearly shows that for any given proposal's life, the deviation of the payback reciprocal from the internal rate also decreases as the internal rate increases. For investment proposals with internal rates of return greater than 30% and with economic lives exceeding ten years (the relevant region for much of U.S. industry), the deviation is negligible, and the payback reciprocal provides a very good estimate of the discounted rate of return. On the other hand, for proposals with relatively low internal rates of return ($R < 8\%$), which is the relevant domain for the regulated industries such as the electric power industry, the deviations remain substantial for all economic lives of less than twenty years, which helps to explain why the payback period has never been popular in such industries. Similarly, proposals with a short life (less than five years) exhibit substantial deviations even for large values of the *IRR*. Thus despite the fact that the payback period is often considered as a conservative rule of thumb which emphasizes liquidity considerations, its use may impart a significant *upward* bias to profitability estimates.

In a similar manner, the relationship between the accounting rate of return and the *IRR* is derived.[8]

$$R_t = \frac{S - D}{I_0} = \frac{S}{I_0} - \frac{I_0/n}{I_0} = R_p - \frac{1}{n}$$

$$R_a = \frac{S - D}{I_0/2} = \frac{2S}{I_0} - \frac{2}{n} = 2\left(R_p - \frac{1}{n}\right)$$

where D is the annual 'straight-line' depreciation, i.e., I_0/n, R_t is the accounting rate of return on the total investment and R_a is the accounting rate of return on the average investment. Substituting the formula for the payback

---

8. If depreciation is not constant, the formula becomes more complicated, but still yields very similar results.

reciprocal which was derived above into these two formulas yields:

$$R_t = \frac{R}{1 - \dfrac{1}{(1+R)^n}} - \frac{1}{n}$$

$$R_a = 2\left[\frac{R}{1 - \dfrac{1}{(1+R)^n}} - \frac{1}{n}\right]$$

The essential properties of the accounting rate of return on total investment R_t are analyzed in Table 6.6, which gives the percentage point deviations of the accounting rate of return on total investment, R_t from the internal rate of return R for a wide range of values of R and n.

In sharp contrast to the payback reciprocal, the sign of the deviation of the accounting rate on total investment from the internal rate is uniformly *negative* for all finite proposal lives greater than one year. The deviations, moreover, *increase* initially as proposal life increases, but after a point, R_t also asymptotically approaches the *IRR* as longer proposal lives are considered. However, in the case of the accounting rate the approach is not nearly as rapid as was true for the payback reciprocal, and over most of the economically relevant range the derivations remain significantly large.

Since the accounting rate of return on average investment R_a is a constant multiple of R_t, the relationship of the former to the internal rate of return is simply a constant vertical displacement of the latter's relationship. For proposals with a life of one year, $R_a = 2R$. As proposal duration increases, R_a first decreases but beyond some critical value of n it increases; as n approaches infinity R_a approaches $2R$. For all other values of n, the sign of the deviation of R_a from R remains positive. Thus the accounting rate of return on average

Table 6.6 Percentage point deviations of the accounting rate of return on total investment R_t from the internal rate of return R for selected values of R and n

Internal rate of return R (%)	Projection duration in n years								
	1	2	5	10	15	20	40	60	100
5	0	−1.2	−1.9	−2.0	−2.0	−2.0	−1.7	−1.4	−1.0
10	0	−2.4	−3.6	−3.7	−3.5	−3.2	−2.3	−1.6	−1.0
15	0	−3.5	−5.2	−5.1	−4.6	−4.0	−2.4	−1.7	−1.0
20	0	−4.6	−6.6	−6.2	−5.3	−4.5	−2.6	−1.7	−1.0
30	0	−6.5	−8.9	−7.6	−6.1	−4.8	−2.5	−1.7	−1.0
40	0	−8.3	−10.9	−8.6	−6.4	−5.0	−2.5	−1.7	−1.0
50	0	−10.0	−12.4	−9.1	−6.6	−5.0	−2.5	−1.7	−1.0
60	0	−11.5	−13.7	−9.4	−6.6	−5.0	−2.5	−1.7	−1.0

investment *overstates*, while the accounting rate of return on total investment *understates* investment proposals' internal rate of return.[9]

_____ **RECONCILING THEORY WITH PRACTICE**

Having determined the formal relationship between the rules of thumb and the *IRR*, let us return to the questions regarding the persistence with which many businesspeople use simple short-cut measures of profitability and the observed trend towards the use of time-discounted methods in the 1960s and 1970s. Before we do this, a preliminary warning may be in order. Despite the systematic nature of the relationship of short-cut methods to the time adjusted internal rate of return, these results have *no* significance for the normative theory of the investment of the firm.[10] Even minor deviations of the rules of thumb from the internal rate may lead to decision errors. However, the systematic nature of the relationship between rules of thumb and the internal rate, and the range over which the deviations remain relatively small, are very relevant for the positive theory of investment. They can help to account for the fact that most successful business firms used short-cut rules of thumb in the past and explain why many still persist in their use today, even in the face of the overwhelming theoretical arguments in favor of time discounting.

Use of rules of thumb

Considerable evidence exists that most of the industrial firms who employed the payback rule operate in the range of project lives and profitability in which the rule of thumb provides a very close approximation of the project's true *IRR*. Almost all of the researchers who reported on the use of the payback rule comment on the fact that firms demanded relatively short payback periods while applying the rule to projects of rather long lives.[11] But these are precisely the conditions (high profitability and long economic life) which ensure a very close approximation of the rule of thumb estimate to the project's true profitability. Thus, the use of the crude measure of profitability need not lead, in such instances, to a *decision error*: that is, to a reversal of the decision which would have been reached using the *IRR*.

Similarly, the results of the analysis can be used to explain the observed use of the accounting rate of return on total investment R_t rather than on average

9. For simplicity the analysis has been carried out in terms of pre-tax cash flows. In Appendix 6A it is shown that these general relationships between the rules of thumb and the *IRR* hold for the after-tax case as well.
10. This section employs Milton Friedman's familiar distinction between normative and positive theories. The term 'normative' refers to propositions concerning what should or ought to be; 'positive' refers to propositions designed to explain or predict reality as it actually exists. See Milton Friedman, *Essays in Positive Economics*, University of Chicago Press, 1953, pp. 3–43.
11. See, for example, Donald F. Istvan, 'The Economic Evaluation of Capital Expenditures,' *Journal of Business*, January 1961.

investment R_a. On the surface, the latter would seem to have the greater appeal – especially for accountants, who might be expected to argue that the investment (denominator of the ratio) should be progressively reduced as the initial outlay is recouped through depreciation allowances.

In this case, the popularity of R_t can be traced to the systematic *downward* bias which it imparts to the profitability estimate. (The reader should recall that the sign of the deviation is always negative.) The use of R_t can only lead to the decision error in which a project which would have been accepted had its *IRR* been calculated, is rejected. Conversely, the use of the conservative R_t formula can never lead to the acceptance of a project which should be rejected. The opposite holds true for R_a, and since most financial executives tend to prefer an 'opportunity loss' to an actual money loss, the preference for R_t is not surprising. The conservative downward bias which results from the use of total, rather than average, investment in the formula for the accounting rate of return can also be rationalized as a crude adjustment for risk and/or timing, both of which are ignored in the rule of thumb calculation.

Shift to time discounting

Now let us turn to the even more perplexing question of why many of these same firms began to make the transition to more sophisticated time-discounted measures of investment worth in the 1960s and 1970s. First, credit must be given to the generation of specialists in corporate finance, managerial economics, and engineering economy who refined and strengthened the theoretical foundations of modern investment analysis. Second, the transition to modern evaluation techniques coincides with a 'revolution' in corporate forecasting capability. The corporations of the post-World War II period had an arsenal of newly created tools at their disposal to help forecast the uncertain future; and soon econometricians and systems analysts began to make their appearance on corporate planning teams and even in the boardroom. Perhaps the best known example of the post-war transition is provided by the Ford Motor Company which appointed a former Harvard University professor of accounting (McNamara) as its president and a former University of Chicago professor of econometrics (Yntema) as its financial vice-president.

In this context the reader should recall that our analysis of the popular rules of thumb rests on the assumption of *equal annual* receipts. As long as business firms were unable to refine their forecasts beyond a ball park estimate of the average annual cash flow and the economic life of the project – e.g. 'a million dollars for ten years' – the rules of thumb worked well. As in fact, considering the trauma which often affects executives when radically new techniques are introduced, there was little economic justification for making the transition to *IRR* or *NPV* until better forecasts became available. However, once a firm is able to estimate both the magnitude and timing of the cash flow, the transition to evaluation methods which reflect the impact of the differential timing of receipts and outlays is almost inevitable. Under these circumstances, rules of thumb become as obsolete as the fabled gray mare, and readers of books like this begin the long trek to positions of corporate responsibility.

Preference for *IRR* over *NPV*

A detailed examination of more recent empirical surveys shows that management has a strong preference for the *IRR* over its other time-discounted counterparts such as *NPV*. Moreover, most large corporations, which still use a rule of thumb such as payback, do so in combination with the internal rate of return. [12] Thus despite the theoretical difficulties which academics have with the *IRR* it is very popular with practitioners. And by the principle of revealed preference, it is clear that, by and large, management is unconcerned with the theoretical and technical shortcomings of the *IRR* which we have spelled out in great detail in Chapter 4.

In this context we should recall that the *theoretical shortcomings* of the *IRR* method relate only to mutually exclusive choice situations. Thus, with respect to many (and perhaps most) capital expenditure decisions, the *IRR* is not inferior to net present value. But, even though it gives good results in most cases why should management prefer the *IRR* when an even better method (i.e., *NPV*) is available?

Unlike the case of payback, one cannot rationalize the use of *IRR* on grounds of simplicity. On the contrary, the *IRR* is actually somewhat more difficult to calculate than the *NPV*; and, moreover, it is plagued on occasion by the technical problem of multiple roots. Nor can we gain much insight from that old textbook dictum about *NPV* requiring an estimate of the cost of capital, for as we have already seen, such an estimate is also required if the *IRR* is to be used as a decision rule. It appears not unlikely, that the preference for *IRR* reflects a very strong, but perhaps subconscious, preference for measures of profitability which are stated in percentage terms. 'Everyone knows what 10% means; what is a positive net present value?' How can the fledgling executive reconcile this with his or her theoretical conscience? There are two alternatives.

1. Give your boss a crash course in capital budgeting; this may temporarily inflate your ego but will probably shorten the duration of your stay with the firm.
2. A more agreeable alternative is to plug for, and use, *IRR* but always make room for an appendix on *NPV* in your feasibility reports in mutually exclusive choice situations.

SUMMARY

This chapter has been devoted to the analysis of nondiscounted methods of evaluating capital investment proposals. Two popular rules of thumb are

12. See Petty and Scott, op. cit.

analyzed: the payback (and its reciprocal) and the nondiscounted accounting rate of return on total investment. (The accounting rate of return on *average* investment is simply twice the latter.)

Despite some obvious defects, a majority of all business firms probably still employ such methods as payback and accounting return, although in recent years more and more larger firms have been making the transition to time-discounted measures of investment worth.

An analysis of the formal relationship between the rules of thumb and the time-discounted *IRR* shows that as long as the firm assumes equal annual receipts, the simple rules of thumb often provide a close approximation to a project's true *IRR* in the domain of project life and profitability which is relevant for the firm in practice. It is only when more sophisticated techniques are used to forecast the components and timing of the cash flow that the use of time-discounted methods becomes an imperative for rational decision-making. Finally, we should mention that although the comparison between the internal rate of return and the rules of thumb ignored corporate taxes, the same basic relationship holds for the post-tax cash flows as well.

SUMMARY TABLE

Rules of thumb

1. Payback period, n_p:

$$n_p = \frac{I_0}{S}: \text{ accept all projects with } n_p < n_0$$

where n_0 is some critical number of years, S is the future annual cash flow, and I_0 is the initial investment. Alternatively, define $R_p = 1/n_p$ and accept if R_p is greater than some critical value.

2. The discounted payback period:
   n_p is given by the number of years that the discounted cash flows exactly cover the initial outlay I_0.

3. Accounting rates of return:

On total investment $R_t = \dfrac{S - D}{I_0}$

On average investment $R_a = \dfrac{S - D}{I_0/2}$

where D denotes the depreciation.
Accept a project if R_t or R_a is greater than some critical value.

Relationship between rules of thumb and *IRR*

1. Payback:

$$R_p = R \Big/ \left[1 - \left(\frac{1}{1+R} \right)^n \right], \text{ always } R_p \geqslant R$$

2. Accounting rules:

On total investment

$$R_t = R \Big/ \left[1 - \left(\frac{1}{1+R} \right)^n \right] - \frac{1}{n}, \text{ always } R_t \leqslant R$$

On average investment

$$R_a = 2R_t = 2R \Big/ \left[1 - \left(\frac{1}{1+R} \right)^n \right] - \frac{2}{n}, \text{ always } R_a \geqslant R$$

where *R* stands for the *IRR* and *n* the project's duration in years.

3. The post-tax relationship is similar to the pre-tax relationship.

_____ **QUESTIONS AND PROBLEMS**

6.1 Define the following terms:

(a) Payback period
(b) Accounting rate of return.

6.2 For each of the following cash flows A–E, calculate the payback period:

Year:	0	1	2	3	4	5	6	7	8
A	−2,000	400	400	400	400	400	400	400	400
B	−9,000	3,000	2,500	2,000	1,500	1,000	500	−	−
C	−12,000	10,000	2,000	−	−	−	−	−	−
D	−12,000	2,400	2,400	2,400	2,400	2,400	14,400	−	−
E	−12,000	2,000	2,000	2,000	2,000	2,400	2,000	2,000	2,000

6.3 What is the payback period of a project which requires $1,000 initial investment, and has receipts of $500 for five years? What will be its payback if the receipts are $500 for two years? What is the economic significance of your answer?

6.4 For each of the following cash flows, calculate the accounting rate of return (on total investment), assuming straight-line depreciation:

Year:	0	1	2	3	4	5	6	7	Duration (years)
F	−1,400	300	300	300	300	300	300	300	7
G	−25,000	12,500	12,500	12,500	12,500	12,500	−	−	5
I	−10,000	4,000	4,000	4,000	4,000	−	−	−	4
J	−2,000	1,500	1,500	−	−	−	−	−	2

6.5 Calculate the payback period and its reciprocal for each of the cash flows appearing in question 6.4. Compare and explain your answer using the two rules of thumb.

6.6 Set out the formal relationships between the following rules of thumb for project evaluation and the internal rate of return:

(a) Payback period (reciprocal).
(b) Accounting rate of return on total investment.
(c) Accounting rate of return on average investment.

6.7 What is the significance of the formal relationship between rules of thumb and the *IRR* for investment decision-making?

6.8 'It is surprising that large U.S. firms often use short payback periods to appraise long-lived projects.' Critically comment on this statement.

6.9 For each of the following projects, calculate the payback reciprocal, the accounting rate of return on total investment, and the internal rate of return. Assume straight-line depreciation:

> Project A: Initial investment of $10,000 and annual gross receipts (before deducting depreciation) of $2,000, for ten years.
> Project B: Initial investment of $10,000 and annual gross receipts of $2,000 for twenty years.
> Project C: Initial investment of $10,000 and annual gross receipts of $2,000 for forty years.

Compare and explain your results.

6.10 For each of the following projects, calculate the payback reciprocal and the accounting rates of return on total and average investment, and the internal rate of return. (Assume straight-line depreciation.)

> Project D: Initial investment of $20,000 and annual gross receipts of $3,000 for ten years.
> Project E: Initial investment of $20,000 and annual gross receipts of $6,000 for ten years.
> Project F: Initial investment of $20,000 and annual gross receipts of $9,000 for ten years.

Compare and explain your results.

6.11 The Gordon Investment Company was established in 1963. The company's policy was to concentrate its investments in industrial firms in an effort to gain control. The parent company created a decentralized management system which gave the managers of the subsidiaries considerable freedom, and as a result different methods of project evaluation are employed by the subsidiaries.

Alpha Company uses the 'payback' criterion, where the cash flow is taken on a 'before interest and depreciation' basis. According to Alpha's criterion, a project is acceptable if the payback period does not exceed four years. Another subsidiary Beta, uses the 'accounting method' which is defined as follows: compute the rate of return by dividing the net receipt (before interest but after depreciation) by the total investment. If this accounting rate of return exceeds 20%, the project is acceptable.

In February 1990, the management of the Gordon Investment Company asked Mr. Smith, a management consultant, for his professional judgement of the methods used by Alpha and Beta. As a first step, Smith chose a sample of invest-ment projects being evaluated by the two subsidiaries.

Projects considered by Alpha

Project 1: An investment of $10,000. The net receipts (after deducting depreci-ation and interest) are $1,600 per annum. The yearly interest charge is $700 and the annual depreciation is $500.

Project 2: An investment of $60,000. The net receipts (after deducting depreci-ation and interest) are $3,000 per annum. The yearly interest and depreci-ation charges are $4,200 and $10,000, respectively.

Project 3: An investment of $150,000. The net annual receipts, after deducting depreciation and interest, are $10,000 during the first five years and $40,000 per annum in the next ten years. The yearly depreciation charge is $10,000 and the yearly interest charge is $15,000.

Projects considered by Beta

Project 1: An investment of $600,000. Net receipts, before interest but after depreciation, are $100,000. The yearly depreciation is $200,000.

Project 2: An investment of $1 million. Net receipts, before interest but after depreciation, are $240,000. The yearly depreciation is $25,000.

Mr. Smith also made the following assumptions:

1. The investment projects are *not* mutually exclusive.
2. The salvage value of all projects at the end of their economic life is zero.
3. Straight-line depreciation is used.
4. Due to differences in risk, the appropriate cost of capital for Alpha is 25% and the appropriate rate for Beta is 20%.
5. Corporate taxes are not payable by the companies and therefore can be ignored.
6. The sample of projects is *representative* of the types of project evaluated by the firms.

Assume that you are Mr. Smith and recommend an optimal decision rule for evaluating investments.

(a) Which rule do you recommend? Why?
(b) In defending your answer compare the decisions reached by the subsidiaries using their methods with the decisions which you reach using the proposed optimal method. Carefully explain your results.

6.12 Consider a project with a pre-tax internal rate of return of 10%, and a duration of five years. The project's initial investment is $100 ($I_0$). Assuming a constant annual cash flow S, solve for the pre-tax and post-tax accounting rate of return (R_a and R_t) and for the payback reciprocal R_p. Assume straight-line depreciation and a corporate tax of 34% ($T_c = 0.34$). (See Appendix 6A.)

6.13 Distinguish between 'opportunity loss' and 'financial loss'. Which rule of thumb leads to each type of loss? Explain your answer.

6.14 A firm considers a project whose economic life is $n = 4$ years. The initial invest-ment is $I_0 = 100, and the annual pre-tax cash now before depreciation is $S = 50. The tax rate $T_c = 34\%$. Calculate the post-tax payback period first by assuming straight-line depreciation and then by assuming *ACRS* depreciation method (see Chapter 5). Assume that the asset is in a 3-year life category for depreciation purposes.

6.15 A project has an initial investment of $I_0 = \$1,000$ and the following cash flows:

Year	1	2	3	4
Cash flow	$500	$500	$500	$500

(a) Calculate the payback period and the implied payback rate of return in percentage terms.

(b) Calculate the discounted payback period and the implied payback rate of return in percentage terms. Assume a cost of capital of 20%.

(c) Calculate the *IRR* of the project.

6.16 The firm faces a project with a constant annual cashflows for $n = 10$ years. It is given that $R \simeq 0.615 R_p$, where R and R_p denote the *IRR* and the payback rate of return, respectively. Calculate R and R_p.

6.17 The following information on a project is given. A constant annual cash flow; the accounting rate of return is $R_t = 20\%$, and the payback rate of return is $R_p = 30\%$. Calculate the project *IRR*.

APPENDIX 6A: POST-TAX RELATIONSHIPS BETWEEN RULES OF THUMB AND INTERNAL RATE OF RETURN

In this appendix the effects of introducing corporate taxes into the analysis are examined. The post-tax relationships between the rules of thumb and the internal rate of return are of crucial importance since it may be presumed that profit-oriented firms are concerned solely with errors in post-tax profitability estimates.[13] Fortunately for our purposes, it can be shown that the relationships among the alternative measures of return depicted in Tables 6.4 and 6.5 of the text remain invariable for any level of taxation. The general proof of this proposition follows the notation and method of analysis used in the pre-tax case.[14]

Retaining the assumptions of equal annual pre-tax cash receipts and straight-line depreciation, and letting T_c equal the corporate tax rate, the net post-tax receipt before depreciation is defined as $(S - D)(1 - T_c) + D$. Hence:

$$I_0 = \frac{(S-D)(1-T_c)+D}{(1+R^*)} + \frac{(S-D)(1-T_c)+D}{(1+R^*)^2} + \cdots + \frac{(S-D)(1-T_c)+D}{(1+R^*)^n}$$

$$= \frac{(S-D)(1-T_c)+D}{(1+R^*)} \times \left[1 - \left(\frac{1}{1+R^*}\right)^n \middle/ \left(1 - \left(\frac{1}{1+R^*}\right)\right) \right]$$

where:

$R^* = $ post-tax internal rate of return
$T_c = $ corporate income tax rate

Simplifying and rearranging terms yields:

$$R^* = \frac{(S-D)(1-T_c)+D}{I_0} \times \left[1 - \left(\frac{1}{1+R^*}\right)^n \right]$$

---

13. Of course, this 'concern' need not (and presumably often does not) exist at a conscious level.
14. Post-tax variables are distinguished from their pre-tax counterparts by an asterisk.

Under the same assumptions, the post-tax payback reciprocal (R_p^*) is defined as:

$$R_p^* = \frac{(S-D)(1-T_c)+D}{I_0}$$

Substituting this definition into the preceding equation and rearranging terms yields:

$$R_p^* = \frac{R^*}{1 - \left(\dfrac{1}{1+R^*}\right)^n}$$

Comparing the relevant pre-tax and post-tax formulas clearly shows that the relationship of the post-tax payback reciprocal to the post-tax internal rate of return is *identical* to the pre-tax relationship and, therefore, has the same general properties. It follows that the deviations given in Table 6.4 of the text hold equally for both the before-tax and after-tax cases.

A similar result can readily be proven for the accounting rates of return as well. Let us define the post-tax accounting rate of return on total investment R_t^* as follows:

$$R_t^* = \frac{(1-T_c)(S-D)}{I_0}$$

Recalling that under the assumption of straight-line depreciation $D = I_0/n$, we can rewrite the post-tax *IRR* as:

$$R^* = \frac{(1-T_c)(S-D)}{I_0} \times \left[1 - \left(\frac{1}{1+R^*}\right)^n\right] + \frac{1}{n} \times \left[1 - \left(\frac{1}{1+R^*}\right)^n\right]$$

Substituting the definition of R_t^* into this equation and rearranging terms gives:

$$R_t^* = \frac{R^*}{1 - \left(\dfrac{1}{1+R^*}\right)^n} - \frac{1}{n}$$

which also has the identical form of the pre-tax relationship.[15] Here again it follows that the deviations presented in Table 6.5 of the text hold for both the before- and after-tax cases. Thus all of the general properties of the pre-tax relationships hold with equal force for the after-tax case as well, *independent* of the tax rate assumed.

_____ **QUESTIONS AND PROBLEMS**

6A.1 For each of the following cash flows, calculate the post-tax payback reciprocal R_p^*, the post-tax accounting rate of return R_t^*, and the post-tax *IRR*, assuming a 34% corporate income tax rate and straight-line depreciation:

Cash flow	*PV* of the investment outlay ($)	Annual pre-tax cash receipts ($)	Duration (years)
A	20,000	9,000	5
B	12,000	4,000	6
C	50,000	11,000	10
D	100,000	30,000	20

15. Since the post-tax accounting rate of return on average investment is a constant multiple of the post-tax rate of return on total investment, this result holds for that relationship as well.

6A.2 The 'Bazak' Company deals with projects with constant annual cash flows whose duration is more than 30 years. The firm uses the payback method and accepts every project with a payback period of five years or less. 'Bazak' pays no corporate taxes.

(a) 'The above method is an unreasonable investment rule, particularly in the case of projects with a long duration.' Do you agree with this statement? Prove your answer.

(b) After the corporate tax rate was reduced in 1986 from 46% to 34%, an economic consultant recommends using the 'accounting method' instead of the payback method. He claims that when the tax is taken into account, the 'accounting method' yields the best approximation to the internal rate of return. Do you agree with this recommendation? Explain carefully.

SELECTED REFERENCES

Agarwal, Raj, 'Corporate Use of Sophisticated Capital Budgeting Techniques: A Strategic Perspective and a Critique of Survey Results,' *Interfaces*, April 1980.

Brigham, Eugene F. and Pettway, Richard H., 'Capital Budgeting by Utilities,' *Financial Management*, Autumn 1973.

Fremgen, James. 'Capital Budgeting Practices: A Survey,' *Management Accounting*, May 1973.

Gitman, Lawrence J. and Forrester, John R. Jr, 'A Survey of Capital Budgeting Techniques Used by Major U.S. Firms,' *Financial Management*, Fall 1977.

Gordon, Lawrence, A., 'Further Thoughts on the Accounting Rate of Return vs. the Economic Rate of Return?' *Journal of Business Finance and Accounting*, Spring 1977.

Hoskins, C. G. and Mumey, G. A., 'Payback: A Maligned Method of Asset Ranking?' *Engineering Economist*, Fall 1979.

Kim, Suk H., 'Capital Budgeting Practices in Large Corporations and Their Impact on Overall Profitability,' *Baylor Business Studies*, November/December 1978, January 1979.

Klammer, T., 'Empirical Evidence of the Adoption of Sophisticated Capital Budgeting Techniques,' *Journal of Business*, July 1972.

Klammer, T. and Walter, M. C., 'The Continuing Increase in the Use of Sophisticated Budgeting Techniques,' *California Management Review*, Fall 1984.

Longbottom, D. A. and Wiper, L., 'Capital Appraisal and the Case for the Average Rate of Return,' *Journal of Business Finance and Accounting*, 4, 4, 1977.

Narayanan, M. P., 'Observability and the Payback Criterion,' *Journal of Business*, July 1985.

Nehauser, John J. and Viscione, Jerry A., 'How Managers Feel About Advanced Capital Budgeting Methods,' *Management Review*, November 1973.

Oblak, David J. and Helm, Roy J. Jr, 'Survey and Analysis of Capital Budgeting Methods Used by Multinationals,' *Financial Management*, Winter 1980.

Petry, Glenn, H., 'Effective Use of Capital Budgeting Tools,' *Business Horizons*, October 1975.

Prakash, A. J., Dandapani, K., and Karels, G. V., 'Simple Resource Allocation Rules,' *Journal of Business, Finance and Accounting*, Autumn 1988.

Rosenblatt, Meir J., 'A Survey and Analysis of Capital Budgeting Decision Processes in Multi-division Firms,' *The Engineering Economist*, Summer 1980.

Schall, L. D., Sundem, G. L., and Geijsbeek, W. R. Jr, 'Survey and Analysis of Capital Budgeting Methods,' *Journal of Finance*, March 1978.

Statman, M., 'The Persistence of the Payback Method: A Principal–Agent Perspective,' *Engineering Economist*, Winter 1982.

Stephen, Frank H., 'On Deriving the Internal Rate of Return from the Accountant's Rate of Return,' *Journal of Business Finance and Accounting*, Summer 1976.

Williams, Ronald B. Jr, 'Industry Practice in Allocating Capital Resources,' *Managerial Planning*, May/June 1970.

7

Managing Working Capital

ARTICLE 13

Preferred Clients

With Big Loans Slow, Major Banks Romance Local Midsized Firms

Lenders Like the Margins, Extended Relationships And Low Rates of Default

Credit Standards Stay Strict

NEW YORK – If there's a credit crunch, it isn't crunching Jack Hartog.

Mr. Hartog is chairman of Hartog Foods International, a distributor of juice concentrates and processed foods. When one of its banks cut its credit lines a few months ago, Hartog Foods found 12 others interested in winning its business. That led the company, whose annual sales are in the range of $150 million, to increase its borrowings.

'We were pleasantly surprised. The competition was active, very aggressive,' says the 64-year-old chairman, who chose Chase Manhattan Bank, Brown Brothers Harriman & Co. and a longtime Hartog lender, Bank of New York Co.

Although few companies are being courted by 12 banks, Mr. Hartog's success does reflect a changed financial climate. With big ticket banking in the doldrums, major banks are trying harder to woo small and midsized local businesses.

High Margins

Once the backwater of corporate bank-ing, the middle market is one of the few high-margin lending businesses left, not having been taken over by securities firms that arrange commercial paper or other offerings. Midsized companies traditionally pay relatively high interest rates, and not many default.

Moreover, the middle market is one of the last bastions of relationship banking, the tradition of long-lasting, mutually beneficial ties between a corporate borrower and its lenders. In re-emphasizing relationships, banks have come a long way from the 1980s, when they financed raids against clients and many saw old ties as old hat.

But banks aren't chasing after middle-market companies the way they used to chase leveraged buy-outs and commercial real estate loans. While increasingly lending to the middle market, banks also are raising their standards in hopes of weeding out shaky borrowers. 'Banks are scared to make bad loans,' says Steven Sklar, chief financial officer of Biocraft Laboratories Inc., who recently arranged a loan with a new lender for the generic-drug maker in Fair Lawn N.J. 'But once you convince them you're a good risk, it's very competitive.'

Loan Demand Light

Right now, many bankers say, loan demand from credit-worthy borrowers is light – and that's partly why New York banks are wooing each other's clients. 'We are booking business, but it's at the expense of our competitors,' Chemical's Mr. Lourenso says. 'The overwhelming majority of our customer base is in a "How do I survive the recession?" state of mind.' Many companies have trimmed inventories and held back on capital spending.

In a January survey, the National Federation of Independent Business found demand for credit at record lows. And only 4% of the business people surveyed called financing their main problem; in the 1980–82 credit crunch, that figure topped 30%. 'Banks have the money to lend. They just don't have the customers,' says William Dunkelberg, the group's chief economist.

For some small and midsized companies, however, finding a new lender has become difficult. Most banks have tightened lending standards and are demanding additional documentation. Many also prefer to make loans for the purchase of equipment or hard assets that can serve as collateral and generate revenue.

Even some borrowers understand why banks are tightening up. James Roenitz, chairman of Landmark Group, a Plymouth, Wis., holding company for some midsized businesses, say his banks have raised their credit standards, but he doesn't believe they are too conservative. In the past, he says, 'many were too damn liberal.'

However, some companies need financing desperately. Norman Spector, chief executive of Norsal Corp., says European American Bank pulled the plug on a $300,000 revolving credit line. That action, he adds, could have sunk the Long Island, N.Y., manufactuer of radar equipment, which has 25 employees and annual sales of $2 million. Chemical came up with a revolving credit but refused an additional short-term loan to help meet seasonal cash-flow needs. However, Chemical let Norsal postpone payments on the principal of the revolving credit for three months.

Source: *Wall Street Journal*, February 26, 1992, p. A1.

As we can see from article 13, the relationship amongst economic activity of the firm, its inventory level, and the firm's bank relationship is quite complex. One bank cut its credit line to Hartog Foods International, while another twelve lenders offer the loan.

When there is a recession, 'many companies trim inventory', and the 'demand for credit [is] at record lows'. In spite of this low demand, banks 'also are raising their standard in hopes of weeding out shaky borrowers,' hence avoiding or minimizing 'bad loans'.

What determines the inventory level, and what determines the level of cash held by the firm? What are credit standards and bad loans? While banks may have bad loans, do business firms also have bad loans? What credit standard can the firm employ to avoid bad loans? And why is short-term asset (e.g., inventory) financed by short-term loan from the bank? Why is it not recommended that the firm should finance its fixed assets by short-term loans? (Imagine what would happen if the bank pulled the plug on these loans.)

Note that to this point the book has concentrated on capital budgeting, i.e., on the long-term investment in plant and equipment. However, as we have seen in Chapter 5, even long-term investments create a need for additional cash balances, inventories of raw materials and finished goods, trade credit, etc. For sheer size alone, few activities can compare in importance with the demand for funds generated by the investment in the short-term assets that provide the firm with working, as contrasted with fixed, capital. This chapter provides an overview of the principles underlying the management of the major working capital components, and discusses the concepts given in article 13.

CHARACTERISTICS OF WORKING CAPITAL

Working capital refers to a firm's current assets. Net working capital is defined as current assets minus current liabilities. Current assets are those which the firm expects to be able to turn into cash within one year (or during its normal operating cycle). A firm's primary current assets are cash itself, short-term marketable securities, accounts receivable (i.e., trade credit extended to its customers), and inventories of raw materials and finished goods. In a similar fashion, those claims against a firm's assets which are payable within one year (e.g., accounts payable and short-term bank loans) are called current liabilities.

You should note, however, that the permanent or fixed assets of one firm are often the current assets of another. For example, a newly produced truck is part of Ford's current assets, but becomes a part of the fixed assets of the firm which acquires it in order to deliver its products. The distinction between current and permanent assets depends on their intended economic use, and not on their physical characteristics. In both instances we are speaking about the same truck.

Working capital is the relatively liquid portion of a firm's total capital, and constitutes a sort of buffer stock for meeting obligations out of the company's ordinary operating cash flow cycle. The current assets comprising a firm's working capital have the following characteristics:

1. *Short life span.* These assets have a short life span, typically less than one year. Exceptions occur in those firms whose production cycle is more than one year. For example, tobacco companies that store their raw-material inventories for as much as three years still report them as 'current assets'.
2. *Rapid transferability into other assets.* The components of working capital can be quickly transformed into other asset forms. Thus, for example, cash is used to replenish inventories, the inventories are run down as sales are made, and are then transformed into accounts receivable, which again become cash as the receivables are collected. This characteristic of working capital can be visualized by looking at Figure 7.1 which shows the firm's 'cash cycle'. Even if the level of working capital is held constant, the components are continuously changing. In our highly simplified example, the production process transforms cash into raw materials and then into finished goods. Credit sales transform the inventories into receivables, and

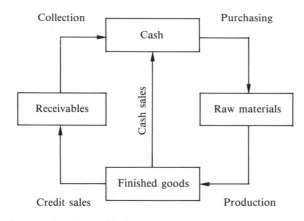

Figure 7.1 Cash cycle of the firm.

when these accounts are collected we once again have a cash balance —
presumably larger than in the beginning, if a profit was made.

3. *Synchronization*. Finally, the size of working capital depends crucially on
the degree of synchronization among production, sales and collections. If
all these activities occurred instantaneously, with perfect synchronization,
the management of working capital would be trivial, and this chapter would
not have been written. However, when an element of uncertainty is added
to the underlying lack of synchronization among a firm's business activities,
the need for the careful management of a firm's working capital requirements becomes obvious.

———————————— FINANCING WORKING CAPITAL: ALTERNATIVE STRATEGIES

Just as there appears to be no universally valid standard of taste or artistic
license, there is no universally accepted strategy for financing working capital.
Japanese firms often view, and therefore solve, their financing problems very
differently from their European or American counterparts. Cigarette manufacturers and steel mills often follow widely differing financing strategies.
Despite these very obvious differences, we can identify a principle which
underlies most, if not all, such strategies.

Working capital financing strategies usually reflect an attempt to maintain
some relationship between the durability of assets and the maturity of the debt
used to finance these assets. One result of this approach is summed up in the
well-known dictum, 'never finance fixed investments with short-term capital.'
The other side of this coin would seem to imply that short-term assets should
only be financed by short-term sources. But, as we see below, this is not generally correct. Of course, in an ideal world in which raw materials are acquired
at the beginning of the year, processed and then sold at the end of the year,
the expenditure on raw materials would be financed by, say, a one-year loan

from the bank. And if we assume that the one-year interest rate is less than the long-term rate, such a strategy also implies the minimization of capital costs.

Figure 7.2 illustrates this simple situation. Resources are acquired at the beginning of the production period, used up during the period, and replenished at the beginning of the next period. For example, suppose a textile firm buys the cotton needed (point a), uses the cotton during the year (point b), and buys cotton again for the next production cycle (point c). Thus the inventory level of cotton has a repeating cycle. These short-term needs are financed by short-term credit (see Figure 7.2); the remaining fixed assets of the firm are financed by long-term capital (long-term debt and equity).

The matching of assets and liabilities has much to be said for it. The matching of maturities reduces risk. When long-term assets are financed by short-term debts, say a one-year loan, the debt must be 'rolled-over' at the end of the year. It is a rare investment indeed which has a cash flow (profits and depreciation) sufficient to retire the entire debt at the end of the first year of operation. If for any reason the bank does not agree to renew the loan, or agrees to finance it at much higher interest rates the firm may face a serious financial problem, even though the underlying investment is sound. Such problems are avoided when investments in fixed plant and equipment are financed by long-term debt or equity. In such a case, interest and capital payments can be paid out of the expected annual cash flow over the lifetime of the investment.

Unfortunately, the real world is not as simple as the example given in Figure 7.2 would seem to imply. The uncertainties of business lead the firm to hold precautionary reserves of cash, raw materials, and finished products. Although these assets are formally listed as 'current' in the balance sheet, they are in a sense the 'fixed' portion of the firm's current assets. Inventories and

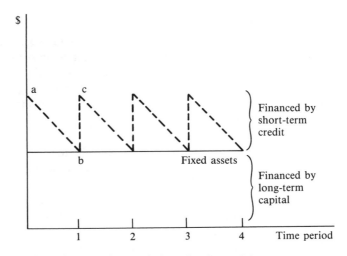

Figure 7.2 Financing working capital: a simple model.

in particular cash, for example, are rarely reduced to zero: some slack always remains to cover unforeseen contingencies. Hence, a more realistic strategy is to employ long-term sources to finance fixed assets plus the *fixed* portion of current assets. Only those current assets which fluctuate over the firm's operating cycle should be financed by short-term funds (see Figure 7.3).

This financing strategy can also be expressed in terms of the firm's balance sheet. Recall that we have defined working capital as 'the excess of current assets over current liabilities'. Put another way, working capital can be defined as the component of current assets which is financed out of long-term sources. This can be seen in Figure 7.4 in which net working capital is represented by the shaded section. This can be verified from Table 7.1 which sets out Bethlehem Steel's 1991 balance sheet. The company's working capital, i.e., excess of current assets over current liabilities, was $26.8 million ($957.8 − $931.0 = $26.8). From the same balance sheet we can also see that $26.8 million corresponds to that part of current assets which is financed by long-term debt and equity, which shows that the two definitions come to the same thing.

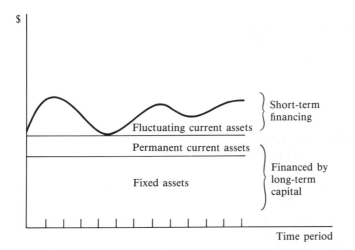

Figure 7.3 Financing working capital under uncertainty.

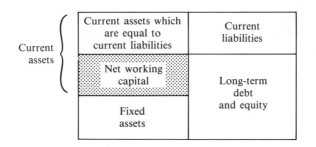

Figure 7.4 Net working capital.

Table 7.1 Bethlehem Steel Corporation
consolidated balance sheet, year
ended December 31, 1991 ($m)

Assets:	
Current assets	957.8
Fixed assets	3,170.5
Total assets	4,128.3
Liabilities and stockholders' equity:	
Current liabilities	931.0
Long-term liabilities	2,522.5
Total equity	674.8
Total liabilities and equity	4,128.3

The financing strategy which has been sketched out above suggests that the firm will try to make its net working capital approximate its best estimate of the 'fixed' component of the firm's current assets. The remaining current assets will be financed out of short-term sources.

THE MANAGEMENT OF WORKING CAPITAL

Effective working capital management implies two closely related types of action. First, basic policy must be set regarding the desired levels for each asset component. Second, an administrative framework must be established for managing and controlling these assets within the policy guidelines.

Because of its quantitative importance, the management of working capital has been the subject of many books and articles on short-term finance, operations research, and applied mathematics. A modern firm's financial management team cannot afford to overlook this important problem, which for many companies represents the largest single use of their financial resources.

Different firms approach the problem of working capital differently. Some firms still rely on the use of simple accounting rules of thumb to determine the efficiency with which short-term resources are allocated. However, the advent of the computer, and the increasing use of financial models, has allowed many firms to apply more formal methods to gauge the effectiveness of their working capital strategy. But whether rules of thumb or formal models, or, most commonly, some combination of the two, are used, the goal of working capital management remains the same. Effective working capital management tries to provide easily implemented rules for routine decisions, as well as a framework for the continuous monitoring and evaluation of policy guidelines.

NEED FOR LIQUID RESERVES

'Nothing is more permanent than the temporary,' and in the business world 'acting' vice-presidents have a tendency to become 'permanent' vice-presidents. Although most of this book is devoted to *long-term* financing and investing decisions, few of the latter are as 'permanent' as a firm's decision to hold reserves of cash and other liquid assets.

All firms (and virtually all individuals) hold liquid reserves. On the surface, the holding of cash (or even short-term interest-bearing securities) appears to involve a loss, because income is forgone on funds which otherwise could have been invested in productive activities. Recognizing this paradox, the English economist John Maynard Keynes, explained the holding of liquid assets in terms of three underlying motives: a transactions motive, a precautionary motive and a speculative motive.

The transactions motive

The need to hold cash arises because receipts and expenditures can never be perfectly synchronized. This is for the same reason that inventories of any commodity have to be kept, and that a water supply company builds a reservoir. When outflows are not exactly matched in time by inflows, a reservoir is needed to absorb routine fluctuations. The same holds true for the firm: for example, a reserve is needed to meet discrepancies in the daily inflow and outflow of cash, end-of-month bulges, etc. Similarly, liquid reserves may be accumulated in advance of specific outlays such as dividend payments or the purchase of fixed assets. Finally, the firm needs cash to facilitate payments: when the firm writes a check against its bank, the financial manager must ensure that the funds will be available when the check arrives for collection.

The precautionary motive

The precautionary motive reflects the need to hold liquid reserves to allow for unforeseen outflows, and/or unanticipated shortfalls due, for example, to a drop in sales. Although Benjamin Franklin taught us that man can count on only three reliable friends – a faithful dog, an elderly wife, and money in the bank – a significant interest return can be earned on liquid reserves by investing part of them in short-term securities. Nevertheless, no matter if one holds money in the bank or short-term securities, both fulfil the precautionary motive for holding liquid assets.

The speculative motive

The last, and by far the most volatile of the three considerations, is the speculative motive. This refers to the holding of liquid reserves in anticipation of future profitable investment opportunities. For example, a firm may accumulate a liquid reserve in anticipation of the opportunity of developing a new product or process in the near future.

The motives for holding liquid reserves are not mutually exclusive and, in fact, it would be difficult and impractical to divide a firm's monetary assets according to the particular purpose for which they are held. Total monetary resources should be regarded as one unit. There is no general rule regarding the division of reserves between cash and marketable securities which can be applied to all firms. The level of monetary assets itself depends on many factors including the firm's ability to obtain credit from banks and other financial institutions on short notice.

MANAGING LIQUID RESERVES

Liquidity means the ability to convert an asset to cash quickly and *without loss* or having to incur a substantial price concession. It is clear from this definition that cash is the perfect liquid asset, but of course its return is zero. Nowadays, banks pay a low interest rate on cash held, provided it is held above some minimum level. Short-term treasury bills have no default risk, and even a pronounced shift in market conditions will not affect their price very much since they have only a few months to maturity. This is not true for long-term bonds whose price fluctuations, and hence the probability of a loss should they have to be sold before maturity, is significantly high. Thus only cash and very high grade securities, with relatively short-term maturities, can be considered liquid assets, if the probability of loss is to be held within tolerable limits.

Since cash and short-term securities account for a significant proportion of many firms' assets, the efficient management of these funds could increase corporate earnings by millions. Recognizing this, many firms have expanded the size of the divisions which deal directly with cash management. In addition, cash management consultants have experienced a boom in their business. To illustrate the importance of the efficient management of liquid reserves, consider the case of IBM which held $5.1 billion in cash and short-term securities at the end of 1991. Suppose, that on *average*, the firm initially earns 5% on these funds (cash included). IBM's annual interest income would be $255 million. Now suppose that a financial expert (perhaps yourself) is hired and succeeds in increasing the total return by just two-tenths of one percent, i.e., from 5% to 5.2%, without adversely affecting liquidity. As a result, IBM's interest income rises to $265.2 million, which represents an increase of $10.2 million.

The increase in the return on total liquid reserves can be achieved either by the investment in securities with higher yields or by a reduction in the proportion of non-interest-bearing cash, or by some combination of the two. The goal of cash management is to reduce the amount of cash on hand, thereby increasing profitability, *without* reducing business activity or exposing the firm to undue risk. However, the firm must be very selective when investing its liquid reserves.

METHODS FOR CONSERVING CASH

As we have seen, the burden of holding liquid reserves can be reduced by seeking investment outlets which offer higher yields without increasing risk beyond tolerable levels. Another way to increase the return on liquid reserves is to minimize the proportion of the reserve which is kept in cash balances. Many firms can achieve significant savings merely by rearranging their commitments to get a better *synchronization* of cash inflows and outflows. In this way the firm can reduce its minimum required cash balance, and/or avoid costly borrowing. Two principal ways that cash can be conserved are:

1. Speeding up its collection of accounts receivable.
2. Slowing down its own payments to suppliers and creditors.

Speeding up collections

Although some customers can be cajoled into making early payments by letters and telephone calls, competition within the industry rarely permits a firm to make significant improvements in the payment habits of its customers. As we shall see below, it is often more effective to offer credit customers an economic incentive, in the form of a cash discount for early payment. However, the implicit interest cost of such discounts can be very high.

The firm still has ample room for improving its cash position, independent of the payment policy of its customers, by improving its collection of cash. This means finding ways to reduce the delay from the moment the paying firm writes its check to the time the funds become available for use in the recipient firm. At first glance, this seems trivial, but a firm receiving payments from a large number of customers spread across the country may find that as much as a week can be lost before the money becomes available.

The left-hand side of Table 7.2 sets out a hypothetical example of a customer in San Francisco making a payment to the selling firm's home office in Boston. In the case of this out-of-town customer, eight working days elapse before his payment becomes available in Boston. The delay reflects the slowness of the mail system and the 'many hands' involved in the clearing process. One improvement might be the establishment of regional offices. In such a case, the customer in California would be instructed to make its payment to

Table 7.2 The check collection process

Present system	Elapsed time	Lock box system	Elapsed time
1. California customer writes and mails check	3 days	1. Customer writes check and mails it	1 day
2. Check received at Boston home office	1 day	2. Check arrives at lock box in customer's city and is picked up by local bank	1 day
3. Check deposited in Boston bank	1 day	3. Check is cleared locally	1 day
4. Boston bank sends to Federal Reserve System for clearing	2 days	4. California bank wires Boston office that funds are available for use	
5. If 'good', funds are transferred to Boston bank	1 day		
6. Money is now available for use			
	8 working days		3 working days

the Boston firm's California regional office, thereby saving perhaps as much as two days. Alternatively, the Boston firm might establish collection accounts at a number of banks in key locations across the country. Customer payments could be received directly in these accounts, thereby saving additional time, since banks are much more efficient in the transfer of funds than is the postal system.

The lock box system

The right-hand side of Table 7.2 illustrates what has proved to be the most widely used device for speeding collections – the *lock box system*. Here the Boston firm rents post office boxes in a number of key cities, which in turn, are managed by local commercial banks acting in its behalf. The local banks monitor the lock boxes around the clock. As soon as the check arrives, it is deposited in the Boston firm's account at the local bank, so that the check-clearing process is started immediately. In essence, the lock box reverses the usual order of events. The check is deposited first, and only later is the accounting entry made at the selling firm's Boston office. In Table 7.2, the California paying firm is assumed to be located in San Francisco, a city in which the Boston firm operates a lock box. Since a Federal Reserve Bank is also located in San Francisco, the delay in the receipt of payment is reduced from eight to three working days. And, considering the great effort which is being made today to develop improved methods and electronic techniques for the transfer of funds, this delay may well be reduced even further in the future.

Slowing down payments

An alternative strategy for conserving cash is to slow down our own firm's payments to its suppliers and other creditors. This might be done in several ways. Just as decentralizing collections can speed up the collection process, making all payments from the corporation's central headquarters allows the firm to take advantage of mailing delays. Alternatively, the corporation might systematically use distant locations when making payments – the New York branch paying the California bills, etc. Another ploy is to use awkward, difficult to handle, but of course legal, means of payment. For example, bills can be paid using a bank draft drawn by the corporation on itself and payable through a specific bank. In this case, the receiving bank must first present the draft to the issuing firm, and only a day later will the necessary funds become available. The use of bank drafts can be rewarding when the corporation has a large payroll, or is paying dividends to a large number of shareholders. Finally, you might consider delaying payment altogether, but this will cost the firm its cash discount.

Playing the float

The name of the game that we have been describing is called 'playing the float'. Float is the difference between the balance shown in the corporation's accounts and its actual balance at the bank. Float can be positive or negative.

In our lock box example, the Boston firm was suffering from negative float, that is, for five days the balance of its bank account was lower than that appearing in the bank itself, because of the delay in collection. Of course, the other side of the coin is that the California company, due to the delay in the receipt of its payment, benefited from positive float: that is, its actual bank balance was larger than the balance on its own books during the period of the delay.

The financial manager is of course interested in the net collected balance at the bank. If he is quick and knowledgeable he can take advantage of the existence of the float by making allowance for the expected delay in clearing the check. But it takes two to 'play the float'. If you are the financial manager of the 'buying' firm, you can be certain that across the country, your counterpart at the selling firm, will be working overtime to reduce your ability to exploit any float to a minimum.

Costs versus benefits

A word of caution to the fledgling financial manager who is about to establish a comprehensive system of nine thousand lock boxes across the country – one in each of the cities or villages in which his firm has a customer. The operation of such a system would cost an awful lot of money. Like any other use of the firm's limited resources, the costs of providing more efficient cash management must be weighed against its benefits.

THE BAUMOL MODEL

The management of cash balances can also be facilitated by applying formal mathematical models. Perhaps the best known example is William Baumol's pioneering application of inventory techniques to the problem of determining the *optimal* size of a firm's cash balance.[1] The Baumol model assumes that the size and timing of cash outflows during the period in question are known with certainty (e.g., payroll, taxes, etc.). The underlying logic of his approach is best illustrated by a concrete example.

Suppose a construction firm is building a power plant for the government. Of the $100 million total cost, the firm receives $75 million in advance. During the construction period, which we assume to be four years, the firm will have to make cash payments for raw materials, wages, salaries etc. What is the *optimal* amount of cash that the construction firm should hold? The company has two basic options:

1. Hold the entire $75 million in cash, withdrawing from these funds as needed. Such a policy *minimizes* the risk of a cash shortage, but also yields a zero return or a low return paid on minimum cash balance.

---

1. See William J. Baumol, 'The Transactions Demand for Cash, An Inventory Theoretic Approach,' *Quarterly Journal of Economics*, November 1952.

2. Invest the $75 million in short-term securities at 1% interest, and withdraw *C* dollars every month from this investment portfolio to meet the cash outflows.

In our example, the time horizon for managing the cash flows is four years, during which time the outflows, for simplicity, are assumed to be known with *certainty*. We denote the total cash flow by *T*, and assume that the firm holds *C* dollars in cash at the beginning of the period to meet its wage bill and other expenses. We further assume that when its initial cash holdings are exhausted, the firm withdraws an additional *C* dollars from its investment portfolio to meet future needs. This process repeats itself until the project has been completed. Figure 7.5 illustrates the withdrawal process. The reader should note that the assumed method of replenishing the cash balance, like the withdrawal of stocks from an inventory, creates a sawtooth pattern with return jumps to the level *C* whenever the cash balance reaches zero.

To find the optimal amount to be withdrawn, denoted as C^*, one must minimize two types of cost. The first is a *fixed cost*, i.e., the fixed transactions cost (e.g., clerical costs, brokerage fees, etc.) associated with converting the securities to cash. In the first option, in which the firm holds the entire $75 million in cash, these costs are zero. The second type of cost is an *opportunity cost* which reflects the interest income forgone. This cost is at a maximum in the first option. For simplicity, we assume that the income from cash balances is zero.

If the firm's total cash outflow during the four years is *T* dollars, the *number* of withdrawals of cash from the firm's investment portfolio is given by T/C. The relevant transactions cost is the fixed cost per transaction denoted by *F*. The total of such costs which are incurred by the firm over the entire planning

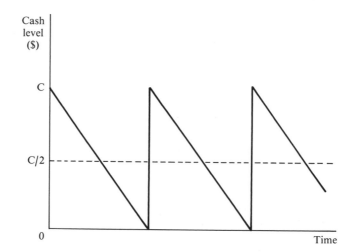

Figure 7.5 The cash withdrawal process.

period is defined as:

$$\text{Total transactions cost} = \frac{T}{C} \times F$$

where:

T = total dollar amount withdrawn during the period
C = dollar amount of each withdrawal, so that T/C is the *number* of transactions
F = fixed cost per transaction.

The total transactions cost also includes a variable component which depends on the size (dollar amount) of the transaction. But this variable cost plays no role in determining the desired size of cash balances and, therefore, is ignored.

The average cash balance held during the period is $C/2$ (see Figure 7.5), and therefore, the *opportunity cost* (foregone interest income) of holding this balance is equal to $(C/2)i$, where i denotes the relevant interest rate on short-term securities.

The total cost incurred by the firm from holding this average cash balance is the sum of the opportunity cost and the direct transactions costs of replenishing the cash balance:[2]

$$\text{Total cost} = \frac{C}{2} \times i + \frac{T}{C} \times F$$

The *optimal* size of the periodic cash withdrawal is given by:

$$C^* = \sqrt{\frac{2 \times \text{Total fixed transaction cost}}{\text{Interest rate}}} = \sqrt{\frac{2TF}{i}}$$

where C^* denotes the *optimal* size of the cash withdrawal, and therefore, $C^*/2$ is the *optimal average* cash balance.

The optimal cash balance varies directly with the fixed transaction cost F, and inversely with the interest rate i. Thus, if the fixed cost per transaction is very high, a firm will wish to decrease the number of transactions by which it replenishes its cash balance, thereby increasing the size of its average cash balance. Conversely, if the interest rate is high, the firm will tend to decrease the size of each transaction. This tends to decrease the proportion of reserves held as cash, i.e., the size of the average cash balance.

The application of the Baumol formula can be illustrated by considering a few numerical examples. For simplicity, assume that during the first three years of the above-mentioned project total outlays are \$25 million per year

2. Take the derivative of total cost with respect to C and equate to zero to obtain:

$$\frac{i}{2} - \frac{TF}{C^2} = 0$$

or

$$C^2 = \frac{2TF}{i} \quad \text{and} \quad C^* = \sqrt{\frac{2TF}{i}}$$

($T = \$25$ million); the current short-term interest rate is 5% per annum; and the fixed transaction cost is \$100. Applying the inventory model, the optimal size of cash withdrawals is \$316,228:

$$C^* = \sqrt{\frac{2 \times \$25 \text{ million} \times 100}{0.05}} \simeq \$316,228$$

As we have already noted, the firm will decrease the number of transactions (thereby increasing the size of periodic withdrawals) if the fixed transactions cost rises. For example, should the transaction cost rise to \$150, the optimal size of withdrawals increases to \$387,298:

$$C^* = \sqrt{\frac{2 \times \$25 \text{ million} \times 150}{0.05}} \simeq \$387,298$$

Conversely, the size of the optimal withdrawal *decreases* if the relevant interest rate rises. Thus in our last example, a rise in interest rates to 6% implies a reduction of the optimal withdrawal to \$353,553:

$$C^* = \sqrt{\frac{2 \times \$25 \text{ million} \times 150}{0.06}} \simeq \$353,553$$

CREDIT POLICY

A second component of a firm's working capital arises from the necessity to extend credit to its customers. A firm's credit policy consists of two inter-related activities: the *granting of credit*, and the *collection of receivables*. Both of these aspects affect the composition of working capital. A more liberal credit policy implies higher levels of credit sales, and as a result, higher levels of accounts receivable. More stringent collection policies, imply a reduction in outstanding receivables.

Credit management involves five basic decisions:

1. *Credit period.* This decision relates to the length of time for which the firm is prepared to grant credit to its customers.
2. *Credit instruments.* Having decided to grant credit, the firm must also decide on the legal form it will take. Should a formal IOU be required or is a simple receipt sufficient?
3. *Credit standards.* Next, credit standards have to be set. This involves the decision as to which customers constitute 'good' or 'bad' credit risks. It also requires the stipulation of a method for determining their credit-worthiness either on the basis of past performance, the analysis of their financial statements, or external reports of banks and/or credit agencies.
4. *Collection policy.* A policy for monitoring outstanding credits must be established, and a decision must be reached in cases of slow payment.
5. *Incentives.* The firm must decide on the extent of the financial (or other) incentives which will be offered for prompt payment.

It is clear from the above that credit policy has a two-fold purpose. At first glance, it might appear that avoiding credit losses is an end in itself. But this is only part, and not necessarily the most important part, of the credit manager's function. Credit policy also has a direct impact on sales. Easing the terms of credit by lengthening the credit period, offering generous cash discounts, or relaxing credit standards will stimulate sales; the opposite can be expected from a tightening of credit policy. The credit problem affects a firm's overall strategy, because the increase in sales is not without cost. Cash discounts and a lengthening of the credit period are equivalent to a reduction in price, and the easing of credit standards can, and often does, lead to bad debts. Hence the additional sales revenue has to be weighed against the additional costs generated by such policies.

_____ THE CREDIT-GRANTING DECISION

The extension of credit is essentially a method of enhancing sales by making it easier for customers to pay for a firm's products or services. It is especially important for those customers who find it impossible, or inconvenient, to borrow. The key decision, of course, is whether credit should be granted at all, but if the answer is affirmative, the firm must also decide how much credit should be extended. It is at this stage that management discretion is exercised. However, the terms of credit, that is, length of period, and size of cash discounts, etc., are often strongly influenced by industry practice. Significant deviations from accepted standards can lead to reprisals from competitors.

_____ EVALUATING CREDIT RISKS

In reaching a decision on whether or not to extend credit, management must assess the risks involved in the request for credit. Hence the measurement of customer credit quality lies at the heart of the decision.

A popular rule of thumb used by credit managers to evaluate the probability of default is to consider the so-called *three Cs* of credit:

1. *Character*. This factor attempts to measure the customer's *willingness* to pay. It raises the fundamental question of whether or not he will *try* to honor his promise to pay. Most managers consider this issue crucial. If the answer to this question is strongly negative, it is unlikely that credit will be granted.
2. *Capital*. This factor refers to the customer's *ability* to pay. Here an attempt is made to determine whether the customer has sufficient financial resources to meet the proposed obligation.
3. *Capacity*. This is a more subjective measure of the customer's *ability to pay*. Here, his previous 'track record' with the firm is crucial.

Two other Cs are sometimes added to the rule of thumb:

4. *Collateral*, which is simply the assets which the customer can offer to secure his debt.
5. *Condition* refers to the customer's vulnerability to changes in business conditions, or other specific events.

A credit assessment based on some combination of these five factors requires information drawn from the firm's previous experience, from the analysis of the customer's financial position, or from external sources. The major external sources are *credit reporting agencies*, such as Dun and Bradstreet, which collect and sell credit information, and in addition, provide credit ratings based on a customer's ability to pay, *credit associations*, such as the National Association of Credit Management, and local industry associations, also provide information on credit customers. Finally, some firms turn to commercial banks to obtain credit references on customers. Although there are no general rules, the subjective weights given to the various sources are usually left to the credit manager's discretion.

If loss of sales is to be avoided, credit investigations must be carried out quickly. And, as we have already emphasized, the avoidance of credit losses is only part of the credit-management function; the other, and perhaps no less important function of credit management, is the promotion of sales.

CREDIT TERMS

The terms of credit granted to customers affect sales volume and the timing of receipts. As a result, credit policy has a significant impact on the present value of a firm's revenues. It is reasonably clear why improved credit terms can induce an increase in sales. For all practical purposes, a lengthening of the payment period is, in terms of present value, fully equivalent to a price reduction. Unfortunately, the influence of credit terms on the pattern of customer payments is not as clear cut.

As we have already noted, the firm has less discretion over the terms of credit. Here the practice of competitors must be considered if unintended losses of sales are to be avoided. Despite this, some room for manoeuver still remains. In many firms, the credit terms offered to customers depend on the outcome of the credit evaluation. For example, very high risk customers may be required to pay cash upon delivery (C.O.D.). If they have a credit record which suggests a danger that their checks may be returned due to insufficient funds, they may even be required to pay cash *before* delivery (C.B.D.).

With respect to credit sales, industry practice is often dominant. The credit period is often dictated by the logic of the business in question; for example, payment terms may reflect the rate of turnover of the customer's inventory. Within these constraints, firms try to control their risk exposure by offering financial incentives for prompt payment. Consider, for example, a firm which requires full payment within 60 days (i.e., it offers two months' credit), but also grants a 2% discount if the account is paid within 30 days. In the jargon of the business world, these terms are written as 2/30 net 60. In essence, the customer is offered the opportunity to earn 2% should he forgo the second 30 days' credit. This is equivalent to an *annual* rate of interest of over 26%:

$$(1.02)^{12} - 1 \simeq 26.8\%$$

Cash discounts in actual practice are often very high. For example, if a cash discount of 5% is offered for early payment, that is, the credit terms are 5/30 net 60, the implicit annual rate of interest is 79.6%:

$$(1.05)^{12} - 1 \simeq 79.6\%$$

In this instance the customer can earn an annual rate of interest of almost 80% simply by forgoing one month's credit.

Numerous examples of cash discounts which imply interest rates of over 100% can be found. For example, the terms of sale 5/10 net 30 permit the customer to earn a 5% discount from the sales price if he pays on the tenth rather than the thirtieth day after the sale. Thus, the customer can earn 5% by forgoing 20 days' credit which, at first glance, seems not unreasonable. Yet this discount is equivalent to an annual rate of interest of almost 144%. Since there are 18.25 twenty-day periods in a year (365/20 = 18.25), the *annual* interest rate calculation becomes:

$$(1.05)^{18.25} - 1 \simeq 143.6\%$$

The existence of such large discounts for early payment raises a perplexing question. Why do firms *offer* such large discounts in the first place? It is difficult to imagine a firm with an interest cost of over 100% per year, yet as we have already pointed out, examples of cash discounts which imply such rates can be found. An easy, but highly dubious explanation can be found by assuming that such firms' credit managers have never had a course in basic finance, or cannot afford to buy a pocket calculator. But this does not appear to be the case. A more satisfying explanation can be found by assuming that the firms *knowingly* offer such discounts as an incentive for early payment in order to control their risk exposure to bad debts. In this view, the firm is prepared to forgo part of its real profit in order to avoid slow payments, because the latter have a nagging tendency to evolve into uncollectible debts.

But yet a third explanation can be found. In this scenario the 'actual' price of the firm's product is the *discounted* price which, owing to the very liberal payment terms, it expects all of its customers to take. The very high rate of forgone interest, implicit in the terms of sale, can then be considered as a sort of penalty on customers who pay later than the discount period. This approach has plausibility, especially in those industries which do *not* impose a penalty for customers who exceed the period for net payments. Thus, in the case of the terms 5/10 net/30, a customer who succeeds by hook or by crook in stretching the payment to 60 days, not only adversely affects his ability to get credit in the future but pays a significant penalty as well. The implicit annual interest rate on the forgone discount is still almost 43% even if an extra 50 days of credit are obtained:

$$(1.05)^{7.3} - 1 = 42.8\%$$

(Note that $365/50 = 7.3$ and we assume that the customer is not penalized for the extra 30 days.)

COLLECTION POLICY

As the popular saying reminds us, good intentions are not sufficient to avoid a sentence to purgatory. Similarly, customers' good intentions are often insufficient to ensure the prompt receipt of payments. The 'stretching' of payables is an old, if not greatly honored, game; and bad debts can probably never be completely avoided. It is the credit department's responsibility to monitor outstanding debts in order to isolate delinquent accounts, to devise a policy for expediting their collection, and finally to suggest procedures for minimizing such delinquencies in the future.

The '*aging*' of customers' accounts receivable is a convenient tool for keeping track of the record of payments. For example, a schedule of overdue accounts might take the form of Table 7.3. Customer A has a 'clean' account, the $50,000 owed is still not due. The second customer, B, is a slow payer; of the $90,000 in credit which he received, he is in arrears in his payments by as much as two months. Finally, we have customer N who owes $100,000, all of which is overdue, with $50,000 overdue by more than two months. The fact that this customer has no outstanding debt *within* the stated collection period suggests that his credit may have already been cut off.

Clearly, procedures have to be devised for handling delinquent accounts, whether it be a strongly worded letter, or telephone call, or both, to the second customer and perhaps turning customer N over to a professional collection agency. However, the continuing nature of the seller–customer relationship implies an additional aspect of the collection process. In many, and perhaps most firms, changes in future credit terms are the main device for controlling delinquent accounts and bad debts. Unlike financial institutions, firms rarely collect interest for late payments and usually have no collateral to secure the debt. As a result, the selling firm often turns to more stringent credit terms, or a reduction of the amount of credit on future purchases, as a penalty for

Table 7.3 Schedule of overdue accounts

	Amount not yet due	1 month overdue	2 months overdue	More than 2 months overdue
Customer A	$50,000			
Customer B	$20,000	$40,000	$30,000	
⋮				
Customer N	–	$25,000	$25,000	$50,000

delinquent payment of current accounts. Legal action is usually taken only in extreme cases.

Credit terms can be tightened in a number of ways. Of course, credit can be withdrawn completely. Short of that, the credit period for net payment can be reduced or the amount of credit which is made available to a late paying customer can be reduced; the remainder being sold on a C.O.D. basis.

Monitoring accounts is a continuous process, and Table 7.4 suggests a useful tool for doing this. The firm can compare its average collection period with industry averages, but more importantly with its own stated credit terms to see how its credit department is actually operating. Table 7.4 sets out the aging schedule of accounts receivable for a hypothetical company. This schedule gives a breakdown of accounts by the length of time they have been outstanding. The interpretation of the data requires some knowledge of the firm's credit terms. For example, if its terms of sale are net 10 days, it may be in deep trouble. If such is the case, 60% of its accounts are overdue. On the other hand, if the firm sells on a 2/10 net 60 basis, almost all of its accounts are on schedule – 40% are still within the discount period and fully 90% are within the 60 day credit period. But if this same schedule is for a firm which sells on a 2/10 net 30 basis, the aging of accounts raises some serious questions. In this case, 30% of the accounts are already overdue, and 10% of the accounts are more than a month overdue and perhaps represent potential bad debts.

Finally, a word of caution may be in order. Credit management should not rely solely on mechanical rules of thumb. An overzealous credit manager can lose good customers. One strategy is always to try and find the underlying reason for delinquent payments, especially when a previously good account appears to have gone sour. But no manager should forget the other side of the coin. Profits generated by credit sales are unearned unless the account is collected. Like so many of the firm's activities, credit management is a 'two-edged' sword. A more liberal credit policy implies higher levels of sales, but increases the resources tied up in receivables. More stringent collection policies may reduce receivables and bad debts, but they also tend to reduce sales.

Table 7.4 Aging schedule of accounts receivable

Age of accounts (days)	Percentage of total receivables outstanding
0–10	40
11–30	30
31–45	10
46–60	10
over 60	10
	100

NATURE OF THE INVENTORY PROBLEM

In principle, the investment in inventory is similar to the fixed investment in machinery, equipment, and buildings. In both cases, an initial outlay is incurred in expectation of earning a future return. However, the investment in inventory differs from fixed investment in at least two important respects:

1. As we have seen in Chapter 5, the investment in inventory is typically only one component of a complex project. For example, investing in a new product requires raw material and finished goods inventories. As a result, it is difficult to measure the direct return on inventory investment. With this in mind, 'models' have been developed to provide for the efficient management of inventory. In other words, the firm does not attempt to maximize the return on its investment in inventory, but rather to *minimize the costs* of holding the inventories.
2. Because inventory decisions are repetitive, the relevant management decisions often relate to *how often*, and by *how much*, inventories should be replenished.

INVENTORY COSTS

Some of the costs involved in the holding of inventories increase as the amount of inventory held rises, while others tend to fall as the inventory level is increased. Hence, changing the inventory level creates conflicting forces: some cost components increase, but others are reduced, which is the reason why inventory creates a management 'problem'.

Costs which vary directly with inventory levels

It is possible to distinguish six main types of carrying cost which rise when the investment in inventory increases, and fall when the level of inventory is decreased.

1. *Capital costs.* This cost stems from the fact that the firm has part of its financial resources tied up in inventory. This cost component depends on the firm's cost of capital, the size of the inventory investment, and the time period over which the inventory is held.
2. *Storage costs.* The capital cost of holding inventories should also reflect the use of buildings and other facilities needed to store the inventory. In cases where space is rented, the rent paid becomes an important component of the total inventory cost. This cost also varies directly with inventory size.
3. *Handling costs.* Inventory must be moved from time to time, or delivered to other departments. Hence inventory costs include the costs of labor and mechanical equipment, such as fork lift trucks. It is worth noting that part of this cost varies proportionally with the amount of inventory held.

Another part, for example, the cost of moving finished goods out of inventory to a firm's retail outlets, depends on the size of sales.

4. *Insurance.* Insurance premiums are typically charged on the average value of the inventory in question; hence the higher the level of inventory, the greater will be the insurance cost.
5. *Property tax.* Property taxes are usually levied as a percentage of the value of the inventory, and therefore, they also vary directly with inventory levels.
6. *Depreciation and obsolescence.* Part of an inventory may lose its value over time as a result of spoilage, damage or obsolescence.

Costs which vary inversely with inventory levels

1. *Ordering costs.* The clerical and administrative work, (typing letters, telephone calls, and so on) associated with the ordering of inventory are for all practical purposes *fixed per order*. The larger the order, and therefore, the larger the average inventory level, the smaller will be the number of orders placed. This results in *smaller* total annual order cost. Shipping costs, up to a given level, also decline with an increase in order size.
2. *Quantity discount loss.* A decrease in average inventory, which means a decrease in order size, may in some instances raise the average unit price due to the loss of quantity discounts. Thus, the larger the order, the larger the inventory held and the lower the cost.
3. *Stockout costs.* When a firm runs out of finished goods, it loses potential revenue and/or consumer goodwill. Stockouts of raw material inventory, on the other hand, often cause serious interruptions and losses in production. Obviously, the larger the inventory, the smaller will be the probability of running out of stock. Thus, stockout costs also *vary inversely* with the size of the inventory.

INVENTORY MODELS

Costs which vary in opposite directions when the level of inventory is changed lie at the heart of the inventory problem. The purpose of an inventory model is to help the firm find the *optimal* level of inventory: that is, the size of inventory which minimizes total inventory costs. For simplicity, consider a 'deterministic model' which assumes that the demand for the firm's products and the lead time (i.e., the time between placing an order and its arrival in stock) are known with certainty.

These assumptions can be relaxed by assuming a probabilistic model in which the demand and/or lead times are subject to a probability distribution. Although probabilistic models describe the realities of business more precisely than do their deterministic counterparts, such models are often complicated and difficult to handle. Moreover, experience shows that the greater part of the potential cost savings can usually be secured by using relatively simple deterministic models.

Figure 7.6 illustrates a typical inventory cost function. On the horizontal axis, inventory size (in units) is measured, while the vertical axis shows the annual costs (in dollars) which are incurred. Curve A includes all those cost components which are fixed per order, and therefore vary *inversely* with inventory size; for example, order costs. Since holding a larger inventory implies a smaller number of orders during the year, such costs fall as the level of inventory rises. Costs, which vary directly with inventory size (e.g., capital costs and insurance), are represented by the rising line B of Figure 7.6. Total costs are denoted by the U-shaped curve, labeled T, which is derived by summing curves A and B. Since the firm's goal is to minimize the total costs associated with the holding of inventory, point Q* represents the *optimal* inventory size. Note that at the optimum, the additional 'type B' variable costs which would be incurred, if the level of inventory is increased by one unit, is just equal to the decline in 'type A' costs.

The problem can be clarified further by writing out the cost function which underlies Figure 7.6. In the case of certainty, there are no stockout costs, hence the total annual inventory cost becomes:

$$\text{Total cost} = \text{Variable cost} + \text{Fixed cost}$$

or in symbols:

$$T_C = C_1\bar{Q} + C_2N$$

where:

T_C = total inventory costs
C_1 = those costs (per unit) which vary directly with the inventory level
$\bar{Q}$ = average inventory held, and $C_1\bar{Q}$ equals the total variable cost (line B of Figure 7.6).

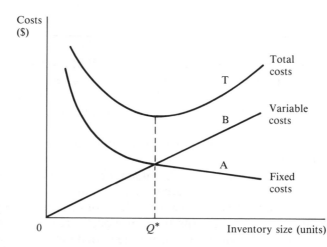

Figure 7.6 A typical inventory cost function.

C_2 = the fixed cost per order

N = number of orders placed during the year, and C_2N is the total annual fixed costs (curve A of Figure 7.6).

Assume that the firm decides to place an order with a supplier for Q units. If the demand for the firm's products is spread evenly over the year, the average inventory held during the year will be $Q/2$. The process is illustrated in Figure 7.7. The opening inventory is given by Q: that is, by the initial lot-size ordered. Since sales are assumed to take place evenly through the year, the inventory decreases gradually, until at point t_1 it is exhausted. But exactly at this point of time, a new shipment of Q units arrives, and the inventory again rises to Q. The process continues, and at points t_2, t_3, additional orders arrive.

In this type of model, stockouts do not occur. Since the quantity sold by the firm is known with certainty, the precise level of inventory at each point of time is also known. By coordinating the order placements with the information on demand, stockouts can be completely avoided. For example, suppose that the order lead time is $t/2$ (see Figure 7.7), and that it is also known with certainty. As a result, the firm will place its order of Q units at time $t/2$ so that the shipment will arrive exactly at point t_1. Only in the extreme case of zero lead time, would the firm place its order exactly at point t_1.

From the above description, you can see that the average inventory held in each period of time, and therefore, during the year as a whole, is $Q/2$ units. Inventory declines from Q units at the beginning of each period to zero at the end of the period, which results in an average inventory of $Q/2$.

Given the assumption of certainty, the optimal order size (or optimal lot

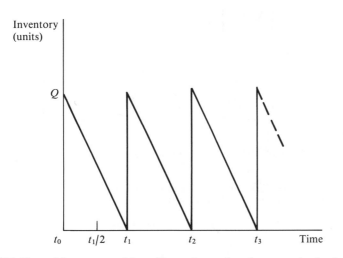

Figure 7.7 Size of inventory with uniform demand and zero order lead time.

size as it is also called) can be calculated from the following formula:[3]

$$Q^* = \sqrt{\frac{2SC_2}{C_1}}$$

where Q^* = optimal order size, S = total quantity (in units) sold during the year, and C_2 and C_1 retain their previous definitions.

UNCERTAINTY AND SAFETY STOCKS

In actual practice, demand and order lead times are rarely known with certainty. The purpose of this section is to discuss the types of problem raised by the existence of uncertainty. Figure 7.8 illustrates an inventory problem in which sales are known with certainty, but order lead times are not. Assume that the firm orders Q units. In periods t_1 and t_2 there is no lag in the lead time, hence no shortage occurs. However, the third order arrives late, and over the period marked a the firm is out of stock. Conversely, Figure 7.9 illustrates a case in which the shipment comes early so that the firm's actual inventory exceeds the optimum quantity required. In period t_2, the shipment arrives a days early, and as a result the average inventory held during period t_2 increases. When sales are uncertain, shortages can occur even if the order lead

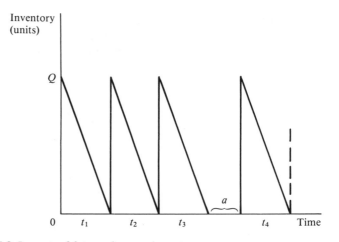

Figure 7.8 Impact of late orders on inventory.

3. Note that $T_C = C_1\bar{Q} + C_2N$, but $S = NQ$ and $\bar{Q} = Q/2$, therefore $T_C = C_1Q/2 + C_2S/Q$. Take the derivative with respect to Q and equate to zero to obtain:

$$\frac{C_1}{2} - \frac{C_2S}{Q^2} = 0 \quad \text{or} \quad Q^2 = 2C_2S/C_1$$

Hence:

$$Q^* = \sqrt{\frac{2C_2S}{C_1}}$$

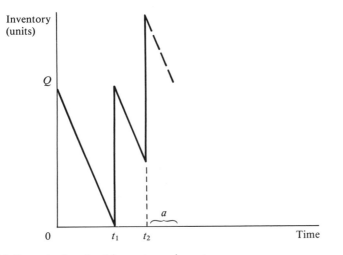

Figure 7.9 Impact of early shipments on inventory.

time is known with absolute certainty. For example, this could result if there is a sudden unforeseen increase in the demand for a product.

Obviously, in a real life situation, both the lead time and the demand (sales) are uncertain, so that stockouts can occur from any combination of these two factors. In order to reduce the risk of a stockout, the firm often holds an extra quantity of inventory as a *safety stock*. The problem which confronts such a firm is how to balance the stockout costs against the cost of carrying the extra inventory.

SUMMARY

This chapter has been devoted to the principles underlying the management of the primary components of a firm's working capital: liquid reserves, inventories, and accounts receivable.

The effective management of working capital requires:

1. Setting of the desired levels for each component.
2. Establishing an administrative framework for monitoring these assets to ensure that they remain within policy guidelines.

A firm's liquid reserve comprises cash and interest-bearing securities. To be considered liquid, an asset must be easily converted into cash *without* loss. Hence only very high grade securities, with relatively short maturities, can be considered appropriate for this purpose.

The goals of liquidity management are two-fold:

1. To reduce the amount of cash on hand without adversely affecting the firm's operations.

2. To increase the return on the invested reserves without impairing the firms liquidity.

Achieving these goals can be facilitated by:

1. Speeding up collections.
2. Use of the lock box system.
3. Slowing down of payments.
4. Playing the float.

In addition mathematical methods, e.g., Baumol's inventory model, can be used to improve the utilization of a firm's liquid reserves.

The chapter goes on to discuss credit policy and the management of accounts receivable. Credit policy involves decisions in five areas:

1. Length of credit period.
2. Formal legal documents (if any) to be required.
3. Setting credit standards.
4. Collection policy.
5. The use of financial (or other) incentives to encourage prompt payment of debts.

Several sources of credit information are available:

1. Previous experience with the customer.
2. Analysis of the customer's financial statements.
3. Reports of commercial credit rating agencies.
4. Credit references of banks and trade associations.

Although the firm has some leeway in setting the terms of credit, industry practice is often a dominant consideration if unintended losses of sales are to be avoided. Credit policy is a two-edged sword. Easy credit terms may lead to higher sales, but also tie up the firm's resources in accounts receivable. More stringent collection policies, and less liberal terms of credit may reduce receivables and bad debts, but also tend to reduce sales. As is true of many corporate decisions, the optimal strategy usually lies somewhere in the middle.

We conclude the chapter with a discussion of the inventory problem. Because of the magnitude of the investment involved, corporations often expend considerable time and resources on the control and management of inventory costs. These costs can be divided into two groups:

1. Costs which vary directly with the level of inventory. These include:

   Capital costs
   Storage costs
   Handling costs
   Insurance
   Property taxes
   Depreciation and obsolescence

   These costs rise when inventories increase, and fall when they decrease.
2. Costs which vary inversely with the size of inventory, i.e., increase when the

inventory level is lower and decrease when inventories are higher. Such costs include:

Ordering costs
Loss of quantity discounts
Stockout costs.

Simple inventory models which can help the firm determine optimal inventory size are presented. Such models are designed to minimize total inventory costs. One such model, the optimal order size formula, is set out, assuming certainty:

$$Q^* = \sqrt{\frac{2SC_2}{C_1}}$$

where:

Q^* = optimal order size
S = total quantity (in units) sold during the year
C_1 = costs (per unit) which vary directly with inventory levels.
C_2 = fixed cost per order.

Since the pattern of demand and order lead times are rarely known with certainty, the inventory models can be adjusted to reflect the underlying uncertainty. The use of 'safety' stocks and lagged order points, for this purpose, are illustrated.

_____ **SUMMARY TABLE**

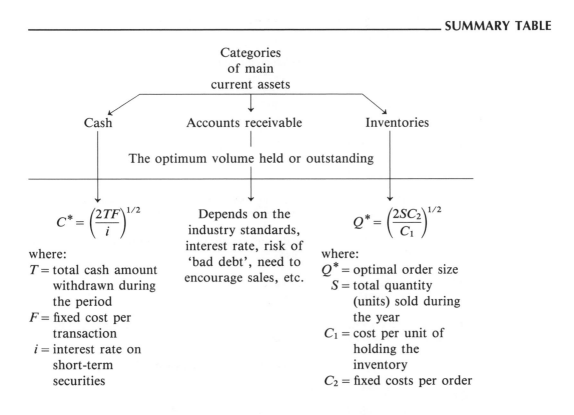

Categories
of main
current assets

Cash   Accounts receivable   Inventories

The optimum volume held or outstanding

$$C^* = \left(\frac{2TF}{i}\right)^{1/2}$$

where:
T = total cash amount
    withdrawn during
    the period
F = fixed cost per
    transaction
i = interest rate on
    short-term
    securities

Depends on the
industry standards,
interest rate, risk of
'bad debt', need to
encourage sales, etc.

$$Q^* = \left(\frac{2SC_2}{C_1}\right)^{1/2}$$

where:
Q^* = optimal order size
S = total quantity
    (units) sold during
    the year
C_1 = cost per unit of
    holding the
    inventory
C_2 = fixed costs per order

QUESTIONS AND PROBLEMS _____

7.1 Define the following terms:

(a) liquidity
(b) float
(c) the Baumol Model
(d) (net) working capital
(e) safety stock
(f) COD
(g) CBD

7.2 What motives can you think of for holding liquid assets?

7.3 Explain the lock box system.

7.4 'We use similar methods to decide on the size of our inventory of spare parts, and on our liquidity reserves.' Is that possible? Justify your answer.

7.5 What is meant by the statement, 'It takes two to play the float'?

7.6 What are the principal characteristics of the assets comprising a firm's working capital?

7.7 What are the pros and the cons of a liberal credit policy? What are the pros and the cons of a stringent credit policy?

7.8 Which are the five basic decisions which need to be taken when a firm decides on its credit policy?

7.9 List and explain the five Cs which credit managers use to evaluate the probability of default.

7.10 Give an example of a cash discount for early payment which implies an interest rate of approximately 100%.

7.11 'Our firm has an interest cost of 15%. Nevertheless, we offer a discount which imply interest rates of a multiple of this amount.' Why do you think the firm has adopted such a policy?

7.12 'We don't fool around: if a customer is in arrears with his payment we immediately go to court.' Why is this not necessarily a good policy?

7.13 List the costs which vary directly with inventory levels. List the costs which vary indirectly with inventory levels.

7.14 'We never had and never will have stockouts?' On what assumptions is such a statement based?

7.15 Which firm do you think holds a larger safety stock (as a percentage of sales): a steel mill or a supermarket? Justify your answer.

7.16 Why is it not advisable to finance fixed investments with short-term capital?

7.17 One definition of net working capital says it is 'the excess of current assets over current liabilities.' Another defines it as 'the component of current assets which is financed out of long-term sources'. Are these two definitions the same? Explain.

7.18 'Our supplier offers a 2% discount if we pay after ten days instead of after thirty days. Since our cost of capital is 8% per year, we never take the discount.' Critically evaluate this statement.

7.19 The Guthry Corporation sells goods to a customer. The terms Guthry offers are 60 days net, or a 1% discount if the bill is settled upon delivery. Guthry knows that the customer's cost of capital is 10%. When can Guthry expect payment?

7.20 The Farwell Corporation needs $2.6 million per year for cash outlays. The short-term interest rate is 6% and the fixed transaction cost for cash withdrawals is $115.50. What is the optimal size of the cash withdrawal? How often will cash be withdrawn?

7.21 The Gerten Company needs $1 million cash a month. The cost of the employee's time which is needed to prepare the transaction is estimated at $20. Furthermore, the bank charges $14.80 for each transaction. The interest rate which Gerten receives on short-term funds is 6.4%. What is the optimal size of each cash withdrawal?

7.22 Consider again Gerten's problem in the previous question. Instead of having an employee prepare the transaction every time, a telephone call to the bank suffices. The cost comes to 70 cents. How does your answer change?

7.23 Marson & Co. is buying a new typewriter. The terms of payment are 2/15 net 30. What is the implicit interest rate which Marson would be charged if they only paid on day 30? (Assume no penalty.)

7.24 Marson & Co. is buying a new typewriter. The terms of payment which they are offered are 60 days net, or a 2% discount if they pay immediately. If Marson chooses to forgo the discount, how high do you think is their cost of capital?

7.25 GTR & Co. has ordered its yearly amount of spare parts. Full payment is required within 30 days, but a 2% discount is offered if the account is settled within 10 days. GTR's cost of capital is 8%. What should it do?

7.26 A mail order firm offers the following payment options: a discount of 1.5% if the invoice is paid upon delivery, or a 1% discount if the account is settled within 15 days. The third option is to pay the net invoice within 40 days.

(a) If your cost of capital is 10% which option will you prefer?
(b) How does your answer change if your cost of capital is 15%?
(c) How does your answer change if your cost of capital is 16%?

7.27 A firm is offered the following terms: 60 days net, or a $\frac{1}{2}$% discount for C.O.D. The firm chooses not to take the discount. Assuming the firm acts rationally, what can you say about its cost of capital?

7.28 Computer City sells 50 home computers per month, at a price of $2,485 each. Capital costs are 8%, insurance is 3%, and warehousing amounts to 6% of the sales price. Whenever an order is placed, a truck has to be sent to the supplier, which costs $220. (The truck can carry at most 150 computers.) Calculate the optimal order size and the time intervals when orders will be placed?

7.29 A drugstore sells 2,500 boxes of a certain expensive pill per year. The price per box is $100. Variable inventory costs, spoilage, and interest amount to 20% of the price of the box. The fixed cost for every order is $10. How many boxes should be ordered at a time?

7.30 Pharmacos & Co. uses 10,000 bags of a chemical compound per year at a cost of $20 each. The fixed cost per order is $208.20. Variable inventory costs are 30% of the price of the box. What is the optimal order size? At what time intervals will the orders be placed?

7.31 Your baby daughter needs four disposable diapers per day. A bag which contains 28 diapers sells for $6. Your cost of capital is 10% and since you have enough space in your garage there are no inventory storage costs. You estimate the cost of driving to the drugstore and back at $3.90. (The cost of your time is zero.) How often will you make the trip per year?

7.32 Your local supermarket delivers all purchases to your house for a flat fee of $1.50. You use goods for $100 per week. 4% of your average inventory is usually lost due to a mouse in your house. Your cost of capital is 8%. How many dollars' worth of goods should you order at a time? How many orders will you place per year.

SELECTED REFERENCES

Batlin, C. A. and Hinko, Susan, 'Lockbox Management and Value Maximization', *Financial Management*, Winter 1981.

Baumol, William J., 'The Transactions Demand for Cash, An Inventory Theoretic Approach', *Quarterly Journal of Economics*, November 1952.

Ben Horim, Moshe and Levy, Haim, 'Management of Accounts Receivable Under Inflation', *Financial Management*, Spring 1983.

Gilmer, R. H. Jr, 'The Optimal Level of Liquid Assets: An Empirical Test,' *Financial Management*, Winter 1985.

Gitman, Lawrence J., Forrester, Keith D. and Forrester, John R., 'Maximizing Cash Disbursement Float', *Financial Management*, Summer 1976.

Hawawini, Gabriel, Viallet, Claude and Vora, Ashok, 'Industry Influence on Corporate Working Capital Decisions,' *Sloan Management Review*, Summer 1986.

Miller, Merton H., and Orr, Daniel, 'The Demand for Money by Firms: Extension of Analytic Results', *Journal of Finance*, December 1968.

Morris, James R., 'The Role of Cash Balances in Firm Valuation,' *Journal of Financial and Quantitative Analysis*, December 1983.

Myers, Stewart C. (ed.), *Modern Developments in Financial Management*, New York: Praeger, 1976.

Nauss, Robert M. and Markland, Robert E., 'Theory and Application of an Optimizing Procedure for Lock Box Location', *Management Science*, August 1981.

Petty, J. William and Scott, David F., 'The Analysis of Corporate Liquidity,' *Journal of Economics and Business*. Spring–Summer 1980.

Van Horne, James C., 'A Risk–Return Analysis of a Firm's Working Capital Position,' *Engineering Economist*, Winter 1969.

PART I SUGGESTIONS FOR FURTHER READING ————————————————

The evolution of the role of financial management and the development of the modern theory of corporate finance are surveyed by Michael C. Jensen and Clifford W. Smith Jr in 'The Theory of Corporate Finance: An Historical Overview,' in *The Modern Theory of Corporate Finance* (McGraw-Hill, New York, 1983).

For a classic statement of the goals of the firm, see Nobel Laureate Herbert A. Simon's 'On the Concept of Organizational Goal,' *Administrative Science Quarterly*, June 1964.

Agency problems were introduced into the finance literature by Michael C. Jensen and William H. Meckling in 'Theory of the Firm: Managerial Behavior, Agency Costs, and Ownership Structure,' *Journal of Financial Economics*, October 1976.

For a detailed discussion of the implications of agency theory for financial management, see Amir Barnea, Robert A. Haugen and Lemma W. Senbet, *Agency* Problems and Financial Contracting (Englewood Cliffs, N.J.: Prentice Hall, 1985) and the *Midland Corporate Finance Journal*, Winter 1985.

The reader with a historical bent can turn to the pioneering articles on capital budgeting by Boulding and Samuelson:

> K. Boulding, 'The Theory of a Single Investment,' *Quarterly Journal of Economics*, May 1935.
> P. A. Samuelson, 'Some Aspects of the Pure Theory of Capital,' *Quarterly Journal of Economics*, May 1937.

The capital budgeting problem was rediscovered at the beginning of the 1950s by:

> J. Dean, *Capital Budgeting*, New York Columbia University Press, 1951.
> F. Lutz and V. Lutz, *The Theory of Investment of the Firm*, Princeton University Press, 1951.

The theoretical foundation for capital budgeting under certainty can be found in:

> J. H. Hirshleifer, 'On the Theory of Optimal Investment Decision,' *Journal of Political Economy*, August 1958.
> M. J. Bailey, 'Formal Criteria for Investment Decisions,' *Journal of Political Economy*, October 1959.
> E. Solomon, *The Management of Corporate Capital*, New York: The Free Press, 1959.

Some tax aspects of capital budgeting are examined in detail by:

> N. Dopuch and S. Sunder, 'FASB's Statements on Objectives and Elements of Financial Accounting: A Review,' *Accounting Review*, January 1980.
> V. C. Lembke and H. R. Toole, 'Differences in Depreciation Methods and the Analysis of Supplemental Current-cost and Replacement Cost Data,' *Journal of Accounting Auditing and Finance*, Winter 1981.

For comprehensive treatment of the U.S. 1986 Tax Reform Act, see:

> *A Complete Guide to the Tax Reform Act of 1986*, Englewood Cliffs, N.J.: Prentice Hall, 1986.
> *Introduction to Federal Taxation*, Englewood Cliffs, N.J.: Prentice Hall, annual editions.

Part II

Risk and Uncertainty

Introduction

Why Settle For The Lowest Rates in 20 Years?
6.69% current yield – 100% no load

T. Rowe price adjustable rate U.S. Government Fund offers higher yields with low volatility

With CD, bank, and money market rates at 20-year lows, you may be looking for ways to get higher yields without a lot of risk.

This Fund is designed for investors who want more income, without the volatility of higher-yielding long-term bond funds.

The advertisement in article 14 by T. Rowe Price Investment Services, Inc., extends to investors an investment vehicle which offers a high yield with low volatility. They suggest that the investor can obtain a 'higher yield without a lot of risk.' The fact that everyone likes high yields (or high returns) is obvious. But why does T. Rowe Price assume that investors do not like volatility? Does volatility imply risk? In this chapter we show that the larger the volatility the worse off the investor since his expected utility (welfare) diminishes.

Indeed, risk or uncertainty lie at the very heart of capital investment decisions. The formal treatment of risk, is often quite complicated; hence we preferred initially to expose the reader to the basic methods of project evaluation, to the importance of the timing of the cash flows and to the analysis of the factors which determine the components of the cash flows. Forearmed with this knowledge, the reader will be better prepared to grapple with the problems created by the existence of uncertainty.

In the following five chapters we examine several alternative ways of explicitly incorporating risk into the analysis of the firm's investment decisions. Our main purpose is to prove beyond any shadow of a doubt the importance of not ignoring uncertainty, rather than suggesting that all firms adopt some of the more sophisticated tools which we shall be using. Technical and administrative difficulties often preclude the use of such methods in actual decision-making, but even if for many firms formal risk analysis is not yet feasible, they must still devise rough but practical rules of thumb for taking uncertainty into account. Hopefully, the methods of risk evaluation presented in this section will at least provide a benchmark for determining actual decision strategies in practice.

Chapter 8 briefly sets out the utility foundations of modern risk analysis; the popular mean variance decision rule is derived in Chapter 9. Chapter 10 discusses some practical applications of risk analysis. Chapter 11 presents the basic elements of modern portfolio analysis, while the capital asset pricing model (*CAPM*) which is derived from the mean variance portfolio analysis, and the arbitrage pricing theory (*APT*) model are described in Chapter 12.

8

Foundations of Risk Analysis

As noted in Part I, the firm's capital investment decisions depend on its estimates of the cash flows of alternative investment opportunities. Forecasting the future is at best a risky business. In this chapter we lay the conceptual foundation for reaching capital budgeting decisions under conditions of risk or uncertainty.

THE ESSENCE OF RISK

A firm's expectations of the possible future gains from an investment must be based in part on past performance, and in part on forecasts of future performance. As a result, management rarely has precise expectations regarding the future profit to be derived from a particular investment. In fact, the best that a firm can reasonably be expected to do is to make some estimate of the range of possible future costs and benefits and the relative chances of earning a high or low profit on the investment.

Formally, we shall distinguish between two states of expectation: certainty and risk (or uncertainty).

Certainty

Strictly speaking, perfect certainty refers to expectations which are single-valued; that is, prospective profits are represented in terms of a single outcome, and not in terms of a range of alternative possible outcomes. We shall use the term *certainty* to describe those situations in which investors' expectations regarding future profits are bounded within a very narrow range. But do such investments actually exist outside of the realm of textbooks? At first glance it may appear that no investment yields a perfectly certain income stream, but on reflection several illustrations can be found. For example, suppose that the firm decides to invest in three-month treasury bills. By investing in these short-term treasury bills, the firm can calculate the exact return which will be received at the end of three months. If we simply ignore the insignificant probability of a revolution or a war which might destroy the existing monetary system, this investment amounts to certainty. We also ignore the important question of inflation and its impact on the real return from investment.[1] Similarly, if we are willing to ignore the remote possibility of bankruptcy or financial default in such giant corporations as General Motors and AT&T, then the short-term liabilities of these companies can also be considered safe investments. Although the opportunity to invest in treasury bills exists for *all* investors (both individuals and corporations alike) this opportunity is irrelevant for most firms since individual investors or shareholders can readily acquire riskless assets directly. As a result, there is no incentive for individuals to purchase shares of a company which simply invests a significant proportion of its equity in riskless assets. Investment companies and mutual funds may invest relatively large proportions of their assets in such riskless assets, but most firms invest in productive assets rather than in financial assets, i.e. most firms are typically confronted by risky investment alternatives.

Risk

The term *risk* (or equivalently *uncertainty*) is used interchangeably to describe an investment whose profit is not known in advance with absolute certainty, but for which an array of alternative outcomes and their probabilities are known.[2] In other words, a risky investment is one for which the *distribution* of profits is known. The distribution may be estimated on the basis of either objective or purely subjective probabilities.

An example of such a frequency distribution is given in Table 8.1 which sets out the historical record of the profit from a hypothetical investment over the past forty years. The data of Table 8.1 were then used to prepare the histogram drawn in Figure 8.1. Historical data of this sort are often available for financial investments, and can be used to facilitate current investment decisions. But even where a long record of past profitability is available, the decision to invest remains complex. There often may be no reason why the future distribution of profits should resemble the past distribution. Before arriving at a decision, all of the factors that might indicate future changes in the distribution must be carefully weighed. Moreover, even if the distribution can be expected to remain unchanged, realizing a high profit (the right-hand side of the histogram) or a loss (the left-hand side of the histogram) in any particular year is largely a matter of chance.

1. The impact of inflation on the decision-making process is discussed in Chapter 5.
2. Frank Knight distinguishes between 'risk' as defined here and 'uncertainty' which he defined as an option for which only the array of possible outcomes, but *not* their probabilities is known. See his *Risk, Uncertainty and Profit*, Houghton Mifflin Company, New York, 1921, chapter 6. The reader should note that the introduction of subjective probability has greatly diminished the significance of the distinction between risk and uncertainty. By assigning *subjective* probabilities to decision problems, an inherent *uncertain* situation can be transformed into a *risky* choice.

Table 8.1 An example of a frequency
distribution of profits

Profit[a]	Frequency (number of years)
− 30.00 to − 20.01	2
− 20.00 to − 10.01	3
− 10.00 to − 0.01	5
0.00 to 9.99	10
10.00 to 19.99	9
20.00 to 29.99	6
30.00 to 39.99	3
40.00 to 49.99	2
Total	40

[a] To facilitate comparison, the returns are
expressed as percentages.

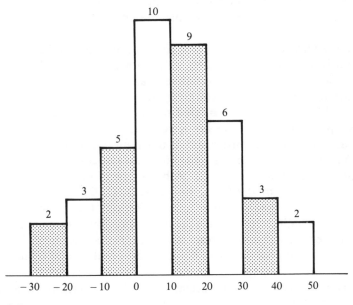

Figure 8.1

Firms with a lot of experience or those dealing with repetitive investments
which are renewed every few years are confronted with situations similar to the
one portrayed in Figure 8.1. However, more often the firm has little or no past
experience to draw upon, particularly when investments in new products or
processes are being considered, and therefore relevant historical data cannot
be found which can serve as a guide for current decisions. In such cases the
firm must base its decision solely on subjective probabilities, i.e. on personal
judgment regarding the chances of gain or loss.

ALTERNATIVE INVESTMENT CRITERIA _____

Having defined risk, let us now turn to the crucial question of devising a relevant decision rule for evaluating investments with risky, i.e. uncertain, returns.

The maximum return criterion (MRC)

Let us initially assume a uniform investment period, for example one year, and let us further assume that the decision-maker can choose only a single investment alternative.[3] What decision rule should the investor apply in order to choose the best possible alternative? To define the problem more precisely consider a firm that is confronted with the five options given in Table 8.2. Two of the proposals (A and B) represent perfectly certain investments, while the other three options (C, D, and E) entail varying degrees of risk. Such a situation is quite realistic: the entrepreneur can typically buy riskless short-term government bonds or deposit his money in a savings bank; alternatively, he can acquire productive facilities, the income and profit from which must be considered as highly uncertain.

Only in the unrealistic case in which the firm restricts itself to 'safe' investments, that is to proposals A and B, is the choice simple. In this instance the company should choose the alternative that offers the highest return (see Chapter 3). In our example, investment B, which affords a return of 10 as compared with the return of 8 offered by alternative A, would be chosen.

Such simple choice situations are hardly representative of the alternatives faced by modern corporations; reality is much more complicated and for that matter much more interesting as well. Firms do not confine themselves solely to safe proposals. A more realistic problem, therefore, is how to select the 'best' investment out of the five options, A, B, C, D, E.

Can we still apply the maximum return criterion? Clearly we cannot do so without major qualifications. Whereas in the previous example, profits were known with certainty (8 and 10 respectively), this does not hold for the other three proposals. Suppose we try to compare proposals B and C: the return of

Table 8.2 Distribution of possible outcomes (return/probability) of five alternative investments

A		B		C		D		E	
Return	Prob.	Return	Prob.	Return	Prob.	Return	Prob.	Return	Prob.
8	1.0	10	1.0	−8	0.25	−4	0.25	−20	0.1
				16	0.5	8	0.5	0	0.6
				24	0.25	12	0.25	50	0.3

3. Discussion of combinations of investments, i.e. the very important portfolio problem is deferred to Chapter 11, while analysis of the no less important multiperiod capital budgeting problem is postponed to Chapter 12.

B is 10 but what can we attribute to C? If we assume a negative return of -8, then project B is clearly preferable; however, if we assume the return of C will be 16 or 24, then it is equally clear that investment C represents the better alternative. Since there is no *a priori* reason to single out any one of three possible outcomes of project C, the maximum return criterion breaks down. Thus once uncertainty is introduced, finding an appropriate investment criterion is unavoidable; the maximum return criterion which is appropriate in a world of perfect certainty is no longer applicable in a realistic setting in which risk prevails.

The maximum expected return criterion (MERC)

To compare the desirability of alternative investments under conditions of risk, we must first devise a measure which can reflect the entire distribution of returns. One possible solution to this problem stipulates that decisions should be reached on the basis of an investment's *expected* profit, where expected profit is defined as the mean of the *return* distribution weighted by the probabilities of occurrence. For example, if we consider project C of Table 8.2 the *expected* return can be calculated as follows:

$$(0.25 \times (-8)) + (0.5 \times 16) + (0.25 \times 24) = 12$$

Similarly, we can readily calculate the expected return for the other alternatives:

Projects	Expected return	
A	8	(1×8)
B	10	(1×10)
C	12	$((0.25 \times (-8)) + (0.5 \times 16) + (0.25 \times 24))$
D	6	$((0.25 \times (-4)) + (0.5 \times 8) + (0.25 \times 12))$
E	13	$((0.1 \times (-20)) + (0.6 \times 0) + (0.3 \times 50))$

Having calculated the expectations for each of the five alternative projects, we can now choose that project with the highest *expected return*; in our example this is project E with an expected return of 13.

The *expected* return criterion can be applied to uncertain investments since each investment can be characterized by a single measure of profitability, and therefore all investment proposals can be ranked according to this criterion. However, the fact that the maximum expected *return* criterion *can* be applied by no means indicates that it *should* be used. On the contrary, in most cases this criterion is inappropriate because it does not take risk explicitly into account. The following example illustrates the drawbacks of using this criterion for evaluating risky investments.

Suppose that the firm has to choose between proposals I and II in Table 8.3. Both projects require an initial outlay of $1,000; however, the demand for the products produced under I (say luxury products) is very vulnerable to general

Table 8.3 Calculation of expected *NPV*

Net receipts	Project I ($)	Project II ($)
Economic recession with probability of 0.2	100	1,100
Economic prosperity (with probability of 0.8)	2,000	1,750
Expected *PV* of net receipts[a]	1,620	1,620
Less initial outlay	−1,000	−1,000
Expected net profit	620	620

[a] The expected net income of project I is $(0.2 \times 100) + (0.8 \times 2,000) = \$1,620$; the expected net income of project II is $(0.2 \times 1,100) + (0.8 \times 1,750) = \$1,620$.

economic conditions: that is to say, in prosperity demand increases rapidly but in recession the demand falls off drastically. On the other hand, the demand for the products of project II (say a basic food item) is less affected by general economic conditions; hence the monetary returns from project I are less stable than those of project II.

The two projects yield the same expected profit, i.e. an expected profit of $620 (i.e. 1,620 − 1,000); but clearly they are not equivalent. The outcome of project I is more uncertain than that of project II; and the fact that their expected profits are identical confirms the contention that the expected return criterion does not take risk into account. As a result the expected return (or profit) criterion, *by itself*, does not provide an appropriate decision criterion when uncertainty prevails.

The fact that project I is riskier than project II can be seen even more clearly if the distributions of expected profit are drawn. Figure 8.2 shows that the

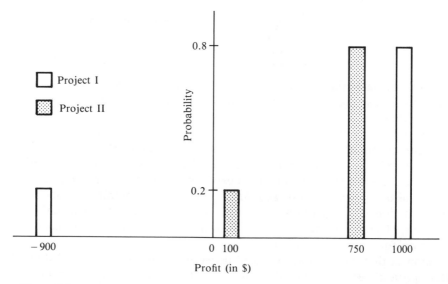

Figure 8.2

possible outcomes under project II are much closer to one another than is true for project I. Moreover, the greater risk inherent in project I is also illustrated by the fact that this project has a 20% chance of a $900 *loss*; the probability of loss is zero should project II be accepted. Hence, while the calculation of expected profit can serve as a measure of profitability, it cannot in itself serve as a measure of risk.

The logic of the above example is equally applicable to a private individual investing in two different types of stock. In this case the cash flows are simply the returns of the two stocks. In the following chapters, we examine several possible measures of risk which can be used along with the expected return when reaching investment decisions under conditions of uncertainty. But first, we turn to the theory of expected utility in order to gain additional insight into the nature of investment risk.

RISK AND UTILITY

Maximum expected utility criterion (MEUC)

The numerical examples of the preceding section suffice to show the inadequacies of a decision criterion based solely on expected return or profit. In their classic book on the theory of games,[4] John von Neumann and Oskar Morgenstern showed that an appropriate criterion can be found if the expected *utility* derived from the monetary income is substituted for the money profits themselves. Such a criterion has the advantage of taking both the profitability and the risk inherent in an uncertain investment project into account simultaneously.

Utility theory recognizes that it is the pleasure or satisfaction that we get from money, and not money itself, which is important. For example, if you learn that upon graduation your annual salary will double from $20,000 to $40,000 a year, does it mean that your satisfaction will double as well? The answer is no. Remember that you use money to buy goods and services. With the first $20,000 you buy the most important goods and services (e.g., food, clothing, and shelter) hence your salary increase will greatly increase your satisfaction but it will not double it.

To understand the concept of utility, consider the case of an individual who must choose between the two alternatives given in Table 8.4. Note that the two investments under consideration have the same expected profit, i.e. $2,000 where net profit is the total return minus the initial investment. A glance at the two options suffices to show that the risk of investment B is greater than that of investment A. We show that despite the equal expected profits, investment A is indeed preferable to investment B. The intuitive explanation for the preference of investment A over investment B can be clarified if we examine the

4. J. von Neumann and O. Morgenstern, *Theory of Games and Economic Behavior*, 2nd edn, Princeton University Press, 1953. A more popular version is given in R. D. Luce and H. Raiffa, *Games and Decisions*, Wiley, New York, 1966.

Table 8.4

	Investment A		Investment B	
	Net profit	Probability	Net profit	Probability
	$		$	
	1,000	0.5	0	0.5
	3,000	0.5	4,000	0.5
Expected profit	2,000		2,000	

difference in the monetary outcomes of the two proposals. Suppose that the investor who tentatively chooses investment A considers shifting from A to B. What changes are induced by such a shift? Clearly, the differences between the two investments can be summarized as follows. In a poor year he will realize $1,000 less on investment B relative to investment A, while in a good year investment B yields $1,000 more. Thus, if the investor changes his decision and shifts from investment A to investment B, he has a 50% chance of gaining $1,000, but he also has a 50% chance of losing $1,000. Is it worth while to shift from investment A to investment B?

In general, most investors will not switch from A to B since the subjective satisfaction (or utility) that they derive from the additional $1,000 is less than the utility that they must give up if they lose $1,000. To help clarify this argument, consider an individual who invests his money for one period and then uses the monetary return to buy consumer goods. For most individuals the additional satisfaction (utility) from consumption diminishes as consumption increases. That is to say, the consumer initially satisfies his more essential needs, and hence the utility that he derives from spending say the first $1,000 is relatively large. Once he satisfies his more basic needs we expect that the additional utility which he derives from spending the second $1,000 will be lower, and so on for additional increments of income.

The concept of *diminishing marginal utility* is illustrated in Table 8.5. As we can see, total utility increases as income rises: that is to say, the higher the income, the larger is the satisfaction derived from the income. However, the marginal utility is diminishing; the utility of the first $1,000 is 1, for the second $1,000 it is 0.8, for the third $1,000 it is 0.7, and for the fourth $1,000 it is only 0.5. Combining the relevant figures from Tables 8.4 and 8.5, Table 8.6 presents investment A and investment B in terms of the utility which is derived

Table 8.5

Income ($)	Utility	Marginal utility
0	0	
1,000	1	1
2,000	1.8	0.8
3,000	2.5	0.7
4,000	3.0	0.5

Table 8.6

	Investment A			Investment B		
	Probability	Profit ($)	Utility	Probability	Profit ($)	Utility
	0.5	1,000	1	0.5	0	0
	0.5	3,000	2.5	0.5	4,000	3.0
Expected net profit		2,000			2,000	
Expected utility[a]		1.75			1.5	

[a] The expected utility of investments A and B is given by $(0.5 \times 1) + (0.5 \times 2.5) = 1.75$ and $(0.5 \times 0) + (0.5 \times 3) = 1.5$, respectively.

from these two proposals. The data of Table 8.6 indicate that while proposals A and B are characterized by the same expected profit, they differ with respect to their expected utility. The expected utility derived from investment A is 1.75 as compared with investment B's expected utility of only 1.5. Thus despite the fact that the expected profit criterion cannot discriminate between investments A and B, the expected utility criterion indicates a clear preference for investment A, which as we have already noted is considerably less risky. Moreover, the ranking of investment A over B holds for all utility functions, so long as the utility function has the property of diminishing marginal utility. This statement can be proved by examining individuals' attitudes towards risk.

ALTERNATIVE ATTITUDES TOWARD RISK

It is convenient for the purposes of the analysis to distinguish between two classes of investors: those who dislike risk whom we call 'risk averters', and those who prefer risky prospects, whom we call 'risk lovers'. Since the bulk of the theoretical and empirical evidence supports the view that the typical investor is risk averse, we concentrate on this broad class of individuals.

Consider the following hypothetical example where an individual is offered the opportunity of purchasing the following investment option for a purchase price of $10:

End-of-period value	Probability
9	0.5
11	0.5

The *expected* end-of-period value of such an investment is $(0.5 \times 9) + (0.5 \times 11) = 10$; that is, the expected value equals the initial purchase price. In other words, the expected monetary profit from the investment is zero. (We continue to ignore the discount factor, which is tantamount to assuming a very short investment period.) Can an individual be expected to purchase such an option? Since we have rejected the principle of expected return or profit and tentatively replaced it with the principle of expected utility, our answer depends on the individual's attitude toward risk: that, is on the degree to which he likes or dislikes to trade a safe prospect for an uncertain one.

Definitions

An individual whose utility function is *concave* will be called a *risk averter*. The utility function $U(X)$ is concave if $U'(X) \geqslant 0$ and $U''(X) \leqslant 0$.

An individual whose utility function is *convex* will be called a *risk lover*. The utility function $U(X)$ is convex if $U'(X) \geqslant 0$ and $U''(X) \geqslant 0$.

(In both cases we require strict inequalities for at least one value of X.)

A concave utility function has the property that the marginal utility of money declines over the entire relevant range. Thus investors whose preferences are characterized by diminishing marginal utility will be called risk averters. It follows that every risk averter prefers a perfectly certain investment to an investment with an equal but uncertain expected return. Taking our example, a risk-averse individual will *not* purchase the above option because in terms of utility, the possible loss of $1 more than offsets the equal possible gain of $1.

This conclusion can be confirmed by using a graphical device. Figure 8.3 sets out the same investment problem: the purchase for $10 of an option whose

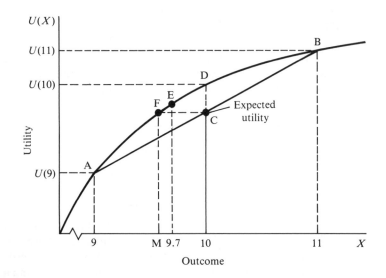

Figure 8.3

end-of-period value has an equal probability of being $9 or $11. The possible end-of-period values are measured along the horizontal axis and utility is measured along the vertical axis. The individual's utility function is drawn in Figure 8.3 as a *concave* curve rising from the origin; this is tantamount to assuming that he is risk-averse. The expected utility is represented graphically by point C of Figure 8.3, the point at which a perpendicular rising from the point marked 10 on the horizontal axis intersects the chord connecting points A and B. The expected utility, given by point C, is equal to $1/2U(9) + 1/2U(11)$ (where U stands for utility). A glance at the diagram shows that the utility of the purchase price, $U(10)$, which corresponds to point D on the utility curve, is greater than the *expected* utility of the investment option, which corresponds to point C. Thus a risk-averse individual will not purchase an uncertain option whose expected value is equal to its purchase price, since the concavity of his utility function translates the *zero monetary gain* into a *utility loss*.

Now let us assume that the same individual is offered the same option, but at a lower price, say $9.70. The expected end-of-period value remains $10 (i.e. $0.5 \times 9 + 0.5 \times 11$) so that the option has a positive expected return ($10 - 9.70 = $0.30). Will the risk-averse individual purchase the option now? Despite the lower price of $9.70, Figure 8.3 clearly shows that he *will not* be willing to purchase the option because the utility of a perfectly certain sum of $9.70 (point E) still exceeds the expected utility of the risky option (point C). How far must the price fall before our risk-averse investor will be willing to acquire it? Again the answer can be readily inferred from Figure 8.3. The maximum price that he will be willing to pay is represented by point M on the horizontal axis. At this price, $U(M)$ (point F) is just equal to the expected utility from the risky investment option. The distance between the outcome of 10 and M measures the *risk premium* required to induce the risk-averse individual to purchase the option.[5] At prices lower than M (points to the left of M on the horizontal axis) the investment option is more attractive since it represents a gain in utility. Conversely, at prices above M, as we have already seen, the risky investment represents a loss of utility for the risk-averse investor. The value M represents the *certainty equivalent* value of the risky option (we make further use of this concept in Chapter 10). Mathematically, M is the value which resolves $EU(X) = U(M)$ where X is a random variable or outcome. The risk premium, π, is given by $\pi = E(X) - M$.

Having discussed the basic properties of risk aversion, let us put the graphical analysis through its paces by returning to the original example given in Table 8.6 above. Recall that we have asserted, but as yet not proven, that *all* risk averters (i.e. individuals characterized by diminishing marginal utility of money) will prefer investment A to B, due to the greater dispersion of the latter

---

5. To be more precise, the investor has to choose between an uncertain income and a certain income. The risk premium is the difference between 10 and the certain income, M. However, the precise definition of the risk premium also depends on the investor's initial wealth. To avoid extra notation and for simplicity, we eliminate the discussion of the wealth effect (see problem 8.13).

for an equal expected profit. Figure 8.4 graphs the data of Table 8.6. Since we are assuming risk aversion, the utility function is drawn as a concave curve rising from the origin. The expected utility of project A is simply $0.5U(1,000) + 0.5U(3,000) = 0.5(1) + 0.5(2.5) = 1.75$ (where U stands for utility). This value corresponds to point A of Figure 8.4; i.e. the intersection of the vertical line rising from point 2,000 on the horizontal axis (which is the expected monetary return) with the appropriate chord on the utility function. Similarly, point B indicates the expected utility from investment B. Since point A lies above point B (and this relationship holds for *all* concave utility functions), it follows that every risk averter will prefer investment A over investment B, independent of the degree of his risk aversion.

The reason for this result can also be inferred from Figure 8.4. Other things being equal, risk averters do not like a wide dispersion of outcomes. From the graph, it is clear that both projects have the same expected profit but the range of outcomes of proposal B is much greater than the range of outcomes of proposal A. Hence all risk averters will prefer investment A over investment B.

Two additional classes of possible investors can be identified. First, we have those optimistic fellows who have a preference, rather than an aversion, for risk. In terms of our analysis such an individual is characterized by a *convex*

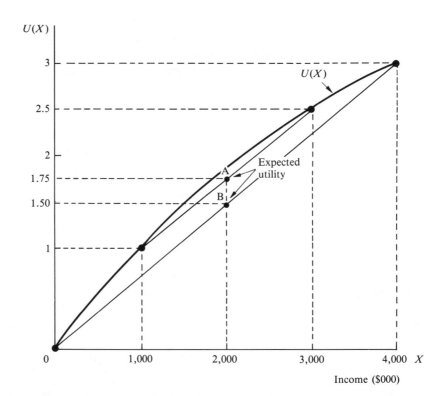

Figure 8.4

utility function, which means that the marginal utility of each additional dollar increases, which upon reflection is not a very realistic assumption.

Second, we have those investors who are 'risk neutral', i.e. are neither risk averters nor risk lovers. Such an individual has a linear utility function, and displays constant marginal utility of money. Risk neutrality constitutes a borderline case between risk lovers and risk averters. A risk-neutral individual chooses his investments solely according to their expected profit, and completely ignores the dispersion of the returns.[6]

The expected utility criterion provides an elegant and theoretically impeccable solution to the problem of investment under uncertainty. However, an individual (or corporation) seeking investment advice will not be grateful for the suggestion that he should maximize his expected utility. The expected utility rule is not operational; in general we do not know the precise shape of the utility function, and hence cannot calculate expected utilities. Moreover, corporations typically have many shareholders, each presumably with a different utility function. Consequently we must look elsewhere for additional investment criteria which are capable of application to actual decision problems; however, in formulating these rules we shall be using the insights which we have derived from the examination of the expected utility criterion.

--- SUMMARY

The purpose of this chapter has been to set out the utility foundation of the theory of investment choice under conditions of risk and uncertainty. A risky (or uncertain) investment is defined as an option whose monetary return is not known with perfect certainty, but for which an array of alternative returns and their (objective or subjective) probabilities are known. After a demonstration that the *maximum* profits and maximum *expected* return (profits) criteria do not provide a straightforward solution to our problem, attention was directed to the theory of expected utility. Three broad classes of risk attitudes, corresponding to three types of investor, were distinguished:

1. Risk averters − individuals with concave utility functions.
2. Risk lovers − individuals with convex utility functions.
3. Risk-neutral individuals − those with linear utility functions.

The introduction of utility into the analysis provides an elegant solution to the investment decision problem under uncertainty by permitting us to assign *unequal weights* to different monetary outcomes. However, the chapter closes with a warning regarding the inability to apply the utility principle directly to decision problems, and therefore we turn in the following chapters to an examination of operational decision rules which, while they reflect the insight gained from the utility analysis, are *not* set out explicitly in terms of immeasurable utilities.

6. We leave the graphical proof of this statement to the reader.

SUMMARY TABLE

Investment criteria

1. MRC – maximum return criterion, applicable only when outcomes are certain.
2. MERC – maximum expected return criterion, applicable to risk or uncertainty, but fails to take into account risk.
3. MEUC – maximum expected utility criterion, incorporates both profitability and risk and therefore represents the appropriate criteria.

Alternative attitudes towards risk

1. Risk-averter – dislikes risk; concave utility function $U(X)$ with $U'(X) \geqslant 0$ and $U''(X) \leqslant 0$.
2. Risk-lover – likes risk; convex utility function $U(X)$, with $U'(X) \geqslant 0$ and $U''(X) \geqslant 0$. (In both (1) and (2) we require a strict inequality for at least one value of X.)
3. Risk-neutral – indifferent to risk; linear utility function $U(X)$, where $U(X) = a + bx$ (where $b > 0$) hence $U'(X) = b > 0$ and $U''(X) = 0$.

Risk premium

1. The expected utility is given by $EU(X)$ where X is a random variable or outcome.
2. The value M for which $U(M) = EU(X)$, is the certainty equivalent of random variable X.
3. The expected monetary value is $E(X)$.
4. The risk premium is defined as π, where $\pi = E(X) - M$.

QUESTIONS AND PROBLEMS

8.1 The following table sets out the annual percentage changes in the Standard & Poor's 500 stock index for 32 years.

Year	Annual change	Year	Annual change
1	11.8	17	7.7
2	−6.6	18	−11.4
3	45.0	19	0.1
4	26.4	20	10.8
5	2.6	21	15.7
6	−14.3	22	−17.4
7	38.1	23	−29.7
8	8.5	24	31.5
9	−3.0	25	19.2
10	23.1	26	−11.5
11	−11.8	27	9.9
12	18.9	28	12.1
13	13.0	29	25.8
14	9.1	30	−9.7
15	−13.1	31	14.8
16	20.1	32	17.3

(a) Calculate the frequency distribution of the annual changes in a table; starting at '− 30.0 to − 20.1' and finishing at '40.0 to 49.9'.

(b) Use the data of part (a) to draw a histogram of the historical record.

8.2 Assume that an individual is confronted with the problem of choosing one of the following investment options (return/probability):

Option A		Option B		Option C		Option D		Option E	
Return	Prob.	Return	Prob.	Return	Prob.	Return	Prob.	Return	Prob.
7	1.0	6	1/2	−12	1/4	− 30	2/10	−16	1/8
		16	1/2	12	1/2	12	4/10	− 4	2/8
				24	1/4	24	3/10	8	2/8
						60	1/10	24	3/8

(a) Which option will be chosen according to the maximum expected return criterion?

(b) What is the major shortcoming of this rule for decision-making under uncertainty?

8.3 Assume that an individual must choose between the following two investment alternatives:

Investment A		Investment B	
Return ($)	Probability	Return ($)	Probability
100	3/10	300	3/10
400	4/10	400	4/10
700	3/10	500	3/10

(a) Which alternative will be chosen according to the maximum expected return criterion?

(b) Calculate the marginal utility of money implied by the utility function in the following table:

Income ($)	Utility
0	0
100	20
200	39
300	57
400	73
500	87
600	98
700	105

(c) Which alternative will the individual choose according to the maximum expected utility criterion. (First determine which investment you believe the individual would choose by evaluating the marginal utility, then calculate the expected utility.)

8.4 'A risk averter never enters a fair game of chance.' Prove this statement graphically. In your answer indicate the 'risk premium' necessary to induce him to agree to play. (Note: a 'fair' game is one in which the price to participate is equal to the mean value of the prize.)

8.5 An investor whose utility function is given by $U(X) = X^{1/2}$, where X denotes money profits, is offered a chance to choose one of the following investment options:

Option A		Option B	
Probability	Profit	Probability	Profit
1/2	16	1/2	81
1/2	196	1/2	121

(a) Which option will be chosen?
(b) Prove your answer graphically.
(c) What is the maximum price that such an investor will be willing to pay for each option? Compare the price you get for each option with its expected profit.
(d) Graph your answer to (c) using the graph you drew in part (b).

8.6 An individual with the utility function $U(X) = (X/10)^2$ is known to be indifferent between two lotteries A and B, which offer the following prizes:

Lottery A		Lottery B	
Probability	Prize	Probability	Prize
1/2	110	p	90
1/2	130	$1-p$	150

Find the value of p.

8.7 'A risk-neutral investor, that is one who has a linear utility function, makes his investment decisions in accordance with the principle of maximum expected return, rather than with that of maximum expected utility.' Is this statement correct? Prove your answer using a graph of the utility function.

8.8 Assume an investor with the following utility function:

Return ($)	Utility
−2,000	−600
−1,000	−150
0	0
1,000	80
2,000	150
3,000	210
4,000	250
5,000	280
10,000	340

(a) Graph the investor's utility function.
(b) Will this investor be willing to execute an investment project that requires an outlay of $2,000 and has an equal chance to be a complete loss or to generate a cash flow with a *PV* of $5,000?
(c) What is the maximum amount the investor would agree to invest in a project with a cash flow with an equal probability of a *PV* of $1,000 or a *PV* of $10,000?
(d) Answer parts (b) and (c) graphically.

8.9 Answer question 8.8, assuming that the investor is risk-neutral.

8.10 Assume that an individual is confronted with the problem of choosing *one* of the following investment options:

Option A		Option B		Option C		Option D	
Probability	Return	Probability	Return	Probability	Return	Probability	Return
1/2	−10	1/8	−10	1/2	0	1/4	−10
1/4	20	1/2	20	3/8	10	1/8	0
1/4	30	3/8	40	1/8	20	5/8	40

The return is per $100 invested and is stated in dollars.

(a) Which option will be chosen according to the principle of maximum expected return?
(b) Which option will be chosen according to the maximum expected utility principle, using the following two alternative utility functions, $U_1(x)$ and $U_2(x)$:

Return (x)	$U_1(x)$	$U_2(x)$
−10	−100	−100
0	0	0
10	86	120
20	150	260
30	200	440
40	232	660

(c) How does your answer to part (b) change if you assume that the individual has the following utility function:

$$U_3(x) = a + \frac{U_2(x)}{b} \quad \text{(where } b > 0\text{)}$$

Solve the problem numerically for the special case where $a = -10$ and $b = +10$, and explain your results.
(d) Graph the above mentioned alternative utility functions, U_1, U_2, U_3, over the domain $(40 > x > -10)$ and indicate which of the functions represents a 'risk averter' and which represents a 'risk lover'.
(e) Why is it impossible for U_2 and U_3 to represent *different* risk attitudes?
(f) Calculate the marginal utilities of money implied by U_1 and U_2. Show your calculations. Are these results consistent with your answer to part (d)?

8.11 Assume the following two investment options:

Option A		Option B	
Probability	Return	Probability	Return
1/2	2	1/2	8
1/2	10	1/2	20

(a) Show numerically and graphically which of the two options will be chosen by an investor whose utility function is given by:

$$U(x) = 1,000 + (x - 10)^3$$

(Hint: begin by graphing the utility function.)

(b) What is the maximum price that such an individual will be willing to pay for each option?

8.12 Consider three options:

Option A		Option B		Option C	
Probability	Return	Probability	Return	Probability	Return
1/2	1	1/4	1	1/4	1
1/2	4	1/2	3	1/2	2
		1/4	4	1/4	4

An individual is considering the choice between A and B or between A and C only. In each of the two choices, assuming initial wealth, $W_0 = \$100$ for all:

(a) Which option will be chosen by an individual making his choice by the principle of maximum expected return?

(b) Which option will be chosen by a risk-neutral individual with utility function $U(W) = W$?

(c) Which option will be chosen by a risk lover with $U(W) = W^2$?

(d) Which option will be chosen by a risk averter with $U(W) = W^{1/2}$?

(e) What should be the middle outcome in option C (instead of 2) so that each individual will be indifferent between A and C? Solve separately for each of the four individuals above. (Hint: Remember that the solution to the quadratic formula is

$$\frac{-b \pm (b^2 - 4ac)^{1/2}}{2a}$$

8.13 A risk averter with the utility function $U(W) = W^{1/2}$ and initial wealth $W_0 = \$100$ has found a lottery ticket with the following prize distribution:

Probability	Prize
α	$0
$1 - \alpha$	$96

(a) Find α if we know that he is willing to sell the lottery ticket for no less than $10.25.

(b) Does α change when the initial wealth changes say to $W_0 = \$10,000$?

8.14 An individual with the utility function $U(X) = X - 0.125 X^2$ is allowed to choose between a certain income ($X_A = \$2$) and an uncertain stream (X_B) with five different outcomes with equal probabilities:

Probability	0.2	0.2	0.2	0.2	0.2
Outcome	0	1	2	3	4

The utility function is not defined for outcomes exceeding $X_B = 4$, i.e., $X_B \leqslant 4$.

(a) Which of the two options will the individual prefer?
(b) What is the minimal certain income that he will accept for 'selling' the uncertain option?

In your answer discuss the constraint on the utility function. What happens if we also have an outcome $X_B = 5$?

8.15 A risk lover with the utility function $U(W) + (W/10)^2$ is indifferent between the following two options:

Option A		Option B	
Probability	Terminal wealth	Probability	Terminal wealth
3/4	100	4/5	95
1/4	120	1/5	x

Find the outcome x.

8.16 An investor owns a car with a value of $10,000. If he does not insure himself against loss, he has a 0.9 probability of retaining his car and a 0.1 probability of totally losing it (i.e. the car is stolen and not found). The investor's utility function is $U(W) = \sqrt{W}$ and has wealth apart from the car of $W = \$10,000$.

(a) What is the maximum amount of money he is willing to pay to insure himself against loss.
(b) How would you change the answer to (a) if the investor's utility function is $U(W) = W$ (i.e., it is linear)?

8.17 An investor whose initial wealth is zero is indifferent between having a certain amount of money having 10 utils and getting the following distribution:

Probability	Outcome	Utilities
1/3	0	0
1/3	$100	10
1/3	$200	$U(200)$

(a) Find the utility of $200, i.e., $U(200)$.
(b) Is the investor a risk lover, a risk neutral, or a risk averter?

8.18 An insurance firm charges an insurance premium of 10% of the value of your car. Suppose that only two events are possible: total loss or no damage at all. The value of your car is $10,000 and your wealth (apart from the car) is $2,000. With the 10% premium rate you are exactly indifferent between purchasing the insurance or not. Your utility function is $U(W) = \log_{10} W$. Calculate the probability of a total loss.

8.19 Investor A has preference $U_A(W)$ while investor B gets twice the utility of any level of wealth, namely $U_B(W) = 2U_A(W)$. Given that investor A is a risk averter, is it possible that investor B is a risk lover?

8.20 The rates of return for a given stock and bond are given by

Stock		Bond	
Return	Probability	Return	Probability
0%	1/2	7%	1/2
30%	1/2	8%	1/2

Assume that all investors are risk averse and are considering putting $1,000 in one of these two options. How do you explain that some investors may buy the bond and some the stock? What investment is preferred by an investor whose utility function is $U(W) = \log_{10}(W)$?

8.21 The rates of return on a AT&T are 5% or 20% with an equal probability. The rates of return or IBM are -2% or 30% with an equal probability.

(a) You have initial wealth of $1,100 and you decided to invest $100 in one of these two stocks. What stock would you select if your utility function is linear? Would you change your choice if you have an initial wealth of $10,100?

(b) Does the size of your investment (e.g., $200 rather than $100) affect your choice?

8.22 An investor has a linear utility function of the form:

$$U(W) = 10 + \tfrac{3}{4}W \quad \text{in the range } W < 100$$
$$U(W) = 35 + \tfrac{1}{2}W \quad \text{in the range } W \geqslant 100$$

Since in both cases the utility function is linear, it seems that this investor will be indifferent between having a wealth of $80 with certainty, or having $40 wealth with a probability of $\tfrac{1}{2}$, and $120 with probability of $\tfrac{1}{2}$ since the average wealth in both cases is $80.

(a) Calculate the expected utility of these two choices.

(b) Explain your results in light of the fact that the utility function has two linear segments.

SELECTED REFERENCES

Amihud, Yakov, 'General Risk Aversion and an Attitude towards Risk,' *The Journal of Finance*, June 1980.

Ang, J. S. and Lewellen, W. G., 'Risk Adjustment in Capital Investment Project Evaluations,' *Financial Management*, Summer 1982.

Baron, D. P., 'On the Utility Theoretic Foundations of Mean–Variance Analysis,' *Journal of Finance*, December 1977.

Beladi, Hamid, Lee, Young-Kwang, and Naqvi, Nadeem, 'The Long-Run Behavior of the Firm under Uncertainty,' *Atlantic Economic Journal*, December 1987.

Bordley, R. F., 'An Additive Group Utility for a Fund Manager,' *Management Science*, 34, 1988.

Busche, K. and Hall, C. D., 'An Exception to the Risk Preference Anomaly,' *Journal of Business*, 61, 1988.

Chen, S. N., 'Simple Optimal Asset Allocation under Uncertainty,' *Journal of Portfolio Management*, Summer 1987.

Cox, J. C. and Epstein, S., 'Preference Reversals Without the Independence Axiom,' *American Economic Review*, 79, 1989.

Currim, I. S. and Sarin, R. K., 'Prospect versus Utility,' *Management Science*, 35, 1989.

de B. Harris, Frederick H., 'Competing Theories of Firm Decision Making Under Risk,' *Southern Economic Journal*, October 1987.

Dotan, Amihud and Raviv, S. Abraham, 'On the Interaction of Real and Financial Decisions of the Firm Under Uncertainty,' *Journal of Finance*, June 1985.

Fishburn, P. C. and LaValle, I. H., 'Transitivity is Equivalent to Independence for States-additive SSB Utilities,' *Journal of Economic Theory*, February 1988.

Friedman, M. and Savage, L. J., 'The Expected Utility Hypothesis and the Measurability of Utility,' *Journal of Political Economy*, December 1952.

Graves, P. E., 'Relative Risk Aversion: Increasing or Decreasing?' *Journal of Financial and Quantitative Analysis*, June 1979.

Hakansson, Nils H., 'Friedman–Savage Utility Functions Consistent with Risk Aversion,' *Quarterly Journal of Economics*, August 1970.

Hanoch, G. and Levy, H., 'The Efficiency Analysis of Choices Involving Risk,' *Review of Economic Studies*, July 1969.

Hey, John D. and Lambert, Peter J., *Surveys in the Economics of Uncertainty*, New York: Basil Blackwell, 1987.

Jean, William H., 'The Geometric Mean and Stochastic Dominance,' *Journal of Finance*, March 1980.

Jewitt, I., 'Choosing between Risky Prospects: The Characterization of Comparative Statics Results, and Location Independent Risk,' *Management Science*, 35, 1989.

Levy, Haim and Sarnat, Marshall, *Portfolio and Investment Selection*, Englewood Cliffs, N.J.: Prentice Hall, 1984.

Meyer, J., 'Mean–Variance Efficient Sets and Expected Utility,' *Journal of Finance*, December 1979.

Miller, Stephen M., 'Measures of Risk Aversion: Some Clarifying Comments,' *Journal of Financial and Quantitative Analysis*, June 1975.

Moore, P. G. and Thomas H., 'Measuring Uncertainty,' *Omega*, December 1975.

Pindyck, Robert S., *Risk Aversion and Determinants or Stock Market Behavior*, Cambridge: N.B.E.R., 1986.

Rubinstein, A., 'Similarity and Decision-making under Risk (Is There a Utility Theory Resolution to the Allais Paradox?),' *Journal of Economic Theory*, October 1988.

Shapiro, Alan C. and Titman, Sheridan, 'An Integrated Approach to Risk Management,' *Midland Corporate Finance Journal*, Summer 1985.

Wagner, Wayne H., 'The Many Dimensions of Risk,' The *Journal of Portfolio Management*, Winter 1988.

von Neumann, J. and Morgenstern, O., *Theory of Games and Economic Behavior*, Princeton, N.J.: Princeton University Press, 1953.

9

Measuring Risk

As we can see from Table 9.1, different securities are characterized by different mean returns as well as different standard deviations. For example, the standard deviation of small stocks is 35.30%, and on U.S. treasury bills (T-bills) it is only 3.36%. While the mean rate of return measures the profitability or the interest, the standard deviation is a type of risk index. Although it ignores covariances with other assets, it constitutes a proxy for the risk involved.

In this chapter, we introduce standard deviation (and variance) as measures of an asset's risk. We also introduce the concept of covariance which will be used extensively in the next chapter.

If the analysis of risk is to be meaningful for the firm, a method must be found to translate the utility analysis of the preceding chapter into operational decision rules which do not depend on the measurement of the elusive will o' the wisp 'utility'. Clearly, there are many ways to incorporate risk into decision problems. Common to almost all of the approaches, however, is the need to develop an index which will *directly* reflect the risk inherent to an

Table 9.1 Statistics for five year holding period returns, nominal, and real

	Nominal		
	Average		Standard deviation
Security type	Geometric	Arithmetic	
Small company stocks	12.07	17.28	35.30
Common stocks	10.38	12.61	20.76
Corporate bonds	5.42	5.67	8.53
Long-term government bonds	4.79	5.09	8.65
Intermediate government bonds	5.14	5.23	5.61
U.S. treasury bills	3.70	3.71	3.36

Source: Derived from data in Ibbotson Associates, *Stocks, Bonds, Bills, and Inflation* (1991).

investment proposal.[1] For simplicity, and in order to focus our attention on the role of uncertainty, we initially ignore the element of time and the need to discount future returns by assuming a very short investment period. In the later sections of the chapter this restriction is relaxed and the analysis is carried out in terms of net present values and their associated risk.

MEASURING RISK BY THE VARIABILITY OF RETURNS

Although in modern parlance the term 'risk' has come to mean hazard or danger of loss, the Latin word *risicum* retained some positive connotations at least up to the Middle Ages. In the earlier form, risk refers to chance or luck — *both* good and bad. Modern investment analysis has returned to the original meaning of risk, identifying the latter with the dispersion of returns, i.e. with possible deviations (both positive and negative) from the expected return.[2] The most widely used method of risk analysis utilizes the expected (mean) profit as an indicator of an investment's anticipated profitability and the variance (or standard deviation) as an indicator of its risk.

Expected profit

The expected value of a project's profitability is given by:

$$E(x) = \sum_{i=1}^{n} Pr_i x_i$$

where:

$E(x)$ = expected value of the project
x_i = ith possible outcome (profit)
Pr_i = probability of obtaining the ith outcome x_i
n = number of possible outcomes

Consider, for example, an investment which offers a 50% chance of earning a net profit of $1,000, a 25% chance of breaking even, and a 25% chance of a $400 loss, so that Pr_i and x_i are as follows:

Pr_i	x_i
0.50	1,000
0.25	0
0.25	− 400

The expected value of the investment is simply the weighted average of the possible outcomes, weighted by the probability of the outcome occurring.

---

1. The implications of combining projects into portfolios are spelled out in Chapters 11 and 12.
2. The case for associating the derivation of the Latin *risicum* from the Arabic *risq*, is argued by Benjamin Z. Kedar, 'Again: Arabic *Risq* Medieval Latin *Risicum*,' *Studi Medievali*, Centro Italiano Di Studi Sull' Alto Medioevo, Spoleto, 1970.

Variance as a measure of risk

The variance, or the standard deviation, of possible outcomes measures the dispersion of profits around the mean (expected) value. It provides information on the extent of the possible deviations of the actual return from the expected return.

The variance of the distribution (σ^2) is given by the formula:

$$\sigma^2(x) = \sum_{i=1}^{n} Pr_i(x_i - E(x))^2 = E(x - E(x))^2$$

To determine the variance we first calculate the deviation of each possible outcome from the expected value, i.e. $(x_i - E(x))$, then raise it to the second power (i.e., square the deviations), and multiply this term by the probability of the return, occurring, i.e., of getting x_i, that is by Pr_i. The summation of all these products serves as a measure of the distribution's variability, and is called the *variance*. The reader should note that since the distribution of future profit x_i is measured in dollars, the dimension of σ^2 is dollars squared, which of course is economically meaningless. Hence we take the square root of the variance, thereby obtaining the standard deviation, σ, which also measures the variability of the distribution but has the further advantage of being set out in terms of dollars (not dollars squared). However, despite this difference in dimensions the reader should note that if investment A is more risky than investment B in terms of the variance, i.e., $\sigma_A^2 > \sigma_B^2$, then its standard deviation must also be greater, i.e., $\sigma_A > \sigma_B$. Thus for ranking investment proposals according to their risk one can use the variance or standard deviation interchangeably.[3]

In practice the actual calculation of the variance is somewhat easier if the following formula is used:

$$\sigma^2(x) = \sum_{i=1}^{n} Pr_i x_i^2 - \left(\sum_{i=1}^{n} Pr_i x_i \right)^2$$

An example
Let us calculate the expected value and the variance of the following distribution:

Probability of occurrence Pr_i	Profits $\$x_i$
0.50	80
0.25	100
0.25	120

3. One might legitimately ask: if we desire a risk index in terms of dollars rather than in terms of dollars squared, why raise all terms to the second power in the first place? Why not directly calculate the term $\sum_{i=1}^{n} Pr_i(x_i - E(x))$ which has the dimension of dollars? However, the reader should note that this term is *always* equal to zero, which explains the need to 'square' the deviations.

The expected profit is given by:

$$E(x) = Pr_1 x_1 + Pr_2 x_2 + Pr_3 x_3$$
$$= (0.5 \times 80) + (0.25 \times 100) + (0.25 \times 200) = \$115$$

and the variance is:

$$\sigma^2(x) = \sum_{i=1}^{3} Pr_i x_i^2 - \left(\sum_{i=1}^{3} Pr_i x_i \right)^2$$
$$= [(0.5 \times 80^2) + (0.25 \times 100^2) + (0.25 \times 200^2)] - 115^2$$
$$= 15,700 - 13,225$$
$$= \$2,475$$

This method of calculation is very simple even for relatively large problems. However, the reader can verify that calculating the variance from its basic definition gives the same results, but the calculations are somewhat more tedious:

$$\sigma^2(x) = \sum_{i=1}^{3} Pr_i (x_i - E(x))^2$$
$$= 0.5(80 - 115)^2 + 0.25(100 - 115)^2 + 0.25(200 - 115)^2$$
$$= (0.5 \times 1,225) + (0.25 \times 225) + (0.25 \times 7,225) = 2,475$$

The standard deviation, which is simply the square root of the variance, is given by:

$$\sigma(x) = \sqrt{2,475} = 49.75$$

COVARIANCE AND THE CORRELATION COEFFICIENT

When more than one investment is purchased, the combination can affect risk. Consider an individual who invests part of his money in the construction industry. Since profits in the industry fluctuate considerably, he may be interested in investing part of his money in another industry to stabilize his income. This stabilization can be facilitated by investing part of his money in an industry whose profits fluctuate either independently or negatively with those of the construction industry. By so doing, the investor can achieve a fairly stable average return; when the return on one type of stock is relatively low, the return from the other stocks will be relatively high, and vice versa. The degree to which diversification stabilizes the return is a function of the relation between the two random variables. The two closely related concepts which serve as quantitative measures of the relation between the fluctuations of two random variables are the *covariance* and the *correlation coefficient*.

Covariance

We define the covariance of two random variables x and y as:

$$\text{Cov}(x,y) = E(x - E(x))(y - E(y))$$

In the discrete case we get:[4]

$$\text{Cov}(x,y) = \sum_{i=1}^{n} (x_i - E(x))(y_i - E(y))Pr_{(ii)}$$

where $Pr_{(ii)}$ stands for the joint probability of getting x_i and y_i simultaneously. The above definition of $\text{Cov}(x,y)$ can be restated as:

$$\text{Cov}(x,y) = E[(x - E(x))(y - E(y))] = E[xy - yE(x) - xE(y) + E(x)E(y)]$$
$$= E(xy) - 2E(x)E(y) + E(x)E(y) = E(xy) - E(x)E(y)$$

or

$$\text{Cov}(x,y) = E(xy) - E(x)E(y)$$

where $E(xy)$ is the expected value of the random variable xy.

We can explain the intuitive meaning of the covariance as follows. Look at the expression $(x - E(x))(y - E(y))$. Suppose $x - E(x) > 0$ (x exceeds $E(x)$) and $y - E(y) > 0$ (y exceeds $E(y)$), then the covariance will be positive, i.e.:

$$(x - E(x))(y - E(y)) > 0$$

We will get a positive value also when both the returns x and y are below their average. However, if:

$$(x - E(x)) > 0 \quad \text{and} \quad (y - E(y)) < 0$$

or

$$(x - E(x)) < 0 \quad \text{and} \quad (y - E(y)) > 0$$

which means that the return on one asset is above its average and the other is below its average, then:

$$(x - E(x))(y - E(y)) < 0$$

Consequently, if we get $\text{Cov}(x,y) = E(x - E(x))(y - E(y)) > 0$, we have to conclude that x and y simultaneously tend either to exceed their respective average or to be below it. However, if $\text{Cov}(x,y) < 0$, we can say that they tend

---

4. In the continuous case we have:

$$\text{Cov}(x,y) = \iint (x - E(x))(y - E(y))f(x,y) \, dx \, dy$$

or

$$\text{Cov}(x,y) = \iint xyf(x,y) \, dx \, dy - \left(\int xf(x) \, dx \int yf(y) \, dy \right)$$

where $f(x,y)$ denotes the joint density function of x and y.

to disperse from their average in opposite directions. That is why our hypothetical investor will try to choose an industry whose returns have a *negative* covariance with the returns in the construction industry.[5]

Correlation coefficient

The covariance has been shown to be an indicator of the direction of the dependence between two variables. This indicator, however, changes with any change in the unit of measurement (cents, dimes, or dollars) of the random variables. We need, therefore, an indicator which will be independent of the units used in measuring the outcomes. Furthermore, we desire information concerning both the direction *and* the power of the relationship between the variables. The index which has the required characteristics is called the correlation coefficient and is given by:

$$R(x, y) = \frac{\text{Cov}(x, y)}{\sigma(x)\sigma(y)}$$

where $\sigma(x)$ and $\sigma(y)$ are the standard deviation of x and y, respectively. This coefficient always satisfies:

$$-1 \leqslant R(x, y) \leqslant 1$$

and is independent of the units of measurement.

When R lies between 0 and +1, the relation between the returns on the two assets is of a positive nature; and the closer we are to +1, the stronger the relationship. When $R + 1$ there is a *perfect positive* correlation. In other words, the relation is linear, which means there are b and a such that:

$$y = a + bx \quad \text{where} \quad b > 0$$

When $0 > R \geqslant -1$ the relation is negative, and the smaller R, the stronger the negative relation. In the extreme case where $R = -1$ we have:

$$y = a + bx \quad \text{with} \quad b < 0$$

The impact of the degree of correlation on portfolio choice is deferred until Chapter 11.

———————————————————————————— **THE MEAN–VARIANCE RULE**

A very popular decision rule has been developed by Harry Markowitz, recipient of the Nobel Prize for Economics in 1990, for evaluating investments

---

5. It is worth mentioning that the relationship between x and y can be written as:

$$y_t = a + bx_t + e_t$$

where a, b are constants, t stands for year t, and e_t is the deviation of y_t from the straight line. The line which minimizes the Σe_t^2 is called the regression line of y on x. By using this 'best' line we find that the slope of the line is:

$$b = \frac{\text{Cov}(x, y)}{\sigma^2(x)}$$

on the basis of their expected return and variance (standard deviation).[6] The 'expected return–variance' or 'mean–variance' rule (also referred to in the literature as the E–V rule) can be defined as follows: project A will be preferred to project B if one of the following two conditions hold:

1. The expected return of A exceeds or is equal to the expected return of B *and* the variance of A is less than the variance of B, *or*
2. The expected return of A exceeds that of B *and* the variance of A is less than or equal to that of B.[7]

Thus the expected return is taken as an indicator of a project's profitability and the variance serves as the index of its risk.

To illustrate the application of the E–V rule, consider the example of the two investments whose distributions of profits are given in Table 9.2. (These are the same two investments which were analysed using the expected utility rule in Table 8.6 of the previous chapter). Both investments A and B have the same expected profit:

$$E(A) = (0.5 \times 1,000) + (0.5 \times 3,000) = 2,000$$
$$E(B) = (0.5 \times 0) \quad + (0.5 \times 4,000) = 2,000$$

The variance of project A is 1,000,000:

$$\sigma^2(A) = 0.5(1,000 - 2,000)^2 + 0.5(3,000 - 2,000)^2 = 1,000,000$$

Hence the standard deviation of investment A which is the square root of the variance is 1,000:

$$\sigma(A) = \sqrt{1,000,000} = 1,000$$

Similarly, the variance and standard deviation of investment B are 4,000,000 and 2,000, respectively:

$$\sigma^2(B) = 0.5(0 - 2,000)^2 + 0.5(4,000 - 2,000)^2 = 4,000,000$$

Table 9.2

	Investment A		Investment B	
	Net profit ($)	Probability	Net profit ($)	Probability
	1,000	0.5	0	0.5
	3,000	0.5	4,000	0.5
Expected profit	2,000		2,000	
Standard deviation	1,000		2,000	

6. See his pioneering article 'Portfolio Selection,' *Journal of Finance*, March 1952.
7. Equivalently in symbols, the E–V preference rule implies preference for A if either:

$$E(A) \geqslant E(B) \quad \text{and} \quad \text{Var}(A) < \text{Var}(B)$$

or

$$E(A) > E(B) \quad \text{and} \quad \text{Var}(A) \leqslant \text{Var}(B)$$

and

$$\sigma(B) = \sqrt{4,000,000} = 2,000$$

Thus if we adopt the Markowitz expected return−variance rule (E−V rule), we can confirm that project A is preferred to project B. Both have the same expected profit (2,000) but project B is more risky in terms of the variance, a result which is consistent with the expected utility solution to the same problem.

The importance of the E−V criterion stems from the fact that it can be derived from the expected utility rule. If we assume that returns are normally distributed so that the mean and the variance provide us with all of the relevant information about their distributions, all risk averters will reach their investment decisions according to the E−V rule.[8] Thus in many important cases the E−V rule can be substituted for the theoretically correct, but non-operational, expected utility analysis. Nevertheless, even when the returns are not normal, the E−V rule serves as an excellent approximation to the expected utility.[9]

VARIANCE OF *NPV* AS A MEASURE OF RISK

A firm can either discount the expected cash flows of a project by the cost of capital or its certainty equivalent by the riskless interest rate. We defer the discussion of the two methods to Chapter 10. Here we demonstrate how to calculate the mean and variance of a project's *NPV*.

Up to this point we have analyzed the problem of risky investment on the assumption that the element of time could be ignored. However, since capital budgeting typically deals with multiperiod investments, some of which constitute mutually exclusive alternatives, expected net present value must be substituted for expected profit as our measure of a project's profitability, and by analogy the variance of net present value is used as the risk indicator.

To simplify the analysis we assume investment projects involving an immediate cash outlay followed by positive net cash inflows in each of two subsequent years. Given this assumption, the expected *NPV* of an investment proposal is defined as the sum of the present values of the expected net cash flows in the first and second years, less the initial investment outlay:

$$NPV = \alpha x_1 + \alpha^2 x_2 - I_0, \text{ and}$$
$$E(NPV) = \alpha E(x_1) + \alpha^2 E(x_2) - I_0$$

8. The same result obtains if we assume a quadratic utility function. For further details of the utility foundations of mean-variance analysis, see Harry Markowitz, *Portfolio Selection*, Wiley, New York, 1959; and Haim Levy and Marshall Sarnat, *Portfolio and Investment Selection*, Prentice Hall International, London, 1984, chapter 7.

9. For the approximation of the E−V rule when distributions are not normal, see H. M. Markowitz and H. Levy 'Approximating Expected Utility by a Function of Mean−Variance,' *American Economic Review*, June 1979; and Y. Kroll, H. Levy, and H. Markowitz, 'Mean−Variance versus Direct Utility Maximization,' *Journal of Finance*, March 1984.

where:

$$E(x_1) = \text{expected value of the net cash flow in the first year}$$
$$E(x_2) = \text{expected value of the net cash flow in the second year}$$
$$I_0 = \text{initial investment outlay}$$
$$\alpha = 1/(1 + r) = \text{a coefficient for capitalizing cash flows over time, where } r$$
$$\text{denotes the riskless interest rate}$$
$$E(NPV) = \text{expected net present value}$$

For simplicity, let us assume that cash flows x_1 and x_2 are statistically independent. (When they are not independent the correlation should be incorporated, see summary table.) Given this:

$$\sigma_{NPV}^2 = \alpha^2 \sigma_1^2 + \alpha^2 \sigma_2^2$$

$$= \frac{\sigma_1^2}{(1 + r)^2} + \frac{\sigma_2^2}{(1 + r)^4}$$

where:

$$\sigma_1^2 = \text{variance of the cash flow distribution in year 1}$$
$$\sigma_2^2 = \text{variance of the cash flow distribution in year 2}$$
$$\sigma_{NPV}^2 = \text{variance of the } NPV$$

Given the assumption of statistical independence (correlation is zero), total variance of *NPV* is equal to the discounted sum of the annual variances. Thus the overall measure of risk depends on the *time-adjusted* risks incurred in each year, with the discounting of all annual risks to their present values serving to make the expected risks of more distant years comparable to those of earlier years. This can be illustrated by considering the following case of a firm confronted by two investment proposals, A and B, each having the same expected *NPV* but different time patterns of *nondiscounted* annual variances:

	σ_1^2	σ_2^2	σ_{NPV}^2
Project A	1	3	4
Project B	3	1	4

Clearly, with a positive discount factor project A is less risky since the greater variability occurs in the second period.

MEASURING RISK BY THE COEFFICIENT OF VARIATION

Occasionally, using the variance or standard deviation as an indicator of risk can be misleading. Clearly, the larger the variance of earnings, the larger the chance that the actual return will deviate significantly from the average or expected return. However, in some cases the expected profit of the proposal under consideration may be so large that the proposal should be considered relatively safe even if it has a large variance.

The expected profit and the standard deviation of two hypothetical investments are given in Table 9.3. As can be seen, the expected profit of project B is $500, i.e., significantly larger than the expected profit of investment A which is only $100. Can we, as a result, say with assurance that project B should be preferred to project A? If we examine the standard deviations of the two proposals, we note that although proposal B is the more profitable on average, it is also the more risky (its standard deviation is 25 as compared with a deviation of only 10 in project A). Thus, the mean–variance (or the mean–standard deviation) rule cannot discriminate between the two proposals, and therefore we cannot determine which proposal is preferable.

This simple example illustrates one of the major drawbacks of using the standard deviation or variance as a risk index. Intuitively we can say that most, if not all, investors will prefer proposal B even though the E–V rule does not indicate a clear-cut preference over A. And, as we shall see, this is one instance in which our intuition, rather than our arithmetic, should be relied upon. The reason is straightforward: project B's profitability is so high that it more than compensates for its greater risk (variability). For example, should the earnings of proposal B deviate by four standard deviations[10] to the left-hand side of its distribution (i.e., a very pessimistic result) and the profit of proposal A by four standard deviations to the right side (i.e., a very optimistic outcome), an individual would be better off with investment B. Even if this very unlikely combination of deviations should occur, the return on B would be still $400 ($500 - (4 \times 25)$) as compared with A's profit of only $140 ($100 + (4 \times 10)$).[11]

This simple numerical example is sufficient to show that in some cases the standard deviation (or variance) does not provide an appropriate measure of risk. In order to overcome these shortcomings, some writers have advocated that the *coefficient of variation*, defined as $c = \sigma/E$, be used instead of the standard deviation as the measure of an investment's risk. (The reader should note that the coefficient of variation is defined simply as the standard deviation divided (i.e., normalized) by the expected profit.) Indeed, if we replace the standard deviation by the coefficient of variation in our numerical example,

Table 9.3

	Expected profit	Standard deviation	Coefficient of variation (σ/E)
Investment A	100	10	0.10
Investment B	500	25	0.05

10. Note that the probability of such a large deviation is extremely small. For example, if the distribution is normal, the probability of such a deviation is only 0.003%.
11. A similar line of reasoning has been used by William J. Baumol in an attempt to develop an efficiency criterion which can replace the E–V rule. See his 'Expected Gain–Confidence Limit Criterion for Portfolio Selection,' *Management Science*, October 1963. See also Paul Halpern and Yehuda Kahane, 'A Pedagogical Note on Baumol's Gain–Confidence Limit Criterion for Portfolio Selection and the Probability of Ruin,' *Journal of Banking and Finance*, June 1980.

intuition is vindicated, and proposal B is clearly preferable to proposal A. Looking back at Table 9.3 we note that project B has both a *higher* expected profit and a *lower* coefficient of variation. Thus if we employ the expected return–coefficient of variation rule, it follows that an investor will be better off by choosing proposal B rather than proposal A.

Does the replacement of the standard deviation by the coefficient of variation overcome all the difficulties encountered in measuring risk? The answer is clearly no. Although the coefficient of variation can serve as a better measure of risk in some cases, [12] it by no means resolves *all* the problems relating to the meaning of risk. This contention is illustrated in Table 9.4 which sets out the relevant data for two alternative investments.

Again the E–V rule cannot distinguish between the two proposals; investment B is the more profitable but is also the more risky. Nor does the expected profit–coefficient of variation rule help resolve the issue; the coefficient of variation of project B is also larger than that of A (0.5 as compared with zero). Thus neither the expected profit–standard deviation criterion nor the expected profit–coefficient of variation criterion can choose between the two proposals, even though upon reflection common sense alone is sufficient to indicate that investment B is preferable to investment A. Every rational individual would choose project B rather than project A, because even the *worst* possible outcome of investment B ($5) is higher than the profit offered by alternative A ($2). Clearly the decision-maker must exercise considerable caution when using either of these two popular measures of investment risk, if paradoxical choices are to be avoided. In Appendix 9A we suggest a stochastic dominance rule which relies on the entire distribution of outcomes rather than just the

Table 9.4

	Investment A		Investment B	
	Profit	Probability	Profit	Probability
	2	1	5	0.5
			15	0.5
Expected profit (E)		2		10
Variance (σ^2)		0		25
Standard deviation		0		5
Coefficient of variation (σ/E)		0		1/2

The expected values of proposals A and B are given by $1 \times 2 = \$2$, and $(0.5 \times \$5) + (0.5 \times \$15) = \$10$ respectively. Similarly, the variance of the two proposals is given for A and B, respectively, by:

$$1(2 - 2)^2 = 0$$

and

$$0.5(5 - 10)^2 + 0.5(15 - 10)^2 = 25$$

12. For example, the coefficient of variation is the theoretically correct measure of risk if we assume a log-normal distribution of returns and risk-averse investors; see Haim Levy, 'Stochastic Dominance among Log-normal Prospects,' *International Economic Review*, October 1973.

mean and variance alone. Indeed, the stochastic dominance rule reveals the preference for investment B.

_____ **SENSITIVITY ANALYSIS**

Having clarified somewhat the underlying concepts of risk, we turn in this section to a pragmatic way of handling project risk. Probably the most common method of evaluating a project's risk in practice is *sensitivity analysis* in which the firm makes its best estimate of the revenues and costs involved in a project, calculates the project's *NPV* (or the *IRR* for that matter), and then checks the sensitivity of the *NPV* to possible estimation errors of the gross revenue and the various cost items.

For example, what will be the *NPV* of a project should the estimate of the annual revenue be overstated by 5% or 10%? If a small error proves critical, in the sense that the *NPV* becomes negative, the project is considered very risky since small estimation errors are very likely to occur. On the other hand, suppose that for errors in the range of 1%–15% the *NPV* remains positive. In this instance the *NPV* is relatively insensitive to errors in the estimate of future cash flows and therefore the project will be considered to have low risk. Even if one overestimates the revenue by as much as 14%, the project's *NPV* is still positive.

A numerical example
To illustrate the way that sensitivity analysis is carried out with a numerical example, consider a project with zero initial outlay (e.g., renting or leasing a machine). The annual gross revenue and costs are set out in Table 9.5.

Let us further assume that the proposal's economic duration is ten years ($n = 10$) and the cost of capital is 10% ($k = 0.1$). Hence, the firm's best estimate of the project's *NPV* is:

$$NPV = \sum_{t=1}^{10} \frac{13.2}{(1+0.1)^t} = (13.2)(6.145) \approx 81.114 \text{ million}$$

(Recall that in the specific case, $I_0 = 0$; hence $NPV = PV$.)

Table 9.5 Best estimate of future annual cash flows ($ million)

Gross revenue, *Rev*	100.0
Costs:	
Labor, C_1	10.0
Energy, C_2	60.0
Materials, C_3	5.0
Other, C_4	5.0
Total annual costs, ΣC_i	80.0
Annual income (before tax)	20.0
Tax (at 34%)	6.8
Net annual income	13.2

The *NPV* can be written in general form as follows:

$$NPV = \sum_{t=1}^{n} \frac{(1 - T_c)Rev}{(1 + k)^t} - \sum_{t=1}^{n} \frac{(1 - T_c)C_1}{(1 + k)^t} - \sum_{t=1}^{n} \frac{(1 - T_c)C_2}{(1 + k)^t} - \sum_{t=1}^{n} \frac{(1 - T_c)C_3}{(1 + k)^t}$$

$$- \sum_{t=1}^{n} \frac{(1 - T_c)C_4}{(1 + k)^t}$$

The advantage of this decomposition is that the firm can examine the sensitivity of the *NPV* to changes in revenue or in each of the cost components. For example, suppose that there is an error of $\alpha\%$ in the estimate of the revenue (*Rev*) but there is no change in any of the other components. We obtain a new estimate of the project's net present value, NPV_α, which is given by:

$$NPV_\alpha = NPV + (1 - T_c) \sum_{t=1}^{n} \frac{\alpha Rev}{(1 + k)^t}$$

If $\alpha > 0$, $NPV_\alpha > NPV$ and if $\alpha < 0$, $NPV_\alpha < NPV$. In a similar manner, the sensitivity of the project's profitability to errors in the estimates of each of the cost components can be examined.

Table 9.6 presents the results of the sensitivity analysis. The table gives the new *NPV*, i.e., *NPV* after a change of $\alpha\%$ has been made in one of the various components. For example, if the revenue is reduced by 10% ($\alpha = -10\%$) then the *NPV* drops from \$81.114 million to \$40.557 million. However, an increase in energy costs (C_2) by 10% decreases the *NPV* from \$81.114 to \$56.779.

An examination of the sensitivity matrix permits the firm to reach a number of conclusions relating to the project's riskiness:

1. Even if the gross revenue is overestimated by as much as 20%, the NPV_α is still positive.
2. The price of energy may go up in the future, but as long as the price rise is 33% or less, the project remains profitable.

Table 9.6 Sensitivity analysis of hypothetical project (\$ million)

Estimation error α	Revenue *Rev*	Labor cost C_1	Energy cost C_2	Material cost C_3	Other costs C_4
-50%	-121.671	101.393	202.785	91.253	91.253
-40%	-81.114	105.448	178.451	89.225	89.225
-30%	-40.557	93.281	154.117	87.198	87.198
-20%	0.0	89.225	129.782	85.170	85.170
-10%	40.557	85.170	105.448	83.142	83.142
0	81.114	81.114	81.114	81.114	81.114
$+10\%$	121.671	77.058	56.780	79.086	79.086
$+20\%$	162.228	73.003	29.496	77.058	77.058
$+30\%$	202.785	68.947	8.111	75.030	75.030
$+40\%$	243.342	64.891	-16.223	73.003	73.003
$+50\%$	283.899	60.836	-40.557	70.974	70.974

$$NPV = \sum_{t=1}^{10} \frac{13.2}{(1 + 0.1)^t} = \$81.114 \text{ million}$$

3. The project's desirability is not seriously affected by the other cost components.

Since NPV_α is a linear function of α, one can write for example:

$$NPV_\alpha = NPV + \alpha(1 - T_c) \sum_{t=1}^{n} \frac{Rev}{(1+k)^t}$$

Further, as the after-tax present value of revenue is constant (for any given initial *Rev*), we can simply write:

$$NPV_\alpha = NPV + b\alpha$$

where:

$$b \equiv (1 - T_c) \sum_{t=1}^{n} \frac{Rev}{(1+k)^t}$$

In the same way, each of the cost components can be set out as a linear equation. This allows us to present the sensitivity analysis in a simple diagram.

Figure 9.1 summarizes the sensitivity of the project to changes in revenue

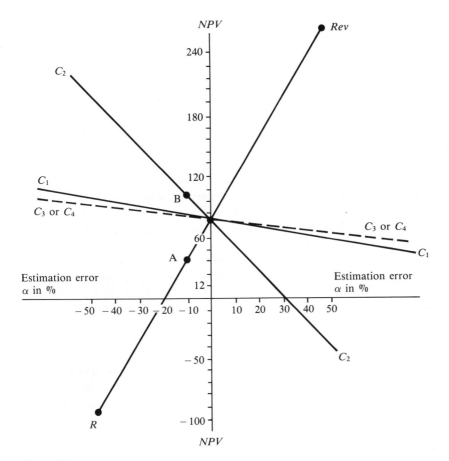

Figure 9.1

(*Rev*) as well as to each of the cost components. It is clear from the diagram that changes in each of the cost components of C_1, C_3, and C_4 have only a minor impact on the project's *NPV*. (The straight lines corresponding to these cost items are relatively flat.) On the other hand, lines for *Rev* and C_2 are relatively steep, and here the firm would be well advised to take greater pains when predicting these two items. An error here could mean serious losses.

The linear property of the sensitivity relationship has two principal advantages: (a) by extending the lines, the firm can consider all levels of α up to any α which it considers to be relevant without additional calculation; (b) errors in various components can be combined. For example, suppose that the sales are overestimated by 10%, but if the firm sells less, it also consumes about 10% less energy. Thus, a reduction of 10% in *Rev* decreases the *NPV* from about $81 million to about $40 million (point A), but the parallel reduction in energy costs (C_2) increases the *NPV* from $81 million to about $105 million (point B). The net effect of the reduction in revenue, therefore, would be a decrease in the *NPV* of about $14 million, and so the project would remain profitable, i.e., its *NPV* is still positive.

ELECTRONIC SPREADSHEETS

For illustrative purposes, we have assumed very simple relationships among the various items in the above sensitivity analysis. For example, if revenue or a cost item changes in one year, it changes in all years, i.e., all cash flows are of the equal-annual variety. The availability of microcomputers and finance-related software packages makes such simplification unnecessary. Electronic spreadsheets are offered by a wide variety of companies under different names and with somewhat differing features.

If we try to conduct a more complex sensitivity analysis in the traditional way, it is useful to work with a large sheet of paper, a pencil and a good eraser. You would then divide the sheet up into, say, ten columns, one column for each year, or you could divide the sheet into yearly columns for the next twenty years, or even into fifty-two weekly columns (provided wide enough paper can be found). Across the top of this sheet the appropriate heading for each column (1995, 1996, etc.) would be written. Each line would also be labeled, e.g., revenue, labor costs, energy costs, etc. Thus a 'matrix' is created into which the estimates can be entered. The real work starts now: what happens to *NPV* if revenue remains stable for two years, and then is expected to rise by 10% per year after that? Or what happens if energy costs fall by 10% a year? In the pre-electronic age, the eraser would now come into use. The old figure would be taken out, new figures would be entered and the results computed. This can be quite tedious and very, very smudgy, especially if many changes need to be made, possibly simultaneously. And remember, it is good management practice to consider and try out as many realistic options as possible.

Electronic spreadsheets operate on the same principle: namely a matrix is created on the computer into which figures (and text) can be entered, and then altered; however, the results are now recomputed almost instantly, and without any effort on the manager's part. In our example, its use permits an easy simulation of a large variety of assumptions relating to revenues and costs. In particular, there is no longer any need to make the simplifying assumptions regarding the manner in which costs and revenues can change. Moreover, the revenue and cost items can be broken down into as many subdivisions as management deems desirable.

_____ SUMMARY

This chapter has examined the popular mean–variance (E–V) rule for reaching investment decisions. When returns can be assumed to be normally distributed the mean–variance analysis provides a decision rule which is compatible with the maximization of expected utility. Moreover, in many cases the E–V rule serves as an excellent approximation to expected utility, even when the distributions are not normal.

Despite its widespread use, the variance does not always provide a meaningful definition of risk; as a result, decision-makers must still exercise considerable caution when using this popular measure of investment risk, if decision errors are to be avoided. In cases where returns are not normally distributed, decisions can be improved by considering the entire cumulative probability distribution. Two decision criteria, based on the total distribution, are spelled out in Appendix 9A.

Despite these limitations, the variance of returns is still by far the most popular and convenient measure of investment risk. Although in some situations more appropriate risk indexes than the variability of returns can be found, there is no other *operational* risk indicator which in general is better than the variance of the returns. In many important cases the variance is the best possible measure of risk, while in other cases it can usefully serve as a proxy for the risk inherent in an investment. In both instances, the risk-averse entrepreneur will seek an investment strategy which will stabilize his returns, i.e., which will minimize the variance of returns, for a given expected profit. However, in practice a great many firms try to solve some of the riskiness of projects by applying sensitivity analysis to the major components of the cash flow.

_____ SUMMARY TABLE

The characteristics of the random variable

If the return which we denote by x is a random variable, then:

1. Expected return:

$$E(x) = \sum_{i=1}^{n} Pr_i x_i$$

2. Variance:

$$\sigma^2(x) = \sum_{i=1}^{n} Pr_i(x_i - E(x))^2$$

3. Standard deviation:

$$\sigma(x) = \sqrt{\sigma_x^2}$$

4. Coefficient of variation:

$$c = \sigma/E$$

5. Cumulative probability:

$$F(x) = Pr(X \leqslant x)$$

Expected *NPV* and the variance of *NPV* of a two-year project

1. Expected *NPV*:

$$E(NPV) = \alpha E(x_1) + \alpha^2 E(x_2) - I_0$$

2. Variance of *NPV*:

$$\text{Var}(NPV) = \alpha^2 \sigma_1^2 + \alpha^4 \sigma_2^2 + 2\alpha^3 R(x_1, x_2)\sigma_1 \sigma_2$$

where $\alpha = 1/(1 + r)$, $r =$ the riskless interest rate, and the coefficient of correlation is given by:

$$R(x_1, x_2) = \text{Cov}(x_1, x_2)/\sigma_1 \sigma_2$$

Selecting among risky projects

1. By the E−V criterion: choose x if $E(x) \geqslant E(y)$, $\sigma(x)^2 \leqslant \sigma(y)^2$
2. By the E−C criterion: choose x if $E(x) \geqslant E(y)$, $\sigma(x)/E(x) \leqslant \sigma(y)/E(y)$.

To avoid trivial cases we require at least one inequality in (1) and (2) above.

3. By FSD and SSD criteria (see Appendix 9A).

QUESTIONS AND PROBLEMS

9.1   Consider the following two investments:

Investment A		Investment B	
Return ($)	Probability	Return ($)	Probability
500	1/8	800	1/8
1,000	3/4	1,000	3/4
1,500	1/8	1,200	1/8

(a) Calculate the expected return of each investment.
(b) Calculate the variance and the standard deviation of each.
(c) Which investment would you prefer using the mean–variance rule?

9.2 Examine the following two investment proposals, each with an initial investment of $5,000. The net cash flow of the proposals is as follows:

	Project A				Project B		
	Year 1		Year 2		Year 1		Year 2
Prob.	Cash flow ($)	Prob.	Cash flow ($)	Prob.	Cash flow ($)	Prob.	Cash flow ($)
1/10	2,000	1/3	2,000	1/3	2,000	1/10	2,000
8/10	3,000	1/3	3,000	1/3	3,000	8/10	3,000
1/10	4,000	1/3	4,000	1/3	4,000	1/10	4,000

Assume that in each project the net cash flow in the second year is statistically independent of the first year's outcome.

(a) Calculate each project's expected net present value and variance of *NPV*, assuming a discount rate of 8%.
(b) Which project do you prefer? Explain.

9.3 The Nelson Company is considering selling one of its machines. The selling price of the machine is dependent on the results of a public tender, the possible outcomes of which, after taxes, are:

$14,700 with a probability of 0.1
$ 8,000 with a probability of 0.8
$ 4,300 with a probability of 0.1

The alternative is to use the machine in the company. The cash flows generated by the machine are not known with certainty, and are listed below on an after-tax basis:

Year 1		Year 2	
Cash flow ($)	Probability	Cash flow ($)	Probability
3,500	0.4	3,000	0.5
6,000	0.6	5,000	0.25
		9,000	0.25

(Note that if the company sells the machine, it receives the money at once. Note also that once the company submits a formal offer to sell, it cannot change its mind.) Assuming an after-tax discount rate of 6%:

(a) Calculate each alternative's expected net present value and variance of *NPV*.
(b) Which alternative is preferable according to the mean–variance criterion?
(c) Assume now that the after-tax cost of capital rises to 8%. Will the firm choose to sell the machine? Briefly explain your results.

9.4 'Risk deferment always pays.' Evaluate this statement.

9.5 Express the expected value, the variance and the standard deviation of a variable y, in terms of x on the assumption that $y = a + by$.

9.6 The Multiplier Investment Company can invest in one of two mutually exclusive projects. The two proposals have the following probability distributions of net present value:

Project C		Project D	
Probability	*NPV* ($)	Probability	*NPV* ($)
8/25	3,000	2/25	800
9/25	5,000	21/25	4,800
8/25	7,000	2/25	8,800

(a) Which project will be chosen according to the mean–variance rule?
(b) Which project will be preferred according to the expected return–coefficient of variation rule?

9.7 Consider the following investments:

Investment A		Investment B	
NPV ($)	Probability	*NPV* ($)	Probability
700	2/9	1,700	1/2
1,000	5/9	2,300	1/2
1,300	2/9		

(a) Which alternative will be preferred according to the mean–variance criterion?
(b) Which alternative will be preferred according to the expected return coefficient of variation rule?
(c) According to your intuition, which alternative would be preferred by most investors? Explain.

9.8 A project's economic life n is 10 years. The variance of the annual cash flow is given by σ_t^2, $t = 1, 2, ..., 10$. It is known that there is zero correlation between the return of any pair of years, and that $\sigma_t = \sigma_0 = 1$ for all t. Assuming a risk-free annual interest rate of 10%, find the variance of the project's *NPV*.

9.9 A project's cash flow for two years is as follows:

First year	Second year	Joint probability
5	15	1/3
10	15	1/3
15	15	1/3

(a) Write down the general formula for the expected value and the variance of the *NPV* of the project.
(b) Using $r = 0.10$, calculate $E(NPV)$ and $\text{Var}(NPV)$. What is the interpretation of the results? (Hint: note that the covariance of the two years' cash flows is zero.)

9.10 How would you change your answer to question 9.9 if the cash flows in the two years are substitutes for each other?

9.11 The following one year project is considered by the firm.

Cash flow	Probability
-5	$1/4$
0	$1/4$
5	$1/4$
10	$1/4$

Calculate the expected net present value, the variance of the *NPV* and the coefficient of variation. Assume $r = 0.10$ and the initial investment is $I_0 = \$5$.

9.12 The firm estimates its gross revenue *Rev* to be equal to $200. The firm's cost of production is $C = \$100$. It is further known that C and *Rev* are perfectly correlated, namely each 1% change in *Rev* is accompanied by a 1% change in C, and the changes are in the same direction. Assume a cost of capital $k = 0.1$, a project life $n = 10$ years, and an initial investment $I_0 = \$200$. Draw a graph of the project's *NPV* when C and *Rev* change simultaneously. What will be the *NPV* if the production cost increases by 20%?

9.13 Suppose that you have the following income, X:

X	Probability
2	$1/2$
4	$1/2$

(a) Calculate the mean and variance of X.
(b) Now suppose that you have to pay taxes at a rate of 34% on your income from X such that your net income is $Y = (1 - 0.34)X$. Calculate the mean and variance of Y.
(c) Calculate the coefficient of variation of X and Y. Do you prefer the distribution of X or Y?

9.14 You invest in treasury bills which mature and give you $r = 6\%$ return on your investment at the end of the year. Calculate the mean, variance, and the coefficient of variation on your investment.

9.15 You have an initial wealth of $10 and are facing the following two options: (1) to buy a lottery ticket for $1 which gives you $0 with probability of 1/2 and $2 with probability of 1/2; or (2) not to purchase a lottery ticket at all.

(a) Calculate the mean and variance of the two options.
(b) According the E–V rule, which option do you prefer?
(c) Assume that you have a utility function $U(W) = W^{1/2}$. Calculate the expected utility of the two options. Is your result consistent with the E–V rule?

9.16 The variance of an investment is known to be equal to $\sigma_x^2 = 100$. Also, $\sum_{i=1}^{n} Pr_i x_i^2 = 100$. What is the mean return on this investment?

9.17 The rate of return on the S&P index and on treasury bills for the next year have the following distributions:

Treasury bills		S&P index	
Return	Probability	Return	Probability
6%	1	-10%	1/3
		0	1/3
		$+30\%$	1/3

Calculate the covariance of the return on these two investments.

9.18 You have the income streams from x and y with the following:

Correlation: $R_{xy} = +0.5$
Variance: $\sigma_x^2 = 1$
Variance: $\sigma_y^2 = 100$

What is the covariance between x and y?

9.19 It is given that the return on stock A is X with $\text{Var}(X) = 1$. Another stock yields a return $Y = -2X$. Calculate the standard deviation of Y.

9.20 The rate of return on stock A is given by X. The return on stock B is given by $Y = a + bX$. 'Then the correlation between X and Y must be $+1$.' Do you agree? Prove your result.

9.21 Suppose that you have a project with two-year cash flows, and the first and second year cash flows are perfectly negatively correlated, namely $R(X_1, X_2) = -1$. Also the variances of the cash flows in each year are equal $\sigma_1^2 = \sigma_2^2 = \sigma_0^2$

(a) Suppose that the discount rate is 0. Is it possible that the variance of the *NPV* will be 0?
(b) How do you change your answer to (a) above where the discount rate is positive but $\sigma_1^2 = \sigma_2^2 = \sigma_0^2$ still holds?
(c) How do you change your answer to (a) above where the discount rate is 0 but $\sigma_1^2 \neq \sigma_2^2$ where σ_i^2 ($i = 1, 2$) is the ith year cash flow's variance?

9.22 You have a project with a two-year cash flows where the correlation between the two years' cash flows is $R = 0$. The variance of the *NPV* is $\text{Var}(NPV) = 100$. The variance of each year cash flow is $\sigma_1^2 = \sigma_2^2 = 60$. Calculate the discount rate.

APPENDIX 9A: CUMULATIVE DISTRIBUTIONS AND RISK _____

As we noted in the text, if investment returns are normally distributed one can safely use the E–V rule as the decision criterion. Given this assumption, the expected profit and the variance of the profit provide us with all the required information regarding the distribution of outcomes. The E–V rule can also be used without imposing any restriction on the distributions of returns if we assume preferences are characterized by a quadratic utility function. In this case we have:

$$U(x) = x + \beta x^2 \quad \text{with} \quad U' = 1 + 2\beta x > 0 \quad \text{and} \quad U'' = 2\beta < 0$$

Assuming such a utility function, we have for two investments x and y:

$$EU(x) = E(x) + \beta E(x^2) = E(x) + \beta(E(x))^2 + \beta\sigma_x^2$$

and

$$EU(y) = E(y) + \beta(E(y))^2 + \beta\sigma_y^2$$

If x is better than y, then by the E–V rule we have:

$$E(x) > E(y)$$
$$\sigma_x < \sigma_y$$

It follows that in this case $EU(x) > EU(y)$ for *all* quadratic utility functions. To see this we employ the fact that for a quadratic function $\partial EU/\partial E > 0$ (based on the property that $U' > 0$) and $\partial EU/\partial\sigma^2 < 0$ (using the property $U'' < 0$). However, this utility function has its drawbacks. First, for all values of $x > -1/(2\beta)$ it declines, and second it is characterized by an increasing risk premium as wealth increases which is quite contrary to observed investor behavior. But these inadequacies of quadratic utility functions bring us back to the assumption that returns are distributed normally. However, in cases where the returns are not distributed normally, the mean–variance rule can often be misleading.

Recognition of such a possibility led Frederick Hillier and David Hertz to the conclusion that investment decision-making might be improved by examining the *entire* cumulative distribution of possible outcomes. [13] With the tools at their disposal, Hillier and Hertz succeeded in analyzing investment problems in which the cumulative distributions of alternative proposals do *not* intersect, but experienced considerable difficulty in interpreting their results when such intersections did occur. The purpose of this appendix is to extend their work by applying some relatively new techniques which permit us (in a number of important instances) to make an unambiguous choice among investment alternatives even if their cumulative distributions intersect. But first let us digress for a moment and refresh our memories regarding some of the basic properties of probability distributions.

The probability distribution and the cumulative distribution functions

The probability distribution provides information regarding the probability that a random variable will get some value x. We can use this information, in turn, to define the *cumulative distribution function*, or in short the *distribution function*, which sets out the probability that the random variable will attain a value smaller or equal to some x, that is $P_r(X \leqslant x)$. A common notation for the cumulative distribution is $F(x) = P_r(X \leqslant x)$. In this section we familiarize ourselves with the chief characteristics of this type of probability distribution which will then be used to study problems of investment choice.

An example
Assume the following probability distribution of net present value for a hypothetical

13. See F. S. Hillier, 'The Derivation of Probabilistic Information for the Evaluation of Risky Investments,' *Management Science*, April 1963, and David B. Hertz, 'Risk Analysis in Capital Investment,' *Harvard Business Review*, January/February 1964.

investment proposal:

Return ($x)	Probability $P_r(x)$
80	0.2
90	0.2
110	0.4
120	0.2

If we want to know the probability that the project's *NPV* will be 'smaller or equal' to any particular value, the answer can be derived from the following cumulative probability function:

$$F(x) = P_r(X \leqslant x) = \begin{cases} 0 & x < 80 \\ 0.2 & 80 \leqslant x < 90 \\ 0.4 & 90 \leqslant x < 110 \\ 0.8 & 110 \leqslant x < 120 \\ 1 & x \geqslant 120 \end{cases}$$

For example, if one wants to know the probability that the return will be smaller than (or equal to) $112.5 the appropriate interval ($110 \leqslant x < 120$) can be examined and a probability of 80% is the answer. Graphical representations of the probability distribution and the cumulative probability distribution are given in Figure 9A.1. The reader should note that this particular cumulative distribution is a 'step-function' which reflects the fact that we used an example of a *discrete* random variable. With respect to a continuous random variable, such as the normal distribution, the cumulative distribution rises continuously in a smooth (rather than stepwise) fashion.

Distribution free investment analysis

Now let us use the concept of a cumulative distribution to analyze investment choice.

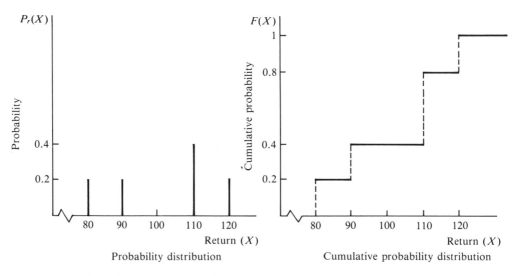

Probability distribution   Cumulative probability distribution

Figure 9A.1

Consider again the simple example given at the end of Chapter 9 in which investment A yields a profit of $2 with a probability of 1, while alternative B yields a profit of $5 with a probability of 1/2, or $15 with a probability of 1/2. As we have already pointed out, neither the E–V nor the mean coefficient of variation rules can distinguish between these two alternative investments, despite the fact that investment B is obviously preferable to A, since *all* possible outcomes of B exceed the outcome of A.

The superiority of investment B is easily demonstrated by examining the cumulative distributions of the two investments. In Figure 9A.2 the cumulative probability distribution of B lies to the right of that of investment A. In the simple case considered, in which the cumulative distributions do not intersect, a decision which is consistent with the expected utility rule can always be identified, without recourse to the shapes of individuals' utility functions, by applying the following general rule of *first degree stochastic dominance* (*FSD*) which is set out in terms of monetary outcomes and their probabilities and not in terms of utilities:[14]

> Any investment B is preferable to investment A if $F_B(x) \leqslant F_A(x)$, for all values of x (and a strict inequality holds for some value x), i.e., if the cumulative probability distribution of B lies to the right of that of A.

This is tantamount to the requirement that the two cumulative probability distributions do not intersect. This condition also means that the probability of receiving a return greater than or equal to some level x must always be *higher* in alternative B than in investment A. Since the chance of earning higher returns is always greater, investment B will be preferred by all investors.

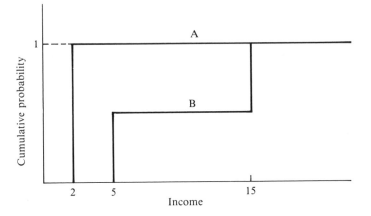

Figure 9A.2

14. For the derivation of this technique see J. P. Quirk and R. Saposnik, 'Admissibility and Measurable utility Functions,' *Review of Economic Studies*, February 1962; J. Hadar and W. R. Russell, 'Rules for Ordering Uncertain Products,' *American Economic Review*, March 1969, and G. Hanoch and H. Levy, 'The Efficiency Analysis of Choices Involving Risk,' *Review of Economic Studies*, July 1969. A detailed discussion of the implications of stochastic dominance for financial analysis is given in H. Levy and M. Sarnat, *Portfolio and Investment Selection: Theory and Practice*, Prentice Hall, London, 1984, chapter 6.

Some numerical examples

In order to demonstrate the simplicity of the stochastic dominance technique, let us examine a specific numerical example.

Example 1

Consider the two alternative investments A and B in Table 9A.1. A comparison of investments A and B clearly shows that investment B is preferable to investment A since investment B offers an equal probability of double the income. This is equivalent to confronting an individual with the choice of betting on either of two unbiased roulette wheels, one of which pays the winner double the amount of the other for the same wager. Clearly all rational persons would choose to play on the roulette wheel having the equal probability of the larger payoffs (represented by alternative B), since common sense alone suffices to tell us that this option is preferable. Despite this, the E–V rule cannot discriminate between the two options: investment A has both a higher expected return and a greater risk (variance).

Now let us check to see if the use of cumulative distributions can help to eliminate this anomaly. The cumulative probability distributions of both options are given in Table 9A.1 and these figures were used to construct Table 9A.2 which sets out the relevant data for *comparing* the cumulative probability functions of the two investments.

Table 9A.1

Investment A			Investment B		
Return (x)	Prob. (p)	Cum. prob.	Return (x)	Prob. (p)	Cum. prob. F_B
5	0.33	0.33	10	0.33	0.33
10	0.33	0.67	20	0.33	0.67
15	0.33	1	30	0.33	1

Table 9A.2

Income	Cumulative probability of investment A F_A	Cumulative probability of investment B F_B	F_A minus F_B
−5	0	0	0
0	0	0	0
5	0.33	0	0.33
7	0.33	0	0.33
10	0.67	0.33	0.33
12	0.67	0.33	0.33
15	1	0.33	0.67
17	1	0.33	0.67
20	1	0.67	0.33
22	1	0.67	0.33
25	1	0.67	0.33
28	1	0.67	0.33
30	1	1	0
35	1	1	0

The left-hand column includes all attainable returns from investments A and B, as well as several values of returns which are not attainable in either of the options.[15]

From the right-hand column of Table 9A.2 we can see that $F_A(x) - F_B(x) > 0$ for all levels of x; or alternatively we can write $F_A(X) \leqslant F_B(X)$. This result is shown in Figure 9A.3 which plots the cumulative probability functions for the two investments. The 'roulette wheel' with the smaller payoffs is denoted by B and the other alternative by A. Since the cumulative distribution of B lies to the right of A the first degree stochastic dominance criterion is fulfilled, and investment B (the roulette wheel with the larger payoff) is preferable to, i.e. dominates, investment A, independent of the shape of the utility function, which is as it should be.

Unfortunately the firm is not always confronted with simple choice situations which are characterized by nonintersecting cumulative distributions. In general, as Hillier and Hertz found, the distributions often intersect once or even a number of times. In such situations the decision is somewhat more complicated, but if we make the usual assumption of risk aversion, we can discriminate between projects in a number of important cases, even though their distributions do intersect, by applying the following risk-aversion criterion, or *second degree stochastic dominance* (*SSD*) as it is often called:

> Investment A is preferable to investment B for all risk-averters if the cumulative difference between F_B and F_A is non-negative over the entire domain of x.[16]

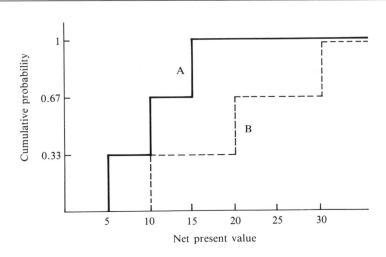

Figure 9A.3

15. The reader can verify that the cumulative probability distributions are not affected by considering the unattainable levels of return. In other words, the cumulative probability distribution of a discrete random variable is a step function, remaining constant for those values of x which have a zero probability and rising in jump fashion at those values of x for which probability is positive.
16. That is if the following condition holds: $\int_{-\infty}^{x} [F_B(t) - F_A(t)] \, dt \geqslant 0$ for all values of x, and a strict inequality holds for some value x_0. See Hadar and Russell, *op. cit.*, Hanoch and Levy, *op. cit.*, and Levy and Sarnat, *loc. cit.* If, in addition to risk aversion, we assume a decreasing absolute risk premium the third derivative will be non-negative. For this case Whitmore has derived a stochastic dominance rule which asserts that A is preferred over B if $E_A(X) \geqslant E_B(X)$ and in addition:

$$\int_{-\infty}^{x} \left(\int_{-\infty}^{v} [F_B(t) - F_A(t)] \, dt \right) dv \geqslant 0 \text{ for all values } x$$

See G. A. Whitmore, 'Third Degree Stochastic Dominance,' *American Economic Review*, 60, 1970, pp. 457–59.

If the risk-aversion criterion is fulfilled, the expected utility of project B is higher than the expected utility of project A (for all risk averters). Thus we can choose between the two alternatives in a manner which is consistent with expected utility theory, but *without* the need to know the detailed shape of the utility function beyond the realistic assumption of risk aversion. Hence such a rule is doubly blessed: it is consistent with the utility theory which underlies most of modern risk analysis while at the same time it provides a practical tool for actual decision analysis.

The meaning of this criterion can readily be visualized by considering the two investments A and B whose (continuous) cumulative probability distributions have been drawn in Figure 9A.4. According to the risk-aversion criterion, the cumulative probability distributions may intersect, but the cumulative difference between F_A and F_B must remain non-negative over the entire domain of X. In Figure 9A.4 the differences between the two distributions are marked with a plus sign where $F_A > F_B$ and with a minus sign where $F_B > F_A$. A glance at the diagram suffices to show that over the entire range of returns the cumulative area between the two distributions always remains positive. Hence the risk-aversion criterion is fulfilled and investment B *dominates* investment A for all risk averters. This is true since up to X_0 the distribution of A lies above that of B and therefore the area under A exceeds the area under B. And while it is true that between X_0 and X_1 distribution B lies above A, the preceding shaded area marked with a plus sign is larger than the area marked with a minus sign. Since beyond X_1, A again exceeds B, the *cumulative* shaded areas always exceed the areas marked with a minus sign over the entire range of X.

In order to clarify this investment rule, we now apply it to the specific numerical examples given in Table 9A.3. From this table we have computed the cumulative probability distributions for the two alternatives; these distributions are plotted in Figure 9A.5. Since the two distributions intersect, options A and B do *not* dominate each other by the first degree stochastic dominance criterion. But if we invoke the risk-aversion criterion, investment B is clearly preferable to investment A: it is clear by inspection that the cumulative shaded area under A is always greater than the cumulative area under B.

Of course, it may not always be an easy matter to verify the dominance of one investment over another by inspection, especially in cases where the probability distributions intersect a number of times. In such instances the area under the cumulative probability

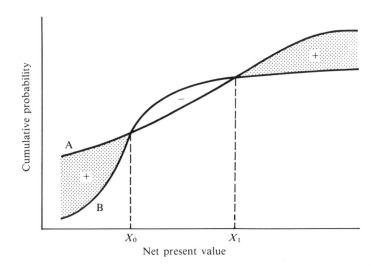

Figure 9A.4

Table 9A.3

Investment B			Investment A		
Return	Prob.	Cum. prob.	Return	Prob.	Cum. prob.
1	0.25	0.25	1/2	0.1875	0.1875
2	0.25	0.50	3/2	0.1875	0.375
			5/2	0.2500	0.625
9	0.25	0.75	7/2	0.1875	0.8125
10	0.25	1.00	9/2	0.1875	1.00

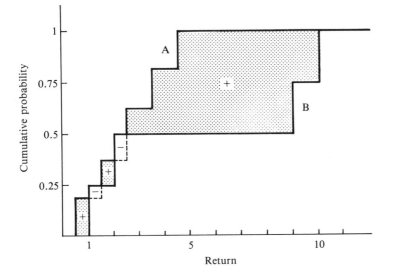

Figure 9A.5

distributions can be calculated by hand, or a simple computer program can be utilized for screening the projects by this choice criterion.

_____ QUESTIONS AND PROBLEMS

9A.1 A publisher tries to estimate the sales of a new book in the current month relying on the sales figures during the preceding month. He expects that the sales will have the following distribution:

Probability $P_r(X_2)$	Number of copies which will be sold in the current month X_2
1/10	$X_1 - 1,000$
2/10	$X_1 - 500$
4/10	X_1
2/10	$X_1 + 500$
1/10	$X_1 + 1,000$

where X_1 denotes the quantity of copies of the book sold during the preceding month.

(a) Calculate the expected number of copies, $E(X_2)$, which will be sold in the current month.
(b) Calculate the variance of X_2.
(c) Calculate the cumulative probability function of X_2, assuming that $X_1 = 1,500$. (Graph your results.)
(d) Use the cumulative probability function you calculated in (c) to find the probability that X_2 will be smaller or equal to 1,600.

9A.2 (a) Define the first degree stochastic dominance (FSD) criterion.
(b) Consider the following two investment options:

Option A		Option B	
Probability	Return	Probability	Return
2/5	10	1/5	5
1/5	15	2/5	10
2/5	30	1/5	15
		1/5	30

Which option is preferable by the first degree stochastic dominance criterion? Prove your answer graphically.

9A.3 Consider the following two investment options:

Option C		Option D	
Probability	Return	Probability	Return
1/8	10	1/8	5
2/8	15	1/8	8
1/8	20	1/8	15
3/8	30	2/8	22
1/8	35	3/8	25

Which option is preferable by the FSD criterion? Prove your answer graphically.

9A.4 Consider the following two investment options:

Option A		Option B	
Probability	Return	Probability	Return
2/10	4	3/10	8
3/10	12	4/10	18
5/10	26	3/10	30

Which option is preferable by the risk-aversion criterion? Prove your answer graphically.

9A.5 'If investment A is preferable to investment B by the FSD rule then necessarily A is preferable to B by the risk-aversion criterion.' Appraise this statement.

9A.6 Consider the following two investment options:

Option C		Option D	
Probability	Return	Probability	Return
1/2	10	1	15
1/2	20		

(a) Which option is preferable by the FSD criterion?
(b) Which option is preferable by the risk-aversion criterion? Prove your answer graphically.
(c) Is your approach to part (b) consistent with the expected utility approach?

SELECTED REFERENCES

Aharony, Joseph and Loeb, Martin, 'Mean–Variance vs. Stochastic Dominance: Some Empirical Findings on Efficient Sets,' *Journal of Banking on Finance*, June 1977.

Ali, M. M., 'Stochastic Dominance and Portfolio Analysis,' *Journal of Financial Economics*, June 1975.

Arditti, Fred D., 'Risk and the Required Return on Equity,' *Journal of Finance*, March 1967.

Bawa, Vijay S., Bodurtha, James N., Jr, Rao, M. R., and Suri, Hira L., 'On Determination of Stochastic Dominance Optimal Sets,' *Journal of Finance*, June 1985.

Ben-Horim, M. and Levy, H., *Statistics: Decisions and Applications in Business on Economics*, New York: Random House, 1981.

Balachandran, B. V., Nagarajan, A. J., and Rappaport, A., 'Threshold Margins for Creating Economic Value,' *Financial Management*, Spring 1986.

Clarke, Richard N., 'Certainty Equivalence and the Theory of the Firm under Uncertainty,' *International Economic Review*, June 1985.

Cooley, P. L., Roenfeldt, R. L., and Modani, N. K., 'Interdependence of Market Risk Measures,' *Journal of Business*, July 1977.

Cooper, D. F. and Chapman, C. B., *Risk Analysis for Large Projects: Models, Methods and Cases*, New York: Wiley, 1987.

Darvish, Tikva and Eckstein, Shlomo, 'A Model of Simultaneous Sensitivity Analysis of Projects,' *Applied Economics*, January 1988.

DeJong, Douglas and Collins, Daniel W., 'Explanations for the Instability of Equity Beta: Risk-free Rate Changes and Leverage Effects,' *Journal of Financial and Quantitative Analysis*, March 1985.

Dybvig, H. and Ingersoll, J. E. Jr, 'Mean–Variance Theory in Complete Markets,' *Journal of Business*, April 1982.

Ehrhardt, M. C., 'A Mean–Variance Derivation of a Multi-factor Equilibrium Model,' *Journal of Financial and Quantitative Analysis*, June 1987.

Fisher, Lawrence and Kamin, Jules H., 'Forecasting Systematic Risk: Estimates of "Raw" Beta that Take Account of the Tendency of Beta to Change and the Heteroskedasticity of Residual Returns,' *Journal of Financial and Quantitative Analysis*, June 1985.

Gehr, A. K. Jr, 'Risk and Return,' *Journal of Finance*, September 1979.

Gilmer, R. H. Jr., 'Risk and Return: A Question of Holding Period,' *Journal of Economics and Business*, May 1988.

Huang, C. C., Vertinsky, I. and Ziemba, W. T., 'On Multiperiod Stochastic Dominance,' *Journal of Financial and Quantitative Analysis*, March 1978.

Huberman, K. G. and Kandel, S., 'Mean–Variance Spanning,' *Journal of Finance*, September 1987.

Jarrow, Robert, 'The Relationship between Arbitrage and First Order Stochastic Dominance,' *Journal of Finance*, September 1986.

Jean, William H. and Helms, Billy P., 'Stochastic Dominance as a Decision Model,' *Quarterly Journal of Business and Economics*, Winter 1986.

Johnson, K. H. and Burgess, R. C., 'The Effects of Sample Sizes on the Accuracy of EV and SSD Efficiency Criteria,' *Journal of Financial and Quantitative Analysis*, December 1975.

Kandel, Samuel and Stambaugh, Robert F., 'On Correlations and Inferences about Mean–Variance Efficiency,' *Journal of Financial Economics*, March 1987.

Kearns, R. B. and Burgess, R. C., 'An Effective Algorithm for Estimating Stochastic Dominance Efficient Sets,' *Journal of Financial and Quantitative Analysis*, September 1979.

Kim, S.-H. and Elsai, H. H., 'Estimation of Periodic Standard Deviations under the PERT and Derivation of Probabilistic Information,' *Journal of Business, Finance and Accounting*, Winter 1988.

Kon, Stanley J., 'Models of Stock Returns – A Comparison,' *Journal of Finance*, March 1984.

Kroll, Y., Levy, H., and Markowitz, H. M., 'Mean–Variance versus Direct Utility Maximization,' *Journal of Finance*, March 1984.

Kryzanowski, Lawrence and Chau To, Minh, 'The E–V Stationarity of Security Returns: Some Empirical Evidence,' *Journal of Banking and Finance*, March 1987.

Lehmann, B. N., 'Orthogonal Frontiers and Alternative Mean–Variance Efficiency Tests,' *Journal of Finance*, July 1987.

Levy, H., 'Stochastic Dominance among Log-normal Prospects,' *International Economic Review*, October 1973.

Levy, H., 'Two-moment Decision Models and Expected Utility Maximization,' *American Economic Review*, 1989.

Levy, H. and Kroll, Y., 'Ordering Uncertain Options with Borrowing and Lending,' *Journal of Finance*, May 1978.

Levy, H. and Markowitz, H. M., 'Approximating Expected Utility by a Function of Mean and Variance,' *American Economic Review*, June 1979.

Markowitz, Harry M., *Mean–Variance Analysis in Portfolio Choice and Capital Markets*, Oxford: Blackwell, 1987.

McEnally, R. W. and Upton, D. E., 'A Re-examination of the Ex Post Risk Return Tradeoff on Common Stocks,' *Journal of Financial and Quantitative Analysis*, June 1979.

Meyer, J., 'Further Applications of Stochastic Dominance to Mutual Fund Performance,' *Journal of Financial and Quantitative Analysis*, June 1977.

Modigliani, Franco and Pogue, Gerald A., 'An Introduction to Risk and Return,' *Financial Analysts Journal*, March/April 1974; part II, May/June 1974.

Murphy, Joseph E. Jr and Osborne, M. F. M., 'Games of Chance and the Probability of Corporate Profit or Loss,' *Financial Management*, Summer 1979.

Myers, Stewart and Ruback, Richard, *Discounting Rules for Risky Assets*, Cambridge: N.B.E.R., 1987.

Porter, R. B., Bey, R. P., and Lewis, D. C., 'The Development of a Mean–Semivariance Approach to Capital Budgeting,' *Journal of Financial and Quantitative Analysis*, November 1975.

Pratt, J. W. and Hammond, J. S. III, 'Evaluating and Comparing Projects: Simple Detection of False Alarms,' *Journal of Finance*, December 1979.

Reichenstein, William, 'On Standard Deviation and Risk,' *The Journal of Portfolio Management*, Winter, 1987.

Sarnat, M., 'On the Use of Risk Analysis for the Evaluation of Industrial R&D Expenditures,' *Managerial and Decision Economics*, September 1987.

Saunders, A., Ward, C., and Woodward, R., 'Stochastic Dominance and the Performance of the UK Unit Trusts,' *Journal of Financial and Quantitative Analysis*, June 1980.

Scott, Robert C. and Horvath, Philip, A., 'On the Direction of Preference for Moments of Higher Order than the Variance,' *Journal of Finance*, September 1980.

Shanken, Jay, 'On the Exclusion of Assets from Tests of the Mean–Variance Efficiency of the Market Portfolio: An Extension,' *The Journal of Finance*, June 1986.

Stein, W. E., Pfafenberger, R. C. and French, D. W., 'Sampling Error in First Order Stochastic Dominance,' *Journal of Financial Research*, Fall 1987.

Tehranian, H., 'Empirical Studies in Portfolio Performance Using Higher Degrees of Stochastic Dominance,' *Journal of Finance*, March 1980.

Tew, Bernard and Reid, Donald, 'More Evidence on Expected Value–Variance Analysis versus Direct Utility Maximization,' *Journal of Financial Research*, Fall 1987.

Vickson, R. C. and Altmann, M., 'On the Relative Effectiveness of Stochastic Dominance Rules: Extension to Decreasingly Risk-averse Utility Functions,' *Journal of Financial and Quantitative Analysis*, March 1977.

Wachowicz, John M. Jr and Shrieves, Ronald E., 'An Argument for "Generalized" Mean–Coefficient or Variation Analysis,' *Financial Management*, Winter 1980.

Whitmore, G. A., 'The Theory of Skewness Preference,' *Journal of Business Administration*, Spring 1975.

Whitmore, G. A., 'Third Degree Stochastic Dominance,' *American Economic Review*, 60, 1970.

10

Applications of Risk Analysis

ARTICLE 15

Managing

...Moreover, the equity attributable to a particular business should be adjusted to reflect the fact that some activities within a firm are riskier than others. And because risks change – frequently and sometimes significantly in the case of trading sophisticated financial instruments – the equity ideally ought to be reallocated almost constantly, rather than, as is the current practice, once a quarter or once a year or not at all. According to Charles Bralver of Oliver Wyman & Co., a consultant to the banking and securities industries, some Wall Street firms implicitly factor in this flux when measuring the performance of individual business units, but few do so explicitly or consistently.

'Important: Open only when Merrill Lynch makes our ROE goal. Don't hold your breath.'

The consensus is that Morgan Stanley and Merrill Lynch manage measurement issues better than most other firms do. Merrill Lynch's standards for judging performance reflect an unusual devotion to weighing the relative risks inherent in different businesses. The company regularly analyzes its reasonable worst-case exposure to loss in about 60 different activities, including those like interest rate swaps that require off-balance-sheet capital commitments.

The firm sees to it that the business unit has enough capital to survive such a loss, increasing (or decreasing) the equity account as necessary. Individual units are expected to aim for the same 15% after-tax return on this 'risk-adjusted' equity. By putting all units on the same footing, Merrill can compare the performances of different businesses more efficiently.

Source: *Fortune*, April 6, 1992, p. 72.

As shown in article 15, Merrill Lynch is active in about sixty activities which are characterized by different levels of risk. Each individual unit is expected to earn a 15% risk-adjusted return on equity. What is meant by 'risk-adjusted' return on equity? Should the cash flows be adjusted for risk, or should the discount rate used in calculating the *NPV* of the investment be increased? In this chapter we show that risk can be considered either in the cash flows (numerator of our *NPV* calculation), or in the discount rate (denominator of our *NPV* calculation). In particular, if Merrill Lynch has one very risky and one very safe activity, should both projects be discounted at the same discount rate? The answer is, of course, no – the adjustment for risk should be made to each project before they are compared, just as Merrill Lynch claims in the article. In addition, while risk is a function of the activities of the individual units, it is also a function of the way the activities are financed.

To this point we have focused attention on the *principles* of risk measurement in an attempt to determine the fundamental properties of some of the better-known risk indices and decision rules. With the theoretical background to build upon, let us turn now to the no less important problems concerning the use of risk analysis in practice.

This chapter is devoted to the practical application of risk analysis. Two *indirect* methods for adjusting the *NPV* calculation for risk are discussed:

1. The *certainty equivalent method*.
2. The *adjusted discount method*, which is a popular rule of thumb used by many firms.

After showing that the rule-of-thumb method is equivalent to the more sophisticated techniques based on the discounting of certainty-equivalent cash flows, the remainder of the chapter is devoted to two practical applications of *direct* adjustments for risk for those firms which are able to estimate the probability distributions of individual projects:

1. Simulation analysis.
2. Decision trees.

INDIRECT ADJUSTMENT FOR RISK

In the preceding chapter it was implicitly assumed that each investment project could be characterized by two indices: one which measures the investment's profitability and a second which reflects its risk. This type of approach is a *direct method* of incorporating risk into the decision-making process since we attempt to measure directly the risk of each investment proposal or combination of proposals. One example of such an approach is the E–V (expected *NPV*–variance of *NPV*) rule.

An alternative way to incorporate risk into the decision-making procedure is to include it *indirectly* in the discount rate used in calculating the *NPV*. In this type of approach we characterize each project by a *single* indicator of investment worth, i.e., its 'risk-adjusted' net present value. Thus the measure of attractiveness, in this instance the project's *NPV*, contains an indirect or implicit factor which reflects the project's risk, and no attempt is made explicitly to express the risk of each proposal or portfolio of proposals.

In order to isolate the theoretical properties of the rule of thumb adjustment of the discount rate, we first set out an alternative theoretical method for adjusting a project's cash flow for risk, based on the expected utility principle.

This 'certainty-equivalent' method will then be used as a benchmark for evaluating the popular rules of thumb.

Certainty-equivalent method

Suppose that an investor is offered the following future net receipt: $5 with a probability of 0.5 and $15 with a probability of 0.5. What is the present value of his return? One way to answer this question is to find the *certainty equivalent* amount of this probability distribution. In principle, the certainty equivalent depends on the investor's preferences, i.e., on his utility function. Let us assume that point E of Figure 10.1 represents the distribution's expected utility to our hypothetical investor. Note that point E is simply the weighted average of the utility of the two possible outcomes ($0.5U(5) + 0.5U(15)$) and, as discussed in Chapter 9, is given by the intersection of the vertical line rising from $10 (which is the expected monetary return) with the chord connecting the two alternative outcomes on the utility function.

Now, suppose that we offer the investor a *perfectly certain* sum of money instead of the uncertain distribution. What is the amount of money which must be offered to ensure that the investor will be indifferent between the risky and perfectly certain alternatives? As explained in Chapter 9, the answer is: that sum which provides the *same level of utility*, i.e., $8 in the example given in Figure 10.1. Hence, $8 is the *certainty-equivalent* of a risky distribution which offers an equal probability of receiving $5 or $15.

Now, what is the present value of this risky prospect? Since, as we have just seen, the certainty equivalent of the distribution is $8, its present value will be $8/(1 + r)$, where r denotes the *riskless* interest rate. We discount the cash flow using the riskless interest rate, because we first reduced the cash flow (i.e., the

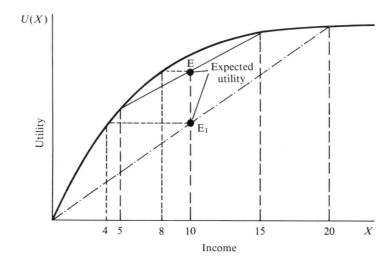

Figure 10.1

numerator of the equation) to its certainty equivalent (refer to the discussion of certainty equivalence in Chapter 9).

An example
Another example may help clarify this line of reasoning. Suppose that the initial outlay of a given investment proposal is $50 and that its net annual cash flow for the next twenty years is $5 with a probability of 0.5 and $15 with a probability of 0.5. Hence, the certainty equivalent of the annual cash receipt again is $8. Assuming a riskless interest rate of 5%, the proposal's risk-adjusted net present value is:

$$\$8 \times 12.462 - \$50 = \$99.70 - \$50 = \$49.70$$

where 12.462 is the appropriate present value interest factor of an annuity for twenty periods at 5%, given in the present value table used in Chapter 3.

Note that the *expected* annual cash flow is:

$$(0.5 \times 5) + (0.5 \times 15) = \$10$$

Thus, the proposal's *expected* net present value is given by:

$$10 \times 12.462 - 50 = \$74.62$$

which is higher than the *risk-adjusted* net present value ($49.70). The difference can be interpreted as follows. The *NPV* of $74.62 is *not* adjusted for risk and therefore only measures the proposal's expected profitability; the previous calculation of $49.70 measures the net present value *adjusted for risk*. It follows that the *difference* between $74.62 and $49.70 measures the 'value' of the risk inherent in the investment in question. In principle, the investor (or firm) would be willing to pay $24.92 to induce an insurance company to underwrite, and thus assume, this risk.

The higher the variability of the future outcomes, the greater the risk, and therefore we would expect the risk-adjusted *NPV* to decline even further as variability increased. For example, suppose we replace the previous distribution by an equal probability of earning $20 or nothing. The average annual cash flow remains $10 as before, but the variability (variance) of the possible outcomes is increased considerably. This new proposal is represented by the dot/dashed line in Figure 10.1. As can be seen from the diagram, the expected utility of the more risky cash flow, denoted by E_1, has a certainty equivalent of only $4. The project's risk-adjusted net present value (again using a horizon of twenty years and a 5% riskless discount rate) is given by:

$$(\$4 \times 12.462) - \$50 = \$49.8 - \$50 = -\$0.20$$

Thus for a given *expected* net present value, the larger the dispersion (variance), the lower will be the certainty-equivalent cash flow, and hence the lower will be the risk-adjusted *NPV*. This result of the certainty-equivalent approach is consistent with both the expected utility and mean–variance methods which were discussed in earlier chapters, although clearly it utilizes a very different technique for carrying out the risk adjustment.

Adjusting the discount rate

As we have just seen, the risk-adjusted *NPV* can be calculated using the risk-less rate of interest as the discount rate, if the future cash flow is first reduced to its certainty-equivalent value. Alternatively, this adjustment can be carried out by increasing the discount rate, i.e., by adjusting the denominator rather than the numerator of the *NPV* equation. Clearly, the greater the risk, the higher will be the adjusted discount rate and therefore the lower will be the project's risk-adjusted *NPV*. In this case, the difference between the risk adjusted discount rate and the riskless rate measures the required *risk premium*.

An example

Consider an investment proposal which requires an initial outlay of $100 and provides an equal probability of earning a net annual cash flow of $50 or $150 for ten years, i.e., an expected (mean) annual cash receipt of $100:

$$(0.5 \times \$50) + (0.5 \times \$150) = \$100$$

If we again assume a 5% riskless rate of interest, the *unadjusted NPV* of this proposal is $672.20:

$$(\$100 \times 7.722) - \$100 = \$772.20 - \$100 = \$672.20$$

where 7.722 is the appropriate present value coefficient assuming a 5% discount rate and a ten-year cash flow. However, since the future cash flow is *not* known with certainty, let us assume that the firm requires an additional 5% as a premium to compensate for the risk incurred and therefore calculates the *NPV* of the project using a 10% discount rate. In this case, the *risk-adjusted NPV* is only $514.50:

$$(\$100 \times 6.145) - \$100 = \$614.50 - \$100 = \$514.50$$

Thus, even though the project's expected *NPV* is $672.20, due to its risk, the firm values the proposal at only $514.50.

Now suppose that we hold the average receipt constant at $100, but increase its variability. For example, suppose that for the same initial outlay we have another project which provides an equal probability of receiving an annual cash flow of either $200 or nothing for ten years. Note that the expected (mean) annual cash flow remains $100. Since the variance increases, we can assume that the required risk premium will also be larger, say 15%, and as a result the adjusted discount rate will be 20% (5% riskless interest rate plus 15% risk premium). In this case the risk-adjusted *NPV* is only $319.20.

$$(\$100 \times 4.192) - \$100 = \$419.20 - \$100 = \$319.20$$

where 4.192 is the appropriate present value coefficient for a 20% discount rate and a ten-year cash flow. Thus the higher the variance, the greater will be the discount rate, and hence the lower will be the risk-adjusted *NPV*. Once again this result is consistent with the expected utility and mean–variance principles.

Certainty equivalent vs. discount rate adjustment

The certainty equivalent method adjusts the project's cash flow, while in the second rule-of-thumb method the discount rate is adjusted. Although it may not be intuitively obvious, the two methods are equivalent in the sense that they provide the *same NPV* if the respective risk adjustments are carried out in an appropriate manner. To show this, consider a case in which the expected net cash receipt one year hence is $\bar{C}$ dollars. Now assume that the certainty equivalent of this sum is C^*, which, of course, must be smaller than $\bar{C}$. Thus, one can always write:

$$C^* = q\bar{C}$$

where $0 < q < 1$. The risk-adjusted present value of the cash receipt, using the certainty equivalent approach, is

$$\frac{C^*}{1 + r}$$

where r denotes the riskless interest rate. But as $C^* = q\bar{C}$, the present value can be rewritten as follows

$$\frac{q\bar{C}}{1 + r} = \frac{\bar{C}}{(1 + r)/q} = \frac{\bar{C}}{1 + k}$$

where $1 + k = (1 + r)/q$.

By definition, k must be greater than r, so the expression $\bar{C}/(1 + k)$ can be interpreted as the risk-adjusted present value when the adjustment is effected by raising the discount rate. Thus, if the adjusted discount rate is determined by the relationship $(1 + r)/q = 1 + k$, the two methods will yield the same adjusted present values. For example, if $r = 5\%$ and $q = 0.9$, the adjusted discount rate can be calculated as follows:

$$k = (1.05 \div 0.9) - 1 = 16.7\%$$

If, on the other hand, the risk is larger and hence q is smaller, say $q = 0.8$, the adjusted discount rate is approximately 31%:

$$(1.05 \div 0.8) - 1 = 31.3\%$$

In summary, the larger the risk, the smaller the certainty equivalent C^* in comparison to the mean cash flow $\bar{C}$ and, therefore, the factor q must also be smaller. This in turn implies a higher adjusted discount rate.[1]

Thus the popular rule-of-thumb adjustment of the discount rate is conceptually equivalent to the more sophisticated techniques based on the discounting of certainty-equivalent cash flows, which are advocated in the theoretical literature.[2] Of course, the question of determining k remains. This is discussed in Chapter 16.

---

1. Although the algebra is somewhat more complicated, this equivalence holds for multiperiod projects as well.
2. This is of considerable importance, not only for interpreting the actual practices of firms, but for the theory of finance as well; see Part III.

APPLYING PROBABILITY MEASURES IN PRACTICE _____

Now let us turn our attention to that subset of firms who are able to apply the more sophisticated techniques of direct risk analysis already discussed. It is noteworthy that the various measures of risk and return which have been proposed share an important characteristic: all the indices and decision rules require the prior assignment of a probability to each of the possible outcomes of the risky investment option. As we have seen, one straightforward way to handle this problem is to assign probabilities to different outcomes in terms of the proposal's net present value. These probabilities may be objective, subjective, or what is probably more often the case, some mixture of objective information regarding the possible outcomes with a large measure of subjective judgement.

Simulation analysis

In order to improve the process by which the probabilities are assigned, one should recall that a project's *NPV* is a sort of summary outcome of the proposal's prospects which is based on forecasts of sales, market prices, costs, etc. Once we explicitly recognize the economic roots which determine the *NPV*, the analysis becomes considerably more complex because a probability distribution must be assigned to each of the relevant economic factors, and this requires sophisticated forecasting techniques. The probability distribution of the *NPV*, in turn, is derived from the distributions of the underlying real economic factors. Of course, the larger the number of economic factors considered, the more difficult it becomes to derive the *NPV* distribution. However, it must be emphasized that such an analysis of the basic factors which determine the project's *NPV* is necessary for improving our estimate of the project's chances of success or failure.

In order to help overcome the technical difficulties of handling and evaluating so many economic factors, David Hertz proposed the use of a simulation technique to evaluate the profitability of investment projects when their probability distributions are derived from the probability distributions of underlying economic factors.[3] Hertz distinguishes between market analysis, investment analysis and cost analysis (see Figure 10.2). Each of these categories is subdivided; for example under the heading 'market analysis' we find the following subdivisions: market size, selling price, market growth rate, and market share. To each of these factors one has to assign some probability distribution. For

3. David B. Hertz, 'Risk Analysis in Capital Investment,' *Harvard Business Review*, January/February 1964, pp. 95–106; and 'Investment Policies that Pay Off,' *Harvard Business Review*, January/February 1968, pp. 96–108.

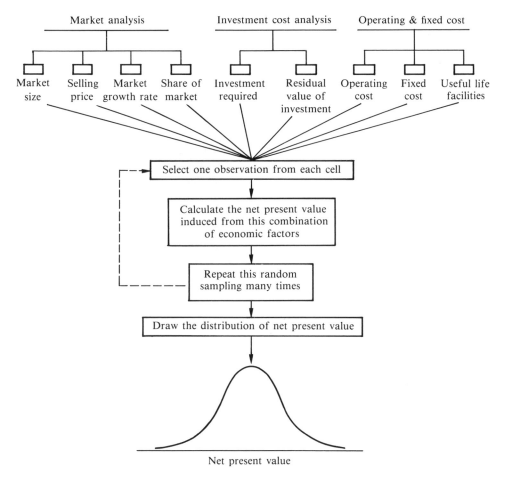

Figure 10.2

example, suppose that the firm assigns the following probabilities to the selling price of the product under consideration:

Selling price ($)	Probability
5	0.05
6	0.10
7	0.10
8	0.50
9	0.10
10	0.10
11	0.05

Suppose also that the following probabilities are assigned to the firm's market share:

Market share (units)	Probability
100,000	0.25
150,000	0.50
200,000	0.25

Now suppose that we spin two roulette wheels. The first is a proxy for the selling price and has 100 numbers; numbers 1 to 5 stand for a price of $5, numbers 6 to 15 for a market price of $6, and so on. The other roulette wheel also has 100 numbers, with numbers 1 to 25 standing for sales of 100,000 units, numbers 26 to 75 representing 150,000 units of sales, and numbers 76 to 100 sales of 200,000 units.

Now assume that after spinning both wheels, the first stops at number 9, which means that we are in the $6 price zone, and the other wheel stops at number 23, which means that sales will be 100,000 units. As a result, gross revenue will be $6 × 100,000 = $600,000. Of course, we should have many other 'roulette wheels', one for each of the factors which determine the net profit. Spinning all the wheels simultaneously, we can calculate the profit or the net present value. Now we repeat this procedure many times and obtain the frequency distribution, i.e., the statistical distribution of outcomes of *NPV* resulting from various combinations of the underlying economic factors. Obviously, once we have more than two economic factors to consider, it helps to use a computer to carry out the simulation.

Finally, two warnings are in order. First, the economic factors set out in Figure 10.2 are, in general, statistically dependent. For example, market size and especially the firm's market share are related to its operating costs, which

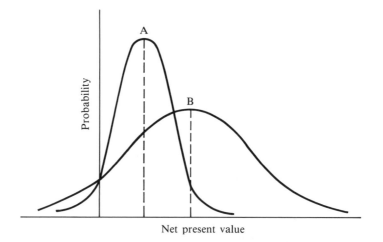

Net present value

Figure 10.3

often decline significantly as output increases. This can, and should, be handled by allowing for interdependencies between the statistical distributions of the relevant factors. Second, one should remember that the simulation approach facilitates, and hopefully improves, the estimate of the statistical distribution of *NPV*; however, it does not absolve the firm from evaluating this distribution in terms of its profitability and risk. For example, suppose that the firm desires to evaluate two mutually exclusive investments, A and B. Running the simulations for the two projects results in the two distributions drawn in Figure 10.3. Both the expected *NPV* and risk (variance) of project B are larger than their counterparts in investment A. Thus, the firm must weigh the implied tradeoff between the higher expected profit and greater risk when choosing between these two investment alternatives. The simulation provides us with better estimates of the distributions but cannot by itself reach a decision. The computer simulation facilitates the process of decision-making but does *not* replace the decision-maker, which perhaps explains why you are reading this book.

DECISION TREE

The decision flow diagram, or 'decision tree' as it is often called, is another technique which can facilitate investment decision-making when uncertainty prevails, especially when the problem involves a sequence of decisions.[4] In a sequential decision problem, in which the actions taken at one stage depend on actions taken in earlier stages, the evaluation of investment alternatives can become very complicated. In such cases, the 'decision tree' technique facilitates project evaluation by enabling the firm to write down all the possible future decisions, as well as their monetary outcomes, in a systematic manner. As is true of simulation analysis, the use of decision trees does not obviate the need to reach decisions regarding projects having different expected profit–risk profiles. However, the use of the decision tree does make the implications of alternative possible courses of action more transparent, especially when the firm is confronted by a complex sequence of decisions.

Perhaps the best way to explain the decision tree is to demonstrate its use by a specific example. Suppose that an oil company owns drilling rights in a given area and that the company initially faces a decision of whether or not to make a seismic test which would indicate the chances of finding oil in the area. Hence, making the test (which of course costs money) or avoiding it, is the *first decision* in our sequence of decisions. In stage 2, the firm again faces two alternatives: either to sell its drilling rights to another company, or to drill with the hope of finding oil. However, as one can see from Figure 10.4, these

---

4. The reader who wishes to pursue this subject further can consult John F. Magee, 'Decision Trees for Decision Making,' *Harvard Business Review*, July/August 1964; and 'How to Use Decision Trees in Capital Investment,' *Harvard Business Review*, September/October 1964; or Howard Raiffa, *Decision Analysis: Introductory Lectures on Choices Under Uncertainty*, Addison Wesley, Reading, Mass., 1968.

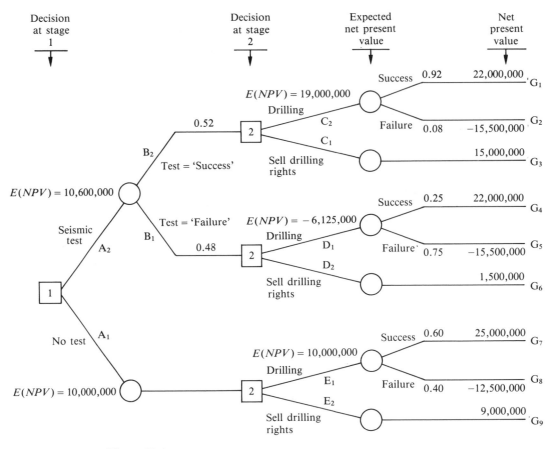

Figure 10.4

two simple alternatives yield radically different monetary rewards, depending on the action taken in stage one, i.e., whether or not the seismic test is made, and on its success or failure in the event that the firm decides to make the test. Hence, the first stage is characterized in Figure 10.4 by two branches of possible action denoted by A_1 and A_2. The present value of the cash flow forecasts under each scenario is summarized in Table 10.1. If the firm decides to make the seismic test (i.e., follow branch A_2) it will, in the second stage, again be confronted by two branches of possible decisions (branches B_1 and B_2). Thus each successive decision in the sequence has its own branch to represent further decisions; hence the name decision 'tree'.

Now let us turn to the specific numerical example of the oil company given in Figure 10.4. If the firm decides not to carry out the seismic test, it can sell the drilling rights for $9 million (see branch G_9). Alternatively the company can drill for oil without making the seismic test. In the latter event, the monetary outcome depends solely on whether or not oil is found. Suppose that the oil company estimates the probability of finding oil at 0.6, and the probability of a dry hole at 0.4. If we assume that the drilling cost is \$12,500,000, there is a probability of 0.4 of losing this sum (see branch G_8). On the other hand, there is a probability of 0.6 of striking oil, in which case the firm will earn an *NPV* (after deducting the drilling and other costs) of \$25 million (see branch G_7). The *expected NPV*, should the firm decide to drill, without a seismic test, is \$10 million:

$$E(NPV) = (0.6 \times \$25,000,000) + (0.4 \times (-\$12,500,000)) = \$10,000,000$$

Table 10.1 Present value of cash flow forecasts of oil exploration project

I. *PV* of cash flows if seismic test is *not* performed (branch A_1)

PV of cash flows:

If oil is found	(prob. 0.6)	\$37,500,000
If oil is not found	(prob. 0.4)	0

PV of costs:

Drilling costs	\$12,500,000

NPV:

If oil found (37,500,000 − 12,500,000)	\$25,000,000
If oil not found	−12,500,000

E(NPV):

If drill $E(NPV) = (0.6 \times 25,000,000) + (0.4 \times (-12,500,000))$	= \$10,000,000
If sell drilling rights $E(NPV) = NPV$	= \$9,000,000

II. *PV* of cash flows if seismic test *is* performed (branch A_2) and results *are* successful

PV of cash flows:

If oil is found	(prob. 0.92)	\$37,500,000
If oil is not found	(prob. 0.08)	0

PV of costs:

Drilling costs	\$12,500,000
Seismic test	3,000,000

NPV:

If oil found (37,500,000 − 15,500,000)	\$22,000,000
If oil not found (total costs)	−15,500,000

E(NPV):

If drill $E(NPV) = (0.92 \times 22,000,000) + (0.08 \times (-15,500,000))$	= \$19,000,000
If sell drilling rights $E(NPV) = \$18,000,000 - 3,000,000$	= \$15,000,000

III. *PV* of cash flows if seismic test *is* performed (branch A_2) and results *are not* successful (failure)

PV of cash flows:

If oil is found	(prob. 0.25)	\$37,500,000
If oil is not found	(prob. 0.75)	0

PV of costs:

Drilling costs	\$12,500,000
Seismic test	3,000,000

NPV:

If oil found (37,500,000 − 15,500,000)	\$22,000,000
If oil not found (total costs)	−15,500,000

E(NPV):

If drill $E(NPV) = (0.25 \times 22,000,000) + (0.75 \times (-15,500,000))$	= − \$6,125,000
If sell drilling rights $E(NPV) = \$4,500,000 - 3,000,000$	= \$1,500,000

Let us turn now to the monetary consequences of following branch A_2, i.e., we now shall assume that the firm decides to make the seismic test in the first stage. We further assume that this seismic test costs $3 million and that there exists a probability of 0.52 that the test will yield good results (denoted as 'success' in Figure 10.4), and a probability of 0.48 that it will fail. The decision in stage 2 obviously will depend on the test results. Should the company decide to sell the drilling rights after the seismic test fails, it will realize a lower price than it could have obtained without the seismic test. Clearly the poor results of the test (which we assume are public knowledge) decrease the market value of the drilling rights.

Let us assume that if the test fails the firm can sell its concession for $4,500,000, which will net the firm only $1,500,000 because we have assumed that the seismic test costs $3 million (see branch G_6). On the other hand, the firm might still decide to drill despite the failure of the seismic test. However, as a result of the failure of the test, the company revises its estimates of the probability of finding oil. The probability of hitting oil is now estimated to be only 0.25 (as compared with 0.6 without the additional information provided by the seismic test). Should the firm fail to find oil, the loss will be $15,500,000 – the assumed drilling cost of $12,500,000 plus the $3 million cost of the seismic test (see branch G5). Should the firm strike oil the net present value will be $22 million, which reflects a present value of $25 million from the net oil revenues minus the cost of the seismic test (see branch G_4). The *expected NPV*, should the firm decide to drill even if the seismic test fails, is – $6,125,000:

$$E(NPV) = (0.25 \times \$22,000,000) + (0.75 \times (-\$15,500,000)) = -\$6,125,000$$

The second possibility, i.e., the case of a successful seismic test, is described by branch B_2. Clearly, a successful test will increase the value of the drilling rights, say to $18 million, and since the company spent $3 million on the seismic test, its net income from selling the rights would be $15 million (see branch G_3). Obviously, a successful seismic test also increases the probability of finding oil so we assume that the firm now estimates this probability at 0.92 (branch G_1). Thus the expected *NPV*, should the firm decide to drill following a successful seismic test, is $19 million:

$$E(NPV) = (0.92 \times \$22,000,000) + (0.08 \times (-\$15,500,000)) = \$19,000,000$$

Having obtained the monetary outcomes from all possible branches of Figure 10.4, which decision sequence is optimal? Clearly, the decision depends on the utility that the firm attributes to each possible outcome. However, in order to demonstrate the use of the decision-tree technique, let us first assume, for simplicity, that the firm reaches its decisions according to the maximum expected *NPV* criterion. Following this rule, we calculate the expected *NPV* for each branch of Figure 10.4 and that course of action represented by the branch with the highest expected *NPV* will be chosen. However, this is not as simple as it might seem. First we must examine the *NPV*s of stage 2 in order to choose the optimal course of action (branch) for stage 2; only then can we 'fold back' the tree and choose the optimal decision for stage 1.

To illustrate the type of calculation required, let us examine the specific problem given in Figure 10.4. Our first step is to compare the expected *NPV*s of the branches in stage 2. Assuming that the firm makes the seismic test, the expected *NPV* of branch C_2 ($19 million) is higher than the *NPV* from selling the contract (branch C_1); hence the course of action denoted by branch C_1 can be discarded and should be ignored in our further calculations. Similarly, branch D_2 results in a higher expected *NPV* than does branch D_1, and therefore D_1 can also be discarded. If on the other hand, the firm decides not to make the seismic test, branch E_1 has a higher expected *NPV* than E_2 and therefore the latter can be discarded.

Having made these eliminations in the second-stage decisions, we can then evaluate the first-stage decision as follows. The expected *NPV* of the seismic test becomes $10,600,000:

$$(0.52 \times \$19,000,000) + (0.48 \times \$1,500,000) = \$10,600,000$$

Note that this calculation of stage 1 exploits the previous screening of the alternatives of stage 2. If the test is successful, branch C_2 is chosen, so the expected *NPV* of that alternative is $19 million with a probability of 0.52. If the test is unsuccessful, the best path to follow is branch D_2, which results in an *NPV* of $1,500,000 with a probability of 0.48. Similarly, if we 'fold back' the other branches, the maximum expected *NPV*, if the seismic test is *not* made, is the $10 million which results from the option of drilling without the test.

Examining our results, we find that the optimal decision in the first stage, using the maximum expected *NPV* criterion, is to make the seismic test. If successful, the firm will go ahead in stage 2 with the decision to drill for oil. Should the test prove unsuccessful, the optimal second-stage decision will be to sell the drilling rights. In terms of Figure 10.4, the optimal path follows branches A_2, B_2, and C_2 if the test is a success; and branches A_2, B_1, and D_2 should it fail. Note that in both cases we start with branch A_2, i.e., with the decision to make the seismic test; the next decision in the sequence being taken only after the results of the test have been obtained. In summary, the decision-tree technique permits us to transport ourselves in 'conceptual time' to the extremities of the tree where expectations were calculated in terms of the alternative outcomes and their probabilities of occurrence. Then we worked our way back by folding back, so to speak, the branches of the tree, choosing only those paths which yield the *maximum* expected *NPV* at each decision junction.

If the specific utility function is known, one can replace the maximum expected *NPV* rule and employ the maximum expected utility criterion to find the best sequential decisions.

SUMMARY

This chapter has been devoted to the practical application of risk analysis. As is true of capital budgeting techniques in general, the adoption of sophisticated risk analysis by business firms has lagged behind the theoretical literature. However, it should be noted that the percentage of firms using risk evaluation techniques is steadily rising, although the majority of such firms still prefer an *indirect*, rule-of-thumb adjustment of the discount rate to the more sophisticated method of directly estimating the probability distributions of individual projects.

Two *indirect* methods of adjusting *NPV* calculations for risk are discussed:

1. The certainty equivalent method.
2. The adjusted discount method.

The former adjusts the projects' cash flow and discounts the stream using the riskless rate of interest. In the latter method, the discount rate, rather than the cash flow, is adjusted. Although it is not intuitively obvious, the two methods are equivalent, in the sense that they provide the *same NPV* if the respective adjustments are carried out appropriately. Thus, the popular rule-of-thumb adjustment of the discount rate is conceptually equivalent to the more sophisticated techniques based on the discounting of certainty-equivalent cash flows.

The remainder of the chapter is devoted to two practical applications of the 'direct' adjustment for risk for those firms which estimate the probability distributions of their investment projects:

1. *Simulation analysis.* A method for deriving the probability distribution of underlying economic factors.
2. *Decision tree.* A decision flow diagram which can facilitate investment decision-making when uncertainty prevails, especially when the problem involves a sequence of decisions.

Neither of these two techniques eliminates the need to reach decisions regarding the tradeoff between the higher expected *NPV* and greater risk which characterizes so many investment alternatives, but they can provide us with better estimates of the distributions, thereby clarifying the implications of alternative courses of action. However, no matter how sophisticated the analytical technique, it *cannot* replace the decision-maker.

SUMMARY TABLE

Adjustment for risk

(a) Discounting $q\bar{C}$ by risk-free interest rate:

$$NPV = \frac{q\bar{C}}{1+r} - I_0$$

where $\bar{C}$ is the mean cash flow, $0 < q < 1$ is a risk adjustment factor, and $q\bar{C}$ is the certainty equivalent of the cash flow's distribution.

(b) Discounting $\bar{C}$ by k where $k > r$:

$$NPV = \frac{\bar{C}}{1 + k} - I_0$$

(c) The two adjusting methods yield identical results if:

$$1 + k = (1 + r)/q$$

(d) For a given utility function, the larger the variability of return, the lower q, hence the larger the risk premium $k - r$.

Simulation analysis

Examine the whole distribution by looking at various combinations of events.

Decision tree

Applicable when the firm has to make a sequence of decisions at various points of time of the project's life.

_____ QUESTIONS AND PROBLEMS

10.1 Define and explain the certainty-equivalent method.

10.2 Assume an investor with the following utility function:

Dollars	Utility
−1,000	− 30
0	0
1,000	20
2,000	38
3,000	54
4,000	68
5,000	70
10,000	105

The investor is faced with a project which requires an initial outlay of $15,000 and yields a net annual cash flow of $2,000 with a probability of 1/2 and $5,000 with a probability of 1/2, for the following eight years. Assume a 6% riskless interest rate.

(a) Calculate the annual risk-adjusted net cash flow, using the *certainty-equivalent method*.
(b) Calculate the risk-adjusted net present value of the project. Should the investor accept this project?
(c) Find the 'value' of the risk inherent in the project.

10.3 The ABC Food Company is confronted with the following two investment proposals, A and B:

1. Proposal A requires an initial outlay of $100,000 and provides an equal probability of earning a net annual cash flow of $12,000 or $28,000 for fifteen years.
2. Proposal B requires the same initial outlay and provides an equal probability of earning a net annual cash flow of $5,000 or $45,000 for fifteen years.

Assume that the riskless interest rate is 6% and that the firm requires a risk premium of 1.5% for every 10% of coefficient of variation (σ/E) of the annual cash flows.

(a) Calculate the unadjusted net present value of each proposal.
(b) Which investment proposal will be preferred if the firm uses the *adjusted discount rate* method?

10.4 The Melkor Tool Corporation is examining the following project. The initial outlay is $400,000 and the net annual cash flow for the next ten years is $60,000 with a probability of 2/3 and $150,000 with a probability of 1/3. Assume a 7% riskless interest rate.

(a) What is the *risk premium* (in terms of the discount rate) required by the firm, if you know that the project has a risk-adjusted *NPV* of $35,000?
(b) What is the *maximum* risk premium the firm could demand and still accept the project?

10.5 Assume a project which requires $30,000 as an initial outlay and its *expected* net cash receipt is $36,000 for one year. Assume also that the certainty equivalent of this sum is $33,300, and that the riskless interest rate is 7%.

(a) Calculate the risk-adjusted net present value of the project (using the certainty equivalent method).
(b) Find the adjusted discount rate that will yield the same adjusted *NPV*.
(c) What would be the appropriate discount rate under the assumption that the risk of the project is larger and hence the certainty equivalent of its expected receipt is only $30,600?

10.6 You are asked to examine the following proposal. An investment outlay of $3,500 and one year's net receipts of $1,600 or $6,400 with equal probability. Suppose that your utility function is determined by $U(x) = \sqrt{x}$. Assuming a 6% riskless interest rate:

(a) Would you accept this proposal?
(b) Find the adjusted discount rate that will yield the same adjusted *NPV* as the certainty-equivalent method.

10.7 Define and explain the use of the following two techniques in decision-making:

(a) Simulation analysis.
(b) The decision tree.

10.8 The Nefton Oil Company owns drilling rights in a given area for ten years and has two possibilities: either to drill with the hope of finding oil, or to sell its drilling rights to another company.

Suppose that the company estimates the probability of finding oil ('success') 0.55 and the probability of a dry hole ('failure') 0.45. Assume that the drilling cost is $14 million, so that in the case of failure, the company loses this sum, but in the case of striking oil, the company will earn a net present value (after deducting the drilling and other costs) of $36 million.

The oil company initially is faced with a decision whether or not to make a seismic test, which would add more information on the chances of finding oil. Assume that this test costs $4 million and there is an equal probability that the test will succeed or fail.

1. The probability of a successful test *and* striking oil is 45%.
2. The probability of a successful test *and* striking a dry hole is 5%.
3. The probability of an unsuccessful test and striking oil is 10%.
4. The probability of an unsuccessful test and not finding oil is 40%.

Denoting a successful test as 'T_S', an unsuccessful test as 'T_f', striking oil as 'S', and not striking oil as 'F', the probability of striking oil given that the test succeeds, i.e. $P(S \mid T_S)$, is 90%. The probability of not finding oil even though the test succeeds $P(F \mid T_S)$, is 10%. The probability of a success in finding oil although the test fails, $P(S \mid T_f)$, is 20% and the probability of not finding oil when the test fails, $P(F \mid T_f)$, is 80%.

The company can sell the drilling rights, but the price realized depends on its timing:

1. If the firm decides not to carry out the seismic test, it can sell the drilling rights for $12 million.
2. If the firm proposes to sell the drilling rights after it carries out the test and the results are a success, the firm can realize $24 million. But if the test fails, the poor results of the test decrease the market value of the rights and the firm can sell its concessions for only $6 million.

(Note that if the firm carries out the seismic test, any price must be decreased by the cost of the test, which is $4 million.)

(a) Draw a decision tree which describes the sequence of decisions which follows from the initial decision whether to make a seismic test or not.
(b) What is the optimal decision using the maximum expected *NPV* criterion?

10.9 The Starlight Electronic Corporation (SEC) is confronted with the problem of building a large or small plant for producing a newly developed product which has an expected economic life of ten years. The decision depends, among other things, on the size of the market for the new product. The demand may be high in the first three years, but if many of the potential users find that the product does not fulfill their wishes, the demand may then fall to a lower level. On the other hand, an initial high demand may point to the possibility of a permanent market.

The marketing manager developed the following market forecast:

1. The probability of high demand in the first three years (marked as H_3) and high demand for the last seven years (H_7) is 45%.
2. The probability of a high demand in the first three years (H_3) followed by low demand in the last seven years (L_7) is 15%.
3. The probability of low demand in the first three years (L_3) and low demand in the last seven years (L_7) is 30%.
4. The probability of L_3 and H_7 is 10%.

If the firm sets up a big plant now, it has to continue running it for the next ten years, regardless of the demand, but if the firm builds a smaller plant, it will have the option to expand it after the first three years. The financial vice-president provided the following financial appraisal:

1. With a high demand, a big plant will realize a net annual cash flow of $1,600,000.
2. The net annual cash flow of a big plant with low demand will be only $200,000, because of the high overhead costs and inefficiency.
3. In case of low demand a small plant will be the more efficient one, and will yield a net annual cash flow of $500,000.
4. The net annual cash flow of a small plant in a high-demand market will be $700,000. (This reflects the possibility of raising prices.)
5. If the small plant is expanded after three years and if the market demand is high during the last seven years, the net annual cash flow will be $1,500,000 (in three years). We assume that the plant will be slightly less efficient than a large plant which is built today.
6. If the small plant is expanded after three years, but the demand is low through the remaining seven years, the net annual cash flow will be only $100,000 in each of these years.

According to the engineering estimates, the cost of building a big plant will be $3 million; a small plant will cost only $1,500,000, but if expanded after three years it will cost an additional $2 million.

Mr. McNeal, the chief executive officer of SEC, has to prepare a recommendation to the board of directors.

(a) Draw the decision tree which describes the sequence of decisions, implied by the initial decision whether to build a big or a small plant.
(b) What will be the chief executive officer's optimal decision if he uses a 10% discount rate and the maximum expected *NPV* criterion? (Ignore taxes.)

(Hint: note that the probability of a high demand in the last seven years given a low demand in the first three years is:

$$P_r(H_7 \mid L_3) = \frac{0.10}{0.40} = 25\%$$

Similarly,

$$P_r(H_7 \mid H_3) = \frac{0.45}{0.60} = 75\%,$$

$$P_r(L_7 \mid L_3) = \frac{0.30}{0.40} = 75\% \text{ and } P_r(L_7 \mid H_3) = \frac{0.15}{0.60} = 25\%$$

where P_r denotes probability and '|' means conditional.)

10.10 CBA firm employs simulation analysis to analyze its projects. After considering all revenue and cost components the firm found the following relationship regarding the net cash flows of two alternative projects A and B:

	Project A		Project B	
NPV	Probability		*NPV*	Probability
−10	1/5		−10	2/5
0	1/5		+5	1/5
+20	3/5		+20	2/5

Which project should be selected? (Hint: it may help to graph the cumulative probabilities of each project. See Appendix 9A.)

10.11 Suppose that the cost function of a given project and the gross revenue are given by:

Cost	Probability	Revenue	Probability
10	1/4	100	1/2
20	1/4	200	1/2
30	1/4		
40	1/4		

The cost and the revenue are independent. What is the *NPV* probability function?

(Additional information: This is a one-year project, cash flows are obtained at the end of the year, the discount rate is $r = 0.1$, and the initial investment is $I_0 = \$50$.)

10.12 An investor is facing the following investment: the initial outlay is $I_0 = \$100$, the cash flow at the end of the first year is $+50$ and $+400$ with equal probability. The risk-free interest rate is $r = 0.10$, and the investor's utility function is $U(x) = \log_e x$ (where x is the cash flow).

(a) Should the investor accept this project?
(b) Find the *NPV* of the project by using the certainty equivalent approach.
(c) What is the individual's cost of capital k?

10.13 An investor whose utility function is given by $U(x) = \sqrt{x}$ faces the following two investments:

Project A		Project B	
Cash flow	Probability	Cash flow	Probability
100	1/2	0	1/2
200	1/2	400	1/2

The cash flow is received at the end of the year, the initial investment is $I_0 = \$100$ (for both projects).

(a) Which project is preferred by the expected utility approach?
(b) Assuming that the risk-free interest rate is $r = 0.10$, calculate the cost of capital that should be assigned to each of the two projects.
(c) Calculate the *NPV* of each project by discounting the mean cash flow.

10.14 How would you change your answer to 10.13 when:

(a) $U(x) = x$
(b) $U(x) = x^2$

Explain your results.

10.15 The following cash flow is received in the next two years:

Cash flow	Probability
9	1/2
36	1/2

The investor's utility function is $U(x) = \sqrt{x}$. The risk-free interest rate is $r = 0.10$.

(a) Determine the cost of capital that should be applied to the first and second year cash flows, respectively.

(b) Calculate the project's present value.

10.16 An investor is considering taking an investment with the following cash flows: 0 and 9 with equal probability. The utility function is $U(x) = x - (1/20)x^2$. Calculate the value of q, where $q\bar{x} = x^*$, where $\bar{x}$ is the mean return and x^* is the certainty equivalent.

10.17 'When the risk-free interest rate is equal to zero the adjusted cost of capital k is also equal to zero.' Evaluate this statement.

10.18 An investor's utility function is $U(X) = 10 + 5X$, where X is the cash flow. Calculate the certainty equivalent of the following distribution:

X	Probability
0	1/2
10	1/2

Explain your results.

10.19 The risk-free interest rate is $r = 10\%$, and the firm's adjusted cost of capital is infinity. 'This implies that the project under consideration has a zero mean cash flow.' Evaluate this statement.

10.20 You have two investments with the following uncertain income:

Investment A		Investment B	
Return	Probability	Return	Probability
0	1/2	0	1/4
10	1/2	5	1/2
		10	1/4

Which investment would have the higher certainty-equivalent cash flow when it is known that investors are risk averse? Do you need to know the precise utility function, U, to answer this question? Why?

10.21 Suppose that the utility function is $U(X) = X^2$. The risk-free interest rate is $r = 10\%$. The cash flows from the project one year hence is $X_1 = 10$ or $X_2 = 30$ with an equal probability.

(a) Employing the certainty-equivalent approach, calculate the *PV* of these cash flows.

(b) What is the investor's cost of capital? Explain your results.

10.22 Suppose that you get with equal probability $9 or $36 one year from now. Your utility function is $U(X) = X^{1/2}$. The risk-free interest rate is 10%.

(a) Find the certainty equivalent of these cash flows and solve for your risky discount rate. How much premium did you add to the risk-free interest rate?

(b) Answer part (a) where you get the above cash flow ten years from now. How do you explain the differences in your answers to (a) and (b)?

SELECTED REFERENCES

Adler, F. Michael, 'On Risk-adjusted Capitalization Rates and Valuation by Individuals,' *Journal of Finance*, September 1970.

Bar-Yosef, S. and Mesznik, R., 'On Some Definitional Problems with the Method of Certainty Equivalents,' *Journal of Finance*, December 1977.

Bernhard, Richard H., 'Risk-adjusted Values, Timing of Uncertainty Resolution, and the Measurement of Project Worth,' *Journal of Financial and Quantitative Analysis*, March 1984.

Blatt, John M., 'Investment Evaluation under Uncertainty,' *Financial Management*, Summer 1979.

Bogue, Marcus, C. and Roll, Richard, 'Capital Budgeting of Risky Projects with "Imperfect" Markets for Physical Capital,' *Journal of Finance*, May 1974.

Castagna, A. D. and Matolcsy, Z. P., 'The Relationship between Accounting Variables and Systematic Risk and the Prediction of Systematic Risk,' *Australian Journal of Management*, October 1978.

Celec, S. E. and Pettway, R. H., 'Some Observations on Risk-adjusted Discount Rates: A Comment,' *Journal of Finance*, September 1979.

Constantinides, G. M., 'Market Risk Adjustment in Project Valuation,' *Journal of Finance*, May 1978.

Cozzolino, John M., 'Controlling Risk in Capital Budgeting: A Practical Use of Utility Theory for Measurement and Control of Petroleum Exploration Risk,' *The Engineering Economist*, Spring 1980.

Ekern, Steinar, 'On the Inadequacy of a Probabilistic Internal Rate of Return,' *Journal of Business Finance and Accounting*, 6(2), 1979.

Frankfurter, G. M. and Frecker, T. J., 'Efficient Portfolios and Superfluous Diversification,' *Journal of Financial and Quantitative Analysis*, December 1979.

Fuller, Russel J. and Lang-Hoon, Kim, 'Inter-temporal Correlation of Cash Flows and the Risk of Multi-period Investment Projects,' *Journal of Financial and Quantitative Analysis*, December 1980.

Gitman, L. J., 'Capturing Risk Exposure in the Evaluation of Capital Budgeting Projects,' *The Engineering Economist*, Summer 1977.

Gregory, D. D., 'Multiplicative Risk Premiums,' *Journal of Financial and Quantitative Analysis*, December 1978.

Hoskins, C. G., 'Capital Budgeting Decision Rules for Risky Projects Derived from a Capital Market Model Based on Semivariance,' *The Engineering Economist*, Summer 1978.

Hsiao, F. S. T. and Smith, W. J., 'An Analytic Approach to Sensitivity Analysis of the Internal Rate of Return Model,' *Journal of Finance*, May 1978.

Keeley, Robert H. and Westerfield, Randolph, 'A Problem in Probability Distribution Techniques for Capital Budgeting,' *The Journal of Finance*, June 1972.

Klammer, T. P. and Walker, M. C., 'The Continuing Increase in the Use of Sophisticated Capital Budgeting Technique,' *California Management Review*, Fall 1984.

Kudla, Ronald J., 'Some Pitfalls in Using Certainty-equivalents: A Note,' *Journal of Business Finance and Accounting*, Summer 1980.

Lewellen, W. G., 'Some Observations on Risk Adjusted Discount Rates,' *Journal of Finance*, September 1977.

Lockett, A. G. and Gear, A. E., 'Multistage Capital Budgeting under Uncertainty,' *Journal of Financial and Quantitative Analysis*, March 1975.

Miller, Edward M., 'Uncertainty Induced Bias in Capital Budgeting,' *Financial Management*, Autumn 1978.

Obel, B. and van der Weide, J., 'On the Decentralized Capital Budgeting Problem under Uncertainty,' *Management Science*, September 1979.

Parkinson, M., 'The Extreme Value Method for Estimating the Variance of the Rate of Return,' *Journal of Business*, January 1980.

Perrakis, Stylianos, 'Certainty Equivalents and Timing Uncertainty,' *Journal of Financial and Quantitative Analysis*, March 1975.

Petty, William J. and Bowlin, Oswald D., 'The Financial Manager and Quantitative Decision Models,' *Financial Management*, Winter 1976.

Ross, S. A., 'A Simple Approach to the Valuation of Risky Streams,' *Journal of Business*, July 1978.

Schwab, Bernhard, 'Conceptual Problems in the Use of Risk-adjusted Discount Rates with Disaggregated Cash Flows,' *Journal of Business Finance and Accounting*, Winter 1978.

Sick, Gordon A., 'Certainty Equivalent Approach to Capital Budgeting,' *Financial Management*, Winter 1986.

Whisler, W. D., 'Sensitivity Analysis of Return,' *Journal of Finance*, March 1976.

Zin, C. D., Lesso, W. G. and Motazed, B., 'A Probabilistic Approach to Risk Analysis in Capital Investment Projects,' *The Engineering Economist*, Summer 1977.

11

Decreasing Risk by Diversification: The Portfolio Approach

ARTICLE 16

'You Can Lower Your Risk ... And Still Pursue Growth'

Investors should understand that the market's daily ups and downs mean not only high potential rewards but also greater risk. As a result, you may have a gain or loss when you sell your shares. ... Although the market will experience ups and downs, the Fund is managed to moderate the effects of market fluctuations while remaining poised for long-term growth.

Diversification Made Simple: Fidelity Asset Manager™

Now there's an easier way to diversify across a broad range of securities ... in one simple investment. Fidelity Asset Manager seeks high total return with reduced risk over the long term by allocating its assets among stocks, bonds, and money market instruments. You simply make one investment with **no sales charge**, and join a diversified portfolio which is carefully watched and gradually adjusted by Fidelity professionals who seek to enhance your return in any market environment.

Source: based on a Fidelity investments advertisement appearing in the *Wall Street Journal*, April 3, 1992. p. M1.

What can we learn from Fidelity Investments' advertisement? First, that this mutual fund which managed more than $60 billion of assets is considering two important factors in selecting the investments: reward (growth or mean return) and risk.

Second, risk is identified with market ups and downs, or market fluctuations. While growth is desirable, the fluctuation (risk) is not desirable and the Fund is managed to 'moderate the effects of market fluctuations.'

Third, this goal of a high total return with small risk is achieved by diversifying in stocks, bonds, and money market instruments. What Fidelity suggests is consistent with the old maxim, 'Don't put all of your eggs into one basket.' In the preceding three chapters alternative investments were treated as independent individual projects; the interaction between them was not taken into account. In this chapter we focus attention on the possibility of such interaction. Here we emphasize the possibility that risk diversification can be facilitated by combining investments into a *portfolio*.

The theory of portfolio selection was originally developed for the analysis and management of financial assets, such as securities.[1] In this chapter we set out the basic elements of the theory explicitly in terms of the expected returns and variance (or standard deviation) of the returns from securities. The portfolio approach will then be applied to the analysis of capital market equilibrium and problems of capital budgeting at the level of the firm in Chapter 12.

MEASURING THE RETURN ON FINANCIAL INVESTMENTS

In Part I the net present value method was used to determine the feasibility of capital expenditures. Because of the nature of financial securities, investment in them tends to differ from investment in physical assets: financial assets tend to be highly divisible – you cannot build two-thirds of a bridge but you can buy one-millionth of a share in the ownership of AT&T. Thus for all practical purposes, scale problems can usually be ignored when analyzing the return on securities.

The investment in (physical) goods usually involves a long-term commitment of resources over a fixed number of years (that is, disinvestment is costly and often uneconomic); most securities, independent of their date of maturity (if any),[2] can be held for as short or as long a period as is desired; in other words, investments in securities are highly reversible. Finally, while the firm is often faced with mutually exclusive alternatives, the decision to purchase a share of AT&T does not generally preclude the purchase of GM stock.

Thus, when analyzing investments in securities, differences in scale and duration among alternative investments can safely be ignored. This property of financial investments is of considerable importance since we seek a measure which can rank investments by return without determining their individual discount rates. (The vast number of investors in a financial market precludes any attempt at making meaningful *NPV* calculations of stocks and bonds.) What is required is an index which provides an objective measure of financial investments' profitability for all investors. The measure of return which has this

1. The theory was first set out in the pioneering work of Harry Markowitz, 'Portfolio Selection,' *Journal of Finance*, March 1952. Important extensions have been made by Markowitz, *Portfolio Selection*, Wiley, New York, 1959; James Tobin, 'Liquidity Preference as Behaviour Towards Risk,' *Review of Economic Studies*, February 1958; William F. Sharpe, 'Capital Asset Prices: A Theory of Market Equilibrium under Conditions of Risk,' *Journal of Finance*, September 1964; John Lintner, 'The Valuation of Risk Assets and the Selection of Risky Investments in Stock Portfolios and Capital Budgets,' *Review of Economics and Statistics*, February 1965.
2. Common stock or preferred stock as well as perpetual bonds have no formal redemption dates.

property[3] is the *holding period rate of return* (*HPR*). The underlying idea is to specify the holding period (e.g., one year) and then assume that all benefits received during the period are *reinvested*.

Consider, for example, the one-year *HPR* on a share of common stock:

$$1 + HPR = \frac{\text{Value at end of holding period}}{\text{Value at beginning of holding period}} = \frac{V_t}{V_{t-1}}$$

The value at the beginning of the year (ignoring transaction costs) is simply the market price of the share. Its value at the end of the year is found by multiplying the end of year price by the *number* of shares held. Recall that cash dividends, stock dividends, etc., have been assumed to be reinvested. A numerical example can help clarify this type of calculation.

Consider a stock which sold for $35 at the beginning of the year, paid a cash dividend of $1.50 per share on the last day of the year, split 2 for 1 in the July of that year and sold for only $17.75 on the last day of the year. What is the *HPR* of that stock? The initial value is clearly $35; but the end-of-period value is certainly not $17.75. Due to the 2 : 1 split of the stock in July, our hypothetical investor holds *two* shares at the end of the year, and moreover he receives a dividend of $1.50 on *each* of the two shares held. Hence the end of period value is $38.50 (2 × $17.75 + 2 × $1.50 = $38.50) and the *HPR* is 10%:

$$HPR = \frac{38.50}{35.00} - 1 = 0.10$$

For multiperiod investments the *HPR* can readily be converted to an equivalent return *per period* by calculating the *compounded* average rate of return ($\overline{HPR}$). This is accomplished by taking the geometric mean of the single period returns and subtracting one:

$$\overline{HPR} = \sqrt[N]{[(1 + HPR_1)(1 + HPR_2) \ldots (1 + HPR_N)]} - 1$$

where:

$\overline{HPR}$ = compounded per period rate of return
$1 + HPR_i$ = holding period return in period i
N = number of periods.

These holding period returns are the basic building blocks of the portfolio model, and will be used below to calculate the expected returns, variances, and covariances which are the inputs of the portfolio selection model.

_____ IMPROVING THE RISK–RETURN RELATIONSHIP BY DIVERSIFICATION

Underlying the portfolio approach to decision-making is the contention that by combining a number of securities into a 'portfolio', some degree of income

3. For a proof of the equivalence between *NPV* and *HPR* rankings, see Haim Ben-Shahar and Marshall Sarnat, 'Reinvestment and the Rate of Return on Common Stock,' *Journal of Finance*, December 1966.

stabilization can be achieved without impairing the expected profit. This proposition can be illustrated by considering the example of two securities given in Table 11.1. For simplicity, let us assume that the individual can either invest all of his resources in one of the two securities, A or B; or alternatively, he can diversify his investment by putting half of his resources in A and the other half in B. For emphasis, the distribution of the returns on security A is assumed to be *identical* to the distribution of returns on security B. (The distributions given in Table 11.1 reflect an investment of 100% of the the investor's resources, say $100, either in A or in B.) The investor must decide whether to put all his resources ($100) in one of the two securities or diversify his investment between the two alternatives. If he invests the entire amount in a single security (either A or B) he has a 50% chance of losing $20 and a 50% chance of earning $30. In both A and B the expected return is $5 with a variance of $625 (i.e., a standard deviation of $25).

Now, what are the relevant expected earnings and risk should our hypothetical investor decide to diversify his holdings, say by investing $50 in A and $50 in B? The answer depends on the *statistical relationship* between the two distributions. Let us initially assume that the income streams of the two securities are statistically independent of each other; in other words, that the correlation between the returns from the two securities is zero. In such a case the probability of getting any pair of returns from the two securities is equal to the product of their individual probabilities. For example, the *joint probability* that the return on both investments will be $-$\$20$ is $0.5 \times 0.5 = 0.25$, so by diversifying equally between A and B our entrepreneur has only a 25% chance of losing $20.[4]

Using this approach, we can calculate the probability distribution of the returns on a *mixed portfolio* comprised of equal proportions in securities A and B (see Table 11.2). The expected return of such a portfolio is $5, that is the same as each of the individual securities; however, the variance is reduced considerably. In addition to the extreme results ($+30$ and -20) which are attainable from each of the single investments, the portfolio provides an

Table 11.1

	Security A		Security B	
	Return	Probability	Return	Probability
	-20	0.5	-20	0.5
	30	0.5	30	0.5
Expected return	5		5	
Variance of returns	625		625	
Standard deviation of returns	25		25	

4. Note that there is a 25% chance that the outcome of investment A will be $-$\$20$ and a similar chance that the outcome of investment B will be $-$\$20$. But since the investor 'buys' only half of each security, he will lose $10 in A and $10 in B, so that his total loss will be $20 with a probability of 25%.

Table 11.2 A mixed portfolio: 50% invested in A and 50% in B

	Return	Probability
	− 20	1/4
	+ 5	1/2[a]
	+ 30	1/4
Expected return	+ 5	
Variance of return[b]	312.5	
Standard deviation	17.7	

[a] Since the two alternatives are independent events the probability of earning $5 results from a 0.25 chance that A will lose $20 while B earns $30, and from a 0.25 probability that A will earn $30 while B loses $20.

[b] The variance is given by $0.25(-20-5)^2 + 0.5(5-5)^2 + 0.25(30-5)^2 = 312.5$.

intermediate result (+ 5) as well. Thus, the diversified portfolio reduces the dispersion of outcomes, and the chance of suffering a major loss (− $20) is lowered from a probability of 0.5 for each single investment to a probability of only 0.25 for the mixed portfolio. Moreover, this risk reduction property of portfolio diversification exists even though we assume that the two projects have *identical* earnings and risk characteristics.

The above example demonstrates how an investor can improve his risk-return position by diversifying when the income streams in question are assumed to be statistically independent. In practice, however, the analysis is somewhat more complicated: the income streams of individual securities (or projects) are not necessarily statistically independent, but as long as they are not *perfectly* (positively) correlated, diversification can reduce risk. The degree of risk reduction depends on the degree of the statistical interdependence between the income streams of the different investments and on the number of securities over which the investor can spread his risk. The lower the interdependence and the greater the number of investments, the greater will be the potential gain from diversification. Let us turn now to the more general analysis of the portfolio selection problem.

THE CONCEPT OF AN EFFICIENT PORTFOLIO

To analyze the portfolio effects of combining the returns of different investments, let us assume that an individual is confronted by two securities A and B. The expected return and standard deviation of security A are denoted by μ_A and σ_A respectively, and of security B by μ_B and σ_B respectively. These two securities are plotted as points A and B in Figure 11.1. Should the individual decide to diversify his investment by purchasing a portfolio in the proportions p_A of A and p_B of B ($p_B = 1 - p_A$), the expected return μ on such a portfolio

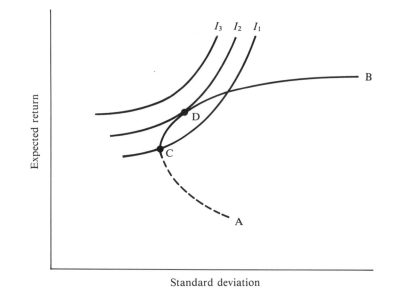

Figure 11.1

is given by:

$$\mu = p_A\mu_A + p_B\mu_B = p_A\mu_A + (1 - p_A)\mu_B$$

with a variance of:

$$\text{Var}(x) = p_A^2\sigma_A^2 + (1 - p_A)^2\sigma_B^2 + 2p_A(1 - p_A)\text{Cov}(x_A, x_B)$$

where the random variables x_A and x_B denote the returns on securities A and
B respectively, and $\text{Cov}(x_A, x_B)$ denotes the covariance between x_A and x_B. The
equation for the variance can also be written as:

$$\text{Var}(x) = p_A^2\sigma_A^2 + (1 - p_A)^2\sigma_B^2 + 2p_A)(1 - p_A)R\sigma_A\sigma_B$$

where R denotes the coefficient of correlation between the returns of the two
securities.

Let us now examine the effects of combining the two securities in a portfolio, under varying assumptions regarding the coefficient of correlation, R.
When $R = 0$ the transformation curve, which represents the pairs of expected
return and variance which result from combining the two securities in all possible proportions, takes the form of the locus ACB of Figure 11.1. This curve
has its minimum variance (standard deviation) at point C. All the portfolios
(points) on curve ACB correspond to the different proportions in which the
amount invested is divided between the two securities.

Only the solid portion of the curve represents *efficient* portfolios of

---

5. Since the coefficient of correlation $R = \text{Cov}(x_1x_2)/\sigma_1\sigma_2$ the two equations are equivalent.

securities A and B, an efficient portfolio being defined as a combination of securities which maximizes the expected return for a given variance (or standard deviation). The dashed segment AC is irrelevant, since these portfolios are by definition inefficient: alternatives exist which offer higher expected returns for the same levels of risk. The statement can readily be proven by examining Figure 11.2. For every point on section AC a corresponding point which is preferable can be found on section BC. For example, Point G' dominates G since it has a higher mean than G but the same variance. Therefore, section AC represents inefficient portfolios which will never be chosen by a rational investor.

To complete the graphical representation of investment choice, the indifference curves of a hypothetical risk-averse investor have been superimposed on the transformation curve of Figure 11.1. The indifference curves rise from left to right, which indicates that the investor must be compensated with a higher expected return as the variance increases. The curves are drawn convex downwards on the assumption that additional increments of variance (risk) require increasingly larger increments of expected return to compensate the individual. The investor's *final* choice out of the efficient set depends on his tastes. Moreover, in accordance with the expected utility maxim, the investor will choose that portfolio which permits him to reach the highest indifference curve, because the higher the indifference curve, the greater his utility. The *optimal* portfolio for the hypothetical investor of Figure 11.1 is denoted by point D which lies on indifference curve I_2. We now turn to an analysis of the impact of the degree of correlation between securities on the variance of the portfolio.

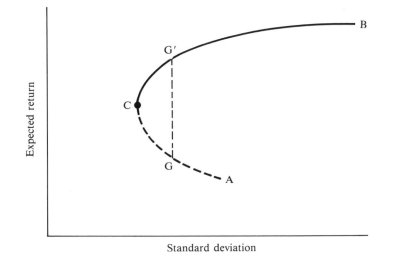

Figure 11.2

CORRELATION AND THE GAINS FROM DIVERSIFICATION _____

How to Build a Stock Portfolio Even If You Aren't a Moneybags

Seeking Unrelated Industries

'You don't want more than one company in an industry, and you don't want companies in related industries,' says Mr. Lipson. For example, an auto manufacturer and a steel company that supplies auto manufacturers will move together. Further, 'you also don't want industries that respond to the economic cycle the same way, such as trucking and basic manufacturing,' he says.

While Mr. Lipson believes that investors need at least 15 stocks to be adequately diversified, other advisers are comfortable with a smaller number. 'It's not so much the number of names that makes you diversified, but how you spread them out,' says George Vanderheiden, who heads the equity growth group for Fidelity Investments.

International Stocks

Investors can add to their diversification by including some international exposure. 'To be really well diversified, you need 10% of your portfolio in inter-

national stocks,' says John Markese, president of the American Association of Individual Investors, an investor-education group based in Chicago.

Kenneth Jessen, 53, an engineer for Hewlett-Packard Co. in Loveland, Colo., follows much of this advise. He holds at least 10 stocks and diversifies into emerging sectors like waste management, and foreign stocks. Right now, he says his research has led him to two British companies: Hanson PLC ('20 years of consistent increase in earnings per share,') and Glaxo Holdings PLC.

While it makes sense to buy only the kinds of stocks you understand, beware of the familiarity factor. 'People tend to buy McDonald's, Toys 'R' Us and drug companies,' says Michael Stolper, president of Stolper & Co., a San Diego firm that evaluates money managers.

Source: based on an article by Ellen E. Schultz, *Wall Street Journal*, April 10, 1992, pp. C1 and C13. (All quotes from p. C13.)

As demonstrated in article 17, the experts who manage portfolios believe that selecting stocks from 'unrelated industries' is more important than selecting a large number of stocks for the portfolio. In addition, since some stocks are traded in various countries outside the U.S. stockmarket, it is also recommended to incorporate some international stocks in the portfolio.

The concept of 'related' or 'unrelated' stocks has to do with co-movement of prices or the correlation between the returns on the various stocks. The 'related' concept is measured by the correlation coefficient. When it is zero. we say that the stocks are unrelated, hence a large risk reduction is achieved. When the correlation is positive and large, the gain is limited. If we can find stocks with negative correlation, this is preferable because the risk reduction is enhanced. However, since in reality it is hard to find stocks with a negative correlation, the experts recommend to find only 'unrelated' stocks (that is, with zero correlation). We turn to analyze the effect of the correlation on risk reduction.

As we noted in the above example, the degree to which a two-security portfolio reduces the variance of returns depends on the degree of correlation between the returns of the securities. To quantify this relationship let us assume the following expected returns and variances for two hypothetical securities A and B:

$$\begin{array}{cc} A & B \\ \mu_A = 10 & \mu_B = 20 \\ \sigma_A^2 = 100 & \sigma_B^2 = 900 \end{array}$$

where:

μ_A = mean return on security A
μ_B = mean return on security B
σ_A^2 = variance of the return on security A
σ_B^2 = variance of the return on security B

The expected returns and variances for portfolios of varying proportions and for four alternative assumptions regarding the degree of correlation between returns are given in Table 11.3. The data clearly show that diversification can reduce the portfolio variance of returns, and moreover, the lower the coefficient of correlation, the greater the reduction in the variance. For example, if we choose the proportions p_A and p_B which minimize the variance, in the case $p_A = 3/4$ and $p_B = 1/4$, and assume $R = -1$, the portfolio variance can be reduced to zero:

$$\begin{aligned} \sigma^2 &= p_A^2 \sigma_A^2 + p_B^2 \sigma_B^2 + 2(-1)p_A p_B \sigma_A \sigma_B \\ &= \tfrac{9}{16} \times 100 + \tfrac{1}{16} \times 900 - 2 \times \tfrac{3}{4} \times \tfrac{1}{4} \times 10 \times 30 \\ &= \frac{900 + 900 - 1800}{16} = 0 \end{aligned}$$

In general, diversification will reduce the minimum attainable variance if the correlation coefficient is less than the ratio of the standard deviation of the security with the smaller deviation to the security with the larger deviation.

Table 11.3

Proportion of portfolio invested in security A	Expected return on portfolio[a]	Variance of returns for alternative coefficients of correlation[b]				
		$R = +1$	$R = +1/2$	$R = 0$	$R = -1/2$	$R = -1$
0	20	900	900	900	900	900
1/5	18	676	628	580	532	484
2/5	16	484	412	340	268	196
3/5	14	324	252	180	108	36
4/5	12	196	148	100	52	4
1	10	100	100	100	100	100

[a] The mean is independent of R, and is obtained from the formula:

$$\mu = p_A \mu_A + (1 - p_A)\mu_B$$

[b] The formula for the variance is:

$$\text{Var}(x) = p_A^2 \sigma_A^2 + (1 - p_A)^2 \sigma_B^2 + 2p_A(1 - p_A)R\sigma_A \sigma_B$$

The inverse relationship between the degree of correlation and the degree of variance reduction can be seen more clearly in Figure 11.3, which presents a family of transformation curves for varying assumptions regarding the degree of correlation. Diversification in this diagram reduces variance except in the extreme case where the returns are perfectly correlated ($R = +1$). On such an assumption the transformation curve reduces to a straight line joining points A and B.[6] As the correlation coefficient is reduced from $+1$ to $+1/2$, 0, and $-1/2$, the transformation curve bulges out further and further to the left, and if we were to superimpose a set of indifference curves on the same plane, we could readily see that the risk-averse investor reaches higher levels of utility (i.e., a higher indifference curve), the smaller is the coefficient of correlation. It should also be noted that in the case of perfect negative correlation between the returns of the two securities, the transformation curve will at one point touch the vertical axis, which means that there exists a portfolio which can completely eliminate the variance (or standard deviation). Of course, the final decision to choose the minimum variance (or standard deviation) portfolio or some other point on the curve depends on individuals' tastes (that is, on the slope of the indifference curves).

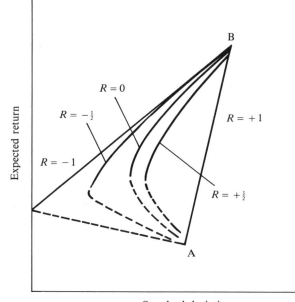

Figure 11.3

6. In the particular case where $R = +1$ the variance of the portfolio is given by $\sigma^2 = p_A^2\sigma_A^2 + p_B^2\sigma_B^2 + 2p_Ap_B\sigma_A\sigma_B = (p_A\sigma_A + p_B\sigma_B)^2$, and hence $\sigma = p_A\sigma_A + p_B\sigma_B$. The last equation describes a straight line connecting points A and B.

In the other extreme case of perfect negative correlation in which $R = -1$, the portfolio variance is given by $\sigma^2 = p_A^2\sigma_A^2 + p_B^2\sigma_B^2 - 2p_Ap_B\sigma_A\sigma_B = (p_A\sigma_A - p_B\sigma_B)^2$. The investment proportions which minimize the variance are given by $p_A/p_B = \sigma_B/\sigma_A$. In this case the variance of the portfolio is equal to zero; hence AB touches the vertical axis.

In reality, the returns on investment are not perfectly correlated, either positively or negatively. In most cases, some positive correlation, reflecting general economic conditions, exists, and at best the cash flows may have zero, or slightly negative correlation. As a result, portfolio diversification can help to stabilize the returns, but cannot entirely eliminate the fluctuations (variance) of investment returns. In general, diversification reduces, but does not completely eliminate, risk.

─────────── THE NUMBER OF SECURITIES AND THE GAINS FROM DIVERSIFICATION

ARTICLE 18

How to Build a Stock Portfolio Even If You Aren't a Moneybags

You don't need a mountain of cash to buy individual stocks.

Would-be investors are often told that unless they have more than $100,000 to put into stocks, they should stick with mutual funds.

'People espousing this are worried that you won't get enough diversification and that transaction costs on small portfolios are too high,' says Arthur Micheletti, chief economist at Bailard, Biehl & Kaiser, a money-management firm in San Mateo, Calif.

But he and other investment advisers and portfolio managers say individuals can build an adequately diversified, high quality portfolio of individual stocks with as little as $25,000.

People who buy even as few as 10 stocks can be adequately diversified, if they buy securities in different industries and use a variety of selection criteria. And they can keep transaction costs low by buying round lots, using discount brokers and keeping trading to a minimum.

How do you build a small portfolio?

First consider the number of stocks needed. Academic research on diversification suggest that individuals need 10 to 20 securities. 'So if you assume an average stock price of $20, you could buy 15 stocks in round lots of 100 shares for $30,000,' says Elliot Lipson, president of Horizon Financial Advisors.

One Investment Advisor's Model Portfolio

Elliot Lipson, president of Horizon Financial Advisors, illustrates how a small portfolio of stocks can achieve a lot of diversification, if the stocks come from industries that respond differently to economic and other factors.*

STOCK	INDUSTRY
PepsiCo	Beverage
Bird Corp.	Bldg. Materials
Turner 'B'	Broadcasting
Bear Stearns	Brokerage
Everex Systems	Computer
Groundwater Tech.	Environmental
Humana	Hospital
American Bankers Insurance Group	Insurance
Asarca	Metals, misc.
Petroleum & Resources	Oil
United Dominion Realty	Real Estate
GTE	Telephone
Casey's General Stores	Retail Grocery
UST Inc.	Tobacco
Gleason	Tools

* Buying 100 shares of each stock would cost about $33,000. For added diversification, Mr Lipson would put $5,000 into each of two mutual funds: Vanguard Explorer, a small-stock fund, and Harbor International, a fund that buys stocks of companies outside the U.S. *Source*: based on an article of this title by Ellen E. Schultz, *Wall Street Journal*, April 10, 1992, p. C1.

For This Top Money Manager, a Handful of Stocks Is Enough

Say you have $200 million to invest. How many stocks would you buy?

Joan E. Lappin thinks a good portfolio holds about 10 stocks, 15 at the outside. Following that strategy of concentrated investments has helped the New York money manager roll up annual gains averaging 45% over the last five years — including about 37% so far this year.

That kind of investment concentration flies in the face of the fundamental advice that investors should always diversify their holdings, either by buying a large number of stocks or by purchasing mutual funds with extensive stock portfolios.

Source: based on James A. White's article, *Wall Street Journal*, December 10, 1991, p. C1.

We discuss below how the number of assets in the portfolio affects the gains from diversification. Do we really need to include thousands of stocks in the portfolio to enjoy the reduction in risk? (See articles 18 and 19.)

In order to examine the relationship between the number of projects included in the portfolio and the gain from diversification, let us assume that we are confronted by three securities, A, B, and C, the price of each of which is $100. The expected return and variance of each of these securities are given in Table 11.4. For the sake of convenience we shall assume zero coefficients of correlation between the returns of each pair of securities. We also assume that the investments are completely divisible, that is the investor can combine the securities in any proportion.

The three-security case is illustrated in Figure 11.4. The investor is confronted with three mutually exclusive alternatives:

1. Invest in a portfolio which includes all three securities.
2. Confine himself to a two-security portfolio.
3. Put all of his money into a single security.

Curve I of Figure 11.4 represents the transformation curve of portfolios comprising differing proportions of securities A and B; curves II and III are the relevant transformation curves for portfolios which include B and C, and A and C, respectively. Curve IV represents the transformation curve for portfolios which include all possible combinations of all three securities. In the latter case, the investor is offered an additional degree of freedom, and is in a

Table 11.4

	Securities		
	A	B	C
Expected return	10	20	30
Variance of returns	100	900	2,500

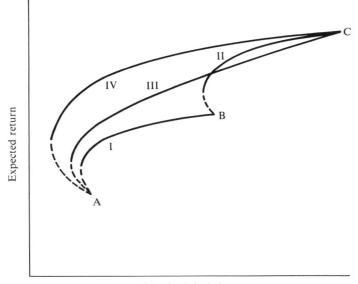

Figure 11.4

better position to reduce the variance for any given expected return: that is, curve IV lies to the left of the other three curves. This *additional* possibility for diversifying his investment can only increase, and not decrease, an investor's utility since he still remains free to put his money into only two of the three securities. This relationship holds for portfolios which include four, five, or more securities.

It would seem to follow that investors who select their portfolios according to the mean–variance rule and who desire to benefit from diversification should tend to build large portfolios. In practice, however, the degree of diversification is often limited, for one or more of the following reasons:[7]

1. Sometimes an investor has only a small amount of money at his disposal so that diversifying over a large number of securities would mean investing very small amounts in each security.
2. An individual investor may find it difficult and expensive to keep track of a large number of securities; even a cursory check of the past performance and future outlook of a large number of securities is likely to prove a difficult and tedious task for most investors. Thus outside of the realm of

---

7. Empirical studies, based on the capital asset pricing model (see Chapter 12) have shown that randomly chosen portfolios with as few as 10 to 15 securities capture almost all of the potential reduction of risk through diversification. See J. Evans and S. H. Archer 'Diversification and the Reduction of Dispersion: An Empirical Analysis,' *Journal of Finance*, December 1968; and K. H. Johnson and D. S. Shannon, 'A Note on Diversification and the Reduction of Dispersion,' *Journal of Financial Economics*, December 1974. Compare also Bruno Solnik, 'Why not Diversify Internationally Rather than Domestically?' *Financial Analysts Journal*, July/August 1974.

textbooks, investors usually restrict themselves to a small number of securities. However, the individual investor can, and often does, hold a larger number of securities in his portfolio *indirectly* by investing in the shares of mutual funds or investment companies.

Obtaining shares of a mutual fund is one way to benefit from the potential gains of diversifying in a large number of assets. However, mutual funds charge some form of management fee for their services, and investors may decide to avoid these fees even if it means holding no more than ten or so stocks in their portfolio. Holding a very large number of assets may not be crucial since most of the gains of diversifying can be achieved by holding a small number of assets. To demonstrate, assume that an investor faces n identical and independent securities, all with the same mean and variance. It is easy to show in this case that diversifying by placing $1/n$ in each asset yields a portfolio variance of $\sigma_p^2 = \sigma^2/n$ where σ^2 is the variance of each individual asset.[8]

Table 11.5 shows that if $\sigma_p^2 = 100$, including two assets in the portfolio reduces the variance to 50, whereas including three assets reduces it to $33\frac{1}{3}$, and so on. The marginal reduction in the variance of the portfolio by the successive addition of each asset decreases, but most of the gain is achieved when 10–15 stocks are considered, as recommended in article 19. Indeed, the property of the interaction between the variance of a portfolio and the number of assets included in the portfolio explains the popular slogan 'a little diversification goes a long way.'

THE EFFICIENT FRONTIER WITH BORROWING AND LENDING

A further significant increase in utility can be achieved if investors are permitted to borrow or lend money at some *riskless* interest rate r. To illustrate, suppose that some risky security A exists with an expected return $E(A)$ and standard deviation $\sigma(A)$ (see Figure 11.5). An investor might confine himself

Table 11.5 The portfolio variance as a function of the number of assets when all assets are independent

Number of assets in the portfolio	Portfolio variance σ_p^2/n ($\sigma_p^2 = 100$)	Marginal reduction in the variance
1	100	—
2	$100/2 = 50$	50
3	$100/3 = 33\frac{1}{3}$	$16\frac{2}{3}$
4	$100/4 = 25$	$8\frac{1}{3}$
5	$100/5 = 20$	5
$\vdots$	$\vdots$	$\vdots$
10	$100/10 = 10$	1.11

8. In the case of n independent assets, σ_p^2 is given by:

$$\sigma_p^2 = \left(\frac{1}{n}\right)^2 \sigma_1^2 + \left(\frac{1}{n}\right)^2 \sigma_2^2 + \cdots + \left(\frac{1}{n}\right)^2 \sigma_n^2 = \frac{\sigma^2}{n}$$

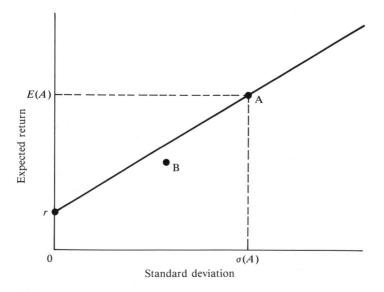

Figure 11.5

to the risky asset; however, given the opportunity to borrow or lend at $r\%$, he can also combine A with riskless bonds (or with debt). Denoting by y the return generated by a portfolio which blends the risky asset A with riskless bonds (or debt), we can write the return on such a portfolio as follows:

$$y = pr + (1-p)A$$

where p denotes the proportion invested in bonds (or in debt if p is negative), $(1-p)$ denotes the proportion invested in security A, and y is a random variable which denotes the return of the new portfolio. The expected return and standard deviation of the new portfolio are given by:

$$E(y) = pr + (1-p)E(A)$$
$$\sigma(y) = (1-p)\sigma(A)$$

and hence $(1-p) = \sigma(y)/\sigma(A)$ and $p = 1 - (\sigma(y)/\sigma(A))$.

Substituting these expressions for p and $1-p$ in the formula for the expected portfolio return yields:

$$E(y) = r + \frac{E(A)-r}{\sigma(A)}\sigma(y)$$

All the combinations of $E(y)$ and $\sigma(y)$ lie on a straight line and represent the set of efficient portfolios (see Figure 11.5). If the investor chooses to be at point A he neither borrows nor lends, and the optimal investment proportion in bonds is $p = 0$. If he chooses a point on the line to the right of point A, this signifies a levered portfolio, i.e., he borrows money at r and invests his own resources plus the borrowed money in A (i.e., $p < 0$). If, on the other hand, his optimal choice is a point located to the left of point A, this means that the investor prefers to diversify his investment between the risky asset A and the riskless bonds (i.e., $p > 0$). Finally, should he choose to be at point r, this would represent a case of extreme risk aversion in which all of his resources are invested in the riskless asset.

Obviously, if given the opportunity to invest in another asset, say B, the investor could construct another straight line of attainable mixed or levered portfolios by blending this new risky asset with riskless bonds (or with debt). However, in general investors will prefer to diversify their holdings over both risky assets as well as riskless bonds (debt). This is illustrated in Figure 11.6 which sets out the risk–return characteristics of each of the two securities, A and B, as well as the curve of portfolios of varying combinations of A and B. It is clear that the efficiency frontier which connects point r with point N represents the best possible alternative for all risk-averse investors. For every point on line rA or rB one can find a point on line rN which promises a higher expected return for the same risk. If we recall that point N itself represents a mixed portfolio of risky securities A and B, we can summarize Figure 12.6 as follows. If an individual chooses to be at point N he places all of his resources in the portfolio of risky assets and neither buys bonds (lends) nor borrows. If he chooses a point to the left of N, this signifies the blending of the risky portfolio N with riskless bonds; points to the right of N represent levered portfolios in which money is borrowed and invested in the risky portfolio represented by N.

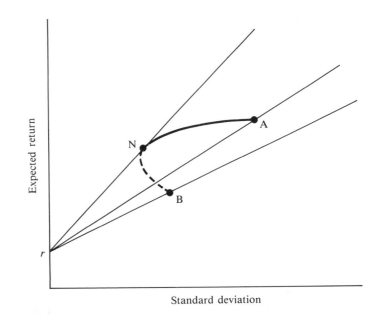

Figure 11.6

This chapter has presented a graphical analysis of the portfolio selection process. In general, risk can be reduced by combining individual securities in a portfolio; the degree of risk reduction depending on the degree of correlation among returns and the number of securities included in the portfolio. The lower the correlation and the greater the number of securities, the greater are the gains from diversification. Investors' utility can also be increased by permitting them the additional option of borrowing and/or lending at a riskless interest rate. In this case, the efficient frontier is linear, a property which will be used in the following chapter which extends the E−V analysis to the market as a whole.

_____ SUMMARY TABLE

Efficient portfolios

1. Calculate the portfolio mean:
$$\mu = p_1\mu_1 + (1 - p_1)\mu_2$$

2. Calculate the portfolio variance:
$$\text{Var}(x) = p_1^2\sigma_1^2 + (1 - p_1)^2\sigma_2^2 + 2p_1(1 - p_1)R\sigma_1\sigma_2$$

By varying the investment proportion p_1 we get an infinite set of portfolios.
3. A given portfolio is called 'efficient' if there is no other portfolio which has a higher (or equal) mean and a lower (or equal) variance.

The gains from diversification

1. The gain is larger the lower the correlation coefficient R.
2. The gain is larger the larger the number of securities in the portfolio. However, most of the gain is achieved by diversifying in a small number of securities.
3. If $R = -1$, the efficient set is a straight line, and a portfolio with zero variance may be achieved.
4. If $R = +1$, the efficient set is a straight line.

Borrowing and lending

When borrowing and lending at r is allowed, the efficient set is a straight line given by:

$$E(y) = r + \frac{E(A) - r}{\sigma(A)}\,\sigma(y)$$

where $(E(A), \sigma(A))$ is the tangency point of the line with risky assets frontier.

QUESTIONS AND PROBLEMS

11.1 Assume that an individual can either invest all of his resources in one of the two securities A or B; or alternatively, he can diversify his investment between the two. The distributions of the returns are as follows:

Security A		Security B	
Return	Probability	Return	Probability
−10	1/2	−20	1/2
50	1/2	60	1/2

Assume that the correlation between the returns from the two securities is zero.

(a) Calculate each security's expected return, variance, and standard deviation.
(b) Calculate the probability distribution of the returns on a *mixed portfolio* comprising equal proportions of securities A and B. Also calculate the expected return, variance, and standard deviation.
(c) Calculate the expected return and the variance of a mixed portfolio comprising 75% of security A and 25% of security B.

11.2 The securities of companies Z and Y have the following expected returns and standard deviations:

	Company Z	Company Y
Expected return (%)	15	35
Standard deviation (%)	20	40

Assume that the correlation between the returns of the two securities is 0.25.

(a) Calculate the expected return and standard deviation for the following portfolios:

    (1) 100%Z
    (2)   75%Z + 25%Y
    (3)   50%Z + 50%Y
    (4)   25%Z + 75%Y
    (5) 100%Y

(b) Graph your results.
(c) Which of the portfolios in part (a) is optimal? Explain.

11.3 Distinguish between an *efficient portfolio* and an *optimal portfolio*.

11.4 Given the following two securities A and B:

	A	B
Expected return (%)	12	24
Standard deviation (%)	6	36

(a) Will an individual ever concentrate all of his investment in security A?
(b) Will he ever concentrate all of his investment in security B?

11.5 Given the following securities C and D:

	Security C	Security D
Expected return (%)	8	20
Standard deviation (%)	18	24

(a) Calculate the expected return and the variance for the following portfolios, assuming that the returns are perfectly correlated ($R = +1$):

(1) 100%C
(2) 75%C + 25%D
(3) 50%C + 50%D
(4) 25%C + 75%D
(5) 100%D

Use these points to graph the transformation curve between C and D.
(b) Answer part (a), assuming that $R = +0.5$.
(c) Answer part (a) for the case of zero correlation between the two securities ($R = 0$).
(d) Graph the transformation curve for the two cases $R = -0.5$ and $R = -1$.
(e) Can you find the proportions of C and D in the mixed portfolio that reduce the portfolio's variance to zero? (Assume $R = -1$.)

11.6 What is the general relationship between the gains from diversification and the correlation among security returns?

11.7 'In the case of perfect positive correlation between two securities ($R = +1$), an investor will never diversify his investment between the two.' Do you agree? In your answer, analyze several alternative situations and use diagrammatic proofs.

11.8 What is the relationship between the number of available securities and the gains from diversification? Does that have any implications for the small investor?

11.9 Given the following three securities:

	A_1	A_2	A_3
Expected return (%)	10	15	20
Standard deviation (%)	20	30	40

(a) Calculate the expected return and the variance (assuming that the correlation for each pair of securities (R_{ij}) is equal to zero) for each of the following two-security portfolios:

(1) $p_1 = 2/5$	(2) $p_1 = 2/5$	(3) $p_1 = 0$
$p_2 = 3/5$	$p_2 = 0$	$p_2 = 3/5$
$p_3 = 0$	$p_3 = 3/5$	$p_3 = 2/5$

where p_i denotes the proportion of security i in the portfolio.
(b) Find, for each of the above portfolios, the three-security portfolio that gives the same expected return as the two-security portfolio.
(c) Calculate the variance of returns for each one of the three-security portfolios and compare your results with your results of (a).

11.10 Assume that an investor wishes to invest $1,000 in a portfolio which includes only one common stock. The rate of interest on riskless bonds (r) is 7% and the expected return and standard deviation of the single stock are 17% and 25% respectively.

(a) Graph the frontier of efficient portfolios for this case.
(b) Suppose that the investor selects a portfolio composed of 60% stock and 40% bonds. What is the expected return and standard deviation of this portfolio?
(c) Suppose now that the investor found it optimal to invest in a portfolio with a 20% standard deviation. How much (in dollars) must he invest in stock and how much in bonds to achieve this risk level? What is the expected return of this portfolio?

11.11 Assume four investment options with the following relationships between their expected returns, ER_i, and their standard deviations, σ_i:

$$ER_1 < ER_2 < ER_3 < ER_4 \quad \text{and} \quad \sigma_1 < \sigma_2 < \sigma_3 < \sigma_4$$

that is, all four options are M–V-efficient. It is claimed that all risk-neutral investors will choose option 4.

(a) Is this claim correct?
(b) If it is, does it contradict the M–V rule?
(c) Does such a result contradict the expected utility principle?

11.12 The following table gives the annual return per $100 invested in four mutually exclusive investment options during the years 1–6:

Year	A	B	C	D
1	20	22	6	10
2	40	21	8	12
3	30	18	5	18
4	22	16	4	20
5	36	20	6	15
6	46	22	10	14

Assuming that these data constitute the entire population for each option:

(a) Calculate the expected returns and standard deviations of each investment.
(b) Determine the M–V efficient and inefficient sets.

11.13 Assume that four securities have an *equal probability* of earning the following rates of return:

A	B	C	D
40	−16	60	5
−10	50	−30	5
20	−12	120	5
−6	22	−40	5

(a) Assuming that the investor is constrained to a single-security portfolio, what are the M–V efficient options? Draw the efficient set for this case.
(b) Answer part (a) assuming that the investor also can construct portfolios

which include two securities in equal proportions. Assume that the returns on the four securities always occur in combinations as shown in the above table, i.e. a return of 40 on security A is always observed when security C has a return of 60, etc.

(c) Determine the efficient set for the case when the investor is allowed to construct portfolios consisting of three securities in equal proportions.

(d) Draw the three efficient sets from (a), (b), and (c) on one diagram. Explain and analyse your results.

11.14 The following table lists the returns available on four mutual funds.

	Return on mutual fund (%)			
Year	Amcap Fund	Chemical Fund	Fidelity Trend Fund	Kemper Growth Fund
1	16.4	−8.1	−3.8	2.4
2	22.4	11.9	9.7	17.8
3	51.9	24.9	26.3	40.8
4	27.9	30.9	25.5	44.1
5	6.2	−4.3	−5.2	−11.5

Source: Wiesenberger, *Investment Companies*.

(a) Assuming that the investor is constrained to a single fund portfolio, what are the E−V efficient options?

(b) Assuming that the investor can invest in a portfolio composed of equal proportions in two funds, determine the E−V efficient options.

(c) Assuming that the investor can invest in a portfolio composed of two funds, with the objective of minimizing the portfolio variance, which pair of mutual funds will he choose from mean−variance considerations? What are the particular investment proportions minimizing the variance? What are the mean return and the variance of the chosen portfolio? (Hint: to solve this part, you will need to calculate the covariances or the correlation coefficients of all the pairs of mutual funds.)

11.15 The following are the expected return, standard deviation of and correlation between returns on Monsanto and Motorola stock.

	Monsanto		Motorola
Expected return	11.28%		16.35%
Standard deviation	32.19%		45.16%
Correlation coefficient		0.40	

Source: CRSP monthly returns tape.

(a) Calculate six points on the efficient frontier for $p_1 = 0, 0.1, 0.3, 0.8, 0.9, 1.0$, where p_1 is the proportion invested in Monsanto stock. Draw the efficient frontier in the mean−standard deviation plane.

(b) Find the investment proportions which minimize the portfolio variance. What is the variance and the expected return of the minimum−variance portfolio?

(c) How would your answer to (b) change if the correlation coefficient were negative, −0.40?

11.16 Suppose that there are two identical and independent securities ($R_{ij} = 0$), with a mean of 10 and variance of 20. What is the optimal portfolio composition? Do you need the investor's indifference curve to answer this question? And if you do need it, why do you need it? Similarly, if you do not need, why do you not need it?

11.17 Suppose that there are n identical securities where all correlations are zero, the mean return on all n securities is μ_0 and the variance is σ_0^2. What investment proportions minimize the variance of the portfolio? Prove your answer.

11.18 Suppose that there are n identical securities where for each security $\mu = \mu_0$ and $\sigma^2 = \sigma_0^2 = 10$. All correlations are zero. You invest equal amounts of money in each security. Calculate the variance for the following alternatives: $n = 1, 2, 5,$ 10, 100, and 1,000. What can you learn from this result?

11.19 There are two securities with the following means and variances:

Security A		Security B	
Mean	6	Mean	10
Variance	5	Variance	8

The correlation is $R_{AB} = +1/2$. A portfolio consisting of these two securities has a variance of 4. What are the investment proportions of these two stocks?

11.20 There are two stocks with a perfect negative correlation $R = -1$. The variance of stock 2 is four times larger than the variance of stock 1, namely, $\sigma_2^2 = 4\sigma_1^2$

   (a) Write the formula for the portfolio variance in this specific case when P_1 or P_2 denote the investment proportions.
   (b) Find the investment proportions which will minimize the portfolios variance.
   (c) What are the investment proportions which minimize the portfolio variance if the correlation is $R = +1$?

11.21 Suppose that there is one risky asset and one riskless asset. The mean rate of return on the risky asset is 10% and its standard deviation is 5%. Is it possible that the following two points lie on the capital market line?

   Point A: $E(X_1) = 30\%,$ $\sigma_1 = 25\%$
   Point B: $E(X_2) = 15\%,$ $\sigma_2 = 20\%$

SELECTED REFERENCES

Alexander, Gordon J. and Resnick, Bruce G., 'More on Estimation Risk and Simple Rules for Optimal Portfolio Selection,' *Journal of Finance*, March 1985.

Baron, D. P., 'Investment Policy, Optimality, and the Mean–Variance Model: Review Article,' *Journal of Finance*, March 1979.

Barry, C. B. and Winkler, R. L., 'Nonstationarity and Portfolio Choice,' *Journal of Financial and Quantitative Analysis*, June 1976.

Bettis, Richard A. and Mahajan, Vijay, 'Risk/Return Performance of Diversified Firms,' *Management Science*, July 1985.

Blume, Marshall E., 'Portfolio Theory. A Step Towards its Practical Application,' *Journal of Business*, April 1970.

Board, J. L. Q. and Sutcliffe, C. M. S., 'Optimal Portfolio Diversification and the Effects of Differing Intra Sample Measures of Return,' *Journal of Business Finance and Accounting*, Winter 1985.

Brealey, R. A. and Hodges, S. D., 'Playing with Portfolios,' *Journal of Finance*, March 1975.

Brennan, M. J., 'The Optimal Number of Securities in Risky Asset Portfolios Where There are Fixed Costs of Transacting: Theory and Some Empirical Results,' *Journal of Financial and Quantitative Analysis*, September 1975.

Brito, N. O., 'Portfolio Selection in an Economy with Marketability and Short Sales Restrictions,' *Journal of Finance*, May 1978.

Burgess, Richard C. and Bey, Roger P., 'Optimal Portfolios: Markowitz Full Covariance versus Simple Selection Rules,' *Journal of Financial Research*, Summer 1988.

Chen, S.-N., 'Simple Optimal Asset Allocation under Uncertainty,' *Journal of Portfolio Management*, Summer 1987.

Cheung, C. S. and Kwan, C. C. Y., 'A Note on Simple Criteria for Optimal Portfolio Selection,' *Journal of Finance*, March 1988.

Dhingra, Harbans L., 'Effects of Estimation Risk on Efficient Portfolios: A Monte Carlo Simulation Study,' *Journal of Finance and Accounting*, Summer 1980.

Dybvig, P. H., 'Distributional Analysis of Portfolio Choice,' *Journal of Business*, 61, 1988.

Elton, E. J., Gruber, M. J., and Padberg, M. W., 'Simple Criteria for Optimal Portfolio Selection: Tracing out the Efficient Frontier,' *Journal of Finance*, March 1978.

Frankfurter, George M. and Phillips, Herbert E., 'Portfolio Selection: An Analytic Approach for Selecting Securities from a Large Universe,' *Journal of Financial and Quantitative Analysis*, June 1980.

Frost, Peter A. and Savarin, James E., 'Portfolio Size and Estimation Risk,' *The Journal of Portfolio Management*, Summer 1986.

Gonzalez, N., Litzenberger, R., and Rolfo, J., 'On Mean Variance Models of Capital Structure and the Absurdity of their Predictions,' *Journal of Financial and Quantitative Analysis*, June 1977.

Gressis, N., Philippatos, G. C., and Hayya, J, 'Multiperiod Portfolio Analysis and the Inefficiency of the Market Portfolio,' *Journal of Finance*, September 1976.

Harpaz, Giora, 'Optimal Risk Sharing Policies,' *The American Economist*, Fall 1986.

Jacob, Nancy L., 'A Limited Diversification Portfolio Selection Model for the Small Investor,' *Journal of Finance*, June 1974.

Jahera, J. S. Jr, Lloyd, W. P., and Page, D. E., 'Firm Diversification and Financial Performance,' *Quarterly Review of Economics and Business*, Spring 1987.

Jose, Manuel L., Nichols, Len M., and Stevens, Jerry L., 'Contributions of Diversification, Promotion and R & D to the Value of Multiproduct Firms: A Tobin's q Approach,' *Financial Management*, Winter 1986.

Khaksari, S., Kamath, R., and Grieves, R., 'A New Approach to Determining Optimum Portfolio Mix,' *Journal of Portfolio Management*, Spring 1989.

Levy, H., 'Does Diversification Always Pay?' in E. Elton and M. Gruber (eds), *TIMS Study in Management Science Essays in Honor of Harry Markowitz*, 1979.

Li, Y. and Ziemba, W. T., 'Characterizations of Optimal Portfolios by Univariate and Multivariate Risk Aversion,' *Management Science*, 35, 1989.

McEntire, Paul L., 'Portfolio Theory for Independent Assets,' *Managerial Science*, August 1984.

McLaren, K. R. and Upcher, M. R., 'Testing Further Restrictions on Portfolio Models, *Australian Economic Papers*, December 1986.

Milonas, N. T. and Papaioannou, G. J., 'Thinness and Portfolio Diversification Benefits: The Case of the Greek Stock Exchange,' *Rivista Internazionale di Scienze Economiche e Commerciali*, December 1986.

Nawrocki, D. and Staples, K., 'A Customized LPM Risk Measure for Portfolio Analysis,' *Applied Economics*, 21, 2, 1989.

Pastore, Mario, 'Mean–Variance Analysis of Portfolios of Dependent Investments: An Extension,' *Journal of Economics and Business*, May 1988.

Rosenthal, Leonard and Sullivan, Timothy, 'Some Estimates of the Impact of Corporate Diversification on the Valuation and Leverage of USA Firms,' *Journal of Business Finance and Accounting*, Summer 1985.

Rubinstein, Mark E., 'A Mean–Variance Synthesis of Corporate Financial Theory,' *Journal of Finance*, March 1973.

Schneller, M. I., 'Mean–Variance Portfolio Composition When Investors' Revision Horizon is Very Long,' *Journal of Finance*, December 1975.

Schwartz, R. A. and Whitcomb, D. K., 'The Time–Variance Relationship: Evidence on Autocorrelation in Common Stock Returns,' *Journal of Finance*, March 1977.

Senbet, L. W. and Thompson, H. E., 'The Equivalence of Alternative Mean–Variance Capital Budgeting Models,' *Journal of Finance*, May 1978.

Sengupta, J. K. and Sfeir. R. E., 'Evaluation of Investment Portfolios: Some Tests of Robustness and Diversification,' *Applied Economics*, February 1987.

Simkowitz, M. A. and Beedles, W. L., 'Diversification in a Three-moment World,' *Journal of Financial and Quantitative Analysis*, December 1978.

Statman, M., 'How Many Stocks Make a Diversified Portfolio?' *Journal of Financial and Quantitative Analysis*, September 1987.

Williams, J. T., 'A Note on Indifference Curves in the Mean–Variance Model,' *Journal of Financial and Quantitative Analysis*, March 1977.

12

The Capital Asset Pricing Model and Arbitrage Pricing Theory

ARTICLE 20

How Savvy Fund Investors Tally the Risk

Looking for a stock mutual fund? Chances are you're already knee-deep in performance figures. But many experts say you shouldn't stop with total return, which is price changes and reinvested dividends. Calculating risk is just as critical.

When experienced investors want to size up risk, they use at least one statistical measure that most individuals overlook: 'beta.' The meaning isn't immediately self-evident, but this gauge goes a long way toward assessing a fund's volatility.

Commonly associated with measuring volatility of individual stocks, beta tracks how closely a fund follows the ups and downs of the stock market. It's calculated by looking at the month-to-month fluctuations of a fund's total return over a three-year period, compared with similar movements of the S&P 500-stock index. For purposes of comparison, the S&P 500 is assigned a beta of 1.00. A fund with a beta of less than 1.00 is less volatile than the broader market. A figure higher than 1.00 means a fund is more volatile, and thus its risk – and potential reward – is higher.

'Beta' measures a fund's volatility against the S&P 500

A look at the top performers so far this year illustrates how beta can be used. The Janus Fund generated a total return of 47.2% through Sept. 8, making it the eighth-best performer; according to Chicago-based Morningstar. Better yet, its beta is 0.71, the lowest of the top 10 funds. By contrast, the Twentieth Century Giftrust Investors fund, which generated a slightly higher return of 49.6%, has a beta of 1.36 – meaning it is 36% more volatile than the market. So in a market downturn, it's more likely to lose more value. Janus investors receive almost identical returns, while taking less risk.

Expert Opinion

There are drawbacks to beta. For one, it isn't statistically valid in comparing specialized funds, such as gold funds, which can move inversely to the stock market in response to bullion prices. Also, beta, pegged to the S&P, is designed only to measure the U.S. equities market.

Bond funds' betas are calculated using Shearson Lehman Hutton's Government/ Corporate Bond Index. But for some,

(continued)

McCAW CELLULAR 'A' OTC-MCAWA

| VALUE LINE | 763 |

	Target Price	Range
	1997	1998
1966		

RECENT PRICE **35**

P/E RATIO **NMF** (Trailing: NMF Median: NMF)

RELATIVE P/E RATIO **NMF**

DIV'D YLD **NIL**

Range 1998
100
80
64
48
40
32
24
20
16
12
8
6

TIMELINESS **3** Average
(Relative Price Performance Next 12 Mos.)
SAFETY **5** Lowest
(Scale: 1 Highest to 5 Lowest)
BETA 1.80 (1.00 = Market)

1996-98 PROJECTIONS
	Price Gain	Ann'l Total Return
High	105 (+200%)	32%
Low	55 (+55%)	12%

Insider Decisions
	M J J A S O N D J
to Buy	0 0 0 0 0 0 1 0 0
Options	0 0 0 0 0 0 0 0 0
to Sell	0 0 0 0 0 1 0 0 0

Institutional Decisions
	2Q'92	3Q'92	4Q'92
to Buy	60	56	76
to Sell	45	59	54
Hld's(000)	76991	73880	80586

| | High: | 35.5 | 47.3 | 28.1 | 26.0 | 30.3 | 35.5 | 36.0 | 41.3 | |
| | Low: | | 25.8 | 16.3 | 11.0 | 15.0 | 11.0 | 20.3 | 31.5 | |

— Relative Price Strength

15.0 × "Cash Flow" p. sh

Shaded areas indicate recessions

Percent	9.0
shares	6.0
traded	3.0

Options: CBOE, ASE

EMPIRE DISTRICT NYSE-EDE

| VALUE LINE | 713 |

	Target Price	Range
	1997	1998
1966		

RECENT PRICE **23**

P/E RATIO **16.7** (Trailing: 18.3 Median: 9.5)

RELATIVE P/E RATIO **1.05**

DIV'D YLD **5.7%**

Range 1998
50
40
32
24
20
16
12
10
8
6
4
3

TIMELINESS **5** Lowest
(Relative Price Performance Next 12 Mos.)
SAFETY **2** Above Average
(Scale: 1 Highest to 5 Lowest)
BETA .45 (1.00 = Market)

1996-98 PROJECTIONS
	Price Gain	Ann'l Total Return
High	25 (+10%)	7%
Low	18 (−20%)	1%

Insider Decisions
	M J J A S O N D J
to Buy	1 0 1 1 0 1 0 0 0
Options	0 0 0 0 0 0 0 0 0
to Sell	0 1 0 0 0 0 0 1 1

Institutional Decisions
	2Q'92	3Q'92	4Q'92
to Buy	5	9	10
to Sell	12	9	8
Hld's(000)	1665	1651	1630

| | High: | 15.8 | 16.1 | 15.9 | 17.0 | 18.0 | 12.3 | 9.9 | 8.7 | 23.3 | 24.8 | 24.1 |
| | Low: | 13.6 | 13.3 | 13.8 | 13.7 | 11.6 | 9.3 | 7.4 | 6.8 | 20.9 | 20.1 | 14.8 |

2 for 1 split

1.09 × Dividends p sh divided by Interest Rate

— Relative Price Strength

Shaded areas indicate recessions

Percent	3.0
shares	2.0
traded	1.0

Options: None

such as junk-bond funds, beta isn't meaningful, since there is little relation between their behavior and the broader bond market.

Calculating beta takes an expert. It's best to consult mutual fund directories, available at brokerage house and libraries. You can also find statistics on volatility in services provided by firms such as Morningstar (800 876-5005). Morningstar's *Mutual Fund Values* costs $55 for three monthly sets of detailed information on 1,100 funds. And on computer disk, *Business Week*'s Mutual Funds Scoreboard – compiled by Morningstar – also includes a volatility measure.

Although 'beta' as a measure of risk is controversial, it is commonly used in many publications. For example, *Value Line* reports it for their individual firm analyses as illustrated below.
Source: Meeltan, John, *Business Week*, October 2, 1989, p. 118. Tables from *Value Line*, April 16, 1993.

Article 20 discusses beta as a measure of risk. What is beta? Why is it a measure of risk or safety? How is it related to the mean rate of return on the securities under consideration? If the McCaw Cellular Company has a beta of 1.80, what are the implications regarding the required mean rate of return for the firm's stock? Is 1.80 considered to be very high, very low, or moderate risk? Is beta of Empire District of 0.45 considered to be very low? Why is the safety of a firm with a beta of 1.80 considered to be below average, whereas a company with a beta of 0.45 is considered to be safer? In order to introduce the concept of beta, we must first examine the equilibrium pricing model known as the *capital asset pricing model* (CAPM) where beta plays an integral role.

Before we discuss the meaning of beta as a risk index, we need an equilibrium model of stock evaluation. Recall that, throughout the book we have taken the maximization of the market value of the existing shareholders' equity as the goal of the firm. A direct implication of this assumption is that the firm should choose its investment program and financing policy so as to maximize the price (value) of its common stock. This in turn requires some sort of model of the forces which influence and determine stock prices. This chapter is devoted to a model of the securities market based explicitly on the portfolio analysis of the preceding chapter. In this chapter we examine the equilibrium relationship between expected return and risk; this relationship will be derived from a formal model, known in the literature as the capital asset pricing model (CAPM) and in particular we discuss the risk index beta. In Part III, this model is used to help determine the discount rate (cost of capital) to be used in firms' financial decisions.

An important advantage of this model lies in the fact that it takes uncertainty directly into account and, therefore, allows us to study the dual impact of profitability and risk upon the value of a firm's shares. A shortcoming of the model is the fact that it rests on very restrictive assumptions; however, the capital asset pricing model does provide significant insights into the problem of capital budgeting under uncertainty. Moreover, the logic which underlies the model can help the firm devise operational rules of thumb for reaching investing and financing decisions in practice. In the second part of this chapter we present the *arbitrage pricing theory* (APT) model, which relies on less severe assumptions and which is less criticized on empirical grounds.[1]

THE MODEL

Today's securities market is a complex mechanism incorporating thousands of decision variables, and therefore any attempt to gain insight into the workings of such a market requires a high degree of abstraction from reality. Thus the fascinating world of brokers, speculators, and market tips will be ruthlessly shunted aside in order to focus our attention on the all-important relationship between risk and return. We assume that securities are traded in a hypothetical 'perfect' capital market in which:

1. There are no transaction costs or taxes.
2. All relevant information regarding securities is freely available to all investors simultaneously.
3. All investors can borrow or lend any amount in the relevant range without affecting the interest rate, and there is no risk of bankruptcy.
4. There is a given uniform investment period for all investors.
5. Investors are risk averse and reach their decisions using the mean–variance rule.

For simplicity, let us initially assume that the market comprises only five securities, A, B, C, D, E. Figure 12.1 sets out the risk–return characteristics of each of these securities; the shaded area represents the various combinations of two or more of the risky securities in portfolios of differing proportions. Now let us consider an investor who for some reason restricts himself to a portfolio which includes only securities A and E: curve I, connecting points A and E, represents all the attainable risk–return combinations from this two-security portfolio, with each point on the curve representing a different set of investment proportions. (Note that only the solid part of the curve represents efficient portfolios; the dashed part of the curve represents inefficient combinations, i.e. each point represents a lower attainable return for a given level of risk.) Similarly, transformation curve II is the appropriate curve for portfolios which include various proportions of D and E. Clearly, similar curves could also be generated for other two-security combinations or for portfolios which include three, four or more securities.

If we permit the investor to build his portfolio as he wishes, the envelope curve of the five-security portfolios will lie to the left of the transformation curves of the constrained portfolios which include four or fewer securities.

1. The capital asset pricing model was developed in William F. Sharpe, 'Capital Asset Prices: A Theory of Market Equilibrium under Conditions of Risk,' *Journal of Finance*, September 1964; John Lintner, 'Security Prices Risk and Maximal Gains from Diversification,' *Journal of Finance*, December 1965 and Jan Mossin, 'Equilibrium in a Capital Asset Market,' *Econometrica*, October 1966. The APT model was developed by Stephen Ross, 'The Arbitrage Theory of Capital Asset Pricing,' *Econometrica*, 1976.

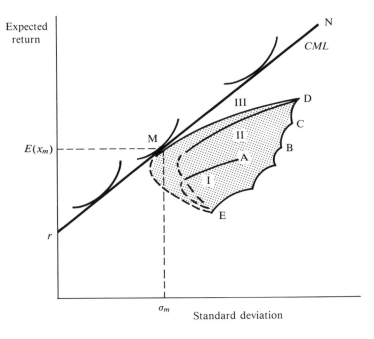

Figure 12.1

Choosing to hold any proportion of all the five securities assumed to comprise the market, the envelope curve for the five-security case is denoted as III in Figure 12.1. This curve sets out all of the combinations of expected return and standard deviation which can be obtained by freely building a portfolio of risky assets using all of the securities available in the market. The shaded area to the right of curve III represents portfolios which are *inefficient* relative to the portfolios on the solid part of curve III. Here again the lower, dashed part of the curve is also inefficient since these portfolios are dominated by the upper segment of curve III (see Chapter 11 for a complete discussion).

THE CAPITAL MARKET LINE

Now let us assume that the investor can borrow or lend (buy bonds) at the riskless rate of interest, r. This option, which is represented in Figure 12.1 by the *capital market line* (CML) denoted as rN, which rises from the interest rate r on the vertical axis and which is tangent to transformation curve III at point M, sets out all the alternative combinations of the risk portfolio M with riskless borrowing and lending. The segment from point r to point M includes the mixed portfolios of risky securities and bonds. Levered portfolios (combinations of M with riskless loans) are represented by points along the line beyond point M. Point M represents the risk–return characteristics of the *market portfolio* which has optimal proportions of the five risky securities. This portfolio is optimal since given the option of riskless borrowing or lending at rate r, portfolio M permits the investor to reach the highest market line, thereby permitting him to reach his highest possible indifference curve. Note that the optimal risk portfolio, represented by point M, has the property of maximizing the angle formed when a straight line is drawn from point r to any point on the transformation curve. Thus the line rN has the highest possible slope of any market line drawn to any point on the transformation curve.

If an investor's indifference curve is tangential to point M, this individual will invest all of his resources in risky securities only. Of course, the indifference curves of most investors will *presumably not* be tangential at point M. Tangency solutions which lie on the segment rM represent mixed portfolios which combine risky securities and riskless bonds. Those which occur on the segment MN represent levered portfolios: that is, the risk portfolio M which is financed partly by loans. However, it must be emphasized that in our idealized market all investors must have one important characteristic in common. Whether he chooses a pure risk, mixed, or levered portfolio, an investor who chooses to invest in risky assets invariably builds a risk portfolio which has the optimal proportions represented by point M. *Hence the proportions of each security in the risky portion of the portfolios of all investors are the same, independent of their individual tastes.* Despite the differences in tastes, all individuals will diversify the risky portion of their portfolios in the same proportions among the individual securities. Differences in individual tastes are operative only in determining the proportion of bonds (loans) which the investor buys (takes). The indifference curves enter the analysis only after the optimal proportions of the risk portfolio (represented by point M) have been established, and serve to determine the tangency point with the market line rN, but do not alter the tangency of the market line with point M itself.

The capital market line indicates that the expected return and risk (standard deviation) of all *efficient portfolios* lie on a straight line rN (see Figure 12.1). To show this relationship, we denote the expected return and the standard deviation of *efficient portfolios* by E_p and σ_p, respectively. Since an efficient portfolio is a simple mixture of the riskless asset and the portfolio M, we have

$$E_p = pr + (1 - p)E(x_m)$$
$$\sigma_p = (1 - p)\sigma_m$$

where p denotes the proportion invested in the riskless asset. By substituting $(1 - p) = \sigma_p/\sigma_m$ from the second equation into the first, we can derive the capital market line, CML:

$$E_p = r + \frac{E(x_m) - r}{\sigma_m}\sigma_p$$

All efficient portfolios lie on the straight line. Obviously, in the specific case where the efficient portfolio is the market portfolio (which is also efficient) we have $\sigma_p = \sigma_m$ and hence $E_p = E(x_m)$. The other extreme case is that of the riskless asset. By definition the riskless asset is also efficient with $\sigma_p = 0$ and hence $E_p = r$.

As we have just seen, in an idealized perfect capital market in which riskless lending and borrowing opportunities are available without transaction costs, all investors will desire to hold the same proportions of risky securities in their portfolios. This raises two questions: which securities are held, and in what proportions? The answer to the first question is straightforward. In a perfect market, in which all lenders and borrowers face the same (riskless) interest rate, the risky portfolios of all investors will include the same securities independent of their tastes. Thus if a particular security is not included in portfolio M, no investor holds it. But if no investor desires to hold a security, its price must fall, thereby increasing its return, until it becomes sufficiently attractive to be included in portfolio M. It follows that in equilibrium, *all* available securities will be included in the risk portfolios of all investors. The answer to the second question regarding the proportions in which the securities are held is somewhat more difficult, and requires additional analysis.

In order to find the optimal proportion of securities that are included in M, we must first analyze the process by which the optimal point M is derived. Let $E(x_0)$ and σ_0 denote the expected return per dollar investment and standard deviation of any risky portfolio; the formulae for these two measures of portfolio return and risk are given by:

$$E(x_0) = \sum_{i=1}^{n} p_i E(x_i)$$

and

$$\sigma_0^2 = \sum_{i=1}^{n} p_i^2 \sigma_i^2 + 2 \sum_{\substack{i=1 \\ j>i}}^{n} p_i p_j \, \mathrm{Cov}(x_i, x_j)$$

where:

p_i = proportion of an investor's wealth invested in the ith security
n = number of different securities available in the market
σ_i^2 = variance of returns (per dollar invested) in the ith security
$E(x_i)$ = expected return (per dollar invested) in the ith security
$\mathrm{Cov}(x_i, x_j)$ = covariance between securities i and j

The expression $\mathrm{Cov}(x_i, x_j)$ in the formula for the portfolio variance represents the covariance between all pairs of securities; thus it reflects the correlation between the fluctuations in the returns of any two securities from period to period. Note that since the above formula holds for any portfolio, the investment proportions p_i need *not* be optimal.

In general, $\Sigma_{i=1}^{n} p_i \neq 1$, that is the investment proportions will not add up to 1 because the investor may also buy riskless bonds or borrow. When the latter two possibilities are taken into account, the investment proportions (including riskless bonds or loans) must add to 1: $\Sigma_{i=1}^{n} p_i + p_r = 1$, where p_r denotes the proportion invested in riskless bonds (or loans). If the investor borrows, $p_r < 0$ and $\Sigma_{i=1}^{n} p_i > 1$; if the investor buys bonds, $p_r > 0$ and $\Sigma_{i=1}^{n} p_i < 1$; and if the investor neither borrows nor lends, $p_r = 0$ and $\Sigma_{i=1}^{n} p_i = 1$. The latter possibility represents the special case where the indifference curve is tangential to the market line at point M itself.

Recalling our discussion of Figure 12.1 the problem confronting the investor is how to choose a point $(E(x_0), \sigma_0)$ on the envelope curve so that the capital market line (CML) connecting it to the point r on the vertical axis forms a maximum angle α thereby permitting him to reach the highest possible indifference curve. In analytical terms, the investor must find the investment proportions p_i which maximize the following expression:

$$tg\ \alpha = \frac{E(x_0) - r}{\sigma_0} = \frac{\sum_{i=1}^{n} p_i E(x_i) - r}{\left[\sum_{i=1}^{n} p_i^2 \sigma_i^2 + 2 \sum_{\substack{i=1 \\ j>i}}^{n} p_i p_j\, \mathrm{Cov}(x_i, x_j) \right]^{1/2}}$$

Portfolio M in the example given in Figure 12.1 maximizes this expression, and therefore represents the optimum unlevered risk portfolio. The investment proportions of this portfolio are optimal for all investors. Note that we are discussing the first stage of the decision process in which the optimal risk portfolio is determined: that is, we are locating the optimal point on the efficiency curve, and *not* the tangency of the curve to an indifference curve.

CAPITAL ASSET PRICING MODEL (CAPM)

The preceding formula can now be used to derive the following equilibrium condition between the risk and return of a security:[2]

$$E(x_i) = r + \frac{E(x_m) - r}{\sigma_m^2}\, \mathrm{Cov}(x_i, x_m)$$

where $E(x_m)$ and σ_m^2 denote, respectively, the expected return and variance of the optimal portfolio of risky securities, the proportions of which are fixed for all investors. This portfolio, which we call the *market portfolio*, corresponds to point M of Figure 12.1. The equilibrium relationship between expected return and risk must hold for *every security i* in the market. Thus the expected return of each security reflects the pure riskless interest rate plus a risk *premium* which is related to that security's contribution to the overall risk of the market portfolio. From the formula it is also clear that the *higher* the association between the return on the individual security and the return on the market portfolio, the greater is the required risk premium.

The model by which every investor maximizes the slope of the line $(tg\alpha)$ and, as a result, by which prices are determined such that the above risk–return relation holds, is called the *capital asset pricing model* (CAPM). The CAPM

2. The formal derivation is given in Appendix 12A.

was developed by Sharpe (1964) and Lintner (1965) for which Sharpe received the 1990 Nobel Prize in Economics. Also the relationship between the expected return of each risky asset and its risk is called the *security market line* (SML), which constitutes a linear relationship between expected return and risk. Denoting the market price of risk (as measured by the variance) by:

$$\frac{E(x_m) - r}{\sigma_m^2} \equiv \lambda$$

the last equation can be rewritten as:

$$E(x_i) = r + \lambda \, \text{Cov}(x_i, x_m)$$

Thus, $E(x_i)$, the expected rate of return on the ith security, is equal to the risk-free rate plus the market price of risk λ multiplied by the contribution of the ith security to the portfolio risk, i.e., $\text{Cov}(x_i, x_m)$. Since λ is a constant factor for all securities, one can put $E(x_i)$ on the vertical axis and $\text{Cov}(x_i, x_m)$ on the horizontal axis and derive a linear relationship between $E(x_i)$ and $\text{Cov}(x_i, x_m)$.

However, the most common way to present the linear relationship between $E(x_i)$ and risk is as follows. First recall that if one runs the following time series regression:

$$x_{it} = \alpha_i + \beta_i x_{mt} + e_t$$

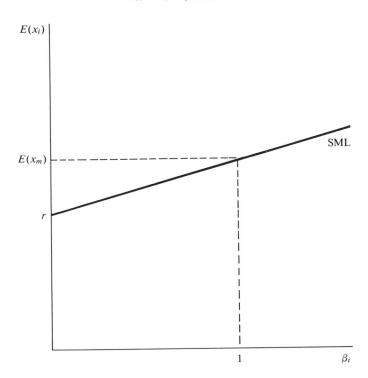

Figure 12.2

then by definition of the regression slope we have:

$$\beta_i = \frac{\text{Cov}(x_i, x_m)}{\sigma_m^2}$$

where x_{it} and x_{mt} denote the rate of return on security i and the market portfolio in period t, respectively. Substituting β_i for $\text{Cov}(x_i, x_m)/\sigma_m^2$ in the risk return equation, we get the following *security market line* (SML):

$$E(x_i) = r + (E(x_m) - r)\beta_i$$

The linear relationship between mean return ($E(x_i)$) and risk (β_i) is called the capital asset pricing model. Figure 12.2 illustrates this linear relationship.

Note that if $\beta_i = 1$ the security has the same risk as the market portfolio and hence:

$$E(x_i) = r + (E(x_m) - r) \times 1 = E(x_m)$$

If $\beta_i = 0$, the ith security makes a zero contribution to the portfolio's risk, and hence the expected return on the security is equal to the riskless rate r. In general, $E(x_i)$ increases linearly with increases in β_i.

SYSTEMATIC AND NONSYSTEMATIC RISK

The risk of each security (or of a portfolio) can be decomposed into two parts. The first component is that part of a security's risk which can be eliminated by combining it in a diversified portfolio. This *diversifiable* component of risk is often called the *nonsystematic risk*, since no systematic relationship exists between this portion of the security's risk and the market. The *nondiversifiable* component of a security's risk, i.e., the part of the risk on its return which *cannot* be eliminated by including the security in a diversified portfolio, is usually called the *systematic risk*. The latter stems from the general market fluctuations, or more specifically from that component of a security's risk which reflects the relationship of its fluctuations to those of the market portfolio. It is this nondiversifiable portion of the risk which gives rise to the risk premium; the nonsystematic risk requires no such premium since it can be eliminated through diversification. The higher a security's beta (other things being constant), the higher is its nondiversifiable risk, and therefore the higher is the expected return on this security.

In order to identify the two risk components and their impact on a security's risk premium, let us write the two linear equations of the CML and of the SML. By the CML we have:

$$E_p = r + \frac{E(x_m) - r}{\sigma_m} \sigma_p$$

where p denotes an efficient portfolio. By the SML, however, we have the following equation:

$$E(x_i) = r + (E(x_m) - r)\beta_i$$

which holds for all individual securities and portfolios alike, whether efficient or not.

Dividing and multiplying the SML by σ_m, we rewrite it as:

$$E(x_i) = r + \frac{(E(x_m) - r)}{\sigma_m} (\beta_i \sigma_m)$$

which is the same as the CML with the exception that $(\beta_i \sigma_m)$ is written instead of σ_p and hence it is this factor that determines the individual security's risk premium. Thus, the risk component of the individual security which determines the risk premium is the factor $\beta_i \sigma_m$.

Let us discuss securities with positive β, which is the most common phenomenon. For these securities, each individual stock's standard deviation σ_i can be decomposed into two components: the systematic risk $\beta_i \sigma_m$ and the nonsystematic risk σ_i^{NS}:[3]

$$\sigma_i^{NS} = \sigma_i - \beta_i \sigma_m$$

To summarize, we define the following notations for security i:

$\sigma_i^D \equiv$ diversifiable risk

$\sigma_i^{NS} \equiv$ nonsystematic risk

$\sigma_i^{ND} \equiv$ nondiversifiable risk

$\sigma_i^S \equiv$ systematic risk

and we have

$$\sigma_i^{ND} \equiv \sigma_i^S = \beta_i \sigma_m$$

and

$$\sigma_i^D \equiv \sigma_i^{NS} = \sigma_i - \beta_i \sigma_m$$

The graphical decomposition of a security's standard deviation into the systematic and nonsystematic risk is illustrated in Figure 12.3 which depicts the capital market line, the market portfolio M, an efficient portfolio P, and security i.

Portfolio P and security i both have the same expected rate of return, thus $E(x_p) = E(x_i)$. Since for efficient portfolios we have $E(x_p) = r + [(E(x_m) - r)/\sigma_m] \sigma_p$ and for the ith security we have $E(x_i) =$

---

3. It is more common in the financial literature to decompose the variance rather than the standard deviation:

$$\sigma_i^{2NS} = \sigma_i^2 - \beta_i^2 \sigma_m^2$$

However, as can be seen from the equilibrium equation, $\beta_i \sigma_i$ and not $\beta_i^2 \sigma_m^2$ determines the risk premium, and hence $\beta_i^2 \sigma_m^2$ cannot serve as the systematic risk index. Moreover, suppose that you have two securities with $\beta_i = +\frac{1}{2}$ and $\beta_j = -\frac{1}{2}$, respectively. The decomposition of its standard deviation can distinguish between the systematic risk of these two stocks, but $\beta_i^2 \sigma_m^2 = \beta_j^2 \sigma_m^2$ and hence the decomposition of σ^2 is inappropriate since it indicates that the two stocks have the same systematic risk. See M. Ben Horim and H. Levy, 'Total Risk, Diversifiable Risk and Nondiversifiable Risk: A Pedagogic Note,' *Journal of Financial and Quantitative Analysis*, June 1980.

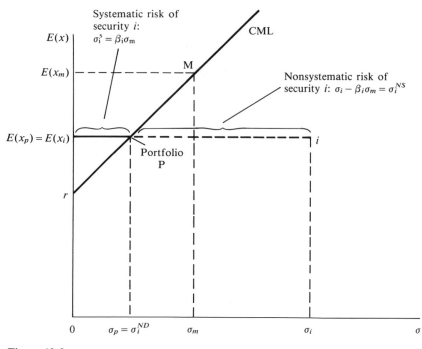

Figure 12.3

$r + [(E(x_m) - r)/\sigma_m](\beta_i\sigma_m)$, for the case when $E(x_i) = E(x_p)$ we also must have $\beta_i\sigma_m = \sigma_p$, and then $\beta_i\sigma_m = \sigma_i^{ND} = \sigma_i^S$.

Thus the nondiversifiable, systematic risk of a security is measured by the horizontal distance of the vertical axis from the CML, at the security's expected rate of return. In order to measure the security's risk component which determines the risk premium $(E(x_i) - r)$, we draw a line from point i (representing the security's mean and standard deviation) to the CML, parallel to the horizontal axis. At the point of intersection with the CML we reach σ_p, which is identical to the ith security's systematic risk. The nonsystematic risk is simply the total risk σ_i minus the systematic risk, or:

$$\sigma^{NS} = \sigma_i - \beta_i\sigma_m$$

This analysis shows that for all cases where $\beta \geq 0$, the terms 'diversifiable risk' and 'nondiversifiable risk' best convey their own meaning. Some readers, however, may find the terms 'nonsystematic risk' and 'systematic risk' more appropriate, especially for the cases where $\beta < 0$. A negative systematic risk is perhaps best understood as negative systematic co-movement of the rate of return of the security under consideration with that of the market portfolio.

Equilibrium value of risky assets

A security's rate of return is given by:

$$x_i = \frac{R_i}{P_{i0}} - 1$$

where R_i denotes the (uncertain) end-of-period *return* (and not the rate of return) and P_{i0} is the equilibrium price of the ith stock at the beginning of the period. From the risk–return relationship of the CAPM we obtain:

$$E\left(\frac{R_i}{P_{i0}} - 1\right) = r + \lambda \, \text{Cov}\left[\left(\frac{R_i}{P_{i0}} - 1\right), x_m\right]$$

Since P_{i0} is a constant and $\text{Cov}(-1, x_m) = 0$, we get:

$$\frac{E(R_i)}{P_{i0}} - 1 = r + \lambda\left(\frac{1}{P_{i0}}\right)\text{Cov}(R_i, x_m)$$

Finally, after rearrangement of terms:

$$P_{i0} = \frac{E(R_i) - \lambda \, \text{Cov}(R_i, x_m)}{1 + r}$$

Thus, the equilibrium price of a risky asset whose future (uncertain) return is R_i is the certainty equivalent, $E(R_i) - \lambda \, \text{Cov}(R_i, x_m)$ discounted at the risk-free interest rate r. Obviously, if R_i denotes the return from a risky asset, then P_{i0} is the equilibrium price (value) of this asset. Note that if we have risky bonds then B_{i0} would replace P_{i0} and one can apply the same formula to derive the equilibrium price of bonds B_{i0}.

In order to obtain the *total* equilibrium value of a corporation's equity, S_{i0}, we should substitute the *total* return of equity, i.e., the end-of-period net earnings or income Y_i, for the return R_i in the above formulas.

THE ZERO BETA MODEL

One of the CAPM assumptions is that unlimited borrowing and lending is available. In practice, it is reasonable to assume that unlimited lending is available, but it is unlikely that unlimited borrowing is available. This shortcoming is not a severe limitation of the CAPM since a similar model is obtained when limited borrowing is assumed. When the riskless asset is not available, Black[4] showed that the following linear relationship holds:

$$E(x_i) = E(z) + (E(x_m) - E(z))\beta_i$$

4. Fischer Black, 'Capital Market Equilibrium with Restricted Borrowing,' *Journal of Business*, July 1972.

This is similar to the CAPM with the exception that $E(z)$ replaces the risk-free interest rate. Portfolio z is a portfolio with a zero beta within the market portfolio (namely, $\text{Cov}(z, x_m) = 0$), hence the name *zero beta model*.

CALCULATING BETA IN PRACTICE

In order to apply the capital asset pricing model, a method must be found for estimating each firm's *future* beta, i.e., the component of its risk which cannot be eliminated through diversification. Although beta might be estimated solely on the basis of subjective probability beliefs, it is the common practice to use past data to estimate future betas. However, where one expects the historical relationship between the rates of return on a given security and the rates of return on the market portfolio to be materially different in the future, the observed *ex-post* relationship should be modified to reflect such changes.

The method for estimating beta can be illustrated using the hypothetical data of Table 12.1 which sets out the rates of return for an individual security and for the market portfolio during the past ten years. If we further assume that the risk-free interest rate is equal to $r\%$ per year, the systematic risk of the security can be estimated on the basis of the historical data using the following regression equation:

$$x_{it} = \alpha_i + \beta_i x_{mt} + e_t$$

where:

x_{it} = rate of return on the ith security in year t in excess of the risk-free interest rate

x_{mt} = rate of return on the market portfolio in year t in excess of the risk-free interest rate

α_i = regression line intercept

e_t = residual error about the regression line

β_i = ith security's systematic risk[5]

The estimate of the systematic risk, denoted by $\hat{\beta}_i$ is given by the standard formula

$$\hat{\beta}_i = \frac{\text{Cov}(x_i, x_m)}{\sigma_m^2} = \frac{\sum_{t=1}^{10} (x_{it} - \bar{x}_i)(x_{mt} - \bar{x}_m)}{\sum_{t=1}^{10} (x_{mt} - \bar{x}_m)^2}$$

where $\bar{x}_i$ and $\bar{x}_m$ denote the arithmetic annual average rate of return of the ith security and market portfolio respectively, and 10 represents the number of years in this specific example.

5. Although the systematic risk is given by $(\beta_i \sigma_m)$, σ_m is constant for all individual assets; hence, it is common practice to identify the systematic risk with β_i alone.

Table 12.1

Year	Rate of return on security in excess of the interest rate x_i (1)	Rate of return on market portfolio in excess of the interest rate x_m (2)	x_m^2 (2) × (2)	$x_i x_m$ (1) × (2)
1	5.2	7.4	54.8	38.5
2	7.3	8.2	67.2	59.9
3	10.1	12.3	151.3	124.2
4	15.4	16.9	285.6	260.3
5	19.8	19.1	364.8	378.2
6	24.9	22.5	506.3	560.3
7	29.7	25.1	630.0	745.5
8	35.2	26.4	697.0	929.3
9	40.1	29.8	888.0	1,195.0
10	42.6	30.3	918.1	1,290.8
Total	230.3	198.0	4,563.1	5,582.0
Annual average	23.0	19.8		

Employing some algebraic manipulation, this equation can be rewritten as:

$$\hat{\beta}_i = \frac{\sum_{t=1}^{10} x_{it} x_{mt} - 10 \bar{x}_i \bar{x}_m}{\sum_{t=1}^{10} x_{mt}^2 - 10 \bar{x}_m^2}$$

Plugging in the data from Table 12.1, we obtain an estimate of the security's future beta, $\hat{\beta}_i = 1.6$:

$$\hat{\beta}_i = \frac{5582.0 - 10 \times 23 \times 19.8}{4563.1 - 10 \times 392} = \frac{1028}{643.1} = 1.6$$

Note that we defined x_{it} and x_{mt} as returns in excess of the risk-free interest rate. However, if the risk-free interest rate is *constant over time*, the same estimate for the systematic rate is obtained even when x_{it} and x_{mt} are the returns and not the excess returns. This stems from the fact that for any two random variables x and y the following holds:

$$\beta_i = \frac{\text{Cov}(x, y)}{\sigma_y^2} = \frac{\text{Cov}(x - r, y - r)}{\sigma_{y-r}^2}$$

when r is a constant, e.g., the risk-free interest rate.

THE CHARACTERISTIC LINE

The regression line of x_i on x_m, or *characteristic line* as it is usually called, is plotted in Figure 12.4. The reader should note that the characteristic line which is appropriate for the hypothetical example of Table 12.1 has a slope (β) equal to 1.6. (The ten dots represent the ten annual plots of the

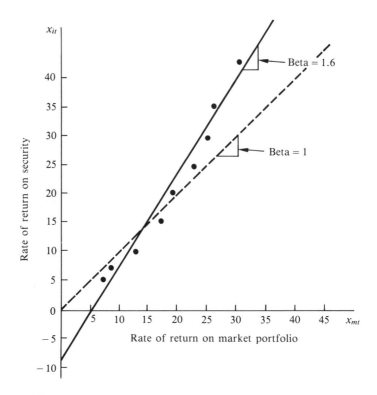

Figure 12.4

relationship between the individual security's rate of return with that of the market portfolio.) The second characteristic line, denoted as $\beta = 1$ has a slope of $45°$ and is appropriate for any security having the *same* risk as the market portfolio since the return in such security fluctuates, on the average, in the same way as the market as a whole.

The concept of a characteristic line also suggests the possibility of classifying companies by their systematic risk. Stocks having a beta greater than one ($\beta > 1$) are classified as *aggressive stocks* since they go up faster than the market in a 'bull', i.e., rising, market, but fall faster in a 'bear', i.e., falling, market. Stocks with betas less than one ($\beta < 1$) are *defensive*; their returns fluctuate less than the market as a whole. Finally, the limiting case of stocks with betas equal to unity are *neutral stocks*; they fluctuate, on the whole, along with the market.

The classification of stocks by their systematic risk is illustrated in Table 12.2. Using the regression technique described above and substituting the average return on all New York Stock Exchange stocks for the market portfolio, betas were derived using the historical rates of return for a sample of firms over twenty-eight years. The betas of a sample of five extremely defensive stocks and five extremely aggressive stocks out of these 200 firms is given in Table 12.2. The betas of the defensive stocks ranged from 0.39 for Texas

Table 12.2

Defensive stocks ($\beta < 1$)	β
Texas Utilities	0.39
Baxter International	0.50
Unisys Corporation	0.50
Commonwealth Edison	0.58
Idaho Power	0.59
Aggressive stocks ($\beta > 1$)	β
Helene Curtis	2.00
Zenith Electronics	2.32
Fedders Corp.	2.42
Loews Corp.	2.45
Avent	2.71

Utilities to 0.59 for Idaho Power. With respect to the aggressive securities, beta ranges between 2.00 and 2.71. Since the expected rate of return on common stock, in the context of the capital asset pricing model, is linked to systematic risk, we use the estimated betas of Table 12.2 as a basis for calculating the required return on equity in Chapter 17.[6]

CAPITAL ASSET PRICING MODEL AND CAPITAL BUDGETING

The implications of the capital asset pricing model for capital budgeting are straightforward. In a perfect capital market, combining investment projects whose cash flows have little, or even negative, correlation does not necessarily create opportunities for risk diversification over and beyond what was previously possible for individual (and institutional) investors.[7] In such a market, portfolio diversification and corporate risk diversification are perfect substitutes, and as a result, the contribution of the project to the firm's variance can be ignored since the diversifiable unsystematic portion of the risk can be eliminated indirectly by the investors themselves when building their portfolios. Thus, given the assumption of a perfect capital market, each project should be evaluated solely in terms of its own expected return and undiversifiable systematic risk, i.e., appropriate discount rate is equal to the risk-free interest rate plus a risk premium which depends solely on the project's beta.

If we recall the equilibrium condition for individual securities, the required

6. Current estimates of beta for a wide variety of companies are available on a commercial basis. For example, *Value Line* and Merril Lynch, Pierce, Fenner and Smith provide updates of estimted betas for the stocks of many corporations.
7. A number of authors have offered proofs of this proposition. See Jan Mossin, 'Equilibrium in a Capital Asset Market,' *Econometrica*, October 1966; Stewart C. Myers, 'Procedures for Capital Budgeting under Uncertainty,' *Industrial Management Review*, Spring 1968; Haim Levy and Marshall Sarnat, 'Diversification, Portfolio Analysis and the Uneasy Case for Conglomerate Mergers,' *Journal of Finance*, September 1970.

rate of return for each individual project is given by $E(x_i)$:

$$E(x_i) = r + (E(x_m) - r)\beta_i$$

where β_i now denotes the systematic risk of the ith project. Recognizing that $(E(x_m) - r)/\sigma_m^2 = \lambda$ represents the market price of risk, i.e., market tradeoff between return and risk, the required rate of return on the ith project can be rewritten as:

$$E(x_i) = r + \lambda \operatorname{Cov}(x_i, x_m)$$

Applying this concept we can explain some extreme cases which have plagued the capital budgeting literature. For example, should the firm consider the possibility of investing in riskless bonds, the required rate of return reduces to $E(x_i) = r$, i.e., to the interest rate itself, because the covariance between the return on a riskless bond and the return on the market portfolio is zero. On the other hand, if $\beta_i = 1$, the required rate of return is:

$$E(x_i) = r + (E(x_m) - r) \times 1 = E(x_m)$$

Thus the required rate of return on a project whose returns fluctuate exactly like the market as a whole is the same as the expected return on the market portfolio. Moreover, in a case of negative betas, i.e., for projects whose returns fluctuate inversely with the market, the required rate of return may be *less* than the riskless interest rate, once their superior risk-reducing properties are recognized. In conclusion, the higher a project's systematic risk (beta) the higher will be the required rate of return. The remainder of the project's variance which emanates from random fluctuations which are not systematically associated with the market can be ignored.

APPLICATION TO CAPITAL BUDGETING: IMPERFECT MARKETS

Of course, in the real world, capital markets are less than perfect and investor's diversification is *not* a perfect costless substitute for corporate diversification. In reality, stabilizing the firm's income stream is often an important (and valid) goal of corporate financial strategy.[8] If the firm is well diversified with many projects, bankruptcy risk decreases and therefore results in a reduction of lenders' risk, which may lead to significant cost savings when raising capital either by reducing the interest rate required on a given amount of capital, or by increasing the proportion of debt capital which can be raised at a given interest rate.[9] In addition, because of transaction costs, the individual investor

8. The importance of recognizing the correlations among investment opportunities is almost intuitively obvious. Numerous examples of risk-reducing combinations of investments can be found: manufacturers of machine tools and other highly cyclical products often tend to diversify into consumer goods to help stabilize the income stream; risk reduction also provides one of the explanations for the recent surge of conglomerate mergers.

9. An analogous argument with respect to conglomerate mergers has been presented by Levy and Sarnat, ibid., and by W. G. Lewellen, 'A Pure Financial Rationale for the Conglomerate Merger,' *Journal of Finance*, May 1971.

is unable to diversify across many stocks and would benefit if the firm diversi-fied its investments. For example, in the extreme case in which investors hold only single-security portfolios, rather than the market portfolio, project risk is measured by the *variance* of the returns, and the portfolio selection model of Chapter 11 can be applied directly to the capital budgeting problem using a project's *expected NPV* and the variance of *NPV* as the index of return and risk respectively.

As is true of the individual investor in securities, the firm is faced with the problem of choosing an optimal combination (portfolio) of projects out of the subset of efficient combinations (portfolios); and because of possible covari-ance between the cash flows of new investment proposals and those generated by existing projects, the combinations should include existing cash flows as well as newly proposed investments. These efficient investment combinations facing the firm can be illustrated by the envelope curve in Figure 12.5. All of the remaining interior combinations should not be chosen since they represent *inefficient* options, in the sense that the firm can always improve its position (increase return with no increase in risk, or reduce risk without sacrifice of return) by choosing a different combination on the efficiency curve.[10]

If we recall that the distribution of the expected income stream accruing to shareholders reflects the past and present capital investment projects

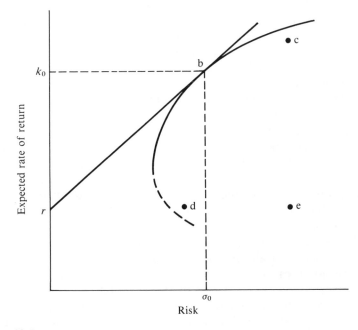

Figure 12.5

10. In the case of the firm the efficient frontier may not be continuous owing to the indivisibility of investment projects. It should also be noted that a point on the efficiency curve cannot include more than one project out of a set of *mutually exclusive* alternatives.

undertaken by the firm the slope of the opportunity line confronting the firm, rb of Figure 12.5, measures the market price of a unit of risk to the firm in an imperfect market where the investor holds only a single stock in his portfolio. This measure of the tradeoff between expected return and risk can be used to determine the firm's *optimal* capital budget; i.e., the point of tangency between the opportunity line and the curve of efficient combinations (point b) represents the *optimal* investment combination for our hypothetical firm. [11]

The explicit application of the mean–variance criterion to capital expenditure decisions can shed further light on the paradoxical cases considered earlier. If the firm is confronted with projects of varying risk, the mean–variance model suggests that the optimal portfolio (point b of Figure 12.5) might have been achieved by combining two projects having the characteristics of points such as c and d (note that the first project has a higher expected rate of return than k_0 and a higher risk than σ_0). The second project has an expected rate of return lower than the mean rate of return k_0, and also a risk lower than σ_0. Thus the explicit application of the mean–variance framework to the capital budgeting problem immediately suggests the possibility that situations may arise in which it pays the firm to accept a low-risk project even though its *NPV* is negative when discounted at the rate of k_0 that is the firm's average cost of capital (for example, a project of the type represented by point d in Figure 12.5).

At first glance this result seems startling, but on reflection it can readily be explained. Most firms holding low-risk assets such as bonds would find that the net present value of such investments is negative when discounted at the firm's opportunity cost of capital, since the latter reflects the average risk to the firm, and is therefore higher (and usually substantially higher) than the interest rate on bonds.

The appropriateness of using one discount rate to calculate the *NPV* of all projects becomes even more dubious once we recognize the possibility of statistical interdependence between the cash flows of the various investment projects. In such circumstances it may pay to accept a project with a *negative NPV* even though its variance is higher than σ_0^2. (Such a project is represented by point e in Figure 12.5.) Clearly, the negative covariance of such a project with other proposals might conceivably be sufficient to combine them into an 'efficient' combination. Of course, if the firm was faced with the problem of choosing only one project, an alternative with the risk–return characteristics denoted by point e would be rejected by the mean–variance rule since it represents an inefficient alternative as compared with point d.

The application of a single-valued risk-adjusted discount rate to *all* individual projects represents a sort of rule-of-thumb solution. Such a rule assumes that the individual characteristics of the alternative projects do not change the average risk level of the firm. However, where the firm must choose among investment opportunities with risk characteristics which materially change the average risk level to the firm, both the optimal investment mix and

11. The firm and stockholders can move along the line (see Figure 12.5) by borrowing or lending.

the appropriate discount rate must be simultaneously determined. Namely, each project is calculated with its own risk-adjusted discount rate. If this is done, all accepted projects would have a positive *NPV*.

THE GENERALIZED CAPM (G-CAPM)

The CAPM implies that at the optimum all investors should hold the market portfolio composed of all risky marketable assets. However, due to transactions costs, indivisibility of investment, or even asymmetric information, it has been found that investors hold only a few assets in their portfolios. Realizing that in practice only a few assets are held by investors, Levy, Merton and Markowitz developed a variant of the CAPM called the *generalized CAPM (G-CAPM)* which is an equilibrium risk–return relationship in a segmented market.[12] By the G-CAPM, the kth investor may hold only n_k risky assets, creating a portfolio whose return is R_k with a mean of $E(x_k)$ and risk $\beta_{i,k}$ where $\beta_{i,k}$ is the beta of the ith asset, calculated against the return on the kth investor's optimum portfolio R_k. In this case, the kth investor and all other investors who hold portfolio R_k have a *segmented* market of risky assets with a 'little CAPM' in which the following risk–return relation holds:[13]

$$E(x_i) = r + (E(x_k) - r)\beta_{i,k} \qquad i = 1, 2, ..., n_k$$

Denoting the initial wealth invested by the kth investor in the market by T_k, the G-CAPM asserts that in equilibrium we have the following risk–return relationship:

$$E(x_i) = r + \Sigma T_k (E(x_k) - r)\beta_{i,k} / \Sigma T_k$$

where $E(x_i)$ is the mean rate of return on portfolio k selected by the kth investor. The G-CAPM model or segmented market equilibrium has the following properties:

1. When transactions costs are assumed to be zero and information is symmetric, all investors will hold the same portfolio. In this case, $\beta_{i,k} = \beta_i$ and $E(x_k) = E(x_m)$, and the CAPM is a specific case of the G-CAPM (hence the term 'generalized' CAPM).
2. Since by the G-CAPM investors hold only a few assets in their portfolios, the stock's own variance σ_i^2 is not mitigated away and may therefore explain mean returns. Indeed, in the following section we show that the variance σ_i^2 or residual variance $S_{e,i}^2$ is important in explaining stock prices and is consistent with the G-CAPM.

---

12. See Haim Levy, 1978, *op. cit.*; Robert Merton, 'A Simple Model of Capital Market Equilibrium with Incomplete Information,' *Journal of Finance*, 1987; and Harry Markowitz, 'Risk Adjustment,' *Journal of Accounting, Auditing, and Finance*, 1990. For an elaboration and comparative analysis of the CAPM see William Sharpe, *op. cit.*
13. The derivation is similar to the derivation of the CAPM with the distinction that only a few assets n_k are involved, see Levy (1978).

THE CAPITAL ASSET PRICING MODEL: THE EMPIRICAL EVIDENCE _____

The CAPM relates the expected return of a security, $E(x_i)$ to its systematic risk β_i in the following way:

$$E(x_i) = r + (E(x_m) - r)\beta_i$$

The validity of the CAPM can be tested in two ways:

1. By checking if the underlying assumptions of the model are logical and fit investors' behavior;
2. By testing empirically the degree to which the CAPM explains, i.e., predicts, the behavior of security prices.

Many of the model's assumptions (e.g., no transaction costs, perfect divisibility of investments, homogeneous expectations regarding the future, uniform investment horizons, etc.) clearly do not hold in reality. However, one should not reject the CAPM solely on these grounds. Perhaps these deviations from reality are not crucial, so that the CAPM may still explain price behavior. As Milton Friedman[14] has emphasized, the 'realism' of a theory's assumptions can be judged only by the degree to which the theory provides valid and meaningful explanations and predictions, and this requires an examination of the logical consequences of the theory against observed reality. In fact, to be meaningful and useful, the assumptions must be descriptively unrealistic in the sense that they must abstract from a complex reality. Few would argue that the hair color of the president of the New York Stock Exchange is germane to the problem of explaining the determination of prices in that market. But how 'unrealistic' can the assumptions be? We have no recourse but to test the model's predictions empirically.

There are many ways of testing the CAPM. Let us first describe the most simplistic procedure. In order to test the degree to which the CAPM explains stock price behavior, one normally uses *ex-post* data to estimate the *ex-ante* parameters of the model. Typically, a time series regression of the following form is used:

$$x_{it} = \alpha_i + \beta_i x_{mt} + e_t$$

where x_{it} and x_{mt} are the rates of return on the ith security and on the market portfolio in period t, and α_i and β_i are the regression coefficients and e_t is a residual term. Let us denote the estimate of the ith security's systematic risk by $\hat{\beta}_i$. Suppose that we include 100 securities in our sample, and for each one we have 20 observations of their annual rates of return. We then run 100 regressions (time series regressions of each security against the market portfolio x_{mt}) and the output of these 100 regressions are 100 matched pairs $(\bar{x}_i, \hat{\beta}_i)$ which are the average rate of return on the ith security and the estimate

---

14. See Milton Friedman, 'The Methodology of Positive Economics,' in *Essays in Positive Economics*, University of Chicago Press, 1953.

of its systematic risk. We then run a cross-section regression of the type:

$$\bar{x}_i = \gamma_0 + \gamma_1 \hat{\beta}_i + u_i$$

(u_i denotes the error term). This regression is very similar to the theoretical relationship asserted by the CAPM, that is:

$$E(x_i) = r + (E(x_m) - r)\beta_i$$

with the following differences:

1. In the regression analysis we use the *ex-post* average return $\bar{x}_i$ as an estimate of the expected rate of return $E(x_i)$.
2. We also use the *ex-post* estimate $\hat{\beta}_i$ instead of the *ex-ante*, and unknown, true systematic risk β_i.

If the CAPM provides a good approximation of stock price behavior, we would expect to find the following empirical results:

1. γ_0 would not be significantly different from the risk-free interest rate r.
2. γ_1 would not be significantly different from $(E(x_m) - r)$. However, since $E(x_m)$ is not observable and therefore is not known, it is common to compare the estimate γ_i to the average *ex-post* excess return $(\bar{x}_m - r)$.
3. Obviously, we also expect to find a reasonable value for the square of the correlation coefficient, R^2.

The number of studies which have tried to verify empirically the validity of the CAPM in this way (or by some other variation of the method explained above) is so numerous that we will not attempt to catalogue all of them.[15] However, in general the results offer only limited support of the CAPM. To be specific, the following findings characterize most of the empirical efforts:

1. γ_0 is much larger than the risk-free interest rate which prevailed in the period covered by the relevant study.
2. γ_1 is positive as implied by the CAPM, but is much smaller than $(\bar{x}_m - r)$.
3. The R^2 (using individual stocks rather than grouped data) is quite low, usually only around 20% if one uses annual rates of return; and is very close to zero when monthly rates of return are used.

15. See, for example, Irwin Friend and Marshall Blume, 'Measurement of Portfolio Performance under Uncertainty,' *American Economic Review*, September 1970; Marshall Blume and Irwin Friend, 'A New Look at the Capital Asset Pricing Model,' *Journal of Finance*, March 1973; Irwin Friend and Randolph Westerfield, 'Risk and Capital Asset Pricing,' *Journal of Banking and Finance*, September 1981; Fischer Black, Michael C. Jensen, and Myron Scholes, 'The Capital Asset Pricing Model: Some Empirical Tests,' in *Studies in the Theory of Capital Markets*, Praeger, New York, 1972; Merton H. Miller and Myron Scholes, 'Rate of Return in Relation to Risk: A Reexamination of Some Recent Findings,' in M. C. Jensen (ed.) *Studies in the Theory of Capital Markets*, Praeger, New York, 1972; Haim Levy, 'Equilibrium in an Imperfect Market: A Constraint on the Number of Securities in the Portfolio,' *American Economic Review*, September 1978; and Eugene F. Fama and J. MacBeth, 'Risk, Return and Equilibrium: Empirical Test,' *Journal of Political Economy*, May/June 1973.

While in most empirical tests the regression coefficient of beta is positive and significant, as predicted by the CAPM, Lintner's work (reported in Douglas (1968, 1969)) as well as Miller and Scholes (1972) and Levy (1978) indicate that when the following regression is run, γ_2 turns to be significantly positive, which contradicts the CAPM:[16]

$$\bar{x}_i = \gamma_0 + \gamma_1 \beta_i + \gamma_2 S_{e,i}^2 + u_i$$

where $S_{e,i}^2$ is the residual variance (see the definition of unsystematic risk where $\sigma_i^2 = \beta_i^2 \sigma_m^2 + S_{e,i}^2$).

Fama and MacBeth (1973), using a different methodology, find opposite results to those of Lintner, Douglas, and Levy. To be more specific, they find that the regression coefficient of the residual variance is not significantly different from zero, and the coefficient of beta is significantly positive supporting the CAPM linear relationship.

Gibbons (1982), Stambaugh (1982), and Kandel and Stambaugh (1987) develop a different methodology to test the CAPM with conflicting results.[17] While Gibbons rejects the CAPM, Stambaugh finds evidence supporting the CAPM linear relationship.

While there is a plethora of articles written on tests of the CAPM, most support the linear relationship.[18] However, in a recent article, Fama and French (1992)[19] show that when firm size and the ratio of book-to-market value are considered, the regression coefficient of beta completely disappears. This is evidence against the CAPM linear relationship.

However, recall that all of the tests on the CAPM employ *ex-post* data. The CAPM is an equilibrium model which is based on *ex-ante* (not *ex-post*) parameters. If the *ex-post* estimates of beta are not stable over time, it is possible that the CAPM still holds even if tests with *ex-post* data refute it.

Thus, the empirical findings lend only partial support for the CAPM in its

16. See George Douglas, 'Risk in the Equity Market: An Empirical Appraisal of Market Efficiency, University Microfilms, Inc., Ann Arbor, Michigan, 1968; Haim Levy, *op. cit.*; and Miller and Scholes, *op. cit.*
17. See Michael Gibbons, 'Multivariate Tests of Financial Models: A New Approach,' *Journal of Financial Economics*, March 1982; Robert Stambaugh, 'On the Exclusion of Assets From Test of the Two-parameter Model: A Sensitivity Analysis,' *Journal of Financial Economics*, November 1982; and S. Kandal and R. Stambaugh, 'On the Correlations and Sensitivity of Interferences about Mean–Variance Efficiency,' *Journal of Financial Economics*, 1987.
18. For a test of the consumption-based CAPM see D. Breeden, 'An Intertemporal Asset Pricing Model with Stochastic Consumption and Investment Opportunities,' *Journal of Financial Economics*, 7, 1979; D. Breeden, 'Consumption Risk in Future Markets,' *Journal of Finance*, 35, 1980; and D. Breeden, M. Gibbons, and R. Litzenberger, 'Empirical Test of the Consumption-oriented CAPM,' *Journal of Finance*, 44, 1989. For testing the post-tax form of the CAPM see Black, F. and Scholes, M., 'The Effects of Dividend Yield and Dividend Policy on Common Stock Prices and Returns,' *Journal of Financial Economics*, 1, 1974; and R. H. Litzenberger, and K. Ramaswamy, 'The Effect of Personal Taxes and Dividends on Capital Asset Prices: Theory and Empirical Evidence,' *Journal of Financial Economics*, June 1979.
19. See Eugene Fama and Kenneth French, 'The Cross-section of Expected Stock Returns,' *Journal of Finance*, 1992.

pure form.[20] Indeed, if one recalls that the typical investor holds a small non-diversified portfolio consisting of less than four stocks on average[21] it is obvious that β which measures the covariability of the return of a given stock with a market portfolio (which no-one holds!) can play only a limited role in measuring a security's risk. Indeed, if one substitutes the ith security's variance for β and runs the naive regression:

$$\bar{x}_i = \gamma_{0t} + \gamma_i \hat{\sigma}_i^2 + u_i$$

the coefficient of correlation actually increases from about 20% (when $\hat{\beta}_i$ is used) to about 40% when it is replaced by $\hat{\sigma}_i^2$. This is a result which makes sense only if investors hold extremely nondiversified portfolios.

However, recall that $\hat{\sigma}_i^2$ by itself cannot serve as the risk index unless each investor holds only *one* stock in his portfolio. As mentioned above, investors do diversify to some extent, which implies that the true measure of risk lies somewhere between σ_i^2 and β_i, but probably closer to σ_i^2 since investors' portfolios are closer to a pure non-diversified portfolio than to a fully diversified one comprised of all available marketable risky assets.[22]

Is the CAPM testable?

In a well-known paper, Richard Roll presents a serious methodological criticism of empirical tests of the CAPM.[23] Roll questions the very testability of the CAPM. He shows that the absence of a perfect linear fit using empirical data merely implies that the selected market portfolio is mean–variance inefficient. Hence the failure of the empirical test may be simply a result of the researcher having chosen an inappropriate index for the market portfolio. Since, in theory, the market portfolio should include *all* risky assets[24] (e.g., stocks, bonds, land, gold coins, human capital, etc.) it is difficult, if not impossible, to test the CAPM empirically.

Yet, even if a proxy to the market portfolio is selected which is highly correlated with the true market portfolio, one may still get very different results.

20. Clearly the use of predictions based on *ex-post* data is fraught with difficulties. See, for example, Edwin H. Elton and Martin J. Gruber, 'Estimating the Dependence Structure of Share Prices: Implications for Portfolio Selection,' *Journal of Finance*, December 1973.

However, the substitution of *ex-ante* data drawn directly from financial institutions does not change the conclusion that investors' assessments of a security's risk are not closely connected to its beta coefficient as implied by the CAPM; see Irwin Friend, Randolph Westerfield, and Joao Ferreira, 'The CAPM and Mean–Variance Efficient Portfolios: *Ex-Ante* and *Ex-Post* Data,' Working Paper No. 10-80, Rodney L. White Center for Financial Research, University of Pennsylvania, October 1980.

21. See Marshall Blume, Jean Crockett, and Irwin Friend, 'Stock Ownership in the United States: Characteristics and Trends,' *Survey of Current Business*, November 1974.

22. For a theoretical equilibrium model of prices subject to the constraint that investors do *not* hold all risky assets see Levy, 1978, *op. cit.*

23. See Richard Roll, 'A Critique of Asset Pricing Theory's Tests,' *Journal of Financial Economics*, March 1977.

24. See David Mayers, 'Non-marketable Assets and the Capital Market Equilibrium under Uncertainty,' in *Studies in the Theory of Capital Markets*, Praeger, New York, 1972.

Shanken (1987) develops a procedure which simultaneously tests the relationship between the proxy to the market portfolio and the true market portfolio as well as the CAPM. Even this procedure requires knowledge of the correlation between the proxies (e.g., the S&P 500) and the true and unobservable market portfolio. Information which is, of course, unknown.

By now you may well be ready to ask, 'If the CAPM is so bad, why is it so popular in academic circles?' The answer can be found in a famous dictum of George Stigler, who in a completely different context, pointed out that 'a theory can only be replaced by a better ... theory.' Although the CAPM provides important insights, we shall be extremely cautious about applying it uncritically to corporations' capital investment decisions, involving as they do millions of shareholders' dollars. The need for caution is reflected in management's observed reluctance to utilize techniques based on the CAPM when evaluating capital investments. In a survey of large U.S. corporations, 52% of the executives polled indicated that the concept of systematic risk seldom influences policy decisions, while another 40% stated flatly that the CAPM has no effect on corporation decisions.[25]

ARBITRAGE PRICING THEORY (APT) MODEL

In the light of the above deficiencies of the CAPM, another testable model of the risk–return tradeoff – the *arbitrage pricing theory* (APT) – was developed. The APT, which was developed by Stephen Ross,[26] is actually a different model which competes outright with the CAPM, rather than extending it.

In the derivation of this equilibrium model, Ross does not assume risk aversion, and in particular does not assume that investors make their decisions in the mean–variance framework. Instead, he assumes that the securities' rates of return R_i are generated by the following process:

$$R_i = E(R_i) + \beta_i(I - E(I)) + e_i$$

where:

R_i = the rate of return on security i ($i = 1, 2, ..., n$, when we have n securities), with mean $E(R_i)$

I = the value of the factor generating security returns, whose mean is $E(I)$

β_i = a coefficient measuring the effect of changes in the factor I on the rate of return R

e_i = the random deviation (noise)

Note that I is a *common factor* to all securities: for example, the gross national product (GNP), the Dow-Jones Stock Index, or any other factor

---

25. See J. William Petty II and David F. Scott Jr, 'Capital Budgeting Practices in Large American Firms: A Retrospective Analysis and Update,' *Journal of Economics and Businsses*, Spring 1980.
26. See Stephen A. Ross, 'The Arbitrage Theory of Capital Asset Pricing,' *Journal of Economic Theory*, December 1976.

which one perceives to be appropriate for the generation of security rates of return.

The basic idea of the APT Model is that investors can create a zero beta portfolio with zero net investment (hence the name 'arbitrage' pricing theory). If the zero beta portfolio constructed with zero investment yields a nonzero (positive) return, a sure profit can be made by arbitraging. To be more specific, construct a portfolio with proportions p_i such that:

$$\sum_{i=1}^{n} p_i \beta_i = 0 \quad \text{and} \quad \sum_{i=1}^{n} p_i = 0$$

The first condition stipulates that this is a zero beta portfolio, and the second condition indicates that a zero amount is invested in this portfolio. Obviously, such a portfolio can be constructed only when some of the stocks are held short (negative p_i), and some are held long (positive p_i) and the investors who receive the proceeds of the short sales invest them in other securities.

Multiply by p_i the return generating process for security i:

$$p_i R_i = p_i E(R_i) + p_i \beta_i (I - E(I)) + p_i e_i$$

and sum over all the assets ($i = 1, 2, ..., n$) to obtain the portfolio rate of return:

$$\sum_{i=1}^{n} p_i R_i = \sum_{i=1}^{n} p_i E(R_i) + (I - E(I)) \sum_{i=1}^{n} p_i \beta_i + \sum_{i=1}^{n} p_i e_i$$

or

$$R_p = E(R_p) + (I - E(I)) \sum_{i=1}^{n} p_i \beta_i + \sum_{i=1}^{n} p_i e_i$$

Here R_p and $E(R_p)$ stand for the portfolio rate of return and the portfolio mean rate of return, respectively. Now since:

$$\sum_{i=1}^{n} p_i \beta_i = 0 \quad \text{(by construction)}$$

and for a very large portfolio the average noise is approximately zero, i.e.:

$$\sum_{i=1}^{n} p_i e_i \simeq 0,$$

we obtain a constant rate of return $R_p = E(R_p)$, i.e., a portfolio with zero variability is constructed with zero net investment (recall the condition that $\sum_{i=1}^{n} p_i = 0$).

In equilibrium, the mean return on such a portfolio must be zero, $E(R_p) = 0$. Otherwise with no risk and no investment, a sure profit can be made by buying (or selling short) such a portfolio. Suppose that this is not so and that the mean return is, say, $E(R_p) = \$3$, and we have, $R_p = E(R_p) = \$3$. With zero investment ($\sum_{i=1}^{n} p_i = 0$), one can earn \$3 with certainty. Investors will continue to buy such a portfolio, its price will go up, and the rate of return will go down until $R_p = E(R_p) = 0$. Thus, in equilibrium, no arbitrage opportunities are available.

In summary, by construction we have:

$$\sum_{i=1}^{n} p_i = 0 \quad \text{and} \quad \sum_{i=1}^{n} p_i \beta_i = 0$$

which implies that:

$$E(R_p) = \sum_{i=1}^{n} p_i E(R_i) = 0 \quad \text{and} \quad R_p = \sum_{i=1}^{n} p_i E(R_i) = 0$$

since the portfolio has zero variability and the mean return is equal to the return itself.

By a standard theorem of linear algebra, the three equations:

$$\sum_{i=1}^{n} p_i \times 1 = 0, \quad \sum_{i=1}^{n} p_i \beta_i = 0, \quad \text{and} \quad \sum_{i=1}^{n} p_i E(R_i) = 0$$

imply that $E(R_i)$ can be written as a linear combination of 1 and β_i as follows:

$$E(R_i) = a_0 + a_1 \beta_i \qquad (i = 1, 2, ..., n)$$

where a_0 and a_1 are the coefficients of a straight line. We now turn to the determination of the coefficients a_0 and a_1. First, consider a portfolio with zero beta and with: $\sum_{i=1}^{n} p_i = 1$. Then, multiplying the linear equation above by p_i and summing over all i ($i = 1, 2, ..., n$) we obtain:

$$E(R_p) = \sum_{i=1}^{n} p_i E(R_i) = a_0 \sum_{i=1}^{n} p_i + a_1 \sum_{i=1}^{n} p_i \beta_i = (a_0 \times 1) + (a_1 \times 0)$$

or $E(R_p) = a_0$. Since by construction:

$$\sum_{i=1}^{n} p_i = 1 \quad \text{and} \quad \sum_{i=1}^{n} p_i \beta_i = 0$$

our portfolio is a *zero beta portfolio* denoted by z, and so $R_p = R_z$. Note that:

$$\sum_{i=1}^{n} p_i \beta_i$$

is the portfolio β_p, which is equal to zero by construction. Thus, $E(R_p) = E(R_z)$ and so $E(R_z) = a_0$. We have determined the intercept a_0 to be equal to the zero beta portfolio mean rate of return.

Now let us look at a portfolio with:

$$\sum_{i=1}^{n} p_i \beta_i = 1 \quad \text{and} \quad \sum_{i=1}^{n} p_i = 1$$

Plugging $E(R_z)$ for a_0 in the linear equation we obtain:

$$E(R_i) = E(R_z) + a_1 \beta_i$$

Multiply by p_i and sum over all i $(i = 1, 2, ..., n)$ to obtain:

$$E(R_p) = \sum_{i=1}^{n} p_i E(R_i) = E(R_z) \sum_{i=1}^{n} p_i + a_1 \sum_{i=1}^{n} p_i \beta_i$$

Since $\sum_{i=1}^{n} p_i = 1$ and $\sum_{i=1}^{n} p_i \beta_i = 1$, we obtain:

$$E(R_p) = E(R_z) + a_1$$

Hence $a_1 = E(R_p) - E(R_z)$, where $E(R_p)$ is the mean rate of return on the portfolio with $\beta = 1$.

Substituting for a_0 and a_1 in the equation $E(R_i) = a_0 + a_1 \beta_i$, we finally get:

$$E(R_i) = E(R_z) + (E(R_p) - E(R_z))\beta_i$$

where $E(R_p)$ is the mean rate of return of a portfolio with beta equal to 1 and $E(R_z)$ is the mean rate of return on the zero beta portfolio.

However, by the return-generating process, the mean rate of return on the portfolio with beta equal to 1 must be equal to the mean of the index $E(I)$ (expressed in appropriately standardized units). Substituting $E(I)$ for $E(R_p)$ we get:

$$E(R_i) = E(R_z) + (E(I) - E(R_z))\beta_i$$

This is the risk–return relationship implied by the APT.

Taking the market portfolio with rate of return R_m as the returns generating factor I, we obtain as a specific case of the APT the CAPM result without a riskless asset:

$$E(R_i) = E(R_z) + (E(R_m) - E(R_z))\beta_i$$

where R_z is the return on a zero beta portfolio.

Before we turn to a numerical example, let us pinpoint the assumptions of the APT model. First, a necessary condition for the derivation is that the average portfolio noise is zero, i.e.:

$$\sum_{i=1}^{n} p_i e_i \simeq 0$$

Thus, a basic assumption of the APT model is that investors hold a very large number of assets in their portfolios.

The second assumption is that short sales are allowed and all the proceeds from the short sales are received by the investor. It should be emphasized that these two assumptions are also characteristics of the classical CAPM. The APT is testable since one can use any index for I, not necessarily the market portfolio. Let us consider a specific example.

Example
We show in this example how one can create a zero beta portfolio and that the linear function $E(R_i) = a_0 + a_1 \beta_i$ holds as claimed above.

Assume that we have three risky assets with the following parameters:

$$E(R_1) = 0.10 \qquad E(R_2) = 0.40 \qquad E(R_3) = 0.70$$
$$\beta_1 = 1 \qquad\qquad \beta_2 = 2 \qquad\qquad \beta_3 = 3$$

We would like to construct a zero beta portfolio with zero investment, i.e.:

$$\sum_{i=1}^{3} p_i\beta_i = 0 \quad \text{and} \quad \sum_{i=1}^{3} p_i = 0$$

These two constraints can be rewritten in expanded form as follows:

$$p_1 + p_2 + p_3 = 0 \quad \text{or} \quad p_3 = -p_1 - p_2 \qquad \text{(i.e., zero investment)}$$

and

$$p_1\beta_1 + p_2\beta_2 + p_3\beta_3 = 0 \quad \text{or} \quad p_1 + 2p_2 + 3p_3 = 0 \qquad \text{(i.e., zero beta)}$$

Substituting in the last equality $p_3 = (-p_1 - p_2)$, we obtain:

$$p_1 + 2p_2 + 3(-p_1 - p_2) = 0 \quad \text{or} \quad -2p_1 - p_2 = 0$$

which implies that:

$$p_1 = -\tfrac{1}{2}p_2$$

Take, for instance, $p_2 = 1$, hence:

$$p_1 = -\tfrac{1}{2} \quad \text{and} \quad p_3 = -p_1 - p_2 = -1 - (-\tfrac{1}{2}) = -\tfrac{1}{2}$$

For the portfolio $p_1 = -\tfrac{1}{2}$, $p_2 = 1$, and $p_3 = -\tfrac{1}{2}$, we have:

$$\sum_{i=1}^{3} p_i = 0 \quad \text{and} \quad \sum_{i=1}^{3} p_i\beta_i = 0$$

as required. We also note that if:

$$\sum_{i=1}^{n} p_i = 0 \quad \text{and} \quad \sum_{i=1}^{n} p_i\beta_i = 0$$

the rates of return on the individual assets must adjust so that in equilibrium:

$$E(R_p) = \sum_{i=1}^{n} p_i E(R_i) = 0$$

We selected $E(R_i)$ such that the equilibrium condition holds and no arbitrage profit is available, since:

$$\sum_{i=1}^{n} p_i E(R_i) = (-\tfrac{1}{2} \times 0.10) + (1 \times 0.40) + (-\tfrac{1}{2} \times 0.70) = 0$$

Also, we indicated that in such a case $E(R_i)$ can be written as a linear function of the β_i. First, let us find the slope of the line:

$$E(R_i) = a_0 + a_1\beta_i$$

Using the parameters of the securities 2 and 3 the slope a_1 is given by:

$$a_1 = \frac{E(R_3) - E(R_2)}{\beta_3 - \beta_2} = \frac{0.70 - 0.40}{3 - 2} = 0.30$$

Hence, $a_1 = 0.3$. Since $E(R_3) = a_0 + 0.3\beta_3$, we have $0.7 = a_0 + 0.3 \times 3$, which yields $a_0 = -0.2$.

It is left to show that security 1 lies on the straight line with the coefficients $q_0 = -0.2$, $a_1 = 0.3$ or:

$$E(R_i) = -0.2 + 0.3\beta_i$$

Since $\beta_i = 1$ and $E(R_1) = 0.1$, it is easy to verify that security 1 indeed lies on the same straight line. Thus, in general, under the conditions of this model $E(R_i)$ is given as a linear function of β_i.

The main advantage of the APT model is that we are not confined to the market portfolio and any factor can be included in the return-generating process. Actually, more than one factor can be included. In general, the model can be written as:

$$R_i = E(R_i) + \beta_{i1}(I_1 - E(I_1)) + \beta_{i2}(I_2 - E(I_2)) + \cdots + \beta_{in}(I_n - E(I_n)) + e_i$$

where I_i is the it return-generating factor and β_{ik} is the security i beta with respect to factor k.

EMPIRICAL TESTS OF THE APT

There are basically two ways to test the APT:

1. Formulate hypotheses regarding the relevant factors which generate the return. For example, the inflation rate, interest rate, or change in production. Then use these factors to run a regression to see whether they explain the return of the security. Of course, this is an ad hoc method since it is absent of a theory explaining why these factors (versus other unnamed factors) are more relevant in explaining returns.
2. Employ factor analysis which simultaneously determines the number of factors which are priced as well as their coefficients.

To date, empirical tests of the APT yield conflicting results. While Roll and Ross (1980) find that only a few factors (approximately five) are significant, Dhrymes *et al.* (1984) show that the number of significant factors is a function of the size of the group of assets analyzed: it is three significant factors for a group consisting of fifteen securities, and seven for a group consisting of sixty securities (which is the largest group analyzed). There are many other studies which have been conducted on the APT or some modification of the basic model.[27] Although in general the empirical studies indicated that more than one factor is significant, there is conflicting empirical evidence regarding the number of relevant factors, and even more disagreement regarding the identification of these factors.

Market efficiency and portfolio selection

The market is considered to be efficient if all information is reflected in the stock price. In efficient markets one cannot use a time series of historical data, accounting figures or other available information to make an *abnormal return* on an asset. Once the information appears in the press (e.g., the U.S. Federal Reserve cuts the interest rate or General Motors plans a new public issue), the stock price has already adjusted to reflect this information. Experts are divided about whether markets are efficient as well as about the degree to which markets are efficient. Most academics claim that the market is efficient and therefore abnormal profits cannot be earned. Wall Street, however, is crowded with 'chartists' and 'technicians' who believe that by looking at various time series of historical data (e.g., earnings, stock price changes, volume of trading, and short interest positions outstanding), future price changes can be predicted. Also, some experts practice 'active asset allocation' and believe they can predict the best time to switch between securities (when to move from cash positions to stocks or bonds and vice versa).

The truth probably lies somewhere between these two views – the market may not be completely efficient, but is not extremely inefficient. Moreover, if there are assets in the market which are underpriced, these experts are probably the first to locate and then buy these assets. In turn, they will push the price to its fair market value. The sophisticated and diligent investor is therefore the one who reaps the profit.

We discuss below several concepts and definitions of market efficiency. We then go on to analyze the impact of market efficiency on the role of portfolio selection.

Efficient market hypothesis (EMH)

There are three basic definitions of market efficiency. These three definitions

27. See S. J. Brown and M. I. Weinstein, 'A new Approach to Testing Asset Pricing Models: The Bilinear Paradigm,' *Journal of Finance*, June 1983; Bruce Lehmann and David Modest, 'The Empirical Foundations of the Arbitrage Pricing Theory I: The Empirical Tests,' *Journal of Financial Economics*, 1988; R. Roll and S. A. Ross, 'An Empirical Investigation of the Arbitrage Pricing Theory,' *Journal of Finance*, December 1980; D. Chinhyung Cho, Edwin J. Elton, and Martin J. Gruber, 'On the Robustness of the Roll and Ross Arbitrage Pricing Theory,' *Journal of Financial and Quantitative Analysis*, March 1984; G. Connor and R. Korajczyk, 'Performance Measurement with the Arbitrage Pricing Theory: A New Framework for Analysis,' *Journal of Financial Economics*, 15, 1986. See also W. Sharpe, 'Factors in NYSE Security Returns, 1931–1979,' *Journal of Portfolio Management*, Summer 1982; and Edwin Burmeister and Marjorie McElroy, 'Joint Estimation of Factor Sensitivities and Risk Premia for the Arbitrage Pricing Theory,' *Journal of Finance*, July 1988.

are primarily concerned with determining the degree to which markets are efficient.

1. Weak-form efficiency

The weak-form efficiency hypothesis asserts that all historical data, in particular historical rates of return, are reflected in the price of a stock. Thus, one cannot use a time series of past performance to discern a pattern of price changes to predict a stock's future rate of return. Weak-form efficiency implies that stock price changes behave like a 'random walk' or a process with no memory. To illustrate, suppose that we flip a fair coin. Whenever heads appears the stock price will go up 1% and when tails appears the stock price will go down by $\frac{1}{2}$%. Suppose that you look at the last five stock price changes and find the following series: +1%, +1%, −1%, −1/2%, and −1/2%. Can you predict the next price change? Of course, the answer is no: the next flip has an equal probability of being heads or tails, and the outcome is independent of the previous toss. The next price change is random and independent of the previous result. The random walk hypothesis asserts that the price changes behave like a random walk which is independent of past changes. An analysis of past patterns of price changes is an unproductive endeavor. Note, however, that a random walk with a positive drift may occur; namely, on average you may be able to make money in the stock market, but still not predict the future price change by looking at the past price change.

2. Semi-strong efficiency

The semi-strong efficiency hypothesis asserts that all public information is reflected in the stock's price. The publicly available information ranges from a time series of past data and forecasts of future earnings to the health of the CEO. Thus, if you hear rumors in the press of friction between members of the firm's board of directors, it is too late for you to make an abnormal profit based on this information.

3. Strong-form efficiency

The strong-form efficient market hypothesis is the most stringent hypothesis. It asserts that *all* information, both public and private, is reflected in the current price of the stock. For example, insiders may possess information on the firm's future earnings. According to this hypothesis, insiders cannot use this information to make abnormal profits since it is already reflected in the price of the stock.

While most would agree that the market is not strong-form efficient, it is questionable whether it is semi-strong or weak-form efficient. If the market is not efficient, one can make an abnormal profit on an investment. But how is an 'abnormal profit' defined? The common definition of an abnormal profit is the excess return that one can obtain after adjusting the return for risk. The common way of adjusting for risk is to employ the CAPM discussed earlier in this chapter. To elaborate, suppose that $r = 5\%$, $\mu_m = 15\%$, and $\beta_i = 0.9$.

According to the CAPM, the risk adjusted rate of return on the stock is: $\mu_i = 0.05 + 0.9(0.15 - 0.05) = 0.14$ or 14%. If you can earn 16% on the stock on average (since you possess superior information), then you can earn an excess return of 2% (16% − 14%). Of course, we have to consider several cases to see if you can indeed make an excess return on average. Consider the following example.

Example
Many firms announce that they are repurchasing some of their stock. Some people claim that whenever the information on a stock repurchase is publicly available, the stock price increases and an abnormal return can be earned. How can this abnormal return be measured? The procedure to measure the excess return is called an *event study* and is conducted as follows. Take a sample of firms who repurchase their stock over a given number of years. Measure the actual rate of return for each stock, say in the few days after the information becomes public. Compare this actual return with one calculated using the CAPM. As we discussed above, this difference is called the excess return. If you have many firms in your sample who repurchased their stocks, you can calculate the average excess return earned by all of the firms. If the average excess return of the firms in your sample is statistically significant, then it implies that an abnormal return can be earned in the days following the stock repurchase announcement. Of course, having this abnormal return does not mean that the market is inefficient. It is possible that the abnormal return occurred very quickly on the announcement date, and when you learn about it and attempt to profit from this information by buying the stock it is too late. You can only purchase the stock at a higher price and thus cannot realize the extra return; and when transaction costs are incorporated then this is particularly true.

So, do arbitrage opportunities imply the market is inefficient? Arbitrage is a situation where for zero investment one can earn nonnegative returns in the future and at least one positive return. Suppose that, based on historical and current information, you can create an arbitrage portfolio. In such a case we say that the market is inefficient: there is no need to adjust for risk because no risk is involved by definition of an arbitrage opportunity. The degree of market inefficiency depends on the sort of information employed to construct such a portfolio. If it is based solely on the historical series of data, the market is weak-form inefficient. If it is based also on other public information, the market is semi-strong inefficient, and if only insiders can create such an arbitrage profit, the market is strong-form inefficient.

Portfolio selection and the EMH

One may wonder whether there is a contradiction between EMH and portfolio selection. If the market is efficient, is there any need to burden ourselves with portfolio theory? While under EMH, the analysis conducted by technicians, fundamentalists, and chartists is worthless, this is not the case for portfolio managers. To elaborate, suppose that two stocks 1 and 2 each trade for $10. You flip two coins, one corresponding to each stock. If heads is revealed the stock price increases to $13 and if tails appears it falls to $9. Of course, stock price changes conform to weak-form market efficiency since the price changes are dependent on a random coin toss and does not depend on historical or public information. If you do not diversify between the two stocks, for your $10 investment, the future mean and variance of each stock is as follows:

Mean: $(\frac{1}{2} \times 13) + (\frac{1}{2} \times 9) = 11$
Variance: $[\frac{1}{2} \times (13 - 11)^2] + [\frac{1}{2} \times (9 - 11)^2] = 4$

Can we gain from diversification in such a market? Absolutely! To see this, assume we invest $5 in stock 1 and $5 in stock 2. Since the two stocks are independent (the coin tosses are independnt), you get the following returns:

Stock 1		Stock 2		Portfolio	
$\frac{1}{2} \times 13$	+	$\frac{1}{2} \times 13$	=	$13	(with probability of $\frac{1}{4}$)
$\frac{1}{2} \times 13$	+	$\frac{1}{2} \times 9$	=	$11	(with probability of $\frac{1}{4}$)
$\frac{1}{2} \times 9$	+	$\frac{1}{2} \times 13$	=	$11	(with probability of $\frac{1}{4}$)
$\frac{1}{2} \times 9$	+	$\frac{1}{2} \times 9$	=	$9	(with probability of $\frac{1}{4}$)

where $\frac{1}{2}$ represents the proportion of investment in which stock ($5/10 = \frac{1}{2}$). The portfolio mean return is:

$$(\frac{1}{4} \times 13) + (\frac{1}{4} \times 11) + (\frac{1}{4} \times 11) + (\frac{1}{4} \times 9) = \$11$$

which is exactly the same as investing in just stock 1 or 2 alone. Note, however, that the variance of the portfolio is lower:

$$[\frac{1}{4} \times (13 - 11)^2] + [\frac{1}{4} \times (11 - 11)^2] + [\frac{1}{4} \times (11 - 11)^2] + [\frac{1}{4} \times (9 - 11)^2] = 2$$

Thus, we reduce the risk from 4 to 2 by choosing to diversify.

Some believe that the EMH implies that all stocks are correctly priced and therefore you can select stocks at random, for example, by throwing a dart at a list of stocks obtained from the *Wall Street Journal*. This is not correct. While you cannot predict which stock will go up and which will go down, you can reduce your risk. If you ignore this diversification, you are exposing yourself to higher risk with no compensation in the form of a higher expected return. Note that in the above example, your variance decreased through diversification from 4 to 2, but your expected return remained the same.

The above simple example can be extended to many assets with positive and negative correlation. For example, suppose that you have a stock with a high variance but low beta (e.g., $\beta_i = 0.5$). By the CAPM, the mean rate of return on the stock will be relatively low. The reason is that this stock is negatively correlated with other securities and hence portfolio risk is reduced. If you do not diversify and you hold only one stock, you pay a relatively high price for the stock, you expose yourself to high risk, and do not enjoy the benefits of the risk-reduction possibilities due to the negative correlation.

In summary, if EMH holds, technical and fundamental analysis is economically worthless. However, portfolio analysis remains, and in fact, more effort should be allocated to portfolio analysis.

SUMMARY

This chapter sets out the basic principles of the capital asset pricing model (CAPM) and the arbitrage pricing theory (APT). The CAPM assumes a perfect capital market in which investors hold portfolios which comprise *all* securities available in the market. This very strong assumption permits us to define a number of important concepts:

1. The *capital market line* (CML) on which all efficient portfolios lie.
2. The *security market line* (SML) which sets out the linear relationship between expected return and risk.
3. The analysis also permits the dichotomization of a security's risk into two components: the *diversifiable* component, or *nonsystematic risk* as it is often called. The nonsystematic risk (diversifiable component) can be eliminated by combining the security in a diversified portfolio; but the *systematic risk* (nondiversifiable component) cannot be eliminated through portfolio diversification.

Although it was originally developed for the security market, the CAPM also provides some important insights into the capital budgeting process. Applied to individual projects, the appropriate discount rate is given by the riskless interest rate plus a premium which is determined by the projects' non-diversifiable (systematic) risk. However, in an extremely imperfect market in which investors hold only single-security portfolios, the firm's optimal capital budget can be found using the mean–variance rule. Clearly, the truth lies somewhere between these two extreme assumptions. In fact, empirical evidence drawn from the New York Stock Exchange suggests that a typical portfolio includes only a few individual common stocks.

To address the deficiencies of the CAPM, the arbitrage pricing theory (APT) was developed. The APT rests on the idea that in equilibrium, arbitrage profits (i.e., with zero investment, nonnegative returns are obtained in every state of nature and at least one positive return can be earned) do not exist. Unlike the CAPM, APT does not depend on a single factor (i.e., the market portfolio) to determine stock returns; however, it falls short in identifying those factors which should be employed.

If the market is efficient we expect no arbitrage profit opportunities. Also, fundamental and technical analysis is economically worthless. However, portfolio selection still plays a central role even if markets are efficient.

It is to be hoped that the reader has emerged from his baptism of fire in a world of risk and uncertainty with some additional insight and a degree of 'risk aversion' and skepticism for quick and easy formulae which are appropriate for a future corporate executive. With that in mind we turn in Part III to the forces which determine the corporation's cutoff rate for investments, i.e., the cost of capital.

Portfolio parameters

1. Expected return:

$$E(x_0) = \sum_{i=1}^{n} p_i E(x_i)$$

2. Portfolio variance:

$$\sigma_0^2 = \sum_{i=1}^{n} p_i^2 \sigma_i^2 + 2 \sum_{\substack{i=1 \\ j>i}}^{n} p_i p_j \, \mathrm{Cov}(x_i, x_j)$$

which can be rewritten also as:

$$\sigma_0^2 = \sum_{i=1}^{n} p_i^2 \sigma_i^2 + 2 \sum_{\substack{i=1 \\ j>i}}^{n} p_i p_j R_{ij} \sigma_i \sigma_j$$

where $E(x_0)$ and σ_0^2 are the portfolio expected return and variance, respectively, and R_{ij} is the correlation coefficient between the ith and jth security's return.

Capital market line (CML)

$$E(x_p) = r + \frac{E(x_m) - r}{\sigma_m} \, \sigma_p$$

It holds *only* with respect to efficient portfolios.

Security market line (SML)

$$E(x_i) = r + (E(x_m) - r)\beta_i$$

It holds for portfolios and individual securities alike, where:

$$\beta_i = \mathrm{Cov}(x_i, x_m)/\sigma_m^2$$

Decomposition of total risk (for positive β)

1. Non-diversifiable risk (σ_i^{ND}) = systematic risk (σ_i^S), where:

$$\sigma_i^{ND} = \sigma_i^S = \beta_i \sigma_m$$

2. Diversifiable risk (σ_i^D) = non-systematic risk (σ_i^{NS}), where:

$$\sigma_i^D = \sigma_i^{NS} = \sigma_i - \beta_i \sigma_m$$

3. Total risk given by:

$$\sigma_i = \sigma_i^{ND} + \sigma_i^D \quad \text{or} \quad \sigma_i = \sigma_i^S + \sigma_i^{NS}$$

The arbitrage pricing theory (APT) model

1. Rate of return generating mechanism:

$$R_i = E(R_i) + \beta_i(I - E(I)) + e_i$$

where I is the common factor generating the asset's rates of return.

2. The equilibrium relationship:

$$E(R_i) = E(R_z) + (E(I) - E(R_z))\beta_i$$

where $E(R_z)$ is the expected rate of return on the zero beta portfolio, such that $\text{Cov}(I, R_z) = 0$.

QUESTIONS AND PROBLEMS

12.1 In what sense does a perfect market separate the investment process into two stages?

12.2 What is the equilibrium relationship between return and risk which must hold for every risky asset in a perfect market?

12.3 Define 'systematic' and 'nonsystematic risk'.

12.4 The 'betas' of four stocks in a perfect market are as follows:

$$\beta_A = -1; \quad \beta_B = 0; \quad \beta_C = 1; \quad \beta_D = 2$$

Assume that the market is in equilibrium; that the riskless interest rate is 6%; and that the expected return on the 'market portfolio' is 14%. Calculate the expected return on shares A, B, C, and D.

12.5 In what circumstances may a firm rationally decide to accept an investment which has a negative *NPV*, where the *NPV* is calculated with the firm's current cost of capital.

12.6 Assume a perfect capital market in which investors are constrained to building single-stock risky portfolios, that borrowing or lending at a riskless interest rate is possible, and that in *equilibrium* the following relationship between two risky securities i and j holds:

	Security i	Security j
Expected return (%)	26	18
Standard deviation (%)	15	9

(a) What is the riskless rate of interest in this market? (Hint: In equilibrium under the above conditions both securities must lie on the same market lines, i.e. the following equation must hold:

$$\frac{E(x_i) - r}{\sigma_i} = \frac{E(x_j) - r}{\sigma_j}$$

(b) If the investor wishes to hold a portfolio with a standard deviation of only 6% what would be his investment strategy?

(c) What would his investment strategy be if he wanted to reach an expected return of 24%?

12.7 Assume the following rates of return:

Year	Market portfolio	Stock i	Stock j
1	10	9	22
2	32	24	48
3	20	14	30
4	18	−2	−20
5	17	16	29
6	3	4	−3
7	12	8	21
8	−5	0	−15
9	18	12	28
10	21	15	36

(a) Calculate the betas of each stock.

(b) Is stock i an aggressive, defensive, or neutral stock?

(c) Is stock j an aggressive, defensive, or neutral stock?

(d) Draw the characteristic line for each stock on the same graph.

12.8 The annual rate of return on the market portfolio x_m and the annual rate of return on a security j, x_j, for a period of eight years are given below:

Year	x_j	x_m
1	0.045	0.020
2	0.050	0.060
3	0.070	0.080
4	0.020	−0.030
5	0.050	0.010
6	0.090	0.080
7	0.040	0.060
8	0.020	−0.040

Estimate the beta coefficient of security j, interpret it and classify the security as 'aggressive' or 'defensive'.

12.9 Assume that the firm's current income Y_0 is equal to $10,000. The firm is making investment $I_0 = $2,000$, and the next-period income is uncertain. The expected next-period income is $\overline{Y}_1 = $10,000$ and its covariance with the return on the market portfolio is $\text{Cov}(Y_1, x_m) = 250$; the expected return on the market portfolio is $\overline{x}_m = 0.10$ and the standard deviation of the market return $\sigma_m = 0.10$; the risk-free interest rate is $r = 0.04$. There are no taxes. Calculate the value of the firm's equity.

12.10 A common stock (j) is expected to yield a (gross) return $R_j = \$40$. The following quantities are given: the expected rate of return on the market portfolio $\overline{x_m} = 0.10$; the standard deviation of the market return $\sigma_m = 0.08$; the covariance of the stock-j return with the market portfolio $\text{Cov}(R_j, x_m) = 0.50$; the risk-free interest rate $r = 0.04$. What is the stock's equilibrium value?

12.11 Assume that the capital market is in equilibrium. The riskless rate is 6% and you buy a common stock (i) whose expected gross return is $120. You pay $100 for the stock. Is $\text{Cov}(R_i, x_m)$ positive or negative? Explain.

12.12 Assume that the capital market is in equilibrium. The risk-free interest rate is $r = 0.04$; the expected rate of return on the market portfolio is $x_m = 0.10$; and the standard deviation of the market return is $\sigma_m = 0.09$.

(a) Write out and draw the capital market line (CML).
(b) Consider three securities whose returns (x_1, x_2, x_3) have the following covariances with the return on the market portfolio:

$$\text{Cov}(x_1, x_m) = \quad 0.0108$$
$$\text{Cov}(x_2, x_m) = -0.0027$$
$$\text{Cov}(x_3, x_m) = \quad 0.0054$$

Write out and draw the security market line (SML), and determine the expected value of the above securities. Also, identify them on the SML.
(c) Define the beta coefficients of the three securities.
(d) If the standard deviations of the three securities are $\sigma_1 = 0.20$, $\sigma_2 = 0.05$. and $\sigma_3 = 0.16$, what is the *diversifiable* risk of each of these securities? (Decompose the standard deviation rather than the variance.)

12.13 Let S_0 be the value of a company's shares *just after current dividends are paid*. Assume no taxes, the expected next period's income is $\overline{Y}_1 = \$1,000$ and $\text{Cov}(Y_1, x_m) = 40$. Also assume that the expected rate of return on the market portfolio is $\overline{x}_m = 0.10$, its standard deviation $\sigma_m = 0.10$, and the risk-free interest rate $r = 0.04$.

(a) Determine the value S_0 under the assumption that the firm is liquidated at the end of the period and all its assets are paid out as dividends D_1.
(b) Answer question (a) assuming that $\text{Cov}(Y_1, x_m) = 0$.

12.14 The annual rates of return (in percent) of two securities, i and j, and of the market portfolio for four years were as follows:

Year	Security i	Security j	Market portfolio
1	− 20	+ 30	+ 40
2	0	+10	+ 20
3	+ 20	−10	0
4	0	+10	+12

Assume a riskless interest rate $r = 5\%$.

(a) Calculate the standard deviations of returns of securities i and j and the covariances between the returns of the two securities and between the returns of each security and the market.

(b) Calculate the systematic (nondiversifiable) risk of the two securities σ_i^S and σ_j^S, and show graphically the location of the two securities and of the market portfolio in the average rate of return–systematic risk plane.

(c) Suppose that the market is in equilibrium. What would be the expected rate of return on the two securities? How can you account for the deviation of the above data from the calculated figures?

12.15 The table below provides the annual rates of return on General Motors, American Motors Corporation, and the S&P Five Hundred Index, which is a proxy for the market portfolio. Assuming a riskless interest rate of $r = 3\%$ answer the following questions.

Year	GM	AMC	Market portfolio
1	14.4	121.2	11.9
2	− 22.2	− 33.9	0.4
3	47.5	3.7	26.9
4	7.7	3.1	− 8.6
5	42.8	17.2	22.8
6	30.7	−16.9	16.5
7	11.4	− 32.8	12.5
8	− 32.5	− 30.4	−10.06
9	30.5	114.0	23.9
10	1.8	− 3.7	11.1
11	− 6.2	− 33.0	− 8.5
12	22.3	− 33.2	3.9
13	4.3	21.6	14.3
14	6.5	17.8	19.1
15	− 37.8	7.5	−14.7
16	− 27.6	− 62.3	− 26.5
17	97.1	65.4	37.3
18	45.85	− 28.02	23.8
19	−11.25	− 6.33	−7.15
20	− 4.7	26.67	12.16

(a) Calculate the systematic risk $\beta_i \sigma_m$, the nonsystematic risk $(\sigma_i - \beta_i \sigma_m)$ and the total risk σ_i of the stocks of GM and AMC.

(b) For risk-free interest rate of $r = 3\%$ draw the CML and illustrate graphically the decomposition of the risk of GM into the two components.

(c) Draw the SML and show the location of the two stocks on the line.

(d) Use the systematic risk σ^S to calculate the equilibrium risk-premiums of GM and AMC. What was the actual estimate of the risk-premium during the last twenty years? How do you explain the difference in the expected risk-premium?

12.16 Suppose that a firm operates for one period and at the end of the period shareholders get the liquidation value of the firm. Let Y be a random variable which denotes the total income for the shareholders at the end of the period. The joint probability to get income $Y = Y_i$ and that the rate of return on the market portfolio will be $x_m = x_{mj}$ is given by P_{ij} in the table:

		Total income (Y_i)		
		1,000	6,000	8,000
x_{mj} (%)	−20	0.05	0.00	0.00
	10	0.05	0.05	0.10 } P_{ij}
	40	0.15	0.50	0.10

Note that the total probability $\Sigma_i \Sigma_j \, P_{ij} = 1$.

The risk-free interest rate is 6%. In the absence of corporate tax answer the following questions:

(a) The firm intends to issue bonds with a face value of $2,000 and coupon interest rate of 10%. Is the bond riskless? Why? What is the total equilibrium market value of the bonds?

(b) Assume that the bonds as described in part (a) are the only debt the firm has. What is the value of the firm's stock in equilibrium?

(c) Suppose that the firm decides *not* to issue bonds, what is the market value of the stock? Is there any relationship between your answers to (a), (b) and (c)?

Hints: 1. If income is below $2,200, bondholders get whatever is available and the shareholders get nothing.

2. The total investment in physical assets remains constant. Thus, issuing bonds implies that fewer shares are issued.

3. $\text{Cov}(x_{mj}, Y_i) = \Sigma_i \Sigma_j \, P_{ij} x_{mj} Y_i - E(x_m) E(y)$

where $p_{ij} = Pr(x_m = x_{mj} \text{ and } Y = Y_i)$

12.17 The future after-tax income of the firm one year from now is a random variable Y_1^T. The joint distribution of the firm's after-tax future income Y_1^T (where $Y_1^T = (1 - T_c)$ (revenue-expenses-depreciation)) and the return on the market portfolio x_m (also a random variable) is given by the following table:

		Y_1^T	
x_m	$6,000	$10,000	$14,000
		Joint probabilities	
−0.10%	0.10	0.15	0.05
0.10%	0.10	0.20	0.10
0.30%	0.05	0.15	0.10

In addition, assume a tax rate $T_c = 0.34$, *current* after-tax income $Y_0^T = \$6,000$, current investment $I_0 = \$5,000$, and the risk-free interest rate $r = 0.06$. The investment is fully depreciated in the one period and its residual value at $t = 1$ is zero.

(a) Determine the value of the firm (assume that current income has not been distributed yet) Assume zero debt at time $t = 0$. (Hint: Recall that the depreciation tax shelter is certain.)

(b) Now assume that there are no taxes and no depreciation, and that the above figures represent the firm's future cash flows. Suppose the firm is increasing the current dividend out of the proceeds of a one-period bond issue, i.e., the new issue is not being used to finance an increase in the firm's activities. The bonds have $6,000 face value and a coupon rate of 7%. Are the bonds a risky asset? Find their market equilibrium value, B_0.

12.18 Assume a perfect capital market in which investors are constrained to holding portfolios that consist of a single stock (a risky asset) and the riskless asset. Two risky securities in this market were observed to have the following parameters *in equilibrium*:

	Stock *i*	Stock *j*
Expected return (%)	18	25
Standard deviation (%)	8	12

(a) What is the riskless interest rate in this market?
(b) Assume that the investor is confronted with two mutually exclusive alternatives:

  1. A portfolio of $900 worth of stock *i*.
  2. A portfolio of $600 worth of stock *j* plus $300 worth of the riskless asset.

Which of the two alternatives is preferable?

12.19 Assume a perfect capital market in which the investors are constrained to holding portfolios that consist of a single stock (a risky asset) and the riskless asset. Two risky securities in this market were observed to have the following parameters *in equilibrium*:

	Stock A	Stock B
Expected return (%)	18	22
Standard deviation (%)	6	8

(a) Determine the riskless rate of return in this market.
(b) Find the optimal investment strategy of the two individuals characterized by the following indifference maps:

  1. $E(R) = a + 0.10\sigma^2$
  2. $E(R) = a + 0.25\sigma^2$

Assume that both are seeking to invest $100 in securities. Demonstrate your answer numerically and graphically.
(c) Since the individuals are allowed to hold only one risky asset in their portfolios, enterprising businesspeople applied for a government licence to set up a mutual fund that will include stocks A and B in equal proportions. The individual investors will then be allowed to diversify between fund shares and the riskless asset. Find the market line characteristic of the mutual fund and compare it with the market line of the two separate stocks. How would you characterize the gains from diversification in this case? Assume zero correlation coefficient between the two stocks included in the mutual fund.
(d) Estimate the maximum management fee (for the zero correlation case) that the fund managers can charge their shareholders. The management fee in effect reduces the mean return that the fund yields to the investors. How will the management fee be affected if the correlation coefficient is negative (say, $-2/3$) rather than zero?

12.20 Hypothetical rates of return (in percentages) on three securities and on the market portfolio are as follows:

Year	Securities 1	Securities 2	Securities 3	Market profile (*m*)
1	5	8	10	5
2	10	4	8	10
3	0	3	−10	−10
4	40	20	20	40

(a) Estimate the beta of each security by running the appropriate first-pass regressions.

(b) Run the second-pass regressions and test the hypothesis that $\hat{\gamma}_1 = 0$, where $\hat{\gamma}_1$ is the slope of the second-pass regression.

12.21 Assume that the entire market consists of three securities only, with betas given by $\beta_1 = 1/2$, $\beta_2 = 1$, and $\beta_3 = 4$, respectively.

(a) Find the investment proportions p_1, p_2, p_3 of the zero beta portfolio with zero net investment (i.e., $\Sigma\, p_i = 0$).

(b) Find the investment proportions p_1, p_2, p_3 fulfilling the constraints $\Sigma\, p_i\beta_i = 1$, and $\Sigma\, p_i = 0$.

12.22 The following describes the mean return and betas of DuPont, Dow Chemical, and Union Carbide.

	DuPont	Dow Chemical	Union Carbide
Mean return (%)	4.6	10	11.2
Beta	0.86	0.74	0.71

Determine the arbitrage portfolio with zero investment and a zero beta. Is there room for arbitrage profit?

12.23 Suppose that Xerox beta is 1.8 and the Utility Pacific beta is 0.9. It is also given that in equilibrium the mean rate of return on Xerox stock is twice as large as the mean rate of return on Utility Pacific. Given this information, and assuming that the market is in equilibrium, calculate the risk-free interest rate.

12.24 There are three stocks in the market and the CAPM holds. The parameters of these stocks are as follows:

	Stock A	Stock B	Stock C
$E(X_i)$	15%	20%	30%
β_i	1/2	1	?

What should be β_3 such that the CAPM holds? What is the mean rate of return on the market portfolio? What is the risk-free interest rate?

APPENDIX 12A: DERIVATION OF THE CAPITAL ASSET PRICING MODEL

This appendix provides a formal demonstration of the derivation of the primary equilibrium condition of the capital asset pricing model (CAPM): that is, the proposition that in equilibrium the expected return on any risky asset (in a perfect capital market) will be given by:

$$E(x_i) = r + (E(x_m) - r)\beta_i$$

where:

$E(x_i)$ = expected return on asset i
r = risk-free interest rate
$E(x_m)$ = expected return on the market portfolio (e.g., Standard & Poors' index)
β_i = ith asset's systematic risk

Optimal investment proportions

As noted in the text each individual investor in the market attempts to reach the highest feasible market line, for example, the line rN of Figure 12.1 which is reproduced here (Figure 12A.1). The market line can be found by minimizing the standard deviation (σ_0) for any given portfolio's expected return $(E(x_0))$:

$$E(x_0) = \sum_{i=1}^{n} p_i E(x_i) + \left(1 - \sum_{i=1}^{n} p_i\right) r$$

$$\sigma_0 = \sqrt{\sum_{i=1}^{n} p_i^2 \sigma_i^2 + 2 \sum_{\substack{i=1 \\ j>i}}^{n} p_i p_j \, \text{Cov}(x_i, x_j)}$$

where p_i denotes the proportion of the portfolio invested in the ith asset.

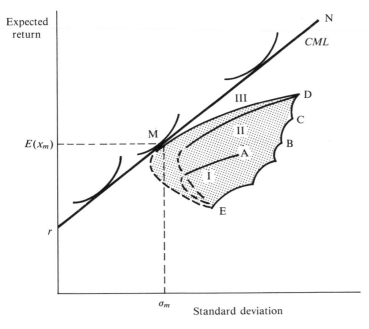

Figure 12A.1

Clearly the availability of riskless bonds (or loans) influences, and therefore appears, in the formula for the expected return. However, the inclusion of such bonds (loans) does *not* affect the standard deviation of the overall portfolio since the variance of a perfectly certain income (payments) stream r is zero. Hence the covariance of the bonds (loans) with the portfolio's risky assets (e.g., common stock) is also zero.

Now let us define the function C, as follows:

$$C = \sigma_0 + \lambda_1 \left[E(x_0) - \sum_{i=1}^{n} p_i E(x_i) - \left(1 - \sum_{i=1}^{n} p_i\right) r \right] \tag{1}$$

where $\lambda_1 =$ a Lagrange multiplier.

The problem is to determine the vector of investment proportions which *minimizes* the overall portfolio standard deviation for all values of $E(x_0)$. This is tantamount to finding the market line rN of Figure 12.1, since by definition, that market line represents the feasible efficient set of alternatives facing the investor. Thus, each point on the line represents the overall portfolio (equities plus bonds or loans) which minimizes the standard deviation, given the expected return. The market line can be generated analytically by differentiating equation (1) with respect to each p_i and with respect to the Lagrange multiplier λ_1, and setting the first derivatives equal to zero. This yields the following set of $n + 1$ equations:

$$\frac{\partial C}{\partial p_1} = \tfrac{1}{2}(\sigma_0^2)^{-1/2} \left[2p_1\sigma_1^2 + 2 \sum_{j=2}^{n} p_j \, \text{Cov}(x_1, x_j) \right] - \lambda_1(E(x_1) - r) = 0$$

$$\frac{\partial C}{\partial p_2} = \tfrac{1}{2}(\sigma_0^2)^{-1/2} \left[2p_2\sigma_2^2 + 2 \sum_{\substack{j=1 \\ j \neq 2}}^{n} p_j \, \text{Cov}(x_2, x_j) \right] - \lambda_1(E(x_2) - r) = 0$$

$$\vdots \qquad \vdots \qquad \vdots \qquad \vdots \qquad \vdots \tag{2}$$

$$\frac{\partial C}{\partial p_n} = \tfrac{1}{2}(\sigma_0^2)^{-1/2} \left[2p_n\sigma_n^2 + 2 \sum_{j=1}^{n-1} p_j \, \text{Cov}(x_n, x_j) \right] - \lambda_1(E(x_n) - r) = 0$$

$$\frac{\partial C}{\partial \lambda_1} = E(x_0) - \sum_{i=1}^{n} p_i E(x_i) - \left(1 - \sum_{i=1}^{n} p_i\right) r = 0$$

Multiplying the first equation by p_1, the second equation by p_2, etc., and summing over all the equations yields:[28]

$$\sigma_0 = \lambda_1 \left(\sum_{i=1}^{n} p_i E(x_i) - \sum_{i=1}^{n} p_i r \right)$$

$$= \lambda_1 \left[\sum_{i=1}^{n} p_i E(x_i) + \left(1 - \sum_{i=1}^{n} p_i\right) r - r \right]$$

At the specific point where $\Sigma_{i=1}^{n} p_i = 1$ we obtain:[29]

$$\sigma_m = \lambda_1(E(x_m) - r)$$

and hence:

$$1/\lambda_1 = \frac{(E(x_m) - r)}{\sigma_m}$$

where m denotes the market portfolio, which is optimal for all investors (see Figure 12A.1).

----

28. Note that the left side of this summation is simply σ_0.
29. Note that the slope of the market line is identical at all points. Thus, finding the highest slope by looking at the specific point where $\Sigma_{i=1}^{n} p = 1$ does not restrict the results, since the same slope holds for all other points.

As we have already noted, the expression $(E(x_m) - r)/\sigma_m$ defines the slope of the market line (rN of Figure 12A.1). The reciprocal of the Lagrange multiplier ($1/\lambda_1$) measures the price of a unit of risk, that is, the required increase in expected return when one unit of risk (in terms of the standard deviation) is added to the portfolio.

Let us now use the above results to determine the equilibrium relationship between an individual asset's expected return and its risk. Recall that in this context 'risk' reflects not only the standard deviation of returns on the asset itself but also the covariance with the returns of all other risky assets in the market.

Since this set of equations, from which we derive the equilibrium conditions for the individual investor, must hold simultaneously for all investors independently of their tastes, we can also use equations (2) to derive the general relationship among the expected returns of all shares and their risk.

In general, the ith equation of (2), at the point $\Sigma_{i=1}^n p_i = 1$, can be rewritten as:

$$E(x_i) = r + \frac{1}{\lambda_1 \sigma_m} \left[p_i \sigma_i^2 + \sum_{\substack{i=1 \\ j \neq i}}^n p_j \, \text{Cov}(x_i, x_j) \right]$$

Recalling the definition of λ_1, we obtain:

$$E(x_i) = r + \frac{E(x_m) - r}{\sigma_m^2} \left[p_i \sigma_i^2 + \sum_{\substack{i=1 \\ j \neq i}}^n p_j \, \text{Cov}(x_i, x_j) \right]$$

But since by definition, the return on the market portfolio is given by $x_m = \Sigma_{i=1}^n p_i x_i$, it can be shown[30] that the expected return on any risk can be written as:

$$E(x_i) = r + \frac{E(x_m) - r}{\sigma_m^2} \, \text{Cov}(x_i, x_m)$$

or alternatively:

$$Ex_i = r + (E(x_m) - r)\beta_i$$

where

$$\beta_i = \frac{\text{Cov}(x_i, x_m)}{\sigma_m^2}$$

which is precisely the equilibrium relationship which was presented in the text.

QUESTIONS AND PROBLEMS

12A.1 Assume that there are only three stocks in the market, and that the optimal investment proportion in each stock A, B, and C is $1/3$. Also assume:

$$\sigma_A^2 = 10, \quad \sigma_B^2 = 8, \quad \sigma_C^2 = 20$$
$$\text{Cov}(A, B) = 8, \quad \text{Cov}(B, C) = -10, \quad \text{Cov}(A, C) = 4$$

Calculate:

(a) $\text{Cov}(A, M)$, $\text{Cov}(B, M)$, and $\text{Cov}(C, M)$ where M denotes the market portfolio.
(b) The systematic risk (beta) for each of the above three stocks.

----

30. $\text{Cov}(x_i, x_m) = \text{Cov}[x_i, (p_1 x_1 + \cdots p_n x_n)] = p_i \sigma_i^2 + \sum_{\substack{j=1 \\ j \neq i}}^n p_j \, \text{Cov}(x_i, x_j)$.

12A.2 Assume that there are only two stocks (A and B) in the market, and that the risk-free interest rate is 5%. Also assume:

$$E(x_A) = 10, \quad \sigma_A^2 = 10$$
$$E(x_B) = 20, \quad \sigma_B^2 = 20, \quad \text{Cov(A, B)} = 0$$

(a) Find the optimal investment proportions in these two stocks on the assumption that the individual invests 100% of his resources in the two stocks.

(b) Find the optimal investment proportions for an individual who decides to invest 50% of his resources in these two stocks, and 50% in the riskless asset.

(c) What is the market price of risk? Show your calculation in detail.

SELECTED REFERENCES

Alexander, Gordon J. and Chervany, Norman L., 'On the Estimation and Stability of Beta,' *Journal of Financial and Quantitative Analysis*, March 1980.

Barry, C. B., 'Effects of Uncertain and Non-stationary Parameters upon Capital Market Equilibrium Conditions,' *Journal of Financial and Quantitative Analysis*, September 1978.

Beja, Avraham and Goldman, Barry, 'On the Dynamic Behavior of Prices in Disequilibrium,' *Journal of Finance*, May 1980.

Ben-Horim, Moshe and Levy, Haim, 'Total Risk, Diversifiable Risk: A Pedagogic Note,' *Journal of Financial and Quantitative Analysis*, June 1980.

Bera, A. K. and Kannan, S., 'An Adjustment Procedure for Predicting Systematic Risk,' *Journal of Applied Econometrics*, October 1986.

Best, Michael J. and Grauer, Robert R., 'Capital Asset Pricing Compatible with Observed Market Weights,' *Journal of Finance*, March 1985.

Bos, T. and Newbold, P., 'An Empirical Investigation of the Possibility of Stochastic Systematic Risk in the Market Model,' *Journal of Business*, January 1984.

Bower, Dorothy H., Bower, Richard S., and Logue, Dennis E., 'Arbitrage Pricing Theory and Utility Stock Returns,' *Journal of Finance*, September 1984.

Boyer, Marcel, Storoy, Sverre, and Sten, Thore, 'Equilibrium in Linear Capital Market Networks,' *Journal of Finance*, December 1975.

Breeden, D. T., 'An Intertemporal Asset Pricing Model with Stochastic Consumption and Investment Opportunities,' *Journal of Financial Economics*, June 1979.

Brenner, Menachem and Smidt, Seymour, 'Asset Characteristics and Systematic Risk,' *Financial Management*, Winter 1978.

Brown, Keith, C. and Brown, Gregory, 'Does the Market Portfolio's Composition Matter?' *Journal of Portfolio Management*, Winter 1987.

Brown, S. L., 'Autocorrelation, Market Imperfections, and the CAPM,' *Journal of Financial and Quantitative Analysis*, December 1979.

Chen, K. C., Cheng, David C., and Hite, Gailen L., 'Systematic Risk and Market Power: An Application of Tobin's *q*' *Quarterly Review of Economics and Business*, Autumn 1986.

Cheng, Pao L. and Grauer, Robert R., 'An Alternative Test of the Capital Asset Pricing Model,' *American Economic Review*, September 1980.

Cho, D. Chinhyung, Elton, Edwin J., and Gruber, Martin J., 'On the Robustness of the Roll and Ross Arbitrage Pricing Theory,' *Journal of Financial and Quantitative Analysis*, March 1984.

Collins, D. W., Ledolter, J., and Rayburn, J. D., 'Some Further Evidence on the Stochastic Properties of Systematic Risk,' *Journal of Business*, July 1987.

Cornell, B. and Dietrich, J. K., 'Mean–Absolute-Deviation versus Least-Squares Regression Estimation of Beta Coefficients,' *Journal of Financial and Quantitative Analysis*, March 1978.

Dowen, Richard, 'Beta, Non-systematic Risk and Portfolio Selection,' *Applied Economics*, February 1988.

Dowen, Richard J. and Bauman, W. Scott, 'A Fundamental Multifactor Asset Pricing Model,' *Financial Analysis Journal*, July/August 1986.

Dukes, William P., Boulin, Oswald D., and MacDonald, S. Scott, 'The Performance of Beta in Forecasting Portfolio Returns in Bull and Bear Markets using Alternative Market Proxies,' *Quarterly Journal of Business and Economics*, Spring 1987.

Dybvig, Philip H. and Ross, Stephen A., 'Differential Information and Performance Measurement using a Security Market Line,' *Journal of Finance*, June 1985.

Elton, Edwin J. and Gruber, Martin J., 'Non-standard C.A.P.M.s and the Market Portfolio,' *Journal of Finance*, July 1984.

Epstein, Larry, G. and Turnbull, Stuart M., 'Capital Asset Prices and the Temporal Resolution of Uncertainty,' *Journal of Finance*, June 1980.

Fabozzi, F. J. and Francis, J. C., 'Beta as a Random Coefficient,' *Journal of Financial and Quantitative Analysis*, March 1978.

Fama, Eugene F., 'Risk, Return, and Equilibrium: Some Clarifying Comments,' *Journal of Finance*, March 1968.

Ferson, W. E., Kendel, S., and Stambaugh, R. F., 'Tests of Asset Pricing with Time-Varying Expected Risks Premiums and Market Betas,' *Journal of Finance*, June 1987.

Foster, T. W. III, Hanson, Don and Vickrey, Don, 'Additional Evidence on the Abatement of Errors in Predicting Beta Through Increases in Portfolio Size and on the Regression Tendency,' *Journal of Business Finance and Accounting*, Summer 1988.

Franke, Gunter, 'Conditions for Myopic Valuation and Serial Independence of the Market Excess Return in Discrete Time Models,' *Journal of Finance*, June 1984.

Frankfurter, G. M., 'The Effect of "Market Indexes" on the *Ex-post* Performance of the Shape Portfolio Selection Model,' *Journal of Finance*, June 1976.

Garven, James A., 'CML to SML: An Alternative Approach,' *Journal of Business Finance and Accounting*, Summer 1988.

Gentry, James and Pike, John, 'An Empirical Study of the Risk–Return Hypothesis Using Common Stock Portfolios of Life Insurance Companies,' *Journal of Financial and Quantitative Analysis*, June 1970.

Giovannini, A. and Jorion P., 'The Time Variation of Risk and Return in Foreign Exchange and Stock Markets,' *Journal of Finance*, June 1989.

Green, Richard C., 'Benchmark Portfolio Inefficiency and Deviations from the Security Market Line,' *Journal of Finance*, June 1986.

Harpaz, Giora, 'Firm Learning and Systematic Risk,' *Research in Finance*, 5, 1985.

Harris, Richard G., 'A General Equilibrium Analysis of the Capital Asset Pricing Model,' *Journal of Financial and Quantitative Analysis*, March 1980.

Heaney, W. John and Cheng Pao L., 'Continuous Maturity Diversification of Default Free Bond Portfolios and a Generalization of Efficient Diversification,' *Journal of Finance*, September 1984.

Huang, Roger D. and Kracaw, William, 'Stock Market Returns and Real Activity: A Note,' *Journal of Finance*, March 1984.

Huffman, Gregory W., 'Adjustment Costs and Capital Asset Pricing,' *Journal of Finance*, July 1985.

Jarrow, Robert and Rosenfeld, Eric R., 'Jump Risks and the Intertemporal Capital Asset Pricing Model,' *Journal of Business*, July 1984.

Jensen, Michael C. (ed.), *Studies in the Theory of Capital Markets*, New York: Praeger, 1972.

Jobson, J. D. and Korkie, Bob, 'On the Jensen Measure and Marginal Improvements in Portfolio Performance: A Note,' *Journal of Finance*, March 1984.

Kandel, S. and Stambaugh, R. F., 'A Mean–Variance Framework for Test of Asset Pricing Models,' *Review of Financial Studies*, 2(2), 1989.

Kraus, Alan and Litzenberger, Robert H., 'Market Equilibrium in a Multiperiod State Preference Model with Logarithmic Utility,' *Journal of Finance*, December 1975.

Kroll, Y., Levy, H., and Rapoport, A., 'Experimental Tests of the Separation Theorem and the Capital Asset Pricing Model,' *American Economic Review*, June 1988.

Kymn, K. O. and Page, W. P., 'A Microeconomic and Geometric Interpretation of Beta in Models of Discrete Adaptive Expectations,' *Review of Business and Economic Research*, Spring 1978.

Lakonishok, Josef and Shapiro, Alan C., 'Systematic Risk, Total Risk and Size as Determinants of Stock Market Returns,' *Journal of Banking and Finance*, March 1986.

Landskroner, Y., 'Intertemporal Determination of the Market price of Risk,' *Journal of Finance*, December 1977.

Lee, C. F. and Jen, F. C., 'Effects of Measurement Errors on Systematic Risk and Performance Measure of a Portfolio,' *Journal of Finance and Quantitative Analysis*, June 1978.

Levy, H., 'Equilibrium in Imperfect Market: A Constraint on the Role of Securities in the Portfolio,' *American Economic Review*, September 1978.

Levy, H., 'The CAPM and Beta in an Imperfect Market,' *Journal of Portfolio Management*, Winter 1980.

Levy, H., 'Measuring Risk and Performance over Alternative Investment Horizons,' Financial Analyst Journal, March/April 1984.

Levy, H., 'Another Look at the Capital Asset Pricing Model,' *Quarterly Review of Business and Economics*, Summer 1984.

Levy, H., 'The Capital Asset Pricing Model: Theory and Empiricism,' *Economic Journal*, March 1983.

Lewellen, Wilbur G., Lease, Ronald C., and Schlarbaum, Gary G., 'Portfolio Design and Portfolio Performance: The Individual Investor,' *Journal of Economics and Business*, Spring/Summer 1980.

Lin, Winston T. and Jen, Frank C., 'Consumption, Investment, Market Price of Risk, and the Risk-free Rate,' *Journal of Financial and Quantitative Analysis*, December 1980.

Lintner, John, 'Security Prices, Risk and Maximal Gains from Diversification,' *Journal of Finance*, December 1965.

Litzenberger, Robert H. and Joy, O. M., 'Target Rates of Return and Corporate Asset and Liability Structure under Uncertainty,' *Journal of Financial and Quantitative Analysis*, March 1971.

Litzenberger, Robert H. and Budd, Alan P., 'Corporate Investment Criteria and the Valuation of Risk Assets,' *Journal of Financial and Quantitative Analysis*, December 1970.

Markowitz, H. M., 'Risk Adjustment,' *Journal of Accounting Auditing and Finance*, Winter/Spring, 1990.

MacKinlay, A. C. 'On Multivariate Tests on the CAPM,' *Journal of Financial Economics*, June 1987.

McEntire, Paul L., 'Portfolio Theory for Independent Assets,' *Management Science*, August 1984.

Merton, R. C., 'Theory of Finance from the Perspective of Continuous Time,' *Journal of Financial and Quantitative Analysis*, November 1975.

Mossin, Jan, 'Equilibrium in a Capital Assets Market,' *Econonmetrica*, October 1966.

Mullins, D. W., Jr., 'Does the Capital Asset Pricing Model Work?,' *Harvard Business Review*, January/February 1982.

Officer, R. R., 'Seasonality in Australian Capital Markets: Market Efficiency and Empirical Issues', *Journal of Financial Economics*, March 1975.

Perold, Andre F., 'Large-scale Portfolio Optimization,' *Management Science*, October 1984.

Perrakis, Stylianos, 'Capital Budgeting and Timing Uncertainty within the Capital Asset Pricing Model,' *Financial Management*, Autumn 1979.

Rabinovitch, R. and Owen, J., 'Nonhomogeneous Expectations and Information in the Capital Asset Market,' *Journal of Finance*, May 1979.

Reilly, Frank K. and Wright, David J., 'A Comparison of Published Betas,' *Journal of Portfolio Management*, Spring 1988.

Rendleman, Richard J. Jr, 'Ranking Errors in CAPM Capital Budgeting Applications,' *Financial Management*, Winter 1978.

Rhee, S. Ghon, 'Stochastic Demand and a Decomposition of Systematic Risk,' *Research in Finance*, 6, 1986.

Roenfeldt, R. L., Griepentrof, G. L., and Pflaum, C. C., 'Further Evidence on the Stationarity of Beta Coefficients,' *Journal of Financial and Quantitative Analysis*, March 1978.

Roll, R., 'A Critique of the Asset Pricing Theory's Tests. Part I: On Past and Potential Testability of the Theory,' *Journal of Financial Economics*, March 1977.

Roll, R. and Ross, S., 'An Empirical Investigation of the Arbitrage Pricing Theory,' *Journal of Finance*, December 1980.

Ross, S. A., 'The Capital Asset Pricing Model (CAPM), Short-sale Restrictions and Related Issues,' *Journal of Finance*, March 1977.

Ross, S. A., 'The Current Status of the Capital Asset Pricing Model (CAPM),' *Journal of Finance*, June 1978.

Ross, S. A., 'The Arbitrage Theory of Capital Asset Pricing,' *Econometrica*, 1976.

Sareewiwatthana, Paiboon and Malone, R. Phil, 'Market Behavior and the Capital Asset Pricing Model in the Securities Exchange of Thailand: An Empirical Application,' *Journal of Business Finance and Accounting*, Autumn 1985.

Scott, Louis, O., 'The Stationarity of the Conditional Mean of Real Rates of Return on Common Stocks: An Empirical Investigation,' *Journal of Financial and Quantitative Analysis*, June 1984.

Scott, E. and Brown, S., 'Biased Estimators and Unstable Betas,' *Journal of Finance*, March 1980.

Shanken, Jay, 'Multivariate Tests of the Zero Beta CAPM', *Journal of Financial Economics*, September 1985.

Sharpe, William, F., 'Capital Asset Prices: A Theory of Market Equilibrium,' *Journal of Finance*, September 1964.

Sharpe, W., 'Capital Asset Prices With and Without Negative Holdings,' *Journal of Finance*, June 1991.

Smith, K. V., 'The Effect of Intervaling on Estimating Parameters of the Capital Asset Pricing Model,' *Journal of Financial and Quantitative Analysis*, June 1978.

Stapleton, R. C. and Subrahmanyam, M. G., 'Marketability of Assets and the Price Risk,' *Journal of Financial and Quantitative Analysis*, March 1979.

Theobald, Michael and Price, Vera, 'Seasonality Estimation in Thin Markets,' *Journal of Finance*, June 1984.

Trauring, M., 'A Capital Asset Pricing Model with Investors' Taxes and Three Categories of Investment Income,' *Journal of Financial and Quantitative Analysis*, September 1979.

Turnbull, S. M., 'Value and Systematic Risk,' *Journal of Finance*, September 1977.

Umstead, D. A. and Bergstrom, G. L., 'Dynamic Estimation of Portfolio Betas,' *Journal of Financial and Quantitative Analysis*, September 1979.

Ushman, Neal, 'A Comparison of Cross-section and Time Series Beta Adjustment Techniques' *Journal of Business, Finance and Accounting*, Autumn 1987.

Van Zijl, T., 'Risk Decomposition: Variance or Standard Deviation – A Reexamination and Extension,' *Journal of Finaneial and Quantitative Analysis*, June 1987.

Williams, J. T., 'Capital Asset Prices with Heterogenous Beliefs,' *Journal of Financial Economics*, November 1977.

The reader who has become interested in probability might still profit from the classic survey by Keynes:

J. M. Keynes, *A Treatise on Probability*, London: Macmillan, 1921.

The utility foundations of modern risk analysis can be found in:

J. von Neumann and O. Morgenstern, *Theory of Games and Economic Behavior*, 2nd edn, Princeton University Press, 1947.

K. Borch, *The Economics of Uncertainty*, Princeton University Press, 1968.

K. J. Arrow, *Essays in Risk Bearing*, Amsterdam: North-Holland, 1970.

Useful collections of articles are to be found in:

K. Borch and J. E. Mossin (eds), *Risk and Uncertainty*, London: Macmillan, 1968.

W. Edwards and A. Tversky, *Decision Making*, Harmondsworth: Penguin, 1967.

The mean–variance portfolio approach to decision-making was first set out in the classic works of Harry Markowitz and James Tobin:

H. M. Markowitz, 'Portfolio Selection,' *Journal of Finance*, March 1952.

H. M. Markowitz, *Portfolio Selection: Efficient Diversification of Investments*, New York: Wiley, 1959.

H. M. Markowitz, *Mean–Variance Analysis in Portfolio Choice and Capital Markets*, New York: Basil Blackwell, 1987.

J. Tobin, 'Liquidity Preference as Behavior Towards Risk,' *Review of Economic Studies*, February 1958.

Building on this foundation, the capital asset pricing model was developed in the mid-1960s:

W. F. Sharpe, 'Capital Asset Prices: A Theory of Market Equilibrium,' *Journal of Finance*, September 1964.

J. Lintner, 'The Valuation of Risk Assets and the Selection of Risky Investments in Stock Portfolios and Capital Budgets,' *Review of Economics and Statistics*, February 1965.

J. Mossin, 'Equilibrium in a Capital Assets Market,' *Econometrica*, October 1966.

E. F. Fama, 'Risk Return and Equilibrium: Some Clarifying Comments,' *Journal of Finance*, March 1968.

Later extensions have been made by:

F. Black, 'Capital Market Equilibrium with Restricted Borrowing,' *Journal of Business*, July 1972.

R. C. Merton, 'An Inter-temporal Capital Asset Pricing Model,' *Econometrica*, 1973.

S. A. Ross, 'The Arbitrage Theory of Capital Asset Pricing,' *Econometrica*, 13, 1976.

Less technically demanding introductions to portfolio theory and capital asset pricing can be found in:

R. A. Brealey, *An Introduction to Risk and Return from Common Stocks*, Cambridge, Mass.: MIT Press, 1969.

W. F. Sharpe, *Portfolio Theory and Capital Markets*, New York: McGraw-Hill, 1971.

E. J. Elton and M. J. Gruber, *Modern Portfolio Theory and Investment Analysis*, New York: Wiley, 1981.

H. Levy and M. Sarnat, *Portfolio and Investment Selection*, Englewood Cliffs, N.J.: Prentice Hall, 1984.

The empirical evidence and problems regarding its interpretation are surveyed by:

I. Friend, 'Recent Developments in Finance,' *Journal of Banking and Finance*, 1, 2, 1977.

R. Roll, 'A Critique of the Asset Pricing Theory's Tests. Part 1: On Past and Potential Testability of the Theory,' *Journal of Financial Economics*, March 1977.

Specific applications of risk analysis and portfolio theory to capital budgeting can be found in:

C. J. Grayson Jr, *Decisions Under Uncertainty: Drilling Decisions by Oil and Gas Operators*, Boston, MA: Division of Research, Harvard Business School, 1960.

S. C. Myers, 'Procedures for Capital Budgeting Under Uncertainty,' *Industrial Management Review*, Spring 1968.

R. H. Litzenberger and A. P. Budd, 'Corporate Investment Criteria and the Valuation of Risk Assets,' *Journal of Financial and Quantitative Analysis*, December 1970.

R. S. Hamada, 'Investment Decisions with a General Equilibrium Approach,' *Quarterly Journal of Economics*, November 1971.

R. C. Stapleton, 'Portfolio Analysis, Stock Valuation and Capital Budgeting for Risky Projects,' *Journal of Finance*, March 1971.

M. E. Rubinstein, 'A Mean–Variance Synthesis of Corporate Financial Theory,' *Journal of Finance*, March 1973.

Part III

Long-term Financial Decisions

Introduction

To this point we have avoided a direct confrontation with financing decisions and the concept of the cost of capital. In the preceding chapters which were devoted to the analysis of investment decisions (under certainty and uncertainty) we explicitly assumed that the cost of capital problem was solved, thereby permitting the use of a given 'riskless' or 'risky' discount rate, as the analysis required. Questions relating to the economic determinants of the cost of capital and its measurement were carefully swept under a by now bulging carpet. However, postponement of the discussion until now should *not* be construed as an indication that the cost of capital has only a secondary impact on financial decision-making. On the contrary, the cost of capital is of crucial importance since it serves as one of the direct determinants of the acceptability of capital investments within the individual firm, and therefore constitutes a key determinant of the economy's aggregate level of investment as well. Postponement of the analysis merely reflects the subject's complexity, and our hope is that the reader will be better prepared to handle this controversial subject now that he has the fundamental tools of financial analysis under his belt.

Chapters 13 through 15 are devoted to the analysis of the impact of financial leverage on shareholders' earnings and risk; the relationship of financial structure to the value of the firm's securities; and the factors determining the firm's *optimal* financing mix, i.e., the financial structure which maximizes the market value of the firm. In Chapter 16 we define the cost of capital, which, of course, is a function of the firm's market value, and hence also depends directly on the choice of financial structure. In Chapter 17 a method for measuring the cost of capital is spelled out, thereby providing a practical solution to the problem of determining a firm's cutoff rate on new investments. Chapter 18 discusses the recurring problem of dividend policy. Chapter 19 is devoted to options and futures, which have become very popular in the past decade. Chapter 20 analyzes the lease or buy decision. Chapter 21 is devoted to mergers and acquisitions. Finally, Chapter 22 considers international finance.

13

Financial Leverage

ARTICLE 21

Break-even or Net Seen by Document Technologies Soon

MOUNTAIN VIEW, Calif. – **Document Technologies Inc.**, which has had losses every quarter since its inception in 1988, expects to break even or become profitable in its third quarter, Dwight Ryan, chairman and chief executive officer, said.

Mr. Ryan said the company, which produces software, circuit boards and components that allow desktop computers to record and display printed documents, currently has a backlog of $800,000 in orders. The company expects during the third week in June to announce a "significant contract," he said in an interview.

Because operating costs were being tightly controlled and orders were increasing, Mr. Ryan said, "I expect to break even in the third quarter of this year." In the year-ago third quarter, the company had a net loss of $686,000 on revenue of $787,000. Document was a privately held company until the first quarter of this year and didn't report per-share earnings.

For the first quarter, Mr. Ryan said he expects the company to report losses about the same as the year-earlier quarter. In the 1991 first quarter, Document had a net loss of $840,000 on revenue of $469,000. Mr. Ryan indicated that for the second quarter of this year, Document's net loss is expected to narrow compared with a year ago. In the 1991 second quarter, Document's net loss was $1 million on revenue of $554,000.

Document, which announced in March an initial public offering of 750,000 common shares sold entirely by the company for $6 a share, raised proceeds to the company of $4.05 million. The funds will be used for working capital and research and development, Mr. Ryan said. Document's stock is traded over the counter. The company was launched with $6 million raised from private investors.

Source: Wall Street Journal, June 5 1992.

In the preceding chapters we assumed that the firm's risk–return profile could be changed only by altering its investment program. In this chapter we deal with an alternative means of influencing earnings and risk: by changing the firm's financial mix. Here we take the firm's investment program and its business risk as given, and seek to determine the influence of changes in capital structure on the rate of return, with a view to finding the particular capital structure which affords the best expected return–risk combination. Special attention is given to the impact of leverage on the break-even analysis and corresponding risk.

While firms try to maximize profitability, not being below the break-even point is important since, as the above article indicates, it implies losing money. Such questions as how the issuance of stocks by Document Technologies, Inc. affects the firm's break-even point, or the effect the issuing debt rather than equity has on the firm's break-even point are examined. In this chapter, the concept of break-even analysis and its effect on profitability, as well as the impact of the financial mix adopted by the firm on its break-even point, are introduced. As we shall see, being below the break-even point does not necessarily mean earnings are negative, but rather implies that earnings on equity are less than the interest rate.

FINANCIAL LEVERAGE AND EARNINGS

What effect does financial leverage, i.e., the introduction of fixed-interest bearing debt (or preferred stock), have on the return to the firm's shareholders and on the risk level of its common stock? To answer this we start by considering a new company which faces a decision regarding its capital structure: that is, a decision with respect to the best debt–equity mix with which to finance its operations. For simplicity, let us initially assume that there are only two mutually exclusive alternatives: (A) financing the firm with 100% equity (stocks), and (B) financing the firm with equal amounts of debt and equity (stock and bonds); and that there are no taxes levied on the income of either the firm or the shareholders. Throughout this chapter we assume that the un-levered firm issues n shares of stock. When the levered firm finances $p\%$ of its investment by debt, it finances $(1 - p)\%$ of the investment by equity, hence the number of shares issued drops proportionally. The stock price is unaffected by the use of leverage. In Chapter 14 we relax this assumption and analyze various possible impacts of leverage on the stock price and on the number of stocks issued. Nevertheless, for the break-even analysis presented here, one can analyze earnings per share or alternatively earnings per dollar of investment (see Appendix 13A). When the stock price is unchanged with leverage, earnings per share and earnings per dollar of investment yield the same results.

Table 13.1 sets out the relevant data for these two alternatives. Since we are discussing two alternative financial plans for the same company, the operating income (earnings before interest) remains constant in both. Note also that the distribution of the operating income, and therefore the degree of business risk attached to these earnings, must be the same in both alternatives. The net income in alternative B declines from $1,000 to $750 since (by assumption) 5% interest must be paid on the $5,000 of capital raised via bonds. As fewer shares are issued in alternative B, though, *earnings per share* (*EPS*), which is the relevant return to the shareholders, rise in alternative B from $1.00 to $1.50. The change in EPS induced by the use of fixed payment securities (e.g., debt) to finance a company's operations is often referred to as *financial leverage*: the

Table 13.1

	Alternative A (100% equity) ($)	Alternative B (50% bonds, 50% equity) ($)
Net operating income (NOI)	1,000	1,000
Interest (5% on bonds)	–	250
Net income (NI)	1,000	750
Capitalization:		
Stock	10,000	5,000
Bonds	–	5,000
Total stocks and bonds	10,000	10,000
Number of shares	1,000	500[a]
Earnings per share (EPS)	1.00	1.50

[a] Since 50% of the investment is financed by debt, the number of shares issued is reduced by 50%.

bonds in this example serving as a lever, so to speak, which raises EPS for a given *net operating income* (*NOI*). The reason for this is not hard to find; although the company pays 5% interest on the bonds, it earns a return of 10% on the capital invested, thereby raising the return to the common shareholders. Since we are considering a case without taxes, substitution of a 5% preferred shares for the bonds will result in the same leverage effect as the bonds.

If we introduce corporate taxes (say at the rate of 34%), net income will be reduced in both examples and EPS (after taxes) will be $0.66 and $0.99 in alternatives A and B respectively. The general line of reasoning remains the same; although the firm pays out 5% on the bonds, the effective cost in terms of after-tax income is only $(1 - T_c)r$, where T_c denotes the corporate tax rate and r the rate of interest. This reduction in the cost of debt follows directly from the tax deduction afforded interest payments. In our particular example the after-tax cost of the debt is $(1 - 0.34) \times 0.05 = 3.3\%$. Since the firm earns a net *after-tax* return of 6.6% without leverage, the leverage effect again results from the difference between the effective (after-tax) rate of outlay on the bonds,[1] 3.3%, and the (after-tax) rate of return earned by the company on the capital invested, 6.6%.

FINANCIAL LEVERAGE AND RISK

Financial leverage is a two-edged sword. In the previous example, we saw that the introduction of fixed-interest bearing securities in the capital structure can raise EPS, but upon reflection it might in certain circumstances also decrease EPS. This possibility of *negative* leverage creates a new type of financial risk,

---

1. Note, however, that in the after-tax example cited, substituting a 5% preferred stock payment no longer creates the same leverage effect because the dividend paid on preferred stock is *not* tax deductible.

in addition to the business risk already inherent in the company's operations. How does negative leverage arise?

Surely, the firm does not *plan* to reduce EPS. The possible negative effects of leverage can be seen more clearly if we explicitly recognize that the firm's net operating income is not usually constant. Consider again the example given in Table 13.1. (For simplicity only, we shall continue to use the example of a world without taxes.) Although the company expects an average annual income of $1,000, this expectation usually does not hold with certainty. In general, earnings will fluctuate, so that in any given year the income from operations may be greater or less than $1,000. Of course there might also be some probability (presumably small) of incurring a loss in a particular year.

Let us assume that the firm's expectation regarding future net operating income can be characterized by the following distribution: $1,000 with a probability of 0.5 and $250 with a probability of 0.5. This assumption is incorporated explicitly in Table 13.2. Note that each alternative now has two outcomes (columns) corresponding to the two possible outcomes of future NOI. As can be seen from Table 13.2, introducing debt into the capital structure increases the *expected value* of the earnings per share from $0.625 to $0.75, but the leverage also has an impact on risk. If the net operating income turns out to be $1,000, leverage increases the EPS from $1.00 to $1.50. However, there is also a 50% likelihood of a less favorable result, i.e., of a net operating income of only $250. Should this occur, the use of debt will decrease the EPS from $0.25 to zero.

In general, we must take both the 'bad' and the 'good' into account if the financial decision is properly to reflect the underlying uncertainty of business

Table 13.2

	Alternative A (100% equity) ($)		Alternative B (50% bonds, 50% equity) ($)	
Probability	0.5	0.5	0.5	0.5
Net operating income	1,000	250	1,000	250
Interest (5% on bonds)	–	–	250	250
Net income	1,000	250	750	0
Capitalization:				
Stock	10,000	10,000	5,000	5,000
Bonds	–	–	5,000	5,000
Total stocks and bonds	10,000	10,000	10,000	10,000
Number of shares	1,000	1,000	500	500
Earnings per share (EPS)	1.00	0.25	1.50	0
Expected value of EPS[a]	0.625		0.75	
Variance of EPS[a]	0.14		0.56	

[a] The expected value of the EPS of firm A is given by $(0.5 \times 1) + (0.5 \times 0.25) = \$0.625$ and its variance is calculated as follows: $0.5(1 - 0.625)^2 + 0.5(0.25 - 0.625)^2 = 0.14$. Similarly the expected value and variance of the EPS of firm B are given by $(0.5 \times 1.50) + (0.5 \times 0) = \$0.75$ and $0.5(1.50 - 0.75)^2 + 0.5(0 - 0.75)^2 = 0.56$ respectively.

life. Hence we calculate the variance (or standard deviation) of EPS as well as its expected value. Table 13.2 shows that the levered alternative is characterized by both a higher expected EPS and a higher variance, i.e., a greater variability of earnings. This result confronts financial management with the difficult problem of finding a way to weigh and compare the advantages and disadvantages of leverage. A first step in this direction is to evaluate the interaction between the firm's business and financial risks.

BUSINESS RISK VERSUS FINANCIAL RISK

A firm's *business* or *economic risk* is related to the industry to which it belongs and to the general conditions of the economy. For example, the business risk of public utilities is usually significantly less than that of manufacturing firms. This reflects the tendency for fluctuations in the demand for the services provided by utilities, such as telephone companies, to be small relative to those experienced by industrial firms, the demand for whose products tends to be more unstable. This instability often reflects changes in fashion, or in the real income of consumers, or shifts in the level of competition. Even if we assume that firms never issue debt, we would still expect to find a higher variability in the earnings per share of industrial firms than of utilities. Thus we usually say that industrial firms have greater *business risk* than public utilities. Moreover this risk is a function of general economic conditions and is *not* related to the firm's financial structure. Therefore, the variability of net operating income (or NOI per share), which is the firm's income *before* any interest payments, is an appropriate measure of such risk.

As we have noted, introducing financial leverage intensifies the variability of EPS, and we shall denote the *additional* variance of earnings induced by leverage as *financial risk*. The decision of a firm to enter a particular line of economic endeavor or to undertake a particular investment program affects its economic risk; the decision to finance the investment (partially or completely) with debt determines the firm's financial risk. Clearly, the individual who holds the firm's stock is vulnerable to total risk, i.e., to the firm's business risk as well as its financial risk. In Table 13.2, the variance of alternative A, which represents a case of pure equity financing, is 0.14. This variance of the unlevered earnings measures the firm's business risk. Alternative B gives the results for the same firm, should it decide to introduce 50% debt. The variability of the EPS in the latter case is higher, i.e., 0.56, since this variance reflects *both* the economic as well as the financial risk.[2] However, only the 0.14 variance is due to business risk; the additional 0.42 is generated by the financial risk incurred from the use of debt.

---

2. For a discussion of leverage in the context of the capital asset pricing model, see Chapter 14.

GRAPHICAL EXPOSITION _____

As we have seen, introducing financial leverage usually increases the average profitability of the firm as well as its risk. In good economic years the impact of financial leverage will most likely be positive; however, the leverage effect may be negative in relatively bad years, as we see when we discuss dividend policy and the case of Oryx Energy Co. shortly. One of the crucial tasks of management is to attempt to evaluate the risks of leverage by forecasting the changes of 'good' versus 'bad' economic conditions. This task can be facilitated by using a special version of a well-known tool – break-even analysis – in order to simulate the impact of financial leverage on EPS for varying levels of output and sales, or alternatively, for different levels of net operating income. [3]

Table 13.3 sets out the earnings per share for the two alternative financing plans (A = 100% equity, and B = 50% equity and 50% bonds) over a wide range of possible levels of future net operating incomes. A glance at Table 13.3 shows that financial leverage is positive (raises EPS) for NOI greater than $500, but is negative (decreases EPS) for cases in which the NOI is less than $500. Leverage is neutral (leaves EPS unchanged) for the cases in which NOI = $500. Hence, the 'break-even' point in this example is $500. For levels of NOI above $500, the firm earns a rate of return on invested capital in excess of the 5% paid to the bondholders, thereby raising the EPS to its common shareholders. Conversely, should net operating earnings fall below $500, the firm will earn less than 5% on its assets, so the bondholders can be compensated only at the 'expense' of the shareholders, which reduces EPS.

The differential impact of financial leverage is illustrated in Fig. 13.1 which graphs EPS as a function of NOI. The dashed line ZZ' which goes through

Table 13.3

A: 100% equity (unlevered)							
Net operating income	1,500	1,250	1,000	750	500	250	0	− 500
Interest	−	−	−	−	−	−	−	−
Net income	1,500	1,250	1,000	750	500	250	0	− 500
Number of shares	1,000	1,000	1,000	1,000	1,000	1,000	1,000	1,000
Earnings per share	1.50	1.25	1.00	0.75	0.50	0.25	0	− 0.50

B: 50% equity, 50% bonds (levered)							
Net operating income	1,500	1,250	1,000	750	500	250	0	− 500
Interest	250	250	250	250	250	250	250	250
Net income	1,250	1,000	750	500	250	0	− 250	− 750
Number of shares	500	500	500	500	500	500	500	500
Earnings per share	2.50	2.00	1.50	1.00	0.50	0	− 0.50	−1.50

3. A more general exposition of the derivation of the break-even point is given in Appendix 13A.

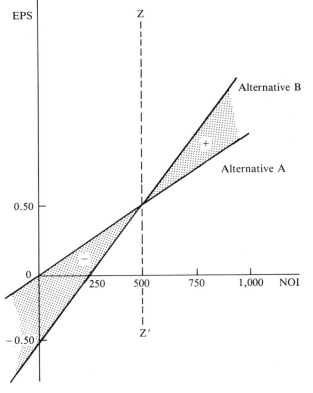

Figure 13.1

the break-even point divides the chart into two sections; all points to the right of this line representing positive leverage (+), and all points to the left representing negative leverage (−). Since risk is associated with the degree of fluctuation, the graph shows that the financial risk associated with the mixed capital structure (alternative B) is greater than that associated with the all equity structure (alternative A). The greater risk is reflected in the *steeper* slope of line B; for each unit change in NOI, the induced change in EPS is greater in the case of the levered capital structure. Despite the identical economic risk (we are making alternative assumptions about the financing of the same company) the introduction of leverage magnifies the fluctuations of EPS, thereby increasing the risk associated with the investment in common stock. It follows that the riskiness of an investment in the shares of a company with a levered capital structure exceeds the risk associated with the same shares when the capital structure is unlevered. The derivation of the general relationship between the EPS generated by levered and unlevered firms is derived in Appendix 13A.

This relationship can be seen even more clearly from Figure 13.2 which plots the hypothetical fluctuations of EPS over time. The solid line, labeled A,

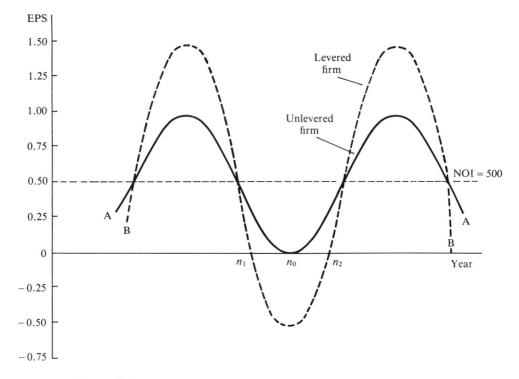

Figure 13.2

represents the assumed fluctuations when the company is financed solely by common stock; the dotted line, marked B, represents the fluctuations in EPS for the same operating incomes when the firm is financed by equal proportions of bonds and stock. Note that the introduction of leverage magnifies the variability of the income stream to the shareholders in both directions. Once again, the leverage break-even point is given by NOI = $500, which corresponds to the point EPS = 0.50 on the vertical axis of Figure 13.2. (The line marked NOI = 500 has been added to identify the critical points where the leverage changes from positive to negative.) Note also that while the firm never suffers an operating loss (we assume zero profits in only one year: point n_0 on the horizontal axis), when leverage is introduced, losses are incurred during the period between n_1 and n_2.

FACTORS DETERMINING THE CHOICE OF FINANCIAL STRUCTURE _____

In a fanciful world of no risk, in which the future volume of sales, prices, costs, and hence profits are known with absolute certainty, the use of financial leverage presents no particular difficulty. Given these unrealistic assumptions, management would know the exact point on the horizontal axis of Figure 13.1

which denotes a future year's NOI. If the leverage is positive, the firm would use a maximum of debt to finance its investments, since in such a case the greater the leverage the higher will be the EPS. On the other hand, if we knew *with certainty* that the NOI is located to the left of the break-even point, i.e., the leverage is negative, the optimal solution would be to finance the firm with 100% equity.

These two extreme solutions really have no practical significance: the actual problem facing the financial manager is to choose a financial strategy (capital structure) in a realistic setting in which future sales, prices, costs, and hence net operating income, are uncertain. That is to say, the NOI will not necessarily always lie to the right of the break-even point. Consequently, the firm cannot be certain that financial leverage will be positive.

Essentially, the impact of financial leverage, given the realistic assumption that uncertainty prevails, can be reduced to three alternative scenarios:

1. Situations in which leverage increases risk, but at the same time decreases expected EPS.
2. Neutral situations in which the increase of risk following the introduction of leverage leaves expected EPS unchanged.
3. Situations in which the introduction of leverage increases expected EPS and risk simultaneously.

These alternative situations are described schematically in Figure 13.3. The three solid curves in the diagram describe the EPS probability distributions of a firm financed by 100% equity; thus, these curves present a pictorial description of the firm's expected profit and business risk. Future EPS is not known with certainty, and the solid curves set out the probabilities of occurrence for various alternatives of EPS.

The dashed curves in the same diagram represent the probability distribution of EPS when leverage is introduced. In all three cases leverage increases the variability of earnings, i.e., leverage increases shareholders' risk. Diagrammatically, the dashed curves are flatter, which reflects the fact that leverage *increases* variability (risk). However, the three curves which are drawn in Figure 13.3 differ with respect to the degree of impact that leverage has on the expected (mean) earnings.

Figure 13.3(a) depicts a situation in which leverage increases risk but decreases expected EPS. This can occur if the mean post-tax unlevered EPS is less than the post-tax interest cost. In such an instance one would expect the firm to adopt an unlevered financial strategy. The second alternative is illustrated in Figure 13.3(b). In this case, introducing leverage increases the variability of the EPS but the mean EPS is unaffected. This can occur should the mean unlevered EPS be just equal to the after-tax interest cost. Again, the optimal strategy is to eschew the use of leverage, since introducing debt does *not* raise profitability, but does increase risk.

Although the first two cases could conceivably occur in real life, they are relatively uninteresting: in both instances the firm would simply forgo debt financing completely. The only relevant, and by far the most challenging

situation confronting financial management is the third alternative in which
the use of leverage increases both EPS and risk. This type of scenario is
depicted in Figure 13.3(c). Here, the introduction of leverage increases
expected EPS and risk simultaneously. In this instance, the expected EPS of
the unlevered firm exceeds the after-tax interest cost; hence any increase in the
degree of leverage increases expected profitability. In terms of Figure 13.3(c),
the mean of the levered alternative (dashed curve) lies to the right of the mean

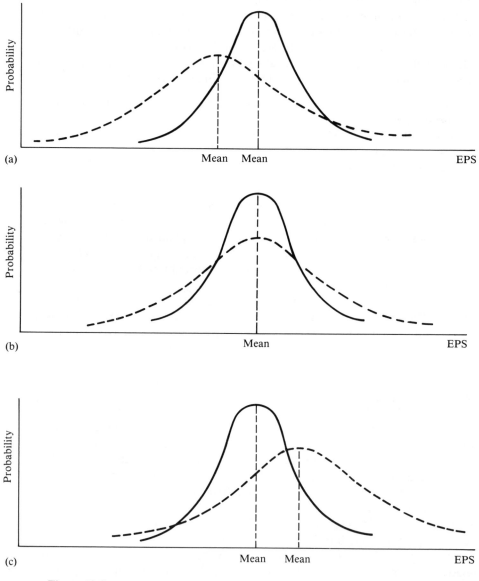

Figure 13.3

of the unlevered distribution (solid curve). Again the increase in variance is reflected by the relative flatness of the dashed curve. Unfortunately, the solution to the financing problem in this case, which incidentally characterizes almost all firms, is neither straightforward nor simple. The analysis of the tradeoff between the increased profitability and greater risk engendered by the use of leverage occupies us for the remainder of this chapter and in Chapter 14. Here we briefly discuss some of the basic factors which can affect a firm's financing policy; a more rigorous analysis of capital structure, which requires considerations of stock valuation, is postponed until Chapter 14.

In reality a firm's long-term financing policy can be influenced by a variety of considerations. Among these are the following.

Location of earnings distribution

The willingness of a firm to accept the increased risk which is engendered by the use of financial leverage depends on the characteristics of the distribution of earnings. Other things being equal, the lower the probability of negative leverage, the greater the opportunity to use financial leverage. Thus firms with relatively high rates of operating profit can better afford to undertake the risk of employing greater leverage, which in turn further magnifies their net earnings. Financial leverage, on the other hand, can become a dangerous strategy when employed by a firm with an inadequate operating profit base.

Stability of sales and earnings

Another key factor which determines the range of earnings, and hence the amount of debt that the firm borrows, is the stability of sales, which in turn influences the stability of operating earnings. The more stable the earnings, the better the chances that the firm can meet its fixed charges and obligations. Thus we expect firms having relatively stable earnings to finance a larger proportion of their investments with debt.

Figure 13.4 describes two firms whose average earnings before interest and taxes are identical, but which differ in the stability of their earnings streams. Three alternative financing strategies (100% pure equity, 25% debt, and 50% debt) are assumed for each of the two firms. The shaded areas of Figure 13.4 denote the anticipated *range* of possible operating results. The reader should note that the range of outcomes is considerably greater in the case of firm B which reflects the assumption that that firm has less stable operating earnings.

Now let us suppose that both firms adopt the same financial strategy of financing their operations with 50% debt. (Such a policy is represented in Figure 13.4 by the two lines marked '50% debt'.) A comparison of the two cases shows that the probability of the first firm's EPS being negative is zero; hence it is certain that its fixed interest charges will be covered out of normal operating income. Clearly this conclusion does not hold for firm B. Should that firm adopt a 50% leverage ratio there would exist a relatively large probability that the NOI will fall in the range of operating events for which EPS is

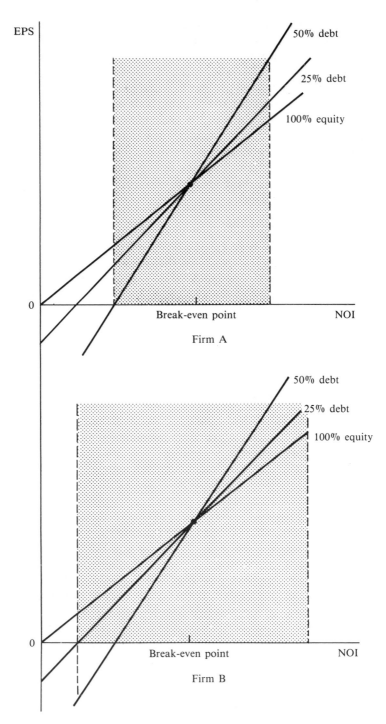

Figure 13.4

negative, which implies that the firm would be unable to pay its fixed interest charges out of current operating earnings. In order to achieve a comparable degree of certainty regarding the coverage of its fixed interest payments, firm B would have to reduce the proportion of debt in its capital structure to 25% (see Figure 13.4).

Risk of bankruptcy

The risk of bankruptcy[4] is strongly associated with the stability of sales and earnings. A firm with highly unstable earnings will be reluctant to adopt a high degree of leverage, since conceivably it might be unable to meet its fixed obligations. Negative earnings in any one year do not usually induce bankruptcy,

ARTICLE 22

Oryx, Plagued By Debt, Cuts Payout by 66%

Oryx Energy Co., plagued by high debt and sluggish oil prices, slashed its quarterly dividend 66% and said it would intensify restructuring efforts.

The dividend will fall to 10 cents from 30 cents, but the move doesn't affect the quarterly dividend declared by directors May 4, payable June 10. Oryx said the reduction will save about $70 million a year.

The oil and gas company, based in Dallas, said it plans to sell about $300 million of either common stock or unspecified equity-related securities "as market conditions permit." Oryx also said it will boost the value of its planned asset sale, announced last year, to $500 million from $400 million.

Oryx expects asset sales to result in second-quarter gains totalling about $35 million. In the year-earlier quarter, the company had a net loss of $15 million, or 23 cents a share, on revenue of $341 million.

"This is something they need to do to generate more cash flow and some breathing room," said Thomas Driscoll, an analyst at Salomon Brothers Inc.

In late trading on the New York Stock Exchange yesterday, Oryx tumbled $2.625 to $20.125.

Oryx is one of the most highly leveraged oil companies; its $2.4 billion in debt is equal to 53% of its assets. Oryx took on $1 billion in debt when it was spun off from Sun Co., Radnor, Pa., in 1988. It accrued additional debt through acquisitions of foreign oil properties and through a stock buy-back program.

The debt, combined with lingering low oil prices, has been a drag on performance. The company had a first-quarter loss of $16 million, or 23 cents a share, compared with net income of $82 million, or 94 cents a share, after a gain on the sale of assets, a year earlier. Revenue tumbled 41% to $332 million from $561 million.

Proceeds of the sales of equity and assets will be used to reduce debt. The company previously said it plans to reduce debt to about $1.5 billion.

Oryx said it isn't clear how much the increased asset sales may reduce its payroll. The company said last October it planned to trim 1,000 jobs, or 40% of its world-wide payroll, and it said yesterday that 775 employees are already gone. A spokesman said more jobs may be cut with the planned sale of assets, but it isn't clear how many.

Source: *Wall Street Journal*, June 5, 1992, p. C17.

---

4. Bankruptcy risk is analyzed in Chapter 15.

but a firm which experiences a loss over several consecutive years may find itself in serious financial distress. Clearly, for a given pattern of sales and earnings, the higher the financial leverage, the higher the probability that the firm will face such a series of losses, and hence the higher is the risk of bankruptcy.

The chances of bankruptcy do not depend solely on the statistical distribution of earnings, but also on the firm's assets and borrowing power. For example, some firms can more readily sell off some of their assets in order to meet debt charges which also enhances the collateral value of such assets, thereby increasing the firm's borrowing power as well; while others hold relatively large cash reserves. In general, the greater the firm's liquidity, either from holding cash assets or from the convertibility of its other assets to cash, the smaller will be its vulnerability to bankruptcy and the greater will be its willingness to undertake the risks of leverage. For a discussion on the relationship between liquidity and bankruptcy, see Chapter 15.

From article 22 we see that leverage, profit, dividend policy, and stock prices are highly related in practice. The high amount of leverage employed by Oryx Energy Co. results in its profit being highly sensitive to changes in revenue (or NOI). As shown, they could not maintain their dividend policy and announced that they must cut the dividend 66%. The market responded to this unfavorable announcement by lowering the stock price by more than 15%.

Dividend policy

Although the analysis of a firm's dividend policy is deferred to Chapter 18, it is noteworthy that most firms attach great importance to achieving an 'unbroken' dividend record, i.e., one in which the dividend payment is never skipped or even temporarily reduced; and if the dividend is cut, as in the case of Oryx Energy Co., the market reacts unfavorably. The implications of such an objective for financial policy are straightforward – for any given dividend rate, the higher the leverage ratio, other things being equal, the greater is the chance that the firm will be unable to meet its dividend payments out of current operating income.

The relationship between leverage and dividend policy is illustrated in Figure 13.5 which sets out the break-even chart for a hypothetical firm, assuming three alternative financing strategies – 100% pure equity, 25% debt, and 50% debt; and two alternative dividend policies – cash dividends of 45 cents and 1 dollar per share. Figure 13.5 clearly shows that the greater the leverage ratio the higher is the chance of not meeting the cash dividend out of operating earnings. For example, under the pure equity option, the 45 cent dividend will not be covered if NOI falls in the range labeled 0A on the horizontal axis. However, as debt financing is successively increased to 25% and 50%, larger operating incomes are required to ensure dividend coverage. In the case of 25% leverage, NOI must exceed 0B; should a 50% leverage ratio be adopted the NOI must lie to the right of point C. Similarly, a higher dividend payout, say one dollar per share, also shifts the 'dividend coverage point' to the right.

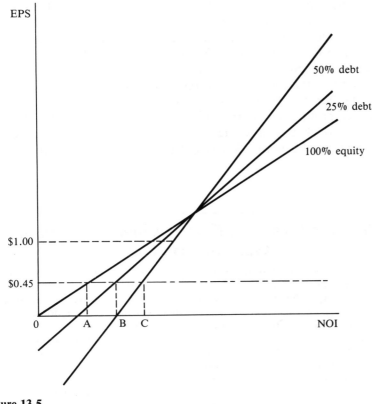

Figure 13.5

Thus, if Oryx had had less leverage, it is likely that they would not have found it necessary to cut their dividend so drastically.

Control

In some cases, firms may resort to the use of intensive leverage in order to retain effective control over the corporation. A loss of control might occur, for example, should the company issue additional shares of stock to the public. In such an instance the firm might well prefer to use additional debt rather than to issue equity even though the debt increases the risk beyond what otherwise might be considered a critical maximum.

Agency costs

In general, there is a clear distinction between the firm's managers and the firm's shareholders. The firm's managers do not necessarily make decisions which maximize the value of the stock. For example, consider a case where shareholders would consider 75% debt as their optimal financial leverage.

However, the managers of the firm realize that with such high leverage, the firm may have a sequence of two to three years of negative income which, in turn, may result in a loss of their jobs. Thus, they choose a lower degree of leverage, say 50%, even though 75% would maximize the value of the firm. The shareholders' monetary loss due to the fact that the managers do not necessarily act in the best interest of the shareholders is called 'agency costs'.

To see it differently, the bonuses paid to top management following extraordinarily high profit generally fall short of the penalty involved when the firm is in the red, which may cause the top managers to lose their jobs. Hence, top management may be more risk averse than the shareholders would like them to be.

ARTICLE 23

GM Replaces President, Finance Chief At GMAC Unit in Wake of Loan Losses

DETROIT — **General Motors** Corp. cleaned house at its General Motors Acceptance Corp. finance unit and pledged tougher internal controls after incurring huge losses on loans to a Long Island, N.Y., car dealer.

GM replaced GMAC's president and its chief financial officer, shuffled or replaced executives in almost a dozen other headquarters positions, and disciplined more than 15 other lower-level managers.

GMAC, which has $101.5 billion in assets and is larger than all but five U.S. banks, also vowed to beef up its internal audit procedures. The unit, which contributed $1.37 billion in profit to GM last year, also will name an executive to a new position in charge of watch-dogging large and "unusual" loans.

The top to bottom shake-up of GM's staid finance arm is the latest demonstration of the new culture of accountability at the No. 1 auto maker. For years, GM was loath to dismiss or publicly brand executives whose operations went awry. That clubby ethic was shattered when GM's board abruptly forced the demotions of the auto maker's president

and chief financial officer April 6, in the wake of 1991's record $4.5 billion loss.

"I think it's a very clear signal that there's a new way of doing business at GM," said Wertheim, Schroder analyst John Casesa, who called the moves positive. "Executives in charge will be held responsible for their actions."

···

The action, announced yesterday, started at the top.

GM said John R. Rines, 44 years old, will become GMAC's new president and chief operating officer, succeeding William J. Lovejoy, 52 years old, who was put on "special assignment."

···

GMAC said three other senior executives will be leaving the company. Gene P. Whitlinger, executive vice president for operations, will be on "special assignment" until his retirement Sept. 1. Harry W. Yergey, formerly area vice president for Eastern U.S. and Canada, will retire, as will Peter Van Cott, vice president for Western U.S. operations.

Source: Wall Street Journal, June 1992, p. A3.

In many cases extraordinary losses can cause top managers their jobs! As article 23 indicates, General Motors replaced its president and chief financial officer, as well as other top executives of General Motors Acceptance Corporation, for incurring large loan losses at a car dealership in New York. Generally, when a top executive fails to achieve acceptable performance, he/she is either laid off or put on 'special assignment'.

Although the 1990s are characterized by increased media attention on the accountability of executives for the profitability of the firm, holding them responsible for their actions is not new. In 1984 Continental Illinois, the seventh largest bank holding company showed a $1.1 billion second-quarter loss, the largest loss in U.S. banking history. The government announced in mid-1984 a rescue operation, but also announced at the same time that it was going to replace David G. Taylor, chairman and chief executive, and the president, Edward S. Bottum. These are only two out of countless casualties in the Continental drama. Another example was the unplanned resignation of John H. Filer in 1984, the chairman and chief executive of Aetna, the largest shareholder-owned insurer in the United States. Although no specific reasons have been given for the resignation, it was well-known among financial analysts that Aetna's recent years' earnings had suffered because of several strategic errors. The successful management of Mr. Filer since 1972 did not save the chief executive when earnings declined for a number of consecutive years. In a more recent example, on August 30, 1988, the *Wall Street Journal* reported the call for the resignation of the chief executive officer of American Medical International, Inc. by the company's largest shareholders. While the company's net income had risen 10% in the nine months ending May 31, 1988 (which translated to $1.17 per share), the chief executive officer was quoted as saying that some of the large shareholders were unhappy with the 'pace and emphasis' of the company's restructuring plan. It seems that the chief executive in this example was more risk averse and less aggressive than some of the company's shareholders desired.

To sum up, chairmen and financial executives' payoff resulting from a given act does not necessarily coincide with the payoff to the shareholders; hence, top management decisions are not always in the best interest of the shareholders. Thus, in choosing financial leverage, top managers know they are exposed to a higher risk, a factor which influences the selected amount of debt.

OPERATING LEVERAGE VERSUS FINANCIAL LEVERAGE

A major disadvantage of financial leverage is that it increases the variability of earnings. Hence, in establishing its financial strategy each firm is confronted with a difficult decision regarding the amount of risk which it is willing to undertake. In this context it is worth noting that any given risk level can be achieved in principle either by changing the firm's financial structure or by changing its asset structure. The larger the proportion of its fixed assets, the greater its *operating leverage*, and such a firm might be expected to adopt a relatively conservative financial leverage ratio.[5]

5. For evidence of the relationship between operating leverage and risk, see Baruch Lev, 'On the Association between Operating Leverage and Risk.' *Journal of Financial and Quantitative Analysis*, September 1974.

Figure 13.6 sets out operating leverage charts for two firms which differ only in the composition of their assets. Both firms sell the same product at the same price and hence have the same total revenue. However, firm A has a higher operating leverage: its variable cost is lower and its fixed investment is higher than those of firm B. The fact that firm A has *lower* variable costs is reflected in the smaller slope of its 'total cost' function, which for diagrammatic simplicity is assumed to be linear.

Clearly, the operating break-even points of the two firms are *not* identical. Moreover, a per unit shift of sales induces a relatively greater change in the profit (or loss) of firm A. This follows from our assumption that the difference between the slopes of the total revenue and the total cost lines of firm A is

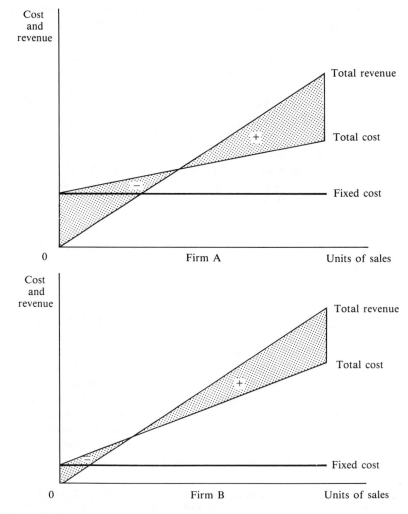

Figure 13.6

greater than the difference between the slopes of the relevant revenue and cost lines of firm B. Firms with high fixed costs and operating leverage, and which, as a result, are also characterized by high variability of operating earnings, might reach their desired risk levels by adopting a conservative debt policy. Conversely, firms with lower operating leverage might conceivably reach the same target risk level with a far larger debt–equity ratio: the willingness to undertake the additional financial risk, reflecting, in this instance, the greater stability of the underlying operating earnings stream.

The 'tradeoff' between operating and financial leverage is demonstrated in Table 13.4 by means of a simple numerical example. In practice, of course, these two strategies are not perfect substitutes, as the oversimplified example might seem to imply; however, both do affect the variability of earnings per share in the same direction. In the example we have assumed that there is an equal probability of sales being 100,000 or 500,000 units. Each unit is sold for $1 and hence the total revenue is either $100,000 or $500,000. Firm A has a larger operating leverage, since its fixed costs are $50,000, as compared with only $35,000 for firm B. However, firm A is a pure equity company; the firm issued 108,000 shares at $4.63 each, i.e., its total equity equals $500,000. Firm B, on the other hand issued only 86,400 shares of $4.63 each, and an additional $100,000 of bonds bearing interest at the rate of 5%. Note that we assume that the stock price is unchanged with leverage hence the number of shares is reduced proportionally to amount of debt employed. We shall relax this assumption in Chapter 14. The variable cost of firm A is assumed to be 50 cents per unit, while the variable cost of firm B (with the low fixed cost) is higher at 60 cents per unit. Taking all this data into account, the earnings per share of both firms will be either zero or $1.22, depending on the actual sales realized.

Thus, the two firms offer the same variability of earnings to their shareholders. This goal is achieved in the case of firm B through the use of more

Table 13.4

	Firm A		Firm B	
	'Bad' year ($)	'Good' year ($)	'Bad' year ($)	'Good' year ($)
Sales	100,000	500,000	100,000	500,000
Fixed cost not including interest	50,000	50,000	35,000	35,000
Interest	–	–	5,000	5,000
Total fixed cost	50,000	50,000	40,000	40,000
Variable cost	50,000	250,000	60,000	300,000
Total cost	100,000	300,000	100,000	340,000
Net earning before tax	0	200,000	0	160,000
Corporate tax (34%)	0	68,000	0	54,400
Net earning after corporate tax	0	132,000	0	105,600
Number of shares	100,000	108,000	80,000	86,400
Earnings per share	0	1.22	0	1.22

intensive financial leverage, and in firm A by a combination of a higher operating leverage with a lower level of debt financing. However, choosing between financial and operating leverage is not as simple as it might seem. In many cases the firm has only limited discretion regarding its plant and equipment, and in other instances the variable costs are not linear, a fact which greatly complicates the firm's calculations. The modest objective of the above example is merely to point out that the firm must consider the impact of *both* kinds of leverage when setting its financial strategy, and that a good rule to remember is the higher the operating leverage, the more risky is the recourse to financial leverage.

SUMMARY

This chapter has been devoted to the analysis of financial leverage. As we have seen financial leverage is a two-edged sword: if the leverage is *positive* the use of debt raises EPS; however, should it be *negative*, EPS can fall. Although, in general, we may assume that on balance leverage is positive, the use of debt also increases the fluctuations of EPS, thereby increasing financial risk. Hence financial management is confronted with the difficult task of weighing the advantages and disadvantages of levering the firm's financial structure. To this end it is convenient to differentiate a firm's business risk from its financial risk. The former is related to the industry to which a company belongs, to its operating leverage and to the general conditions prevailing in the economy. The variability of the firm's net operating income or NOI per share (i.e., earnings before interest and taxes) is an appropriate measure of its business risk. Financial risk, as we have already noted, is associated with the firm's use of leverage. An appropriate measure of this element of risk is the *additional* variance in earnings per share (EPS) induced by leverage.

A rather simple device, the financial break-even chart, provides an efficient and useful tool for visualizing the alternative choice situations confronting the firm. Combined with some basic probability concepts, this type of analysis can be used to identify and evaluate some of the factors which may affect a firm's financing strategy.

1. *Location of earnings distribution.* Other things being equal, the use of leverage is inversely related to the probability that the leverage will be negative.
2. *Stability of sales and earnings.* The more stable a firm's sales and earnings, the greater is the probability that it will be able to meet its fixed charges out of operating income. Hence we expect such a firm to finance a relatively large proportion of its assets out of debt.
3. *Risk of bankruptcy.* Risk of bankruptcy is perhaps the greatest single deterrent to the use of leverage. The degree of such risk again depends on the stability of the earnings distribution as well as on the liquidity of its assets.
4. *Dividend policy.* Another deterrent to the use of leverage is the strong desire

of many firms never to skip or reduce a regular dividend payment. Since leverage increases the variability of EPS, higher leverage ratios increase the probability that the firm will be unable to cover its dividend payment out of current operating revenues.

5. *Control*. The desire to retain effective control of a company, and to avoid issuing additional voting stock could, on the other hand, conceivably lead management into adopting a higher debt ratio than would otherwise be desirable.

6. *Agency costs*. Afraid of losing their job, managers may choose a debt–equity ratio much smaller than the optimal debt–equity ratio.

We conclude this chapter with a brief analysis of the tradeoff between financial and operating leverage. Although the two strategies are not substitutes – many firms find it difficult if not impossible to alter significantly their operating leverage – both affect the variability of EPS (and therefore risk) in the same direction. Hence, we may presume that a high degree of instability of earnings due to operating leverage will have a mitigating effect on the firm's willingness to undertake the additional financial risk inherent in a high debt–equity ratio.

We have now carried the analysis of leverage as far as we can without introducing considerations of valuation. In the following two chapters we examine the impact of financial leverage on the value of the firm's securities in order to isolate the factors which determine its optimal financing strategy, i.e., that financial structure which maximizes the market value of the firm to its shareholders.

SUMMARY TABLE

Type of risk

1. *Business risk*
   Function of firm's
   activity

2. *Financial risk*
   Function of
   financial leverage

3. *Total risk*
   Function of the
   firm's activity and
   financial leverage

Factors affecting the choice of the amount of debt

1. Stability of sales and earnings.
2. Bankruptcy risk.
3. Dividend policy.
4. Control.
5. Agency costs.

Break-even point (see Appendix 13A)

1. In terms of NOI:

$$\frac{\text{NOI}}{C} = r$$

2. In terms of EPS:

$$\text{EPS} = (1 - T_c)r$$

where C is the number of shares equal to the firm's investment.
3. The break-even point does not change with changes in leverage.

QUESTIONS AND PROBLEMS

13.1 A new firm is faced with three mutually exclusive alternatives for financing its investments:

1. Issuing 10,000 shares at $20 each.
2. Issuing 7,500 shares at $20 each and an additional $50,000 of bonds bearing interest at the rate of 5%.
3. Issuing 5,000 shares at $20 each and an additional $100,000 of 5% bonds.

Assume that the net operating income is $25,000.

(a) Calculate the EPS for each alternative, assuming no corporate tax.
(b) How do you explain the fact that the larger the proportion of the bonds, the higher is the EPS?
(c) Calculate the EPS for each alternative, assuming a corporate tax of 34%.

13.2 With respect to question 13.1, assume now that the firm issues preferred stock instead of the bonds.

(a) Calculate the post-tax EPS for each alternative, assuming the substitution of a 5% preferred stock for the bonds.
(b) How can you explain the difference in your results when preferred stock is used?
(c) Calculate the post-tax EPS, for each alternative, assuming that the firm issues preferred stock which pays dividends at the rate of 8.25%. Explain your results.

13.3 Assume a firm whose expectation regarding future net operating income can be characterized by the following distribution: $24,000 with a probability of 1/4, $14,000 with a probability of 1/2, and $4,000 with a probability of 1/4.

Assume also that the firm has only two mutually exclusive financing alternatives: (1) 100% equity, i.e., 10,000 shares at $10 each, and (2) equal amounts of stock and bonds, i.e., 5,000 shares at $10 each, and $50,000 bonds bearing interest at the rate of 8%.

(a) Define 'economic risk' and 'financial risk'.
(b) Calculate the expected value and variance of EPS for each alternative, ignoring corporate taxes.
(c) Measure the economic risk and the financial risk.

13.4 Does a bakery or a cosmetics manufacturer normally have a greater economic risk? Explain.

13.5 How might you explain the fact that mining companies are characterized by a debt component of almost 30%, industrial companies by a debt component of about 50%, and utility companies by a debt component of almost 80%?

13.6 Distinguish between 'location of earnings distribution' and 'stability of sales and earnings'. Discuss each using the following information:

Distribution for location of earnings			
A		B	
Probability	Earnings	Probability	Earnings
1/4	$100	1/4	$500
1/2	200	1/2	600
1/4	300	1/4	700

Distribution for stability of earnings			
A		B	
Probability	Earnings	Probability	Earnings
1/4	$100	1/4	$400
1/2	500	1/2	500
1/4	900	1/4	600

13.7 'Firms with relatively stable sales and earnings tend to use relatively high proportions of debt.' Appraise this statement.

13.8 'Firms who forgo financial leverage are in a better position to protect their dividend.' Appraise this statement.

13.9 (a) Define *operating leverage*. What impact does operating leverage have on the riskiness of the firm?
(b) In what way are operating leverage and financial leverage substitutes?
(c) What is the connection between a firm's business risk and its operating leverage?

13.10 'A firm which desires to increase its financial leverage only slightly should consider issuing preferred stock rather than bonds.' Critically appraise this statement.

13.11 A firm examines two mutually exclusive alternatives: (1) financing the firm with 100% equity, i.e., 10,000 shares at $10 per share, and (2) financing the firm with 5,000 shares at $10 per share and $50,000 bonds bearing an interest rate of 8%.

(a) Ignoring corporate tax, calculate the EPS for the two alternatives as a function of NOI, for the following values of NOI: $24,000; $20,000; $16,000; $12,000; $8,000; $4,000; $0; − $4,000.
(b) Graph EPS as a function of NOI for each alternative.
(c) Find the break-even point.

(d) How can you explain the statement: 'financial leverage is a two-edged sword' in view of the results you obtained above?

13.12 Three firms, A, B, and C, face two mutually exclusive alternatives:

1. Financing the firm with 100% equity (10,000 shares of $10 each); or
2. Financing the firm with equal amounts of stock and bonds (5,000 shares of $10 each, $50,000 bonds bearing interest at the rate of 8%). The probabilities of the net operating income of the three firms are given in the following table:

NOI	0	4,000	8,000	12,000	16,000
Firm			Probability		
A	2/8	1/8	2/8	1/8	2/8
B	2/8	3/8	1/8	1/8	1/8
C	1/8	1/8	1/8	3/8	2/8

Which financing alternative should firm A adopt? Which alternative should firm B and firm C adopt? (Assume that the firms use the mean–variance criterion and ignore corporate tax.)

13.13 A firm is faced with three mutually exclusive financing alternatives:

1. 10,000 shares at $10 per share.
2. 7,500 shares at $10 per share and $25,000 in bonds (8%).
3. 5,000 shares at $10 per share and $50,000 in bonds (8%).

Assume that the firm expects the following values of NOI: $16,000; $14,000; $12,000; $10,000; $8,000; $6,000; $2,000; $0, and − $2,000; with equal probability. (There is no corporate tax.)

(a) Calculate the EPS for each alternative as a function of NOI.
(b) Graph EPS as a function of NOI for each alternative.
(c) Assume that the firm pays a dividend of 20 cents per share, and that it seeks a probability of *at least* 70% to meet this dividend payment out of current income. Which alternatives are capable of fulfilling this goal?
(d) Suppose, now, that the firm wants to increase its dividend payment to 60 cents per share and it desires a chance of *at least* 60% of achieving this goal. Which alternatives are relevant in this case? Graph your answers to (c) and (d) on the diagram of part (b) above.

13.14 Two firms, Alpha and Beta sell the same product at the same price − $5 per unit. Alpha has fixed costs (not including interest) of $150,000 compared with only $80,000 for Beta. The variable cost of Alpha is assumed to be $2 per unit while the variable cost of Beta is $3 per unit.

Alpha is a pure equity company − the firm issued 75,000 shares at $10 each. Beta, on the other hand, issued only 50,000 shares of $10 each and an additional $250,000 of bonds bearing interest at the rate of 8%.

(a) Draw the operating leverage charts for the two firms, ignoring interest expenses, and find the operating break-even point for each firm.
(b) Draw (on the same diagram) the operating leverage charts taking interest into account.

(c) Assume that there is equal probability of sales being 50,000 units ('bad' year) or 200,000 units ('good' year) and a corporate tax of 34%, and calculate the EPS for each firm in a 'good' year and in a 'bad' year.

(d) Explain your results to (a).

13.15 A firm needs $10 million of assets. The financial manager considers two financing options:

1. Issue 10 million shares for $1 per share.
2. Issue 5 million shares for $1 per share and $5 million of debt.

In the absence of taxes, calculate the break-even point in terms of EPS under the following scenarios:

(a) The firm borrows the $5 million at an interest rate $r = 5\%$.
(b) The firm borrows the $5 million at an interest rate $r = 10\%$.
(c) The firm borrows $2.5 million at $r = 5\%$ and the additional $2.5 million at $r = 10\%$.

Compare and analyze your results.

13.16 The Gunn Company has total assets of $10 million. Earnings before interest and taxes were $2 million in 1989 and the tax rate was 34%. Given the following leverage ratios and corresponding interest rates, calculate Gunn's rate of return on equity (i.e., net income/equity) for each level of debt. Assume that, regardless of leverage, total assets remain $10,000.

(Debt/total assets)	Interest rates
0%	0%
10	10
30	10
50	12
60	15

13.17 The Goodyear Corporation produces automobile tires. It is a mildly levered firm. Suppose that Goodyear decides to purchase two other firms: a toy firm which is highly levered, and a food firm which is a pure equity firm. How does purchase of each of these two firms affect Goodyear's business risk? Its financial risk?

13.18 A firm pays $1 per share as an annual dividend and anticipates that the probability of a dividend cut will not exceed 10%. Suppose that the interest rate goes down from 6% to 3% and that the firm calls back its 6% bonds and issues 3% bonds. The firm takes advantage of the low interest rate and issues many more bonds than were issued before. Does the probability of a future dividend cut go up or down with this firm's action in the bond market?

_____ **APPENDIX 13A: BREAK-EVEN CHARTS AND FINANCIAL ANALYSIS**

In this chapter we defined the financial break-even point using a numerical example. In this appendix we derive the general relationship between the EPS generated by levered and unlevered capital structures. Consider a firm that requires C dollars for investment, the outlay on which can be financed either by equity or by a mixed financial strategy – the proportion p of bonds, bearing r percent interest, and the remaining proportion $(1-p)$ in the form of common stock. For simplicity, we shall further assume that the issue price of the stock equals \$1, so that C shares are required in the unlevered pure equity financing option, while $(1-p)C$ shares are required for the levered financing option.

Denoting the *pre-tax* net operating income (net earnings before interest and taxes) by NOI, we can write the *post-tax* earnings per share (EPS) of the unlevered strategy as follows:

$$\text{EPS} = \frac{(1 - T_c)\text{NOI}}{C}$$

where T_c denotes the corporate tax rate. The relevant formula for the levered option is:

$$\text{EPS} = \frac{(1 - T_c)(\text{NOI} - rpC)}{(1 - p)C}$$

where rpC denotes the total interest expense, and $(1-p)C$ denotes the levered firm's equity, as well as the number of its shares. Since NOI appears in both equations, the break-even point, i.e., the value of NOI for which the EPS of both the levered and unlevered alternatives are equal can be derived by equating the two equations:

$$\frac{(1 - T_c)\text{NOI}}{C} = \frac{(1 - T_c)(\text{NOI} - rpC)}{(1 - p)C}$$

Multiplying both sides of this equation by $C/(1 - T_c)$ yields:

$$\text{NOI} = \frac{\text{NOI} - rpC}{1 - p}$$

which can be written as:

$$(1 - p)\text{NOI} = \text{NOI} - rpC$$

Rearranging terms we have:

$$p\text{NOI} = rpC$$

If we cancel out p, which appears on both sides of the equation, we find that the break-even value of the pre-tax operating income is given by $\text{NOI} = rC$, or:

$$r = \frac{\text{NOI}}{C}$$

Thus, if the firm's pre-tax operating rate of return on total investment (assets) is just equal to the interest rate, the use of leverage will not affect the return to shareholders, i.e., its EPS.

Similarly, we can derive the break-even point in terms of *post-tax EPS*, rather than pre-tax NOI. Recall that for the unlevered firm we have the following relationship:

$$\text{EPS} = \frac{(1 - T_c)\text{NOI}}{C}$$

Dividing each side of this equation by $(1 - T_c)$, and substituting this result in the preceding equation, we obtain:

$$r = \frac{\text{EPS}}{1 - T_c}$$

or

$$\text{EPS} = (1 - T_c)r$$

Thus, financial leverage will have no impact on EPS, provided the *post-tax* EPS of the unlevered firm equals the *post-tax* interest rate. The low after-tax break-even point reflects the tax deductibility of the interest charges. Hence, for an interest rate of 5% and corporate tax rate of 34%, the post-tax break-even return on total assets is 3.3%. The firm 'pays' only 3.3% out of its net after-tax earnings; the remaining 1.7% being deducted from taxes, and therefore being 'paid', so to speak, by the government.

The break-even point is *not* a function of the degree of financial leverage, i.e., of the proportion of debt (p) in the capital structure. But despite the fact that the proportion of debt has no impact on EPS at the break-even point, it remains one of the most important determining factors of EPS. A little manipulation of the formal relationship between EPS and the degree of leverage suffices to show that the variability of EPS

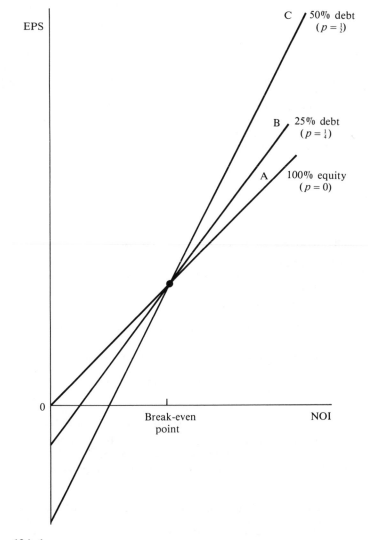

Figure 13A.1

increases as the leverage ratio p is increased:

$$EPS = \frac{(1 - T_c)(NOI - rpC)}{(1 - p)C}$$

Separating terms and cancelling out C, yields:

$$EPS = -\frac{1 - T_c}{1 - p}(rp) + \frac{1 - T_c}{(1 - p)C}(NOI)$$

Since the EPS is a linear function of the NOI, this equation can be rewritten in the familiar linear form:[6]

$$EPS = a + bNOI$$

where:

$$a = -\frac{1 - T_c}{1 - P}(rp) \quad \text{and} \quad b = \frac{1 - T_c}{(1 - p)C}$$

For a given corporate tax rate T_c, interest rate r, and investment outlay C, a higher debt ratio p implies a lower value of the intercept a. (The reader should note the minus sign in the definition of the intercept a.) On the other hand, the higher the debt–equity ratio, the greater will be the slope of the leverage line; an increase in p implying a rise in b. These results are illustrated in Figure 13A.1 which sets out the by now familiar break-even chart for three levels of leverage: zero leverage, i.e. 100% equity financing, 25% debt and 50% debt. Figure 13A.1 confirms the mathematical relationships: the higher the debt ratio, the steeper is the EPS line, and all lines intersect at the same break-even point, i.e., the latter is independent of the degree of leverage.

QUESTIONS AND PROBLEMS

13A.1 Assume that the interest rate on bonds has risen.

    (a) What happens to the post-tax EPS when the rate of interest (r) increases?

    (b) How much is the post-tax EPS changed when r increases by 1%?

    (c) What is the change in the break-even point caused by a 1% increase in r, in terms of pre-tax NOI?

13A.2 (a) Draw the break-even point in terms of post-tax EPS as a function of the rate of interest, for the following values of T_c: 0%, 25%, 50%, 75%.

    (b) Find on the diagram the appropriate EPS for a rate of interest of 8% for each value of T_c.

    (c) Find on the diagram the appropriate rate of interest for an EPS of 3%, for each value of T_c.

13A.3 The corporate tax rate decreased recently from 46% to 34%.

    (a) What is the change in the break-even point (BEP), in terms of pre-tax NOI, caused by the decline in the corporate tax rate?

    (b) What is the change in the BEP in terms of post-tax EPS?

---

6. This equation can be used to draw the break-even chart. For each value of p, the two parameters a and b can be calculated, nad then used to draw the appropriate linear EPS–NOI relationship; each individual line illustrating the potential impact of a given financing strategy on shareholders' earnings.

13A.4 What is the impact of the proportion of debt in the capital structure on the break-even point in terms of post-tax EPS? Prove your answer mathematically and diagrammatically.

13A.5 (a) Express the *expected value* of a levered strategy's post-tax EPS as a function of an unlevered strategy's post-tax EPS.

(b) Express the *variability* of a levered firm's post-tax EPS as a function of an unlevered firm's post-tax EPS.

13A.6 (a) Suppose that the interest rate $r = 0$. 'Then, independent of the corporate tax rate, or the proportion of leverage employed by the firm, the break-even line must pass through the origin.' Appraise this statement.

(b) 'Suppose that the share price is \$1. If the corporate tax rate is $T_c = 0.34$ and the firm finances 0.34 of its investment by debt, then the slope of the break-even line is $1/C$ when C is the number of shares issued.' Appraise this statement.

<hr>

SELECTED REFERENCES

Aivazian, V. A. and Callen, J. L., 'Corporate Leverage and Growth: The Game-Theoretic Issues,' *Journal of Financial Economics*, December 1980.

Ang, J. S., 'A Note on the Leverage Effect on Portfolio Performance Measures,' *Journal of Financial and Quantitative Analysis*, September 1978.

Arditti, Fred D. and Peles, Yoram C., 'The Regulatory Process and the Firm's Capital Structure,' *Financial Review*, Winter 1980.

Ashton, R. K. 'Personal Leverage vs. Corporate Leverage: An Extension to the Debate' *Journal of Business, Finance and Accounting*, Winter 1986.

Bierman, H. Jr and Oldfield, G. S. Jr, 'Corporate Debt and Corporate Taxes,' *Journal of Finance*, September 1979.

Billingsley, Randall S., Lamy, Robert E., and Thompson, G. Rodney, 'The Choice Among Debt, Equity and Convertible Bonds,' *Journal of Financial Research*, Spring 1988.

Boquist, J. A. and Moore, W. T., 'Inter-industry Leverage Differences and the DeAngelo–Masulis Tax Shield Hypothesis,' *Financial Management*, Spring 1984.

Bowen, R. M., Daley, L. A., and Huber, C., 'Leverage Measures and Industrial Classification: Review and Additional Evidence,' *Financial Management*, Winter 1982.

Bowman, Robert G., 'The Importance of a Market-value Measurement of Debt in Assessing Leverage,' *Journal of Accounting Research*, Spring 1980.

Brick, I. E. and Fung, W. K. H., 'Taxes and the Theory of Trade Debt,' *Journal of Finance*, September 1984.

Brooks, R. and Levy, H., 'Financial Break-even Analysis and the Value of the Firm,' *Financial Management*, Autumn 1986.

Chung, K. H., 'Debt and Risk: A Technical Note,' *Journal of Business Finance and Accounting*, Winter 1989.

De Angelo, Harry and De Angelo, Linda, 'Management Buyouts of Publicly Traded Corporations,' *Financial Analysts Journal*, May/June 1987.

Ellsworth, R. R., 'Subordinate Financial Policy to Corporate Strategy,' *Harvard Business Review*, November/December 1983.

Friedman, B. M., *Corporate Capital Structure in the United States*, Chicago University Press, 1985.

Gahlon, J. M. and Gentry, J. A., 'On the Relationship Between Systematic Risk and the Degrees of Operating and Financial Leverage,' *Financial Management*, Summer 1982.

Gehr, A. K. Jr, 'Financial Structure and Financial Strategy,' *Journal of Financial Research*, Spring 1984.

Haley, Charles W. and Schall, Lawrence D., *The Theory of Financial Decisions*, New York: McGraw-Hill, 1973.

Harris, J. M., Roenfeldt, R. L., and Cooley, P. L., 'Evidence of Financial Leverage Clienteles,' *Journal of Finance*, September 1983.

Jones, W. H. and Ferri, M. G., 'Short-term Leverage and Attributes of the Firm,' *Review of Business and Economic Research*, Fall 1979.

Kim, E. H., Lewellen, W. and McConnell, J., 'Financial Leverage Clienteles: Theory and Evidence,' *Journal of Financial Economics*, March 1979.

Lanser, H. P., 'Valuation, Gains from Leverage, and the Weighted Average Cost of Capital as a Cutoff Rate,' *Engineering Economist*, Fall 1983.

Lev, Baruch and Pekelman, Dov, 'A Multiperiod Adjustment Model for the Firm's Capital Structure,' *The Journal of Finance*, March 1975.

Litzenberger, Robert H. and Sosin, Howard B., 'A Comparison of Capital Structure Decisions of Regulated and Non-regulated Firms,' *Financial Management*, Autumn 1979.

Mandelker, G. N. and Rhee, S. G., 'The Impact of the Degrees of Operating and Financial Leverage on Systematic Risk of Common Stocks,' *Journal of Financial and Quantitative Analysis*, March 1984.

Marsh, P., 'The Choice Between Equity and Debt: An Empirical Study,' *Journal of Finance*, March 1982.

Martin, Linda J. and Henderson, Glen, V. Jr, 'The Effect of ERISA on Capital Structure Measures,' *Financial Review*, Spring 1980.

Piper, T. R. and Weinhold, W. A., 'How Much Debt is Right for Your Company?,' *Harvard Business Review*, July/August 1982.

Remmers, Lee, Stonehill, Arthur, Wright, Richard, and Beekhuisen, Theo, 'Industry and Size as Debt Ratio Determinants in Manufacturing Internationally,' *Financial Management*, Summer 1974.

Scott, D. F. Jr and Johnson, D. J., 'Financing Policies and Practices in Large Corporations,' *Financial Management*, Summer 1982.

Shalit, Sol S., 'On the Mathematics of Financial Leverage,' *Financial Management*, Spring 1975.

Shashua, L. and Goldschmidt, Y., 'Break-even Analysis under Inflation,' *Engineering Economist*, Winter 1987.

Taggart, Robert A., 'Corporate Financing: Too Much Debt?' *Financial Analysts Journal*, May/June 1986.

Turnbull, S. M., 'Debt Capacity,' *Journal of Finance*, September 1979.

Vickers, Douglas, 'Disequilibrium Structures and Financing Decisions in the Firm,' *Journal of Business Finance and Accounting*, Autumn, 1974.

Whittington, Ray and Wittenburg, Gerald, 'Judicial Classification of Debt Versus Equity: An Empirical Study,' *The Accounting Review*, July 1980.

Williams, Joseph, 'Prerequisites, Risk and Capital Structure,' *Journal of Finance*, March 1987.

Zechner, Josef and Swoboda, Peter, 'The Critical Implicit Tax Rate and Capital Structure,' *Journal of Banking and Finance*, October 1986.

14

Capital Structure and Valuation

ARTICLE 24

With Corporate Debt Hangover Easing, Leveraged Firms' Shares Are Taking Off

Corporate America is starting to recover from the debt binge of the 1980s. And the stock market is starting to take notice.

In the past six months, junk-bond defaults have fallen 65% from the same six-month period a year earlier, according to the Bond Investors Association in Miami Lakes, Fla., which publishes *Defaulted Bonds Newsletter*. The total amount of bonds in default also has begun to decline after a huge run-up from 1988 through much of 1991.

With the economy on the mend and junk-bond prices rallying, stocks of heavily indebted companies are outperforming the market as a whole. Last year, an index of 200 leveraged stocks complied by Shearson Lehman Brothers rose 39.2% in price compared with 26.3% for the Standard & Poor's 500-stock index.

This year, a 2.8% gain in the same leveraged index has beaten the market by more than four percentage points. Among the biggest movers in that index have been cyclical companies such as **Chrysler**, up 65%, **Black & Decker**, up 37%, and **Union Carbide**, up 33%. Earnings of all three companies should rebound strongly in a recovery.

To be sure, some leveraged giants such as **R. H. Macy** and **Olympia & York Developments** are still teetering. Sectors including real estate, retailing and oil services remain under pressure. And longer-term debt woes will continue to plague insurance companies and, to a lesser degree, banks.

Source: Wall Street Journal, April 28, 1992, p. 360.

CrossLand Proposal To Convert to Equity Cleared by Regulators

NEW YORK – **CrossLand Savings** said it reached a long-sought agreement with federal regulators that allows it to convert debt and preferred stock to equity in order to raise its capital levels.

... the thrift expects to have the plan submitted in about two weeks. The 3%

level is standard for thrifts, he said, but CrossLand will increase to 5% because of the higher level of risk associated with its loan portfolio.

Source: *Wall Street Journal*, December 24, 1990.

GM Is Planning $2.9 Billion Issue of New Stock – Auto Maker to Consolidate Three Production Units in Broad Restructuring

In sweeping moves Friday, GM said it wants clearance from federal securities regulators to issue as much as $2.9 billion of new common stock in one of the largest common stock public offerings ever. For GM, its first new issue of basic common shares since 1955...

GM plans to issue as many as 69.5 million new common shares.

... All together, the shares represent a potential 11% dilution of GM's common outstanding.

Source: *Wall Street Journal*, April 27, 1992, p. A3.

From the above three articles, we see that firms in different industries which are in different phases of their economic cycle employ different debt-to-equity mixes. In the 1980s, American businesses suffered from what is being called a 'leverage hangover.' For example, IBM issued the largest industrial bond issue in the history of the U.S. Articles 2 and 3 indicate that the trend is reversing. For example, CrossLand obtained permission to convert existing preferred stock and debt to equity in an effort to increase the ratio of equity to assets to 5% in 1994. General Motors, which has not issued stock since 1955, stunned the market when it announced that it received approval to issue $2.9 billion in new equity – the largest in history.

These articles trigger the following questions. What is the optimal mix of debt and equity? Why do some firms have high equity-to-asset ratios while others have low ratios? Why do firms change either debt-to-equity mix over time? Does the value of a firm change with a change in its debt-to-equity ratio?

In the preceding chapter we saw that financial leverage can be either positive or negative, depending on the relationship between the rate of return on invested capital and the rate of interest payable to the firm's debtors. Where the former exceeds the latter the leverage effect was defined as positive since

EPS is enhanced; where the rate of return is less than the rate of interest paid on the debt, we defined the leverage as negative because EPS is thereby decreased. Since a firm that does not succeed in earning a return in excess of the interest rate presumably will not survive for long, financial leverage appears, on balance, to be positive in almost all instances. However, as we have already noted, the increase in expected EPS has its 'price', i.e., the increase in the variability of the income stream to the common shareholders. Or in other words, financial leverage increases the total risk associated with the investment in the company's shares.

Since leverage increases expected return and risk simultaneously, this raises the question of the *net* impact of leverage on shareholders' economic welfare. Off hand, it is not clear which of these two factors outweighs the other. Since we have taken the goal of the firm to be the maximization of shareholders' wealth, i.e., the maximization of the market value of its common stock, the only unambiguous way to measure the relative strength of these two factors is to examine the behavior of the market price of the shares themselves. Should the market price of the stock *fall* as a result of the introduction of financial leverage, this would indicate that the increase in shareholders' risk outweighs the increase in expected earnings per share. The opposite conclusion holds if the market value of the stock should rise. The firm's optimal financing strategy (capital structure) is that which maximizes the market value of its outstanding common stock. By definition, any deviation in either direction from the optimal financing mix will induce a decline in value of the common stock and hence in the market value of the firm.

MODIGLIANI AND MILLER ANALYSIS

Franco Modigliani and Merton H. Miller (hereafter referred to as M & M), in a series of justly famous articles, provided a rigorous analysis of the relationship between the value of a firm and its capital structure.[1] We present their analysis by means of simple numerical examples followed by their general 'arbitrage' proof – initially assuming a world without taxes, then when firms are subject to corporate taxation, and finally when both corporate and personal taxes exist.

Before examining the M & M propositions in detail, a prefatory remark is in order. In their original 1958 article, a set of very restrictive assumptions was required to establish the relationship between leverage and the value of a firm's shares. Subsequently, owing to further work, much of it by M & M themselves, it has been shown that the original propositions hold under far less severe assumptions than were originally thought necessary. Consequently, we no longer need many of the implicit and explicit restrictions of the original

1. The original article, 'The Cost of Capital, Corporation Finance, and the Theory of Investment,' appeared in the *American Economic Review*, June 1958.

paper, and shall replace them with the following three assumptions:

1. Individuals and firms can borrow or lend at the same market rate of interest.
2. There is no risk of bankruptcy.
3. There are no transaction costs or other barriers to the free flow of information in the security markets.

These three assumptions are sufficient to derive M & M's first proposition.[2]

The no-tax case: proposition I

M & M argue that in a world without taxes, firms cannot gain from leverage. Proposition I states that in the absence of corporate taxes the value of the firm is *independent* of its capital structure, i.e. of the debt-equity mix:[3]

$$V_L = V_U$$

where:

$V_U \equiv S_U =$ the market value of an unlevered firm's securities, which is equal to the market value of the unlevered firm's stock (equity)

$V_L \equiv S_L + B_L =$ the market value of a levered firm

$S_L =$ the market value of a levered firm's stock (equity)

$B_L =$ the market value of a levered firm's bonds (debt)

While the formal proof is given in the appendix to this chapter, we demonstrate this proof here by a numerical example, and then show the economic forces which cause $V_L = V_U$, in more general terms.

A numerical example

Suppose that there are two firms, A and B, which are *identical* in all respects except for their capital structures. Let us further assume that both firms have just started their operations and require an investment of $1,000 which will return $50 (annually) with probability of 0.5 or $150 with probability of 0.5. Firm A raises the required money by issuing 100 shares of common stock at a price of $10 per share; firm B raises the required $1,000 by issuing 50 shares at $10 per share and issues $500 of 6% bonds. The essence of the M & M proposition is that if we ignore corporate taxes, the market value of the two firms must be the same, despite the fact that they differ in their capital structures. In this specific example, the stock price of both firms is identical, $10, but this is not always necessary. The emphasis is that both firms have the same market values, while the stock price is a function of the number of stocks issued. M & M argue that economic forces exist which ensure the equality of

2. See J. E. Stiglitz, 'A Re-examination of the Modigliani–Miller Theorem,' *American Economic Review*, December 1969.
3. A formal proof of proposition I is given in Appendix 14B.

the market value of the two firms and hence in this example, of their stock price, even though the difference in the capital structures confronts investors with different distributions of return. Table 14.1 summarizes the distribution of earnings per share for the two firms.

Since firm A's cash flow is comprised of $50 with probability 0.5 and $150 with probability 0.5, and it issued 100 shares, the return per share is 50 cents with probability 0.5 and $1.50 with probability 0.5. Similarly, the second firm's cash flow is characterized by an equal probability of earning either $50 or $150. However, in the case of firm B, should $50 be realized from operations, the return per share *after* the payment of interest (6% of $500 = $30) will be only 40 cents ($20 ÷ 50 shares = 40 cents), i.e., in such an event the effect of the leverage is negative and EPS falls from 50 to 40 cents. If, on the other hand, $150 is realized from operations, the net return per share equals $2.40 ($150 − $30 = $120 and $120 ÷ 50 shares = $2.40).

In *contradistinction* to the M & M analysis, let us assume for the moment that investors are *unable* to borrow or lend money, and that they are offered, free of charge, the choice of either distribution A or distribution B. Which alternative will be chosen? Clearly, this depends on an investor's preferences, or in terms of Chapter 8, on his utility function. Figures 14.1 and 14.2 set out the utility functions of two different investors. The expected utility from the results of firms A and B are identified in each diagram by the letters *a* and *b* respectively. Note that the investor whose utility function is given in Figure 14.1 prefers firm B to A (point *b* lies above point *a*), while the opposite holds for the investor whose preferences are drawn in Figure 14.2. The latter prefers the cash flow of firm A (point *a* lies above point *b* in Figure 14.2). Clearly, the market value of firm A might differ from the market value of firm B; the exact relationship between the prices of their common stock depends on the weighted average of the preferences of investors (in terms of the dollar amount of investment rather than the number of individuals). Thus equilibrium in such a market depends on individuals' preferences for particular income streams, i.e., for particular capital structures.

Now let us drop the restriction against borrowing and lending, and explicitly incorporate M & M's assumption that individuals can borrow and lend at the same interest rate available to firms. In terms of our numerical example, this

Table 14.1

	Firm A (100% Equity)		Firm B (50% Equity, 50% Debt)	
	Return per share	Probability	Return per share	Probability
	0.50	0.5	0.40	0.5
	1.50	0.5	2.40	0.5
Expected (average) return [a]	$1.00		$1.40	

[a] The expected return of firm A is given by $(0.5 \times 0.50) + (0.5 \times 1.50) = \$1.00$.
The expected return of firm B is given by $(0.5 \times 0.40) + (0.5 \times 2.40) = \$1.40$.

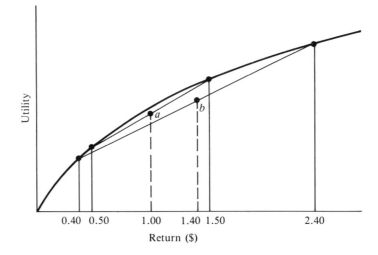

Figure 14.1

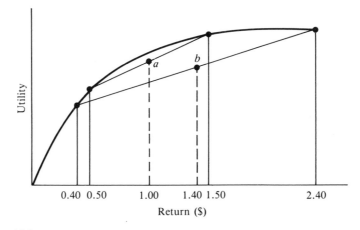

Figure 14.2

means that individuals can borrow or lend at 6%. Given this assumption, M & M argue that the market values of the two firms must be identical and independent of investors' preferences. This also implies, of course, that capital structure does not matter, since all financing will result in the same market value for the two firms.

This can be proven using the previous numerical example. Consider the case of an investor with the preferences depicted in Figure 14.1. Recall that his personal preference is for the income stream generated by the levered firm, B. Let us further assume that the market price of firm B's shares is greater than the share price of firm A, i.e., $P_B > P_A$, where P_A and P_B denote the market price of one share of the stock of firms A and B respectively. On the surface, this situation seems to make sense since, by assumption, the investor prefers the income stream of B to that of A and hence one would expect that he should be willing to pay more for a share of firm B's stock. However, despite its apparent plausibility this is not the case. The price differential in favor of firm B (i.e., $P_B > P_A$) cannot persist even in the extreme situation in which *every* investor in the market is assumed to prefer the income stream of firm B to that of A.

Let us assume for convenience that $P_A = \$10.00$; hence the total market value of firm A equals \$1,000 (100 shares $\times$ \$10 = \$1,000). If $P_B > P_A$, an investor who owns one share of the stock of firm B can sell it for more than \$10, say \$11. (Recall P_B is greater than P_A by assumption.) He can then borrow \$10 at 6% and use the proceeds of the sale *and* the loan to buy two shares of stock in the unlevered firm A (at a price of \$10 per share), putting aside the \$1 premium which he earned by selling his share in firm B. The investor's return before and after these transactions is given in Table 14.2. Clearly, the suggested switch of shares provides the investor with the *identical* income stream as before, but with a saving of the \$1 which he puts aside, i.e., his net investment is \$1 smaller. The difference $P_B - P_A$ is the measure of his profit on this transaction, and therefore he will continue to sell shares in firm B and buy those of A (thereby lowering the price of B and raising the price of A), as long as the price of B exceeds that of A (i.e., as long as $P_B > P_A$). This process will continue until the prices of the shares are equalized.

The reader should recall that when we imposed the constraint that investors are not permitted to borrow or lend, the market values of the otherwise identical levered and unlevered firms were not necessarily the same. But when the assumption that investors can freely lend or borrow on the same terms as firms is introduced, this conclusion changes drastically. In particular, given this assumption, firms cannot increase their market values by employing financial leverage. Since the opportunity to lever themselves (i.e., borrow) is also open to individuals, investors will not be willing to pay a 'premium' in the form of an enhanced market price, for the shares of a levered firm: they can achieve the same income stream by borrowing themselves and thereby 'levering' the income stream of the unlevered firm. Given the assumption of no taxes, this *'homemade leverage'* is a perfect substitute for corporate leverage, and therefore the latter will have no impact on the value of the firm.

Table 14.2

Investment	Income stream	
	Probability	Return
1. Initial position	⎰0.5	\$0.40
One share of B	⎱0.5	\$2.40
2. New position	⎰0.5	$(2 \times 0.50) - 0.60 = \$0.40$
Two shares of A plus \$10 loan	⎱0.5	$(2 \times 1.50) - 0.60 = \$2.40$

As we have just seen, the levered firm's shares cannot command a premium in the market, if investors can freely substitute personal borrowing for corporate borrowing. However, the question arises as to whether the opposite possibility, i.e., $P_A > P_B$, can exist. Once again let us take an extreme case in which every investor in the market is assumed to prefer the return of A to that of B. (That is to say, they are characterized by the preferences illustrated in Figure 14.2). Using the same techniques as before, we can easily show that in equilibrium, the price of the unlevered shares P_A *cannot* exceed the price of the shares of the levered firm P_B.

To demonstrate this, let us initially assume that the price per share of A is $11 and that of firm B is only $10, i.e., a premium for 'safety' exists in the market which reflects investors' assumed preferences for more stable returns. Now assume for numerical convenience that an individual who owns two shares of the unlevered stock A, sells his shares using the proceeds from the sale ($2 \times \$11 = \$22$) to purchase one share of B at $10 and $10 worth of bonds of firm B. His total investment outlay is only $20 so he can put $2 aside. The investor's returns both before and after these transactions are given in Table 14.3. Once again this transaction permits the investor to achieve the identical income stream as before, but with savings of $2 which he puts aside. This 'profit' can be earned as long as P_A exceeds P_B. Thus, the price differential $P_A > P_B$ will generate market forces which will raise the price of B and lower the price of A; this process will continue until equality between the share prices is restored. In equilibrium, the share prices of levered and unlevered firms must be equal; or in other words, in M & M's world of no taxes, no bankruptcy, and perfectly efficient securities markets, leverage cannot affect the value of the firm. Hence no optimal financing strategy can be identified and the firm is indifferent to the use of debt.

'Homemade leverage' and 'undoing leverage': a general treatment
Another approach, which will be particularly helpful when taxes are introduced is as follows. Suppose that the firm neither borrows nor lends money. Also, the firm distributes its earnings to the shareholders hence the value of this unlevered firm is,

$$V_U = \frac{\overline{X}}{k}$$

Table 14.3

Investment	Income stream	
	Probability	Return
1. Initial position		
One share of A	$\begin{cases} 0.5 \\ 0.5 \end{cases}$	$1.00 $3.00
2. New position		
Two shares of B plus $10 of bonds	$\begin{cases} 0.5 \\ 0.5 \end{cases}$	$0.40 + 0.60 = \$1.00$ $2.40 + 0.60 = \$3.00$

where $\bar{X}$ is the average annual cash flow and k is the appropriate discount rate.

Now suppose that the firm borrows at the beginning of the first period (time $t = 0$) the amount B_L, hence the net investment in the firm would be $S_L = V_L - B_L$. For simplicity, assume that the loan never matures (or, alternatively, is renewed every year). In this case, the shareholders' future cash flow will be reduced in each of the future years by $B_L r$, where r is the interest rate on borrowing and B_L is the amount borrowed. Thus, the cash flow to the shareholders of the levered firm will be:

Period:	0	1	2	3	...
Cash flow:	$W - S_L$	$X - B_L r$	$X - B_L r$	$X - B_L r$	...

where X is the return to the unlevered firm whose mean is $\bar{X}$ and W is the investors' initial wealth which is reduced by their amount of investment, S_L. Let us denote the present value of the new cash flow stream by V_L. Is it possible that $V_L > V_U$, or $V_L < V_U$? Let us analyze each case separately.

Suppose that $V_L > V_U$. This implies that there are investors who like leverage since they are willing to pay a higher price for the levered firm. Namely, we can assert that for these investors

$$U(W - V_U, X, X, X, ...) < U(W - S_L, X - B_L r, X - B_L r, ...)$$

where U is the investor's utility function and $W - V_U$ is the wealth remaining in the unlevered firm (and $V_U = S_U$).

We show that in spite of this preference, no rational investor would be willing to pay a higher price for the levered firm, since he can create 'homemade leverage' and get the preferred cash flow stream at a lower price. To see this, consider the following financial transaction. Sell S_L (hence the cash flow at $t = 0$ is W) and buy the cheaper firm V_U, and borrow B_L. Hence the cash flow stream will be

Period:	0	1	2	3	...
Cash flow due to the investment in the unlevered firm: (1)	$W - V_U$	X	X	X	...
Cash flow due to the borrowing: (2)	$+ B_L$	$- B_L r$	$- B_L r$	$- B_L r$	...
Net cash flow: (3) = (1) + (2)	$W - V_U + B_L$	$X - B_L r$	$X - B_L r$	$X - B_L r$	...

Thus we obtain the same cash flow we had before, but paid a lower price. Since $V_L > V_U$, by assumption $V_L = S_L + B_L > V_U$ (or $S_L > V_U - B_L$), then $W - S_L < W - V_U + B_L$. Thus the same cash flow in period $t = 1, 2, 3, ...$ is achieved and a higher wealth at $t = 0$ (i.e., a lower investment) and the investor is better off as a result of this arbitrage. Since no investor who likes leverage would be willing to buy the stock of the levered firm as long as $V_L > V_U$, we conclude that this inequality cannot hold in equilibrium.[4]

Suppose now that $V_U > V_L$ (this may occur when investors do not like leverage). The cash flow streams to the equity-holders of the levered and unlevered firms are as follows:

Period	0	1	2	3	
Unlevered firm:	$W - V_U$	X	X	X	...
Levered firm:	$W - S_L$	$X - B_L r$	$X - B_L r$	$X - B_L r$	...

From the assumption that $V_U > V_L$ we conclude that there are some investors who dislike leverage, hence they are willing to pay a higher price for the stocks of the unlevered firm. We claim that $V_U > V_L$ cannot hold in equilibrium. To see this, suppose that all investors indeed derived a higher utility from the cash flow provided by the unlevered firm. Namely, if:

$$U(W - V_U, X, X, X, ...) > U(W - S_L, X - B_L r, X - B_L r, X - B_L r, ...)$$

will the investors pay a higher price for the unlevered firm, hence inducing the inequality $V_U > V_L$? The answer is no. The reason is that investors can achieve this favorable cash flow stream simply by buying the stocks of the levered firm (i.e., at a lower price, since by assumption $V_U > V_L$) and by lending B_L dollars. Let us demonstrate this financial transaction:

Period:	0	1	2	3	
Buy levered firm: (1)	$W - S_L$	$X - B_L r$	$X - B_L r$	$X - B_L r$	...
Lend B_L dollars: (2)	$- B_L$	$+ B_L r$	$+ B_L r$	$+ B_L r$	...
Net cash flow:					
(3) = (1) + (2)	$W - S_L - B_L$	X	X	X	...

Since by assumption $V_U > V_L = S_L + B_L$, we have $W - V_U < W - S_L - B_L$, thus we get the more favorable cash flow stream (the same income stream in years $1, 2, 3, ...$ for a higher wealth at $t = 0$) simply by buying the 'cheapest' (levered) firm, and by 'undoing' its leverage. We 'undo' the leverage by lending the amount B_L. Thus, no one will hold the unlevered firm as long as $V_U > V_L$. To be more specific, an investor who holds V_U would be better off selling V_U, buying V_L and making a sure profit of $V_U - V_L$. Since we have shown that neither $V_U > V_L$ nor $V_U < V_L$ may hold in equilibrium, we can safely conclude that, in the absence of taxes, in equilibrium the equality $V_L = V_U$ must hold. The advantage of this approach is that it incorporates the case where interest rates on borrowings vary over time but they are identical for firms and individuals (see problem 14.20).

---

4. Note that we assume that the total investment in physical assets under V_U and V_L is constant, hence we have identical net operating income X. We also assume the investor buys the whole firm but the same analysis holds if we assume that he invests $1 either in the levered firm or in the unlevered firm.

The no-tax case: proposition II

From their first proposition which relates the value of the firm to its capital structure, M & M derive a second proposition which deals with the relationship of the required rate of return on equity to leverage. In a previous discussion we suggested by means of a numerical example that the required rate of return (yield) on equity rises with leverage. Utilizing the M & M apparatus, it is possible to spell out the exact functional relationship between the return on equity and leverage.

Denoting a firm's net operating income by X, the rate of return on equity of an unlevered firm (Y_U) is given by

$$Y_U = \frac{X}{V_U}$$

while the rate of return on the equity of a levered firm (Y_L) is given by:

$$Y_L = \frac{X - rB_L}{V_L - B_L} = \frac{X - rB_L}{S_L} = \frac{X}{S_L} - \frac{rB_L}{S_L}$$

where r is the interest rate on the firm's bonds, assumed to be riskless. Multiplying and dividing the first term on the right-hand side by V_U, we get:

$$Y_L = \left(\frac{X}{V_U}\right) \frac{V_U}{S_L} - \frac{rB_L}{S_L}$$

and by adding and subtracting $(X/V_U)(B_L/S_L)$, and using the fact that $V_U - B_L = S_L$, we obtain:

$$Y_L = \frac{X}{V_U} \left(\frac{V_U}{S_L} - \frac{B_L}{L_L}\right) + \left(\frac{X}{V_U} - r\right) \frac{B_L}{S_L} = \frac{X}{V_U} + \left(\frac{X}{V_U} - r\right) \frac{B_L}{S_L}$$

Hence:

$$Y_L = Y_U + (Y_U - r)B_L/S_L$$

Taking the mean of both sides of our equation we obtain:

$$\overline{Y}_L = \overline{Y}_U + (\overline{Y}_U - r) \frac{B_L}{S_L}$$

Therefore, the rate of return on the equity of a levered firm ($\overline{Y}_L$) is equal to the rate of return on an unlevered firm's shares $\overline{Y}_U$, plus a risk premium $(\overline{Y}_U - r)(B_L/S_L)$, which depends on the degree of leverage. The higher the proportion of debt in the capital mixture, B_L/S_L, the greater is an investor's risk, and hence the higher is the required return on equity.

One can interpret M & M's two propositions in the no-tax case as follows. By increasing the proportion of debt in its capital structure, a firm cannot affect its total value, and therefore no change occurs in the stock price (proposition I). On the other hand, by proposition II, increasing the proportion of debt in the capital structure increases the mean rate of return on the firm's equity ($\overline{Y}_L$). When these two propositions are examined simultaneously, we can say that any increase in the proportion of low-cost debt increases the mean return on equity but it also increases investors' risk, therefore raising their required rates of return, i.e., the cost of equity (see Chapters 16 and 17). Since these two influences exactly cancel one another in an M & M world without taxes and bankruptcy, the value (price) of a firm's shares is invariant to leverage.

IMPACT OF CORPORATE TAXES

The invariance of the value of the firm to leverage was established on the explicit assumption that taxes are not imposed on earnings. In this section we shall deal with the much more realistic and hence much more important case, which assumes the existence of a corporate income tax. Table 14.4 shows the net operating income *after taxes* for three financing alternatives assuming a 4% interest rate and 34% corporate income tax. Although, as we have just seen, a firm cannot benefit from the use of debt in a tax-free world, no question arises regarding the advantages of debt once the effects of corporate taxes are recognized. As can be seen from Table 14.4, the after-tax net operating income, and not just EPS, increases as the proportion of bonds in the capital structure rises. This also implies an increase in the value of the firm's common stock as the proportion of debt is increased.[5] The reader should note that the net NOI increases from $1,320,000 in the case of pure equity financing to $1,456,000 when we assume $10 million of debt.

The relationship between the post-tax income of the firm and its capital structure is shown graphically in Figure 14.3. Note that in sharp contrast to the pre-tax case, the total income of the firm depends on the proportion of debt in the capital structure. To be more explicit, the use of debt can potentially increase the income of the firm so long as the deduction of interest for tax purposes is permitted. It is shown below that for a given corporate tax rate the higher the debt-to-equity ratio, the higher the value of the firm.

Table 14.4

	A 100% equity ($)	B $5 million debt ($)	C $10 million debt ($)
1. Operating income	2,000,000	2,000,000	2,000,000
2. Interest (4% on bonds)	—	200,000	400,000
3. Taxable net income	2,000,000	1,800,000	1,600,000
4. Income tax at 34%	680,000	612,000	544,000
5. Net income after taxes	1,320,000	1,188,000	1,056,000
6. Net operating income (line 5 + line 2)	1,320,000	1,388,000	1,456,000

5. For a detailed discussion of the relationship between maximizing the total value of the firm and maximizing the market price of the firm's common stock, see Appendix 14A.

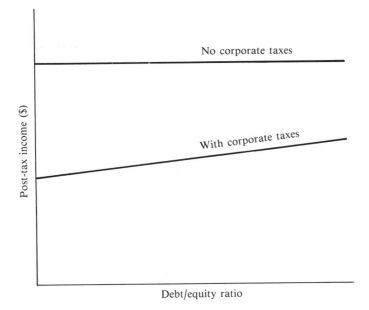

Figure 14.3

M & M also provide a rigorous analysis of the impact of corporate taxation. Retaining the three previous assumptions regarding the borrowing and lending opportunities open to individual investors, the absence of bankruptcy and the absence of all transactions (and information) costs in the capital market, they provide a formal arbitrage proof of the contention that shareholders can gain when the firm introduces leverage as long as corporate earnings are taxed.[6]

The introduction of taxes destroys the necessary equivalence between the total market values of otherwise identical levered and unlevered firms. In fact, M & M show that with corporate taxation the equilibrium relation is given by:

$$V_L = V_U + T_c B_L$$

where T_c is the corporate income tax rate.

It is clear from this relationship that a market premium $T_c B_L$ (which depends on the tax rate and the proportion of debt) is created by the levered firm, and therefore the levered firm's market value is higher than the market value of its unlevered counterpart.[7] Moreover, the greater the proportion of debt in the capital structure, the higher is the value of the firm. Thus a firm

6. The formal arbitrage proof is given in Appendix 14B.
7. In a world with corporate taxation, M & M's second proposition can also be derived. The after-tax rate of return on equity (Y_L^*) becomes:

$$Y_L^* = Y_U^* + (1 - T_c)(Y_U^* - r)\frac{B_L}{S_L}$$

where the asterisks denote after-tax values. The formal derivation of this proposition is given in Appendix 14B.

which takes advantage of the tax deductibility of interest payments can increase its value by levering its capital structure.

Although the rigorous incorporation of risk in the leverage model greatly enhances our understanding of basic financial relationships, it leaves many important questions unresolved. In particular, the M & M analysis leads to an extreme *corner solution* in the more important post-corporate tax case, that is, a firm's optimal capital structure comprises mainly debt. Clearly, such an unrealistic result is unsatisfactory, and we return to the perplexing question of the firm's financing mix at the end of this chapter as well as in the next chapter.

Why do corporate taxes induce a benefit?

Suppose that we have two firms identical in all respects apart from their capital structures. The following figures show their income statements:

	Firm A	Firm B
EBIT	200.0	200.0
Interest	—	10.0
Taxable income	200.0	190.0
Taxes (34%)	68.0	64.6
Net income	132.0	125.4

Firm A is a pure-equity firm while firm B is a levered firm. Firm B borrows $100 at $r = 10\%$, and hence pays $10 interest. Since interest is tax-deductible, the effective interest which the firm pays is only $6.6 and the other $3.4 is paid by the Internal Revenue Service, namely by a reduction in the tax burden. Indeed, the net profit only went down from $132 to $125.4, even though firm B has the extra expense of $10 interest, in comparison with firm A.

In principle, the cash flow streams provided to the shareholders by the levered and unlevered firm differ, and *a priori* it is not clear which cash flow stream is preferred. However, it is easy to demonstrate the gain from leverage by going to the extreme case where we assume that all investors do not like leverage. Therefore, suppose that $V_L = S_L + B_L < V_U + T_c B_L$ (or $S_L < V_U - (1 - T_c)B_L$), that is, M & M's post-tax proposition does not hold. This can be rewritten as $S_L + (1 - T_c)B_L < V_U$ or $W - S_L - (1 - T_c)B_L > W - V_U$ (see below).

Even in this case investors can 'undo' the leverage and still gain from the fact that the firm levered itself. Let us be more specific by showing the two firms' cash flows:

	Period				
	0	1	2	3	...
Cash flow from unlevered firm:	$W - V_U$	$(1 - T_c)X$	$(1 - T_c)X$	$(1 - T_c)X$	...
Cash flow from a levered firm:	$W - S_L$	$(1 - T_c)(X - B_L r)$	$(1 - T_c)(X - B_L r)$	$(1 - T_c)(X - B_L r)$	...

Suppose that shareholders do not like leverage. Namely:

$$U(W - V_U, (1 - T_c)X, (1 - T_c)X, ...)$$
$$> U(W - S_L, (1 - T_c)(X - B_L r), (1 - T_c)(X - B_L r), ...)$$

where U is the investor's utility function, W is his initial wealth, and S_L and $V_U \, (= S_U)$ are the investments in the two alternatives. The investor can buy the levered firm and 'undo' the leverage by lending $(1 - T_c)B_L$ dollars. His cash flow stream (recall, no personal taxes yet) is:

		Period		
	0	1	2	3
Cash flow from buying the levered firm:	$W - S_L$	$(1 - T_c)(X - B_L r)$	$(1 - T_c)(X - B_L r)$	$(1 - T_c)(X - B_L r)$ ...
Cash flowing from lending B_L:	$-B_L(1 - T_c)$	$B_L r(1 - T_c)$	$B_L r(1 - T_c)$	$B_L r(1 - T_c)$ ...
Net cash flow	$W - S_L - (1 - T_c)B_L$	$(1 - T_c)X$	$(1 - T_c)X$	$(1 - T_c)X$

Hence, by investing in the levered firm and by undoing the leverage, we get the same cash flow, $(1 - T_c)X$ and a higher wealth at $t = 0$, since $V_L < V_U + T_c B_L$ implies that $W - S_L - (1 - T_c)B_L > W - V_U$. By similar arguments we can show that $V_L > V_U + T_c B_L$ also cannot hold.

M & M's after-tax proposition indicates that leverage is advantageous. This gain stems from the fact that the firm pays only an effective after tax interest of $(1 - T_c)r$, while the investor gets r when he lends, hence a net profit of $T_c r$ is induced. Since investing in the levered firm and 'undoing' its leverage creates a profit, investors,will be willing to pay a higher price for the levered firm. Hence, the higher the leverage, the higher will be the value of the firm as stated by the formula $V_L = V_U + T_c B_L$.

Separation of the firm's cash flow

Another way to show the relationship $V_L = V_U + T_c B_L$ is by separating the firm's cash flow and discounting each component separately. Denote the after corporate tax discount rate by k^*. Hence, the value of the unlevered firm is given by:

$$V_U = \frac{(1 - T_c)\bar{X}}{k^*}$$

The mean cash flow of the levered firm (which belongs to its shareholders and bondholders combined) is given by:

$$(1 - T_c)(\bar{X} - rB_L) + rB_L = (1 - T_c)\bar{X} + T_c r B_L$$

where B_L is the amount of debt issued by the levered firm. Since we assume no bankruptcy, the tax shelter component $T_c r B_L$ is considered to be certain, hence should be discounted at the risk-free discount rate r. The component $(1 - T_c)\bar{X}$ is identical to the cash flow of the unlevered firm, hence it has the same risk profile and should be discounted at k^*. Thus:[8]

$$V_L = \frac{(1 - T_c)\bar{X}}{k^*} + \frac{T_c r B_L}{r} = V_U + T_c B_L$$

which is the equilibrium relationship between the levered and unlevered firm as asserted by M & M.

CAPM AND CAPITAL STRUCTURE

The preceding M & M analysis assumes that investors hold a portfolio comprised of the shares of the firm in question plus bonds (or borrowing). Let us now turn to the question of the impact of leverage on the value of the firm in a world in which investors hold *fully diversified* portfolios of shares plus bonds (or borrowing).

Invoking the capital asset pricing model (CAPM) the following equilibrium relationship between expected return and systematic risk holds:[9]

$$E(x_i) = r + (E(x_m) - r)\beta_i$$

where:

$E(x_i)$ = expected return on stock i
$E(x_m)$ = expected return on the market portfolio
r = risk-free rate of interest
β_i = systematic risk of the ith stock

Let us assume that we have two firms which are identical in every respect except for their capital structure. The above relationship between (systematic) risk and return has important implications for the relationship between the value of the firm and its capital structure. We begin the analysis under the assumption of no corporate taxation and then go on to the analysis of capital structure with corporate taxation.

Analysis without taxes

Consider two firms, one levered and the other unlevered, who differ only in their capital structures. Since the two firms are otherwise identical, they both have the same earnings before interest payments, i.e., the same net operating income. However, the rate of return on investment to shareholders is

8. Arditti has shown that when one of the cash flow components is certain and the other uncertain one is allowed to discount each component separately. For more details see F. D., Arditti, 'Discounting the Components of an Income Stream,' *Journal of Finance*, June 1974.
9. For convenience, and to avoid unnecessary confusion, we shall use the CAPM notation as set out in Chapter 12. Hence the return on shares will be denoted by x rather than y.

calculated differently for each firm.

(1) $x_L = \dfrac{(\text{NOI} - rB_L)}{S_L}$ for the levered firm

(2) $x_U = \dfrac{\text{NOI}}{V_U}$ for the unlevered firm

where

x_U = return on equity of the unlevered firm
x_L = return on equity of the levered firm
S_L = value of the levered firm's stock
V_U = value of the unlevered firm ($= S_U$ value of its stock)
B_L = amount of debt

From the first equation we obtain:

$$x_L = \left(\frac{\text{NOI}}{V_U}\right) \frac{V_U}{S_L} - \frac{rB_L}{S_L} = \frac{x_U V_U}{S_L} - r \frac{B_L}{S_L}$$

Taking the expected value of this expression yields:

$$E(x_L) = E(x_U) \frac{V_U}{S_L} - r \frac{B_L}{S_L}$$

The systematic risk, β_U, of the unlevered firm is given by:

$$\beta_U = \frac{\text{Cov}(x_U, x_m)}{\sigma_m^2} = \frac{\text{Cov}(\text{NOI}/V_U, x_m)}{\sigma_m^2}$$

where x_m is the rate of return on the 'market portfolio', and σ_m^2 is its variance. The systematic risk of the levered firm, β_L, is:[10]

$$\beta_L = \frac{\text{Cov}(x_L, x_m)}{\sigma_m^2} = \frac{\text{Cov}\left[(\text{NOI} - rB_L)/S_L, x_m\right]}{\sigma_m^2}$$

$$= \frac{1}{\sigma_m^2} \text{Cov}\left(\frac{\text{NOI}}{S_L}, x_m\right) - \frac{1}{\sigma_m^2} \text{Cov}\left(\frac{rB_L}{S_L}, x_m\right)$$

since r is *not* a random variable the last term is zero, which leaves the following expression:

$$\beta_L = \frac{1}{\sigma_m^2} \text{Cov}\left(\frac{\text{NOI}}{V_U} \times \frac{V_U}{S_L}, x_m\right) = \frac{V_U}{S_L} \frac{1}{\sigma_m^2} \text{Cov}\left(\frac{\text{NOI}}{V_U}, x_m\right)$$

Hence, it is clear, by the definition of beta that:

$$\beta_L = \frac{V_U}{S_L} \beta_U$$

---

10. Recall that: (a) $\text{Cov}(x + y, m) = \text{Cov}(x, m) + \text{Cov}(y, m)$. Since r, B_L, and S_L are given at that point of time they are constants and therefore have zero covariance with x_m; (b) for any constant c, $\text{Cov}(cx, m) = c\text{Cov}(x, m)$.

Clearly, the systematic risk of the levered firm differs from that of the otherwise identical firm which is unlevered by a constant which reflects the degree of financial leverage.

Now let us examine the implication of the CAPM for the analysis of the relationship between leverage and the value of the firm. For any security i we have,

$$\frac{E(x_i) - r}{\beta_i} = E(x_m) - r$$

Thus, we expect that $[E(x_i) - r]/\beta_i$ will be constant for *all* securities. This holds true for our two hypothetical firms as well, hence:

$$\frac{E(x_U) - r}{\beta_U} = \frac{E(x_L) - r}{\beta_L}$$

Substituting for $E(x_L)$ and β_L we get:

$$\frac{E(x_U) - r}{\beta_U} = \left[\frac{V_U}{S_L} E(x_U) - r \frac{B_L}{S_L} - r\right] \bigg/ \frac{V_U}{S_L} \beta_U$$

We can multiply both the numerator and the denominator of the right-hand side by S_L/V_U without affecting its value:

$$\frac{E(x_U) - r}{\beta_U} = \left[E(x_U) - r \frac{B_L}{V_U} - r \frac{S_L}{V_U}\right] \bigg/ \beta_U$$

This equality, which is implied by the CAPM, holds only if:

$$-r = -r \frac{B_L}{V_U} - r \frac{S_L}{V_U}$$

or

$$r\left(\frac{B_L}{V_U} + \frac{S_L}{V_U}\right) = r$$

But this, in turn, implies:

$$V_U = S_L + B_L = V_L$$

This is merely a restatement of M & M proposition I in the CAPM framework, which asserts that in the absence of corporate taxes, the value of unlevered and levered firms will be the same. In other words, the value of the firm is invariant to changes in its financial structure. However, the reader should note that the *systematic risk* of the levered firm is larger than the systematic risk of the unlevered firm:[11]

$$\beta_L = \beta_U \frac{V_U}{S_L}$$

The relationship between beta and leverage can be clarified by considering

---

11. The equality $V_U = V_L = S_L + B_L$ implies $V_U > S_L$.

a numerical example. Let us assume that the distribution of the rates of return on the shares of an unlevered firm (x_U) and on the market portfolio (x_m) are as follows:

x_U	x_m
0.10	0.10
0.10	0.15
0.21	0.30
0.23	0.38
0.27	0.40

Let us further assume that each *pair* of returns has an equal probability of occurrence. The beta coefficient of the unlevered shares is given by the following formula:

$$\beta_U = \frac{\text{Cov}(x_U, x_m)}{\text{Var}(X_m)} = \frac{\Sigma x_U x_m - [(\Sigma x_U)(\Sigma x_m)]/N}{\Sigma x_m^2 - N\bar{X}_m^2}$$

$$= \frac{0.283 - 0.242}{0.4269 - 0.3538} = 0.5609$$

Now suppose that the firm has been financed by 50% debt (i.e., $B_L/V_L = 0.5$). What would be its beta coefficient? Since we know that:

$$\beta_L = \frac{V_U}{S_L} \beta_U$$

and, as we have already proven $V_L = V_U$, it follows that $\beta_L = (V_L/S_L)\beta_U$. Hence, with 50% debt, $V_L/S_L = 2$ and $\beta_L = 2\beta_U = 1.122$. For any amount of debt, one may use the following simple formula to find the value of V_L/S_L that one should multiply by β_U in order to get β_L.

$$\frac{V_L}{S_L} = \frac{V_L}{V_L - B_L} = \frac{V_L/V_L}{(V_L/V_L) - (B_L/V_L)} = \frac{1}{1 - (B_L/V_L)}$$

Table 14.5 sets out the precise numerical relationship between leverage and beta on the specific assumption that $\beta_U = 0.5$.

Analysis with corporate taxes

The post-tax rate of return per dollar of investment in the unlevered firm is given by:

$$x_U^* = \frac{(1 - T_c)\text{NOI}}{V_U}$$

For the levered firm we have:

$$x_L^* = \frac{(1 - T_c)(\text{NOI} - rB_L)}{S_L} = \frac{(1 - T_c)\text{NOI}}{V_U} \frac{V_U}{S_L} - (1 - T_c)r \frac{B_L}{S_L}$$

Table 14.5

(1)	(2)	(3)
Leverage ratio (B_L/V_L)	$\dfrac{V_L}{S_L} = \dfrac{1}{1 - (B_L/V_L)}$	$\beta_L = \beta_U(V_L/S_L)$
No leverage	1.00	0.50
0.1	1.11	0.56
0.2	1.25	0.63
0.3	1.43	0.72
0.4	1.67	0.84
0.5	2.00	1.00
0.6	2.50	1.25
0.7	3.33	1.67
0.8	5.00	2.50
0.9	10.00	5.00

where the asterisk denotes a *post-tax* variable. Thus:

$$x_L^* = \frac{V_U}{S_L} x_U^* - (1 - T_c)r \frac{B_L}{S_L}$$

Taking expected values of both sides of the last equation we get:

$$E(x_L^*) = \frac{V_U}{S_L} E(x_U^*) - (1 - T_c)r \frac{B_L}{S_L}$$

Similarly, for the systematic risk of the unlevered firm:

$$\beta_U^* = \frac{\text{Cov}(x_U^*, x_m)}{\sigma_m^2}$$

Using the same technique as in the pre-tax analysis we find the following relationship for the levered firm:

$$\beta_L^* = \frac{\text{Cov}(x_L^*, x_m)}{\sigma_m^2} = \frac{V_U}{S_L} \frac{\text{Cov}(x_U^*, x_m)}{\sigma_m^2}$$

Thus, as before we find:

$$\beta_L^* = \frac{V_U}{S_L} \beta_U^*$$

Note that we again use the functional relationship between x_U^* and x_L^* and the fact that the covariance between $r(B_L/S_L)$ and x_m is zero to obtain this result.
  In equilibrium the following must hold:

$$\frac{E(x_U^*) - r}{\beta_U^*} = \frac{E(x_L^*) - r}{\beta_L^*}$$

Substituting, as before, for $E(x_L^*)$ and β_L^*,

$$\frac{E(x_U^*) - r}{\beta_U^*} = \left[\frac{V_U}{S_L} E(x_U^*) - \frac{(1 - T_c)rB_L}{S_L} - r \right] \bigg/ \frac{V_U}{S_L} \beta_U^*$$

Multiplying all the terms on the right-hand side by S_L/V_U we obtain:

$$\frac{E(x_U^*) - r}{\beta_U^*} = \left[E(x_U^*) - (1 - T_c)r \frac{B_L}{V_U} - r \frac{S_L}{V_U} \right] \bigg/ \beta_U^*$$

This equation holds only if:

$$-r = -(1 - T_c)r \frac{B_L}{V_U} - r \frac{S_L}{V_U}$$

which reduces to:

$$V_U = (1 - T_c)B_L + S_L$$

or

$$V_U + T_c B_L = B_L + S_L$$

But, as by definition $B_L + S_L \equiv V_L$, we can rewrite this as:

$$V_U + T_c B_L = V_L$$

which is the M & M proposition for the case of corporate taxes. Hence the CAPM result leads to the same disturbing conclusion, i.e., that the firm should maximize its value by taking on as much debt as possible.

--- **IMPACT OF PERSONAL TAXES**

In real life, apart from corporate tax T_c, individuals pay personal income taxes at rate T_p, and a capital gains tax at rate T_g. Let us start our analysis by assuming that T_c, T_p, and T_g are fixed. We further assume that the firm wishes to minimize the total tax burden, hence it distributes all earnings as capital gains. Thus, stockholders pay personal capital gain taxes at rate T_g which is lower than the income tax rate T_p, which applies to interest income.

Before the U.S. tax code changes in 1986, T_g was less than T_p. Since 1986 $T_p = T_g$. However, because the tax payment can still be deferred, there is still an implicit advantage to capital gains over cash dividends; hence, in effect $T_g < T_p$, but the difference is much narrower now. We begin our analysis by assuming that $T_g < T_p$ and then analyze the impact of personal taxes in the light of the 1986 U.S. tax code changes. We shall also analyze the case in which there is no tax deferral advantage, i.e., $T_g = T_p$.

The expected cash flow of the unlevered firm, after corporate and personal taxes is given by:

$$(1 - T_c)(1 - T_g)\bar{x}$$

and the value of the unlevered form is given by:

$$V_U = \frac{(1 - T_c)(1 - T_g)\bar{x}}{k^{**}}$$

where k^{**} is the appropriate after corporate and personal taxes discount rate.

The levered firm's cash flow is given by:

$$(1 - T_c)(1 - T_g)(\bar{x} - rB_L) + (1 - T_p)rB_L$$

The first component is the stockholder's expected income, while $(1 - T_p)rB_L$ is income received by the bondholders, who pay personal income tax at rate T_p on the received interest. This cash flow can be rewritten as:

$$(1 - T_c)(1 - T_g)\bar{x} + rB_L[(1 - T_p) - (1 - T_c)(1 - T_g)]$$

The first component is identical to the unlevered firm's cash flow, has the same risk profile and, hence, should be discounted at k^{**}. The second component is the bondholder's income, and the after tax reduction in the firm's income due to borrowing. Since we assume no bankruptcy, this reduction as well as the bondholder's income is certain and should be discounted at the after personal tax risk less interest rate $(1 - T_p)r$. Recall that investors can invest this certain cash flow at r, which yields after tax $(1 - T_p)r$. Thus, $(1 - T_p)r$ reflects the individual after tax alternative cost, which by definition is the appropriate discount rate for certain cash flows.

Since we have a perpetuity, the value of the levered firm is given by:

$$V_L = V_U + \frac{B_L r}{(1 - T_p)r} [(1 - T_p) - (1 - T_c)(1 - T_g)]$$

or

$$V_L = V_U + B_L \left[1 - \frac{(1 - T_c)(1 - T_g)}{(1 - T_p)} \right]$$

Arditti, Levy, and Sarnat proved that this is an equilibrium relationship between the value of the levered and unlevered firms. In essence, one can carry out the same arbitrage, as performed under the assumption of no taxes or no corporate tax, to show that this is an equilibrium relationship between the levered and the unlevered firm.[12]

The economic implication of the above equilibrium relationship between the levered and unlevered firms is not very encouraging since it leads, once again, to a corner solution:

if $1 > \dfrac{(1 - T_c)(1 - T_g)}{(1 - T_p)}$ issuing 100% debt is optimal

if $1 < \dfrac{(1 - T_c)(1 - T_g)}{(1 - T_p)}$ a zero debt policy is optimal

and

if $1 = \dfrac{(1 - T_c)(1 - T_g)}{(1 - T_p)}$ capital structure does not matter

---

12. Arditti, Levy, and Sarnat proved this relationship using an arbitrage argument. For more details, see F. Arditti, H. Levy, and M. Sarnat, 'Taxes, Uncertainty and Optimal Dividend Policy,' *Financial Management*, 1977.

Hence for fixed T_p and T_g, we are almost certain to attain a corner solution, i.e., either 100% or zero debt as an optimal policy.

A numerical example

Assume that $T_c = 0.34$, $T_p = 0.28$, and due to the ability to defer taxes, the effective capital gains tax rate, $T_g = 0.20$. We have two firms identical in all respects apart from their capital structures. The following figures characterize these two firms:

	Firm A	Firm B
EBIT	$200.0	$200.0
Interest	—	10.0
Taxable income	200.0	190.0
Corporate tax ($T_c = 0.34$)	68.0	64.6
Net income	132.0	125.4
Personal tax ($T_g = 0.20$)	26.4	25.08
Net income after corporate and personal taxes	105.6	100.32

We assume that firm B borrowed $100 at $r = 10\%$ hence pays $10 interest. This example reveals the following interesting points which clarify the relationship between V_L and V_U when corporate and personal taxes are incorporated.

1. The unlevered firm's stockholder income is:

$$(1 - T_c)(1 - T_g)x = (1 - 0.34)(1 - 0.2)200 = \$105.60$$

Recall that in our case (the random variable) x is equal to $200.
2. The levered firm's stockholders' income is $100.32, which is given by:

$$(1 - T_c)(1 - T_g)(x - rB_L) = (1 - 0.34)(1 - 0.02)(200 - 10) = \$100.32$$

3. Firm B pays $10 interest. However, its net income is reduced only by $5.28. The reason is that the corporate tax is reduced, and the personal tax is too. Indeed, after all taxes, the interest paid is only $5.28, since:

$$(1 - T_c)(1 - T_g)rB_L = (1 - 0.34)(1 - 0.2)\$10 = \$5.28$$

where $rB_L = 0.1 \times 100 = \$10$.
4. Suppose, for simplicity only, that the same investor is the stockholder as well as the bondholder of the firm. His income from equity is $100.32 which can be rewritten as:

$$(1 - T_c)(1 - T_g)(x - rB_L) = (1 - T_c)(1 - T_g)x - (1 - T_c)(1 - T_g)rB_L$$
$$= 105.6 - 5.28 = 100.32$$

5. Since we assume no bankruptcy, the reduction in his income from equity ($5.28) is certain. However, he also has certain income from his bonds equal to:

$$(1 - T_p)rB_L = (1 - 0.28)10 = \$7.20$$

Thus, the total certain income which the investor obtains is:

$$(1 - T_p)rB_L - (1 - T_c)(1 - T_g)rB_L$$
$$= (1 - 0.28)0.1 \times 100 - (1 - 0.34)(1 - 0.2)0.1 \times 100$$
$$= \$7.20 - \$5.28 = \$1.92$$

Thus in this example, by financing the firm with debt, we reduce the tax burden, hence the post-tax income increases.

6. In evaluating the firm we have to assume that $\bar{x}$ is known. Let us assume now that \$200 represents the mean income $\bar{x}$ of both firms (for that matter any other figure can be selected). Assume further that $k^{**} = 0.20$. The value of the unlevered firm is thus:

$$V_U = \frac{105.6}{0.2} = \$528$$

7. The value of the levered firm: since the investor's post-tax discount rate is $(1 - T_p)r = (1 - 0.28) \times 0.10 = 0.072$, the present value of the certain income is $\$1.92/0.072 = \$26.67$. The value of the risky component is $\$105.6/0.2 = \$528$, hence:

$$V_L = \$528 + \$26.67 = \$554.67$$

Indeed we obtain in this example the relationship:

$$V_L = V_U + B_L \left[1 - \frac{(1 - T_c)(1 - T_g)}{(1 - T_p)} \right]$$

or

$$554.7 = 528 + 100 \left[1 - \frac{(1 - 0.34)(1 - 0.2)}{(1 - 0.28)} \right]$$

$$= 528 + 100 \left[1 - \frac{0.66 \times 0.8}{0.72} \right]$$

$$528 + 100(1 - 0.733) = \$554.7$$

Personal taxes: Miller's argument

Before discussing Merton Miller's results, it should be mentioned that when Miller published his results in 1977, we had $T_c = 0.46$ and a marginal personal tax rate, T_p, which could reach as high as 0.50%. It was possible, therefore, to observe:

$$T_p \gtreqless T_c$$

depending on the level of income. We begin by discussing Miller's results and then turn to analyzing the impact of the 1986 tax code changes on Miller's analysis. In his 1977 presidential address,[13] Miller claims that under certain

---

13. See M. Miller, 'Debt and Taxes,' *Journal of Finance*, 1977, pp. 261–75.

assumptions, when corporate and personal taxes are incorporated, capital structure does not matter, i.e., we return to the pre-tax result $V_L = V_U$. Basically, Miller obtained the same formula that Arditti, Levy, and Sarnat proved. However, unlike Arditti and colleagues who assumed that T_p and T_g are fixed, Miller makes the more realistic assumption that there are many investors with various marginal tax rates T_p. However, he makes the following additional assumptions:

1. Perfect certainty, hence no bankruptcy.
2. The tax rate on equity income is zero.
3. There are municipal bonds whose return is tax-free and certain.
4. Firms and individuals can borrow and lend at the same pre-tax interest rate. Thus, there is no discrimination in the capital market.

The aggregate demand for bonds is given by the curve D of Figure 14.4. Investors have the option to buy tax-free municipal bonds whose interest rate is r_0. Hence the firm should issue bonds with a higher pre-tax interest rate such that the after (personal) tax interest to the bondholder will not fall short of r_0. Namely, we require that:

$$(1 - T_p)r = r_0 \quad \text{or} \quad r = r_0/(1 - T_p)$$

where T_p is the personal tax rate and r is the interest on corporate bonds. If the firm wishes to raise more money by issuing bonds, it should increase r so that investors with a higher marginal tax rate, T_p, will be willing to buy the

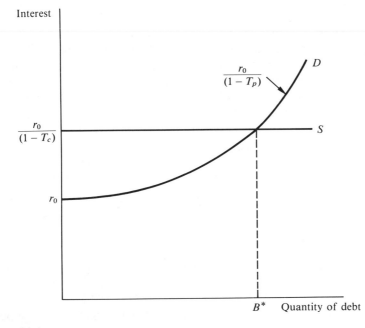

Figure 14.4

firm's bonds. The supply function for bonds is given by line S (see Figure 14.4), where this line intersects the horizontal axis at $r_0/(1 - T_c)$. The intersection point of curves D and S reveals that the optimum amount of borrowing by the whole industry is B^*.

To illustrate, suppose that $r_0 = 0.10$, hence at the intersection point $r = r_0/(1 - T_c) = 0.10/(1 - 0.34) = 0.152$. If the equilibrium interest rate is less than 15.2%, say 14%, the firm will be willing to borrow an infinite amount at this rate, paying the after-tax effective rate of only $(1 - T_c)\,14\% = 9.24\%$ (assuming $T_c = 0.34$). Thus the firm can invest the money in tax-free municipal bonds, making 10% which yields a net 0.76% sure profit.

Similarly, if $r > 15.2\%$, say 16%, the firm would not borrow at all. At $r = 16\%$, the firm pays post-tax interest of 10.56%, but can make 10% by buying tax-free municipal bonds. Hence, an interest rate of $r_0/(1 - T_c) = 15.2\%$ represents the equilibrium pre-tax interest rate.

Since at the intersection point:

$$r_0/(1 - T_p) = r_0/(1 - T_c)$$

Miller concludes that in equilibrium $T_p = T_c$, Since by assumption equity holders pay zero taxes (i.e., $T_g = 0$) we obtain in equilibrium:

$$\frac{(1 - T_c)(1 - T_g)}{(1 - T_p)} = \frac{(1 - T_c)(1 - 0)}{(1 - T_p)} = \frac{(1 - T_c)}{(1 - T_p)} = 1$$

hence $V_L = V_U$ and capital structure does not matter.

Thus, there is an optimum debt in the aggregate (see point B^* in Figure 14.4), but for each individual firm, at the optimum point $(1 - T_c)(1 - T_g) = (1 - T_p)$, hence debt does not induce any benefit to the firm.

The basic idea of Miller can be easily extended to the case where $T_g > 0$. To see this, suppose that the firm has $1 of EBIT. The firm can distribute this $1 either as capital gain (i.e., by financing its investment in equity) or as interest (by issuing debt). To illustrate, once again suppose that the same investor is the firm's stockholder and bondholder. What would he prefer: an income in the form of interest or in the form of capital gain? The answer is, of course, a function of the individual marginal tax rate T_p as is shown below:

	$1 of EBIT	
	If financed by equity	If financed by debt
Corporate tax	T_c	0
Net of corporate tax	$1 - T_c$	1
Personal tax	$T_g(1 - T_c)$	T_p
Income net of corporate and personal tax	$(1 - T_c) - T_g(1 - T_c) = (1 - T_c)(1 - T_g)$	$(1 - T_p)$

Note that on equity income the tax rate is T_g while on interest the personal tax rate is T_p.

As can be seen from this table, there are three partners who share the 'cake' produced by the firm: stockholders, bondholders, and the Internal Revenue Service (IRS).

Since the stockholders and bondholders are the owners of the firm, the firm's goal is to minimize the 'slice' taken by the IRS. Thus if $(1 - T_c)(1 - T_g) > (1 - T_p)$, the firm should issue less debt and more equity, hence increasing the firm owners' slice and decreasing the IRS slice. However, by issuing less debt, T_p goes down (since we attract only those investors with low T_p, see Figure 14.4), $(1 - T_p)$ goes up until we reach the point where $(1 - T_c)(1 - T_g) = (1 - T_p)$. Similarly, if $(1 - T_c)(1 - T_g) < (1 - T_p)$ investors would be better off by shifting funds from equity to debt hence increasing their net income. This shift implies that we attract more bondholders, with a high T_p, hence T_p goes up, $(1 - T_p)$ goes down until we get, once again the equilibrium relationship $(1 - T_c)(1 - T_g) = (1 - T_p)$. Miller claims that, in equilibrium, this equality holds for all firms, hence for each individual firm capital structure does not matter, namely $V_L = V_U$.

Thus, Miller speculates that we will find a 'clientele effect'. Firms which have a high proportion of debt in their capital will attract those investors whose T_p is low. On the other hand, firms with a high proportion of equity will attract those investors with a high tax rate T_p. Another interesting implication of Miller's analysis is that some tax-free institutions (e.g. universities) and investors with low T_p enjoy what he calls a 'bondholder's surplus.' In our example, all investors obtain $r_0/(1 - T_c) = 15.2\%$ pre-tax interest rate. Thus tax-free institutions obtain a 15.2% interest rate while the interest on tax-free municipal bonds is only $r_0 = 10\%$. The difference $(r_0/(1 - T_c) - r_0)$ is the bondholder's surplus. Miller assumes that bondholders enjoy this surplus and the equity holders cannot benefit from it.

Miller's paper has stimulated a lot of research in this area. Almost all researchers reach the conclusion that when some of Miller's assumptions are relaxed, debt is advantageous, at least up to a given point.

Miller's analysis yields unacceptable results in the more realistic case where $T_g > 0$. To see this, recall that Miller assumes that stockholders pay no taxes, i.e., $T_g = 0$. Consider the pre-1986 tax situation where indeed $T_g < T_p$, and at the maximum $T_p > T_c$. Suppose that investors pay only 10% on this income from equity ($T_g = 0.10$). In this case we obtain that debt is irrelevant only if the following holds:

$$(1 - T_c)(1 - T_g) = (1 - T_p)$$

Since the corporate tax rate before 1986 was $T_c = 0.46$, we get $(1 - 0.46)(1 - 0.1) = 1 - T_p$ or $0.54 \times 0.9 = 0.486 = 1 - T_p$ hence $T_p = 0.514$ or 51.4%. This result is unacceptable since the highest marginal income tax in the United States was only 50%. If $T_g = 0.20$, which was not an unreasonable figure, the implied T_p is, $T_p = 1 - 0.54 \times 0.8 = 0.568$, which is, of course, once again an unacceptable figure, even given the pre-1986 tax situation. Since 1986, $T_c = 0.34$ and $T_p = T_g = 0.28$. Given these new rates, $(1 - T_c)(1 - T_g) = (1 - 0.34)(1 - 0.28) = 0.47$, which is always smaller than

$(1 - T_p) = (1 - 0.28) = 0.72$; hence Miller's argument breaks down since $T_p = T_c$ will never hold.

Thus, some of Miller's assumptions must be relaxed in order to obtain a more realistic model. In particular, one should consider the following main factors:

1. Uncertainty of income.
2. Bankruptcy risk – in particular, the cost involved when bankruptcy occurs.
3. Portfolio considerations – investors do not wish to specialize in one firm (as implied by the clientele effect) but to diversify their investment across many firms.
4. A positive income tax on equity income ($T_g > 0$).
5. The borrowing rate for individuals is higher than the firm's borrowing rate which induces a benefit due to leverage.
6. Non-debt tax shelters (e.g., depreciation) as substitutes for debt tax shelters.

In the more realistic framework, when all these factors are taken into account, the firm benefits from leverage, hence $V_L > V_U$. In particular, the firm normally borrows at a much lower rate than individuals, which makes the use of debt advantageous. However, beyond a given point it is no longer advantageous to increase debt since the bankruptcy risk becomes too large. This implies an optimal interior capital structure for the firm.

In the next chapter we assume that debt increases the value of the firm. However, we introduce bankruptcy costs and show that this factor by itself induces an optimum capital structure for the firm.

In general we have the relationship:

$$V_L = V_U + B_L \left[1 - \frac{(1 - T_c)(1 - T_g)}{(1 - T_p)} \right]$$

and since $T_p = T_g$ we return to $V_L = V_U + T_c B_L$. That is, incorporating personal taxes in the 1986 tax framework does not change the post-corporate tax results.

It is now time to reconcile the theoretical results discussed so far with the results of the above articles. Having analyzed the firm's capital structure decision incorporating corporate as well as personal taxes, how can the behavior of the firm in the above article be explained? Why do some firms issue more debt while others pursue a goal of increasing their debt-to-equity ratio? How does the level of interest rates affect a firm's capital structure decision?

Using the formula:

$$V_L = V_U + B_L \left[1 - \frac{(1 - T_c)(1 - T_g)}{(1 - T_p)} \right]$$

it seems that all firms should adopt the same optimal capital structure. Specifically, if the term in square brackets is zero then capital structure does not matter; if the term is positive then all firms should issue debt, and if it is negative all firms should issue no debt. However, we do not observe this behavior in practice. Some firms issue equity in order to obtain a 'healthy' capital

Simple Truths About International Competition
A Discussion With A Select Group of Business Executives

A group of forward-looking senior executives met recently at the Harris Bank to discuss the challenges and complexities of international competition.

Two simple truths emerged:

1. Many issues affecting global competition are beyond our control.
2. U.S. business leaders must focus on the competitive factors they can immediately influence.

Excerpts from their conversation follow:

'It's clear that meeting the international challenge is not necessarily well understood in Washington.'

First Executive: While the Japanese and the Europeans have differing degrees of economic sanctuary, we have to overcome domestic hurdles to international competition.

For example, in 1986 Congress created Section 864(e) in the Tax Code. The interest expense allocation formula in this section basically assumes that a U.S. company with overseas assets that borrows money in the United States does so to fund offshore operations in order to get a bigger interest deduction and lower tax bill here.

The formula's net effects are, first, to increase a company's U.S. tax bill by decreasing the amount of deductible interest expense, which can add up to several million dollars; and second, to drive U.S. companies away from the international marketplace by making offshore investments less attractive.

No European country does this to its companies. And the Japanese certainly don't.

'Another issue is that the cost of capital is substantially lower in other countries than it is here'.

Second Executive: Japanese public companies can get much different multiples on earnings, so they can raise public money incrementally at a much lower effective cost in terms of earnings averages.

Also, Japanese banks make capital available much more readily and cheaply since frequently they're major equity holders in Japanese companies. There's more to gain when they can participate in a company's growth, so they're much more willing to provide capital.

'Lower capital costs mean the Japanese can take a completely different view on returns'.

Third Executive: We're in a 50/50 joint venture with a Japanese company. Our Japanese partner's cost of capital is one-quarter of ours. Given the time value of money, we must make a higher return up front. There's no way to catch up if a project goes beyond six or seven years with an 18 percent rate.

'We've created these short-term pressures and accepted a short-term view. So it's a tough, tough cycle to stop'.

Seventh Executive: We do quarterly reports that show how good we are as managers of the company. Then there's stock price. We raise money, make acquisitions, and pay managers with stock, so we say we must have that return to keep stock prices climbing.

We're never going to be able to compete with the Japanese cost of capital. It's a totally different system and always will be. But we can, and need to, really slow down and look at things from a longer-term perspective. Corporate America would be better off it we could inject some patience.

'Simple Truths' is the sixth in a series of *Harris Conversations for the 90s.*

Other topical roundtables that can help Harris customers be more competitive will follow.

Source: Fortune, April 20, 1992, p. 252.

structure, whereas other firms take advantage of lower interest rates and issue more debt. From the above formula we see that the level of interest rates does not affect the firm's decision about the use of leverage. The only relevant variables are the tax rates T_c, T_p, and T_g.

However, article 27 asserts that Japanese banks 'make capital available much more readily and cheaply' to Japanese firms, which gives them an advantage relative to American firms. Thus, it seems that the lower the interest rate the more advantageous it is to borrow – contrary to the above valuation formula.

The above article highlights a few important points:

1. Even though we do not have a crystal clear formula for determining a firm's capital structure, in practice capital structure matters.
2. The corporate tax structure is not simple. Companies in the U.S. with assets overseas are penalized relative to European and Japanese firms and hence have less incentive to borrow.
3. The interest rate facing a firm can affect its competitive edge and hence probably its desire to borrow – contrary to the valuation formula.

To reconcile the behavior we observe with the behavior predicted in theory, bankruptcy costs (both direct and indirect) must be introduced. For example, suppose that the Federal Government cuts the interest rate. The productivity and risk of the firm's projects do not change. Then $V_U = \bar{x}/k$ would probably increase since $\bar{x}$ does not change and $k = r + \text{risk premium}$ would decrease since the interest rate r decreases. However, in theory this should not affect the firm's capital structure decision since:

$$V_L = V_U + B_L \left[\frac{(1 - T_c)(1 - T_g)}{(1 - T_p)} \right]$$

does not incorporate the interest rate into the decision. While this is true in theory, it does not hold in practice since firms do not ignore bankruptcy costs (ignored in the above formula).

Recall that bankruptcy is declared whenever the operating income x is lower than the interest liability rB_L. The firm chooses an optimum capital structure after considering the probability of bankruptcy as well as the interest tax shield advantage. When r goes down, the probability of bankruptcy goes down and the firm has an incentive to increase its borrowing, B_L. Bankruptcy is discussed in the next chapter.

SUMMARY

This chapter has been devoted to measuring the impact of financial leverage on shareholders' earnings and risk. As we have seen financial leverage is a two-edged sword: if the leverage is *positive* the use of debt raises EPS; however, should it be negative EPS falls. Although in general we may assume that, on balance, leverage is positive, the use of debt also increases the fluctuations of EPS, thereby increasing financial risk. Hence financial management is confronted with the difficult task of weighing the advantages and disadvantages of levering the firm's financial structure.

Since leverage affects both expected return and risk, a way must be found to evaluate the tradeoff between risk and return. The only unambiguous way to measure the relative strength of the two factors is to measure their combined impact on the price of the firm's shares.

A rigorous analysis of the impact of leverage on the market value of a firm's equity has been provided by Modigliani and Miller (M & M) both for a taxless world and one with corporate taxes. In a world without corporate taxes, no bankruptcy or liquidation costs and perfectly efficient capital markets, M & M demonstrate that leverage *cannot* affect the value of the firm, and, therefore, an *optimal* capital structure cannot be identified. Under these assumptions the firm is indifferent to the use of debt or equity to finance its investments. In the more important case of corporate taxation the M & M analysis leads to an extreme 'corner solution', that is the firm's *optimal* financial structure is made up almost exclusively of debt.

When corporate as well as personal taxes are considered, Miller showed that under a set of restrictive assumptions (and with the tax rates prevailing before the 1986 tax reform) capital structure does not matter. Relaxing some of Miller's assumptions, and exploiting the 1986 tax code (which does not distinguish between income from interest, dividends or capital gains, $T_p = T_g$) indicates that leverage is advantageous at least up to a given point.

Application of the CAPM to the analysis reinforces the basic M & M proposition. In the pre-tax case the value of the firm is invariant to changes in the debt–equity mix; and in the post-tax case the CAPM framework again implies a maximum use of debt. In terms of the CAPM this also implies that a firm's systematic risk (beta coefficient) rises with the degree of leverage.

_____ **SUMMARY TABLE**

Capital structure and valuation

1. Assumptions:
   (a) Firms and individuals can borrow and lend at the same rate, *r*.
   (b) No transaction costs,
   (c) No bankruptcy.

2. Valuation relationships:

No taxes	Corporate taxes only (T_c)
↓	↓
$V_L = V_U$	$V_L = V_U + T_c B_L$
↓	↓
Capital structure is irrelevant	Optimal capital structure: 100% debt

Corporate taxes (T_c) as well
as personal taxes (T_p and T_g)

↓

$$V_L = V_U + B_L\left[1 - \frac{(1 - T_c)(1 - T_g)}{(1 - T_p)}\right]$$

↙ ↘

If $1 = \dfrac{(1 - T_c)(1 - T_g)}{(1 - T_p)}$	If $1 \neq \dfrac{(1 - T_c)(1 - T_g)}{(1 - T_p)}$
Capital structure is irrelevant	We obtain a corner solution (either 100% or zero debt)

Miller's results

1. Assumptions:
   (a) All assumptions mentioned in (a) above.
   (b) $T_g = 0$, no taxes on income from equity.
   (c) Certainty.
2. Results:
   (a) $V_L = V_U \Rightarrow$ capital structure is irrelevant.
   (b) In equilibrium $T_p = T_c = 0.34$.
   (c) 'Clientele' effect.

Extension of Miller's model to uncertainty

1. With the 1986 tax code, $T_p = T_g = 0.28 < T_c = 0.34$, hence we obtain $V_L = V_U + T_c B_L$ even when personal taxes are considered.
2. When firms can borrow at a lower rate than individuals the debt is advantageous, i.e., $V_L > V_U$. However, in the presence of possible bankruptcy costs, an interior optimal capital structure is obtained (see Chapter 15).

14.1 Define the term 'homemade leverage'.

14.2 Modigliani and Miller claim that in a world without taxes, firms cannot benefit from leverage. Prove that statement by using a numerical example. Explain carefully the arbitrage transaction.

14.3 Assume a world of no taxes and two firms which are identical in all respects apart from their capital structures. Firm A issues 1,000,000 shares of stock at a price of $1 per share and no debt. Firm B issues $500,000 of debt at a 5% interest rate and 1,000,000 shares of stock. Given that the two firms are characterized by the same distribution of NOI and that M & M's proposition, $V_L = V_U$, holds, answer the following questions:

(a) What is the price of the stock of firm B?
(b) How would you change your answer if the interest rate changed to 10%?
(c) How would you change your results if firm B issued 500,000 shares of stock?

14.4 Firms A and B are identical in all respects apart from their capital structures. Firm A issues 100 shares of stock at a price of $1 per share. Firm B issues $50 of debt and 25 shares of stock. In the absence of taxes what is the maximum price that firm B can sell its shares?

14.5 Suppose that we have two firms identical in all respects apart from their capital structure. With regard to the unlevered firm we have $\overline{Y}_U = \overline{X}/V_U$, which in this case is $\overline{Y}_U = \$10/\$100$. $\overline{Y}_U$ is defined as the mean rate of return of the unlevered firm. The levered firm finances 50% of its assets by issuing bonds bearing a 5% interest rate. In the absence of all taxes, what is the mean rate of return to the equity holders of the levered firm?

14.6 Assume that $V_U = V_L$ and the rate of return to the equity holders of the levered firm (with $B_L/S_L = 2$) is: $Y_L = 0$ with probability $1/2$ and $Y_L = 0.20$ with probability $1/2$. The interest rate is 5%. What is the distribution of the rates of return to the investors in the unlevered firm? Calculate the mean and variance of the two distributions, i.e., the distribution of the levered and unlevered firms. What conclusion can you draw from a comparison of the two distributions? (Assume no taxes.)

14.7 Assume that there are two firms, Alpha and Beta, which have just commenced operations and both of which require an initial investment of $4 million. Furthermore assume that these firms are *identical* in all respects except for their capital structures.

Alpha raises the required money by issuing 200,000 shares of common stock at a price of $20 per share, while Beta raises the required $4 million by issuing 120,000 shares at $20 per share and by using $7\frac{1}{2}$% bonds for the remainder.

Assume that both firms expect a return of $240,000 on their investment with a probability of $1/3$ and $960,000 with a probability of $2/3$. Answer the following questions, ignoring taxes:

(a) Assuming that investors are *unable* to borrow and lend, is it possible that the market price of Beta's shares will be greater than the share price of Alpha?
(b) Is it possible that the price of Alpha's shares will be higher than the price of Beta's shares? Prove your answers to (a) and (b).
(c) In equilibrium, can Beta's share price be greater than Alpha's under M & M's

assumption that individuals can borrow or lend at the same market rate of interest as firms? (In your answer, show the details of the arbitrage (selling and buying) process.)

14.8 With respect to question 14.7, assume that the equilibrium price of Beta's stock = $20. Can Alpha's share price be greater than Beta's given M & M's borrowing and lending assumption? (In your answer, show the details of the arbitrage process.)

14.9 Assume a world of no taxes. M & M's proposition 1 states that when investors and firms face the same interest rate then $V_L = V_U$.

(a) Does this imply that the share price of the unlevered firm's stock is equal to the share price of the levered firm's stock? Illustrate your answer with a numerical example.
(b) Formulate the specific condition under which $V_U = V_L$ implies that the share prices of the two firms are identical.

14.10 A new firm which expects $800,000 in operating income before taxes is confronted with four mutually exclusive alternatives for financing its required investment:

1. By 100% equity ($5 million in shares of stock).
2. By $4 million in shares of stock and $1 million of 7.5% bonds.
3. By $3 million in shares and $2 million of bonds.
4. By $2 million in shares and $3 million of bonds.

Assume a corporate tax rate of 34% and answer the following questions:

(a) Calculate the net income and the net operating income after taxes for each of the above alternatives.
(b) Calculate for each one of the four alternatives the value of the firm according to M & M's post-tax equilibrium relationship. (Assume that the capitalization rate for unlevered firms is 10%.)
(c) Graph the value of the firm as a function of the debt/equity ratio.

14.11 The Aladin Lamp Company has this year an operating income of $6,000,000. The firm has 1,600,000 shares of stock and no bonds.

(a) Calculate the total value of the firm and the value per share, using the NOI method and capitalization rate of 15%.
(b) What would your answer be to part (a) if the firm has $15,000,000 of debt (bonds) with an 8% interest charge and 1,000,000 shares of stock?
(c) What would your answer to part (a) be if the firm has $30,000,000 of debt (bonds) and 400,000 shares of stock?

14.12 In a world without corporate taxes, M & M claim that firms cannot benefit from leverage. Prove this statement using the following numerical example. Consider two firms with the same operating income, i.e., $X = $20 million. One of the firms has 2 million shares of stock and no debt (i.e., it is unlevered); the other firm is capitalized by 1 million shares of stock and $10,000,000 in bonds paying a 10% coupon rate of interest.

14.13 Consider two corporations A and B, identical in all respects except for their financial structures. While firm A has debt in its capital structure, firm B finances all its operations only with equity. The earnings before interest and tax of each firm (EBIT) is a random variable denoted by X. The following data describe the two firms and the random variable X

The market value of the stock of firm B is \$20,000,000, and the interest rate that firm A pays on its debt is 7%.

(a) In the absence of corporate taxes can the share price of firm A be higher than the share price of firm B, or vice versa? Prove your answer by means of a numerical example using two-way arbitrage.

	Firm A	Firm B
Number of shares of Common stock (N)	1,000,000	2,000,000
Long term debt (B_L)	\$10,000,000	—

Distribution of EBIT for the two firms:

X	$Pr(X)$
\$2,000,000	0.5
\$1,200,000	0.25
\$ − 500,000	0.25

(b) Now assume a corporate tax of $T_c = 0.34$. What should be the price of corporation A stock, given that the price of stock of corporation B is \$10? Prove your answer by carrying out the two-way arbitrage and show that the price that you suggest is indeed an equilibrium price.

14.14 Assume two firms exist which differ *only* by their capital structures. If the corporate tax rate is T_c, it is claimed that the following equilibrium condition holds:

$$V_L = V_U + T_c B_L$$

where:

V_L = market value of the levered firm
V_U = market value of the unlevered firm
B_L = the market value of bonds issued by the levered firm
T_c = corporate tax rate

Prove this by assuming that the unlevered firm is financed by 3,000,000 shares of common stock having a market price of \$10 a share; the levered firm has 2,000,000 shares of stock and \$10 million in long-term debt bearing interest at a rate of 10% (i.e., $r = 10\%$). Also assume that $T_c = 34\%$. In your answer, use detailed tables to show the precise arbitrage mechanism which ensures that deviations from the above equality cannot be permanent (Hint: see Appendix 14B).

14.15 What is the optimal capital structure that will be chosen by a firm's manager, who adopts the M & M model in the presence of corporate taxes? Do firms in practice behave according to the M & M model?

14.16 Define and prove M & M's proposition II in the absence of income taxes. What is the relationship of the pre-tax proposition II to its post-tax counterpart? (See Appendix 14B.)

14.17 Assume an unlevered firm whose net operating income is equal to \$700,000 and its total market value is \$5,000,000.

(a) What will be the required rate of return on the equity of a levered firm in equilibrium in the absence of taxes, if the interest rate on the firm's bonds is 8%, and the proportion of the debt in the capital structure $B_L/(B_L + S_L)$ is 20%? 40%? 60%? 80%?

(b) Illustrate graphically the rate of return on the levered firm's equity as a function of the debt/equity ratio (B_L/S_L).

(c) Answer the above in post-tax terms assuming a 34% corporate tax rate. (See Appendix 14B.)

14.18 John McKinney Jr is planning to establish an electronics company which will require an initial capital investment of $12,500,000. His financial manager offers five mutually exclusive alternatives for financing this investment (the interest rate is 7.5%).

1. 1 million shares and no debt.
2. 800,000 shares and $2,500,000 worth of bonds.
3. 600,000 shares and $5 million worth of bonds.
4. 400,000 shares and $7,500,000 worth of bonds.
5. 200,000 shares and $10 million worth of bonds.

If he issues only shares he is going to use all of the money received to finance his investment. However, if he issues a mix of debt and stocks, the cash inflow will be larger than $12,500,000. The firm will distribute amounts larger than this sum immediately as cash dividends. Assume a corporate income tax rate of 34% and answer the following questions:

(a) Calculate the market value of the firm for each financing alternative using the M & M post-tax equilibrium formula before the cash dividend is paid.

(b) Calculate the maximum possible price per share, for which the firm can sell its shares, in each alternative before the cash dividend is paid.

(c) Calculate the amount of the dividend paid in each alternative and the stock price after the cash is distributed.

(d) Suppose an investor who wishes to invest $2.5 million either in the unlevered firm or in the levered firm with $5,000,000 in debt. With which investment is he better off? (Do not forget the cash dividend!).

(e) What is the meaning of a 'corner solution' in the above case? Why is such a solution unsatisfactory?

14.19 Assume two firms identical in all respects apart from their capital structures. The NOI of the two firms is denoted X and does not change over time. However, the interest rate (for firms and individuals alike) varies over time and is denoted r_1 for the interest rate in the first year, r_2 in the second year, etc. That is, the firm borrows B_L at r_1 for the first year, then returns the loan and borrows B_L in the second year for r_2 etc. Assume no taxes and also that $V_L = \$100$ (with $S_L = \$50$ and $B_L = \$50$) and $V_U = \$80$, where V_L is the value of the levered firm, V_U is the value of the unlevered firm. S_L and B_L stand for the value of the equity and the debt of the levered firm, respectively. In the absence of taxes, the investor holds α of the stock of the levered firm. Given the above, what arbitrage would you carry out? Show the profit from your arbitrage.

14.20 Similarly to question 14.19 above, assume that the interest rate varies over time. Also assume a corporate tax rate of $T_c = 0.34$, and the following values

$$V_L = \$150, \quad V_U = \$100, \quad B_L = \$100, \quad S_L = \$50$$

Which firm, if any, is overvalued? Assume that you hold $\alpha = 0.1$ of the stock of the levered firm. What arbitrage would you undertake such that your annual income would not be affected? How much would you save?

14.21 Assume a world with no taxes and two identical firms apart from their capital structure, where $V_L = \$100$, $S_L = \$50$, $B_L = \$50$ and $V_U = \$80$. Also assume that the net operating income is a random variable which varies over time, denoted by $X_1, X_2, X_3, \ldots$ and in general X_t, where t denotes the year t. 'Since distributions change over time M & M's irrelevancy of capital structure does not hold.' Evaluate this assertion. If you do not agree, what arbitrage would you undertake to support your answer.

14.22 Assume that firms can borrow and lend at r. Individuals can lend at r but can borrow only at $r_1 > r$. In a world of no taxes, does M & M's proposition that $V_L = V_U$ hold? If not, what can be said about the relationship between V_L and V_U.

14.23 Consider the following data concerning the income and investment of a given firm and some market parameters (assume no-tax framework).

Current income $X_0 = \$5,000$; current investment $I_0 = \$3,000$; expected rate of return on the market portfolio $\bar{r}_m = 0.14$; standard deviation of the market rate of return $\sigma_m = 0.12$; risk-free interest rate $r = 0.06$; expected end-of-period income $\bar{X}_1 = \$6,000$; $\text{Cov}(\tilde{X}_1, \tilde{r}_m) = 100$.

(a) Determine the value of the firm at t_0.
(b) Suppose the firm issues (at time t_0) debt which yields return $\tilde{y}^b$ with the following characteristics:

$$\tilde{y}^b = \$2,000$$
$$\text{Cov}(\tilde{y}^b, \tilde{r}_m) = 10$$

In other words, the firm does not change its investment but finances it partly by debt which is risky and partly by stock. Determine the value of the debt, and the value of the firm at t_0. Does the value of the firm change as a result of the debt issue?

14.24 (a) Given that $\beta_U = 1$ (unlevered), calculate β_L for a levered firm with 50% debt in its capital mix. Assume a corporate tax rate equal to zero.
(b) Now answer the same question assuming a 34% corporate tax.

14.25 Suppose there are no taxes. Calculate the beta of a levered firm with a 25% debt to equity ratio given the following data.

Year	Rate of return on the unlevered firm X_U	Rate of return on the market portfolio X_m
1	0.1	0.08
2	0.12	0.06
3	0.05	0.10
4	0.02	0.12

14.26 Given the following data, calculate β_U and β_L assuming a *debt to equity* ratio of 0.5. Explain your results.

Year	Rate of return on the unlevered firm X_U	Rate of return on the market portfolio X_m
1	0.1	0.5
2	0.05	0.075
3	0.025	0.15
4	0.0415	0.05

14.27 The Reagan administration in 1986 reduced the corporate and personal income tax rates. In particular the corporate rate was reduced from 46% to 34%. Suppose that the corporate tax rate is reduced to 30% but there is *no change* in the personal income tax rates. What would be the impact of this change on:

(a) The value of the levered firm? The value of the unlevered firm? The gap between V_L and V_U?
(b) The total borrowing in the economy?
(c) The optimal capital structure of a specific firm, e.g., Xerox Corporation?
(d) What will be your answer to (b) and (c) in the actual case where personal income tax rate is 28% (flat rate) and where the capital gain tax is also 28%?

14.28 Modigliani and Miller assert that in a world without taxes the value of the firm is independent of its capital structure. Assume the following three cash flows (CFs) for two firms, one levered and one unlevered, a 5% risk-free interest rate and the cost of capital is known for sure to be 10% for the unlevered firm.

	CF_1	CF_2	CF_3
Dollar amount	−5	0	35
Probability	$\frac{1}{3}$	$\frac{1}{3}$	$\frac{1}{3}$

Firm I is not levered and its current price is $1.20 per share and 100 shares outstanding. Firm 2 is levered and its current price is $1.00 per share, 25 shares outstanding and $75 worth of debt.

(a) In the M & M framework, which firm is not in equilibrium? Why?
(b) Assuming $\alpha = 0.10$, prepare a table showing the arbitrage opportunity for each cash flow.
(c) Show your results graphically by drawing the probability of returns before and after the arbitrage. Explain.

14.29 Assume the following (unrealistic) tax rates $T_c = 0.34$, $T_p = 0.60$, and $T_g = 0.30$. The value of the unlevered firm is $V_U = 100$. What is the equilibrium value of the levered firm which issued debt $B_L = \$100$ and is it identical in all respects to the unlevered firm apart from its capital structure.

14.30 The beta for the Drip Company is 0.8 if it employs no leverage in its capital structure and the tax rate is 34%. The manager of Drip uses the following expression to calculate the influence of leverage on beta:

$$\beta_L^* = \beta_U^*[1 + (B_L/S_L)(1 - T_c)]$$

[Note also that $\beta_L^* = \beta_U^*(V_U/S_L)$)] where B_L is the debt employed, S_L is the value of equity, and β_U^* and β_L^* stand for the beta of the unlevered and levered firm, respectively.

(a) Several alternative target leverage ratios are being considered. What will be the beta on the common stock of Drip Company if the following leverage ratios are employed: $B_L/S_L = 0.4$, 0.8, 1.0, 1.2, and 1.4?

(b) If the financial manager uses the SML (discussed in Chapter 12) to estimate the mean rates of return on equity, what are the mean rates of return on equity at each of the above leverage ratios. (The estimated risk-free return is 6%, and the market risk premium is 5%.)

14.31 Suppose that there are no bankruptcy costs and no personal or corporate taxes. How does a cut in interest rates affect the value of the unlevered firm? The value of the levered firm? Return on equity of the levered and the unlevered firm?

14.32 In article 27 the American executives claim that the Japanese firms face lower interest rates which makes their cost of capital lower, and hence makes it difficult for the American firms to compete with them. Though the executives argument refers to a world of uncertainty, to simplify the analysis go back to Chapter 4 and assume certainty. Also assume no taxes and that the American and Japanese face the same production function. Explain why projects with positive *NPV* from the Japanese point of view has a negative *NPV* from the American point of view. Which country will produce more? Do you think this analysis can be extended to a world with taxes and uncertainty?

——— APPENDIX 14A: ALTERNATIVE FORMULATIONS OF THE GOAL OF THE FIRM

In this book we have assumed that the firm takes as its goal the maximization of the wealth of its existing shareholders. Several variants of this objective have been referred to in the course of our discussion of leverage. Depending on the particular context, the objective of the firm [14] has also been defined in terms of the maximization of the value of the firm; the price per share of its common stock, or the value of the owners' equity. The purpose of this appendix is to show that the three alternatives come to the same thing and that all three imply the maximization of stockholders' wealth.

Let us start by demonstrating the equivalence between maximizing the total market value of the firm and the maximization of share price. [15] Consider an unlevered firm whose total capitalization consists of n_0 shares of common stock with a market price per share of P_0. The total value of this firm is given by:

$$V_0 = n_0 P_0$$

Now, suppose the firm considers an alternative capital structure, which includes B_0 dollars of bonds, the remainder to be financed by equity. As a result, the firm can maintain the same level of economic activity by issuing a smaller number of shares. Denoting the required number of shares by n_1 we can determine the number of shares needed when B_0 dollars of bonds are issued as follows:

$$n_1 = \frac{V_0 - B_0}{V_0} \times n_0$$

14. The appendix follows the proof set out in Haim Levy and Marshall Sarnat, 'A Pedagogic Note on Alternative Formulation of the Goal of the Firm,' *Journal of Business*, October 1977.
15. Obviously the number of shares, and hence their price, can be changed arbitrarily by stock splits or stock dividends. In such an event, the 'price' per share would have to be adjusted to reflect these alterations.

Denoting the price of the shares of the levered alternative by P_1, the total market value of the levered firm, V_1, can be written as follows:

$$V_1 = n_1 P_1 + B_0 = \frac{V_0 - B_0}{V_0} \times n_0 P_1 + B_0$$

Since by definition $n_0 = V_0/P_0$ we can rewrite this expression as:

$$V_1 = (V_0 - B_0)\frac{P_1}{P_0} + B_0$$

Now, if leverage increases the value of the firm, so that $V_1 > V_0$, we have:

$$V_1 \equiv (V_0 - B_0)\frac{P_1}{P_0} + B_0 > V_0$$

But this relationship can hold *if and only if* $P_1 > P_0$, i.e., if the price of the shares of the levered alternative is higher than the share price of the unlevered strategy. Hence the financial policy which maximizes the value of the firm also maximizes the price of the firm's common stock. Thus, we use interchangeably the objective functions 'maximizing of the value of the firm' and 'maximizing the value per share'.

A numerical example might prove helpful. Suppose that the firm wants to raise \$100,000 by selling 1,000 shares of common stock at a price of \$100 per share. Now let us assume that the firm decides on an alternative financial policy, say issuing \$50,000 of bonds. In order to make the relevant comparison, the firm should issue only 500 shares $((V_0 - B_0)/V_0 \times n_0 = 500)$ since it needs to raise only half of the equity that it previously required. If the 'levered' firm succeeds in selling its stock for more than \$100 per share, the leverage is *positive* and the total market value of the firm (bonds plus stock), as well as the price per share of stock increase.[16]

Note that the maximization of the price per share is not identical in the above example to the maximization of the total market value of the equity, since for a given investment (i.e., a given size of the firm), the higher the proportion of debt employed the lower is the total required equity. Thus it is not intuitively obvious that the maximization of the market value of the firm (share price) implies the maximization of the value of owners' wealth (or equity).

In order to clarify this question, let us consider the case of an unlevered firm which repurchases 50% of its outstanding shares at the going market price P_0, using for this purpose the proceeds of a new debt issue. Let us further assume that the debt issue is announced one day after the repurchase agreement, which is tantamount to assuming that the change in financial policy (increase in leverage) is not anticipated by the market on the day the shares are repurchased. To show in this case that the maximization of the value of the firm is consistent with the maximization of equity (or wealth) of its *existing* shareholders, we shall employ a simple device. Consider the previous example. A firm which issues n_0 shares at a market price of P_0; hence its total market value is again given by $V_0 = n_0 P_0$. Now assume that the firm considers repurchasing $n_0/2$ of its shares, at the going price of P_0. Since the firm wishes to maintain the same level of operations, it raises an additional amount of debt, $B = V_0/2$, to finance the partial repurchase of its shares. Recalling that $n_0 = V_0/P_0$, the total value of the firm after these transactions can be written as $V_1 = n_0/2 \times P_1 + B = n_0/2 \times P_1 + V_0/2 = V_0/2 \times P_1/P_0 + V_0/2 = V_0(P_1/P_0 + 1)/2$, where P_1 denotes the new price of shares after the

---

16. The reader should note that if the firm raises \$50,000 by means of a bond issue and also issues 500 shares at a price $P_1, P_1 > P_0$, the total capital raised will exceed \$100,000. In order to hold the level of investment unchanged, we assume that the firm immediately distributes any excess as a dividend to its shareholders. The need to preserve a given level of overall economic activity is a sine qua non for the rigorous analysis of problems involving leverage, as has been emphasized by Franco Modigliani and Merton H. Miller in their pioneering 1958 article, and in their subsequent work (see Modigliani and Miller, 'The Cost of Capital, Corporation Finance and the Theory of Investment,' *American Economic Review*, June 1958.)

introduction of debt into the capital structure. Clearly, if $V_1 > V_0$ this again implies that $P_1 > P_0$. Hence, each *existing* stockholder who held two shares before the bonds were issued received P_0 for one share (through the firm's repurchase of 50% of the outstanding shares); in addition, his second share is now worth P_1, $P_1 > P_0$, and as a result the shareholder's total wealth is also enhanced because $(P_0 + P_1) > 2P_0$.

Now let us consider a somewhat more plausible scenario in which the firm first incurs debt and only later uses the proceeds to repurchase 'some' of its outstanding shares. In this instance we cannot stipulate with certainty the exact number of shares, B/P_1, which will be repurchased; the market can be expected to react to the 'new information' regarding the firm's new financial policy, and as a result, the repurchase will be effected at a new market price P_1, $P_1 \gtreqless P_0$. In this case the value of the firm after the transactions (debt issue and share repurchase) becomes:

$$V_1 = \left(n_0 - \frac{B}{P_1}\right)P_1 + B = n_0 P_1 - B + B = n_0 P_1$$

Recalling that $V_0 = n_0 P_0$, we once again find that $V_1 > V_0$ if and only if $P_1 > P_0$. Moreover, since shareholders' total wealth prior to the debt issue was $V_0 = n_0 P_0$ and following the share repurchase their total wealth is given by $n_0 P_1 - B = V_1 - B$ *plus* B which was received in payment for the repurchased shares, total wealth increases if and only if $V_1 > V_0$, or equivalently if $P_1 > P_0$.

As we have just seen, the total value of equity (held by the firm *and* the shareholders) rises when the market price per share and the total value of the firm increases. Thus, when our problem is correctly stated, the three alternative goals of the firm are: maximum total market value, maximum share price, and maximum value of owners' equity are identical after all, and all three imply the maximization of the wealth of the firm's existing shareholders.

APPENDIX 14B: A FORMAL PROOF OF THE MODIGLIANI AND MILLER PROPOSITIONS

In the text we have illustrated the M & M analysis, in the absence of taxation, by means of specific numerical examples. However, by employing the arbitrage mechanism which characterizes a perfectly efficient capital market, the general proof of their argument is straightforward.

Proposition I: no taxes

M & M's first proposition states that the value of the firm is independent of its capital structure. In other words, *other things being equal*, the value of a levered firm will be exactly equal to its unlevered counterpart. To prove this statement,[17] let us first define the following notations:

$V_U \equiv S_U$ = market value of an unlevered firm's securities (shares)
$V_L \equiv S_L + B_L$ = market value of a levered firm's securities
$\quad S_L$ = market value of a levered firm's shares
$\quad B_L$ = market value of a levered firm's bonds (debt)
$\quad r$ = interest rate
$\quad X$ = net operating income, which is identical for both the levered and unlevered firms. This income stream is gross of interest payments (if any), but net of other operating expenses.

---

17. The proof is taken from F. Modigliani and M. H. Miller, 'Reply to Heins and Sprenkle,' *American Economic Review*, September 1969.

Proposition I can be proved by showing that if V_U does not equal V_L, then it would be possible for holders of the shares of the 'overvalued' firm to achieve a better investment combination by selling their shares and buying the shares of the undervalued firm, and that this shift will continue until the following equilibrium relationship is restored:

$$V_L = V_U$$

Consider an investor who holds any fraction α of the shares of the unlevered firm. His investment is $\alpha S_U \equiv \alpha V_U$ and his return is αX. If $V_U > V_L$, the investor can build a new portfolio which increases his return, without increasing his investment. Table 14B.1 describes the suggested transaction. Before the change in the investment portfolio the investor received a return αX for an investment $\alpha S_U = \alpha V_U$. Following the change in the portfolio he still receives a return of αX, but his investment outlay is αV_L. Now, if we assume that $V_U > V_L$, it will be worth while to sell the shares of the unlevered firm and to use the proceeds from the sale to buy the stocks and bonds of the levered firm. But this process will tend to raise the market price of the levered firm's shares, while at the same time the price of the unlevered firm's shares will tend to fall. This can be expected to continue until $V_L = V_U$, at which time equilibrium will have been restored. For when $V_U = V_L$ investors have no further incentive to change their portfolios.

Let us now examine the reverse case, in which we assume that $V_L > V_U$. In order to show that this inequality cannot hold in equilibrium, we shall assume initially that an investor holds a fraction α of the levered firm's stock. Hence his investment is αS_L, or equivalently, $\alpha(V_L - B_L)$, and his return equals $\alpha(X - rB_L)$. Table 14B.2 shows that if $V_L > V_U$, as assumed, the investor can gain by switching his investment from the levered firm to the unlevered firm. In this manner the investor still receives the same return $\alpha(X - rB_L)$ that he had before, but his investment is now $\alpha(V_U - B_L)$ rather than $\alpha(V_L - B_L)$. As long as $V_U < V_L$ it is worth while to shift to the shares of the unlevered firm, thereby obtaining the *same* stream of returns for less cost. By switching from the overvalued firm to the undervalued firm, market forces are again created which, in equilibrium, restore the equality $V_L = V_U$.

Table 14B.1

	Investment required	Return produced
Initial position	αV_U	αX
Transaction		
(a) Buy the fraction α of the shares in the levered firm	$\alpha S_L \equiv \alpha(V_L - B_L)$	$\alpha(X - rB_L)$
(b) Buy the fraction α of the bonds of the levered firm	αB_L	αrB_L
Total investment (a + b)	αV_L	αX

Table 14B.2

	Investment required	Return produced
Initial position	$\alpha S_L = \alpha(V_L - B_L)$	$\alpha(X - rB_L)$
Transaction		
(a) Buy the fraction α of the shares in the unlevered firm	$\alpha S_U = \alpha V_U$	αX
(b) Borrow αB_L on personal account	$-\alpha B_L$	$-\alpha rB_L$
Total investment (a + b)	$\alpha(V_U - B_L)$	$\alpha(X - rB_L)$

To summarize, the arbitrage mechanism of a perfect capital market ensures that in equilibrium neither $V_L > V_U$ nor $V_L < V_U$ can persist, and therefore, V_L must equal V_U. This means that the value of the firm is independent of its capital structure, which is the proposition that we set out to prove. This formal proof confirms the numerical examples given in the text.

It should be noted that we have assumed here, as before, that the two firms are characterized by the same level of profitability (X) and by the same economic risk, and that they differ only in their capital structures. However, there is really no need to think about two firms at all; we seek to determine the impact of a change in the capital structure of a given firm on the value of its securities. Thus the relevant example would be to consider the same firm in two different hypothetical situations rather than two different firms in a given time period. The use of two firms serves only a convenient expository device, and is not necessary for the argument.[18]

Proposition I: with corporate taxes

Taking corporate taxes into account, M & M argue that the equilibrium value of the levered firm will be higher than its unlevered counterpart. The precise equilibrium relationship is given by their post-tax proposition I:

$$S_L + B_L \equiv V_L = V_U + T_c B_L$$

This can be proved as follows. Denoting the corporate tax rate by T_c, the net income of the shareholders of the unlevered firm is $(1 - T_c)X$, while the net income to the shareholders of the levered firm is $(X - rB_L)(1 - T_c)$. Consider first a case in which we assume that $S_L + B_L \equiv V_L > V_U + T_c B_L$, which implies that $S_L > V_U - (1 - T_c)B_L$. An investor who owns αS_L of the levered firm's shares can gain by making the portfolio switch that is spelled out in Table 14B.3. The return to the investor, both before and after the transaction, is the same, and is given by $\alpha(X - rB_L)(1 - T_c)$. But by switching to the unlevered firm, and borrowing on his personal account, his outlay is $\alpha[V_U - (1 - T_c)B_L]$, which by assumption is smaller than his previous outlay αS_L. Thus he can gain by selling the levered firm's shares and buying the unlevered firm's shares, so long as $V_L > V_U + T_c B_L$. Thus in equilibrium the last inequality can not hold, and V_L must equal $V_U + T_c B_L$.

To complete the post-tax presentation, we must prove that $V_L < V_U + T_c B_L$ also cannot hold. Let us assume that an investor owns a fraction α of the unlevered firm's shares; that is, his investment outlay is $\alpha S_U \equiv \alpha V_U$ which affords him a return of $\alpha X(1 - T_c)$. But if the investor carries out the switch indicated in Table 14B.4, that is,

Table 14B.3

	Investment required	Return produced
Initial position	αS_L	$\alpha(X - rB_L)(1 - T_c)$
Transaction		
(a) Buy the fraction α of the shares in the unlevered firm	$\alpha S_U \equiv \alpha V_U$	$\alpha X(1 - T_c)$
(b) Borrow $\alpha(1 - T_c)B_L$ on personal account	$-\alpha(1 - T_c)B_L$	$-\alpha(1 - T_c)rB_L$
Total investment (a + b)	$\alpha[V_U - (1 - T_c)B_L]$	$\alpha(1 - T_c)[X - rB_L]$

18. As Stiglitz, *op. cit.*, has shown, this enables us to dispense with the awkward device of postulating the so-called equal risk classes which plagued earlier proofs of the M & M propositions.

Table 14B.4

	Investment required	Return produced
Initial position	$\alpha S_U \equiv \alpha V_U$	$\alpha X(1 - T_c)$
Transaction		
(a) Buy the fraction α of the shares in the levered firm	$\alpha S_L = \alpha(V_L - B_L)$	$\alpha(X - rB_L)(1 - T_c)$
(b) Buy a fraction $\alpha(1 - T_c)B_L$ of the bonds of the levered firm	$\alpha B_L(1 - T_c)$	$\alpha rB_L(1 - T_c)$
Total investment (a + b)	$\alpha(V_L - T_c B_L)$	$\alpha X(1 - T_c)$

selling the shares of the overvalued unlevered firm and purchasing the shares and bonds of the levered firm, he can achieve the same level of return at a reduced investment outlay. And since this shift will be worth while so long as $V_L < V_U + T_c B_L$ market forces are again created which will restore the equilibrium equality between V_L and $V_U + T_c B_L$.

Proposition II

In a world of taxes M & M's second proposition can also be derived. Denoting the *after-tax* rate of return on the unlevered and levered firm by Y_U^* and Y_L^*, respectively, we obtain the following post-tax relationships:

$$Y_U^* = \frac{(1 - T_c)X}{V_U}$$

$$Y_L^* = \frac{(1 - T_c)(X - rB_L)}{V_L^* - B_L} = \frac{(1 - T_c)(X - rB_L)}{S_L}$$

$$= \frac{(1 - T_c)X}{S_L} - \frac{(1 - T_c)rB_L}{S_L}$$

Multiplying and dividing the first term on the right-hand side by V_U, we have:

$$Y_L^* = \frac{(1 - T_c)X}{V_U} \cdot \frac{V_U}{S_L} - \frac{(1 - T_c)rB_L}{S_L} = Y_U^* \frac{V_U}{S_L} - \frac{(1 - T_c)rB_L}{S_L}$$

Now if we add and subtract:

$$\frac{Y_U^*(1 - T_c)B_L}{S_L}$$

we obtain:

$$Y_L^* = Y_U^* \left[\frac{V_U}{S_L} - \frac{(1 - T_c)B_L}{S_L} \right] + Y_U^* \frac{(1 - T_c)B_L}{S_L} - \frac{(1 - T_c)rB_L}{S_L}$$

Since by Proposition I, $V_U - B_L + T_c B_L = S_L$, we have:

$$Y_L^* = Y_U^* + (1 - T_c)(Y_U^* - r) \frac{B_L}{S_L}$$

Thus the post-tax yield on the equity of the levered firm is equal to the post-tax yield of the unlevered firm plus a risk premium which is a function of leverage, the interest rate, and the corporate tax rate.

Proposition II, for both the no-tax and post-tax cases, is represented graphically in Figure 14B.1. The line $Y_U a$ shows the required rate of return on equity as a function

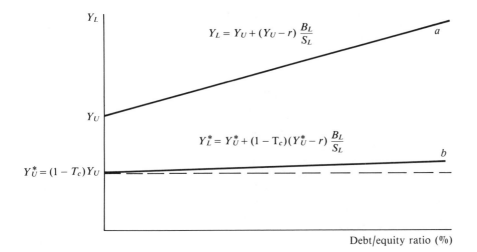

$$Y_L = Y_U + (Y_U - r)\frac{B_L}{S_L}$$

$$Y_L^* = Y_U^* + (1 - T_c)(Y_U^* - r)\frac{B_L}{S_L}$$

$$Y_U^* = (1 - T_c)Y_U$$

Debt/equity ratio (%)

Figure 14B.1

of the degree of leverage for the no-tax case. The higher B_L/S_L, the higher is the required rate of return. The slope of this line $(Y_U - r)$ represents the required risk premium when B_L/S_L is changed by one unit.

The line $Y_U^* b$ sets out this relationship for the corporate tax case. Since by definition $(1 - T_c) < 1$ and $(Y_U^* - r) < Y_U - r)$, the slope of line $Y_U^* b$ is smaller than before. Thus because of the tax advantage of debt, the required risk premium is much lower than in the no-tax case. For example, assuming $Y_U = 10\%$, $r = 4\%$, and $T_c = 50\%$, the slope of line $Y_U a$ is 6% as compared with a slope of only $\frac{1}{2}\%$ for line $Y_U^* b$.

SELECTED REFERENCES

Arditti, F. and Levy, H., 'Valuation, Leverage and the Cost of Capital in the Case of Depreciable Assets,' *Journal of Finance*, June 1973.

Bradley, M., Jarrell, G. A., and Kim, E. H., 'On the Existence of an Optimal Capital Structure: Theory and Evidence,' *Journal of Finance*, July 1984.

Barnea, A., Talmor, E., and Haugen, R. A., 'Debt and Taxes: A Multiperiod Investigation,' *Journal of Banking and Finance*, March 1987.

Becker, J., 'General Proof of Modigliani–Miller Propositions I and II Using Parameter-preference Theory,' *Journal of Financial and Quantitative Analysis*, March 1978.

Bhandari, Laxmi Chand, 'Debt/Equity Ratio and Expected Common Stock Returns: Empirical Evidence,' *Journal of Finance*, June 1988.

Boness, A., Chen, Andrew H., and Jatusipitak, Som, 'On Relations Among Stock Price Behavior and Chances in the Capital Structure of the Firm,' *Journal of Financial and Quantitative Analysis*, September 1972.

Booth, Laurence D., 'Capital Structure, Taxes and the Cost of Capital,' *Quarterly Review of Economics and Business*, Autumn 1980.

Boquist, John A. and Moore, William T., 'Inter-industry Leverage Differences and the DeAngelo–Masulis Tax Shield Hypothesis,' *Financial Management*, Spring 1984.

Brennan, Michael J. and Schwartz, Eduardo S., 'Optimal Financial Policy and Firm Valuation,' *Journal of Finance*, July 1984.

Brewer, D. E. and Michaelson, J., 'The Cost of Capital, Corporation Finance and the Theory of Investment: Comment,' *American Economic Review*, January 1965.

Brick, Ian and Fisher, Lawrence, 'Effects of Classifying Equity or Debt on the Value of the Firm under Uncertainty,' *Journal of Financial and Quantitative Analysis*, December 1987.

Conine, Thomas E. Jr, 'Corporate Debt and Corporate Taxes: An Extension,' *The Journal of Finance*, September 1980.

Cordes, J. and Sheffrin, S., 'Estimating the Tax Advantage of Corporate Debt,' *Journal of Finance*, March 1983.

Cornell, B. and A. C. Shapiro, 'Financing Corporate Growth, *Journal of Applied Corporate Finance*, Summer 1988.

De Angelo H. and Masulis, R. W., 'Optimal Capital Structure under Corporate and Personal Taxation,' *Journal of Financial Economics*, May 1980.

Dubofsky, David A. 'The Effects of Maturing Debt on Equity Risk,' *Quarterly Review of Economies and Business*, Autumn 1985.

Eckbo, B. Espen, 'Valuation Effects of Corporate Debt Offerings,' *Journal of Financial Economics*, January/February 1986.

Finnerty, J. E., 'Stock-for-debt Swaps and Shareholders Returns,' *Financial Management*, Autumn 1985.

Friedman, B. M., *Financing Corporate Capital Formation*, University of Chicago Press, 1986.

Golbe, Devra L. and Schachter, 'The Net Present Value Rule and an Algorithm for Maintaining a Constant Debt–Equity Ratio,' *Financial Management*, Summer 1985.

Gorman, Raymond and Shields, Elizabeth, 'Capital Structure, Corporate Taxes and the Clientele Effect,' *Journal of Midwest Financial Association*, 15, 1986.

Hamada, Robert S., 'The Effect of the Firm's Capital Structure on the Systematic Risk of Common Stocks,' *Journal of Finance*, May 1972.

John, K., 'Risk-shifting Incentives and Signalling through Corporate Capital Structure,' *Journal of Finance*, July 1987.

Kane, Alex, Marcus, Alan J., and McDonald, Robert L., 'Debt Policy and the Rate of Return Premium to Leverage,' *Journal of Financial and Quantitative Analysis*, December 1985.

Kim, E. H., 'Miller's Equilibrium Shareholder Leverage, Clienteles, and Optimal Capital Structure,' *Journal of Finance*, May 1982.

Kim, Wi Saeng and Sorensen, Eric H., 'Evidence on the Impact of the Agency Costs of Debt on Corporate Debt Policy,' *Journal of Financial and Quantitative Analysis*, June 1986.

Kolodny, Richard and Suhler, Diane Rizzuto, 'Changes in Capital Structure, New Equity Issues and Scale Effects,' *Journal of Financial Research*, Summer 1985.

Kraus, Alan and Litzenberger, Robert H., 'A State-preference Model of Optimal Financial Leverage,' *Journal of Finance*, September 1973.

Krouse, Clement G., 'Optimal Financing and Capital Structure Programs for the Firm,' *Journal of Finance*, December 1972.

Lee, W. L., Thakor, A. V., and Vora, G., 'Screening, Market Signalling, and Capital Structure,' *Journal of Finance*, December 1983.

Lewellen, Wilbur G. and Emery, Douglas, R., 'Corporate Debt Management and the Value of the Firm,' *Journal of Financial and Quantitative Analysis*, December 1986.

Lloyd-Davis, P. R., 'Optimal Financial Policy in Imperfect Markets,' *Journal of Financial and Quantitative Analysis*, September 1975.

Mandelker, Gershon N. and Rhee, S. Ghon, 'The Impact of the Degrees of Operating and Financial Leverage on Systematic Risk of Common Stock,' *Journal of Financial and Quantitative Analysis*, March 1984.

Melnyk, Lew Z., 'Cost of Capital as a Function of Financial Leverage,' *Decision Sciences*, July–October 1970.

Miller, Merton H., 'Debt and Taxes,' *Journal of Finance*, May 1977.

Modigliani, Franco and Miller, Merton H., 'The Cost of Capital, Corporation Finance, and the Theory of Investment,' *American Economic Review*, June 1958.

Myers, S. C., 'The Capital Structure Puzzle,' *Journal of Finance*, July 1984.

Osterberg, William P., *Tobin's q. Investment and the Endogenous Adjustment of Financial Structure*, Cleveland: Federal Reserve Bank, 1988.

Patterson, Cleveland S. 'Debt and Taxes: Empirical Evidence,' *Journal of Business Finance and Accounting*, Summer 1985.

Peavy, John W. III and Scott, Jonathan, 'A Closer Look at Stock-for-debt Swaps *Financial Analysts Journal*, May/June 1985.

Peles, Yoram C. and Sarnat, Marshall, 'Corporate Taxes and Capital Structure: Some Evidence Drawn from the British Experience,' *Review of Economics and Statistics*, February 1979.

Pinegar, J. Michael and Lease, Ronald C., 'The Impact of Preferred-for-common Exchange Offers on Firm Value,' *Journal of Finance*, September 1986.

Resek, Robert W., 'Multidimensional Risk and the Modigliani-Miller Hypothesis,' *Journal of Finance*, March 1970.

Robichek, Alexander A., Higgins, Robert C., and Kinsman, Michael D., 'The Effect of Leverage on the Cost of Equity Capital of Electric Utility Firms,' *Journal of Finance*, May 1973.

Rogers, Ronald C. and Owers, James E., 'Equity for Debt Exchanges and Stockholder Wealth,' *Financial Management*, Autumn 1985.

Ross, S. A., 'The Determination of Financial Structure: The Incentive-signalling Approach,' *Bell Journal of Economics*, Spring 1977.

Schneller, M. I., 'Taxes and the Optimal Structure of the Firm,' *Journal of Finance*, March 1980.

Senbet, L. and Taggart, R., 'Capital Structure Equilibrium under Market Imperfections and Incompleteness,' *Journal of Finance*, March 1984.

Senchack, A. J. Jr, 'The Firm's Optimal Financial Policies: Solution, Equilibrium and Stability,' *Journal of Financial and Quantitative Analysis*, November 1975.

Stapleton, Richard C. and Burke, Christopher M., 'European Tax Systems and the Neutrality of Corporate Financing Policy,' *Journal of Banking and Finance*, June 1977.

Stiglitz, Joseph E., 'On the Irrelevance of Corporate Financial Policy,' *American Economic Review*, December 1974.

Sundararajan, V. 'Debt–Equity Ratios of Firms and Interest Rate Policy: Macroeconomic Effects of High Leverage in Developing Countries,' *International Monetary Fund Staff Papers*, September 1985.

Taggart, Robert A. Jr, 'Taxes and Corporate Capital Structure in an Incomplete Market,' *Journal of Finance*, June 1980.

Talmor, Eli, 'The Determination of Corporate Optimal Capital Structure under Value Maximization and Informational Asymmetry,' *Journal of Economics and Business*, February 1984.

Titman, Sheridan and Wessels, Roberto, 'The Determinants of Capital Structure Choice,' *Journal of Finance*, March 1988.

Wrightsman, D., 'Tax Shield Valuation and the Capital Structure Decision,' *Journal of Finance*, May 1978.

15

Bankruptcy Risk and the Choice of Financial Structure

ARTICLE 28

Continental Has 4 Potential Suitors Studying Its Books

HOUSTON – Continental Airlines, operating under Chapter 11 bankruptcy-law protection since December 1990, has four potential investors examining its books, sources close to the committee of unsecured creditors confirmed.

. . . Continental, a unit of **Continental Airlines Holdings** Inc., froze pay for management in September 1990, and reduced pay to officers at the level of vice president and above in September 1991. In November, Continental announced

a six-month wage freeze for non-management employees, and it extended that in May, with the exception of some one-time merit raises for certain workers.

The planned pay cut suggests that Continental's previous efforts to reduce expenses haven't gone far enough. Last August and September, the company eliminated 1,400 jobs, grounded 22 jets and trimmed its capacity 6%.

Source: *Wall Street Journal*, June 17, 1992, p. A4.

ARTICLE 29

Child World, Inc.

Child World, Inc., Avon Conn., received U.S. bankruptcy court approval to liquidate its assets and go out of business if it cannot find a buyer.

The toy retailer, however, gave no indication in court that it has abandoned a last-minute effort to find a buyer or financing needed for a proposed merger with Philadelphia-based **Lionel** Corp., another toy retailer in Chapter 11 bankruptcy court proceedings.

Merger talks between Child World and Lionel "are continuing," George

Padgett, a Lionel attorney confirmed following the hearing on Child World's case.

Lionel, operating with approximately $55 million in debtor-in-possession financing, is seeking to reorganize and emerge from bankruptcy protection. Child World, which filed for bankruptcy protection May 6, hasn't been able to find new financing. It is running out of cash and is seeking a merger to survive.

Source: *Wall Street Journal*, June 16, 1992, p. B13.

When a firm cannot meet its financial obligations, bondholders may ask that the firm be declared bankrupt. However, the court (special bankruptcy court) may allow the firm to continue operation in an attempt to recover from the financial distress. This is called Chapter 11 and serves to protect a firm from its bondholders. Indeed, as the article above indicates, Continental Airlines has been operating under the protection of Chapter 11 since December 1990.

The second article discusses a firm which encountered a more serious situation. Child World, Inc. received court approval to liquidate its assets. It is interesting that in the article we see that Lionel is 'seeking to reorganize and emerge from bankruptcy protection.' Thus while Chapter 11 may assist some firms, others are unable to recover and hence must liquidate. But what are the costs of liquidation? What is the interaction between liquidation costs and a firm's capital structure?

In order to analyze this issue, recall that we ended the previous chapter by concluding that when one relaxes some of Miller's assumptions, debt is advantageous. The debt benefit may vary from one firm to another. For example, consider a case where one firm can borrow at 5%, the other at 8%, while individuals must borrow at 10%. In this case, it is obvious that debt is advantageous, but it is equally clear that debt is more advantageous to the first firm which can borrow at 5%. In this chapter, we assume that debt is advantageous, namely $V_L = V_U + \alpha B_L$ where α is some positive figure reflecting the debt advantage. This seems to lead to a 100% debt corner solution. We demonstrate in this chapter how the introduction of bankruptcy risk and liquidation costs guarantee an interior optimum capital structure which may vary across firms.

Note that α may have different values depending on the possible scenario assumed. For example, if we assume corporate taxes but no personal taxes, then in the absence of bankruptcy:

$$V_L = V_U + T_c B_L = V_U + \alpha B_L$$

hence:

$$\alpha = T_c$$

Another possible scenario is that corporate and personal taxes exist at fixed rates T_p, T_g, and T_c. In this case, in the absence of bankruptcy, we obtain:

$$V_L = V_U + B_L \left[1 - \frac{(1 - T_c)(1 - T_g)}{(1 - T_p)} \right]$$

hence:

$$\alpha = \left[1 - \frac{(1 - T_c)(1 - T_g)}{1 - T_p} \right].$$

(We assume $\alpha > 0$, i.e., debt is advantageous.)

With the 1986 change in the tax code we have $T_g = T_p$, hence $\alpha = T_c$ even with personal taxes. However, since tax rates change over time (indeed the personal tax rate has been increased to 31%), we will retain the general formula with personal taxes which will thus incorporate the future possibility of $T_p \neq T_g$ (which is currently under consideration). If personal taxes are not fixed at given rates (Miller's framework) α still may be positive due to the fact that firms can borrow at lower rates than individuals.

For simplicity we adopt the formula $V_L = V_U + T_cB$, i.e., we assume that corporate taxes exist but no personal taxes, hence $\alpha = T_c$. However, precisely the same analysis can be repeated without any change in the conclusions for any other value α which measures the debt benefit, as long as $\alpha > 0$.

THE PROBLEM OF EXTREME CORNER SOLUTIONS

As we noted at the end of the preceding chapter, the Modigliani and Miller analysis of a firm's capital structure, in the case in which the firm is assumed to pay corporate taxes, leads to an extreme 'corner solution' in the sense that a firm's capital structure comprises nearly 100% debt. The fact that the M & M analysis implies such a solution can easily be verified from the equilibrium relationship which states that $V_L = V_U + T_cB_L$. In the numerical example given in Table 15.1 and graphed in Figure 15.1, we have used their equilibrium condition to determine the maximum price at which the firm can sell its common stock. (Note that for a given firm's activity, the higher the debt, the higher debt/equity ratio.[1]) Suppose that a new firm decides to sell 20,000 shares and to use the proceeds to finance some specific business activities. The firm issues no debt and, of course, tries to sell its shares at the highest possible price. Let us assume that it succeeds in selling its stock at a net price of $1 per share; hence the total amount of money available for investment is $20,000. Now suppose that the same firm considers the possibility of financing the same operations by borrowing $5,000 and issuing only 15,000 shares. Assuming a 34%

Table 15.1

	Alternative financing policies[a]			
	Zero debt ($)	$5,000 debt ($)	$10,000 debt ($)	$15,000 debt ($)
Value of the firm	20,000	21,700	23,400	25,500
Total value of debt	—	5,000	10,000	15,000
Total value of stock	20,000	16,700	13,400	10,100
Number of shares	20,000	15,000	10,000	5,000
Price per share	$1	$1.11	$1.34	$2.02

[a] Assuming a corporate tax rate of 34%.

1. Since the value of the firm increases, it has more cash than it needs for the $20,000 worth of business activities. This is possible if the additional money in excess of the $20,000 is held in cash, thereby not creating any additional return. Alternatively, the firm can distribute the excess cash as a dividend or repurchase some of its stock (see problem 14.18).

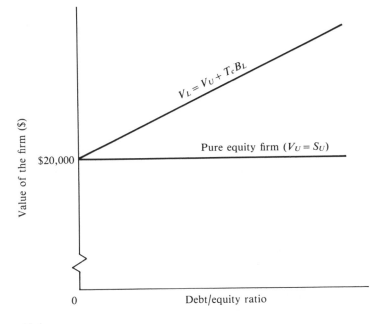

Figure 15.1

corporation tax rate and applying the M & M *post-tax* equilibrium condition $(V_L = V_U + T_c B_L)$, we find that:

$$V_L = \$20,000 + (0.34 \times \$5,000) = \$21,700$$

Since the value of the debt is $5,000, it follows that the value of stock is $16,700, i.e., the firm can sell 15,000 shares at a price of $1.11 per share ($16,700/15,000 = $1.11) compared with a price of $1 in the unlevered case. Similarly, should the firm decide to borrow $10,000 and issue only 10,000 shares it can succeed in selling the shares for $1.34 per share. The firm will maximize its market value, and hence the market price of a share of its stock, if management adopts an extreme policy of issuing nearly 100% debt. Such a 'corner solution' is, of course, an unsatisfactory result in the positive sense, because in reality firms do not, and in fact cannot, achieve anywhere near this degree of leverage. Clearly, the analysis of the previous chapter did not capture all of the relevant factors influencing the financing decision.

_____ **RISK OF BANKRUPTCY**

In practice, a firm is confronted with rising interest rates beyond fairly low levels of the debt/equity ratio, since lenders and borrowers are sensitive to the possibility of 'gamblers ruin', i.e., bankruptcy, which as we have already noted is ruled out in the M & M analysis. Similarly, the M & M analysis assumes that investors and firms can borrow at the same interest rate. In effect this means that the investor will be indifferent between the leverage achieved by the firm and the so-called homemade leverage which he can achieve by borrowing on his own account. Once again this reflects the absence of possible bankruptcy risk in the model, for unless this assumption holds, considerations of limited liability will logically lead the investor to prefer corporate to homemade leverage. Thus to the degree that substantial differences in borrowing rates exist, which is tantamount to the introduction of differential bankruptcy risk into the model, one can expect a firm's optimal capital structure to fall far short of the extreme corner solution. The actual degree of leverage used will reflect the particular firm's ability to absorb the financial risk inherent in the use of debt without incurring a penalty from the financial community in the form of increased interest rates and/or a fall in the price of its stock.

THE NATURE OF FINANCIAL FAILURE

Broadly speaking, we shall denote by the term *economic failure*[2] a firm whose net rate of return, adjusted for risk, is significantly lower than the prevailing rate of interest. A corporation is a *legal failure* if the corporation's assets are not sufficient to meet the legally enforceable claims of its creditors. These two concepts of business failure are not identical: the former measures success or failure in terms of earnings on invested capital; the latter uses a corporation's ability to meet its legally enforceable liabilities as the benchmark of performance.[3]

Two other terms are commonly used with respect to financial failure:

1. *Technical insolvency.* This refers to a state in which a firm finds itself unable to meet its current obligations even though its total assets exceed its total liabilities.
2. *Bankruptcy (or, equivalently, insolvency in an equity sense).* A firm is bankrupt or insolvent in an equity sense when its total liabilities exceed a fair valuation of its total assets.

For convenience we shall use the term 'failure' to include both of these aspects of the problem.

CHAPTER 11 OF THE BANKRUPTCY CODE

Under Chapter 11 of the Federal Bankruptcy Code, a company operates with court protection from creditor suits while it works out a plan to pay its debt. Thus, a firm which misses interest payments to its debtholders may petition for court protection. This protection allows the firm to try to raise money to pay

2. This section relies on the classic analysis of Arthur Stone Dewing, *The Financial Policy of Corporations*, 5th edn., Ronald Press, New York, 1953 (1st edn. 1919).
3. The reader should note that the term 'legal failure' is somewhat misleading since this condition can exist even in the absence of any formal legal proceedings.

its obligations and thus attempt to avoid bankruptcy. For example, on August 9, 1988, the *Wall Street Journal* reported on the Chapter 11 filing of the Western Company of North America. Western was seeking to reduce its senior unsecured debt from $545 million to $175 million through giving senior unsecured creditors approximately $30 million in cash and about two hundred acres of land.

Maybe one of the more famous filings for Chapter 11 is the conglomerate LTV. This firm received court protection for more than two years and in September 1988, LTV suggested reorganization with only partial compensation to its creditors (e.g., 50 cents for each one dollar of debt to be paid in the form of the firm's stock). For more recent Chapter 11 cases as well as liquidation decisions, see the article at the beginning of the chapter.

Underlying causes of failure

The usual 'causes' given for financial failure, e.g., lack of capital, faulty accounting, poor planning, etc., are more often not causes but rather rationalizations or excuses for the poor performance of the company. The underlying cause of most failures can best be summarized by the term *management incompetence*. It is the lack of managerial skills which appears to be the fundamental cause of business failure, independent of the size or nature of the business undertaking. Ultimately, business success or failure depends on the quality of a firm's management.[4]

Scope of financial failures[5]

As we have already mentioned, the extreme corner solution implied by the M & M analysis must be rejected because it does not reflect the essential properties of the capital structure decision, and therefore fails to 'explain' (i.e., account for) the behavior patterns of actual firms. The source of much of this distortion of economic reality and theory can be traced to the failure of the M & M model to reflect the risks and costs associated with the possibility of financial failure. The significance of this omission can be gauged by examining the data of Table 15.2. From 1925 to 1989 the rate of corporation failure ranged from a low of 4 per 10,000 during World War II to a high of 154 per 10,000 during the Great Depression of the 1930s. If, for illustrative purposes only, we take the average failure rate during the decade of the 1970s, i.e., slightly more than 35 per 10,000, this means that if one chooses a firm at random from the corporations constituting that population, there exists a probability of $\frac{1}{3}\%$ that the firm chosen will go bankrupt during the year. If we

---

4. Dun and Bradstreet lists management incompetence as the cause in almost 90% of all business failures. See *The Failure Record Through 1969*.

5. For a comprehensive analysis of the trends in corporate bankruptcy in the United States, see Edward I. Altman, *Corporate Bankruptcy in America*, Heath Lexington Books, Lexington, Mass., 1971. Altman also sets out a multivariate statistical model designed to explain the aggregate failure rate and liability experience. For a technique to predict financial failure, see Appendix 15A.

Table 15.2

Year	Number of failures	Failure rate per 10,000 listed concerns	Average liability per failure ($)
1925	21,214	100	20,918
1926	21,773	101	18,795
1927	23,146	106	22,471
1928	23,842	109	20,534
1929	22,909	104	21,094
1930	26,355	122	25,357
1931	28,285	133	26,032
1932	31,822	154	29,172
1933	19,859	100	23,038
1934	12,091	61	27,621
1935	12,244	62	25,366
1936	9,607	48	21,148
1937	9,490	46	19,310
1938	12,836	61	19,204
1939	14,768	70	12,359
1940	13,619	63	12,239
1941	11,848	55	11,488
1942	9,405	45	10,713
1943	3,221	16	14,076
1944	1,222	7	25,908
1945	809	4	37,361
1946	1,129	5	59,654
1947	3,474	14	58,898
1948	5,250	20	44,690
1949	9,246	34	33,323
1950	9,162	34	27,099
1951	8,058	31	32,210
1952	7,611	29	37,224
1953	8,862	33	44,477
1954	11,086	42	41,731
1955	10,969	42	40,968
1956	12,686	48	44,356
1957	13,739	52	44,784
1958	14,964	56	48,667
1959	14,053	52	49,300
1960	15,445	57	60,772
1961	17,075	64	68,843
1962	15,782	61	76,898
1963	14,374	56	94,100
1964	13,501	53	98,454
1965	13,514	53	97,800
1966	13,061	52	106,091
1967	12,364	49	102,332
1968	9,636	39	97,654
1969	9,154	37	125,000
1970	10,748	40	176,000
1971	10,326	42	186,000
1972	9,566	38	209,000
1973	9,345	36	246,000
1974	9,915	38	308,000
1975	11,432	43	383,000
1976	9,628	35	313,000
1977	7,919	28	391,000
1978	6,619	24	356,000

Table 15.2 (Continued)

Year	Number of failures	Failure rate per 10,000 listed concerns	Average liability per failure ($)
1979	7,564	28	352,639
1980	11,742	42	394,744
1981	16,794	61	414,147
1982	24,908	88	627,000
1983	31,334	110	512,957
1984	52,078	107	562,022
1985	57,067	114	584,856
1986	61,616	120	725,850
1987	61,111	102	568.212
1988	57,098	98	685,243
1989	50,389	65	878,386
1990	50,361	75	1,059,770

Source: *U.S. Statistical Abstracts*, 1979, 1985, 1987, and 1990.

apply the average failure rate for the period as a whole, this probability rises to 1%. Clearly, even a relatively small probability of a disaster such as financial failure will be a cause of great concern to management and, therefore, will affect the financial decision-making process.

ARTICLE 30

As New Bond Defaults Taper Off...

In billions, bond defaults

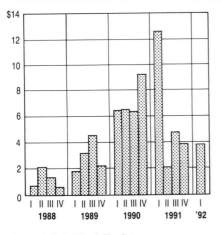

Total Bonds In Default Start To Fall

In billions, bonds remaining in default

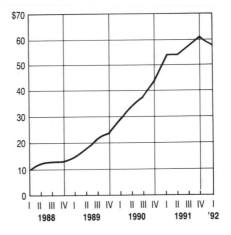

Source: Defaulted Bonds Newsletter

One reason for dwindling defaults: leveraged buy-out activity peaked in 1988 and 1989, three years ago. Most of the buy-outs that were going to get into trouble already have. As Mr. Ross puts it, 'There is a three-year infant mortality cycle.'

Also, declining short-term interest rates

have eased companies' interest burdens. And scores of heavily indebted companies from **Time Warner** to **RJR Nabisco**, have been able to sell stock to reduce debt in the past year. Jerome Fons, an economist at Moodys Investors Service, Inc., the bond rating service says junk-bond rating upgrades are exceeding the number of downgrades for the first time in three years.

. . . William Dudley, a fixed-income analyst at Goldman Sachs, says that 'non-performing loans seem to have plateaued' at big banks. As a result of lower interest rates, he said, 'the level of stress on corporate America is very much diminished.'

Robert Albertson, a Goldman analyst who follows banks, notes that the debt-related improvement also extends to individuals. Consumer debt as a percentage of disposable personal income has fallen from a peak of 18.9% in 1986 to 17.2%. 'The consumer has deleveraged as well,' he says.

Source: Wall Street Journal, April 28, 1992, p. C1.

As article 30 shows, leveraged buy-outs caused significant financial defaults (and bankruptcies) in 1988 and 1989. By the end of 1991 and start of 1992, however, bond defaults declined, due in part to a drop in interest rates which served to ease the financial stress facing American firms. What is the relationship between leverage and the probability of bankruptcy? What role do interest rates play? We now turn our attention to these and other related issues.

BANKRUPTCY RISK AND OPTIMAL CAPITAL STRUCTURE _____

Corporations Rush to Issue New Debt on Drop In Rates, but Offerings Are Seen as Too Pricey

NEW YORK – Corporate treasurers issued more than $1.7 billion of new notes and bonds yesterday as they rushed to take advantage of declining interest rates. . . . But the focus in the market clearly was the avalanche of new corporate debt, the bulk of which was sold by utilities and banks.

Source: Wall Street Journal, June 17, 1992, p. C19.

While the general level of interest rates affects the behavior of all firms, there are also characteristics unique to individual firms which can explain why, on the same day, one firm will decide to issue equity, while another will issue debt or preferred stocks. For example, if a firm has declining profits and is losing money (e.g., General Motors which lost more than $6 billion dollars in 1990) and the firm's future profit potential is discouraging, then it is probably better that it issues equity. However, if a firm has stable income and a bright future it can sustain increasing debt. Thus the brighter the forecast, the smaller the probability that $X < rB_L$, and the greater the firm's incentive to issue bonds. This may explain why, on the same day, for a given interest rate we observe one firm issuing bonds and the other in the same industry issuing equity.

This chapter is devoted to the delicate balance between bankruptcy costs and the tax advantage of borrowing. We return to the effect of interest rates on a firm's cost of capital in Chapter 16.

Let us turn our attention to the question of how the probability of bankruptcy can be expected to affect the firm's financial structure decision. Clearly, the probability of going bankrupt depends on many economic factors; however, the two most important for our purposes are the firm's economic and financial risks. Economic risk is associated mainly with the industry to which the firm belongs and with the general conditions of the overall economy. Hence even competent management can do very little to reduce economic risk once the underlying decision regarding the type of economic activity to be pursued is made. Financial risk, on the other hand, is subject almost completely to the discretionary control of management. By reducing the use of leverage the firm can decrease the variability of earnings, thereby decreasing the probability of not being able to meet fixed charges (interest and redemptions) during a series of consecutive years. By increasing its use of leverage the firm also increases its financial risk and thereby the probability of financial failure.

Fortunately, the probability of bankruptcy and its impact on financial decision making can be incorporated in the basic capital structure model developed in Chapter 14 by utilizing a convenient hypothetical device. Suppose that each year the firm pays a premium to an insurance company (or to the government) in order to insure itself against the possibility of bankruptcy (e.g., banks paying a premium to the Federal Deposit Insurance Corporation, FDIC). Such an arrangement implies that the insurance company will pay the interest (and other fixed charges) to the firm's creditors in years in which losses are sustained. This assumption allows us to retain the M&M assumption of no bankruptcy, while also reflecting the costs of avoiding this risk. This, in turn, implies a significant change in the valuation equation, because the payments involved in the insurance transaction also affect the value of the firm. Another possibility is to incorporate bankruptcy by recognizing that it is not costless but rather involves a loss of approximately 23% of the firm's assets (see Table 15.6). We can thus subtract from our equation, $V_L = V_u + T_c B_L$, the cost of bankruptcy times its probability of occurrence. These two approaches (extra premium and administrative costs) lead to similar solutions, i.e., an optimal interior capital structure.

The essential feature of the insurance arrangement lies in the fact that the insurance company pays the firm in years of negative cash flow but also receives an annual premium from the firm. In the unlikely event that the expected value of the cash receipts from the insurance company is equal to the stream of insurance premiums paid by the firm, no change will occur in the valuation equation for the firm, and therefore the corner solution will persist. However, under the more realistic assumption that the insurance company sets its premium sufficiently high to cover administrative costs and to provide a return on its investment, the net expected value of the insurance transaction is negative from the firm's viewpoint. Since bankruptcy is not costless (see Table 15.7), the firm is prepared to pay the 'extra' premium required to cover the expenses and provide the insurance company's required profit. But this premium in excess of the expected value of the insurance coverage constitutes a net outlay from the firm to the insurance company and therefore must be deducted from the firm's cash flow, thereby changing its market value.

An explanation for the firm's willingness to pay the extra premium is that in the case of bankruptcy the firm incurs substantial liquidation costs which are deducted from the firm's assets (fee to accountants, attorneys, etc.; see Table 15.6). The firm is therefore willing to pay the insurance company an 'extra' premium with the aim of avoiding bankruptcy and thus avoiding the liquidation costs. Let us illustrate this with a simple example (Table 15.3).

For simplicity, we assume no taxes and that the interest payout is $24 in a case of 25% leverage and $48 in the case of 50% leverage. We also assume that when the cash flow is negative, bankruptcy occurs and the firm loses 12% of its assets (which are say, $V_L = \$1500$) as liquidation costs. The insurance company pays the firm the negative cash flow if this occurs, hence avoiding bankruptcy. If the contract were a fair game, the insurance company would charge the following insurance premium:

0% leverage: None
25% leverage: $\frac{1}{3} \times 24 = \$8$
50% leverage: $(\frac{1}{3} \times 48) + (\frac{1}{3} \times 8) = \$18\frac{2}{3}$

These are the premiums charged only if the insurance firm is precluded from making any profit (on average) on the transaction. However, the insurance firm needs to cover its costs and make a profit from its services. The firm will be willing to pay more to avoid bankruptcy, even in a case of risk neutrality (namely, all charges are calculated by the mean cash flows) and the maximum 'extra' premium the firm will be willing to pay is a function of the liquidation costs which can be avoided, namely:

0% leverage: $0 \times 12 = \$0$
25% leverage: $\frac{1}{3} \times 12 = \$4$
50% leverage: $(\frac{1}{3} \times 12) + (\frac{1}{3} \times 12) = \$8$

Hence, the higher the financial leverage, the higher the probability of bankruptcy and thus the higher the extra premium the firm will be willing to

Table 15.3

Firm's cash flows ($1000)					
No leverage		25% debt		50% debt	
Cash flow	Probability	Cash flow	Probability	Cash flow	Probability
0	1/3	−24	1/3	−48	1/3
40	1/3	+16	1/3	−8	1/3
150	1/3	126	1/3	102	1/3

pay to avoid bankruptcy. If we deduct the extra premium from the value of the firm $V_L = V_U + T_c B_L$, a corner solution may be avoided.

Since the insurance company's required return reflects its perception of the firm's risk, we expect that for a *given* level of business risk, the size of the excess premium will depend on the firm's financial risk, i.e., on the degree to which it uses leverage. The higher the financial leverage ratio and the higher the interest rate on the bonds issued by the firm, the higher the risk of bankruptcy: hence the higher will be the extra premium. Figure 15.2 illustrates a typical situation in which this payment is assumed to be quite moderate for low debt/equity ratios but increases at an accelerated rate as the firm resorts to more and more financial leverage.

Figure 15.3 illustrates the impact of deducting the present value of the extra insurance premium on the M & M valuation model. If one deducts from the basic after-tax valuation formula ($V_L = V_U + T_c B_L$) the present value of the costs of avoiding bankruptcy, the corner solution is precluded. The line V_L of Figure 15.3 sets out the relationship between the value of the firm and its financial leverage as postulated in the non-bankruptcy case. As we have previously shown, this model implies an extreme capital structure comprised largely of debt. The curve denoted by V_B in Figure 15.3 is derived by deducting the present value of the excess premium paid to avoid bankruptcy from the line

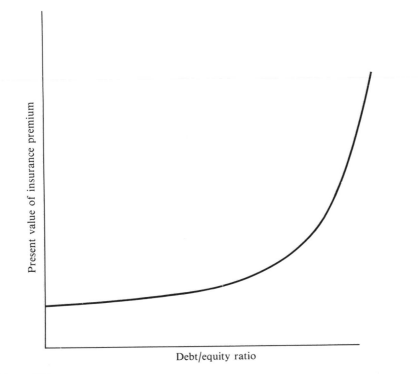

Figure 15.2

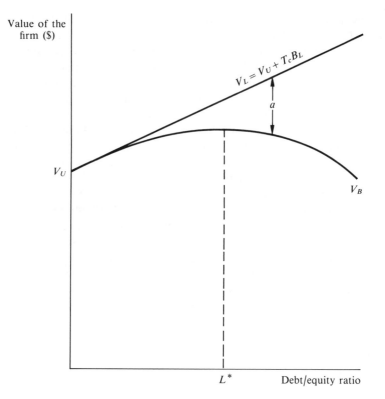

Figure 15.3

V_L. The particular shape of the V_B curve reflects our assumption that the risk of bankruptcy (and, therefore, the size of this premium) rises at an *increasing* rate as additional leverage is employed. Another interpretation of the distance *a* is that it represents the administrative costs in the case of bankruptcy, times the probability of bankruptcy. Since the administrative costs are given (see Table 15.6), the further we move to the right the greater the probability of bankruptcy occurring, hence the larger the distance *a*.

The striking feature of explicitly incorporating bankruptcy risk in the M & M valuation model is that it permits us to avoid the extreme corner solutions. Up to point L^* of Figure 15.3 the value of the firm rises as debt is introduced into the capital structure; however, beyond this point, increasing the use of leverage lowers the value of the firm. It follows that such a firm will not (and should not) strive to maximize the use of debt in its capital structure. Increasing leverage raises expected profits and owing to the tax effect it increases the value of the firm as well (line V_L); but the introduction of debt also increases the risk of financial failure. For moderate degrees of debt the overall impact of leverage is positive (i.e., the value of the firm rises), but beyond some point the risk of bankruptcy becomes dominant and the impact of further increases in debt is negative. Such a critical turning point, denoted by L^* in Figure 15.3, defines the firm's *optimal* capital structure. And in general it can safely be expected to fall far short of a 99% debt level.

The incorporation of bankruptcy risk can also serve to resolve another paradoxical result of the M&M model. The original valuation model (ignoring bankruptcy) implies not only an extreme corner solution, but also that this extreme debt/equity ratio is optimal for all firms, independent of their economic activity. Once again, this implication stands in sharp contrast to reality. Table 15.4 sets out a rough measure of the actual debt/equity ratios in eight industries. The data confirm the well-known fact that public utilities tend to employ relatively more debt than do manufacturing concerns.[6] The ratio of long-term debt to equity is 0.82 for the former and 0.58 for the latter.

The reason for the variation in debt/equity ratios is easy to find. Utilities are less vulnerable to the risk of economic failure: the demand for their services is relatively stable, i.e., their economic risk is relatively low, although one should always bear in mind that some risk always exists. On the other hand, the economic risk in mining and manufacturing is much greater: due to changes in fashion or to the introduction of new products, the demand for industrial products, for example, is far less stable. This difference by itself can help to explain the variety of financial policies followed by various industry groups. Figure 15.4 illustrates two firms that would command the same market value if they did not use debt at all (V_U). Assume that the curve labeled A represents a mining or manufacturing firm and the curve denoted by B is a public utility. Ignoring bankruptcy risk, the two firms would adopt a policy of maximum debt financing and both would have the same market value as described by line V_L. However, once the risk of bankruptcy is recognized, the manufacturing firm can be expected to use far less debt than does the public utility, i.e., the optimal debt/equity ratio of the former L_A lies to the left of the optimal debt/equity mix of the latter, L_B. This result follows from the

Table 15.4 Capital structure in selected industries

	(1) Long-term debt ($ billion)	(2) Equity	(3) Long-term debt/equity ratio (%)
Agriculture, forestry, and fishery	16.21	20.27	0.80
Mining	48.72	111.83	0.44
Construction	42.87	62.52	0.69
Manufacturing	727.54	1,253.27	0.58
Transportation and public utilities	428.20	519.39	0.82
Wholesale and retail trade	248.67	331.97	0.75
Finance, insurance and real estate	678.90	1,779.47	0.38
Services	160.62	128.12	1.25

Source: Department of the Treasury, Internal Revenue Service, *Statistics of Income, 1988, Corporation Income Tax Returns*.

6. The data of Table 15.4 reflect only long-term debt. However, the inclusion of short-term debt does not change the basic conclusion that the degree of leverage used by utilities is significantly greater than that in manufacturing and mining.

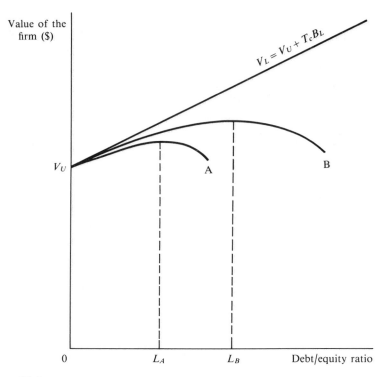

Figure 15.4

assumption that the *economic risks* in manufacturing are greater than those of a public utility. Thus even though both firms are confronted by the risk of financial failure, the degree of risk is greater for the manufacturing concern. In terms of our convenient insurance device, both firms can insure themselves against failure, but the excess premium charged to the manufacturing firm will be significantly higher than that required of the utility. Thus, the explicit incorporation of bankruptcy risk into the model bridges the gap between the theoretical results and empirical observation; the revised valuation model, which incorporates the penalty for financial failure, can serve as a useful guide and benchmark for corporate financial strategy.

Though this type of insurance against bankruptcy is hypothetical,[7] this type of insurance contract (though not identical) has recently been observed. For example, in 1984 Citicorp purchased $900 million of insurance against losses on loans which it gave five South American nations. Thus, the bank pays a premium to an insurance company and the insurance company, in turn, will pay the bank the loaned money should the borrowers go bankrupt. Suppose

---

7. Note that the device of insurance is employed as a means of formally incorporating bankruptcy risk into the model. The risk exists even though a firm does not actually insure itself, the hypothetical premium serving as a convenient proxy for the economic costs of bearing a given level of bankruptcy risk.

that if Citicorp does not get back the loans it will go bankrupt. Thus, by insuring the loans, it really insured itself against bankruptcy exactly as explained in this chapter. Though this was the first bank which purchased such insurance, it is not unlikely that more banks and firms will follow this strategy in the future.

Numerical example

In order to make the crucial role of default risk even more transparent, let us consider a specific numerical example. Table 15.5 reproduces the four financing options originally set out in Table 15.1. In this particular example, the value of the unlevered firm, V_U, equals \$20,000. The unadjusted valuation formula, $V_L = V_U + T_c B_L$ (assuming $T_c = 34\%$), was then used to calculate the value of the firm for three degrees of leverage. These values are given in line 1 of Table 15.5. In order to simplify the exposition, we further assume that the firm can insure itself against bankruptcy, and that the size of the annual *extra premium* is \$4,000 (\$2,640 on an after-tax basis) multiplied by the probability of bankruptcy. Clearly, the higher the latter, the higher will be the required premium which reflects the insurance company's higher required return on the riskier undertaking.

This annual excess premium for firm A is given in line 5 of Table 15.5.[8] To calculate the net present value of the firm, with bankruptcy risk eliminated, one must deduct the present value of the extra premium from line 1 (the value of the firm using the unadjusted M & M model). Namely, $V_L^* = V_L - PV$ (extra

Table 15.5

	Alternative financing policies			
	Zero debt	\$5,000 debt	\$10,000 debt	\$15,000 debt
1. Value of the firm $V_L = V_U + T_c B_L$	20,000	21,700	23,400	25,100
2. Total value of debt	–	5,000	10,000	15,000
3. Total value of shares	20,000	16,700	13,400	10,100
		Firm A		
4. Probability of failure (in %)	1	5	$7\frac{1}{2}$	15
5. After-tax excess premium paid (\$2,640) × (4)	26.4	132	198	396
6. Present value of the excess premium (at 10% discount rates[a])	264	1,320	1,980	3,960
7. Net value of firm (1)–(6) (V^*)	19,736	20,380	21,420	21,140
		Firm B		
8. Probability of failure (in %)	5	10	20	30
9. After-tax excess premium paid (\$2,640) × (8)	132	246	528	792
10. Present value of the excess premium (at 10% discount rate)	1,320	2,460	5,280	7,920
11. Net value of firm (1)–(10) (V^*)	18,680	19,240	18,120	17,180

[a] Assuming a perpetuity.

8. To be consistent with M & M analysis, we assume that the assets beyond \$20,000 are held in cash or are paid as a cash dividend (see footnote 1).

premium) where V_L^* is the market value of the levered firm when insured against bankruptcy. This present value has been calculated using a 10% discount rate and assuming a perpetual cash flow premium. The net present value of the firm when the possibility of financial failure is taken into account is given in line 7.

The reader should note that while the original M & M hypothesis leads to an extreme debt policy, successive increments of debt to the capital structure increase the value of the firm (line 1); once the economic costs of bankruptcy are taken into account this 'corner solution' disappears. An examination of line 7 reveals that the value of the firm increases with leverage up to the $10,000 debt alternative but declines when $15,000 of debt is employed. Hence $10,000 of debt represents the *optimal* financial policy for firm A. This result was obtained by explicitly incorporating the cost of bankruptcy risk into the M & M valuation model, using the very realistic assumption that the probability of financial failure *increases* as the financial leverage ratio increases (see lines 4 and 8 of Table 15.5).

Table 15.5 also presents a parallel set of calculations for a second firm denoted as B. This firm is similar in all respects to the first firm with the

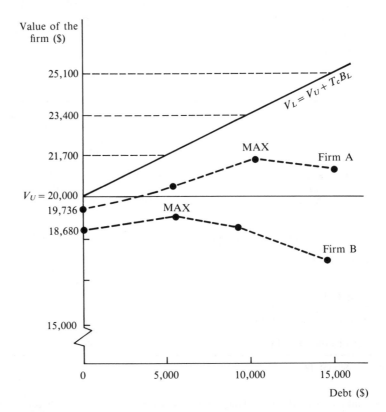

Figure 15.5

exception that its economic risk is assumed to be much higher. The probability of failure in the unlevered alternative is 5% for firm B as compared with only 1% for firm A (compare lines 4 and 8). As a result, the total risk of bankruptcy in firm B becomes quite large as leverage is introduced.

The relationship between firms A and B is illustrated graphically in Figure 15.5. In the original M & M model (ignoring bankruptcy risk) the continuously rising line V_L sets out the value of *both* firms for various financing alternatives. When bankruptcy costs are explicitly included in the valuation model, the value of firm A reaches a maximum at a $10,000 debt level, while that of B reaches a maximum at a lower level of debt, i.e., $5,000. Once again this illustrates the fact that, other things being equal, firms with higher economic risks (e.g., mining companies) will tend to use proportionately less debt than firms with lower levels of economic risk (e.g., public utilities).

To sum up the discussion so far, the higher the business risk, leverage, and interest rate then the higher the probability of bankruptcy. Thus, we expect more failures when the use of leverage is intense, and we expect fewer when the market interest rate goes down, as experienced in 1991 and 1992 (see the article at the beginning of the chapter).

Bond ratings and bankruptcy risk

The risk of bankruptcy differs from one firm to another and even for a given firm over time. Indeed, Moody's and Standard and Poor's (S&P's) upgrade and downgrade firms periodically.

ARTICLE 32

A Financial Rise and Fall

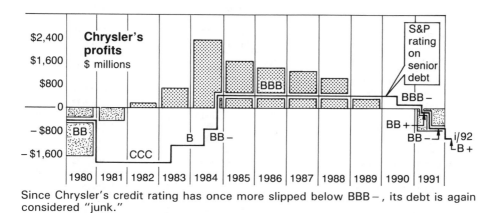

Since Chrysler's credit rating has once more slipped below BBB−, its debt is again considered "junk."

Fortune Chart/Source: Standard & Poors

Source: Fortune, April 20, 1992, p. 70.

For example, as can be seen from the chart in article 32, in 1980 Chrysler Corp. was rated BB by S&P's and was later downgraded to CCC in 1981 and 1982. When Chrysler showed positive profits, its rating was upgraded to B and eventually to BBB — the best rating it had earned in 1980–81. In 1990, Chrysler faced new financial stress and declining profits resulting in another downgrading.

Investors look at a firm's financial statements and debt rating to infer the probability of bankruptcy. The lower the bond rating, the larger the financial distress and hence the larger the interest rate required by bondholders to compensate them for the risk.

LIQUIDATION COSTS

Even with the possibility that the firm may go bankrupt, it can be shown that given certain restrictive assumptions the relationship between the value of the firm and its leverage as proposed by M & M still holds. The most restrictive and unrealistic assumption necessary for this result is that bankruptcy be costless.

In order to better understand the assumption, recall that bankruptcy is the financial state that bondholders may choose to precipitate when the firm fails to meet the interest and principal payments on its debt as those payments come due. If the firm's failure to meet its cash obligations results in bondholders suing for the interest and principal owed them, a state of bankruptcy is entered. The firm's assets are liquidated, the fees of lawyers representing both sides are paid, and the residual funds obtained from liquidation are distributed

Table 15.6 Administrative expenses of bankruptcy cases in U.S. district courts, fiscal years 1969 and 1976

	1969	%	1976	%
Total realization	$113,137,000	100.00	$229,535,533	100.00
Total administrative expenses	26,446,000	23.4	52,584,678	22.9
Receivers' commissions	777,000	0.7	835,466	0.4
Receivers' expenses	234,000	0.2	414,900	0.2
Trustees' commissions	4,009,000	3.5	7,133,560	3.1
Referees' salary and expense fund	2,808,000	2.5	7,630,861	3.3
Reporting and transcribing testimony	339,000	0.3	626,657	0.3
Accountants' fees	576,000	0.5	1,234,297	0.5
Auctioneers' fees	1,611,000	1.4	3,174,835	1.4
Appraisers' fees	462,000	0.4	711,973	0.3
Attorneys for creditors	460,000	0.4	359,104	0.2
Attorneys for trustees	7,268,000	6.4	15,497,324	6.8
Attorneys for receivers	781,000	0.7	840,231	0.4
Attorneys for bankrupts	1,314,000	1.2	1,762,663	0.8
Attorneys for others	560,000	0.5	1,566,256	0.7
Rental expenses	1,241,000	1.1	2,239,956	1.0
Trustees for all other expenses	4,014,000	3.5	8,506,595	3.7

[a] The figures relate to liquidation from July 1–June 30 of the following year.
Source: Table of Bankruptcy Statistics, Washington D.C., Administrative Office of the United States Courts, 30 June 1969 and 30 June 1976.

among security holders with bondholders having prior claim. Thus, bankruptcy involves costs: liquidation costs are estimated to comprise anywhere from 30% to 70% of the asset's going-concern value. Table 15.6 shows that the administrative expenses associated with bankruptcy alone can consume almost a quarter (about 23%) of the asset's realized value. Note also that administrative expenses contributed a constant percentage of liquidated assets in 1969 and 1976 even though the value of the liquidated assets themselves increased from about $113 million in 1969 to $229 million in 1976. Although such detailed bankruptcy data are not collected any more, there is no reason to believe that the percentage costs are significantly different now.

The breakdown of the total realization of assets induced by bankruptcy does not vary much across years. Figure 15.6 illustrates a typical year assets realization breakdown. The pie chart reveals that 12.1% of the realization goes to priority creditors, 33.8% to secured creditors and 26.6% was paid to unsecured creditors. The administrative expenses and the 'other payment' category account for 27.5% of the total realization. Thus, going bankrupt involves significant costs which are deducted from the firm's assets. Only what is left after the deduction of these costs is distributed to the creditors; and only

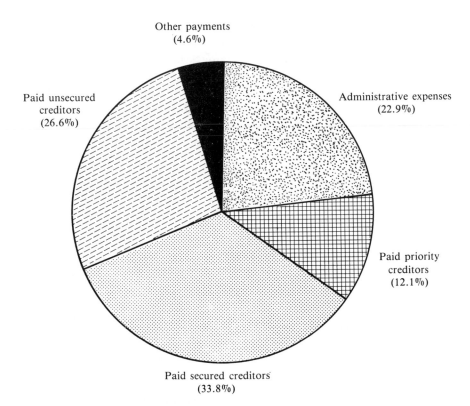

Figure 15.6 Percentage of total realization in asset cases. *Source*: Administrative Office of the United States Courts.

the remaining assets realization left after paying the creditors as well as the administrative charges is distributed to the shareholders.

A recent study by Altman[9] strongly supports the notion that bankruptcy costs are far from trivial. Altman studied a sample of 18 industrial firms which went bankrupt over the period 1970–78 and a second sample of seven large bankrupt companies in the 1980s. For the sample of 18 firms the total bankruptcy costs are estimated to be 16.7% of the value of the firm. Table 15.7 presents some information on the indirect costs for seven bankruptcies of large firms.

On the average, the indirect bankruptcy costs were 17.7%. Note that indirect bankruptcy costs include forgone sales and lost profits. In order to get the total bankruptcy costs one has to add the direct bankruptcy costs which include explicit costs paid in the reorganization or liquidation process. Since most of the seven companies were still involved in the reorganization process when this study was conducted it was impossible to collect these direct costs. Thus, one can say that, on the average, the bankruptcy costs were at least 17.7% of the firm's assets.

Clearly, cost considerations of such a magnitude vitiate the M & M proposition about the relationship between leverage and the value of the firm. In the real world firms do not adopt extremely leveraged positions which increase the possibility of bankruptcy beyond acceptable levels. Moreover, even if bankruptcy were costless, managers would still tend to lose their jobs once bankruptcy occurs, which again implies that firms normally will not willingly take on the extreme amounts of debt that is implied by the M & M theory with corporate taxation. The tax advantages lost due to the fact that the manager (who maximizes his expected utility) is not willing to increase the firm's leverage, are called 'agency costs'.[10]

Table 15.7 Estimate of bankruptcy costs of seven large firms

Firm	Date of bankruptcy	Indirect cost as percent of the value of the firm
Braniff International	May 1982	27.9
Itel Corp.	January 1981	31.9
Lionel Corp.	February 1982	0.6
McLout Steel	December 1981	20.5
Sambo's Restaurants	June 1981	23.0
White Motor Co.	September 1980	1.7
Wickes Cos.	April 1982	18.4
Average:		17.7

Source: Edward I. Altman 'A Further Empirical Investigation of the Bankruptcy Cost Question,' *Journal of Finance*, September, 1984.

9. Edward I. Altman, 'A Further Empirical Investigation of the Bankruptcy Cost Question,' *Journal of Finance*, September 1984.
10. See Chapter 13 for a detailed discussion of agency costs.

The preceeding two chapters have surveyed the factors affecting the firm's financing mix, including: location of the earnings distribution; stability of sales and earnings; dividend policy; control; and the risk of bankruptcy. The latter consideration appears to be most crucial in precluding the excess use of debt.

The inclusion of bankruptcy risk in the M & M valuation model permits us to explain and account for two features of the observed financial policies of corporations:

1. Despite the tax advantages attached to the use of debt, firms in practice do not adopt extremely levered capital structures.
2. The degree to which leverage is employed depends inversely on the firm's underlying economic risk: the greater the economic risk the smaller will be the financial leverage ratio.

Finally, even without bankruptcy, low income (which may be due to extensive leverage) may induce a dismissal of the firm's manager; therefore he would be inclined not to adopt an extreme, although possibly optimal, leverage policy.

_____ SUMMARY TABLE

Debt benefit with no bankruptcy costs

In the absence of bankruptcy cost, the value of the levered firm is related to the value of the unlevered firm by the following formula:

$$V_L = V_U + \alpha B_L, \quad \text{where } \alpha > 0$$

We have:

1. $\alpha = T_c$ when we assume corporate but no personal taxes.

2. $\alpha = 1 - \dfrac{(1 - T_c)(1 - T_g)}{(1 - T_p)}$ with corporate and personal taxes.

   Given the 1986 tax code $T_g = T_p$, hence case (1) and (2) coincide with the case where $\alpha = T_c$.
3. α can be determined by a large number of factors (taxes, imperfections in capital markets, portfolio considerations, etc.). It also may change as a function of B_L but we assume that it is a positive constant.

Bankruptcy cost

$$V_L^* = V_L - PV(P) = V_U + \alpha B_L - PV(P)$$

where V_L^* is the value of the levered firm when insured against bankruptcy,

$PV(P)$ in the present value of extra premium paid to insurance companies, and αB_L is the debt benefit. Another interpretation of $PV(P)$ is that it represents the reduction in the value of the firm due to administrative costs in the case of bankruptcy.

Properties of $PV(P)$

1. $PV(P)$ is an increasing function of the degree of leverage – inducing an interior optimum capital structure.
2. Firms with high business risk will be charged a higher rate, hence reaching their optimum at a lower debt-to-equity ratio.

QUESTIONS AND PROBLEMS

15.1 Explain how the removal of the 'no bankruptcy' assumption affects the M & M conclusion regarding leverage and valuation.

15.2 Distinguish between 'economic failure' and 'legal failure'.

15.3 Explain how the following numerical example depicts a firm which is bankrupt or insolvent in an equity sense:

Equity	
Common stock	$25,000,000
(1,000,000 shares at $25 par value)	
Retained earnings	($5,000,000)
Current liabilities	$10,000,000
Long-term debt	
Bonds ($1,000 par value)	$50,000,000
Total liabilities and capital	$80,000,000

Assume the market price of the firm's stock is $9.00 per share and the market value of its bonds is $760 per bond.

15.4 Give a numerical example of a firm which is bankrupt or insolvent in an equity sense.

15.5 'If firms were able to insure themselves against bankruptcy by paying a premium in excess of the expected value of the contract, M & M's post-tax result would hold, and the optimal capital structure would comprise nearly 100% debt.' Critically evaluate this statement.

15.6 The New Electronic Laboratories Corporation (NELCO) asked the L&S Insurance Company, which specializes in bankruptcy insurance, to underwrite its risk of failure. The insurance company undertook an obligation to pay a required constant sum to the firm's creditors in years in which losses are sustained, for an annual premium on this sum. The 'excess' insurance premium required to induce the insurance company to underwrite the risk varies as a function of the rate of the debt in the capital structure as set out in the table. NELCO had five alternatives for financing its initial required investment of $10 million:

1. No debt and 10 million shares at $1 per share.
2. $2 million of debt and 8 million shares.
3. $4 million of debt and 6 million shares.
4. $6 million debt and 4 million shares.
5. $8 million debt and 2 million shares.

Percentage of debt in the capital structure $B_L/(B_L + S_L)$	Annual 'extra' premium (% of the $10 million)
0.0	0.05
0.1	0.2
0.2	0.25
0.3	0.35
0.4	0.5
0.5	0.7
0.6	1.0
0.7	1.45
0.8	2.0
0.9	2.7

Thus as the firm increases the proportion of debt, the number of shares issued decreases proportionally. However, the value of the firm increases by the formula $V_L = V_U + T_c B_L$. Thus, with leverage the firm obtains more than the required $10 million. Assume that the excess assets are distributed as a cash dividend. Assume also that the corporate tax rate is 34% and that the discount rate (for present value calculations) is $6\frac{2}{3}\%$.

(a) Plot the present value of the insurance premium offered to NELCO as a function of the debt/equity ratio $[B_L/(B_L + S_L)]$.
(b) Calculate for each alternative the net value of the firm, before the cash dividend is paid, with bankruptcy risk eliminated, i.e., $(V_L = V_U + T_c B_L - PV(P))$.
(c) Find the optimal financial policy for NELCO from the above five alternatives.
(d) Plot the value and the net value of NELCO as a function of its financial leverage ratio.
(e) What is the amount of each dividend paid by the firm for various degrees of leverage.

15.7 Another company – COMP – was offered a similar arrangement by L & S, with the same conditions as NELCO, except for the premium rates, which were higher:

Percentage of debt in the capital structure $B_L/(B_L + S_L)$	Annual 'extra' premium (%)
0.0	0.1
0.1	0.25
0.2	0.35
0.3	0.5
0.4	0.75
0.5	1.15
0.6	1.7
0.7	2.4
0.8	3.2
0.9	4.2

Except for its economic risk, COMP is similar in all respects to NELCO (i.e., in its initial investment, the sum of money needed to avoid bankruptcy, the tax rate and the discount rate). Answer the following question assuming that COMP has the same financial alternatives as NELCO:

(a) Plot the present value of the insurance premium offered to COMP as a function of the debt/equity ratio.
(b) Calculate, for each alternative, the net value of the firm with bankruptcy risk eliminated.
(c) Find the optimal financial policy for COMP.
(d) Plot the value and the net value of COMP as a function of its financial leverage ratio.
(e) Compare your results in 15.6 with those of 15.5. How do you account for the differences in optimal financial strategies?

15.8 The following quotation is taken from the *Wall Street Journal*, September 5, 1984.

'Coleco Industries Inc. said it had sweetened the terms of a $41.5 million debenture offering made in May and raised an additional 13.5 million from the same institutional investors and others.

'The company said it sold $13.5 million of 11% convertible debentures in a private placement. It also retired $41.5 million of 10% convertible debentures and exchanged them for $41.5 of 11% convertible debentures due 1989. Coleco didn't identify the investors.

'Morton E. Handel, executive vice president, said the company exchanged the old debentures for more costly debentures because the price of Coleco's stock has slipped and because "it helped make the deal".

'Coleco shares, which traded as high as $16.875 in May, closed in composite trading on the New York Stock Exchange yesterday at $14, up 25 cents.'

(a) What factors may account for the increase in the interest rate from 10% to 11%?
(b) What is, in your view, the relationship between the interest rate charged by bondholders and Coleco stock price?

15.9 Assume no personal tax, a corporate tax of $T_c = 0.34$, and no bankruptcy. Also assume that $V_U = \$10$. It is given that without bankruptcy we have $V_L = V_U + T_c B_L$.

(a) Assume now that the firm may be bankrupt. However, it can insure itself against such an event. The present value of the insurance cost is a function of the firm's debt and is given by $\alpha(B_L) \times B_L$, when $\alpha(B_L)$ is a positively increasing function of B_L. Find the optimal amount of debt and the optimal capital structure stated in terms of the function $\alpha(B_L)$.

(b) Now suppose that $\alpha(B_L) = 0.34$. What is the optimal capital structure of the firm in this specific case?

(c) Answer (b) when $\alpha(B_L) = 0.01\, B_L^2$. What is the value of the levered firm? Illustrate your results graphically.

15.10 Assume that the value of the unlevered firm is $V_U = \$100$ (all figures are in millions). Another firm is considering issuing debt of $B_L = \$30$ or $B_L = \$50$. The tax rate is $T_c = 0.34$. Assume both the levered firm and unlevered firm are identical in all respects apart from the capital structures, and that the levered firm distributes all tax shelter benefits immediately as a cash dividend. That is, both firms invest only $100 in projects.

(a) In the absence of bankruptcy, what is the value of the levered firm under the two alternative levels of leverage? What is the total amount of cash dividends distributed under the two leverage alternatives?

(b) Now suppose that bankruptcy is possible. Bankruptcy is not costless and the administrative costs are 25% of the value of the firm (see Table 15.6). Assuming that all investors have linear utility functions, what is the value of the levered firm when $B_L = \$30$ and the probability of bankruptcy is 0.10, and alternatively when $B_L = \$50$ and the probability of bankruptcy is 0.80? Would the firm adopt a leverage policy which is a corner solution?

15.11 Assume that the earnings before interest and taxes (EBIT) which is denoted X has the following distribution:

X	Probability
0	1/3
5	1/3
25	1/3

The corporate tax is $T_c = 0.34$ and the firm goes bankrupt when income is negative (i.e., it cannot service its debt obligations).

(a) What is the probability of bankruptcy when the firm is unlevered and $V_U = \$100$?

(b) What is the probability of bankruptcy when the firm finances its investment by $50 worth of bonds bearing an 8% interest rate? With $70 worth of bonds at 8% interest rate? (Note: the firm's size and before tax income do not change with leverage.)

15.12 The Nylon firm is unlevered and the value of its investment is $100. The firm's annual cashflow is given by (all figures in millions of dollars)

Cash flow (X)	Probability
1	1/3
5	1/3
20	1/3

The firm is considering repurchasing some of its stock and financing it with debt such that the activity level (or cash flow before interest X) is kept unchanged. Having 25% leverage the firm has to pay after-tax $5 = R$ as interest and at 75% leverage the firm has to pay after-tax $8 = R$ as interest. Bankruptcy occurs whenever the cash flow $y + X - R$ is negative. In the case of bankruptcy, the firm would lose $3 in administrative costs. Assume that all parties are risk neutral.

(a) Calculate the premium the insurance company would charge for the two levels of leverage given that they have zero costs in managing their firm.

(b) For the two levels of leverage calculate the maximum premium that the firm would be willing to pay to the insurance company at the corresponding 'extra' premium.

15.13 Suppose that the firm faces the following net operating income which will occur one year hence:

State of the world	Probability	Operating income
Recession	1/2	− $100 million
Expansion	1/2	+ $400 million

A bank considers giving $50 one-year loan to this firm. In case of a recession, the bank would lose the principal as well as the interest. The riskless interest rate is 10% per annum. Suppose that the bank's manager behaves as a risk-neutral. What interest rate should he charge on this loan?

15.14 Rework question 15.13 on the assumption that the bank behaves as a risk averter with a utility function of $U(W) = \sqrt{W}$. Assume that the bank has an initial wealth of $1,000. The other data given in question 15.13 are unchanged.

APPENDIX 15A: PREDICTING FINANCIAL FAILURE

One of the best known approaches to the problem of predicting financial failure is that of Edward Altman who combines a number of financial ratios simultaneously in an effort to determine a firm's failure potential. This technique is called the Z-score model[11] and the weights given to each ratio are appropriate for manufacturing firms. The model is expressed as follows:

$$Z = 1.2X_1 + 1.4X_2 + 3.3X_3 + 0.6X_4 + 0.99X_5$$

where:

X_1 = working capital/total assets
X_2 = retained earnings/total assets
X_3 = earnings before interest and taxes/total assets
X_4 = market value of preferred and common equity/total liabilities
X_5 = sales/total assets

X_1 − *Working capital/total assets.* The ratio of working capital (current assets less current liabilities) to total assets is a ratio which reflects liquidity and size character-

---

11. See Edward I. Altman, *Corporate Financial Distress*, Wiley, New York, 1983. Numerous variants of the Z-score model have been developed, but unlike the original model they are not in the public domain. The weights assigned to each ratio were derived by Altman using multivariate discriminant analysis.

istics. A firm which suffers continuing operating losses will find its working capital shrinking relative to its total assets.

X_2 – *Retained earnings/total assets*. This ratio measures a firm's cumulative profitability over time. As such, it also reflects a firm's age. Typically, a young firm will have a low ratio since it has not had the time to accumulate retained earnings. Hence the analysis is biased against young firms which have a greater chance of displaying a *low* retained earnings to total assets ratio than do older firms. But this accurately reflects the empirical evidence. The incidence of financial failure is significantly higher during firms' earlier years.

X_3 – *EBIT/total assets*. This ratio measures the productivity of a firm's assets after abstracting from tax and financing effects. In essence, it measures a firm's earning power which of course is the ultimate safeguard against financial failure.

X_4 – *Market value of equity/total liabilities*. The numerator of this ratio is calculated by multiplying the number outstanding of each type of share (common and preferred) by their market prices. The denominator is the book value of current plus long-term liabilities. This ratio measures the degree to which the value of the firm can decline before it becomes insolvent. Since market value appears to provide a more effective predictor of bankruptcy, the market value of equity is substituted for the more commonly used book value of accounting net worth.

X_5 – *Sales/total assets*. This turnover ratio measures a firm's ability to generate sales, and presumably reflects its ability to deal effectively with competitive conditions. [12]

The interpretation of the Altman model is straightforward; the lower the Z score, the higher is a firm's failure potential. Any firm with a Z-score below 1.8 is considered a prime candidate for bankruptcy. To clarify the use of the model, we apply it, in Table 15A.1 to the data of a hypothetical corporation, the Metro Manufacturing Company. As can be seen from the table, Metro's Z-score is a robust 3.8185, i.e., comfortably above the critical value of 1.8.

Table 15A.1 Analysis of Metro Manufacturing Company using the Z-score model

Ratio (1)	Value in current year (2)	Z-score model coefficient (3)	Contribution to Z-score $(2) \times (3) = (4)$
X_1	$\dfrac{2{,}841}{30{,}715} = 0.0925$	1.2	0.1110
X_2	$\dfrac{14{,}453}{30{,}715} = 0.4706$	1.4	0.6588
X_3	$\dfrac{4{,}788}{30{,}715} = 0.1559$	3.3	0.5145
X_4	$\dfrac{19{,}453}{11{,}262} = 1.7273$	0.6	1.0364
X_5	$\dfrac{46{,}470}{30{,}715} = 1.5129$	0.99	1.4978
		Z-score	3.8185

Analysis based on the assumption that Metro's shares were selling in the market at their book value.

12. Curiously, this ratio taken by itself is the least significant of the five; however, when combined with the other four, it ranks second in its contribution to the aggregate discriminating ability of the model.

The Z-score model, or variants on the same theme, have been applied not only in the United States, but in many other countries as well, e.g., Australia, Brazil, Canada, England, France, Germany, Ireland, Japan and the Netherlands.[13] Although there is considerable variation among the scores of the different countries, in all cases the 'failed groups' have much lower Z-scores than their 'non-failed' counterparts. And in all countries, the overall average Z-score of firms, which subsequently failed, is below the critical value of 1.8.

SELECTED REFERENCES

Aharony, Joseph and Swary, Itzhak, 'A Note on Corporate Bankruptcy and the Market Model Risk Measures,' *Journal of Business Finance and Accounting*, Summer 1988.

Aharony, Joseph, Jones, Charles P., and Swary, Itzhak, 'An Analysis of Risk and Return Characteristics of Corporate Bankruptcy using Capital Market Data,' *Journal of Finance*, September 1980.

Altman, E. I., Haldeman, Robert G., and Narayanan, P., 'ZETA Analysis: A New Model to Identify Bankruptcy Risk of Corporations,' *Journal of Banking and Finance*, June 1977.

Altman, E. I., Baidya, T. K. N., and Ribeiro Dias, L. M., 'Assessing Potential Financial Problems for Firms in Brazil,' *Journal of International Business Studies*, Fall 1979.

Altman, E. I., 'A Further Empirical Investigation of the Bankruptcy Cost Question,' *Journal of Finance*, September 1984.

Ang, J. S., Chua, J. H., and McConnell, J. J., 'The Administrative Cost of Corporate Bankruptcy: A Note,' *Journal of Finance*, March 1982.

Ang, James S. and Petersen, David, 'Optimal Debt versus Debt Capacity: A Disequilibrium Model of Corporate Debt Behavior,' *Research in Finance*, 6, 1986.

Arbel, A., Kolodny, R., and Lakonishok, J., 'The Relationship between Risk of Default and Return on Equity: An Empirical Investigation,' *Journal of Financial and Quantitative Analysis*, November 1977.

Asofby, P. H. and Tatloc, W., 'Bankruptcy Tax Act Radically Alters Treatment of Bankruptcy and Discharging Debts,' *Journal of Taxation*, February 1981.

Baron, D. P., 'Default Risk and the Modigliani–Miller Theorem: A Synthesis,' *American Economic Review*, March 1976.

Castanias, R., 'Bankruptcy Risk and Optimal Capital Structure,' *Journal of Finance*, December 1983.

Darrough, Masako N. and Stoughton, Neal M. 'Moral Hazard and Adverse Selection: The Question of Financial Structure,' *Journal of Finance*, June 1986.

Davis, E. P., *Rising Sectorial Debt/Income Ratios: A Cause for Concern?* Basle: Bank for International Settlements, 1987.

Feder, Gershon, 'Note on Debt, Assets and Lending under Default Risk,' *Journal of Financial and Quantitative Analysis*, March 1980.

Flath, D. and Knoeber, C. R., 'Taxes, Failure Costs and Optimal Industry Capital Structure: An Empirical Test,' *The Journal of Finance*, March 1980.

Franks, J. R. and Torous, W. N., 'An Empirical Investigation of U.S. Firms in Reorganization,' *Journal of Finance*, July 1989.

Haugen, Robert A. and Senbet, Lemma W., 'Bankruptcy and Agency Costs: Their Significance to the Theory of Optimal Capital Structure,' *Journal of Financial and Quantitative Analysis*, March 1988.

13. See Edward I. Altman, *The Success of Business Failure Prediction Models: An International Survey, Occasional Paper*, No. 5, Salomon Brothers Center for the Study of Financial Institutions, Graduate School of Business Administration, New York University, 1983.

Kalaba, R. E., Langetieg. T. C., Rasakhoo, N., and Weinstein, M. I., 'Estimation of Implicit Bankruptcy Costs,' *Journal of Finance*, July 1984.

Kim, E. H. and Schatzberg, J., 'Voluntary Liquidations: Causes and Consequences,' *Midland Corporate Finance Journal*, Winter 1988.

Lawler, Thomas A., 'Yield Spreads, Relative Yield Spreads and Default Risk,' *Financial Review*, Winter 1980.

Morris, J., 'Taxes, Bankruptcy Costs and the Existence of an Optimal Capital Structure,' *Journal of Financial Research*, December 1982.

Ohlson, James A., 'Financial Ratios and the Probabilistic Prediction of Bankruptcy,' *Journal of Accounting Research*, April 1980.

Ramaswamy, K., 'Stock Market Perception of Industrial Firm Bankruptcy,' *Financial Review*, May 1987.

Scott, J., 'The Probability of Bankruptcy: A Comparison of Empirical Predictions and Theoretical Models,' *Journal of Banking and Finance*, September 1981.

Smith, C. W. Jr and Warner, J. B., 'Bankruptcy, Secured Debt, and Optimal Capital Structure: Comment,' *Journal of Finance*, March 1979.

Stiglitz, Joseph E., 'Some Aspects of the Pure Theory of Corporate Finance: Bankruptcies and Takeovers,' *Bell Journal of Economics and Finance*, Autumn 1972.

Viscione, Jerry A., 'Assessing Financial Distress,' *Journal of Commercial Bank Lending*, July 1985.

Warner, J. B., 'Bankruptcy, Absolute Priority, and the Pricing of Risky Debt Claims,' *Journal of Financial Economics*, May 1977.

16

Defining the Cost of Capital

ARTICLE 33

A group of forward-looking senior executives met recently at the Harris Bank to discuss the challenge and complexity of international competition ... 'Another issue is that the cost of capital is substantially lower in other countries than it is here ... Japanese public companies can get much different multiples on earnings, so they can raise public money incrementally at a much lower cost in terms of earnings averages. Also, the Japanese banks make capital available much more readily and cheaply...'

Source: adapted from *Fortune*, April 20, 1991, p. 252.

What is the cost of capital? How is it defined? What is the relationship between the cost of capital and earnings particularly earnings multiplies? Are high earnings multiples indicative of healthy firms? How do interest rates affect the cost of capital? If foreign competitors like Japan indeed face a lower cost of capital, does this give them a competitive edge?

In the preceding chapter we concluded that, up to a limit, the use of financial leverage can potentially increase the value of the firm. If we denote the proportions of debt and equity which correspond to this limit by the letter L^*, the latter represents the firm's *optimal* capital structure. And as we have assumed that the goal of the firm is to maximize its market value (thereby maximizing the market value of the stockholders' equity), it follows that the firm should strive to achieve that financing mix which it believes to be optimal in the long run.

In this chapter we turn our attention to the problem of defining the cost of capital: that is, a firm's minimum required rate of return on new investment. We discuss in detail the cost of the two sources of financing discussed in the above article. Initially we set out the theoretical arguments supporting the use of a *weighted average* of the various sources of financing as the measure of the cost of capital, the weights being determined by the proportion of each source in the optimal capital structure, L^*. In the following chapter we discuss the ways in which each individual type of financing (debt, preferred stock, common stock, retained earnings, etc.) can be measured, and conclude the discussion by setting out a practical method for calculating the cost of capital using General Electric and IBM as examples.

We concentrate in this chapter and in the next on defining and measuring the cost of equity, debt, and preferred stock. The analysis of the cost of other sources of funds (e.g., accounts payable) is left to the end-of-chapter problems.

FIRM'S COST OF CAPITAL VERSUS INDIVIDUAL PROJECT'S COST OF CAPITAL

The cost of capital and the discount rate are two concepts which are used interchangeably throughout the book. However, there is a distinction between the *firm's* cost of capital and *specific project's* cost of capital. Let us elaborate.

Firm's cost of capital

The firm's cost of capital is the rate employed to discount the firm's average cash flow, hence obtaining the value of the firm. It is also the weighted average cost of capital, as we shall see below. The weighted average cost of capital should be employed for project evaluation (i.e., calculating the *NPV*) only in cases where the risk profile of the new project is a 'carbon copy' of the risk profile of the firm.

Specific project's cost of capital

In any case where the risk profile of the individual project differs from that of the firm, an adjustment should be made in the required discount rate to reflect this deviation. To illustrate: suppose that the firm's weighted average cost of capital is 20% and the risk-free interest rate is 10%. The firm should discount the project's average cash flows, in general, at the 20% discount rate. However, consider a case where the firm faces a project whose cash flow is certain. What is the minimum required rate of return on this certain project? In this case it is clearly the 10% risk-free rate which reflects the opportunity cost that the firm could earn by investing its money in other safe assets. Similarly, if the project under consideration is characterized by very high risk, the 20% discount rate may be insufficient and a higher discount rate should be employed.

A formal analysis

For simplicity we assume a perpetual cash flow stream and no taxes. However, the same results can be obtained for a non-perpetual cash flow stream and when taxes exist. Let the firm's average cash flow be $\bar{x}$ and its market value be V. Hence there is some discount rate k which fulfils the following equality:

$$V = \frac{\bar{x}}{k}$$

Suppose now that the firm is considering a new investment whose initial outlay is I_0. Should the firm accept the new project? The decision is, of course, dependent on the average additional cash flow $\Delta \bar{x}$ due to the new project as well as its risk profile. Suppose that as a result of accepting the new project, we obtain a new value for the firm V_1 given by:

$$V_1 = \frac{\bar{x}_1}{k_1} = \frac{\bar{x} + \Delta \bar{x}}{k + \Delta k}$$

where $\bar{x}_1 = \bar{x} + \Delta \bar{x}$ and $k_1 = k + \Delta k$ are the appropriate new average cash flow and discount rate of the firm.

The condition $V_1 \geqslant V_0$ (where V_0 is the value of the firm before the investment) is not a sufficient condition to accept the project. The reason is that the firm invested \$$I_0$, hence the project should be accepted only if the value of the firm increases at least by I_0. Thus, the project should be accepted if and only if:

$$V_1 = \frac{\bar{x} + \Delta \bar{x}}{k + \Delta k} \geqslant V_0 + I_0 \quad \text{(or if } V_1 - V_0 \geqslant I_0)$$

This condition can be rewritten as:

$$\bar{x} + \Delta \bar{x} \geqslant k V_0 + k I_0 + \Delta k V_0 + \Delta k I_0$$

Dividing all terms by I_0 we obtain:

$$\frac{\bar{x}}{I_0} + \frac{\Delta \bar{x}}{I_0} \geqslant \frac{k V_0}{I_0} + k + \frac{\Delta k V_0}{I_0} + \Delta k$$

However, by definition we have, $V_0 = \bar{x}/k$ which implies that $k V_0 = \bar{x}$. Substitute $\bar{x}$ for $k V_0$ to obtain:

$$\frac{\bar{x}}{I_0} + \frac{\Delta \bar{x}}{I_0} \geqslant \frac{\bar{x}}{I_0} + k + \frac{\Delta k}{I_0} V_0 + \Delta k$$

Cancelling out $\bar{x}/I_0$ from both sides finally yields:

$$\frac{\Delta \bar{x}}{I_0} \geqslant k + \Delta k + \frac{\Delta k}{I_0} V_0$$

Since $\Delta \bar{x}/I_0$ is the additional required return on the new investment, we can write an equality sign to obtain the minimum *required rate of return* on the new investment:

$$\frac{\Delta \bar{x}}{I_0} = k + \Delta k + \frac{\Delta k}{I_0} V_0$$

To sum up, if $\Delta \bar{x}/I_0$ is equal to the sum of terms on the right-hand side, one is exactly indifferent to accepting or rejecting the project since in this case V_1

is exactly equal to $V_0 + I_0$. In other words, the *NPV* of the project given by $(V_1 - V_0) - I_0$ is precisely zero. If $\Delta \bar{x}/I_0$ is greater than this value, we obtain a positive *NPV*, namely $V_1 > V_0 + I_0$ and the project should certainly be accepted.

Let us analyze this implied cost of capital from the project. First note that if $\Delta k = 0$, then the new project is very similar in its risk profile to the firm's risk, hence the shareholders do not change their required discount rate. In this specific case where the project's risk is a carbon copy of the firm's risk, we have $\Delta \bar{x}/I_0 = k$, and the firm's discount rate which prevailed before taking the new investment also serves as the project's cost of capital.

If, on the other hand, $\Delta k > 0$, then in order to justify the acceptance of the project we should earn, in addition to k, a risk premium equal to $\Delta k + (\Delta k/I_0) V_0$, to compensate for the additional risk due to the new project.

Example
Assume that $k = 0.10$, $\bar{x} = \$10$, hence $V_0 = \bar{x}/k = 10/0.10 = \$100$. The firm considers a new investment whose initial cash flow is $I_0 = \$50$. It is further known that this project is very risky which will cause stockholders to increase their discount rate from 0.10 to $k_1 = k + \Delta k = 0.10 + 0.05 = 0.15$. What is the *minimum* required rate of return that the firm must earn on the new project?

Using our formula we obtain:

$$\frac{\Delta \bar{x}}{I_0} = k + \Delta k + \frac{\Delta k}{I_0} V_0$$

$$= 0.10 + 0.05 + \frac{0.05}{50} 100 = 0.15 + 0.10 = 0.25$$

Since the firm invests $I_0 = \$50$, a 25% return implies that $\Delta \bar{x}$ should be at least $\$12.5$ (since $\$12.5/\$50 = 0.25$) in order to make the project acceptable. Let us check this result. If indeed $\Delta \bar{x} = 12.5$, we obtain:

$$V_1 = \frac{\bar{x}_1}{k_1} = \frac{\bar{x} + \Delta \bar{x}}{k + \Delta k} = \frac{10 + 12.5}{0.10 + 0.05} = \frac{22.5}{0.15} = \$150$$

where V_1 is the value of the firm in the case where the new project is executed.

Thus, we indeed observe that at this critical point where the project's *NPV* is exactly equal to zero $V_1 = V_0 + I_0 = 100 + 50$. If $\Delta \bar{x} > \$12.5$ the project is characterized by a positive *NPV* which implies that $V_1 > V_0 + I_0$, and the firm should accept the project.

The above analysis reveals that the specific project's cost of capital is given by:

$$\frac{\Delta \bar{x}}{I_0} = k + \Delta k + \frac{\Delta k}{I_0} V_0$$

which varies from one project to another in accordance with the project's risk profile. However, if the new project does not change the firm's risk profile, we obtain:

$$\frac{\Delta \bar{x}}{I_0} = k$$

where $V_0 = \bar{x}/k$. Hence, the discount rate (which we identify later as the firm's weighted average cost of capital) is also the project's cost of capital.

While academicians as well as practitioners agree that each project has its own risk profile and hence its own discount rate, it is equally agreed upon that it is difficult, if not impossible, to estimate a separate cost of capital for each individual project. This is particularly true in light of the fact that the future variability of the cash flows of a potential project are unknown (namely, Δk is unknown). Thus, it is common to estimate the weighted average cost of capital of the firm, as a first approximation. In many cases (where $\Delta k = 0$) this estimate of the weighted average cost of capital is the suitable discount rate to be employed. However, when management considers a project to be relatively risky ($\Delta k > 0$), an additional risk premium should be added to the weighted average cost of capital. Similarly, if a project is less risky than the firm's risk ($\Delta k < 0$), a 'safety premium' should be deducted from the firm's weighted average cost of capital. While we state various statistical methods (in the next chapter) to estimate the firm's cost of capital, the adjustments made by management for a specific risk profile for the project under consideration remain mainly an art based on intuition and experience rather than scientific statistical methods.

In most of this chapter we assume that the project has the same risk profile as characterizes the firm (i.e., $\Delta k = 0$). We explain why the weighted average cost of capital is the appropriate discount rate, keeping in mind some changes in the figure may be needed to reflect the specific risk profile of the project under consideration.

The relationship between the cost of capital and firm's capital structure is analyzed by means of a numerical example in the next section.

WEIGHTED AVERAGE COST OF CAPITAL

Numerical example

For simplicity, let us first assume that all new investments are financed in the exact proportions of debt and equity given by the optimal financial structure, L^*. What is the cost of capital (discount rate) that the firm should use when evaluating a new project? Table 16.1 illustrates the case of a firm which has adopted a policy of financing investments with 40% debt and 60% equity, presumably on the assumption that this capital structure is optimal, given the firm's risk-return profile. Thus its initial capital structure (column 1 of Table 16.1) comprises $6 million of common stock yielding 15% in dividends, and $4 million of bonds on which it pays 5% interest. To simplify the discussion we assume that the firm distributes *all* of its net earnings as dividends; hence

Table 16.1

	Before the new investment ($)	New investment ($)	After the new investment ($)
Capital structure:			
Bonds (5%)	4,000,000	400,000	4,000,000
Stock	6,000,000	600,000	6,600,000
Total	10,000,000	1,000,000	11,000,000
Cash flows:			
Net operating income	1,100,000	110,000	1,210,000
Interest	200,000	20,000	220,000
Dividends	900,000	90,000	990,000

the required rate of return by the stockholder (for the given capital structure) is equal to the dividend yield.

Ignoring corporate taxes for the moment, we assume in Table 16.1 that the firm earns $1,100,000 on its $10 million of capital, paying out $200,000 (5% × $4 million) as interest to its bondholders and the remaining $900,000 as dividends to its common stockholders. Hence, the yield on the existing equity is 15% ($900,000/$6,000,000 = 15%).

Column 2 of Table 16.1 sets out the expected results of a proposed new investment. An additional $1 million is required to finance the investment, and the firm decides to raise 40% of this sum by issuing 5% bonds and the remaining 60% by issuing additional common stock, i.e., the firm desires to preserve its existing debt/equity ratio (2/3 in this example). What is the minimum required rate of return on the new investment, i.e., the rate of return which will leave the value of the existing shareholder equity unchanged?

In order to answer this question let us analyze the cost component of each element of the financing mix. Clearly one component of the required return consists of the $20,000 (5% × $400,000 = $20,000) which the firm must pay the new bondholders. In addition, though, Table 16.1 shows that the firm must earn an additional $90,000 if it does not want to reduce the earnings (dividends) on the existing equity. The $90,000 represents a 15% return on the new equity ($90,000/$600,000 = 15%) which will enable the firm to pay a 15% dividend to the new shareholders without affecting the dividends of the old shareholders. In other words, the new investment must earn $20,000 + $90,000 = $110,000 if the value of the existing equity is to remain unchanged by the new investment. If the operating returns are *less* than $110,000 the investment should be rejected; if it yields more than $110,000 it should be accepted since the position of the existing shareholders would be improved.

This contention can be illustrated using the data in column 3 of Table 16.1 which gives the firm's capital structure and cash flows *after* the new investment is accepted, on the explicit assumption that the critical amount, i.e., $110,000, is earned on the new project. As can be seen, the $110,000 is just sufficient to leave the position of the old stockholders unchanged; the earnings available for dividends for all classes of shareholder is $990,000, which represents an unchanged dividend (earnings) yield of 15% ($990,000/$6,600,000 = 15%). Should the firm earn less than this amount on the new investment, say only $44,000 rather than $110,000, the earnings available for dividends, after interest is paid, will be only $924,000 ($900,000 + 24,000); hence the dividend yield will decline from 15% to 14% ($924,000/$6,600,000 = 14%). Similarly, should the return on the new investment be more than $110,000, say $176,000, the existing stockholders will be better off. In this case, the firm again pays $20,000 to the new bondholders leaving $156,000 as the contribution of the new investment of the firm's shareholders. Thus, the total earnings available for distribution to the stockholders is $1,056,000 ($900,000 + $156,000) and the new dividend yield rises to 16% ($1,056,000/$6,600,000 = 16%).

Now let us turn to the analogous question of the discount rate which this firm should apply when evaluating an investment proposal's net present value (*NPV*). For the sake of convenience we assume that the project in our example involves an initial outlay of $1 million and generates a perpetual cash flow of $110,000 per year. Denoting the discount rate by k, the *NPV* calculation reduces to:

$$NPV = \frac{110,000}{k} - 1,000,000$$

To be consistent with our previous analysis, we must make the further stipulation that for the case in which $110,000 is earned, the *NPV* must be zero: otherwise the existing shareholders will not be indifferent to the project. Imposing this condition we have:

$$NPV = \frac{110,000}{k} - 1,000,000 = 0$$

The discount rate which equates the *NPV* to zero is given by:

$$k = \frac{110,000}{1,000,000} = 11\%$$

Thus in this example, the cost of capital is 11%. If the annual cash flow of the new project is greater than $110,000, the *NPV* (at 11%) will be positive and the firm should accept the project. If the annual cash flow is less than $110,000, the *NPV* calculated at the 11% cost of the capital will be negative, and the project should be rejected. These results are consistent with the previous analysis and confirm our conclusion that for earnings exceeding $110,000 the existing shareholders are better off; for earnings below $110,000 they are worse off; and for earnings exactly equal to $110,000 the shareholders are indifferent to the proposal. This relationship between the interests of existing shareholders and the *NPV* calculation of project acceptability can be ensured, in our example *if, and only if* the discount rate is set at 11%.

How should the 11% discount rate be interpreted? An examination of Table 16.2 shows that the 11% rate represents a *weighted average* of the required rate of return of the individual sources of financing, with each type of financing

Table 16.2

	Amount raised (in dollars) (1)	Proportion of total money raised (2)	Cost of the specific components (3)	Contribution to the cost of capital (4) = (2) × (3)
Debt	400,000	0.40	5%	0.40 × 5% = 2%
Stocks	600,000	0.60	15%	0.60 × 15% = 9%
			Weighted average cost of capital	11%

being given its proportionate weight in the firm's long-run target capital structure. Alternatively, the 11% can be viewed as the weighted average of the cost components. Since debt accounts for 40% of the firm's total financing mix, the contribution of the debt component to the cost of capital is 2% $(0.40 \times 0.05 = 0.02 = 2\%)$. Similarly, the contribution of the equity component is 9% $(0.60 \times 0.15 = 0.09 = 9\%)$. Combining the two components gives an overall cost of capital equal to 11%. The justification for using a discount rate (cost of capital) which reflects the costs of the individual sources of financing, weighted by their share in the firm's optimal (target) capital structure, reflects the fact that such a calculation ensures that the value of the existing owners' equity will be maximized. Setting a lower rate, as our numerical example showed, would induce the firm to accept projects which are not in the existing shareholders' best interest; setting the rate above the weighted average, on the other hand, would lead the firm to forgo projects whose acceptance would increase the value of the existing shareholders' equity.

Formal derivation

It is easy to show in a more formal way, that the project's cost of capital is the weighted average of the cost of equity and the cost of debt. First recall that we have shown earlier in this chapter that the project's cost of capital is given by:

$$\frac{\bar{x}}{V_L} = k$$

where the value of the firm is given by $V_L = \bar{x}/k$ and the subscript L indicates that we deal with a levered firm (that is, a firm which is partially financed with debt). Namely, the cost of capital is given by $k = \bar{x}/V_L$. Let us expand this term as follows:

$$k = \frac{\bar{x} - rB_L + rB_L}{V_L} = \frac{\bar{x} - rB_L}{V_L} + \frac{rB_L}{V_L}$$

which can also be rewritten as:

$$k = \frac{\bar{x} - rB_L}{S_L} \left(\frac{S_L}{V_L}\right) + r\left(\frac{B_L}{V_L}\right)$$

where S_L is the market value of the equity of the levered firm, B_L stands for the firm's debt, and by definition $V_L = S_L + B_L$. Note that the value of the equity is nothing but:

$$S_L = \frac{\bar{x} - rB_L}{k_e}$$

where k_e is the appropriate cost of equity and $\bar{x} - rB_L$ is the average cash flow which belongs to the stockholders (that is, net of the cash flow to bond-holders). Thus, one can write the shareholder's cost of capital as:

$$k = k_e\left(\frac{S_L}{V_L}\right) + r\left(\frac{B_L}{V_L}\right)$$

which is the weighted average cost of equity k_e and cost of debt r, and the weights are the proportions of equity (S_L/V_L) and debt (B_L/V_L) in the firm's capital structure. Another justification of the weighted average cost of capital and its relation to Modigliani and Miller's proposition II is given in Appendix 16A.

Corporate taxes and the weighted average cost of capital

The after-tax average cash flow of the levered firm is given by $\bar{x}_t$ where:

$$\bar{x}_t = (1 - T_c)(\bar{x} - rB_L) + rB_L = (1 - T_c)\bar{x} + T_crB_L$$

and the value of the firm V_L is given by:

$$V_L = \frac{\bar{x}_t}{k^*} = \frac{(1 - T_c)\bar{x} + T_crB_L}{k^*}$$

where k^* is the post-tax cost of capital. This equation can be rewritten as:

$$k^* = \frac{(1 - T_c)\bar{x}}{V_L} + \frac{T_crB_L}{V_L}$$

Add and subtract $(1 - T_c)rB_L/V_L$ to obtain:

$$k^* = \frac{(1 - T_c)(\bar{x} - rB_L)}{V_L} + \frac{(1 - T_c)rB_L}{V_L} + \frac{T_crB_L}{V_L}$$

or

$$k^* = \frac{(1 - T_c)(\bar{x} - rB_L)}{S_L}\left(\frac{S_L}{V_L}\right) + r\left(\frac{B_L}{V_L}\right)$$

where S_L is the value of equity. Since $(1 - T_c)(\bar{x} - rB_L)/S_L$ is the after-tax cost of equity, which we denote by k_e^*, we finally obtain:

$$k^* = k_e^*\left(\frac{S_L}{V_L}\right) + r\left(\frac{B_L}{V_L}\right)$$

Thus, we find that k^* is the weighted average cost of the equity and cost of debt. Note that the cost of debt in this formulation is r and not $(1 - T_c)r$. The reason is that the tax advantage of the debt is already taken into account in the cash flow (rT_cB_L – i.e., in the project's numerator) and hence should not be taken, once again, in the denominator.

Alternatively, one may choose not to include the interest tax shelter on the cash flow (numerator). In this case the interest tax-shelter will be taken into account in the denominator, namely in the discount rate. The cost of debt in this case will be $(1 - T_c)r$ rather than r. To see this, once again let us write the value of the firm as follows:

$$V_L = \frac{(1 - T_c)\bar{x}}{k^*}$$

(Recall the interest tax shelter is precluded from the numerator.) Hence:

$$k^* = \frac{(1 - T_c)\bar{x}}{V_L} = \frac{(1 - T_c)(\bar{x} - rB_L)}{V_L} + \frac{(1 - T_c)rB_L}{V_L}$$

which can be written as:

$$k^* = \frac{(1 - T_c)(\bar{x} - rB_L)}{S_L}\left(\frac{S_L}{V_L}\right) + (1 - T_c)r\left(\frac{B_L}{V_L}\right)$$

or

$$k^* = k_e^*\left(\frac{S_L}{V_L}\right) + (1 - T_c)r\left(\frac{B_L}{V_L}\right)$$

which is the weighted average cost of capital with $(1 - T_c)r$ rather than r as the cost of debt component.

Project evaluation and post-tax weighted average cost of capital

In project evaluation, one may choose either to include the interest tax shelter in the numerator and to discount it by:

$$k^* = k_e^*\left(\frac{S_L}{V_L}\right) + r\left(\frac{B_L}{V_L}\right)$$

or to preclude the interest tax-shelter from the cash flow and to discount it by lower cost of capital:

$$k^* = k_e^*\left(\frac{S_L}{V_L}\right) + (1 - T_c)r\left(\frac{B_L}{V_L}\right)$$

The two approaches yield precisely the same *NPV* for the project as long as the capital structure in every year of the project's life is held constant. However, since ignoring the tax shelter in the numerator and discounting the cash flow by

$$k_e^*\left(\frac{S_L}{V_L}\right) + (1 - T_c)r\left(\frac{B_L}{V_L}\right)$$

proved to be computationally much more simple, in the rest of the book we employ this approach.

Example

Let us assume the following parameters:

$$k_e^* \equiv \text{cost of equity} = 0.15$$
$$r \equiv \text{interest rate} = 0.10$$
$$T_c \equiv \text{tax rate} = 0.34$$

$$\frac{S_L}{V_L} = \frac{B_L}{V_L} \equiv \text{optimal capital structure} = 0.50$$

The firm is considering an investment of $I_0 = \$100$ whose annual net cash flow (not including the tax shelter) is $100 a year for two years. We show below that the two methods of treating the interest tax shield yield the same *NPV*, as long as the capital structure is kept constant.

Method I: incorporating the tax shield in the discount rate

In this case the firm's cost of capital is:

$$k^* = k_e^*\left(\frac{S_L}{V_L}\right) + (1 - T_c)r\left(\frac{B_L}{V_L}\right)$$

$$= (0.15 \times 0.5) + (0.66 \times 0.10) \times (0.5) = 0.108$$

or 10.8%, where the superscript indicates post-tax variable. The project's *NPV* is:

$$NPV = -100 + \frac{100}{1.108} + \frac{100}{(1.108)^2} \approx \$71.709$$

and the project's present value is given by:

$$PV = \frac{100}{1.108} + \frac{100}{(1.108)^2} = \$171.709$$

Method II: incorporating the tax shield in the numerator

In this case, the firm's cost of capital is given by:

$$k^* = k_e^*\left(\frac{S_L}{V_L}\right) + r\left(\frac{B_L}{V_L}\right) = (0.15 \times 0.5) + (0.10 \times 0.5) = 0.125 \text{ or } 12.5\%$$

The table below reveals the project's cash flows.

Time	$t = 0$	$t = 1$	$t = 2$
1. Cash flow not including the interest tax shelter	−100	+100	+100
2. Present value of remaining cash flow	171.71	90.25	0
3. Debt	85.855	45.125	0
4. Interest tax shelter ($T_c r B_L$)	0	2.9087	1.53425
5. Total cash flow including the interest tax shelter (5) = (1) + (4)	−100	102.9087	101.53425

The project's *NPV* when the interest tax shelter is taken into account in the cash flow is:

$$NPV = -100 + \frac{102.9087}{1.125} + \frac{101.53425}{(1.125)^2} = \$71.708$$

which is approximately the same as obtained under method I (the 0.01 difference is due to rounding). Note that the project's *PV* is \$171.71. Thus, in order to keep a constant debt/equity ratio, the firm has to borrow, at $t = 0$, half of that sum, namely \$85.855. At $t = 1$, the remaining *PV* of the project is only 90.25 which is the present value of the \$100 obtained at $t = 2$. Thus the firm should decrease its borrowing to half of this sum, \$45.125. The interest tax shelter, $T_c r B_L$, is obtained only at the end of each year, hence we get $2.9087 = 0.34 \times 0.1 \times 85.855$ at $t = 1$ and $1.53425 = 0.34 \times 0.1 \times 45.125$ at $t = 2$. It is quite obvious from this example that method II is computationally more involved, which explains why method I is more commonly used.

Adjusted net present value (ANPV) *approach*
According to this approach there are two steps in evaluating projects:

1. Calculate the project's *NPV* by assuming that it is financed purely by equity, and use the firm's cost of equity as the discount rate:

$$NPV = \sum_{t=1}^{n} \frac{(1 - T_c)S_t + T_c D_t}{(1 + k_U)^t} - I_0$$

where k_U is the cost of equity of the unlevered firm and D_t is the annual depreciation.
2. Adjust the *NPV* by adding (or subtracting) to it any benefit which this project induces. For example, if this project is relatively safe and allows the firm to borrow more money, one should credit this project with the interest tax shelter due to the potential borrowing power created by this project. For example, if due to the acceptance of the new project we can borrow more, \$B, without incurring any more risk, the adjusted net present value (denoted by *ANPV*) will be

$$ANPV = \sum_{t=1}^{n} \frac{(1 - T_c)S_t + T_c D_t}{(1 + k_U)^t} + \sum_{t=1}^{n} \frac{T_c r B_L}{(1 + r)^t} - I_0$$

In principle, this method should lead to a correct decision but it is difficult, if not impossible, to implement. This approach requires the firm to be able to specify in great detail the risk level attached to each project and its 'credit power', namely, how much the firm can borrow due to the new project without increasing its risk. This task is not simple and in practice is determined mainly by relying on experience and intuition and not on any quantitative method.

FINANCING A NEW PROJECT IN PRACTICE _____

We have assumed in the preceding analysis that the firm finances each new project by 40% debt and 60% equity, i.e., it was assumed that the firm finances *each* project in the same proportions as its optimal (target) capital structure. However, it is well known that in practice firms do not issue stocks and bonds simultaneously every time a need for additional long-term financial resources arises. This is especially true when the firm raises relatively small amounts of money, since often it is not economical to split such sums, by raising part of it by a bond issue and the rest by a stock issue. Thus, even a firm which has set a target financial structure will tend to deviate from this optimal mix from time to time. Figure 16.1 illustrates the financing policy of a hypothetical firm with a target capital structure of 40% debt and 60% equity. As can be seen from the graph, the proportion of debt decreases in the first two years. This does not necessarily mean that the firm issued common stock in these years; the decline in the share of debt in the total financing mix might reflect an increase in retained earnings during these same years, or the retirement of part of the firm's outstanding debt. In year 3 the firm 'corrects' for these deviations from its target capital structure by issuing bonds, thereby restoring the proportion of debt in the capital structure to 40%. This financing mix is retained in year 4, however, due perhaps to unusually favourable market conditions the firm raises additional debt in year 5, and the proportion of debt rises above the 40% target. In the future the firm presumably will meet its financial requirements by raising additional equity, once again restoring the long-run target capital structure. Thus even though the firm has set a specific debt policy, it will probably deviate in the short run from its target debt/equity ratio, because practical considerations (flotation costs, market considerations, etc.) make the alternative of raising capital each year by issuing a financing 'package', in fixed proportions of debt and equity, undesirable.

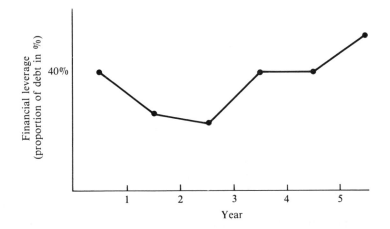

Figure 16.1

Should the fact that firms tend to deviate from their long-run optimal financial structure change our conclusion that the weighted average cost of capital be used as the discount rate for evaluating new investments? In order to answer this question let us once again turn to the numerical example given in Table 16.1, in which the cost component of debt is assumed to be 5%, the cost component of equity is 15% and the firm's target financial structure has been set at 40% debt and 60% equity. As noted in Figure 16.1, the firm does *not* issue bonds and stock each year, and as a result it tends to deviate temporarily from the optimal financial structure. Now suppose that the firm considers a project whose internal rate of return is 7% and which will be financed by a bond issue. Should the project be accepted? If we compare the project's internal rate of return (7%) with the cost of the debt component (5%) the project is clearly acceptable. However, if the internal rate of return is compared with the *weighted average* cost of capital of 11% (see Table 16.2), the project will be rejected. The question remains: which is the appropriate discount rate?

It is the accepted view that the firm should ignore temporary deviations from its long-run policy and use the weighted average cost of capital as a discount rate (i.e., 11% in our example). Thus the above project, whose internal rate of return is 7%, should be rejected, even though it is financed with the proceeds of a 5% bond issue. To clarify this line of reasoning, the reader should recall that the raising of low cost debt capital to finance this particular project will tend to raise the proportion of debt in the firm's capital structure above the target level of 40%. This, in turn, implies an increase in risk so that the firm will have to finance its projects in future years with relatively expensive equity capital, if the optimal debt level is to be restored. Should the firm use the specific interest rate, rather than the weighted average, it might conceivably accept a project with an internal rate of return of 7% in the years in which bonds are issued, while a project with a 14% rate of return might be rejected in a year in which equity capital was being raised.

To avoid such an error, firms should ignore transitory deviations from their target debt/equity ratios. Since increasing the proportion of debt this year *implies* that the firm must issue additional equity in the future, both of these sources must be taken into account when evaluating a new project. By using the weighted average cost of capital, the firm can avoid situations in which relatively low-return projects are accepted, while high-return projects are rejected, solely because of timing. In our example, using the 11% weighted average cost of capital, the project with a 7% rate of return will be rejected even though it is financed by debt, and the project with a 14% internal rate of return will be accepted even though the firm finances it with high cost equity.

To sum up, the individual types of financing constitute a 'joint product' which must be evaluated together if the firm is to optimize its investment decisions.[1]

---

1. See also Appendix 16A.

LEVERAGE AND THE SPECIFIC COSTS OF FINANCING

So far we have tried to show that the firm should employ a cutoff rate for new investment which reflects the weighted average of the costs of its specific sources of financing (debt, equity, and so on). However, it is crucial to recognize that *these individual costs are neither constant over time nor independent of the firm's overall financial strategy*. In general, all of the specific costs tend to rise as leverage is increased. Bondholders settle for a fixed annual income. However, for intense degrees of leverage, the risk of bankruptcy rises; hence the bondholders may lose all or part of their interest income and/or principal. The larger the risk of bankruptcy the higher will be the interest rate required to compensate the bondholders for incurring the greater risk. Thus, even relatively small firms who do not ordinarily influence money market rates will be confronted by an upward sloping supply curve for loans. The higher the proportion of debt, the higher the risk from the bondholders' point of view, and hence the higher will be the required interest rate. By an analogous argument we also expect the cost of preferred stock to rise with leverage. The higher the risk of bankruptcy, the higher will be the required return and hence the higher will be the specific cost of preferred stock. Similarly, as we pointed out in Chapter 14, the variability of per-share earnings increases with leverage. Since most, if not all, shareholders are risk-averse, *the greater the variability of the earnings stream, the higher will be the average required return on equity*. And needless to add the common shareholders are the most vulnerable to bankruptcy as well. Thus we also expect the cost of equity to rise with leverage.

In general, the greater the risk, the larger will be the required return, and therefore the higher will be the financing cost. However, one should remember that financial leverage is only one of the risk factors which affect the cost of capital. A second factor is the firm's economic or business risk. Each specific cost component is composed of the riskless interest rate (representing the time value of money) plus a risk premium. This risk premium, in turn, is determined by the firm's economic risk (which exists even when financial leverage is zero) plus its financial risk. Thus each specific source can be decomposed into two parts:

$$k_i = r + BRP + FRP$$

where:

k_i = ith cost component
r = riskless interest rate
BRP = business risk premium
FRP = financial risk premium

Does the above analysis necessarily imply that the firm's weighted average cost of capital must also rise with leverage? As can be seen from Table 16.3, the firm's cost of capital can have U-shaped properties even when the cost of each individual component increases with leverage. This reflects the fact that the firm's cost of capital is a *weighted average* of the individual sources. Up to a point, the inclusion of relatively low-cost debt in the capital structure reduces the average cost. However, for highly levered financing structures, both the cost of debt and of equity rise sharply, and these factors combine to reverse the impact of the inclusion of additional debt in the capital structure.

The numerical example of Table 16.3 is illustrated in Figure 16.2 which graphs the relationship between the cost of capital and financial leverage. Although both the cost of debt and equity are assumed to rise with leverage, the firm's weighted average cost of capital is U-shaped: initially decreasing to a leverage ratio of 40% and then rising. Since the goal of the firm is to minimize its cost of capital, thereby maximizing the value of the firm, 40% debt represents the *optimal* financial leverage in our specific example.[2]

CAPM approach

As we have seen, the firm's cost of equity can be decomposed into two components: the risk-free interest rate and a risk premium. This premium depends on the firm's risk level; the higher the risk the greater is the required rate of return on equity. Clearly a firm's business risk as well as the intensity of its financial leverage have a direct impact on the risk premium. Following this approach we found that the variability of a firm's earnings per share constitutes the appropriate measure of its riskiness.

Table 16.3

Capital structure		Cost of debt component	Cost of equity component	Weighted average cost of capital
Debt (1)	Equity (2)	(3)	(4) (in %)	(5) = (1) × (3) + (2) × (4)
0.1	0.9	5.0	15.0	14.00
0.2	0.8	5.0	16.0	13.80
0.3	0.7	6.0	17.0	13.70
0.4	0.6	7.0	18.0	**13.60**
0.5	0.5	8.0	20.0	14.00
0.6	0.4	9.0	22.0	14.20
0.7	0.3	10.0	25.0	14.50
0.8	0.2	12.0	28.0	15.20
0.9	0.1	15.0	35.0	17.00

2. For detailed discussion of the relationship of the minimization of the cost of capital to the maximization of the value of the firm, see F. D. Arditti, 'The Weighted Average Cost of Capital: Some Questions on its Definition, Interpretation and Use,' *Journal of Finance*, September 1973.

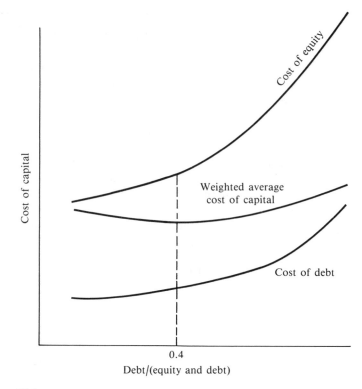

Figure 16.2

An alternative approach, based on the capital asset pricing model (*CAPM*) takes into account not only a firm's own earnings variability, but also the covariability of its earnings with those of other firms. Using this approach we assume that investors in the stock market hold a portfolio of stocks of many firms. Hence even though the variability of a firm's own earnings may be relatively high, its stock might still not be considered very risky due to the negative covariance with other securites in the portfolio.

Recalling the results of Chapter 12, the firm's risk, using the CAPM approach, is measured by its systematic risk, i.e., beta and not by its variance alone. Thus, the required rate of return on equity is given by k_{e_i}:

$$k_{e_i} = r + (Ex_m - r)\beta_i$$

where

r = the risk-free interest rate
Ex_m = the expected rate of return on the market portfolio
β_i = the ith firm's systematic risk
k_{e_i} = the required rate of return on equity of the ith firm.

Finally note that the CAPM approach does not ignore the variability of earnings, since the latter is included in beta. However, in the CAPM approach the variance is only one component of the systematic risk; beta reflects many covariances which may have a much stronger impact on the size of beta than does the firm's own variance. However, it is noteworthy that empirical studies have shown that a strong positive correlation often exists between the firm's beta coefficients and its variability. This implies that even if one accepts the underlying logic of the CAPM approach, variance can still be used as a useful proxy of the firm's systematic risk.

Historical mean return

Table 16.4 shows the historical record of rates of return distributions on various financial investments for the years 1926–91. Though the cost of capital is an *ex-ante* variable, one of the methods to estimate the cost of equity is simply by looking at the *ex-post* mean return. Table 16.4 reveals three important phenomena:

1. The long-term geometric mean rate of return, which can serve as an estimate for k_e, is 9.9% for common stocks and 12.1% for small stocks, where small stocks represent stocks of relatively small firms, i.e., more risky stocks.
2. Looking at the standard deviation and the distributions on the right-hand side, it is clear that there is a positive relationship between the distribution dispersion and the required mean rate of return. Since the standard deviation σ_i and β_i are highly correlated, the mean rate of return also increases as β_i increases, as predicted by CAPM.
3. The mean rate of return on treasury bills is about 3.5% per annum, hence the estimate of the risk-premium $(E(x_m) - r)$, which is an input employed to estimate k_e, is in the region 6.4–8.5% depending on the selected mean (arithmetic or geometric).

Thus, one may use the historical record either to estimate the risk premium $(E(x_m) - r)$, or directly to estimate k_e by looking at the *ex-post* geometric mean rate of return.

Dividend growth approach

The stock price is nothing but the present value of all future cash dividends:

$$P_0 = \sum_{t=1}^{\infty} \frac{d_t}{(1 + k_e)^t}$$

Assuming that dividends will grow each year at g%, we obtain:

$$P_0 = \frac{d_1}{1 + k_e} + \frac{d_1(1 + g)}{(1 + k_e)} + \frac{d_1(1 + g)^2}{(1 + k_e)^3} + \cdots = \frac{d_1}{k_e - g}$$

Table 16.4 Basic series: summary statistics of annual total returns 1926–91

Series	Geometric mean	Arithmetic mean	Standard deviation	Distribution
Common stocks	10.4%	12.4%	20.8%	
Small company stocks[a]	12.1	17.5	35.3	
Long-term corporate bonds	5.4	5.7	8.5	
Long-term government bonds	4.8	5.1	8.6	
Intermediate-term government bonds	5.1	5.3	5.6	
U.S. treasury bills	3.7	3.8	3.4	
Inflation	3.1	3.2	4.7	
				−90% 0% 90%

[a] The 1933 small company stock total return was 142.9%
Source: Ibbotson Associates.

Hence the cost of equity k_e is given by:

$$k_e = \frac{d_1}{P_0} + g$$

We elaborate on the assumptions which underlie this approach in the next chapter.

Price/earnings approach

A very simple approach is to look at the price/earnings ratio P_0/E where E is the last published earning per share and P_0 is the current stock price. Hence $k_e = E/P_0$ serves as an estimate of cost of equity. This approach yields an identical result to the dividend model approach in case of moderate growth. (See the next chapter for more details.)

Both the dividend approach and earnings per share approach rely on the

Table 16.5 Percentage of respondent firms using different methods of estimating cost of equity capital

Model	Percentage
1. Dividend growth model	20
2. Capital asset pricing model and dividend growth model	14
3. Earnings to current market price ratio	12
4. Bond yield plus risk premium	10
5. Accounting return on equity	8
6. Historical common stock return	4
7. Capital asset pricing model	2
8. Other (including judgemental and no response)	30
Total	100

Source: Blume, Friend and Westerfield, *op. cit.*

firm's earnings. Recall that if a firm pays out a fixed proportion of its earnings as dividends, the higher the dividends the higher the earnings per share E. Thus, it implies the lower E/P_0 the lower the cost of equity. Alternatively, the higher P_0/E the lower the cost of equity. This is exactly what the American executives claim in the earlier article. They claim that the Japanese firms sell equity at higher multiples of P/E and therefore their cost of equity is lower than that of American firms.

Methods used in practice

In their survey of the largest firms whose stocks are listed on the NYSE, Blume, Friend and Westerfield included a question regarding the method employed by the firm in estimating their cost of equity.

Table 16.5 reveals that many firms use more than one method. However, by far the dominant method is the dividend growth model; 20% rely solely on this method and more than 14% use this method as well as the CAPM. Only 2%, however, rely solely on the CAPM.

_____ CHANGES IN LONG-TERM FINANCIAL POLICY

At the beginning of this chapter we distinguished between a firm's long-run optimal financial strategy and temporary deviations around its target ratio (see Figure 16.1). Although purely transitory deviations can properly be ignored, this does *not* mean that the firm should not re-examine from time to time its long-term financial policy. Capital market conditions, government policy, the tax structure, and a myriad of other influences can, and do, change over time, often generating significant changes in the relative cost of alternative sources of funds. The need for such a revaluation of financial policy is illustrated in Table 16.6 which reproduces the data of Table 16.3 with one difference: we now assume that the interest rate has fallen by two percentage points. As a direct result, the weighted average cost of capital given in Table 16.6 is lower than that in the previous illustration. Moreover, as we can see from Figure

Table 16.6

Capital structure (%) Debt (1)	Equity (2)	Cost of debt component (%) (3)	Cost of equity (%) (4)	Weighted average cost of capital (5) = (1) × (3) + (2) × (4)
0.1	0.9	3.0	15.0	13.80
0.2	0.8	3.0	16.0	13.40
0.3	0.7	4.0	17.0	13.10
0.4	0.6	5.0	18.0	12.80
0.5	0.5	5.5	20.0	**12.75**
0.6	0.4	6.0	24.0	13.20
0.7	0.3	7.0	28.0	13.30
0.8	0.2	10.0	30.0	14.00
0.9	0.1	13.0	35.0	15.20

16.3 the proportion of debt in the optimal capital structure also changes. Prior to the fall in interest rates, the optimal proportion of debt was 40%; following the drop in interest rates, this proportion rises to 50%. Thus significant changes in the required returns on debt and equity not only change the absolute magnitude of the cost of capital, but the proportions of the optimal capital structure as well. Similarly, economic and social changes which affect the character of the firm's operations, particularly those which significantly

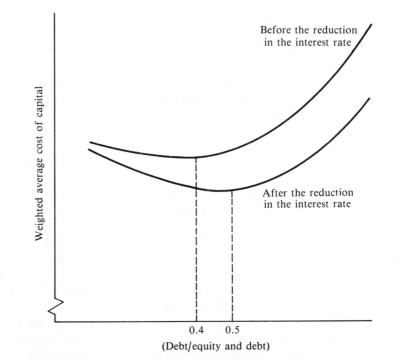

Figure 16.3

change its business risk, can have a parallel effect on its long-term financial strategy. All of these dynamic considerations suggest the dangers of getting 'locked-in' to a particular financial strategy, and the need for a periodic reassessment of the firm's long-term financial policies.

Competition between American and Japanese firms

Referring back to the article at the beginning of this chapter in which American executives claim that Japanese firms have a lower cost of equity (high P/E multiples) and also a lower cost of debt (are able to borrow at lower interest rates), why does this affect the competition between American and Japanese firms? Like in Figure 16.2 or 16.3, the cost of capital is a weighted average of the two sources of financing – equity and debt. Since both costs are lower for Japanese firms, the weighted average cost of capital (WACC) is always lower than the WACC of American firms (see Figure 16.4). For example, for simplicity assume that both Japanese and American firms have an optimal debt ratio of 0.50. The WACC is therefore 10% for the Japanese firms and 12% for the American. Now suppose that both firms directly compete in manufacturing cars and the internal rate of return (IRR) of producing the cars (considering all costs) is 11% for both the American and Japanese firms. Due to the differing WACC, the project is a positive NPV project for the Japanese firms (11% versus 10%) while it is a negative NPV project for the American firms (11% versus 12%). This is the point which is made in the article. (The causes of the lower cost of capital for Japanese firms are discussed in the next chapter.)

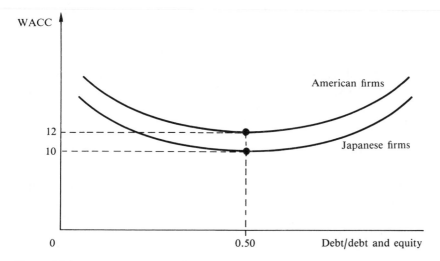

Figure 16.4

MARKET VALUE VERSUS BOOK VALUE

A firm's weighted average cost of capital can be calculated either on the basis of book (i.e., accounting values) or on the basis of market values. However, considerable confusion can be avoided if we emphasize from the very outset that market value provides the only acceptable method for estimating the cost of capital. Market values should be used when calculating each specific cost component; market weights should be used for calculating the weighted average. Perhaps the easiest way to justify the reliance on market values, rather than accounting values, is to consider a highly simplified yet not unrealistic example. Consider the case of a firm which issued a $100 bond bearing 5% interest a number of years ago. For the sake of simplicity we shall assume no corporate taxes or flotation costs, and that the bond (like the famous consols issued by Britain at the time of Napoleon) is a perpetuity having no maturity. The interest yield of the debt, therefore, is 5%:

$$100 = \frac{5}{1 + k_d} + \frac{5}{(1 + k_d)^2} + \cdots = \frac{5}{k_d} \quad \text{and} \quad k_d = \frac{5}{100} = 5\%$$

where k_d denotes the interest yield.

Now let us assume that after a number of years, world-wide inflation induces a sharp rise in domestic interest rates. To be specific let us assume that the interest rate on bonds of similar risk and duration doubles to 10%. Now given these circumstances, what do you expect the *market* price of the old bond to be? Clearly, they must now afford investors a return of 10% rather than 5% or no-one will hold them; but since the firm's interest payment is fixed (forever) at $5 per bond, the only way that this can be achieved is by a fall in the market price to $50. Hence in a free and competitive securities market, bondholders will try to sell the bonds as long as the price is over $50 (and the yield below 10%) but no investor will buy them until the price falls to $50 (and the yield equals the going market rate of 10%).

What impact does the above price change have on the interest cost of debt? If we use historical accounting book values, the issue price remains $100 and, therefore, the yield remains 5% as before. However, if we use the new market price of $50, the interest cost rises to 10%:

$$50 = \frac{5}{1 + k_d} + \frac{5}{1 + k_d} + \cdots = \frac{5}{k_d} \quad \text{and} \quad k_d = \frac{5}{50} = 10\%$$

Which of these two calculations, that is, the 5% or the 10%, is appropriate for our purposes? Recall that we have defined the cost of capital as the minimum required rate of return on investment, i.e., the discount rate to be used when evaluating new capital investment projects. Assuming for a moment a *hypothetical world in which all investment is financed by debt*, the use of accounting values suggests that investments should be accepted if they earn a return of more than 5%. The market value approach would stipulate 10% as the correct cutoff rate. However, only the latter is correct, because the firm can always earn more than 5% simply by repurchasing two of its own bonds in the market for $100 (recall that their market price is now $50) thereby saving $10 in interest payments and earning a rate of return of 10%. Thus the cost of the debt component cannot be less than its opportunity cost to the firm which in this case is 10%. Historical accounting costs and prices are simply irrelevant.

An analogous argument can readily be found to support the use of market prices when evaluating preferred and common stocks. Since market values are used in calculating each cost component, market weights should be used in calculating the weighted average cost of capital. Note that market values rather than accounting values should be used *even if the firm does not plan a new issue*. Retirement of existing debt or the repurchase of its own securities always represent alternative investment options to the firm. Although market values are the only conceptually correct figures to be used, it would be uneconomic and impractical to revise the calculation of the cost of capital daily, i.e., every time the market price of its securities changes. A compromise with reality is required in which the *average* market price or trend is identified; temporary deviations around the trend line can, and should, be ignored.[3]

_____ SUMMARY

We have shown in this chapter that the project's cost of capital which is also the minimum required rate of return, $\Delta \bar{x}/I_0$, is a function of the project's risk. This discount rate, in principle, varies from one project to another. In practice, we assume as a first benchmark that the project's risk does not change the risk profile of the firm. In this case, the weighted average cost of capital is equal to the firm's cost of capital, and this discount rate should be applied to project evaluation. If, however, the project under consideration is riskier (or less risky) than the risk profile of the firm, an adjustment should be made in the discount rate to reflect this extra risk (or extra safety).

_____ SUMMARY TABLE

Project's cost of capital

1. Project cost of capital is equal to $\Delta \bar{x}/I_0$ given by:

$$\frac{\Delta \bar{x}}{I_0} = k + \Delta k + \frac{\Delta k}{I_0} V_0$$

　　where:

3. In practice the book and market values of equity often differ markedly so that the use of book values would impart a serious bias to the estimate of the cost of capital. This is not usually true for debt, and in many instances substituting the book value of debt for its market value does not materially change the analysis.

$\Delta \bar{x}/I_0 = $ the minimum required rate of return on the new project

$k = $ discount rate applied to the firm, before the project is undertaken

$k_1 = k + \Delta k = $ new cost of capital given if the project is accepted

$V_0 = $ value of the firm before the new investment

2. If the project does not change the firm's risk profile we have, $\Delta k = 0$, hence cost of capital $\Delta \bar{x}/I_0 = k$, where $k = \bar{x}/V_0$.

Weighted average cost of capital

1. Pre-corporate tax:

$$k = k_e \left(\frac{S_L}{V_L}\right) + r\left(\frac{B_L}{V_L}\right)$$

2. Post-corporate tax: two variants:

$$k^* = k_e^* \left(\frac{S_L}{V_L}\right) + r\left(\frac{B_L}{V_L}\right) \qquad\qquad k^* = k_e^* \left(\frac{S_L}{V_L}\right) + (1 - T_c)r\left(\frac{B_L}{V_L}\right)$$

$\downarrow$ $\downarrow$

Interest tax shelter should be included in the cash flow

Interest tax shelter should not be included in the numerator

Post-corporate tax cost of equity

1. Dividend growth approach: $k_e^* = (d_1/P_0) + g$
2. CAPM approach: $k_{e_i}^* = r + (E(x_m) - r)\beta_i$
3. Historical geometric mean return: $k_e^* = \sqrt[n]{\prod_{t=1}^n (1 + R_t)} - 1$ where R_t is the rate of return on the stock in year t
4. Earnings/price ratio: $k_e^* = E/P_0$

QUESTIONS AND PROBLEMS

16.1 Assume a firm with an initial capital structure comprised of $15 million of common stock, yielding 18% in dividends and $5 million of bonds on which it pays 6% interest. Assume also that the firm distributes all of its net earnings as dividends. Answer the following questions, ignoring corporate taxes:

(a) How much is the net operating income of the firm?
(b) Suppose that the firm needs $4 million to finance new investments but desires to preserve its existing debt/equity ratio. What is the minimum required *NOI* on new investment?

16.2 A firm which pays 40% corporate tax desires to raise $2 million by issuing bonds at an interest rate of 7.5%.

(a) How much must the firm earn on the additional capital in order to preserve the return on equity?
(b) What is the specific after-tax cost of bonds?

16.3 Extraplast Colors, Inc. was established at the end of 1985. The initial required investment was $5,400,000 and the firm issued 120,000 shares of common stock at a price of $30 per share and $1,800,000 of bonds. The retained earnings at the end of 1986 were $600,000 and the firm was considered a new common stock issue in 1993. The financial policy of the firm during the years from 1986 till 1993 is summarized in the following table:

| Year | Retained earnings after tax ($) | Common stock issues | | Debt issues |
		Number of shares	Price per share ($)	Amount of money raised by bonds ($)
1985	600,000	–	35	–
1986	400,000	30,000	38	–
1987	700,000	–	40	2,000,000
1988	1,200,000	–	48	600,000
1989	500,000	50,000	50	–
1990	600,000	–	56	1,700,000
1991	1,400,000	40,000	60	–
1992	1,000,000	–	65	2,100,000
1993	1,500,000	–	70	–

(a) Calculate for each year the capital structure of the firm in dollars and in %.
(b) Illustrate graphically the financial policy of the firm.
(c) Did the firm follow a consistent policy? Explain.

16.4 'A firm which pays 7.5% as interest on debt should always accept a project whose internal rate of return is 13% as long as it can be financed by a bond issue.' Critically evaluate this statement.

16.5 Consider the following balance sheet and profit and loss statement of Gamma Corporation:

Balance sheet ($000)

Assets		Liabilities	
Cash	20,000	Bonds ($1,000 par value)	60,000
Inventories	180,000	Short-term loan	10,000
Plant and equipment	50,000	Common stock ($1 par value)	180,000
	250,000		250,000

Income statement ($000)

Earnings before interest and tax	100,000
Operating expenses	69,577
Operating income	30,423
Interest payments	3,150
Net income	27,273
Less 34% tax	9,273
Net income after tax	18,000
Net earnings per share	$0.10

The market price of a share of stock is $1.25
The market price of a bond is $750

Suppose that Gamma distributes all of its net earnings as dividends and that the specific cost of debt = interest after tax ÷ market price of a bond.

(a) Should the firm accept a project whose after-tax internal rate of return is 7%?
(b) Should the project be accepted if the firm's long-term target capital structure is 50% debt and 50% equity?

16.6 Suppose that we have a pure equity firm whose cost of capital is given by:

$$k_{e_i} = r + (E(x_m) - r)\beta_i$$

where $r = 0.05$, $E(x_m) = 0.10$, and $\beta_i = 1$.

(a) What is the firm's cost of capital?
(b) The firm is considering a new project. Suppose that β for the firm (including the new project) jumps to 2. Ignoring taxes, what is the minimum required rate of return from the new project?
   Additional information: value of the firm before taking the investment is $V_0 = \$1,000$, and the new investment is $I_0 = \$500$.

16.7 A firm whose market value is $V_0 = \$200$ and whose expected cash flow is $\bar{x} = \$20$ is considering taking a new project whose initial outlay is $I_0 = \$100$. The new project is less risky than the existing projects, and the discount rate for the firm would be *reduced* by 2 percentage points, should the firm decide to take the project. It is further given that 50% of the firm's resources consists of debt and 50% consists of equity.

(a) Find the minimum required rate of return that should be applied to the new project. Prove the formula that you employ.
(b) Suppose now that the project's *IRR* is larger by 8% in comparison to the minimum required rate of return that you have obtained in (a) above. Calculate the *NPV* of the new project. By how much does the value of the firm increase?
(c) Repeat your answer to (a) above when $V_0 = \$2,000$ rather than $200 and $\bar{X} = \$200$ rather than $20. Explain carefully your results.

16.8 The value of a firm is given by:

$$V_0 = \frac{\bar{x}}{k} = \frac{20}{0.1} = \$200$$

The firm considers a new investment whose initial outlay is $I_0 = \$100$. The project is very risky and the firm estimates that, if taken, the shareholders' discount rate will increase to $k_1 = 0.20$. Calculate the minimum required rate of return from the new project and show that for the marginal project (i.e., $NPV = 0$), $V_1 = V_0 + I_0$ where V_1 is the value of the firm if the project is taken.

16.9 Modigliani and Miller claim that after corporate tax (and no personal tax), the average cost of capital is given by k_L^*, where:

$$k_L^* = k_U^* \left[1 - T_c \frac{B_L}{V_L} \right]$$

where k_U^* is the cost of capital of pure equity firm, T_c the tax rate, B_L the value of debt, and V_L the value of the levered firm. (The superscript indicates post-tax variables.) Prove that Modigliani and Miller's after tax cost of capital k_L^* is nothing but

$$k^* = k_e^*\left(\frac{S_L}{V_L}\right) + (1 - T_c)r\left(\frac{B_L}{V_L}\right)$$

16.10 The value of the firm is given by $V = \bar{x}/k$. A new investment denoted by I_0 is considered.

(a) It is asserted that the investment should be taken only if $dV/dI_0 \geqslant 0$. Is this a correct assertion? (dV/dI_0 is the derivative of V with respect to I_0.)

(b) It is asserted that the investment should be taken only if $dV/dI_0 \geqslant 1$. Is this assertion correct?

(c) Take the derivative dV/dI_0 in order to calculate the minimum required rate of return from the new project. In what respect does it differ from the value given in Chapter 16? Explain the reason for the difference.

16.11 It is given that:

$$V_0 = \frac{\bar{x}}{k} = \frac{100}{0.1} = \$1,000$$

The firm is considering investing \$1,000 in a risk free asset. The interest on the risk free asset is $r = 0.05$. Employing the formula given in the text for $\Delta\bar{x}/I_0$, find the minimum required return on the new investment.

16.12 Show numerically that the *NPV* of the following project is identical if calculated under the two alternative methods: (a) tax shelter is incorporated in the numerator, and (b) tax shelter is incorporated in the denominator. Assume $I_0 = \$1,000$, $n = 10$ years, annual after tax (but without considerations of the interest, namely $(1 - T_c)\bar{X}$) cash flow $CF = \$100$, risk-free interest rate $r = 0.1$, cost of equity $k_e = 0.3$, $B_L/V_L = 0.75$, and $T_c = 0.34$.

16.13 The firm's cost of debt is given by:

$$k_d = r_0 + a_1(B_L/V_L)$$

and the firm's cost of equity is given by

$$k_e = k_0 + a_2(B_L/V_L)$$

where $a_1 > a_2 > 0$ and B_L is the value of the firm's debt, V_L, is the value of the firm, S is the value of equity and it is given that $V_L = B_L + S_L$.

(a) Let Y be the weighted average cost of capital. Write the formula for Y.

(b) Draw the graph of the cost function of each component and the cost of capital Y where B_L/V_L is measured along the horizontal axis.

(c) Find the capital structure B_L/V_L which minimizes the weighted average cost of capital stated in terms of a_1, a_2, k, and r.

(d) Solve for this capital structure when $k_0 = 0.10$, $r_0 = 0.05$, $a_2 = 0.04$, and $a_1 = 0.05$.

(e) How would you change your answer to (d) when $a_1 = a_2 = 0.04$? Explain.

16.14 The firm faces the following cost of debt function:

$$r = r_0 + a_1(B_L/V_L) + a_2(B_L/V_L)^2$$

where $r_0 = 0.10$, $a_1 = 0.05$, $a_2 = 0.01$ and B_L/V_L is the firm's capital structure parameter. The firm's management pays on its borrowing the marginal interest rate of $r = 0.1275$ (or 12.75%). Determine the firm capital structure B_L/V_L.

16.15 In 1993 the Federal Reserve increased the interest rate from 6 to 6.5%. As a result, the risk-free borrowing interest rate for a given firm increased from 7 to

8%. Assume two firms, one with systematic risk of $\beta = 0.5$ and the other with $\beta = 2$. Calculate each firm's cost of equity before and after the change in interest rate. Discuss your results. Assume that $E(x_m) = 10\%$ (i.e., the expected return on the market is 10%) and is not affected by the change in the interest rate.

16.16 In 1992 a firm pays a cash dividend of $1 per share, and this dividend is expected to grow every year by 10% forever. The firm's cost of equity $k_e = 20\%$. What is the current price (present value) of the firm's stock?

16.17 A firm paid in the past five years the following dividends per share:

Year	Dividend per share
1	$0.0
2	1.1
3	1.21
4	1.33
5	0.73

It is also known that the firm split its stock in a ratio $2:1$ in year 5. The current stock price is $P_0 = \$7.3$. Estimate the firm cost of equity k_e.

16.18 Assume that the after-tax cost of capital of the unlevered firm is $k_U^* = 10\%$. The capital structure of the levered firm is characterized by $B_L/V_L = 0.5$. Apply M & M's relationship between the levered and unlevered cost of capital to find:

(a) The cost of capital of the levered firm when the corporate tax rate is $T_c = 0$.
(b) The cost of capital of the levered firm when the corporate tax is $T_c = 0.48$, namely, before the reduction of the corporate tax rate in 1986.
(c) The cost of capital after the 1986 tax reduction to $T_c = 0.34$.

16.19 There are two firms identical in all respects apart from the capital structure. The value of the unlevered firm is:

$$V_U = \frac{(1 - T_c)\bar{X}}{K_U^*} = \frac{(1 - 0.34)100}{0.1} = \$660$$

Suppose that the corporate tax rates are increased from 34% to 46%. As a result of this change the value of the unlevered firm drops to $V_U = \$500$. The levered firm has a capital structure of $B_L/V_L = 0.5$.

(a) What is the levered firm's cost of capital before the tax rate increase?
(b) What is the levered firm's cost of capital after the tax rate increase?

16.20 Assume a world with no taxes and two firms identical in all respects apart from their capital structures. The rate of return on the pure equity, unlevered firm is given by $Y_U = X/V_U$ and the rate of return on the equity of the levered firm is given by $Y_L = X/S_L$ where S_L is the market value of the stock of the levered firm and X is the firm's EBIT (a random variable).

(a) What is the mean rate of return on the equity of the unlevered firm?
(b) What is the mean rate of return on the equity of the levered firm. Prove that the following relationship holds:

$$E(Y_L) = E(Y_U) + [E(Y_U) - r]B_L/S_L$$

where B_L is the value of debt of the levered firm.

(c) Show that the mean rates of return found in (a) and (b) above are consistent with the CAPM equilibrium relationship.

16.21 Two firms, one Japanese and one American, compete in a blind international auction to establish a new car manufacturing firm in Russia. The initial investment is $500 million and the net revenue after all costs (but interest) is assumed to be $100 million annually for 8 years. The cost of equity of the American firm is 14% and the cost of debt is 6%. The cost of equity of the Japanese firm is 10% and the cost of debt is 2%. Both firms have 50% debt and 50% equity financing policy. The firms offer (in the blind auction) the Russian Government $X for the right to have this project. The firm which offers the higher amount $X will win in the auction. Who do you think will win? What is the highest value of X that the Japanese can write down in their offer and what is the highest value X that the American firm can afford?

16.22 In 1992 the interest rate (or yield to maturity) on a 30 year triple A bond of IBM was 8%; the interest rate (yield to maturity) on a 'junk' bond of Koor Corporation was 40%. However, when Koor issued its bond, the yield to maturity was only 20%

(a) How can you explain the differences in the yield on IBM and Koor?
(b) How can you explain the jump from 20% to 40% of the yield of Koor's bonds?
(c) What is the current cost of debt of Koor, 20% or 40%?

_____ **APPENDIX 16A: WEIGHTED AVERAGE COST OF CAPITAL**

In the text we have presented the argument on behalf of the use of the weighted average cost of capital by means of numerical examples. In this appendix we present the Modigliani–Miller analysis of the appropriate cutoff rate for new investments – their proposition III.

Ignoring corporate taxes, the value of the unlevered firm is given by $V_U = \bar{x}/k$, where $\bar{x}$ is the average net operating income and k is the discount rate of the unlevered firm (which is equal to the yield Y_U on the stock of a pure equity firm). M & M's Proposition III asserts *that k should also be used as the cost of capital for a levered firm*. To illustrate this proposition it is sufficient to consider the extreme case in which a levered firm finances a new investment of I_0 dollars solely out of debt.

Since by proposition I (see Appendix 14B):

$$V_L = S_L + B_L = V_U$$

the value of the equity before the new investment was

$$S_L = V_U - B_L$$

Assume that the rate of return on the new investment is R, hence the new net operating income is $\bar{x} + RI_0$ and the value of the firm becomes

$$V_L = \frac{\bar{x} + RI_0}{k} - I_0 = V_U + \frac{RI_0}{k} - I_0$$

and the value of equity after the investment (S_L) is given by:

$$S_L = V_U + \frac{RI_0}{k} - B_L - I_0 = S_L + I_0\left(\frac{R}{k} - 1\right)$$

Thus the value of the equity rises only if $R > k$, i.e., if the internal rate of return on the new project exceeds k, hence k should be used as the cost of capital of levered, as well as unlevered, firms. The same conclusion holds when the firm finances the new investment I_0 by equity or by any combination of debt and equity.

Now let us turn to the question of whether the proposed discount rate, k, is indeed the weighted average cost of equity and debt.

A levered firm has a capital structure with the proportion B_L/V_L of debt and S_L/V_L of equity. Since the cost of debt is $r\%$, and the cost of equity is $Y_L = Y_U + (Y_U - r)B_L/S_L$ (by proposition II), the weighted average cost of capital is given by:

$$\frac{B_L}{V_L} r + \frac{S_L}{V_L} Y_L = \frac{B_L}{V_L} r + \left[\frac{S_L}{V_L} Y_U + (Y_U - r) \frac{B_L}{B_L}\right]$$

$$= \frac{B_L}{V_L} r + \frac{S_L}{V_L} Y_U + \frac{S_L}{V_L} \frac{B_L}{S_L} Y_U - \frac{S_L}{V_L} \frac{B_L}{S_L} r$$

$$= Y_U\left(\frac{S_L}{V_L} + \frac{B_L}{V_L}\right)$$

but since $V_L = S_L + B_L$, the weighted average cost of capital is simply equal to Y_U. If we recall that $Y_U = \bar{x}/V_U$ or $V_U = \bar{x}/Y_U$, which can be rewritten as $V_U = \bar{x}/k$, when $k = Y_U$. Thus, the weighted average cost of capital Y_U is the proper cutoff rate, k, that should be used in project evaluation.

SELECTED REFERENCES

Agmon, T., Ofer, A. R., and Tamir, A., 'Variable Rate Debt Instruments and Corporate Debt Policy,' *Journal of Finance*, December 1980.

Arditti, Fred D. and Levy, Haim, 'The Weighted Average Cost of Capital as a Cutoff Rate: A Critical Analysis of the Classical Textbook Weighted Average,' *Financial Management*, Autumn 1977.

Ben-Horim, Moshe, 'Comment on the Weighted Average Cost of Capital as a Cutoff Rate,' *Financial Management*, Summer 1979.

Benzion, U., Rapoport, A., and Yagil, J., 'Discount Rates Inferred From Decisions: An Experimental Study,' *Management Science*, 1989.

Block, Stanley and Block, Marjorie, 'The Financial Characteristics and Price Movement Patterns of Companies Approaching the Unseasoned Securities Market in the Late 1970s,' *Financial Management*, Winter 1980.

Bodie, Z. and Friedman, B. M., 'Interest Rate Uncertainty and the Value of Bond Call Protection,' *Journal of Political Economy*, February 1978.

Butler, J. S. and Schaschter, B., 'The Investment Decision: Estimation Risk and Risk Adjusted Discount Rates,' *Financial Management*, Winter 1989.

Chen, Andrew H. and Kensinger, John W., 'Innovations in Corporate Financing: Tax Deductable Equity,' *Financial Management*, Winter 1985.

Craine, R. N. and Pierce, J. L., 'Interest Rate Risk,' *Journal of Financial and Quantitative Analysis*, November 1978.

Fabozzi, F. J. and Hershkoff, R. A., 'The Effect of the Decision to List on a Stock's Systematic Risk,' *Review of Business and Economic Research*, Spring 1979.

Fox, A. F., 'The Cost of Retained Earnings – A Comment,' *Journal of Business Finance and Accounting*, 4, 4, 1977.

Friend, Irwin and Tokutsu, Ichiro, 'The Cost of Capital to Corporations in Japan and the U.S.A.,' *Journal of Banking and Finance*, June 1987.

Gentry, James A. and Pyhrr, Stephen A., 'Stimulating an EPS Growth Model,' *Financial Management*, Summer 1973.

Gordon, M. J. and Gould, L. I., 'The Cost of Equity Capital: A Reconsideration,' *Journal of Finance*, June 1978.

Harris, Robert S., 'The Refunding of Discounted Debt: An Adjusted Present Value Analysis,' *Financial Management*, Winter 1980.

Henderson, Glenn V. Jr, 'Shareholder Taxation and the Required Rate of Return on Internally Generated Funds,' *Financial Management*, Summer 1976.

Ibbotson, R. G., 'Price Performance of Common Stock New Issues,' *Journal of Financial Economics*, September 1975.

Johnson, K. B., Morton, T. G., and Findlay, M. C. III, 'An Empirical Analysis of the Flotation Cost of Corporate Securities, 1971–1972,' *Journal of Finance*, September 1975.

Lakonishok, Joseph and Ofer, Aharon R., 'The Value of General Price Level Adjusted Data to Bond Rating,' *Journal of Business Finance and Accounting*, Spring 1980.

Livingston, M., 'The Pricing of Premium Bonds,' *Journal of Financial and Quantitative Analysis*, September 1979.

Makhya, Aril K. and Thompson, Howard E., 'Comparison of Alternative Models for Estimating the Cost of Equity Capital for Electric Utilities,' *Journal of Economics and Business*, February 1984.

Mandelker, G. and Raviv, A., 'Investment Banking: An Economic Analysis of Optimal Underwriting Contracts,' *Journal of Finance*, June 1977.

McDonald, John G. and Osborne, Alfred E. Jr, 'Forecasting the Market Return on Common Stocks,' *Journal of Business Finance and Accounting*, Summer 1974.

Merton, Robert C., 'On the Pricing of Corporate Debt: The Risk Structure of Interest Rates,' *Journal of Finance*, May 1974.

Ofer, A. R. and Taggart, R. A. Jr, 'Bond Refunding: A Clarifying Analysis,' *Journal of Finance*, March 1977.

Shiller, R. J. and Modigliani, F., 'Coupon and Tax Effects on New and Seasoned Bond Yields and the Measurement of the Cost of Debt Capital,' *Journal of Financial Economics*, June 1979.

Smirlock, Michael and Yawitz, Jess, 'Asset Returns, Discount Rate Changes and Market Efficiency,' *Journal of Finance*, September 1985.

Smith, C. W. Jr, 'Alternative Methods for Raising Capital: Rights versus Underwritten Offerings,' *Journal of Financial Economics*, December 1977.

Soldofsky, Robert M. and Miller, Roger L., 'Risk–Premium Curves for Different Classes of Long-term Securities, 1950–66,' *Journal of Finance*, June 1969.

Stoll, H. R., 'The Pricing of Security Dealer Services: An Empirical Study of NASDAQ Stocks,' *Journal of Finance*, September 1978.

Weinstein, M. I., 'The Effect of a Rating Change Announcement on Bond Price,' *Journal of Financial Economics*, December 1977.

White, R. W. and Lusztig, P. A., 'The Price Effects of Rights Offerings,' *Journal of Financial and Quantitative Analysis*, March 1980.

Wilcox, J. W., 'The P/B–ROE Valuation Model,' *Financial Analyst Journal*, July/August 1984.

Yawitz, J. B., 'Risk Premia on Municipal Bonds,' *Journal of Financial and Quantitative Analysis*, September 1978.

Zanker, F. W. A., 'The Cost of Capital for Debt-financed Investments,' *Journal of Business Finance and Accounting*, 4, 3, 1977.

Zwick, B., 'Yields on Privately Placed Corporate Bonds,' *Journal of Finance*, March 1980.

17

Measuring the Cost of Capital

ARTICLE 34

Stocks at the End of Recessions

As previous recessions ended, stocks were generally priced low compared with earnings, dividends, or book value (companies' assets minus liabilities). They aren't now. Figures are for the Standard & Poor's 500-stock average, one month after each recession ended.

	Ratio of stock prices to		Short-term interest rates	Earnings growth following year
	Earnings	Dividends		
1949	7	15	1.3%	22%
1954	11	20	1.4	31
1958	14	25	1.5	17
1961	21	34	1.6	15
1970	18	29	2.4	11
1975	10	24	3.2	24
1980	8	22	4.6	3
1982	11	20	5.8	10
Now	26	34	3.6	41*

*Projected growth in 1992 from 1991.
Sources: Ned Davis Research Inc., Standard & Poor's, Ibbotson Associates, Institutional Brokers Estimate System. Adapted from *Wall Street Journal*, April 16, 1992, p. C1.

The figures given in article 34 report the ratio of price to earnings (P/E), ratio of price to dividends (P/d), and short-term interest and growth rates projected in 1992. Although these figures correspond to the S&P Index (an average of 500 stocks), the same type of data exists for individual firms. Which of these figures measure the firm's cost of capital? Can we use the E/P ratio (the reciprocal of the P/E ratio) as the cost of equity? Do we obtain a better measure by employing the ratio d/P plus the growth in earnings? Can we use short-term interest rates as the cost of debt plus the growth rate (denoted by g) as the cost of equity? Should we use the interest rate on long-term instruments as a measure of debt? Moreover, if one uses the last approach, is it enough to measure the growth in earnings for one year or would a better measure be an estimate using the last five or ten years of growth in earnings? Is the relevant growth the growth in earnings or dividends?

We analyze issues like the ones given above: does the fall in the stock's price affect the firm's cost of capital? What about a fall in the bond's price?

Having surveyed the theoretical arguments supporting the use of a weighted average cost of capital as the cutoff rate for evaluating new investments, we turn in this chapter to the prosaic, but no less important, question of its measurement. We shall first discuss the ways in which the cost of each individual type of financing (debt, preferred stock, common stock, and retained earnings) can be estimated, *given the firm's target capital structure*. Answering such questions, we then set out a practical method for calculating the firm's weighted average cost of capital using General Electric and IBM as examples. The cost of capital estimation of other firms (e.g., AMC, Contelo, Xerox, etc.) is left as problem assignments.

COST OF INDIVIDUAL COMPONENTS

The specific cost of each component is the minimum rate of return required by the suppliers of capital. For example, the specific cost of the bond component of the financing mix is the yield required by bondholders. Clearly the payment of interest *without* dilution of earnings per share implies that the firm must earn at least this rate on its investment. The minimum rate of return, which ensures no dilution of shareholders' earnings, constitutes the 'specific cost' of debt or the 'cost of debt component'. A similar definition will be used for the equity component.

To avoid any confusion the reader should note that these specific costs should *not* be used as the cutoff rate in project evaluation. The former are estimated solely for the purpose of calculating the weighted average cost of capital; and it is the weighted average which constitutes the appropriate cutoff point (i.e., discount rate) when evaluating the feasibility of investments. Thus the specific costs of debt and equity presented in this chapter are the appropriate costs to be used when calculating the weighted average cost of capital.

SPECIFIC COST OF DEBT

Given the firm's target debt/equity ratio L^*, let us first turn our attention to the calculation of the specific cost which is to be assigned to the debt component of the weighted average cost of capital. Suppose that a firm raises $1 million by issuing 1,000 bonds at a unit price of $1,000 and at an interest rate of 8%, i.e., the firm pays the holder of each bond $80 interest at the end of each year. Also assume that these bonds will be redeemed after ten years. Hence, at the end of the tenth year the firm pays the bondholder $80 interest plus an additional $1,000 to retire the bond's principal. Ignoring corporate taxes for a moment, Table 17.1 shows that the firm must earn *at least* $80,000, i.e., 8% on the $1 million raised by the bond issue in order to meet the interest payments without incurring or generating any dilution of earnings. If the firm invests the proceeds of the bond issue at exactly 8%, net operating income will be increased by $80,000, i.e., by an amount just sufficient to pay the bond interest. As a result net income is again $1 million and therefore the rate of return on the initial investment is not affected by the new investment or its financing which remains 10%. Hence the minimum rate of return on the new investment which preserves the return on existing investment is 8%. In terms of this chapter, 8% is the 'specific cost' of the debt component which should be used when calculating the weighted average cost of capital.

Table 17.1 sets out the cash flow for only one year. The entire financing picture can be seen more clearly when we consider the firm's aggregate cash outflows to the bondholders. Over the entire life of the bonds, the firm must pay the bondholders the following stream of cash payments:

First year	Second year	...	Tenth year
$80,000	$80,000	...	$1,080,000

The bondholders receive $80,000 interest per year over a period of ten years, plus an additional $1 million at the end of the tenth year which represents the redemption of the principal. Since we assume that each bond is sold for $1,000, we can now analyze the cash flow of a single bond in order to determine the specific cost of the bonds. Clearly, the new investment must yield sufficient funds to meet the cash outflows to the bondholders. Denoting the specific cost of the debt component by k_d, we have:

$$1,000 = \frac{80}{1 + k_d} + \frac{80}{(1 + k_d)^2} + \cdots + \frac{1,080}{(1 + k_d)^{10}}$$

The discount rate, k_d, which solves this equation is exactly 8%. If the firm earns 8% on the new investment it will just be able to pay the interest and principal of the bonds out of the proceeds of the investment. Any project whose internal rate of return is lower than 8% will not generate sufficient cash flows to pay the interest and principal to the bondholders, and therefore will reduce

Table 17.1

	Before the bond issue ($)	After the bond issue ($)
Initial investment	10,000,000	10,000,000
Additional investment	–	1,000,000
Total	10,000,000	11,000,000
Net operating income	1,000,000	1,080,000
Interest	–	80,000
Net income	1,000,000	1,000,000
Rate of return on equity	10%	10%

earnings per share. In this sense, 8% represents the specific cost to be assigned to the debt component of the weighted average cost of capital.

Adjustment for corporate taxes

To this point we have ignored corporate taxes. In reality, the specific cost of debt is significantly lower, because in the USA corporate interest payments are deductible for tax purposes. Table 17.2 illustrates the calculation of the after-tax of debt, assuming a 34% corporate tax rate. (We again employ the basic data of Table 17.1). Column 1 of Table 17.2 sets out the firm's financial condition *before* the new bond issue, but *after* the payment of corporate taxes. Due to the impact of the corporate tax, the rate of return on invested capital is only 6.6% compared with the pretax return of 10%. Column 2 of Table 17.2 isolates the *changes* in the financial figures generated by the new $1 million bond issue on the assumption that, for the moment at least, the firm does not invest the proceeds of the bond issue. As a result, operating income remains unchanged at $1 million. However, as the firm must pay interest on the debt, earnings after interest are reduced by $80,000 to $920,000. Since interest payments are tax-deductible, the firm's tax bill is only $312,800, and the after-tax rate of return on existing equity falls from 6.6 to 6.072%.

How can we account for the fact that although the firm pays $80,000 interest to the bondholders, its post-tax flow is reduced by only $52,800? Although the bondholders do receive $80,000 each year as interest, only $52,800 is payable out of net profits, the remaining $27,200 coming from the reduction in corporate taxes. The firm pays the bondholders $52,800 and the Internal Revenue Service, so to speak, pays the other $27,200, because of its willingness to recognize corporate interest payments as a tax-deductible expense.

If we denote the annual pre-tax interest payment by the letter C and the corporate tax rate by the letters T_c, the annual *after-tax* interest cost to the firm is only $(1 - T_c)C$. The specific after-tax cost of the debt component is given by that rate of discount, k_d^* which equates the after-tax cash flow generated by

Table 17.2

	Before the bond issue ($) (1)	After the bond issue but before the investment ($) (2)	After the bond issue and the investment ($) (3)
Total investment	10,000,000	10,000,000	11,000,000
Operating income	1,000,000	1,000,000	1,080,000
Interest	–	80,000	80,000
Earnings after interest	1,000,000	920,000	1,000,000
Corporate tax (34%)	340,000	312,800	340,000
Net after-tax earnings	660,000	607,200	660,000
Existing investment	10,000,000	10,000,000	10,000,000
New debt	–	1,000,000	1,000,000
After-tax rate of return on equity	6.6%	6.072%	6.6%

the bond with its initial purchase price:

$$1,000 = \frac{(1 - T_c)80}{1 + k_d^*} + \frac{(1 - T_c)80}{(1 + k_d^*)^2} + \cdots + \frac{(1 - T_c)80}{(1 + k_d^*)^{10}} + \frac{1,000}{(1 + k_d^*)^{10}}$$

Assuming $T_c = 34\%$, the discount rate which solves the equation is 5.28%. If the proceeds of the bond issue are invested to yield either 8% on a pre-tax basis, *or equivalently* 5.28% on an after-tax basis, the firm's return on equity will remain unchanged. This is illustrated in column 3 of Table 17.2. Hence the after-tax specific cost of debt is 5.28%, or more generally:

$$k_d^* = (1 - T_c)k_d$$

where k_d denotes the pre-tax specific cost of debt, k_d^* denotes the after-tax cost and T_c denotes the corporate tax rate. Other things being equal, the higher the corporate tax rate, the lower will be the effective cost of using debt, since the Internal Revenue Service will cover a large share of the total interest cost. Moreover, it should be emphasized that it is the after-tax cost of debt financing which is relevant to the firm and its shareholders. On occasion, we employ 'pre-tax', or 'no tax', examples for simplicity or for illustrative purposes only. In actual practice, however, no firm can afford to ignore the tax implications of its investment and financing policies.[1]

Flotation costs

In general, a new issue of any type of security will incur flotation costs which reflect the administrative expenses, registration and legal fees, and risks associated with the raising of capital, as well as the need to underprice the issue relative to outstanding securities in order to induce investors to acquire the new securities. The effect of these costs is to reduce the proceeds to the firm, thereby raising the specific cost of the capital raised. Using our previous example of the 8% bond issue, let us now assume that the 'spread' between the price the public pays for the bonds (i.e., $1 million) and the net proceeds to the firm is $52,800, that is, the flotation costs are $52.8 per bond. The latter sum reflects all of the costs (including any underpricing) necessary to float the bond issue. How does this affect the cost of the bonds? The after-tax specific cost is now given by the solution of the following formula:

$$947.2 = \frac{(1 - T_c)80}{(1 + k_d^*)} + \frac{(1 - T_c)80}{(1 + k_d^*)^2} + \cdots + \frac{(1 - T_c)80 + 1000}{(1 + k_d^*)^{10}}$$

and k_d^* rises from 5.28% (see previous example which ignored flotation costs) to 5.997%. Thus the effective after-tax cost of the bond component is increased by the necessity to cover the expenses incurred during bond issue, and in general the higher the flotation costs, the higher will be the specific cost of the capital.

---

1. See for example, F. D. Arditti and H. Levy, 'Pre-tax and Post-tax Discount Rates,' *Journal of Business Finance*, 1971.

The impact of a given flotation cost on the specific cost of the bonds also depends on the maturity of the debt. Figure 17.1 illustrates the relationship for 2% and 10% flotation costs and the length to maturity. For simplicity, we continue to assume a bond with a face value of $1,000 which pays 8% annual interest after taxes, i.e., annual after-tax interest of $80. The curve marked 2% describes the case in which the net proceeds to the firm are $980 for each bond sold; the graph marked 10% sets out the case in which the net proceeds to the firm are only $900. For short-term bonds, the specific cost of debt rises sharply. For example, for a one-year bond, the cost rises from 8% to 10.2% when flotation costs are 2% and to 20% when flotation costs are assumed to be 10%. However, in the relevant range for long-term debt, say twenty years, the specific cost rises only moderately to 8.21% when flotation costs are 2% and

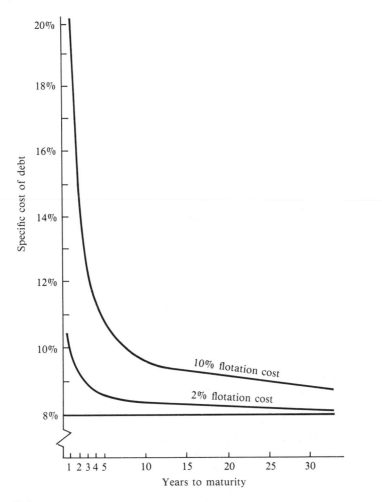

Figure 17.1

to 9.1% when flotation costs are assumed to be 10%. In general, the greater the number of years to maturity, the smaller is the impact of a given spread on the cost of the debt component.

SPECIFIC COST OF PREFERRED STOCK _____

Preferred stock is a hybrid security in the sense that it has some properties of bonds and others which are similar to common stock. Like bondholders, preferred shareholders typically receive a *fixed* annual income, called the preferred dividend; but as is true of common stock, failure to pay the preferred dividend will not cause bankruptcy. On the other hand, in the event that the firm fails, preferred shareholders are in an inferior position to the firm's debtors; the latter are compensated *before* the preferred shareholders, although as the name itself suggests, preferred stockholders have a prior claim to the firm's income and assets *vis-à-vis* the holders of common stock.

For the purposes of calculating the weighted average cost of capital, the specific cost of a preferred stock will be defined as follows:

$$k_p^* = \frac{d}{P_0}$$

where d denotes the fixed annual dividend and P_0 is the *net* issuing price (after deducting flotation costs). Assuming a net price of $95 and a dividend of $5, the specific cost of the preferred stock would be:

$$k_p^* = \frac{5}{95} = 5.26\%$$

Because a preferred stock represents a greater risk to the investor than a perpetual bond, the dividend yield of preferred stocks will usually be greater than the interest yield on long-term bonds. This gap is even greater from the viewpoint of the firm because dividends, unlike interest, are *not* tax deductible. The tax consideration is illustrated in Table 17.3 which reproduces our previous numerical example of a firm confronted with a $1 million investment with an 8% internal rate of return. In column 2 of Table 17.3 we assume that the project is financed by a bond issue yielding 8% interest. As we have already noted, the specific after-tax cost of debt is 5.28%. Since the project also earns 5.28% *after taxes*, earnings per share are not diluted by this investment-financing combination. Column 3 analyzes the cash flows when the same project is financed by 8% preferred stock. In this case the pre-tax internal rate of return on the project does not suffice to cover the 8% preferred dividend and, as a result, the rate of return to the firm's existing shareholders falls to 6.32%. Column 4 repeats the experiment assuming a project return of 12.12%. In this instance, the annual *pre-tax* return of $1,121,200 is just sufficient to cover the *post-tax* 8% preferred dividend, leaving the existing investor's return unchanged at 6.6%. Unlike the case of the 8% bond, whose *after-tax* specific cost is only 5.28%, the *after-tax* specific cost of an 8%

Table 17.3

	Before the new investment ($) (1)	After the new investment		
		Pre-tax rate of return = 8%		Pre-tax rate of return = 12.12%
		Financed by bonds ($) (2)	Financed by preferred stock ($) (3)	Financed by preferred stock ($) (4)
Total investment	10,000,000	11,000,000	11,000,000	11,000,000
Operating income	1,000,000	1,080,000	1,080,000	1,121,200
Interest (8%)	–	80,000	–	–
Earnings after interest	1,000,000	1,000,000	1,080,000	1,121,200
Corporate tax (34%)	340,000	340,000	367,200	381,208
Net earnings after interest and taxes	660,000	660,000	712,800	739,992
Dividend on preferred stock (8%)	–	–	80,000	80,000
Net earnings available for common stock	660,000	660,000	632,800	659,992
Equity	10,000,000	10,000,000	10,000,000	10,000,000
Bonds	–	1,000,000	–	–
Preferred stock	–	–	1,000,000	1,000,000
Rate of return on equity	6.6%	6.6%	6.32%	6.6%[a]

[a] The small difference is due to rounding.

preferred share remains 8%, because the firm must earn 8% *after-tax* to meet its obligation to the preferred shareholders. Dividends, unlike interest, must be paid out of net after-tax profits. Analogously we might say if k_p^* denotes the *after-tax* specific cost of a preferred stock, its pre-tax specific cost is given by:

$$\frac{k_p^*}{1 - T_c}$$

In our numerical example in which $k_p^* = 8\%$ and $T_c = 34\%$, we find that the pre-tax specific cost k_p is 12.12%:

$$k_p = \frac{k_p^*}{1 - T_c} = \frac{0.08}{0.66} = 12.12\%$$

These relationships are summarized in Table 17.4. A 34% corporate tax rate greatly enhances the desirability of using debt. In the case of preferred stock the firm must earn $1.52 (before taxes) for every $1 of dividends just to break even. In the case of a bond, $1 of (pre-tax) earnings is sufficient to pay $1 of interest. The explanation is straightforward; the Internal Revenue Service simply refuses to share in the cost of equity financing, thereby creating a strong bias in favor of debt financing. In terms of our analysis, the specific cost of preferred stock will usually be substantially greater than that of debt.

Table 17.4

	Bonds	Preferred stock
Pre-tax specific cost	k_d	$k_p^*/(1 - T_c)$
Post-tax specific cost	$(1 - T_c)k_d$	k_p^*
Numerical example assuming same 8% interest and dividend payments		
Pre-tax specific cost	8.00%	12.12%
Post-tax specific cost	5.28%	8.00%

COST OF EQUITY

ARTICLE 35

LDI Corp. Postpones Offering

CLEVELAND – **LDJ** Corp., citing a recent decline in its stock price, said it is postponing a $50 million public offering of convertible subordinated debentures.

LDI's common closed at $15 a share on Feb. 18, when the offering was filed with the Securities and Exchange Commission. It was quoted at $12 yesterday in national over-the-counter trading.

Robert S. Kendall, chairman, said however, that he is encouraged about the technology integration company's prospects and believes the stock price doesn't "accurately reflect LDI's growth potential."

Source: *Wall Street Journal*, April 16, 1992, p. C19.

As we see in article 35, LDI Corporation postponed their equity offering. The stock price was $15.00 per share on February 18 when the offering was filed with the Security and Exchange Commission, but had fallen to $12.00 per share by June. Does this drop in price affect the firm's cost of equity or weighted average cost of capital? We shall see in this chapter that if the earnings and growth potential of LDI is unchanged as the chairman claims in the article, then the price decline implies a significant increase in the firm's cost of capital and hence explains why the offering was postponed. However, if potential earnings and growth have declined, it is possible that the cost of equity will remain unchanged. We discuss how price changes may affect the cost of equity in the following sections.

A firm's equity includes both common stock and retained earnings.[2] Hence a firm can increase its equity either by selling additional stock or by retaining part of its current profits. These two modes of financing essentially are two components of the same financing source, i.e., owners' equity. However, due to flotation costs, the specific cost of raising new equity capital in the market

---

2. We define 'equity' to *exclude* preferred stock. The reader should note that the term 'retained earnings' refers to that part of current earnings which is reinvested in the business rather than being paid out as dividends, and *not* to the 'accumulated surplus' of the balance sheet.

will be somewhat greater than that of retained earnings, but the principle remains the same in both cases.

Let us initially assume that investors in the common stock of the Omega Company expect to receive an annual dividend of $10, and that they also expect the market price of the stock will rise to $110 by the end of the year. Given these hypothetical expectations, investors are willing to pay $100 for this stock in today's market. Ignoring flotation costs for the moment, what is the required rate of return on Omega's common stock? The answer is given by the discount rate, k_e, which solves the following equation:[3]

$$\$100 = \frac{\$10}{1 + k_e} + \frac{110}{1 + k_e} = \frac{120}{1 + k_e}$$

In this case $k_e = 0.2$ or 20%. Unlike the cost of debt or cost of preferred stock, we discuss below only post-tax cost of equity. To simplify the notation we denote the cost by k_e rather than k_e^*. The reader should keep in mind that dividends are paid only after tax has been paid to the IRS, hence k_e is the post-tax cost of equity. Thus if the firm issues additional common stock at the going market price of $100 per share, it must realize at least 20% on new investment in order to provide the minimum rate of return required by shareholders. Hence 20% is the specific cost of equity which should be used when calculating the weighted average cost of capital. Suppose now that investors do not change their expectations but attribute greater uncertainty to the firm's ability to earn this expected profit. Since the firm's shares are now perceived to be more risky, investors will be willing to buy the stock only at a lower price, say $95. What is the specific cost of equity in this instance? The cost of equity in this case is given by that rate of discount which equates the present value of the expectations with the current price, i.e., with $95:

$$\$95 = \frac{\$120}{1 + k_e}$$

Hence:

$$k_e = 26.3\%$$

Because the firm can sell new shares for only $95, a higher rate of return (26.3%) must be earned on the investment in order to cover the shareholders' required rate of return. Just the opposite result holds should the shareholders attribute a greater degree of certainty to their future expectations. In such a case shareholders will be ready to pay a higher price for the stock, say $110; and the specific cost becomes:

$$\$110 = \frac{\$120}{1 + k_e}$$

---

3. Since we capitalize dividends, which by definition represent a cash flow *after* the payment of corporate tax k_e denotes the *post-tax* discount rate. However, to simplify the notation we have dropped the asterisk from the specific costs of equity and debt for the remainder of the chapter.

Hence:

$$k_e = 9.1\%$$

So far, we have assumed that the stock is held for one year and then sold. In reality, shareholders can hold their shares for an unrestricted number of years, thereby obtaining a stream of future dividends. If the firm sells new stock for a net price P_0, the specific cost of common stock is given by:

$$P_0 = \frac{d_1}{1 + k_e} + \frac{d_2}{(1 + k_e)^2} + \cdots = \sum_{t=1}^{\infty} \frac{d_t}{(1 + k_e)^t}$$

and if we further assume that the dividend stream is expected to remain constant, i.e. $d_1 = d_2 = \cdots = d$, this equation reduces to:[4]

$$P_0 = \frac{d}{k_e}$$

and the specific cost of common stock is given by the dividend yield:

$$k_e = \frac{d}{P_0}$$

However, as we shall see below, a constant annual dividend implies that the firm pays out all of its earnings every year, and that the earnings themselves are constant over time. Hence in this case the cost of equity is given by:

$$k_e = \frac{d}{P_0} = \frac{E}{P_0}$$

where E denotes earnings per share.

Let us leave aside this special case in which the firm distributes all its earnings as dividends and examine the more realistic case in which firms retain some proportion of their annual earnings, distributing the rest as dividends. If we denote net earnings per share (after deduction of depreciation, interest, and taxes) by E, and cash dividends by d the first year dividend is given by:

$$d_1 = (1 - b)E$$

where b denotes the fraction of earnings which the firm desires to reinvest $(0 \leqslant b \leqslant 1)$. It is clear from this definition that if the firm follows a policy of reinvesting a *fixed* proportion of its annual earnings, dividends in the following years will not remain constant. This can readily be seen from the following calculation of the earnings available for distribution in the second year, assuming that the firm earns an average rate of return R on the reinvested portion

---

4. This follows from the summation of an infinite geometric progression:

$$P_0 = \frac{d}{1 + k_e} + \frac{d}{(1 + k_e)^2} + \cdots + \frac{d}{(1 + k_e)^n} + \cdots$$

$$= \frac{d}{1 + k_e} \times \frac{1}{1 - \dfrac{1}{1 + k_e}} = \frac{d}{k_e}$$

of the previous year's earnings:

$$E_2 = E + RbE = E(1 + bR)$$

If the firm follows the assumed policy of paying out a fixed proportion $(1 - b)$ of its annual earnings as dividends, the second-year dividend, d_2 becomes:

$$d_2 = (1 - b)E_2 = (1 - b)E(1 + bR)$$

In the third year the earnings available for allocation equals the earnings of year 2 plus the additional earnings on the investments financed out of the retention of part of the previous year's earnings. Thus the level of earnings per share in the third year will be:

$$E_3 = E_2 + bE_2 R = E(1 + bR) + bE(1 + bR)R$$

which can also be written as:

$$E(1 + bR)(1 + bR) = E(1 + bR)^2$$

and the dividend in the third year becomes:

$$d_3 = (1 - b)E(1 + bR)^2$$

Given the investment policy, the dividend will go on increasing from year to year at a rate bR. If we assume that the firm retains 50% of its earnings ($b = 0.5$) and earns 10% on the average on new investments, the dividends will grow at a 5% rate each year ($bR = 0.5 \times 0.10 = 0.05$).

Having identified the components of the dividend flow, we can compute the present value of the future dividend stream, using the post-corporate tax required rate of return k_e as the discount rate:

$$P_0 = \frac{(1 - b)E}{1 + k_e} + \frac{(1 - b)E(1 + bR)}{(1 + k_e)^2} + \frac{(1 - b)E(1 + bR)^2}{(1 + k_e)^3} + \cdots$$

Denoting bR by g, for growth rate, and the first year dividend $(1 - b)E$ by d, we derive the Gordon dividend growth model:[5]

$$P_0 = \frac{(1 - b)E}{k_e - bR} = \frac{d}{k_e - g}$$

Recalling that P_0 is the observed market price of the stock, i.e. *the maximum*

---

5. The equation is an infinite geometric progression with the common factor $(1 + bR)/(1 + k_e)$. Summing the progression yields:

$$P_0 = (1 - b)E \frac{1}{1 + k_e} \left[1 + \frac{(1 + bR)}{(1 + k_e)} + \frac{(1 + bR)^2}{(1 + k_e)^2} + \cdots \right]$$

$$= (1 - b)E \frac{1}{1 + k_e} \times \frac{1}{1 - (1 + bR)/(1 + k_e)} = \frac{(1 - b)E}{k_e - bR}$$

Note that $bR < k_e$ constitutes a necessary condition for the convergence of the geometric progression. Since, in general, $b < 1$ (that is, dividends are paid) R can be greater or smaller than k_e. The specific model presented in the text was developed by Myron J. Gordon, *The Investment, Financing and Valuation of the Corporation*, Homewood, Ill., Irwin, 1962.

price per share for which the firm can sell additional shares, k_e is the specific cost of common stock. Rewriting the above formula we get:

$$k_e = \frac{d}{P_0} + g$$

Thus in the more general case, the cost of equity is equal to the dividend yield d/P_0 plus the growth rate of future earnings, which for a given retention policy, b, also constitutes the growth rate of dividends. Although it is quite clear that the discount rate k_e which equates the present value of future dividends with the market price of the stock is the specific cost of common stock, a numerical example may be helpful.

Suppose that a firm which is financed only by equity earns \$10 per share each year and pays all of this amount to the shareholders as a dividend. If the market price of the stock is, say \$100, k_e is given by:

$$\$100 = \frac{10}{1 + k_e} + \frac{10}{(1 + k_e)^2} + \cdots = \frac{10}{k_e}$$

and

$$k_e = \frac{10}{100} = 10\%$$

Assume now that at the end of the first year the firm needs \$10 per share to finance a new investment. Should the firm undertake this project? The answer of course depends on whether the market price of the stock will rise or fall as a result of the new investment. In other words, it depends on whether the net present value calculated at the appropriate discount rate is positive or negative. In order to show that the appropriate discount rate for the new investment is k_e (and, therefore, k_e is indeed the specific cost of common stock), let us assume that the firm omits its dividend payment at the end of the first year, and uses the money to finance the new investment, which yields $R\%$ every year thereafter. Let us further assume that commencing in the second year, the firm returns to its previous policy of paying out all earnings as dividends. The new dividend equals $\$10 + 10R$, i.e., \$10 plus the additional earnings from the new investment, and the share's market price is given by:[6]

$$P_0 = \frac{0}{(1 + k_e)} + \frac{(10 + 10R)}{(1 + k_e)^2} + \frac{(10 + 10R)}{(1 + k_e)^3} + \cdots = \frac{10}{k_e} \times \frac{(1 + R)}{(1 + k_e)}$$

But as $k_e = 10\%$ we get:

$$P_0 = \frac{10}{0.1} \times \frac{(1 + R)}{1.1} = \$100 \times \frac{(1 + R)}{1.1}$$

6. Again summing the infinite progression we derive:

$$P_0 = \frac{(10 + 10R)}{(1 + k_e)} \times \frac{1}{1 - 1/(1 + k_e)} = \frac{10 + 10R}{k_e(1 + k_e)} = \frac{10}{k_e} \times \frac{(1 + R)}{(1 + k_e)^2}$$

Since the market price of the stock before undertaking the new investment was $100, we can verify that the market price of the stock will rise only if $R > 10\%$, i.e., only if the internal rate of return on the new investment is greater than the specific cost of common stock. If we use k_e as the discount rate for evaluating the new project, it will have a positive *NPV* only if $R > k_e$ and therefore any project with a positive *NPV*, calculated at k_e, also induces a rise in the market price of the stock. Hence, by definition, k_e is the minimum rate of return required by shareholders and should be used as the cost of the equity component when calculating the weighted average cost of capital.

Thus, the cost of capital of a pure-equity firm is k_e. The firm should not take a project whose return is lower than k_e even if it possesses an excess amount of cash. If the firm possesses excess cash and has no profitable projects, it should pay the excess cash out as a dividend (or repurchase its stock and thus earn k_e). The shareholders can then invest their dividends elsewhere. The following citation taken from the *Wall Street Journal*, September 13 1984 explains why k_e sets the cutoff rate:

'Pioneer Corp. said it repurchased about 12% of its common shares outstanding for $134 million.

About 2.6 million shares were purchased recently in privately negotiated transactions and about two million shares were bought on the open market in July and August. The company now has about 33.3 million shares outstanding, a spokesman said.

The spokesman added that the company was repurchasing shares because it was the best use of its excess cash. Pioneer said the repurchasing may continue.'

Thus, Pioneer Corp. had excess cash and probably did not have profitable projects. So, instead of taking projects which yield less than k_e, the firm simply repurchased its own stock yielding k_e on its investment. Thus, repurchasing the stock as an investment option proves to be useful in practice and not only in theory.

PRICE/EARNINGS RATIO (*P/E*) AND SUPER-GROWTH COMPANIES

It is common practice, especially among financial analysts, to capitalize future earnings rather than dividends when evaluating common stocks. Despite the popularity of such calculations, it must be emphasized that replacing dividends with earnings in the valuation formula is conceptually incorrect and may lead to a serious error: the relevant cash flow to the investor is the dividend stream. Moreover, discounting current earnings (part of which are reinvested) would constitute *double counting* the retained earnings, the return on which, R, already is reflected in the growth rate of future earnings, bR. One explanation for the widespread use of earnings in valuation is that a very simple version of the present value of earnings provides a good rule of thumb approximation of the cost of capital for companies with only moderate growth prospects.

In order to examine the relationship between earnings and dividend valuation models, let us rewrite the dividend growth model on the explicit assumption that the average rate of return on reinvested earnings, R, is exactly equal to the specific cost of equity, k_e:

$$P_0 = \frac{(1-b)E}{k_e - bR} = \frac{(1-b)E}{k_e - bk_e} = \frac{(1-b)E}{(1-b)k_e} = \frac{E}{k_e}$$

Given this assumption, the price of the stock, as derived from the dividend model, is equivalent to the price that would be derived from the calculation of the present value of a fixed stream of future earnings. And the firm's cost of capital is equal to the earnings yield, E/P_0:

$$k_e = \frac{E}{P_0}$$

where E denotes earnings per share in the *first year*. However, since we derived our results from the dividend growth model, we can equivalently set out the cost of capital as follows:

$$k_e = \frac{E}{P_0} = \frac{d}{P_0} + g$$

In this specific case $(R = k_e)$, the cost of equity is given by the reciprocal of the price/earnings ratio which is widely used by firm managements and financial analysts alike. Thus for the class of firms under consideration, i.e., those for whom the average rate of return on reinvested earnings equals the specific cost of equity capital $(R = k_e)$, the easily calculated and very popular earnings yield provides a good estimate of the cost of common stock.

Do these results necessarily imply that the per share earnings of such a company are constant, i.e., that the growth rate is zero? The answer is no. We have defined this class of companies in terms of the relationship between R and k_e, but earnings per share (and dividends) can increase over time even if extraordinary profit opportunities $(R > k_e)$ do not exist. For example, a high retention policy in itself can cause an expansion of earnings even though the rate of return on reinvestment is only moderate. In such a case we would still refer to such a company as a 'moderate-growth' firm despite the significant rate of increase in its earnings over time.

To clarify this argument, assume that a firm which earns $1 per share in the current year adopts a policy of retaining 50% of its earnings $(b = 50\%)$. In order to emphasize the role played by the retention policy, let us further assume that the reinvested profits earn only 5%. Given this relatively low rate of return, will future earnings grow? Clearly, the answer is in the affirmative. Next year's earnings per share will increase to $1.025 ($1 as before plus 5% of $0.50 = 2\frac{1}{2}$ cents). Similarly next year's dividend, given the fixed retention policy, will also grow at the same rate, i.e., from 50 cents to $51\frac{1}{4}$ cents per share. Thus, both earnings and dividends will grow at the rate $g = bR$, which is $2\frac{1}{2}\%$ per year in our example. Moreover, this growth rate can be increased to 4% per year merely by increasing the retention rate to 80%, even though we assume that the additional funds are reinvested at a very low rate of return.

It follows that even relatively unprofitable firms might display relatively high growth rates if they retain high proportions of their earnings.

A more meaningful distinction between firms can be made on the basis of the gap between the average reinvestment rate R, and the required return of shareholders, k_e. Firms characterized by a relatively small difference between R and k_e should be considered as 'moderate-growth' companies. On the other hand, firms like IBM whose average rate of return R is considerably greater than the cost of equity capital will be defined as 'super-growth' stocks. (This super-growth which has characterized IBM in the last few decades has diminished in the last few years.) Alternatively, we can distinguish between stocks by comparing the 'rule of thumb' and 'dividend growth model' estimates of the cost of capital:

$$k_e = \frac{E}{P_0} \quad \text{and} \quad k_e = \frac{d}{P_0} + g$$

respectively. If the difference between the two estimates is negligible we are dealing with a *moderate-growth* stock, no matter how high the actual growth rate; if the E/P_0 rule of thumb provides a poor estimate of $d/P_0 + g$ then we are dealing with a *super-growth stock*.

The value P_0/E is called the earnings multiple and the higher the multiple, in general, the lower the firm's cost of equity. Let us go back to article 35 on page 518. If indeed the earnings per share remains unchanged, then in February $k_e = E/15$ and in June $k_e = E/12$. For illustration, suppose that $E = \$2$. This implies that the cost of equity increased from $2/15 = 13.3\%$ in February to $2/12 = 16.7\%$ in June. However, if the future earnings were expected to decline to \$1.59 (from \$2), then the cost of capital would remain unchanged $1.59/12 = 13.3\%$. The same argument holds when one employs $d/P_0 + g$ to estimate the cost of equity. Thus, we see how earnings, prices, and earnings multiplies (P_0/E) are conceptually related in determining a firm's cost of equity.

SUPER-GROWTH FOR A LIMITED PERIOD

Using the formula $k_e = d/P_0 + g$ to estimate the firm's cost of equity may lead to a paradoxical result, i.e., to an unreasonably high cost of equity. Let us illustrate the point using the case of Xerox Corporation. Suppose that one wants to estimate the firm's cost of equity at the end of year 10, using the adjusted EPS for ten years to estimate the growth rate $\hat{g}$. Moody's Industrial Manual reveals the following figures:

Year	1	2	3	4	5	6	7	8	9	10
Adjusted EPS (\$)	0.045	0.093	0.33	0.38	0.63	0.93	1.24	1.49	1.73	2.08

For simplicity we use the geometric mean and not the logarithmic regression (see Appendix 17A) to obtain the estimated growth rate, $\hat{g}$:

$$\hat{g} = \left(\frac{EPS^{10}}{EPS^1}\right)^{1/9} - 1 = \left(\frac{2.08}{0.045}\right)^{1/9} - 1 = 53.1\% \cong 53\%$$

Since d/P_0 for Xerox at the end of the tenth year was about 1%, the cost of equity for Xerox, applying the dividend growth model can be estimated as follows:

$$k_e = \frac{d}{P_0} + \hat{g} = 1\% + 53\% = 54\%$$

Does it make sense that the cost of equity even of this supergrowth firm was 54% in the tenth year?

Recalling that by definition the cost of equity consists of the riskless interest rate plus a risk premium, such a high cost of equity is reasonable only if the probability of default is very high, and in such a case the stock price should be very low. Obviously this is not the case of most supergrowth firms and certainly not of Xerox. Although supergrowth firms suffer from high stock price fluctuations relative to non-growth firms, 54% a year seems to be excessive considering the risk involved.

The apparent paradox can be resolved if we note that a firm cannot earn extraordinarily high profits forever. As new firms enter the highly profitable industry the extraordinary profits will tend to disappear after a few years. Even in the case of a firm which earns extraordinary profits due to an invention protected by patent, the reader should note that patents have finite lives. Hence, one should always consider the possibility of a reduction in future growth and not rely solely on past data when applying the dividend growth formula. This is crucial in the case of supergrowth firms.

Let us now develop a formula to estimate the cost of equity for the case of limited growth periods. Suppose that profits and dividends are expected to grow at an extraordinary rate g_1 for $n - 1$ years and then will continue to grow at a normal rate g_2, where $g_2 < g_1$. Applying the dividend growth approach, the stock price is given by:

$$P_0 = \frac{d}{(1 + k_e)} + \frac{d(1 + g_1)}{(1 + k_e)^2} + \cdots + \frac{d(1 + g_1)^{n-1}}{(1 + k_e)^n}$$

$$+ \frac{d(1 + g_1)^{n-1}(1 + g_2)}{(1 + k_e)^n(1 + k_e)} + \frac{d(1 + g_1)^{n-1}(1 + g_2)^2}{(1 + k_e)^n(1 + k_e)^2} + \cdots$$

This can be rewritten as:

$$\sum_{t=1}^{n} \frac{d(1 + g_1)^{t-1}}{(1 + k_e)^t} + \frac{d(1 + g_1)^{n-1}}{(1 + k_e)^n} \sum_{i=1}^{\infty} \frac{(1 + g_2)^i}{(1 + k_e)^i}$$

Using the summation formula for an infinite geometric progression, this equation can be rewritten as:

$$P_0 = \sum_{t=1}^{n} \frac{d(1 + g_1)^{t-1}}{(1 + k_e)^t} + \frac{d(1 + g_1)^{n-1}}{(1 + k_e)^n} \times \frac{(1 + g_2)}{(1 + k_e)} \times \frac{1}{[1 - (1 + g_2)/(1 + k_e)]}$$

which after multiplying through becomes:

$$P_0 = \sum_{t=1}^{n} \frac{d(1+g_1)^{t-1}}{(1+k_e)^t} + \frac{d(1+g_1)^{n-1}}{(1+k_e)^n} \cdot \frac{1+g_2}{k_e - g_2}$$

Since P_0 (the stock's current price) and d (its current dividend) are given, the cost of equity, k_e, is a function of the super-growth rate g_1, the normal growth rate g_2, and the duration of the super-growth period, $n-1$ years.

Numerical example

Let $P_0 = \$100$, $d = \$1$, and $g_1 = 50\%$ for 9 years (i.e., $n - 1 = 9$). After the 10th year the firm's patent will expire, so that the earnings and dividends will grow at $g_2 = 5\%$ per year. If the growth rate is 50% *forever*, the cost of equity would be:

$$k_e = \frac{d}{P_0} + g = \frac{1}{100} + 50\% = 51\%$$

which does not make sense. However, applying the above formula which takes into account that the extraordinary growth rate will be reduced in the future to 5%, we obtain:

$$\$100 = \sum_{t=1}^{10} \$1 \times \frac{(1.5)^{t-1}}{(1+k_e)^t} + \$1 \times \frac{(1.5)^9}{(1+k_e)^{10}} \times \frac{1.05}{(k_e - 0.05)}$$

By trial and error one can plug in values for k_e until the present value of future dividends is just equal to $100. In this special case, $k_e \simeq 17.2\%$, which is a much more reasonable estimate of the cost of equity.

So far we have assumed that the super-growth phase will last for nine years at the rate $g_1 = 50\%$ per annum. How sensitive is the cost of equity k_e to errors in the length of the super-growth period or in the growth rate estimate? Table 17.5 gives the value of k_e obtained by the same trial-and-error method for alternative values of n and g_1 (assuming that g_2, the normal growth rate remains 5%). In general, as the length of the super-growth period increases, the discount rate increases, approaching in the limit the theoretical infinite growth value $k_e = (d/P_0) + g_1$. As the super-growth period becomes shorter, the discount rate decreases steeply, but always remains higher than the permanent growth rate, which in this case is assumed to be 5%.

Let us return to the case of Xerox Corporation. Suppose that the high growth rate of about 50% was expected to continue for the next 9 years and

Table 17.5 The value of k_e for various values of g_1 and n (%)

$g_1 \backslash n$	1	3	5	10	15	20	50	100
5	6.0	6.0	6.0	6.0	6.0	6.0	6.0	6.0
10	6.0	6.1	6.2	6.5	6.8	7.2	8.9	9.9
25	6.0	6.4	6.9	9.3	12.0	14.0	22.0	24.5
50	6.0	7.0	8.8	17.2	26.0	32.0	45.0	49.0

that a normal growth of 5% was expected thereafter. Since the price of the firm's stock at the end of the tenth year was about $100, Table 17.5 indicates that the cost of equity is 17.2% and not 51% as noted previously (recall that $n = 10$ implies a growth rate of g_1 for $n - 1 = 9$ years). In reality, growth rates tend to decrease gradually over time; the per share earnings of Xerox after year 10 were as follows:

Year	Adjusted EPS	Year	Adjusted EPS	Year	Adjusted EPS
11	2.40	16	3.07	21	7.33
12	2.71	17	4.51	22	7.08
13	3.16	18	5.06	23	4.34
14	3.80	19	5.77	24	4.35
15	4.18	20	6.69		

which constitutes an average growth rate of about 4.7% per annum over the thirteen-year period:

$$\hat{g}_2 = \left(\frac{\text{EPS}_{24}}{\text{EPS}_{11}}\right)^{1/13} - 1 = \left(\frac{4.35}{2.40}\right)^{1/13} - 1 \simeq 4.7\%$$

The super-growth which prevailed in the first 10 years did not persist. Thus, when future growth opportunities, rather than *ex-post* growth, are taken into account in estimating the cost of equity the cost of equity *paradox* is resolved.

To sum up, the dividend model must be based on a realistic estimate of *future growth rates*. However, for many mature firms which have reached a stable development, the past growth rate serves as a good estimate of the future growth in profits and dividends. But for supergrowth firms, e.g., firms with temporary monopoly power or patents, basing our analysis solely on past growth can lead to a gross overestimate of the true cost of equity.

ADJUSTING EARNINGS PER SHARE (EPS)

Since we are primarily concerned with the past record of a firm's earnings in order to help us estimate the crucial growth rate, some adjustment of the EPS figures may be necessary. The need to adjust the EPS figures in order to ensure comparability between the years can be illustrated by the hypothetical example given in Table 17.6. Although net after-tax profits remained the same between years 1 and 2, the number of shares doubled in year 2, thereby reducing EPS

Table 17.6 Earnings per share for a hypothetical company

Year	Net earnings	Number of shares	Earnings per share
1	100,000	50,000	2
2	100,000	100,000	1

by 50%, that is, from $2 per share in year 1 to $1 per share in year 2. How should we interpret this drop in EPS?

To the degree that the company issued new shares to the public, and that sufficient time has elapsed for the new investments financed by the issue to reach fruition, the conclusion that profitability dropped drastically seems justified. If the company issued new shares and the funds were not properly used, this is tantamount, from the investor's point of view, to acquiring a new partner who adds nothing to the company's overall profitability but shares in the earnings. However, if the drop in EPS is due to a 2 for 1 stock split, no additional capital was raised, but neither have the former shareholders acquired new partners. For every share owned in year 1 a shareholder now has two shares, so EPS did not really drop but remained stable at $2 per *adjusted* share in year 1. Hence, if paradoxical results are to be avoided, EPS figures must be adjusted.

Adjusting EPS for stock splits and stock dividends

In a stock dividend or split, a company's shareholders are given additional shares to represent their ownership interest. No additional investment on the part of the shareholders is required and, of course, no additional capital is raised by the corporation. The difference between the stock dividend and the split is technical and need not concern us here; in a split, as the name suggests, the par or stated value of the stock is reduced, while in a stock dividend the par or stated value remains unchanged, and a transfer is effected from earned surplus to the capital account. In both instances no transaction takes place, and the split or stock dividend represents a bookkeeping entry.[7]

To clarify the procedure for adjusting EPS for splits or stock dividends, let us consider the example given in Table 17.7 of a company which declared a 10% stock dividend in year 3 and a 2 for 1 split (equivalent for our purposes

Table 17.7 Unadjusted earnings per share and stock dividends (splits) of a hypothetical company

Year	Net earnings after tax (1)	Number of shares (2)	Unadjusted earnings per share (3)	Spilts and stock dividends (4)
1	1,000	1,000	1.00	–
2	1,100	1,000	1.10	–
3	1,200	1,100	1.09	10%
4	1,500	1,100	1.36	–
5	1,500	2,200	0.68	2:1
6	1,600	2,200	0.73	–

7. Large stock dividends and splits may broaden the market for a firm's stock by lowering the per unit price, thereby lowering the minimum investment required to secure the preferential commission on 100 share round lots. The case for a small stock dividend or split is far less clear, although where the cash dividend rate remains unchanged it affords management the opportunity of 'announcing' a dividend increase in advance.

to a 100% stock dividend) in year 5. As a first step, a base year is chosen; in our example it is denoted 'year 1'. An 'index' of the number of shares a shareholder owns in each of the following years, *without additional investment*, is constructed. Such an index is given in Table 17.8. For simplicity, consider a shareholder with 100 shares in year 1. In year 3, following the 10% stock dividend, the *number* of shares which he owned increases to 110, without any additional investment, and the index is set at 110 from year 3 on. In year 5, following the 2 for 1 split, the number of shares which he owned increased to 220 (not 200, since he held 110 shares when the split occurred). From that date the index becomes 220. When calculating the adjusted EPS, Table 17.9, the observed EPS (column 1) is multiplied by the index (column 2), and the resulting product (column 3) represents the EPS, adjusted for stock splits and stock dividends.[8]

The need for the adjustment becomes clear when we compare the record of unadjusted earnings per share for the company (column 1 of Table 17.9) with its adjusted EPS (column 3 of Table 17.9). These fluctuations in *unadjusted* EPS which were induced by the accounting manipulations clearly are of no significance to the investor and must be offset when the *rate of growth in*

Table 17.8

Year	Number of shares at beginning of each year	Splits and stock dividends	Number of shares at end of each year
1	100	–	100
2	100	–	100
3	100	10%	110
4	110	–	110
5	110	2 : 1	220
6	220	–	220

Table 17.9

Year	Unadjusted earnings per share (1)	Index (2)	Adjusted earnings per share $(1) \times (2)/100 = (3)$
1	1.00	100	1.00
2	1.10	100	1.10
3	1.09	110	1.20
4	1.36	110	1.50
5	0.68	220	1.50
6	0.73	220	1.61

8. Alternatively, year 6 could be chosen as the base year and the index constructed backwards by *dividing* the annual unadjusted earnings-per-share data by 1 plus the relevant percentage change in the number of shares. This is the procedure commonly employed by Moody's and other reporting services when adjusting for splits or stock dividends.

earnings is being calculated. The company did not experience a 27% drop in profitability between years 1 and 6, as the unadjusted EPS figures suggest. On the contrary, a glance at Table 17.9 suffices to show that the company's profits (for a given investment) *increased* by 61% (adjusted EPS were $1.61 in year 6 compared with $1.00 in year 1) during those years. Similarly the increase in profitability between years 1 and 3 was 20% (adjusted) and not 9% as the unadjusted figures suggest. Since we are examining the past record of EPS in order to descern *trends* in the rate of growth, only the *adjusted* record is relevant for this purpose.[9]

Adjusting EPS in practice: Georgia–Pacific Corporation

To illustrate the EPS adjustments in practice, let us consider an actual case of a corporation which declared stock dividends and split its stock. The Georgia–Pacific Corporation is an integrated manufacturer and distributor of forest products and chemicals. It is the largest domestic producer of softwood and plywood. Table 17.10 lists the basic financial data taken from the firm's annual statements which show a negative growth rate of about -8% per year during a 12-year period. Denoting the growth rate by g, we have $EPS_{12} = EPS_1(1 + g)^n$, where $n = 11$ in this specific case. Taking the nth root we obtain:

$$g = \left(\frac{EPS_{12}}{EPS_1}\right)^{1/11} - 1 = \left(\frac{0.97}{2.43}\right)^{1/11} - 1 = -8\%$$

But -8% is not the true growth rate in earnings per share. In order to calculate the true rate of growth the EPS figures must be adjusted for stock

Table 17.10 Georgia–Pacific Corporation, earnings per share

Year	Net income (millions $) (1)	Number of common shares (million shares) (2)	EPS (3) = (1)/(2)	Annual growth rate in EPS (%)
1	$129	53	$2.43	–
2	163	54	3.02	24.3
3	164	56	2.93	−3.0
4	148	60	2.47	−15.7
5	215	99	2.17	−12.1
6	262	103	2.54	17.1
7	302	103	2.93	15.4
8	327	105	3.11	6.1
9	244	104	2.35	−24.4
10	160	105	1.52	−35.3
11	52	106	0.49	−67.8
12	105	108	0.97	98.0

9. A similar adjustment should be made for the stock dividend component of a rights offering as well. See Haim Levy and Marshall Sarnat, *Portfolio and Investment Selection: Theory and Practice*, Prentice Hall International, 1984, chapter 2.

dividends and splits. Table 17.11 provides the basic information on stock dividends and splits and the standard share index. Georgia–Pacific distributed stock dividends of 2–4% a year and in year 5 split its stock 3 for 2 which is equivalent to a 50% stock dividend. Starting with 100 shares and denoting the adjustment factor by α, the index at the end of year 2 is:

$$100(1 + \alpha) = 100 \times 1.02 = 102$$

At the end of year 3 it is $102 \times 1.02 \times 1.02 = 106.12$ since it reflects two additional 2% stock dividends in that year and the stock issued in March was entitled to receive the stock dividend declared in September. In the same way, the appropriate standard share index is calculated each year. The index at the end of year 12 was 172.3. Thus an investor who held 100 shares of stock in year 1 had accumulated 172.3 shares by the end of year 12 without additional investment.

Table 17.12 sets out the 'reported' and 'adjusted' EPS of Georgia–Pacific; Figure 17.2 plots the two EPS series. Clearly the impact of the adjustment is significant, and therefore, it is common practice always to refer to the *adjusted* earnings per share whenever the results of several years are compared. The true (adjusted) growth rate for the period is:

$$\left(\frac{1.67}{2.43}\right)^{1/11} - 1 = -3.4\% \text{ and not } -8\%$$

We have performed a *forward* adjustment from the base year (year 1) to the current year (year 12). This is the most convenient procedure; for each additional year we only have to determine the additional adjustment factor. Most investment analysts do a 'retroactive' or 'backward' adjustment: the last year's index is set at 100 and the standard share index is adjusted backward by *dividing* the current index by the adjustment factor. The advantage of this method is that the last year's earnings per share are simply computed from the reported results. Its major shortcoming stems from the fact that the entire

Table 17.11 Calculation of the standard share index for Georgia–Pacific Corporation

Year	Standard share index, beginning of period	Stock dividends or stock splits	Adjustment factor	Standard share index, end of period
1	–	–	–	100.00
2	100	2% stock dividend	1.02	102.00
3	102	2% stock dividend March, year 3	1.02	104.04
	104.04	2% stock dividend Sept., year 3	1.02	106.12
4	106.12	2% stock dividend March, year 4	1.02	108.24
	108.24	2% stock dividend Sept., year 4	1.02	110.41
5	110.41	2% stock dividend March, year 5	1.02	112.62
	112.62	3-for-2 stock split August, year 5	1.5	168.92
6	168.92	2% stock dividend August, year 6	1.02	172.30
7	172.30	–	–	172.30

adjusted EPS series has to be recalculated each year, as the base year (index equal to 100) always advances to coincide with the last year. The last two columns in Table 17.12 give the 'backward' standard share index and the 'retroactively' adjusted earnings per share. Note that although the numbers are different, the percentage changes and growth rates are the *same* for both methods.

Table 17.12 Adjusted earnings per share for Georgia–Pacific Corporation

Year	Earnings per share, as reported ($) (1)	Standard share index (2)	Adjusted EPS($) $(3) = \dfrac{(1) \times (2)}{100}$	'Backward' standard share index $(4) = [(2)/172.30] \times 100$	'Retroactively' adjusted EPS($) $(5) = \dfrac{(1) \times (4)}{100}$
1	2.43	100.00	2.43	58.04	1.41
2	3.02	102.00	3.08	59.20	1.79
3	2.93	106.12	3.11	60.38	1.77
4	2.47	110.40	2.73	61.59	1.52
5	2.17	168.92	3.67	62.82	1.36
6	2.54	172.30	4.38	64.08	1.63
7	2.93	172.30	5.05	65.36	1.92
8	3.11	172.30	5.36	98.04	3.05
9	2.35	172.30	4.05	100.00	2.35
10	1.52	172.30	2.62	100.00	1.52
11	0.49	172.30	0.84	100.00	0.49
12	0.97	172.30	1.67	100.00	0.97

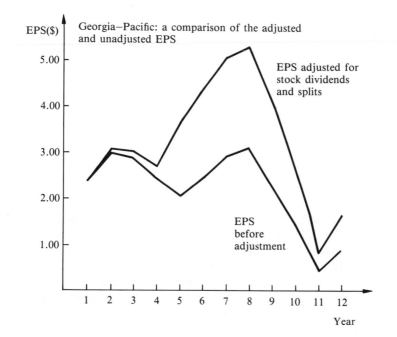

Figure 17.2

SPECIFIC COST OF RETAINED EARNINGS _____

The typical business firm finances a large share of its long-term capital investments internally out of retained earnings. Although such funds might appear to be 'free' in the sense that the firm does not incur an actual outlay cost, there is no conceptual difference between the use of retained earnings or the proceeds of a stock issue to finance new investments. Both of these sources have a well-defined opportunity cost, i.e., the rate of return which stockholders expect from the stock. Retained earnings should be treated like a common stock issue with one notable exception. No flotation costs are incurred when internal, rather than external, funds are employed. Hence, there is no need to deduct such costs from the current market price, P_0, when calculating the specific cost of equity. As a result, the cost of retained earnings will always be somewhat less than the cost of common stock, the exact differential depending on the magnitude of the flotation costs.

CALCULATING THE COST OF CAPITAL IN PRACTICE _____

Now that we have examined the theoretical underpinning of the analysis of the cost of capital in some detail, let us turn to the difficult question of its practical application. More specifically let us see if the procedures outlined in the previous sections can be applied to actual business firms. The question of application is absolutely crucial; for as we have tried to emphasize throughout the book, a theory or analytical apparatus which is 'good in theory but bad in practice' is simply a bad theory. The ultimate test of a theory in corporate finance is not its formal elegance but lies rather in our ability to apply the theoretical concepts to actual business problems. To this end we shall now illustrate the calculation of the weighted average cost of capital for two well-known firms – General Electric (GE) and International Business Machines (IBM).

General Electric (GE)

As a first step in the analysis, we estimate the specific cost of equity capital for GE on March 17, 1992. As we have already noted, this requires the estimation of the future growth of earnings. For the purpose of this analysis, let us estimate the growth rate by means of regression analysis, using historical data on earnings per share over the period 1978–91 (since the estimated growth in earnings was determined on March 17, 1992). Using this approach the annual growth rate per share earnings was estimated to be 10.37%.

Given G.E.'s expected dividend is $2.20, and the market price on March 17, 1992 is $78.625, the specific cost of equity (retained earnings included) is

13.17%. (For simplicity, we shall ignore flotation costs throughout the analysis.)

$$k_e = d/P_0 + g = 2.20/78.625 + 0.1037 = 13.17\%$$

Clearly, 13.17% represents the estimate of GE's *after-tax* specific cost of equity, because the per-share earnings of Table 17.13 have been calculated *net* of corporate taxes.

Let us deviate from our main task for a moment in order to examine one of the basic characteristics of GE stock. Does the 10.37% growth rate indicate that GE should properly be considered a so-called super-growth stock? As we have already noted, the fact that observed earnings increase over time is not in itself sufficient evidence to support an affirmative answer to this question. In fact, in the case of GE we can readily demonstrate that the growth rate of about 10.49% does represent a true growth situation. This contention can be verified by calculating the E/P_0 rule of thumb estimate of GE's specific cost of equity:

$$k_e = 5.65/78.625 = 7.19\%$$

where $5.65 denotes GE's earnings per share in 1992. If we use the published 1991 earnings rather than the 1992 we obtain:

$$k_e = 5.10/78.625 = 6.49\%$$

Since 7.19% is not a good approximation of GE's cost of equity capital as calculated from the $d/P_0 + g$ formula (13.17%), we can conclude the *extraordinarily* profitable investment opportunities have been a major factor accounting for the growth of GE's earnings.

The after-tax specific cost of debt $k_d^* = (1 - T_c)k_d$, was estimated to be 5.20%. Although market prices were employed in the calculation of the specific costs of equity, for simplicity book values were used to estimate the cost of debt.

Table 17.14 sets out the specific costs of debt and common equity and the

Table 17.13 General Electric 10.49% net earnings per share of common stock ($)

Year	Adjusted earnings per share	Year	Adjusted earnings per share	
1978	1.35	1986	2.73	
1979	1.55	1987	2.33	
1980	1.67	1988	3.75	
1981	1.82	1989	4.36	
1982	2.00	1990	4.85	
1983	2.23	1991	5.10	
1984	2.52	1992	5.65	(Estimate)
1985	2.57			

Source: Standard & Poor's *NYSE Stock Reports*.

Table 17.14 General Electric: weighted average cost of capital, 1992

	Capital structure ($ million) (1)	Capital structure (%) (2)	After-tax specific costs (%) (3)	Contribution to the weighted average cost of capital (%) (4) = (2) × (3)/100
Long-term debt[a]	22,682.0	25.03	5.20	1.301
Common equity[b]	45,259.6	74.97	13.17	9.872
Total	67,941.6	100.00	WACC	11.173

[a] Based on book values in 1991.
[b] Based on market values on March 17, 1992.

market value of each source of financing (number of shares outstanding times their market price.)[10] Assuming that the observed capital structure constitutes GE's target. financing mix, its after-tax weighted average cost of capital is approximately 11%, and *the latter should be used as a cutoff rate for evaluating investment projects.* Thus GE is certainly a growth firm and the simple method is misleading.

A word of caution is in order. Our calculation of GE's cost of capital is only illustrative. In particular, the important growth rate was estimated solely on the basis of historical earnings data. Presumably the company's financial analysts and economists would use additional sources of information drawn from general economic, industry and company forecasts, when estimating the future growth pattern of GE's earnings.

IBM: is it still a super-growth firm?

Having estimated the cost of capital of a growth firm (GE), let us now turn to IBM a firm whose very name became a synonym for rapid or super-growth in the 1970s and early 1980s. However, growth in the late 1980s has remained steady for IBM. (IBM's per-share earnings for the period 1978–91 is provided in Table 17.15.) Applying the same regression technique we used before (see Appendix 17A), the estimated annual growth rate of IBM's earnings from 1978 to 1990 is 4.77%. In estimating the growth rate, we eliminated the 1991 earnings considering this as an outlier not representing future earnings. Given its estimated 1992 dividend of $4.84 per share and the market price of its stock on March 13, 1992 of $89.625, the specific cost of equity for IBM (ignoring flotation costs) is:

$$k_e = d/P_0 + g = 4.84/89.625 + 0.0477 = 10.17\%$$

In spite of the elimination of the outlier, can we say that IBM is a growth

10. The reader should note that with regard to equity, the market value of the common stock (number of shares times market price) reflects the full market value of the firm's equity so that there is no need to make any additional calculation of the value of any other balance sheet equity items such as surplus, retained earnings or various reserve accounts.

Table 17.15 IBM: net earnings per share of common stock ($)

Year	Adjusted earnings per share	Year	Adjusted earnings per share
1978	5.32	1987	8.72
1979	5.16	1988	9.27
1980	6.10	1989	6.47
1981	5.63	1990	−10.51
1982	7.39	1991	− 0.99
1983	9.04		
1984	10.77		
1985	10.67		
1986	7.81		

Source: Standard and Poor's *NYSE Stock Reports.*

Table 17.16 IBM: weighted average cost of capital

	Capital structure ($ million) (1)	Capital structure (%) (2)	After-tax specific costs (%) (3)	Contribution to the weighted average cost of capital (%) (4) = (2) × (3)
Debt[a]	13,231	20.54	5.20	1.068
Common equity[b]	51,117	79.45	10.17	8.080
	64,408	100.00	WACC	9.148%

[a] Based on book values in 1991.
[b] Based on market values on March 13, 1992.

stock? To see this, let us calculate the E/P_0 ratio, which is: $E/P_0 =$ 10.51/89.625 = 11.72 when earnings for 1990 are used. This figure is not very different from 10.17, implying that IBM has lost its 'super-growth' status.

Table 17.16 sets out all of the relevant data on specific costs and capital structure required to estimate IBM's weighted average cost of capital on March 13, 1992. The after-tax specific cost of debt was 5.20%. Combining this with the cost of equity results in weighted average of 9.148%. Thus the cutoff rate was lower for IBM (about 9.1%) than for GE (about 11%).

SECURITY ANALYSTS' GROWTH FORECASTS

As explained above one can employ the *ex-post* data to forecast the growth in the firm's earnings per share. Sometimes, however, some basic changes in the firm take place (e.g., change in the product line, more aggressive marketing department, etc.) which imply that one has to incorporate this new information and not merely rely on *ex-post* data. Thus it is sometimes wise to listen to a financial analyst, who, on the one hand knows the firm's past earnings record, but on the other hand, also knows the new developments in the firm.

Table 17.17

Sector/industry/company	Price	Actual EPS	Mean	Actual	Relative	6 mo	% up	% down	Coeff. of var.
				Estimates – Fiscal year 1					
				Percentage change			Revisions		
Technology		1.85	2.46	32.9	0.96	−4.3	9	16	5.0
Computers		2.41	3.09	28.2	0.92	−2.2	9	18	3.7
Computer manufacturers		4.45	5.48	23.0	0.88	0.3	11	18	2.7
Alpha Micro Sys.	8–3	1.46	1.70	16.4	0.84	6.3			0.0
Altos Computer	9–4	0.65	0.99	51.9	1.09	16.1		9	8.7
Amdahl Corp.	13–2	0.96	1.01	5.6	0.76	33.5		36	10.1
Apple Computer	27–0	1.28	0.98	23.3	0.55	30.5	8	13	5.4
Apollo Computer	25–2	0.37	0.75	101.2	1.45	11.4			2.4
Burroughs CP	52–4	4.60	5.65	22.8	0.88	1.1	9	5	3.0
CPT Corp	8–6	1.05	1.25	19.3	0.86	24.9	6	44	10.3
Commodore Intl	32–5	4.66	5.74	23.2	0.89	−5.9			10.5
Compaq Computer	5–1	0.11	0.54	390.9	3.53	NA	20		15.2
Control Data	27–0	4.20	3.55	−15.5	0.61	−29.1		39	12.9
Control Laser	6–4	−1.63	0.50	NM	NM	−23.1			
Convergent Tech.	14–0	0.40	0.59	46.5	1.05	−29.8	29	12	21.0
Cray Resh Inc.	54–0	1.77	2.42	36.7	0.98	−0.2			1.8
Data Gen. Corp.	54–6	0.96	2.44	154.5	1.83	11.8	19	4	4.8

The risk with this approach is that relying on one financial analyst may be too subjective and too biased. However, one can take the mean estimate of the growth rate of many financial analysts to obtain a more objective and more reliable growth rate estimate.

To date, there are at least two services which collect the financial analysts' forecasts. These two services are the Institutional Broker's Estimate Service (IBES) and Zack's Investment Service. Both services gather the financial analysts' forecasts from various sources and provide their subscribers with monthly reports.

Table 17.17 is a sample page from the IBES *Monthly Summary Data*.[11] The table provides the company name and estimates of earnings per share for various periods of time. The most interesting figure for our purpose is, of course, the long-term growth ($\hat{g}$) which appears on the right hand side of the table. The median five-year growth rate we see is 13% for Burroughs Corp. Using this estimated growth rate, one can estimate the cost of equity and the weighted average cost of capital of various firms.

As article 36 shows, Zacks Investment Research publish estimates of future earnings of various firms which can also be employed to estimate the growth rate in earnings. But as the figure shows, these estimates are not without error. For example, the automobile industry's actual earnings were in 1991, 25.6%

11. See *Institutional Brokers Estimate System Monthly Summary Data*, Lynch, Jones and Ryan, New York.

Table 17.17 (cont.)

Sector/industry/company	Mean	Actual	Relative	6 mo	% up	% down	Coeff. of var.	Median	S.D.
				Estimates – Fiscal year 2				Estimated 5-yr growth rate	
		Percent change			Revisions				
Technology	3.19	64.8	0.96	−1.5	8	13	6.5	18	3
Computers	4.08	55.3	0.90	−1.9	8	13	5.1	18	3
Computer manufacturers	6.70	46.5	0.85	−0.5	11	14	4.1	17	3
Alpha Micro Sys.	2.00	37.0	0.80	NA				30	7
Altos Computer								35	6
Amdahl Corp.	1.44	49.6	0.87	−23.7		27	9.6	22	6
Apple Computer	2.21	72.4	1.00	27.4	17	4	15.1	26	7
Apollo Computer	1.32	254.2	2.06	23.9	24		7.7	40	8
Burroughs CP	6.67	45.0	0.84	0.4		5	7.1	13	3
CPT Corp.	1.60	52.4	0.89	NA				20	7
Commodore Intl	7.25	55.6	0.91	NA				25	6
Compaq Computer	0.90	715.2	4.74	NA	33		20.0	28	11
Control Data	4.47	6.5	0.62	24.8		33	8.8	13	3
Control Laser									
Convergent Tech.	1.24	208.8	1.80	−28.6	12	29	16.1	45	14
Cray Resh Inc.	3.06	72.8	1.01	−0.1		15	3.7	25	2
Data Gen Corp.	4.00	316.4	2.42	15.5	12		7.2	20	4

ARTICLE 36

The Biggest Earnings Surprises

Percentage difference between actual earnings (from continuing operations, where applicable) and analysts' average estimated earnings among the Dow Jones Industry Groups for the second quarter of 1992.

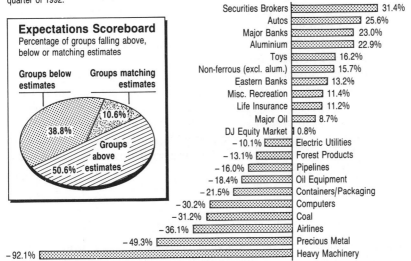

Expectations Scoreboard
Percentage of groups falling above, below or matching estimates

Groups below estimates
Groups matching estimates

10.6%
38.8%
Groups above estimates
50.6%

Securities Brokers 31.4%
Autos 25.6%
Major Banks 23.0%
Aluminium 22.9%
Toys 16.2%
Non-ferrous (excl. alum.) 15.7%
Eastern Banks 13.2%
Misc. Recreation 11.4%
Life Insurance 11.2%
Major Oil 8.7%
DJ Equity Market 0.8%
−10.1% Electric Utilities
−13.1% Forest Products
−16.0% Pipelines
−18.4% Oil Equipment
−21.5% Containers/Packaging
−30.2% Computers
−31.2% Coal
−36.1% Airlines
−49.3% Precious Metal
−92.1% Heavy Machinery

Sources: Zacks Investment Research; adapted from *Wall Street Journal*, August 3, 1992, p. C1.

larger than estimated and for heavy machinery the estimate was 92.1% smaller than estimated. Thus it is not clear whether the estimates are better than a simple 'naive' regression estimate.

MEASURING THE COST OF CAPITAL USING THE CAPITAL ASSET PRICING MODEL

As noted in the theoretical discussion of Part II, the evaluation of a project's desirability must reflect both its contribution to profitability and its contribution to the firm's risk level. In the CAPM approach, the contribution of a new project's risk should be measured by taking its covariance not only with the firm's own earnings, but also the covariance with other firms' earnings as well. The reasoning underlying this approach is based on the assumption that the investor in the stock market holds many securities in his portfolio. Hence from his point of view, risk should be measured by the covariance of the returns on the new project with the market portfolio rather than with the returns on the firm's existing investments. Thus, if the firm evaluates a new project i, with systematic risk β_i, the required rate of return on the new project is k_i:

$$k_i = r + (E(x_m) - r)\beta_i$$

where:

$$r = \text{risk-free interest rate}$$
$$E(x_m) = \text{expected return on the market portfolio}$$

Using the CAPM approach there is no unique cutoff rate that the firm should employ in project evaluation. Each project has its own cutoff point, i.e., its required rate of return, which depends directly on the project's risk as measured by beta. Unfortunately, the implementation of this approach in practice is quite complicated. By its very nature, the investment in physical assets requires a multiperiod analysis; the capital asset pricing model, as we have seen, is a one-period model. [12]

An alternative approach is to use the CAPM to estimate the specific cost of each individual source of financing. For simplicity, we confine our illustration to the case of the specific cost of equity. However, the same technique can be used to estimate the specific costs of preferred stock and debt.

In calculating the weighted average cost of capital, the specific cost of equity was estimated by the present value of future cash flows as measured by the dividend growth model:

$$k_e = \frac{d}{P_0} + g$$

12. For an extension of the CAPM to a multiperiod framework see Robert Merton, 'An Intertemporal Asset Pricing Model,' *Econometrica*, September 1973; and Douglas Breeden, 'An Intertemporal Asset Pricing Model with Stochastic Consumption and Investment Opportunities,' *Journal of Financial Economics*, 1979.

where k_e denotes the required rate of return on equity, d is the annual cash dividend and g is the annual growth rate of earnings (and hence the dividend growth rate as well). The CAPM approach suggests an alternative way to estimate k_e.

Table 17.18 presents estimates of the cost of equity, based on the CAPM, for the five 'aggressive' and five 'defensive' stocks whose betas were estimated in Chapter 12. The analysis refers to a twenty-year period. During this period the average rate of return on the market portfolio was 17.43% and the average risk-free interest rate (on treasury bills) was 3.31%. Applying the formula for the specific cost of equity:

$$k_e = r + (E(x_m) - r)\beta_i$$

and substituting the observed values for $E(x_m)$ and r, we derive the following equation:

$$k_e = 0.0331 + (0.1743 - 0.0331)\beta_i$$

This formula is applied to each of the ten companies in Table 17.18. Column 2 sets out the risk premium for each firm; the specific cost of equity is given in column 3. The cost of equity for 'defensive' stocks ranged from a low of 9.24% for Abbot Laboratory to 16.3% for Union Carbide. (The reader should note that the required return on Union Carbide stock was very close to the return on the market as a whole since its beta was close to one.) The minimum required rates of return (specific cost of equity) for aggressive stocks were all greater than 20%.

Calculating the cost of capital in practice: the CAPM approach

In this subsection we use the CAPM to calculate the cost of capital for General Motors (G.M.). Table 17.19 presents the annual rates of return on the stock of G.M. as well as of the market portfolio for the 20 years (we use Standard

Table 17.18

	(1) Systematic risk β_i	(2) Risk premium $(14.12) \times (1)$	(3) Specific cost of equity $k_i = 3.31 + (2)$
Abbot Laboratory	0.42	5.93	9.24
General Telephone	0.60	8.47	11.78
Greyhound Corporation	0.62	8.75	12.06
R. H. Macy Corporation	0.65	9.18	12.49
Union Carbide Corporation	0.92	12.99	16.30
Bethlehem Steel	1.37	19.34	22.65
Hooper Chemical	1.43	20.19	23.50
Cerro Corporation	1.67	23.58	26.89
Medusa Portland	1.86	26.26	29.57
Conalco inc.	3.44	48.57	51.88

Table 17.19 Annual rates of return on GM and the market portfolio (S&P 500 Index) for a twenty-year period (%)

Year	GM	Market portfolio
1	30.7	16.5
2	11.4	12.5
3	−32.5	−10.1
4	30.5	23.9
5	1.8	11.1
6	−6.2	−8.5
7	22.3	3.9
8	4.3	14.3
9	6.5	19.1
10	−37.8	−14.7
11	−27.6	−26.5
12	97.1	37.3
13	45.9	23.8
14	−11.3	−7.2
15	−4.7	12.2
16	2.3	12.3
17	−5.5	25.8
18	−9.9	−9.7
19	71.1	14.8
20	22.4	17.3

& Poor's 500 as a proxy for the market portfolio). In calculating the cost of capital by the CAPM approach we first estimate the firm's systematic risk, β:

$$\beta_{GM} = \frac{\text{Cov}(x_{GM}, x_m)}{\sigma_m^2} = 1.533$$

where x_m denotes the rate of return on the market portfolio. Now, using this β we can estimate the cost of equity of G.M. as follows:

$$k_e = r + (\bar{x}_m - r)\beta_i$$

where k_e is the estimate of the cost of equity, r the risk-free interest rate, and $\bar{x}_m$ is the average return on the market portfolio.

As an estimate of the risk-free rate, we take the arithmetic mean of treasury bills for this 20-year period,[13] which is 6.8%. Therefore, the cost of equity for G.M. is as follows:

$$k_e = 6.8 + (8.41 - 6.8)1.533 \simeq 9.27$$

where 8.41% is the average rate of return on the S&P 500 Index.

Theoretically, one should use the market values as weights in calculating the average cost of capital. In G.M. employing book values rather than market values yields almost the same results. Thus, we demonstrate below, for

13. Based on R. Ibbotson and R. Sinquefield, *Stocks, Bonds, Bills, and Inflation*, The Financial Analyst Research Foundation (1990) and various issues of the *Wall Street Journal*.

simplicity only, the calculation with book values, and leave the more complicated market value calculations to end-of-chapter problems. [14]

The weighted average cost of capital of G.M. is calculated as follows:

Capital structure (year 20)	Amount ($ million)	%	Specific cost	Contribution to the weighted average cost of capital
Common equity	$26,786.1	0.8411	9.27	7.797
Preferred stock	283.6	0.0089	4.54	0.040
Debt	4,777.0	0.1500	6.10	0.915
	$31,846.7	1.0000	WACC	8.752

The specific cost of debt k_d was calculated as follows:

$$k_d = \frac{\text{interest payment}}{\text{debt}} (1 - \text{tax rate}) = \frac{530}{4,777} (1 - 0.34) = 7.322$$

The specific cost of preferred stock was calculated as follows:

$$k_p = \frac{\text{preferred dividend}}{\text{preferred stock}} = \frac{12.9}{283.6} = 4.54\%$$

Using the CAPM approach we estimate General Motors' cost of capital at about 8.8%, which is the after-tax discount rate which the firm should use for project evaluation.

The cost of capital: US industrial firms

We estimated above the cost of capital of various individual firms. Table 17.20 reveals the cost of various sources of funds as supplied by a sample of large

Table 17.20 Average costs of capital for plant and equipment expenditure programs supplied by largest NYSE corporations

	All industry groups combined (%)
1. After-tax cost of new common equity	17.2
2. After-tax cost of retained earnings	16.6
3. Before-tax cost of debt	12.5
4. After-tax cost of debt	6.4
5. After-tax cost of capital	12.4

Source: Blume, Friend and Westerfield, *op. cit.*

14. See problem 17.27.

firms. The data is taken from managers' response to a survey conducted by Blume, Friend and Westerfield. The cost of common stock equity is 17.2% while the cost of retained earnings is a bit lower, 16.6%, presumably due to the saving of flotation costs. The after-tax cost of debt is 6.4% and the after-tax weighted average cost of capital is 12.4%. This, of course, does not imply that the firm employs this weighted average cost of capital as a discount rate in project evaluation. The firm may adjust this figure and employ a different cutoff rate which reflects the specific project's risk profile.

Finally, please note that though we capture in the above examples the main sources of financing, one illustration is still an oversimplification of the real issues that one may face in estimating the weighted average cost of capital. Let us just mention a few of the issues:

1. What if the book value of bonds is significantly different to its market value?
2. What if bonds and preferred stock are privately placed, hence there is no market price for these financial instruments?
3. How to treat deferred taxes?
4. How to treat accounts payable which are certainly a source of funds?

We leave the analysis of these issues to the end-of-chapter problems where we suggest a solution for each of the above issues.

IMPACT OF THE 1987 CRASH ON THE COST OF CAPITAL

The stock market plays a crucial role in the theory of finance; stock prices are a key determinant of the cost of capital and thereby affect corporate investment decisions. Moreover, as we have emphasized throughout the book, common stock prices also provide a benchmark for evaluating the performance of management. Clearly, this does not mean that daily fluctuations in stock prices should be permitted to influence our analysis; however, the events of October 1987 were so pronounced that some of their implications need to be spelled out explicitly.

Black Monday

On Monday, October 19, 1987, America's longest-lived bull market came to an abrupt and unprecedented end. In one frantic day of trading, the Dow Jones Stock average dropped by 22%, and a half a trillion dollars of stock values were wiped out. The following day stock prices plunged on major stock exchanges around the world. One market, the Hong Kong Stock Exchange, closed shop for the week. In today's electronic world, the capital market never goes to sleep. As trading closes in the United States it moves across the Pacific to Tokyo and the new international financial centers of Hong Kong and Singapore. From there, trading again moves westward to the major financial centers of Europe: London, Frankfurt, and Paris.

Hindsight is always clearer than foresight and numerous candidates for the 'cause' of the crash were immediately mentioned. The one thing that is clear, however, is that a financial collapse of this magnitude must reflect a combination of factors, operating together, to undermine investors' confidence. Among these factors we find:

1. Stock prices had risen in the United States almost continuously since 1982 with the rise being especially pronounced in the nine months prior to the fall. This invoked the old stock market rule that what goes up must eventually come down.
2. The United States budget deficit had reached record levels, and its financing posed a major problem.
3. Similarly, the United States was running a large deficit in its balance of trade, i.e., imports to the United States greatly exceeded American exports. As a result, the value of the dollar against major foreign currencies had been falling.
4. The persistence of the gap in the U.S. balance of trade, and the need to attract foreign capital to finance the budget deficit, induced expectations of rising interest rates and the possibility of economic recession.
5. The 'globalization' of stock trading and the rapid transfer of stock market trends from market to market as well as technological and financial innovations, such as the widespread use of computers and the interaction between future and spot trading, were viewed by some analysts as destabilizing.
6. And, of course, the politicians came in for their share of responsibility with the U.S. Treasury Secretary and the German Finance Minister being singled out for criticism for their public pronouncements (and policies) prior to the crash.

The stock market crash and firms' cost of capital

As we have already noted, transitory fluctuations in stock prices are not usually allowed to affect the analysis of corporate investment behavior. However, a 22% drop in the stock market average in one day cannot be ignored. In particular, we must address the question of the impact of such a change on real economic activity. For example, what does the sharp fall in stock prices imply for the firm's investment in new plant and equipment? The answer to this question lies in the stock market's impact on the firm's cost of capital.

To simplify the discussion, consider a hypothetical firm which finances its investments solely out of equity. Assume further that the company in question has 100 shares outstanding and stable annual earnings of $100, all of which are distributed as dividends. Hence earnings per share (EPS) are $1. If the share price is assumed to be $10, the firm's cost of capital is 10%. Now let us assume that the firm is considering the possibility of issuing an additional 100 shares to finance a new investment project. What is the minimum required return on the new project? Ignoring any flotation costs, you can easily verify that the required return, i.e., the firm's cost of capital, is 10%. The company raises an additional $1,000 of equity (100 shares at a price of $10 per share). A 10% cost of capital implies that the new project, if it is to be accepted, must earn a profit of at least $100 per year. At this minimum rate of profit there is no dilution of earnings: the EPS after the investment remains $1 ($200/200 = $1). Thus, by definition, the firm's cost of capital is 10%.

Now assume that due to the stock market crash, the price of the firm's shares falls from $10 to $6. If the firm can sell the 100 new shares for only $6, it will have only $600 to invest (100 shares × $6 = $600). Since the firm must earn $100 on these additional shares to avoid the dilution of earnings, its cost of capital has risen sharply to 16.7% ($100/$600 = 16.7%). Other things being equal, this will have an inhibiting effect on new investment.

How does our analysis change if the firm in the preceding example does not intend to raise additional equity? Will its cost of capital rise even in the absence of new equity financing? Although it may not be intuitively obvious we can again show that the cost of capital following the fall in stock price is 16.7%, independent of the firm's financing decisions. Recall that, in the specific example above, EPS is $1 and the stock price (after the crash) is assumed to be $6. Should the firm decide to repurchase one of its shares for $6 the remaining shareholders will 'earn' 16.7% ($1/$6 = 16.7%). Hence, the firm should accept projects only if they offer a return of at least 16.7%. Thus, even without additional financing, the firm's cost of capital rises to 16.7%.

The logic underlying this result can be clarified by a simple example. Assume for simplicity that there are only two shareholders in the firm in question, one of whom sells his shares to the firm at a price of $6 per share. The second shareholder retains his shares. Thus, the second shareholder gives up $6 out of the firm's cash inflow which is used to repurchase the shares. However, he gains an additional earnings stream of $1 per share which otherwise would go to the first shareholder. Hence, the return to the remaining shareholder on the repurchase is 16.7% ($1/$6 = 16.7%).

The stock market crash and share repurchase

We are now in a position to understand the flood of corporate repurchases which occurred following the crash. Among the firms which announced their intention to buy back their own shares we find USX, Citicorp, IBM, Honeywell, United Technologies, and many others. Their decision reflects the underlying belief that the outlook for future corporation earnings does not justify the fall in share price. Hence, the higher return on share repurchase represented an attractive investment opportunity. This implies that the firms in question either did not expect future corporation profits to fall as a result of the crash, or at worse, expected that any decline in future earnings would be smaller than the fall in share price.

Dividend growth model

This conclusion can be clarified further by applying the dividend growth model which sets out the firm's cost of capital as:

$$k_e = \frac{d}{P_0} + g$$

where:

k_e = cost of equity
d = the expected dividend
P_0 = current market price of a share
g = the expected growth rate of earnings and dividends

If we assume the following values:

d = $5
P_0 = $100
g = 7%

the cost of capital is 12%:

$$k_e = \frac{\$5}{\$100} + 0.07 = 12\%$$

Now if there is a sudden fall in share price to say $60, but expectations regarding future earnings remain unchanged, the cost of capital, as we pointed out in the previous example, will rise sharply:

$$k = \frac{\$5}{\$60} + 0.07 = 15.3\%$$

However, if the fall in stock price is accompanied by a downward revision of expectations regarding future corporate profits (and therefore growth rates) the change in the cost of capital becomes ambiguous and depends on the relationship of the fall in stock price to the decline in the expected growth rate.

Capital asset pricing model (CAPM)

Finally, we can also examine the behavior of corporations following the stock market decline within the context of the CAPM, which estimates the firm's cost of capital as follows:

$$k_e = r + (E(x_m) - r)\beta_i$$

where:

k_e = cost of equity
r = riskless interest rate
$E(x_m)$ = expected return on the market portfolio
β_i = firm's beta (systematic) risk

If we assume that there was no meaningful change in the risk-free interest rate, the only variables affecting the cost of capital are the systematic risk (β_i) and the expected return on the market portfolio.

Since β_i measures the *relative* deviation of the individual stock's return (price) to deviations in the market as a whole, a *general decline* in the market cannot be expected to change these relative deviations. Of course, a specific β_i may change, but on average the betas can be expected to remain the same. This is clear if we recall that the average of all individual betas must always be equal to one no matter what happens to the absolute level of stock prices. Once again expected corporate profits provide the key variable affecting the firm's cost of capital. If expected corporate profits do not change, the fall in stock price will raise the expected return on the market portfolio, $E(R_m)$, and the individual firm's cost of capital k_i will increase thereby making the repurchase of its shares attractive.

SUMMARY

This chapter has presented an operational method for measuring the weighted average cost of capital in actual practice. The principles underlying the measurement of the specific cost of the individual components are discussed and the necessary adjustments to reflect corporate taxation and flotation costs are spelled out. After analyzing the impact of growth on the calculations, estimates of the cost of capital were presented for General Electric and for IBM. We conclude the chapter with an illustration of how the capital asset pricing model can be used to estimate the cost of equity capital, using for this purpose data on the returns of five 'aggressive' and five 'defensive' stocks over a 20-year period.

SUMMARY TABLE

Cost of debt

1. *Pre-tax cost.* The value k_d which solves:

$$P_0 = \sum_{t=1}^{n} \frac{C_t}{(1 + k_d)^t} + \frac{P_n}{(1 + k_d)^n}$$

where C_t is the coupon (interest), P_0 the bond's current price, and P_n the terminal (face) value of the bond.

2. *Post-tax cost.* The value k_d^* which solves:

$$P_0 = \sum_{t=1}^{n} \frac{(1 - T_c)C_t}{(1 + k_d^*)^t} + \frac{P_n}{(1 + k_d^*)^n}$$

3. If the bonds are sold at par, $P_0 = P_n$ and we have the relationship: $k_d^* = (1 - T_c)k_d$. If the bonds are not sold at par, some adjustment should be made in the formulas.

Cost of preferred stock

1. Pre-tax:

$$k_p = \frac{d/(1 - T_c)}{P_0}$$

2. Post-tax:

$$k_p^* = \frac{d}{P_0}$$

Hence the relationship $k_p^* = (1 - T_c)k_p$

Cost of equity

1. The CAPM:

$$k_{e_i} = r + (\bar{x}_m - r)\beta_i$$

2. For constant growth firm:

$$k_e = \frac{d}{P_0} + g$$

3. If the reinvestment rate is equal to k_e, we have:

$$k_e = \frac{d}{P_0} + g = \frac{E}{P_0}$$

where E is the current earnings per share.

4. If dividend is growing at g_1, for $n - 1$ year (super-growth period) and at a lower (normal) growth, g_2 thereafter, the cost of equity is the value which solves:

$$P_0 = \sum_{t=1}^{n} \frac{d(1 + g_1)^{t-1}}{(1 + k_e)^t} + \frac{d(1 + g_1)^{n-1}}{(1 + k_e)^n} \cdot \frac{1 + g_2}{k_e - g_2}$$

5. The growth rate g is estimated based on adjusted earnings per share (or adjusted dividends).

_____ QUESTIONS AND PROBLEMS

17.1 What is the specific cost of a $500 *perpetual* bond paying $45 in interest each year?

17.2 How much must a firm which pays 34% corporation tax earn on a new investment of $2 million which is financed by 7.5% bonds if the common shareholder's rate of return is to remain unchanged? What is the specific after-tax cost of the debt component?

17.3 What is the effective specific after-tax cost of a five-year bond with a face value of $500 which pays $72.50 interest *before tax* if the flotation costs are 4% and the corporate tax rate is 34%?

17.4 What is the effective specific after-tax cost of a ten-year bond with a face value of $500 which pays 7% interest, if the flotation costs are:

(a) 2%
(b) 4%
(c) 6%
(d) 8%

Assume a 34% corporation tax rate.

17.5 Assume no corporate taxes and that flotation costs are 5%. The interest rate is 10% on a bond with a face value of $100. What is the cost of debt if the bond matures in one year? In 10 years?

17.6 Suppose that in a given country the tax rate is 55%. How much must a firm which pays 55% corporate tax earn on a new investment of $5 million which is financed by preferred stock yielding a dividend of 9%, if the common stock-holder's return is to remain unchanged? How much must it earn if the same investment is financed by 9% bonds? Explain your results.

17.7 Investors in the common stock of Amgal Corporation expect to receive an annual dividend of $12.50 and also expect that the market price of the stock will rise to $105 by the end of the year. Ignoring flotation costs:

(a) What is the required rate of return on Amgal's common stock if the current market price of the stock is $100?
(b) What is the specific cost of equity if the current market price of the stock is $94?

17.8 Derive the dividend valuation model on the assumption that earnings are expected to increase at a given rate over time.

17.9 The Gamma Company earns 25% on new investments and pays 40% of its earnings as dividends.

(a) Calculate the growth rate of its future earnings according to the dividend growth model.
(b) Find Gamma's current earnings yield (E/P_0), assuming that the specific cost of its equity is equal to 20%.
(c) Is Gamma a 'moderate-growth' or 'super-growth' company? Explain.

17.10 What is the maximum price you will be willing to pay for a share of common stock that is paying $1.80 annual dividend, if you expect the dividend to grow at a rate of 7% in perpetuity and your required rate of return is 10%?

17.11 A high-technology electronics firm and a national food manufacturer both pay an annual dividend of $4 per share. Both firms have no debt and a stable earnings record and pay all their earnings as cash dividend. Neither firm anticipates changing the expected dividend in the future, but such changes cannot be completely ruled out. Yet the market price of the electronics stock is $32 per share whereas the food manufacturer's stock sells at $40. What is the required rate of return of the two stocks implied by these figures? How can we account for the difference?

17.12 Two chemical corporations, both equity financed with no debt, are essentially in the same business and therefore have the same risk and the same required rate of return. However, whereas one of the corporations has a stable earnings and dividend record, paying out all its earnings in dividends, the other is a growth stock increasing its earnings and dividends annually through a different management strategy. The current dividend is $5 per share for both corporations. The stable corporation's stock trades for $40 per share, whereas the price of the growth stock is $50.

Estimate the investors' required rate of return on these stocks and the steady future growth rate of the growing corporation as perceived by the market.

17.13 The following table lists some selected financial data of CBM for six years. The last column gives the consumer price index (CPI) for the corresponding period.

Year	Cash dividend ($000)	Net income ($000)	Number of shares	CPI
1	654,554	1,575,467	146,712,688	116.3
2	824,320	1,837,939	148,259,260	130.5
3	973,986	1,989,877	149,844,582	139.6
4	1,205,552	2,398,093	150,694,548	146.3
5	1,474,709	2,719,414	147,470,876	156.3
6	1,679,731	3,110,568	145,810,364	170.4

(a) Calculate the EPS and the dividend per share and estimate the geometric mean growth rate over the period in nominal and in real (inflation-adjusted) terms.

(b) Assuming that the reported earnings indeed represent the true economic income, which of the two growth rates would you use to estimate CBM's cost of capital? (Hint: look at the payout ratio.)

(c) Suppose that due to inflation the reported earnings overestimate the true economic income. What can you say about the payout ratio trend? Which growth rate is the most relevant in this case?

17.14 The following two excerpts from the CBM annual reports for 1991 and 1992 show an apparently puzzling contradiction: The 1991 *annual* cash dividend is stated as $11.52 in the annual report and as $2.88 in the 1992 annual report. A closer look reveals that the 1991 cash dividends in the 1992 report were 'adjusted for 1992 stock split'.

	From 1992 Report		From 1991 Report	
	1992	1991	1991	1990
First quarter	$0.86	$0.72	$2.88	$2.50
Second quarter	0.86	0.72	2.88	2.50
Third quarter	0.86	0.72	2.88	2.50
Fourth quarter	0.86	0.72	2.88	2.50
	$3.44	$2.88	$11.52	$10.00

(a) Using the dividend figures before and after adjustment, determine the ratio in which the stock was split.

(b) Use the result of (a) to adjust the 1990 cash dividend and calculate the average growth rate of cash dividends over the three years.

17.15 The following table shows the net income and the number of common stock shares of Philippia Petroleum Company for 10 years:

Year	10	9	8	7	6	5	4	3	2	1
Net income ($ millions)	891	718	531	412	335	388	212	148	132	111
No. of shares of common stock (million shares)	154.4	154.4	76.8	76.4	76.4	76.4	76.0	76.0	76.0	76.0

In year 8 the stock was split two-to-one.

(a) Calculate the stated earnings per share (EPS) and adjust the EPS for the stock split in year 8.
(b) Use the adjusted EPS series to calculate the average annual growth rate for the 10 years as the geometric mean over the period.

17.16 How would you formulate the dividend valuation model for a case in which earnings are expected to increase for the next five years and to remain stable from the sixth year on and that the firm pays all of its earnings as dividends?

17.17 Consider the following balance sheet and the income statement of Delta Inc.

Balance sheet ($000)

Assets		Liabilities	
Cash	11,000	Current liabilities	20,000
Receivables	20,000	Long-term debt[a] bonds	80,000
Inventories	139,000	Equity common stock[b]	160,000
Plant and equipment	90,000		
Total assets	260,000	Total liabilities	260,000

[a] $1,000 par value
[b] $10 par value

Income statement ($000)

Operating revenue	140,000
Operating expense	76,000
Net operating income	64,000
Interest payments	6,400
Net income	57,600
Taxes (34%)	19,584
Net income after taxes	38,016

Assume that the market price of Delta's stock is $12, the market price of its bonds is $800 and that the bonds have 100 years to maturity.

(a) Suppose that Delta is a 'non-growth' company. Should it accept a project with an after-tax internal rate of return of 12%?
(b) How will your answer to (a) be affected if you know that the financing mix (in book values) is the firm's optimal (target) capital structure?

17.18 The CBM company is operating outside the United States where the corporate tax rate is approximately 46%. Use the accounting data of CBM below to carry

CBM Selected Accounting Data

	Year 1	Year 2	Year 3	Year 4	Year 5
	($000 except per share amounts)				
Gross income from sales, rentals and services:					
Sales	$ 9,472,649	$ 8,754,794	$ 7,090,157	$ 5,959,475	$ 4,545,359
Rentals and services	13,390,127	12,321,295	11,043,027	10,344,858	9,891,182
	22,862,776	21,076,089	18,133,184	16,304,333	14,436,541
Cost of sales	3,266,605	2,838,225	2,256,135	1,959,631	1,630,978
Cost of rentals and services	5,146,353	4,645,800	4,042,448	3,865,813	3,717,709
Selling, development and engineering, and general and administrative expenses	9,205,367	8,151,129	7,177,080	6,409,315	5,664,897
Interest on debt	140,487	55,175	40,350	44,950	62,607
Other income, principally interest	449,295	411,808	475,243	494,469	360,527
Earnings before income taxes	5,553,259	5,797,568	5,092,414	4,519,093	3,720,877
U.S. Federal and non-U.S. income taxes	2,542,000	2,687,000	2,373,000	2,121,000	1,731,000
Net earnings	$ 3,011,259	$ 3,110,568	$ 2,719,414	$ 2,398,093	$ 1,989,877
Per share[a]	$5.16	$5.32	$4.58	$3.99	$3.34
Average number of shares outstanding[a]	583,373,269	584,428,584	594,298,448	601,701,768	596,177,708
Cash dividends paid	$ 2,007,572	$ 1,684,612	$ 1,487,627	$ 1,203,791	$ 968,989
Per share[a]	$3.44	$2.88	$2.50	$2.00	$1.63
Number of shares outstanding[a]	583,594,543	583,241,454	589,883,503	602,778,192	599,378,326
Net investment in plant, rental machines and other property	$ 12,193,019	$ 9,302,228	$ 7,889,326	$ 6,962,908	$ 6,695,043
Long-term debt	$ 1,589,358	$ 285,534	$ 255,776	$ 275,127	$ 295,115
Working capital	$ 4,405,877	$ 4,510,789	$ 4,864,073	$ 5,838,125	$ 4,751,829
Number of shareholders	696,918	580,572	581,513	577,156	586,470

[a] Adjusted for stock split in year 1.

XEROX CORPORATION: FIVE YEARS IN REVIEW ($ million except per share data)	15	14	13	12	11
Per share data					
Income per common share					
Continuing operations	$4.42	$4.34	$6.77	$6.55	$6.04
Discontinued operations	–	66	31	14	08
Net income per common share	4.42	5.00	7.08	6.69	6.12
Dividends declared per common share	3.00	3.00	3.00	2.80	2.40
Operations					
Income					
Rentals, service and sales	$8,464	$8,456	$8,510	$8,037	$5.852
Equity in net income of financial services businesses	197	39	25	3	–
Other income	141	162	143	144	139
Total	8,802	8,657	8,678	8,184	6,991
Research and development expenses	555	565	526	430	367
Income from continuing operations	466	368	572	553	508
Discontinued operations	–	56	26	12	7
Net income	466	424	598	565	515
Net income applicable to common stock	420	424	598	565	515
Financial position					
Current assets	$3,655	$3,814	$3,616	$3,560	$3,152
Rental equipment and related inventories	3,987	4,196	4,621	4,845	4,601
Accumulated depreciation of rental equipment	2,458	2,555	2,715	2,879	2,796
Land, buildings and equipment	2,778	2,641	2,565	2,460	2,151
Accumulated depreciation of buildings and equipment	1,308	1,201	1,127	1,050	894
Investment in financial services businesses, at equity	2,017	225	161	79	–
Total assets	9,297	7,668	7,674	7,514	6,716
Current liabilities	2,306	2,175	2,081	2,085	1,775
Long-term debt	1,461	850	870	898	913
Outside shareholders' interests in equity of subsidiaries	438	445	496	540	483
$5.45 cumulative preferred stock	442	–	–	–	–
Common and class B shareholders' equity	4,222	3,724	3,728	3,630	3,259
Additions to rental equipment and related inventories	810	876	1,112	997	914
Additions to land, buildings and equipment	325	329	321	335	300
Selected data and ratios					
Average common shares outstanding (thousands)	94,897	84,697	84,503	84,424	84,125
Common shareholders of record at year-end	107,180	109,136	102,139	106,293	111,877
Employees at year-end[a]	104,007	109,940	117,930	117,247	112,678
Book value per common share	$44.51	$44.12	$44.27	$43.13	$38.92
Return on assets[b]	5.0%	4.9%	7.8%	8.0%	8.3%
Return on equity[c]	10.1%	9.9%	15.6%	16.0%	16.3%
Total debt[d] to total capitalization[e]	28.2%	25.2%	22.0%	22.2%	21.9%
Total debt and preferred stock to total capitalization	34.4%	25.2%	22.0%	22.2%	21.9%

[a] Certain income statement data have been restated to adjust for classifications adopted in year 15. Excludes employees.

[b] Return on assets is calculated by dividing income from continuing operations by average assets of continuing operations.

[c] Return on equity is calculated by dividing income from continuing operations less preferred stock dividends by average common and class B shareholders' equity.

[d] Total debt is defined as the sum of notes payable, current portion of long-term debt, and long-term debt.

[e] Total decapitalization is defined as the sum of total debt outside shareholders' interests in equity of subsidiaries $5.45 cumulative preferred stock and common and class B shareholders' equity.

XEROX CORPORATION: TEN YEARS IN REVIEW	10	9	8[c]
Yardsticks of progress			
Income (loss) per common share			
Continuing operations	$5.77	$5.03	$4.49
Discontinued operations	–	–	–
Extraordinary income	0.15	–	–
Net income per common share	5.92	5.03	4.49
Dividends declared per common share	2.00	1.50	1.10
Operations ($ millions)			
Total operating revenues	$5,902	$5,082	$4,418
Rentals and services	4,015	3,714	3,495
Sales	1,887	1,368	923
Cost of rentals, services, and sales	2,400	2,057	1,805
Depreciation of rental equipment	509	484	502
Depreciation and amortization of buildings and equipment	155	149	144
Research and development expenses	311	269	226
Operating income	1,142	995	878
Interest expense	123	111	134
Income before income taxes	1,067	913	805
Income taxes	515	441	376
Outside shareholders' interests	87	68	69
Income from continuing operations	465	404	360
Income (loss) from discontinued operations[a]	–	–	–
Extraordinary income (net of income taxes)	12	–	–
Net income	477	404	360
Financial position ($ millions)			
Current assets	$2,567	$2,269	$2,059
Rental equipment and related inventories at cost	4,071	3,909	3,800
Accumulated depreciation of rental equipment	2,595	2,512	2,386
Land, buildings, and equipment at cost	1,763	1,662	1,596
Accumulated depreciation and amortization of buildings and equipment	738	633	548
Total assets	5,578	5,047	4,803
Current liabilities	1,339	1,146	1,081
Long-term debt	908	1,020	1,176
Outside shareholders' interests	349	315	301
Shareholders' equity	2,786	2,460	2,173
Additions to rental equipment and related inventories	696	552	456
Additions to land, buildings, and equipment	190	168	198
General and ratios			
Average common shares outstanding	80,517,659	80,343,003	80,342,521
Shareholders at year-end	117,924	125,549	129,077
Employees at year-end – continuing operations	104,736	103,977	97,558
Income before income taxes to total operating revenues	18.1%	18.0%	18.2%
Net income to average shareholders' equity	18.2%	17.4%	17.7%
Long-term debt to total capitalization[b]	22.5%	26.9%	32.2%

7ᶜ	6ᶜ	5ᶜ	4	3	2	1
$4.29	$4.37	$3.76ᵈ	$3.50	$2.95	$2.64	$1.89
(1.22)	(0.23)	(0.19)	(0.26)	(0.28)	(0.22)	0.15
—	—	—	—	—	—	—
3.07	4.14	3.57ᵈ	3.24	2.67	2.42	2.04
1.00	1.00	0.90	0.84	0.80	0.65	0.58⅓
$4,054	$3,505	$2,915	$2,338	$1,896	$1,636	$1,357
3,316	2,866	2,430	1,904	1,541	1,324	1,073
738	639	485	434	355	312	284
1,648	1,309	1,024	558	459	398	417
460	391	325	291	231	192	174
122	98	73	46	35	32	27
198	179	154	117	96	87	101
844	865	766	645	537	496	381
149	111	66	37	35	32	22
757	788	692	621	516	474	361
341	363	328	291	244	233	192
74	77	61	53	39	33	22
342	348	298⁴	277	233	208	147
(98)	(19)	(15)	(21)	(22)	(18)	11
—	—	—	—	—	—	—
244	329	283ᵈ	256	211	190	158
$1,687	$1,632	$1,276	$1,053	$918	$825	$649
3,574	3,221	2,452	1,928	1,626	1,322	1,068
2,058	1,706	1,354	1,063	869	696	549
1,443	1,253	999	668	542	432	353
447	376	299	215	172	144	116
4,614	4,207	3,209	2,484	2,145	1,844	1,516
1,127	1,050	852	659	556	492	419
1,279	1,167	703	445	426	359	263
259	221	155	114	108	89	71
1,898	1,733	1,475	1,249	1,041	883	726
582	862	595	438	382	312	267
269	281	226	125	121	89	76
79,550,021	79,548,124	79,388,281	79,228,281	78,821,232	78,591,401	77,712,417
135,578	137,471	138,314	143,666	143,640	146,605	129,981
93,532	97,399	90,200	72,237	62,638	55,367	49,335
18.7%	22.5%	23.7%	26.6%	27.2%	29.0%	26.6%
13.4%	20.5%	20.8%	22.4%	21.9%	23.6%	24.0%
37.2%	37.4%	30.1%	24.6%	27.0%	27.0%	24.8%

ᵃ The revenues, costs and expenses of discontinued operations for year 7 and prior years have been excluded from the respective captions and the income (loss) from discounted operations is reported separately. Income (loss) from discontinued operations is net of income tax and outside shareholders' interests.

ᵇ Total capitalization is defined as the sum of long-term debt, outside shareholders' interests in equity of subsidiaries, and shareholders' equity.

ᶜ Certain data have been restated for the years 5 through 9 to give effect to the retroactive change in the method of accounting for capital leases and to reflect changes in the classification of components of operating revenues and related costs and the change in the classification of service expense to cost of rentals and services from the selling, administrative and general expense category.

ᵈ Income from continuing operations, net income, and related per share amounts reflect a decrease of $5 million ($0.06 per share) for the cumulative effect at the beginning of year 5 of retroactively applying the new method of accounting for capital leases.

out the following calculations:

(a) Calculate the growth rate in the earnings per share for the years 1–5.
(b) Estimate post-tax cost of equity for year 1, using the growth rate of EPS as an estimate to the growth rate of dividends.
(c) Estimate the post-tax cost of debt for year 1.
(d) Calculate the weighted average cost of capital for year 1.

In your answer to (d) use book value of debt and market value of equity as weights. Additional information:

Stock price for year 1 is $64.25.
Earnings per share adjusted for stock splits (which do not appear in the five years data):

Year	$
10	3.12
9	2.70
8	2.76
7	2.35
6	2.23

Dividend in year 1 is $3.44.
Long-term debt including current portion = $1,628,198,000.

CBM Selected Accounting Data, 1986–1990.

17.19 The Xerox Corporation has asked you to estimate its cost of capital and you decide to rely upon Xerox's annual reports, excerpts from which are given on pp. 554–6. In addition, you will find that the number of outstanding shares on the last day of year 15 was 95,048,322 and, that the amount of interest Xerox paid on its long-term debt was $122,800,000. The price of Xerox common stock is currently $34.75.

(a) Estimate the growth rate of Xerox using historical data on earnings per share over the past 15 years.
(b) Ignoring flotation costs, calculate the after-tax weighted average cost of capital. (Assume that the existing proportions of debt and equity are optimal. Also assume that the firm plans to raise more money in the same proportion of debt/equity which currently exists and that the corporate tax rate is $T_c = 0.34$.)
(c) Calculate the after-tax average cost of capital, assuming that half of the equity comes from new issues with a flotation cost of 5% (and half from retained earnings) and that the flotation cost of bonds is 3%.
(d) Suppose now that as a result of inflation, the future rate of interest is expected to rise to 10%, and that the target capital structure changes to 28.45% debt and 71.55% equity. Ignoring flotation costs, calculate the after-tax weighted average cost of capital.

17.20 Define the specific cost of equity using the CAPM approach. Using this same approach, how would you define the specific cost of preferred stock?

17.21 Assume that the riskless interest rate (r) is 6%; the expected return on the market portfolio ($E(x_m)$) is 14%; and the coefficients of the systematic risk (β_i) for five firms are as follows:

$$\beta_A = 0.25; \ \beta_B = 0.75; \ \beta_C = 1; \ \beta_D = 1.45; \ \beta_E = 2.25$$

(a) Calculate the specific cost of equity for each firm.
(b) What is the relationship between beta and the specific cost of equity? Explain.

17.22 (a) Calculate the systematic risk (beta) for the following three firms, A, B, and C, whose specific costs of equity are: $k_A = 10\%$; $k_B = 12\%$; and $k_C = 16\%$, assuming that $r = 7\%$ and $E(x_m) = 12\%$.
(b) Which firm's stocks are 'aggressive'? Which are defensive? Explain.

17.23 A firm is considering two investment projects, each with several alternative levels of activity corresponding to different amounts of investment and different return distributions (the firm may choose only one activity level in each project). The projects are specified by the following schedule (x_m is the return on the market portfolio):

Project 1			Project 2		
Investment ($)	Expected return ($)	Covariance with x_m	Investment ($)	Expected return ($)	Covariance with x_m
100	300	8	100	150	4
200	500	16	200	360	8
300	650	24	300	560	12
400	730	32	400	730	16
500	800	40	500	800	20

The following market parameters are given: the expected return of the market portfolio $E(x_m) = 0.15$; standard deviation of the market return $\sigma_m = 0.10$; risk-free interest rate $r = 0.05$.

(a) Using the CAPM certainty equivalent cash flow, how much should the firm invest in each project?
(b) Suppose you want to apply the risk-adjusted discount rate (k) to projects 1 and 2. What rate should be applied to each project at each level of investment? (You have to derive 10 different rates.)
(c) Estimate the cost of capital by the formula:

$$k_i = r + (E(x_m) - r)\beta_i = r + \lambda \ \text{Cov}(x_i, x_m)$$

where x_i is the return per $1 of investment so that k_i is in percent. Carry out this calculation only for the first investment of project 1. Compare your result to (b) above. Explain the differences.

Hint: recall that the SML holds only for assets in equilibrium; in equilibrium the NPV must be equal to zero.

17.24 Using the dividend growth model, we find that the cost of equity for IBM and General Motors is a function of the selected period of estimating the growth rate.

In particular we obtain

	IBM	GM
Estimate of $\hat{g}$ based on 1983–1992	14.3	0.047
Estimate of $\hat{g}$ based on 1983–1993	14.4	0.047
Cost of equity ($d/P_0 + g$) end of 1992	15.62	10.18
Cost of equity ($d/P_0 + g$) end of 1993	16.22	16.08

How can you explain the drastic change in the equity cost of GM in comparison to the small change in the cost of equity of IBM?

Additional information: During the second half of 1993 the energy crisis began. All petroleum exporting nations sharply increased the price of oil. The demand for cars drastically declined.

While the price of IBM almost did not change from the end of 1992 to the end of 1993, the price of GM went down from $81.125 to $46.125.

17.25 The following announcement appeared in the *Wall Street Journal* on September 14, 1984.

'Pan American World Airways said it will make a public offering in Switzerland next week of Swiss franc convertible bonds due 1994 amounting to the equivalent of about $20 million.

The airline has been reporting losses in recent years, including a deficit of $120 million on revenue of $1.8 billion for the first half of this year. Despite the losses, Pan Am has been able to improve its balance sheet, with cash and short-term securities currently amounting to $450 million. The Swiss offering would improve the airline's finances further.

Pan Am said the Swiss bonds will bear an interest rate of 6.5% and will be convertible January 4, 1985 into common stock of Pan Am Corp., the parent holding company of the airline, at a rate of one common share for each $5.50 of bonds. Pan Am is restructuring into a holding company, with the restructuring expected to become effective today.

In composite trading on the New York Stock Exchange yesterday, Pan Am closed at $4.75, unchanged.'

It is also given that firms with a similar risk to that of Pan Am issued in the U.S. market in September, 1984, long-term bonds yielding 12%.

(a) What do you think should be the impact of the recent Pan Am losses on the interest rate at which the firm borrows?

(b) How can you explain the fact that Pan Am issued bonds bearing 6.5% interest while other firms in the same risk class issued bonds in the U.S. Market, bearing a 12% interest rate?

17.26 The table below presents some data regarding firm A.

Year	Earnings per share	Dividends	Stock dividends
1989	$1.00	$0.50	–
1990	1.10	0.55	–
1991	0.40	0.20	100%
1992	0.50	0.40	–

The stock price is $4.00 and the firm has 50% debt and 50% equity in its capital.

(a) Estimate the firm's cost of equity.
(b) Suppose that one investor estimates the growth rate by using the earnings data and another investor uses the dividend data. Which data yield a more accurate estimate of the firm's growth rate?

17.27 On January 1, 1992, the finance vice-president of Contelo asked you to calculate their weighted average cost of capital. Preliminary data gathering reveals the following information.

Background

In 1986 Contelo altered its overall strategy by diversifying into telecommunications and information processing as opposed to previously just telephone operations. By following this strategy, Contelo is now composed of five business groups: (1) telephone operations, (2) small business systems, (3) information services (commercial and governmental), (4) communications engineering and construction, and (5) network services (satellites). In 1991, over 30% of revenues came from non-telephone businesses.

The company's emphasis is on technological advances and their subsequent implementation. Contelo, a regulated telephone company, is presently in a rapidly changing regulatory market.

Accounting as financial data

The following was collected concerning Contelo:

Right-hand side of the balance sheet ($000) for the last year

Current liabilities:	
Commercial paper	15,000
Interim borrowings	49,792
Accounts payable	199,436
Other	349,313
	613,541
Deferred credits:	
Deferred income taxes	665,756
Long-term debt	1,631,984
Redeemable preferred stock	103,278
Common equity:	
Common stock and paid-in capital	628,808
Retained earnings less translation adjustments	584,771
	1,213,579
Total	4,228,138

The long-term debt and the preferred stock were sold mainly through a private placement hence there is no price to these two classes of assets. Both the bonds and the preferred stocks are rated Baa by Moody's.

The table reveals some information regarding rates of return and earnings of Contelo for nine years (which serves as a base in calculating the systematic risk):

| Year | Annual rates of return (%) | | Adjusted[a] EPS ($) |
	Contelo	S&P 500	
1	0.312	0.315	1.23
2	0.548	0.192	1.57
3	−0.063	−0.115	1.73
4	0.010	0.011	1.97
5	0.211	0.123	2.10
6	0.082	0.259	2.13
7	0.178	−0.097	2.34
8	0.122	0.147	2.32
9	0.332	0.173	2.42

[a] Adjusted for stock dividends, splits, etc.

There is no publicly available price for all of Contelo's bonds and preferred stock. However, the yield on the same class of assets as published in the financial news media is found to be:

Moody's Baa 20-year bond yield	14.05%
Moody's Baa preferred stock yield	12.05%

Also, the interest payment on long-term debt paid by Contelo was $150 million in year 9 and the dividend on preferred stock is $5,490,000. The estimated corporate tax rate is 34%.

Assume for 'deferred income taxes' that half is from accelerated depreciation of some specific projects (so Contelo has reserved funds) and half is from a general delay in the tax payment not related to specific projects.

For 'accounts payable' assume the firm buys at 2/10 − net 30. That is, a 2% discount if paid during the first ten days and no interest charges if paid on or before the 30th day. Contelo's policy is to pay 50% of accounts payable on the 10th day and 50% on the 30th day.

The average interest rates in year 9 for interim borrowings and commercial paper are 9.8% and 10.1%, respectively. Assume that the 'other' category has the same cost as interim borrowings. Also it is given that the market values of the short-term liabilities are approximately equal to their corresponding book value.

Contelo paid $1.62 cash dividends per share in year 7. Its common stock price is $P_0 = 21\frac{3}{8}$ and 69,874,067 common shares are outstanding in year 9. The one-year treasury bill rate is 9.99%.

Calculate the weighted average cost of capital of Contelo using *market values* (and not book values). However, for short-term liabilities assume that the book value is equal to the market value. For cost of equity, calculate it using both methods ($d/P_0 + g$ and CAPM).

17.28 Use the CAPM approach to calculate American Motors Corporation's (AMC) weighted average cost of capital. Estimate by using the following market values:

	Amount ($ millions)
Common equity	177.7
Preferred stock	100.0
Debt	833.1
Total	$1,110.8

The annual rates of return for AMC and the S&P 500 Index for twenty years are as follows:

Year	AMC	S&P	Year	AMC	S&P
1	−16.9	16.5	11	−62.3	−26.5
2	−32.8	12.5	12	65.4	37.3
3	−30.4	−10.1	13	−28.0	23.8
4	114.0	23.9	14	−6.3	−7.2
5	−3.7	11.1	15	26.7	12.2
6	−33.0	−8.5	16	47.7	12.3
7	−33.2	3.9	17	−43.0	25.8
8	21.6	14.3	18	−38.7	−9.7
9	17.8	19.1	19	179.0	14.8
10	7.5	−14.7	20	−5.7	17.3

Additional Information: Interest payments in year 20 totaled $108.45 million, the tax rate is 34%, preferred dividend payments amounted to $9.70 million and the average rate on treasury bills for this period is 6.8%.

17.29 Suppose that the current dividend is $1 per share and will grow by 20% each year in the next two years. Then the growth rate will be 10% per year and continue at this rate forever. Assuming that the current stock price is $20 which reflects the present value of all future cash dividends, calculate the firm's cost of equity.

17.30 A firm's WACC was 15% last year. This year the WACC is measured as 17%. What might be the reason for this increase in the WACC?

17.31 Firm A, whose beta is $\beta_A = 1$, buys firm B, whose beta is $\beta_B = 4$. The market value of firm A is four times larger than the market value of firm B. Thus, the new merged firm is five times bigger than firm B. Firm A and firm B are pure equity firms. The cost of capital of firm A is 10% and of firm B is 30%. What is the cost of capital of the new combined firm? In your answer use the CAPM to estimate the cost of capital.

APPENDIX 17A: ESTIMATING THE GROWTH RATE FROM HISTORICAL DATA _____

As noted in the text, the growth rate of earnings per share constitutes one of the most important components in the analysis of the cost of equity capital. This appendix spells out a simple regression procedure for estimating the growth rate from *ex-post* data using the standard statistical technique of least-squares regression.

Since the growth rate has a cumulative effect on earnings, the relationship between the earnings per share in any year t (E_t), and the earnings per share in the base year (E_0) can be formulated as follows:

$$E_t = E_0(1 + g)^t$$

where g denotes the compounded average annual growth rate. In order to estimate the growth rate statistically, we first take the natural log of both sides of the above equation, which gives:[15]

$$\ln E_t = \ln E_0 + t \ln(1 + g)$$

This equation is linear in logarithms, and has a slope equal to $\ln(1 + g)$.

Using the least-squares regression technique we can now estimate $\ln(1 + g)$. Denoting the ith observation of the log of earnings per share by x_i, the estimate of the slope of the regression line [i.e. $\ln(1 + g)$] is given by:

$$\ln(1 + g) = \frac{\sum_{i=1}^{n} (x_i - \bar{x})(t_i - \bar{t})}{\sum_{i=1}^{n} t_i^2 - n\bar{t}^2}$$

where t_i denotes the ith year, bars denote averages, and n is the total number of years included in the study. Subtracting the average year $\bar{t}$ from all the variables t_i, the average of the derived series, i.e., the average of $(t_i - \bar{t})$, becomes zero and we obtain the expression:

$$\ln(1 + g) = \frac{\sum_{i=1}^{n} x_i t_i^*}{\sum_{i=1}^{n} t_i^{*2}}$$

we apply this formula to estimate the growth rate of General Electric and IBM.

PROBLEM

17A.1 Use your results for problem 17.15 to recalculate the average annual growth rate of the Philippia Petroleum earnings per share in the 10-year period by the logarithmic regression method. Compare the result to the geometric mean growth in problem 17.15. How do you account for the difference in the two figures?

SELECTED REFERENCES

Aivazian, V. A. and Callen, J. L., 'Investment, Market Structure, and the Cost of Capital,' *Journal of Finance*, March 1979.

Ang, J. S., 'Weighted Average is True Cost of Capital,' *Financial Management*, Spring 1974.

---

15. If the earnings are negative for a given year, $\ln E$ is not defined and some modification should be done, e.g., eliminating the negative earnings year (outlier) or grouping several years' earnings together.

Arditti, Fred D., 'The Weighted Average Cost of Capital: Some Questions on its Definition and Use,' *Journal of Finance*, September 1973.

Arditti, Fred D., Levy, Haim, and Sarnat, Marshall, 'Taxes, Capital Structure, and the Cost of Capital: Some Extensions,' *Quarterly Review of Economics and Business*, Summer 1977.

Arditti, Fred D. and Pinkerton, J. M., 'The Valuation and Cost of Capital of the Levered Firm with Growth Opportunities,' *Journal of Finance*, March 1978.

Arzac, E. R. and Marcus, M., 'Flotation Cost Allowance for the Regulated Firm: A Reply,' *Journal of Finance*, March 1984.

Benzion, Uri and Yagil, Joseph, 'On the Price–Earnings Ratio Model,' *The Investment Analyst*, April 1987.

Bjerring, J. H., Lakonishok, J., and Vermaelen, T., 'Stock Prices and Financial Analysts' Recommendations,' *Journal of Finance*, March 1983.

Bloch, Ernest, *Inside Investment Banking*, Homewood, Ill.: Dow Jones/Irwin, 1986.

Boudreaux, Kenneth J. and Long, Hugh W., 'The Weighted Average Cost of Capital as a Cutoff Rate: A Further Analysis,' *Financial Management*, Summer 1979.

Brennan, Michael J., 'A New Look at the Weighted Average Cost of Capital,' *Journal of Business Finance*, Spring 1973.

Brigham, Eugene F. and Tapley, T. Craig, 'Financial Leverage and the Use of the Net Present Value Investment Criterion: A Reexamination,' *Financial Management*, Summer 1985.

Budd, A. F. and Litzenberger, R. H., 'Changes in the Supply of Money, the Firm's Market Value and Cost of Capital,' *Journal of Finance*, March 1973.

Capstaff, J., 'PE Ratios and Growth,' *The Investment Analyst*, October 1985.

Coggin, T. D. and Hunter, J. E., 'Analysts EPS Forecasts Nearer Actual than Statistical Models,' *Journal of Business Forecasting*, February 1983.

Conine, Thomas E. Jr and Tamarkin, Maurry, 'Divisional Cost of Capital Estimation: Adjusting for Leverage,' *Financial Management*, Spring 1985.

DeJong, Douglas and Collins, Daniel W., 'Explanations for the Instability of Equity Beta: Risk-free Rate Changes and Leverage Effects,' *Journal of Financial and Quantitative Analysis*, March 1985.

Elliot, Walter J., 'The Cost of Capital and U.S. Capital Investment: A Test of Alternative Concepts,' *Journal of Finance*, September 1980.

Emanuel, D., 'A Theoretical Model for Valuing Preferred Stock,' *Journal of Finance*, September 1983.

Estep, Preston W., 'A New Method for Valuing Common Stocks,' *Financial Analysts Journal*, November/December 1985.

Ezzamel, Mahmoud A., 'Estimating the Cost of Capital for a Division of a Firm and the Allocation Problem in Accounting: A Comment,' *Journal of Business Finance and Accounting*, Spring 1980.

Farrell, James L. Jr, 'The Dividend Discount Model: A Primer,' *Financial Analysts Journal*, November/December 1985.

Fielitz, Bruce D. and Muller, Frederick L., 'A Simplified Approach to Common Stock Valuation,' *Financial Analysts Journal*, November/December 1985.

Findlay, M. Chapman III, 'The Weighted Average Cost of Capital and Finite Flows,' *Journal of Business Finance and Accounting*, 1977.

Gitman, L. J. and Mercurio, V. A., 'Cost of Capital Techniques used by Major U.S. Firms: Survey and Analysis of Fortune's 1000,' *Financial Management*, Winter 1982.

Gordon, Myron J. and Halpern, Paul J., 'Cost of Capital for a Division of a Firm,' *Journal of Finance*, September 1974.

Green, Richard C. and Talmor, Eli, 'Asset Substitution and the Agency Cost of Debt Financing,' *Journal of Banking and Finance*, October 1986.

Howe, Keith M., 'Flotation Cost Allowance for the Regulated Firm: A Comment,' *Journal of Finance*, March 1984.

Jahnke, Gregg, Klaffke, Stephen, and Oppenheimer, Henry R., 'Price Earnings Ratios and Security Performance,' *Journal of Portfolio Management*, Fall 1987.

Jarrett, Jeffrey E., 'Estimating the Cost of Capital for a Division of a Firm, and the Allocation Problem in Accounting,' *Journal of Business Finance and Accounting*, Spring 1978.

Keane, Simon M., 'The Cost of Capital as a Financial Decision Tool,' *Journal of Business Finance and Accounting*, Autumn 1978.

Kim, Moon H., 'Weighted Average vs. True Cost of Capital,' *Financial Management*, Spring 1974.

Lewellen, Wilbor G., 'A Conceptual Reappraisal of Cost of Capital,' *Financial Management*, Winter 1974.

Linke, Charles M., 'Weighted Average vs. True Cost of Capital,' *Financial Management*, Spring 1974.

Litzenberger, Robert H. and Rao, C. U., 'Portfolio Theory and Industry Cost-of-Capital Estimates,' *Journal of Financial and Quantitative Analysis*, March 1972.

Long, Michael S. and Rasette, George A., 'Stochastic Demand, Output and the Cost of Capital,' *Journal of Finance*, May 1974.

Miles, James A. and Ezzell, John R., 'The Weighted Average Cost of Capital, Perfect Capital Markets and Project Life: A Clarification,' *Journal of Financial and Quantitative Analysis*, September 1980.

Nantell, Timothy J. and Carlson, Robert C., 'The Cost of Capital as a Weighted Average,' *Journal of Finance*, December 1975.

Rappaport, Alfred, 'The Affordable Dividend Approach to Equity Valuation,' *Financial Analysis Journal*, July/August 1986.

Ruback, Richard S., 'Calculating the Market Value of Riskless Cash Flows,' *Journal of Financial Economics*, March 1986.

Shapiro, Alan C., 'In Defense of the Traditional Weighted Average Cost of Capital as a Cutoff Rate,' *Financial Management*, Summer 1979.

Siegel, Jeremy J., 'The Application of the DCF Methodology for Determining the Cost of Equity Capital,' *Financial Management*, Spring 1985.

Weston, J. E. and Lee, W. Y., 'Cost of Capital for a Division of a Firm: Comment,' *Journal of Finance*, December 1977.

Zhu, Yu and Friend, Irwin, 'The Effects of Different Taxes on Risky and Risk-free Investment and on the Cost of Capital,' *Journal of Finance*, March 1986.

18

Dividend Policy

A Tax-efficient Bonanza

The shareholders of Berkshire Hathaway were asked in May 1985 if they wanted to receive a dividend. Since 1969, when Warren Buffett became CEO of the company, they had never been given one. Instead, as Buffett has eloquently explained in his annual reports, all retained earnings, shorn of corporate taxes, have been reinvested to maximize shareholder returns. Did those same "owner-partners" as he calls them, want him to continue that policy or not?

An overwhelming 88% wisely urged him to stay the course. Says CFO Verne McKenzie: "In the last three years Berkshire's net worth has doubled. If we had paid out all that net worth as a dividend, I'm not sure our shareholders could have collectively doubled their investments."

In the past ten years, Berkshire returned an average of 32.1% per year, almost twice the return of Standard & Poor's 500-stock index. Says John Tilson, who runs the top-performing Pasadena Growth Fund: "For a company with Berkshire's high returns, and its strong franchise, paying dividends is absurd." Tilson loves Berkshire Hathaway, which at a recent price of $8,900 a share is still 5% to 10% undervalued by his estimates. *Source*: *Fortune*, April 20, 1992, p. 30.

The shareholders of Berkshire Hathaway prefer not to receive dividends since in doing so they pay lower taxes. In some years, capital gains taxes were lower than taxes on dividends. Nowadays there is a relatively smaller advantage given the tax rates in the U.S. are the same, but there is an advantage of tax deferral – you pay tax as capital gains only when you sell the stock.

Despite the obvious advantages of owning low-dividend, high-growth stocks, individual investors still hold big pieces of high-dividend equities. About two-thirds of the outstanding stock in **General Motors** is in Joe and Jane Smith's hands. Small investors also own more than half of Big Blue's shares. Presumably some of those folks hold the stock through tax-exempt accounts, such as IRAs, but many don't.

Just why investors love high-dividend-paying stocks is something of a conundrum among the experts. Nobel Prize winners Merton Miller and Franco Modigliani studied the investment value of dividends in the early 1960s and found that even in a tax-free world, dividends offer no value to the investor. Once you account for income taxes, dividends are at a distinct disadvantage to capital gains. His findings were particularly stinging at a time when investors paid taxes as high as 91% on dividends, but paid only 25% on capital gains.

Nowadays, with tax rates lower and the differential between the rates on capital gains and ordinary income all but gone, the disadvantage of dividends is less. But Miller is still no touter of dividends. Says he: "A new argument holds that the dividend is important because at least the shareholder gets the money, and the managers, who may otherwise pour the money down their rat holes on misguided projects and acquisitions, don't. One would hope there would be other ways to discipline management."

John Childs, a senior vice president of Kidder Peabody and a noted authority on dividend policy, points out that, logical or not, investors want dividends for a panoply of reasons. One of the biggest is the wish to wring some cash out of the stock while waiting for capital appreciation.

Sounds sensible. But it turns out that many investors in high-yielding stocks simply take their dividends, incur the tax, and plow the cash right back into the company through a dividend reinvestment program. About a third of IBM's individual shareholders reinvest their dividends. These investors are taking big tax hits on income that they clearly don't need.

If you *do* need spending money from your investments, you may be better off if you cut your stake in two. Relegate part to tax-free municipal bonds, recently yielding a fat 6.8%, and the rest to low- or even no-dividend growth stocks. It will take fewer dollars to generate the same amount of cash from the bond, and you will have better diversification and no annual tax bite.

Source: *Fortune*, April 20, 1992, p. 31.

ARTICLE 39

Mazda Motor Corp.

Japan's **Mazda Motor** Corp. reported a 60% plunge in unconsolidated, or parent company, pretax profit to 19.67 billion yen ($151 million) in the year ended March 31, from 49.13 billion yen in the previous year. It cited the slump in the global auto market, rising operating costs and the yen's appreciation for the drop in earnings.

Net income, meanwhile, dropped 66% to 9.27 billion yen from 27.01 billion yen a year earlier. Sales edged up 3.5% to 2.304 trillion yen from 2.226 trillion yen. The dividend was unchanged at 7.5 yen a share.

For the current fiscal year, Mazda said

it sees unconsolidated pretax profit falling 24% to 15 billion yen. Net profit is also expected to drop, by 14% to 8.0 billion yen. But sales are projected at 2.430 trillion yen, up 5.5%.

Mazda noted Japan's auto market continued to be sluggish in fiscal 1991 as improved demand for midsize cars couldn't offset the generally weak demand for subcompact and micro-mini cars. Exports were sluggish amid increased local production and softer demand in the U.S., Europe and Southeast Asia.

Source: *Wall Street Journal*, May 26, 1992, p. B4.

As can be seen from article 39, Mazda's net income dropped 66% and its future is not bright with the current year's profit expected to drop an additional 24%. Yet, the firm decided not to change its dividend policy which remains as 7.5 yen per share. Why does Mazda not reduce its dividend? Is it important for a firm to keep a constant dividend when it is facing unprofitable years? What signal does Mazda send to its investors regarding the future profit potential of the firm?

As we have already seen, the firm is continually faced with two crucial and interrelated problems: the capital investment and long-term financing decisions. Along with its investment and financing policies, the firm must also decide on its dividend policy: that is, the proportion of earnings which should be distributed to its shareholders in the form of cash dividends.

While Berkshire's policy seems to be convincing, many shareholders in other companies insist on being paid dividends even if it increases their tax burden. From the two articles above we see that dividend policy is not a simple and straightforward issue. It involves the following issues:

1. What tax burden is imposed on shareholders?
2. Is there disagreement between shareholders, with some wanting a high dividend whereas others want no dividend?
3. How should changes in tax rates imposed on dividends be incorporated, if at all? The dividend disadvantage in the U.S. used to be substantial when a 91% tax on dividends but only a 25% capital gains tax was imposed.
4. If management could be 'disciplined' so that they could act in accordance with shareholders' preferences, is it possible that shareholders would prefer dividends not be paid?

In this chapter we focus attention on a question which has occupied the attention of leading financial experts for more than two decades: why do firms almost universally pay out a substantial portion of their earnings as cash dividends?

The key to this problem can be found in the answer to two additional, albeit related, questions:

1. What impact (if any) does dividend policy have on the market price of a firm's common stock? Essentially this question asks whether dividend policy is a significant factor in determining the market value of the shareholders' investment.
2. If dividend policy does affect shareholders' wealth (the market value of common stock), what constitutes the firm's *optimal* dividend policy?

Dividend policy has been (and remains today) a subject of considerable controversy. Much ink and invective have been spilled, yet operational solutions to the problem of dividend policy are far from perfect, and qualitative judgemental factors, the so-called intangibles of financial decisions, remain of considerable importance in determining dividend policy. The purpose of this chapter is not to resolve the irresolvable; our more modest goal is to clarify some of the more important issues so that an intelligent choice can be made among alternative theories. For example, when Mazda's profit went down and it maintained its dividend payout, a higher proportion of earnings was being paid as dividends. If the firm did not change its investment plans, this implies that more money should be raised in the capital markets.

The goal is to improve, not to replace, judgement! To this end we analyze dividend policy under various assumptions regarding the degree of competition and uncertainty prevailing in the securities markets, *not* it should be emphasized, in the hopeless quest for the grail of the optimum but rather in order to help achieve a better foundation on which to base corporate dividend decisions.

DIVIDENDS AND VALUATION: NO EXTERNAL FINANCING

To help clarify the underlying theoretical foundation of the dividend decision, let us initially imagine a world in which no taxes are levied on current income or capital gains. For simplicity, we shall also assume the absence of a new issue market for securities, so that firms must finance their investment programs solely from internally generated sources.

The analysis of the impact of dividend policy on the value of a firm's common stock requires a prior stipulation of a formal valuation model. Numerous variants exist, but perhaps the best known of these models defines the price of a firm's common stock as the present value of all future dividend payments:

$$P_0 = \frac{d_1}{(1 + k_e)} + \frac{d_2}{(1 + k_e)^2} + \cdots = \sum_{t=1}^{\infty} \frac{d_t}{(1 + k_e)^t}$$

where:

P_0 = initial price of a share of common stock

d_t = cash dividend per share distributed in year t. (Note that in this chapter we make the distinction between d_t, the dividend per share, and D_t, the total cash dividend paid by the firm)

k_e = cost of equity capital

According to this view the underlying earnings are only a means to an end: if the retained portion of earnings are reinvested for the benefit of the shareholders they too will produce future dividends and therefore will be reflected in the cash flow. If they do *not* produce future dividends, such reinvested earnings are correctly excluded from the discounted value of future benefits. Or as John B. Williams unforgettably expressed it in the form of some sage advice of an old farmer to his son:

> A cow for her milk,
> A hen for her eggs,
> And a stock by heck,
> For her dividends.

> An orchard for fruit,
> Bees for their honey,
> And stocks, besides,
> For their dividends. [1]

Now let us follow the farmer's advice, and use the dividend valuation formula to analyze the impact of a change in dividend policy on stock prices. For example, let us assume that the firm decides to forgo its cash dividend in the first year in order to reinvest the additional sum d_1, *for one year*, distributing in the second year $d_2 + d_1(1 + R)$; that is the company increases its second-year dividend by d_1 plus the one-year return on this additional investment, Rd_1.

Obviously, shifting the dividend from the first year to the second year constitutes a change in dividend policy. But what is the impact of this change on the value of the company's stock? To answer this question we rewrite the valuation equation in a form which explicitly reflects the above change in dividend policy. The new valuation formula, following the dividend change, is given by:

$$P_0' = \frac{0}{1 + k_e} + \frac{d_2 + d_1(1 + R)}{(1 + k_e)^2} + \sum_{t=3}^{\infty} \frac{d_t}{(1 + k_e)^t}$$

where:

$P_0' =$ new stock price
$R =$ rate of return on reinvestment in year 1

Subtracting the previous equation from this formula we derive the change in the value of the stock (ΔP) which results from the assumed change in dividend policy:

$$\Delta P = P_0' - P_0 = \frac{d_1(1 + R)}{(1 + k_e)^2} - \frac{d_1}{(1 + k_e)} = \frac{d_1}{(1 + k_e)} \left[\frac{(1 + R)}{(1 + k_e)} - 1 \right]$$

$$= \frac{d_1}{(1 + k_e)} (R - k_e)$$

If $R = k_e$ (that is, if the reinvestment rate R is equal to the market required rate of return k_e), then the change in dividend policy has no impact on the value of the stock, that is, $P_0' - P_0 = 0$. On the other hand, if $R > k_e$, the

---

1. See John B. Williams, *The Theory of Investment Value*, Cambridge, Mass., Harvard University Press, 1938, p. 58. Williams continues: 'The old man knew where milk and honey came from, but he made no such mistake as to tell his son to buy a cow for her cud or bees for their buzz'. *Ibid.*

reinvestment of the first year 'dividend', d_1, increases the market value of the shares. Conversely, should R be less than k_e, the price of the stock will fall.

The reader should recall the assumption underlying this highly simplified model, i.e., that no external sources of financing are available to the firm. In such a case a decision by the firm to increase its investment induces a parallel change in its dividend policy and vice versa. Thus dividend policy is tied to investment policy, and apart from the special case in which $R = k_e$, changes in dividend policy can be expected to have a substantial and direct impact on the value of the firm.

These results can easily be generalized to cover the case of constant growth. Recall that in this case we assume that the firm retains a constant fraction b of its earnings per share, earns a rate of return, R, on its investments, and employs no external sources of financing. Given these assumptions, per share earnings and dividends will grow at a compounded average annual rate equal to bR and the price of a share, that is the present value of future dividends, is given by:

$$P_0 = \frac{(1-b)E}{(1+k_e)} + \frac{(1-b)E(1+bR)}{(1+k_e)^2} + \frac{(1-b)E(1+bR)^2}{(1+k_e)^3} + \cdots$$

where:

$$E = \text{current earnings per share}$$
$$b = \text{fraction of retained earnings which is reinvested}$$
$$(1-b)E \equiv d = \text{current dividend per share}$$
$$R = \text{rate of return on reinvested earnings}$$
$$k_e = \text{cost of equity}$$

As we have shown in Chapter 17, the summation of all the terms on the right-hand side of the equation yields the solution:

$$P = \frac{(1-b)E}{(k_e - bR)}$$

Since b, the fraction of earnings per share which is reinvested, represents the firm's dividend policy, it is clear that in the growth model dividend policy 'counts', that is share price depends on a firm's dividend policy. The relationship of share price to alternative dividend policies (alternative values of b) can be seen in Table 18.1 which sets out the solutions of the valuation equation on the assumption that earnings per share in the first year (E) are \$10, and k_e, the discount rate, is 20%: solutions for two alternative values of the reinvestment rate of return, R (25% and 10%), are given.

An examination of Table 18.1 shows that a share's market price rises as the percentage retained, b, increases when the rate of return on reinvestment is greater ($R = 25\%$) than the cost of equity. The opposite relationship holds when $R = 10\%$, that is when R is less than the discount rate. In the simple dividend growth model, valuation depends on dividend policy, and on the relationship between k_e and R. If the company expects to earn a rate of return on reinvested profits which is higher than the alternative cost of the distributed

Table 18.1 Theoretical share prices for alternative retention ratios (b) and rates of return (R)

Retention ratio as % of earnings (b)	Reinvestment rate (P)	Share price in $[a] ($P_0$)
0	$R = 25\%$	50.00
0.1		51.40
0.2		53.30
0.5		66.70
0	$R = 10\%$	50.00
0.1		47.40
0.2		44.40
0.5		33.30

[a] Calculated from the formula: $P_0 = (1 - b)E/(k_e + bR)$ on the assumption that $k = 20\%$ and $E = \$10$.

profits (dividends) to the shareholders, the increase in the proportion of retained earnings is desirable. However, if the investment opportunities confronting the firm are relatively poor ($R < k_e$), a decrease in retained earnings (increase in the dividend payout ratio) increases the value of the firm.

Finally, in cases where $R = k_e$, the valuation equation can be rewritten as follows:

$$P_0 = \frac{(1 - b)E}{k_e - bR} = \frac{(1 - b)E}{k_e - bk_e} = \frac{(1 - b)E}{(1 - b)k_e} = \frac{E}{k_e}$$

The dividend term itself as well as the dividend policy variable b are eliminated from the valuation formula, which indicates that when $R = k_e$, dividend policy is irrelevant for valuation purposes since it has no effect on shareholders' wealth. The intuitive explanation for this phenomenon is straightforward: the shareholders' opportunity cost is k_e, but since the firm can earn exactly the same rate of return ($R = k_e$) on its retained earnings, the shareholders are indifferent as to whether the firm reinvests the earnings for them, or whether they receive cash dividends and reinvest them elsewhere themselves – assuming, of course, the absence of transaction costs and taxes.

DIVIDENDS AND VALUATION: WITH EXTERNAL FINANCING

To this point we have assumed retained earnings are the only source which the firm can draw upon to finance new investment projects. This, of course, forges a link, as we have seen, between a firm's investment and dividend policies – the only way to finance investment projects is through retention of earnings, and given the level of earnings, the only way to increase retention is by raising the proportion retained, thereby decreasing dividends. In practice such situations might, and undoubtedly do, exist. In the short run, access to outside financing may become difficult or impossible, and for a variety of reasons (for example, family control) a firm may find itself constrained to retained earnings even in the long run.

The typical corporation, however, usually has recourse to alternative means of financing its investment projects, and is not necessarily restricted to the use of retained earnings. The availability of external sources of financing breaks the link between dividend and investment policies. Given the ability to raise outside capital, the firm can simultaneously increase investment and dividends.[2] In such a situation the previously analysed *tradeoff* between investment and dividends no longer obtains since the firm can always raise additional funds to finance its investment program and the payment of dividends simultaneously.

Miller and Modigliani model

Perhaps the best known advocates of the incorporation of external financing in valuation models are Merton Miller and Franco Modigliani (hereafter referred to as M & M)[3] who have used this approach to show that the price of a firm's common stock is *independent* of its dividend policy in a perfect riskless capital market in which no individual trader or firm can influence the price of securities; information is freely and immediately available to all; there are no transactions costs or other legal and institutional impediments to investment; and there is no differential taxation of personal income (i.e., dividends) and capital gains. It is interesting to note that the tax assumption is closer to actual tax rates today than when M & M advocated their theory.

In order to focus attention on the crucial role played by the existence of external sources of financing, let us initially assume a world of perfect certainty. To prove the M & M invariance theorem, we define the following notation:

$d_{j(t)}$ = dividend per share paid by firm j on the *last* day of period t
$P_{j(t)}$ = price (ex-any-dividend in $t-1$) of a share of firm j at the *start* of period t

As we assume *certainty* and a perfect capital market, the price of each share must be such that the rate of return to investors $r_{(t)}$ on every share will be the same over any given interval of time; and equal to the riskless interest rate[4] that is:

$$r_{(t)} = \frac{d_{j(t)} + P_{j(t+1)} - P_{j(t)}}{P_{j(t)}}$$

2. However, the reader should note that many major corporations, such as IBM and Xerox, have issued common stock only once in the post-World War II period.
3. See Merton H. Miller and Franco Modigliani, 'Dividend Policy, Growth, and the Valuation of Shares,' *Journal of Business*, October 1961.
4. Hence we denote the rate of return by r rather than by the Greek letter ρ which was used in M & M's original article.

and, therefore:

$$P_{j(t)} = \frac{1}{1 + r_{(t)}} (d_{j(t)} + P_{j(t+1)})$$

for every firm's shares.[5]

Market forces assure that the last two equations will hold. If the rate of return on one firm's shares is lower than that of another firm's shares, investors will sell the shares yielding the low return and buy the shares which offer the higher return, and this process will continue until the rate of return on all shares is equal to r. To analyze the impact of dividend policy on stock valuation, let us reformulate the valuation equation in terms of the total value of the firm rather than in terms of an individual share. Without loss of generality we drop the subscript j and introduce the following additional notations:

$n_{(t)}$ = number of shares on record at the start of period t

$m_{(t+1)}$ = number of new shares sold during t at the ex-dividend closing price $P_{(t+1)}$

It is clear from these definitions that $n_{(t+1)} = n_{(t)} + m_{(t+1)}$.

$V_{(t)} = n_{(t)}P_{(t)}$ = total value of the enterprise at the start of period t

$D_{(t)} = n_{(t)}d_{(t)}$ = total dividends paid at the end of t to shareholders on record at the start of period t

Using these symbols and the relationship: $n_{(t)}P_{(t+1)} = V_{(t+1)} - m_{(t+1)}P_{(t+1)}$, the valuation equation can be rewritten as:

$$V_{(t)} = \frac{1}{1 + r_{(t)}} (D_{(t)} + n_{(t)}P_{(t+1)}) = \frac{1}{1 + r_{(t)}} (D_{(t)} + V_{(t+1)} - m_{(t+1)}P_{(t+1)})$$

Hence the end-of-year dividend $D_{(t)}$, the terminal value $V_{(t+1)}$, and the term $m_{(t+1)}P_{(t+1)}$ would appear to be the factors which determine $V_{(t)}$. It would appear, therefore, that dividend policy really affects share values since the value of the firm ($V_{(t)}$) depends, *inter alia* on $D_{(t)}$. Nevertheless, M & M have succeeded in proving the irrelevance of dividend policy. Suppose now that the company decides to invest $I_{(t)}$ dollars in year t. The company may finance this investment by reducing $D_{(t)}$ or by raising external capital, thereby increasing $m_{(t)}P_{(t+1)}$. As we can see from the valuation equation the dividend policy decision affects the value of firm $V_{(t)}$ in two ways: (1) directly through the dividend payment, $D_{(t)}$, and (2) indirectly through the amount of outside capital required to finance the investment program, $-m_{(t+1)}P_{(t+1)}$. The latter is determined by the relationship:

$$m_{(t+1)}P_{(t+1)} = I_{(t)} - (X_{(t)} - D_{(t)})$$

where $X_{(t)}$ is the firm's total net profit for the period t. This relationship reflects the fact that the portion of investment not covered by retained earnings

---

5. Since M & M assume a perfect market and complete certainty, there is no need to distinguish between bonds and stocks.

must be financed by raising external capital. Substituting this expression for $m_{(t+1)}P_{(t+1)}$ in the valuation formula yields:

$$V_{(t)} = n_{(t)}P_{(t)} = \frac{1}{(1 + r_{(t)})} (X_{(t)} - I_{(t)} + V_{(t+1)})$$

Thus the value of the firm depends on earnings $X_{(t)}$, investment $I_{(t)}$, and $V_{(t+1)}$, but does not depend on the current dividend $D_{(t)}$. However, if we assume that future dividends are independent of the first-year dividend $D_{(t)}$, and that they are known with certainty, it follows that $V_{(t+1)}$ is also independent of the current dividend $D_{(t)}$, but still might be dependent on future dividends. However, we can repeat the same line of reasoning for $V_{(t+1)}$ and show that this value is also independent of $D_{(t+1)}$, and similarly that $V_{(t+2)}$ is independent of $D_{(t+2)}$, and so on. Therefore, the current value of the firm, $V_{(t)}$ is also independent of all future dividends. In sum, the level of future earnings $X_{(t)}$ is the key variable which determines the value of the firm. In the absence of a link between dividend and investment decisions dividend policy in a riskless perfect capital market is irrelevant.[6]

INTERNAL AND EXTERNAL FINANCING: A RECONCILIATION

The dividend growth model and the results of M & M can be reconciled by noting that dividend changes do not affect share prices in both cases when the investment effect is neutralized. In order to isolate the impact of dividend policy on valuation, M & M hold firms' net investment constant: that is, they compare situations with identical investment programs but which differ in

6. It is clear from the M & M analysis that $D_{(t)} = X_{(t)} - I_{(t)} + EF_{(t)}$, where $EF_{(t)}$ denotes the firm's external financing during the period. Thus the firm should first find its *optimal* level of investment and then adjust its dividend policy and external financing to the desired level. It follows that the irrelevancy of dividend policy under conditions of certainty can be derived directly from the investment-consumption analysis of Chapter 4. Simply replace the consumption in the two periods, C_0 and C_1 (see Table 4.14), by the dividends in each period, D_0 and D_1. The separation property between investment and financial decisions remains. As a result, any dividend policy is optimal so long as the firm follows the *NPV* rule when evaluating its investments. If some shareholders have a preference for a different dividend policy (combination of D_1 and D_2) they can borrow or lend thereby adjusting the cash flow to their preferences. The particular dividend policy chosen by the firm is, under these circumstances, irrelevant.

Note that in this type of analysis we assume liquidation of the firm at the end of the period. The value of the firm today (V_0) is:

$$V_0 = (X_0 - I_0) + \frac{X_1^*}{(1 + r)}$$

where:

X_0 = the return today
X_1^* = tomorrow's return *after* the investment
I_0 = today's investment

Given the assumption of liquidation this is also equal to

$$V_0 = d_0 + \frac{d_1}{1 + r}$$

their dividend policies. In the growth model, on the other hand, investment varies with changes in dividend policy. In order to neutralize the effects of investment in the dividend growth model, we must set the present value of any new investment equal to zero. [7] Thus investment can be permitted to differ but only as long as $R = k_e$.

Consider the following example of a firm which pays out all of its earnings as dividends. In such a case the value of the company's shares is given by:

$$P_0 = \frac{E}{(1 + k_e)} + \frac{E}{(1 + k_e)^2} + \cdots + \frac{E}{(1 + k_e)^t} + \cdots$$

where E denotes the company's expected earnings all of which it expects to pay out as cash dividends and k_e is the cost of equity capital. Now assume that the firm suspends its first-year dividend and reinvests that same amount in an annuity yielding an annual rate of return on R which is exactly equal to k_e. In this case no dividend is paid in the first year and the firm earns an additional RE per annum in perpetuity all of which is paid out as future dividends:

$$P_0' = \frac{0}{(1 + k_e)} + \frac{(E + RE)}{(1 + k_e)^2} + \cdots + \frac{(E + RE)}{(1 + k_e)^t} + \cdots$$

Recall that investment is neutralized, as we have already shown, so long as $R = k_e$. Hence P_0' is exactly equal to P_0 and dividend policy has no effect on share prices.

The same result can be reached using the growth model formula:

$$P_0 = \frac{(1 - b)E}{(k_e - Rb)}$$

Given the assumption $R = k_e$, this can be rewritten as:

$$P_0 = \frac{(1 - b)E}{(k_e - k_e b)} = \frac{(1 - b)E}{(1 - b)k_e} = \frac{E}{k_e}$$

Since b can be eliminated from the valuation formula, dividend policy is again irrelevant for valuation.

Thus, given the assumption of certainty and of perfect capital markets, *both* the dividend growth and the M & M models assert that once investment policy is neutralized dividend policy can have no effect on share prices. [8] However, this should not be interpreted to mean that dividend policy is not important.

---

7. See Myron J. Gordon, 'Optimal Investment and Financing Policy,' *Journal of Finance*, May 1961.

8. They do disagree with respect to the impact of uncertainty. However, it has been shown that the two approaches can also be reconciled in the case of uncertainty, see M. J. Brennan, 'A Note on Dividend Irrelevance and the Gordon Valuation Model,' *Journal of Finance*, December 1971.

_____ **FACTORS AFFECTING DIVIDEND DECISIONS**

The assumption that securities are traded in frictionless capital markets under conditions of perfect certainty clearly is intended only as an approximation of reality. Real-life capital markets are neither perfect nor riskless. In this section we examine some of the implications of relaxing these assumptions before tackling the formidable task of introducing taxation into the theoretical models.

Flotation and transaction costs

The irrelevancy of dividend policy in a perfect market assumes of course zero flotation costs. Thus a firm is indifferent between the financing of its new project either out of the retained earnings or by issuing new securities. However, in practice these two sources of finance are not perfect substitutes: external financing is the more extensive alternative due to the existence of flotation costs which reflect the need to cover the cost of underwriting. Other things being equal, the smaller the firm, or the smaller the new issue, the larger will be the proportion of such costs. Again, this is a factor which favors the use of retained earnings, that is, a low-dividend payout.

Another factor which may favor retained earnings is the existence of transaction costs. Thus a shareholder who desires to increase his investment in the firm would prefer not to receive cash dividends, thereby increasing his investment in the firm without paying commissions which are proportionately high, particularly when the amount of investment is relatively small. However, this sword cuts two ways. Investors who desire to decrease their investment in the firm, say in order to increase current consumption, will by an analogous argument prefer to receive dividends thereby avoiding the commission fees which apply to the alternative of selling off part of their shares.

Control

Many firms, particularly small family-owned firms, operate under a self-imposed constraint which limits the amount of external financing which can be raised; the reason is that management is afraid of losing control of the firm. New issues of common stock dilute control, while after a point further increases in debt become undesirable or even impossible. Thus, after some point, dividend and investment decisions are tied to one another. In such a situation the dividend growth model is appropriate and offers useful insight with respect to the optimal payout ratio (dividend policy).

Informational content of dividends

Many researchers place special emphasis on the so-called informational content of dividends.[9] In the real world the relevant information regarding a firm's future prospects is neither readily available nor costless. In such a situation dividends can be (and probably are) important purveyors of information to investors. Thus shifts in dividend policy may affect an investor's expectations regarding the future prospects of the firm, thereby affecting its current share price as well. According to this approach, increases in a firm's dividend rate will be interpreted as an optimistic signal from management regarding the expected level of future profits. Conversely, decreases in the dividend rate will be treated as harbingers of ill tidings. And these two effects need not be offsetting. Cuts in dividends are likely to have a greater negative impact on share prices than a corresponding increase in dividends, which reflects the fact that the current price of most shares already includes a significant premium for some future growth.

Stability of earnings

A firm's cash position is another important factor that must be taken into account when determining long-run dividend policy. A rapidly expanding and very profitable firm is often faced with a chronic shortage of cash. Such a firm usually prefers to set a relatively low payout ratio, and to plow back most of its earnings in order to finance further growth. Although it is true that the firm could turn to the capital market for funds, the uncertainty engendered by rapid expansion often leads such a firm to set a 'safe' payout ratio, that is one which it can maintain should the rate of growth in earnings decline in the future.

In general the greater the risk of larger fluctuations in future earnings, the greater is the probability that the firm will adopt a policy of setting a relatively low payout ratio. The line of reasoning which underlies such a policy is as follows:

1. Most firms are anxious to avoid the negative 'information content' of a decline in the cash dividend rate. One way to minimize the risk that large fluctuations in earnings will force a cut in dividends is to set a low payout ratio which can be maintained even in the face of a relatively serious or prolonged decline in earnings.
2. The existence of large fluctuations in earnings materially increases the risk of default and as a result the firm will try to avoid a high proportion of debt in its capital structure, thereby limiting its access to this source of external

---

9. See M & M, *op. cit.*; R. Watts, 'The Information Content of Dividends,' *Journal of Business* April 1973; Stephen Ross, 'The Determination of Financial Structures: The Incentive Signalling Approach', *Bell Journal of Economics*, Spring 1977; and Sudipto Bhattacharya, 'Imperfect Information, Dividend Policy, and "The Bird in the Hand" Fallacy,' *Bell Journal of Economics*, Spring 1979.

financing. A parallel policy of paying out a low proportion of earnings as dividends is especially appropriate for such a firm since it helps provide the relatively large proportion of equity capital required to finance its investment program.

_____ TAXES AND DIVIDENDS

To this point we have ignored taxes – a strategy which cannot be recommended (for long) either in theory or practice. The introduction of the taxes (which existed before the 1986 tax reform) raised a fundamental question. In view of the differential taxation of dividend income and capital gains, why should firms pay dividends at all?[10] How can the different dividend policies shown in the articles at the beginning of this chapter be explained? Current dividends were taxed at marginal personal income tax rates while retained earnings incur no immediate personal tax liability. Any increase in the value of a firm's shares which stems from the reinvestment of income was (pre-1986) taxed as a capital gain only when the shares are sold, i.e., at a rate lower than the marginal personal tax rate. Since many investors were in relatively high personal tax brackets this could be expected to create a strong preference for capital gains. Despite this, U.S. corporations distributed a substantial part of their real earnings as dividends. Hence the expression 'dividend puzzle'.

Clearly no problem arises in a world without taxes. As we have just seen, the M & M analysis suggests that investors would be indifferent to dividends, i.e. no systematic preference for retained earnings would exist.[11] But once taxes are recognized, the nagging question of why firms do not eliminate (or at least sharply reduce) their cash dividends crops up. Several, not necessarily mutually exclusive, ways to resolve the dividend dilemma have been suggested.

Transaction costs

As we have already noted, investors who desire to receive a steady income stream from their equity holdings might prefer the receipt of periodic dividends to the alternative of selling off a portion of their shares from time to time, thereby reducing the costs of such transactions.

---

10. The question of *why corporations pay dividends* has been raised explicitly by Fischer Black and Myron Scholes, 'The Effects of Dividend Yield and Dividend Policy on Common Stock Prices and Returns,' *Journal of Financial Economics*, 1974; Fischer Black, 'The Dividend Puzzle,' *Journal of Portfolio Management*, Winter 1975; Merton Miller and Myron Scholes, 'Dividends and Taxes,' *Journal of Financial Economics*, December 1978; and Martin Feldstein and Jerry Green, 'Why Do Companies Pay Dividends?' *American Economics Review*, 1983.
11. But even here the M & M analysis does not account for the observed stability of corporate dividend policy, see p. 589.

The clientele effect

The idea alluded to in the beginning of the chapter that different classes of investors might have differing 'tastes' regarding dividend policy is not new. In their 1961 article, M & M suggested that the differential taxation of capital gains and dividends might conceivably lead to a tendency for each corporation to attract a particular 'clientele' comprising those investors who have a preference for its dividend policy (payout ratio). Given such a distribution of shareholders among corporations, a firm would be indifferent between alternative payout ratios. However, once a particular dividend policy has been established, the firm would be reluctant to change its payout ratio since this would lead to clientele shifts, and the latter generate undesirable transactions costs for investors.

Perhaps the best known attempt to measure the clientele effect was made in 1970 by Elton and Gruber [12] who used the average decline of share prices as a stock goes *ex-dividend* to estimate the marginal tax bracket of investors. Using data from April 1966 to March 1967, they found that this tax bracket was 36.4%. Elton and Gruber also presented empirical evidence supporting the existence of a clientele effect, which indicates that, in general, the higher a firm's dividend payout ratio, the lower the tax bracket of its shareholders. However, their general conclusion must be qualified, for although they found a negative correlation between investors' tax brackets and firms' dividend payouts, there are departures from the general rule. Thus, Table 18.2 shows that as one systematically moves from low to high dividend-payout firms, investors in some of the higher tax brackets *prefer* dividends to retentions. For example,

Table 18.2 Mean dividend payouts and implied tax bracket of investors

Decile	Dividend payout mean	Implied tax bracket
1	0.204	0.4883
2	0.316	0.4945
3	0.371	0.3889
4	0.409	0.4245
5	0.447	0.4108
6	0.486	0.4848
7	0.533	(unavailable)
8	0.594	0.1889
9	0.674	0.0806
10	1.040	0.2245

Source: E. J. Elton and M. J. Gruber, 'Marginal Stockholder Tax Rates and the Clientele Effect', *Review of Economics and Statistics*, February 1970.

12. E. J. Elton and M. J. Gruber, 'Marginal Stockholder Tax Rates and the Clientele Effect,' *Review of Economics and Statistics*. February 1970.

a move from the fifth dividend-payout decile to the sixth is accompanied by an *increase* in the implied personal tax rate. After 1986, we expect the clientele phenomenon to diminish substantially since there is only a slight advantage to capital gains, since capital tax gains are only paid with profit realization.

Supportive evidence of the clientele effect can be found in Table 18.3, which is based on 1985 income returns. Without a clientele effect one would expect that the higher the income the wealthier the individuals, hence, the higher will be the income from dividend and interest given as a percentage of the total income. However, Table 18.3 reveals that this figure falls from 15.2% for low income to 7.4% for income levels of $40,000–$49,994 (for higher income, this tendency is reversed). Thus, at least up to income of $50,000, individuals protect themselves by taking investments which yield a higher capital gain and less interest and dividends. Recall that in 1985, income tax rates were progressive, hence the higher the income, the higher the incentive to switch from securities which pay high dividends and interest to securities (and maybe other investments) which were based heavily on capital gains or tax-free (e.g., municipal bonds), which were subject to a lower or no income tax.

The Miller–Scholes thesis

Merton Miller and Myron Scholes[13] used an often overlooked feature of U.S. tax law to restore the equivalence between dividend income and capital gains. Since 1969, individuals' deductions for interest on investments (i.e., excluding interest paid on mortgages and business loans) have been limited to their investment income plus $25,000. Thus each extra dollar of dividend income increases the allowable interest tax deductions by one dollar. Clearly, for the relevant investor the additional dollar of income is exactly offset by the additional dollar of deduction which leaves his taxable income unchanged. Thus such an individual will be indifferent between the receipt of dividends or a capital gain via the firm's repurchase of its shares, if he can offset the tax effect

Table 18.3 Dividend and interest as percentage of income at different income levels in ($ billion)

Income level	Under 10,000	10,000 to 19,999	20,000 to 29,999	30,000 to 39,999	40,000 to 49,999	50,000 to 99,999	100,000 and over
1. Adjusted gross income	106.4	360.9	399.9	399.8	269.9	440.0	255.1
2. Interest plus dividends	16.2	38.2	29.7	25.4	20.0	43.9	46.6
3. Percentage of dividends and interest of gross income [(3) = (2)/(1)]	15.2	10.6	7.4	6.3	7.4	10.0	18.3

Source: U.S. Internal Revenue Service, *Statistics of Income Bulletin*, Spring 1987.

13. Miller and Scholes, *op. cit.*, 1978.

by borrowing.[14] Unfortunately, two empirical findings limit the usefulness of this ingenious, albeit somewhat convoluted, argument.

1. Since the limit on interest deductions was only introduced in 1969, the Miller–Scholes approach does not provide an explanation for observed dividend policy before that year.
2. Few investors with dividend income make sufficiently large interest payments on debt to make the constraint binding.[15]

Portfolio approach

Another alternative explanation for observed dividend behavior can be found by applying the portfolio principle. Feldstein and Green[16] use the idea that shareholders' risk-aversion provides a limit to corporate growth. They consider an economy with shareholders in diverse tax situations, i.e., two groups of taxable individuals and untaxed institutions, but the same line of reasoning holds for investors in 'low' and 'high' tax brackets. Firms can either distribute their profits as dividends or reinvest them and grow larger, eventually distributing these funds to shareholders as capital gains. Under a scenario of certainty, this would lead to a segmented market in which taxable individuals invest only in firms which forgo dividend payments, while untaxed institutions would prefer the firms which pay dividends. However, if we assume that investors regard each firm's return as uncertain, they will desire to diversify their holdings. Feldstein and Green demonstrate that in such a market share, price maximization implies that each firm must attract both types of investor, and this in turn implies that some fraction of earnings must be distributed as dividends. Market equilibrium of the segmented form can take place only in the case of little or no uncertainty, or if we assume a constraint on investors' ability to diversify risk.

Information signalling approach

Finally, an intuitively appealing explanation for observed dividend payments, in the face of differential taxation, can be found by considering one of the many implications of the separation of ownership and management. According to this approach management employs dividends to convey information regarding the *sustainable* level of its real income.[17]

---

14. Miller and Scholes show how this can be accomplished through borrowing and simultaneously investing in risk-free assets. Clearly this implies some level of transactions costs, but the basic point remains – much if not all of the marginal personal tax on dividends can be avoided.
15. See Feldstein and Green, *op. cit.*
16. *Ibid.*
17. See Fred Arditti, Haim Levy, and Marshall Sarnat, 'Taxes, Uncertainty and Optimal Dividend Policy,' *Financial Management*, Spring 1976; Stephen Ross, 'The Determination of Financial Structures: The Incentive Signalling Approach,' *Bell Journal of Economics*, Spring 1977; and Sudipto Bhattacharya, 'Imperfect Information, Dividend Policy and "The Bird in the Hand" Fallacy,' *Bell Journal of Economics*, Spring 1979.

In the highly uncertain world confronting investors, the use of dividend changes as a proxy for the trend in earnings is readily understandable and makes good sense. Reported earnings per share can be manipulated by means of 'imaginative' accounting (or worse) even by a firm in dire financial straits. The same cannot be said for cash dividends, which represent a drain on the firm's real resources. While a firm might conceivably raise dividends in the face of declining earnings or even losses, this process cannot continue indefinitely. Investors are likely to treat an increase in reported earnings, which is *confirmed* by a corresponding change in the dividend rate, with far greater confidence, presumably on the grounds that such a dual increase represents a higher level of *sustainable* earnings and not just a transitory fluctuation of profits.

UNCERTAINTY AND DIVIDEND POLICY

In reality there is probably some truth in all of the above explanations. Dividend policy, like financial management in general, is a multifaceted activity. In this section, however, we shall focus attention on the information-signalling effect and demonstrate, in a formal manner, how the explicit introduction of uncertainty of information[18] can account for the observed policy of paying dividends even when personal tax rates exceed the rate of tax on capital gains. We assume that the personal tax rate is higher than the capital gains rate. While this difference was substantial before 1986, recall that after 1986 the difference became much smaller since the two tax rates are now equal. A slight differential still exists since you can defer payment on any capital gain.

In a perfect capital market

Let us initially turn to the question of the impact of dividends on the market value of the firm in a perfect capital market, using the following notation:

S_L = market value of a firm's common stock

B_L = market value of a firm's debt

X = random variable representing a firm's earnings before interest and taxes but after the deduction of depreciation expense

T_c = corporate tax rate

T_p = personal tax rate, assumed to be the same for all individuals

T_g = capital gains tax rate, assumed to be the same for all individuals and applicable to any gains from the price appreciation of common stock (we assume $T_g < T_p$)

q = dividend/payout (or dividend/earnings) ratio; while $(1 - q)$ represents that fraction of after-tax earnings not paid out as dividends, which we assume results in an equivalent increase in the market value of the firm's equity

---

18. This follows the approach of Arditti, Levy, and Sarnat, *op. cit.*

r = riskless rate of interest; all interest income is taxed at T_p and interest payments are tax deductible against personal income

Given our assumptions and the above notation, it follows that $q(1 - T_p)$ denotes that part of each dollar of the firm's *after-tax* income paid as dividends, which accrues to the shareholder after the payment of his personal income tax. The fraction of each dollar of the firm's after-tax income that is retained $(1 - q)$, generates a capital gains tax payment by the shareholder equal to $(1 - q)T_g$, so that the residual amount accruing to the shareholder is $(1 - T_g)(1 - q)$. Hence, out of each *post-tax* corporate dollar earned by the firm, the amount received by the shareholders, after the payment of all taxes (corporate, personal, and capital gains), denoted by w, is given by the expression:

$$w = q(1 - T_p) + (1 - T_g)(1 - q)$$

or equivalently

$$w = (1 - T_g) - q(T_p - T_g)$$

Clearly, w decreases as the dividend payout ratio increases, when the personal tax rate exceeds the rate of tax on capital gains. Let us demonstrate with the tax rates which prevailed in the United States prior to 1986. For example, if $T_p = 0.46$ and $T_g = 0.20$, then a payout ratio of 40% ($q = 0.40$) results in an after-tax income of 69.6 cents ($w = 0.696$); but if the dividend payment, q, is increased to 60%, then investors' after-tax income is reduced to 64.4 cents ($w = 0.644$). Hence a firm's best policy, under the above assumptions, is to pay zero dividends. The reasoning behind this result is as follows: an investor who receives one dollar in a *perfect capital market* attaches the same degree of risk to the dollar of future income independent of the way it is received. Hence, a dollar of capital gains or a dollar of dividends are of equal value. But the existence of differential taxation destroys this equality: because of taxation, greater value will be attached to low dividend payouts which leads to the conclusion that the lowest dividend payout, namely zero, will be optimal.[19] Obviously, after the 1986 tax law change the difference between T_p and T_g became much smaller, but still provides some incentive not to pay cash dividends.

In an imperfect capital market

As we have just seen, the taking into account of personal and capital gains taxes, in addition to corporate taxes, implies an optimal dividend payout of zero. Clearly, it is the fact that the tax rate on capital gains is lower than the tax rate on income which induces this corner solution. However, even the most

19. See D. E. Farrar and L. L. Selwyn, 'Taxes, Corporate Financial Policy and Return to Investors,' *National Tax Journal*, December 1967; and S. C. Myers, 'Taxes, Corporate Financial Policy and Return to Investors: Comment,' *National Tax Journal*, December 1967. For a formal proof see Arditti, Levy, and Sarnat, *op. cit.*

cursory empirical examination suffices to show the inadequacy of such a result; in reality the typical corporation retains only a part of its earnings, the remainder being paid out to its shareholders as dividends. Thus the explanatory property of such a model is seriously impaired.

A solution to the dilemma created by the discrepancy between observed corporate behavior in the real world and the prescription for such behavior spelled out by the formal theoretical model presented above can be found by relaxing the assumption of a perfect capital market. More specifically, we introduce an assumption which reflects the differential risk which a corporate shareholder may impute to the two components of corporate profits — dividends and retained earnings.

We assume that due to management's ability to influence or even manipulate reported earnings, the typical shareholder will view that portion of reported earnings which is not 'confirmed' by a dividend payment as a less reliable indicator of a firm's true earning power. Numerous examples can be given of management's ability to influence the relationship of a firm's reported accounting profits to its underlying economic earnings. For example, the allowance for bad debts and the reserve for outstanding claims which are important components of the earnings statement of banks and insurance companies are highly subjective estimates made by management. Similarly, the degree of management discretion in determining the reported earnings of a highly diversified conglomerate firm has been a cause of much concern in the Securities and Exchange Commission.

ARTICLE 40

Tale of Deceit

Why Arthur Andersen Was So Slow to Detect Chicanery at Frigitemp

---

Biggest Accountant in U.S. Audited Concern's Books But Missed Irregularities

---

One may think that manipulating the reported earnings by the firm's management is impossible since its books are audited by an independent and objective accountant. The *Wall Street Journal* dated September 21, 1984 gives us only one example showing that this is not the case. The title of the article which appears in the *Wall Street Journal* is reproduced as article 40. For some readers this title is enough to convince them that reported earnings are not always reliable even if audited by independent accountants.

The reported earnings of Frigitemp had been distorted for many years. The firm abused the common accounting rules for reporting long-term income and hence consistently reported on income which actually did not exist. In particular, the firm declared income from long-term construction projects before the income was actually received. This unaccepted accounting method accelerated

Frigitemp's reported income stream, but did not accelerate the actual income stream, hence a big discrepancy between reported and actual earnings emerged. There were many other irregularities in this firm, yet Arthur Andersen, which is one of the 'Big Eight' accounting firms, failed to detect them. Though the firm had provided distorted reported earnings for many years, it finally declared bankruptcy. Many shareholders who relied on the distorted reported earnings lost their money. This supports our view that firms can manipulate their earnings for a long period of time but cannot do it with cash dividends, hence the latter are more valuable to the investors.

Incidentally, Arthur Andersen paid almost $7 million to settle four lawsuits alleging they were 'recklessly negligent' in failing to detect the company's irregularities.

Numbers Game

How Miniscribe Got Its Auditor's Blessing On Questionable Sales

Coopers & Lybrand Allowed Computer Firm to Make Suspicious Adjustments

Coopers Says It was Misled

On the last Friday of March five years ago, Raymond MacFee, a partner at the giant accounting firm of Coopers & Lybrand, was looking forward to a quiet weekend. He had finally finished the audit of MiniScribe Corp.'s 1986 financial results — or so he thought.

But then Mr. MacFee's boss unexpectedly called him to a meeting in their Denver office on Saturday. To help overcome a cash crunch, MiniScribe, a Longmont, Colo., computer disk-drive maker, was rushing to finish a prospectus to sell $97.7 million in bonds the following month. The company needed Coopers's approval on some unusual last-minute adjustments to its 1986 financial report. Mr. MacFee, who already had reservations about some of MiniScribe's numbers, was struck ill at the meeting and didn't return to work for three days. By that time, MiniScribe had its adjustments and a clean opinion from Coopers.

Behind the Good News

As it turned out, MiniScribe's financial report was anything but clean. The company actually had deep financial, operating and marketing problems. The highflying MiniScribe had announced seven consecutive record-breaking quarters, and its stock had quintupled in the past 18 months. But MiniScribe's superlative record was actually fabricated: Some shipments were booked as sales; reserves were manipulated; and growth figures were grossly exaggerated.

The company had "perpetrated a massive fraud," according to an investigation by its outside directors two years later. MiniScribe then restated its 1986 profits, slashing them to $12.2 million from the $22.7 million that Coopers, one of the nation's most prestigious accounting firms, had certified.

. . .

Recent settlements over accounting malpractice "call into question the entire audit process," says John Shank, an accounting professor at the Amos Tuck school of business at Dartmouth College. *Source: Wall Street Journal*, May 14, 1992, p. A1.

While the Frigitemp case appeared in the *Wall Street Journal* in 1984, unfortunately, inflated earnings and fraud are reported frequently in the financial media. Article 41 from the *Wall Street Journal* in May 1992 shows the MiniScribe Corp. obtained its auditor's blessing on questionable sales which distorted the firm's reported profit. This 'massive fraud' created a profit of $22.7 million.

The point to learn from articles 40 and 41 is that revenue and earnings can be manipulated and thus a degree of uncertainty regarding the reliability of reported performance exists. Dividends, however, are cash-in-hand and hence are verifiable cash flows from an investor's point of view.

In essence, we propose to relax a key part of the perfect capital market assumption, namely that all market participants have equal and costless access to all information. Here it is suggested, that since shareholders are in an inferior 'information position' *vis-à-vis* management because of management's ability to influence accounting magnitudes they will view reported earnings with suspicion. Cash dividends, on the other hand, require an actual expenditure of a firm's resources, and, in the long run, should reflect underlying profitability. Thus by paying a dividend the firm provides investors with some additional information regarding the estimated permanence of earnings. In other words, the cash dividend distribution is employed as a signalling device. The firm signals to its stockholders that it is indeed as profitable as the accounting statements received. *This reduces the conditional variability of deviations of reported accounting earnings from underlying economic profits*, since such uncertainty relates only to the retained portion of earnings. Hence, the variance of earnings narrows as the payout ratio increases.

Simultaneously considering the personal-capital gains tax differential and the uncertainty attached to undistributed earnings, the investor's expected return-risk opportunity is given by:[20]

$$\bar{Y} = E(1 - T_p) + E\frac{(T_p - T_g)\sigma_Y}{(1 - T_g)\sigma_{E''}}$$

where $\bar{Y}$ denotes the expected value of shareholders' after-tax income; E = reported EPS (which is equal to the expected value); σ_Y = standard deviation of Y; and $\sigma_{E''}$ = maximum standard deviation of earnings per share when all earnings are retained.

A simple graphical device can now be employed to illustrate the dividend policy problem. The above equation describes a straight line in the $\bar{Y}$ and σ_Y plane; each point on this line corresponding to a given value of q, i.e., to a particular dividend policy. For the value of $q = 1$, $\bar{Y} = (1 - T_p)E$ and $\sigma_Y = 0$. On the other hand, for $q = 0$, i.e., when all earnings are retained, $\sigma_Y = (1 - T_g)\sigma_{E''}$ and $\bar{Y} = (1 - T_g)E$, which are the *maximum* expected earnings and *maximum* risk points. Figure 18.1 illustrates such a transformation line (*aa'*) superimposed on a set of indifference curves for a typical risk averter. The tangency point P^* represents that dividend policy which this

---

20. The derivation of this equation is given in Appendix 18A.

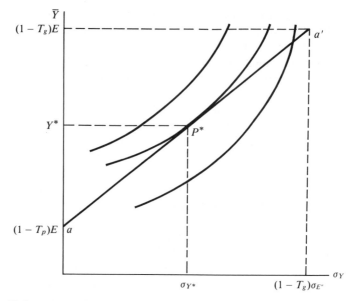

Figure 18.1

individual considers optimal – the value q that corresponds to $\overline{Y}^*$ and σ_{Y^*}. In general the optimal point will *not* lie at a corner of the transformation line.

It is also instructive to look at the transformation lines as a function of the tax rates T_p and T_g. In a world in which there are no personal or capital gains taxes, the transformation curve simply becomes a horizontal line (for example the line Eb of Figure 18.2) and the optimal dividend payout is $q^* = 1$, shown as point E in Figure 18.2. If we consider the other extreme case in which personal taxes exist but $\sigma_{E''} = 0$, i.e., there is no uncertainty, then the vertical line mm' which lies on the vertical axis of Figure 18.2 portrays the transformation curve, and its locus of points is defined by:

$$\overline{Y} = E(1 - T_g) + qE(T_g - T_p)$$

In this instance, the optimal point is given by m' which means that the optimal payout ratio, q^*, is zero. However, when both taxes and uncertainty are considered, the transformation curve is again a rising line such as ma in Figure 18.2, and the optimal dividend payout typically lies *between* zero and one. Obviously, after 1986 the difference in the effective tax rates T_g and T_p shrank, hence the line ma in Figure 18.2 will be much flatter.

The introduction of signalling in an imperfect information setting which stipulates that shareholders do not know a firm's true economic profits with certainty results in an optimal dividend policy which calls for the distribution of part of a firm's earnings to shareholders. To obtain this result there is no need to assume that management knows precisely the firm's true profits. Due to measurement problems, arbitrary cost allocations, etc., this is rarely the case. However, for our purpose, it is sufficient to assume that the firm's

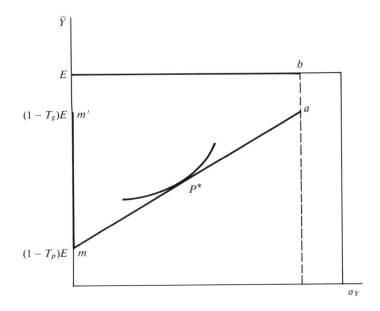

Figure 18.2

management is in a better position than its shareholders to estimate economic profits. While such an assumption complicates the presentation of the argument, it does not alter any of the conclusions.

DIVIDEND POLICY IN PRACTICE

Normally, the fluctuations in earnings are much more pronounced than the fluctuations in dividends. A downturn in earnings is not followed by a downturn in dividends, unless the downturn in earnings persists for a long time period. Thus, managers know that the market reacts negatively to dividend downturns, hence they try to avoid such a decline. One may find many firms with negative earnings which distribute cash dividends, hoping to have positive earnings in the future. By paying dividends in years with negative earnings, management signals to the investors that the decline in earnings is temporary, and that positive earnings are expected to prevail in the future. This phenomenon is illustrated in Table 18.4 which presents data on total dividends and earnings of private U.S. corporations for selected years during the period 1929–87. In the years of the Great Depression earnings were very low or even negative; however, corporations in the aggregate declared dividends in excess of earnings. For example, in 1933 although the firms lost $2.1 billion, cash dividends amounting to $2.1 billion were paid to shareholders. But no matter how strong the desire to maintain dividends, firms cannot continue to distribute earnings at the same pace in the face of losses during a number of consecutive years. And as Table 18.4 shows, U.S. firms, taken in the aggregate,

Table 18.4 Profits after taxes and dividends, all
private U.S. corporations selected
years from 1929–91 ($ billion)

Year	Corporate profits after taxes	Dividends
1929	8.2	5.8
1933	−2.1	2.0
1939	4.0	3.8
1940	5.9	4.0
1941	6.7	4.4
1942	8.3	4.3
1945	9.0	4.6
1950	17.0	8.8
1955	25.1	10.3
1960	26.8	12.9
1965	50.4	19.1
1970	41.7	22.5
1975	83.9	29.6
1980	152.3	54.7
1981	145.4	63.6
1982	106.5	66.9
1983	130.4	71.5
1984	146.1	79
1985	127.8	83.3
1986	115.3	91.3
1987	148.4	98.2
1988	180.5	110
1989	172.6	124
1990	218.7	149.3
1991	210.7	146.5

Source: Department of Commerce, Bureau of
Economic Analysis, The National Income and Products
Accounts of the United States, 1929–91, and *Survey of
Current Business*, July issues.

cut their dividends drastically, albeit not by the same amount as the decline
in earnings, during the first half of the 1930s. It was only in the latter half of
the 1940s that total corporate dividends again reached their 1929 level, even
in nominal terms.

Partial adjustment hypothesis

The historical pattern of dividends and earnings has fascinated economists and
specialists in business finance for many years. The seminal work in this area
is John Lintner's pioneering 1956 empirical study,[21] in which he proposed a
lagged model to explain individual firms' dividend policies, as well as dividends in the aggregate. On the basis of field interviews, Lintner hypothesized
the following relationship to explain dividend decisions:

$$\Delta d_{it} = a_i + c_i(d_{it}^* - d_{i(t-1)}) + u_{it}$$

21. J. Lintner, 'Distribution of Incomes of Corporations Among Dividends Retained Earnings
and Taxes,' *American Economic Review*, May 1956.

where d_{it}^* is the target payout ratio, Δd_i is the change in dividend payments, and d_t and d_{t-1} are the amounts of dividends paid in the year t. The subscript i identifies the individual company and d_{it}^* represents the dividends which the company would have paid in the current year if its dividends were based simply on its fixed target payout ratio applied to current profits. The parameter c_i indicates the fraction of the difference between this 'target' dividend d_{it}^*, and the actual payment made in the preceding year $d_{i(t-1)}$. The lagged Lintner model views current dividends as a function not only of current earnings but of past dividends as well. This reflects the firms' desire to avoid increasing current dividends to levels which cannot be maintained, a policy which might force the firm to cut dividends in the future. According to Lintner, corporations follow a policy of setting a *target* dividend payout ratio which they apply to earnings. However, due to the strong bias against dividend cuts, increases in earnings are translated into increases in dividends only gradually so as to avoid the necessity of future downward revisions. The lag in the adjustment of current dividends to increases in earnings is a sort of safety device designed to make dividends a function of *permanent* rather than transitory earnings which cannot be sustained. [22]

Consider a case in which a firm earns an unusual profit in a given year, but management knows that there is only a slight probability that the high level of profit will be maintained in the future. Let us further assume that the company in question pays cash dividends of two dollars per share. In such cases a firm desiring to increase dividends in the profitable year, will often prefer to declare an 'extra' dividend, say, of one dollar per share rather than to raise its 'regular' dividend rate. The motive underlying such a policy is not to disappoint the shareholder should earnings and dividends return to their previous levels in the following year. Such behavior, and Lintner's lagged adjustment hypothesis in general, are clearly consistent with the theoretical view which emphasizes the importance of the *informational content* of dividends in a capital market which is less than perfect.

Another argument in favor of regularity of dividend payments is that such a policy not only enhances the investment position of the company's stock, but also its credit standing when raising debt capital in the open market. A strong dividend record is often an important consideration for institutional investors when the firm's bonds are being examined. Moreover some regulated financial

---

22. John A. Brittain has modified the basic Lintner model by treating dividends as a function of the cash flow (earnings and depreciation). The rationale for such a procedure is that changes in the liberality of depreciation allowances for tax purposes during wartime and economic recessions makes net profits a poor measure of firms' 'ability' to pay dividends. See J. A. Brittain, *Corporate Dividend Policy*, The Brookings Institution, Washington, D.C., 1966. Another variation on this same theme has been presented by Keith V. Smith who hypothesizes that a company faced with a serious and prolonged secular decline in earnings will prefer a once-and-for-all large cut in its payout ratio rather than a gradual series of cuts in its payout ratio over a period of years. According to this so-called *increasing stream of dividends hypothesis*, dividend increases will lag behind the rise in earnings, but should a cut in dividends become unavoidable, the firm will prefer large rather than a small downward revision of its dividend policy. See Keith V. Smith, 'Increasing Stream Hypothesis of Corporate Dividends Policy,' *California Management Review*, Fall 1971, pp. 56–64.

institutions are not allowed to buy stock of firms which pay irregular cash dividends, hence a strong case for keeping an unbroken dividend stream.

DIVIDENDS AND VALUATION: THE EMPIRICAL EVIDENCE _____

It is clear enough that in a perfect capital market in which external financing is *freely* available, rational investors would be indifferent between the components of their return: dividends and capital gains. However, it is equally clear that in an imperfect market the firm should consider the possible effects of the differential tax brackets of its shareholders, dilution of control, flotation and transaction costs, the stability of earnings, etc., when reaching its dividend decisions. Under these circumstances, it is not clear if dividends would be preferred to capital gains or vice versa.

In order to examine the impact of dividends on share prices, the following type of regression equation has been applied, empirically, to cross-sections of common stock:

$$P_i = a + b_1 d_i + b_2 (E_i - d_i) + u_i$$

where:

P_i = price of the ith company's shares
d_i = dividend per share of the ith company
$E_i - d_i$ = retained earnings of the ith company's shares
u_i = error term

Most empirical studies using the above type of regression equation have found that $b_1 > b_2$, and have concluded, therefore that cash dividends are systematically preferred to retained earnings: that is, in real-life dividend policy seems to count. However, Irwin Friend and Marshall Puckett[23] have raised serious doubts regarding the interpretation of such empirical results. For example, they argue that where $b_1 > b_2$, firms could clearly increase their market values by gradually increasing their dividend payout ratios until $b_1 = b_2$. The latter equality is a necessary condition for a firm to reach its optimal dividend policy. Hence empirical studies which find b_1 significantly higher than b_2 indicate either that a permanent state of disequilibrium exists in the market or that the above type model is inadequate to capture the essentials of the valuation process.

In their critical analysis, Friend and Puckett stress the statistical limitations of the regression model which imparts serious bias to the results. Although we cannot go into all their arguments in any detail, one particular source of bias appears to be of crucial importance. The above simple regression model is obviously incomplete in the sense that it does not include all of the relevant variables which may affect valuation.

23. Irwin Friend and Marshall Puckett, 'Dividends and Stock Prices,' *American Economic Review*, September 1964.

The most important of these omitted variables is a firm's given risk. As we have already mentioned, firms which are characterized by high degrees of uncertainty regarding future earnings (that is, by large fluctuations in their earnings) tend to adopt low dividend payout ratios, since such a policy reduces the probability that the firm will be forced to cut its dividends at some future time due to a drop in earnings. Thus, high-risk firms tend to have low payout ratios. This negative correlation between the omitted variable (risk) and the payout ratio creates a bias in favor of cash dividends. We know that, other things being equal, high risk lowers a share's market price. But as high-risk firms also adopt low payout ratios, the regression analysis findings that firms with low payout ratios are characterized by low market prices may well reflect, as Friend and Puckett have suggested, the negative correlation between payout ratios and risk, rather than investors' preference for dividends.

This analysis suggests that the inclusion of a risk variable in the regression equations should eliminate the bias, and hence the preference for dividends induced by the bias should also disappear.[24] However, after making a number of corrections in the regression model and adding risk and other variables, Friend and Puckett found the evidence on the effects of dividend policy tenuous and inconclusive. While little support can be found for the hypothesis that a strong market preference exists for cash dividends rather than retained earnings, a moderate preference was found in non-growth industries. The opposite preference (that is favoring retained earnings) seemed to hold for growth companies. Friend and Puckett conclude their work with a warning that the empirical validation of the existence or absence of an optimal dividend payout ratio will require more sophisticated techniques than have been applied hitherto to such empirical studies.

_____ **THE CON EDISON EXPERIENCE**

The combination of complex alternative theoretical models with, at best, controversial empirical evidence would seem to provide little solace for a worried financial executive in a world of extreme uncertainty. And clearly dividend policy remains one of the more difficult decisions confronting the business firm. Although magic answers to management's dilemmas are not likely to jump out of a computer printout, the preceding analysis, by pointing out the significance of the information content of unanticipated dividend changes in an uncertain world, can provide a framework for analyzing actual decisions.

A case in point is provided by Con Edison which in the wake of the oil crisis stunned Wall Street[25] with an announcement that it would *not* pay any

24. It is noteworthy that Fred Arditti has obtained some results which support the analysis of Friend and Puckett. In a regression analysis which omits risk variables a preference for cash dividends is observed. However, when he adds the risk factor, thereby correcting for the statistical bias, the regression coefficient of the payout variable becomes insignificant. See Fred D. Arditti, 'Risk and the Required Return on Equity,' *Journal of Finance*, March 1967.
25. See *Wall Street Journal*, April 24, 1974.

dividend in the second quarter of 1974. The decision marked the first time since the concern was formed in 1881 (i.e., 89 years) that the Company had failed to make a regular dividend payment, and served to disprove a favorite Wall Street axiom that utilities *always* pay their dividends.

The suspension of cash dividend payments reinforced the parallel announcement that operating profits had fallen by 21% in the same quarter. The market's reaction was not long to follow. After a delayed opening, the price of Con Edison's shares fell by 32% on a turnover which placed it at the top of the New York Stock Exchange's most active list for the day.

INTEGRATING DIVIDEND POLICY AND CAPITAL STRUCTURE _____

ARTICLE 42

BP's Horton Quits As Chief and Chairman

Mr. Horton, 52 years old, was also at the center of rumors of a boardroom split earlier this year over his reported insistence on continuing BP's dividend in the face of declining earnings and burgeoning debt, now put at £8 billion. BP officials insisted yesterday that the company's dividend policy remains unchanged, but some stock analysts in New York said the $4.25 annual dividend might be in jeopardy with Mr. Horton's departure.

'A Very Uncertain Feeling'
"The question of the dividend will come to the fore," said Eugene Nowak, an analyst with Dean Witter Reynolds Inc. "This gives investors, no question, a very uncertain feeling."

Mr. Horton will be replaced as chairman by Lord Ashburton, 63, a former director of the Bank of England and nonexecutive director of BP since 1982. The chief executive's post will be filled by Deputy Chairman David Simon, a 30-year BP veteran who will take over the day-to-day running of the company.

Source: Wall Street Journal, June 26, 1992, p. A3.

From article 42 we see that debt, earnings, and dividend policy are related. British Petroleum experienced declining earnings and substantial debt, causing uncertainty regarding the firm's ability to maintain its dividend policy. Nevertheless, the officials of British Petroleum insisted 'that the divided policy remains unchanged.' Since shareholders do not like dividend cuts, and management prefers to maintain a given dividend policy, how does the firm's operating risk and leverage affect its dividend policy and the probability that the firm must cut dividends in the future? We turn to this issue next.

The desire to avoid such shocks helps account for much of actual dividend behavior. Risk aversion is a powerful force in the corporate boardroom, and we are now in the position to integrate the previous analysis of the effect of leverage on risk with the dividend decision. Figure 18.3 reproduces the, by now, familiar break-even chart for a firm under two alternative assumptions regarding its financial mix – all equity or 50% debt. We have also superimposed on the graph the probability distribution for the firm's operating

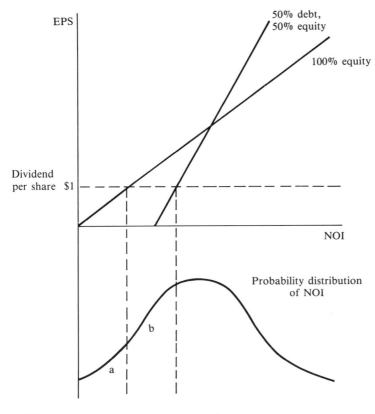

Figure 18.3

earnings. This firm is in the particularly enviable position that there is practically no probability of its losing money. Perhaps it is a regulated industry. But there does exist a positive probability (area 'a' under the curve) that operating earnings will be too low to meet its dividend payments, which we have assumed to be one dollar per share, even when it follows a policy of pure equity financing. Should the firm lever its capital structure, say by introducing 50% debt, the probability that the net operating income (NOI) will not be sufficient to pay the one dollar per share dividend rises, and is measured by the area a + b. This reflects the fact that interest payments take precedence over dividends.

Although such a graph is rarely (if ever) drawn on the wall of a board chairman's office, it does illustrate the type of thinking which underlies what often appear on the surface to be purely judgemental decisions.

_____ **SUMMARY**

This chapter has examined a number of problems relating to both the theoretical and practical aspects of dividend policy. Attention was initially directed to the impact of dividend policy on the market valuation of the firm's shares in an effort to determine the theoretically optimal policy to be followed by a firm desiring to maximize owners' wealth.

When external sources of financing are *not* available the firm's decisions to invest are tied to its dividend policy: in such a case a decision by the firm to increase its investment induces a parallel change in its dividend policy. As a result changes in dividend policy can be expected to have a direct impact on the valuation of common stock, except in the limiting case in which the net present value of the additional investment is zero. This conclusion holds both for *growth* and *non-growth* situations. Hence, dividend policy is of special significance to a firm which for one reason or another is constrained to financing its further expansion solely out of retained earnings. In such situations a proposed increase in dividends must be carefully weighed against the incremental return of any forgone investment.

The availability of external sources of financing breaks the link between dividend and investment policies, since given the ability to raise outside capital, the firm can simultaneously increase investment and dividends.

Real-life capital markets are not perfect. The firm is confronted, in practice, by numerous factors which are often neglected in the theoretical models. Differential taxation of capital gains and dividends (mainly before 1986), flotation and transaction costs, control, the psychological impact of dividend changes on investors, the stability of earnings and the possibility of bankruptcy and the information conveyed by dividend payments in an uncertain world are all factors which must be given consideration when setting a firm's dividend policy. When all of the dimensions of the dividend decision are recognized, it is clear that dividend policy remains one of the most difficult financial decisions facing the firm.

Due to the complexity of the factors affecting actual dividend decisions, it is not clear from the theoretical analysis whether investors systematically prefer dividends to capital gains, or vice versa. Numerous empirical studies have been conducted; however, the results of these regression analyses are not conclusive because of the statistical limitations of the underlying models. Attempts to correct for the statistical bias of the earlier studies have been made, but given the present state of the art in statistics, empirical analysis has only succeeded in narrowing, but not in closing, the gap which exists between the alternative hypotheses regarding the impact of dividend policy on valuation. In practice, the picture is somewhat brighter. Despite the considerable controversy regarding the theoretical aspects of dividends and the interpretation of the empirical record, important practical insights can be derived from the academic models. In particular, the need to avoid 'negative information' signals provides a useful guideline for practical decision-making at the level of the firm.

The general valuation formula for any cash dividend stream is:

$$P_0 = \sum_{t=1}^{\infty} \frac{d_t}{(1 + k_e)^t}$$

with a constant dividend growth we have:

$$d_{t+1} = d_t(1 + g)$$

$$\downarrow$$

$$P_0 = \frac{(1 - b)E}{k_e - bR}$$

No-external financing   External financing

$k_e \neq R$ $k_e = R$ and $P_0 = \dfrac{E}{k_e}$ $V_t = \dfrac{1}{1 + r} [X - I_0 + V_{t+1}]$

$\downarrow$ $\downarrow$ $\downarrow$

Dividend   Dividend policy   Dividend policy does not
policy   does not matter   matter irrespective of the
does   relationship between R and k_e.
matter

Risk–return relationship

The risk–return relationship when reported earnings are considered to be more uncertain than cash dividend is

$$\bar{Y} = E(1 - T_p) + E \frac{(T_p - T_g)\sigma_Y}{(1 - T_g)\sigma_{E''}}$$

Where ($\bar{Y}$, σ_y) stand for the mean and standard deviation of the return, T_p, T_g, are the personal income tax rate and capital gains tax rate, respectively. E is the earnings per share, and $\sigma_{E''}$ is the maximum standard deviation of earnings per share when all earnings are retained.

18.1 What will be the impact (the change in the value of the firm's stock) of shifting a cash dividend of $6.05 from the first year to the second, if the rate of return on reinvestment is 14% and the relevant discount rate is 10%? (In your answer, assume that no external sources of financing are available to the firm.)

18.2 Answer question 18.1, assuming that the rate of return on reinvestment in year 1 is equal to 8%.

18.3 Calculate the theoretical stock prices for the following alternative retention ratios (b) and rates of return (R) using the Gordon valuation model. (Assume that earnings per share in the first year (E) are \$6 and the discount rate (k) is 15%.)

(a) $R = 20\%$; $b = 0$, 15%, 25%, 50%, 60%

(b) $R = 10\%$; $b = 0$, 15%, 25%, 50%, 60%

18.4 In what sense does the dividend valuation model lead to a 'corner solution'? How can this shortcoming be overcome?

18.5 What is meant by the 'information content' of dividends?

18.6 Several studies have been carried out (prior to the 1986 tax reform) to test investors' preferences for dividends as opposed to capital gains. A regression model of the following type has been used in most of these studies:

$$P_i = a + b_1 d_i + b_2(E_i - d_i) + u_i$$

Discuss the statistical limitations of this model.

18.7 The equity of Hagayon Ltd. consists of $N = 50,000$ shares of common stock. The price of the stock on January 1, 1994 is \$130 and the expected net income in 1994 is \$500,000. The discount rate used by the shareholders of this firm is $k = 10\%$. Ignore personal taxes on cash dividends.

(a) Suppose that the firm will not pay cash dividend in 1994. What is the expected price of its stock on December 31, 1994. What is the expected price at the end of the year if the firm pays 10% stock dividend but no cash dividend?

(b) Make now the alternative assumption that the firm pays on December 31, 1994 a cash dividend of \$4 per share. What is the ex-dividend expected price of the stock? What is the impact of the distribution of the cash dividend on the shareholders' wealth?

(c) Assume that at the end of the year the firm distributes a cash dividend of \$4 per share and a few hours later also a 10% stock dividend. What is the impact of this distribution on the investors' wealth?

(d) Suppose that the firm decides to invest at the end of the year in a new project which requires an initial outlay of \$500,000, but still to pay cash dividend of \$4 per share. The project is highly profitable. Would you recommend the firm to skip the payment of the cash dividend and to use the retained earnings to finance the new project? Prove your answer.

(e) Suppose that a financial consultant advises the firm to pay a cash dividend of \$4 per share. How many shares should the firm issue in order to finance the new project?

18.8 A given share is sold for \$30 just before time t_0. If the firm pays a \$3 dividend per share, the price will immediately drop to \$27. Suppose you own 100 shares. If the firm decides not to distribute the dividends, you would need to sell 10 shares (at \$30 a share) since you need to have a \$300 cash income (pre tax). Assume that the shares were originally bought for \$20 each.

(a) If both ordinary personal tax rate and capital gains tax are 28%, what is your after-tax wealth under the two alternative situations?

(b) Answer part (a) again, this time assuming the pre-1986 differential tax rates. Assume that the ordinary income tax is 40%, while the capital gains tax is 25%.

18.9 The firm is capitalized by 100,000 shares of common stock which trade at the beginning of the period at $10 per share. The expected net income in period one is $X_1 = \$200,000$ and the firm has declared a cash dividend of $1 per share, to be paid at the end of the period. The firm's cost of equity is 20%. Ignore personal taxes.

(a) What is the ex-dividend share price? What would have been the end-of-period stock price if the firm skipped the dividend?

(b) How many shares of common stock will the firm have to sell at the ex-dividend price in order to undertake an investment project which requires an investment $I_1 = \$200,000$?

(c) What is the value of the firm just after the new issue? What would have been the value of the firm if it skipped the dividend and used the retained earnings to finance the investment?

18.10 Assume a situation in which the firm will be liquidated one period from now (thus, now is time t_0 and one period from now is time t_1). Also assume perfect certainty, perfect capital markets and no taxes. Suppose earnings at time t_0 are $X_0 = \$100,000$, investment is $I_0 = \$40,000$ and earnings plus liquidation value at time t_1 are $X_1 = \$200,000$. The interest rate for borrowing and lending is $r = 8\%$. Determine the cash dividends D_0 and D_1 for the following alternative amounts of external financing (EF) that the firm decides to borrow at time t_0: $EF = \$10,000$, $\$50,000$, and $\$80,000$. Also determine the value of the firm V_0 at time t_0. Is it a function of the dividend policy?

18.11 The XYZ Corporation is a non-growth firm which traditionally pays out around 40% of its annual earnings in cash dividends. Up to last year it had had 100,000 shares of common stock outstanding and an annual level of $X_0 = \$500,000$. Last year the XYZ Corporation went to the market and sold another 50,000 shares of common stock for $1,000,000 in order to finance new promising investments.

(a) What was the cash dividend per share prior to the new stock issue?

(b) The XYZ Corporation will want to maintain the same cash dividend per share after the new stock issue. Assuming that the investment has not yet affected this years earnings and they remain at the previous level, what will be the new payout ratio?

(c) What should be the future earnings in order to enable the XYZ Corporation to maintain the same cash dividend per share without exceeding the traditional payout ratio of 40%?

(d) Assume that the investment will indeed raise the earnings to the new level you calculated in (c) and maintain it indefinitely. What is the after-tax internal rate of return on the investment? Compare it to the last year's *dividend yield* and to the earnings per $1 of equity.

(e) Now assume that because of transaction costs (underwriters' premiums, brokerage fees, etc.) the net proceeds to the firm are only 90% of the gross stock issue. What should be the internal rate of return on investment in this case in order to maintain the same earnings and dividends per share?

18.12 A shareholder owns 1,000 shares of ABC Corporation's common stock, trading on January 1, 1994 at $10 per share (cum dividends). A cash dividend of $2 per share is declared, which will be distributed to the stockholders on February 1, 1994.

(a) What is the value of the shareholder's ABC stock valued at the ex-dividend price? How can the shareholder maintain the previous value of his holdings (before the dividend was declared)? Ignore personal tax and transaction costs.

(b) Instead of distributing a cash dividend, the firm considers declaring an 'equivalent' stock dividend. What stock dividend will produce the same ex-dividend share price as in (a)? What is the number of ABC shares that the shareholder owns after the stock dividend? What is the value of his holding?

(c) Now assume that there is a transaction cost of 2% of the price of each share purchased (although there are no personal taxes). What is the difference between the cash dividend and the stock dividend option in this case?

18.13 The long-term investment plan of a firm calls for an investment of $I_0 = \$100,000$ in the current period. The annual income of the firm is $X_0 = \$100,000$. The firm traditionally pays out 40% of its net income as cash dividend to its shareholders.

Can the firm keep up with its dividend payments and undertake the entire investment as planned?

Show the firm's sources and uses of funds on the assumption that it maintains the same dividend and undertakes the planned investment.

18.14 Assume a one-period situation with full certainty and perfect capital markets. Also let:

$$X_0 = 400$$
$$X_1 = 600$$
$$r = 20\%$$
$$\Delta X_1 = 100 + 100 \ln I_0 \ (I_0 \geqslant 0)$$

Here, time $t = 0$ is now and $t = 1$ is one year from now. Also X_0 and X_1 stand for the firm's current income and the income one year from now if no additional investment is made at t_0. I_0 is the investment and ΔX_1 is the additional income one year from now resulting from the new investment. Thus, if investment I_0 is undertaken now, the total income one period from now will be $X_1^* = X_1 + \Delta X_1$. After reaching the optimal investment, the firm distributes as dividends all cash available now (d_0) and one period from now (d_1). Assume complete certainty where r is the relevant discount rate.

(a) Find the optimal investment and the cash dividends d_0, d_1. What is the value of the firm V_0?

(b) If $d_0 = \$500$, determine the external financing EF_0 (borrowing) and the dividend d_1 and calculate the value of the firm. Compare with your result in (a) above.

18.15 Consider a one-period case with full certainty and perfect capital markets. Firms and individuals can borrow and lend at 5%. Assume $X_0 = 0$, and X_1 is a function of the investment I_0 as follows:

$$X_1 = 1,000 - 1,000 \ e^{-0.002 I_0}$$

Here X_0 and X_1 is the firm's income now and one year from now respectively.

(a) What is the optimal amount to be invested at time t_0?
(b) What is the value of the firm?
(c) What must be the cash dividends d_0 and d_1 if they are to be of equal amounts (i.e., if $d_0 = d_1$)?
(d) Determine the external financing EF_0 required to sustain the dividend policy of (c).

18.16 Consider a two-period case with full certainty and perfect capital markets (note that now there are *three* relevant points in time: t_0, t_1, and t_2). Investment at time t_0 will yield *net* return at time t_1 *only*, in accordance with the following schedule:

Marginal investment at t_0 ($)	Marginal *net* return at t_1 ($)
100	80
100	50
100	20
100	6
100	1

Investment at time t_1 will yield *net* return at time t_2 *only*, in accordance with the following schedule:

Marginal investment at t_0 ($)	Marginal *net* return at t_1 ($)
100	50
100	40
100	30
100	20
100	10
100	10

If the firm does not invest, its income in all three periods is zero, namely $X_0 = X_1 = X_2 = 0$.

The firm decides to undertake some of the above investments. Furthermore, it adopts a dividend policy such that dividends increase each year by 20%. At the end of period t_2 the firm is liquidated and its liquidation value is distributed to shareholders.

Determine the optimal investment, the dividends and the external financing for times t_0, t_1, and t_2 assuming a borrowing and lending rate of 12% in both periods.

18.17 One important consequence of equal borrowing and lending rates facing the individual, as we have seen in Chapter 4, is that the wealth of an individual depends on his or her investment decision, not consumption decision. This problem deals with the implication of the above conclusion to the firm by illustrating that one can apply the investment–consumption analysis of Chapter 4 to the question of the impact of dividend policy in perfect and imperfect markets. Assume a framework of one model under *full certainty* where transactions take place at the beginning of the period and the firm is liquidated at the end of the period. Past investments will give the firm income at the beginning of the period (time t_0) in an amount equal to $X_0 = \$10,000$. If no additional investment takes place at time t_0, then the income at the end of the period (time t_1) will be $X_1 = \$5,000$. However, if new investment is made at time t_0, the income at t_1 will be $X_1^* = X_1 + \Delta X_1$, where ΔX_1 is the return (at t_1) on the investment that was made at t_0. The firm faces the following investment projects – all independent of one another:

Project	Investment required at t_0 ($)	Return at t_1 ($)
A	800	1,200
B	1,500	1,600
C	700	800
D	2,300	3,200
E	400	600
F	350	500
G	1,000	1,400

Assume that the lending and borrowing rate is 20%. The firm is 100% equity financed and it has no liabilities.

(a) If the firm makes no investment at the current time (time t_0), what is the total value of the firm?

(b) Which investment projects should the firm undertake and which should it reject? What is the total investment amount at the current time, and what will be the total return on this investment at time t_1? What is the total value of the firm after making the investments?

(c) Suppose the firm distributes all its income except amounts allocated to new investment to shareholders as dividends. If no investment is made at the current time, what will be the current dividend (d_0) and the end-of-period dividend (d_1)? Using the *PV* of dividends what is the present value of this dividend stream and how does it compare with the value of the firm?

(d) Now suppose the firm undertakes and invests in all the profitable investment projects out of A through G. If the firm does not engage in any borrowing, what is the current dividend (d_0) and the future dividend (d_1)? Using the *PV* of dividends what is the value of the firm in this case?

(e) It is known that stockholders prefer high dividends at t_0. In order to satisfy the shareholders the firm decides to borrow $5,000 at time t_0. The money will be used to finance the investment and any left-over will be distributed as dividends. What are d_0 and d_1 in this case? What is the value of the firm? Compare your answers with parts (c) and (d).

(f) Suppose now that the market is imperfect and the firm and shareholders cannot borrow at all (and cannot issue stock), but they can lend at 20%. The firm decides to pay out $d_0 = $8,250. What investments does it make? What is d_1? Does the dividend policy affect the value of the firm in this case? Why? Can you indicate the optimum dividend policy?

(g) Suppose now that the firm can borrow and lend money. However, for each $100 (or a fraction of $100) that it borrows it pays apart from the 20% interest also transaction costs (banker's fee or commission) of $10. The shareholders do not face such transaction cost. What projects would you suggest the firm to undertake? What is the *NPV* of the firm if it pays out $d_0 = $5,150? What is the *NPV* of the firm if it pays out $d_0 = $8,250? Is dividend policy relevant in this case? If yes, what is the optimal dividend policy? Illustrate your answer graphically.

18.18 (a) Write down all the models that you know for stock valuation. What is the relationship between them?

(b) In calculating the *PV* of the earnings per share we 'double count' some of the profit. Give a hypothetical example where such double counting exists and one example where the double counting does not exist.

(c) 'If all investors intend to hold the stock for only one year, Gordon's dividend model breaks down.' Do you agree with this assertion? Prove your answer.

18.19 Suppose that an investor holds the stock of a firm which he bought for $1,000 at time period t_0. The firm is considering two alternative dividend policies. (1) Pay $100.00 cash dividend at the end of the first year, t_1, and $100.00 at the end of the second year, t_2, and then liquidate itself hence paying back the $1,000.00 value of the assets to the shareholder. (2) Pay no dividend at the end of the first year, but rather invest the retained earnings at the interest rate of $r = 10\%$, hence paying a cash dividend of $210.00 ($100 + 100(1 + r)$) in the second year plus the liquidation value of $1,000.00. Assume that the capital gains and personal tax rates are identical, $T_g = T_p = 0.28$.

Suppose that the investor wishes to maximize his wealth at the end of the second period, t_2. He can invest, like the firm, any interim cash flows at 10%. Which dividend policy would he prefer? What is the *effective* tax rate that he pays on any capital gains if policy two is adopted? (Hint: capital gains tax is paid only at the time of the realizations of the project.)

18.20 Suppose that there is no external financing and you employ the dividend growth model to evaluate a firm's stock. The firm retains $b\%$ of its earnings every year. Due to an increase in risk, stockholders increase their required cost of equity, k_e. Also the firm increases its required rate of return from investments R; k_e and R increase by the same proportion. What is the effect of the increase in risk on the stock's price?

18.21 Limbo, a toy firm has a policy to pay $1 per share as dividends. Cutting the cash dividends below $1 would be perceived as a bad signal by the shareholders. There are 1 million shares outstanding. The firm's net income is $2 million with a probability of 1/4, $1.5 million with a probability of 1/4, $1.2 million with a probability of 1/4, and $1 million with a probability of 1/4. Limbo is a pure equity firm. Each share is traded for $10.

(a) What is the probability that Limbo will have to cut the dividend next year?
(b) Limbo considering a debt issue of $500,000, of 10% interest debt. The cash flow from the debt will not create additional profit next year. What is the probability that Limbo will have to cut the dividend next year? (Assume no taxes.)
(c) How would you change your answer to (b) if Limbo issues $500,000 equity by issuing 50,000 shares at $10 per share?

18.22 Assume that the data from problem 18.21 is intact with the following exception. Limbo issued debt of $5 million bearing 10% interest rate and uses the money to repurchase half of its shares namely 500,000 shares at $10 per share. The firm's income before deducting interest remains the same. Assume no taxes.

(a) Calculate the minimum EPS of Limbo. What is the probability of a need to cut the cash dividends?
(b) How would you change your answer to (a) above knowing that Limbo issued $5 million junk bonds paying 15% interest a year rather than the above 10% interest bonds? What is the probability of a need for a dividend cut in this case?

APPENDIX 18A: DERIVATION OF INVESTOR'S OPPORTUNITY SET _____

In order to formalize this discussion, we assume a one-period model in which the firm knows its true economic earnings of the past period with certainty, but the shareholder does not. E' denotes the true earnings per share figure known by the firm, and E symbolizes the earnings figure reported to shareholders. Now let us assume that the firm declares a dividend of M dollars per share, such that:

$$M = q'E' \tag{A1}$$

where q' is some number that represents the proportion of true earnings paid out as dividends. Symbolizing the shareholder per share after-tax income by Y, we obtain:

$$Y = (1 - T_p)q'E' + (1 - T_g)(1 - q')E' = (1 - T_g)E' + (T_g - T_p)q'E' \tag{A2}$$

Note that in spite of the fact that q' and E' are unknown to the shareholders, the product $q'E'$ is known with certainty since it is the cash dividend, M, paid by the firm. However, since E' remains unknown, shareholders view Y as a random variable.

The expected value of Y is then given by:

$$\bar{Y} = (1 - T_g)\bar{E}' + (T_g - T_p)M \tag{A3}$$

where the bar indicates the expected value. Assuming for simplicity, and without loss of generality, that $\bar{E}' = E$, and considering that M is by definition also equal to reported earnings per share, E, multiplied by the reported dividend payment, q, equation (A3) can be rewritten as follows:

$$\bar{Y} = (1 - T_g)E + (T_g - T_p)qE \tag{A4}$$

A glance at equation (A2) above indicates that the variability of E' determines the variability of Y. Thus, from equation (A2) we have:

$$\sigma_Y = (1 - T_g)\sigma_{E'} \tag{A5}$$

where σ_Y denotes the standard deviation of Y. (Recall that $q'E' = M$ is known to the investor with certainty.) Following our argument in the text that one can view the variability of E' as a conditional variability that decreases as the reported dividend payout, q, increases, we write:

$$\sigma_{E'} = (1 - q)\sigma_{E''} \tag{A6}$$

where $\sigma_{E''}$ denotes the maximum value attained by the standard deviation of E' when the firm retains all earnings. Substituting equation (A6) into equation (A5) yields:

$$\sigma_Y = (1 - T_g)(1 - q)\sigma_{E''} \tag{A7}$$

Employing (A4) and (A7) to eliminate q, we obtain:

$$\bar{Y} = E(1 - T_p) + E\frac{(T_p - T_g)}{(1 - T_g)}\frac{\sigma_Y}{\sigma_{E''}} \tag{A8}$$

SELECTED REFERENCES _____

Aharony, Joseph and Swary, Itzhak, 'Quarterly Dividend and Earnings Announcements and Stockholders' Returns: An Empirical Analysis,' *Journal of Finance*, March 1980.

Ambarish, R., John, K., and Williams, J., 'Efficient Signalling with Dividends and Investments,' *Journal of Finance*, June 1987.

Ang, James S., 'Dividend Policy: Informational Content or Partial Adjustment?' *Review of Economics and Statistics*, February 1975.

Arditti, Fred, Levy, Haim, and Sarnat, Marshall, 'Taxes, Uncertainty and Optimal Dividend Policy,' *Financial Management*, Spring 1977.

Asquith, Paul and Mullins, David W. Jr 'Signalling with Dividends, Stock Repurchases and Equity Issues,' *Financial Management*, Autumn 1986.

Bagwell, L. S. and Shoven, J. B., 'Cash Distribution to Shareholders,' *Journal of Economic Perspectives*, Summer 1989.

Baker, Kent, Farrelly, Gail E. and Edelman, Richard B., 'A Survey of Management Views on Dividend Policy,' *Financial Management*, Autumn 1985.

Bar-Yosef, Sasson and Huffman, Lucy, 'The Information Content of Dividends: A Signalling Approach,' *Journal of Financial and Quantitative Analysis*, March 1986.

Bar-Yosef, Sasson and Kolodny, Richard, 'Dividend Policy and Capital Market Theory,' *Review of Economics and Statistics*, May 1976.

Benzion, U. and Shalit, S. S., 'Size, Leverage and Dividend Record as Determinants of Equity Risk,' *Journal of Finance*, September 1975.

Bhattacharya, Sudipto, 'Imperfect Information, Dividend Policy and "The Bird in the Hand" Fallacy,' *The Bell Journal of Economics*, Spring 1979.

Bierman, H. Jr and Hass, J. E., 'Investment Cut-off Rates and Dividend Policy,' *Financial Management*, Winter 1983.

Black, Fischer and Scholes, Myron, 'The Effects of Dividend Yield and Dividend Policy on Common Stock Prices and Returns,' *Journal of Financial Economics*, Vol. 1, 1974.

Black, Fischer, 'The Dividend Puzzle,' *Journal of Portfolio Management*, Winter 1976.

Blume, Marshall E., 'Stock Returns and Dividend Yields: Some More Evidence,' *The Review of Economics and Statistics*, November 1980.

Booth, L. D. and Johnston, D. J., 'The Ex-dividend Day Behavior of Canadian Stock Prices: Tax Changes and Clientele Effects,' *Journal of Finance*, June 1984.

Bradford, David, 'The Incidence and Allocation Effect of a Tax on Corporate Distribution,' N.B.E.R. Working Paper No. 349, May 1979.

Brennan, Michael J., 'A Note on Dividend Irrelevance and the Gordon Valuation Model,' *Journal of Finance*, December 1971.

Charest, G., 'Dividend Information, Stock Returns and Market Efficiency – II,' *Journal of Financial Economics*, June/September 1978.

Chen, Carl, R., 'The Dividend and Investment Decisions of Firms: A Varying Parameter Approach,' *Journal of the Midwest Finance Association*, Vol. 9, 1980.

Choudhury, G. and Miles, D. K., *An Empirical Model of Companies' Debt and Dividend Decisions: Evidence from Company Accounts Data*, London: Bank of England, 1987.

Crutchley, C. E. and Hansen, R. S., 'A Test of the Agency Theory of Managerial Ownership, Corporate Leverage, and Corporate Dividends,' *Financial Management*, Winter 1989.

De Allessi, L. and Fishe, R. P. H., 'Why Do Corporations Distribute Assets? An Analysis of Dividends and Capital Structure,' *Journal of Institutional and Theoretical Economics*, March 1987.

DeAngelo, Harry and Masulis, Ronald W., 'Leverage and Dividend Irrelevancy Under Corporate and Personal Taxation,' *Journal of Finance*, May 1980.

Dharan, Bala G. 'The Association Between Corporate Dividends and Current Cost Disclosures,' *Journal of Business Finance and Accounting*, Summer 1988.

Dielman, T. E. and Oppenheimer, H. R., 'An Examination of Investor Behavior During Periods of Large Dividend Changes,' *Journal of Financial and Quantitative Analysis*, June 1984.

Durand, D., Afterthoughts on a Controversy with MM, Plus New Thoughts on Growth and the Cost of Capital, *Financial Management*, Summer 1989.

Eades, Kenneth, Hess, Patrick J. and Kim, Han E., 'On Interpreting Security Returns during the Ex-dividend Period,' *Journal of Financial Economics*, March 1984.

Easterbrook, F. H., 'Two Agency-cost Explanations of Dividends,' *American Economic Review*, September 1984.

Einhorn, S. G. and Shangquan, P., 'Using the Dividend Discount Model for Asset Allocation,' *Financial Analyst Journal*, July/August 1984.

Elton, Edwin and Gruber, Martin, J., 'Marginal Stockholder Tax Rate and the Clientele Effect,' *Review of Economics and Statistics*, February 1970.

Elton, Edwin, Gruber, Martin J., and Rentzlen Joel, 'The Ex-dividend Day Behavior of Stock Prices, A Re-examination of the Clientele Effect: A Comment,' *Journal of Finance*, June 1984.

Feldstein, M. and Green, J., 'Why Do Companies Pay Dividends,' *American Economic Review*, 13, 1983.

Foster, T. W. III and Vickrey, D., 'The Information Content of Stock Dividend Announcements,' *Accounting Review*, April 1978.

Franks, J. R. and Landskroner, Y., 'Dividends, Taxes and Financial Intermediaries,' in Marshall Sarnat and Giorgio P. Szego, *Essays in Financial Economics in Memory of Irwin Friend, Studies in Banking and Finance*, 5, 1988.

Fung, William K. H. and Theobald, Michael F., 'Dividends and Debt under Alternative Tax Systems,' *Journal of Financial and Quantitative Analysis*, March 1984.

Gordon, Myron J., *The Investment, Financing and Valuation of the Corporation*, Homewood, Ill.: Richard D. Irwin, 1964.

Gordon, Myron J., 'Why Corporations Pay Dividends,' in Marshall Sarnat and Giorgio P. Szego, *Essays in Financial Economics in Memory of Irwin Friend, Studies in Banking and Finance*, 5, 1988.

Gordon, M. J., Corporate Finance Under the MM Theorems,' *Financial Management*, Summer 1989.

Hakansson, Nils H., 'To Pay or Not to Pay Dividends,' *Journal of Finance*, May 1982.

Handjinicolaou, George and Kalay, Avner, 'Wealth Redistributions or Changes in Firm Value: An Analysis of Returns to Bondholders and Stockholders around Dividend Announcements,' *Journal of Financial Economics*, March 1984.

John, Kose and Williams, Joseph, 'Dividends, Dilution and Taxes: A Signalling Equilibrium,' *Journal of Finance*, September 1985.

Kalay, Avner and Subrahmanyam, Marti G., 'The Ex-dividend Day Behavior of Option Prices,' *Journal of Business*, January 1984.

Kane, A., Lee, Y. K. and Marus, A., 'Earnings and Dividend Announcements: Is There a Corroboration Effect?' *Journal of Finance*, September 1984.

Lakonishok, Josef and Vermaelen, Theo, 'Tax Induced Trading Around Ex-Dividend Days,' *Journal of Financial Economics*, July 1986.

Lee, C. F. and Kau, J. B., 'Dividend Payment Behavior and Dividend Policy on REITs,' *Quarterly Review of Economics and Business*, Summer 1987.

Lintner, John, 'Distribution of Incomes of Corporations Among Dividends, Retained Earnings and Taxes,' *American Economic Review*, May 1956.

Litzenberger, R. H. and Ramaswamy, K., 'The Effect of Dividends on Common Stock Prices: Tax Effects or Information Effects?' *Journal of Finance*, May 1982.

Lobo, Gerald J., Nair, R. D., and Song, In Man, 'Additional Evidence on the Information Content of Dividends,' *Journal of Business Finance and Accounting*, Winter 1986.

Long, J. B. Jr, 'The Market Valuation of Cash Dividends: A Case to Consider,' *Journal of Financial Economics*, June/September 1978.

Mayne, Lucille S., 'Bank Dividend Policy and Holding Company Affiliation. Preliminary Programme of the 15th Annual Conference of the Western Finance Association,' *Journal of Financial and Quantitative Analysis*, June 1980.

McDonald, Robert and Soderstrom, Naomi, *Dividend and Share Exchanges: Is There a Financing Hierarchy?* Cambridge, Mass: N.B.E.R., 1986.

Mehta, D. R., 'The Impact of Outstanding Convertible Bonds on Corporate Dividend Policy,' *Journal of Finance*, May 1976.

Metriner, K., 'How to Attract the Right Shareholders,' *Financial Executive*, May 1983.

Michel, Allen, 'Industry Influence on Dividend Policy,' *Financial Management*, Autumn 1979.

Miller, Merton H. and Rock, Kevin, 'Dividend Policy under Asymmetric Information,' *Journal of Finance*, September 1985.

Miller, Merton H. and Modigliani, Franco, 'Dividend Policy, Growth and the Valuation of Shares,' *Journal of Business*, October 1961.

Modigliani, Franco, 'Debt, Dividend Policy, Taxes, Inflation and Market Valuation,' *Journal of Finance*, May 1982.

Moore, Basil, 'Equity Values and Inflation: The Importance of Dividends,' *Lloyds Bank Review*, July 1980.

Morgan, I. G., 'Dividends and Capital Asset Prices,' *Journal of Finance*, September 1982.

Ofer, A. R. and Siegel, D. R., 'Corporate Financial Policy, Information and Market Expectations: An Empirical Investigation of Dividends,' *Journal of Finance*, September 1987.

Ofer, A. R. and Thakor, A. V., 'A Theory of Stock Price Responses to Alternative Corporate Cash Disbursement Methods: Stock Repurchases and Dividends,' *Journal of Finance*, June 1987.

Palmon, Dan and Yaari, Uzi, 'Retention and Tax Avoidance: A Clarification,' *Financial Management*, Spring 1981.

Partington, Graham H., 'Dividend Policy and its Relationship to Investment and Financing Policies: Empirical Evidence,' *Journal of Business Finance and Accounting*, Winter 1985.

Patell, James M. and Wolfson, Mark A., 'The Intraday Speed of Adjustment of Stock Prices to Earnings and Dividend Announcements,' *Journal of Financial Economics*, June 1984.

Petit, R. R., 'Taxes, Transactions Costs and the Clientele Effect of Dividends,' *Journal of Financial Economics*, December 1977.

Poterba, James M., 'The Market Valuation of Cash Dividends: The Citizens Utilities Case Reconsidered,' *Journal of Financial Economics*, March 1986.

Poterba, James and Summers, Lawrence T., 'New Evidence that Taxes Affect the Valuation of Dividends,' *Journal of Finance*, December 1984.

Richardson, Gordon, Sefcik, Stephan E., and Thompson, Rex, 'A Test of Dividend Irrelevance Using Volume Reactions to a Change in Dividend Policy,' *Journal of Financial Economics*, December 1986.

Sarig, O. H., 'Why Do Companies Pay Dividends? Comment,' *American Economic Review*, Vol. 74, 1984.

Shefrin, Hersh M. and Statman, Meir, 'Explaining Investor Preference for Cash Dividends,' *Journal of Financial Economics*, June 1984.

Smirlock, M. and Marshall, W., 'An Examination of the Empirical Relationship Between the Dividend and Investment Decisions: A Note,' *Journal of Finance*, December 1983.

Stapleton, R. C. and Burke, C. M., 'Taxes, the Cost of Capital and the Theory of Investment. A Generalization of the Imputation System of Dividend Taxation,' *Economic Journal*, December 1975.

Wansley, J. W. and Fayez, E., 'Stock Repurchases and Security-holders Returns: A Case of Teledyne,' *Journal of Financial Research*, Summer 1986.

West, Kenneth, 'Dividend Innovations and Stock Price Volatility' *Econometrica*, January 1988.

Wilkes, F. M., 'Dividend Policy and Investment Appraisal in Imperfect Capital Markets,' *Journal of Business Finance and Accounting*, Summer 1977.

Williams, John B., *The Theory of Investment Value*, Cambridge, Mass: Harvard University Press, 1938.

Woolridge, J. Randall and Gosh, Chinmoy, 'Dividend Cuts: Do They Always Signal Bad News?' *Midland Corporate Finance Journal*, Summer 1985.

19

Options and Futures

ARTICLE 43

Exploring the Uses of Derivatives Should Be Satisfying, Not Mystifying

Derivatives don't make risk disappear, but they do make it possible to exchange a risk you'd rather not take for one you're more willing to accept. Options, swaps, and other derivatives are simple in essence, but since they're so versatile, evaluating their various uses can be complex. That's especially true with newer derivatives linked to commodity and equity indices. But it's not our style to magnify complexity. Our success has always been based on helping clients think through every situation fully and clearly. Then we draw on the technical resources of our global network to design the specific tactic that fits your particular strategy. By taking the mystery out of derivatives, we make it easier to take advantage of these important financial tools. It's a key reason we've become a leader in the full range of risk management products.

Source: Business Week, June 15, 1992, p. 101.

What are 'derivatives' or 'derivative assets'? Are these assets too complex to understand? Are they risky in comparison to stocks and bonds? Can derivative assets be used to decrease rather than increase the risk of a portfolio? There is no question regarding the importance of derivative assets. While some people are intimidated by their complexity and others are enthusiastic about the opportunities these assets provide, no-one can afford to overlook the use of these assets: they are everywhere.

In 1973, the year that the Chicago Board of Options Exchange (CBOE) opened, only eighteen stocks had options listed. Today, alongside the CBOE, several other exchanges (American, Philadelphia, and Pacific) list options and the number of stocks with options is well over two hundred. The trading volume in options also increased rapidly and it now exceeds the total volume on the American Stock Exchange.

The rising popularity of option trading in the investment community has been accompanied by rising interest in option valuation among the academic community. Various option valuation models have been developed, some of which are actually used by practitioners to spot mispriced options.

While options can be purchased for speculative purposes, and hence could be considered as gambling rather than investing, their role in corporate decision-making is steadily increasing. For example, put options can be employed for portfolio insurance. Also, stocks can be considered as call options and hence can be evaluated by the call option model. Similarly, issuing callable bonds and insuring the assets can be considered as options as we elaborate later in this chapter. Recently, option trading began on foreign currencies. Thus, multinational firms, importers and exporters can rely on this market to hedge against fluctuations in the foreign currency exchange rates. While options were originally short-term securities (see Table 19.3) nowadays there are options with durations of several years (see Table 19.4).

Futures contracts on commodities have existed for a long time, and in 1976 futures on financial assets were introduced. Next, options on futures were developed. The popularity of futures contracts on financial assets increased dramatically over the years. In September 1988 Japan introduced futures on a stock index.

We discuss in this chapter various types of option and show that many financial assets can be considered a type of option. Then we discuss futures contracts, and options on futures. Finally, we discuss the Black and Scholes option valuation model.

TYPES OF OPTION

Options are contracts to buy or sell a particular underlying asset for a fixed price on or before a specified date in the future. Although there are only two basic options types – a call and a put – the number of possible investment strategies in the options market is quite large and keeps increasing with the introduction of new investment combinations. We describe in this section the main financial instruments available in the options market.

Before starting with option valuation analysis, the basic terminology of the options market must be introduced:

Underlying stock is the asset (stock) involved in the option contract.

Exercise price (or *striking price*) is the price at which the underlying stock may be bought (for a call option) or sold (for a put option).

Expiration date (or *maturity date*) is the latest date when the option may be exercised.

European option is an option that can be exercised only on the maturity date.

American option is an option that can be exercised at any time no later than the maturity date.

We now proceed to describe the main types of options available to the investor, which are known as *calls* and *puts*. Although most of the traded options are American options (in the sense of the above definition), the valuation models mostly focus on European options because of their fixed exercise date. Moreover, we show below that it does not pay to exercise an American option before maturity, so that in effect American options are generally treated like European options. In some cases, however, the early exercise feature of American options is valuable, and these cases are also discussed below.

Call options

American calls constitute the most prominent type of option. A *call* option is a right (but not an obligation) to buy a given number of shares of the underlying stock at a given price (striking price) on or before a specific date (the expiration date).

Examples

On July 31, 1992, a call on Upjohn Corporation stock traded for $5\frac{3}{4}$. The expiration date was the Saturday following the third Friday in August 1992, the striking price was $30, and the market price of the underlying stock on that date was $35\frac{3}{8}$.

Thus the holder of the call option was entitled to buy a share of Upjohn stock for $30 at any date before the end of August 1992. The options are traded in the market and in our particular example the price of the call on Upjohn stock was $5\frac{3}{4}$. The price of the option plus the striking price was slightly higher than the market price of Upjohn stock ($35\frac{3}{4}$ compared to $35\frac{3}{8}$).[1]

On July 31, 1992 the price of the stock of Upjohn Corporation was $35\frac{3}{8}$. The call price on an October 1992 call with a striking price of $45 was $\frac{3}{16}$. The call price in this case is very close to zero since there is a very small chance that the market price of the stock will rise in a relatively short period of about one month from less than $35\frac{3}{8}$ to over $45. Recall that a call option is the *right* to buy the underlying stock, but not an obligation. Thus, if until October 1992 the price of Upjohn stock remains below $45 the call value will drop to zero since no rational investors will exercise the option at a striking price of $45 when they can buy the stock in the market for less than $45.

More than one call written on the same stock may be traded in the market. For example, on July 31, 1992, four different calls on Upjohn stock were traded on the CBOE as shown in Table 19.1. Obviously, the market price of the underlying stock is the same for all calls, $35\frac{3}{8}$. However, the striking price and the expiration date vary from one contract to another. For a given stock price, the lower the striking price the higher is the chance of making a profit

---

1. In general call options are protected against splits and stock dividends, but not against cash dividend distributions. Thus, if a stock dividend reduces the stock price, the exercise price of the option is also appropriately adjusted to allow for the stock dividend, while no such adjustment is made following cash dividend distribution. In general the expiration date of an option is the third Saturday of the month. For simplicity we will call this date as the end of the month.

Table 19.1 Calls on Upjohn stock

Stock price ($)	Striking price ($)	Call price for various expiration date ($)		
		Aug. 1992	Sept. 1992	Oct. 1992
$35\frac{3}{8}$	30	$5\frac{3}{4}$	r	$5\frac{3}{4}$
$35\frac{3}{8}$	35	$1\frac{1}{8}$	$1\frac{11}{16}$	2
$35\frac{3}{8}$	40	$\frac{3}{16}$	$\frac{3}{8}$	$\frac{5}{8}$
$35\frac{3}{8}$	45	s	s	$\frac{3}{16}$

r = not traded; s = no option offered.
Source: *Wall Street Journal*, August 3, 1992.

by exercising the option, and hence as expected, the market price of the option increases as the striking price decreases for options with the same expiration date. For example, for options with an August 1992 expiration date, the call price was $5\frac{3}{4}$ for $30 striking price dropping to $\frac{3}{16}$ for $40 striking price (see Table 19.1).

A second interesting phenomenon revealed by the Upjohn example is that the option price is higher for later expiration dates. Namely, for two call contracts which are identical in all respects except the maturity date, the call with the longer time to expiration will have the higher market price. Thus in Table 19.1, the call with $35 striking price on Upjohn stock expiring at the end of August 1992 (in about three weeks from the date of the market date) trades for $1\frac{1}{8}$, whereas the same call expiring in September 1992 trades for $1\frac{11}{16}$; for an October 1992 expiration date it trades for $2. The reason for this is quite simple: the longer the time remaining until expiration, the greater is the chance that the price of the underlying stock will move up, and this clearly increases the profit potential of the option. This property holds for European as well as American options, yet with American options the intuitive explanation is more transparent: indeed, if investors have a choice of buying an option that can be exercised during the next month, or alternatively during the next two months, they will always prefer the latter, since it includes the first month's opportunity to exercise *plus* a right to exercise the option during one additional month. Thus, investors will be willing to pay more for options with longer maturities.

Put options

A *put* is a right (but not an obligation) to sell a given number of shares of the underlying stock at a specified price on or before a specific date.

The put option differs from the call option in that the word 'buy' is replaced with 'sell.' For example, on July 31, 1992, the price of the put written on IBM stock was $\frac{11}{16}$ for a July 31, 1992 expiration date. The striking price was $85 while the market price of IBM stock on that day was $94\frac{5}{8}$. The put holder has the right to sell one share of IBM at $85 at any time before the end of October 1992. In our specific case the striking price is much greater than the market price, hence the larger value ($\$\frac{11}{16}$) of the put. As long as the price of IBM remains below the striking price the put will not be exercised since it is more profitable to sell the stock at the market price. Unlike call options, other things being equal, the *higher* the striking price the *higher* is the put price. To understand this, recall that with put options the investor *sells* the stock at the striking price rather than buys it, so that for a given price of the underlying stock the profit potential is higher for a higher striking price.

As with the call option, however, the longer the time remaining to expiration, the higher is the put price since the investor is allowed a longer period of time in which to exercise the put.

We demonstrate these two properties of the put options in Table 19.2 using the CBOE data on IBM puts. The IBM put figures reveal the following: (1) for a given maturity, the higher the striking price, the higher is the option market price; (2) for a given striking price, the longer the time remaining until the expiration date, the higher is the put price.

In the next section, we analyze these basic properties of calls and puts in terms of the future price distribution of the underlying stock.

Calls and puts: graphical exposition

The put and call prices and their relationship to the price of the underlying stock can be illustrated by graphical means. Suppose that the future price distribution of the underlying stock is as shown in Figure 19.1. For a European call, we define $f(S_t)$ as the probability distribution density of the stock price S_t at some future point of time t. For an American call, $f(S_t)$ represents all the possible values which the stock price S_t may take from the present to some future exercise date t. S_0 denotes the current market price of the stock and E_x is the exercise price. Assuming that the option is held until the expiration date, the holder of the call will make a profit by exercising the call only if the stock price at expiration S_t is higher than E_x (see Figure 19.1(a)). If the stock price at maturity is less than the striking price, the call is worthless: it is cheaper to buy the stock in the market for S_t than to exercise the call paying E_x for the same stock. The potential profit of the call-holder is thus given by the shaded

Table 19.2 Puts on IBM stock

		Put price for various expiration dates ($)		
Stock price ($)	Striking price ($)	Aug. 1992	Sept. 1992	Oct. 1992
$94\frac{5}{8}$	85	$\frac{1}{8}$	$\frac{5}{16}$	$\frac{11}{16}$
$94\frac{5}{8}$	90	$\frac{3}{8}$	$1\frac{1}{16}$	$1\frac{13}{16}$
$94\frac{5}{8}$	95	$2\frac{3}{8}$	$3\frac{1}{4}$	$3\frac{7}{8}$
$94\frac{5}{8}$	100	$6\frac{1}{2}$	r	r
$94\frac{5}{8}$	105	r	r	r

r = not traded; s = no option offered.
Source: *Wall Street Journal*, August 3, 1992.

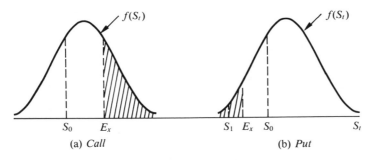

(a) *Call*   (b) *Put*

Figure 19.1

area in panel (a), which is the right tail of the distribution. Clearly, as the striking price is reduced, the point E_x shifts to the left and the shaded area (the potential profit) increases. Since the potential profit increases as E_x decreases, the investor should be willing to pay a higher price for a call with a lower exercise price.

Figure 19.1(b) illustrates the case of a put option. The investor has the right to sell the stock at exercise price E_x. If the stock price is greater than E_x at the expiration date t, the value of the put is zero: it is better to sell the stock in the market than to exercise the put. However, if the market price of the underlying stock falls below E_x on expiration, the put-holder can exercise the option and make a profit. Suppose that the stock price falls to S_1. In this case the profit is $E_x - S_1$: even if the investor does not have the stock, he can buy it for S_1 and sell it for the higher price E_x, as stated in his contract, thus making the profit $E_x - S_1$. The potential profit from holding a put option is illustrated by the left tail of the distribution in Figure 19.1(b), the shaded area left to E_x. Obviously, the higher the striking price E_x, the larger is the shaded area and hence the larger is the potential profit from holding a put, so that investors should be willing to pay a higher price for the put as the striking price increases. This is consistent with the data on IBM put options in Table 19.2.

The prices of various options are published by the financial papers. The full list of traded options is much too long to be included in this chapter. Thus Table 19.3 presents data on a sampling of the options traded on August 3, 1992 to familiarize the reader with the way in which the options' data are published.

While options were originally short-term securities (expiring in 6–9 months), nowadays long-term options exist. For example, Table 19.4 shows the data on June 1992 options which exercise in 1995.

Given the stock price distribution (which can be estimated subjectively), the data published in the financial newspapers are sufficient in order to draw the right tail of the price distribution relevant to the holder of a call and the left tail of the stock price distribution relevant to the holder of the put. The striking price is known for the various options, and if the stock price distribution $f(S_t)$ has been estimated, the tails of the distribution can be drawn. Recall that $f(S_t)$ (and hence the tails) are a function of the time

Table 19.3 Sample columns from the *Wall Street Journal*, August 3, 1992

LISTED OPTIONS QUOTATIONS

Friday, July 31, 1992

Options closing prices. Sales unit usually is 100 shares.
Stock close is New York or American exchange final price.

American

Option	NY Close	Strike	Calls-Last Aug	Calls-Last Sep	Calls-Last Oct	Puts-Last Aug	Puts-Last Sep	Puts-Last Oct
ArcoCh		50	r	r	1/2	r	r	r
Adaptc	23 7/8	20	r	4 7/8	r	r	r	r
	23 7/8	22 1/2	1	r	3 5/8	r	r	3/16
	23 7/8	25	r	1 7/8	2 1/4	r	r	r
Advnta	22	17 1/2	4 1/2	2 7/16	r	r	r	r
	22	20	2 7/16	r	r	r	s	r
	22	22 1/2	r	r	1 5/8	r	r	r
Aetna	43 1/4	35	r	s	8 3/4	r	s	r
	43 1/4	40	3 3/8	3 1/8	r	r	3/8	3 3/4
	43 1/4	45	3/8	3/4	1 1/4	r	r	7/8
Ahman	17	15	r	r	r	r	r	r
	17	17 1/2	1/4	1/2	5/8	r	r	r
AlaskA	28 7/8	20	r	r	3/8	r	r	r
ABrck	28 7/8	25	4	4 3/8	r	r	4	s
	28 7/8	30	r	r	1 3/8	r	r	s
Am Cya	40 1/8	55	r	2 5/8	7 1/2	r	r	r
	61 3/8	60	2	1/2	3 3/8	1 3/4	r	r
	61 3/8	65	1/4	r	1	r	r	r
Am Exp	23	20	3	r	r	r	s	r
	23	22 1/2	7/8	1 1/4	1 5/8	r	s	s
	23	25	1/8	5/16	7/16	r	r	s
Am Hom	74 7/8	65	10 1/2	r	r	r	r	r
	74 7/8	70	r	r	r	r	r	r
	74 7/8	75	1 3/8	2 1/2	3 1/8	s	7/8	r
	74 7/8	80	r	r	1	r	r	s
Amgen	65 1/2	50	r	s	r	r	r	r
	65 1/2	55	s	s	11	r	s	s

Option	NY Close	Strike	Calls-Last Aug	Calls-Last Sep	Calls-Last Oct	Puts-Last Aug	Puts-Last Sep	Puts-Last Oct
	65 1/2	60	5 1/2	r	7	3/8	1	1 3/4
	65 1/2	65	2 1/8	2 7/8	3 3/4	1 1/2	2 3/4	3 1/4
	65 1/2	70	5/16	1 1/8	1 5/8	5 7/8	r	6 3/4
Apple	47	40	7	r	4 1/4	1/16	r	2 1/16
	47	45	2 3/4	3 5/8	4 1/4	5/8	1 1/2	r
	47	50	7/16	1 3/16	2	3 1/16	r	r
	47	55	r	r	r	r	r	r
	47	60	s	s	7/8	s	r	r
Ballrd	26	22 1/2	4 1/8	3 5/8	r	r	3/8	1 1/2
BausLm	26	25	2 7/16	2	7/8	s	3/8	3/4 1
BellSo	52 3/4	45	r	r	r	1/4	r	r
	52 3/4	50	3 3/8	3 3/8	3 3/4	r	r	r
	52 3/4	55	3/4	1/2	7/8	r	7/8	r
Belmac	12 1/2	12 1/2	3/4	1 1/8	r	6 3/4	r	1/4
	12 1/2	15	r	11/16	r	r	r	1 1/8
Biogen	29 1/2	25	4	r	r	r	r	4 1/8
	29 1/2	30	3 3/4	1 1/2	1 3/8	s	s	r
	29 1/2	35	r	1/2	1/2	s	s	r
Block	35	35	r	r	1 5/8	r	r	14
BoxEnB	13	12 1/2	3/16	1 1/2	r	1	1 1/4	2 3/8
	13	15	9 3/8	r	1/4	1 3/8	5 1/8	r
Cabltr	54 1/4	45	r	r	r	1/8	2 1/4	2 1/8
	54 1/4	50	1 1/16	3/4	9/16	1 3/8	2 7/8	r
Calgne	13 1/4	12 1/2	1 1/16	17/8	r	1/2	1 1/4	1 1/4
	13 1/4	15	r	2 1/4	s	9/16	1 1/2	r
Centel	30 1/4	17 1/2	13/16	r	r	1/4	r	s
	30 1/4	30	r	2	r	r	r	r
Chips	5	35	r	9/16	r	r	r	r
Chiron	45	5	s	3/4	1/16	r	r	r

(Continued)

Table 19.3 *Continued*

Friday, July 31, 1992
Options closing prices. Sales unit usually is 100 shares.
Stock close is New York or American exchange final price.

CNA Fn	85	r	$7\frac{3}{4}$	r	r	$1\frac{3}{8}$	r
Cadenc	$17\frac{1}{2}$	r	r	r	r	r	$1\frac{3}{8}$
19	20	$\frac{5}{8}$	r	r	r	r	r
19	$22\frac{1}{2}$	r	r	r	$3\frac{3}{8}$	r	r
CaesrW	$22\frac{1}{2}$	r	s	$9\frac{1}{2}$	r	s	r
$31\frac{3}{4}$	25	$6\frac{7}{8}$	r	$7\frac{5}{8}$	$\frac{1}{16}$	r	r
$31\frac{3}{4}$	30	$2\frac{3}{8}$	$3\frac{1}{4}$	$4\frac{1}{4}$	$\frac{11}{16}$	$1\frac{1}{4}$	r
$31\frac{3}{4}$	35	$\frac{1}{2}$	$1\frac{1}{8}$	$1\frac{15}{16}$	$3\frac{1}{4}$	r	r
$31\frac{3}{4}$	40	$\frac{1}{16}$	s	r	r	s	r
Caterp	50	$5\frac{1}{8}$	r	r	$\frac{1}{8}$	$\frac{1}{2}$	r
$55\frac{1}{4}$	55	r	r	r	$1\frac{1}{8}$	r	r
$55\frac{1}{4}$	60	$\frac{1}{4}$	$\frac{1}{2}$	$1\frac{1}{4}$	r	r	r
ChkDrv	30	$1\frac{3}{16}$	$2\frac{1}{4}$	r	r	r	r
$29\frac{1}{2}$	35	r	$\frac{11}{16}$	r	r	r	r
ClerCd	$12\frac{1}{2}$	$3\frac{1}{4}$	r	$3\frac{3}{4}$	r	r	r
$15\frac{5}{8}$	15	$1\frac{1}{4}$	2	$2\frac{3}{4}$	$\frac{11}{16}$	$1\frac{3}{8}$	$1\frac{7}{8}$
$15\frac{5}{8}$	$17\frac{1}{2}$	$\frac{5}{16}$	$\frac{3}{4}$	$1\frac{3}{8}$	r	$3\frac{1}{8}$	r
$15\frac{5}{8}$	20	r	s	$\frac{7}{8}$	$4\frac{1}{4}$	s	$4\frac{3}{4}$
$15\frac{5}{8}$	$22\frac{1}{2}$	r	s	r	$7\frac{1}{8}$	s	$7\frac{1}{4}$
Collgn	$17\frac{1}{2}$	$3\frac{7}{8}$	r	r	r	r	r
$21\frac{1}{2}$	20	$1\frac{1}{2}$	$2\frac{1}{8}$	$3\frac{5}{8}$	r	r	r
$21\frac{1}{2}$	$22\frac{1}{2}$	$\frac{3}{8}$	$1\frac{3}{8}$	r	r	r	r
$21\frac{1}{2}$	25	r	s	$1\frac{3}{8}$	r	s	r
ColuGs	15	$3\frac{1}{2}$	r	$3\frac{3}{4}$	r	r	r
$18\frac{5}{8}$	$17\frac{1}{2}$	$1\frac{1}{8}$	r	r	$\frac{1}{4}$	r	r
$18\frac{5}{8}$	20	$\frac{1}{4}$	r	$\frac{3}{4}$	r	r	r
Cnseco	25	$4\frac{1}{2}$	r	r	$\frac{1}{4}$	r	r
$29\frac{5}{8}$	30	r	$2\frac{5}{8}$	$3\frac{7}{8}$	2	r	r
$29\frac{5}{8}$	$21\frac{1}{2}$	$\frac{1}{2}$	s	r	r	s	r
Con Ed	30	$1\frac{1}{8}$	r	$1\frac{1}{2}$	r	r	r
Cytogn	15	r	r	r	r	r	$1\frac{1}{8}$
19	$17\frac{1}{2}$	r	r	r	r	$1\frac{1}{4}$	r
19	20	$\frac{7}{8}$	$1\frac{3}{4}$	$2\frac{1}{2}$	r	r	r
19	$22\frac{1}{2}$	r	$\frac{7}{8}$	$1\frac{7}{8}$	r	r	r
Depren	$7\frac{1}{2}$	r	r	$1\frac{9}{16}$	r	r	r
DunBrd	55	$3\frac{7}{8}$	r	$4\frac{7}{8}$	r	$\frac{11}{16}$	r
$58\frac{1}{2}$	60	r	$1\frac{3}{16}$	2	r	$2\frac{7}{8}$	r

FounHl	35	$1\frac{3}{16}$	$2\frac{1}{8}$	$3\frac{3}{4}$	r	r	r
GidLew	20	r	r	r	r	r	$\frac{3}{4}$
Glaxo	$22\frac{1}{2}$	$5\frac{1}{8}$	s	r	r	s	$\frac{1}{4}$
$27\frac{5}{8}$	25	$2\frac{1}{2}$	$2\frac{7}{8}$	$3\frac{1}{4}$	$\frac{1}{8}$	$\frac{5}{16}$	$\frac{13}{16}$
$27\frac{5}{8}$	30	$\frac{1}{8}$	$\frac{3}{8}$	$\frac{3}{4}$	$2\frac{1}{2}$	$2\frac{7}{8}$	$3\frac{3}{8}$
$27\frac{5}{8}$	35	$\frac{1}{16}$	s	s	r	s	s
Grace	35	$2\frac{1}{8}$	r	r	$\frac{1}{4}$	r	r
$37\frac{1}{8}$	40	r	$\frac{1}{2}$	$\frac{7}{8}$	r	r	r
Hershy	35	9	s	r	r	s	r
$43\frac{3}{4}$	40	r	r	r	$\frac{1}{8}$	r	r
$43\frac{3}{4}$	45	r	r	$1\frac{1}{4}$	r	r	r
IBP	15	$3\frac{1}{4}$	r	r	r	r	r
$18\frac{3}{8}$	20	$\frac{3}{16}$	r	r	r	r	r
Infrmx	35	$3\frac{3}{8}$	r	r	r	r	$3\frac{1}{8}$
$37\frac{3}{4}$	40	$1\frac{1}{8}$	2	4	$2\frac{1}{8}$	r	r
Lennar	30	r	r	$2\frac{1}{2}$	$\frac{3}{4}$	$1\frac{5}{8}$	r
$30\frac{1}{2}$	35	r	r	$\frac{5}{8}$	r	$4\frac{7}{8}$	r
LaPac o	$43\frac{3}{8}$	$2\frac{3}{8}$	s	r	r	s	r
LaPac	45	$1\frac{1}{2}$	r	r	$\frac{15}{16}$	r	r
Mirage	20	$6\frac{5}{8}$	s	r	r	s	r
$26\frac{3}{4}$	25	$2\frac{3}{8}$	r	r	$\frac{5}{8}$	$1\frac{1}{4}$	$2\frac{1}{8}$
$26\frac{3}{4}$	30	r	r	$1\frac{1}{2}$	$3\frac{5}{8}$	r	r
NMedE	10	r	s	r	r	s	$\frac{3}{16}$
$14\frac{3}{4}$	$12\frac{1}{2}$	$2\frac{1}{8}$	$2\frac{1}{2}$	r	$\frac{3}{16}$	$\frac{3}{8}$	$\frac{5}{8}$
$14\frac{3}{4}$	15	$\frac{7}{16}$	$\frac{3}{4}$	$1\frac{1}{16}$	1	$1\frac{3}{16}$	$1\frac{9}{16}$
$14\frac{3}{4}$	$17\frac{1}{2}$	r	$\frac{1}{8}$	$\frac{3}{8}$	$3\frac{5}{8}$	r	$3\frac{3}{8}$
NoblAt	15	$2\frac{1}{2}$	r	r	r	r	r
Novell	45	r	r	r	$\frac{1}{8}$	r	$1\frac{1}{4}$
55	50	$5\frac{1}{2}$	6	r	$\frac{3}{8}$	$1\frac{3}{8}$	$2\frac{3}{4}$
55	55	$1\frac{15}{16}$	r	$5\frac{1}{2}$	$1\frac{13}{16}$	$3\frac{5}{8}$	r
55	60	$\frac{5}{16}$	1	$2\frac{7}{8}$	$5\frac{1}{2}$	7	r
55	65	r	s	$1\frac{1}{4}$	r	s	r
Olin	35	$10\frac{3}{4}$	s	s	r	s	s
		Aug	Sep	Dec	Aug	Sep	Dec
Alcan	20	r	r	$1\frac{3}{8}$	r	r	$1\frac{1}{4}$
$19\frac{3}{4}$	$22\frac{1}{2}$	r	r	$\frac{1}{2}$	r	r	r
Amax	20	r	r	$1\frac{7}{16}$	r	r	$1\frac{5}{8}$

$20\frac{1}{4}$	$22\frac{1}{2}$	r	r	$\frac{3}{4}$	r	r	r
AmBrnd	40	r	r	r	r	r	$\frac{1}{2}$
$48\frac{1}{8}$	50	r	$\frac{1}{2}$	$1\frac{3}{8}$	r	$3\frac{1}{8}$	r
$47\frac{1}{8}$	55	r	r	$\frac{3}{8}$	r	r	r
ArowEl	20	$\frac{7}{8}$	$1\frac{5}{8}$	$2\frac{3}{8}$	r	r	r
$20\frac{1}{4}$	$22\frac{1}{2}$	r	r	$1\frac{1}{2}$	r	r	r
Asarco	20	s	r	s	s	$\frac{1}{16}$	s
Bikbst	$12\frac{1}{2}$	$\frac{7}{16}$	r	r	r	r	r
$12\frac{7}{8}$	15	r	r	$\frac{1}{2}$	r	r	r
BwnFer	$22\frac{1}{2}$	$\frac{3}{4}$	1	$1\frac{5}{8}$	r	r	r
$22\frac{3}{4}$	25	r	$\frac{3}{16}$	$\frac{3}{4}$	r	r	r
Catels	10	r	r	r	r	r	$3\frac{1}{4}$
Chase	$22\frac{1}{2}$	r	$3\frac{1}{2}$	r	r	r	r
25	25	$\frac{5}{8}$	$1\frac{3}{16}$	$2\frac{1}{4}$	$\frac{5}{8}$	1	$2\frac{1}{8}$
25	30	$\frac{1}{16}$	$\frac{1}{4}$	$\frac{5}{8}$	r	5	r
ChemBk	35	$\frac{13}{16}$	$1\frac{1}{2}$	$2\frac{11}{16}$	$\frac{13}{16}$	r	$2\frac{1}{2}$
$34\frac{7}{8}$	40	r	$\frac{3}{16}$	$\frac{3}{4}$	$5\frac{3}{8}$	$5\frac{1}{2}$	r
ChemW	$17\frac{1}{2}$	$\frac{5}{16}$	r	$1\frac{3}{8}$	r	r	r
Chevrn	60	s	r	r	s	r	$\frac{3}{8}$
$71\frac{3}{8}$	65	6	r	r	r	r	$1\frac{1}{2}$
$71\frac{3}{8}$	70	$1\frac{5}{8}$	$2\frac{3}{8}$	$3\frac{7}{8}$	$\frac{15}{16}$	r	r
$71\frac{3}{8}$	75	$\frac{1}{8}$	$\frac{1}{2}$	$1\frac{1}{4}$	r	5	$6\frac{1}{4}$
Circus	35	r	r	r	r	r	$\frac{3}{8}$
$44\frac{7}{8}$	40	r	$5\frac{1}{2}$	$6\frac{7}{8}$	r	$\frac{1}{4}$	1
$44\frac{7}{8}$	45	1	$1\frac{3}{4}$	3	r	$1\frac{3}{4}$	r
$44\frac{7}{8}$	50	r	$\frac{3}{8}$	$1\frac{1}{8}$	r	r	r
Coastl	30	r	r	r	r	$2\frac{1}{4}$	r
ConAgr	25	r	$2\frac{1}{2}$	r	r	$\frac{1}{4}$	r
$27\frac{1}{2}$	30	r	$\frac{1}{4}$	r	r	r	r
$27\frac{1}{2}$	35	s	r	s	s	$7\frac{2}{8}$	s
Copytl	10	r	$1\frac{1}{4}$	r	r	r	r
$10\frac{1}{4}$	$12\frac{1}{2}$	r	r	$1\frac{1}{4}$	r	r	r
CytRx	5	r	r	r	$\frac{3}{8}$	r	r
5	$7\frac{1}{2}$	r	r	$\frac{1}{4}$	r	r	r
Datscp	20	r	r	r	r	$\frac{3}{8}$	r
Deere	40	$2\frac{5}{8}$	$2\frac{15}{16}$	r	r	$\frac{7}{8}$	r
42	45	r	$\frac{7}{8}$	$1\frac{13}{16}$	r	$3\frac{1}{4}$	$4\frac{1}{2}$

(*Continued*)

Table 19.3 *Continued*

Friday, July 31, 1992
Options closing prices. Sales unit usually is 100 shares.
Stock close is New York or American exchange final price.

Donely	55	r	$3\frac{1}{2}$	r	r	r	r	$64\frac{5}{8}$	70	r	r	$1\frac{3}{8}$	r	r	r	RoyApl	10	$\frac{7}{16}$	$\frac{7}{8}$	$1\frac{1}{2}$	r	r	$1\frac{11}{16}$
Dover	45	r	$\frac{3}{8}$	$1\frac{1}{2}$	r	r	r	Laidtb	10	r	r	$\frac{9}{16}$	r	1	$1\frac{1}{8}$	$9\frac{7}{8}$	$12\frac{1}{2}$	$\frac{1}{16}$	r	r	r	r	r
Duracl	30	r	$\frac{1}{2}$	r	r	r	r	MGI Ph	$7\frac{1}{2}$	$\frac{1}{8}$	r	r	r	r	r	SPl Ph	20	$2\frac{1}{4}$	$2\frac{9}{16}$	r	r	r	r
EmrsEl	50	$1\frac{3}{4}$	$2\frac{1}{8}$	r	$\frac{1}{2}$	$\frac{7}{8}$	r	MGIC	40	r	$1\frac{1}{4}$	$2\frac{3}{8}$	$1\frac{1}{16}$	r	r	$21\frac{3}{4}$	$22\frac{1}{2}$	$\frac{7}{8}$	$1\frac{5}{16}$	r	r	r	r
FishPr	15	r	r	$8\frac{1}{2}$	r	r	r	MNC	$12\frac{1}{2}$	$\frac{7}{16}$	r	r	r	r	r	$21\frac{3}{4}$	25	$\frac{1}{8}$	r	r	r	r	r
FrMcRP	20	r	r	r	$\frac{1}{8}$	r	r	McCaw	25	r	r	$3\frac{1}{2}$	r	r	r	SFePac	$12\frac{1}{2}$	r	r	$\frac{15}{16}$	r	$\frac{5}{8}$	r
GTE	$22\frac{1}{2}$	s	$12\frac{1}{8}$	s	s	r	s	MrdnBc	25	r	$3\frac{1}{2}$	r	r	r	r	Sbarro	20	r	r	$3\frac{1}{2}$	r	r	r
$34\frac{7}{8}$	30	$4\frac{7}{8}$	$4\frac{7}{8}$	r	r	$\frac{1}{8}$	$\frac{7}{16}$	$28\frac{3}{4}$	r	$\frac{11}{16}$	r	r	r	r		$21\frac{3}{8}$	$22\frac{1}{2}$	r	r	$1\frac{13}{16}$	r	r	r
$34\frac{7}{8}$	35	$\frac{7}{16}$	$\frac{11}{16}$	$1\frac{7}{16}$	r	$1\frac{1}{8}$	$1\frac{5}{8}$	NiagMP	20	r	r	$\frac{1}{2}$	r	r	r	$21\frac{3}{8}$	25	r	r	1	r	r	r
GenRe	85	r	r	$6\frac{3}{4}$	$\frac{11}{16}$	r	r	Pfizer	65	13	$12\frac{5}{8}$	r	r	r	$\frac{3}{4}$	Seagte	$12\frac{1}{2}$	r	r	r	r	r	$\frac{1}{2}$
$87\frac{1}{2}$	90	r	$1\frac{5}{8}$	$3\frac{3}{4}$	r	r	r	$78\frac{1}{4}$	70	8	$8\frac{3}{8}$	10	$\frac{1}{8}$	r	$1\frac{5}{8}$	$15\frac{3}{8}$	15	$\frac{3}{4}$	$1\frac{1}{4}$	$2\frac{1}{8}$	r	$\frac{3}{4}$	r
Gillet	50	$2\frac{1}{2}$	$3\frac{1}{4}$	r	$\frac{1}{4}$	$\frac{7}{8}$	r	$78\frac{1}{4}$	75	$3\frac{5}{8}$	$4\frac{1}{2}$	$6\frac{5}{8}$	$\frac{5}{8}$	$1\frac{7}{16}$	$3\frac{3}{8}$	$15\frac{3}{8}$	$17\frac{1}{2}$	r	$\frac{3}{8}$	$\frac{15}{16}$	r	r	r
$52\frac{1}{2}$	55	r	$\frac{3}{4}$	$1\frac{3}{4}$	r	r	r	$78\frac{1}{4}$	80	$\frac{11}{16}$	$1\frac{9}{16}$	$3\frac{1}{2}$	3	$3\frac{3}{4}$	r	Shawmt	$12\frac{1}{2}$	r	$3\frac{3}{8}$	r	r	r	r
Hecla	10	$\frac{1}{4}$	$\frac{3}{8}$	r	$\frac{5}{16}$	$\frac{9}{16}$	$\frac{13}{16}$	$78\frac{1}{4}$	85	s	r	2	s	r	r	16	15	$1\frac{1}{4}$	$1\frac{3}{4}$	r	r	r	1
Hercul	45	s	12	s	s	r	s	Ph Mor	60	s	$19\frac{3}{4}$	s	s	r	s	16	$17\frac{1}{2}$	$\frac{1}{4}$	$\frac{5}{8}$	$1\frac{1}{16}$	r	r	r
$57\frac{1}{8}$	55	r	$2\frac{3}{4}$	r	r	r	r	80	65	r	r	r	r	r	$\frac{1}{2}$	16	20	r	$\frac{3}{16}$	$\frac{3}{4}$	r	r	r
$57\frac{1}{8}$	60	r	r	$1\frac{5}{8}$	r	r	r	80	70	$9\frac{1}{2}$	$10\frac{1}{4}$	r	$\frac{1}{16}$	$\frac{1}{4}$	1	SumitT	25	$2\frac{1}{4}$	$3\frac{1}{8}$	r	$\frac{3}{4}$	r	r
Imunex	25	$8\frac{1}{4}$	r	r	r	r	r	80	75	$5\frac{1}{4}$	$5\frac{3}{4}$	7	$\frac{1}{4}$	$\frac{3}{4}$	$2\frac{1}{4}$	$26\frac{7}{8}$	30	$\frac{5}{16}$	1	$2\frac{3}{4}$	r	r	r
34	30	$4\frac{3}{8}$	r	r	$\frac{5}{8}$	$1\frac{1}{8}$	r	80	80	$1\frac{1}{4}$	$2\frac{1}{4}$	$4\frac{1}{8}$	$1\frac{3}{8}$	$2\frac{1}{2}$	$4\frac{1}{8}$	Telef	35	r	r	$1\frac{1}{8}$	$2\frac{1}{2}$	r	r
34	35	$1\frac{1}{4}$	$2\frac{1}{4}$	4	r	r	r	80	95	$\frac{1}{8}$	$\frac{5}{8}$	$2\frac{1}{8}$	r	6	r	UNUM	45	r	$1\frac{1}{4}$	r	$\frac{3}{4}$	r	r
34	40	r	$\frac{5}{8}$	$2\frac{5}{8}$	r	r	r	80	90	r	$\frac{1}{8}$	$\frac{13}{16}$	r	r	r	UHltCr	80	r	r	r	$\frac{5}{16}$	r	r
Invacr	$22\frac{1}{2}$	$\frac{7}{8}$	r	r	r	r	r	PionHi	30	r	r	r	$3\frac{1}{8}$	r	r	92	85	$7\frac{1}{2}$	r	r	$\frac{7}{8}$	$2\frac{5}{16}$	r
$22\frac{1}{2}$	25	s	$\frac{3}{4}$	2	s	r	r	PfdHlth	15	r	$\frac{3}{8}$	r	r	r	r	92	95	r	$3\frac{3}{8}$	$7\frac{1}{2}$	r	r	r
Kellog	50	s	r	r	rs	$\frac{1}{16}$	r	QuakSt	15	$\frac{1}{8}$	r	$\frac{5}{8}$	r	1	r1	92	100	$\frac{5}{8}$	r	$5\frac{1}{4}$	r	r	r
$64\frac{5}{8}$	60	r	r	r	r	$\frac{7}{8}$	$1\frac{5}{8}$	RJB Nb	$7\frac{1}{2}$	$1\frac{5}{16}$	$1\frac{7}{16}$	$1\frac{5}{8}$	r	r	r								
$64\frac{5}{8}$	65	r	$1\frac{3}{4}$	r	r	$2\frac{7}{8}$	$3\frac{3}{4}$	$8\frac{3}{4}$	10	r	r	$\frac{5}{16}$	$1\frac{1}{4}$	r	$1\frac{5}{16}$								

Table 19.4 Long-term options

Option/Exp/Strike	Last	Option/Exp/Strike	Last	Option/Exp/Strike	Last	Option/Exp/Strike	Last	Option/Exp/Strike	Last
CBOE		Citicp Jan 94 17½ p	1 7/8	FordM Jan 94 35	9 5/8	IBM Jan 94 85 p	5 1/4	Oracle Jan 95 20	5 5/8
AT&T Jan 94 35 p	1 5/8	Citicp Jan 94 20	4 3/8	FordM Jan 94 35 p	3 1/8	IBM Jan 94 105	7 1/2	PepsiC Jan 94 40	3 1/4
AT&T Jan 94 40 p	2 7/8	Citicp Jan 94 20 p	3	FordM Jan 94 40	7 1/4	IBM Jan 95 85	20	PepsiC Jan 95 35 p	4 1/8
AT&T Jan 94 45	4 3/4	Citicp Jan 94 22½	3 3/4	FordM Jan 94 40 p	5	IBM Jan 95 105	11 1/2	Sears Jan 94 30 p	1 9/16
AT&T Jan 94 50	3	Citicp Jan 94 22½ p	4 3/8	FordM Jan 94 45	5 1/8	IBM Jan 95 105 p	18	Sears Jan 94 45	3 1/8
AT&T Jan 95 40 p	3 5/8	Citicp Jan 95 20	6 1/8	FordM Jan 94 50	3 1/2	IBM Jan 95 135	4 1/8	Sears Jan 95 35	8 1/8
AT&T Jan 95 45	6 3/4	Citicp Jan 95 22½	5 1/8	FordM Jan 94 50	4	IBM Jan 95 135 p	38 1/8	Sears Jan 95 45	4 1/8
BnkAm Jan 94 30	16	Citicp Jan 95 22½ p	4 3/8	FordM Jan 95 35 p	4 3/8	JohnJn Jan 94 45	7 3/8	Syntex Jan 93 35	3 1/2
BnkAm Jan 94 40	10 5/8	CocaCl Jan 94 32½ p	1 1/4	FordM Jan 95 55	13 1/2	JohnJn Jan 94 55	3 3/8	Syntex Jan 93 35 p	3 3/8
BnkAm Jan 94 40 p	3 7/8	CocaCl Jan 94 47½	3 3/4	Gap Jan 93 30	6 1/2	JohnJn Jan 95 40 p	3 5/8	Syntex Jan 93 40	1 5/8
BnkAm Jan 94 50	5 1/2	CocaCl Jan 95 30	16	Gap Jan 93 40	2 9/16	JohnJn Jan 95 50	7 1/2	Syntex Jan 93 50	7/16
BnkAm Jan 94 50 p	9 1/4	CocaCl Jan 95 50 p	9 1/4	Gap Jan 94 30	3 5/8	K mart Jan 93 20	3 1/8	Syntex Jan 93 65	1/8
Boeing Jan 94 40	7 3/4	DeltaA Jan 94 50 p	4 5/8	Gap Jan 94 40	5	K mart Jan 93 20 p	1 1/8	Syntex Jan 94 30	8 3/8
Boeing Jan 94 40 p	4 1/4	DeltaAr Jan 94 60	7	GenEl Mar 93 55	23 3/8	K mart Jan 93 25	1	Syntex Jan 94 35	6 1/4
Boeing Jan 94 50	3 3/8	DeltaA Jan 95 60	10 1/8	GenEl Jan 94 75	10 1/2	K mart Jan 94 20	4 5/8	Syntex Jan 94 40	4 3/8
Boeing Jan 94 60	1 1/2	DeltaAr Jan 95 70	6 3/8	GenEl Jan 95 60	23 3/8	K mart Jan 94 25	2 1/16	Syntex Jan 95 35	7 3/4
Boeing Jan 95 35 p	3 1/4	DowCh Mar 93 40 p	9/16	GenEl Jan 95 75	13 3/8	K mart Jan 95 20	6	Texins Jan 94 30	10 1/8
Boeing Jan 95 50	5 3/8	DowCh Mar 93 55 p	4 3/4	GnMotr Mar 93 25 p	3/16	Limitd Jan 95 27½	2 5/8	Texins Jan 94 40	4 3/8
BrMySq Mar 93 60	9 5/8	DowCh Jan 94 55	1	GnMotr Mar 93 30	11	Limitd Jan 95 22½	5 5/8	Texins Jan 95 40	6 1/2
BrMySq Mar 93 60 p	2 1/8	EKodak Jan 95 40 p	7 1/8	GnMotr Mar 93 30 p	5 1/8	McDonl Mar 93 25	3 5/8	Upjohn Jan 94 30	6
BrMySq Mar 93 75	2 1/16	FordM Jan 93 20	21 3/8	GnMotr Mar 93 40	4 3/8	McDonl Jan 95 45	21 3/4	Upjohn Jan 94 30 p	3 1/4
BrMySq Jan 94 60	12	FordM Jan 93 25 p	1 1/8	GnMotr Mar 93 40 p	3 3/8	Merck Jan 94 41 5/8	10 1/8	Upjohn Jan 94 45	1 5/8
BrMySq Jan 94 85	2 3/8	FordM Jan 93 30	12 1/4	GnMotr Mar 93 45	2 3/8	Merck Jan 94 41 5/8 p	12 3/8	Upjohn Jan 95 30	7 1/4
BrMySq Jan 95 60	14 1/4	FordM Jan 93 35	7 1/2	GnMotr Mar 94 45 p	6 1/2	Merck Jan 95 30	2	Upjohn Jan 95 30 p	4 1/8
BrMySq Jan 95 75	7 7/8	FordM Jan 93 35 p	1 1/8	GnMotr Jan 94 30 p	1 5/8	Merck Jan 95 35	7 1/2	Upjohn Jan 95 35	5 1/4
BrMySq Jan 95 85	4 7/8	FordM Jan 93 40	5 5/8	GnMotr Jan 94 40	6 1/4	Merck Jan 94 50	5 1/8	WalMart Jan 95 65	7 1/2
BrMySq Jan 95 85 p	19 7/8	FordM Jan 93 40 p	2 1/4	GnMotr Jan 94 40 p	4 7/8	Merck Jan 94 58¾	4	WalMt Jan 93 50	7 5/8
Centr Jan 94 10	6	FordM Jan 93 45	2 5/8	GnMotr Jan 94 50	3	Merck Jan 95 40	15 1/2	WalMt Jan 93 50 p	1 13/16
Centr Jan 94 10 p	2 3/8	FordM Jan 93 45 p	5 1/8	Heinz Jan 93 35	14	Merck Jan 95 50	10 5/8	WalMt Jan 93 60	2 1/8
Centr Jan 94 20	2 3/4	FordM Jan 93 50	1 3/8	IBM Jan 94 70	9 1/8	Mobil Jan 94 65	6 1/4	WalMt Jan 93 60 p	6 1/4
Centr Jan 94 30	1 3/4	FordM Jan 94 70	9 5/8	IBM Jan 94 85	17 1/4	Mobil Jan 94 80	5 1/8	WalMt Jan 93 70	7/16
Citicp Jan 94 17½	6	FordM Jan 94 30 p	1 11/16			Mobil Jan 95 50 p	2 1/2	Call vol 1,748 Opint 274,648	
								Put vol 1,755 Opint 369,549	

(continued)

Table 19.4 *Continued*

Option/Exp/Strike	Last
AMEX	
AMR Dec 93 80	6
AMR Jan 95 55 p	$5\frac{3}{4}$
AMR Jan 95 65 p	$9\frac{1}{4}$
ASA Dec 93 35 p	3
ASA Jan 95 55	$3\frac{7}{8}$
AmExp Dec 93 15	$9\frac{1}{2}$
AmExp Dec 93 20	$5\frac{1}{2}$
AmExp Dec 93 20 p	$1\frac{3}{4}$
Amgen Jan 94 75	9
Amgen Jan 94 75 p	$18\frac{3}{4}$
Amgen Jan 94 100	$3\frac{1}{2}$
Amgen Jan 95 45 p	$4\frac{3}{4}$
Amgen Jan 95 55	$21\frac{1}{4}$
Amgen Jan 95 70	15
AppleC Dec 93 50	$7\frac{3}{4}$
AppleC Dec 93 50 p	$9\frac{1}{2}$
AppleC Dec 93 80	$1\frac{3}{4}$
AppleC Jan 95 40	$15\frac{1}{4}$
AppleC Jan 95 40 p	$6\frac{1}{4}$
BellSo Jan 94 45 p	$3\frac{1}{8}$
Chase Dec 93 20 p	$1\frac{1}{4}$
Chase Jan 95 25	$7\frac{1}{2}$
Chevrn Dec 93 75	$3\frac{1}{8}$
Chevren Jan 95 55	16
Chevrn Jan 95 70 p	10
Chevrn Jan 95 85	$3\frac{5}{8}$
ColGas Jan 95 $12\frac{1}{2}$	$7\frac{3}{4}$
Digital Dec 93 40	$5\frac{3}{8}$
Digital Dec 93 40 p	$8\frac{3}{4}$
Digital Dec 93 60	$1\frac{3}{4}$
Digital Dec 93 60 p	$26\frac{1}{2}$
Digital Jan 95 40	$7\frac{3}{4}$
Disney Dec 93 25	$12\frac{3}{8}$
Disney Dec 93 $37\frac{1}{2}$	5
Disney Dec 93 50	$1\frac{1}{2}$
Disney Jan 95 30 p	$3\frac{1}{8}$
Disney Jan 95 40	$5\frac{3}{4}$
Disney Jan 95 50	$3\frac{1}{2}$
DuPont Dec 93 30	20
GTE Dec 93 35	$1\frac{5}{8}$
GTE Jan 95 30	5
Glaxo Jan 94 25	$4\frac{3}{8}$
Glaxo Jan 94 25 p	$3\frac{1}{4}$
Glaxo Jan 94 35	$1\frac{1}{2}$
Glaxo Jan 94 45	$\frac{9}{16}$
Glaxo Jan 95 20	9
Glaxo Jan 95 20 p	2
Glaxo Jan 95 25	$6\frac{1}{8}$
Glaxo Jan 95 25 p	$4\frac{1}{4}$
Glaxo Jan 95 35	$2\frac{5}{8}$
Pfizer Dec 93 45	$32\frac{7}{8}$
Pfizer Dec 45 p	$\frac{3}{4}$
Pfizer Dec 93 70	14
PhilMr Dec 93 60	$21\frac{1}{4}$
PhilMr Dec 93 60 p	2
PhilMr Dec 93 80	$9\frac{1}{4}$
PhilMr Dec 93 80 p	9
PhilMr Jan 95 60	$24\frac{1}{2}$
PhilMr Jan 95 80	13
PhilMr Jan 95 80 p	11
PhilMr Jan 95 100	$6\frac{1}{2}$
ProctG Dec 93 45	$7\frac{1}{4}$
ProctG Dec 93 45 p	3
ProctG Jan 95 50	$8\frac{1}{8}$
ProctG Jan 95 60	4
RJR Nab Jan 95 10	$2\frac{3}{8}$
RJR Nab Jan 95 $12\frac{1}{2}$	$1\frac{1}{2}$
RJR Nb Jan 93 $7\frac{1}{2}$	$2\frac{7}{16}$
RJR Nb Jan 93 10	$\frac{3}{4}$
RJR Nb Jan 93 $12\frac{1}{2}$	$\frac{1}{4}$
RJR Nb Jan 94 $7\frac{1}{2}$	$3\frac{1}{4}$
RJR Nb Jan 94 10	$1\frac{5}{8}$
RJR Nb Jan 94 $12\frac{1}{2}$	$\frac{7}{8}$
Texaco Dec 93 50	$13\frac{3}{4}$
TritEn Jan 95 50	5
UCarb o Dec 93 15	$11\frac{5}{8}$
UCarb o Dec 93 25	$4\frac{1}{4}$
US Sur Jan 94 75 p	6
US Sur Jan 94 100	24
US Sur Jan 94 100 p	$16\frac{5}{8}$
US Sur Jan 94 130	$11\frac{1}{2}$
US Sur Jan 94 170	$3\frac{7}{8}$
US Surg Jan 95 75 p	$10\frac{1}{4}$
US Surg Jan 95 100 p	$20\frac{1}{8}$
USWst Jan 94 30	$7\frac{1}{4}$
USXMar Jan 94 15	7
USXMar Jan 94 25 p	$5\frac{5}{8}$
USXUSS Jan 95 40	7
WellsF Jan 94 70	$15\frac{1}{8}$
WstgEl Jan 95 15	$4\frac{7}{8}$
WstgEl Jan 95 $17\frac{1}{2}$	$3\frac{7}{8}$
WstgEl Jan 95 $22\frac{1}{2}$	$2\frac{1}{8}$
viColGs Jan 94 20	$2\frac{3}{4}$
Call vol 3,604 Opint	282,488
Put vol 1,145 Opint	286,256
PHILADELPHIA	
Option/Exp/Strike	Last
AbtLab Jan 94 20	$12\frac{1}{8}$
AbtLab Jan 94 25	$6\frac{7}{8}$
AbtLab Jan 95 25	$8\frac{3}{8}$
AbtLab Jan 95 30	$6\frac{3}{8}$
AldSgnl Jan 94 55 p	$6\frac{3}{4}$
Anheus Jan 93 70	$\frac{7}{16}$
BkBost Jan 95 20	$9\frac{3}{8}$
DomRsc Oct 92 40	$\frac{7}{16}$
FedNM Jan 94 40	$25\frac{5}{8}$
FedNM Jan 94 70	$7\frac{7}{8}$
FedNM Jan 94 70 p	$11\frac{3}{8}$
FedNM Jan 94 85	$3\frac{7}{8}$
HmeDp o Jan 94 $23\frac{3}{8}$	$23\frac{7}{8}$
HmeDp o Jan 94 $23\frac{3}{8}$ p	$\frac{3}{4}$
HmeDp o Jan 94 30	$18\frac{1}{4}$
HomeDp Jan 94 45 p	$5\frac{5}{8}$
HomeDp Jan 94 55	5
Marriot Jan 95 20	$2\frac{13}{16}$
Morgan Jan 94 50	$12\frac{3}{4}$
NCNM Jan 94 50	7
QuakrO Jan 94 50	$11\frac{1}{2}$
RJR Nab Jan 95 10	$2\frac{3}{8}$
RJR Nb Jan 93 $7\frac{1}{2}$	$2\frac{7}{16}$
RJR Nb Jan 93 10	$\frac{13}{16}$
RJR Nb Jan 94 10	$1\frac{5}{8}$
RJR Nb Jan 94 $12\frac{1}{2}$	$\frac{7}{8}$
Salomn Jan 94 25	$13\frac{1}{4}$
Salomn Jan 94 30 p	$1\frac{7}{8}$
Salomn Jan 94 35	6
TimeW Jan 93 115	$8\frac{3}{4}$
TimeW Jan 94 85	36
TimeW Jan 95 100 p	$9\frac{5}{8}$
TimeW Jan 95 115 p	$15\frac{3}{8}$
Waste Jan 94 40	$3\frac{1}{4}$
Waste Jan 94 50	$1\frac{5}{16}$
Wolwth Jan 94 20	9
Cal vol 289 Opint	63,053
Put vol 150 Opint	18,107
p-Put.	
PACIFIC	
AMD Jan 95 10	$2\frac{5}{8}$
Compq Jan 94 25	$5\frac{5}{8}$
Compq Jan 94 25 p	$4\frac{1}{2}$
Compq Jan 94 45	$1\frac{5}{8}$
ConrPr Jan 94 20 p	$4\frac{3}{8}$
GnMill Jan 94 80	$3\frac{1}{2}$
Micsft Jan 94 $83\frac{3}{8}$	11
Micsft Jan 94 100	6
Nike B Jan 94 55	14
PacTel Jan 95 35 p	$2\frac{5}{8}$
SchrPl Jan 94 40 p	1
SchrPl Jan 94 55	$7\frac{3}{4}$
SmtB eq Jan 94 60	19
Call vol 149 Opint	14,559
Put vol 36 Opint	5,252
NEW YORK	
Option/Exp/Strike	Last
CampSp Jan 94 30 p	$1\frac{1}{2}$
Chubb Jan 94 60 p	2
Chubb Jan 94 90	$3\frac{1}{2}$
Nynex Jan 94 65 p	$2\frac{1}{2}$
Call vol 12 Opint	1,800
Put vol 17 Opint	2,898
p-Put.	

Source: *Wall Street Journal*, July 7, 1992, p. C12

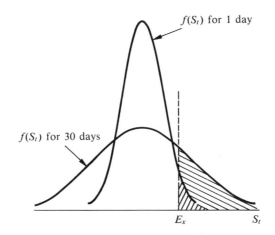

$f(S_t)$ for 1 day

$f(S_t)$ for 30 days

E_x S_t

Figure 19.2

remaining to maturity. Hypothetical stock price distributions relevant for a call option with one day to maturity and a call option with 30 days to maturity are shown in Figure 19.2. The longer the time remaining to maturity, the greater is the uncertainty in future stock prices, so the stock price distribution is more widely spread (has higher variance). Thus, the shaded area right to point E_x is larger for the 30 day option and hence the price of this call option will be greater. The same argument applies to the left tail determining the put price.

OPTION TRADING

The transactions in options are not carried out directly between sellers and buyers. All options are bought or written on the exchange through the Option Clearing Corporation. The anonymity of the participants in the transactions creates a current market for options which allows each investor to buy or sell an option in the market at any time.

Normally the option contracts are in units of 100 shares (round lot). Thus, if the published quotation of a call is, say, $2 and the exercise price is $30, the holder of the call will have to pay $30 × 100 = $3,000 for 100 shares of the underlying stock when the option is exercised and the market price of the call entitling the buyer to this privilege is $2 × 100 = $200.

The transactions are made through a brokerage firm which, of course, charges a commission. The commission is negotiable and hence varies from one broker to another and from one customer to another. All option trades are taxed as capital gains which, due to the 1986 U.S. tax law changes, is at the same rate as the investor's marginal tax rate. Since most listed options have maturities of less than 12 months, the short-term capital gains rule applies.

Finally, unlike stocks, purchases of options must be paid for in full and no margin is allowed.

PROFILE PROFILES OF CALLS AND PUTS _____

For each investor buying a call, there must be an investor who sells the call. The latter is known to the financial community as the 'writer' (seller) of the call. Since holding a call and writing a call are opposite transactions, it is clear that whenever one side makes a profit, the other side must incur a loss. Let us describe the payoff matrix of each side:

Holder of a call		Writer of a call	
$-C$	if $S_t \leqslant E_x$	C	if $S_t \leqslant E_x$
$(S_t - E_x) - C$	if $S_t > E_x$	$C - (S_t - E_x)$	if $S_t > E_x$

If the stock price on expiration date, S_t is less than the exercise price, i.e. $S_t < E_x$, the holder of the call will allow it to expire without exercising it and his loss is equal to the entire amount C paid when he purchased the call. If conversely $S_t > E_x$, the holder will exercise the call by paying the striking price E_x for a share of stock worth S_t: his profit will be $S_t - E_x$ minus his initial investment C. Denoting by y_t the call-holder's profit (or loss), we see that y_t can be rewritten as:

$$y_t = \begin{cases} -(C + E_x) + S_t & \text{if } S_t > E_x \\ -C & \text{if } S_t \leqslant E_x \end{cases}$$

The slope of the line corresponding to the segment $S_t > E_x$ is $+1$ and the vertical intercept is a negative number $-(C + E_x)$, representing the total 'investment' in the stock.

For a call-writer we have exactly the opposite cash flows: if $S_t \leqslant E_x$, the call is not exercised so that he makes a profit equal to the initial proceeds from writing the call, C. If on the other hand $S_t > E_x$ and the call is exercised, the call-writer is obligated to deliver a stock worth S_t for a price E_x. Thus, the call writer's profit (or loss) in this case is $C - (S_t - E_x)$, which may be rewritten as:

$$y_t = \begin{cases} (C + E_x) - S_t & \text{if } S_t > E_x \\ +C & \text{if } S_t \leqslant E_x \end{cases}$$

For the segment $S_t > E$, this is again a straight line as a function of the stock price S_t but with a negative slope of -1 and positive vertical intercept $C + E_x$, representing the total 'receipts' from the transaction.

Example

Figure 19.3 illustrates the profit profiles of a call-writer and a call-holder for the following example:

Call price	$C = \$1$
Exercise price	$E_x = \$10$
Stock price at expiration date	$S_t =$ an unknown random variable
	(plotted along the horizontal axis)

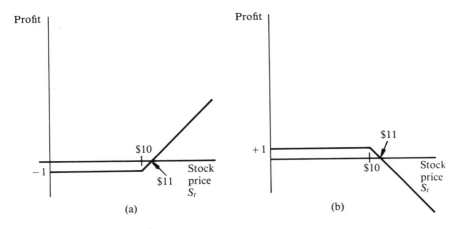

Figure 19.3 (a) Call-holder. (b) Call-writer.

Note that for the call-holder (Figure 19.3(a)), the profit line intersects the horizontal axis at $S_t = \$11$, since for $S_t = \$11$ his profit from exercising the stock $S_t - E_x = \$11 - \$10 = \$1$ exactly offsets his initial investment $C = \$1$. At the break-even point we always have $y_t = 0$ or $S_t = E_x + C$, which in our case gives $S_t = \$10 + \$1 + \$11$. Each dollar of increase in S_t above \$11 produces a \$1 increase in the profit of the call-holder, hence the slope of the profit line is $+1$. A similar argument has been employed to draw the profit profile of a call writer (Figure 19.3(b)). His break-even point is given by $y_t = (C + E_x) - S_t = 0$ or $S_t = C + E_x = \$1 + \$10 = \$11$. The call-holder and the call-writer thus have the same break-even point, on either side of which their profiles are mirror images of one another.

Let us now turn to describe the cash flow profile of a put:

Holder of a put		Writer of a put	
$-P$	if $S_t > E_x$	P	if $S_t > E_x$
$(E_x - S_t) - P$	if $S_t \leqslant E_x$	$P - (E_x - S_t)$	if $S_t \leqslant E_x$

The put-holder loses the entire investment P if $S_t > E_x$: it is better to sell in the market than to exercise. Conversely, if $S_t < E_x$, he makes a profit of $(E_x - S_t)$, less his initial investment P. Thus if the put is exercised, the put holder's return y_t is given by

$$y_t = \begin{cases} -P + (E_x - S_t) = (E_x - P) - S_t & \text{if } S_t \leqslant E_x \\ -P & \text{if } S_t > E_x \end{cases}$$

For the segment $S_t \leqslant E_x$ the line has a negative slope of -1 and a (positive) vertical intercept $E_x - P$. The put-writer conversely makes a profit of P if $S_t > E_x$, since the option is not exercised and he gets the cash proceeds P from writing the put. If, however, $S_t < E_x$, he loses $(E_x - S_t)$ by selling for E_x a

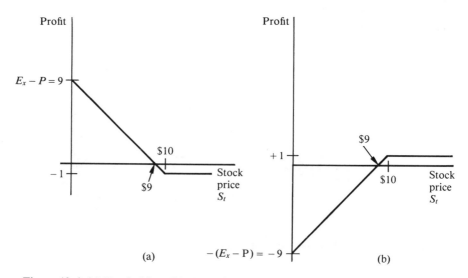

Figure 19.4 (a) Put-holder. (b) Put-writer.

share of stock worth S_t in the market. Therefore, the function y_t is:

$$y_t = \begin{cases} P - (E_x - S_t) = -(E_x - P) + S_t & \text{if } S_t \leqslant E_x \\ P & \text{if } S_t > E_x \end{cases}$$

which is again, for $S_t \leqslant E$, a linear function, of the stock price S_t, with a slope of $+1$ and a (negative) vertical intercept $-(E_x - P)$.

Example

Figure 19.4 illustrates the profit profiles of a put-holder (Figure 19.4(a)) and a put writer (Figure 19.4(b)) for the following specific example: $E_x = \$10$, $P = \$1$, and S_t is an unknown random variable plotted along the horizontal axis.

Note that if the stock price falls from $10 to $9, both the put-holder and the put-writer exactly break even, since the cash flow for both sides involved in the transaction vanishes:

Put-holder: $-P + (E_x - S_t) = -1 + (10 - 9) = 0$
Put-writer: $+P - (E_x - S_t) = +1 - (10 - 9) = 0$

LEVERAGE AND OPTIONS

Suppose that an investor considers investing a given sum (say $100) either in a stock or in the corresponding call. If the stock price at the expiration date is below the exercise price, the terminal wealth of the option holder is zero (namely a loss of 100%) and holding the stock rather than the call proves to be a better investment strategy. However, if $S_t > E_x$ on the expiration date, investment in the option is much more profitable: for each $1 profit on the stock, we can make $1 profit by holding the call, but since the call initially costs much less than the stock, the percentage rate of return on the call is much higher. Thus, a relatively small investment in the call guarantees that the investor gets the same absolute profit as the stockholder. This implies that the investment in the option is highly leveraged or option magnify gains in percentage terms.

Example

Let us demonstrate the leverage component of call options by looking at some data on a stock and the corresponding call price changes recorded on the CBOE.

The quotation for the Boeing call and for the corresponding stock price on Friday, July 31, 1992, and on Monday, August 3, 1992 were:

	July 31, 1992	August 3, 1992
Stock price	$39\frac{7}{8}$	$40\frac{1}{4}$
Call price	$5\frac{3}{8}$	$5\frac{1}{2}$

The exercise price was $35 and the option expiration date was the end of September 1992.

The investor who invested in Boeing stock on July 31, 1992 made $\frac{3}{8}$ over one day, which is approximately 0.94% $((\frac{3}{8}/39.875) \times 100 = 0.0094)$ on the investment. An investigator who purchased the call rather than the stock (investing $5\frac{3}{8}$ instead of $39\frac{7}{8}$) was $\frac{1}{8}$ which is 2.33% on the investment. Thus, when the stock price is above the exercise price, any rise in the stock price is followed by a higher percentage rise in the call price. However, as in corporate capital structure, leverage is a 'two-edged sword'. When the price of the stock falls, a much sharper percentage loss is incurred by the option holder. For example, the following figures characterize the Dow Chemical stock and calls between the same dates:

	July 31, 1992	August 3, 1992
Stock price	$57\frac{7}{8}$	$57\frac{1}{8}$
Call price	$1\frac{1}{8}$	$\frac{3}{4}$

The striking price was $60 and the expiration date was in September 1992. It is easy to verify that the loss on the stock in one day was $(\frac{6}{8} \div 57.875) \times 100 \simeq 1.30\%$, while the loss on the call was much greater $(\frac{3}{8} \div \frac{9}{8}) \times 100 \simeq 33.33\%$.

Thus, the percentage price movements of the option are much larger than the corresponding percentage price movements of the underlying stock.

BOUNDS ON OPTION VALUE

In deriving bounds on option value, we first assume that the option cannot be exercised before expiration date (a European option).

As we shall see, the call price C satisfies the following inequality:

$$C \geqslant S_0 - \frac{E_x}{1 + r}$$

where

S_0 = current market price of the underlying stock
E_x = exercise price
r = risk-free interest rate (for the period until expiration date)

To derive this lower bound on call price, consider the two alternative investment strategies in Table 19.5 where S_1 is the stock price at the expiration date. From this table we see that if $S_1 > E_x$, the two strategies provide the same payoff, S_1, and if $S_1 < E_x$, portfolio A provides a higher payoff, E_x. Thus if the initial investment in the two portfolios is the same, portfolio A will dominate portfolio B and no investor will purchase the stock. Therefore, in reality the initial investment required to build portfolio A must be *larger* than the initial investment in portfolio B, otherwise all investors will switch from portfolio B to portfolio A (by a process known as arbitrage). Thus we must have in equilibrium:

$$C + E_x/(1 + r) \geqslant S_0$$

Hence $C \geqslant S_0 - E_x/(1 + r)$.

Example
On July 31, 1992 we find the following information regarding the IBM stock and call option:

Stock price $\quad S_0 = \$94\frac{5}{8}$
Call price $\quad C = \$6$
Exercise price $\quad E = \$90$
Expiry date $\quad$ October 1992

Since the riskless interest rate for $2\frac{2}{3}$ months (the period remaining to expiration) was approximately $r \simeq 1\%$ in July 1992, we find that the call price must be greater than \$5.52:

$$\$6 = C \geqslant 94\tfrac{5}{8} - \frac{90}{1.01} \simeq 5.52$$

The actual market price of the call was $C = \$6$, which of course obeys this lower bound condition.

Since in principle the difference $S_0 - E_x/(1 + r)$ may be negative, while the

Table 19.5 Cash flows from two alternative portfolios, I

	Investment	Future cash flow expiration date	
		if $S_1 > E_x$	if $S_1 \leqslant E_x$
Portfolio A			
Buy one call	$-C$	$S_1 - E_x$	0
Buy bonds bearing interest r	$-E_x/(1+r)$	E_x	E_x
Total	$-[C + E_x/(1+r)]$	S_1	E_x
Portfolio B			
Buy one share of the underlying stock	$-S_0$	S_1	S_1

call price at worst can drop to zero, we conclude that:

$$C \geqslant \max[0, S_0 - E_x/(1+r)]$$

Also since the call is an option to buy the underlying stock, the call price C can never exceed the stock price. Otherwise, investors can buy the stock directly at a cheaper price and no one will purchase the option. So we must have the following upper bound:

$$C \leqslant S_0$$

Collecting these results we have the following upper and lower bounds on the call price:

$$S_0 \geqslant C \geqslant \max[0, S_0 - E_x/(1+r)]$$

The option value C can vary in this range. As we have seen, other things being equal, C increases (i.e. moves closer to the upper bound) as the exercise price E_x increases and the time to expiration increases.

Put–call parity

Investors can create two alternative strategies which yield the same income, regardless of the future stock price at expiration S_1. These two strategies which we call portfolios A and B are specified in Table 19.6. The following standard notation is used in Table 19.6:

C = call price
P = put price
E_x = exercise price (the same for the put and the call)
r = interest rate (for the period to expiration)
S_0 = current stock price
S_1 = stock price at time 1, i.e., at the expiration date
$E_x/(1+r)$ = the amount borrowed, calculated to ensure repayment of
$\quad (1+r)E_x/(1+r) = E_x$ at expiration date.

Table 19.6 Cash flows from two alternative portfolios, II

	Investment	Future cash flow	
		if $S_1 > E_x$	if $S_1 \leqslant E_x$
Portfolio A			
Buy stock	$-S_0$	S_1	S_1
Buy put	$-P$	0	$E - S_1$
Borrow at interest rate r	$+E_x/(1+r)$	$-E$	$-E_x$
Total	$-S_0 - P + E_x/(1+r)$	$S_1 - E_x$	0
Portfolio B			
Buy call	$-C$	$S_1 - E_x$	0

Since the two portfolios yield the same cash flows irrespective of the future stock price, the initial investment in these two portfolios must also be identical. Otherwise if, say, the investment in portfolio B is higher, an investor who owns a call can sell it, borrow money, buy a put and the underlying stock, and thus create a portfolio with a lower investment and yet with the same future cash flows. If the investment in portfolio A is higher, an investor who holds portfolio A can sell the stock and the put, lend out a corresponding sum (to cancel the borrowing), and buy a portfolio B reducing the investment without any change in the future cash flows. If the investor does not own any of these portfolios he can always sell short the overpriced one, and buy the underpriced one: hence the difference represents his profit. This process is known as arbitrage. Thus, in equilibrium, when no arbitrage opportunities exist, we expect to find the following relationship, which is known as the *put–call parity*,

$$C = S_0 + P - E_x/(1+r)$$

Obviously, this relationship is exact in a perfect market with no transaction costs and with the same interest rate for borrowers and for lenders. In real life we do have transaction costs, the borrowing rate is higher than the lending rate, and the switch from one portfolio to another is not costless. Hence, we do not find this exact parity between the put and the call prices in reality.

Example

Let us look at the put–call relationship of the Dow Chemical options listed on the Chicago Exchange. On July 31, 1992 we find the following prices:

Stock price $S_0 = \$57\frac{7}{8}$
Call price $C = \$3$
Put price $P = \$\frac{7}{16}$
Striking price $E_x = \$55$ (the same for the put and call)

The expiration date is August 1992 so we have approximately $\frac{2}{3}$ of a month to expiration.

Since there are many different interest rates (for borrowers, lenders, etc.), we will use the put–call parity equation to solve for r, and see if we get a reasonable figure. Using our example, we find:

$$3 = 57\tfrac{7}{8} + \tfrac{7}{16} - 55/(1 + r)$$

Hence $1 + r = 0.994$ and r is negative.

Is this figure reasonable? The prevailing riskless rate was 2.9% in August 1992. Although the put–call parity assumes a perfect market, the market is far from perfect and the borrowing interest rate is substantially higher than the lending rate, which may account for the gap. Thus the put–call parity formula should be used with great caution. Indeed, in earlier periods when the interest rate was higher (e.g., 5.14% in 1988), r estimated from the put–call parity was positive (3.5%), but also lower than the market interest rate.

_____ EUROPEAN VERSUS AMERICAN CALLS: EARLY EXERCISE DOES NOT PAY

The difference between European and American call options is that while an American call can be exercised any time before (or at) the expiration date, the European call can be exercised only at the expiration date.

The common option valuation models were developed for European calls. However, the valuation models can be applied also to American calls since in fact it never pays to exercise a call before the expiration date.[2] Thus, if an investor behaves rationally, an American call can be treated exactly as a European call. But what if the call-holder needs cash before expiration? We show that it is always more profitable for the investor to sell the call in the market rather than to exercise it before expiration. To prove this rather surprising claim, first note that other things being equal, the value of the more restrictive European call cannot be greater than the value of an American call, which allows greater freedom of choice. Since we have shown that with respect to the European call:

$$C > \max[0, S_0 - E_x/(1 + r)]$$

and since an American call is worth at least as much as a European call, the above inequality holds also with respect to American calls.

If an American call is exercised at a given date t before expiration, the investor gets $S_t - E_x$, where S_t is the stock price at date t. Since:

$$S_t - E_x < S_t - E_x/(1 + r)$$

the investor in need of cash is better off selling the call at the market price, which is never less than $S_t - E_x/(1 + r)$ (S_t being the current price at that date), rather than exercising the call and selling the stock, which gives him only $S_t - E_x$ in cash proceeds.

---

2. This is true only for stocks which do not pay cash dividends. Otherwise it may pay to have an early exercise depending on dividend policy.

The intuitive explanation for this formal proof is that the market call price has two components:

1. The immediate profit in case of exercise, $S_t - E_x$.
2. The additional potential profit if the stock will go up from the present date until the expiration date.

If the option is exercised, the investor gets benefit 1 above, but gives up benefit 2, which is worth money. Thus, it always pays not to have an early exercise, which accounts for the dictum 'a call option is worth more alive than dead'.

Early exercise of an American call may be desirable if underlying stock pays cash dividends and the call option is not protected against the decrease in ex-dividend stock prices. To be more specific, suppose that a holder of an American call expects the price of the stock to be $S_t = \$100$ on December 31, which is the expiration date. Also we know that $E_x = \$90$, so that the call holder expects a $10 profit on the expiration date. If the corporation does not pay any cash dividends, it pays to hold the call until the very latest moment, i.e., until the expiration date, as we have shown above.

Now suppose that the corporation pays a cash dividend of $20 per share on December 15. The ex-dividend stock price will fall roughly by $20 immediately after the cash dividend is distributed and in all probability it will not exceed the exercise price ($90) on expiration. As a result the call will be worthless on expiration. On the other hand, if the stock price is $S_t = \$98$ on December 14, just before the dividend distribution, the investor can exercise the call and make a profit of $S_t - E_x = \$98 - \$90 = \$8$. Thus, in reality, with corporations paying cash dividends to their stockholders, an American call with its early exercise option may have a definite advantage over the European call which is not exercisable until the expiration date.

FINANCIAL ASSETS AS OPTIONS

Stocks and bonds as options

Suppose that the total value of the firm's assets is $1,000, the value of its stocks is $S = \$200$, and the value of its bonds is $B = \$800$. Thus the firm's balance sheet, in terms of market value, is given by:

	Assets		Liabilities
	$1,000	Bonds	$ 800
		Stocks	200
Total	$1,000	Total	$1,000

Suppose also that the face value of the bonds is also $800. If the firm has to pay its debt immediately, the bondholders will get $800 and the stockholders will get $200.

Suppose now that the firm has to pay its debt one year from now. However, the current market value of its assets dropped to $500. Knowing that the firm owes its debt holders $800, will the value of the stock drop to zero? Not necessarily. The reason is that the firm has to pay its debt one year from now, and it is possible that at the maturity date, the value of the firm's assets will be more than $800. Thus, the firm's balance sheet may look like this (all in market values):

	Assets		Liabilities
	$500	Bonds	$400
		Stocks	100
Total	$500	Total	$500

Namely, the stock value is $100 in spite of the fact that the asset's value is less than the face value of the debt.

In order to understand this phenomenon, consider the following situation. Suppose that the value of the firm's assets at the maturity date of the debt is given by the distribution in Figure 19.5. Since there is a chance that the value of the assets will exceed $800, the stock price today does not fall to zero, reflecting this positive probability which is located to the right of point $800 (see Figure 19.5).

Thus, we can say that a firm which issues debt with a face value of B_0 (in our example, $800) indeed sold its assets to the bondholders but the stockholders have a call option on the firm's assets with a striking price B_0. The market value of the stock is equal to the value of a call option on the firm's assets. Thus, holding stocks of a levered firm is equivalent to holding a call option on the firm's assets. To show this in more detail, consider two firms identical in all respects apart from their use of financial leverage. Firm 1 is unlevered and one buys a call option on its assets with striking price B_0. Firm 2 is levered where the face value of the debt is B_0. We claim that as long as the striking price of the call option is equal to the face value of the debt (B_0), the two streams of cash flows, to the option holder and to the equity holder of the levered firm, are identical. Table 19.7 reveals hypothetical figures regarding the value of the firm's assets at the expiration date.

We, of course, assume that at expiration the value of the assets of the

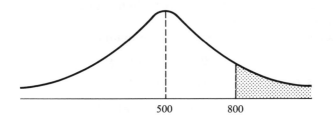

500   800

Figure 19.5

Table 19.7 Cash flows at expiration to the call option holder and equity holder

Value of firm's assets (same for both firms)	Firm 1 (unlevered)			Firm 2 (levered)	
	Striking price	Option holder cash flow		Debt	Stockholder cash flow
400	800	0		800	0
500	800	0		800	0
800	800	0		800	0
1,000	800	200		800	200
2,000	800	1,200		800	1,200
2,500	800	1,700		800	1,700

unlevered firm is equal to the value of its stocks. Thus, since we get the same cash flow streams at expiration, stock of the levered firm can be considered a call option on the stock of the unlevered firm. We can assert that the bondholders are indeed the owners of the firm, but they sold a call option to the stockholders with a striking price of B_0.

Denoting the value of the firm's assets at expiration by A, we get the following relationships:

1. $C = S$

   Namely, the value of equity (S) is equal to the value of a call option on the firm's assets with an exercise price B_0. Recall that we have shown that the cash flows to call option holders and to the stockholders are identical. Thus, the market value of these assets must be equal.

2. $B = A - C$

   where B is the value of bonds and A the value of the assets. This relationship reflects the fact that the bondholders may be considered as the owners of the firm, hence the assets A belong to them. However, the stockholders have a call option on the assets; therefore the bond's value is equal to the asset's value less a call option on the asset (of course, with a striking price of B_0).

3. From the put–call parity, we know that:

   $$C = A - B_0/(1 + r) + P$$

   where P is the put value on the firm's assets and B_0 is the striking price and A replaces the stock value S in the put–call parity equation discussed earlier. (Recall that puts and calls are written in this case on the firm's assets and not on the firm's stock.)

4. But since $B = A - C$ (see (2) above), we obtain:

   $$B = B_0/(1 + r) - P$$

5. Since $C = S$ (see (2) above), we obtain:

   $$S = A - B_0/(1 + r) + P$$

The interpretation of these results is as follows. The stock value is equal to the assets value at expiration, A, minus the present value of the cash outflow to the bondholders $B_0/(1 + r)$. However, the firm has a limited liability on its asset and in the case that A is less than B_0, bondholders cannot claim the stockholders' personal assets. Thus, the limited liability property has economic value to the stockholders and this value is equal to P, the put value on the firm's assets with striking price B_0.

Similarly, the value of the bonds is:

$$B = B_0/(1 + r) - P$$

which is the present value of the future receipt $B_0/(1 + r)$ minus the value of the limited liability property, P. Thus, while the limited liability property is advantageous to the stockholders it is disadvantageous to the bondholders.

Warrants

Warrants are similar to call options in the following respect: the holder of a warrant has the right to exercise the warrant on or before the expiration date at some predetermined exercise price. However, unlike call options, warrants are issued by business corporations and thus involve cash flows between corporations and investors, and not between two investors as with call or put contracts. Also warrants can have maturities of several years, unlike the majority of the options which usually expire in less than 12 months. Thus, the difference between call options and warrants can be summarized as follows:

1. The maturity of warrants in general is longer.
2. In general, it is the issuing corporation that receives the proceeds from selling the warrants.
3. On exercise, the holders of warrants pay the corporation the exercise price for its stock.
4. When a warrant is exercised, the corporation issues stocks and the number of outstanding shares goes up. The corporation gets back the warrant and hence the number of outstanding warrants decreases, completely vanishing if all investors exercise their warrants.

Warrants are thus another type of financial instrument used for raising money by corporations. Unlike calls and puts, which are negotiated directly between investors, warrants have an impact on the corporation's cash flows and capital structure. From the investor's point of view, however, a warrant is an investment with some characteristics which are similar to the call option, since the warrants will be exercised only if the stock price is higher than the exercise price.

Rights

Many firms raise money by issuing rights. There are a few parameters which characterize a right issue.

1. The subscription price, P_s, which is normally set below the market price of the stock.
2. The allocation ratio, N: if N is, say, 5, this asserts that a holder of 5 old stocks is entitled to buy during a given period of time (normally a few weeks) a new stock at price P_s, namely at a discount. There is daily trade in these rights up to the expiration date. Thus, a right is nothing but a call option on the stock with striking price of P_s.

Insurance

Suppose that you own a house. If it is not insured and fire breaks out, the remaining value of the house is its salvage value. Thus, the value of your asset is a random variable. You can buy a fire insurance contract which guarantees that you obtain a value A^* (the insured value) no matter what is the value of your house A; namely, no matter if fire breaks out or not. Thus, buying an insurance policy is like buying a put option on the house with a striking price A^*.

Callable bonds

To illustrate, suppose that the interest rate is $r = 10\%$ on a bond with 20 years to maturity. The firm would like to issue 20-year bonds. However, the firm would like to protect itself against a possible decline in the interest rate. So, the firm will issue a bond say at \$100, but this bond is callable, say at \$105. If the interest rate goes down, the firm can call its bonds at 105, and issue new bonds at a lower rate. Thus, the firm has a call option to buy the bonds at a striking price of 105. Hence option models can be used to evaluate the callability property of a bond.

Foreign exchange options

Consider a multinational firm of exporters who are involved in international trade. An American who sells products to Germany will get his income according to the term of the sales agreement 30 days from now. However, since his sales are in German marks, his income in dollars is a random variable reflecting the future unknown exchange rate. If the German mark declines *vis-à-vis* the dollar, his dollar income will decline. To protect himself against such events, the American investor can buy a call option to buy the U.S. dollar (or a put option to sell German marks). Recently trading in options for foreign currencies has begun, but it is not as developed as the option market for stocks.

We have mentioned in this section only a few examples. In day-to-day decision-making the management of the firm faces many financial transactions which can be considered as options.

INDEX OPTIONS AND PORTFOLIO INSURANCE

Nowadays there are options on a portfolio of stocks, known as *index options*. These are options on various indexes, e.g., S&P 100 stock index, S&P 500 stock index, NYSE index, etc. Table 19.8 illustrates the most popular S&P 100 stock index option, taken from the *Wall Street Journal*, August 3, 1992. For example, on July 31, 1992, one could buy a call option on this index for $7\frac{1}{4}$ with a striking price of $390 and with an August 1992 maturity date. The S&P 100 stock index was $395.80 at the close of trading on July 31, 1992. Index options fulfill an important economic need. If one wishes to buy options on many stocks (a portfolio) there is no need to buy hundreds of different options but rather one option on a given index. They facilitate in particular the portfolio insurance discussed next.

Portfolio insurance arrived in the market in 1984 and grew rapidly, at least until the October 1987 crash. Portfolio insurance can be executed in various ways, including via the index options market and works in the following manner. Suppose that a mutual fund or a pension fund holds hundreds of stocks. The manager would like to protect himself against a downward movement in the price. Theoretically, he can do so by buying a put option on each single security in his portfolio. Practically speaking, this is impossible simply because put options are not traded in the market for many securities. The fund manager can achieve the same insurance goal simply by buying a put option on an index. The higher the correlation between the returns on the selected index and the pension fund portfolio, the better the protection of the purchased insurance.

For example, consider a mutual fund which holds a portfolio which is very similar in its investment composition to the S&P 100 index. The current price of the shares of the mutual fund is the same as the S&P 100 index, namely $395.80. Suppose that from the manager's point of view, it would be considered disastrous if the share price dropped below $385. To avoid this

Table 19.8 Chicago Board S&P 100 Index, August 3, 1992

Strike price	Calls – last		Puts – last	
	Aug.	Sept.	Aug.	Sept.
365	–	–	$\frac{5}{16}$	–
375	–	–	$\frac{5}{8}$	–
385	$11\frac{1}{4}$	–	$1\frac{3}{8}$	–
390	$7\frac{1}{4}$	$10\frac{1}{4}$	$2\frac{1}{2}$	–
395	$4\frac{1}{4}$	–	$4\frac{1}{2}$	–
400	$2\frac{1}{16}$	$4\frac{1}{2}$	$7\frac{5}{8}$	–
405	$\frac{15}{16}$	–	–	–
410	$\frac{7}{16}$	–	–	–

Source: *Wall Street Journal*, August 3, 1992.

disaster, the manager can buy an August put option for $1\frac{3}{8}$ (see Table 19.8). Should the price drop to say $300, the manager can sell his put for $385, hence guaranteeing that the mutual fund's wealth will not drop below this $385 lower bound.

Portfolio insurance can also be achieved by choosing the appropriate mix of riskless and risky assets. For example, a mutual fund with assets of $100 million may hold $80 million in riskless assets bearing a 10% interest rate and $20 million in stocks. In this case, the lower bound is $88 million. Even if the stock prices drop to zero, the end-of-period wealth will be $88 million.

To achieve a desired level of protection, portfolio insurance policies are programmed to sell the stock when the price falls and to buy the stock when price rises. Hence, portfolio insurance policies which have grown in popularity quite rapidly, along with the automatic orders to buy or sell by computers have been blamed for the 1987 crash in the stock market. This portfolio insurance well known as 'dynamic hedging' is done by a mechanical formula which asserts that in order to protect the investment from losses, one has to sell stocks index futures and/or stocks, after the market has fallen and buy them after it has risen. By October 19, 1987 some $60–$90 billion of assets were 'insured'; all these assets were managed by the same mechanical formula called 'program trading'. Basically, program trading is similar to the well-known 'stop-loss' order, a policy under which the broker gets a prearranged order to sell stocks when the share's price falls to a certain price. However, unlike stop-loss orders, program trading was adopted by many funds managers, and when all of them wished to sell on the same day, no buyers could be found, and the price fell sharply.

Some practitioners and academics argue that once stock prices started to fall, many pension funds and institutional investors automatically executed sell orders which intensified the stock price plunge. This, in turn, triggered more sell orders and so on. As a result, portfolio insurance was unable to provide the financial protection it promised.

The newspapers and many experts blamed program trading as the cause or at least an important factor affecting the October 1987 crash. Indeed, realizing the horror of program trading (at least as perceived by potential investors) Shearson Lehman spent $1 million on prime time television to tell about 130 million viewers watching the 1988 football Super Bowl that it stopped program trading on its accounts. Thus, there was an urgent need to restore the confidence of potential investors, who fled the market after the stock market crash. Thus, while the role that portfolio insurance strategy played in the 1987 crash is hard to quantify, the reader should keep in mind that portfolio insurance is a powerful tool which can be employed either directly with put options or by a combination of stocks and bonds.

BLACK AND SCHOLES OPTION VALUATION FORMULA _____

In this section we discuss the well-known option valuation formula developed by Black and Scholes which is widely used by both academics and practitioners.[3] The derivation of this formula is very complicated and is beyond the scope of this book. However, we explain the underlying principles of the derivation, show how to use this formula, and identify the determinants of the option value.

Let us first introduce the assumptions employed by Black and Scholes in deriving their formula:

1. There are no transaction costs and no taxes.
2. The risk-free interest rate is constant.
3. The market operates continuously.
4. The stock prices are continuous, i.e., there are no jumps in the stock prices; if one plots a graph of the stock price against time, the graph must be smooth.[4]
5. The stock pays no cash dividends.
6. The option is European (exercisable only at expiration).
7. Stocks can be sold short without penalty and short sellers receive the full proceeds from the transaction.

If all these assumptions hold, Black and Scholes proved that the current call price C_0 is given by:

$$C_0 = S_0 N(d_1) - E_x e^{-rt} N(d_2)$$

where:

S_0 = current stock price

E_x = exercise price

e = base of natural logarithms = 2.7128

r = continuously compounded annual riskless rate of interest (so that the end-of-year value of \$1 invested in the riskless asset is e^r, and not $(1 + r)$ as in the discrete-compounding case)

t = remaining time to the expiration of the call expressed as a fraction of a year

$N(d_1)$; $N(d_2)$ = the values of the cumulative normal distribution at points d_1 and d_2 respectively, where:

$$d_1 = \frac{\ln(S_0/E_x) + (r + \frac{1}{2}\sigma^2)t}{\sigma\sqrt{t}}$$

$$d_2 = \frac{\ln(S_0/E_x) + (r - \frac{1}{2}\sigma^2)t}{\sigma\sqrt{t}} = d_1 - \sigma\sqrt{t}$$

σ = standard deviation of the continuously compounded annual rate of return, representing the volatility of the stock price

3. See F. Black and M. Scholes, 'The Pricing of Options and Corporate Liabilities,' *Journal of Political Economy* (May/June 1973).
4. To be more specific the stock price follows a so-called Ito process with a constant drift. This implies that for any finite time interval the stock price is lognormally distributed.

From this formula we see that the parameters S_0, E_x, r, t, and σ determine the option value. Surprisingly, the one single parameter which intuitively appears to be most important for valuation – the expected rate of return on the stock – does not enter the Black and Scholes formula. The absence of the expected return from the valuation formula can be explained by the fact that, in this model, the equilibrium value of the option is attained by creating a hedged portfolio (consisting of the option and its underlying stock) that yields a certain income regardless of the future stock price. Whatever the return on the stock, it has no impact on the return of the hedged portfolio which consists of the option and its underlying stock.

The higher the current stock price S_0, and the lower the exercise price E_x, the higher will be the call option value C_0. Also, the longer the time to expiration t, the greater is the chance that a profit will be made on the call and hence the higher is the call value. Though the impact of r and σ^2 on the call price C_0 is not obvious from the Black and Scholes formula, we can determine that the higher r and σ^2, the higher is the call price C_0. A partial intuitive explanation of the relationship between r and C_0 is as follows: as the interest rate r increases, the present value of the exercise price E_x/r becomes smaller and the call price C_0 rises. Once again this is not obvious from the Black and Scholes formula but can be illustrated by using the bounds on the call value. We have seen before that type following bounds hold:

$$S_0 \geqslant C_0 \geqslant S_0 - E_x/(1+r)$$

As r increases, $S_0 - E_x/(1+r)$ increases and the lower bound on the call price increases. As r approaches infinity, we get the highest value for the call $C_0 = S_0$.

The interrelationship between C_0 and σ can also be intuitively (and at least partially) explained: suppose that we have two stocks and two corresponding options. Everything is identical regarding these two pairs apart from the stock variance σ^2. Figure 19.6 illustrates two density functions of stock price distributions which we denote by $f_1(S_t)$ and $f_2(S_t)$, respectively.

Recall that we have the same exercise price E_x in both cases. Which call

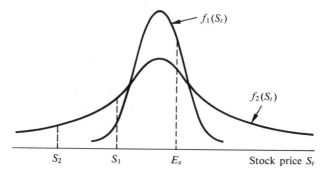

Figure 19.6

option is worth more, C_1, or C_2? In risk–return analysis the usual intuitive answer is that $f_1(S_t)$, which has a smaller risk with the same expected return, is preferable and hence the option corresponding to $f_1(S_t)$ is worth more. This is not true here, and in fact just the opposite holds: the option on the riskier stock (that with the higher variance) is worth more, $C_2 > C_1$. To explain this assertion, recall that investment in a call option can be represented as an asymmetric game: if the stock deviates to the right (increasing above the exercise price E_x), the profit is $S_t - E_x$ and it increases with the magnitude of the upward deviation. However, a deviation to the left (below E_x does not increase our loss, which remains total. Regardless of whether the stock price is S_1 or S_2 (see Figure 19.6 – both below E_x), the call value will be zero, and the loss will be identical for these two events. Thus, a high variability of the stock price provides a possibility of high potential profit without increasing the potential loss. Hence the higher σ, the higher is the call value (all other parameters held constant).[5]

These properties of the call price can be summarized as follows:

$$C_0 = f(\overset{+}{S_0}, \overset{-}{E_x}, \overset{+}{\sigma}^2, \overset{+}{t}, \overset{+}{r})$$

where f is the valuation function, ' + ' means that an increase in the appropriate parameter is followed by an increase in the call value, ' – ' implies that an increase in the parameter is followed by a decrease in the call value.

The Black and Scholes formula needs five input parameters. Of these five parameters, four are readily available: S_0, E_x, t are parameters of the underlying stock and the corresponding option, published in the financial media. For the interest rate r we can take the yield on treasury bills with maturity equal to the expiration of the option under consideration. One parameter, σ^2, however, has to be estimated. We can take the *ex-post* stock price data and calculate the *ex-post* variance. However, there is no guarantee that the stock variability will remain constant in the future. Thus option valuation is subject to statistical errors in estimating stock price variability.

Using the Black and Scholes formula

Let us examine two numerical examples that demonstrate how the Black and Scholes formula is used in practice.

Calculating the call price C_0

Suppose that the current stock price is $S_0 = \$100$, the exercise price is $E_x = \$125$, and the time to expiration is three months, or $t = \frac{1}{4} = 0.25$ if expressed as a fraction of a year. The continuously compounded annual interest rate is taken as $r = 0.12$ (or 12%) from the prevailing yields in the bond

---

5. This argument is incomplete. It is conceivable that the potential earnings increase with the variance, but the probability of obtaining this higher profit (i.e., the probability that $S_t > E_x$ is smaller for high-variance distributions. Thus, in order to complete the argument, we have to prove that the derivative $\partial C/\partial\sigma > 0$. The proof is tedious and is therefore omitted.

market. The Black and Scholes formula now takes the form:

$$C_0 = 100N(d_1) - 125e^{-0.12 \times 0.25}N(d_2)$$

where:

$$d_1 = \frac{\ln(100/125) + (0.12 + 0.5\sigma^2) \times 0.25}{\sigma\sqrt{0.25}}$$

$$d_2 = \frac{\ln(100/125) + (0.12 - 0.5\sigma^2) \times 0.25}{\sigma\sqrt{0.25}}$$

In order to complete the calculations we need the standard deviation σ of the continuously compounded annual rates of return on the stock. This parameter is not known, but it can be estimated from the past record of holding period rates of return:

$$R_t = (S_t - S_{t-1})/S_{t-1}$$

calculated for sufficiently short periods (a month or shorter), or alternatively from the past record of stock prices using the formula for the continuously compounded monthly rates of return:[6]

$$R_t = \ln(S_t/S_{t-1})$$

Once a time series of monthly returns has been obtained in this way, its standard deviation can be calculated. The result is the standard deviation of *monthly* rates of return, and it should be multiplied by the square root of 12 to obtain the annual estimate of σ for the Black and Scholes formula.[7]

---

6. It is easily seen that when the period from $t - 1$ to t is short (a month or less), so that the change from S_{t-1} to S_t is small (a few percent at most), the continuously compounded rate of return and the holding rate of return are approximately equal. Indeed for positive y close to 1, $\ln y$ can be expanded in a series as $\ln y = (y - 1) + (y - 1)^2/2 + \cdots$. Omitting the small terms of second order and higher, we obtain the approximate equality $\ln y \approx y - 1$. In our case, S_t/S_{t-1} is close to 1 (the change in S_t is small over a short period), so that $\ln(S_t/S_{t-1}) \approx (S_t/S_{t-1}) - 1 = (S_t - S_{t-1})/S_{t-1}$, which is equal to the holding rate of return for the same period.

7. Let R be the continuously compounded rate of return on the stock over one month, i.e., $S_t = S_{t-1}e^R$, where t is the month index. Then $S_t/S_{t-1} = e^R$ and $R = \ln(S_t/S_{t-1})$. Estimating the continuously compounded rate of return R_t for each month t, we can calculate the variance of the continuously compounded monthly rates of return $\sigma_1^2 = \Sigma_{i=1}^n (R_i - \bar{R})^2/n$, where n is the number of months used in estimation and the subscript 1 identifies the one-month period. What is the relationship between the monthly variance and the annual variance of continuously compounded rates of return? Denote by R_a the annual rate of reutrn and by S_{12} the price at the end of the year (after 12 months). Then we have:

$$S_{12} = S_0 e^{R_1} e^R \ldots e^{R_{12}}$$

where $R_1, R_2, \ldots, R_{12}$ are the continuously compounded monthly rates of return for the 12 successive months in the year. Thus $S_{12} = S_0 \exp(R_1 + R_2 + \cdots + R_{12})$ and $\ln(S_{12}/S_0) = R_a = R_1 + R_2 + \cdots + R_{12}$. Assuming independence of the monthly rates of return, we obtain for the variance of the annual rate of return $\text{Var } R_a = \text{Var } \ln(S_{12}/S_0) = \text{Var } R_1 + \text{Var } R_2 + \cdots \text{Var } R_{12}$. If we further assume that the distribution of the monthly rates of return is stationary over time, so that $\text{Var } R_1 = \text{Var } R_2 = \cdots = \text{Var } R_{12} = \sigma_1^2$, then we obtain

$$\text{Var } R_a = 12\sigma_1^2$$

and the standard deviation of the annual rates of return is equal to the standard deviation of the monthly rates of return times the square root of 12, $\sigma = \sigma_1\sqrt{12}$.

Table 19.9 lists 13 monthly stock price observations from which 12 monthly rates of return are calculated by the two alternative techniques. The standard deviation of the monthly returns is virtually the same, $\sigma_1 = 0.18 - 0.19$. For the estimate of the corresponding annual parameter in the Black and Scholes formula we thus take $\sigma = 0.18 \times \sqrt{12} = 0.62$: the standard deviation of the continuously compounded annual rates of return is thus estimated at 62%. Substituting this estimate in the expressions for d_1, d_2 we obtain:

$$d_1 = \frac{\ln(0.80) + [0.12 + 0.5(0.62)^2] \times 0.25}{0.62 \times 0.5} = \frac{-0.2231 + 0.030 + 0.0481}{0.31}$$

$$= \frac{-0.1450}{0.31} = -0.4677$$

$$d_2 = \frac{-0.2231 + 0.030 - 0.0481}{0.31} = -0.7781$$

The call price is thus given by:

$$C_0 = 100N(-0.47) - 125e^{-0.03}N(-0.78)$$

Here the values of d_1 and d_2 are rounded to two decimal places. Taking the corresponding cumulative probabilities from these tables we obtain the final result:

$$C_0 = (100 \times 0.3192) - (125 \times 0.9704 \times 0.2177) = 31.92 - 26.41 = \$5.51$$

If the Black and Scholes formula is valid, the option should trade at \$5.51, given the other values and parameters as specified and estimated above.

Table 19.9

Month	Stock price S_t	Continuously compounded monthly rate of return $\ln(S_t/S_{t-1})$	Holding period monthly rate of return $(S_t - S_{t-1})/S_{t-1}$
1	$100		
2	120	0.1823	0.2000
3	160	0.2877	0.3333
4	140	-0.1335	-0.1250
5	160	0.1335	0.1429
6	150	-0.0645	-0.0625
7	130	-0.1431	-0.1333
8	160	0.2076	0.2308
9	120	-0.2877	-0.2500
10	130	0.0800	0.0833
11	110	-0.1671	-0.1538
12	120	0.0870	0.0909
13	100	-0.1823	-0.1667
Standard deviation of monthly rates of return		0.1852	0.1879

Table 19.10

σ	d_1	d_2	$N(d_1)$	$N(d_2)$	C_0
0.1	-3.84	-3.89	0.0001	0.0001	0
0.2	-1.88	-1.89	0.0301	0.0239	$0.11
0.3	-1.21	-1.36	0.1131	0.0869	$0.77
0.4	-0.87	-1.07	0.1922	0.1423	$1.96
0.5	-0.65	-0.90	0.2578	0.1841	$3.45
0.6	-0.49	-0.79	0.3121	0.2148	$5.15

Estimating stock volatility

We saw in the previous example that the major difficulty in practical application of the Black and Scholes formula is estimation of the standard deviation σ. The Black and Scholes formula can be used 'in reverse' to estimate the implied standard deviation if the market call price is known. Suppose that $S_0 = \$100$, $E_x = \$125$, $r = 0.12$, and $t = 0.25$ (three months) as in the previous example. Also given is the call price $C_0 = \$2.00$. *If the Black and Scholes formula is assumed to be valid*, this C_0, given all the other quantities, corresponds to a certain unique σ. To estimate this implied σ, we calculate the call price from the Black and Scholes formula for various assumed values of the standard deviation and try to match the market price $C_0 = \$2.00$.

The relevant calculations are summarized in Table 19.10. For different values of σ from 0.1 to 0.6, we calculate the corresponding values of d_1, d_2 using the formula:

$$d_{1,2} = \frac{-0.2231 + (0.12 \pm 0.5\sigma^2) \times 0.25}{0.5\sigma} = \frac{-0.1931 \pm 0.125\sigma^2}{0.5\sigma}$$

$N(d_1)$, $N(d_2)$ are then obtained from the normal distribution tables and C_0 is calculated from the same formula as in the previous example.

From the last column in Table 19.10 we see that if the Black and Scholes formula is valid, the implied standard deviation of the annual rates of return on the stock is slightly higher than $\sigma = 0.40$ or 40%.

Note that for very small standard deviations (0.1 and 0.2), the call price is virtually zero: given such small standard deviations of annual returns, the chance that the stock price will rise in only three months from $S_0 = \$100$ to more than \$125 (the exercise price E_x) is very slight indeed and the option is, therefore, virtually worthless.

FUTURES AND OPTIONS ON FUTURES

A futures contract is an order, given in advance, to buy (or sell) a given commodity or financial asset on some future date at a fixed price which is agreed upon today. Commodity futures have existed for a long time. However, futures in financial assets, which started in 1977, constituted a major development in the U.S. financial markets. Since 1977 the volume of transactions in financial futures has grown at a staggering rate.

Trading in commodity future contracts includes many commodities such as corn, oats, soybeans, wheat, cotton, orange juice, crude oil, silver, gold, etc. Among the many financial assets which have been traded through futures contracts are contracts in foreign currencies (e.g. British pound, yen, Swiss franc and German mark), and contracts in securities (e.g. Bond index, S&P 500 stock index, NYSE Composite index, etc.).

In September 1988, Japan started trading in stock index futures contracts in Tokyo and Osaka. Also it is anticipated that Japan will be trading in futures contracts on U.S. Treasury bonds in the near future.

Before illustrating futures contracts with a few examples, let us discuss the mechanics of futures contract trading and the economic need that this market fulfills.

Hedging with futures

Suppose that a farmer grows cotton, which will be ready for sale in October. The farmer may be very efficient in his production, yet he may lose money due to future changes in the price of cotton. To avoid such an event, the farmer sells a futures contract in cotton. Thus, he is hedging against future price uncertainty. Looking at the *Wall Street Journal*, the farmer finds that the cotton futures contract price for delivery in October is 55 cents per pound. Thus, he sells a cotton future contract. This means that no matter what the spot price of cotton is in October, the farmer is guaranteed 55 cents per pound; thus he is 'protected' against cotton price fluctuations.

On the other side of this transaction, we may find a fabric manufacturer who uses cotton in his manufacturing process. The manufacturer would like to avoid the uncertainty in the costs of the raw materials used in production, hence he buys a futures contract in cotton. He is thus certain that he will pay 50 cents per pound for cotton in October, regardless of the spot price of cotton on this date. Selling the futures in this case is termed holding a *short position* or *short hedge* and buying the futures is termed holding a *long position* or *long hedge*.

In the above example, both parties eliminate their price uncertainty by executing a transaction in the futures market. Note however that the farmer does not have to actually deliver the cotton in October. He can also buy a futures contract for delivery in October, hence offsetting his short position.

We illustrated above the role of the futures market in reducing price uncertainty. However, there are also speculators in this market. Speculators, who neither have nor need the actual cotton, may sell (or buy) cotton futures if they believe that the price of this futures will go down (or up). Thus, in this market we have both hedgers and speculators.

Trading in futures

Although the price (and the date) in the futures contract transaction is predetermined, the payment is made only on the future date. The futures transaction, however, involves a payment of margin and daily cash settlement. This daily cash settlement is also known as *mark-to-market*. For example, suppose the farmer sells a cotton futures contract of 50,000 pounds at 50 cents per pound. One day later, the price drops to 48 cents per pound. Then the farmer gets a check from the exchange clearinghouse for his profit in dollars of 50,000 (0.50 − 0.48) = $1,000. Obviously, the fabric manufacturer, who is holding a long hedge in cotton futures, loses from a drop in the cotton future, hence he pays $1,000. Such cash settlements are done everyday until the expiration of the futures contract.

Suppose that a speculator believes that the cotton price will go down. He sells a futures contract and makes $1,000. Then he buys a futures contract at 48 cents a pound to offset his position. The net profit in one day to the speculator is $1,000, without his having to make any commitment to buy or sell in the future.

Note that the futures price is generally different from the spot price where the spot price is the price of an immediate delivery of the commodity or of the financial assets. This difference is well known as the *basis*. However, as one approaches the expiration date of the contract the two prices approach each other and finally reach equality, a case where the basis is zero.

Futures contracts in financial assets

As mentioned above, financial futures contracts play a central role in the United States (and probably will soon play a central role also in Japan). Table 19.11 demonstrates the futures price of S&P stocks as recorded on July 31, 1992.

The S&P index (spot price) was $424.22. The futures price with March 1993 maturity was $424.30. An investor who wanted to invest in the index could buy the futures contract for $424.30. If in March 1993 the S&P was priced at, say, $452.30, a profit of $28 would be made. A big advantage of buying the futures rather than the spot is that only a small margin has to be paid on the purchase date (which can be in the form of treasury bills on which the investor earns interest), hence with a small amount of money one can control a large volume of interest. Looking once again at Table 19.11 we see that as expected for a maturity close to July 31, 1992, the gap between the future price and spot price diminishes (compare $423.90 and $424.44).

Table 19.11 Futures prices of S&P 500 stocks

	Open	High	Low	Settle
September	423.90	425.05	422.50	423.90
December	424.35	425.40	423.10	424.35
March 1993	424.30	425.90	423.80	425.00

Source: *Wall Street Journal*, August 3, 1992.

Once futures had been developed, the next logical step was to develop instruments on these futures contracts. Table 19.12 presents the July 31, 1992 prices of call and put options on the futures S&P 500 stock contract. For example, when the expiration date is October 1992 and the striking price is $415, the call option has a market price of $15.80 while the value of the corresponding put option is $6.50. As expected, the call price increases with maturity and decreases with an increase in the striking price.

Futures prices are very sensitive to world events. For example, with the severe drought that hit the Midwest agricultural belt in the summer of 1988, it was estimated that corn crop production would fall by 30%. The prices of corn futures contracts subsequently soared.

Another interesting phenomenon occurred when Hurricane Gilbert, the strongest storm of this century, hit the Mexican Gulf and the shores of Texas. Before the hurricane was over land, it was predicted that the oil rigs would be directly hit, hence affecting the future supply of oil. The immediate market reaction was a surge in the price of oil futures. The hurricane passed the oil area without damaging the oil fields, which induced a drop in the oil futures. Obviously, speculators who received the information first on the hurricane's change in direction benefited from the market fluctuation in the futures contract prices.

Futures versus cash markets: transaction costs

Stock index futures are traded in 500 units; if, for example, the S&P Index is selling for approximately $200, the smallest transaction in futures is $500 \times 200 = \$100,000$. This characteristic of the stock index futures rules it out for many small investors. However, for pensions and mutual funds and many other large investors the transaction costs in the futures market are lower than the transaction costs in the cash market. First, in the cash market the minimum bid–ask spread is $\frac{1}{8}$ of a dollar. If a stock is selling on average for $50, this means that one 'loses' 0.25% to the broker. The spread is much narrower in the futures market. It is one 'tick' or $25 for a S&P contract, which is worth

Table 19.12 S&P 500 Stock Index (CME) ($500 × premium)

	Calls–settle			Puts–settle		
Stock price	Aug.–c	Sept.–c	Oct.–c	Aug.–c	Sept.–p	Oct.–p
415	10.60	13.15	15.80	1.70	4.30	6.50
420	6.85	9.70	12.40	2.95	5.80	8.10
425	3.95	6.85	9.50	5.05	7.95	–
430	2.00	4.85	6.90	8.10	10.60	12.50
435	09.0	2.80	4.90	–	13.85	15.50
440	0.35	1.60	3.35	–	17.60	

Source: *Wall Street Journal*, August 3, 1992.

approximately $100,000. Percentage-wise, it is only 0.025% ($25 : $100,000) in the futures market versus approximately 0.25% ($8 : $50) in the cash market.

The same holds true for commissions. To illustrate, suppose that an institutional investor who is considering buying either the S&P 500 future contract or the underlying shares. Suppose that the S&P is selling for $200. Hence, the value of the transaction in the futures market is $200 × 500 = $100,000, and the commission on such a futures contract is about $25. Now suppose that the institutional investor is considering buying shares in the cash market. Assuming on average a price of $50 per share, the investor buys 100,000 : 50 = 2,000* shares. An institutional investor pays a commission of about 5 cents per share. Hence, they will pay 2,000 × 0.5 = $100, which is much more than the commission in buying the futures contract. The larger the number of transactions that the investor carries out during the year, the more significant is the advantage of futures contracts, in comparison with transactions in the cash market.

The relationship between spot and forward (or futures) prices

Forward transactions are similar to futures contracts with the exception that there is no daily market to the forward contract hence the transaction must be completed at an agreed future date. A forward contract is tailor-made to fit the needs of the two parties which make the agreement. We demonstrate below the relationship between forward and spot prices in the foreign exchange market. A similar relationship holds with respect to spot and future prices.

Example
Suppose the spot exchange rate is £1 = $2.00, the three-month forward rate is $1 = $2.05 and the three-month riskless interest rate on both dollars and pounds is 8% per annum, i.e., about 4% for the six-month period. Any investor can carry out the following arbitrage: borrow, say, $100, convert this sum into pounds, invest the pounds at the 4% riskless rate of interest, convert the proceeds back into dollars via the forward market and make a riskless profit. At the end of the period the investor would pay $104.00 (interest plus principal) on the loan while earning:

$$\frac{\$100}{2.00} \times (1.04)(2.05) = \$106.60$$

on the investment in pounds. Since the investor covered his loan in the forward market, his riskless profit on this transaction would be $2.60. However, if many people engage in such a transaction, we would expect the exchange rates (spot and forward) and/or the interest rates to change, until equilibrium is restored.

More formally, we use the following symbols: S = the spot exchange rate (in dollars per pound); F = the forward or futures exchange rate; r = the riskless interest rate on pounds; r^* = the riskless interest rate on dollars. In equilibrium we expect the following equation to hold:

$$\frac{S(1 + r^*)}{F(1 + r)} = 1$$

If this equation holds, no profit can be made by arbitraging. Indeed, in our example, $S = \$2.00$, $F = \$2.05$, and by assumption the interest rate is the same on both currencies, i.e., $r = r^* = 0.04$. As a result of this assumption, the equilibrium equation above does not hold $((\$2.00 \times 1.04)/(2.05 \times 1.04) = 0.9756 \neq 1)$ and investors can profit by arbitraging, as shown. Now suppose that the sterling interest rate is $r = 0.04$, as before, while the dollar interest rate, r^*, is such that the above equation is satisfied:

$$1 + r^* = F(1 + r)/S = 2.05 \times 1.04/2.00 = 1.066$$

or

$$r^* = 6.6\%$$

Let us try to arbitrage as before: borrow \$100 at the three-month dollar interest rate of 6.6%, we will have to repay \$106.60 at the end of three months (and not \$104 as before). But this is precisely the dollar equivalent of our investment in pounds, and the arbitrage profits have been completely wiped out by the adjustment of the interest rates.

Futures, index arbitrage, and the October 1987 crash

Index arbitrage is nothing but an arbitrage between stock index futures and the spot (stocks) market. For example, suppose that stock index futures fall by 10%; investors can buy the futures and sell the underlying shares, pocketing the difference between the prices of the two. Of course, index arbitrageurs create a link between the prices of the stock index futures and the underlying assets.

Futures were blamed for the October 1987 crash and two exchanges, the Board of Trade and the Chicago Mercantile Exchange, were forced to defend their role before Congress. The truth is that index arbitrage brings the cash market and futures market into line, and is therefore beneficial. The problem in October 1987 was that the futures and share markets became unhinged because brokers could not cope with the volume of sell orders. By the morning of October 20, 1987 shares were not being traded on the NYSE. This transferred sell orders to the futures market, and the stock index futures were selling at a 22% discount. In normal days, arbitrageurs could make enormous profit by buying the stock futures index and selling the underlying shares. However, on October 20, they could not make the profit since they were unable to sell shares that morning. The arbitrageurs were afraid to carry out this arbitrage because they did not know at what price they would be able to sell the shares later on during the day. Thus, the panic itself was in the cash market, and the futures market simply reflected this panic. Futures trading did not cause the crash, and arbitrageurs simply constituted a link between the cash and futures markets, but played no role in causing the crash. Today, virtually all experts agree that futures markets play a positive role and arbitrageurs create a healthy economic link between futures and cash markets.

SUMMARY

This chapter dealt with various contingent claims (derivative assets). Though rights and warrants are well-established financial instruments, options are relatively new and it is only since the establishment of the Chicago Board of Options Exchange that the interest in options among academicians and practitioners has been steadily growing.

Options are written on a given stock, and so there is a certain relationship between the option value and the price of the underlying stock. Although the absolute value of the fluctuations in option price may be close to that of the fluctuations in the price of the underlying stock, the *percentage* fluctuations are much larger because of the lower option price. Hence options are highly levered instruments, and as such considered very risky.

We distinguish between American calls and European calls. The difference between the two options is that American calls can be exercised at any time up to the expiration date, while European calls are exercisable only at the expiration date. Surprisingly enough, in the absence of cash dividends, this flexibility advantage of the American calls has no economic value, since it never pays to exercise an American call before the expiration date. Hence the dictum that options are worth more 'alive than dead'.

Equilibrium models of option valuation are based on the notion of a hedged portfolio. Investors can create combinations of options with their underlying stocks which guarantee a certain return. In equilibrium this certain return must yield the risk-free interest rate, and using this fact, the option valuation models are derived.

The five factors that determine the call price in the Black and Scholes model are S_0, E_x, r, t, and σ^2. The call price increases with every increase in S_0, r, t, σ^2 and with every decrease in E_x. Unlike the value of most financial investments, the call price is independent of the expected return on the underlying stock. Out of these five basic factors, four (S_0, E_x, r, t) are readily available, but σ^2 has to be estimated. Any error in the estimate of σ^2 may lead to an error in the derived equilibrium call price C_0.

Futures on commodities, and particularly on financial assets, have attracted a rapidly growing number of investors. Futures contracts are employed to hedge risk, as well as for speculation.

1. Notation:

C = call price
P = put price
y_t = profit (or loss) in dollars
E_x = exercise price (striking price)
r = risk-free interest rate (for the period until expiration)
S_0 = current price of the underlying stock (known)
S_t = future price of the underlying stock (a random variable)

2. Profit profiles of a call:

Call-holder: $\quad y_t = -(C + E_x) + S_t \quad$ if $S_t > E_x$
$\qquad\qquad\quad\; y_t = -C \qquad\qquad\quad$ if $S_t \leqslant E_x$

Call-writer: $\quad y_t = (C + E_x) - S_t \quad$ if $S_t > E_x$
$\qquad\qquad\quad\; y_t = C \qquad\qquad\qquad$ if $S_t \leqslant E_x$

3. Profit profiles of a put:

Put-holder: $\quad y_t = (E_x - P) - S_t \quad$ if $S_t \leqslant E_x$
$\qquad\qquad\quad y_t = -P \qquad\qquad\quad$ if $S_t > E_x$

Put-writer: $\quad y_t = -(E_x - P) + S_t \quad$ if $S_t \leqslant E_x$
$\qquad\qquad\quad y_t = P \qquad\qquad\qquad$ if $S_t > E_x$

4. Bounds on the call price:

$$S_0 \geqslant C \geqslant \max[0, S_0 - E_x/(1 + r)]$$

5. Put–call parity in a perfect market:

$$C = S_0 + P - E_x/(1 + r)$$

6. Exercise call only if $S_t > E_x$.
   Exercise put only if $S_t < E_x$.
7. European calls can be exercised only at maturity while American calls can be exercised at any date before or on the maturity date. However, in the absence of cash dividends, it does not pay to exercise calls before the maturity date.
8. The Black and Scholes valuation model:

   (a) $$C_0 = S_0 N(d_1) - E_x e^{-rt} N(d_2)$$

   where:

   N = cumulative normal distribution

   $$d_1 = \frac{\ln(S_0/E_x) + (r + \frac{1}{2}\sigma^2)t}{\sigma\sqrt{t}}$$

$$d_2 = \frac{\ln(S_0/E_x) + (r - \frac{1}{2}\sigma^2)t}{\sigma\sqrt{t}} = d_1 - \sigma\sqrt{t}$$

e = base of natural logarithms (= 2.7128)
t = time to expiration (in fractions of a year)
r = continuously compounded annual riskless interest rate
σ = standard deviation of the continuously compounded annual rates of return on the underlying stock
S_0 and E_x as defined in (1) above

(b) The effect of the various factors on call option price:

$$C_0 = f(\overset{+}{S_0}, \overset{-}{E_x}, \overset{+}{\sigma^2}, \overset{+}{t}, \overset{+}{r})$$

(c) Estimating σ, we can solve the equation for C_0 (since all the other parameters are given).

(d) Using the observed market call price as C_0, we can use the Black and Scholes formula to estimate the stock price variability as represented by σ^2.

(e) In equilibrium with no arbitrage profit we have

$$\frac{S}{F} \frac{(1 + r^*)}{(1 + r)} = 1$$

where:

S = spot exchange rate (in dollars per pound)
F = forward exchange rate (in dollars per pound)
r = riskless interest rate on pounds
r^* = riskless interest rate on dollars

QUESTIONS AND PROBLEMS

19.1 Two call options on the stock of Delta Airlines with exercise prices of $30 and $35 and with maturities of 90 days sold for $3¼ and $1, respectively. Can you explain the difference in the prices of the two call options?

19.2 The *Wall Street Journal* records the following information on Bristol Myers stock:

Stock price	$65⅛
Exercise price	$55
Price of call option	$11¼ (one month's maturity)
	$12 (four months' maturity)

What caused the difference in the two call prices?

19.3 Two put options on the stock of Eastman Kodak with exercise prices of $70 and $75 sold for $1⅛ and $2⁹⁄₁₆, respectively. Explain the difference in the prices of the put options.

19.4 The *Wall Street Journal* lists the price of Dow Chemical stock as $25\frac{3}{4}$. A put option on the stock with exercise price of $25 expiring with one month's maturity, had a price of $\frac{5}{8}$, while a similar put option with the same exercise price of $25 expiring in four months had a price of $1\frac{3}{4}$. How do you account for the difference in prices?

19.5 An investor holds stock of Texas Instruments priced at $86\frac{5}{8}$. He buys a put option and sells a call option on the stock with 90-day maturities at prices of $8 and $4\frac{1}{2}$, respectively. The exercise price of both the put option and the call option is $85. Graph the value of his portfolio as a function of the stock price.

19.6 What are the differences between options and warrants?

19.7 The following table lists the price of IBM stock and of its corresponding call option with a 30-day maturity and with an exercise price of $60, over a 12-day trading period. Would you expect the percentage change in the stock price or in the option price to be greater? Confirm your answer by calculating the mean and the standard deviation of the change in price of the stock and of the option. Draw a frequency histogram of the change in the stock price and in the option price.

Day	Stock price ($)	Option price ($)
1	$60\frac{5}{8}$	$1\frac{5}{8}$
2	$60\frac{5}{8}$	$1\frac{1}{2}$
3	60	$1\frac{1}{8}$
4	$60\frac{3}{4}$	$1\frac{3}{8}$
5	$60\frac{7}{8}$	$1\frac{1}{2}$
6	$61\frac{5}{8}$	$1\frac{15}{16}$
7	$62\frac{3}{8}$	$2\frac{1}{2}$
8	$63\frac{1}{2}$	$3\frac{1}{8}$
9	$64\frac{5}{8}$	$4\frac{5}{8}$
10	$66\frac{1}{2}$	$6\frac{5}{8}$
11	$66\frac{3}{4}$	$6\frac{3}{4}$
12	$66\frac{1}{2}$	$6\frac{7}{8}$

19.8 Using the following data:

Date of information	November 30
Stock price	$50
Call price	$8
Exercise price	$45
Expiration date	December 31
Risk-free interest rate (annual)	5%

Does the call price lie within its expected lower and upper bounds?

19.9 Assuming that the put–call parity holds, calculate the value of a put option using the information given in problem 19.8.

19.10 What is the difference between European and American call options?

19.11 (a) Prove that the following inequality holds for a put option:

$$P \geq \max\left[0, \frac{E_x}{1+r} - S_0\right]$$

where S_0 is the security's current price, P is the price of the put option, E_x is the option's exercise price, and r is the riskless interest rate (for the period until maturity).

(b) Can the price of a put option ever exceed the price of the underlying stock?

19.12 (a) Show that a call option, the underlying stock, and riskless bonds can be combined to result in the same payoff as a put option.

(b) Derive the put–call parity from the investment strategy in (a).

19.13 An investor purchased an American call on CBM stock a month ago, and is suddenly in urgent need of cash. Assume that the current price of CBM stock is $S_0 = \$50$, the exercise price is $E_x = \$40$, and that the stock does not pay cash dividends. The current price of the call is \$12.

(a) Should the investor exercise the option? Explain.

(b) The investor received some inside information according to which the CBM corporation has suffered a heavy loss on its overseas operations. He therefore expects the CBM stock price to plunge to \$30 a share. He decides to sell the CBM stock short (at the present price of \$50 a share). Should the investor keep the call option? Explain.

19.14 Show by an example that if the stock pays cash dividends, early exercise of the option may be profitable.

19.15 Suppose that a call and a put with six months to expiration are traded with the same exercise price E_x. We observe the following market prices:

Call price $C = \$10$
Put price $P = \$8$
Stock price $S_0 = \$100$

The interest rate for six months is $r = 5\%$. What should be the exercise price if the put–call parity holds?

19.16 The stock price is $S_0 = \$100$ and the price of the corresponding call is $C = \$10$. It is given that any change in the future stock price S_t is accompanied by the same absolute change in the future call price C_t. Assume that an investor weighs whether to invest \$100 in the stock (i.e. buying one share) or to purchase 10 calls.

(a) Write out the relationship between the expected return and the variance of the two alternative strategies.

(b) Draw the cumulative distribution of the return on the two alternative investments. Is either strategy preferred by SSD? (See Appendix 9A). Explain your results.

19.17 The following data represent a stock and a call option written on that stock. The current stock price is $S_0 = \$100$, the exercise price is $E_x = \$120$, the annual risk-free interest rate is 10%, and the standard deviation of the continuously compounded annual rate of return is $\sigma = 0.8$. The time remaining to expiration is six months. Use the Black and Scholes formula to calculate the equilibrium call option value.

19.18 Use the data of problem 19.17 to calculate the call value for the following alternative values of standard deviation: $\sigma = 0.1$, $\sigma = 0.5$, $\sigma = 1$, $\sigma = 2$. Discuss your results.

19.19 Use the data of problem 19.17 to calculate the value of the call option for alternative values of t, $t = 0.25$, $t = 0.75$, $t = 1$. Discuss your results.

19.20 'Other things being equal, a $1 decrease in the exercise price E_x induces a $1 increase in the equilibrium call value.' Appraise this statement.

19.21 'When the risk-free interest rate approaches infinity, the call price approaches the current stock price.' Appraise this statement.

19.22 'In a case where the risk-free interest rate is zero an increase in the current stock price S_0 accompanied by an identical increase in the exercise price E_x will leave the equilibrium call value unchanged.' Appraise this statement.

19.23 What effect do the following have on the lower bound of the price of a call option? Explain.

(a) The stock price S_0 increases
(b) The exercise price E_x increases
(c) The risk-free interest rate decreases.

19.24 Given the following information about General Motors' stock and its corresponding call option, calculate the call option value using the Black and Scholes option valuation formula.

Stock price	$S = \$58\frac{5}{8}$
Exercise price	$E_x = \$40$
Time to maturity	$t = 3$ months
Yield on 90 day treasury bill	$r = 7.93\%$ (on annualized basis)
Variance of annual rates of return	$\sigma^2 = 0.0987$

(Calculated from historical data on stock price from the CRSP monthly returns data tapes.)

19.25 The *Wall Street Journal* lists the following information on the stock of National Cash Register and its corresponding option:

Stock price	$S = \$86$
Exercise price	$E_x = \$55$
Time to maturity	$t = 3$ months
Call option price	$C_0 = \$32\frac{3}{8}$
Yield on 90 day treasury bill	$r = 7.93\%$ (annualized)

Calculate the implied standard deviation of the stock price.

19.26 Suppose that the current stock price is $S_0 = \$100$. A call option is written on this stock with an exercise price $E_x = \$110$. The annual interest rate is 20%, and the standard deviation of the stock price is $\sigma = 0$. The time to expiration is $t = 0.5$ years. What is the equilibrium call value?

19.27 'The value $N(d_1)$ in the Black and Scholes formula is always greater than the value $N(d_2)$.' Do you agree with this statement? Explain.

19.28 From the following table the *monthly* rates of return on a stock can be calculated six consecutive months. It is also known that the current stock price is $100, and the annual risk-free interest rate is 5%. A call option is written on this stock with an exercise price $E_x = \$130$ and six months to expiration:

End of month	1	2	3	4	5	6
Stock price ($)	100	90	80	110	120	110

(a) Estimate the continuously compounded *annual* standard deviation of the stock's rate of return.

(b) Compute the equilibrium price of the call option.

19.29 The following data from the *Wall Street Journal* correspond to General Motors' call options: $S_0 = \$49.75$; $E_x = \$45$; $C_0 = \$7.75$; $t = 0.51$. The annual standard deviation of the return on the GM stock is estimated to be 0.3, and the riskless interest rate is approximately 13.5%

(a) Can you determine whether the GM option is in equilibrium?

(b) If the option is not in equilibrium, how do you account for the difference between the actual and the equilibrium price of the option?

19.30 Suppose an American exporter is expecting to receive £10,000 in three months' time. The current exchange rate (S_0) is £1 = $2. The exchange rate in three months is a random variable S_3, with mean $E(S_3) = 2.1$ and standard deviation $\sigma(S_3) = 1.5$. The three months forward exchange rate, F_3, is £1 = $1.9. The exporter is a risk-averter with the following utility function:

$$U(\mu, \sigma) = \mu^2 - \sigma^2$$

where μ is the expected value of wealth and σ the standard deviation.

(a) Does the utility function specified above seem logical? What restrictions must be placed on the investment alternative for it to have economic sense?

(b) Which of the following two alternatives would the exporter prefer:

(i) bearing the foreign exchange risk on the entire £10,000;
(ii) selling the £10,000 forward.

(c) Suppose the exporter may diversify, i.e., sell part of the £10,000 forward while bearing the foreign exchange risk on the rest. What would his optimal strategy be?

(d) Answer (c) under the assumption that the exporter expects to receive £20,000. How does the total wealth affect the optimal strategy?

19.31 Assume that the German mark spot exchange rate, S, is $1 = DM2, the three months forward exchange rate, F, is also $1 = DM2, the three months riskless interest rate on marks, r, is 2%, and the three months riskless interest rate on dollars, r^*, is 4%. Assume, further, that there are no transaction costs.

(a) What arbitrage opportunities exist in this market?

(b) Can these conditions persist for long? If not, which forces will bring about a change, and what are the equilibrium conditions in the market?

_____ SELECTED REFERENCES

Adams, Paul D. and Wyatt, Steve B., 'On the Pricing of European and American Foreign Currency Call Options,' *Journal of International Money and Finance*, September 1987.

Ball, Clifford A. and Torous, Walter N., 'The Maximum Likelihood Estimation of Security Price Volatility: Theory, Evidence and Application to Option Pricing,' *Journal of Business*, January 1984.

Barone-Adese, Giovanni and Whaley, Robert E., 'The Valuation of American Call Options and the Expected Ex-dividend Stock Price Decline,' *Journal of Financial Economics*, September 1986.

Bhattacharya, Mihir, 'Price Changes of Related Securities: The Case of Call Options and Stocks,' *Journal of Financial and Quantitative Analysis*, March 1987.

Bhattacharya, S., 'Notes on Multiperiod Valuation and the Pricing of Options,' *Journal of Finance*, March 1981.

Black, Fischer and Scholes, Myron, 'The Pricing of Options and Corporate Liabilities,' *Journal of Political Economy*, May/June 1973.

Block, S. B. and Gallagher, T. J., 'How Much Do Bank Trust Departments Use Derivatives?' *Journal of Portfolio Management*, Fall 1988.

Blomeyer, Edward C. and Johnson, Herb, 'An Empirical Examination of the Pricing of American Put Options,' *Journal of Financial and Quantitative Analysis*, March 1988.

Blomeyer, Edward C., 'An Analytical Approximation for the American Put Price for Options on Stocks with Dividends,' *Journal of Financial and Quantitative Analysis*, June 1986.

Bookstaber, Richard and Clarke, Roger 'Option Portfolio Strategies: Measurement and Evaluation,' *Journal of Business*, 1984.

Boyle, P. and Anathanarayanan, A. L., 'The Impact of Variance Estimation in Option Valuation Models,' *Journal of Financial Economics*, December 1977.

Boyle, Phelm, 'A Lattice Framework for Option Pricing with Two State Variables,' *Journal of Financial and Quantitative Analysis*, March 1988.

Breeden, D. T. and Litzenberger, R. H., 'Prices of State-contingent Claims Implicit in Option Prices,' *Journal of Business*, October 1978.

Brenner, Menachem and Galai, Dan, 'On Measuring the Risk of Common Stocks Implied by Options Prices: A Note,' *Journal of Financial and Quantitative Analysis*, December 1984.

Brick, Ivan E. and Wallingford, Buckner A., 'The Relative Tax Benefits of Alternative Call Features in Corporate Debt,' *Journal of Financial and Quantitative Analysis*, March 1985.

Brill, Edward and Harriff, Richard B., 'Pricing American Options: Managing Risk with Early Exercise,' *Financial Analysts Journal*, November/December 1986.

Brooks, R., Levy, H., and Yoder, J., 'Using Stochastic Dominance in Evaluating the Performance of Portfolio with Options,' *Financial Analysts Journal*, Autumn 1986.

Chang, Jack S. K. and Shanker, Latha, 'Option Pricing and the Arbitrage Pricing Theory,' *The Journal of Financial Research*, Spring 1987.

Choie, K. S. and Novomestky, F., 'Replication of Long-term With Short-term Options,' *Journal of Portfolio Management*, Winter 1989.

Courtadon, G., 'The Pricing of Options on Default-free Bonds,' *Journal of Financial and Quantitative Analysis*, March 1982.

Cox, J., Ross, S., and Rubinstein, M., 'Option Pricing: A Simplified Approach,' *Journal of Financial Economics*, September 1979.

Dimson, E., 'Option Valuation Nomograms,' *Financial Analysts Journal*, November/December 1977.

Evnine, Jeremy and Rudd, Andrew, 'Index Options: The Early Evidence,' *The Journal of Finance*, July 1985.

Evnine, Jeremy and Losq, Etienne, 'Asset Allocation and Options,' *The Journal of Portfolio Management*, Fall 1987.

Farkas, K. L. and Hoskins, R. E., 'Testing a Valuation Model for American Puts,' *Financial Management*, Autumn 1979.

Ferri, Michael G., Moore, Scott B., and Schrim, David C., 'Investor Expectations about Callable Warrants,' *Journal of Portfolio Management*, Spring 1988.

Fischer, S., 'Call Option Pricing When the Exercise Price is Uncertain, and the Valuation of Index Bonds,' *Journal of Finance*, March 1978.

Galai, Dan and Maulis, R. W., 'The Option Pricing Model and Risk Factor of Stock,' *Journal of Financial Economics*, January/February 1976.

Gastineau, G. L. and Madansky, A., 'Why Simulations are an Unreliable Test for Option Strategies,' *Financial Analysts Journal*, September 1979.

Geske, Robert and Johnson, H. E., 'The American Put Option Valued Analytically,' *Journal of Finance*, December 1984.

Geske, Robert and Roll, Richard, 'On Valuing Ameriean Call Options with the Black–Scholes European Formula,' *Journal of Finance*, June 1984.

Gilster, John E. and Lee, William, 'The Effects of Transaction Costs and Different Borrowing and Lending Rates on the Option Pricing Model: A Note,' *Journal of Finance*, September 1984.

Grinblatt, Mark and Johnson, Herb, 'A Put Option Paradox,' *Journal of Financial and Quantitative Analysis*, March 1988.

Gultekin, N. B., 'Option Pricing Model Estimates: Some Empirical Results,' *Financial Management*, Spring 1982.

Haugen, R. A. and Senbet, L. W., 'Resolving the Agency Problems of External Capital Through Options,' *Journal of Finance*, June 1981.

Hilliard, J. E. and Leitch, R. A., 'Analysis of the Warrant Hedge in a Stable Paretian Market,' *Journal of Financial and Quantitative Analysis*, March 1977.

Ho, Thomas S. Y. and Macnis, Richard G., 'Dealer Bid–Ask Quotes and Transaction Prices: An Empirical Study of Some AMEX Options,' *Journal of Finance*, March 1984.

Jones, E. Philip, Mason, Scott P., and Rosenfeld, Eric, 'Contingent Claims Analysis of Corporate Capital Structures: An Empirical Investigation,' *Journal of Finance*, July 1984.

Kishimoto, N., 'Pricing Contingent Claims under Interest Rate and Asset Price Risk,' *Journal of Finance*, July 1989.

Letane, H. A. and Rendleman, J. R. Jr, 'Standard Deviations of Stock Price Ratios Implied on Option Prices,' *Journal of Finance*, May 1976.

Leabo, D. A. and Rogalski, R. L., 'Warrant Price Movements and the Efficient Market Model,' *Journal of Finance*, March 1975.

Leland, H. E., 'Who Should Buy Portfolio Insurance?,' *Journal of Finance*, May 1980.

Levy, H., 'Upper and Lower Bounds of Put and Call Option Value,' *Journal of Finance*, September 1985.

Levy, H. and Yoder, J., 'Applying the Black–Scholes Model After Large Market Shocks,' *Journal of Portfolio Management*, Fall 1989.

Litzenberger, R. H. and Sosin, H. B., 'The Theory of Recapitalization and the Evidenee of Dual Purpose Funds,' *Journal of Finance*, December 1977.

MacBeth, J. D. and Melville, L. J., 'Tests of the Black–Scholes and Cox Call Option Valuation Models,' *Journal of Finance*, May 1980.

Manaster, S. and Koehler, G., 'Calculation of Implied Varianees from the Black–Scholes Model,' *Journal of Finance*, March 1982.

Manaster, S. and Rendleman, R. L. Jr, 'Option Prices as Predictors of Equilibrium Stock Prices,' *Journal of Finance*, September 1982.

Margrabe, W., 'The value of an Option to Exchange One Asset for Another,' *Journal of Finance*, March 1978.

Marsh, P., 'Variation of Underwriting Agreements for UK Rights Issues,' *Journal of Finance*, June 1980.

Martin, D. W. and French, Dan W., 'The Characteristics of Interest Rates and Stock Variances Implied in Option Prices,' *Journal of Economics and Business*, August 1987.

McDonald, Robert and Siegel, Daniel, 'Option Pricing when the Underlying Asset Earns a Below Equilibrium Rate of Return: A Note,' *Journal of Finance*, March 1984.

Merton, Robert C., 'Theory of Rational Option Pricing,' *Bell Journal of Economics and Management Science*, Spring 1973.

Merton, R. C., Scholes, M. S., and Gladstein, M. L., 'The Returns and Risks of Alternative Put Option Portfolio Investment Strategies,' *Journal of Business*, January 1982.

Mueller, P. A., 'Covered Options: An Alternative Investment Strategy,' *Financial Management*, Autumn 1981.

Nachman, D. C., 'Spanning and Completeness with Options,' *Review of Financial Studies*, Fall 1988.

O'Brien, Thomas, 'Portfolio Insurance Mechanics,' *Journal of Portfolio Management*, Spring 1988.

Officer, D. T. and Trennepohl, G. L., 'Price Behavior of Corporate Securities Near Option Expiration Dates,' *Financial Management*, Summer 1981.

Page, Frank H. and Sanders, Anthony B., 'A General Derivation of the Jump Process Option Pricing Formula,' *Journal of Financial and Quantitative Analysis*, December 1986.

Patell, J. M. and Wolfson, M. A., 'Ex-ante and Ex-post Price Effects of Quarterly Earnings Announcements Reflected in Option and Stock Prices,' *Journal of Accounting Research*, Autumn 1981.

Perrakis, Stylianos and Ryan, Peter, 'Option Pricing Bounds in Discrete Time,' *Journal of Finance*, June 1984.

Rendleman, R. J. Jr and Bartter, B. J., 'Two-state Option Pricing,' *Journal of Finance*, December 1979.

Rendleman, Richard J. Jr and McNally, Richard W., 'Assessing the Costs of Portfolio Insurance,' *Financial Analysts Journal*, May/June 1987.

Ritchken, Peter, 'Enhancing Mean–Variance Analysis with Options,' *Journal of Portfolio Management*, Spring 1985.

Ritchken, Peter and Kuo, Shyanjaw, 'An Unconditional Asset-pricing Test and the Role of the Firm Size as an Instrumental Variable for Risk,' *Journal of Finance*, June 1988.

Rubinstein, Mark, 'A Simple Formula for the Expected Rate of Return of an Option over a Finite Holding Period,' *Journal of Finance*, December 1984.

Rudd, A., 'Using Options to Increase Reward and Decrease Risk,' *Journal of Banking Research*, Autumn 1981.

Schmalensee, R. and Trippi, R. R., 'Common Stock Volatility Expectations Implied by Option Premia,' *Journal of Finance*, March 1978.

Scott, Louis, 'Option Pricing When the Variance Changes Randomly: Theory, Estimation and an Application,' *Journal of Financial and Quantitative Analysis*, December 1987.

Shastri, Kuldeep and Tandon, Kishre, 'An Empirical Test of a Valuation Model for American Options on Futures Contracts,' *Journal of Financial and Quantitative Analysis*, December 1986.

Shashtri, Kuldeep and Tandon, Kishre, 'Options on Futures Contracts: A Comparison of European and American Pricing Models,' *Journal of Futures Markets*, December 1986.

Smith, C. W., 'Option Pricing: A Review,' *Journal of Financial Economics*, January/March 1976.

Spatt, Chester S. and Sterbenz, Frederic P., 'Warrant Exercise, Dividends, and Reinvestment Policy,' *Journal of Finance*, June 1988.

Stapelton, R. C. and Strahmanyan, M. G., 'The Valuation of Options when Asset Returns are Generated by a Binomial Process,' *Journal of Finance*, December 1984.

Swindler, Steven and Zivney, Terry L., 'An Empirical Analysis of the Early Exercise Premium,' *Review of Futures Markets*, 6, 1, 1987.

Tilley, James A. and Latainer, Gary D., 'A Synthetic Option Framework for Asset Allocation,' *Financial Analysts Journal*, May/June 1985.

Trennepohl, Gary L., Booth, James R., and Tehranian, Hassan, 'An Empirical Analysis of Insured Portfolio Strategies Using Listed Options,' *Journal of Financial Research*, Spring 1988.

Whaley, Robert E., 'On Valuing American Futures Options,' *Financial Analysts Journal*, May/June 1986.

Zhu, Yu and Kavee, Robert C., 'Performances of Portfolio Insurance Strategies,' *Journal of Portfolio Management*, Spring 1988.

20

The Lease or Buy Decision

ARTICLE 44

Sideswiped by Taxes and Frugal Buyers, Luxury-Car Makers Take Discount Route

DETROIT — At a time when most auto companies are trying to put the brakes on discounts, makers of luxury cars are cutting some of the most aggressive deals ever.

One stellar example is Mercedes-Benz of North America Inc. The U.S. sales arm of Germany's **Daimler-Benz** AG is touting a discount deal it calls the 'Win/Win' lease. The offer: Drive a Mercedes-Benz 300E sedan for just $630 a month for 36 months. That is a $120-a-month savings from the old monthly payment and allows the lessee to pay $22,600 over three years to drive a car it would cost $50,000 to buy.

"We're responding to the market,"

says Mercedes-Benz spokeswoman Linda Paulmeno. "The market was calling more and more for leasing."

The call has also been heard by competitors. The Cadillac Seville, star of Detroit's new models last fall, now comes with a discount lease, something **General Motors** Corp. had hoped it wouldn't need to offer so soon after the car's introduction. BMW's U.S. sales arm has slapped a $10,000 dealer incentive on the 1991 model 750iL, which comes with a $74,000 price tag. There are even discounts available on Ferraris.

Source: *Wall Street Journal*, June 29, 1992, p. B1.

Why buy a Mercedes-Benz for $50,000 if you can lease it for $630 a month? Is the alternative of leasing the car rather than using your equity or borrowing the money preferred? Throughout the book we have assumed that the firm acquires needed assets by purchasing them. But for many years, the leasing of assets has been a significant alternative to outright ownership. In general, a lease can be defined as a contractual relationship in which the owner of the asset or property (the *lessor*) grants to a firm or person (the *lessee*) the use of the property's services for a specified period of time. Thus in a lease contract, the firm is able to use the leased assets without assuming ownership. Although the idea that leasing can provide an alternative to the use of long-term debt to acquire assets has been around for many years, it was not until the early 1950s that the leasing of capital equipment became a generally accepted method. At present, industrial leasing companies are prepared to offer almost any type of asset. The use of land, warehouses, manufacturing facilities, retail stores, jet engines, computers, trucks, or even beer kegs can be acquired by lease. A popular variant is the so-called 'sale and lease-back' – an arrangement in which an institutional investor, such as an insurance company or university endowment fund, buys an asset from a firm and then leases it back to the firm on a long-term basis (twenty years or more).

Some idea of the magnitude of the leasing industry can be gained from an examination of the rental revenues of International Business Machines, the world's leading lessor of computers. During the second half of the 1970s, income from rentals and services amounted to $57 billion and accounted for over 60% of IBM's total operating income. In 1987, IBM generated over $11 billion of income by leasing arrangements.

TYPES OF LEASE

In general, the types of lease offered in the market today can be classified into two categories: *operating leases* and *financial leases.*

Operating lease

An operating lease is not financial in nature and is written for a short period of time, usually for a period substantially shorter than the equipment's useful life. Durations of this type of lease run typically from a few months to a few years; some, however, run for as short as a few hours. Under an operating lease, the lessor assumes most or all of the responsibilities of ownership including maintenance, service, insurance, liability and property taxes. The lessee can cancel an operating lease on short notice. Thus, the operating lease does not involve the long-term fixed future commitment and is similar to renting. A good example of this type of lease is provided by the rental of an office copying machine.

Financial lease

A financial lease, or 'capital lease' as it is also called, is a contract by which the lessee agrees to pay the lessor a series of payments whose sum equals or exceeds the purchase price of the asset. Typically, the total cash flows from the lease payments, the tax savings and the equipment's residual value will be sufficient to pay back the lessor's investment and provide a profit.

Most financial leases are 'net' leases, i.e., the fundamental ownership responsibilities such as maintenance, insurance, property and sales taxes are placed upon the lessee. And, since the agreement entered into with the lessor is long-term, financial leases cannot be cancelled by either party. Some contracts, however, provide that in case of unforeseen events, the contract can be cancelled, but the lessor imposes a substantial pre-payment penalty which will assure the return of his investment and a profit. Upon termination of the financial lease, the equipment is returned to the lessor, or in some cases, the lessee is given the option to purchase the asset. In this chapter we devote our attention to the analysis of the long-term financial lease. Given the character of such contracts, the emphasis will be on the analysis of leasing as a 'financial decision', i.e., as a substitute for long-term debt-financing.

TAX TREATMENT OF LEASES

The tax status of a lease is of crucial importance. To this end, the contract must be of a form which the tax authorities will accept as a genuine lease, and not simply an instalment loan called a lease. In the United States, a lease having the following characteristics is likely to be approved by the Internal Revenue Service (IRS), thereby permitting the deduction for tax purposes of the full amount of the annual lease payment:

1. The lease term should exceed 75% of of the property's estimated economic life.
2. The terms of the lease must provide the lessor with a reasonable rate of return.
3. The contract must contain a bona fide renewal option and this requirement can best be met by granting the lessee the prior option to meet an equal bona fide outside offer.
4. There should be no repurchase offer, but if there is, the lessee should not be given more than parity with equal outside offers.

The reason for the Internal Revenue Service's concern is clear. Without any restrictions, 'lease' contracts could be drawn up which permit very rapid payments, all of which would be considered tax deductions. In effect, this would permit firms to use such arrangements to depreciate equipment over a much shorter period than its useful life. Thus, by increasing the tax deductions of early years, the firm would be receiving an interest-free loan from the IRS. And of course the firm's gain on such a transaction is the government's loss. [1]

ACCOUNTING TREATMENT OF LEASES

Leasing has been called 'off the balance sheet' financing, because in the past many lease contracts permitted a firm to ignore both the asset and the lease

---

1. A 1981 tax law introduced 'safe harbor' leasing in order to stimulate corporate investment. The safe harbor rules permitted the transfer of tax benefits from one party to another even though the transfer had no other economic substance. The huge tax benefits (estimated at $37 billion) enjoyed in 1981 and 1982 by large U.S. corporations led to a drastic reduction (in mid-1982) of permissible safe harbor transactions; in 1988 the IRS commenced a sweeping investigation of possible abuses of the safe harbor rules. See *Wall Street Journal*, September 6 1988.

liability in its balance sheet. Consider, for example, two identical firms, both of which have 50% debt and whose balance sheets appear in Table 20.1. Now assume that both firms acquire the same asset, but firm A finances its purchase with a loan while firm B acquires the use of the asset under a long-term financial lease. The proportion of debt rises in firm A from 50 to 67%, but in the case of firm B, the assets remain unchanged and the proportion of debt in its capital structure also stays unchanged at 50%. This is unacceptable since the fixed lease payments may be considerably higher than the loan payments. In such a case, the enhanced leverage which is *implicit* in the lease may actually increase the firm's financial risk by more than the loan. But whatever the size of the lease payments, they certainly do affect the firm's financial risk.

In order to correct this situation, the Financial Accounting Standards Board (FASB) issued, in November 1976, its Statement of Accounting Standards No. 13, *Accounting for Leases*. Statement 13 requires firms that enter into financial (capital) leases to report the present value of the future lease payments in their balance sheet as a fixed asset and as a liability. Firms which do not comply with Statement 13 will not receive an *unqualified* auditor's report. The above procedure, which is usually called 'capitalizing the lease,' eliminates the balance sheet differences between firms such as A and B of Table 20.1.

The logic underlying Statement 13 is straightforward and conforms with the analysis of leverage in Chapters 13 and 14. An agreement to make a series of fixed payments under a lease contract is no less binding than a debt-contract, and *both* increase the firm's financial leverage. But as we have already seen in Chapter 13, the increased leverage also increases the firm's financial risk. Recognizing this increase in riskiness, the FASB reasoned that failure to report the lease on the firm's balance sheet could mislead shareholders and potential investors by understating the firm's effective leverage, thereby understating its true risk as well. In the absence of the FASB requirement, we would conclude that firm A which borrowed to purchase its asset has a greater risk than firm B which leased the same asset (see Table 20.1). But this is not true. Both firms are, in essence, in the same position, once we realize that the fixed lease payments can be (and should be) restated as an equivalent debt obligation.

From the standpoint of the lessee, Statement 13 defines a financial (capital)

Table 20.1 Effect of leasing on the balance sheet

		Before the increase in assets			
		Firms A and B			
		Debt	50		
		Equity	50		
Total assets		100	100		

		After increase in assets			
Firm A			Firm B		
(which borrows and buys)			(which leases)		
	Debt	100		Debt	50
	Equity	50		Equity	50
Total assets	150	150	Total assets	100	100

lease, which must be capitalized, as a contract that contains *at least one* of the following conditions:

1. Ownership of the property is transferred to the lessee by the end of the term of the lease contract.
2. The lessee is offered the option of buying the property *below* its true market value upon expiration of the lease.
3. The term of the lease is 75% or more of the property's estimated economic life.
4. The present value of the lease payments is equal to or greater than 90% of the property's fair market value at the beginning of the lease.

Leases which do not meet any of the above requirements are classified by Statement 13 as *operating leases*, and are also subject to very strong disclosure rules. However, in the case of an operating lease, the disclosure of the terms of the lease obligation appears as a footnote rather than in the balance sheet itself. But given the sophistication of today's financial analysts, such disclosure is likely to be sufficient to prevent anyone from being deceived by lease financing. In particular, it is not very likely that the use of leases, in place of debt, allows the firm to increase its optimal (target) capital structure.

POSSIBLE ADVANTAGES OF LEASING

Many reasons have been offered for leasing rather than purchasing assets, but not all of them can be supported. The following are some of the chief claims which have been made on behalf of leasing.

Shift of ownership risk

At first glance, the lease appears to allow the firm to avoid completely the substantial risk of owning obsolete equipment. Thus, if the firm leases a computer and the agreement contains a cancellation clause, the risk of obsolescence appears to have been passed back to the lessor. However, the lessor obviously includes an estimate of the cost of obsolescence when calculating the rental payment. But the cost of 'insuring' the lessor against the risk of obsolescence may be significantly lower than the comparable cost to the lessee, especially in cases where the leased equipment has alternative uses in other firms or industries. Moreover, like an insurance company, the lessor can spread the risk of obsolescence over many contracts.

Flexibility

Relatively short-term operating leases permit the firm to acquire the use of equipment as needed. Thus, the cost of idle equipment can be avoided by not renewing the lease. Hence it is often very convenient to utilize a lease arrangement. However, this advantage does not hold for long-term leases in which the firm is obligated to continue its rental payments until the lease is terminated.

Maintenance

Under a full-service lease the lessor provides maintenance; in many cases he may be in a better position to provide such service. But, once again, part or all of the benefits of such service will be reflected in the lease payments.

Tax advantage

A tax advantage may be gained if the term of the lease is shorter than the depreciation period which the tax authorities would allow if the assets were owned, but still meets the IRS lease requirements. In other cases, one party may be in a better position than the other party to use the tax shields generated by the asset. Consider the case of a firm which does not have sufficient income to exploit all the deductions. In such a case, part of the 'tax saving' accruing to the lessor may be passed on to the lessee in the form of lower lease payments.

Relief from debt restrictions

Although skilled analysts are quick to recognize the fixed charges implicit in a long-term lease, some relief may be afforded from the restrictions on further borrowing, on the use of assets, or on the payment of dividends, which are often imposed when the assets are financed by a bond issue or term loan.

Bankruptcy risk

The lease is conceptually similar to borrowing since it represents an obligation to make a series of fixed rental payments. The impact of these payments on the firm's per share earnings is similar to that of the payment schedule of interest and principal on borrowed money. But from the lessee's point of view there is one further advantage to the lease arrangement. Legal title to the equipment remains with the lessor. Hence, in the case of financial difficulty, the leasing company can simply take back the equipment rather than demand the bankruptcy of the lessee.[2] However, should the equipment's market value be less than the present value of the future lease payments, the lessor will have to wait his turn along with the firm's other unsecured creditors in order to recover the difference.

2. In practice, the situation is often more complicated. For example, in some bankruptcy proceedings the court may order the lessor to refrain from recovering the equipment, thereby permitting the lessee to continue operations. In such cases, the lessor will continue to receive lease payments during the bankruptcy proceedings which essentially puts him in a more favorable position than the bankrupt firm's other secured creditors.

Clearly these 'advantages' of leasing have a price, and the degree to which the firm can benefit from them depends on the terms of the lease contract. This raises the problem of evaluating the desirability of leasing from the standpoint of the firm which is considering the financing of equipment or property by a lease contract.

Let us first turn to the problem of determining the cash flows which are relevant for the analysis of the lease or buy decision. Although the valuation of the desirability of a leasing arrangement appears, on the surface at least, to be straightforward and perhaps even simple, nothing could be further from the truth. Some of the difficulty in evaluating a lease proposal reflects an underlying ambiguity regarding the relevant alternative that should be used as the benchmark for comparison with the lease.

On the surface, it would appear that the choice between the two alternatives – lease or buy – is relatively simple. Assuming that both options have *positive* net present values, it might be argued that the firm should follow the alternative with the higher *NPV*. If the net present value of the lease is greater than the net present value of the purchase option, the machine should be leased, and conversely in the case in which the *NPV* of the purchase exceeds the *NPV* of the lease. But despite the apparent plausibility of this approach such a solution is incorrect.

Comparing the net present values of the buy or lease alternatives involves us in a comparison of apples and oranges, because the two cash flows differ in a fundamental sense. The lease arrangement is like borrowing in that it commits the firm to a series of fixed rental payments. Thus, even if the lease alternative has a greater *NPV*, it may also use more of the firm's borrowing capacity, thereby exposing the firm's shareholders to greater financial risk. The differential financial risk can be identified by carefully specifying the cash flows of the two alternatives.

Cash flow of a lease

We first consider the cash flow of the lease. For convenience, we assume that the lease is for the economic life of the asset, there is no residual value, the firm which leases the equipment pays rent of L_t in year t, and that the firm earns revenue from the sale of the machine's output equal to S_t, in year t. The production cost associated with this output is C_t, (labor, raw materials, electricity, etc.). The firm has no depreciation cost since it does not actually own the machine. Hence the *net* cash flow engendered by the lease can be written as follows:

$$(1 - T_c)(S_t - C_t - L_t) = (1 - T_c)(S_t - C_t) - (1 - T_c)L_t$$

where T_c denotes the appropriate corporate tax rate.

Thus the annual net after-tax cash flow generated by the lease of an asset is:

NET AFTER-TAX INCOME FROM THE USE OF THE ASSET	LESS	AFTER-TAX LEASE PAYMENT

Cash flow of a purchase

Suppose now that the firm decides to *buy*, rather than lease, the machine. Assuming a purchase price of I_0 dollars, and an annual depreciation allowance of D_t, the relevant cash flow of the purchase option in year t is given by:

$$(1 - T_c)(S_t - C_t - M_t - D_t) + D_t$$

Note that we first subtract the depreciation expense, D_t, in order to calculate the corporate tax liability, but then add it back because depreciation is not a cash outflow. We also deduct M_t, which denotes any additional maintenance, insurance or other costs engendered by the decision to buy rather than lease the machine. For simplicity, we shall assume that the sum of all these costs (i.e., M_t) is zero. Hence the net cash flow in year t of the purchase option reduces to:

$$(1 - T_c)(S_t - C_t - D_t) + D_t$$

which can be rewritten as:

$$(1 - T_c)(S_t - C_t) + T_c D_t$$

Thus the annual after-tax cash flow of the purchase option is:

NET AFTER-TAX INCOME FROM THE USE OF THE ASSET	PLUS	DEPRECIATION TAX SHIELD

COMPARING ALTERNATIVES

The present value of the income generated by the use of the asset is not relevant for the comparison of the leasing and purchasing alternatives since it is *not* affected by the method of acquiring the asset. (We are assuming that the *NPV* of the operating income generated from the use of the asset is positive; therefore, here we are only choosing the best method of financing the acquisition.)[3]

---

3. The present value of the income stream is of course very relevant for the decision as to whether or not the asset should be acquired in the first place. But once its *NPV* has been determined to be positive, the choice of *method of financing* (borrowing to purchase or lease) does not depend on the asset's operational cash flow.

The *differential* annual cash flow for any year which is engendered by the decision to lease rather than buy is derived by subtracting the *annual* purchase cash flow from the *annual* lease cash flow:

$$- [(1 - T_c)L_t + T_c D_t]$$

Thus, the differential annual cash flow is equal to:

AFTER-TAX LEASE PAYMENT	PLUS	DEPRECIATION TAX SHIELD

Before a meaningful analysis of the two alternatives can be made, risk must be held constant when comparing the two alternatives. Only if the risks incurred in the purchase and lease alternatives are equated, can their present values be used as a guide for action. However, as we have already seen, the lease option commits the firm to a stream of rental payments, fixed in advance, which implies the using up of some of the firm's borrowing capacity. In order to neutralize the financial risk differential, the analysis of the purchase alternative requires that it be partially financed by a loan which commits the firm to a stream of fixed payments (principal plus interest) exactly equal to that implied by the lease alternative.

The critical *risk-equating* payments stream on such a loan is equal to the stream of the differential annual cash flows:[4]

$$- [T_c D_t + (1 - T_c)L_t]$$

The decision to lease can be evaluated by deducting the present value of this stream of payments from the initial purchase price, I_0. Since the payment stream is after-tax, *the after-tax* interest rate, $(1 - T_c)r$ is used as the discount rate:

$$NPV \text{ of lease decision} = I_0 - \sum_{t=1}^{n} \frac{T_c D_t + (1 - T_c)L_t}{[1 + (1 - T_c)r]^t}$$

If the *NPV* is positive, i.e., if the present value of the stream of payments on the implicit loan is less than the purchase price, the asset should be leased; if it is negative, the equipment should be purchased. Recall that the present value of $T_c D_t + (1 - T_c)L_t$ is nothing but the amount the firm can borrow with this annual cash outflow. If the present value is greater than I_0 (i.e., *NPV* is negative), the firm can borrow money and purchase the machine. In other words, the firm borrows a certain sum (less than I_0) without affecting its annual cash outflow commitment.

---

4. The proof that this procedure actually neutralizes the differential riskiness of the two alternatives is given in Appendix 20A. It is taken from H. Levy and M. Sarnat, 'On Leasing, Borrowing and Financial Risk,' *Financial Management*, Winter 1979.

A numerical example of lease evaluation

Assume that the firm has already decided to acquire a given machine, but is considering whether it should be purchased or leased. The price of the machine (I_0) is $10,000 and its estimated economic (and accounting) life span (n) is 10 years. The after-tax interest rate is 5%, the corporate tax rate (T_c) is 34%, the annual straight-line depreciation charge ($D_t = I_0/n$) is equal to $1,000; and, if leased, the annual rental payment (L_t) would be $1,500.

Should the firm buy or lease the machine? The annual differential cash flow is given by:

$$T_c D_t + (1 - T_c)L_t = (0.34 \times 1,000) + (0.66 \times 1,500)$$
$$= 340 + 990 = 1,330$$

Its present value over the ten-year period, at 5%, is given by:

$$7.722 \times 1,330 = 10,270$$

Plugging this into the *NPV* formula we get:

$$NPV = 10,000 - 10,270 = -270$$

Since the present value of the differential cash flow exceeds the purchase price, the *NPV* is negative and the machine should be purchased rather than leased.

But suppose that the firm is offered the same leasing arrangement at a lower cost, for example for an annual lease payment of only $1,000. In this case the annual differential cash flow is:

$$T_c D_t + (1 - T_c)L_t = (0.34 \times 1,000) + (0.66 \times 1,000)$$
$$= 340 + 660 = 1,000$$

The present value of the 10-year cash flow is:

$$7.722 \times 1,000 = 7,722$$

The purchase price now exceeds the present value of the differential cash flow. Hence, the *NPV* is positive ($10,000 - 7,722 = +2,278$); the machine should therefore be leased rather than purchased.

THE LOGIC OF THE LEASE OR BORROW APPROACH _____

The 'lease or buy' decision really comes down to 'lease or borrow'. If leasing represents a better financing alternative than borrowing, it becomes the preferred alternative. Underlying this approach is the idea that the implicit additional debt financing generated by the lease must be compared not simply with the purchase of the asset, but with the relevant alternative of borrowing rather than leasing. If the present value of the differential implicit fixed payments generated by the lease [$(1 - T_c)L_t + T_c D_t$] is greater than the initial purchase price of the property (I_0), the *NPV* will be negative and the asset should be purchased. In this case, the implicit annual cash flow generated by the decision to lease (lease rentals plus loss of the depreciation tax shield) would be sufficient to borrow an amount greater than the purchase price, I_0. Thus, the purchase should be financed by an *equivalent* loan, and the firm would still have money left over. Conversely, if the present value of the differential cash flow is less than I_0, so that the *NPV* is positive, the lease option represents the better alternative. In this case, the present value of the implicit annual payments stream is smaller than that of an equivalent loan. For example, if $(1 - T_c)L_t + T_cD_t = \$50$ and $I_0 = \$1,000$, and the present value of the $\$50$ is $\$1,200$, this means that the firm can borrow $\$1,200$ with the same annual commitment of $\$50$ a year which it pays to the bank. Thus the firm purchases the machine for $\$1,000$ and saves $\$200$ without affecting the annual cash outflow, which remains at $\$50$.

FINDING THE CRITICAL BREAK-EVEN LEASE PAYMENT

A correct, and incidentally practical, way to choose between the two alternatives is to find the critical level of lease payment that leaves the firm indifferent between the lease and buy strategies. The maximum annual lease payment L_t^* that the lessee can offer can be found by first equating the present value of the differential cash flow to the purchase price of the asset:

$$\sum_{t=1}^{n} \frac{T_cD_t + (1 - T_c)L_t^*}{[1 + (1 - T_c)r]^t} = I_0$$

If we assume, for simplicity, constant annual lease payments the critical level of lease payments can be found by solving this expression[5] explicitly for L^*:

$$\frac{I_0 - \sum_{t=1}^{n} T_cD_t / [1 + (1 - T_c)r]^t}{\sum_{t=1}^{n} (1 - T_c) / [1 + (1 - T_c)r]^t}$$

Should the firm choose the buy or lease alternative? If the proposed lease payments are less than L^*, the equipment in question should be leased; for lease payments greater than L^*, the purchase option is preferable. This is illustrated in Figure 20.1. For lease payments greater than L^* the gain in *NPV* from purchasing is positive, but for lease payments below L^*, purchasing involves a loss of *NPV* and the lease alternative should be chosen.

5. This formula can also be derived from the valuation formula set out in S. C. Myers, D. A. Dill and A. J. Bautista, 'Valuation of Financial Lease Contracts,' *Journal of Finance*, June 1976, pp. 799–819. For evidence of the use of this method in practice, see T. J. O'Brien and B. H. Nunnally Jr, 'A Survey of Corporate Leasing Analysis,' *Financial Management*, Summer 1983.

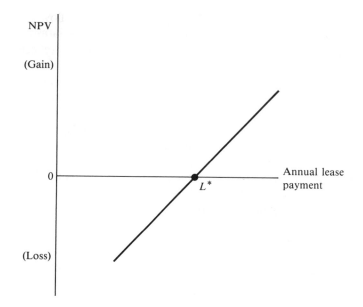

Figure 20.1 *NPV* gain (or loss) from purchasing rather than leasing equipment.

A NUMERICAL EXAMPLE

Now let us apply the lease evaluation formula to a concrete numerical example. Assume that the firm has already decided to acquire a given machine, but is considering whether it should be purchased or leased. The price of the machine (I_0) is \$10,000 and its estimated economic (and accounting) life span (n) is 10 years. The *after-tax* interest rate is 5%; the corporate tax rate (T_c) is 34%; the annual straight-line depreciation charge ($D_t = I_0/n$) is \$1,000; and, if leased, the annual rental payment (L_t) would be \$2,000.

Should the firm buy or lease the machine? Plugging in the data of this example we solve the lease evaluation formula for the critical 'break-even' rental payment L^*; that is, for the maximum annual rental payment which the firm can offer:

$$L^* = \frac{I_0 - PV \text{ of the depreciation tax shelter at 5\% discount}}{PV \text{ of}(1 - T_c) \text{ at 5\% discount}}$$

The coefficient of present value of a 10-year annuity, using the 5% *after-tax* interest rate, equals 7.722. Hence the critical lease payment, in this instance, is \$1,446.8:

$$L^* = \frac{10,000 - 2,625.5}{0.66 \times 7.722} = \frac{7,374.5}{5.097} = 1,446.8$$

Since the terms of the lease call for an annual rental of \$2,000, which exceeds the critical break-even point, the machine should be purchased rather than leased in this case.

LEVERAGED LEASES

Until relatively recently only two parties, the lessor and the lessee, were involved in lease contracts. Today a new type of lease, the *leveraged lease*, has come into widespread use. A leveraged lease is an arrangement in which the lessor borrows a substantial part of the purchase price of the asset which is to be leased. Such a lease can best be explained in terms of a simple diagram (see Figure 20.2).

In essence, there is no difference between leveraged leases and the financial lease contracts that we have been discussing. Strictly speaking, the lessor always obtains the asset to be leased with a combination of debt and equity, but a third party is not involved. In the leveraged lease, lenders (other than the lessor) provide debt capital, usually secured by a first mortgage on the leased asset; in addition, the lease payments are usually assigned to the lender (or a trustee). The lender deducts interest and the instalment on the loan principal and then sends the balance to the provider of equity. Once again the equity may be provided by the lessor himself or indirectly by third parties. The

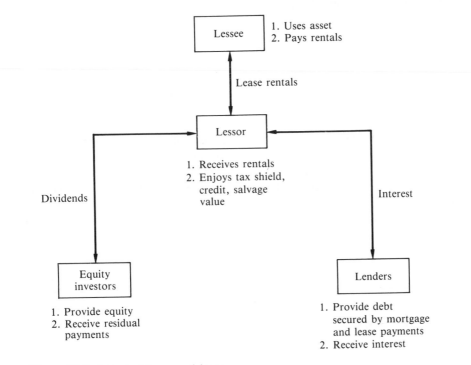

Figure 20.2 A typical leveraged lease.

lessor has the benefits of the depreciation tax shield, any salvage value, the deductibility of interest payments on the loan, and the return on equity if he also provides the equity.

The leveraged lease can be a very useful tool in the case of very large transactions, and/or when one company is not in a position to exploit all of the possible tax benefits from the transactions. The leveraged lease provides a flexible tool for dividing the risk and tax benefits among a group of investors, no one of whom could, or would be willing, to effect the transaction by itself.

The classic and often quoted example of the leveraged lease, was Anaconda's decision to finance most of a new $138 million aluminium plant through lease arrangements. The company had previously suffered a $365 million tax deductible loss when its Chilean copper mines were expropriated. Anaconda was not in a position to take advantage of the investment tax credit (which then existed) or the depreciation tax shields from the new investment. As a result, a leveraged lease of over $110 million was arranged with the First Kentucky Trust Company acting as lessor. A number of banks and financial institutions put up $38.7 million of equity and received the lease payments (net of debt service payments); three insurance companies put up an additional $72 million of debt capital secured by a mortgage on the new plant and a prior claim to the lease payments. However, it was a *non-recourse* loan, i.e., it was *not* secured by the lessor or by the equity holders. If Anaconda had defaulted, the lender's only claim was against the value of the mill (first mortgage) and a general claim against Anaconda's other assets.

SUMMARY

This chapter has attempted to analyse a problem that has been growing in importance as more and more types of assets become available for long-term rental. Although at first glance the lease or buy question appears relatively simple, a correct decision requires an appraisal of almost all aspects of financial decision-making. The lease or buy decision is a type of capital budgeting problem requiring the application of present value techniques. It also has tax implications, and the relevant after-tax cash flows of the two alternatives must be set out with great care. And, finally, the correct solution requires a neutralization of the differential financial risk implicit in the lease versus purchase comparison.

SUMMARY TABLE

Lease versus buy: the annual cash flows

Lease:

$$(1 - T_c)(S_t - C_t) - (1 - T_c)L_t$$

Buy:

$$(1 - T_c)(S_t - C_t) + T_c D_t$$

Differential annual cash flow:

$$- [(1 - T_c)L_t + T_c D_t]$$

Lease versus buy: the decision

$$NPV(\text{lease}) = I_0 - \sum_{t=1}^{n} \frac{T_c D_t + (1 - T_c)L_t}{[1 + (1 - T_c)r]^t}$$

If $NPV > 0$ lease the equipment
If $NPV < 0$ purchase the equipment

Finding break-even value of lease payment

$$L^* = \frac{I_0 - \sum_{t=1}^{n} T_c D_t / [1 + (1 - T_c)r]^t}{\sum_{t=1}^{n} (1 - T_c) / [1 + (1 - T_c)r]^t}$$

If $L_t < L^*$ lease the equipment
If $L_t > L^*$ purchase the equipment

where:

L_t = the actual lease payment
L^* = the critical value

QUESTIONS AND PROBLEMS

20.1 In what sense can leasing be considered as a hedge against obsolescence?

20.2 The Sisra Textile Company is considering the leasing of a machine for ten years at an annual rental of $35,000. The alternative is to purchase the machine for $190,000. Assume a corporate tax rate of 34%, an *after-tax* interest rate of 4%, straight-line depreciation, and zero salvage value. Also assume that no other costs (e.g., maintenance, insurance, etc.) are engendered by the decision to purchase.

(a) Should Sisra buy or lease the machine?
(b) What is the maximum lease payment that Sisra can offer before the purchase alternative becomes preferable.

20.3 Suppose that a firm is confronted with two mutually exclusive alternatives: to buy a machine which costs $25,000 and has an economic life of ten years; or to lease it for $4,500 a year. Assume straight-line depreciation, 34% corporate tax, and an *after-tax* interest rate of 6%

(a) Should the firm 'buy or lease' the machine?
(b) How much will the firm gain (or lose) if it decides to buy the machine rather than lease it?
(c) Answer parts (a) and (b) assuming now that the rental payments are $3,500 a year.
(d) Illustrate graphically the relationship between the gain (or loss) from the decision to buy rather than lease and the level of lease payments.

20.4 Calculate the 'break-even' annual rental for problem 20.3.

20.5 With regard to problem 20.3, assume now that the after-tax interest rate is 8% and answer the following questions:

(a) Should the firm buy or lease the machine (assume that annual rental payments are $4,500)?
(b) Calculate the gains (or losses) incurred if the firm should decide to buy the machine rather than lease it, for the following levels of lease payments: $4,500, $5,000, and $5,500.
(c) Illustrate graphically the relationship between the gain (or loss) from the decision to buy rather than lease and the level of lease payments. Compare this relationship with that of the 6% interest case.

20.6 The United Carton Corporation has decided to acquire a cutting machine which is required for its current production. The company is considering whether to purchase the machine or to lease it. The price of the machine is $40,000 and its economic and (accounting) life is 8 years. If the machine is leased, the annual rental payments would be $9,000.

Assume that the company uses straight-line depreciation, the (after-tax) interest rate is 8%, and the corporate tax rate is 34%. Should the company buy or lease the machine? To solve this problem, answer the following questions:

(a) What are the annual payments of interest and principal required to equalize the annual cash flows of *both* alternatives?
(b) Find the size of the loan which the company should take in order to *neutralize* the leverage implicit in the annual lease payments. (Hint: calculate the present value of the annual payments of principal and interest required to neutralize the leverage, at the *post-tax* discount rate.)
(c) Prove, using a table of principal and interest payments, that the loan you found in part (b) requires *equal annual* payments of principal and after-tax interest which are equal to the amounts you found in part (a).

20.7 Answer problem 20.6 assuming that the annual lease payment is $7,000.

20.8 With reference to problem 20.6, find the *critical value* of the lease payment (L^*).

20.9 Assume that you are considering leasing versus buying a machine. For a given tax rate T_c, interest rate r, initial investment I_0 and straight line depreciation, you solved for the critical lease level L^* and found that $L^* = \$1000$. Now suppose that the initial investment I_0 is doubled. How will your answer regarding the critical lease value be changed? Explain.

20.10 Suppose that Congress passed a new law which stipulated that depreciation is *not* tax deductible. What would be the impact of such a law on the willingness of firms to lease equipment?

20.11 You have a small business. You can buy a Mercedes-Benz for your firm for $50,000 or you can lease it for $7,500 a year for the next 10 years. The interest rate is 10% and the corporate tax rate is 34%. The salvage value of the car after 10 years is zero. Would you buy or lease the car?

20.12 Suppose that in deciding to buy or lease a machine you take all parameters and find that you are exactly indifferent between the two options. Due to change in the tax laws, the government does not allow you to deduct depreciation for tax purposes. How would this change your decision. Prove it formally.

_____ APPENDIX 20A: PROOF OF THE FORMULA WHICH SOLVES L^*

In this appendix we derive the equations which solve for L^* of the text. First we show a method where the interest tax shield is incorporated in the numerator, and then a method where it is not. However, the two methods yield the same solution for L^*.

Let us denote by B_t the balance of a loan outstanding at the end of period t. Hence, for any n period project, $B_n = 0$, and B_0 is the total amount borrowed. In the text it is argued that in order to equate the riskiness of the lease and buy options, the firm should borrow a sum that requires a total payments stream (repayment of principal and after-tax interest) which is just equal to:

$$(1 - T_c)L_t + T_c D_t \qquad \text{(A1)}$$

Thus the neutralization of the differential risk in year t implies that the following relationship should hold:

$$B_{t-1} - B_t + (1 - T_c)rB_{t-1} = (1 - T_c)L_t + T_c D_t \qquad \text{(A2)}$$

That is, the debt repayment $(B_{t-1} - B_t)$ plus after-tax interest payment $(1 - T_c)rB_{t-1}$ should equal the after-tax lease payment plus depreciation shelter. From equation (A2) we derive:

$$B_{t-1} = \frac{(1 - T_c)L_t + T_c D_t + rT_c B_{t-1} + B_t}{1 + r} \qquad \text{(A3)}$$

Note that the interest tax shield $rT_c B_{t-1}$ is incorporated in the cash flow and the discount rate is r rather than $(1 - T_c)r$. Since, by definition, $B_n = 0$, we obtain for $t = n - 1$:

$$B_{n-1} = \frac{(1 - T_c)L_n + T_c D_n + rT_c B_{n-1}}{1 + r} \qquad \text{(A4)}$$

Using (A3) and (A4) we have:

$$B_{n-2} = \frac{(1 - T_c)L_{n-1} + T_c D_{n-1} + rT_c B_{n-2} + B_{n-1}}{1 + r}$$

$$= \frac{(1 - T_c)L_{n-1} + T_c D_{n-1} + rT_c B_{n-2}}{1 + r} + \frac{B_{n-1}}{1 + r}$$

Substituting the right-hand side of equation (A4) for B_{n-1} yields:

$$B_{n-2} = \frac{L_{n-1}(1 - T_c) + T_c D_{n-1} + T_c B_{n-2}r}{1 + r} + \frac{L_n(1 - T_c) + T_c D_n + T_c B_{n-1}r}{(1 + r)^2}$$

which simplifies to:

$$B_{n-2} = \sum_{t=n-1}^{n} \frac{L_t(1 - T_c) + T_c D_t + T_c B_{t-1} r}{(1 + r)^{t-(n-2)}} \tag{A5}$$

Continuing this substitution procedure we finally obtain:

$$B_0 = \sum_{t=1}^{n} \frac{L_t(1 - T_c) + T_c D_t + T_c B_{t-1} r}{(1 + r)^t} \tag{A6}$$

To find the critical lease payment, L_t^*, which leaves the firm indifferent between the buy and lease options, we simply substitute $B_0 = I_0$ and solve for L_t^*:

$$I_0 = \sum_{t=1}^{n} \frac{L_t^*(1 - T_c) + T_c D_t + T_c B_{t-1} r}{(1 + r)^t} \tag{A7}$$

Thus, one can incorporate the interest tax shield $T_c B_{t-1} r$ in the numerator and discount the cash flows by r. This formula is rather difficult to solve since B_{t-1} varies over time. The formula given in the text is much simpler since the interest tax shield, which varies over time, is not included in the numerator.

In order to show the equivalence (A7) to the equation not in the text, let us write (A2) as follows:

$$B_{t-1}(1 + r) - T_c B_{t-1} r = L_t(1 - T_c) + T_c D_t + B_t \tag{A8}$$

Hence:

$$B_{t-1} = \frac{L_t(1 - T_c) + T_c D_t + B_t}{1 + (1 - T_c)r} \tag{A9}$$

Using the same substitution procedure as above, and recalling that $B_n = 0$, the critical lease payment L_t^* can be found from the following equation:

$$B_0 = I_0 = \sum_{t=1}^{n} \frac{(1 - T_c)L_t^* + T_c D_t}{[1 + (1 - T_c)r]^t} \tag{A10}$$

which is identical to the equation of the text. Since equations (A7) and (A10) yield the same estimate of the critical lease payment, L^*, they lead to the *same* decision regarding the relative desirability of the lease and buy alternatives. The only difference is that in equation (A7), the fact that interest is tax deductible is taken into account in the numerator; in equation (A10) it is taken into account in the denominator, i.e., by discounting the cash flow by $(1 - T_c)r$ rather than r.

SELECTED REFERENCES

Allen, C. L., Martin, J. D., and Anderson, P. F., 'Debt Capacity and the Lease–Purchase Problem: A Sensitivity Analysis,' *Engineering Economist*, Winter 1978.

Ang, James and Peterson, Pamela P., 'The Leasing Puzzle,' *Journal of Finance*, September 1984.

Ashton, D. J., 'The Reasons for Leasing – A Mathematical Programming Framework,' *Journal of Business Finance and Accounting*, Summer 1978.

Athanasopoulos, P. and Bacon, P., 'The Evaluation of Leveraged Leases,' *Financial Management*, Spring 1980.

Bayless, Mark E. and Diltz, David, 'An Empirical Study of the Debt Displacement Effects of Leasing,' *Financial Management*, Winter 1986.

Bloomfield, E. C. and Ronald, M. A., 'The Lease Evaluation Solution,' *Accounting and Business Research*, Autumn 1979.

Bower, Richard S., 'Issues in Lease Financing,' *Financial Management*, Winter 1973.

Bowman, R. G., 'The Debt Equivalence of Leases: An Empirical Investigation,' *Accounting Review*, April 1980.

Brealey, R. A. and Young, C. M., 'Debt, Taxes and Leasing – A Note,' *Journal of Finance*, December 1980.

Copeland, T. and Weston, J. F., 'A Note on the Evaluation of Cancellable Operating Leases,' *Financial Management*, Summer 1982.

Crawford, P., Harper, C., and McConnell, J., 'Further Evidence on Terms of Financial Leases,' *Financial Management*, Autumn 1981.

Doenges, R. Conrad, 'The Cost of Leasing,' *Engineering Economist*, Fall 1971.

Fawthrop, R. A. and Terry, Brian, 'Debt Management and the Use of Leasing Finance in UK Corporate Financing Strategies,' *Journal of Business Finance and Accounting*, Autumn 1975.

Finnerty, J. E., Fitzsimmons, Rick N., and Oliver, Thomas W., 'Lease Capitalization and Systematic Risk,' *Accounting Review*, October 1980.

Finucane, T. J., 'Some empirical Evidence on the Use of Financial Leases,' *Journal of Financial Research*, Winter 1988.

Franks, J. R. and Hodges, S. D., 'Lease Valuation when Taxable Earnings Are a Scarce Resource,' *Journal of Finance*, September 1987.

Gordon, Myron J., 'A General Solution to the Buy or Lease Decision: A Pedagogical Note,' *Journal of Finance*, March 1974.

Grimlund, R. and Capettini, R., 'A Note on the Evaluation of Leveraged Leases and Other Investments,' *Financial Management*, Summer 1982.

Hindin, R., 'Lease Your Way to Corporate Growth,' *Financial Executive*, May 1984.

Hochman, S. and Rabinovitch, R., 'Financial Leasing under Inflation,' *Financial Management*, Spring 1984.

Hodges, Stewart D., 'The Valuation of Variable Rate Leases,' *Financial Management*, Spring 1985.

Honic, Lawrence E. and Colley, Stephen C., 'An "After-tax" Equivalent Payment Approach to Conventional Lease Analysis,' *Financial Management*, Winter 1975.

Hull, J. C., 'The Bargaining Positions of the Parties to a Lease Agreement,' *Financial Management*, Autumn 1982.

Johnson, Keith B. and Hazuka, Thomas B., 'The NPV–IRR Debate in Lease Analysis,' *Mississippi Valley Journal*.

Johnson, Robert W. and Lewellen, Wilbur G., 'Analysis of the Lease or Buy Decision,' *Journal of Finance*, September 1972.

Keller, Thomas F. and Peterson, Russel J., 'Optimal Financial Structure, Cost of Capital and the Lease-or-Buy Decision,' *Journal of Business Finance and Accounting*, Autumn 1974.

Kim, E. H., Lewellen, W. G., and McConnell, J. J., 'Sale-and-leaseback Agreements and Enterprise Valuation,' *Journal of Financial and Quantitative Analysis*, December 1978.

Lewellen, W. G., Long, M. S., and McConnell, J. J., 'Asset Leasing in Competitive Capital Markets,' *Journal of Finance*, June 1976.

Lowenstein, Mark A. and McClure, James E., 'Taxes and Financial Leasing,' *Quarterly Review of Economics and Business*, Spring 1988.

McConnell, J. and Schallheim, J. S., 'Valuation of Asset Leasing Contracts,' *Journal of Financial Economics*, August 1983.

Moore, W. T. and Chen, S. N., 'The Decision to Lease or Purchase under Uncertainty: A Bayesian Approach,' *Engineering Economist*, Spring 1984.

Morgan, Eleanor, Lowe, Julian, and Tomkins, Cyril, 'The UK Financial Leasing Industry – A Structural Analysis,' *Journal of Industrial Economics*, June 1980.

O'Brien, T. J. and Nunnally, B. H. Jr, 'A 1982 Survey of Corporate Leasing Analysis,' *Financial Management*, Summer 1983.

Peller, P. R., Stewart, J. E., and Neuhausen, B. S., 'The 1981 Tax Act: Accounting for Leases,' *Financial Executive*, January 1982.

Perg, Wayne, F., 'Levered Leasing: The Problem of Changing Leverage,' *Financial Management*, Autumn 1978.

Peterson, P. P. and Ang. J., 'The Leasing Puzzle,' *Journal of Finance*, September 1984.

Smith, Clifford W. and Wakeman L. MacDonald, 'Determinants of Corporate Leasing Policy,' *Journal of Finance*, July 1985.

Smith, B., 'Accelerated Debt Repayment in Leveraged Leases,' *Financial Management*, Summer 1982.

Stephens, W. L., 'The Lease or Buy Decision: Make the Right Choice,' *Financial Executive*, May 1983.

Wiar, Robert C., 'Economic Implications of Multiple Rates of Return in the Leveraged Lease Context,' *Journal of Finance*, December 1973.

Wolfson, Mark, 'Tax Incentive and Risk-sharing Issues in the Allocation of Property Rights: The Generalized Lease or Buy Problem,' *Journal of Business*, April 1985.

21

Mergers

The following four articles are taken from the 1992 *Economic Yearbook*.[1]

Two **Spanish banks**, Central and Hispano Americano, announced a merger. It would create the country's biggest bank, with assets of $85 billion, overtaking the recently announced state mergers that would produce Corporacion Bancario de Espana.

While the Spanish bank mergers seem to be a simple process, more complicated is the case of Continental and Pirelli. First we have a tough and final rejection by the German firm but after a short period of time we have better conditions for the takeover and a partial victory for the Pirelli firm.

Continental, the Germany tyre manufacturer, issued a tough and final rejection of the merger approach from Pirelli, the Italian tyre company. Pirelli insisted its bid was "friendly", but pressed on with it despite the decision of the Continental board to break off talks.

Shareholders of *Continental*, a German tyre maker, voted to lift restrictions on the voting rights of the firm's shares. Italy's Pirelli claimed a partial victory in its efforts to take over Continental, even though the firm's shareholders also rejected a proposal for a merger between the two firms.

Sometimes, though, takeover bids are not so 'friendly': sometimes there are

1. *The Economic Yearbook*, Addison-Wesley, New York 1992, pp. 142, 144, 149, 147 and 172, respectively.

struggles involving 'poison pill' votes:

America's media and entertainment conglomerate, **Time Warner**, dropped its anti-takeover defence. Shareholders had threatened to use the poison-pill vote at the firm's September annual meeting to show disapproval of a controversial $3.5 billion rights issue.

Takeover bids are spreading now to the East European countries:

Unilever, an Anglo-Dutch detergent and food group, said it would but 80% of a **Polish detergent maker** for $20m. Pollena Bydgoszcz, to be renamed Lever Polska, was auctioned by the Polish government, which retained 20% of the privatized firm. In another deal, America's **Procter & Gamble** agreed to pay $44m for Rakona, a big Czechoslovakian detergent maker.

What leads a firm in the prime of life to seek the assets of its neighbor? What are friendly mergers, hostile takeovers, and poison pills? What do 'greenmail', 'golden parachutes', and 'white knights' have in common? What are the underlying motives for corporate takeovers? And who, if anyone, benefits from them? In short, how can we explain the 'urge to merge' which overcomes some very stout, middle-aged dowager companies as well as high-flying conglomerates.

Clearly, two of the prime objectives of business activity – profitable growth and risk diversification – can be achieved either internally, by means of capital investments, or externally, through the acquisition of existing productive and marketing facilities of other firms. The earlier chapters of the book were devoted to internal growth. They examined the way a firm allocates its physical and financial resources. In this chapter we take a long look at the alternative strategy of achieving growth by means of the acquisition of another firm.

TYPES OF MERGER

For the purposes of our discussion, *mergers*, *consolidations*, and *acquisitions* will be treated as synonyms, although the term 'merger' is often restricted to corporate combinations in which one of the combined firms loses its corporate existence. Consolidation often refers to the formation of an entirely new company, that is, a combination in which both of the combining firms lose their separate corporate identities. Three types of merger can be usefully distinguished.

Horizontal merger

In a horizontal merger the assets of two companies which are engaged in similar lines of activity are combined. The Great Trusts, which were established at the turn of the century (for example, the American Tobacco Company) provide examples of such mergers. Economies of scale in production, research, and management are often cited as the underlying motives for this type of merger. However, the enhancement of market power, following the elimination of competing firms, appears to have been a primary motive for many horizontal mergers.

Sometimes it is expedient to distinguish a special type of horizontal merger, the so-called *circular combination*. These are mergers in which firms, whose products use the same channels of distribution, are combined. General Foods and Standard Brands are among the better-known examples of this type of merger.

Vertical merger

A vertical merger is one in which a firm acquires the sources of its supply of raw materials, or other inputs of the productive process, or alternatively, acquires control over the sales outlets for its products. In essence, such combinations represent the replacement of part of the market allocation mechanism by internal organization and control within the firm.[2] As is also true of horizontal mergers, vertical integration raises perplexing questions with respect to the possible creation of market power and restriction of competition.

Conglomerate merger

The conglomerate merger is one in which firms whose economic activities are fairly unrelated are combined. Such mergers often appear to have the diversification of risk, rather than the achievement of scale economies, for their primary objective. These mergers created a new type of company, the so-called conglomerate firm. Textron, Litton Industries, Ling-Temco-Vought, Gulf & Western, International Telephone & Telegraph, and Teledyne are examples of conglomerate firms.

TRENDS IN MERGER ACTIVITY

At one time or another the U.S. economy has witnessed periods of accelerated merger activity of all types. Three distinct historical merger waves can easily be identified; a fourth and most recent wave of merger activity is still going on.[3]

2. A comprehensive analysis of the pros and cons of vertical integration is given by Oliver E. Williamson, 'The Vertical Integration of Production: Market Failure Considerations,' *American Economic Review*, May 1971.
3. For a critical review of merger activity in the United States, see Baruch Lev, 'Observations on the Merger Phenomenon and a Review of the Evidence,' *Midland Corporate Journal*, Winter 1983.

Turn of the century

From 1893 to 1904, a wave of horizontal mergers, motivated by the desire to acquire monopoly power, swept the United States. This merger wave created many of the now familiar corporate giants: U.S. Steel Corporation, the original Standard Oil Company, the American Tobacco Company, and many others. This was the golden age of the 'Great Trusts', and while scale economies played a role, monopolization and promoters' profits were the prime movers behind many of the most famous and largest of the mergers. In many ways this was the most important of the merger movements. In retrospect it shaped the structure which characterizes much of U.S. industry to this day. Prior to 1890, many of the nation's more important industries were made up of many small and medium-sized firms; subsequent to the mergers, they were transformed into industries dominated by a single firm or small group of large enterprises.[4] This early wave of merger activity was brought to an end by the Supreme Court's Northern Trust decision which clearly prohibited the creation of monopoly power through merger and acquisitions.

The 1920s

Following World War I, the consolidation process was given a further boost by a renewed wave of mergers. If the first wave represents an attempt at 'monopolization', the mergers of the 1920s have been characterized by Nobel Prize laureate George Stigler as 'mergers for oligopoly'. These combinations attempted to restore the concentration which had become diluted over the years in many industries. However, only rarely did the percentage of the market controlled by the new firm approach that of the first wave, in which the leading firms seldom merged less than 50% of an industry's output. The Great Depression of the 1930s and World War II brought an effective end to merger activity, but not before government had intervened to discourage increases in concentration and the creation of market power.

Mid-1950s to 1970

Merger activity continued to increase during the 1950s, and by the middle of the decade had again reached the level of the 1920s. But it was in the second half of the 1960s that a virtual explosion of mergers and acquisitions (over 8,000) took place. This is about double the number of mergers which took place during the first half of the decade.

From the standpoint of financial management, considerable interest attached to this wave of mergers ushered in the 'age of the conglomerate'. Motivated by the Celler–Kefauver Merger Act of 1950, which had an adverse

---

4. This earliest merger wave also played a crucial role in fostering the development of the New York Stock Exchange, see Ralph L. Nelson, *Merger Movements in American Industry: 1895–1956*, National Bureau of Economic Research, Princeton University Press, 1959.

effect on horizontal combinations, and perhaps by the theory of risk diversification (see Part II), the bulk of the acquired assets during this period are accounted for by conglomerate mergers. This merger wave came to an end in 1970, which coincides with a decline in the stock market.

The merger mania of the 1980s

The most recent merger wave began at the end of the 1970s and has continued on into the 1980s[5] and early 1990s. This latest merger wave has not been as widespread as its predecessor of the 1960s, but it has produced a number of very large combinations.[6]

Although many of the mergers of this period have again been of the conglomerate type, it also marks the reappearance of horizontal and vertical mergers. Two significant changes in government policy sparked the latest increase in merger activity:

1. The removal, in 1982, of the anti-trust rule against vertical mergers and the relaxing of the U.S. Justice Department's rule against horizontal mergers in the same year, and again in 1984.
2. The deregulation of specific industries since 1978. For example, the deregulation of the banking, transportation, and communications industries has permitted a greater combination of assets than had hitherto been possible. As a result, recently deregulated industries accounted for a significant share of merger and acquisition activity during the first half of the 1980s.

Both of these changes reflect the Reagan Administration's view that 'big is not necessarily bad.' As can be seen from Table 21.1, which lists the seven largest mergers of all time, the mergers of this period have involved a great deal of money. During the years 1981–84 alone, there were at least 45 transactions of over a billion dollars each. Before this period there were only a dozen or

Table 21.1 The largest mergers, 1981–85

Acquiring company	Target company	Value ($m)	Date
Chevron Corp.	Gulf Corp.	13,300	June 1984
Texaco Inc.	Getty Oil	10,125	Feb. 1984
Du Pont	Conoco	6,924	Aug. 1981
U.S. Steel	Marathon Oil	6,150	Mar. 1982
Mobil Corp.	Superior Oil	5,700	Sept. 1984
Royal Dutch/Shell Group	Shell Oil	5,670	June 1985
R. J. Reynolds	Nabisco Brands	4,904	Sept. 1985

5. A detailed review of the latest merger boom can be found in Lynn E. Browne and Eric S. Rosengren, 'The Merger Boom: An Overview,' Federal Reserve Bank of Boston, *New England Economic Review*, March/April, 1988
6. See Hal R. Varian, 'Symposium on Takeovers,' *Journal of Economic Perspectives*, Winter 1988.

so transactions of this size. [7] As a result, financial managers often devote considerable time and resources searching for, and analyzing the economic value of, suitable candidates for acquisition. Similarly, as a result of the recent wave of *hostile* takeovers, some firms also devote considerable time to worrying about the possibility that some other company may attempt to acquire them.

Finally, the current merger boom has been characterized by a large number of so-called bust up takeovers, i.e., takeovers of diversified companies and the subsequent sale of the components. The latest merger wave has also witnessed the widespread use of debt-financed acquisitions.

MOTIVES FOR MERGER

As we have already noted, external growth via merger is a substitute for growth generated internally by the firm's own capital investment projects. However, a merger differs from the typical capital investment project. More often than not, a merger represents a strategic decision to enter a new market over a prolonged period of time. What, then, are the corporate motives for choosing the option of external growth via acquisition?

Numerous reasons for seeking a merger are often cited in the financial literature. These include the desire to grow, integration of production process,

Table 21.2 Merger motives

1. Efficiency	Managerial efficiency
	    acquire more efficient management
	    replace inefficient management

	Operating synergy
	    scale economies
	    acquire technical know-how
	    exploitation of markets
	    reduction of risk
	    improved liquidity

	Financial synergy
	    reduction of debt costs
	    increase in debt capacity

	Market power

2. Managerial	Agency considerations
	    managerial risk diversification
	    executive compensation
	    power, size and growth

3. Target undervaluation	Better analysis Insider information
4. Tax considerations	Loss carryovers Dividends vs. acquisitions

7. See Hal R. Varian, *op. cit.*

acquisition of marketing facilities, and so on. Although all of these are legitimate goals for management, it should be noted that a merger may *not* be a necessary condition for their fulfilment. In principle, these objectives are achievable via the alternative route of internal expansion. If the firm decides to expand via a merger, it should do so because the acquisition of the existing enterprise is more attractive than alternative methods of achieving the desired expansion. For example, despite the often lengthy and tedious legal negotiations necessary to conclude a merger, the acquisition of productive and marketing facilities, via merger, may still be considerably faster than trying to produce them from scratch. This can be of major importance when a firm desires to take advantage of market opportunities.

Motives cannot be observed and measured, and as a result, a wide variety of explanations for choosing the merger path have been put forth. The motivation for merger can be divided into four major categories: efficiency, managerial considerations, undervaluation, and taxes (see Table 21.2).

EFFICIENCY

The quest for efficiency is perhaps the most general and straightforward of all merger motives; but its generality poses a problem. Clearly the profit-seeking firms, other things being equal, will always prefer efficiency to inefficiency. It is, therefore, our task to differentiate that subset of efficiencies which can best be achieved by a merger, rather than by internal growth.

Acquisition of more efficient management

For many firms, management and other specialized personnel constitute a limited resource. Acquisition of another firm's management or production team, therefore, is often a primary motive for a merger. If the level of efficiency of the combined firm, after the merger, rises, such a merger represents a gain both to the firm and the economy as a whole.

Replacement of incompetent management

Mergers can, in some instances, be viewed as a way of eliminating bad management, if the takeover is accompanied by corporate reorganization.[8] In such a case, the merger represents a sort of 'civilized alternative to bankruptcy'. It is a kind of voluntary liquidation which transfers assets from a weaker/failing firm, to a stronger and more efficient one.

8. This aspect of the merger process has been examined by Andre Shleifer and Robert Vishny, 'Value maximization and the acquisition process,' *Journal of Economic Perspectives*, Winter 1988.

Operating synergy

Synergy, or the 'two plus two equals five' hypothesis, as it is sometimes called, concerns motives which are based on the claim that a merger may create a net gain to the merged firm. As a result, the combined value of the merged firm is greater than the sum of the two parts. *Operating synergy* refers to operating economies which may result in horizontal and vertical mergers. This type of synergy, to the degree that it exists, usually stems in horizontal mergers from economies of scale. More efficient utilization of capacity after the merger, cost savings from the elimination of duplicate facilities, better organization, etc. have all been mentioned as possible sources of operating synergy.

In a vertical combination, the source of the operating synergy may be more efficient coordination of the different levels of operation following the merger. Finally, by definition, we do not expect operating synergy from a conglomerate merger. The possibility of *financial synergy* will be examined in the section on conglomerate mergers below.

Managerial motives

It has been suggested that managers may be motivated by a desire to increase the size of their firms, because they believe their compensation will rise as a result of the increase in the size of the firm. In this context it should be noted that executive compensation is significantly correlated to profitability and not to size *per se*. On the other hand, managers may well have a desire to diversify their own employment risk by means of mergers which diversify the firm's activities, thereby stabilizing the corporation's income stream and reducing bankruptcy risk. From this viewpoint, the corporate managers' principal asset is their own 'human capital' and reputation. Since no market exists in which the risk attaching to such human capital can be diversified, managers may be motivated to diversify the firm by means of conglomerate mergers.[9]

Target undervaluation

If stock prices are sufficiently depressed, the acquisition of existing plant and equipment by merger may constitute a bargain relative to the alternative of investing in entirely new facilities. In terms of capital budgeting, the net present value of the acquisition of existing facilities is higher than that of the investment in new plant and equipment, and therefore, the merger should be preferred. This argument hinges on the existence, over a significantly long period of time, of imperfections in the capital market.

9. This hypothesis is suggested and empirically tested in Yakov Amihud and Baruch Lev, 'Risk Reduction as a Managerial Motive for Conglomerate Mergers,' *Bell Journal of Economics*, Autumn 1981.

Table 21.3 Factors considered in acquisitions

	Degree of importance[a]		
	Very important	Moderately important	Not important
1. Tax considerations	23.9%	52.1%	18.%
2. Opportunity to increase profitability through changes in management	21.2	46.7	27.4
3. Expansion into new markets and technology	66.8	20.1	8.1
4. Undervaluation to the prospective firm by the general market	40.9	47.1	8.1
5. Synergies due to economies of production	52.5	35.1	8.1
6. Increased market share	36.3	43.2	15.1
7. Diversification	26.6	37.5	31.3

[a] The percentages across an industry or size group may not add up to 100% because of nonresponse to this question.
Source: Marshall E. Blume, Irwin Friend, and Randolph Westerfield, 'Factors Affecting Capital Formation,' Rodney L. White Center for Financial Research, The Wharton School, University of Pennsylvania, December 1984.

Tax benefits

Corporate income taxes and inheritance taxes have often provided the underlying motive for a merger. A firm with a large tax loss carry-forward is ripe for a merger with a firm with sufficient current profits to ensure that the tax benefits will not expire due to insufficient earnings. Similarly the anticipated need to pay inheritance taxes may lead a profitable, but closely held family firm, to seek a merger with a larger firm which has more readily marketable common stock. After the merger, the owners of the family-held firm typically will hold the larger firm's stock which can be more readily sold when the need arises.

In 1984, a sample of U.S. firms was surveyed on their willingness to expand by means of the acquisition of existing companies rather than the purchase of new assets (see Table 21.3). The proportion of firms preferring the merger route was over 40%. The surveyed firms were also asked to indicate the factors which influenced the choice between the two methods of expansion. The firms indicated that the most important reason to acquire control of another firm rather than to purchase new plant and equipment was to provide for expansion into new markets and technology. Potential synergies due to economies of production, research or marketing were next in importance, followed by undervaluation of the targeted firms by the general market.

RISK DIVERSIFICATION AND CONGLOMERATE MERGERS

The rapid rise of the inter-industry conglomerate giants raises questions which are difficult to answer within the traditional framework of merger theory. That horizontal and vertical mergers can potentially produce real economic gains is nowhere denied; in fact, the central problem of antitrust policy stems from the possible existence of economies strong enough to offset the socially unacceptable features of some of these mergers. Expansion by means of such mergers may create significant economies of scale in production, research, distribution and management; the case of a conglomerate merger is less clear. The traditional analysis relating to the possible creation of economies of scale is not relevant for the *pure* conglomerate.

The portfolio diversification and valuation model presented in Part II of the book provides a convenient vehicle for analyzing the potential gains from conglomerate growth.[10] The essence of the portfolio approach is that a purely conglomerate merger between *unrelated* firms can help stabilize overall corporate income, because the variability of the combined income streams will be reduced following the combination of statistically independent or negatively correlated income streams. At first glance, it would seem that the pooling of unrelated income streams as a result of a conglomerate merger should produce an improved risk–return position for investors. In an efficient capital market, however, these same advantages of risk diversification can be achieved by means of individual shareholder portfolio diversification. Thus, the diversification argument depends on the existence of some sort of imperfection in the capital market.[11]

Real-life capital markets are not perfectly efficient. For example, substantial economies of scale exist in the new issues market; large firms have better access to the capital markets and also enjoy significant cost savings when securing their financial needs. These cost savings presumably reflect, at least in part, the reduction in bankruptcy risk achieved through diversification. If we assume that in any given year (or run of years) there exists for each individual firm some positive probability of suffering losses large enough to induce financial failure, it can be shown that the joint probability of such an event is reduced by a conglomerate merger. The possibility that the critical level of losses will occur simultaneously for each of the component companies making up the merger is less (and often very much less) than the individual probabilities.

An example

Suppose that firms A and B have the following future cash flows (in million dollars):

Firm A		Firm B	
Probability	Cash flow (x)	Probability	Cash flow (y)
1/3	−10	1/3	−10
1/3	20	1/3	20
1/3	30	1/3	30

10. The potential gains from conglomerate growth are analyzed in greater detail in Appendix 21A.
11. The following three paragraphs are based on Haim Levy and Marshall Sarnat, 'Diversification, Portfolio Analysis and the Uneasy Case for Conglomerate Mergers,' *Journal of Finance*, September 1970.

For simplicity, also assume that the cash flow is negative if the firm is bankrupt. Therefore, we have,

Probability of A going bankrupt: $P_A(x \leqslant 0) = 1/3$
Probability of B going bankrupt: $P_B(y \leqslant 0) = 1/3$

Suppose now that firms A and B merge and the cash flows x and y are statistically independent, which fits the conglomerate merger. After the merger we have the cash flow $z = x + y$, given as follows:

Cash flow of firm A + B	
Probability	Cash flow $z = x + y$
1/9	− 20
2/9	+10
2/9	+ 20
1/9	+ 40
2/9	+ 50
1/9	+ 60

Hence, the probability of bankruptcy is given by:

$$P_{B+C}(z \leqslant 0) = 1/9$$

Thus, the probability of bankruptcy is dramatically reduced after the merger. One may claim that the reduction in the probability of bankruptcy is due to the fact that the investment in A + B is double the investment in A or in B. This is a false claim. To see this, suppose that firms A and B are identical in size. An investor is considering buying firm A (or B) or half of the merged firm A + B. In the latter case, his cash flow will be half of the cash flow z, and the probability of bankruptcy is still 1/9, in comparison with 1/3 in the case that he buys firm A.

Thus, we can safely conclude that the merger reduces the probability of bankruptcy. The fact that merger reduces the probability of bankruptcy can be illustrated graphically. Figure 21.1 shows three cases of mergers. The

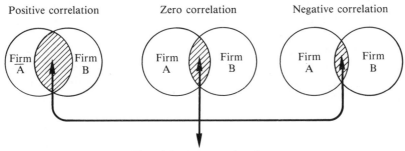

Figure 21.1 Probability of bankruptcy before and after the merger.

probability of bankruptcy of A (or B) is given by the circle. The shaded area indicates the probability of bankruptcy of the merged firm A + B. Obviously, the lower the correlation between the cash flow A and B, the lower the shaded area, hence the smaller the probability that the merged firm will go bankrupt. The intuitive explanation is straightforward; with a negative correlation, a negative value of x is likely to be followed with a positive value of y, hence $z = x + y > 0$ and bankruptcy is avoided. On the other hand, with a positive correlation, a negative value of x is likely to be followed with a negative (or low) value of y, hence bankruptcy is not reduced as much as in the negative correlation case.

In this instance, diversification can be expected to create a true economic gain to the shareholders. The combination of the financial resources of the two firms making up the merger reduces the costs of bankruptcy risk while combining each of the individual shares of the two companies in investors' portfolios does not. Since in this case capital market diversification is *not* a perfect substitute for corporate diversification, the latter provides a source of potential gain to investors.

A parallel argument on behalf of conglomerate mergers can be made in terms of enhanced borrowing power. The lowering of the firm's bankruptcy risk, following the merger, permits an increase of the firm's borrowing capacity, i.e., an increase in the optimal debt/equity ratio. Thus the combined firm can increase the degree of leverage employed beyond what was possible before. As we have already seen in Chapter 15, this will increase the market value of the firm's shares.

VALUATION IN MERGERS

Assuming that for any of the above-mentioned reasons, two firms have decided upon a merger, several formal conditions must be fulfilled. Obviously the proposed merger must be approved by the respective boards of directors, and perhaps, less obviously, it must also be ratified by the shareholders (usually by two-thirds majority) of both firms. This clears the way for putting through the proposal. However, even at this late stage the Antitrust Division of the Department of Justice, or the Federal Trade Commission can seek an injunction against the merger under Section 7 of the Clayton Act on the grounds that it lessens competition.

In essence, two alternatives are open to the merging firms: one can either purchase the assets of the second, or alternatively, it can assume responsibility for both the assets and the liabilities of the acquired firm by purchasing its stock. Only in the latter instance does the acquired company necessarily cease to exist as a separate corporate entity. In either case, payment by the acquiring company can be made either in cash or in securities. The advantage of the latter form of payment lies in the deferment of tax until the securities are sold.

Assume that for tax purposes, or for any other reasons, firm A acquires firm B by exchanging its stock for the stock of B. This establishes a *ratio of exchange*, that is the price of B's stock in terms of the stock of A. Several different benchmarks have been suggested at one time or another to help the firm's management in such negotiations.

Net asset value

One possibility would be to measure a firm's value by net asset value per share, or *book value* as it is usually called. But the use of book values has some very serious drawbacks as a measure of value. Since accounting values depend on assets' historical costs, inflation makes their use all but meaningless. The sole remaining function of this approach apparently is to serve as a convenient straw man to be killed off periodically by the writers of textbooks. A more sophisticated approach would be to estimate the current *replacement value* of the firm's assets, deduct the liabilities, thereby deriving a book value figure which has been adjusted for changes in price levels. But even such a procedure is unsatisfactory. Not all of the assets listed in the balance sheet have value, and, conversely, not all of the firm's valuable assets appear in its balance sheet. Thus, for example, the adjusted book value approach may overstate the true value of the firm by including assets which may become obsolete after the merger. On the other hand, it may understate value by excluding all intangible assets for which original cost is nil, for example, mineral deposits, business connections, management know-how, and so on.

Earnings per share

Another possibility would be to examine the impact of the merger on the earnings per share (EPS) of the acquiring company. For simplicity, consider the following example of firm A which is considering the acquisition of the stock of firm B:

	Firm A	Firm B
Current earnings ($)	10,000,000	1,000,000
Number of shares	5,000,000	1,000,000
EPS ($)	2.00	1.00
Stock price ($)	30.00	10.00
Price/earnings ratio	15	10

What is the maximum price that firm A can offer for firm B's shares, without incurring an *initial dilution* of per share earnings of the merged firm? If firm A offers $12 per share (that is a 20% premium over B's current market price) the exchange ratio will be $12/$30 which is 0.4 shares of A for each share of B. Hence A will issue 400,000 new shares to the former shareholders of company B. Assuming no change in earnings of the combined firm, earnings per share of the merged company become:

Total earnings	$11,000,000
Number of shares	5,400,000
EPS	$2.04

Thus the EPS of the combined firms rises to $2.04 at the expense, so to speak of company B's shareholders, each of whom receives 0.4 shares of stock of A for every share of B formerly held. As a result, the EPS of these shareholders falls from $1.00 to $0.82 ($0.4 \times 2.04$) following the merger. Should firm A offer $20 per share for the stock of company B the opposite result occurs. In this case, the exchange ratio is $20/$30 or about 0.667 shares of A for every share of B; hence 667,000 shares of A must be issued in payment for the shares of B and initial earnings per share of the combined firm become:

Earnings	$11,000,000
Number of shares	5,667,000
EPS	$1.97

In this case, the EPS of the combined firm falls from $2.00 to $1.97; this time at the expense of the shareholders of firm A. No dilution for either party takes place when company A offers the shareholder of B a price compatible with its own price/earnings ratio, in our example $15. At this price 500,000 new shares are issued and the earnings per share before and after the merger remain the same for all parties concerned.

Despite the popularity of such calculations in practice, the impact of a merger on current earnings per share is a *very deficient* guide for managerial decisions, for the following reasons:

1. As we have emphasized throughout the book, *future* earnings and not current earnings should be considered in the valuation of a firm's stock.
2. Concentration on the merger's initial impact on EPS tacitly assumes that a merger is a purely additive process. This can be misleading in cases where complementarities are expected to lead to 'synergistic' growth: that is, the sum of the parts following the merger is expected to be greater than the sum of the individual contributions.
3. Finally, and by far the most important deficiency, stems from the fact that EPS comparisons tacitly assume that the earnings of the two firms are of the same quality, that is, they have the same risk. But this is often *not* the case.

Market price comparisons

A straightforward solution to the above-mentioned problems would be to compare the market prices of the two firms' stocks, since these prices presumably reflect the market's evaluation of the shares' future growth potential and risk. In our numerical example, the exchange ratio, using the market price rule, would be set at $10/$30 and each shareholder in firm B would receive one-third of a share of the stock of company A for every share of B held. But once again, difficulties are encountered. Technical problems may also arise regarding which particular price should be used – that of a particular day, an average over a particular month, and so on. Also, the prices of the individual firms' shares may not reflect the full extent of the potential increases in the combined market value of the two companies following the merger. Clearly, much room remains for negotiation, and as a rule the 'buying firm' will have to offer the sellers a premium over current market price to induce them to enter the merger.

PRESENT VALUE ANALYSIS

Merger is a subject for which market values may not be a reliable indicator of value. For example, the value of the target as a separate entity can be significantly different from its value in a merger. This, of course, is the source of the *premium* over market price which buying firms are often willing to pay to acquire the target firm.

One way to handle this dilemma is to treat the acquisition of another firm by merger as a special type of capital budgeting problem. From the standpoint of the acquiring firm, this requires the estimation of the merger's impact on the cash flow of the combined firm. If the present value of the benefits exceeds the price paid to the target firm's shareholders, the merger is desirable. The target company's shareholders, of course, will accept the merger offer if they deem that the proposed price exceeds the present value of the cash flows which will be generated by the target company *without the merger*.

On the surface the present value approach appears relatively simple, but in practice, this is not the case. In order to reach a correct evaluation of the target, the acquiring firm must solve a number of problems:

1. Operating synergies, which are often the motivating force for the merger, are difficult to estimate.
2. Similarly, the full impact of the replacement of inefficient managers is also hard to gauge in advance.
3. A tendency also exists for buyers to overstate the value of the target's assets. For example, not all of its inventories may actually be saleable, nor all of its receivables collectable.
4. It is difficult to tell just how the target's key personnel will adapt to the acquiring firm's management style. Moreover, a post-merger decision to trim excess staff may evoke opposition or even a strike.
5. Even if the cash flow is correctly assessed, its riskiness must still be estimated in order to arrive at the appropriate discount rate.

FINANCING CORPORATE MERGERS WITH CONVERTIBLES _____

In the previous sections we often assumed that if a merger is effected by means of an exchange of securities, the target firm's shareholders receive the stock of the surviving corporation in payment. Clearly this need not be the case. The deferment of taxation, inherent in an exchange of common stock, can also be realized when other types of security are offered in payment. One popular expedient has been the use of convertible bonds or convertible preferred stock to finance corporate mergers. The use of a convertible fixed-income security has several advantages:

1. It permits a reconciliation of divergent dividend policies of the acquiring and acquired firms. For this purpose it is sufficient to consider the case of an acquiring firm which pays no dividend and an acquired firm whose shareholders wish to continue to receive their regular dividend payment after the merger.
2. Convertible debentures can also be used to avoid the dilution of earnings which occurs, when after the merger, the earnings per share of one of the firms fall. However, it should be emphasized that the Securities and Exchange Commission requires companies to report their 'fully diluted earnings,' i.e., the EPS based on the assumption that all outstanding convertible securities are converted to common stock.

SOME ACCOUNTING CONSIDERATIONS _____

As is so often the case in finance, mergers also have some implications for the firm's accounting staff. In general, two alternative accounting treatments are available. The combination of the two firms in a merger can be handled as a *pooling of interests* or as a *purchase*. In the latter case, any payment beyond the tangible book value of the acquired firm must be shown as *goodwill* in the balance sheet and written off over a reasonable period of time. Since the depreciation of goodwill is not deductible for tax purposes, further net income will be reduced as the goodwill is amortized, which constitutes a psychological and perhaps an economic disadvantage of this type of treatment. A pooling of interests, on the other hand, avoids this disadvantage by combining the balance sheets of the two firms, i.e., the assets and liabilities are simply added together. In this approach neither goodwill, nor charges against future income, are created. Unfortunately, this type of accounting treatment has led to some abuse; in particular so-called 'dirty pooling', i.e., the altering of asset value at the time of merger. As a result of such abuse, the pooling of interests method has been legally restricted to mergers of firms of roughly the same size in which both managements continue to function in the merged firm.

Up to this point, we have assumed a simple scenario in which one of the parties to a merger (the acquiring firm) decides to acquire another firm, which we have called the target firm. Implicitly we have been assuming a *friendly merger*. In such cases, the acquiring company approaches the target firm with a proposal to merge. The two firms' managements then sit down to try and work out suitable terms for the merger. If they succeed, the merger plan is submitted to both firm's shareholders along with managements' recommendation that the merger be approved. If the shareholders, in turn, approve the merger, the acquiring firm buys the target firm's shares (in accordance with the terms of the agreement) paying for them with their own securities (shares or bonds) or with cash.

The above description no longer characterizes the 'merger mania' of the 1980s. More and more frequently, target companies have attempted to fight off attempts at acquisition, either because they feel the merger is not in the best interests of the shareholders, or perhaps out of fear for their own jobs. But whatever the motivation, we denote such a situation as a *hostile merger*. Since a joint agreement of the merger terms is not possible in such cases, the acquir-- ing company will usually make a *takeover bid* to the target firm's shareholders.

Takeover bids

Since negotiation between managements (and boards of directors) of the interested firms is not possible in a hostile merger, the acquiring firm can circumvent the target company's management by appealing directly to its shareholders. Such an appeal is known as a *takeover bid* or *tender offer*. Usually, it takes the form of one company approving, with great publicity, its offer to purchase the shares of the target company for a price which usually involves a substantial premium over the prevailing market price. Alternatively, the acquiring company might offer a package of its own securities in return for the target stock. Of course, the target company's management, if it objects, can employ counter-tactics.

In some cases, the acquiring firm may make a so-called *two-tier offer*. This is a takeover bid that provides better terms to the shareholders who tender their shares early. For example, a two-tier takeover bid might provide a cash price for sufficient shares to obtain control of the corporation, and a lower non-cash (securities) price for the remaining stock. Thus in the U.S. Steel Corporation's bid for Marathon Oil (see Table 21.1), a cash price was offered for 51% of the stock on a first come basis. The remaining stock could only be exchanged for bonds, which presumably induced many shareholders to offer their stock immediately to ensure the receipt of cash rather than bonds. Similarly, in the summer of 1981, DuPont offered Conoco's shareholders cash for 40% of the outstanding shares plus 1.7 shares of DuPont for the balance.

Partial takeovers

The hostile mergers of the 1980s led to an additional phenomenon – the *partial stock buyout*. In a partial buyout an investor or group of investors buys a sizeable stake in a company which it considers undervalued, and therefore, a good candidate for a takeover by another firm. If the investor guesses correctly, and a takeover bid with a significant premium over the target stock's market price is forthcoming, the investor stands to make a substantial profit. This type of speculation has been called *risk arbitrage*. But at least one of the principal practitioners of this art decided to take the risk out of risk arbitrage by obtaining information in advance of impending mergers. However, the use of such insider information is illegal under U.S. security laws, and in November 1986, Ivan Boesky, one of Wall Street's leading risk arbitrageurs, agreed to pay a $100 million fine to the SEC and later went to jail for the abuse of insider information obtained from an investment banker.

Merger defenses

The merger wars which swept the United States in the 1980s consumed enormous amounts of time, cash and corporate resources. Embattled managements, trying to avoid takeovers, created a virtual maze of defenses. They also created a new lexicon – the language of takeovers (see Table 21.4). With the help of outside advisors (investment bankers and law firms specializing in mergers) many target firms in an unfriendly merger scenario attempted to fight off the takeover by recourse to so-called *shark repellents*. These are anti-takeover corporate charter amendments, such as super-majority requirements for approving a nonuniform two-tier takeover bid which has not been approved by the board of directors.

Another policy which has been used frequently is so-called *greenmail*. This is the premium paid by a target firm to an acquiring firm (or individual) in exchange for its own shares. Alternatively, the acquiring firm may pay a premium to another competing acquiring firm (or individual) to get hold of its holdings of the target firm's shares. Thus, for example, in the Texaco – Getty merger (see Table 21.1), Texaco bought the Bass Brothers' immense holdings of Texaco stock at a 20% premium over market price, apparently out of a fear that the Bass Brothers might attempt to gain control of Texaco. Many analysts consider this purchase to have amounted to the payment of *greenmail* by Texaco's management.

Another anti-takeover tactic is the *lockup defense*. In this strategy, management gives a third party the right to buy the firm's assets in order to persuade the acquiring firm to drop its bid. This ploy is particularly effective when the targeted company offers for sale its *crown jewel*, i.e., the most valued asset held by the target firm.

Yet another tactic is the *Pac-Man defense*, in which a targeted company tries to buy up its 'attacker's' stock. Thus, for example, after Bendix made an 'unfriendly' attempt to take over Martin Marietta, the latter counterattacked by buying up Bendix stock. This case is of special interest, because a third party, Allied Corporation, came to Bendix's defense by buying enough Bendix stock to preclude Martin Marietta's gaining control of Bendix. In the language of takeovers this made Allied a *white knight*, a partner solicited by the management of a target firm to help fight off the attempted takeover.

Table 21.4 The language of corporate takeovers

Crown jewel: The most valued asset held by an acquisition target; divestiture of this asset is frequently a sufficient defense to dissuade takeover.

Fair price amendment: Requires super majority approval of nonuniform, or two-tier, takeover bids not approved by the board of directors; can be avoided by a uniform bid for less than all outstanding shares (subject to prorationing under federal law if the offer is oversubscribed).

Going private: The purchase of publicly owned stock of a company by the existing or another competing managment group; the company is delisted and public trading in the stock ceases.

Golden parachutes: The provisions in the employment contracts of top-level managers that provide for severance pay or other compensation should they lose their jobs as a result of a takeover.

Greenmail: The premium paid by a targeted company to a raider in exchange for his shares of the targeted company.

Leveraged buyout: The purchase of publicly owned stock of a company by the existing management with a portion of the purchase price financed by outside investors: the company is delisted and public trading in the stock ceases.

Lockup defense: Gives a friendly party (see white knight) the right to purchase assets of a firm, in particular the crown jewel, thus dissuading a takeover attempt.

Maiden: A term sometimes used to refer to the company at which the takeover is directed (target).

Poison pill: Gives stockholders other than those involved in a hostile takeover the right to purchase securities at a very favorable price in the event of a takeover.

Proxy contest: The solicitation of stockholder votes generally for the purpose of electing a slate of directors in competition with the current directors.

Raider: The person(s) or corporation attempting the takeover.

Shark repellents: Anti-takeover corporate charter amendments such as staggered terms for directors, super-majority requirement for approving a merger, or mandate that bidders pay the same price for all shares in a buyout.

Standstill agreement: A contract in which a raider or firm agrees to limit its holdings in the target firm and not attempt a takeover.

Stripper: A successful raider who, once the targer is acquired, sells off some of the assets of the target company.

Target: The company at which the takeover attempt is directed.

Targeted repurchase: A repurchase of common stock from an individual holder or a tender repurchase that excludes an individual holder; the former is the most frequent form of greenmail, while the latter is a common defensive tactic.

Tender offer: An offer made directly to shareholders to buy some or all of their shares for a specified price during a specified time.

Two-tier offer: A takeover offer that provides a cash price for sufficient shares to obtain control of the corporation, then a lower non-cash (securities) price for the remaining shares.

White knight: A merger partner solicited by management of a target who offers an alternative merger plan to that offered by the raider which protects the target company from the attempted takeover.

Source: *Federal Reserve Bank of St. Louis Review*, 67, 10, December 1985, p. 17.

The targeted firm can also employ a *poison pill*. This gives shareholders of a firm not involved in the takeover the right to buy the target firm's securities at a favourable price if the takeover goes through, and so on.

Even if management gives up the fight, they can still award themselves *golden parachutes*. These are provisions in the executives' employment contracts which call for the payment of severance pay, or other compensation, should they lose their jobs as a result of a successful takeover.

WHO GAINS FROM MERGERS?

Mergers in general, and the merger mania of the 1980s in particular, is a controversial subject. Greenmail, corporate raiding, shark repellents, and the time wasted on short-term merger and anti-merger strategies have all come under attack at one time or another. Moreover, the insider trading abuses which accompanied the latest merger wave have been the subject of government litigation. On the positive side, takeovers seem to promote a more efficient use of resources in target firms, thereby contributing to the efficient working of capital markets.

The quantitative measurement of the impact of mergers is very difficult but the following generalizations can be supported by the available empirical evidence: [12]

1. The market value of target firms tends to rise in takeover attempts. Selling shareholders almost always receive a substantial premium over market price. Thus, it is the shareholders of the acquired firm who stand to gain in a merger. The average premium over market price enjoyed by target firms' shareholders has been estimated at between 20 and 35%. [13]
2. The evidence is less clear with respect to the buyers. Even if we assume that they do gain from the mergers, their gain is proportionately much less than that of the sellers.
3. The empirical evidence suggests that attempts to fight off a takeover attempt by means of shark repellents and poison pills has a depressing effect on stock prices. [14]

12. The literature on mergers is voluminous. The empirical evidence on the economic impact of takeovers is summarized in: Michael C. Jensen and R. Ruback, 'The Market for Corporate Control: The Scientific Evidence,' *Journal of Financial Economics*, April 1983; and Gregg A. Jarrel, James A. Brickley, and Jeffrey M. Netter, 'The Market for Corporate Control: The Empirical Evidence Since 1980,' *Journal of Economic Perspectives*, Winter 1988.
13. *Ibid*. These figures probably underestimate the gains since many empirical studies ignore price increases prior to the formal announcement of the takeover bid.
14. See, for example, Michael Ryngaert, 'The Effect of Poison Pill Securities on Shareholder Wealth,' *Journal of Financial Economics*, 20, 1988.

To this point we have examined situations in which one firm decides to acquire the productive assets of another. Divestitures, spinoffs, and going private are kinds of reverse merger phenomenon in which a firm is interested in getting rid of some of its assets.

A divestiture is a sale by the firm of a division or a subsidiary to another firm, usually in exchange for cash and notes. Thus in one sense, a divestiture can be thought of as a sort of partial merger in which a part of the selling firm has been merged into the buying firm. The sale by International Paper of its Canadian subsidiary to Canadian Pacific, and U.S. Steel's sale of part of its coal facilities to Standard Oil of Ohio, are two examples of corporate divestitures.

Many motives have been suggested for corporate divestitures:

1. An important motive for many divestitures is the desire to generate cash for other purposes. For example, the selling firm may wish to reduce its debt to expand into other lines of activity, to build a war chest for a contemplated takeover bid, or even to build up a cash reserve in order to fight off a hostile takeover.
2. Some companies are motivated by a desire to divest themselves of an unprofitable line of business activity, or a business which does not fit their long-run strategic design.
3. Some firms feel that they are undervalued by the market. The sale of part of their assets at their true market value is designed to induce the market to recognize this error and raise the firm's stock price.

'Going private' refers to the purchase of a company from its shareholders by a group of private owners which may include the firm's existing managers. After the transaction, the shares are delisted and public trading in the stock ceases. Going private enables a firm to avoid listing costs which can be significant for a small firm. Secondly, by concentrating ownership, more effective monitoring of managerial performance becomes possible, and this can be expected to have a positive impact on management performance.

Considerable interest has been generated by a special type of managerial buyout – the leveraged buyout (LBO). An LBO is a type of divestiture in which the existing management joins with other investors to buy a firm from its shareholders using loans to finance the purchase. Following the buyout, public trading in the stock ceases, although the new owners can again 'go public' at some later date. The key feature of LBOs has been the extremely high degree of leverage employed. A classic example of such an LBO is provided by RCA's sale of Gibson Greeting Cards to a group of investors, which included Gibson's own management team, for $81 million. The purchasers put up only $1 million dollars in cash; the remaining $80 million was raised by bank loans. This particular scenario had a 'happy ending' – at least for Gibson's buyers, if not for RCA. A year after the LBO, Gibson went public and the purchasing group's original equity investment of $1 million dollars was worth more than one hundred times its original cost in the market.

A spin-off is a special type of divestiture in which no cash is involved and there is no shift in ownership. In a spin-off, the divested division is *given* to the shareholders of the parent firm. The parent corporation issues shares to its present shareholders who remain the owners of both the parent and its off-spring. The newly-created entity is operated as a separate corporation with its own board of directors, officers, etc.

The motivation for a spin-off is not always clear. Some may be undertaken to avoid certain regulatory or institutional constraints. Setting up a separate entity may also improve owners' ability to assess managerial performance, thereby providing a positive incentive to management.

HOLDING COMPANIES

In addition to the three types of company mergers, a frequently encountered form of corporate organization is the holding company. A holding company is simply a firm whose purpose is to hold a controlling interest in one or more other corporations, known as its subsidiaries. The controlling interest need *not* be 51% of the outstanding stock. Given the dispersion of ownership of most large modern firms, holding as little as 10% of the voting stock often provides effective control. In many respects, a holding company shares both the advantages and disadvantages of other large-scale operations, such as mergers, consolidations, or a single, large company with multiple national divisions. However, the holding company is unique in several aspects. On the positive side, it permits a high degree of leverage through fractional ownership; isolation of risk due to the preservation of legal distinctions among its subsidiaries; and the ability to gain control of other firms without obtaining formal shareholder or management approval. On the other hand, the holding company is subject to multiple taxation, since dividends received from subsidiaries constitute taxable income; is often more expensive to administer than a single, unified corporation; and due to its high leverage, profitability is extremely volatile.

SUMMARY

This chapter distinguishes three types of business consolidation:

1. Horizontal mergers in which the assets of two or more competing firms are combined.
2. Vertical mergers in which one firm acquires control over the sources of its raw materials or over the sales outlets for its final products.
3. Conglomerate mergers in which otherwise economically unrelated firms are consolidated.

Many business firms seek profitable growth, risk diversification, integration of productive facilities, and the acquisition of marketing facilities. However, these objectives, in principle, can be achieved either internally via capital investments or externally by means of the acquisition of other firms. The principal motives for choosing the second alternative are: efficiency, managerial considerations, undervaluation, diversification, and taxes.

At one time or another the U.S. economy has witnessed waves of mergers of all three types: horizontal, vertical, and conglomerate. In the mid-1960s conglomerate forms of combination became dominant. The absence in a pure conglomerate merger of the traditional economies of scale in production, research, distribution and management raises doubts about the potential gains from such acquisitions. In fact, in a *perfectly efficient* security market the risk diversification created by a conglomerate merger would not lead to a true economic gain. However, in practice, security markets are not absolutely perfect, and the possibility of gain is restored by considerations relating to the reduction of bankruptcy risk and the economies of scale in the raising of new capital which such a reduction implies.

Several methods were examined that can be used to help management set a price for the target company's shares: net asset value, earnings per share, comparisons of market prices, and present value of cash flows.

The 1980s and 1990s witnessed a flood of 'unfriendly' mergers in which the takeover attempts have been actively opposed by the target firms. These merger battles raised serious questions regarding the economic impact of such combinations. They also have created a colorful new language: 'greenmail', 'white knights', 'shark repellents', etc.

_____ SUMMARY TABLE

Types of merger

1. Horizontal – between two similar businesses.
2. Vertical – acquisition of source of raw materials or sales outlets.
3. Conglomerate – between two unrelated businesses.

Motives for mergers

1. Efficiency.
2. Managerial.
3. Target undervaluation.
4. Tax considerations.

Synergy – the net gain which result from a merger

1. Operating synergy (scale economies, acquisition of technological know-how, exploitation of markets, risk reduction).
2. Financial synergy (increased debt capacity, lower cost of capital).

Defensive tactics against takeover bids

1. Shark Repellents – anti-takeover amendments in a company's charter.
2. Green mail – premium paid to an acquiring firm by the target firm for the purchase of its own stock.
3. Lockup defense – rights given to a third party by the target firm to acquire shares in order to thwart the ambitions of an acquiring firm.
4. Sale of the crown jewel – sale of a target firm's most valued asset.
5. 'White knight' defense – solicitation of an additional partner on the part of the target firm to help fight off a hostile acquisition bid.
6. 'Poison pills' – rights given to a third party to acquire shares at a favorable price should the merger go through.
7. Pac-Man defense – acquisition of the acquiring firm's shares by the target firm.
8. 'Golden parachutes – provisions in the employment contracts of top executives for generous compensation arrangements should they lose their positions as a result of a takeover.

QUESTIONS AND PROBLEMS

21.1 Explain briefly the nature of the *potential* gain in horizontal, vertical, and conglomerate mergers.

21.2 'Nobody would want to buy a firm with a large loss carry-forward, since this is an indication of an unprofitable business.' Critically evaluate this statement.

21.3 What synergies exist in: (a) horizontal mergers, (b) vertical mergers, (c) conglomerate mergers?

21.4 'Our conglomerate simply buys firms whose stock is undervalued.' What implicit assumptions are necessary to make this a reasonable strategy?

21.5 'In order to improve the risk–return position of investors, companies should merge into conglomerates.' Under what conditions is this statement incorrect?

21.6 Why might a conglomerate pay lower interest rates than one of its individual components?

21.7 Assume a capital market which meets all of the conditions of a perfect market with the exception of the absence of taxation. Can an investor gain from a pure conglomerate merger in such a situation? Explain.

21.8 In the absence of any synergy, could you expect a purely conglomerate merger between two very large firms? Explain.

21.9 What problems arise when present value analysis is used for the valuation of a merger target?

21.10 Why would an acquiring firm make a two-tier offer?

21.11 Can a 'golden parachute' be employed to defend against a hostile takeover?

21.12 There are three identical firms each with cash flow of;

       $-\$10$ million with probability of $1/5$
       $+\$15$ million with probability of $4/5$

The three firms' cash flows are statistically independent. Whenever the cash flow is negative, the firm goes bankrupt. Suppose that two of the three firms merged. What is the joint probability of bankruptcy. What is the probability of bankruptcy if all three firms merge?

21.13 Repeat question 21.12, this time assume that only two firms merge and when the cash flows are: (a) fully positively correlated, (b) fully negatively correlated.

21.14 Two firms A and B merged. Each firm has the following income cash flow before interest:

       $\$+5$ million with a probability of $1/5$
       $\$+15$ million with a probability of $4/5$

However, firm A has interest debt payment of $6 million while firm B has no debt at all. Whenever the income is lower than the interest bill, bankruptcy is declared.

(a) Calculate the probability of bankruptcy of each firm before the merger.
(b) What is the probability of bankruptcy of the merged firm?

Assume that the cash flows are independent.

APPENDIX 21A: PORTFOLIO ANALYSIS OF CONGLOMERATE DIVERSIFICATION

Let us assume a pure conglomerate merger between two completely unrelated companies. Thus, the correlation of the returns on the two firms is assumed to be zero. The same analysis also holds, however, for a nonzero correlation case. In the absence of synergistic effects, the post-merger rate of return to shareholders in the new firm will be the weighted average of the returns of each of the individual firms making up the merger. In terms of the expected rate of return we have:

$$E = PE_1 + (1 - P)E_2$$

where:

    E_1 and E_2 = expected rates of return of the two firms making up the merger
           E = expected rate of return after the merger
           P = relative size of the first firm
    $(1 - P)$ = relative size of the second firm

Thus, if an investor diversifies $1 in proportion P and $(1 - P)$ in the two firms, his expected rate of return would be given by E.

Since we are assuming zero correlation between the returns of the two individual firms, the total post-merger variance (σ^2) will be lower than the simple sum of the individual variances:

$$\sigma^2 = P^2\sigma_1^2 + (1 - P)^2\sigma_2^2$$

As we have also assumed that the expected return after the merger is a weighted average of the individual expected returns, the risk—return characteristics of the new firm represents an 'efficient' combination.

Gain from diversification: perfect capital market

It would appear to follow, that the shares of the new firm should sell at a premium *vis-à-vis* the weighted sum of the pre-merger prices of the shares of the individual firms. However, such a premium will *not* be forthcoming in a perfectly efficient capital market because the superior post-merger risk—return combination could have been achieved by investors, even in the absence of the merger, by combining the individual shares of the two firms in their portfolios in the proportions P and $(1 - P)$. Despite the stabilizing diversification effect, a conglomerate merger *per se*, does not necessarily create opportunities for risk diversification over and beyond those which were available to individual (and institutional) investors prior to the merger. In a perfect security market, the pre-merger equilibrium price of the shares would reflect the possibility of all such combinations and, therefore, no increase in the combined market value of the two firms, after the merger has been effected, is to be expected, or in fact, is even possible.[15]

This proposition is illustrated in Figure 21A.1. For simplicity, we assume a securities

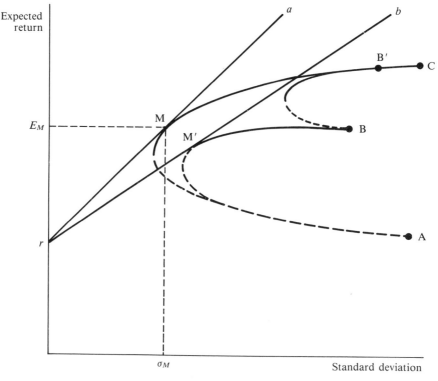

Figure 21A.1

15. A formal proof of the 'neutrality' of a pure conglomerate merger in a perfect capital market is given in Haim Levy and Marshall Sarnat, 'Diversification, Portfolio Analysis and the Uneasy Case for Conglomerate Mergers,' *Journal of Finance*, September 1970.

market in which the shares of only three companies are traded.[16] AMC is the envelope curve of efficient combinations of the three companies (A, B, C) assumed to comprise the market; the market opportunity line, *ra*, rising from the riskless rate of interest *r*, reflects the assumption that lending or borrowing, at the rate *r*, can take place. Applying the CAPM, the slope of this line uniquely determines the tradeoff between expected return and risk for all investors, independent of their tastes.[17] And as we have seen in Chapter 12, the proportions of investment in each share included in portfolio M are optimal for every investor in the market. Since a pure conglomerate merger does not alter the optimal proportions of investment in the various shares, point M represents both the pre-merger and post-merger equilibrium risk portfolio. Thus, in the absence of synergism, the stabilization of returns induced by such a merger, does not produce a clear-cut economic gain in a perfect capital market.

Gain from diversification: imperfect capital market

Given the neutrality of conglomerate mergers in a perfect capital market, we now turn to the possible influence of market imperfections on the economic effects of such mergers. In practice, investors do not include all available securities in their portfolios because of differential transactions costs, costs of acquiring information and the difficulties of keeping track of numerous investments. The New York Stock Exchange Shareholders' Surveys show that individual investors, on the average, typically hold less than four stocks in their portfolios.

For simplicity we shall assume that for all, or some, of the above reasons, an investor confines his portfolio to *two shares only*, A and B. The impact of such restrictions on optimal portfolios can also be seen in Figure 21A.1. All possible efficient combinations of A and B lie on the envelope curve AM'B, with M' on this curve representing the optimal unlevered portfolio, given the constraint that the investor restricts his portfolio to these two shares only. The new optimum portfolio is tangent to the market opportunity line, *rb*, which lies *below* the *ra* line. Thus all attainable positions under the two share constraint are inferior to the three share case, and represent a reduction of utility to the investor.

Despite the two share constraint, the investor, following a merger of companies B and C, can again invest in all of the shares of the market, that is, in the new merger (B + C) and in company A. To determine whether the merger has improved the investor's position, we first find the combination of shares B and C that the merger permits the investor to add to his portfolio. This combination lies on the envelope curve BB'C which is constructed with no special restriction on the proportions of investment in shares B and C. But, after the merger the proportions of B and C are *fixed*, and the envelope curve BB'C reduces to a point, such as B'. The post-merger point B' represents a new composite security with fixed proportions which reflect the relative size of the two companies making up the merger.

Following the merger, the investor can combine shares B' and A when constructing his portfolio. A new envelope curve representing the efficient combinations of share A and the 'composite' merger share B' is formed. If the new envelope curve crosses the *rb* market line the investor will have improved his position. Thus, unlike the case of the perfect market, the conglomerate merger in an imperfect market does allow a degree of additional diversification which the investor hitherto could not achieve himself due to the constraint on the size of the portfolio, and this added degree of freedom may, as we have seen, translate itself into an economic gain for the investor.

---

16. The use of three, rather than *n* companies, does not impair the generality of the argument since the third company's shares can be thought of as representing the 'rest of the world'.
17. The slope of the line *ra* is given by $(E_M - r)/\sigma_M$, where E_M = expected return on the unlevered market portfolio, and σ_M = standard deviation of the market portfolio (see Chapter 12).

But, upon reflection, it is equally clear that the investor may *not* gain, and in fact may even lose, from this type of merger. Although he can now invest 'indirectly' in the shares of company C, he has *lost* the option of investing only in the shares A and B. Recall that the investment in B and C is constrained by the fixed proportions given by the relative size of the merged firms. This fixed proportions constraint may entail a loss in comparison to the option to invest only in A and B in any proportion one chooses. Thus should the new envelope curve lie below the line *rb*, the new equilibrium position would represent a loss of utility to the investor following the merger.[18] Hence, as we have already indicated in the text, the most substantial argument supporting conglomerate mergers rests on the possible reduction of bankruptcy risk and expansion of a firm's debt capacity following such mergers.

SELECTED REFERENCES

Allen, P. R. and Sirmans, C. F. 'An Analysis of Gains to Acquiring Firm's Shareholders: The Special Case of REITS,' *Journal of Financial Economics*, March 1987.

Amihud, Yakov, Dodd, Peter, and Weinstein, Mark, 'Conglomerate Mergers, Managerial Motives and Stockholder Wealth,' *Journal of Banking and Finance*, October 1986.

Amoako-Adu, Ben and Yagil, Joseph, 'Stock Price Behavior between the Base, Announcement, and Consumation Dates of the Merger,' *Journal of Economics and Business*, May 1986.

Asquith, P. and Kim, E. Han, 'The Impact of Merger Bids on the Participants and the Firms' Security Returns,' *Journal of Finance*, December 1982.

Auerbach, Alan J. (ed.), *Mergers and Acquisitions*, Chicago: University Press, 1988.

Auerbach, Alan J. (ed.), *Corporate Takeovers: Causes and Consequences*, Chicago: University Press, 1988.

Barnes, Paul, 'UK Building Societies – A Study of the Gains from Mergers,' *Journal of Business Finance and Accounting*, Spring 1985.

Becketti, Sean, 'Corporate Mergers and the Business Cycle,' *Economic Review*, Federal Reserve Bank of Kansas City, May 1986.

Bierman, Harold Jr, 'Neglected Tax Incentive for Merger,' *Financial Management*, Summer 1985.

Black, B. S. and Gundfest, J. A., 'Shareholder Gains From Takeovers and Restructurings,' *Journal of Applied Corporate Finance*, Spring 1988.

Bradley, Michael and Wakeman, L. Macdonald, 'The Wealth Effects of Targeted Share Repurchases,' *Journal of Financial Economics*, April 1983.

Brown, Keith C. and Raymond, Michael V., 'Risk Arbitrage and the Prediction of Successful Corporate Takeovers,' *Financial Management*, Autumn 1986.

Bumpass, Donald L., 'The Trade-off between Market Power Increases and Efficiencies in Horizontal Mergers,' *Atlantic Economic Journal*, December 1987.

Chang, P. C., 'Merger Waves and Stock Market Fluctuations: A Test of Causality,' *Atlantic Economic Journal*, March 1987.

Chaplin, Brian and Wright, Mike, *The Logic of Mergers: The Competitive Market in Corporate Control in Theory and Practice*, London: Institute of Economic Affairs, 1987.

Cooke, Terrence, *Mergers and Acquisitions*, London: Basil Blackwell, 1986.

18. The possibility of loss assumes that the fixed proportions of B and C represented by the merger are, in this instance, sufficiently different from the preferred combination to allow the loss of B to offset completely the gains from adding B + C to the portfolio. In this context, it should be emphasized that in an imperfect capital market the composition of the optimum unlevered portfolio is *not* necessarily the same for all investors. For further details, see Haim Levy and Marshall Sarnat, *Portfolio and Investment Selection*, Prentice Hall, Englewood Cliffs, J.J., 1984.

Dann, Larry Y. and De Angelo, Harry, 'Corporate Financial Policy and Corporate Control: A Study of Defensive Adjustments in Asset and Ownership Structure,' Working Paper, Managerial Economics Research Center of the University of Rochester, August 1986.

Davidson, L. R., 'Takeover Partitioning Gains and Pareto Improvements in a Rational Market with Asymmetric Information,' *Journal of Business Finance and Accounting*, Autumn 1985.

De Angelo, Harry and Rice, Edward M. 'Antitakeover Charter Amendments and Stockholder Wealth,' *Journal of Financial Economics*, April 1983.

Dennis, D. K. and McConnell, J. J. 'Corporate Mergers and Security Returns,' *Journal of Financial Economics*, June, 1986.

Dodds, J. C. and Queh, J. P., 'Effect of Mergers in the Share Price Movement of the Acquiring Firm: A UK Study,' *Journal of Business Finance and Accounting*, Summer 1985.

Dunn, James R., 'Determinants of Interindustry Mergers – An Update,' *Proceedings of the American Statistical Association Business and Economic Statistics Section*, 1984.

Eckbo, B. Epsen, 'Mergers and the Market for Corporate Control, the Canadian Evidence,' *Canadian Journal of Economics*, May 1986.

Firth, M., *Share Prices and Mergers*, Aldershot: Gower, 1986.

Fisher, M. Franklin, 'Horizontal Mergers: Triage and Treatment,' *Journal of Economic Perspectives*, Fall 1987.

Fruhan, Willam E. Jr, 'Corporate Raiders: Head 'Em Off at Value Gap,' *Harvard Business Review*, July/August, 1988.

Harris, R. G. and Sullivan, L. A., 'Horizontal Merger Policy: Promoting Competition and American Competitiveness,' *Antitrust Bulletin*, Winter 1986.

Hasbrouck, Joel, 'The Characteristics of Takeover Targets, q and Other Measures,' *Journal of Banking and Finance*, September 1985.

Hite, G. L., Owers, J. E. and Rogers, R. C., 'The Market for Interfirm Asset Sales: Partial Sell-offs and Total Liquidations,' *Journal of Financial Economics*, June 1987.

Ho, Michael J., 'Share Rights Plans: Poison Pill, Placebo or Suicide Tablet?' Master's thesis, M.I.T. Sloan School of Management, 1986.

Holly, Sean and Longbottom, Andrew, 'Company Acquisitions, Investment and Tobin's Q: Evidence for the United Kingdom' *Journal of Economics and Business*, May 1988.

Hughes, A. and Singh, A., 'Takeovers and the Stock Market,' *Contributions to Political Economy*, March 1987.

Jarrel, Gregg A. and Poulson, Annette, 'Shark Repellents and Poison Pills: Stockholder Protection – From the Good Guys or the Bad Guys?' *Midland Corporate Finance Journal*, Summer 1986.

Jarrel, Gregg A., 'The Wealth Effects of Litigating by Targets: Do Interests Diverge in a Merge?' *Journal of Law and Economics*, April 1985.

Jensen, Michael C., 'The Takeover Controversy: Analysis and Evidence,' *Midland Corporate Finance Journal*, Summer 1986.

Jensen, Michael C. and Ruback, Richard S., 'The Market for Corporate Control: The Scientific Evidence,' *Journal of Ffnancial Economics*, April 1983.

Jorde, Thomas, 'Restoring Predictability to Merger Guidelines Analysis,' *Contemporary Policy Issues*, July 1986.

Keenen, Michael and White, Lawrence, *Mergers and Acquisitions: Current Problems in Perspective*, Lexington, Mass.: Heath, 1982.

Knoeber, Charles, 'Golden Parachutes, Shark Repellents and Hostile Tender Offers,' *American Economic Review*, March 1986.

Lease, Ronald, McConnell, John J., and Mikkelson, Wayne H., 'The Evidence on Limited Voting Stock: Motives and Consequences,' *Midland Corporate Finance Journal*, Summer 1986.

Lewellen, Wilbur, Loderer, Claudio, and Rosenfeld, Ahron, 'Merger Decisions and Executive Stock Ownership in Acquiring Firms,' *Journal of Accounting and Economics*, April 1985.

Linn, Scott C. and McConnell, John J., 'An Empirical Investigation of the Impact of Anti-takeover Amendments in Common Stock Price,' *Journal of Financial Economics*, April 1983.

Litzenberger, Robert H., 'Some Observations on Capital Structure and the Impact of Recent Recapitalizations on Share Prices,' *Journal of Financial and Quantitative Analysis*, March 1986.

Lowenstein, L., 'Management Buyouts,' *Columbia Law Review*, May 1985.

Malatesta, Paul H. and Thompson, Rex, 'Stock Price Reactions to Partially Anticipated Events: Evidence on the Economic Impact of Corporate Acquisition Attempts,' *Research in Finance*, 6, 1986.

Mariotti, S. and Ricotta, E., 'Diversification, Agreements Between Firms and Innovative Behavior,' *Ricerche Economiche*, October December 1986.

Maupin, Rebekah, Bidwell, Clinton, and Ortegren, Alan K., 'An Empirical Investigation of the Characteristics of Publicly Quoted Corporations which Change to Closely Held Ownership through Management Buyouts,' *Journal of Business Finance and Accounting*, Winter 1984.

McConnell, John J. and Nantell, Timothy J., 'Common Stock Returns and Corporate Combinations: The Case of Joint Ventures,' *Journal of Finance*, June 1985.

Melicher, Ronald W., Ledolter, Johannes, and D'Antonio, Louis J., 'A Time Series Analysis of Aggregate Merger Activity,' *Review of Economics and Statistics*, August 1983.

Michel, Allen and Shaked, Israel, 'Corporate Takeovers: Excess Returns and the Multiple Bidding Phenomena,' *Journal of Business Finance and Accounting*, Summer 1988.

Partch, Megan, 'The Creation of a Class of Limited Voting Common Stock and Shareholder Wealth,' Working Paper, University of Oregon, May 1986.

Pettway, Richard H. and Yamada, Takeshi, 'Mergers in Japan and their Impacts upon Stockholders' Wealth,' *Financial Management*, Winter 1986.

Pound, John A., 'Takeover Defeats Hurt Stockholders: A Reply to the Kidder–Peabody Study,' *Midland Corporate Finance Journal*, Summer 1986.

Powers, Imelda Yeung, 'A Game Theoretic Model of Corporate Takeovers by Major Stockholders,' *Management Science*, April 1987.

Ravenscraft, David T. and Scherer, F. M., *Mergers, Sell-offs and Economic Efficiency*, Washington: Brookings Institution, 1987.

Rege, U. P., 'Accounting Ratios to Locate Take-over Targets,' *Journal of Business,' Finance and Accounting*, Autumn 1984.

Rosenfeld, James D., 'Additional Evidence on the Relation between Divestiture Announcements and Shareholder Wealth,' *Journal of Finance*, December 1984.

Roy, Asim, 'Partial Acquisition Strategies for Business Combinations,' *Financial Management*, Summer 1985.

Samuels, J. M., *Readings on Mergers and Takeovers*, London: Paul Elek Booth, 1972.

Sawyer, M. 'Mergers: A Case of Market Failure?' *British Review of Economic Issues*, Autumn 1987.

Schipper, Katherine and Smith, Abbie, 'A Comparison of Equity Carve Outs and Seasoned Equity Offerings: Share Price Effects and Corporate Restructuring,' *Journal of Financial Economics*, January/February 1986.

Settle, John W., Petry, Glen H., and Hsia, Chi-Cheng, 'Synergy, Diversification and Incentive Effect of Corporate Merger on Bondholder Wealth,' *Journal of Financial Research*, Winter 1984.

Shugart, William F. II and Tollison, Robert, 'The Random Character of Merger Activity,' *Rand Journal of Economics*, Winter 1984.

Stoughton, Neal M., 'The Information Content of Corporate Merger and Acquisition Offers,' *Journal of Financial and Quantitative Analysis*, June 1988.

Teresa, John A., 'Mergers and Investment Incentives,' *Journal of Financial and Quantitative Analysis*, December 1986.

Torabzadeh, Khalil M. and Bertin, William J., 'Leveraged Buy-outs and Shareholder Returns,' *The Journal of Financial Research*, Winter 1987.

Travlos, N. G., 'Corporate Takeover Bids, Methods of Payment, and Bidding Firms' Stock Returns,' *Journal of Finance*, September 1987.

Varaiya, Nikhil and Ferris, Kenneth R., 'Overpaying in Corporate Takeovers: The Winner's Curse,' *Financial Analysts Journal*, May/June 1987.

Wansley, James W., Roenfeldt, Rodney, L., and Cooley, Phillip L., 'Abnormal Returns from Merger Profiles,' *Journal of Financial and Quantitative Analysis*, 1983.

Wright, M. and Coyne, J., *Management Buy-outs*, London: Croom Helm, 1985.

Yen, Gili, 'Merger Proposals, Managerial Discretion and Magnitude of Shareholders' Wealth Gains,' *Journal of Economics and Business*, August 1987.

22

International Financial Management

Denmark's Rebuff Hurts European Markets

Denmark may be a nation of only 5.1 million people. But Danish voters' rejection Tuesday of the Maastricht treaty on European economic and political integration sent shivers yesterday through Europe's bond, stock and currency markets.

Because each of the 12 nations of the European Community must ratify the treaty that was agreed to by European leaders last December, traders and investors interpreted the Danish snub as a strong setback to the prospect for economic unification in Europe. And they said it dashed expectations that a European-wide commitment to low inflation would continue to lead to a convergence of European interest rates.

Hardest hit were European bond markets, where prices tumbled and yields rose. Among the worst performers were Spanish and Italian government bonds. In Spain, government bonds yields surged to 11.10% yesterday from 10.83% on Tuesday before the results of the Danish referendum were known. In Italy, yields rose to 12.53% from 12.32%.

Bonds denominated in European currency units, or ECUs, also fell hard, with yields climbing to 8.82% from 8.58% on Tuesday.

'On balance, this whole business spells bad news' for European markets, 'at least for the time being; markets never like lack of confidence and uncertainty,' said George Magnus, chief international fixed income economist at S. G. Warburg & Co. in London. 'Nothing much has changed in terms of economic fundamentals, but the prospect of seeing the whole convergence argument fall on its head has unnerved people. And the specter of possible [currency] devaluations in Europe is also something people feel very uncomfortable about.'

Until the full impact of the Danish rebuff is clear – something that analysts say could take months – money managers on both sides of the Atlantic advise investors to stay away from the so-called high-yielding bond markets – particularly Spain and Italy – and increase their holdings in the government bonds of Germany and the Netherlands, whose central banks are committed to strong anti-inflation policies. Outside of Europe, money managers recommend that American investors look at North America and Japan.

'I would think that prudent fund managers are reallocating funds out of Europe and into the U.S., Canada and Japan right now', said Jeph Gundzik, a portfolio manager at Freedom Capital Management Corp. in New York. 'The U.S. offers currency stability relative to

Europe. Even with questions over the extent of the U.S. recovery, you can't say that Europe offers more stability right now with the results of the Danish referendum that throws into question European monetary union (EMU) and convergence' of European bond yields towards those in Germany.

Source: *Wall Street Journal*, June 4, 1992, p. C1.

How European Bond Markets Reacted

Yields and price change based on J. P. Morgan government bond indexes

			Wednesday's change	
	Yield 6/3/92	Yield 6/2/92	Yield (%)	Price* (percent)
Belgium	8.891%	8.878%	+0.013	−0.134%
Britain	9.144	9.013	+0.131	−0.690
Denmark	9.114	8.819	+0.295	−1.244
France	8.785	8.667	+0.118	−0.539
Germany	8.248	8.235	+0.013	−0.056
Itay	13.122	12.859	+0.263	−0.840
Netherlands	8.388	8.364	+0.024	−0.131
Spain	11.667	11.375	+0.292	−0.940
Sweden	9.857	9.633	+0.224	−0.956

Based on local currency index.
Source: J. P. Morgan & Co.

In June 1992, Denmark's vote questioned the monetary unification of Europe. If complete unification is achieved, can we treat all twelve European countries as one domestic capital market?

The figures in article 49 indicate that in June 1992 Europe was far from monetarily unified. The yield on government bonds in Italy was 13.1%, while in Germany it was only 8.2%. Why would investors not rush to buy the 'high yield' bonds in Italy? The reason is that returns and yields should be compared after possible changes in the foreign exchange rates are incorporated. Indeed, this is the dimension of risk that must be taken into account. Indeed, the article recommends that investors 'stay away from the so-called high yielding bond market − particularly Spain and Italy − and increase their holding in Germany and the Netherlands.' Thus, high yields in terms of local currency do not necessarily imply a high yield in terms of other currencies such as the U.S. dollar.

International financial management differs from the domestic treatment of finance because of currency, tax, and capital market variations between currencies that do not exist within a country. These differences reflect the unique cultural heritage of individual countries which have shaped their values and attitudes toward business enterprise. Indeed, if all countries used the same currency, the same tax system, and had perfectly integrated capital markets, international finance would simply be an extension of the domestic model.

Although fluctuations in foreign exchange rates have always been a source of potential financial risk, in the two decades prior to 1970 the exchange rates of developed nations were relatively stable. Because the exchange rates of most major trading countries were expected to remain fixed *vis-à-vis* the dollar, there was little need for diversification of foreign currencies even for multi-national, let alone domestic, firms. However, since that time financial managers have been faced with increasing difficulties. Fluctuations in the external value of the dollar can no longer be ignored, and exchange risk, if anything, can be expected to increase during the foreseeable future. This chapter takes a look at the structure of the international financial community and the options that are available to a corporation which wishes either to avoid, or at least to contain within manageable levels, its exposure to the risk of change in the exchange rates of foreign currencies. We try to see how the international environment can be exploited, and how the firm can protect itself from the increased risk and complexities of 'going international'.

INTRODUCTION TO EXCHANGE RATES

Foreign currency is a good, just like wheat, gold, or Toyotas. The demand for foreign currency reflects the need to acquire that currency to finance the purchase of goods, or to make investments, in the country in question. Like any other good, foreign currency has a price, which is called its exchange rate.

The *exchange rate* for foreign currency is the price of a unit of the foreign currency in terms of the domestic currency. Just as one might quote the price of wheat at $4 per bushel, one might quote the price of a British pound as $2 per British pound. The exchange rate for wheat is $4 per bushel, and the exchange rate for British pounds is $2 per British pound. Onions may cost $0.40 per pound, while one German mark (DM) is $0.50. The exchange rate of onions is $0.40 per pound, and the exchange rate for German marks is $0.50 per DM. Calculating exchange rates in this manner is called a direct quote. It divides the amount of dollars required to purchase foreign currency by one unit of the foreign currency:

Direct quotes:
$4|bu wheat $2/British pound
$0.40/1b onions $0.50/DM

Prices of any commodity can also be quoted the other way. For example, the price of wheat can be quoted as one quarter bushel per dollar rather than $4 per bushel. Similarly, the price of a British pound can be quoted as 0.50 British pounds (= 50 pence) per dollar, or the German mark can be quoted as DM2 per dollar. This type of exchange rate is called an indirect quote:

Indirect quotes:
1/4 bu wheat/$ 0.50 British pounds/$
2.5 lb onions/$ 2 DM/$

Foreign currency quotations are a bit difficult to understand. Most of us make them infrequently, e.g. when traveling to Europe on vacation. Moreover, the price of foreign exchange, as we have just seen, involves *two currencies.* In a direct quote, foreign currency (British pounds, German marks, etc.) is priced in terms of dollars, i.e. U.S. dollars are the unit of account. In an indirect quote dollars are being priced in terms of foreign currency, i.e., British pounds or German marks serve as the unit of account.

One easy rule to remember is to always give the unit of account first; the unit of currency being priced comes last. For example, in the direct quote for German marks: ($0.50/DM) the unit of account is the U.S. dollar and the currency priced is the German mark. Hence we can say the German mark is selling for half a dollar.

Alternatively, in the case of an indirect quote (2DM/$) the unit of account is the German mark and it is the U.S. dollar which is being priced. Hence, we can also say a U.S. dollar is selling for two German marks.

Exchange rates are published daily in the leading newspapers all over the world. Table 22.1 gives some sample quotations on July 28, 1992. Column 1 gives the *indirect quotation* for that day, i.e., the amount of foreign currency per U.S. dollar. Column 2 gives the *direct quotation*, i.e., the amount of U.S. dollars required to buy one unit of foreign currency. (The name of each country's currency unit is also given.)

Table 22.1 Exchange rates, July 28, 1992

New York rates	Foreign currency per dollar			
	Tues.	Mon.	6 month ago	Year ago
Australian dollar	1.3449	1.3449	1.3358	1.2880
Austrian shilling	10.36	10.52	11.29	12.28
Belgian franc[a]	30.53	30.51	33.15	36.00
British pound[b]	0.5188	0.5215	0.5585	0.5952
Canadian dollar	1.1877	1.1886	1.1742	1.1522
Dutch guilder	1.6715	1.6715	1.8113	1.9700
French franc	4.9735	5.0010	5.4900	5.9480
German mark	1.4740	1.4825	1.6003	1.7515
Greek drachma	181.20	184.00	184.85	192.25
Hong Kong dollar	7.7398	7.7345	7.7578	7.7500
Irish punt	0.5533	0.5565	0.5999	0.6545
Israeli shekel	2.4600	2.4600	2.3110	2.3155
Italian lira	1114.50	1123.50	1207.00	1304.70
Japanese yen	127.40	127.70	125.03	137.70
Mexican peso[c]	3114.51	3117.00	3067.00	3034.51
Norwegian krone	5.8260	5.8260	6.3155	6.8150
Singapore dollar	1.6158	1.6160	1.6350	1.7477
South Korean won	786.80	787.16	763.20	726.30
Spanish peseta	94.30	95.60	100.70	109.30
Swedish krona	5.3815	5.3815	5.8380	6.3310
Swiss franc	1.3054	1.3120	1.4280	1.5288
Taiwan dollar	25.18	24.61	25.08	26.92
Morgan Gnty. Index[d]	81.6	81.8	83.8	88.3

[a] Commercial rate.
[b] Dollars per pound: 1.9275.
[c] Floating rate.
[d] Dollar vs. group of key currencies.
Source: First American Bank of New York; reproduced from *U.S.A. Today*, July 29, 1992.

It is now almost the universal practice in the foreign currency markets to quote all exchange rates on an indirect basis in which the dollar is priced in terms of foreign currency (see Table 22.1). There is one notable exception to this rule. It is an accepted convention to quote the British pound on a direct basis, i.e., as dollars per pound.

Cross-currency quotes

All exchange rates are quoted in terms of dollars. Even if you are a resident of Germany and interested in trading marks to buy British pounds, the exchange rate will be quoted to you in terms of dollars. If you wish to find the number of British pounds (£) that you can get for a German mark (DM), you multiply the rates as follows:

$$\text{Cross rate} = \frac{\text{Pounds}}{\text{Dollars}} \times \frac{\text{Dollars}}{\text{DM}} = \frac{\text{Pounds}}{\text{DM}}$$

Using the exchange rate for the British pound (0.5215) and that of the German mark (0.6745) we get:

$$\text{Cross rate} = 0.5215 \times 0.6745 = 0.351$$

Thus the price of a German mark in terms of British pounds is 0.351. This sort of exchange rate, where one currency is quoted in terms of another currency, and neither currency is the dollar, is called a *cross-rate*. Since the exchange rates of all currencies are quoted in terms of the dollar, all of the cross-rates can easily be computed in this manner. A representative sample of actual exchange cross rates between major foreign currencies is given in Table 22.2. The cross-rate between the German mark and the British pound, i.e., 0.351, appears in line 3 of column 1.

Table 22.2 Exchange cross-rates, July 24, 1992

Exchange cross rates

July 24	£	$	DM	Yen	F Fr.	S. Fr.	N Fl.	Lira	C$	B Fr.	Pta.	Ecu
£	1	1.900	2.850	242.5	9.620	2.525	3.213	2159.0	2.264	58.65	181.1	1.398
$	0.526	1	1.500	127.6	5.063	1.329	1.691	1136.0	1.192	30.87	95.32	0.736
DM	0.351	0.667	1.000	85.09	3.375	0.886	1.127	757.5	0.794	20.58	63.54	0.491
Yen	4.124	7.835	11.750	1000.0	39.67	10.41	13.25	8903.0	9.336	241.90	746.8	5.765
F Fr.	1.040	1.975	2.963	252.1	10.	2.625	3.340	2244.0	2.353	60.97	188.3	1.453
S Fr.	0.396	0.752	1.129	96.04	3.810	1.000	1.272	855.0	0.897	23.23	71.72	0.554
N Fl.	0.311	0.591	0.887	75.47	2.994	0.786	1.000	672.0	0.705	18.25	56.36	0.435
Lira	0.463	0.880	1.320	112.3	4.456	1.170	1.488	1000.0	1.049	27.17	83.88	0.648
C$	0.442	0.839	1.259	107.1	4.249	1.115	1.419	953.6	1.000	25.91	79.99	0.617
B Fr.	1.705	3.240	4.859	413.5	16.40	4.305	5.478	3681.0	3.860	100.00	308.8	2.384
Pta	0.552	1.049	1.574	133.9	5.312	1.394	1.774	1192.0	1.250	32.39	100.0	0.772
Ecu	0.715	1.359	2.039	173.5	6.881	1.806	2.298	1544.0	1.619	41.95	129.5	1.000

Yen per 1,000: French Fr. per 10: Lira per 1,000: Belgian Fr. per 100: Pesta per 100.
Source: Financial Times, July 27, 1992.

Pricing foreign goods

The exchange rates of Table 22.1 can be used to find the cost of an American product in terms of a foreign currency. Assume that a German wants to buy a U.S. computer which costs $5,000. What is its equivalent price in German marks, i.e., how many DM will the German purchaser have to pay for the computer? The exchange rate for the dollar was DM 1.4740 per dollar (see Table 22.1). Hence the cost of the computer in German marks is DM 7,370:

$$\$5,000 \times DM\ 1.474/\$ = DM\ 7,370$$

Appreciation and depreciation of exchange rates

If the value of domestic currency declines in terms of foreign currency, it is said to have depreciated. When the value of the domestic currency declines, it takes more of that currency to purchase a unit of the other currency. Conversely, it takes less of the other currency to buy one unit of the depreciated domestic currency. For example, if the dollar exchange rate goes from $0.5/DM to $0.6/DM, the dollar has depreciated relative to the German mark. Whereas one used to be able to buy a German mark for fifty cents, it now takes sixty cents. The dollar has thus depreciated by 20%. Conversely, in terms of the indirect quote, the exchange rate has gone from DM2/$ to DM1.66/$. It used to take two marks to buy a dollar; it now takes only one and two-thirds marks.

The effect of a currency depreciating relative to another currency is the same as the currency depreciating relative to the price of goods. If the price of onions goes from $0.40/lb to $0.50/lb, then the dollar has depreciated relative to onions. There has been price inflation in the goods market for onions − it takes more dollars to buy a given amount of onions. The depreciation of the dollar relative to foreign currencies means that there has been inflation in the dollar relative to other currencies − it takes more dollars to buy a unit of any given foreign currency.

_____ **EXCHANGE RATE DETERMINATION**

As we have seen, the exchange rate is nothing more than the price of a foreign currency in terms of the domestic currency. If we treat the foreign currency like any other good, its price will be determined by the supply and demand for the foreign currency. If there is more of the currency being supplied than is being demanded at the going price (i.e., if there is excess supply for the currency) then the price of the foreign currency will fall in terms of the domestic currency until demand and supply are equated. This drop in price means that the foreign currency will depreciate relative to the domestic currency. This decline in the value of the foreign currency is the same as the decline in the value of wheat if more wheat is produced. If the supply of wheat increases and the demand for wheat stays unchanged, the only way that the wheat market will clear is if the price of wheat drops.

If the exchange rate is treated as the price that clears the market for a given currency, then we must ask what determines the supply and demand of the currency. The *traditional approach* to exchange rate determination, using the supply and demand framework, views the exchange rate as the price which equilibrates the demand and supply for domestic currency in exchange for foreign currency. These 'demands and supplies' in turn reflect international transactions in goods, services, and financial assets.

International trade and exchange rates

When the United States buys goods from Germany, it pays for them in currency or in barter. If it exports as much to Germany as Germany exports to the United States, the balance of trade between the two countries is in equilibrium and no further currency transactions are needed. But if the United States exports *less* than it imports, then it must make up the deficit. If Germany will accept dollars as payment, then the United States can pay the difference between its imports and exports with dollars. The larger the deficit, the greater is the supply of dollars that finds its way into the German market. But the Germans only have a demand for so many dollars. As the United States gives them more and more dollars to meet its deficit, an excess supply of dollars is created, and the dollar must *depreciate* relative to the mark.

If Germany does not want all the dollars, it can still sell them to another country that has an excess demand for dollars. Such an excess demand will occur if that country imports more from the United States than they export and, therefore, the dollars are needed to make up the difference. Germany will sell its excess dollars at whatever price the market for dollars will bear. The world price for dollars will be determined by the net world demand for dollars compared with the net world supply of dollars. If the United States is faced with a trade deficit with all countries, then all countries will eventually find that they are holding more dollars than they want at the going exchange rate. For example, Germany may try to sell its dollars to Britain, only to find that Britain also has more dollars than it wants. The only way Germany can get rid of its excess supply of dollars is to sell them at a discount. Instead of trading them to Britain at the going rate of say $1.50 per pound, they must sell them at say $1.601/£. Thus, in such a case, the dollar has also depreciated relative to the British pound.

The exchange rate for the dollar will depreciate until the supply and demand are equated. If the United States continues to finance its trade with dollars rather than with exports of goods and services, then it will continue to increase the supply of dollars abroad, and the dollar will continue to depreciate.

Monetary approach

The monetary approach to exchange rate depreciation emphasizes the role of financial transactions in producing exchange rate changes. In this view, exchange rates fluctuate as a result of the willingness of individuals to hold the outstanding stock of money, rather than as a result of the flow of payments due to international trade. The monetary model emphasizes the effects of three variables on exchange rate depreciation: (a) inflation; (b) the real interest rate, and (c) aggregate income.

Purchasing power parity

The depreciation or appreciation of a currency is closely linked to the rate of inflation. This link comes about through a relationship called purchasing power parity, or PPP. Assume, for example, that Germany and the United States both produce a compact car. The cars are identical, and are recognized by most consumers as being identical. This implies that the two cars must sell for the same price in the market, or else one of the two will take away the market from the other.

Suppose that last year, the U.S. car was selling for $4,000 in the United States, the German car was selling for DM8,000 in Germany, and the exchange rate between the two currencies was $0.5/DM. Hence, the two cars were also selling for the same price in each of the two countries:

U.S. car:	$4,000
German car:	DM8,000 × $0.5/DM = $4,000

Now, assume that the inflation rate over the next year was higher in the United States than in Germany; say 10% in the United States and 5% in Germany. As a result, the price of the U.S. car will rise to $4,400 and the price of the German car will rise to DM8,400. If the exchange rate stays at $0.5/DM, the new price of the two cars in the U.S. market will be:

U.S. car:	$4,400
German car:	DM8,400 × $0.55DM/ = $4,200

Thus the German car will be cheaper in the U.S. market. It is also easy to see that the U.S. car will be more expensive than the German car in the German market:

U.S. car:	$4,400 × DM2/$ = DM8,800
German car:	DM8,400

The net effect will reduce demand for the U.S. car, both at home and abroad, and increase demand for the German car at home and abroad. In order to keep the two markets competitive, the exchange rate must change. Specifically, it must change to equate the price of the two cars given the shift in the relative inflation rates. That is, we must have the new exchange rate, such that

$$DM8,400 \times \$X_1/DM = \$4,400$$

This implies a new rate of \$0.5238/DM. Thus the dollar will depreciate relative to the DM.

The purchasing power parity (PPP) argument generalizes this relationship. It states that the required change in the exchange rate is related to the ratio of the relative change in the inflation rates of the two countries:

$$(1 + X) = \frac{(1 + h_d)}{(1 + h_f)}$$

where:

X = percentage change in the exchange rate.
h_d = inflation rate in the domestic country.
h_f = inflation rate in the foreign country.

Plugging in the inflation rates and the exchange rate change, it is easy to verify this formula from the example above:

$$\frac{0.5238}{0.5} = \frac{1.10}{1.05}$$

This then is the purchasing power parity argument. It states that the country with the higher inflation rate will experience depreciation in its currency, and that the change in exchange rates is equal to the relative *difference* between the rates of inflation in the two countries. However, the PPP argument has some serious shortcomings:

1. It applies only to traded goods. Haircuts, housing, and other goods that are not easily imported are exempt from this argument, since they cannot be substituted from abroad.
2. It is a *long-run* argument. As inflation makes the domestic goods more expensive, there will be an incentive to substitute the less expensive foreign good for the domestic one. But this will take time: time to recognize the price difference, to evaluate the relative quality of the good, to make marketing arrangements, and to increase the foreign production of the good for export. As a result, large and prolonged deviations from PPP have persisted.

Decreasing the interest rate

If the real interest rate in the United States is lowered, investment money will leave the country. Foreigners and U.S. citizens will invest elsewhere, since their return will be higher than in the United States. This capital outflow will cause an increase in the supply of dollars abroad, as investors try to cash in their dollars for the currency of a country with more attractive investments. This will cause the dollar to depreciate relative to the other currencies.

Increase in aggregate income

If the aggregate income in the United States increases relative to the income of other countries, it will import more from abroad, since the demand for all goods, both foreign and domestic, will increase. But the demand abroad for U.S. goods will not increase by an equal amount, because the income in these other countries has not increased. As a result, the U.S. trade deficit will rise, leading to a depreciation in the dollar.

To sum up, three relationships can lead to a depreciation of the domestic currency:

1. Having a higher rate of inflation.
2. Having its (real) interest rate fall relative to that of the foreign country.
3. Having its income grow faster.

One point worth noting is that it is the *relative* changes that are important. If both countries have the same rates of inflation, or if both countries experience the same shift in income or in real interest rates, there will be no adjustment necessary in the exchange rate.

THE MARKET FOR FOREIGN EXCHANGE

Like a stock exchange, the foreign exchange market is not a meeting place for the ultimate suppliers and demanders of the currency in question. Typically, transactions are carried out by an intermediary; in this case often by a bank. Nor is the foreign exchange market a physical location. Today, the foreign exchange market spans the globe. Like the British Empire in the nineteenth century, the sun literally never sets on foreign exchange trading. Trading starts each morning in the Far East, moves west to Europe, from there to New York, and from there to the U.S. West Coast. Among the major trading centers are Tokyo, Sidney, Hong Kong, Singapore, Frankfurt, Paris, London, and New York. Moreover, modern communications technology connects these centers by telephone, telex and on-line computers. Thus, the foreign exchange market is a highly sophisticated communications network that connects the major market participants with one another.

Market participants

The market comprises four major categories of participant:

1. Banks and non-bank *dealers* in foreign exchange who buy and sell foreign exchange for their customers. They earn their profits from the difference between the 'bid' price at which they buy the currency and the slightly higher 'ask' price at which they sell the currency. By their willingness to buy and sell foreign exchange, these dealers 'make the market'.
2. Individuals and firms who use the market to facilitate their commercial or

financial transactions, or as we shall see below, to 'hedge' their foreign exchange risks. This group includes exporters, importers, international portfolio investors, multinational firms, and tourists.

3. Speculators and arbitrageurs who profit from trading in the market itself. The former seek their profits by anticipating a change in exchange rates, while the arbitrageur tries to profit from the existence of simultaneous differences in the price quotation for a given currency in different markets.

4. Central banks who buy and sell currencies in order to influence the exchange rates of their own currency. Thus, for example, should the market rise too sharply, the *Bundesbank*, which is Germany's central bank, might intervene by using marks to buy dollars. And conversely, it might sell dollars should the mark fall below the level which it deems desirable. The central banks are not profit-motivated. They seek to influence exchange rates in order to promote the economic interests of their citizens.

Figure 22.1 sets out the various linkages between the market participants. (The diagram includes the links with currency futures and options markets which will be discussed below.) Only the head or major regional offices of the larger banks are actively engaged in the foreign exchange market on their own account. Those banks which are willing to buy and sell foreign currencies more or less continuously are known as 'market makers'. For very large transactions, foreign exchange brokers are used to help find partners for the deal. Unlike the stock market makers, these brokers do not trade on their own account; their specialty is setting up very large foreign currency transactions for which they charge a commission.

Most small banks and the local branches of the larger banks do not deal directly with the inter bank foreign exchange market. Hence, a typical transaction between a customer and his commercial bank requires an extra step (see Figure 22.1). After receiving the customer's order, the local branch in turn deals with its head office or with a major bank to complete the transaction.

Trading in the foreign exchange market

A key to understanding foreign exchange trading is to remember that, with the exception of speculation and arbitrage, foreign exchange transactions are derived from transactions in commodity and investment markets. Trade in currencies is needed because people want to trade in commodities and assets. Thus, the American importer of Mercedes cars buys German marks in order to pay for the cars. Or if you want to buy shares in Daimler Benz, rather than their cars, you have to buy German marks in the foreign exchange market in order to pay for your purchase of stock on the Frankfurt Stock Exchange. A second point to remember is that you *cannot* be a demander of one currency in the foreign exchange market without being the supplier of another. Thus, in our example above, the U.S. importer and investor are both suppliers of dollars and demanders of German marks in the $/DM market.

Despite this, many foreign exchange transactions appear to be unrelated to any underlying commodity or investment decision. However, since an

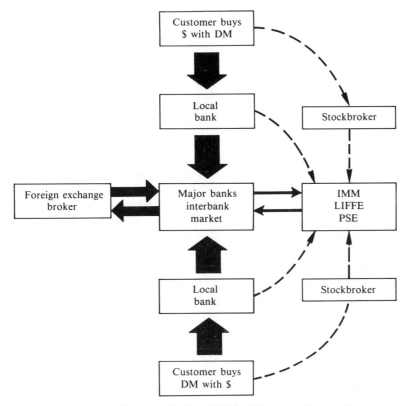

Note: The International Money Market (IMM) Chicago trades foreign exchange futures and DM futures options. The London International Financial Futures Exchange (LIFFE) trades foreign futures. The Philadelphia Stock Exchange (PSE) trades foreign currency options.

Figure 22.1 Structure of foreign exchange markets. *Source*: *Federal Reserve Bank of St. Louis Review*, March 1984.

efficiently functioning foreign exchange market facilitates international trade and investment, transactions which permit the smooth functioning of the exchange markets play a very useful role. *Arbitrage* is one such transaction. The existence of foreign exchange markets in various locations, and the wide array of cross rates to which they give rise, create opportunities for 'arbitrage profits'. An arbitrage transaction is defined as the simultaneous purchase and sale of a currency in two markets in an attempt to profit from a price discrepancy between the two markets. Competition among arbitrageurs quickly corrects any discrepancies and is the force which keeps the various price quotations and markets consistent with one another.

The forward market

Foreign exchange transactions are made on both a 'spot' and 'forward' basis. A *spot transaction* is one in which foreign currency is purchased for delivery and payment on the second following business day. (Same day deliveries are possible at slightly different prices.) A *forward transaction* is one which stipulates the delivery of a specific amount of one currency on a specified date in the future, at an exchange rate fixed in advance. The contract is signed today but future payment and delivery are effected at a known exchange rate. Such contracts, as we see below, can eliminate uncertainty regarding the future course of exchange rates.

For major currencies such as the British pound and German mark it is common to quote three forward rates (30, 90, and 180 days) in addition to the spot exchange rate. The forward rates can be expressed in actual prices, the *outright rate*, or in terms of the differential between the forward rate and the spot rate. The latter is called a *swap rate*, and is used by professional traders in the interbank market.

If the forward rate, expressed in dollars, is higher than the spot rate, then that currency is selling at a premium in the forward market. Conversely, if the forward rate is below the spot rate, the currency is at a discount in the forward market.

A swap rate can easily be converted into an outright rate by adding (or subtracting) the premium (discount) point differential to the spot rate. For example, if the spot rate for the British pound is $1.75350 and the three month swap rate is quoted at a premium of 0.01465, the outright three-month forward rate for the pound against the dollar is 1.76815. The annualised forward premium (discount) can also be expressed in percentage terms using the following formula:

$$\frac{\text{Forward premium}}{\text{(discount)}} = \frac{\text{Forward rate} - \text{Spot rate}}{\text{Spot rate}} \times \frac{12}{\text{Forward contract in months}}$$

In our example of the British pound:

$$\frac{\text{Forward premium}}{\text{(discount)}} = \frac{1.76815 - 1.75350}{1.7535} \times \frac{12}{4} = 3.34\%$$

FOREIGN EXCHANGE RISK

As we have already noted, the system of pegged exchange rates which was established during World War II under the Bretton Woods Agreement was replaced in the mid-1970s by a regime of floating exchange rates. Today all the major currencies are free to fluctuate (at least to some extent) against the dollar. Figure 22.2 which graphs the monthly percentage change in the exchange rates of eight major currencies (British pounds, Swiss francs, Italian lira, French francs, Japanese yen, German marks, Dutch guilders, and Belgian francs) clearly shows the dramatic change in the variability of exchange rates. For example, up to 1967 the exchange rate between the U.S. dollar and the British pound was completely stable; however, since November

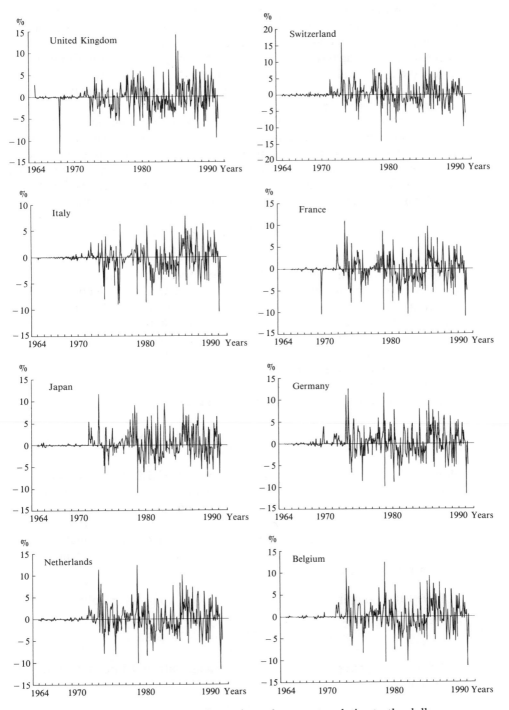

Figure 22.2 Monthly percentage change in exchange rate relative to the dollar.

1967, when the pound sterling was officially devalued, the exchange rate has fluctuated significantly. Thus if an American firm (or investor) holds pounds, or some other financial asset denominated in pounds, and the exchange value of the pound rises against the dollar, an *exchange profit* is made. Conversely, should the pound fall relative to the dollar, an *exchange loss* will be incurred. Figure 22.2 shows clearly that these potential gains and losses from the holding of foreign currencies can be very large.

The result of these greatly enhanced exchange rate movements has been to increase both the potential gains and losses from international transactions. Today, exporters, importers and multinational corporations are exposed to a new type of risk – exchange risk. In order to quantify the exchange rate fluctuations, the monthly rates of return on the holding of foreign currencies, from the viewpoint of an American investor, can be calculated as follows:

$$R_{jt} = \frac{M_{jt} - M_{jt+1}}{M_{jt+1}} = \frac{M_{jt}}{M_{jt+1}} - 1$$

where M_{jt} denotes the exchange rate of the jth country's currency in month t expressed in terms of that currency per U.S. dollar and R_{jt} denotes the rate of return earned by an American investor from holding the jth country's currency in period t. For example, suppose that we wish to calculate the profit to an American investor who holds British pounds. Let $M_t = 0.75$, i.e., assume that at the beginning of the period the exchange rate was 75 pence (0.75 pounds) per dollar. At the end of the investment period let us assume that the exchange rate was 50 pence per dollar ($M_{t+1} = 0.50$). The gain (loss) to the American investors from the exchange rate change is given by:

$$R_t = \frac{M_t}{M_{t+1}} - 1 = \frac{0.75}{0.50} - 1 = 0.50 = 50\%$$

Now consider an American investor who purchased 1,000 British pounds at time t and then converted his holdings to dollars at time $t + 1$. At the beginning of the period, the exchange rate was 0.75 pounds per dollar, so the investor paid \$1,333 to obtain \$1,000. When he converts his money back to dollars he gets \$2,000 (1,000/0.50 = 2,000). Thus he earns a rate of return equal to 50%.

Consider the following transactions, which are also illustrated in Figure 22.3. An American investor:

1. Buys 1,000 pounds at an exchange rate of 0.75 pounds per dollar at time t,

$$1,000 \times \frac{1 \text{ dollar}}{0.75 \text{ pounds}} = 1,333 \text{ dollars}$$

2. Converts his pounds to dollars at an exchange rate of 0.5 pounds per dollar at time $t + 1$:

$$1,000 \text{ pounds} \times \frac{1 \text{ dollar}}{0.5 \text{ pounds}} = 2,000 \text{ dollars}$$

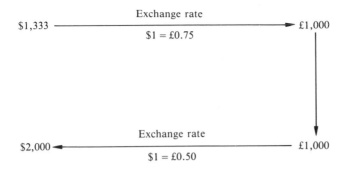

Figure 22.3

3. Earns a rate of return of 50% on the transaction:

$$R_t = \frac{\text{Exchange gain (loss)}}{\text{Initial investment}} = \frac{2,000 - 1,333}{1,333} = 0.5 = 50\%$$

The American investor (firm) who holds pounds gains as the pound becomes more expensive ($2 versus $1.33); conversely, a British investor who holds a position in dollars, *loses* as the dollar falls in value (0.75 pounds per dollar to 0.5 pound per dollar).

For simplicity we have restricted the discussion to non-interest-bearing holdings of foreign currencies. But clearly, firms or individual investors who hold foreign currency typically receive interest on their deposits in addition to the gain (or loss) from exchange rate fluctuations. As we have already seen, gain (loss) is simply the positive (or negative) return generated by fluctuations in the exchange rate. However, if we further assume that the holding of foreign currency earns interest at the rate of $r_{j,t}$ the unit of foreign currency holdings increases (in terms of the foreign currency j) to $M_{jt}(1 + r_{jt})$ during the period. When this end-of-period amount is converted into U.S. dollars at the rate M_{jt+1} the investor nets a *total* return of:

$$\frac{M_{jt}(1 + r_{jt})}{M_{jt+1}} - 1 = \left[\frac{M_{jt}}{M_{jt+1}} - 1\right](1 + r_{jt}) + r_{jt}$$

$$= R_{jt}(1 + r_{jt}) + r_{jt}$$

$$= R_{jt} + r_{jt} + R_{jt} \times r_{jt}$$

Thus, the total return is the sum of the exchange rate return R_{jt} the interest rate on currency j for the holding period, r_{jt}, and the cross product $R_{jt}r_j$ which represents the exchange rate gain (or loss) on interest income.

If we now assume that the investor in our previous example earns 1% interest on his holdings of British pounds, the total rate of return becomes 51.5%

$$0.50 + 0.01 + (0.50 \times 0.01) = 51.5\%$$

Once again the relevant transactions can be illustrated by a simple diagram (see Figure 22.4).

Table 22.3 Total gain or loss (in percent) to a U.S. investor from the holding of non-interest-bearing foreign currencies, selected periods, 1959–92

Currency	Feb. 1959–Dec. 1961	Jan. 1966–Dec. 1968	Jan. 1971–July 1973	Aug. 1973–Dec. 1973	Jan. 1971–Dec. 1973	Jan. 1974–Jan. 1980	Jan. 1980–Aug. 1981	Aug. 1981–Jan. 1982	Feb. 1982–May 1992
Belgian francs	0.44	−1.00	38.49	−13.90	20.22	34.01	−45.86	4.50	18.75
French francs	0.00	−1.01	33.72	−12.32	17.25	20.82	−48.12	2.61	10.11
German marks	4.50	0.25	55.10	−12.99	34.96	38.04	−45.10	8.38	45.13
Italian lire	0.13	0.19	6.50	−3.78	2.48	−21.83	−54.57	1.36	3.22
Japanese yen	−0.50	0.89	35.76	−5.91	27.73	20.41	1.79	3.89	80.04
Dutch guilders	4.72	0.00	38.40	−7.97	27.37	34.57	−46.00	9.57	41.49
Swiss francs	−0.23	0.47	50.59	−11.65	33.05	51.57	−36.05	14.99	27.30
U.K. pounds	0.00	−14.29	4.98	−7.55	−2.95	−0.57	−19.65	3.72	−2.60

Source: calculated from data in IMF *International Financial Statistics*, various issues.

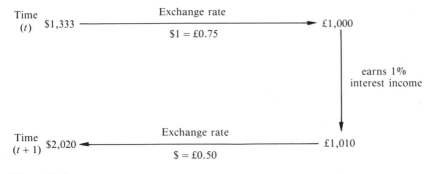

Figure 22.4

Table 22.3 quantifies the *cumulative* profit or loss on the holding of non-interest-bearing foreign currencies for selected periods during the years 1959–92. The two early periods 1959–61 and 1966–68 illustrate the argument that, prior to the monetary crisis, the changes in exchange rates were of only secondary importance. On the other hand, during the two-year period, from 1971–73, American firms or investors could have earned a significant profit by holding all but two of the eight foreign currencies included in our sample. However, in the last five months of 1973, the holding of foreign currencies produced a loss relative to the dollar in all cases.

The fluctuations in foreign exchange rates did not abate after 1973; indeed, the uncertainty regarding both the magnitude and the direction of exchange rate fluctuations has continued to be a significant factor in international investment and trade. For example, from 1974–79, the foreign currencies included in our sample, with the exception of Italy and the United Kingdom, rose in value relative to the dollar, but these gains were more than wiped out in 1980 and the first half of 1981. The sharp fall in the dollar in recent years again made the holding of foreign currencies attractive. Table 22.4 sets out the gain to U.S. firms and investors from holding foreign currencies during the month of May 1992. The gain is impressive: the Japanese yen rose by 3.86% relative to the dollar in that month alone. The relevant figures for the German mark and British pound were 2.19% and 2.42%, respectively. The magnitude of the potential gains and losses can be gauged if we convert the monthly figures to compounded annual rates. Thus, the monthly rise in the Japanese yen

Table 22.4 Percentage monthly gain to U.S. investors from holding non-interest-bearing foreign currencies in May 1992

Belgian francs	0.94	Japanese yen	3.86
French francs	2.65	Dutch guilders	2.22
German marks	2.19	Swiss francs	2.94
Italian lire	1.99	U.K. pounds	2.42

Source: International Financial Statistics, June 1992.

represents a 58% return on an annual basis:

$$(1.0386)^{12} - 1 = 58\%$$

Even the 2.19% gain on the holding of German marks in May corresponds to an annual rate of 30%. Of course, the other side of this coin comprises of the equivalent losses suffered by European and Japanese firms and investors who held U.S. dollars during this same period.

As article 50 shows, in 1992 the European bond market outperformed the U.S. when returns are measured in terms of U.S. dollars. The opposite may, of course, occur in 1993 or 1994. Given the possible fluctuation, should American investors invest in Europe or should European investors invest in the U.S.? That is, should an investor consider a global portfolio? The answer is yes, and as the article states: 'Global market funds can dampen the volatility of an investor's portfolio and boost returns.'

ARTICLE 50

Europe Beckons, as High-Yield Bonds Get Called

U.S. investors spinning the globe in search of high-yielding, government-guaranteed bonds are likely to find Europe very tempting right now.

European bonds are offering investors significantly higher yields than U.S. Treasurys. Italian bonds due in about 10 years offer a tantalizing yield of about 12.7%, compared with 7.1% on similar U.S. bonds. British 10-year bonds, called gilts, yield about 9.2%, Danish bonds about 8.8%, and French issues about 8.6%.

But while some European markets look like bargains, others are treacherous right now, investment managers warn. The key is to find countries where the outlook is for falling interest rates and low inflation.

Among the countries whose bonds fit the bill these days, international money managers say, are Germany, Britain, France and Denmark. Moreover, diversifying into European bonds, or global mutual funds, can damp the volatility of an investor's portfolio and boost returns.

Searching for safe investments with attractive yields will be especially important for many U.S. investors this week. That's because more than $8 billion of municipal bonds will be 'called', or redeemed early, on Wednesday, and

investors will be looking for places to re-invest that money. Many of those municipals were issued a decade or so ago, when U.S. interest rates were in double-digit territory, and investors now have to go overseas to get government-guaranteed returns anywhere near that level.

In fact, U.S. investors could have earned higher total returns – including price changes and interest income – over the past $5\frac{1}{2}$ years by diversifying into some European bonds than by investing solely in the U.S. bond markets, statistics compiled by J. P. Morgan & Co. and Salomon Brothers Inc. show.

Another reason to look to Europe: U.S. interest rates are likely to edge higher this year or in 1993, predicts Ian Kelson, director in charge of fixed-income investments for Morgan Grenfell Investment Services Ltd. in London. And when interest rates rise, bond prices fall.

So far this year, British government bonds have been the star European performers, providing U.S. investors with more than four times the total return of the U.S. bond market, according to J. P. Morgan. British government bonds represent the best buys in Europe, contends John ...

Source: *Wall Street Journal*, June 29, 1992, p. C1.

European Bond Market Score Card

Total returns, including interest income and price changes, on selected European government bond indexes through June 25, in percent

Country	Year to date		Since Dec. 31, 1987	
	In U.S. dollars	In local currency	In U.S. dollars	In local currency
United Kingdom	8.97%	7.61%	59.26%	58.67%
Spain	3.88	4.32	86.49	68.64
The Netherlands	3.68	5.28	30.33	28.20
France	3.01	3.04	59.14	55.19
Belgium	2.83	4.24	48.14	42.46
Germany	2.35	3.92	27.20	24.88
Italy	2.31	3.71	73.27	74.21
Denmark	2.29	2.47	65.52	61.44
Europe index*	3.57	4.34	46.90	44.05
U.S. index	2.17		55.08	

*Includes the eight countries shown.
Source: J. P. Morgan Global Research

_____ RATE OF RETURN IN THE INTERNATIONAL EQUITY MARKET

Table 22.5 reveals the differences between the rates of returns for various contries in terms of both local currencies and U.S. dollars. The biggest difference

Table 22.5 Price performance of selected stock markets through June 22 (%)

	Since Dec. 31	
	In local currency	In U.S. dollars
Developed countries		
Canada	−4.9%	−8.1%
France	+8.4	+6.7
Germany	+9.9	+6.5
Hong Kong	+38.1	+39.0
Italy	−1.7	−4.5
Japan	−28.3	−29.6
Switzerland	+11.8	+7.5
United Kingdom	+3.1	+2.8
Emerging countries		
Brazil	+239.8%	+10.1%
Indonesia	+33.3	+30.9
Mexico	+17.1	+15.5
U.S. Market		
DJ Industrial Avg	+3.5%	
S&P 500	−3.3	

Source: Morgan Stanley Capital International; reproduced from the *Wall Street Journal*, June 24, 1992, p. C1.

is for Brazil where the rate of return in terms of local currency is 239.8%, but in terms of U.S. dollars is only 10.1%. While 10.1% is a relatively high return for 6 months, it falls short of 239.8%. To see how to calculate the rate of exchange, consider the U.S. dollar versus the Brazilian currency. For simplicity, suppose that on December 31, the ratio was 1:1 (U.S.-to-Brazil). If an investor invested $100 in Brazilain currency, he would initially receive 100 units of Brazilian currency and from his investment receive 339.8 units. However, from the table we see that in terms of U.S. dollars his profit is only 10.1% and hence in terms of dollars he would increase his wealth from $100 to $110.1. Therefore, for 339.8 units of Brazilian currency he would receive $110.1 which implies an exchange rate of 339.8/110.1 = 3.086. Thus the difference in the returns in local currency and U.S. dollars can be explained by the sharp decrease in the value of the Brazilian currency relative to the dollar.

PORTFOLIO APPROACH TO INTERNATIONAL FINANCIAL MANAGEMENT

The gain from international diversification in the bond as well as the stock market has been examined in numerous studies. The most recent study was conducted by Chow, Riely, and Formby covering a ten year period from 1978 to 1988 and twenty-five countries.[1] Table 22.6 reports the mean and standard deviation of the monthly returns on these twenty-five countries. The highest mean return is on Japanese stocks (almost 2% a month) and the greatest risk is on Israel stocks with a standard deviation of almost 12%.

Figure 22.5 presents the efficient frontiers on assuming various diversification

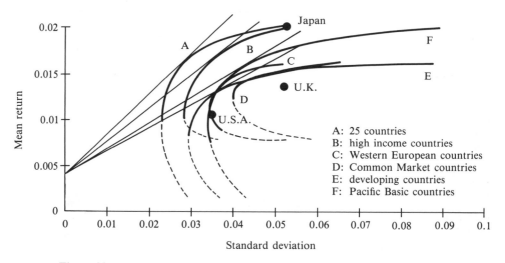

Figure 22.5

1. See K. V. Chos, W. B. Riely, and J. P. Formby, 'International Portfolio Selection and Efficiency Analysis,' *Review of Quantitative Finance and Accounting*, March 1992.

Table 22.6 Distribution parameters of 25 countries (120 monthly returns)

	Mean	Std. dev.
1. U.S.	0.0093916	0.0395002
2. Austria	0.0082681	0.0569132
3. Belgium	0.0099316	0.0588748
4. Denmark	0.0093629	0.0579826
5. France	0.0153146	0.0804667
6. Germany	0.0078624	0.0485672
7. Netherlands	0.0099926	0.0435453
8. Norway	0.0143707	0.0795749
9. Sweden	0.0161177	0.0606704
10. Switzerland	0.0096057	0.0492316
11. Canada	0.0108623	0.0632055
12. Japan	0.0199013	0.0513422
13. Finland	0.0186522	0.0445687
14. Ireland	0.0096748	0.0640525
15. Spain	0.0126623	0.0756978
16. Australia	0.0102335	0.0694655
17. New Zealand	0.0161626	0.0522237
18. South Africa	0.0069619	0.0784494
19. Chile	0.0147604	0.0832542
20. Venezuela	− 0.0004293	0.0769916
21. Israel	0.0103322	0.1197132
22. India	0.0059466	0.0470976
23. South Korea	0.0085567	0.0580903
24. Philippines	− 0.0035597	0.0856387
25. U.K.	0.0126753	0.0519974

strategies. Obviously, diversification in all twenty-five countries yields the largest gain with an efficient frontier highest and farthest to the left. For illustration, Japan, the U.S. and the U.K. are given in the figure. For example, Japan dominates the U.K. in terms of mean and variance. However, this does not mean that the U.K. should be eliminated. On the contrary. Including Japan, the U.K. as well as the remaining twenty-three countries enhances the gain from international diversification. It is worth noting that the U.S. investor can reduce risk and increase mean return by investing internationally.

The sharply-increased exchange rate fluctuations of the 1970s and 1980 has prompted many American firms to reconsider their policy of holding all their liquid balances in U.S. dollars. Unfortunately, some financial institutions were tempted by the new monetary situation and tried to make a quick profit by speculating in foreign currency; but obviously this new opportunity which reflects the underlying international monetary instability is a two-edged sword and one bank, the eighth largest in the United States, collapsed. For firms as well as individuals, the exchange fluctuations provide a new, albeit risky, vehicle of investment, but nonetheless one with important potential if properly understood and managed.

Under the Bretton Woods system of pegged exchange rates, the markets for foreign currency tended to be inefficient in the sense that economically unrealistic rates were often maintained by central banks, or by direct exchange controls, over relatively long periods of time. Although central banks still intervene in the market, and hence the popularity of the terms 'managed' or 'dirty' float, the weight of empirical evidence strongly suggests that today's foreign exchange markets are efficient. Thus, it appears reasonable to assume that the observed exchange rates reflect all relevant information, and as a result, the structure of interest rates across countries will prevent firms or other investors from systematically exploiting past information on exchange rate trends to increase their return. Similarly, the empirical evidence also supports the notion that the forward exchange markets are also efficient. Thus, the return on a domestic security (say treasury bill) and the return on a fully hedged foreign treasury bill (or its equivalent) should be the same.

In such a market a firm cannot 'gain' in expected returns arbitraging, but it can achieve a more efficient risk–return balance (in the sense of Chapter 10) by applying the portfolio principle to the management of its liquid reserves. The portfolio approach to the management of foreign currencies provides a way to mitigate (but not completely eliminate) losses (and gains) due to fluctuations in exchange rates for those who are heavily exposed to this new type of risk.

Cash management and diversification in practice

'Companies are no longer looking at a bank balance, they are looking at a portfolio.' This statement by Geoffrey Bell, senior advisor to the J. Henry Schroeder Bank & Trust Company and head of its Reserve Asset Management Group, accurately describes the new approach of many corporations to cash management.[2] Up to the early 1970s, firms held their liquid reserves in bank accounts, short-term government securities, etc. However, since that time fluctuations in the value of the dollar against many foreign currencies have led many firms, especially those with international dealings, to view their cash assets in terms of a portfolio consisting of foreign currencies and securities. Although in doing so, firms rarely apply a precise formal model to determine the optimal diversification of their cash reserves, they clearly apply what can be termed as the portfolio principle to cash management problems.

The global outlook to cash management which is implied by the portfolio approach is not the figment of some overworked academic's imagination. The unsettling events which rocked the international financial structure during the 1970s have left a permanent imprint on corporate strategy and practice. Many firms have sought new and more aggressive ways to invest their cash, more often than not turning to foreign currencies, foreign certificates of deposit and even maturing high grade foreign bonds. One such company, National Cash Register, held 20% of its cash reserves in domestic commercial paper (mostly 90-day maturities), 20% in domestic certificates of deposit and 60% in the Euromarket and Caribbean offshore market where interest rates were

2. The following review of actual business practice draws on the survey of corporate financial managers reported in 'Cash Management,' *Business Week*, 13 March 1987, pp. 62–8.

generally higher than in the United States. These outside investments were well diversified; the firm held about one hundred different positions of 2–3 million dollars each. The company's treasurer, Robert C. James, explained, 'Our thought is that whatever the risk is, if we ever lose anything, we won't lose a big hunk.' Reflecting this approach, NCR's policy *vis-à-vis* foreign holdings was never to have more than $50 million invested in any one country.

Another firm which diversifies its cash balances among foreign currencies is Litton Industries. As early as 1978, Litton invested one-third of its cash portfolio in foreign certificates of deposit; at the time, the certificates were yielding more than those available in the United States. Another third of their funds was invested in time deposits denominated in German marks and Swiss francs yielding only 4.6% and 1.37%, respectively. Litton's treasurer, Charles Black, explained that even though the interest rate was low, investing in 'strong' currencies such as marks and Swiss francs offset risks associated with investing in 'weak' currencies such as U.S. and Canadian dollars. Clearly Litton expected an exchange gain, relative to the dollar, from the holding of marks and Swiss francs which would materially enhance the low interest yield on the foreign time deposits.

Another firm which pursued an even more aggressive policy is Dow Chemical which invested in a levered portfolio of foreign currencies, sometimes borrowing in the United States to back the investments. The idea behind the strategy is that any unforeseen cash needs can be quickly met by short-term borrowing in the United States while cash funds should seek the highest yield. Dow did not hedge its investment in the forward market, thereby bearing a higher risk but also enjoying the possibility of a higher return on investment as well.

Even this brief review of cash management in practice clearly underscores the fact that traditional methods of cash management are giving way to more aggressive forms of investment with a broader perspective. Firms have learned the value of diversification and now hold investments in many currencies as opposed to the traditional notion of holding cash assets in the home (base) currency only. Some firms use the forward market extensively to further reduce, or eliminate, their exposure to risk of exchange rate fluctuations and hence seek only interest rate differentials among different countries. More aggressive firms expose themselves to some of the inherent risks of exchange rate fluctuations speculating that the gains will overshadow the losses. Such firms mitigate these risks by holding a portfolio of 'naked', i.e., uncovered foreign currency investments.

MANAGING EXCHANGE RISK

Almost all firms view foreign exchange management as a form of risk management. Few will condone undertaking foreign currency transactions which are unconnected with operations, i.e., they do not permit outright speculation. But that is about the extent of the agreement. Each firm tends to develop its own management style with respect to the central questions of exchange risk:

1. How should exchange risk exposure be defined?
2. To what extent should exchange risks be hedged?
3. If hedged, what particular strategy should be adopted?

A firm's answers to these questions depends on its overall corporate philosophy, the structure of its business and the goals it sets for its foreign operations.

Defining exchange risk

Foreign exchange exposure relates to the potential impact of a change in exchange rates on the firm's cash flows, profitability and market value. Three principal types of foreign exchange exposure can be identified: economic, translation, and transaction.

Economic exposure reflects the possibility that a change in exchange rates may affect the net present value of the firm's expected cash flows. The change in *NPV* can be positive or negative depending on the effect of the exchange rate change. For example, consider a U.S. firm which exports to Germany. How will a fall in the German mark affect its operations? This depends on the economic analysis of the impact of the devaluation of the mark. The devaluation of the mark discourages U.S. exports to Germany by making them more expensive in terms of marks. Hence the competitiveness of U.S. exports to Germany is reduced.

Translation exposure, or accounting exposure as it is also called, stems from the need to report income from foreign operations according to accepted accounting principles. Consider, for example, a multinational U.S. firm with subsidiaries operating in a number of foreign countries. Each country requires the subsidiary corporation to report its income and expenses in local currency. However, in order to prepare the consolidated financial statements of the parent corporation, the local currency accounts of each subsidiary must be 'translated' to U.S. dollars.

Accepted accounting practice requires U.S. corporations to include the profit (loss) from changes in the value of foreign currency in their reported earnings per share. The method for carrying out the translation is set out in *Statement of Financial Accounting Standards Number 52 (FASB #52)*. Translation is a highly controversial subject, but one thing is clear. Firms with international operations (export, import, foreign subsidiaries, etc.) are exposed to very significant translation risks, i.e., to the possibility that the method of translation of foreign revenues and assets to the home currency may have a pronounced negative impact on reported consolidated earnings.

Transaction exposure arises when a firm agrees to make a payment or receive a payment denominated in a foreign currency. For example, suppose a U.S. firm exports its products to France on open bank account for 5 million French francs, payable in 60 days. If at the end of 60 days the franc *appreciates* by 10%, relative to the dollar, the U.S. firm will gain, i.e., the

5 million francs will be converted into more dollars than could be obtained at the current exchange rate. Conversely, should the exchange rate for the franc fall, the 5 million francs will be converted into fewer dollars than could be obtained in the spot market at the current exchange rate.

What exposures should be covered?

Once the firm's risk exposure has been defined and estimated, it still must decide why (if any) of the exchange rate risks should be covered. Cover refers to a strategy by which exchange risk embodied in an exposed position is eliminated or reduced. Covering foreign exchange risks is something like insurance. At first glance, it seems as if all risks should be covered. After all we assume firms to be risk-averse. But coverage, like insurance, has its price and the benefits of coverage must be weighed against its cost. This again is a controversial subject, but many firms limit their coverage decisions to transaction exposure, preferring not to expend real resources to offset accounting risks.

OTHER METHODS OF ELIMINATING EXCHANGE RISK

Many of the risks created by the instability of foreign exchange rates can be avoided if the firm (or investor) forgoes any chance of gain. But like insurance contracts, the institutional arrangements for avoiding exchange risk are not costless.

Hedging in the forward market

Exchange rate risk can be hedged, at a cost, by recourse to the forward market; the cost of the 'cover', i.e., insurance against foreign exchange risk, depends on the difference between the *spot* rate, and the spread between the relevant 'bid' and 'ask' prices. Hence, modern financial risk management requires a working knowledge of the *forward contract*. Consider, for example, a firm which invests part of its liquid resources in short-term Japanese bonds, which yield 8.74%. The firm must first acquire the yen through a spot purchase at the prevailing exchange rate for the yen. But by the time the bond matures, the value of the yen may have changed. To hedge against this possibility of changing exchange rates, assume that the firm, when it acquired the yen, also sold a forward contract which stated that the firm would deliver a certain amount of yen in exchange for dollars at a future date at a specified price. This is what is meant by 'selling yen forward'. The forward transaction, in this case, allows the firm to eliminate the uncertainty of any future change in the exchange rate. No matter what happens to the yen's value, the firm is completely *hedged* against this risk and receives, as a result, an 8.74% return on the Japanese utility bond, *less* the cost of the forward transaction.

If the firm had expected a rise in the yen's value, *and was willing to take the risk*, it could have abstained from hedging with a forward contract or might have covered only a proportion of the total amount instead. A hedge which covers only part of the exposure is called a '*variable hedge*' . The latter permits a firm to bear as much risk as it sees fit.

To see how a forward market works, consider the following simplified example. A U.S. manufacturer purchases electronic components from a Japanese electronics firm for 229 million yen. Assuming a current spot exchange rate of 229 yen per dollar, the U.S. importers' cost is equal to $1 million (229 million ÷ 229 = 1 million). The invoice is payable (in yen) in 90 days. If the importer takes advantage of the trade credit and waits 3 months, he must bear the transaction risk. Should the yen appreciate in value relative to the dollar, e.g., to an exchange rate of 200 yen per dollar, the U.S. importer will have to pay $1,145,000 at the new spot price in order to acquire the 229 million yen. The additional cost of $145,000 might conceivably wipe out the entire profit on the transaction. If the importer is sufficiently worried about such a possibility, he can purchase 229 million yen on the forward market for delivery in 90 days, say at a rate of 225 yen per dollar. Thus, his dollar cost will be $1,017,778 (229 million ÷ 225 = 1,017,778) no matter what the spot exchange rate happens to be 3 months later. This is what is meant by covering a transaction exposure (in this case a trade payable) by a *hedge* in the forward market.

Until recently, forward contracts were unavailable for periods greater than one year. Hence a corporation which wanted to hedge its exchange rate over a longer period had to find another firm or financial institution willing to participate in a currency exchange, usually called '*swap*' or '*back-to-back loans*'. But finding such a partner was both cumbersome and expensive. Today, many large banks offer forward contracts for periods extending up to five years for U.S. and Canadian dollars, German marks, British pounds, and Swiss francs. As a result, the long-term forward market has tended to replace the swaps in these currencies. However swaps remain an important hedging device for lesser traded currencies and for transactions extending beyond five years.

Currency futures markets

Forward contracts are typically created by banks and serve the purposes of many large international corporations. Access to the forward market is limited to those firms that have a regular banking relationship with banks that offer forward contracts. Smaller firms, or those firms and investors who wish to speculate in the market, are largely excluded from this market. However, this type of investor can turn to the futures market.

Futures trading in foreign currencies was introduced by the Chicago Mercantile Exchange which established, in 1972, the *International Monetary Market* (*IMM*) as an alternative to the regular forward contracts offered by commercial banks. On the IMM, contracts are available in the leading trading currencies and other financial instruments. Unlike the forward market, trading on the IMM takes place in an organized exchange. The IMM clearing house guarantees performance of the contract even if one party defaults. To this end, the IMM requires participants to deposit a required margin.

Local currency borrowing

Exposure to foreign exchange risk can be offset by borrowing the needed money directly in the local currency market of the country in question, or by lending (i.e., purchasing a security in that country's money market). Alternatively, large multinationals achieve a similar effect by inter-company transactions.

'Leads and lags'

This is the practice followed by some firms of accelerating their payments of accounts payable which are denominated in a strengthening currency ('leads'), while delaying for as long as possible payments of accounts which are set out in terms of a weakening currency ('lags').

Numerous variants of the above methods are available. For example, some firms are able to manipulate the 'invoicing' currency for their transactions; others attempt to manage their balance sheets to achieve a balance of assets and liabilities by currency denomination.

INTERNATIONAL FINANCIAL MARKETS

International financial activity is concentrated in certain cities which can be identified as international financial centers. London and New York are the most important of these, but Amsterdam, Geneva, Paris, Tokyo, and Zurich have also emerged as important centers for international finance. Since the end of the 1950s, another important international marketplace has evolved. This is the Eurocurrency market which today plays a significant role in both the money and long-term capital markets.

Eurocurrency market

The Eurocurrency market is an international money and capital market that deals in currencies outside their countries of origin. *Eurodollars* are U.S. dollars deposited in banks outside the borders of the United States. An example would be the deposit of dollars with a London bank or the London branch of an American or German bank. Originally the dollar was virtually the only currency used in the Euromarket. Today, all major western currencies are represented in the Eurocurrency market. Thus, a Euro-DM is created by the deposit of German marks in banks outside the Federal Republic of Germany, and Euro-yen are Japanese yen deposited outside Japan.

Most Eurocurrency deposits are placed with the bank for a specific maturity and at a fixed interest rate. The maturities range from overnight funds to maturities of up to five years. The remaining deposits take the form of a negotiable certificate of deposit. The advantage of, say, a London Eurodollar deposit (or CD) stems from its geographical location. Since it is held outside the United States, the Eurodollar deposit is *not* subject to control and regulation by U.S. monetary authorities. This reduces the cost of such funds to the bank, which in turn permits the payment of interest rates which are higher than their equivalent U.S. rates. These higher interest rates have proved a major attraction for corporations and public institutions that wish to hold part of their liquid assets in dollar-denominated deposits.

Loans offered on the Euromarket range from 24 hours to one year. Longer-term loans of up to 5–10 year maturity are also available. Both interest rates on Eurodollar loans and deposits are tied to a standard rate, in this case LIBOR – the London Inter-Bank Offer Rate. This is the rate of interest paid to large banks on their deposits with the largest London banks.

SUMMARY

This chapter has been devoted to international financial management in the turbulent atmosphere of volatile exchange rate fluctuations. The decades of the 1970s and 1980s have witnessed a remarkable change in the international economic order. The Bretton Woods System of fixed exchange rates was replaced by freely fluctuating exchange values. Today, all the major currencies are free to fluctuate, at least to some extent, against the dollar. This shift has not only created additional risks, but has also confronted corporate financial managers with a challenge in the form of new investment opportunities.

The exchange rate, like any other price, is determined by the forces of demand and supply for the foreign currency in question. These demands and supplies, in turn, reflect a multitude of influences:

1. If the United States imports more than it exports to a particular country the supply of dollars will increase (in order to pay for the import surplus) and the exchange rate for the dollar will depreciate.
2. In the long run, purchasing power parity (PPP) will tend to make exchange rates adjust so as to reflect the differential rates of inflation between countries.
3. If the *real* interest rate in the United States falls relative to other countries, investors will seek outlets abroad. This tends to increase the supply of dollars and leads to a depreciation of the dollar.
4. If aggregate income in the United States grows at a relatively fast rate, the increased demand for imports will lead to a depreciation of the dollar.

Because of the volatile fluctuations in exchange rates, almost all firms view foreign exchange management as a special case of risk management. Three principal types of exchange risk can be identified:

1. Economic exposure which reflects the possibility that a change in exchange rates may affect the *NPV* of the firm's expected cash flow.

2. Translation (accounting) exposure stems from the legal requirement to report income derived from foreign subsidiaries according to accepted accounting principles. The method for carrying out the translation from foreign currencies to dollars is set out in the *Statement of Financial Accounting Standards Number 52* (*FASB #52*).
3. Transactions exposure arises when a firm agrees to make, or receive, a future payment denominated in a foreign currency.

There are several alternative methods for avoiding exchange risk:

1. Exchange risk can be hedged in the forward market by entering into an appropriate forward contract, by participating in a currency swap, or by transactions in the futures market.
2. Exchange risk can also be offset by borrowing (or lending) in the currency market of the country in question.

SUMMARY TABLE

Direct and indirect quotes

1. *Direct quote* = the amount of dollars required to purchase a unit of foreign currency.
2. *Indirect quote* = 1/the direct quote = the amount of foreign currency required to purchase \$1.

Cross rates

Cross rates = the direct quote of one currency × the indirect quote of a second currency.

Example

$$\frac{\text{Pounds}}{\text{Dollars}} \times \frac{\text{Dollars}}{\text{DM}} = \frac{\text{Pounds}}{\text{DM}}$$

Purchasing power parity (PPP)

The PPP argument claims that the required change in the exchange rate is determined by the relative change in the inflation rates of the two countries:

$$(1 + X) = \frac{(1 + h_d)}{(1 + h_f)}$$

where:

X = percentage change in the exchange value
h_d = inflation rate in the domestic country
h_f = inflation rate in the foreign country

Conversion of swap rates to annualised premium/discount percentages

The swap rate is defined as the differential between the spot and forward rate. While it is generally quoted in absolute terms, it can be expressed in terms of an annual premium/discount as follows:

$$\begin{matrix} \text{Forward} \\ \text{premium} \\ \text{(discount)} \end{matrix} = \frac{\text{Forward rate} - \text{Spot rate}}{\text{Spot rate}} \times \frac{12}{\text{Forward contract in months}}$$

Rate of return on holding foreign currency

$$R_{jt} = \frac{M_{jt} - M_{jt+1}}{M_{jt+1}} = \frac{M_{jt-1}}{M_{jt+1}} - 1$$

R_{jt} = rate of return on holding foreign currency j during period t

M_j = rate of exchange of the jth country's currency at jt beginning of period t

M_{jt+1} = rate of exchange of the jth country's currency at the end of period $t + 1$

Rate of return on interest bearing assets in foreign currency

$$R_{jt} + r_{jt} + R_{jt} \times r_{jt}$$

R_{jt} = rate of return on holding foreign currency j during period t

r_{jt} = rate of interest on foreign currency asset j during time t

QUESTIONS AND PROBLEMS

22.1 Compute the corresponding direct quotes, when the indirect quotes are:

(a) 1.55 Swiss francs per dollar
(b) 6.07 French francs per dollar
(c) 1299 Italian lira per dollar
(d) 6.83 Norwegian krona per dollar
(e) 145 Japanese yen per dollar

22.2 Use the data of the previous problem to compute the following cross rates:

(a) Swiss franc per French franc
(b) Japanese yen per Italian lira
(c) Italian lira per Japanese yen
(d) Norwegian krone per Swiss franc.

22.3 A French textile manufacturer wants to buy a Swiss weaving machine, which costs 84,500 Swiss francs. Use the data given in problem 22.1 to compute how much the manufacturer has to pay in terms of local currency.

22.4 An American importer buys 2,000 men's suits from a Japanese firm at a cost of 17,000 yen per suit, payable in dollars. Use the data of problem 22.1 to compute how much the importer has to pay.

22.5 The exchange rate between the English pound and the U.S. dollar is 0.60 pounds per dollar in 1992. Assume that inflation will amount to 3.5% in the United States, and 7.6% in England, during 1993. What do you expect the exchange rate to be after one year, if the purchasing power parity hypothesis holds?

22.6 On March 1, 1 Swiss franc sells for 1.10 German marks. One year later the rate is 1.20 marks per Swiss franc. In Switzerland there was no inflation during that year. According to the PPP theorem, what was the rate of inflation in Germany?

22.7 On January 15, the exchange rate of the Belgian franc to the dollar was 37.78. On February 15 the rate was 38.21. What exchange profit (converted to an annual basis) was made?

22.8 On April 5, the exchange rate of the U.S. dollar to the Canadian dollar was 1.02. On June 5 the rate was 0.98. What exchange profit (converted to an annual basis) was made by the holder of which currency?

22.9 A German automobile producer sells 500 cars to a U.S. importer at a price of $4,000 each. The invoice is payable in 90 days, in dollars. The spot rate is 2 German marks per dollar, the forward rate is 1.95 per dollar. What transactions take place, if the German firm wants to hedge in the forward market?

22.10 The German automobile producer of the previous problem now wants to cover his exchange risk by borrowing. The yearly interest rates are 6.4% in Germany and 9.5% in the United States. What transactions will be made?

22.11 (a) Assume that the spot rate is DM2 and the forward rate for one year is 1.95. The interest rate prevailing in the United States and Germany as presented in the previous question remains constant. Can an investor combine borrowing and lending activities with foreign currency transactions in both the spot and forward markets to insure himself a guaranteed profit without risking any of his own capital?

(b) How would the assumption that a 0.5% commission is taken for each conversion (spot and purchase/sale forward) change your answer.

22.12 A Dutch investor feels that a devaluation of the Dutch florin *vis-à-vis* the American dollar is imminent and has purchased dollars in accordance to his expectations. Unexpectedly he is faced with a need for cash but is unable to secure immediate credit from any source. He is expecting future receipts in Dutch florins. How can this investor maintain his position in dollars yet at the same time meet his current cash needs?

22.13 An American manufacturer imports raw materials from Britain and sells the finished products to Japan. Prices for both imports and exports are quoted in the supplier's/customer's local currency. He receives 90 days' credit from his British suppliers and extends 60 days' credit to his Japanese customers. How can this manufacturer use the forward market to neutralize the exchange risk inherent in his business activities?

22.14 Assume that the rate of return in the British stock market was in a given year 20% and the rate of return in the U. S. market 10%. The exchange rate between the pound and dollar at the beginning of the year is $1.70 per pound, and at the end of the year $1.60 per pound.

(a) Calculate the rate of return to the American who invested in this year in the U.K.

(b) Calculate the rate of return to the British investor who invested in this year in the U.S.

22.15 Use the data of question 22.14 with the following additional information. The American investor, fearing that the British pound will weaken, buys a put option to sell £50 at $1.70 in June 1992. The price of the put option is $5.

(a) Calculate the rate of return to the American investor on the $105 invested when he invests $100 in the U. K market and pays $5 for the put option. Was it worth buying the put option?

(b) How would you change your answer to (a) if the exchange rate at the end of the year is £1 = $1.4?

APPENDIX 22A: THE INTERNATIONAL MONETARY SYSTEM _____

It is difficult to think of another area in which change has been so dramatic as the emergence of the 'new economic order' during the 1970s and 1980s. These two decades have witnessed a veritable revolution of the international monetary system.

Gold standard

For almost five thousand years – from the time of the Pharoahs and the Ancient Greeks and Romans to the outbreak of World War I – gold served as an almost universally accepted standard of international value. Gold coins were used as a medium of exchange and store of value. However, because carrying gold was inconvenient, the major trading countries in the nineteenth century used paper money whose par value was defined in terms of gold and which could be redeemed, upon demand, for gold. One of the last countries to adhere to the gold standard was the United States, which did not go on the gold standard until 1879.

The gold standard virtually fixed the exchange rates between countries. (Deviations beyond the cost of transporting gold bullion could be arbitraged away.) However, in effect, the gold standard was actually a 'sterling standard'. Prior to World War I, London was the world's financial center and receivables, bills of exchange, etc. were usually denominated in British pounds. This was convenient because the pound was almost universally used as the standard of account, and moreover, was fully convertible to gold at the Bank of England. However, few traders spoke of convertibility. After all, as the historians have put it: in the nineteenth century there was nothing 'better' into which pounds could be converted.

Modified gold standard

Like so many other things, World War I destroyed the old economic order and the gold (or sterling) standard as well. During the war and the early 1920s, currencies fluctuated both in terms of gold and in terms of each other. Several unsuccessful attempts were made during the 1920s to restore the gold standard, but the Great Depression of the 1930s led most of the major trading countries to abandon the gold standard completely. The chief exception was the United States, which in 1934 established a modified gold standard: gold was priced at $35 an ounce but was traded only with official central banks and *not* with private citizens. From the mid-1930s to the end of World War II all of the major currencies floated against the U.S. dollar which was convertible into gold.

Gold exchange standard: 1944–71

In 1944, representatives of the allied powers met in Bretton Woods, New Hampshire, to establish a 'gold exchange standard'. The Bretton Woods Conference also created the International Monetary Fund (IMF) and the International Bank for Reconstruction and Development (World Bank). Under the Bretton Woods Agreement, all member countries were required to fix the par value of their currencies in terms of gold; however there was no obligation to convert the various currencies into gold upon demand. The exception was the U.S. dollar which was convertible to gold at the official price of $35 per ounce. In practice, each country decided on the rate of exchange to the dollar which they wanted, and then calculated the gold par value of their currency which would result in the desired dollar exchange rate. It was also agreed that all other currencies would be permitted to deviate from their gold par values within a very narrow band of $\pm 1\%$. Responsibility for maintaining the exchange rates was placed on each country's central bank which would buy or sell foreign exchange or gold as needed. Larger deviations required the approval of the IMF.

In 1959, the major trading nations returned to the full convertibility of their currencies, but not all of the countries could maintain their exchange rates within the 2% band. In 1967, the United Kingdom was forced, by its growing trade deficit, to devalue the pound. France followed in 1969 with a devaluation of the franc. A devaluation is the official announcement that a country is reducing the value of its currency relative to other currencies. For example, the 1967 devaluation of the British pound reduced its value (exchange rate) from $2.80 per pound to $2.50 per pound. This made British exports cheaper abroad while raising the cost of imports, thereby reversing the trade deficit. Conversely, countries with very strong currencies could *revalue* their currencies. A revaluation is the official announcement that a country is *raising* the value of its currency relative to other countries. This was done by Germany during the 1960s.

The net result of the Bretton Woods system was that the exchange rates of the major trading nations were relatively stable. Changes due to devaluation or revaluation were large, but infrequent.

The financial crisis of 1971

In 1971, the Bretton Woods system came to an end. Inflation, plus a weakening of the dollar's acceptability as an international currency led to a massive attack on the dollar and a large-scale outflow of gold from the United States. On August 15, 1971, President Nixon suspended the dollar's convertibility to gold. This, in effect, brought the gold exchange standard to an end. The system of pegged exchange rates which had been established at Bretton Woods could not be maintained and the exchange rates of the leading trading nations were allowed to float against the dollar.

Numerous attempts were made to restore the old economic order. A series of international agreements were negotiated for the purpose of reintroducing a measure of exchange rate stability.

Smithsonian Agreement. In December 1971, the world's leading industrial nations, the 'Group of Ten', reached an agreement:

1. They agreed to revalue their currencies upwards with respect to the dollar;
2. The trading band around the new par value was expanded from 2% to 4.5%, i.e. maximum movements of 4.5% relative to the dollar were permitted before the central bank's intervention

3. The United States devalued the dollar, in terms of gold, to $38 per ounce.

The 'snake'. In the spring of 1972, the members of the European Economic Community (EEC), along with the prospective members (Denmark, Ireland, Norway, and the United Kingdom) entered into the European Joint Float Agreement, popularly known as the 'snake'. Under this agreement:

1. Members' currencies were restricted to a 2.25% trading band *vis-à-vis* one another.
2. Jointly, they were allowed to trade relative to the dollar within the Smithsonian 4.5% band.

This rather complex arrangement was referred to as 'the snake within the tunnel'. But subsequent to the agreement, some countries, notably the United Kingdom, withdrew.

In March 1979, the nine members of the EEC launched a new experiment – the *European Monetary System* (*EMS*) – which replaced the old 'snake'. The EMS is more flexible than the snake, and has proved more durable. Its major features are:

1. A new 'composite currency', the *European Currency Unit* (*Ecu*), was created. The Ecu is not a circulating currency; it exists only on the book of the EMS members, and is used to settle accounts among member countries. Its value is based on a weighted average of the value of individual member countries' currencies with the weights reflecting the volume of trade and size of GNP.
2. Each country values its currency in terms of the Ecu.
3. Deviations from these par rates are permitted within a band (which is not the same for all countries). Beyond these limits, members intervene to restore the old rates.
4. However, if the deviation is extreme, the country in question must take action to correct the situation and/or devalue (or revalue) its currency's Ecu value.

The floating exchange rate system

All efforts to restore the fixed exchange rate system failed. By 1973, the United States was again forced to devalue the dollar to $42.22 per gold ounce, and the fixed trading bands could not be held in the face of massive speculative pressures. World-wide inflation and the oil crisis of 1973 sounded the final death knell of the fixed exchange rate system.

In 1976, the IMF meeting in Jamaica laid down the rules for a new agreement. The main provision was that floating exchange rates were officially accepted and member countries were no longer required to maintain fixed bands around their par values. However, they were permitted to intervene in trading in order to offset unwarranted fluctuations caused by speculation. Under the present *floating rate system*, exchange rates are determined by the forces of demand and supply and fluctuate daily against one another. But it is also a *managed floating* system. Although exchange rates are no longer restricted by international agreements regarding permissible trading bands, central banks, can, and often do, intervene to influence trading. Hence, the expression 'managed float', or in popular slang, 'dirty float'. Moreover, the current floating system still retains 'regional' agreements such as the EMS – which restrict the fluctuations of member countries' currencies among themselves.

The forces of supply and demand, and therefore, exchange rate fluctuations are strongly influenced by world events. The major events since the 1976 Jamaica Agreement were as follows:

1. The dollar crisis in 1977–78 and the sharp increase in U.S. interest rates by the Carter Administration. During this period the dollar lost about 10% of its value relative to major European currencies.
2. The oil crisis of 1974. The Organization of Oil Exporting Countries (OPEC) reacted to the weakness of the dollar by doubling the price of oil, which triggered a new

world-wide recession. In addition, the Iran–Iraq war in the 1980s has further affected oil production and prices.

3. In the second half of the 1980s, exchange rates were strongly influenced by the growing U.S. trade deficit. This led to a sharp decline in the value of the dollar relative to the major European currencies and especially relative to the Japanese yen.

SELECTED REFERENCES

Abdullah, Fuad A. and Wingender, John R., 'Multinational Financial Management: Exchange Exposure and International Cash Management,' *Journal of the Midwest Finance Association*, 16, 1987.

Abuaf, Niso, 'The Nature and Management of Foreign Exchange Risk,' *Midland Corporate Journal*, Fall 1986.

Adler, Michael and Dumas, Bernard, 'International Portfolio Choice and Corporation Finance: A Synthesis,' *Journal of Finance*, June 1983.

Adler, Michael and Simon, David, 'Exchange Risk Surprises in International Portfolios,' *Journal of Portfolio Management*, Winter 1986.

Agmon, T. and Lessard, D. R., 'Investor Recognition of Corporate International Diversification,' *Journal of Finance*, September 1971.

Beenstock, M., 'Arbitrage, Speculation and Official Forward Intervention: The Cases of Sterling and the Canadian Dollar,' *Review of Economics and Statistics*, February 1979.

Bookstaber, R. M., 'Corporate Production and Sales Decisions in Achieving International Diversification,' *Review of Business and Economic Research*, Winter 1980/81.

Boothe, P. M. and Glassman, D. A., 'The Statistical Distribution of Exchange Rates: Empirical Evidence and Economic Implications,' *Journal of International Economics*, May 1987.

Boughton, James, M., 'Exchange Rate Movements and Adjustment in Financial Markets: Quarterly Estimates for Major Currencies' *International Monetary Fund Staff Papers*, September 1984.

Brewer, H. L., 'Investor Benefits from Corporate International Diversification,' *Journal of Financial and Quantitative Analysis*, September 1981.

Callier, P., 'One Way Arbitrage, Foreign Exchange and Securities Markets,' *Journal of Finance*, December 1981.

Calvo, G. A., 'Real Exchange Rate Dynamics with Nominal Parities: Structural Changes and Overshooting,' *Journal of International Economics*, February 1987.

Carrington, Samantha and Crouch, Robert, 'A Theorem on Interest Rate Differentials, Risk and Anticipated Inflation,' *Applied Economics*, December 1987.

Cholerton, Kenneth, Pieraerts, Pierre, and Solnik, Bruno, 'Why Invest in Foreign Currency Bonds,' *Journal of Portfolio Management*, Summer 1986.

Christelow, Dorothy, 'International Joint Ventures: How Important Are They?' *Columbia Journal of World Business*, Summer 1987.

Cohn, R. A. and Pringle, J. J., 'Imperfections in International Financial Markets: Implications for Risk Premia and the Cost of Capital to Firms,' *Journal of Finance*, March 1983.

Cornell, B., 'The Denomination of Foreign Trade Contracts Once Again,' *Journal of Financial and Quantitative Analysis*, November 1980.

Cotner, J. S. and Seitz, N. E., 'A Simplified Approach to Short-term International Diversification,' *Financial Review*, May 1987.

Cumby, Robert E., *Is It Risk? Explaining Deviations from Uncovered Interest Parity*, Cambridge: N.B.E.R., 1987.

De Grauwe, Paul, *Exchange Rate Theories and Near-rational Behavior*, Leuven: Katholieke Universiteit, 1988.

Eaker, Mark R. and Grant, Dwight, 'Optimal Hedging of Uncertain and Long-term Foreign Exchange Exposure,' *Journal of Banking and Finance*, June 1985.

Ehrlich, E. E., 'International Diversification by United States Pension Funds,' *Federal Reserve Bank of New York*, Autumn 1981.

Eitman, D. K. and Stonehill, A. I., *Multinational Business Finance*, 3rd ed., Reading, Mass: Addison-Wesley, 1982.

Engel, Charles M., 'On the Correlation of Exchange Rates and Interest Rates', *Journal of International Money and Finance*, March 1986.

Errunza, Vihang and Losq, Etienne, 'International Asset Pricing under Mild Segmentation: Theory and Test,' *Journal of Finance*, March 1985.

Eun, Cheol S. and Jankiramanan, S., 'A Model of International Asset Pricing with a Constraint on the Foreign Equity Ownership,' *Journal of Finance*, September 1986.

Eun, Cheol S. and Resnick, Bruce G., 'Currency Factor in International Portfolio Diversification', *The Columbia Journal of World Business*, Summer 1985.

Feige, E. L. and Singleton, K. J., 'Multinational Inflation Under Fixed Exchange Rates: Some Empirical Evidence for Latent Variable Models,' *Review of Economics and Statistics*, February 1981.

Freidman, A. J. and Sharma, R. M., 'Portfolio Risk Reduction through Foreign Stock,' *Pension World*, September 1980.

Frenkel, J. A. and Levich, R. M., 'Covered Interest Arbitrage: Unexploited Profit?' *Journal of Political Economy*, 1975.

Frenkel, J. A. and Mussa, M. L., 'Efficiency of Foreign Exchange Markets and Measures of Turbulence,' *American Economic Review*, May 1980.

Grauer, F. L. A., Litzenberger' R. H. and Stehle, R. E., 'Sharing Rules and Equilibrium in an International Capital Market under Uncertainty,' *Journal of Financial Economics*, June 1976.

Grauer, R. R. and Hakansson, N. H., 'Gains from International Diversification: 1968–85 Returns on Portfolios of Stocks and Bonds,' *Journal of Finance*, July 1987.

Grubel, Herbert G., 'Internationally Diversified Portfolios: Welfare Gains and Capital Flows,' *American Economic Review*, December 1968.

Hawawini, G., *European Equity Markets: Price Behavior and Effciency*, Monograph 1984–5, Solomon Brothers Center, New York University, 1984.

Herring, Richard J. (ed.) *Managing International Risk*, Cambridge: University Press, 1983.

Hodgson, J. S. and Phelps, P., 'The Distributed Impact of Price-level Variation on Floating Exchange Rates,' *Review of Economics and Statistics*, February 1975.

Hodrick, Robert J., *Risk, Uncertainty and Exchange Rates*, Cambridge: N.B.E.R., 1987.

Huang, Roger D., 'Expectations of Exchange Rates and Differential Inflation Rates: Further Evidence on Purchasing Power Parity in Efficient Markets,' *Journal of Finance*, March 1987.

Huzinga, John, 'An Empirical Investigation of the Long-run Behavior of Real Exchange Rates,' *Carnegie–Rochester Conferences Series on Public Policy*, Autumn 1987.

Ibbotson, R., Siegel, L. and Love, K., 'World Wealth: Market Values and Returns,' *Journal of Portfolio Management*, Fall 1985.

Ibbotson, R., Carr, R. and Robinson, A., 'International Equity and Bond Returns,' *Financial Analysts Journal*, July/August 1982.

Jorion, Philippe, 'International Portfolio Diversification with Estimation Risk,' *Journal of Business*, July 1985.

Kidwell, David S., Marr, M. Wayne and Thompson, G. Rodney, 'Eurodollar Bonds: Alternative Financing for U.S. Companies,' *Financial Management*, Winter 1985.

Larrain, M. R., 'Portfolio Stock Adjustment and the Real Exchange Rate: The Dollar-Mark (DM) and Mark-Sterling,' *Journal of Policy Modeling*, Winter 1986.

Lee, Adrian F., 'International Asset and Currency Allocation,' *Journal of Portfolio Management*, Fall 1987.

Lessard, D. R., 'International Portfolio Diversification: A Multivariate Analysis for a Group of Latin American Countries,' *Journal of Finance*, June 1973.

Levy, Haim, 'Optimal Portfolio of Foreign Currencies with Borrowing and Lending,' *Journal of Money, Credit and Banking*, August 1981.

Levy, Haim and Sarnat, Marshall, 'International Diversification of Investment Portfolios,' *American Economic Review*, September 1970.

Levy, Haim and Sarnat, Marshall, 'Devaluation Risk and the Portfolio Analysis of International Investment,' in Elton and Gruber (eds), *International Capital Markets*, Amsterdam: North-Holland, 1975.

Levy, Haim and Lerman Zvi, 'Internationally Diversified Bond and Stock Portfolios,' *Financial Analysts Journal*, 1989.

Madura, Jeff, 'Currency Cocktail Bonds and Exchange Rate Risk,' *The Investment Analyst*, October 1985.

Makin, J. H., 'Portfolio Theory and the Problem of Foreign Exchange Risk,' *Journal of Finance*, 1981.

Maldonado, R. and Saunders, A., 'International Portfolio Diversification and the Inter-temporal Stability of International Stock Market Relationships,' *Financial Management*, Autumn 1981.

Mathis, F. J. and Maslin, D. C., 'RMA Survey of the Management of International from Portfolio Diversification,' *Journal of Commercial Banking*, March 1981.

Mathur, Ike (ed.), *Managing Foreign Exchange Risks (Managerial Finance)*, 11, 2, 1985.

Moenig, Wolfgang F. and Tease, Warren J., 'Covered Interest Parity in Non-dollar Euromarkets,' *Review of World Economics*, 123, 4, 1987.

Penati, Alessandro and Pennacci, George, *Optimal Portfolio Choice and the Collapse of a Fixed Exchange Rate Regime*, Philadelphia: University of Pennsylvania, Wharton School, 1986.

Rankel, Jefferey and Meese, Richard, *Are Exchange Rates Excessively Variable?* Cambridge: N.B.E.R., 1987.

Sarnat, Marshall and Szego, P. Giorgio, *International Finance and Trade*, Cambridge, Mass.: Ballinger, 1979.

Senbet, L. W., 'International Capital Market Equilibrium and the Multinational Firm Financing and Investment Policies,' *Journal of Financial and Quantitative Analysis*, September 1979.

Shapiro, Alan C. 'Currency Risk and Country Risk in International Banking,' *Journal of Finance*, July 1985.

Sibert, Anne, *The Risk Premium in the Foreign Exchange Market*, Kansas City: Federal Reserve Bank, 1987.

Soenen, Luc A., 'Risk Diversification Characteristics of Currency Cocktails,' *Journal of Economics and Business*, May 1988.

Solnik, Bruno, *International Investments*, Reading, Mass: Addison-Wesley, 1988.

Solnik, Bruno, 'Why not Diversify Internationally rather than Domestically,' *Financial Analysts Journal*, July 1974.

Solnik, Bruno, 'International Pricing of Risk: An Empirical Investigation of the World Capital Market Structure,' *Journal of Finance*, 1974.

Solnik, B. and Noetzlin, B., 'Optimal International Asset Allocation,' *Journal of Portfolio Management*, Fall 1982.

Stehle, R. E., 'An Empirical Test of the Alternative Hypotheses of National and International Pricing of Risky Assets,' *Journal of Finance*, May 1977.

Stern, R., 'Insurance for Third World Currency Inconvertibility Protection,' *Harvard Business Review*, May/June 1982.

Stulz, R. 'The Pricing of Capital Assets in an International Setting: An Introduction,' *Journal of International Business Studies*, Summer 1984.

Swanson, P. E., 'Capital Market Integration Over the Past Decade: The Case of the U.S. Dollar,' *Journal of International Money and Finance*, June 1987.

Tapley, Mark (ed.), *International Portfolio Management*, London: Euromoney, 1986.

Taylor, Mark, 'Risk Premia and Foreign Exchange: A Multiple Time Series Approach to Testing Uncovered Interest Rate Parity,' *Review of World Economics*, May 1988.

Thompson, R. S., 'Risk Reduction and International Diversification: An Analysis of Large U.K. Multinational Companies,' *Applied Economics*, June 1985.

Von Furstenberg, G. M., 'Incentives for International Currency Diversification by U.S. Financial Investors,' *IMF Staff Papers*, September 1981.

Wallingford, B. A., 'International Asset Pricing: A Comment,' *Journal of Finance*, May 1974.

_____ PART III SUGGESTIONS FOR FURTHER READING

The reader who wishes to examine the impact of capital structure on the value of the firm at greater length can well start with the classic article by Franco Modigliani and Merton Miller and then go on to the extensive literature which has emerged in recent years:

F. Modigliani and M. H. Miller, 'The Cost of Capital, Corporation Finance and the Theory of Investment,' *American Economic Review*, June 1958.

F. Modigliani and M. H. Miller, 'Reply to Heins and Sprenkle,' *American Economic Review*, September 1969.

E. F. Fama and M. H. Miller, *The Theory of Finance*, New York: Holt, Rinehart & Winston, 1972.

The significance of bankruptcy risk for financial decision-making is analysed by:

E. I. Altman, *Corporate Bankruptcy in America*, Lexington, Mass.: Heath Lexington Books, 1971.

B. D. Baxter, 'Leverage, Risk of Ruin, and the Cost of Capital,' *Journal of Finance*, September 1967.

J. E. Stiglitz, 'On the Irrelevance of Corporate Financial Policy,' *American Economic Review*, December 1974.

D. P. Baron, 'Firm Valuation, Corporate Taxes and Default Risk,' *Journal of Finance*, December 1975.

J. H. Scott Jr, 'A Theory of Optimal Capital Structure,' *Bell Journal of Economics*, Spring 1976.

The weighted average cost of capital is critically examined by:

F. D. Arditti, 'The Weighted Cost of Capital: Some Questions on its Definition, Interpretation and Use,' *Journal of Finance*, September 1973.

M. J. Gordon and P. J. Halpern, 'Cost of Capital for a Division of a Firm,' *Journal of Finance*, September 1974.

For interesting comparisons of leverage and the cost of capital in the United States and Japan, see:

I. Friend and I. Tokutsu, 'The Cost of Capital to Corporations in Japan and the U.S.A.,' *Journal of Banking and Finance*, June 1987.

W. C. Kester, 'Capital and Ownership Structure: A Comparison of United States and Japanese Manufacturing Corporations,' *Financial Management*, Spring 1986.

Dividend policy has also been the subject of numerous articles and books, but the flavour of the debate can be sampled in:

M. H. Miller and F. Modigliani, 'Dividend Policy, Growth and the Valuation of Shares,' *Journal of Business*, October 1961.

M. J. Gordon, 'Optimal Investment and Financing Policy,' *Journal of Finance*, May 1963.

M. J. Brennan, 'A Note on Dividend Irrelevance and the Gordon Valuation Model,' *Journal of Finance*, December 1971.

A critical review of empirical studies of dividend effects is given by:

I. Friend and M. Puckett, 'Dividends and Stock Prices,' *American Economic Review*, September 1964.

T. E. Copeland and J. Fred Weston, *Financial Theory and Corporate Policy*, 3rd edn, Reading, Mass.: Addison-Wesley, 1988.

A critical analysis of options pricing can be found in:

F. Black and M. Scholes, 'The Pricing of Options and Corporate Liabilities,' *Journal of Political Economy*, May/June 1973.

R. M. Bookstaber, *Option Pricing and Strategies in Investing*, Reading, Mass.: Addison-Wesley, 1981.

J. C. Cox and M. Rubinstein, *Option Markets*, Englewood Cliffs, N.J.: Prentice Hall, 1985.

J. C. Cox, S. Ross and M. Rubinstein, 'Option Pricing: A Simplified Approach,' *Journal of Financial Economics*, September 1979.

R. C. Merton, 'Theory of Rational Option Pricing,' *Bell Journal of Economics and Management Science*, Spring 1973.

C. W. Smith, 'Option Pricing: A Review,' *Journal of Financial Economics*, January/March 1976.

A number of excellent textbooks in international finance are available:

D. K. Eitman and A. 1. Stonehill, *Multinational Business Finance*, 3rd edn, Boston: Addison-Wesley, 1982.

M. Levi, *International Finance: Financial Management and the International Economy*, New York: McGraw-Hill, 1983.

R. M. Rodriguez and E. E. Carter, *International Financial Management*, 3rd edn, Englewood Cliffs, N.J.: Prentice Hall, 1984.

B. Solnik, *International Investments*, Reading, Mass.: Addison-Wesley, 1988.

For useful collections of articles on various aspects of international financial management, see:

R. J. Herring (ed.), *Managing Foreign Exchange Risk*, New York: Cambridge University Press, 1983.

D. A. Ricks, *International Dimensions of Corporate Finance*, Englewood Cliffs, N.J.: Prentice Hall, 1978.

M. Sarnat and G. P. Szego, *International Finance and Trade*, Vols I and II, Lexington, Mass., Ballinger, 1979.

Midland Corporate Finance Journal, special issue, Fall 1986.

For empirical evidence on the efficiency of the foreign exchange markets, see:

R. Z. Aliber, *The International Money Game*, rev. ed., New York: Basic Books, 1981.

Two very useful collections of articles on mergers are available, see *Midland Corporate Journal*, Winter 1983 and Summer 1986.

Detailed and thought-provoking summaries of the empirical evidence on mergers can be found in:

D. C. Mueller, 'The Effects of Conglomerate Mergers: A Survey of the Empirical Evidence,' *Journal of Banking and Finance*, September 1977.

T. E. Copeland and J. Fred Weston, *Financial Theory and Corporate Policy*, 3rd edn, Reading: Addison-Wesley, 1988.

The economic impact of the merger mania of the 1980s is examined by:

M. Ott and G. J. Santoni, 'Mergers and Takeovers − The Value of Predictors' Information', *Federal Reserve Bank of St. Lous Review*, December 1985.

Appendix
Tables A–C

Table A Present value of 1

Periods	1%	2%	3%	4%	5%	6%	7%	8%	9%	10%
1	0.990	0.980	0.971	0.962	0.952	0.943	0.935	0.926	0.917	0.909
2	0.980	0.961	0.943	0.925	0.907	0.890	0.873	0.857	0.842	0.826
3	0.971	0.942	0.915	0.889	0.864	0.840	0.816	0.794	0.772	0.751
4	0.961	0.924	0.888	0.855	0.823	0.792	0.763	0.735	0.708	0.683
5	0.951	0.906	0.863	0.822	0.784	0.747	0.713	0.681	0.650	0.621
6	0.942	0.888	0.837	0.790	0.746	0.705	0.666	0.630	0.596	0.564
7	0.933	0.871	0.813	0.760	0.711	0.665	0.623	0.583	0.547	0.513
8	0.923	0.853	0.789	0.731	0.677	0.627	0.582	0.540	0.502	0.467
9	0.914	0.837	0.766	0.703	0.645	0.592	0.544	0.500	0.460	0.424
10	0.905	0.820	0.744	0.676	0.614	0.558	0.508	0.463	0.422	0.386
11	0.896	0.804	0.722	0.650	0.585	0.527	0.475	0.429	0.388	0.350
12	0.887	0.788	0.701	0.625	0.557	0.497	0.444	0.397	0.356	0.319
13	0.879	0.773	0.681	0.601	0.530	0.469	0.415	0.368	0.326	0.290
14	0.870	0.758	0.661	0.577	0.505	0.442	0.388	0.340	0.299	0.263
15	0.861	0.743	0.642	0.555	0.481	0.417	0.362	0.315	0.275	0.239
16	0.853	0.728	0.623	0.534	0.458	0.394	0.339	0.292	0.252	0.218
17	0.844	0.714	0.605	0.513	0.436	0.371	0.317	0.270	0.231	0.198
18	0.836	0.700	0.587	0.494	0.416	0.350	0.296	0.250	0.212	0.180
19	0.828	0.686	0.570	0.475	0.396	0.331	0.277	0.232	0.194	0.164
20	0.820	0.673	0.554	0.456	0.377	0.312	0.258	0.215	0.178	0.149
21	0.811	0.660	0.538	0.439	0.359	0.294	0.242	0.199	0.164	0.135
22	0.803	0.647	0.522	0.422	0.342	0.278	0.226	0.184	0.150	0.123
23	0.795	0.634	0.507	0.406	0.326	0.262	0.211	0.170	0.138	0.112
24	0.788	0.622	0.492	0.390	0.310	0.247	0.197	0.158	0.126	0.102
25	0.780	0.610	0.478	0.375	0.295	0.233	0.184	0.146	0.116	0.092
26	0.772	0.598	0.464	0.361	0.281	0.220	0.172	0.135	0.106	0.084
27	0.764	0.586	0.450	0.347	0.268	0.207	0.161	0.125	0.098	0.076
28	0.757	0.574	0.437	0.333	0.255	0.196	0.150	0.116	0.090	0.069
29	0.749	0.563	0.424	0.321	0.243	0.185	0.141	0.107	0.082	0.063
30	0.742	0.552	0.412	0.308	0.231	0.174	0.131	0.099	0.075	0.057
40	0.672	0.453	0.307	0.208	0.142	0.097	0.067	0.046	0.032	0.022
50	0.608	0.372	0.228	0.141	0.087	0.054	0.034	0.021	0.013	0.009

Table A (cont.)

Periods	11%	12%	13%	14%	15%	16%	17%	18%	19%	20%
1	0.901	0.893	0.885	0.877	0.870	0.862	0.855	0.847	0.840	0.833
2	0.812	0.797	0.783	0.769	0.756	0.743	0.731	0.718	0.706	0.694
3	0.731	0.712	0.693	0.675	0.658	0.641	0.624	0.609	0.593	0.579
4	0.659	0.636	0.613	0.592	0.572	0.552	0.534	0.516	0.499	0.482
5	0.593	0.567	0.543	0.519	0.497	0.476	0.456	0.437	0.419	0.402
6	0.535	0.507	0.480	0.456	0.432	0.410	0.390	0.370	0.352	0.335
7	0.482	0.452	0.425	0.400	0.376	0.354	0.333	0.314	0.296	0.279
8	0.434	0.404	0.376	0.351	0.327	0.305	0.285	0.266	0.249	0.233
9	0.391	0.361	0.333	0.308	0.284	0.263	0.243	0.225	0.209	0.194
10	0.352	0.322	0.295	0.270	0.247	0.227	0.208	0.191	0.176	0.162
11	0.317	0.287	0.261	0.237	0.215	0.195	0.178	0.162	0.148	0.135
12	0.286	0.257	0.231	0.208	0.187	0.168	0.152	0.137	0.124	0.112
13	0.258	0.229	0.204	0.182	0.163	0.145	0.130	0.116	0.104	0.093
14	0.232	0.205	0.181	0.160	0.141	0.125	0.111	0.099	0.088	0.078
15	0.209	0.183	0.160	0.140	0.123	0.108	0.095	0.084	0.074	0.065
16	0.188	0.163	0.141	0.123	0.107	0.093	0.081	0.071	0.062	0.054
17	0.170	0.146	0.125	0.108	0.093	0.080	0.069	0.060	0.052	0.045
18	0.153	0.130	0.111	0.095	0.081	0.069	0.059	0.051	0.044	0.038
19	0.138	0.116	0.098	0.083	0.070	0.060	0.051	0.043	0.037	0.031
20	0.124	0.104	0.087	0.073	0.061	0.051	0.043	0.037	0.031	0.026
21	0.112	0.093	0.077	0.064	0.053	0.044	0.037	0.031	0.026	0.022
22	0.101	0.083	0.068	0.056	0.046	0.038	0.032	0.026	0.022	0.018
23	0.091	0.074	0.060	0.049	0.040	0.033	0.027	0.022	0.018	0.015
24	0.082	0.066	0.053	0.043	0.035	0.028	0.023	0.019	0.015	0.013
25	0.074	0.059	0.047	0.038	0.030	0.024	0.020	0.016	0.013	0.010
26	0.066	0.053	0.042	0.033	0.026	0.021	0.017	0.014	0.011	0.009
27	0.060	0.047	0.037	0.029	0.023	0.018	0.014	0.011	0.009	0.007
28	0.054	0.042	0.033	0.026	0.020	0.016	0.012	0.010	0.008	0.006
29	0.048	0.037	0.029	0.022	0.017	0.014	0.011	0.008	0.006	0.005
30	0.044	0.033	0.026	0.020	0.015	0.012	0.009	0.007	0.005	0.004
40	0.015	0.011	0.008	0.005	0.004	0.003	0.002	0.001	0.001	0.001
50	0.005	0.003	0.002	0.001	0.001	0.001	0.000	0.000	0.000	0.000

Table A (cont.)

Periods	21%	22%	23%	24%	25%	26%	27%	28%	29%	30%
1	0.826	0.820	0.813	0.806	0.800	0.794	0.787	0.781	0.775	0.769
2	0.683	0.672	0.661	0.650	0.640	0.630	0.620	0.610	0.601	0.592
3	0.564	0.551	0.537	0.524	0.512	0.500	0.488	0.477	0.466	0.455
4	0.467	0.451	0.437	0.423	0.410	0.397	0.384	0.373	0.361	0.350
5	0.386	0.370	0.355	0.341	0.328	0.315	0.303	0.291	0.280	0.269
6	0.319	0.303	0.289	0.275	0.262	0.250	0.238	0.227	0.217	0.207
7	0.263	0.249	0.235	0.222	0.210	0.198	0.188	0.178	0.168	0.159
8	0.218	0.204	0.191	0.179	0.168	0.157	0.148	0.139	0.130	0.123
9	0.180	0.167	0.155	0.144	0.134	0.125	0.116	0.108	0.101	0.094
10	0.149	0.137	0.126	0.116	0.107	0.099	0.092	0.085	0.078	0.073
11	0.123	0.112	0.103	0.094	0.086	0.079	0.072	0.066	0.061	0.056
12	0.102	0.092	0.083	0.076	0.069	0.062	0.057	0.052	0.047	0.043
13	0.084	0.075	0.068	0.061	0.055	0.050	0.045	0.040	0.037	0.033
14	0.069	0.062	0.055	0.049	0.044	0.039	0.035	0.032	0.028	0.025
15	0.057	0.051	0.045	0.040	0.035	0.031	0.028	0.025	0.022	0.020
16	0.047	0.042	0.036	0.032	0.028	0.025	0.022	0.019	0.017	0.015
17	0.039	0.034	0.030	0.026	0.023	0.020	0.017	0.015	0.013	0.012
18	0.032	0.028	0.024	0.021	0.018	0.016	0.014	0.012	0.010	0.009
19	0.027	0.023	0.020	0.017	0.014	0.012	0.011	0.009	0.008	0.007
20	0.022	0.019	0.016	0.014	0.012	0.010	0.008	0.007	0.006	0.005
21	0.018	0.015	0.013	0.011	0.009	0.008	0.007	0.006	0.005	0.004
22	0.015	0.013	0.011	0.009	0.007	0.006	0.005	0.004	0.004	0.003
23	0.012	0.010	0.009	0.007	0.006	0.005	0.004	0.003	0.003	0.002
24	0.010	0.008	0.007	0.006	0.005	0.004	0.003	0.003	0.002	0.002
25	0.009	0.007	0.006	0.005	0.004	0.003	0.003	0.002	0.002	0.001
26	0.007	0.006	0.005	0.004	0.003	0.002	0.002	0.002	0.001	0.001
27	0.006	0.005	0.004	0.003	0.002	0.002	0.002	0.001	0.001	0.001
28	0.005	0.004	0.003	0.002	0.002	0.002	0.001	0.001	0.001	0.001
29	0.004	0.003	0.002	0.002	0.002	0.001	0.001	0.001	0.001	0.000
30	0.003	0.003	0.002	0.002	0.001	0.001	0.001	0.001	0.000	0.000
40	0.000	0.000	0.000	0.000	0.000	0.000	0.000	0.000	0.000	0.000
50	0.000	0.000	0.000	0.000	0.000	0.000	0.000	0.000	0.000	0.000

Table A (cont.)

Periods	31%	32%	33%	34%	35%	36%	37%	38%	39%	40%
1	0.763	0.758	0.752	0.746	0.741	0.735	0.730	0.725	0.719	0.714
2	0.583	0.574	0.565	0.557	0.549	0.541	0.533	0.525	0.518	0.510
3	0.445	0.435	0.425	0.416	0.406	0.398	0.389	0.381	0.372	0.364
4	0.340	0.329	0.320	0.310	0.301	0.292	0.284	0.276	0.268	0.260
5	0.259	0.250	0.240	0.231	0.223	0.215	0.207	0.200	0.193	0.186
6	0.198	0.189	0.181	0.173	0.165	0.158	0.151	0.145	0.139	0.133
7	0.151	0.143	0.136	0.129	0.122	0.116	0.110	0.105	0.100	0.095
8	0.115	0.108	0.102	0.096	0.091	0.085	0.081	0.076	0.072	0.068
9	0.088	0.082	0.077	0.072	0.067	0.063	0.059	0.055	0.052	0.048
10	0.067	0.062	0.058	0.054	0.050	0.046	0.043	0.040	0.037	0.035
11	0.051	0.047	0.043	0.040	0.037	0.034	0.031	0.029	0.027	0.025
12	0.039	0.036	0.033	0.030	0.027	0.025	0.023	0.021	0.019	0.018
13	0.030	0.027	0.025	0.022	0.020	0.018	0.017	0.015	0.014	0.013
14	0.023	0.021	0.018	0.017	0.015	0.014	0.012	0.011	0.010	0.009
15	0.017	0.016	0.014	0.012	0.011	0.010	0.009	0.008	0.007	0.006
16	0.013	0.012	0.010	0.009	0.008	0.007	0.006	0.006	0.005	0.005
17	0.010	0.009	0.008	0.007	0.006	0.005	0.005	0.004	0.004	0.003
18	0.008	0.007	0.006	0.005	0.005	0.004	0.003	0.003	0.003	0.002
19	0.006	0.005	0.004	0.004	0.003	0.003	0.003	0.002	0.002	0.002
20	0.005	0.004	0.003	0.003	0.002	0.002	0.002	0.002	0.001	0.001
21	0.003	0.003	0.003	0.002	0.002	0.002	0.001	0.001	0.001	0.001
22	0.003	0.002	0.002	0.002	0.001	0.001	0.001	0.001	0.001	0.001
23	0.002	0.002	0.001	0.001	0.001	0.001	0.001	0.001	0.001	0.000
24	0.002	0.001	0.001	0.001	0.001	0.001	0.001	0.000	0.000	0.000
25	0.001	0.001	0.001	0.001	0.001	0.000	0.000	0.000	0.000	0.000
26	0.001	0.001	0.001	0.000	0.000	0.000	0.000	0.000	0.000	0.000
27	0.001	0.001	0.000	0.000	0.000	0.000	0.000	0.000	0.000	0.000
28	0.001	0.000	0.000	0.000	0.000	0.000	0.000	0.000	0.000	0.000
29	0.000	0.000	0.000	0.000	0.000	0.000	0.000	0.000	0.000	0.000
30	0.000	0.000	0.000	0.000	0.000	0.000	0.000	0.000	0.000	0.000
40	0.000	0.000	0.000	0.000	0.000	0.000	0.000	0.000	0.000	0.000
50	0.000	0.000	0.000	0.000	0.000	0.000	0.000	0.000	0.000	0.000

Table A (cont.)

Periods	41%	42%	43%	44%	45%	46%	47%	48%	49%	50%
1	0.709	0.704	0.699	0.694	0.690	0.685	0.680	0.676	0.671	0.667
2	0.503	0.496	0.489	0.482	0.476	0.469	0.463	0.457	0.450	0.444
3	0.357	0.349	0.342	0.335	0.328	0.321	0.315	0.308	0.302	0.296
4	0.253	0.246	0.239	0.233	0.226	0.220	0.214	0.208	0.203	0.198
5	0.179	0.173	0.167	0.162	0.156	0.151	0.146	0.141	0.136	0.132
6	0.127	0.122	0.117	0.112	0.108	0.103	0.099	0.095	0.091	0.088
7	0.090	0.086	0.082	0.078	0.074	0.071	0.067	0.064	0.061	0.059
8	0.064	0.060	0.057	0.054	0.051	0.048	0.046	0.043	0.041	0.039
9	0.045	0.043	0.040	0.038	0.035	0.033	0.031	0.029	0.028	0.026
10	0.032	0.030	0.028	0.026	0.024	0.023	0.021	0.020	0.019	0.017
11	0.023	0.021	0.020	0.018	0.017	0.016	0.014	0.013	0.012	0.012
12	0.016	0.015	0.014	0.013	0.012	0.011	0.010	0.009	0.008	0.008
13	0.011	0.010	0.010	0.009	0.008	0.007	0.007	0.006	0.006	0.005
14	0.008	0.007	0.007	0.006	0.006	0.005	0.005	0.004	0.004	0.003
15	0.006	0.005	0.005	0.004	0.004	0.003	0.003	0.003	0.003	0.002
16	0.004	0.004	0.003	0.003	0.003	0.002	0.002	0.002	0.002	0.002
17	0.003	0.003	0.002	0.002	0.002	0.002	0.001	0.001	0.001	0.001
18	0.002	0.002	0.002	0.001	0.001	0.001	0.001	0.001	0.001	0.001
19	0.001	0.001	0.001	0.001	0.001	0.001	0.001	0.001	0.001	0.000
20	0.001	0.001	0.001	0.001	0.001	0.001	0.000	0.000	0.000	0.000
21	0.001	0.001	0.001	0.000	0.000	0.000	0.000	0.000	0.000	0.000
22	0.001	0.000	0.000	0.000	0.000	0.000	0.000	0.000	0.000	0.000
23	0.000	0.000	0.000	0.000	0.000	0.000	0.000	0.000	0.000	0.000
24	0.000	0.000	0.000	0.000	0.000	0.000	0.000	0.000	0.000	0.000
25	0.000	0.000	0.000	0.000	0.000	0.000	0.000	0.000	0.000	0.000
26	0.000	0.000	0.000	0.000	0.000	0.000	0.000	0.000	0.000	0.000
27	0.000	0.000	0.000	0.000	0.000	0.000	0.000	0.000	0.000	0.000
28	0.000	0.000	0.000	0.000	0.000	0.000	0.000	0.000	0.000	0.000
29	0.000	0.000	0.000	0.000	0.000	0.000	0.000	0.000	0.000	0.000
30	0.000	0.000	0.000	0.000	0.000	0.000	0.000	0.000	0.000	0.000
40	0.000	0.000	0.000	0.000	0.000	0.000	0.000	0.000	0.000	0.000
50	0.000	0.000	0.000	0.000	0.000	0.000	0.000	0.000	0.000	0.000

Table B Present value of annuity of 1

Periods	1%	2%	3%	4%	5%	6%	7%	8%	9%	10%
1	0.990	0.980	0.971	0.962	0.952	0.943	0.935	0.926	0.917	0.909
2	1.970	1.942	1.913	1.886	1.859	1.833	1.808	1.783	1.759	1.736
3	2.941	2.884	2.829	2.775	2.723	2.673	2.624	2.577	2.531	2.487
4	3.902	3.808	3.717	3.630	3.546	3.465	3.387	3.312	3.240	3.170
5	4.853	4.713	4.580	4.452	4.329	4.212	4.100	3.993	3.890	3.791
6	5.795	5.601	5.417	5.242	5.076	4.917	4.767	4.623	4.486	4.355
7	6.728	6.472	6.230	6.002	5.786	5.582	5.389	5.206	5.033	4.868
8	7.652	7.325	7.020	6.733	6.463	6.210	5.971	5.747	5.535	5.335
9	8.566	8.162	7.786	7.435	7.108	6.802	6.515	6.247	5.995	5.759
10	9.471	8.983	8.530	8.111	7.722	7.360	7.024	6.710	6.418	6.145
11	10.368	9.787	9.253	8.760	8.306	7.887	7.499	7.139	6.805	6.495
12	11.255	10.575	9.954	9.385	8.863	8.384	7.943	7.536	7.161	6.814
13	12.134	11.348	10.635	9.986	9.394	8.853	8.358	7.904	7.487	7.103
14	13.004	12.106	11.296	10.563	9.899	9.295	8.745	8.244	7.786	7.367
15	13.865	12.849	11.938	11.118	10.380	9.712	9.108	8.559	8.061	7.606
16	14.718	13.578	12.561	11.652	10.838	10.106	9.447	8.851	8.313	7.825
17	15.562	14.292	13.166	12.166	11.274	10.477	9.763	9.122	8.544	8.024
18	16.398	14.992	13.754	12.659	11.690	10.828	10.059	9.372	8.756	8.204
19	17.226	15.678	14.324	13.134	12.085	11.158	10.336	9.604	8.950	8.362
20	18.046	16.351	14.877	13.590	12.462	11.470	10.594	9.818	9.129	8.511
21	18.857	17.011	15.415	14.029	12.821	11.764	10.836	10.017	9.292	8.649
22	19.660	17.658	15.837	14.451	13.163	12.042	11.061	10.201	9.442	8.772
23	20.456	18.292	16.444	14.857	13.489	12.303	11.272	10.371	9.580	8.883
24	21.243	18.914	16.936	15.247	13.799	12.550	11.469	10.529	9.707	8.985
25	22.023	19.523	17.413	15.622	14.094	12.783	11.654	10.675	9.823	9.077
26	22.795	20.121	17.877	15.983	14.375	13.003	11.826	10.810	9.929	9.161
27	23.560	20.707	18.327	16.330	14.643	13.211	11.987	10.935	10.027	9.237
28	24.316	21.281	18.764	16.663	14.898	13.406	12.137	11.051	10.116	9.307
29	25.066	21.844	19.188	16.984	15.141	13.591	12.278	11.158	10.198	9.370
30	25.808	22.396	19.600	17.292	15.372	13.765	12.409	11.258	10.274	9.427
40	32.835	27.355	23.115	19.793	17.159	15.046	13.332	11.925	10.757	9.779
50	39.196	31.424	25.730	21.482	18.256	15.762	13.801	12.233	10.962	9.915

Table B (cont.)

Periods	11%	12%	13%	14%	15%	16%	17%	18%	19%	20%
1	0.901	0.893	0.885	0.877	0.870	0.862	0.855	0.847	0.840	0.833
2	1.713	1.690	1.668	1.647	1.626	1.605	1.585	1.566	1.547	1.529
3	2.444	2.402	2.361	2.322	2.283	2.246	2.210	2.174	2.140	2.106
4	3.102	3.037	2.974	2.914	2.855	2.798	2.743	2.690	2.639	2.589
5	3.696	3.605	3.517	3.433	3.352	3.274	3.199	3.127	3.058	2.991
6	4.231	4.111	3.998	3.889	3.784	3.685	3.589	3.498	3.410	3.326
7	4.712	4.564	4.423	4.288	4.160	4.039	3.922	3.812	3.706	3.605
8	5.146	4.968	4.799	4.639	4.487	4.344	4.207	4.078	3.954	3.837
9	5.537	5.328	5.132	4.946	4.772	4.607	4.451	4.303	4.163	4.031
10	5.889	5.650	5.426	5.216	5.019	4.833	4.659	4.494	4.339	4.192
11	6.207	5.938	5.687	5.453	5.234	5.029	4.836	4.656	4.486	4.327
12	6.492	6.194	5.918	5.660	5.421	5.197	4.988	4.793	4.611	4.439
13	6.750	6.424	6.122	5.842	5.583	5.342	5.118	4.910	4.715	4.533
14	6.982	6.628	6.302	6.002	5.724	5.468	5.229	5.008	4.802	4.611
15	7.191	6.811	6.462	6.142	5.847	5.575	5.324	5.092	4.876	4.675
16	7.379	6.974	6.604	6.265	5.954	5.668	5.405	5.162	4.938	4.730
17	7.549	7.120	6.729	6.373	6.047	5.749	5.475	5.222	4.990	4.775
18	7.702	7.250	6.840	6.467	6.128	5.818	5.534	5.273	5.033	4.812
19	7.839	7.366	6.938	6.550	6.198	5.877	5.584	5.316	5.070	4.843
20	7.963	7.469	7.025	6.623	6.259	5.929	5.628	5.353	5.101	4.870
21	8.075	7.652	7.102	6.687	6.312	5.973	5.665	5.384	5.127	4.891
22	8.176	7.645	7.170	6.743	6.359	6.011	5.696	5.410	5.149	4.909
23	8.266	7.718	7.230	6.792	6.399	6.044	5.723	5.432	5.167	4.925
24	8.348	7.784	7.283	6.835	6.434	6.073	5.746	5.451	5.182	4.937
25	8.422	7.843	7.330	6.873	6.464	6.097	5.766	5.467	5.195	4.948
26	8.488	7.896	7.372	6.906	6.491	6.118	5.783	5.480	5.206	4.956
27	8.548	7.943	7.409	6.935	6.514	6.136	5.798	5.492	5.215	4.964
28	8.602	7.984	7.441	6.961	6.534	6.152	5.810	5.502	5.223	4.970
29	8.650	8.022	7.470	6.983	6.551	6.166	5.820	5.510	5.229	4.975
30	8.694	8.055	7.496	7.003	6.566	6.177	5.829	5.517	5.235	4.979
40	8.951	8.244	7.634	7.105	6.642	6.233	5.871	5.548	5.258	4.997
50	9.042	8.304	7.675	7.133	6.661	6.246	5.880	5.554	5.262	4.999

Table B (cont.)

Periods	21%	22%	23%	24%	25%	26%	27%	28%	29%	30%
1	0.826	0.820	0.813	0.806	0.800	0.794	0.787	0.781	0.775	0.769
2	1.509	1.492	1.474	1.457	1.440	1.424	1.407	1.392	1.376	1.361
3	2.074	2.042	2.011	1.981	1.952	1.923	1.896	1.868	1.842	1.816
4	2.540	2.494	2.448	2.404	2.362	2.320	2.280	2.241	2.203	2.166
5	2.926	2.864	2.803	2.745	2.689	2.635	2.583	2.532	2.483	2.436
6	3.245	3.167	3.092	3.020	2.951	2.885	2.821	2.759	2.700	2.643
7	3.508	3.416	3.327	3.242	3.161	3.083	3.009	2.937	2.868	2.802
8	3.726	3.619	3.518	3.421	3.329	3.241	3.156	3.076	2.999	2.925
9	3.905	3.786	3.673	3.566	3.463	3.366	3.273	3.184	3.100	3.019
10	4.054	3.923	3.799	3.682	3.571	3.465	3.364	3.269	3.178	3.092
11	4.177	4.035	3.902	3.776	3.656	3.543	3.437	3.335	3.239	3.147
12	4.278	4.127	3.985	3.851	3.725	3.606	3.493	3.387	3.286	3.190
13	4.362	4.203	4.053	3.912	3.780	3.656	3.538	3.427	3.322	3.223
14	4.432	4.265	4.108	3.962	3.824	3.695	3.573	3.459	3.351	3.249
15	4.489	4.315	4.153	4.001	3.859	3.726	3.601	3.483	3.373	3.268
16	4.536	4.357	4.189	4.033	3.887	3.751	3.623	3.503	3.390	3.283
17	4.576	4.391	4.219	4.059	3.910	3.771	3.640	3.518	3.403	3.295
18	4.608	4.419	4.243	4.080	3.928	3.786	3.654	3.529	3.413	3.304
19	4.635	4.442	4.263	4.097	3.942	3.799	3.664	3.539	3.421	3.311
20	4.657	4.460	4.279	4.110	3.954	3.808	3.673	3.546	3.427	3.316
21	4.675	4.476	4.292	4.121	3.963	3.816	3.679	3.551	3.432	3.320
22	4.690	4.488	4.302	4.130	3.970	3.822	3.684	3.556	3.436	3.323
23	4.703	4.499	4.311	4.137	3.976	3.827	3.689	3.559	3.438	3.325
24	4.713	4.507	4.318	4.143	3.981	3.831	3.692	3.562	3.441	3.327
25	4.721	4.514	4.323	4.147	3.985	3.834	3.694	3.564	3.442	3.329
26	4.728	4.520	4.328	4.151	3.988	3.837	3.696	3.566	3.444	3.330
27	4.734	4.524	4.332	4.154	3.990	3.839	3.698	3.567	3.445	3.330
28	4.739	4.528	4.335	4.157	3.992	3.840	3.699	3.568	3.446	3.331
29	4.743	4.531	4.337	4.158	3.994	3.841	3.700	3.569	3.446	3.332
30	4.746	4.534	4.339	4.160	3.995	3.842	3.701	3.570	3.447	3.332
40	4.760	4.544	4.347	4.166	3.910	3.846	3.703	3.571	3.448	3.333
50	4.762	4.545	4.348	4.167	3.910	3.846	3.703	3.571	3.448	3.333

Table B (cont.)

Periods	31%	32%	33%	34%	35%	36%	37%	38%	39%	40%
1	0.763	0.758	0.752	0.746	0.741	0.735	0.730	0.725	0.719	0.714
2	1.346	1.331	1.317	1.303	1.289	1.276	1.263	1.250	1.237	1.224
3	1.791	1.766	1.742	1.719	1.696	1.673	1.652	1.630	1.609	1.589
4	2.130	2.096	2.062	2.029	1.997	1.966	1.935	1.906	1.877	1.849
5	2.390	2.345	2.302	2.260	2.220	2.181	2.143	2.106	2.070	2.035
6	2.588	2.534	2.483	2.433	2.385	2.339	2.294	2.251	2.209	2.168
7	2.739	2.677	2.619	2.562	2.508	2.455	2.404	2.355	2.308	2.263
8	2.854	2.786	2.721	2.658	2.598	2.540	2.485	2.432	2.380	2.331
9	2.942	2.868	2.798	2.730	2.665	2.603	2.544	2.487	2.432	2.379
10	3.009	2.930	2.855	2.784	2.715	2.649	2.587	2.527	2.469	2.414
11	3.060	2.978	2.899	2.824	2.752	2.683	2.618	2.555	2.496	2.438
12	3.100	3.013	2.931	2.853	2.779	2.708	2.641	2.576	2.515	2.456
13	3.129	3.040	2.956	2.876	2.799	2.727	2.658	2.592	2.529	2.469
14	3.152	3.061	2.974	2.892	2.814	2.740	2.670	2.603	2.539	2.478
15	3.170	3.076	2.988	2.905	2.825	2.750	2.679	2.611	2.546	2.484
16	3.183	3.088	2.999	2.914	2.834	2.757	2.685	2.616	2.551	2.489
17	3.193	3.097	3.007	2.921	2.840	2.763	2.690	2.621	2.555	2.492
18	3.201	3.104	3.012	2.926	2.844	2.767	2.693	2.624	2.557	2.494
19	3.207	3.109	3.017	2.930	2.848	2.770	2.696	2.626	2.559	2.496
20	3.211	3.113	3.020	2.933	2.850	2.772	2.698	2.627	2.561	2.497
21	3.215	3.116	3.023	2.935	2.852	2.773	2.699	2.629	2.562	2.498
22	3.217	3.118	3.025	2.936	2.853	2.775	2.700	2.629	2.562	2.498
23	3.219	3.120	3.026	2.938	2.854	2.775	2.701	2.630	2.563	2.499
24	3.221	3.121	3.027	2.939	2.855	2.776	2.701	2.630	2.563	2.499
25	3.222	3.122	3.028	2.939	2.856	2.777	2.702	2.631	2.563	2.499
26	3.223	3.123	3.028	2.940	2.856	2.777	2.702	2.631	2.564	2.500
27	3.224	3.123	3.029	2.940	2.856	2.777	2.702	2.631	2.564	2.500
28	3.224	3.124	3.029	2.940	2.857	2.777	2.702	2.631	2.564	2.500
29	3.225	3.124	3.030	2.941	2.857	2.777	2.702	2.631	2.564	2.500
30	3.225	3.124	3.030	2.941	2.857	2.778	2.702	2.631	2.564	2.500
40	3.226	3.125	3.030	2.941	2.857	2.778	2.703	2.632	2.564	2.500
50	3.226	3.125	3.030	2.941	2.857	2.778	2.703	2.632	2.564	2.500

Table B (cont.)

Periods	41%	42%	43%	44%	45%	46%	47%	48%	49%	50%
1	0.709	0.704	0.699	0.694	0.690	0.685	0.680	0.676	0.671	0.667
2	1.212	1.200	1.188	1.177	1.165	1.154	1.143	1.132	1.122	1.111
3	1.569	1.549	1.530	1.512	1.493	1.475	1.458	1.441	1.424	1.407
4	1.822	1.795	1.769	1.744	1.720	1.695	1.672	1.649	1.627	1.605
5	2.001	1.969	1.937	1.906	1.876	1.846	1.818	1.790	1.763	1.737
6	2.129	2.091	2.054	2.018	1.983	1.949	1.917	1.885	1.854	1.824
7	2.219	2.176	2.135	2.096	2.057	2.020	1.984	1.949	1.916	1.883
8	2.283	2.237	2.193	2.150	2.109	2.069	2.030	1.993	1.957	1.922
9	2.328	2.280	2.233	2.187	2.144	2.102	2.061	2.022	1.984	1.948
10	2.360	2.310	2.261	2.213	2.168	2.125	2.083	2.042	2.003	1.965
11	2.383	2.331	2.280	2.232	2.185	2.140	2.097	2.055	2.015	1.977
12	2.400	2.346	2.294	2.244	2.196	2.151	2.107	2.064	2.024	1.985
13	2.411	2.356	2.303	2.253	2.204	2.158	2.113	2.071	2.029	1.990
14	2.419	2.363	2.310	2.259	2.210	2.163	2.118	2.075	2.033	1.993
15	2.425	2.369	2.315	2.263	2.214	2.166	2.121	2.078	2.036	1.995
16	2.429	2.372	2.318	2.266	2.216	2.169	2.123	2.079	2.037	1.997
17	2.432	2.375	2.320	2.268	2.218	2.170	2.125	2.081	2.038	1.998
18	2.434	2.377	2.322	2.270	2.219	2.172	2.126	2.082	2.039	1.999
19	2.435	2.378	2.323	2.271	2.220	2.172	2.126	2.082	2.040	1.999
20	2.436	2.379	2.324	2.271	2.221	2.173	2.127	2.083	2.040	1.999
21	2.437	2.379	2.324	2.272	2.221	2.173	2.127	2.083	2.040	2.000
22	2.438	2.380	2.325	2.272	2.222	2.173	2.127	2.083	2.041	2.000
23	2.438	2.380	2.325	2.272	2.222	2.174	2.127	2.083	2.041	2.000
24	2.438	2.380	2.325	2.272	2.222	2.174	2.127	2.083	2.041	2.000
25	2.439	2.381	2.325	2.272	2.222	2.174	2.128	2.083	2.041	2.000
26	2.439	2.381	2.325	2.273	2.222	2.174	2.128	2.083	2.041	2.000
27	2.439	2.381	2.325	2.273	2.222	2.174	2.128	2.083	2.041	2.000
28	2.439	2.381	2.325	2.273	2.222	2.174	2.128	2.083	2.041	2.000
29	2.439	2.381	2.326	2.273	2.222	2.174	2.128	2.083	2.041	2.000
30	2.439	2.381	2.326	2.273	2.222	2.174	2.128	2.083	2.041	2.000
40	2.439	2.381	2.326	2.273	2.222	2.174	2.128	2.083	2.041	2.000
50	2.439	2.381	2.326	2.273	2.222	2.174	2.128	2.083	2.041	2.000

Table C Future value of 1

Periods	1%	2%	3%	4%	5%	6%	7%	8%	9%	10%
1	1.010	1.020	1.030	1.040	1.050	1.060	1.070	1.080	1.090	1.100
2	1.020	1.040	1.061	1.082	1.102	1.124	1.145	1.166	1.188	1.200
3	1.030	1.061	1.093	1.125	1.158	1.191	1.225	1.260	1.295	1.331
4	1.041	1.082	1.126	1.170	1.216	1.262	1.311	1.360	1.412	1.464
5	1.051	1.104	1.159	1.217	1.276	1.338	1.403	1.469	1.539	1.611
6	1.062	1.126	1.194	1.265	1.340	1.419	1.501	1.587	1.677	1.772
7	1.072	1.149	1.230	1.316	1.407	1.504	1.606	1.714	1.828	1.949
8	1.083	1.172	1.267	1.369	1.477	1.594	1.718	1.851	1.993	2.144
9	1.094	1.195	1.305	1.423	1.551	1.689	1.838	1.999	2.172	2.358
10	1.105	1.219	1.344	1.480	1.629	1.791	1.967	2.159	2.367	2.594
11	1.116	1.243	1.384	1.539	1.710	1.898	2.105	2.332	2.580	2.853
12	1.127	1.268	1.426	1.601	1.796	2.012	2.252	2.518	2.813	3.138
13	1.138	1.294	1.469	1.665	1.886	2.133	2.410	2.720	3.066	3.452
14	1.149	1.319	1.513	1.732	1.980	2.261	2.579	2.937	3.342	3.797
15	1.161	1.346	1.558	1.801	2.079	2.397	2.759	3.172	3.642	4.177
16	1.173	1.373	1.605	1.873	2.183	2.540	2.952	3.426	3.970	4.595
17	1.184	1.400	1.653	1.948	2.292	2.693	3.159	3.700	4.328	5.054
18	1.196	1.428	1.702	2.026	2.407	2.854	3.380	3.996	4.717	5.560
19	1.208	1.457	1.754	2.107	2.527	3.026	3.617	4.316	5.142	6.116
20	1.220	1.486	1.806	2.191	2.653	3.207	3.870	4.661	5.604	6.727
21	1.232	1.516	1.860	2.279	2.786	3.400	4.141	5.034	6.109	7.400
22	1.245	1.546	1.916	2.370	2.925	3.604	4.430	5.437	6.659	8.140
23	1.257	1.577	1.974	2.465	3.072	3.820	4.741	5.871	7.258	8.954
24	1.270	1.608	2.033	2.563	3.225	4.049	5.072	6.341	7.911	9.850
25	1.282	1.641	2.094	2.666	3.386	4.292	5.427	6.848	8.623	10.835

Table C (cont.)

Periods	11%	12%	13%	14%	15%	16%	17%	18%	19%	20%
1	1.110	1.120	1.130	1.140	1.150	1.160	1.170	1.180	1.190	1.200
2	1.232	1.254	1.277	1.300	1.322	1.346	1.369	1.392	1.416	1.490
3	1.368	1.405	1.443	1.482	1.521	1.561	1.602	1.643	1.685	1.728
4	1.518	1.574	1.630	1.689	1.749	1.811	1.874	1.939	2.005	2.074
5	1.685	1.762	1.842	1.925	2.011	2.100	2.192	2.228	2.386	2.488
6	1.870	1.974	2.082	2.195	2.313	2.436	2.565	2.700	2.840	2.986
7	2.076	2.211	2.353	2.502	2.660	2.826	3.001	3.185	3.379	3.583
8	2.305	2.476	2.658	2.853	3.059	3.278	3.511	3.759	4.021	4.300
9	2.558	2.773	3.004	3.252	3.518	3.803	4.108	4.435	4.785	5.160
10	2.839	3.106	3.395	3.707	4.046	4.411	4.807	5.234	5.695	6.192
11	3.152	3.479	3.836	4.226	4.652	5.117	5.624	6.176	6.777	7.430
12	3.498	3.896	4.335	4.818	5.350	5.936	6.580	7.288	8.064	8.916
13	3.883	4.363	4.898	5.492	6.153	6.886	7.699	8.599	9.596	10.699
14	4.310	4.887	5.535	6.261	7.076	7.988	9.007	10.147	11.420	12.839
15	4.785	5.474	6.254	7.138	8.137	9.266	10.539	11.974	13.590	15.407
16	5.311	6.130	7.067	8.137	9.358	10.748	12.330	14.129	16.172	18.488
17	5.895	6.866	7.986	9.276	10.761	12.468	14.426	16.672	19.244	22.186
18	6.544	7.690	9.024	10.575	12.375	14.463	16.879	19.673	22.901	26.623
19	7.263	8.613	10.197	12.056	14.232	16.777	19.748	23.214	27.252	31.948
20	8.062	9.646	11.523	13.743	16.367	19.461	23.106	27.393	32.429	38.338
21	8.949	10.804	13.021	15.668	18.822	22.574	27.034	32.324	38.591	46.005
22	9.934	12.100	14.714	17.861	21.645	26.186	31.629	38.142	45.923	55.206
23	11.026	13.552	16.627	20.362	24.891	30.376	37.006	45.008	54.649	66.247
24	12.239	15.179	18.788	23.212	28.625	35.236	43.297	53.109	65.032	79.497
25	13.585	17.000	21.231	26.462	32.919	40.874	50.658	62.669	77.388	95.396

Table C (cont.)

Periods	21%	22%	23%	24%	25%	26%	27%	28%	29%	30%
1	1.210	1.220	1.230	1.240	1.250	1.260	1.270	1.280	1.290	1.300
2	1.464	1.488	1.513	1.538	1.563	1.588	1.613	1.638	1.664	1.690
3	1.772	1.816	1.861	1.907	1.953	2.000	2.048	2.097	2.147	2.197
4	2.144	2.215	2.289	2.364	2.441	2.520	2.601	2.684	2.769	2.856
5	2.594	2.703	2.815	2.932	3.052	3.176	3.304	3.436	3.572	3.713
6	3.138	3.297	3.463	3.635	3.815	4.002	4.196	4.398	4.608	4.827
7	3.797	4.023	4.259	4.508	4.768	5.042	5.329	5.629	5.945	6.275
8	4.595	4.908	5.239	5.590	5.960	6.353	6.768	7.206	7.669	8.157
9	5.560	5.987	6.444	6.931	7.451	8.005	8.595	9.223	9.893	10.604
10	6.727	7.305	7.926	8.594	9.313	10.086	10.915	11.806	12.761	13.786
11	8.140	8.912	9.749	10.657	11.642	12.708	13.862	15.112	16.462	17.922
12	9.850	10.872	11.991	13.215	14.552	16.012	17.605	19.343	21.236	23.298
13	11.918	13.264	14.749	16.386	18.190	20.175	22.359	24.759	27.395	30.288
14	14.421	16.182	18.141	20.319	22.737	25.421	28.396	31.691	35.339	39.374
15	17.449	19.742	22.314	25.196	28.422	32.030	36.062	40.565	45.587	51.186
16	21.114	24.086	27.446	31.243	35.527	40.358	45.799	51.923	58.808	66.542
17	25.548	29.384	33.759	38.741	44.409	50.851	58.165	66.461	75.862	86.504
18	30.913	35.849	41.523	48.039	55.511	64.072	73.870	85.071	97.862	112.455
19	37.404	43.736	51.074	59.568	69.389	80.731	93.815	108.890	126.242	146.192
20	45.259	53.358	62.821	73.864	86.736	101.721	119.145	139.380	162.852	190.050
21	54.764	65.096	77.269	91.592	108.420	128.169	151.314	178.406	210.080	247.065
22	66.264	79.418	95.041	113.574	135.525	161.492	192.168	228.360	271.003	321.184
23	80.180	96.889	116.901	140.831	169.407	203.480	244.054	292.300	349.593	417.539
24	97.017	118.205	143.788	174.631	211.758	256.385	309.948	374.144	450.976	542.801
25	117.391	144.210	176.859	216.542	264.698	323.045	393.634	478.905	581.759	705.641

Table C (cont.)

Periods	31%	32%	33%	34%	35%	36%	37%	38%	39%	40%
1	1.310	1.320	1.330	1.340	1.350	1.360	1.370	1.380	1.390	1.400
2	1.716	1.742	1.769	1.796	1.822	1.850	1.877	1.904	1.932	1.960
3	2.248	2.300	2.353	2.406	2.460	2.515	2.571	2.628	2.686	2.744
4	2.945	3.036	3.129	3.224	3.322	3.421	3.523	3.627	3.733	3.842
5	3.858	4.007	4.162	4.320	4.484	4.653	4.826	5.005	5.189	5.378
6	5.054	5.290	5.535	5.789	6.053	6.328	6.612	6.907	7.213	7.530
7	6.621	6.983	7.361	7.758	8.172	8.605	9.058	9.531	10.025	10.541
8	8.673	9.217	9.791	10.395	11.032	11.703	12.410	13.153	13.935	14.758
9	11.362	12.166	13.022	13.930	14.894	15.917	17.001	18.151	19.370	20.661
10	14.884	16.060	17.319	18.666	20.107	21.647	23.292	25.049	26.925	28.925
11	19.498	21.199	23.034	25.012	27.144	29.439	31.910	34.568	37.425	40.496
12	25.542	27.983	30.635	33.516	36.644	40.037	43.717	47.703	52.021	56.694
13	33.460	36.937	40.745	44.912	49.470	54.451	59.892	65.831	72.309	79.371
14	43.833	48.757	54.190	60.182	66.784	74.053	82.052	90.846	100.510	111.120
15	57.421	64.359	72.073	80.644	90.158	100.713	112.411	125.368	139.708	155.568
16	75.221	84.954	95.858	108.063	121.714	136.969	154.003	173.008	194.194	217.795
17	98.540	112.139	127.491	144.804	164.314	186.278	210.984	238.751	269.930	304.913
18	129.087	148.024	169.562	194.038	221.824	253.338	289.048	329.476	375.203	426.879
19	169.104	195.391	225.518	260.011	299.462	344.540	395.996	454.677	521.532	597.630
20	221.527	257.916	299.939	348.414	404.274	468.574	542.514	627.454	724.930	836.683
21	290.200	340.449	398.919	466.875	545.769	637.261	743.245	865.886	1007.653	1171.356
22	380.162	449.393	530.562	625.613	736.789	866.674	1018.245	1194.923	1400.637	1639.898
23	498.012	593.199	705.647	838.321	994.665	1178.677	1394.996	1648.994	1946.885	2295.857
24	652.396	783.023	938.511	1123.350	1342.797	1603.001	1911.145	2275.611	2706.171	3214.200
25	854.638	1033.590	1248.220	1505.289	1812.776	2180.081	2618.268	3140.344	3761.577	4499.880

Table C (cont.)

Periods	41%	42%	43%	44%	45%	46%	47%	48%	49%	50%
1	1.410	1.420	1.430	1.440	1.450	1.460	1.470	1.480	1.490	1.500
2	1.988	2.016	2.045	2.074	2.102	2.132	2.161	2.190	2.220	2.250
3	2.803	2.863	2.924	2.986	3.049	3.112	3.177	3.242	3.308	3.375
4	3.953	4.066	4.182	4.300	4.421	4.544	4.669	4.798	4.929	5.063
5	5.573	5.774	5.980	6.192	6.410	6.634	6.864	7.101	7.344	7.594
6	7.858	8.198	8.551	8.916	9.294	9.685	10.090	10.509	10.943	11.391
7	11.080	11.642	12.228	12.839	13.476	14.141	14.833	15.554	16.304	17.086
8	15.623	16.531	17.486	18.488	19.541	20.645	21.804	23.019	24.294	25.629
9	22.028	23.474	25.005	26.623	28.334	30.142	32.052	34.069	36.197	38.443
10	31.059	33.334	35.757	38.338	41.085	44.008	47.117	50.422	53.934	57.665
11	43.794	47.334	51.132	55.206	59.573	64.251	69.261	74.624	80.362	86.498
12	61.749	67.214	73.119	79.497	86.381	93.807	101.814	110.444	119.739	129.746
13	87.066	95.444	104.561	114.475	125.252	136.958	149.667	163.457	178.411	194.620
14	122.763	135.530	149.522	164.845	181.615	199.959	220.010	241.916	265.832	291.929
15	173.096	192.453	213.816	237.376	263.342	291.939	323.415	358.035	396.090	437.894
16	244.065	273.284	305.757	341.822	381.846	426.232	475.420	529.892	590.174	656.841
17	344.132	388.063	437.233	492.224	553.676	622.298	698.867	784.240	879.360	985.261
18	485.226	551.049	625.243	708.802	802.831	908.555	1027.335	1160.676	1310.246	1477.892
19	684.169	782.490	894.097	1020.675	1164.105	1326.491	1510.182	1717.800	1952.266	2216.833
20	964.678	1111.135	1278.559	1469.772	1687.952	1936.677	2219.968	2542.344	2908.877	3325.257
21	1360.196	1577.812	1828.339	2116.471	2447.530	2827.548	3263.353	3762.669	4334.227	4987.885
22	1917.876	2240.493	2614.525	3047.718	3548.919	4128.220	4797.129	5568.750	6457.998	7481.828
23	2704.205	3181.500	3738.771	4388.714	5145.932	6027.201	7051.779	8241.750	9622.417	11222.741
24	3812.929	4517.730	5346.442	6319.749	7461.602	8799.714	10366.115	12197.790	14337.401	16834.112
25	5376.230	6415.177	7645.413	9100.438	10819.322	12847.582	15238.189	18052.730	21362.728	25251.168

Index